P9-CDX-318

Government Giveaways for Entrepreneurs

Fourth Edition

by

Matthew Lesko

Best Selling Author of *Information USA* and *Getting Yours*

Editor: Andrew Naprawa

Contributing Editor: Toni Murray

Researchers:
Jennifer Jones
Pam Schultz
Mary Ann Martello
Sarah Churner
Sharon McGinnis
Audry Elias
Charles Lorenz

Production Coordinator: Beth Meserve

Production Assistant: Peggy Yates

GOVERNMENT GIVEAWAYS FOR ENTREPRENEURS, Fourth Edition, Copyright 1994 by Matthew Lesko. All rights reserved. Printed in the United States of America. Published by Information USA, Inc., P.O. Box E, Kensington, MD 20895.

FOURTH EDITION

Cover Design: Sally Whitehead

Cover Cartoon: Galen D. Bailey

Photo: George Tames

Library of Congress Cataloging-in-Publication Date

    Lesko, Matthew

    Government Giveaways for Entrepreneurs Fourth Edition.

ISBN 1878346-01-6

The information in this book is continually updated on-line through the CompuServe Information Service. To subscribe call 1-800-524-3388 and ask for Representative 168.

Acknowledgements

We would like to thank the thousands of bureaucrats who contributed their time and expertise in explaining what opportunities are available to entrepreneurs.

A Word Of Caution To The Reader

We have to warn you that **this book is out of date**. You have to realize that the moment any book is printed, it is out of date. Especially this one with its over 9,000 sources. A book of this size is sure to have some telephone numbers that have changed. But don't be discouraged. You can live with these small inconveniences. If you are calling a government office listed in the book and the telephone number gets you a local diner, or some other wrong number, here's what you can do.

* Call the operator for the area and ask for the number of the office you're after. The directory assistance operator can be located by dialing the area code followed by 555-1212. To inquire about a toll-free number, call directory assistance at 1-800-555-1212.

* Or, call us at 301-942-6303. We will try to help you in any way we can.

You can keep up to date with the information in this book by ordering our new editions when they become available. Each new edition will not only verify all the sources identified in the book but include updated information as well as new chapters and much more. We hope to be publishing updates every year.

You can also keep current by accessing this information online, via computer, through CompuServe. We will be constantly updating this information on this computer service. For subscription information to CompuServe call (800) 524-3388 and ask for Representative 168. Thanks again for your interest in this book. I hope you will feel free to call with your comments and questions.

Happy Hunting,

Matthew Lesko

Other books written by Matthew Lesko:

Getting Yours: The Complete Guide to Government Money

How to Get Free Tax Help

Information USA

The Computer Data and Database Source Book

The Maternity Sourcebook

Lesko's New Tech Sourcebook

The Investor's Information Sourcebook

The Federal Data Base Finder

The State Database Finder

The Great American Gripe Book

Lesko's Info-Power

What To Do When You Can't Afford Health Care

Table Of Contents

Government Giveaways for Entrepreneurs

Table Of Contents

Eleven Lies About Your Government

The biggest problem in getting taxpayers to take advantage of government opportunities is fighting the myths about government that permeate our society. We are a nation of headline readers, and our perceptions of the world come from one-minute sound bites or the first paragraph of a newspaper story. We forget that news means "what's different". Journalists are not going to sell papers if they write about the same old good stuff that happens every day. And thank God the news is still the bad stuff that happens in our society. When good things become news, then we are really in trouble. After all, the journalist's job is to report on what is wrong with our democracy, so that we can change it.

There are 6,000 journalists running around Washington every day trying to find out how the government screwed up. They all have to generate their bad news story for the day. So day in and day out, taxpayers are inundated with news about the government: $5,000 hammers, $10,000 toilet seats, HUD scandals, IRS scandals, etc. These stories are real, and it's relatively easy for journalists to find them. With over 18 million bureaucrats on government payrolls, it's easy to find someone screwing up today. When you go to work tomorrow, look around your office; you'll see 20% of the people screwing up before the day ends. But these screw ups and scandals represent only a small fraction of what is going on in the government.

Another problem is that the only contacts most taxpayers have with the government are with the Internal Revenue Service (IRS) and the Division of Motor Vehicles (DMV). Everyone hates giving money to the IRS, and we have all experienced waiting in line at the DMV and dealing with a clerk who answered the same question 400 times that day. Not using the rest of the government because of a bad experience at your local DMV is like eating only the broccoli at an expensive gourmet meal and thinking everything else tastes just like it.

The government wants you and your business to take advantage of its resources. Why? Because businesses create new jobs. New jobs create a healthy economy. And a healthy economy gets politicians reelected.

You pay for this government whether or not you use it. So let's get rid of some of your misconceptions about it so that you can better take advantage of this powerful resource.

Lie #1:
Reaganomics Cut The Government

This remains one of the country's biggest all-time lies. Total government expenditures have increased every year since 1948. From 1980 to 1990, during the Reagan/Bush Administration, federal expenditures grew at about twice the rate of inflation. Federal expenditures grew over 155%, and inflation was 59% during the same period. Here are what the numbers look like.

Total Government Expenditures				
Year	Total Government (000,000)	% Increase	Federal Government (000,000)	% Increase
1990	$ 1,768,600		$ 1,251,700	
1980	$ 820,200		$ 590,900	
Increase	$ 948,400	115.60%	$ 660,800	112.03%

Source: Budget of the United States Government

The number of bureaucrats also has substantially increased during the past ten years. Here are those numbers.

Number of Civilian Government Employees		
Year	All Government	Federal Government
1990	18,404,000	3,067,000
1980	16,363,000	2,821,000
Increase	2,041,000	246,000

Source: Budget of the United States Government

The total government share of the Gross National Product has even increased from 1980 to 1990 from 30.7% to 32.7%. This means that government is becoming a bigger and bigger share of our lives, and right now it represents close to one third of everything we do in the United States. It's bigger than all the retail stores, bigger than all the wholesale businesses, and over 8 times the size of the automobile industry in the United States.

Lie #2:
All Government Programs That Help
The Average American Have Been Cut

If this were really true, then we wouldn't be in debt. It is true that over the past 10 years some programs were reduced and some even eliminated. But on a whole they continue to grow, and more new ones are being added every year.

60 New Programs

A look at the 1991 Catalog of Federal Domestic Assistance, (published by the U.S. Government Printing Office) gives you the real story. This official document compiled each year by the President's Office of Management and Budget, describes the money programs available from the federal government. It shows that in 1991 60 new programs were added for a total of $3,962,534,790. And only 17 programs were deleted, worth a total of $300,000,000. That's an increase to the annual deficit of over $3.5 billion.

The kinds of funding and new programs that businesses can take advantage of include:

1) $14,700,000 that is set aside for small business nurseries to plant, prune, and water trees and shrubs on government land throughout the country. This money is going to increase to $50,000,000 next year and run at that level for a number of years.

2) Employment agencies, consultants, and job skill trainers can take advantage of a new program to help individuals with handicaps find employment. $20,000,000 in funds was already budgeted for 1991, and $1.9 billion in 1992.

3) There are also 15 new grant programs for people who want to get a college education.

I also keep reading about local programs that haven't been catalogued yet in this official government document. The Tennessee Valley Authority, for example, is offering loans up to $300,000 for employees who lose their jobs and now want to start their own businesses.

And, it is also happening at the state level. The District of Columbia, which is in deep financial trouble, just started a new loan guarantee program to help people launch their own business.

Not only are there dozens of new programs being initiated every year, the value of the existing programs continues to increase. The following is a listing of federal money programs for entrepreneurs that have substantially increased from 1990 to 1991. These increases compare to a 1991 raise in the rate of inflation of approximately 3%. The number next to the description is the program ID from the Catalog of Federal Domestic Assistance.

Increase In Funding For Entrepreneur Programs

Program	1990	1991	% Increase
Emergency Money for Businesses in Rural Areas (10.404)	$ 73,493,000	$ 100,000,000	12%
Buying and Fixing Up Homes in Rural Areas (10.405)	$ 9,379,240	$ 11,287,160	20%
Teenage Entrepreneurs, Aquaculture Businesses and other Rural Enterprises (10.406)	$ 908,747,960	$2,600,000,000	186%
Businesses Who Want to Move to Rural Areas (10.422)	$ 88,472,600	$ 100,000,000	13%
Feasibility Studies for New Businesses (10.854)	$ 1,869,000	$ 6,600,000	253%
Starting a Business in High Unemployment Areas (11.301)	$ 2,235,000	$ 3,200,000	43%
Help for Companies That Were Hurt by Imports (11.313)	$ 6,373,000	$ 12,950,000	103%
Grants to Fishermen Who Damage Their Boats on Off Shore Oil and Gas Equipment (11.408)	$ 668,034	$ 950,000	42%
Grants to Fishermen Whose Boats Were Damaged by Foreign Fishermen (11.409)	$ 881,932	$ 1,050,000	19%
Loans to Buy or Fix Up Fishing Boats (11.415)	$ 35,031,187	$ 70,000,000	100%
Help for Minority Entrepreneurs to Start Their Own Business (11.800)	$ 19,005,133	$ 25,437,000	34%
Money to Help Small Business Get Government Contracts (12.002)	$ 9,384,860	$ 10,579,552	13%
Loans to Start a Hospital (14.128)	$ 25,611,000	$ 388,234,000	1,452%
Investors Who Want to Build or Fixup Rental Housing or Apartment Buildings (14.134)	$ 0	$ 4,567,000	999% +
Investors Who Want to Build 5 or More Rental or Coop Units (14.135)	$ 188,156,466	$ 502,420,000	167%
Grants for High Tech Small Businesses to Work on New Ideas (47.053)	$ 41,555,000	$ 44,199,000	6%
Small Business Computer Companies to Train on Advanced Computer Systems (47.070)	$ 169,842,000	$ 186,115,000	9%
Small Business Loan Guarantees (59.012)	$3,115,043,000	$3,500,000,000	12%
Loans to Vietnam-Era Veterans to Start a Business (59.038)	$ 13,804,000	$ 17,000,000	23%
Help to Women Entrepreneurs (59.043)	$ 1,500,000	$ 2,000,000	33%
Grants to Small Businesses to Work on New Ideas in the Health Care Industry (93.126)	$ 7,906,000	$ 9,189,000	16%

Source: Catalog of Federal Domestic Assistance

With the concern over the budget deficit, don't count on the politicians to publicize the fact that they voted to increase these programs.

Lie #3:
Your Odds Of Getting Government Money Are A Zillion To One

Of course, I would like you to believe that all you have to do is buy my book, make one telephone call and next week get a $100,000 check in the mail. Nothing in life works that easily. Determining what your actual odds are going to be to get money depends upon the government program and on supply and demand. Most of the programs I've personally been involved with have approval rates ranging from 11% to 60%. Here are data from a few programs to give you a better indication of your actual chances. Also notice that the amount of Small Business Loan Guarantees increased 15% over the past 5 years.

Direct Loans from the Small Business Administration

Year	Number of Loan Applications	Number of Approvals	% Approved
1987	3,583	674	18.81%
1988	3,397	671	19.75
1989	3,329	652	19.58%
1990	2,711	540	19.91%
1991	2,945	586	19.89%

Source: U.S. Small Business Administration

Loan Guarantees at the Small Business Administration

Year	Number of Loan Applications	Number of Approvals	% Approved
1987	28,392	16,436	57.88%
1988	27,942	16,468	58.93%
1989	29,397	17,624	59.95%
1990	32,266	18,301	56.71%
1991	32,768	18,853	57.53%

Source: U.S. Small Business Administration

Grants To Small Businesses to Work On New Ideas (SBIR)

Years	Proposals Received	Grants Awarded	% Approved
1983-1990	95,800	14,903	15.55%

Source: U.S. House of Representatives Committee on Small Business

It is interesting to note that the total value of awards was $1.8 billion and the average award was $120,800.

Grants To TV, Film and Radio Producers (45.006)

Year	Applications Received	Grants Awarded	% Approved
1990	831	262	31.52%

Source: Catalog of Federal Domestic Assistance

Grants To Writers, Magazines, and Publishers (45.004)

Year	Applications Received	Grants Awarded	% Approved
1990	2,531	282	11.14%

Source: Catalog of Federal Domestic Assistance

This sounds like pretty good odds to me. People play the state lottery where there is a one in a million chance of hitting the jackpot. Here you get better than a one in two chance of changing your life, plus you get the opportunity to contribute to society in the best way you know how.

Lie #4:
Most Government Money Goes To Minorities

It's true there are special programs for minorities, but they only represent a very small portion of what is available. It must be that these are the programs that get all the media attention. Data are difficult to come by, partly because government laws make it illegal to ask about race on many applications. But, here are some facts to get rid of your paranoia:

Federal Government Contracts Set Aside For Minorities, 8(a) Program

Year	Total Value of Contract	Minority Set Aside	% Minority
1990	$171,300,890,000	$3,359,262,000	1.96%

Source: Federal Procurement Data Center

Recent Loans Made To 308 Small Businesses by the State of California

Am.Indian	Asian	Afro-American	Hispanic	White	Other
2%	17%	22%	11%	45%	3%

Source: California Department of Commerce

SBA Loans To Small Businesses

Year	Total Loans	Total Minority Loans	% Minority
1987	$3,232,000,000	$299,000,000	9.25%
1988	$3,434,000,000	$343,000,000	9.98%
1989	$3,490,000,000	$385,000,000	11.03%
1990	$4,258,000,000	$474,000,000	11.13%

Source: Statistical Abstract of the United States

Lie #5:
I Never Met Anyone In Business Who Got Money
From The Government So They Can't Give Out Very Much

Nonsense. The amount of money given out to business each year equals $46,000 for every business in the United States. There are 6,018,600 businesses in the United States according to the Bureau of the Census's County Business Patterns, and the government has business money programs worth $292 billion. And, it doesn't all go out in big chunks. Last year 23 million different awards were given to businesses. That is an average of four awards for every business. Now, if your business isn't getting your share, it is not because there isn't enough out there. I'd like to note that some may argue with my figure of 6,000,000 businesses in the United States. This number is taken from County Business Pattern data which show establishments which have at least one employee. Self employed people like taxi drivers are not included in this figure. The largest number for business establishments comes from the Internal Revenue Service which counts 18 million, which includes 3.6 million corporations and 13 million sole proprietorships. I'm sure some will argue that this data on establishments are not accurate. But even if I'm wrong by 50%, that's still $23,000 per business.

1990 Money Available to Entrepreneurs From Federal Government

Type of Opportunities	Value of Awards	Number of Awards
Grants, Loans and Loan Guarantees	$101,005,791,089	3,381,447
Contracts Over $25,000	$171,300,890,000	368,372
Contracts Under $25,000	$ 19,897,390,000	19,500,257
Total	$292,204,071,089	23,250,076

Source: Federal Procurement Data Center and Catalog of Federal Domestic Assistance

1990 MONEY AVAILABLE FOR EACH BUSINESS BY STATE

State	Grants/Loans ($000)	Contracts ($000)	Total ($000)	# of Businesses	Avg. $ Per Business
Alabama	1,271,023	3,388,260	4,659,283	84,847	$46,394
Alaska	390,700	529,188	919,888	14,119	65,152
Arizona	2,051,048	3,667,045	5,718,093	85,410	67,271
Arkansas	1,555,499	390,631	1,946,130	52,118	37,425
California	10,056,664	29,499,571	39,556,235	716,949	55,246
Colorado	2,884,455	4,043,389	6,927,844	94,773	73,700
Connecticut	691,916	4,443,344	5,135,260	93,644	55,218
Delaware	179,567	138,357	317,924	17,417	18,701
Dis.of Columbia	146,357	2,935,517	3,081,874	19,842	154,093
Florida	4,433,938	6,616,097	11,050,035	345,045	32,030
Georgia	2,967,428	2,227,821	5,195,249	152,937	34,179
Hawaii	435,837	547,303	983,140	27,938	35,112
Idaho	723,724	862,046	1,585,770	25,060	63,430
Illinois	3,804,606	2,601,344	6,405,950	263,853	24,264
Indiana	1,777,371	1,971,190	3,748,561	123,923	30,230
Iowa	2,612,858	700,372	3,313,230	71,782	46,017
Kansas	1,707,523	1,131,487	2,839,010	65,736	43,015
Kentucky	894,330	2,010,279	2,904,609	76,898	37,722
Louisiana	1,403,173	2,384,117	3,787,290	89,010	42,553
Maine	312,266	942,302	1,254,568	35,064	35,845
Maryland	2,970,516	6,693,535	9,484,051	109,605	87,009
Massachusetts	442,836	8,807,986	9,250,822	161,175	57,458
Michigan	1,804,740	1,698,383	3,503,123	202,125	17,342
Minnesota	4,916,255	2,087,045	7,003,300	108,259	64,845
Mississippi	1,178,377	1,616,057	2,794,434	51,847	53,739
Missouri	2,119,447	6,960,773	9,080,220	126,955	71,497
Montana	846,460	166,912	1,013,372	24,900	40,535
Nebraska	1,139,308	426,338	1,565,646	43,134	36,410
Nevada	973,337	829,487	1,802,824	27,334	66,771
New Hampshire	167,163	430,293	597,456	34,669	17,070
New Jersey	867,554	4,306,983	5,174,537	212,095	24,408
New Mexico	565,032	3,256,469	3,821,501	34,939	109,185
New York	2,600,460	8,621,028	11,221,488	463,177	24,236
North Carolina	2,138,661	1,592,358	3,931,019	158,793	24,723
North Dakota	910,228	163,566	1,073,794	19,134	56,515
Ohio	2,678,485	6,037,689	8,716,174	243,268	35,869
Oklahoma	1,310,515	873,350	2,183,865	74,146	29,511
Oregon	918,721	648,891	1,567,612	78,152	20,097
Pennsylvania	1,743,589	4,152,665	5,896,254	272,434	21,677
Rhode Island	228,195	600,437	828,632	27,871	29,594
South Carolina	1,232,878	2,663,624	3,896,502	76,732	50,603
South Dakota	687,965	119,266	807,231	19,760	40,362
Tennessee	2,048,126	3,308,460	5,356,586	110,444	48,696
Texas	6,890,273	11,203,047	18,093,320	389,383	46,512
Utah	1,105,829	1,543,171	2,649,000	35,846	73,583
Vermont	145,737	106,763	252,500	19,687	12,625
Virginia	3,078,955	10,167,683	13,246,638	142,720	93,286
Washington	2,373,091	6,315,603	6,315,603	123,278	51,346
West Virginia	237,687	325,147	562,834	37,140	15,211
Wisconsin	1,139,316	1,263,372	2,402,688	118,596	20,190
Wyoming	258,810	145,929	404,739	14,525	28,910
	$ 90,669,704	$188,530,640	$279,200,345	6,018,600	Avg. $46,394

Source: Bureau of the Census

Lie #6:
Individuals Get More Money From Government Programs
Like Social Security, Medicare, Food Stamps, Etc.,
Than Businesses Get From Their Programs

This is not true in a per person case. The government gives out $2,800 per adult person and gives out $46,000 per business. Looking at it this way, the average U.S. business is subsidized 16 times more than the individual.

The total amount of money spent on programs that give direct payments to individuals equals $497.7 billion. The number of adults, people over 21, in the United States totals 177 million. This means that programs for individuals provide an average of $2,800 per person.

The total amount of money programs available for businesses have a value of $292 billion. And, the total number of businesses equals 6 million. The average per business equals $46,000. See Lie #5 for more details.

Lie #7:
Real Entrepreneurs Don't Get Government Help

Lee Iacocca, Donald Trump, H. Ross Perot, Steven Jobs and every other great American entrepreneur have used the government to improve their success. Entrepreneurs don't simply roll up their sleeves and do it all by themselves. That's a fantasy and life doesn't work like that anymore in America. When John Wayne opened up America's frontier, on the back lots of MGM studios, his only obstacles were hostile Indians and nasty weather. Today's world is too big and too complicated to tackle it alone. And the smart entrepreneurs know exactly where to get help.

The first thing Lee Iacocca did when he took over Chrysler was go to Washington and get a $1.2 billion loan to turn the automaker around. He even bragged that he returned the money with interest. As a taxpayer, I wanted to remind him that the money he got from the government was a <u>loan</u>, and that he was supposed to pay it all back.

Donald Trump's entire empire was built on government programs to buy property and fix up property. He even brags in his first book how he made his first million on a government property in Cincinnati. His father was so good at getting government money that he was continually being investigated by the government for possible fraud.

H. Ross Perot made billions when he sold his business to General Motors. His business was made up largely of government contracts. Then, the first thing he did when he left the Board of Directors of General Motors was to negotiate a government contract with the U.S. Postal Service.

Even Steven Jobs and his partner, the two young entrepreneurs who didn't have enough credentials to get a job at IBM, started a whole new computer industry by launching Apple Computers in their garage with the help of government money. The reason that these two couldn't get a job at IBM was because they never finished college.

Lie #8:
Only The Rich And Famous
Like Charles Keating Get Government Money

You don't have to take a Congressperson or Senator to lunch to get money from the government. Very few of the hundreds of thousands of businesses which will get checks from the government next year are going to be big shots like Lee Iacocca or Donald Trump. They are more likely to be the type of people you might know, like:

- Suzanne Schwartz of Louisville who got $12,000 from the government to start a craft business in her home,
- Bret Stern who got $210,000 from the government to work on his invention in his apartment in New York City,
- Mr. and Mrs. Roland who got $300,000 from the government to start their own designer brewery, and
- Debra Jefferies of Columbia, Maryland who received $30,000 from the government to start her own video production company, plus another $25,000 worth of government contracts.

Here are some other businesses you might know which got money from the federal government in 1991.

Federal Awardees

Gold's Gym in Anniston, Alabama got $260,000
Magic Tunnel Car Wash in Anniston, Alabama got $205,000
Cloud Nine Motel in Globe Arizona got $535,000
Irene's Cleaners and Alterations in Mesa, Arizona got $67,000
The Shirt Shop in Alpine, California got $25,000
D J's Fun Place in Bakersfield, California got $60,000
Jim Boy's Tacos in Elk Grove, California got $100,000
Home Veterinary Service in Denver, Colorado got $40,000
T & S Billiards in Windsor Locks, Connecticut got $60,000
Creative Business Interiors in Altamonte Springs, Florida got $100,000
Survival Technology Group in St. Petersburg, Florida got $200,000
Discovery Point Child Care in Lawrence, Florida got $825,000
Weight Loss Management Center in Atkins, Iowa got $65,000
Ron's Alignment in Boise, Idaho got $125,000
This is It! Pizza in Arlington Heights, Illinois got $100,000
Han's Hair Design in Champaign, Illinois got $12,000
Happy Time Day Care Center in Mt. Vernon, Illinois got $235,000
Pro Forma Bike Shop in Bremen, Indiana got $55,000
Sug's Home Care in Corbin, Kansas got $6,000
Lone Star Pizza in Cloverport, Kentucky got $21,000
Beaver Creek Resort in Monticello, Kentucky got $1,700,000
Mad Maggies Billiard Parlor in Danvers, Massachusetts got $250,000
Little Professor Book Center in Baltimore, Maryland got $130,000
Johnny's Selected Seeds in Albion, Maine got $600,000
Country-Side Catering in Capac, Michigan got $105,000
Small Wonders Learning Center in Winston-Salem, North Carolina got $255,000
$ and $sense Dry Cleaners in Austin, Texas got $92,000

And don't forget, state governments also give money to businesses. Here are a few companies which were helped by the state of New Jersey:

State Awardees

Ross Electric Supply Distributors in Trenton, New Jersey got $50,000
Popcorn Explosion in Hawthorne, New Jersey got $250,000
Top of the Line Cosmetics in Long Branch, New Jersey got $250,000
Staple Sewing Aids in Grafield, New Jersey got $250,000
Finishing Touch Embroideries in West New York got $250,000
Main Road Bakery in Vineland, New Jersey got $60,000

Lie #9:
Government Creates The Obstacles
That Hinder The Success Of A Business

The obstacles are really created by the private sector, in the form of consultants, lawyers, accountants, and other professionals. And, it's the government that can eliminate them.

Money After Your Bank Says No

If you have a legitimate business idea to create jobs and improve our society but you have a stuffy banker who won't talk to you, this obstacle can be overcome by turning to the government. The government writes over 3,000,000 checks a year to entrepreneurs to start or expand their business, and the majority of these checks are reserved for businesses which have been turned down by traditional commercial money sources.

Free Legal Help Instead of Paying Your Lawyer $700

Let's say today you decide to go out and start your own business. You go to the bank to open up a checking account and the banker asks if you are "Incorporated". You don't know if you are, or if you should be, or what. You ask your banker for advice and she advises you to go see an attorney. You call an attorney and the lawyer scares you into believing that the safest thing in life is to start an "incorporated" business but it will cost $700. You don't have an extra $700 so you put off starting your own business.

The lawyer didn't solve the problem, only created one. This type of roadblock could be removed by one of the Small Business Development Centers around the country created to help you with problems like this. They have free consultants who will sit down and tell you what's good and bad about incorporating. And if you decide to incorporate, they will show you how to do it for **under $100**.

Free Market Studies Instead of Paying Your Consultant A Bundle

Let's say you are currently making blankets in the United States and would like to sell them in Europe. Maybe you go to the library to read up on European countries. That's what most of us have been trained to do in school. You'll soon realize that everything you read is out of date, like encyclopedias. Or, you find only superficial journalistic accounts from magazines and newspapers. So you think your next best bet is to call an international marketing consultant. Most consultants probably won't talk to you for less than $5,000 worth of business. So, the next time you get an extra $5,000 you'll call them back.

This is another roadblock. Instead, you can call the government and get an article about what you need in a way that's better, faster and cheaper. Why trust a journalist's account of what is going on in Europe when that journalist may have only spent a week or so researching the column? Instead, you can contact a government expert who has spent the last 15 years studying Europe and can fax you a report that was updated as of last night. Plus, you can contact government offices who will dispatch U.S. Embassy officials in any country in the world to go out and find three people in that country who are qualified to represent you and your product. And they'll do this for only $90. It will cost you that much just for a consultant to get from the airport to your office.

Instant Relief When Fear Mongers Scare the Hell Out Of You

Let's say you pick up the newspaper one day and read about a new law called the Americans With Disabilities Act that requires almost every business to accommodate employees and customers with disabilities or suffer a steep fine. You worry that a fine like that could put you out of business. You call your favorite management consultant about the law, and he's not sure how and if it affects you. He charges you $100 to get the latest information. A few hundred dollars later he calls to report that you will have to make some structural changes to your workplace, and recommends a good architect. The architect spends your money and then recommends a contractor, and on, and on, and on. Before you're finished, you could easily spend more money on these professionals than what it would cost to pay the fine.

Instead of relying on these $100 an hour consultants to go learn the law for you, you can call a government office and talk to someone who wrote the law, and the consultation is free. They will also send free consultants out to your business to show you the cheapest way to comply with the law.

Real entrepreneuring is not having to rely on a high priced lawyer, consultant or accountant in order to make a business decision. It's knowing how to eliminate these obstacles and get the information you need better and faster, and get it for free.

Lie #10:
All Government Information Is Worthless,
Out-of-Date And Not Worth Using

Government information is more important to entrepreneurs than government money. If someone gave you a million dollars to start or expand a business, you would quickly be out of business if you didn't have the information to spend it wisely. To stay in business you need information about your markets, your competition, legislation, technology, financial conditions and much more. Information is the key to success in our society and you can get it better, faster, and cheaper than anyone else by using the government. Big companies know this and use it to their advantage. All the Fortune 500 companies make billion dollar decisions based on information they get free from the government.

A $60,000 Per Year Pasta Expert

For over 13 years I acted as a marketing consultant to large companies which were buying and selling companies. When Proctor and Gamble was interested in starting a chain of pasta stores, they called me. I found the information they needed in the government. I discovered Bill Janis at the U.S. Department of Commerce and he was wonderful. For over a decade he has been studying pasta and he inundated me with free market studies, reports and special papers telling me what's hot and what's not in the pasta business. He also told me who was making money in the business and who wasn't. As a consultant, what I did was to package all of these materials, take his name off them, and put my name on them. You see, nothing in the government is copyrighted.

When Citicorp called for help to identify where all the rich people live in the United States, we went to the IRS, Bureau of the Census, and the Federal Reserve Board. We collected all the relevant information and sold it to Citicorp for a pretty penny.

When a rich stock investor, who had a million dollars tied up in Maine potatoes on the New York Commodities Exchange called, I found Charlie Porter at the U.S. Department of Agriculture. He was the government's resident economist who specialized in the supply and demand of potatoes. He was right on the money in developing our client's investment strategy.

The government is the largest producer of information and expertise in the world. Information is power. The success or failure of your business relies on information, not on money. No one in the private sector can possibly afford to do what the government does. We are living in an information society; the only thing that stops us from doing what we want to do is the lack of information or presence of misinformation. And there is no reason for this to happen because we all have access to the best information in the world. It's in the government.

$3 Billion Market Study For Free

No one can afford to collect information like the government does. The government recently spent over $3 billion counting all the people and houses in the Decennial Census. That's a $3 billion market study that even Proctor and Gamble can't afford. But that's just a tip of the iceberg. Almost every government department and agency is involved in collecting and analyzing information that will affect you and your business. For example, you can call the government and get:

- a recorded message that will tell you what will be on the front page of tomorrow's *Wall Street Journal*,
- a mailing list of all rich single men over 6 feet tall who live in your zip code,
- an analysis showing the best neighborhoods in which to open up a dental practice for children,
- free help on opening up a day care center in your office,
- financial information on your competitors,
- an analysis of how technology can solve your business problem,
- over 300,000 experts who will do free research for you on most any topic,
- free market studies and analysis of your invention idea,
- free legal help if you get audited, and
- inside information about the future of your business.

Lie #11:
Getting Government Help Isn't Worth The Hassle

This myth could be right. Calling the government can be a hassle, and you can get the bureaucratic run-around. But almost everything in life is that way today, and we have to learn how to deal with it or go live in a hole. Have you ever tried calling the telephone company lately to get your phone number changed? That, too, is going to take you a number of telephone calls to get fixed.

So, because calling the government for help may be a hassle, you may not want to use it for every little problem you may have. If you are looking for the exact time, you can make a number of telephone calls to the government and eventually find the Atomic Clock at the U.S. Observatory. This government timepiece will give you the time within nanoseconds. But is it worth looking for it? Probably not. But if you are looking for $100,000 to start your own video company, or $1,000,000 to improve the productivity of your manufacturing plant, or if you just want to know the best location for a jewelry store, it may be worth a few telephone calls. It may even be worth a few weeks of telephone calls if the information will change your life. What did you do in the last couple of weeks that changed the direction of your life?

The Good And Bad Of Entrepreneuring:
Six Reasons Why
Now Is The Best Time To Start A Business

I believe the current conditions in our country make it an excellent environment for entrepreneuring. Here's why.

1) Big Business Is Forcing Entrepreneurism

Most creative people who work in large companies feel frustrated and believe their real talents go unused. They see that the company they work for is not much different than a government agency. They see that 20% of the people are doing 80% of the work. They also are fed up with having to have 10 months of meetings before any little decision is made.

Few people working in big business feel that their efforts go towards making a difference. Office politics seem to be just as important as actual work. People feel unfulfilled and search for ways to feel needed.

As an entrepreneur you know you are needed from the first day you open up for business. You immediately see the direct correlation between your efforts and the success of your business. It's not office politics or 10 months of meetings that will determine your success; it's going to be hard work, fast decision making mixed with a dose of good luck.

The more big business makes people feel unimportant and just a cog in the wheel, the more they will force entrepreneurs to go out and do it themselves.

2) The Best Tax Shelter

As long as our society is based on capitalism, having your own business offers the best of all tax advantages, no matter how Congress tinkers with the tax code. This is because under the tax laws, money spent in an attempt to generate a sale for your business is tax deductible. This is how people who own their own business write off their house, their car, their country club, their travel, their entertainment, and even their boats.

When I was a young, single entrepreneur, I paid almost no taxes. Almost everything I did was a business expense. But now that I am married with two children, things are a little different. I haven't figured a way to deduct such expenses as computer games and toys.

3) A Bad Economy Helps

Bad economic times show employees that the security of having a job is not secure at all. No matter how good you are at your work, or no matter how high you are up the ladder, you can still lose your job. It is that fear of losing that security that keeps so many people from starting their own business. Life is just as unpredictable whether you are working for yourself or working for someone else. You might as well have fun and be your own boss. This way you'll never be fired again!

The success of your business also will improve if you start it during hard times. If you start a business during a boom, customers can come easily and you'll get fat and happy. Then, when the first economic downturn hits, you may not be able to handle it. You won't know how to operate in a mean and lean mode. This is why a lot of businesses go belly up in bad economic times.

However, if you start your business when times are tough, it will make your business stronger. You will figure out ways to make it work when times are bad and you'll make a bundle when the economy makes a comeback and business get easier. You will also learn how to handle things when the economy turns sour again. You'll be ready to operate a lean and mean company and you won't become a business failure statistic.

4) Opportunities in a Post-Industrial Society

When our country was a growing industrialized society it took a lot of money to get into business. You needed to invest in a factory, equipment, and high priced unionized employees. Now we live in an information and service-based economy, and most of these types of businesses take very little money to start. For many service businesses, all you need is a phone, a desk and business card, and you are in business. The factory for my information business is between my ears. I don't have to invest in a plant, equipment or anything, except computers and paper.

Employees in the post-industrial society are a lot cheaper. People working in the industrialized society made $20 to $30 per hour. You can now get people to work in information and service-based businesses at $5 to $10 per hour. That's a real bargain.

5) Big Business Creates Opportunities For You

As big business gets bigger and bigger it creates more and more opportunities for the small entrepreneur. When my Fortune 500 clients look for new businesses opportunities, the first thing they ask is: "How big will this business eventually be?" And if the answer wasn't at least $100 million, they were not interested. It takes them just as much effort to get into a $100 million business as it does for them to get into a $1 million business. So they concentrate only on the big ones, and leave the $1 million crumbs for the small entrepreneurs. Well, I don't know about you, but a $1 million business is not a bad living. I see myself as an entrepreneur cockroach, living off $1 million crumbs that fall through the cracks of the big guys. And if my history serves me well, the cockroach outlived the dinosaur by a long shot.

6) An Information Explosion Equals An Open Society

The information explosion has greatly expanded what once was just a little club of entrepreneurs. Before the information explosion you had to know someone to get the legal, marketing, technical or competitive information needed to launch a venture. Now you don't have to know someone to get this kind of help, you just have to understand the process of accessing information. Why can anyone tap into this information goldmine? Because this information is in our government, and living in an open democracy we all have the same right to this information whether you're Donald Trump or a street cleaner.

What Entrepreneurs Don't Need

Everybody is always telling entrepreneurs about all the essentials they need. I think it's just as important to tell entrepreneurs what they don't need. After starting four businesses of my own and even after having two failures, here is what I believe you should be extra careful to avoid.

1) Too Much Professional Advice

If you're starting a business with a limited supply of capital, too much professional advice is going to kill you. If you try to surround yourself with all the trappings of business success, you're soon going to go out of business.

Remember, you and your time are the most important resources in your business. Succeeding in business is a "beat the clock" game. If you're spending a lot of your time meeting with lawyers and accountants or choosing fancy "power" furniture, you'll have little time to concentrate on the <u>one</u> thing that is important to your success......getting a client. This is the most critical success factor of any new business. Without a client, everything else is meaningless.

When I started my first business, I got the high priced accountants, the high priced lawyers, the power business cards and power furniture, but I went out of business. And who won? It was the accountants, lawyers, and furniture salesmen. They were all smart enough to get paid and I was out on the street.

Your clients don't care what kind of accounting system you use or what legal structure you have formed. And having the right look, whether it be impressive business cards or furniture, may only affect your business 5% or 10%. This is a very insignificant percentage if you have no business. Furthermore, it's a waste of time if you're spending a half a day choosing furniture when you could be spending a half a day getting a client. And 99% of the clients don't care what kind of furniture you have. The only person who cares about what kind of furniture you have is the furniture salesman.

2) Too Much Money

Anyone can start a business if given $1 million bucks. It doesn't take a lot of creativity to spend money to buy advertising in your local newspaper. But what are you going to do next year when your business doesn't have an extra $1 million around? Instead of learning how to buy space, you should first learn how to get your local paper to write a FREE story about your business! The price is right and it's more effective than advertising because you're also getting a big, respected institution, the newspaper, to endorse you.

Too much money for a novice entrepreneur can make you fat, lazy and uncreative. The key to developing a strong business is learning how to get sales using the least amount of money, not the most amount of money.

3) Too Perfect A Product

A beginner entrepreneur can easily get hung up trying to develop the perfect product. Most of us can never be perfect, but we can still be successful. Entrepreneurs can get easily trapped into believing that their product or service has to be perfect before they offer it to the public.

Trying to be flawless can lead to failure. Being a perfectionist can cause you to go broke before you get to market. Be careful that your perfectionist attitude isn't really a mask for your own insecurities. What your family and friends will think about your product doesn't matter. The object of a product is to sell it to a customer. Your relatives and pals don't have to be your customers. Customers come with all different kinds of needs, and very few are willing to pay for perfection. Go open up your own closets and look at all the mediocre stuff you have purchased.

Until you start asking people for money you really don't know what they will buy. Your product is probably going to change dozens of times before it reaches its final form. And this metamorphosis is due to customer feedback, your most important information source. The most important thing is to introduce your product as soon as possible so that you can stay in business long enough to find out how to improve it.

Few of us are smart enough to read minds but we're all smart enough to listen. If you offer a product to ten people and five of them say they would buy it if it were green, go right out and paint the damn thing green, so you can make a few sales.

If you spend too much time designing the ultimate product you'll probably be wrong anyway and have few resources left to learn from your mistakes. Over designing isn't just a disease of the small entrepreneur. Do your remember the Ford's Edsel or Coca-Cola's New Coke?

4) A Board of Directors

Anytime you get three people in a room to talk about an idea there will always be one naysayer. Finding potential problems is always easy to do. If an idea was perfect, it wouldn't be an idea anymore; it would already be a product or service fulfilled by someone else.

For ideas to work, it usually takes the passion and commitment of one person. This kind of spirit doesn't come from a board of directors which engages in group decision making. Although democratic, this process usually results in ideas where everyone owns a small piece of the end product and no one person is committed to the complete picture.

Also, board meetings can be a waste of time for struggling entrepreneurs. Entrepreneurs have to live from moment to moment, often making quick, reflexive decisions so they can immediately move to the next decision. The temperament required for entrepreneuring is different than the temperament needed to placate a diverse group such as a board of directors.

5) An MBA

I have a BS in Business and an MBA. I believe it took me two failing businesses to unlearn all that I was taught in my six years of business school. I was brainwashed into believing such things as: "if you need money, you go to the bank." When I was starting my businesses I quickly learned that a bank is the last place an entrepreneur with no money should go. Business schools spend a lion's share of the time teaching you how to run big businesses like General Motors. And from the shape that General Motors is in, you can see that they don't do such a good job at that.

The jargon you learn in business school certainly is helpful if you want to get a job in big business. But if you are a small entrepreneur, much of what they teach you will just interfere with your instincts. There is no magic to most operations of running a business. Accounting is keeping a checkbook. Production is making sure that your product costs less than what you sell it for. But, in the beginning marketing can seem magical. Finding a customer is what any new business is all about, and that doesn't take an MBA. It takes a lot of door pounding.

6) Government Forms

Don't tell the government this because I may get in trouble. I believe that entrepreneurs should even forget about government licenses and forms for starting a business.

After I had two businesses that failed, I got rid of the accountants, the lawyers, the power furniture and power business cards, and I also didn't file any local, county, state or federal forms. Don't get me wrong; I did file my tax return. Never mess around with the IRS. The government forms I'm talking about are the permits, licenses and applications to do business. My theory is that filing all these forms takes time and energy. Your time is very important. You'd be better off to concentrate that time on what is the critical success factor of your business.....getting customers.

If you don't file the necessary forms there isn't much that can happen to you. The way the government works, it will take them three years to find you. And by then, you'll either be out of business, or you'll be successful enough to pay the $25 fine and file whatever is necessary.

Choosing The Business That Is Right For You:
Trust Your Heart As Well As Your Head

Choosing the business that is right for you can be a daunting prospect. Take heart, however, there are as many different businesses as there are ideas. One of them is right for you.

To begin with, choose an area that excites you. To succeed, you must love what you do. I know that this sounds deceptively simple, but everything else depends upon this one principle.

Find out if there's a market for your products or services. Study your competition, suppliers and new customers. Once this is done, trust your instincts. Choosing a business is a very personal decision. After all, you may end up spending the rest of your life with this business.

Following your heart, as well as your head, will greatly increase your chances of financial and personal success. I'm not advocating that you rely upon instinct alone, but the elements that lead to success often have little to do with advanced business degrees or perfectly balanced ledgers.

When you love what you do -- magic happens. Your business is no longer work. You may find yourself thinking about your business all the time, not because you have to, but because it is fun, fulfilling, and exciting.

Your chances of success skyrocket because you won't be easily discouraged. If you look around at the people who run businesses, you'll see that it doesn't take a rocket scientist to run a successful company. Most of us are bright enough to run a business if we decide to try.

Perseverance, not intelligence, is the key. If you love what you're doing, you won't give up at the first economic downturn and try to find something more profitable. You'll stay and learn how to make money even when the economy sours. Eventually, you'll become better at what you do than anyone else.

We pride ourselves in making all our decisions "by the numbers." Numbers are safe. Yet, those who meet the needs of our fast changing society look past the numbers. They see beyond the present and anticipate the future.

Steps for Choosing a Business

(1) **Use Your Imagination.** Clear your mind and let your imagination go. Explore new ideas and opportunities. Ask yourself questions such as:

a) What is my fantasy business?
b) What would I do even if I didn't get paid for doing it?
c) What people do I really admire in the world and why do I admire them?

(2) **Research Your Idea NOW.** Reach for that calculator and explore as many ideas as you can. Your job is to take the best ideas that you have at the moment and see how they grow. You can expect a lot of duds. Don't worry if all of your ideas aren't winners. With work and the help of a calculator, your ideas will lead to interesting opportunities. Do the research, study the options. Remember, all the information you need to find out about any business is out there. Start by looking through this book. It will give you plenty of ideas of where to start.

(3) **Trust Your Instincts.** The final decision can be difficult. If you did enough research you probably came up with more than one potentially good idea. But, be sure to make the final decision with your heart as well as your head. You are the one who has to be happy. And when you are, you will work like hell to make that business a success.

Don't Believe In Instant Success

The Glorification of Failure Will Bring More Success

Everybody fails but no one ever tells you about it. I had two failing businesses before I got lucky with what I am doing now. In 1975 I even had a computer software company that failed. Looking back at the growth of the computer business since then, I feel that I must have been the only person in the country with a computer company that didn't make it.

It's not only me, everybody who does anything in the world has to experience failure. We all know that Henry Ford was responsible for manufacturing the first mass produced automobile called the Model T. But very few people are aware that the Model T was not his first automobile. He went through models from A to S that all were failures before he got it right. Coca-Cola was only selling a dozen cases a week for a long time before they got it right. Even Thomas Edison failed over 1,000 different times while working on the filament for the light bulb before he was successful.

Our society should glorify failure the same way it glorifies success. The stories we read about in the general press and in special interest magazines like *Success*, all make success sound easy. They tell you stories of some housewife who was selling her "Can't Beat Em" cookies at school bake sales when her son's teacher suggested she should sell them in stores. Within no time at all she's a millionaire. That's not going to happen to you.

A millionaire friend of mine, Dr. Fad, didn't make his money instantly either. Maybe you've heard about him. He's responsible for the Wacky Wall Walker fad a number of years ago and made a bundle from it. He was successful with the Wall Walker only after dozens of other products failed. His business sounds glamorous now. He's got his own television show and 60 Minutes did a story on him. But, when he started, his little import/export business struggled for years as he lived in an efficiency apartment with his wife and his business shared a one room office. Some of his early failures included importing Japanese fish parts and face masks for industrial use. He struggled with this unglamorous business for years before he hit the jackpot.

Success Merchants Lie To You

Go out and fail.......that is the only way you are going to get anywhere. The odds of being an instant success are about the same as you being hit by lightning. If you live in Florida, where lightning has a habit of striking often, your odds may not be so bad. If you're waiting for the right idea that is sure to be an instant success like you see in the magazines, you'll never do anything. Magazines lie by making you believe that you, too, can be an instant success, just like the people they profile. This is how they sell magazines.

The magazines are not the only liars. I do it too, when I tell success stories on TV Talk shows. And the people on the TV Infomercials are among the worst offenders. They make you believe that instant success will happen to you just like the people they have on their success panel.

Success Stories Can Stop YOUR Success

The problem with these instant success stories is instead of encouraging you, they are more likely to stop you from fulfilling your dream. When the announcer introduces one of the panel members, it's usually something like this....."Do you see Joe and his wife here? Yesterday Joe was a garbage collector in Chattanooga, Tennessee. Last night he listened to my 15-hour "How To Make A Million" success tapes and today Joe owns 15 beautiful properties in Southern California."

Any rational person knows that kind of instant success probably won't happen to him. But now you feel jealous. You're thinking...."If that garbage collector can do it, why can't I?" And then you think about buying the 15-hour cassette program but you don't, because your rational side knows that you can't listen to hours of tapes at night, and own 15 properties by the next morning. If that garbage collector really did it and you can't, you're going to feel dumb. How can a garbage collector be smarter than you? No one wants to know that a garbage collector is smarter than you are so you don't do anything.

Or, if you buy the tapes and listen to them, you get angry because your life didn't change overnight. You get discouraged, throw the tapes in the closet, and hang up your success dreams, leaving it for the folks on TV.

Failure Helps You Unlearn What You Learned in School

It took me two failing businesses to unlearn all I was taught in my 6 years of Business School. I marched out into the world with an MBA in Computer Science and that was why my first two businesses failed. I was trying to put into practice what I learned in school. They were telling me things like....."If you need money go to the bank". No matter how good the economy is, a bank is the last place an entrepreneur with no assets is likely to find money for his or her business.

In my consulting business I was trying to do things like the big consultants; such as preparing mahogany-bound reports and renting fancy offices. I couldn't perform the services of a big consulting firm as well as a big consulting firm could. The clients who expected that from me were not satisfied in the end. What I learned was that I was a small consulting firm, but there were a lot of companies who didn't want a big consulting firm. They wanted someone who was operating out of their bedroom. I discovered my niche and that uniqueness gave me an edge.

Friends, Loved Ones and Teachers Are Bad For Entrepreneurs

We all have misconceptions about the way things work and what will be successful. We are inundated from all sides with opinions. Our associates, friends, families, and teachers all continually tell us why they believe someone is a success. They don't really know. If they did, they would be doing it too. The truth is, what makes one person a success is not likely to make you a success. The reason for your success will be because you are different than anyone else and your product will be different than anyone else's.

Another way all sorts of well-meaning folks hinder your success is by protecting you. All these people who care for you will not want to see you hurt. They will show you 15 ways your idea is likely to fail. Teachers are the worst. It seems that the more schooling you receive in this country, the more reasons you can think of as to why the idea won't work. Remember, the founder of Federal Express first presented his idea as a paper in business school and the professor barely gave him a passing grade because he thought the idea wouldn't work. And that was at Harvard! So trust your instincts and set your idea in motion.

If you want to succeed, most likely you are going to experience failure. And you shouldn't let anyone protect you from it. It's the best springboard to your future success.

Key Pointers When Applying For Money

The following are tips meant to offer advice and encouragement to both the novice and the "old pro" government money seeker.

1) Don't Always Believe A Negative Answer

If you call a government office and ask about a particular money program and they tell you that no such program exists, don't believe them. No one person in the government can know everything. Senator Kerry of Massachusetts recently surveyed all the local Small Business Administration offices to see how they were administering a program which provides money to Vietnam Era veterans starting their own businesses. Only half the offices knew that such a program existed. These are the same offices which are in charge of giving out the money. Other times programs are consolidated under new names. For example, there used to be a program at the U.S. Department of Agriculture which gave money to farmers to build golf courses and tennis courts in their fields so that they could get into the resort business. The program was called the Recreation Facility Loan Program. I think the name made politicians uneasy, so they folded the money into the Farm Operating Loan Program. The lesson here is not to throw up your hands when told that a program does not exist. Keep asking questions like:

- "Did such a program ever exist?"
- "What happened to the program?"
- "Are there any similar programs?"
- "Can I get a descriptive listing of all your current programs?"
- "What other programs or agencies might offer money in similar areas?"
- "Is there anyone who may know more about this program?"

2) Apply To More Than One Program

There is no prohibition which says that you can apply only to one program for your businesses. For example, if you want to build condominiums in a town of less than 50,000, investigate programs at the Small Business Administration, the Department of Housing and Urban Development, the Department of Agriculture as well as programs at the state and city level. The worst that can happen to you is that all of your applications are approved. This is a nice predicament to be in. You may not be able to accept the money from everyone. Many of the applications do not even ask if you are applying for money elsewhere.

3) Don't Be Discouraged If You Think You Are Not Eligible

If you happen to contact a program office and they tell you that the program was changed so that only non-profit organizations can now receive the money, don't let this discourage you. What you can do is find a non-profit or existing organization to work with you. This is done every day in Washington, DC. Entrepreneurs locate federal money programs and find passive partners who will get a percentage of the money.

4) Talk To Those Who Give The Money

Before you actually fill out any application, it is well worth your time to review the forms with the program officials, either in person if at all possible, or over the telephone. Many of the funding agencies have offices throughout the country to assist you. Such contact should help you tailor your answers to meet the government's expectations. It will give them what they want to see.

5) Give Them What They Want

When you prepare your application, give the government exactly what it asks for, even though it may not make much sense to you. Don't fight it. You will need all your energy to get your money. It is unlikely that you will have any chance in changing the government's ways even if you are right.

6) Starting Small Or Big?

You have to be careful about when to ask for a lot of money and when to ask for just a little. This depends upon the program. So before you say how much money you need, be sure you have some understanding of the maximum amount as well as the average amount of monies given to applicants. Each program office listed can give you this information.

7) Try Again

If your proposal is rejected, learn what you did wrong and try again next year, or try with a different program. Many proposals are rejected because of bad timing or a relatively minor hitch. Don't worry. Being turned down will not be held against you. Some programs deny first time applications just for drill. They want to make sure that you are serious about your project.

8) When the Bureaucracy Is Stuck, Use Your Representative

Contact the office of your U.S. Senator or Congressperson only when the bureaucracy comes to a halt on your paperwork. Sometimes this is the only way to get action. Playing constituent is a very effective resource and should be used only when all else fails.

9) Don't Overlook State Programs

Investigate opportunities from the state agencies at the same time you are exploring federal financial assistance. State real estate programs are listed under "Real Estate Ventures" and state business money programs are listed under "State Money and Help for Your Business."

Jumping Over Bureaucratic Hurdles

Remember you are not going to make one telephone call and as a result, some bureaucrat will send you a check. If it were that easy, our mammoth deficit would be 10 times as big as it is now. What normally happens is that bureaucratic hurdles will be put in your way, and how you handle them will determine the success or failure of your getting the money. An example of the ultimate success in overcoming such bureaucratic roadblocks is depicted by a Boston entrepreneur named Steven Stern. His story follows:

A few years ago, Steven Stern saw me on the David Letterman Show one night when I talked about a government program which gave money to teenage entrepreneurs. The next day Steven called my office and asked for more details about the program. He explained that he was 16 years old and wanted to start a lawn mowing business in Boston. I told him that I really didn't know much about the details of the program but I did give him the name and address of the office which runs the program.

Steven called me back about two days later and said that the Washington DC office told him to contact the regional office located in Boston. When he called the regional office, he was told that he could not apply for that program because the money was set aside for teenagers in rural areas. He asked me what he could do now, and I suggested he call Washington back and get a copy of the law which authorizes the program. I told him that the law would give him all the facts.

When Steven got a copy of the law, he was surprised to find that it stated that the money was indeed intended for teenagers in rural areas, but it also said that it could be used to start lawn mower businesses. What a match. So he took a copy of the law to the government office in Boston and rubbed their noses in the facts. The local office then conceded that he should apply for the money, and gave him an application.

But, at this point Steven was stopped again. Just as they handed him an application, they asked if he belonged to a 4-H club. This was another eligibility requirement for the financial assistance. Well, Steven attended to a city high school where students didn't know one end of a cow from another, let alone belong to a 4-H club. But this did not stop Steven. He went to school the next day and rounded up four of his buddies and started what may have been one of the first and only inner city 4-H club.

Now, completely eligible to apply for the money, Steven sent in his application and three months later received $3,000 to start his business. Within two years Steven was making $10,000 a year and able to support himself through Babson College.

Not all cases are going to be as difficult as Steven's, but they can be, and you have to have the stamina to overcome any hurdle the government puts in your path. Remember that someone is going to get the money every year, and it might as well be you.

Tips On Finding Information:
The Art Of Getting A Bureaucrat To Help You

Our greatest asset as information seekers is that we live in a society inhabited by people who are dying to talk about what they do for a living. However, in this world of big bureaucracies and impersonal organizations, it is rare that any of us get a chance to share what we know with someone who is truly interested. Perhaps this is why psychiatrists are in such great demand.

This phenomenon can work to your advantage; almost anyone can find an expert on any topic providing you expect it will take an average of seven telephone calls.

The Value Of Experts In Today's Information Age

Using experts can be your answer to coping with the information explosion. Computers handle some problems of the information explosion because they are able to categorize and index vast amounts of data. However, many computerized databases fail to contain information that is generated by non-traditional sources, for example, documents that are buried in state and federal agencies.

Another problem is that many databases suffer from lack of timeliness because they offer indexes to articles and most publishers have long lead times for getting the material into print. And in our fast changing society, having the most current information is crucial.

Computers also contribute to a more serious problem. Because of their ability to store such large quantities of data, computers aggravate the information explosion by fueling the information overload. If you access one of the major databases on a subject such as Maine potatoes, most likely you will be confronted with a printout of 500 or more citations. Do you have the time to find and read all of them? Can you tell a good article from a bad one?

The first step to cut through this volume of information is to find an expert specializing in Maine potatoes. Yes, such an individual exists. This person already will have read those 500 articles and will be able to identify the relevant ones that meet your information needs. This expert will also be able to tell you what will be in the literature next year, because probably he is in the midst of writing or reviewing forthcoming articles. And if you are in search of a fact or figure, this government bureaucrat might know the answer right off the top of his head. And the best part of this research strategy is that all the information can be accumulated just for the price of a telephone call.

Case Study: How To Find Mr. Potato

The techniques for locating an expert can best be illustrated by a classic story from the days when I was struggling to start my first information brokerage company in 1975.

At the time the business amounted only to a desk and telephone crowded in the bedroom of my apartment. As so often happens in a fledgling enterprise, my first client was a friend. His problem was this: "I must have the latest information on the basic supply and demand of Maine potatoes within 24 hours."

My client represented a syndicate of commodity investors which invests millions of dollars in Maine potatoes. When he called, these potatoes were selling at double their normal price and he wanted to know why. I knew absolutely nothing about potatoes, but thought I knew where to find out. The agreement with my client was that I would be paid only if I succeeded in getting the information (no doubt you've guessed I no longer work that way).

Luck With The First Telephone Call

The first call I made was to the general information office of the U.S. Department of Agriculture. I asked to speak to an expert on potatoes. The operator referred me to Mr. Charlie Porter. At that point I wondered if this Mr. Porter was a department functionary with responsibility for handling crank calls, but the operator assured me that he was an agriculture economist specializing in potatoes. I called Mr. Porter and explained how I was a struggling entrepreneur who knew nothing about potatoes and needed his help to answer a client's request. Charlie graciously gave me much of the information I needed, adding that he would be happy to talk at greater length either over the phone or in person at his office. I decided to go see him.

Only Problem Was Getting Out Of Charlie Porter's Office

For two and one half hours the next morning, the federal government's potato expert explained in intimate detail the supply and demand of Maine potatoes. Charlie Porter showed me computer printouts that reflected how the price had doubled in recent weeks. For any subject that arose during our conversation, Charlie had immediate access to a reference source. Rows of books in his office covered every conceivable aspect of the potato market. A strip of ticker tape that tracked the daily price of potatoes from all over the country lay across his desk.

Here in Charlie's office was everything anyone might ever want to know about potatoes. The problem, it turned out, was not in getting enough information, but how gracefully to leave his office. Once Charlie started talking, it was hard to stop him. It seemed that Charlie Porter had spent his lifetime studying the supply and demand of potatoes and finally someone with a genuine need sought his expertise.

Tips On Finding Information

One Potato....Two Potato....

When I was finally able to let Charlie know I had to leave, he pointed across the hall in the direction of a potato statistician whose primary responsibility was to produce a monthly report showing potato production and consumption in the United States. From the statistician I was to learn about all the categories of potatoes that are tallied. It turns out the U.S. Department of Agriculture counts all the potato chips sold every month, even how many Pringle potato chips are consumed. The statistician offered to place me on the mailing list to receive all this free monthly data.

The Art Of Getting An Expert To Talk

The information explosion requires greater reliance on experts in order to sift through the proliferation of data. Cultivating an expert, however, demands an entirely different set of skills from using a library or a publication. You must know how to treat people so that they are ready, willing and able to give the information you need. It is human nature for almost anyone to want to share their knowledge, but your approach will determine whether you ultimately get the expert to open up. So it is your job to create an environment that makes an individual want to share his expertise. Remember when dealing with both public and private sector experts, they will get the same paycheck whether they give you two weeks worth of free help or if they cut the conversation short.

Expectations: The 7-Phone Call Rule

There is no magic to finding an expert. It is simply a numbers game which takes an average of seven telephone calls. Telephone enough people and keep asking each for a lead. The magic lies in how much information the expert will share once you find that individual. This is why it is essential to remember "the 7-phone call rule".

If you make several calls and begin to get upset because you are being transferred from one person to another, you will be setting yourself up to fail once you locate the right expert. What is likely to happen is that when your "Charlie Porter" picks up his telephone he is going to hear you complaining about how sick and tired you are of getting the runaround from his organization. Well, to Charlie, you don't sound like you are going to be the highlight of his day. He will instantly figure out how to get rid of you.

This explains why some people are able to get information and others fail. Seasoned researchers know it is going to take a number of telephone calls and they will not allow themselves to get impatient. After all, the runaround is an unavoidable part of the information gathering process. Consequently, the first words that come out of your mouth are extremely important because they set the stage for letting the expert want to help you.

Ten Basic Telephone Tips

Here are a few pointers to keep in mind when you are casting about for an expert. These guidelines amount to basic common sense but are very easy to forget by the time you get to that sixth or seventh phone call.

1) Introduce Yourself Cheerfully
The way you open the conversation will set the tone for the entire interview. Your greeting and initial comment should be cordial and cheerful. They should give the feeling that this is not going to be just another telephone call, but a pleasant interlude in his or her day.

2) Be Open And Candid
You should be as candid as possible with your source since you are asking the same of him. If you are evasive or deceitful in explaining your needs or motives, your source will be reluctant to provide you with information. If there are certain facts you cannot reveal such as client confidentiality, explain just that. Most people will understand.

3) Be Optimistic
Throughout the entire conversation you should exude a sense of confidence. If you call and say "You probably aren't the right person" or "You don't have any information, do you?" it makes it easy for the person to say "You're right, I cannot help you." A positive attitude will encourage your source to stretch his mind to see how he might be able to help you.

4) Be Humble And Courteous
You can be optimistic and still be humble. Remember the old adage that you can catch more flies with honey than you can with vinegar. People in general, and experts in particular, love to tell others what they know, as long as their position of authority is not questioned or threatened.

5) Be Concise
State your problem simply. A long-winded explanation may bore your contact and reduce your chances for getting a thorough response.

6) Don't Be A "Gimme"
A "gimme" is someone who says "give me this" or "give me that", and has little consideration for the other person's time or feelings.

7) Be Complimentary
This goes hand in hand with being humble. A well-placed compliment about your source's expertise or insight about a particular topic will serve you well. In searching for information in large organizations, you are apt to talk to many colleagues of your source, so it wouldn't hurt to convey the respect that your "Charlie Porter" commands, for example, "Everyone I spoke to said you are the person I must talk with." It is reassuring to know you have the respect of your peers.

8) Be Conversational
Avoid spending the entire time talking about the information you need. Briefly mention a few irrelevant topics such as the weather, the Washington Redskins, or the latest political campaign. The more social you are without being too chatty, the more likely that your source will open up.

9) Return The Favor
You might share with your source information or even gossip you have picked up elsewhere. However, be certain not to

betray the trust of either your client or another source. If you do not have any relevant information to share at the moment, it would still be a good idea to call back when you are further along in your research.

10) Send Thank You Notes
A short note, typed or handwritten, will help ensure that your source will be just as cooperative in the future.

Case Study: Jelly Beans

In our information society, which produces thousands of databases and other resources every day, it seems that most decision makers rely primarily on traditional information sources. More often than not executives will spend lots of time and money trying to determine the size of a market or information about a competitor, and if the answer cannot be found through conventional sources, the corporate decision is made without the information. This does not have to be the case.

We believe that you can find solid information for almost any problem, no matter how sensitive the issue may be, if you use some unorthodox research techniques. To illustrate this point, here is a step-by-step account of how one of our researchers succeeded in gathering figures on the U.S. market for jelly beans when a Fortune 500 firm came up empty-handed after exhausting all traditional sources. The prevailing view both inside and outside the industry was that this piece of the information puzzle could not be obtained.

It should be said at the outset that the estimates Information USA, Inc. finally obtained must not be regarded as 100% accurate, but they do represent the best available figures and, most likely, come within 10% to 15% of the actual number.

Opening Round

Faced with the problem of finding the U.S. market for jelly beans, we already knew that our client had contacted the major market research firms, did some literature searches, and came up with practically no useful information. As is evident from this case study, this information hunt occurred when Ronald Reagan was President.

1) The first call was to the U.S. Department of Commerce to locate the government's jelly bean expert. We were referred to Cornelius Kenny, the confectionery industry expert. Mr. Kenny was out that day and would call us back when he returned to the office.

2) A search of Gale's *Encyclopedia of Associations* identified four relevant trade associations. However, upon contacting them we were told that they provide information only to their members.

3) The White House seemed like a good bet because of Ronald Reagan's fondness for jelly beans and all the resulting publicity. The Public Affairs office at 1600 Pennsylvania Avenue said that it never obtained statistical information on the industry but could tell us tales about a life-size water buffalo and portraits of the President constructed of jelly beans. However, they suggested that we contact several lobbying organizations. Calls to these groups proved fruitless.

4) A call to the U.S. Bureau of the Census uncovered John Streeter, an analyst who monitors the panned candy industry.

He told us:

* jelly beans have never been counted and there would be no way to get the answer;

* the non-Chocolate Panned Candy category within the Bureau's Annual Confectionery Survey contains jelly beans;

* the seasonal category of the Non-Chocolate Panned Candies, according to his estimates, contains 90% jelly beans because most jelly beans are sold during Easter and they are about the only non-chocolate panned manufactured candy sold on a seasonal basis;

* $37,804,000 worth of non-chocolate panned candy was shipped by U.S. manufacturers in 1984, which represents about 48,354,000 pounds; the figures for total non-chocolate panned candy for 1984 totaled $251,525,000 and 237,308,000 pounds; and

* government regulations prohibited him from revealing the names of jelly bean manufacturers, but he did refer us to two trade associations he thought might help.

So this analyst at the Census Bureau, who tried to discourage us with warnings that no such figure for the jelly bean market exists, actually gave us quite concrete information as well as some valuable leads.

Armed and Dangerous With A Little Information

At this point we had a market estimate from one government expert based on a figure generated by the U.S. Bureau of the Census. It may have sounded like the answer we were after, but taking that figure to our client at this juncture would be premature and possibly irresponsible. The main drawback was the estimate reflected only one person's opinion, and although he was an expert, he was not a true industry observer as one would be if they were actually in the business of selling jelly beans. At this stage our strategy was to find people in the industry who could give us their interpretation of these figures.

The Census expert referred us to one of the trade associations we already had contacted. However, when we called back saying that Mr. Streeter at the Census Bureau suggested we call them, the association promptly responded with a list of the 25 major jelly bean manufacturers. This is an example of how using the name of a government expert can get you in the door. When we phoned several manufacturers, they laughed when we told them of our effort to ascertain the market for jelly beans. Jelly beans had never been counted, they told us, and their advice was to give up.

At this point Mr. Kenny, the confectionery expert at the U.S. Department of Commerce called us back and he, too, said that the market had never been measured. However, he did hazard a guess that the jelly bean market could be roughly 50% of the total Census figure for Non-Chocolate Panned Candy.

A separate call to a private research group which does trend analysis by surveying grocery stores shared its estimate that 90% of all jelly beans are sold at Easter.

Easier To Be A Critic Than A Source

Our lack of success in dealing with a few manufacturers caused us to change tactics. Instead of asking them to estimate the size of the jelly bean market, we began asking them what they thought of the figures we received from the industry analysts at the Commerce Department as well as the Census Bureau. We decided to try to find someone who actually filled out the Census survey and get a reaction to the Census figures. We spoke with the owner of Herbert Candies, a small candy company. He gave us his 1984 jelly bean production and cost statistics, told us he filled out the Census report, and readily explained what he thought the Census statistics meant in terms of jelly bean production and cost. Furthermore, using his calculator, he helped us arrive at national figures for 1984. He also told us which companies manufacture 80% of the jelly beans produced in the country.

Now, armed with actual figures for 1984 jelly bean production, average cost per pound, average number of jelly beans in a pound, and the percentage of jelly beans produced during Easter, we resumed calling manufacturers -- this time to get their opinion of our figures. This was the real turning point in dealing with the manufacturers. Because everyone in the industry knew that there were no exact numbers on the size of the jelly bean market, as professionals, they were afraid to give a figure because anyone could say it was wrong. However, because they were experts in the business, they were not afraid to criticize someone else's information. Reactions from insiders were just what we needed to help hone a good working number. The manufacturers were able to tell us why our figures were good or not and they gave us sound reasons why the numbers should be adjusted, such as "Based on our sales figures your numbers sound a little low," or "Not all manufacturers report to the Bureau of the Census, so that figure may be low."

To show how this tactic prompted many manufacturers to be candid about both the industry and their sales in particular, here are highlights of our conversations with nine companies. What is presented below may seem to be too detailed, but after reviewing them we hope that it proves our point about how open business executives can be about their company.

1)   Owner, Herbert Candies (small manufacturer and retailer)

*   90% of jelly beans are sold at Easter
*   60% of Census seasonal category are jelly beans
*   average cost of jelly beans is $1 per pound
*   when President Reagan first got into office the jelly bean market shot up 150% but now it is back to normal
*   4 companies have 80% of the market with E.J. Brach the largest at 40%, Brock the second largest, followed by Herman Goelitz and Maillard
*   his company sold 30,000 pounds this past year and 90% at

Easter; 10,000 were gourmet beans at $3.20 per pound and 20,000 were regular jelly beans at $2.80 per pound

2)   Marketing Department, Nabisco Confectionery

*   suggested we call SAMI, a private market research firm
*   estimated 90% of jelly beans are sold at Easter
*   confirmed that E.J. Brach has 40% of the market

3)   Vice President of Marketing and Sales, Herman Goelitz (producer of "Bellies", Ronald Reagan's favorite)

*   between 35% and 50% of his jelly beans are sold at Easter
* $1.00 per pound could be the average retail price
*   a retailer can purchase jelly beans at $.60 per pound
*   the retail price ranges between $1.25 and $5 per pound

4)   General Manager, Burnell's Fine Candy (manufacturer of hanging bag jelly beans)

*   75% of jelly beans are sold at Easter
* $.60 to $.75 per pound is average manufacturer's price
* $1.59 is the average retail price
*   75% of Census seasonal category is probably jelly beans

5)   Senior VP of Marketing and Sales, E.J. Brach (largest manufacturer)

*   produces 24 million jelly beans annually at an average price of $.86 per pound
*   there are approximately 100 beans per pound
*   Brach's selling price is about industry average
*   they have about 50% of the market
*   90% of the jelly beans sold at Easter sounds too high

6)   Product Manager of Marketing Department, Brock Candy (second largest manufacturer)

*   85% to 95% of all jelly beans are sold at Easter
*   average price paid by retailers is $.59 to $.99 per pound
*   there are 130 to 140 jelly beans in a pound
*   E.J. Brach has 40% to 50% of the jelly bean business -- 32 to 45 million jelly beans sold in a year sounds correct given Brock's production figures; but probably it is closer to the high side
*   Brock Candy is number 2 in the industry
*   there are not many jelly bean manufacturers and basing total production on E.J. Brach's sales figures is a good way to arrive at an industry estimate

7)   Traffic Manager, Powell Confectionery (medium size producer)

*   75% of jelly beans are sold at Easter judging from Powell's sales
*   average retail price $.75 to $.80 per pound and the average manufacturer's price is $.65 to $.70 per pound

* 35 to 45 million jelly beans per year sounds reasonable
* it seems fair to double E.J.Brach production figures to get the total market because it has about 50% share of the market

8) President, Ferrara Panned Candy (largest panned candy producer)

* familiar with Census data and believes that jelly beans represent about 75% to 80% of the seasonal sales 80% to 90% of all jelly beans are sold at Easter
* 32 to 45 million pounds per year seems a bit low
* E.J. Brach has 50% of the packaged jelly bean market but has less than half of the bulk jelly bean market

9) New Product Development Manager, Farley Candy

* familiar with Census data and believes that the numbers are understated because not all companies report their figures
* an industry estimate of 32 to 50 million pounds per year seems low

So much for all those who discouraged us from even tackling this issue of the market for jelly beans. All the data poured forth during these telephone conversations provided more information than our Fortune 500 client ever expected.

Deciding On An Estimate

As you can see from the interviews outlined above, traffic managers all the way up to company presidents were willing to give us their best estimate of the size of the market and even divulge their own company's sales figures.

After government experts, the figure seemed to cluster around the 45 to 50 million pound range. It may not be that obvious from just reading the highlights of our interviews, but that consensus became apparent after talking with about a dozen people.

Information Exchange Is A People Business

It is just surprising what company executives and government experts are willing to tell you if they are approached in the right way. You can find the answer to any question (or at least a good estimate) as long as you expect to make many phone calls and you treat each person on the other end of the telephone in a friendly, appreciative way.

The biggest difference between those who succeed in their information quest and those who fail boils down to whether or not they believe the information exists. If you persist in thinking the information can be found, nine times out of ten you will get what you need.

Coping With Misinformation

One of the major problems encountered by researchers is determining the accuracy of the information collected. If you are doing traditional market research and using primary sources, accuracy is not that complicated. Traditional market researchers are well aware of survey methods, sampling techniques, and computing errors using statistical standard deviation analysis. However, if you are a desk researcher, like Information USA, Inc. which relies on secondary sources and expert opinion, how do you compute the standard deviation for error? The answer is that you cannot use hard statistical techniques, but you can employ other soft forms of error checking.

Major Causes for Error and Prevention Tactics

Problem #1: Lost In The Jargon

It is not uncommon for researchers to be dealing frequently in areas of expertise where they do not have complete command of the industry jargon. In such situations it is easy to believe that you have found the exact information needed only to find out later that you missed the mark considerably. This is a common trap to fall into when fishing in unfamiliar waters. And if you have to do the job quickly, it is easy to believe that you know more than you really do or to avoid getting the complete explanation of specific jargon because you do not want to waste the time of the expert who is giving you the information. Here is an experience of a U.S. Department of Agriculture expert which illustrates this point.

This government expert received a call one day from an assistant at the White House. This hot shot, who acted pretty impressed with himself, said he was in a meeting with both the President and the head of the Meat Packers Association and needed to know right then the official number of cows in the United States. The livestock expert asked the presidential aide if that was exactly what he meant and then when he impatiently responded "Yes," the bureaucrat told him the figure. Within minutes the White House staffer called back and said the president of the Meat Packers Association laughed at him and claimed that there were twice as many cows. The assistant then realized he needed the number of all cows -- all "male cows" -- as well as all female ones.

The White House aide had a problem with semantics, probably a city slicker who never knew the difference between cows and cattle. This can happen to anyone, not only a self-assured Presidential aide. For example, if you want to know the market for computers, are you talking about free standing units or central processing units?

Solution #1: Act A Little Dumb

In order to prevent this type of embarrassment, you have to find an expert with whom you are comfortable. When I say comfortable, I mean someone you can go to and ask dumb questions. You will get the most help if you act very humble in your approach. If you request information with the arrogance of the over confident White House staffer, you may be given only the facts you ask for and nothing more. However, if you call up an expert and say something like "Oh God, can you please help me? I don't really know much about this, but my boss needs to know how many cows there are in the country." With more than a hint of indecision in your voice and honestly admitting you don't know much about the field, the expert is more likely to ask you some key questions that will ensure that you get the right figures.

Problem #2: Believing The Written Word Or A Computer

This is a more serious problem than the difficulties and confusion surrounding industry jargon. Mastering the terminology just requires a little homework. However, overcoming a deepseated belief that information either from a computer, in published sources, or from the government is always accurate can be like changing your religion. It took me years, as well as dozens of professional embarrassments, to overcome this problem.

Just because a figure is in print does not make it gospel. Remember the saying, "Figures don't lie, but liars can figure." Keep this in mind before betting the farm on anything you read in print, even if it comes out of a computer. A good illustration which follows pertains to Census Bureau information.

A few years ago we were doing a market study on stereo speakers and discovered that the figures the U.S. Bureau of the Census had for this market were off by over 50 percent. No one in the industry complained to the government because the industry was small and couldn't be bothered. But most of the companies involved knew that the figure was misleading and had no use for it. Another case is a Fortune 500 company which told us that for over 5 years it filled out the U.S. Census form under the wrong Standard Industrial Code (SIC). An important caveat -- this firm ranks as the number two manufacturer in the industry.

You have to remember that number crunchers at the Census Bureau and other such organizations are not always interested in the meaning behind the numbers. Much of their work is simply taking a number from block A, adding it to the number in block B, and placing the result in block C. Verifying where the numbers come from is not their job.

Tips On Finding Information

Published sources are an even bigger problem than government data. Many believe that what you read in a magazine or a newspaper or hear on television or radio must be true. Nonsense, anyone and their brother can be interviewed by a magazine or newspaper, and usually what they say will get printed in a magazine or quoted on the air as long as it is not too outrageous. And, sometimes you are more likely to get it into print if it **is** outrageous. After all, most news stories are just accounts of what someone said as interpreted by a journalist.

The more general the media, the less accurate it may be about an industry. In other words, an article in the ice cream industry trade magazine is more likely to be accurate than a similar story in the *New York Times*. The trade journal will have reporters who cover that particular industry and they will more than likely be able to flush out bad data. The newspaper, on the other hand, will do only one ice cream story a year, and will print almost anything it hears. So just because someone is quoted in an article does not mean that the information is correct.

I have seen much of this firsthand when on nationwide book promotion tours. In newspaper interviews or on radio and television talk shows, I can say almost anything and they will print or broadcast it, as is. I will give countless facts and figures based on my own biased research (remember that I am trying to sell books), and hardly ever will I be questioned or seriously challenged before, during, or after the fact, about their authenticity. I don't know if it is laziness, apathy, or just plain lack of time that allows so much unchallenged information to be presented in the media. I have even blatantly lied to a reporter who thought of himself as a clone of CBS' Mike Wallace of "60 Minutes." Before I started doing media interviews, I assumed that any good reporter worth his or her salt could find holes in what I presented and would expose me as some kind of fraud. I did not know how they would do it, but I guess my own insecurity prompted me to prepare for the worst. The reality is that most reporters spend little or no time studying the topic before they interview you, and if you become annoyed or angry, especially with this Mike Wallace type described above, you can blow them away with an exaggerated fact or half-truth that he will never be able to verify.

Solution #2: Find Another Industry Expert

Whether a figure comes from the Census Bureau, a trade magazine or off the tube, your best bet for determining whether the number is accurate and also the one you need is to track down an industry expert, other than the one quoted, and ask him to comment on the figure. What you are seeking is their biased opinion about the accuracy of the stated figure. If the

expert believes the figure is correct but doesn't know why, find another expert.

Problem #3: Trusting An Expert

This may seem to contradict what I just said in the solution to problem #2, but stick with me and you will see the difference.

There are many times when you cannot start with published or printed data and all you can do is pick the brains of experts within the industry. This means that you will be getting facts and figures based on the best available guess from experts. Many times this is the only way to get the information you need.

Getting this type of soft data can be full of danger. After having worked for hours trying to find a friendly soul to share with you his innermost thoughts about the facts and figures of an industry or company, you do not want to turn him off with an antagonistic remark about the accuracy of his data.

Solution #3: Ask Why?

The best way to judge whether a source is knowledgeable about the fact or figure they gave you is to ask them how they arrived at the number. Such a question will likely initiate one of the following responses:

"I don't know. It's the best I can think of."
- A response like this will be a clue that the expert may not know what he is talking about and you should continue your search for a knowledgeable and willing expert.

"This is the figure I read from an industry association study."
- This should lead you to verify that such a study was conducted and to attempt to interview people involved with the report.

"The industry figure is XX because our sales are half that and we are number 2 in the industry."
- This is probably one of the best types of answers you can get. Any time an industry expert gives you a figure based on something he is positive about, you can almost take it to the bank. The best you can do after this is to find other industry analysts and ask them to comment on the figure you were given.

Misinformation can lead to a decision making disaster. Following the simple techniques described above can take you a long way down the road to making near excellent decisions based on near perfect information.

Using Industry Sources And Overcoming The "Negative Researching Syndrome"

When you cannot find company information from traditional sources or government documents, it is necessary to dig around the industry in order to uncover it. This is likely to be the only place you can turn to when you really want:

1) the scoop on a company's pricing policy;
2) facts on distribution channels for a given product;
3) details about a company's potential future strategy; or
4) estimates on the profitability of a privately held company.

We at Information USA, Inc. are seeing many more research projects which fall into this category, and would like to share with you some of our recent experiences in solving this type of problem.

Two Pronged Approach

Unlike traditional research work, hunting for specific information within an industry involves two separate approaches. The first is identifying potential sources. The second and equally difficult job is developing a strategy for interviewing these sources.

Although most researchers probably would think that the biggest problem is figuring out what organizations and companies to contact, we find this not to be the case when dealing with industry sources. We believe that the toughest challenges our researchers face are improving their techniques and attitudes for obtaining information. Other types of research are not as "technique sensitive," because relying on industry sources means getting in close range to the target company. Although technique is the major trouble spot, let's tackle the problem of sources first.

Identifying Industry Sources

When I refer to industry sources, I am talking about those organizations and individuals whose business it is to know what is going on in the overall industry as well as activities among individual companies. These are the sources which can provide sensitive information that you cannot find elsewhere. Those who know their business and industry have to know about pricing, profitability, and even the strategy of those companies which comprise a particular industry. Most likely these individuals have never seen a given company's in-house strategic plan or a private company's profit and loss statement, but they are usually knowledgeable enough to give you estimates which can be as close as plus or minus 15% of the actual figures. They also will be familiar with an industry's "rule of thumb" in terms of operation, and can offer educated guesses on important figures, like sales based on the number of employees, or production based on the size of equipment, or strategy based on purchasing plans and sales literature. A

researcher's job is to find industry people in a position to know and then to get them to share their knowledge with you.

Starting Points For Sources

Here are six major checkpoints for identifying industry sources.

I. Government Experts:

These sources can be the easiest to talk with and also can usually suggest leads to sources who in turn will identify others within the industry. Normally these are analysts within the federal government and sometimes within state government whose job it is to monitor a specific industry either for the purpose of formulating government policy or preparing market analysis which is used by both the public and private sectors.

Examples of U.S. government industry experts whose focus is primarily on policy are Energy Department specialists who study potential applications for wind energy, or biotechnology experts at the Department of Agriculture who stay current on this research field as it pertains to the food industry. In contrast, those federal experts whose orientation is geared toward market analysis are found at the Department of Commerce who produce the annual *U.S. Industrial Outlook*, and the analysts at the U.S. International Trade Commission who investigate the impact of imports on American industry.

Finding policy oriented experts can be difficult because they are scattered throughout the vast federal bureaucracy. Try to determine which agency in the government probably follows a particular industry under which a given company falls. For food products, try the U.S. Department of Agriculture and the U.S. Food and Drug Administration; for products involving pesticides, check with the U.S. Environmental Protection Agency; for companies in new technologies, contact the Office of Technology Assessment on Capitol Hill. Other resources which will help you identify where these policy experts are hiding include:

1) *U.S. Government Manual* (Government Printing Office);

2) *Lesko's Info-Power* by Matthew Lesko, (published by Information, USA);

3) Local Federal Information Center (look in the U.S. government section of your local telephone book under General Services Administration); or

4) The Washington or district office of your U.S. Representative or Senator.

Below are the main telephone numbers for finding the two major offices which have 100 or more experts with market analysis orientation who cover most every industry. Simply call and ask to speak to the expert who studies golf balls or music instruments or whatever industry you are investigating:

- International Trade Administration (ITA), U.S. Department of Commerce, Washington, DC 20230, 202-377-1461: over 100 analysts who monitor all the major industries in the U.S. and the companies within these industries ranging from athletic products to truck trailers; and

- U.S. International Trade Commission (ITC), Office of Industries, 701 E Street, NW, Room 254, Washington, DC 20436, 202-523-0146: experts who analyze the impact of world trade on U.S. industries ranging from audio components to x-ray apparatus.

Refer to the section on "Experts" for a list of these federal industry experts.

There are no concrete rules for locating state industry experts. Every state government works differently, and the level of expertise varies tremendously. However, there is a trend at the state level to accumulate more data especially within those industries, for instance, high-tech companies, which the state sees as having potential for contributing to their economic development. The starting place for finding a specialist is the state department of commerce and economic development. These offices are located in the state capital and are easy to track down by telephoning the state government operator.

II. Industry Observers:

Industry observers may be affiliated either with trade magazines or trade associations. They are in a position to oversee what is going on in the industry and they collect details about specific companies within the industry. Associations can identify the magazines that report on their industry and vice versa. If you have trouble getting started, contact either the federal analysts at the ITA and ITC described above or consult the *Encyclopedia of Associations* (Gale Research Company) at a local library.

You have to be careful whom you talk with when contacting these organizations. Usually when you call a trade association looking for information about the industry, they will connect you with the library; and when you contact a magazine, you are likely to be switched to the research department. These offices are good to touch base with, but they normally know about only the more obvious published material and are not very helpful in getting answers to the more difficult questions.

After you have contacted the libraries or research departments of these organizations, be sure to call back with a different tactic in order to get through to the association executives and editors of trade magazines. These are the people who are immersed in the industry and pick up bits and pieces of information about companies which rarely show up in the published literature.

III. The Distribution Chain:

People within the chain of distribution can be wholesalers, jobbers, distributors or anyone who acts as an intermediary between the manufacturer and the end user. Although not all products are sold through middlemen, many are, and if the company under investigation uses middlemen, it can be an information bonanza. Most people in these kinds of businesses are down to earth types who generally like people and are approachable. What is also advantageous about dealing with distributors is that they normally handle the products of the company you are interested in as well as those of its competitors. As a result they can be very helpful in comparing strategies and assessing market share.

Who do you talk to in these organizations? You try to talk to the buyers or sales reps. This normally does not leave many people in between. How do you find these organizations? Usually it is quite easy. Most trade associations or magazines can provide you with lists. Or, it is also easy to call up your target company and pretend you want to purchase one of their products, at which point they will be more than happy to inundate you with the names and telephone numbers of suppliers.

IV. Customers:

This may sound foolish to some, but for most industries customers are approachable and often prove to be valuable sources of company information. By talking to the buyers of a half dozen major retail chains, you can determine the market for goods ranging from tablecloths to toys. And the buyers at a dozen or so major food chain stores can give you a clear picture of almost any consumer food product.

How do you find a company's customers? If they fall into groups like supermarkets or department stores, their industry will be organized enough so you can contact the relevant trade association or trade magazines for a listing of members. Also, many times the target company's literature will proudly display major clients or customers. Most industries also produce a buyer's guide which will identify these sources. Again the association or trade magazines will be aware of such publications.

V. Competitors:

Contacting the competitors of a target company may be difficult if they are also your competitor. If the company is not in the same industry as your firm, or someone else is doing the research, competitors can often provide all the information sought. Obviously these are the people who really have to know about the target company. They are in the best position to know how well the company is doing compared to them and what their competitor is likely to do in the future.

VI. Suppliers And Complimentary Product Manufacturers:

Don't overlook suppliers to the target company. These companies can be very helpful because the target company is just a customer to them and what they know about a company they are likely to assume that everyone knows. Many suppliers are directly dependent upon the success of their customer and make it their business to know how well they are doing and can offer predictions about future plans. Their livelihood depends upon knowing this information. Tire manufacturers have to know all about automobile companies and the manufacturers of equipment which make shoes have to know all about shoe companies. The same holds true for complementary products like barbecue utensils and charcoal briquettes, or electric popcorn poppers and popcorn kernels.

The same technique described earlier for finding customers can also be used for locating suppliers and complementary product manufacturers.

Preventing Early Pitfalls And Other Techniques

Developing a good technique is crucial when digging for information within an industry. Finding a source is simply a numbers game, and by following the outline presented above anyone doing the research will eventually run into a couple of people who will have most of the answers you need. However, creating the proper atmosphere for that source to want to share information with you is contingent on both attitude and technique. Here are some of the major problems you are likely to encounter.

A bad start leads to depression. I've seen this happen to even the best of researchers. They will start out confident about a project investigating a company's pricing policy or profitability. After spending a half a day on the project and talking to a half dozen industry experts, they are ready to throw in the towel and give up. What normally happens is that the researcher has run into trouble getting through to anyone who knows much about the company or that anyone they did happen to talk with has been full of negative comments such as "There's no way to get that kind of information."

After initial feedback like this, it is natural for researchers to begin to believe what they are hearing and to forget about their past research triumphs. This faulty start can be even more devastating to a novice who has yet to complete a number of research projects. This problem intensifies as the researcher continues because all the negative feedback poisons their relaxed, friendly interviewing style and upbeat attitude about research. This pessimism creeps into their voice when talking to people within the industry. Soon they will start a conversation by saying things like "You don't have any information on company X, do you?"

Once this begins to happen the researcher should stop immediately and get some help. This "Negative Researching Syndrome" will begin to feed on itself and will only get worse and worse unless something drastic happens.

How do you cure "Negative Researching Syndrome"? Well it isn't easy, and unless the researcher is very experienced, it usually requires the help of a senior researcher. What we usually do when we sense a researcher falling into this trap is to tell him that it is a bad time of day to be making these kinds of calls, or to quit for the day. Another approach is to suggest the researcher pick up the next day but only after we have had a chance to get together to talk about the project. However, before our session I try to make sure the researcher is given an easy short term project just to build up confidence. Then we brainstorm about one or all of the following strategies.

1) Try a different segment of the industry. Instead of talking with distributors, switch to retailers; move from customers to government experts and so on. Anything to try and find someone in the industry who may be more willing to talk.

2) Describe past success stories. We will remind the researcher of projects in the past where we started out thinking that we were never going to get anything and how it all eventually came together. I'll even describe some of my own personal experiences doing research where experts said it couldn't be done. And, of course, we'll remind them that this is really the reason we are getting paid. If it was easy, no one would need us.

3) Try a different "story line." This is explained next.

A Bad "Story Line" Can Kill A Project

A bad story line can also be the chief cause of "Negative Researching Syndrome." What do we mean by a story line? It is the explanation, or reason, the researcher gives for needing the information. If the researcher is uncomfortable with the story, a potential source will sense this unease and be reluctant to talk. In most research this is not a problem. In traditional projects conventional reference sources are used for gathering information, and all you have to do is identify yourself and ask whether certain information is available. However, in dealing with industry sources the situation changes markedly; they are not comfortable just knowing the researcher's name and affiliation. Industry sources want to know what you are after and why. And this is when the story line can make or break it.

Being comfortable with a "story line" can be a complicated process. The bottom line is that you are not after information that is proprietary. Consequently, it is essential for **you** to feel comfortable with what you are saying, because if you don't no one will open up.

If you are uneasy that your story line is too far fetched or something you don't know enough details about, you will fail to convince yourself and as a result it will backfire. Saying that you work for the FBI or write for the Nuts and Bolts magazine are the kinds of stories that spell trouble. Furthermore, most researchers are basically too honest to stretch the truth that far and it begins to eat into their guilt. As they do get deeper into the research, this guilt will aggravate the troubling "Negative Researching Syndrome," and the researcher is bound to wind up empty handed.

Here are a few sample explanations that may not be too improbable.

- Your company is doing a market study on all the companies within the industry. [Not just the target company.]

- You are trying to write an article about the industry and plan to submit it to a trade magazine.

- You are a student working on a paper. [Not a highly useful story but usually one that is easy to live with.]

- You have a client or your boss wants you to investigate the possibility of developing a competing brand and you are trying to get industry comments about such an idea. [People will more likely give opinions than information on a company, but their opinions will include company information.]

- You are working on a speech about the industry and trying to get some background material.

Also, if your story is too negative or "predatory," no one will **want** to give you the information. This, too, will show up when you are talking with industry experts and cause a researcher to come up empty handed. In other words, don't call up an industry source and say, "I am with company X, which is a major competitor of company Y. Can you tell me about the pricing strategy of company Y so that we can try to put them out of business." Many researchers worry that this is what they are doing, and this anxiety and belief will lead to "Negative Researching Syndrome" along with no information.

Choosing a right story line can determine the success or failure of your project. Be sure you can live with it and feel comfortable and honest, and that this explanation will make those in the industry comfortable enough to share information with you. If a researcher's story line does not meet these two criteria, be prepared for a long and hard, and more than likely, frustrating and unsuccessful hunting expedition.

What's Good and Bad About Using Computers In The Information Age

Food Processors, PCs and Other Miracle Products

Before you purchase a data base, first think about what you are actually buying. Is it the steak or the sizzle? Many of today's commercial data base vendors are selling their services the way food processor sales reps sold their wares a few years back. Remember the sales pitch that this kitchen appliance could make the entire meal every day of the week. However, after buying this expensive gadget we found that puree of steak did not taste as good as a charcoaled piece of meat and that carrot mousse did not suit our children's taste buds. So now we all have this equipment sitting on the kitchen counter which we use a few times a month to make coleslaw or milk shakes because the blender we bought 10 years ago is stashed away in the attic.

This phenomenon also has struck personal computers. A few years ago buyers were sold on the belief that the world would pass them by if they did not have a PC and, furthermore, that this sophisticated machine would solve all their problems. We were told that daily tasks such as balancing the checkbook or keeping track of recipes would virtually disappear. However, PC owners discovered that if they never balanced their checkbook by hand, they were never going to do it by computer. It actually was more complicated and took longer to use the computer than the old-fashioned way. And, keeping 50 or so recipes in a $1,000 machine that is located at the other end of the house proved inconvenient. People soon realized that the "practical applications," like word processing and spread sheets, were not typical household activities. And, as a result, computer sales began to plummet.

Waiting For The Technology To Mature

One can safely predict that computers will eventually be easier, cheaper and more practical to use as the sophistication of the technology improves. The same pattern occurred with the introduction of the automobile.

When cars first rolled off the assembly line, the primary advantages they offered over the horse as a traditional means of transportation were technology and novelty. An automobile cost at least ten times more than a horse. These complex machines were difficult to start and required special fuel that was hard to come by. Special clothing, goggles and other paraphernalia were necessary for protection against dust and the elements. And cars were very limited in where they could go because of the lack of good roadways. All of these problems could not compare with the simple act of jumping on a horse and going anywhere. It could not be more obvious that the horse still was the fastest, most convenient, and inexpensive mode of transportation. But even then people were willing to be oversold on the use of a new technology. They bought the sizzle instead of the steak. And those who waited until the cost was worth the benefit of the application found that as the

technology improved, the new product was faster, cheaper and easier to use than the original. And with the increase in available software, or highways in the case of automobiles, there were many more uses and applications for the new product than the old one.

By waiting for the technology to evolve into a cost effective alternative for a specific application, consumers who held on to their horses before buying the first automobiles found that they got to their destinations a lot sooner for a lot less money than the new car buyer. And when these patient consumers purchased the later model, their machine could do a great deal more.

Pros And Cons Of Data Bases

Overselling Computerized Data Bases

A similar story continues to unfold with online data bases. Slick sales reps tell us that we can solve all of our information problems with their data bases. Again buyers, because of their infatuation with the technology, are dazzled at the notion of getting the answer to a million dollar question by simply dialing up an all knowing computer. In order to avoid spending money on novelty items, one has to see if the price of obtaining information via high tech is worth the money compared to relying on traditional alternatives.

Helpful With Large Amounts of Info

Data bases are especially good at handling large amounts of information, and there are literally hundreds of computerized systems that perform this function. These services index and abstract everything from all business-oriented periodicals to those which provide such bibliographic help only in a certain area such as energy. If this is your field of interest, you should think about what you will be paying for. Most of these types of data bases are aimed at the professional user and can be expensive. Studies show that the average professional user of data bases spends about $100 per hour. What will you be getting at these prices?

A $100 Seminar On How To Shop At Macy's

Many of the professional data bases are also very complicated to use. It is the only industry where commercial vendors charge their customers for taking a course on how to spend money on their products. Wouldn't it be something if Macy's Department Store charged you to take a class on how to shop at their store? This should be a clue that data bases are not for everyone.

Much of the material that is online is also available in print form. So you may be paying $100 per hour for the convenience of not dropping by your local library to look up the indexes manually. At $100 an hour you can buy a lot of library help.

Non-Discriminating Computers

Also remember that these bibliographic data bases sometimes create more problems than they solve. Searching a large data base on a subject can churn out 500 articles for you to review. The problem now comes in trying to identify the good articles, not to mention actually obtaining those which you select. The computer is attempting to cope with the information explosion by providing the capability to index any and all data that are generated. However, the computer does a very poor job at being selective. It cannot tell you whether an article is good or bad. This problem is only getting worse because anyone with a word processor can be a publisher within days and the commercial vendors are eager to acquire new data bases.

After you get bombarded with some 500 citations racing across the screen, you still may have to make a half dozen telephone calls to locate a real expert in the field who can suggest which are the best and most current articles to read. Or this expert may be able to give you the answer right over the telephone. Or, even better, he may be able to tell you what will be online next year because he is in the midst of writing or reviewing articles and manuscripts on that subject. **Remember, even though a report or survey is contained in a data base, that does not guarantee it is the latest available information.** Many data bases still rely on printed documentation, so many times there may be less expensive and easier ways to get your hands on more timely information. Refer to the section *Finding An Expert On Any Topic*.

Is Speed Worth The Price?

Getting information to you quickly is another function that data bases and telecommunications do exceedingly well. But here again, you must decide whether the convenience is worthy of the expense. Having the Associated Press wire service available during the day at $10 to $20 per hour may not be cost effective. Most of us barely get through the morning newspaper which costs a mere 50 cents and usually contains the highlights of what is reported on the wire service. And it is not yet feasible to scan your newspapers via computer either in bed or while commuting to work. No doubt getting the price of stocks as they are traded on the floor of the exchange at $75.00 per hour may be worth it if you are a big time investor and have to know stock movements minute-by-minute. But for most of our investment decisions, reading the stock quotes in our 50 cent morning paper is usually good enough. There are many professional applications in addition to big time investing in which speed would be worth a significant premium. It is wise to make sure that paying for this convenience is honestly necessary to you and your organization.

Help If You Are Reinventing The Wheel

Another aspect of telecommunications which appears to have much more potential than has been tapped is the ability of like minded people to communicate instantly. The pace at which

civilization develops seems dependent upon the speed at which ideas are refined and shared with others. Thus, one person on one side of the street is not wasting his or her time wrestling with a problem which has already been solved by someone else on the opposite side of the street. Telecommunications can aid in this process.

We once spoke to a veterinarian in Iowa who was faced with treating a three-legged dog and was uncertain how to proceed. As a member of a veterinarian bulletin board, he posed his question to this professional forum via computer. By the next morning there were answers from doctors in Florida and Massachusetts who had treated similar cases. He did not have to wait for the next annual meeting of veterinarians or for a relevant article to be published in the Journal of Veterinarian Medicine. Overnight he had his question answered and was free to tackle other unsolved problems.

Data Bases Are Here To Stay

By presenting all these negative aspects, we hope it is now more obvious that data bases contribute only a few pieces to solving an information puzzle. Many times the cost far exceeds the benefit. However, like the automobile, online data bases are here to stay, and in time, they will become more reasonably priced and offer applications users never dreamed could exist.

The online data base business, like other segments of the information industry, is a buyer's beware market. **Access to a $1,000 computerized information system that one firm is selling may be available for free or a modest charge from some public or non-profit organization.**

Some suggestions about purchasing data bases are described next which are intended to help you save some money while utilizing this current technology.

Money Saving Online Tips

Use The Free Data Base First

This may sound obvious, but the real problem is that you may not be aware of **free online data bases**. The free ones cannot afford to hire an expensive sales team to promote their systems. Here are some examples of how prices may vary widely for the same product.

- Dow Jones will charge up to $75 per hour for stock price information, or you can dial up the Max Uhle & Co. free data base in New York for some of the same data.

- You can tap into weather information on over 7 systems at prices ranging from $3 to $90 per hour, or you can access the National Weather Service's free data base provided by the federal government, which happens to be the basis for all the other sources of weather information.

- Online encyclopedias can cost up to $75 per hour if you are accessing systems like Dow Jones or BRS, or you can pay as little as $6 per hour on CompuServe or Delphi.

And, sometimes, it is the exact same file.

- There are over 7 software locator data bases which can cost as much as $165 on a system like Data Resources or access a free one provided by Searchmart Corp. in North Palm Beach, Florida.

- City or state demographics can cost over $100 per hour from such vendors as DIALOG, BRS or Chase Econometrics, or you can use the free data base offered by Conway Data, Inc. in Atlanta, Georgia.

- Dialcom makes news from the White House available for a minimum of $500 per month, or you can use the free Boston-based bulletin board called Yellowdata that also provides news originating from the Oval Office.

- The latest economic statistics that are sold on such systems as DRI and Chase for as much as $160 per hour can also be accessed for free from an electronic bulletin board maintained by the U.S. Department of Commerce. And the data are probably available sooner.

Lesko's Info-Power, a monthly newsletter published by Information USA, Inc., frequently identifies unadvertised bulletin boards and data bases that are free.

Consider Off-Line Alternatives

Typically what many commercial data base vendors do is find data that are available in other formats, such as hard copy, off-line printout and computer tape. You can often save a lot of money by not accessing online systems but rather getting the information in less high tech ways. Here are some examples:

- Legi-Slate, Commerce Clearing House, and Congressional Quarterly will charge you up to $190 per hour to find out the current status of legislation, or you can telephone for free searches and even obtain computer printouts on all the bills you are monitoring by using a free data base maintained by the U.S. Congress. (Refer to the section on *Legislation*.)

- Services such as Data Resources, I.P. Sharp, and Chase Econometrics will charge you $100 per hour to obtain demographic information on any country in the world, or you can call the International Demographic Center at the U.S. Bureau of the Census and simply request a free printout of the same information, and most likely it will be more current.

- DIALOG charges $45 per hour for information on U.S. exports, and the Trade Information Branch at the U.S. Department of Commerce will give you much of the same for free and the data will be more current because this government office is where DIALOG gets the information it sells.

- Control Data Corp. allows you to access a file called FARPS that will tell you where to get money in the government for your project, or you can contact the U.S. General Services Administration which maintains the file

and this government agency will do free searches for you.

- An energy bibliographic data base maintained by the U.S. Department of Energy in Tennessee is sold by DIALOG or it can be accessed directly from the government for free.

Use Data Base Wholesalers and Intermediaries

Many commercial vendors have initiation fees and monthly minimums which can increase your hourly cost considerably if you are not going to be a large user. One way to cut out these extra fees, at least until you see what your volume will be, is to use a data base wholesaler or intermediary. For example, if you are a subscriber to MCI, you receive access to the Dow Jones service without paying an additional initiation charge. You may begin to see more of these opportunities as the telecommunications industry develops further.

If you are a first time data base user and are interested in the non-consumer oriented electronic systems, it may be wise to have someone else do your searching. Even some so-called "user friendly" data bases are not as easy to use as their vendors claim. Online charges at $100 per hour mean you can ring up a hefty bill if you are just learning the system. Companies called information brokers will usually handle this for you. The best way to find available brokers is to contact your local reference librarian. They are in a good position to tell you what is available locally. If you have trouble with this approach, you may find help by calling: DIALOG Information Services, Customer Service, 1-800-334-2564.

This major commercial data base vendor maintains a list, by city, of those organizations which will provide this service tailored to your needs. Be sure to ask if a nearby public, academic or specialized library perform online retrieval services. If they do, it is probably going to be much cheaper. For example, the Brooklyn Business Library will do data base searches and charge only for direct out of pocket costs. An information broker is likely to cost you three to four times more. The following reference book identifies over 1,000 public and private organizations which are willing to do data base searches:

Online Data Base Search Services Directory, 1987 ($155)
Computer-Readable Data Bases, 1988 ($160)
    Gale Research Co.
    Book Tower, Dept. 77748
    Detroit, MI 48277-0748
    313-961-2242
    1-800-223-GALE
    Contact: Sandy Gore, extension 394

If you have a PC with a modem but have been reluctant to access the more complicated business data bases, you can call EASYNET. This firm will search some 7 major vendors for you and send the results to your computer. EASYNET covers most of the major business data bases and claims that their average search cost is $17.00. Contact by phone or modem:

    EASYNET Telebase Systems, Inc.
    763 W. Lancaster Avenue

1-800-EASYNET (modem number)
1-800-841-9553
215-526-2800

Save With Evening Discounts

Most of the commercial data base vendors offer discounts if you access their systems during the evening hours and other non-prime times. According to a survey of vendors, the average savings amounted to 50%, which means that if you encounter any volume at all, it would pay for you to hire someone to come into your office in the evening just to access certain data bases. Here is a sample of such discounts offered by some of the major vendors:

ADP Network Services	50%
BRS	62% to 80.9%

CompuServe	52%
DataNet	84.4%
Dialog	53.3%
Dow Jones	22% to 78%
Delphi	45%
Mead Data Central	50%
NewsNet	25%
Source	62.7%

Save On Telecommunications Software

The cheapest may be the best. A paper presented at the 1985 National Online Conference concluded that there was little difference between using a free telecommunications product for the IBM-PC called PC-TALK and a $120 product called Instantcom. To obtain a copy of PC-TALK, contact your local IBM users group.

The Freedom Of Information Act

A Citizen's Guide on Using the Freedom of Information Act and the Privacy Act of 1974 to Request Government Records

Introduction

A popular Government without popular information or the means of acquiring it, is but a Prologue to a Farce or a Tragedy or perhaps both. Knowledge will forever govern ignorance, and a people who mean to be their Governors, must arm themselves with the power knowledge gives. -- James Madison

The Freedom of Information Act (FOIA) established a presumption that records in the possession of agencies and departments of the Executive Branch of the United States government are accessible to the people. This was not always the approach to federal information disclosure policy. Before enactment of the Freedom of Information Act in 1966, the burden was on the individual to establish a right to examine these government records. There were no statutory guidelines or procedures to help a person seeking information. There were no judicial remedies for those denied access.

With the passage of the FOIA, the burden of proof shifted from the individual to the government. Those seeking information are no longer required to show a need for information. Instead, the "need to know" standard has been replaced by a "right to know" doctrine. The government now has to justify the need for secrecy.

The FOIA sets standards for determining which records must be made available for public inspection and which records can be withheld from disclosure. The law also provides administrative and judicial remedies for those denied access to records. Above all, the statute requires federal agencies to provide the fullest possible disclosure of information to the public.

The Privacy Act of 1974 is a companion to the FOIA. The Privacy Act regulates federal government agency recordkeeping and disclosure practices. The Act allows most individuals to seek access to federal agency records about themselves. The Act requires that personal information in agency files be accurate, complete, relevant, and timely. The Act allows the subject of a record to challenge the accuracy of the information. The Act requires that agencies obtain information directly from the subject of the record and that information gathered for one purpose not be used for another purpose. As with the FOIA, the Privacy Act provides civil remedies for individuals whose rights have been violated.

Another important feature of the Privacy Act is the requirement that each federal agency publish a description of each system of records maintained by the agency that contains personal information. This prevents agencies from keeping secret records.

The Privacy Act also restricts the disclosure of personally identifiable information by federal agencies. Together with the FOIA, the Privacy Act permits disclosure of most personal files to the individual who is the subject of the files. The two laws restrict disclosure of personal information to others when disclosure would violate privacy interests.

While both the FOIA and the Privacy Act encourage the disclosure of agency records, both laws also recognize the legitimate need to restrict disclosure of some information. For example, agencies may withhold information classified in the interest of national defense or foreign policy, trade secrets, and criminal investigatory files. Other specifically defined categories of confidential information may also be withheld.

The essential feature of both laws is that they make federal agencies accountable for information disclosure policies and practices. While neither law grants an absolute right to examine government documents, both laws provide a right to request records and to receive a response to the request. If a requested record cannot be released, the requester is entitled to a reason for the denial. The requester has a right to appeal the denial and, if necessary, to challenge it in court.

These procedural rights granted by the FOIA and the Privacy Act make the laws valuable and workable. The disclosure of government information cannot be controlled by arbitrary or unreviewable actions.

Which Act To Use

The access provisions of the FOIA and the Privacy Act overlap in part. The two laws have different procedures and different exemptions. As a result, sometimes information exempt under one law will be disclosable under the other.

In order to take maximum advantage of the laws, an individual seeking information about himself or herself should normally cite both laws. Requests by an individual for information that does not relate solely to himself or herself should be made under the FOIA.

Congress intended that the two laws be considered together in the processing of requests for information. Many government agencies will automatically handle requests from individuals in a way that will maximize the amount of information that is disclosable. However, a requester should still make a request in a manner that is most advantageous and that fully protects all available legal rights. A requester who has any doubts about which law to use should always cite both the FOIA and the Privacy Act when seeking documents from the federal government.

Tips On Finding Information

The Scope of the Freedom of Information Act

The federal Freedom of Information Act applies to documents held by agencies in the executive branch of the federal Government. The executive branch includes cabinet departments, military departments, government corporations, government controlled corporations, independent regulatory agencies, and other establishments of the executive branch.

The FOIA does not apply to elected officials of the federal government, including the President, Vice President, Senators, and Congressmen, or the federal judiciary. The FOIA also does not apply to private companies; persons who received federal contracts or grants; tax-exempt organizations; or state or local governments.

All States and some localities have passed laws like the FOIA that allow people to request access to records. In addition, there are other federal and state laws that may permit access to documents held by organizations not covered by the FOIA.

What Records Can Be Requested Under FOIA?

The FOIA requires agencies to publish or make available some types of information. This includes: (1) Description of agency organization and office addresses; (2) statements of the general course and method of agency operation; (3) rules of procedure and descriptions of forms; (4) substantive rules of general applicability and general policy statements; (5) final opinions made in the adjudication of cases; and (6) administrative staff manuals that affect the public. This information must either be published or made available for inspection and copying without the formality of an FOIA request.

All other "agency records" may be requested under the FOIA. However, the FOIA does not define "agency record." Material that is in the possession, custody, or control of an agency is usually considered to be an agency record under the FOIA. Personal notes of agency employees may not be agency records. A record that is not an "agency record" will not be available under the FOIA.

The form in which a record is maintained by an agency does not affect its availability. A request may seek a printed or typed document, tape recording, map, computer printout, computer tape, or a similar item.

Of course, not all records that can be requested must be disclosed. Information that is exempt from disclosure is described below in the section entitled "Reasons Access May Be Denied Under the FOIA."

The FOIA carefully provides that a requester may ask for records rather than information. This means that an agency is only required to look for an existing record or document in response to an FOIA request. An agency is not obliged to create a new record to comply with a request. An agency is not required to collect information it does not have. Nor must an agency do research or analyze data for a requester.

Requesters may ask for existing records. Requests may have to be carefully written in order to obtain the information that is desired. Sometimes, agencies will help a requester identify the specific document that contains the information being sought. Other times, a requester may need to be creative when writing an FOIA request in order to identify an existing document or set of documents containing the desired information.

There is a second general limitation on FOIA request. The law requires that each request must reasonably describe the records being sought. This means that a request must be specific enough to permit a professional employee of the agency who is familiar with the subject matter to locate the record in a reasonable period of time.

Because different agencies organize and index records in different ways, one agency may consider a request to be reasonably descriptive while another agency may reject a similar request as too vague. For example, the Federal Bureau of Investigation has a central index for its primary record system. As a result, the FBI is able to search for records about a specific person. However, agencies that do not maintain a central name index may be unable to conduct the same type of search. These agencies may reject a similar request because the request does not describe records that can be identified.

Requesters should make their requests as specific as possible. If a particular document is required, it should be identified as precisely as possible, preferably by date and title. However, a request does not have to be that specific. A requester who cannot identify a specific record should clearly explain his or her needs. A requester should make sure, however, that the request is broad enough to cover the information that is needed.

For example, assume that a requester wants to obtain a list of toxic sites near his home. A request to the Environmental Protection Agency for all records on toxic waste would cover many more records than are needed. The fees for such a request might be very high, and it is possible that the request might be rejected as too vague.

A request for all toxic waste sites within three miles of a particular address is very specific. But is unlikely that EPA would have an existing record containing data organized in that fashion. As a result, the request might be denied because there is no existing record containing the information.

The requester might do better to ask for a list of toxic waste sites in his city, county, or state. It is more likely that existing records might contain this information. The requester might also want to tell the agency in the request letter exactly what information is desired. The additional explanation will help the agency to find a record that meets the request.

Many people include their telephone number in their requests. Sometimes questions about the scope of a request can be resolved quickly when the agency employee and the requester talk. This is an efficient way to resolve questions that arise during the processing of FOIA requests.

It is to everyone's advantage if requests are as precise and as narrow as possible. The requester benefits because the request can be processed faster and cheaper. The agency benefits because it can do a better job of responding to the request. The agency will also be able to use its scarce resources to respond to more requests. The FOIA works best when both the requester and the agency act cooperatively.

Making an FOIA Request

The first step in making a request under the FOIA is to identify the agency that has the records. An FOIA request must be addressed to a specific agency. There is no central government records office that services FOIA requests.

Often, a requester knows beforehand which agency has the desired records. If not, a requester can consult a government directory such as the *United States Government Manual*. This manual has a complete list of all the federal agencies, a description of agency functions, and the address of each agency. A requester who is uncertain about which agency has the records that are needed can make FOIA requests at more than one agency.

All agencies normally require that FOIA requests be in writing. Letters requesting records under the FOIA can be short and simple. No one needs a lawyer to make an FOIA request. The Appendix to this section contains a sample request letter.

The request letter should be addressed to an agency's FOIA officer or to the head of the agency. The envelope containing the written request should be marked "Freedom of Information Act Request" in the bottom left-hand corner.

There are three basic elements to an FOIA request letter. First, the letter should state that the request is being made under the Freedom of Information Act. Second, the request should identify the records that are being sought as specifically as possible. Third, the name and address of the requester must be included.

In addition, under the 1986 amendments to the FOIA, the fees chargeable vary with the status or purpose of the requester. As a result, requesters may have to provide additional information to permit the agency to determine the appropriate fees. Different fees can be charged to commercial users, representatives of the news media, educational and non-commercial scientific institutions, and individuals. The next section explains the new fee structure in more detail.

There are several optional items that are often included in an FOIA request. The first is the telephone number of the requester. This permits an agency employee processing a request to talk to the requester if necessary.

A second optional item is a limitation on the fees that the requester is willing to pay. It is common for requesters to ask to be contacted if the charges will exceed a fixed amount. This allows a requester to modify or withdraw a request if the cost is too high.

A third optional item sometimes included in an FOIA request is a request for waiver or reduction of fees. The 1986 amendments waived or reduced the rules for fee waivers. Fees must be waived or reduced if disclosure of the information is in the public interest because it is likely to contribute significantly to public understanding of the operations or activities of the government and is not primarily in the commercial interest of the request. Decisions about granting fee waivers are separate from and different from decisions about the amount of fees that can be charged to requesters.

Requesters should keep a copy of their request letter and related correspondence until the request has been fully resolved.

Fees and Fee Waivers

FOIA requesters may have to pay fees covering some or all of the costs of processing their request. As amended in 1986, the law establishes three types of charges that may be imposed on requesters. The 1986 law makes the process of determining the applicable fees more complicated. However, the new rules reduce or eliminate entirely the cost for small, noncommercial requests.

First, fees can be imposed to recover the costs of copying documents. All agencies have a fixed price for making copies using copying machines. Requesters are usually charged the actual cost of copying computer tapes, photographs, or other nonstandard documents.

Second, fees can also be imposed to recover the costs of searching for documents. This includes the time spent looking for material responsive to a request. Requesters can minimize search charges by making clear, narrow requests for identifiable documents whenever possible.

Third, fees can be charged to recover review costs. Review is the process of examining documents to determine whether any portion is exempt from disclosure. Before the effective date of the 1986 amendments, no review charges were imposed on any requester. Effective April 25, 1987, review charges may be imposed on commercial requesters only. Review charges only include costs incurred during the initial examination of a document. An agency may not charge for any costs incurred in resolving issues of law or policy that may arise while processing a request.

Different fees apply to different categories of requesters. There are three basic groups of FOIA requesters. The first includes representatives of the news media, and educational or noncommercial scientific institutions whose purpose is scholarly or scientific research. Requesters in this category who are not seeking records for commercial use can only be billed for reasonable standard document duplication charges. A request for information from a representative of the news media is not considered to be for commercial use if the request is in support of a news gathering or dissemination function.

The second group includes FOIA requesters seeking records for commercial use. Commercial use is not defined in the law, but generally includes profit making activities. Commercial users pay reasonable standard charges for document duplication, search, and review.

The third group of FOIA requesters includes everyone not included in either of the first two groups. People seeking information for their own use, public interest groups, and non-profit organizations are examples of requesters who fall into the third group. Charges for these requests are limited to reasonable standard charges for document duplication and search. No review charges may be imposed. The 1986 amendments did not change the fees charged to these requesters.

Small requests are free to requesters in the first and third groups.

This includes all requesters except commercial users. There is no charge for the first two hours of search time and the first 100 pages of documents. Noncommercial requesters who limit their requests to a small number of easily found records will not pay any fees at all.

In addition, the law also prevents agencies from charging fees if the cost of collecting the fee would exceed the amount collected. This limitation applies to all requests, including those seeking documents for commercial use. Thus, if the allowable charges for any FOIA request are small, no fees are imposed.

Each agency sets charges for duplication, search, and review based on its own costs. The amount of these charges is included in the agency FOIA regulations. Each agency also sets its own threshold for minimum charges.

The 1986 FOIA amendments changed the law on fee waivers. The new rules require that fees must be waived or reduced if disclosure of the information is in the public interest because it is likely to contribute significantly to public understanding of the operations or activities of the government and is not primarily in the commercial interest of the requester.

The new rules for fees and fee waivers have created some confusion. Determinations about fees are separate and apart from determinations about eligibility for fee waivers. For example, a news reporter may only be charged duplication fees and may ask that the duplication fees be waived. There is no need for a reporter to ask for a waiver of search and review costs because search and review costs are not charged to reporters.

Only after a requester has been categorized to determine applicable fees does the issue of a fee waiver arise. A requester who seeks a fee waiver should include a separate request in the original request letter. The requester should describe how disclosure will contribute to the public understanding of the operations or activities of the government. The sample request letter in the Appendix includes optional language asking for a fee waiver.

Any requester may ask for a fee waiver. Some will find it easier to qualify than others. A news reporter who is charged only duplication costs may still ask that the charges be waived because of the public benefits that will result from disclosure. Representatives of the news media and public interest groups are very likely to qualify for a waiver of fees. Commercial users will find it more difficult to qualify.

The eligibility of other requesters will vary. A key element in qualifying for a fee waiver is the relationship of the information to public understanding of the operations or activities of government. Another important factor is the ability of the requester to convey that information to other interested members of the public. A requester is not eligible for a fee waiver solely because of indigence.

Requirements for Agency Responses

Each agency is required to determine within ten days (excluding Saturdays, Sundays, and legal holidays) after the receipt of a request whether to comply with the request. The actual disclosure of documents is required to follow promptly thereafter. If a request for records is denied in whole or in part, the agency must tell the requester the reasons for the denial. The agency must also tell the requester that there is a right to appeal any adverse determination to the head of the agency.

The FOIA permits agencies to extend the time limits up to ten days in unusual circumstances. These circumstances include the need to collect records from remote locations, review large numbers of records, and consult with other agencies. Agencies are supposed to notify the requester whenever an extension is invoked.

The statutory time limits for responses are not always met. Agencies sometimes receive an unexpectedly large number of FOIA requests at one time and are unable to meet the deadlines. Some agencies assign inadequate resources to FOIA offices. The Congress does not condone the failure of any agency to meet the law's limits. However, as a practical matter, there is little that a requester can do about it. The courts have been reluctant to provide relief solely because the FOIA's time limits have not been met.

The best advice to requesters is to be patient. The law allows a requester to consider a request to be denied if it has not been decided within the time limits. This permits the requester to file an administrative appeal. However, this is not always the best course of action. The filing of an administrative or judicial appeal does not normally result in any faster processing of the request.

Agencies generally process requests in the order in which they were received. Some agencies will expedite the processing of urgent requests. Anyone with a pressing need for records should consult with the agency FOIA officer about how to ask for expedited treatment of requests.

Reasons Access May Be Denied Under the FOIA

An agency may refuse to disclose an agency record that falls within any of the FOIA's nine statutory exemptions. The exemptions protect against the disclosure of information that would harm national defense or foreign policy, privacy of individuals, proprietary interests of business, functioning of government, and other important interests.

A record that does not qualify as an "agency record" may be denied because only agency records are available under the FOIA. Personal notes of agency employees may be denied on this basis.

An agency may withhold exempt information, but it is not always required to do so. For example, an agency may disclose an exempt internal memorandum because no harm would result from its disclosure. However, an agency is not likely to agree to disclose an exempt document that is classified or that contains a trade secret.

When a record contains some information that qualifies as exempt, the entire record is not necessarily exempt. Instead, the FOIA specifically provides that any reasonably segregable portions of a record must be provided to a requester after the deletion of the portions that are exempt. This is a very important requirement because it prevents an agency from withholding an entire document simply because one line or one page is exempt.

Exemption 1: Classified Documents

The first FOIA exemption permits the withholding of properly classified documents. Information may be classified to protect it in the interest of national defense or foreign policy. Information that has been classified as "Confidential," "Secret," or "Top Secret" under the procedures of the Executive Order on Security Classification can qualify under the first exemption.

The rules for classification are established by the President and not the FOIA or other law. The FOIA provides that, if a document has been properly classified under the President's rules, the document can be withheld from disclosure.

Classified documents may be requested under the FOIA. An agency can review the document to determine if it still requires protection. In addition, the Executive Order on Security Classification establishes a special procedure for requesting the declassification of documents. If a requested document is declassified, it can be released in response to an FOIA request. However, a document that was formerly classified may still be exempt under other FOIA exemptions.

Exemption 2: Internal Personnel Rules and Practices

The second FOIA exemption covers matters that are related solely to an agency's internal personnel rules and practices. As interpreted by the courts, there are two separate classes of documents that are generally held to fall within exemption two.

First, information relating to personnel rules or internal agency practices is exempt if it is a trivial administrative matter of no genuine public interest. A rule governing lunch hours for agency employees is an example.

Second, internal administrative manuals can be exempt if disclosure would risk circumvention of law or agency regulations. In order to fall into this category, the material will normally have to regulate internal agency conduct rather than public behavior.

Exemption 3: Information Exempt Under Other Laws

The third exemption incorporates into the FOIA other laws that restrict the availability of information. To qualify under exemption three, a statute must require that matters be withheld from the public in such a manner as to leave no

discretion to the agency. Alternatively, the statute must establish particular criteria for withholding or refer to particular types of matters to be withheld.

One example of a qualifying statute is the provision of the Tax Code prohibiting the public disclosure of tax returns and tax law designating identifiable census data as confidential. Whether a particular statute qualifies under Exemption 3 can be a difficult legal determination.

Exemption 4: Confidential Business Information

The fourth exemption protects from public disclosure two types of information: trade secrets and confidential business information. A trade secret is a commercially valuable plan, formula, process, or device. This is a narrow category of information. An example of a trade secret is the recipe for a commercial food product.

The second type of protected data is commercial or financial information obtained from a person and privileged or confidential. The courts have held that data qualifies for withholding if disclosure by the government would be likely to harm the competitive position of the person who submitted the information. Detailed information on a company's marketing plans, profits, or costs can qualify as confidential business information. Information may also be withheld if disclosure would be likely to impair the government's ability to obtain similar information in the future.

Only information obtained from a person other than a government agency qualifies under the fourth exemption. A person is an individual, a partnership, or a corporation. Information that an agency created on its own cannot normally be withheld under exemption four.

Although there is no formal requirement under the FOIA, many agencies will notify a submitter of business information that disclosure of the information is being considered. The submitter can file suit to block disclosure under the FOIA. Such lawsuits are generally referred to as "reverse" FOIA lawsuits because the FOIA is being used in an attempt to prevent rather than to require disclosure of information. A reverse FOIA lawsuit may be filed when a submitter of documents and the government disagree whether the information is confidential.

Exemption 5: Internal Government Communications

The FOIA's fifth exemption applies to internal government documents. One example is a letter from one government department to another about a joint decision that has not yet been made. Another example is a memorandum from an agency employee to his supervisor describing options for conducting the agency's business.

The purpose of the exemption is to safeguard the deliberative policymaking processes of government. The exemption encourages frank discussions of policy matters between agency officials by allowing supporting documents to be withheld from public disclosure. The exemption also protects against premature disclosure of policies before final adoption.

While the policy behind the fifth exemption is well-accepted, the application of the exemption is complicated. The fifth exemption may be the most difficult FOIA exemption to understand and apply. For example, the exemption protects the policymaking process, but it does not protect purely factual information related to the policy process. Factual information must be disclosed unless it is inextricably intertwined with protected information about an agency decision.

Protection for the decision making process is appropriate only for the period while decisions are being made. Thus, the fifth exemption has been held to distinguish between documents that are pre-decisional and therefore may be protected, and those which are post-decisional and therefore not subject to protection. Once a policy is adopted, the public has a greater interests in knowing the basis for the decision.

The exemption also incorporates some of the privileges that apply in litigation involving the government. For example, papers prepared by the government's lawyers are exempt in the same way that papers prepared by private lawyers for clients are not available through discovery in civil litigation.

Exemption 6: Personal Privacy

The sixth exemption covers personnel, medical, and similar files the disclosure of which would constitute a clearly unwarranted invasion of personal privacy. This exemption protects the privacy interests of individuals by allowing an agency to withhold from disclosure intimate personal data kept in government files. Only individuals have privacy interests. Corporations and other legal persons have no privacy rights under the sixth exemption.

The exemption requires agencies to strike a balance between an individual's privacy interests and the public's right to know. However, since only a clearly unwarranted invasion of privacy is a basis for withholding, there is a perceptible tilt in favor of disclosure in the exemption. Nevertheless, the sixth exemption makes it hard to obtain information about another individual without the consent of the individual.

The Privacy Act of 1974 also regulates the disclosure of personal information about individuals. The FOIA and the Privacy Act overlap in part, but there is no inconsistency. Individuals seeking records about themselves should cite both laws when making a request. This ensures that the maximum amount of disclosable information will be released. Records that can be denied to an individual under the Privacy Act are not necessarily exempt under the FOIA.

Exemption 7: Law Enforcement

The seventh exemption allows agencies to withhold law enforcement records in order to protect the law enforcement process from interference. The exemption was amended slightly in 1986, but it still retains six specific subexemptions.

Exemption (7)(A) allows the withholding of law enforcement records that could reasonably be expected to interfere with enforcement proceedings. This exemption protects active law enforcement investigations from interference through premature disclosure.

Exemption (7)(B) allows the withholding of information that would deprive a person of a right to a fair trial or an impartial adjudication. This exemption is rarely used.

Exemption (7)(C) recognizes that individuals have a privacy interest in information maintained in law enforcement files. If the disclosure of information could reasonably be expected to constitute an unwarranted invasion of personal privacy, the information is exempt from disclosure. The standards for privacy protection in Exemption 6 and Exemption (7)(C) differ slightly. Exemption (7)(C) refers only to unwarranted invasions of personal privacy rather than to clearly unwarranted invasions.

Exemption (7)(D) protects the identity of confidential sources. Information that could reasonably be expected to reveal the identity of a confidential source is exempt. A confidential source can include a state, local, or foreign agency or authority, or a private institution that furnished information on a confidential basis. In addition, the exemption protects information furnished by a confidential source if the data was compiled by a criminal law enforcement authority during a criminal investigation or by an agency conducting a lawful national security intelligence investigation.

Exemption (7)(E) protects from disclosure information that would reveal techniques and procedures for law enforcement investigations or prosecutions or that would disclose guidelines for law enforcement investigations or prosecutions if disclosure of the information could reasonably be expected to risk circumvention of the law.

Exemption (7)(F) protects law enforcement information that could reasonably be expected to endanger the life or physical safety of any individual.

Exemption 8: Financial Institutions

The eighth exemption protects information that is contained in or related to examination, operating, or condition reports prepared by or for a bank supervisory agency such as the Federal Deposit Insurance Corporation, or the Federal Reserve, or similar agencies.

Exemption 9: Geological Information

The ninth FOIA exemption covers geological and geophysical information, data, and maps about wells. This exemption is rarely used.

FOIA Exclusions

The 1986 amendments to the FOIA gave limited authority to agencies to respond to a request without confirming the existence of the requested records. Ordinarily, any proper request must receive an answer stating whether there is any responsive information, even if the requested information is exempt from disclosure.

In some narrow circumstances, acknowledgement of the existence of a record can produce consequences similar to those resulting from disclosure of the record itself. In order to avoid this type of problem, the 1986 amendments established three "record exclusions." However, these exclusions do not broaden the ability of agencies to withhold documents.

The exclusions allow agencies to treat certain exempt records as if the records were not subject to the FOIA. Agencies are not required to confirm the existence of three specific categories of records. If those records are requested, agencies may state that there are no disclosable records responsive to the request. However, these exclusions give agencies no authority to withhold additional categories of information from the public.

The first exclusion is triggered when a request seeks information that is exempt because disclosure could reasonably be expected to interfere with a current law enforcement investigation. There are specific prerequisites for the application of this exclusion. First, the investigation in question must involve a possible violation of criminal law. Second, there must be a reason to believe that the subject of the investigation is not already aware that the investigation is underway. Third, disclosure of the existence of the records -- as distinguished from contents of the records -- could reasonably be expected to interfere with enforcement proceedings.

When all three of these conditions are present, an agency may respond to an FOIA request for investigatory records as if the records are not subject to the requirements of the FOIA. In other words, the agency's response does not have to reveal that it is conducting an investigation.

The second exclusion applies to informant records maintained by a criminal law enforcement agency under the informant's name or personal identifier. The agency is not required to confirm the existence of these records unless the informant's status has been officially confirmed. This exclusion helps agencies to protect the identity of confidential informants. Information that might identify informants has always been exempt under the FOIA.

The third exclusion applies only to records maintained by the Federal Bureau of Investigation which pertain to foreign intelligence, counterintelligence, or international terrorism. When the existence of those type of records is classified, the FBI may treat the records as not subject to the requirements of FOIA.

This exclusion does not apply to all classified records on the specific subjects. It only applies when the records are classified and when the existence of the records is also classified. Since the underlying records must be classified before the exclusion is relevant, agencies have no new substantive withholding authority.

In enacting these exclusions, congressional sponsors stated that it was their intent that agencies must inform FOIA requesters that these exclusions are available for agency use. Requesters who believe that records were improperly withheld because of the exclusions can seek judicial review.

Administrative Appeal Procedures

Whenever an FOIA request is denied, the agency must inform the requester of the reasons for the denial and the requester's right to appeal the denial to the head of the agency. A requester may appeal the denial of a request for a document or for fee waiver. A requester may contest the type or amount of fees that were charged. A requester may appeal any other adverse determination including a rejection of a request for failure to describe adequately the documents being requested. A requester can also appeal because the agency failed to conduct an adequate search for the documents that were requested.

A person whose request was granted in part and denied in part may appeal the partial denial. If an agency has agreed to disclose some but not all of the requested documents, the filing of an appeal does not affect the release of the documents that are disclosable. There is no risk to the requester in filing an appeal.

The appeal to the head of an agency is a simple administrative appeal. A lawyer can be helpful, but no one needs a lawyer to file an appeal. Anyone who can write a letter can file an appeal. Appeals to the head of the agency often result in the disclosure of some records that have been withheld. A requester who is not convinced that the agency's initial decision is correct should appeal. There is no charge for filing an appeal.

An appeal is filed by sending a letter to the head of the agency. The letter must identify the FOIA request that is being appealed. The envelope containing the letter of appeal should be marked in the lower left hand corner with the words "Freedom of Information Act Appeal."

Many agencies assign a number to all FOIA requests that are received. The number should be included in the appeal letter, along with the name and address of the requester. It is a common practice to include a copy of the agency's initial decision letter as part of the appeal, but this it not required. It can also be helpful for the requester to include a telephone number in the appeal letter.

An appeal will normally include the requester's arguments supporting disclosure of the documents. A requester may include any facts or any arguments supporting the case for reversing the initial decision. However, an appeal letter does not have to contain any arguments at all. It is sufficient to state that the agency's initial decision is being appealed. The Appendix to this section includes a sample appeal letter.

The FOIA does not set a time limit for filing an administrative appeal of an FOIA denial. However, it is good practice to file an appeal promptly. Some agency regulations establish a time limit for filing an administrative appeal. A requester whose appeal is rejected by an agency because it is too late may refile the original FOIA request and start the process again.

A requester who delays filing an appeal runs the risk that the documents could be destroyed. However, as long as an agency is considering a request or an appeal, the agency must preserve the documents.

An agency is required to make a decision on an appeal within twenty days (excluding Saturdays, Sundays, and federal holidays). It is possible for an agency to extend the time limits by an additional ten days. Once the time period has elapsed, a requester may consider a that the appeal has been denied and may proceed with a judicial appeal. However, unless there is an urgent need for records, this is not always the best course of action. The courts are not sympathetic to appeals based solely on an agency's failure to comply with the FOIA's time limits.

Filing a Judicial Appeal

When an administrative appeal is denied, a requester has the right to appeal the denial in court. An FOIA appeal can be filed in the United States District Court in the district where the requester lives. The requester can also file suit in the district where the documents are located or in the District of Columbia. When a requester goes to court, the burden of justifying the withholding of documents is on the government. This is a distinct advantage for the requester.

Requesters are sometimes successful when they go to court, but the results vary considerably. Some requesters who file judicial appeals find that an agency will disclose some documents previously withheld rather than fight about disclosure in court. This does not always happen, and there is no guarantee that the filing of a judicial appeal will result in any additional disclosure.

Most requesters require the assistance of an attorney to file a judicial appeal. A person who files a lawsuit and substantially prevails may be awarded reasonable attorney fees and litigation costs reasonably incurred. Some requesters may be able to handle their own appeal without an attorney. Since this is not a litigation guide, details of the judicial appeal process have not been included. Anyone considering filing an appeal can begin by reviewing the provisions of the FOIA on judicial review.

The Privacy Act of 1974

The Privacy Act of 1974 provides safeguards against an invasion of privacy through the misuse of records by federal agencies. In general, the Act allows citizens to learn how records are collected, maintained, used, and disseminated by the federal government. The Act also permits individuals to gain access to most personal information maintained by federal agencies and to seek amendment of any incorrect or incomplete information.

The Privacy Act applies to personal information maintained by agencies in the executive branch of the federal government. The executive branch includes cabinet departments, military departments, government corporations, government controlled corporations, independent regulatory agencies, and other establishments in the executive branch. Agencies subject to the Freedom of Information Act (FOIA) are also subject to the Privacy Act. The Privacy Act does not generally apply to records maintained by state and local governments or private companies or organizations.

The Privacy Act grants rights only to United States citizens and to aliens lawfully admitted for permanent residence. As a result, foreign nationals cannot use the Act's provisions. However, foreigners may use the FOIA to request records about themselves.

The only records subject to the Privacy Act are records about individuals that are maintained in a system of records. The idea of a "system of records" is unique to the Privacy Act and requires explanation.

The Act defines a "record" to include most personal information maintained by an agency about an individual. A record contains information about education, financial transactions, medical history, criminal history, or employment history. A system of records is a group of records from which information is actually retrieved by name, social security number, or other identifying symbol assigned to an individual.

Some personal information is not kept in a system of records. This information is not subject to the provisions of the Privacy Act, although access may be requested under the FOIA. Most personal information in government files is subject to the Privacy Act.

The Privacy Act also establishes general records management requirements for federal agencies. In summary, there are five basic requirements that are more relevant to individuals.

First, agencies must establish procedures allowing individuals to see and copy records about themselves. An individual may also seek to amend any information that is not accurate, relevant, timely, or complete. The rights to inspect and to correct records are the most important provisions of the Privacy Act. This section explains in more detail how an individual can exercise these rights.

Second, agencies must publish notices describing all systems of records. The notices include a complete description of personal-data recordkeeping policies, practices, and systems. This requirement prevents the maintenance of secret record systems.

Third, agencies must make reasonable efforts to maintain accurate, relevant, timely, and complete records about individuals. Agencies are prohibited from maintaining information about how individuals exercise rights guaranteed by the First Amendment to the U.S. Constitution unless maintenance of the information is specifically authorized by statute or relates to authorized law enforcement activity.

Fourth, the Act establishes rules governing the use and disclosure of personal information. The Act specifies that information collected for one purpose may not be used for another purpose without notice to or the consent of the subject of the record. The Act also requires that agencies keep a record of some disclosures of personal information.

Fifth, the Act provides legal remedies that permit individuals to seek enforcement of rights under the Act. In addition, there are criminal penalties that apply to federal employees who fail to comply with the Act's provisions.

Locating Records

There is no central index of federal government records. An individual who wants to inspect records about himself or herself must first identify which agency has the records. Often, this will not be difficult. For example, an individual who was employed by the federal government knows that the employing agency or the Office of Personnel Management maintains personnel files.

Similarly, an individual who receives veterans' benefits will normally find the related records at the Veterans Administration or at the Defense Department. Tax records are maintained by the Internal Revenue Service, social security records by the Social Security Administration, passport records by the State Department, etc.

For those who are uncertain about which agency has the records that are needed, there are several sources of information. First, an individual can ask an agency that might maintain the records. If that agency does not have the records, it may be able to identify the proper agency.

Second, a government directory such as the *United States Government Manual* contains a complete list of all federal agencies, a description of agency functions, and the address of the agency and its field offices. An agency responsible for operating a program normally maintains the records related to that program.

Third, a Federal Information Center can help to identify government agencies, their functions, and their records. These Centers, which are operated by the General Services Administration, serve as clearinghouses for information about the federal government. There are several dozen Federal Information Centers throughout the country.

Fourth, the Office of Federal Register publishes an annual compilation of system of records notices for all agencies. These notices contain a complete description of each record system maintained by each agency. The compilation - which is published in five large volumes - is the most complete reference for information about federal agency personal information practices. The information that appears in the compilation is also published occasionally in the *Federal Register*.

The compilation -- formally called Privacy Act Issuance -- maybe difficult to find. Copies will be available in some federal depository libraries and possibly in other libraries as well. Although the compilation is the best single source of detailed information about personal records maintained by the federal agencies, it is not necessary to consult the compilation before making a Privacy Act request.

A requester is not required to identify the specific system of records that contains the information being sought. It is sufficient to identify the agency that has the records. Using information provided by the requester, the agency will determine which system of records has the files that have been requested.

Those who request records under the Privacy Act can help the agency by identifying the type of records being sought. Large agencies maintain dozens or even hundreds of different record systems. A request is processed faster if the requester tells the agency that he or she was employed by the agency, was the recipient of benefits under an agency program, or had other specific contacts with the agency.

Making a Privacy Act Request for Access

The fastest way to make a Privacy Act request is to identify the specific system of records. The request can be addressed to the system manager. Few people do this. Instead, most people address their requests to the head of the agency that has the records or the agency's Privacy Act Officer. The envelope containing the written request should be marked "Privacy Act Request" in the bottom left-hand corner.

There are three basic elements to a request for records under the Privacy Act. First, the letter should state that the request is being made under the Privacy Act. Second, the letter should include the name, address, and signature of the requester. Third, the request should describe as specifically as possible the records that are wanted. The Appendix to this section includes a sample Privacy Act request letter. It is a common practice for an individual seeking records about himself or herself to make the request both under the Privacy Act of 1974 and the Freedom of Information Act. See the discussion in the front of this section about which act to use.

A requester can describe the records by identifying a specific system of records, by describing his or her contacts with an agency, or by simply asking for all records about himself or herself. The broader and less specific a request is, the longer it may take for an agency to respond.

It is a good practice for a requester to describe the type of records that he or she expects to find. For example, an individual seeking a copy of his service record in the Army should state he was in the Army and include the approximate dates of service. This will help the Defense Department narrow its search to record systems that are likely to contain the information being sought. An individual seeking records from the Federal Bureau of Investigation may ask that files in specific field offices be searched in addition to the FBI's central office files. The FBI dose not routinely search field office records without a specific request.

Agencies generally require requesters to provide some proof of identity before records will be disclosed. Agencies may have different requirements. Some agencies will accept a signature; others may require a notarized signature. If an individual goes to the agency to inspect records, standard personal identification may be acceptable. More stringent requirements may apply if the records being sought are especially sensitive.

Agencies will inform requesters of special identification requirements. Requesters who need records quickly should first consult regulations or talk to the agency's Privacy Act Officer to find out how to provide adequate identification.

An individual who visits an agency office to inspect a Privacy Act record may wish to bring along a friend or relative to review the record. When a requester brings another person, the agency may ask the requester to sign a written statement authorizing discussion of the record in the presence of that person.

It is a crime to knowingly and willfully request or obtain records under the Privacy Act under false pretenses. A request for access under the Privacy Act can be made only by the subject of the record. An individual cannot make a request under the Privacy Act for a record about another person. The only exception is for a parent or legal guardian who can request records for a minor or a person who has been declared incompetent.

Fees

Under the Privacy Act, fees can be charged only for the cost of conveying records. No fees may be charged for the time it takes to search for the records or the time it takes to review the records to determine if any exemptions apply. This is a major difference from the FOIA. Under the FOIA, fees can sometimes be charged to recover search costs and review costs. The different fee structure in the two laws is one reason many requesters seeking records about themselves cite both laws. This minimizes allowable fees.

Many agencies will not charge fees for making copies of files under the Privacy Act, especially when the files are small. If paying the copying charges is a problem, the requester should explain in the request letter. An agency can waive fees under the Privacy Act.

Requirements for Agency Responses

Unlike FOIA, there is no fixed time when an agency must respond to a request for access to records under the Privacy Act. It is good practice for an agency to acknowledge receipt of a Privacy Act request within ten days and to provide the requested records within thirty days.

At many agencies, FOIA and Privacy Act requests are processed by the same personnel. When then is a backlog of requests, it takes longer to receive a response. As a practical matter, there is little that a requester can do when an agency response is delayed. Requesters can be patient.

Agencies generally process requests in the order in which they were received. Some agencies will expedite the processing of urgent requests. Anyone with a pressing need for records should consult the agency Privacy Act Officer about how to ask for expedited treatment of requests.

Reasons Access May Be Denied Under the Privacy Act

Not all records about an individual must be disclosed under the Privacy Act. Some records may be withheld to protect important government interests such as national security or law enforcement.

The Privacy Act exemptions are different from the exemptions of the FOIA. Under the FOIA, any record may be withheld from disclosure if it contains exempt information when a request is received. The decision to apply an FOIA exemption is made only after a request has been made. In contrast, Privacy Act exemptions apply not only to records but to systems of records. Before an agency can apply a Privacy Act exemption, the agency must first issue a regulation stating that there may be exempt records in that system of records. Thus, there is a procedural prerequisite for the application of the Privacy Act exemptions.

Without reviewing agency regulations, it is hard to tell whether particular Privacy Act records are exempt from disclosure. However, it is a safe assumption that any system of records that qualifies for an exemption has been exempted by the agency.

Since most record systems are not exempt, the exemptions are not relevant to most requests. Also, agencies do not automatically rely upon the Privacy Act exemptions unless there is a specific reason to do so. Thus, some records that are exempt may be disclosed upon request.

Because Privacy Act exemptions are complex and used infrequently, most requesters need not worry about them. The exemptions are discussed here for those interested in the law's details and for reference when an agency withholds records. Anyone interested in more information about the Privacy Act's exemptions can begin by reading the relevant sections of the Act.

The Privacy Act's exemptions differ from those of the FOIA in another important way. The FOIA is mostly a disclosure law. Information exempt under the FOIA is exempt from disclosure only. That is not true under the Privacy Act. It imposes many separate requirements on personal records. No system of records is exempt from all Privacy Act requirements.

For example, no system of records is ever exempt from the requirement that a description of the system be published. No system of records can be exempted from the limitations on disclosure of the records outside the agency. No system is exempt from the requirement to maintain an accounting for disclosures. No system is exempt from the restriction against the maintenance of unauthorized information on the exercise of First Amendment rights. All systems are subject to the requirement that reasonable efforts be taken to assure that records disclosed outside the agency be accurate, complete, timely, and relevant. Agencies must maintain proper administrative controls and security for all systems. Finally, The Privacy Act's criminal penalties remain fully applicable to each system of records.

1. General Exemptions

There are two general exemptions under the Privacy Act. The first applies to all records maintained by the Central Intelligence Agency. The second general exemption applies to selected records maintained by an agency or component whose principal function is any activity pertaining to criminal law enforcement. Records of these criminal law enforcement agencies can be exempt under the Privacy Act if the records consists of (A) information compiled to identify individual criminal offenders and which consist only of identifying that and notations of arrests, the nature and disposition of criminal charges, sentencing, confinement, release, and parole or probation status: (B) criminal investigatory records associated with an identifiable individual; or (C) reports identifiable to a particular individual compiled at any stage from arrest through release from supervision.

Systems of records subject to these general exemptions may be exempted from many of the Privacy Act's requirements.

Exemption from the Act's access and correction provisions is the most important. Individuals have no right under the Privacy Act to ask for a copy of records that are generally exempt or to seek correction of erroneous records.

In practice, these exemptions are not as expansive as they sound. Most agencies that have exempt records will accept and process Privacy Act requests. The records will be reviewed on a case-by-case basis. Agencies will often disclose any information that does not require protection. Agencies also tend to follow a similar policy for requests for correction.

Individuals interested in obtaining records from the Central Intelligence Agency or from law enforcement agencies should not be discouraged from making requests for access. Even if the Privacy Act access exemption is applied, portions of the records may still be disclosable under the FOIA. This is a primary reason individuals should cite both the Privacy Act and the FOIA when requesting records.

The general exemption from access does not prevent requesters from filing a lawsuit under the Privacy Act when access is denied. The right to sue under the FOIA is not changed because of a Privacy Act exemption.

2. Specific Exemptions

There are seven specific Privacy Act exemptions that can be applied to many systems of records. Records subject to these exemptions are not exempt from as many of the Act's requirements as are the records subject to the general exemptions. However, records exempt under the specific exemptions are exempt from the Privacy Act's access and correction provisions. Nevertheless, since the access and correction exemptions are not always applied when available, those seeking records should not be discouraged from making a request. Also, the FOIA can be used to seek access to records exempt under the Privacy Act.

The first specific exemption covers record systems containing information that is properly classified. Classified information is also exempt from disclosure under the FOIA. Information that has been classified in the interest of national defense or foreign policy will normally be unavailable under either the FOIA or the Privacy Act.

The second specific exemption applies to systems of records containing investigatory material compiled for law enforcement purposes other than material covered by the general law enforcement exemption. The specific law enforcement exemption is limited when -- as a result of the maintenance of the records -- an individual is denied any right, privilege, or benefit to which he or she would be entitled by federal law or for which he or she would otherwise be entitled. In such a case, disclosure is required except where disclosure would reveal the identity of a confidential source who furnished information to the government under an express promise that the identity of the source would be held in confidence. If the information was collected from a confidential source before the effective date of the Privacy Act (September 27, 1975), an implied promise of confidentiality is sufficient to permit withholding of the identity of the source.

The third specific exemption applies to systems of records maintained in connection with providing protective services to the President of the United States or other individuals who receive protection from the Secret Service.

The fourth specific exemption applies to systems of records required by statute to be maintained and used solely as statistical records.

The fifth specific exemption covers investigatory material compiled solely to determine suitability, eligibility, or qualifications for federal civilian employment, military service, federal contracts, or access to classified information. However, this exemption applies only to the extent that disclosure of information would reveal the identity of a confidential source who provided the information under a promise of confidentiality.

The sixth specific exemption applies to systems of records that contain testing or examination of material used solely to determine individual qualifications for appointment or promotion in federal service, but only when disclosure would compromise the objectivity or fairness of the testing or examination process. Effectively, this exemption permits withholding of questions used in employment tests.

The seven specific exemption covers evaluation material used to determine potential for promotion in the armed services. The material is only exempt to the extent that disclosure would reveal the identity of a confidential source who provided the information under a promise of confidentiality.

3. Medical Records

Medical records maintained by federal agencies -- for example, records at Veterans Administration hospitals -- are not formally exempt from the Privacy Act's access provisions. However, the Privacy Act authorizes a special procedure for medical records that operates, at least in part, like an exemption.

Agencies may deny individuals direct access to medical records, including psychological records, if the agency deems it necessary. An agency normally reviews medical records requested by an individual. If the agency determines that direct disclosure is unwise, it can arrange for disclosure to a physician selected by the individual or possibly to another person chosen by the individual.

4. Litigation Records

The Privacy Act's access provisions include a general limitation on access to litigation records. The Act does not require an agency to disclose to an individual any information compiled in reasonable anticipation of a civil action or proceeding. This limitation operates like an exemption, although there is no requirement that the exemption be applied to a system of records before it can be used.

Administrative Appeal Procedures for Denial of Access

Unlike the FOIA, the Privacy Act does not provide for an administrative appeal of the denial of access. However, many agencies have established procedures that will allow Privacy Act requesters to appeal a denial of access without going to court. An administrative appeal is often allowed under the Privacy Act, even though it is not required, because many individuals cite both the FOIA and Privacy Act when making a request. The FOIA provides specifically for an administrative appeal, and agencies are required to consider an appeal under the FOIA.

When a Privacy Act request for access is denied, agencies usually inform the requester of any appeal rights that are available. If no information on appeal rights is included in the denial letter, the requester should ask the Privacy Act Officer. Unless an agency has established an alternative procedure, it is possible that an appeal filed directly with the head of the agency will be considered by the agency.

When a request for access is denied under the Privacy Act, the agency explains the reason for the denial. The explanation must name the system of records and explain which exemption is applicable to the system. An appeal may be made on the basis that the record is not exempt, that the system of records has not been properly exempted, or that the record is exempt but no harm to an important interest will result if the record is disclosed.

There are three basic elements to a Privacy Act appeal letter. First, the letter should state that the appeal is being made under the Privacy Act of 1974. If the FOIA was cited when the request for access was made, the letter should state that the appeal is also being made under the FOIA. This is important because the FOIA grants requesters statutory appeal rights.

Second, a Privacy Act appeal letter should identify the denial that is being appealed and the records that were withheld. The appeal letter should also explain why the denial of access is improper or unnecessary.

Third, the appeal should include the requester's name and address. It is good practice for a requester to also include a telephone number when making an appeal. The Appendix at the end of this section includes a sample letter of appeal.

Amending Records Under the Privacy Act

The Privacy Act grants an important right in addition to the ability to inspect records. The Act permits an individual to request a correction of a record that is not accurate, relevant, timely, or complete. This remedy allows an individual to correct errors and to prevent those errors from being disseminated by the agency or used unfairly against the individual.

The right to seek a correction extends only to records subject to the Privacy Act. Also, an individual can only correct errors contained in a record that pertains to himself or herself. Records disclosed under the FOIA cannot be amended through the Privacy Act unless the records are also subject to the Privacy Act. Records about unrelated events or about other people cannot be amended unless the records are in a Privacy Act file maintained under the name of the individual who is seeking to make the correction.

A request to amend a record should be in writing. Agency regulations explain the procedures in greater detail, but the process is not complicated. A letter requesting an amendment of a record will normally be addressed to the Privacy Act Officer of the agency or to the agency official responsible for the maintenance of the record system containing the erroneous information. The envelope containing the request should be marked "Privacy Act Amendment Request" on the lower left corner.

There are five basic elements to a request for amending a Privacy Act record.

First, the letter should state that it is a request to amend a record under the Privacy Act of 1974.

Second, the request should identify the specific record and the specific information in the record for which an amendment is being sought.

Third, the request should state why the information is not accurate, relevant, timely, or complete. Supporting evidence may be included with the request.

Fourth, the request should state what new or additional information, if any, should be included in place of the erroneous information. Evidence of the validity of the new or additional information should be included. If the information in the file is wrong and needs to be removed rather than supplemented or corrected, the request should make this clear.

Fifth, the request should include the name and address of the requester. It is a good idea for the requester to include a telephone number. The Appendix includes a sample letter requesting amendment of a Privacy Act record.

Appeals and Requirements for Agency Responses

An agency that receives a request for amendment under the Privacy Act must acknowledge receipt of the request within ten days (not including Saturdays, Sundays, and legal holidays). The agency must promptly rule on the request.

The agency may make the amendment requested. If so, the agency must notify any person or agency to which the record had previously been disclosed of the correction.

If the agency refuses to make the change requested, the agency must inform the requester of: (1) the agency's refusal to amend the record; (2) the reason for refusing to amend the request; and (3) the procedures for requesting a review of the denial. The agency must provide the name and business address of the official responsible for conducting the review.

An agency must decide an appeal of a denial of a request for amendment within thirty days (excluding Saturdays, Sundays, and legal holidays), unless the time period is extended by the agency for good cause. If the appeal is granted, the record will be corrected.

If the appeal is denied, the agency must inform the requester of the right to judicial review. In addition, a requester whose appeal has been denied also has the right to place in the agency file a concise statement of disagreement with the information that was the subject of the request for amendment.

When a statement of disagreement has been filed and an agency is disclosing the disputed information, the agency must mark the information and provide copies of the statement of disagreement. The agency may also include a concise statement of its reasons for not making the requested amendments. The agency must also give a copy of the statement of disagreement to any person or agency to whom the record had previously been disclosed.

Finding a Judicial Appeal

The Privacy Act provides a civil remedy whenever an agency denies access to a record or refuses to amend a record. An individual may sue an agency if the agency fails to maintain records with accuracy, relevance, timeliness, and completeness as is necessary to assure fairness in any agency determination and the agency makes a determination that is adverse to the individual. An individual may also sue an agency if the agency fails to comply with any other Privacy Act provision in a manner that has an adverse effect on the individual.

The Privacy Act protects a wide range of rights about personal records maintained by federal agencies. The most important are the right to inspect records and the right to seek correction of records. Other rights have also been mentioned here, and still others can be found in the text of the Act. Most of these rights can become the subject of litigation.

An individual may file a lawsuit against an agency in the federal district court in which the individual lives, in which the records are situated, or in the District of Columbia. A lawsuit must be filed within two years from which the basis for the lawsuit arose.

Most individuals require the assistance of an attorney to file a judicial appeal. An individual who files a lawsuit and substantially prevails may be awarded reasonable attorney fees and litigation costs reasonably incurred. Some requesters may be able to handle their own appeal without an attorney. Since this is not a litigation guide, details about the judicial appeal process have not been included. Anyone considering filing an appeal can begin by reviewing the provisions of the Privacy Act on civil remedies.

Appendix: Sample Request and Appeal Letters

A. Freedom of Information Act Request Letter

Agency Head [or Freedom of Information Act Officer]
Name of Agency
Address of Agency
City, State, Zip Code
Re: Freedom of Information Act Request.

Dear_____:

This is a request under the Freedom of Information Act.

I request that a copy of the following documents [or documents containing the following information] be provided to me: [identify the documents or information as specifically as possible].

In order to help determine my status to assess fees, you should know that I am (insert a suitable description of the requester and the purpose of the request).

[Sample requester descriptions:
a representative of the news media affiliated with the newspaper (magazine, television station, etc.) and this request is made as part of new gathering and not for a commercial use.
affiliated with an educational or noncommercial scientific institution and this request is made for a scholarly or scientific purpose.
an individual seeking information for personal use and not for a commercial use.
affiliated with a private corporation and am seeking information for use in the company business.]

[Optional] I am willing to pay fees for this request up to a maximum of $XXX. If you estimate that the fees will exceed this limit, please inform me first.

[Optional] I request a waiver of all fees of this request. Disclosure of the requested information to me is in the public interest because it is likely to contribute significantly to public understanding of the operations or activities of the government and is not primarily in my commercial interest. [Include a specific explanation.]

Thank you for your consideration of this request.

Sincerely,
Name
Address
City, State, Zip Code
Telephone number [Optional]

B. Freedom of Information Act Appeal Letter

Agency Head or Appeal Officer
Name of Agency
Address of Agency
City, State, Zip Code
Re: Freedom of Information Act Appeal

Dear_____:

This is an appeal under the Freedom of Information Act.

On (date), I requested documents under the Freedom of Information Act. My request was assigned the following identification number: XXXXX. On (date), I received a response to my request in a letter signed by (name of official). I appeal the denial of my request.

[Optional] The documents that were withheld must be disclosed under the FOIA because * * *.

[Optional] I appeal the decision to deny my request for a waiver of fees. I believe that I am entitled to a waiver of fees. Disclosure of the documents I requested is in the public interest because the information is likely to contribute significantly to public understanding of the operations or activities of government and is not primarily in my commercial interests. (Provide details)

[Optional] I appeal the decision to require me to pay review costs for this request. I am not seeking the documents for a commercial use. (Provide details)

[Optional] I appeal the decision to require me to pay search charges for this request. I am a reporter seeking information as part of news gathering and not for commercial use.

Thank you for your consideration of this appeal.

Sincerely,

Name
Address
City, State, Zip Code
Telephone number [Optional]

Tips On Finding Information

C. Privacy Act Request for Access Letter

Privacy at Officer [or System of Records Manager]
Name of Agency
City, State, Zip Code
Re: Privacy Act Request for Access.

Dear____:

This is a request under the Privacy Act of 1974.

I request a copy of any records [or specifically named records] about me maintained at your agency.

[Optional] To help you to locate my records, I have had the following contacts with your agency: [mention job applications, periods of employment, loans or agency programs applied for, etc.).

[Optional] Please consider that this request is also made under the Freedom of Information Act. Please provide any additional information that may be available under the FOIA.

[Optional] I am wiling to pay fees for this request up to a maximum of $ XXX. If you estimate that the fees will exceed this limit, please inform me first.

[Optional] Enclosed is [a notarized signature or other identifying document] that will verify my identity.

Thank you for your consideration of this request.

Sincerely,

Name
Address
City, State, Zip Code
Telephone number [Optional]

D. Privacy Act Denial of Access Letter

Agency Head or Appeal Officer
Name of Agency
City, State, Zip Code
Re: Appeal of Denial of Privacy Act Access Request.

Dear___:

This is an appeal under the Privacy Act of the denial of my request for access to records.

On (date), I requested access to records under the Privacy Act of 1974. My request was assigned the following identification number: XXXXX. On (date), I received a response to my request in a letter signed by (name of official). I appeal the denial of my request.

[Optional] The records that were withheld should be disclosed to me because * * *.

[Optional] Please consider that this appeal is also made under the Freedom of Information Act. Please provide any additional information that may be available under the FOIA.

Thank you for your consideration of this appeal.

Sincerely,

Name
Address
City, State, Zip Code
Telephone number [Optional]

E. Privacy Act Request to Amend Records

Privacy Act Officer [or System of Records Manager]
Name of Agency
City, State, Zip Code
Re: Privacy Act Request to Amend Records

Dear____:

This is a request under the Privacy Act to amend records about myself maintained by your agency.

I believe that the following information is not correct: [Describe the incorrect information as specifically as possible].

The information is not (accurate) (relevant) (timely) (complete) because * * *.

[Optional] Enclosed are copies of documents that show that the information is incorrect.

I request that the information be [deleted] [changed to read:]

Thank you for your consideration of this request.

Sincerely,

Name
Address
City, State, Zip Code
Telephone number [Optional]

F. Privacy Act Appeal of Refusal to Amend Records

Agency Head or Appeal Officer
Name of Agency
City, State, Zip Code
Re: Privacy Act Request to Amend Records

Dear____:

This is an appeal made under the Privacy Act of the refusal of your agency to amend records as I requested.

On (date), I was informed by (name of official) that my request was rejected. I appeal the rejection of my request.

The rejection of my request for amendment was wrong because * * *.

[Optional] I enclose additional evidence that shows that the records are incorrect and that the amendment I requested is appropriate.

Thank you for your consideration of this appeal.

Sincerely,

Name
Address
City, State, Zip Code
Telephone number [Optional]

Federal Money Programs for Your Business

The following is a description of the federal funds available to small businesses, entrepreneurs, inventors, and researchers. This information is derived from the *Catalog of Federal Domestic Assistance* which is published by the U.S. Government Printing Office in Washington, DC. The number next to the title description is the official reference for this federal program. Contact the office listed below the caption for further details. The following is a description of the terms used for the types of assistance available:

Loans: money lent by a federal agency for a specific period of time and with a reasonable expectation of repayment. Loans may or may not require payment of interest.

Loan Guarantees: programs in which federal agencies agree to pay back part or all of a loan to a private lender if the borrower defaults.

Grants: money given by federal agencies for a fixed period of time and which does not have to be repaid.

Direct Payments: funds provided by federal agencies to individuals, private firms, and institutions. The use of direct payments may be "specified" to perform a particular service or for "unrestricted" use.

Insurance: coverage under specific programs to assure reimbursement for losses sustained. Insurance may be provided by federal agencies or through insurance companies and may or may not require the payment of premiums.

* Economic Injury Disaster Loans (EIDL) 59.002

Office of Disaster Assistance
Small Business Administration (SBA)
409 3rd Street, SW
Washington, DC 20416   202-502-6734

To assist business concerns suffering economic injury as a result of certain Presidential, SBA, and/or Department of Agriculture disaster declarations. Types of assistance: Loans. Estimate of annual funds available in 1992: $108,000,000.

* Loans for Small Business (Business Loans 7(a)(11)) 59.003

Director, Loan Policy and Procedures Branch
Small Business Administration (SBA)
409 3rd Street, SW
Washington, DC 20416   202-205-7511

To provide loans to small business owned by low-income persons or located in areas of high unemployment. Types of assistance: Loans, Loan Guarantee. Estimate of annual funds available in 1992: $16,800,000.

* Management and Technical Assistance for Socially and Economically Disadvantaged Businesses (7(j) Development Assistance Program) 59.007

Associate Administrator for Minority Small Business
and Capital Ownership Development
409 3rd Street, SW
Washington, DC 20416   202-205-6423

To provide management and technical assistance through qualified individuals, public or private organizations to existing or potential businesses which are economically and socially disadvantaged or which are located in areas of high concentration of unemployment. Types of assistance: Grants. Estimate of annual funds available in 1992: $8,040,000.

* Physical Disaster Loans (7(b) Loans(DL)) 59.008

Office of Disaster Assistance
Small Business Administration
409 3rd Street, SW
Washington, DC 20416   202-205-6734

To provide loans to the victims of designated physical-type disasters for uninsured loans. Types of assistance: Loans, Loan Guarantee. Estimate of annual funds available in 1992: $358,300,000.

* Small Business Investment Companies (SBIC; SSBICC) 59.011

Director
Office of Investments
Small Business Administration
409 3rd Street, SW
Washington, DC 20416   202-205-6510

To establish privately owned and managed small business investment companies; to provide equity capital and long term loan funds and advisory services. Type of assistance: Loans, Loan Guarantees. Estimate of annual funds available in 1992: $263,539,000.

* Small Business Loans (Regular Business Loans - 7(a) Loans) 59.012

Director
Loan Policy and Procedures Branch
Small Business Administration
409 3rd Street, SW
Washington, DC 20416   202-205-7510

To provide guaranteed loans to small businesses which are unable to obtain financing in the private credit marketplace, but can demonstrate an ability to repay loans granted. Types of assistance: Loan Guarantees. Estimate of annual funds available in 1992: $5,133,352,000.

* Local Development Company Loans (502 Loans) 59.013

Office of Economic Development
Small Business Administration
409 3rd Street, SW, Room 720
Washington, DC 20416   202-205-6485

To make federal loans to local development companies to provide long-term financing to small business concerns located in their areas. Types of assistance: Loan Guarantees. Estimate of annual funds available in 1992: $34,718,000.

* Bond Guarantees for Surety Companies (Surety Bond Guarantee) 59.016

Asst. Administrator
Office of Surety Guarantees
Small Business Administration
409 3rd Street, SW

Washington, DC 20416
Dorothy Kleeschulte   202-205-6540

To guarantee surety bonds issued by commercial surety companies for small contractors unable to obtain a bond without a guarantee. Types of assistance: Insurance. Estimate of annual funds available in 1992: $1,566,000,000.

* Handicapped Assistance Loans (HAL-1 and HAL-2) 59.021

Director, Loan Policy and Procedures Branch
Small Business Administration
409 3rd Street, SW
Washington, DC 20416   202-205-7510

To provide direct loans for nonprofit sheltered workshops and other similar organizations that produce goods and services. Types of assistance: Loans, Loan Guarantees. Estimate of annual funds available in 1992: $11,800,000.

* Service Corps of Retired Executives Association (SCORE) 59.026

National SCORE Office
1825 Connecticut Ave., NW
Washington, DC 20009   202-653-6279

To utilize the management experience of retired and active business executives to counsel and train potential and existing small businesses. Types of assistance: Grants. Estimate of annual funds available in 1992: $1,712,000.

* Veterans Loan Program (Veterans Loans) 59.038

Director, Loan Policy and Procedures Branch
Small Business Administration
409 3rd Street, SW
Washington, DC 20416   202-205-7510

To provide loans to small businesses owned by Vietnam-era and disabled veterans. Types of assistance: Loans. Estimate of annual funds available in 1992: $16,700,000.

* Certified Development Company Loans (504 Loans) 59.041

Office of Economic Development
Small Business Administration
409 3rd Street, SW
Washington, DC 20416   202-205-6485

To assist small business concerns by providing long-term financing for fixed assets through the sale of debentures to private investors. Types of assistance: Loan Guarantees. Estimate of annual funds available in 1992: $682,443,000.

* Business Loans for 8(a) Program Participants (8(a) Program Loans) 59.042

Director
Loan Policy and Procedures Branch
Small Business Administration
409 3rd Street, SW
Washington, DC 20416   202-205-7510

To provide direct and guaranteed loans to small business contractors receiving assistance under the subsection of 7(j) 10 and section 8(a) of the Small Business Act (15 U.S.C. 636 (a)), who are unable to obtain financing on reasonable terms in the private credit marketplace, but can demonstrate an ability to repay loans granted. Types of assistance: Loans. Estimate of annual funds available in 1992: $4,900,000.

* Women's Business Ownership Assistance 59.043

Small Business Administration
Office of Women's Business Ownership
409 3rd Street, SW
Washington, DC 20416   202-205-6673

To promote the legitimate interest of small business concerns owned and controlled by women and to remove, in so far as possible, the discriminatory barriers that are encountered by women in accessing the capital and other factors of production. Types of assistance: Grants. Estimate of annual funds available in 1992: $1,267,000.

* Commodity Loans and Purchases (Price Supports) 10.051

Cotton, Grain and Rice Price
  Support Division
Agricultural Stabilization and Conservation Service
U.S. Department of Agriculture
P.O. Box 2415
Washington, DC 20013   202-720-7641

To improve and stabilize farm income, to assist in bringing about balance between supply and demand of the commodities, and to assist farmers in the orderly marketing of their crops. Types of assistance: Direct Payments, Loans. Estimate of annual funds available in 1992: $7,675,721,000.

* Cotton Production Stabilization (Cotton Direct Payments) 10.052

Deputy Administrator Policy Analysis
Agricultural Stabilization and Conservation Service
U.S. Department of Agriculture
P.O. Box 2415
Washington, DC 20013   202-720-6734

To assure adequate production for domestic and foreign demand for fiber, to protect income for farmers, to take into account federal costs, to enhance the competitiveness of U.S. cotton for domestic mill use and export, and to conserve our natural resources. Types of assistance: Direct Payments. Estimate of annual funds available in 1992: $930,253,000.

* Dairy Indemnity Program 10.053

Emergency Operations and Livestock Program Division
Agricultural Stabilization and Conservation Service
U.S. Department of Agriculture
P.O. Box 2415
Washington, DC 20013   202-720-7673

To protect dairy farmers and manufacturers of dairy products who, through no fault of their own, are directed to remove their milk or dairy products from commercial markets because of contamination from pesticides which have been approved for use by the Federal government. Types of assistance: Direct Payments. Estimate of annual funds available in 1992: $200,000.

* Emergency Conservation Program (ECP) 10.054

Agricultural Stabilization and Conservation Service
U.S. Department of Agriculture
P.O. Box 2415
Washington, DC 20013   202-720-6221

To enable farmers to perform emergency conservation measures to control wind erosion on farmlands, or to rehabilitate farmlands damaged by wind erosion, floods, hurricanes, or other natural disasters. Types of assistance: Direct Payments. Estimate of annual funds available in 1992: $24,612,250.

* Feed Grain Production Stabilization (Feed Grain Direct Payments) 10.055

Deputy Administrator Policy Analysis
Agricultural Stabilization and Conservation Service
U.S. Department of Agriculture
P.O. Box 2415
Washington, DC 20013   202-720-4418

To assure adequate production for domestic and foreign demand, to protect income for farmers, to take into account federal costs, to enhance the competitiveness of United States exports. Types of assistance: Direct Payments. Estimate of annual funds available in 1992: $2,279,453,000.

* Wheat Production Stabilization (Wheat Direct Payments) 10.058

Deputy Administrator Policy Analysis
Agricultural Stabilization and Conservation Service
U.S. Department of Agriculture
P.O. Box 2415
Washington, DC 20013   202-720-4417

To assure adequate production for domestic and foreign demand, to protect income for farmers, to take into account federal costs, to enhance the competitiveness of U.S. exports, to compact inflation, and to conserve our natural resources. Types of assistance: Direct Payments. Estimate of annual funds available in 1992: $1,712,500,000.

* National Wool Act Payments (Wool and Mohair Support Payments) 10.059

Deputy Administrator Policy Analysis
Agricultural Stabilization and Conservation Service
U.S. Department of Agriculture
P.O. Box 2415
Washington, DC 20013   202-720-6734

To encourage continued domestic production of wool at prices fair to both producers and consumers in a way which will assure a viable domestic wool industry in the future. Types of assistance: Direct Payments. Estimate of annual funds available in 1992: $179,600,000.

* Water Bank Program 10.062

Agricultural Stabilization and Conservation Service
U.S. Department of Agriculture
P.O. Box 2415
Washington, DC 20013   202-720-6221

To conserve surface waters; preserve and improve the nation's wetlands; increase migratory waterfowl habitat in nesting, breeding and feeding areas in the U.S.; and secure environmental benefits for the nation. Types of assistance: Direct Payments. Estimate of annual funds available in 1992: $21,113,713.

* Agricultural Conservation Program (ACP) 10.063

Agricultural Stabilization and Conservation Service
U.S. Department of Agriculture
P.O. Box 2415
Washington, DC 20013   202-720-6221

Control of erosion and sedimentation, encourage voluntary compliance with federal and state requirements to solve point and nonpoint source pollution, improve water quality, encourage energy conservation measures, and assure a continued supply of necessary food and fiber for a strong and healthy people and economy. Types of assistance: Direct Payments. Estimate of annual funds available in 1992: $230,147,000.

* Forestry Incentives Program (FIP) 10.064

Agricultural Stabilization and Conservation Service
U.S. Department of Agriculture
P.O. Box 2415
Washington, DC 20013   202-720-6221

To bring private non-industrial forest land under intensified management; to increase timber production; to assure adequate supplies of timber; and to enhance other forest resources through a combination of public and private investments on the most productive sites on eligible individual or consolidated ownerships of efficient size and operation. Types of assistance: Direct Payments. Estimate of annual funds available in 1992: $14,334,176.

* Rice Production Stabilization (Rice Direct Payments) 10.065

Deputy Administrator
Policy Analysis Division
Agricultural Stabilization and Conservation Service
U.S. Department of Agriculture
P.O. Box 2415
Washington, DC 20013   202-720-7923

To assure adequate production for domestic and foreign demand, to protect income for farmers, to take into account federal costs, to enhance the competitiveness of U.S. exports, and to conserve our natural resources. Types of assistance: Direct Payments. Estimate of annual funds available in 1992: $490,200,000.

* Emergency Livestock Assistance 10.066

Emergency Operations and Livestock Programs Division
Agricultural Stabilization and Conservation Service
U.S. Department of Agriculture
P.O. Box 2415
Washington, DC 20013   202-720-5621

To provide emergency feed assistance to eligible livestock owners, in a State, county, or area approved by the Executive Vice President, CCC, where because of disease, insect infestation, flood, drought, fire, hurricane, earthquake, storm, hot weather, or other natural disaster, a livestock emergency exists. Types of assistance: Direct Payments. Estimate of annual funds available in 1992: $82,000,000.

* Grain Reserve Program (Farmer-Held and Owned Grain Reserve) 10.067

Cotton, Grain and Rice Price Support Division
Agricultural Stabilization and Conservation Service
U.S. Department of Agriculture
P.O. Box 2415
Washington, DC 20013   202-720-9886

To insulate sufficient quantities of grain from the market to increase price to farmers. Types of assistance: Direct Payments. Estimate of annual funds available in 1992: $26,000,000.

* Rural Clean Water Program (RCWP) 10.068

Conservation and Environmental Protection Division
Agricultural Stabilization and Conservation Service
U.S. Department of Agriculture
P.O. Box 2415
Washington, DC 20013   202-720-6221

To achieve improved water quality in the most cost-effective manner possible in keeping with the provisions of adequate supplies of food, fiber, and a quality environment, and to help control nonpoint source agricultural pollution. Types of assistance: Direct Payments. Estimate of annual funds available in 1992: $1,235,830.

* Conservation Reserve Program (CRP) 10.069

Conservation and Environmental Protection Division
Agricultural Stabilization and Conservation Service
U.S. Department of Agriculture
P.O. Box 2415
Washington, DC 20013   202-720-6221

To protect the nation's long-term capability to produce food and fiber; to reduce soil erosion; to reduce sedimentation; to improve water quality; to create a better habitat for fish and wildlife. Types of assistance: Direct Payments. Estimate of annual funds available in 1992: $1,739,560,000.

* Colorado River Basin Salinity Control Program (CRBSCP) 10.070

Conservation and Environmental Protection Division
Agricultural Stabilization and Conservation Service
U.S. Department of Agriculture
P.O. Box 2415
Washington, DC 20013   202-720-6221

To provide financial and technical assistance to identify salt source areas; develop project plans to carry out conservation practices to reduce salt loads; install conservation practices to reduce salinity levels; and carry out research, education, and demonstration activities. Types of assistance: Direct Payments. Estimate of annual funds available in 1992: $17,366,164.

* Small Business Innovation Research (SBIR Program) 10.212

SBIR Coordinator
Office of Grants and Program Systems
Cooperative State Research Service
U.S. Department of Agriculture (USDA)
Room 323, Aerospace Bldg.
14th and Independence Ave., SW
Washington, DC 20250-2200   202-401-6852

To stimulate technological innovation in the private sector, strengthen the role of small businesses in meeting federal research and development needs, increase private sector commercialization of innovations derived from USDA supported research and development effort, and foster and encourage minority and disadvantaged participation in technological innovation. Types of assistance: Grants. Estimate of annual funds available in 1992: $5,627,503.

* Sustainable Agriculture Research and Education 10.215

Cooperative State Research Service
U.S. Department of Agriculture
Washington, DC 20520   202-720-4423

To promote scientific investigation and education in order to reduce pesticides, improve low-input farm management, research and take advantage of local agricultural conditions and practices. Types of assistance: Grants. Estimate of annual funds available in 1992: $6,441,709.

* Emergency Loans 10.404

Administrator
Farmers Home Administration
U.S. Department of Agriculture
Washington, DC 20250   202-720-1632

To assist family farmers, ranchers and aquaculture operators with loans to cover losses resulting from major and/or natural disasters. Types of assistance: Loans. Estimate of annual funds available in 1992: $72,000,000.

* Farm Labor Housing Loans and Grants (Labor Housing) 10.405

Multi-Family Housing Processing Division
Farmers Home Administration
U.S. Department of Agriculture
Washington, DC 20250   202-720-1604

To provide decent, safe and sanitary low-rent housing and related facilities for domestic farm laborers. Types of assistance: Loan Guarantees. Estimate of annual funds available in 1992: $11,000,000.

* Farm Operating Loans 10.406

Director, Farmer Programs Loan Making Division
Farmers Home Administration
U.S. Department of Agriculture
Washington, DC 20250   202-720-1632

To enable operators of not larger than family farms through the extension of credit and supervisory assistance, to make efficient use of their land, labor, and other resources. Loans also available to youths. Types of assistance: Loans, Loan Guarantees. Estimate of annual funds available in 1992: $1,600,000,000.

* Farm Ownership Loans 10.407

Administrator
Farmers Home Administration
U.S. Department of Agriculture
Washington, DC 20250   202-720-1632

To assist eligible farmers, ranchers, and aquaculture operators, including farming cooperatives, corporations, partnerships, and joint operations through the extension of credit to become owner-operators of not larger than family farms. Types of assistance: Loans, Loan Guarantees. Estimate of annual funds available in 1992: $555,500,000.

* Rural Rental Housing Loans 10.415

Director, Multi-Family Housing Processing Division
Farmers Home Administration
U.S. Department of Agriculture
Washington, DC 20250   202-720-1604

To provide economically designed and constructed rental and cooperative housing and related facilities suited for independent living for rural residents. Types of assistance: Loan Guarantees. Estimate of annual funds available in 1992: $573,900,000.

* Soil and Water Loans (SW Loans) 10.416

Administrator
Farmers Home Administration
U.S. Department of Agriculture
Washington, DC 20250   202-720-1632

To facilitate improvement, protection, and proper use of farmland by providing adequate financing and supervisory assistance for soil conservation, water resource development, conservation and use. Types of assistance: Loans. Estimate of annual funds available in 1992: $2,544,000.

* Indian Tribes and Tribal Corporation Loans 10.421

Director
Community Facilities Division
Farmers Home Administration
U.S. Department of Agriculture
Washington DC 20250   202-720-1490

To enable tribes and tribal corporations to acquire land for the use of the tribe or its members. Types of assistance: Loan Guarantees. Estimate of annual funds available in 1992: $1,000,000.

* Business and Industrial Loans 10.422

Administrator
Farmers Home Administration
U.S. Department of Agriculture
Washington, DC 20250-0700   202-690-1533

To assist public, private, or cooperative organizations (profit or nonprofit), Indian tribes or individuals in rural areas to obtain quality loans for the purpose of improving, developing or financing business, industry, and employment and improving the economic and environment climate in rural communities including pollution abatement and control. Types of assistance: Loan Guarantees. Estimate of annual funds available in 1992: $101,127,500.

* Industrial Development Grants (IDG) 10.424

Director
Community Facilities Loan Division
Farmers Home Administration
U.S. Department of Agriculture
Washington, DC 20250   202-720-1490

To facilitate the development of small and emerging private business, industry and related employment for improving the economy in rural communities. Types of assistance: Grants. Estimate of annual funds available in 1992: $20,750,000.

* Rural Rental Assistance Payments (Rental Assistance) 10.427

Director
Multi-Housing Services and Property Management Division
Farmers Home Administration
U.S. Department of Agriculture
Washington, DC 20250   202-720-1599

To reduce the rents paid by low-income families occupying eligible Rural Rental Housing (RRH), Rural Cooperative Housing (RCH), and Farm Labor Housing (LH) projects financed by the Farmers Home Administration through its Sections 515, 514, and 516 loans and grants. Types of assistance: Direct Payments. Estimate of annual funds available in 1992: $319,900,000.

* Interest Rate Reduction Program 10.437

County Supervisor
Farmers Home Administrator
(in the county where the farming is located)
Or write FmHA
U.S. Department of Agriculture
Washington, DC 20250

To aid not larger than family sized farms in obtaining credit when they are temporarily unable to project a positive cash flow without a reduction in the interest rate. Types of assistance: Loan Guarantees. Estimate of annual funds available in 1992: $175,000,000.

* Intermediary Relending Program 10.439

Farmers Home Administration
Room 6321
South Agriculture Building
Washington, DC 20250   202-690-4100

To finance business facilities and community development. Types of assistance: Loans. Estimate of annual funds available in 1992: $32,500,000.

* Crop Insurance 10.450

Manager
Federal Crop Insurance Corporation
U.S. Department of Agriculture, Ste. 500

Washington, DC 20250   202-254-8460

To improve economic stability of agriculture through a sound system of crop insurance by providing multi-peril insurance for individual producers of commercially grown commodities against unavoidable causes of loss such as adverse weather conditions, fire, insects or other natural disasters. Types of assistance: Insurance. Estimate of annual funds available in 1992: $1,170,292,796.

* Foreign Agricultural Market Development and Promotion 10.600

Assistant Administrator
Commodity and Marketing Programs
Foreign Agricultural Service
U.S. Department of Agriculture
Washington, DC 20250   202-447-4761

To create, expand, and maintain markets abroad for U.S. agricultural commodities. Types of assistance: Direct Payments. Estimate of annual funds available in 1992: $34,700,000.

* Market Promotion Program (MPP) 10.601

Assistant Administrator
Commodity and Marketing Programs
Foreign Agricultural Service
U.S. Department of Agriculture
Washington, DC 20250   202-447-4761

To encourage foreign agricultural market development, and to counter or offset the adverse effect on the export of a U.S. agricultural commodity or the product thereof due to subsidy, import quota, or other unfair foreign trade practice. Types of assistance: Direct Payments. Estimate of annual funds available in 1992: $200,000,000.

* Rural Electrification Loans and Loan Guarantees (REA) 10.850

Administrator
Rural Electrification Administration
U.S. Department of Agriculture
Washington, DC 20250-1500   202-720-9540

To assure that people in eligible rural areas have access to electric services comparable in reliability and quality to the rest of the nation. Types of assistance: Loan Guarantees. Estimate of annual funds available in 1992: $2,057,550,000.

* Rural Telephone Loans and Loan Guarantees (REA) 10.851

Administrator
Rural Electrification Administration
U.S. Department of Agriculture
Washington, DC 20250   202-720-9540

To assure that people in eligible rural areas have access to telephone service comparable in reliability and quality to the rest of the nation. Types of assistance: Loan Guarantees. Estimate of annual funds available in 1992: $358,875,000.

* Rural Telephone Bank Loans (Rural Telephone Bank) 10.852

Governor
Rural Telephone Bank
U.S. Department of Agriculture
Washington, DC 20250   202-720-9540

To provide supplemental financing to extend and improve telephone service in rural areas. Types of assistance: Loans. Estimate of annual funds available in 1992: $177,045,000.

* Rural Economic Development Loans and Grants 10.854

Administrator
Rural Electrification Administration
U.S. Department of Agriculture
Washington, DC 20250   202-720-9552

To promote rural economic development and job creation projects, including funding for project feasibility studies, start-up costs, incubator projects, and other reasonable expenses for the purpose of fostering rural development. Types of assistance: Loans, Grants. Estimate of annual funds available in 1992: $8,773,000.

* Great Plains Conservation 10.900

Deputy Chief for Programs
Soil Conservation Service
U.S. Department of Agriculture
P.O. Box 2890
Washington, DC 20013   202-720-1868

To conserve and develop the Great Plains soil and water resources by providing technical and financial assistance to farmers, ranchers, and others in planning and implementing conservation practices. Types of assistance: Direct Payments. Estimate of annual funds available: $16,500,109.

* Research and Evaluation Program 11.312

David H. Geddes
Room H-7315
Economic Development Administration
U.S. Department of Commerce
Washington, DC 20230   202-482-4085

To assist in the determination of causes of unemployment; to promote programs that will raise income levels; to alleviate economic distress. Types of assistance: Grants. Estimate of annual funds available: $1,193,000.

* Trade Adjustment Assistance 11.313

Daniel F. Harrington
U.S. Department of Commerce
Trade Adjustment Assistance Division
Economic Development Administration
14th and Constitution Ave. NW
Washington, DC 20230   202-377-3373

To provide trade adjustment assistance to firms and industries adversely affected by increased imports. Types of assistance: Grants. Estimate of annual funds available in 1992: $14,000,000.

* Fishermen's Contingency Fund (Title IV) 11.408

Inspection Services Division
Financial Services Division
National Marine Fisheries Service
1335 East West Hwy.
Silver Spring, MD 20910   301-713-2396

To compensate U.S. commercial fishermen for damage/loss of fishing gear and 50% of resulting economic loss due to oil and gas related activities in any area of the Outer Continental Shelf. Types of assistance: Direct Payments. Estimate of annual funds available in 1992: $989,000.

* Fishing Vessel and Gear Damage Compensation Fund (Section 10) 11.409

Chief, Financial Services Division
National Marine Fisheries Service
U.S. Department of Commerce
1335 East West Hwy.
Silver Spring, MD 20910   301-713-2396

To compensate U.S. fishermen for the loss, damage, or destruction of their vessels by foreign fishing vessels and their gear by any vessel. Types of assistance: Direct Payments. Estimate of annual funds available in 1992: $1,296,000.

* Minority Business Development Centers (MBDC) 11.800

Assistant Director
Office of Program Operations
Room 5063, Minority Business Agency
U.S. Department of Commerce
14th and Constitution Ave., NW
Washington, DC 20230   202-377-8015

To provide business development services for a minimal fee to minority firms and individuals interested in entering, expanding or improving their efforts in the marketplace. Types of assistance: Grants. Estimate of annual funds available in 1992: $22,491,000.

* American Indian Program (AIP) 11.801

Assistant Director
Office of Program Development
Room 5063
Minority Business Development Agency
U.S. Department of Commerce
14th and Constitution Ave., NW
Washington, DC 20230   202-377-8015

To provide business development service to American Indians and individuals interested in entering, expanding or improving their efforts in the marketplace. Types of assistance: Grants. Estimate of annual funds available in 1992: $1,495,000.

* Minority Business and Industry Association-Minority Chambers of Commerce (MB and IA/C of C) 11.802

Theresa Speake, Asst. Director
Office of Program Development
Room 5096, Minority Business Development Agency
U.S. Department of Commerce
14th and Constitution Ave., NW
Washington, DC 20230   202-377-5770

To provide financial assistance for Minority Business and Industry Association/ Minority Chambers of Commerce (MB and IA/C of C) which act as advocates for their members and the minority community. Types of assistance: Grants. Estimate of annual funds available in 1992: $4,601,000.

* Procurement Technical Assistance for Business Firms (Procurement Technical Assistance (PTA)) 12.002

Defense Logistics Agency
Cameron Station
Office of Small and Disadvantaged Business Utilization (DLA-U)
Room 4B130
Alexandria, VA 22304-6100   202-274-6471

To assist eligible entities in the payment of the costs of establishing new Procurement Technical Assistance Programs and maintaining existing Procurement Technical Assistance Programs. Types of assistance: Grants. Estimate of annual funds available in 1992: $12,279,481.

* Interest Reduction Payments-Rental and Cooperative Housing for Lower Income Families (236) 14.103

Director
Office of Multifamily Housing Management
U.S. Department of Housing and Urban Development
Washington, DC 20410   202-708-3730

To provide good quality rental and cooperative housing for persons of low- and moderate-income by providing interest reduction payments in order to lower their housing costs. Types of assistance: Direct Payments. Estimate of annual funds available in 1992: $645,579,000.

* Mortgage Insurance-Construction or Substantial Rehabilitation of Condominium Projects (234(d) Condominiums) 14.112

Insurance Division
Office of Insured Multifamily Housing Development
U.S. Department of Housing and Urban Development
Washington, DC 20410   202-708-2556

To enable sponsors to develop condominium projects in which individual units will be sold to home buyers. Types of assistance: Loan Guarantees. Estimate of annual funds available in 1992: $7,679,000.

* Mortgage Insurance - Homes (203(b)) 14.117

Director
Single Family Development Division
Office of Single Family Housing
U.S. Department of Housing and Urban Development
Washington, DC 20410   202-708-2700

To help families undertake home ownership. Types of assistance: Loan Guarantees. Estimate of annual funds available in 1992: $44,279,662,000.

* Mortgage Insurance-Cooperative Projects (213 Cooperatives) 14.126

Policies and Procedures Division
Office of Insured Multifamily Housing Development
U.S. Department of Housing and Urban Development
Washington, DC 20410   202-708-2556

To make it possible for nonprofit cooperative ownership housing corporations or trusts to develop or sponsor the development of housing projects to be operated as cooperatives. Most cooperative mortgages are now obtained under 221 (d)(3). Types of assistance: Loan Guarantees. Estimate of annual funds available: Contact Office Above.

* Mortgage Insurance-Manufactured Home Parks (207(m) Manufactured Home Parks) 14.127

Policies and Procedures Division
Office of Insured Multifamily Housing Development
U.S. Department of Housing and Urban Development
Washington, DC 20410   202-708-2556

To make possible the financing of construction or rehabilitation of manufactured home parks. Types of assistance: Loan Guarantees. Estimate of annual funds available: Contact Office Above.

* Mortgage Insurance-Hospitals (242 Hospitals) 14.128

Hospital Program
U.S. Department of Housing and Urban Development
Washington, DC 20410   202-708-0599

To make possible the financing of hospitals. Types of assistance: Loan Guarantees. Estimate of annual funds available in 1992: $428,754,000.

* Mortgage Insurance-Nursing Homes, Intermediate Care Facilities and Board and Care Homes (232 Nursing Homes) 14.129

Insurance Division
Office of Insured Multifamily Housing Development
U.S. Department of Housing and Urban Development
Washington, DC 20412   202-708-2556

Types of assistance: Loan Guarantees. Estimate of annual funds available in 1992: $684,098,000.

* Mortgage Insurance-Purchase of Sales-Type Cooperative Housing Units 14.132

Director
Single Family Development Division
Office of Insured Family Housing
U.S. Department of Housing and Urban Development
Washington, DC 20410   202-708-2700

To make available good quality new housing for purchase by individual members of a housing cooperative. Now accepting applications. Types of assistance: Loan Guarantees. Estimate of annual funds available: Contact office above.

* Mortgage Insurance-Purchase of Units in Condominiums (234(c)) 14.133

Director
Single Family Development Division
Office of Insured Single Family Housing
U.S. Department of Housing and Urban Development
Washington, DC 20410   202-708-2700

To enable families to purchase units in condominium projects. Types of assistance: Loan Guarantees. Estimate of annual funds available in 1992: $2,904,209,000

* Mortgage Insurance-Rental Housing for Moderate Income Families and Elderly, Market Interest Rate (221(d)(3) and (4) Multifamily - Market Rate Housing) 14.135

Policies and Procedures Division
Office of Insured Multifamily Housing Development

U.S. Department of Housing and Urban Development
Washington, DC 20410   202-708-2556
To provide good quality rental or cooperative housing for moderate income
families and the elderly. Types of assistance: Loan Guarantees. Estimate of
annual funds available in 1992: $666,648,000.

* Mortgage Insurance-Rental Housing for the Elderly (231) 14.138
Policies and Procedures Division
Office of Insured Multifamily Housing Development
U.S. Department of Housing and Urban Development
Washington, DC 20410   202-708-2556
To provide good quality rental housing for the elderly. Types of assistance: Loan
Guarantees. Estimate of annual funds available in 1992: $2,693,000.

* Mortgage Insurance-Rental Housing in Urban Renewal Areas 14.139
Policies and Procedures Division
Office of Insured Multifamily Housing Development
U.S. Department of Housing and Urban Development
Washington, DC 20410   202-708-2566
To provide good quality rental housing in urban renewal areas, code
enforcement areas, and other areas designated for overall revitalization. Types
of assistance: Loan Guarantees. Estimate of annual funds available in 1992:
$5,674,000.

* Property Improvement Loan Insurance for Improving all Existing Structures and Building of New Nonresidential Structures (Title I) 14.142
Director
Title I Insurance Division
U.S. Department of Health and Human Services   202-708-2880
Washington DC 20410   1-800-733-4663
To facilitate the financing of improvements to homes and other existing
structures and the building of new nonresidential structures. Types of assistance:
Loan Guarantees. Estimate of annual funds available in 1992: $1,440,000,000.

* Rent Supplements--Rental Housing for Lower Income Families 14.149
Office of Multi-Family Housing Management
U.S. Department of Housing and Urban Development
Washington, DC 20410   202-708-3730
To make good quality rental housing available to low income families at a cost
they can afford. Types of assistance: Direct Payments. Estimate of annual funds
available in 1992: $50,139,000.

* Supplemental Loan Insurance-Multifamily Rental Housing 14.151
Policies and Procedures Division
Office of Insured Multifamily Housing Development
U.S. Department of Housing and Urban Development
Washington DC 20411   202-708-2556
To finance repairs, additions and improvements to multifamily projects, group
practice facilities, hospitals, or nursing homes already insured by HUD or held
by HUD. Types of assistance: Loan Guarantees. Estimate of annual funds
available in 1992: $184,370,000.

* Mortgage Insurance for the Purchase or Refinancing of Existing Multifamily Housing Projects (Section 223(f) Insured Under Section 207) 14.155
Office of Insured Multifamily Housing Development
Policies and Procedures Division
U.S. Department of Housing and Urban Development
Washington, DC 20410   202-708-2556
To provide mortgage insurance to lenders for the purchase or refinancing of
existing multifamily housing projects, whether conventionally financed or subject
to federally insured mortgages. Types of assistance: Loan Guarantees. Estimate
of annual funds available in 1992: $418,075,000.

* Housing for the Elderly or Disabled 202- 14.157
Housing for the Elderly and Handicapped People Division
Office of Elderly and Assisted Housing
U.S. Department of Housing and Urban Development
Washington, DC 20410   202-708-2730
To provide for rental or cooperative housing and related facilities (such as
central dining) for the elderly or disabled. Types of assistance: Loans. Estimate
of annual funds available in 1992: $11,105,000.

* Operating Assistance for Troubled Multifamily Housing Projects (Flexible Subsidy Fund) (Troubled Projects) 14.164
Director
Management Operations Division
Office of Multifamily Housing Management
U.S. Department of Housing and Urban Development
Washington, DC 20420   202-708-3730
To provide assistance to restore or maintain the physical and financial soundness
of certain projects assisted or approved for assistance under the National
Housing Act or under the Housing and Urban Development Act of 1965. Types
of assistance: Grants, Direct Payments. Estimate of annual funds available in
1992: $208,500,000.

* Mortgage Insurance-Two Year Operating Loss Loans, Section 22 14.167
Office of Insured Multifamily Housing Development
Policies and Procedures Division
U.S. Department of Housing and Urban Development (HUD)
Washington, DC 20410   202-708-3730
To insure a separate loan covering operating losses incurred during the first two
years following the date of completion of a multifamily project with a HUD
insured first mortgage. Types of assistance: Loan Guarantees. Estimate of annual
funds available in 1992: $8,155,000.

* Mortgage Insurance--Experimental Homes (ExTech 233-Homes) 14.507
Asst. Secretary for Policy Development and Research
Division of Innovative Technology
U.S. Department of Housing and Urban Development
451 7th Street, SW
Washington, DC 20410   202-708-0640
To help finance the development of homes that incorporate new or untried
construction concepts designed to reduce housing costs, raise living standards,
and improve neighborhood design by providing mortgage insurance. Types of
assistance: Loan Guarantees. Estimate of annual funds available: Contact Office
Above.

* Mortgage Insurance--Experimental Projects Other Than Housing (ExTech 233-Projects Other Than Housing) 14.508
Asst. Secretary for Policy Development and Research
Division of Innovative Technology
U.S. Department of Housing and Urban Development
451 7th Street, SW
Washington, DC 20410   202-708-0640
To provide mortgage insurance to help finance the development of group
medical facilities that incorporate new or untried construction concepts intended
to reduce construction costs, raise living standards and improve neighborhood
design. Types of assistance: Loans. Estimate of annual funds available: Contact
Office Above.

* Mortgage Insurance--Experimental Rental Housing 14.509
Asst. Secretary for Policy Development and Research
Division of Innovative Technology
U.S. Department of Housing and Urban Development
451 7th Street, SW
Washington, DC 20410   202-708-0640
To provide mortgage insurance to help finance the development of multifamily

housing that incorporates new or untried construction concepts designed to reduce housing costs, raise living standards, and improve neighborhood design. Types of assistance: Loan Guarantees. Estimate of annual funds available: Contact Office Above.

* National Water Resource Research Program 15.806

Geological Survey
U.S. Department of the Interior
MS 424, National Center
Reston, VA 22092   703-648-6811

To support needed research into any aspect of water resource related problems deemed to be in the national interest. Types of assistance: Project Grants. Estimate of annual funds available in 1992: $1,787,000.

* Earthquake Hazards Reduction Program 15.807

Geological Survey
U.S. Department of the Interior
MS 905, National Center
Reston, VA 22092   703-648-6722

To mitigate earthquake losses that can occur in many parts of the nation by providing earth science data and assessments essential for warning of imminent damaging earthquakes, land-use planning, engineering design, and emergency preparedness decisions. Types of assistance: Project Grants. Estimate of annual funds available in 1992: $10,000,000.

* Geological Survey--Research and Data Acquisition 15.808

Geological Survey
U.S. Department of the Interior
MS 104, National Center
Reston, VA 22092   703-648-4451

To support research in any field of study that helps fulfill the Geological Survey's mission. Types of assistance: Project Grants. Estimate of annual funds available in 1992: $9,000,000.

* Protection of Ships from Foreign Seizure (Fishermen's Protection Act) 19.201

Ronald J. Bettauer
Asst. Legal Adviser for International Claims and Investment Disputes
Office of the Legal Adviser
Suite 402, 2100 K St., NW
Washington, DC 20037-7180   202-632-7810

To reimburse U.S. fishermen whose vessels are seized by a foreign country on the basis of claims to jurisdictions not recognized by the U.S., claims to jurisdictions recognized by the U.S. but exercised in a manner inconsistent with international law as recognized by the U.S., any general claim to exclusive fisher management with conditions and restrictions. Types of assistance: Insurance. Estimate of annual funds available in 1992: $100,000.

* Fishermen's Guaranty Fund (Section 7) 19.204

Office of Fisheries Affairs
Bureau of Oceans and International Environmental
   and Scientific Affairs
Room 5806
U.S. Department of State
Washington, DC 20520-7818   202-647-2009

To provide for reimbursement of losses incurred as a result of the seizure of a U.S. commercial fishing vessel by a foreign country on the basis of rights or claims in territorial waters or on the high seas which are not recognized by the United States. Types of assistance: Insurance. Estimate of annual funds available in 1992: $900,000.

* Airport Improvement Program (AIP) 20.106

Federal Aviation Administration
Office of Airport Planning and Programming
Grants-in-Aid Division
APP-500, 800 Independence Ave., SW
Washington, DC 20591   202-267-3831

To assist sponsors, owners, or operators of public-use airports in the development of a nationwide system of airports adequate to meet the needs of civil aeronautics. Types of assistance: Grants. Estimate of annual funds available in 1992: $1,900,000,000.

* Federal Ship Financing Guarantees (Title XI) 20.802

Associate Administrator for Maritime Aids
Maritime Administration
U.S. Department of Transportation
Washington, DC 20590   202-366-0364

To promote construction and reconstruction of ships in the foreign trade and domestic commerce of the U.S. by providing Government guarantees of obligations so as to make commercial credit more available. Types of assistance: Loan Guarantees. Estimate of annual funds available: Contact Office Above.

* Maritime War Risk Insurance (Title XII, MMA, 1936) 20.803

Edmond J. Fitzgerald, Director
Office of Trade Analysis and Insurance
Maritime Administration
U.S. Department of Transportation
Washington, DC 20590   202-366-2400

To provide war risk insurance whenever it appears to the Secretary of Transportation that adequate insurance for water-borne commerce cannot be obtained on reasonable terms and conditions from licensed insurance companies in the U.S.. Types of assistance: Insurance. Estimate of annual funds available in 1992: $273,000.

* Operating-Differential Subsidies (ODS) 20.804

Associate Administrator for Maritime Aids
Maritime Administration
U.S. Department of Transportation
400 7th Street, SW
Washington, DC 20590   202-366-0364

To promote development and maintenance of the U.S. Merchant Marine by granting financial aid to equalize cost of operating a U.S. flag ship with cost of operating a competitive foreign flag ship. Types of assistance: Direct Payments. Estimate of annual funds available in 1992: $272,210,000.

* Capital Construction Fund (CCF) 20.808

Associate Administrator for Maritime Aids
Maritime Administration
U.S. Department of Transportation
Washington, DC 20590   202-366-0364

To provide for replacement vessels, additional vessels or reconstructed vessels, built and documented under the laws of the U.S. for operation in the U.S. foreign, Great Lakes or noncontiguous domestic trades. Types of assistance: Direct Payments. Estimate of annual funds available in 1992: $256,000.

* Supplementary Training 20.810

Bruce J. Carlton, Director
Office of Maritime Labor and Training
Maritime Administration
U.S. Department of Transportation
Washington, DC 20590   202-366-5755

To train seafarers in shipboard firefighting, diesel propulsion and other such essential subjects related to safety and operations where this training is not or cannot be provided by the industry directly. Types of assistance: Other. Estimate of annual funds available in 1992: $678,000.

* Construction Reserve Fund (CRF) 20.812

Associate Administrator for Maritime Aids
Maritime Administration
U.S. Department of Transportation
Washington, DC 20590   202-366-0364

To promote the construction, reconstruction, reconditioning or acquisition of merchant vessels which are necessary for national defense and to the development of U.S. commerce. Types of assistance: Direct Payments. Estimate of annual funds available in 1992: $72,000.

* Payments for Essential Air Services 20.901
Director
Office of Aviation Analysis, P-50
U.S. Department of Transportation
400 7th St. SW
Washington, DC 20590   202-366-1030
To provide air transportation to eligible communities by subsidizing air service. Types of assistance: Direct Payments. Estimate of annual funds available in 1992: $38,600,000.

* Promotion of the Arts--Design Arts 45.001
Director
Design Arts Program
National Endowment for the Arts
1100 Pennsylvania Ave., NW
Washington, DC 20506   202-682-5437
To promote excellence in architecture, landscape architecture, urban design, historic preservation, planning, interior design, graphic design, industrial design and fashion design. Types of assistance: Grants. Estimate of annual funds available in 1992: $3,777,000.

* Promotion of the Arts--Dance 45.002
Dance Program
National Endowment for the Arts
1100 Pennsylvania Ave., NW
Washington, DC 20506   202-682-5435
To provide support for professional choreographers, dance companies, organizations and individuals that present or serve dance. Types of assistance: Grants. Estimate of annual funds available in 1992: $8,521,000.

* Promotion of the Arts--Literature 45.004
Director
Literature Program
National Endowment for the Arts
1100 Pennsylvania Ave., NW
Washington, DC 20506   202-682-5451
To aid creative writers of fiction and non-fiction, poets, and translators of literary works (into English). Types of assistance: Grants. Estimate of annual funds available in 1992: $4,577,000.

* Promotion of the Arts--Media Arts: Film/Radio/ Television 45.006
Cliff Whitham
Media Arts Program
National Endowment for the Arts
1100 Pennsylvania Ave., NW
Washington, DC 20506   202-682-5452
To provide grants in support of projects designed to advance the media arts and to encourage their practice and wider appreciation. Types of assistance: Grants. Estimate of annual funds available in 1992: $12,397,000.

* Promotion of the Arts--Theater 45.008
Director
Theater Program
National Endowment for the Arts
1100 Pennsylvania Ave., NW
Washington, DC 20506   202-682-5425
To provide grants to aid professional not-for-profit theater companies, individual theater artists, national theater service organizations, professional theater training institutions, and professional not-for-profit theater presenters, including festivals. Types of assistance: Grants. Estimate of annual funds available in 1992: $9,563,000.

* Promotion of the Arts--Visual Arts 45.009
Director
Visual Arts Program
National Endowment for the Arts
1100 Pennsylvania Ave., NW
Washington, DC 20506   202-682-5448
To provide grants to assist visual artists including: painters, sculptors, photographers, crafts artists, printmakers, artists specializing in traditional and new genres. Types of assistance: Grants. Estimate of annual funds available: $5,554,000.

* Promotion of the Arts--Museums 45.012
Director
Museum Program
National Endowment for the Arts
1100 Pennsylvania Ave., NW
Washington, DC 20506   202-682-5442
To provide grants in support of American museums' essential activities and the evolving needs of the museum field. Types of assistance: Grants. Estimate of annual funds available in 1992: $11,080,000.

* Promotion of the Arts--Opera-Musical Theater 45.014
Director
Opera-Musical Theater Program
National Endowment for the Arts
1100 Pennsylvania Ave., NW
Washington, DC 20506   202-682-5447
To support excellence in the performance and creation of professional opera and musical theater. Types of assistance: Grants. Estimate of annual funds available in 1992: $6,063,000.

* Promotion of the Arts--Folk Arts 45.015
Director
Folk Arts Program
National Endowment for the Arts
1100 Pennsylvania Ave., NW
Washington, DC 20506   202-682-5449
To provide grants to assist, foster, and make publicly available the diverse traditional American folk arts. Types of assistance: Grants. Estimate of annual funds available in 1992: $3,160,000.

* Arts and Artifacts Indemnity 45.201
Indemnity Administrator
Museum Program
National Endowment for the Arts
Washington, DC 20506   202-682-5442
To provide for indemnification against loss or damage for eligible art works, artifacts and objects. Types of assistance: Insurance. Estimate of annual funds available: Contact Office Above.

* Computer and Information Science and Engineering (CISE) 47.070
Asst. Director
Computer and Information Science and Engineering
National Science Foundation
1800 G Street, NW, Room 306
Washington, DC 20550   202-357-7936
To support research improving the fundamental understanding of computer and information processing, to enhance the training and education of scientists and engineers who contribute to and exploit that understanding, to enhance the personnel pool for these fields, and to provide access to very advanced computing and networking capabilities. Types of assistance: Grants. Estimate of annual funds available in 1992: $210,940,000.

* Superfund Technical Assistance Grants for Citizen Groups at Priority Sites (Superfund Technical Assistance Grants) 66.806
Murray Newton
Office of Emergency and Remedial Response
5203-G
Environmental Protection Agency
401 M Street, SW
Washington, DC 20460   703-603-8775
To provide resources for community groups to hire technical advisors who can assist them in interpreting technical information concerning the assessment of

potential hazards and the selection and design of appropriate remedies at sites eligible for cleanup under the Superfund program. Types of assistance: Grants. Estimate of annual funds available in 1992: $3,200,000.

* Superfund Innovative Technology Evaluation Program (SITE) 66.807

Richard Nalesnik, Chief
Office of Environmental Engineering Technology Demonstration
Environmental Protection Agency
401 M Street, SW, (RD-681)
Washington, DC 20460   202-260-2583

To promote research and development of alternative and innovative treatment technologies that can be used under the Comprehensive Environmental Response, Compensation and Liability Act (CERCLA) and to provide incentives for the development and use of such technologies. Types of assistance: Grants. Estimate of annual funds available in 1992: $12,493,000.

* Foreign Investment Guaranties 70.002

Daven Oswalt, Information Officer
Overseas Private Investment Corporation
1615 M Street, NW
Washington, DC 20527   202-457-7033

To guarantee loans and other investment made by eligible U.S. investors in friendly developing countries and areas. Types of assistance: Loan Guarantees. Estimate of annual funds available in 1992: $375,000,000.

* Foreign Investment Insurance (Political Risk Insurance) 70.003

Daven Oswalt, Information Officer
Overseas Private Investment Corporation
1615 M Street, NW
Washington DC 20527   202-457-7033

To insure investments of eligible U.S. investors in developing friendly countries and areas, against the risks of inconvertibility, expropriation, war, revolution and insurrection, certain types of civil strife, and business interruption. Types of assistance: Insurance. Estimate of annual funds available in 1992: $2,290,000,000.

* Direct Investment Loans (Dollar Loans) 70.005

Daven Oswalt, Information Officer
Overseas Private Investment Corporation
1615 M Street, NW
Washington DC 20527   202-457-7033

To make loans for projects in developing countries sponsored by or significantly involving U.S. small business or cooperatives. Types of assistance: Loans. Estimate of annual funds available in 1992: $25,000,000.

* Energy-Related Inventions 81.036

George Lewitt, Director
Office of Technology Evaluation and Assessment.
National Institute of Standards and Technology
Gaithersburg, MD 20899   301-975-5500

To encourage innovation in developing non-nuclear energy technology by providing assistance to individual and small business companies in the development of promising energy-related inventions. Types of assistance: Grants. Estimate of annual funds available in 1992: $6,169,365.

* Basic Energy Sciences--University and Science Education (Basic Energy Sciences, High Energy and Nuclear Physics, Fusion Energy, Health and Environmental Research, Program Analysis, Field Operations Management, Superconducting Super Collider, Scientific Computing, and University & Science Education) 81.049

William Burrier
Division of Acquisition and Assistance Management
Office of Energy Research
Office of Energy, Mail Stop G-236
Washington, DC 20545   301-335-5544

To provide financial support for fundamental research, training and related activities in the basic sciences and advanced technology concepts and assessments in fields related to energy. Types of assistance: Grants. Estimate of annual funds available in 1992: $411,621,000.

* Energy Extension Service 81.050

James Demetrops, Director
State Energy Programs Division
U.S. Department of Energy, (CE-522)
Forrestal Building
1000 Independence Ave., SW
Washington, DC 20585   202-586-9187

To encourage individuals and small establishments to reduce energy consumption and convert to alternative energy sources. Types of assistance: Grants. Estimate of annual funds available in 1992: $4,757,000.

* Office of Minority Economic Impact Loans (OMEI Direct Loans for DOE Bid or Proposal Preparation) 81.063

Sterling Nichols
Office of Minority Economic Impact
MI-1, U.S. Department of Energy
Forrestal Bldg., Room 5B-110
Washington, DC 20585   202-586-1594

To provide direct loans to minority business enterprises (MBE) to assist them in financing bid or proposal preparation costs they would incur in pursuing DOE work. Types of assistance: Loans. Estimate of annual funds available: Contact Office Above.

* Industrial Energy Conservation 81.078

Marsha Quinn
Office of Industrial Technologies
CE-14, U.S. Department of Energy
Washington, DC 20585   202-586-2097

To work closely with industry to develop new technologies to improve energy efficiency and fuel flexibility in the industrial sector. To conduct programs to reduce waste generation, increase recycling, improve the use of waste as process feedstocks, and encourage adoption of new technologies. Types of assistance: Grants. Estimate of annual funds available in 1992: $3,000,000.

* Regional Biomass Programs 81.079

Mike Voorhies
Office of Natural Programs
CE-52, U.S. Department of Energy
Washington, DC 20585   202-586-1480

To conduct a long-term research effort to provide generic technology tailored to specific regions for feedstock, production, and conversion technologies, and municipal solid waste. Types of assistance: Grants. Estimate of annual funds available in 1992: $4,523,000.

* Conservation Research and Development (Conservation) 81.086

Barbara Twigg
Office of Management and Resources
Conservation and Renewable Energy
Washington, DC 20585   202-586-8174

To conduct a research effort in the areas of buildings, industry, transportation. Grants will be offered to develop and transfer to the nonfederal sector various energy conservation technologies. Types of assistance: Grants. Estimate of annual funds available in 1992: $8,258,000.

* Renewable Energy Research and Development (Renewable Energy) 81.087

Barbara Twigg
Office of Management and Resources
U.S. Department of Energy
Washington, DC 20585   202-586-8714

To research and develop efforts in energy technologies: solar buildings, photovoltaics, solar thermal, biomass, alcohol fuels, urban waste, wind, ocean, and geothermal. Grants will be offered to develop and transfer to the nonfederal sector various renewable energy technologies. Types of assistance: Grants. Estimate of annual funds available in 1992: $100,000.

* Fossil Energy Research and Development 81.089

Dwight Mottett
U.S. Department of Energy
Fossil Energy Program
FE-122
Germantown, MD 20545   202-903-3008

To support long-term, high risk research and development with high potential payoff to increase domestic production of oil and gas or help shift use of oil and gas to more abundant coal and oil shale resources. Types of assistance: Grants. Estimate of annual funds available in 1992: $53,777,063.

* Socioeconomic and Demographic Research, Data and Other Information 81.091

Georgia R. Johnson
U.S. Department of Energy
Forrestal Building, Room 5B-110
Washington, DC 20585   202-586-1593

To provide financial support for developing and enhancing socioeconomic and demographic research to determine minority energy consumption, minority income spent on energy; develop information to guide policy and assist minority education and business. Types of assistance: Grants. Estimate of annual funds available in 1992: $800,000.

* Nuclear Energy, Reactor Systems, Development, and Technology 81.095

H. Rohm
Office of Nuclear Energy (NE-40)
B-410, Germantown Building
Washington, DC 20545   301-353-6590

To provide financial support for research, design, analysis, and assessments in science and technology in fields related to nuclear energy. Types of assistance: Grants. Estimate of annual funds available in 1992: $3,500,000.

* Clean Coal Technology Program 81.096

C. Lowell Miller
U.S. Department of Energy
Fossil Energy Program
FE-22, Clean Coal Technology
Washington, DC 20585   703-235-2450

To solicit proposals to conduct cost-shared Innovative Clean Coal Technology projects to demonstrate technologies that are capable of being commercialized in the 1990's, that are more cost-effective than current technologies, and that are capable of achieving significant reduction of SO2 and/or NOX emissions from existing coal burning facilities, particularly those that contribute to transboundary and interstate pollution. Types of assistance: Grants. Estimate of annual funds available in 1992: $177,243,200.

* Technology Integration (TIP) 81.103

C. Sink
Office of Technology Development
Environmental Restoration and Waste Management
U.S. Department of Energy (DOE), EM-52
Washington, DC 20545   301-903-7928

To support the mission of TIP by expediting the transfer of technologies/information from DOE to industry and from industry to DOE. Also, to coordinate technological development for environmental restoration and waste management within DOE and between DOE and other government agencies. Types of assistance: Grants. Estimate of annual funds available: $4,000,000.

* Disabled--Innovation and Development (Research and Demonstration Projects in Education for the Disabled) 84.023

Martha Coutinho
Division of Innovation and Development
Office of Asst. Secretary of Education

400 Maryland Ave., NW
Washington, DC 20202   202-205-8156

To improve the education of children with disabilities through research and development projects and model programs (demonstrations). Types of assistance: Grants. Estimate of annual funds available in 1992: $21,000,000.

* Early Education for Children with Disabilities 84.024

James Hamilton
Division of Educational Services
Special Education Programs
Office of Asst. Secretary for Special Education
and Rehabilitation Services
U.S. Department of Education
400 Maryland Ave., SW
Washington, DC 20202   202-205-9084

To support demonstration, dissemination and implementation of effective approaches to preschool and early childhood education for children with disabilities. Types of assistance: Grants. Estimate of annual funds available: $24,202,000.

* Media and Captioning for Individuals with Disabilities 84.026

Ernest Hairston
Division of Educational Services
Special Education Programs
Office of Asst. Secretary of Special Education
and Rehabilitation Services
U.S. Department of Education
Washington, DC 20202   202-205-9172

To maintain free loan service of captioned films for the deaf and instructional media for the educational, cultural, and vocational enrichment of disabled. Provide for acquisition and distribution of media materials and equipment; provide contracts distribution of media material and equipment; provide contracts and grants for research into use of media and technology, train teachers, parents, etc. in media and technology use. Types of assistance: Grants. Estimate of annual funds available in 1992: $17,000,000.

* Educational Research and Development 84.117

Office of Educational Research and Improvement
U.S. Department of Education
555 New Jersey Ave., NW
Washington, DC 20208   202-219-2079

To advance knowledge about and understanding of education policy and practice, and solve, alleviate, or illuminate educational problems. Types of assistance: Grants. Estimate of annual funds available in 1992: $27,700,000.

* Technology, Educational Media and Materials for Individuals with Disabilities (Technical Development) 84.180

Ellen Schiller
Division of Innovation and Development
U.S. Department of Education
400 Maryland Ave., NW
Washington, DC 20202   202-205-8123

To advance the use of new technology, media, and materials in the education of disabled students and the provision of early intervention to infants and toddlers with disabilities. Types of assistance: Grants. Estimate of annual funds available: $5,593,000.

* Food and Drug Administration Research 93.103

Program and Grants Management
Grants and Assistance Agreements
Division of Contracts and Grants
Federal Drug Administration
Public Health Service
U.S. Department of Health and Human Services
HFA-520, Room 340
Parklawn Bldg., 5600 Fishers Lane
Rockville MD 20857   301-443-6170

To assist profit-making organizations, public and others, to research and disseminate information about AIDS, poison control, drug hazards, human and veterinary drugs, medical devices, diagnostic products, biologies, and radiation emitting devices; stimulate technological innovation; use small business to meet Federal R&D needs; increase private sector commercialization of innovations derived from Federal research; foster minority and disadvantaged persons' participation in innovations. Types of assistance: Grants. Estimate of annual funds available in 1992: $10,000,000.

* Adolescent Family Life Research Grants 93.111

Ms. Eckard
Office of Adolescent Pregnancy Program
Office of Asst. Secretary for Health
Public Health Service
U.S. Department of Health and Human Services
Room 736E, Humphrey Bldg.
200 Independence Ave., SW
Washington, DC 20201 202-690-8181

To encourage and support research projects concerning adolescent premarital sexual practices and to resolve the negative consequences. Types of assistance: Grants. Estimate of annual funds available in 1992: $926,000.

* Biological Response to Environmental Health Hazards 93.113

Dr. Schonwalder
Scientific Programs Branch
Division of Extramural Research and Training
NIEHS, National Institutes of Health
Public Health Service
U.S. Department of Health and Human Services
P.O. Box 12233
Research Triangle Park, NC 27709 919-541-7634

To promote understanding of how chemical and physical agents cause pathological changes that manifest as diseases. Types of assistance: Grants. Estimate of annual funds available in 1992: $72,965,000.

* Applied Toxicological Research and Testing (Bioassay of Chemicals and Test Development) 93.114

Dr. Schonwalder
Scientific Programs Branch
Division of Extramural Research and Training
NIEHS, National Institutes of Health
Public Health Service
U.S. Department of Health and Human Services
P.O. Box 12233
Research Triangle Park, NC 27709 919-541-7643

To develop scientific information about potentially toxic and hazardous chemicals and develop methods for predicting human response to toxic agents. Types of assistance: Grants. Estimate of annual funds available in 1992: $6,406,000.

* Biometry and Risk Estimation--Health Risks From Environmental Exposures 93.115

Dr. Schonwalder
Scientific Programs Branch
Division of Extramural Research and Training
NIEHS, National Institutes of Health
Public Health Service
U.S. Department of Health and Human Services
Research Triangle Park, NC 27709 919-541-7643

To conduct a broad-scale effort in biometry and risk estimation of probable health risks of cancer, reproductive and neurological effects, and other adverse effects from exposures to various environmental hazards. Types of assistance: Grants. Estimate of annual funds available in 1992: $6,020,000.

* Acquired Immunodeficiency Syndrome (AIDS) Activity (AIDS) 93.118

Clara Jenkins
Grants Management Branch
Procurement and Grants Office
Centers for Disease Control

Public Health Service
U.S. Department of Health and Human Services
255 E. Paces Ferry Rd., NE
Atlanta, GA 30305 404-842-6575

To develop and implement surveillance, epidemiological research, health education, school health, and risk reduction activities of the human immunodeficiency virus, (HIV) in States and major cities. Types of assistance: Grants. Estimate of annual funds available in 1992: $232,854,000.

* Mental Health Services for Cuban Entrants 93.120

Refugee Mental Health Program
National Institute of Mental Health
Alcohol, Drug Abuse and Mental Health Administration
Public Health Service
U.S. Department of Health and Human Services
Room 18-49, Parklawn Bldg.
5600 Fishers Lane
Rockville, MD 20857 301-443-2130

To support a complete range of treatment settings which are needed for mentally ill and/or developmentally disabled Cuban entrants currently in Federal custody. Entrants needing treatment cover a wide range of diagnostic categories and treatment histories. Types of assistance: Grants. Estimate of annual funds available in 1992: $3,600,000.

* Oral Diseases and Disorders Research 93.121

Ms. Ringler
Extramural Program
National Institute of Dental Research
National Institutes of Health
Public Health Service
U.S. Department of Health and Human Services
Bethesda, MD 20892 301-496-7437

To obtain improved information on the early diagnosis etiology and prevention of dental caries and improved dental care. Types of assistance: Grants. Estimate of annual funds available in 1992: $112,595,000.

* Small Business Innovation Research (SBIR Program) 93.126

Grants Management Officer
National Institute of Drug Abuse
Alcohol, Drug Abuse and Mental Health Administration
Public Health Service
U.S. Department of Health and Human Services
Room 8A-54, Parklawn Bldg.
5600 Fishers Lane
Rockville MD 20857 301-443-6710

To stimulate technological innovation; use small business to meet alcohol, drug, and mental health research and development needs; increase private sector commercialization of innovations derived from federal research and development; and encourage participation by minority and disadvantaged firms. Types of assistance: Grants. Estimate of annual funds available in 1992: $9,997,000.

* Injury Prevention and Control Research Projects 93.136

Mr. Cassell
Grants Management Officer
Procurement and Grants Office
Centers for Disease Control
Public Health Service
U.S. Department of Health and Human Services
255 E. Paces Ferry Rd., NE
Atlanta, GA 30305 404-842-6630

To support injury control research and demonstrations on priority issues. Types of assistance: Grants. Estimate of annual funds available in 1992: $14,500,000.

* Pediatric AIDS Health Care Demonstration Program 93.153

Division of Services for Children with Special Health Care Needs
Maternal and Child Health Bureau

Health Resources and Services Administration
Public Health Service
U.S. Department of Health and Human Services
Room 18A27, Parklawn Bldg.
Rockville, MD 20857   301-443-9051

To support demonstration projects for strategies and innovative models for intervention in pediatric AIDS and coordination of services for child-bearing women and children with AIDS, or who are at-risk of contracting AIDS. Types of assistance: Grants. Estimate of annual funds available in 1992: $19,518,000.

* Rural Health Research Centers 93.155

Dr. Taylor
Office of Rural Health Policy
Office of Administration
Health Resources and Services Administration
Public Health Service
U.S. Department of Health and Human Services
Parklawn Bldg, Room 9-05
5600 Fishers Lane
Rockville, MD 20857   301-443-0835

To support the development of rural health research centers to provide an information base and policy analysis capacity on the full range of rural health issues, including reimbursement, recruitment and retention of health professionals, access to care, and alternative delivery systems. Types of assistance: Grants. Estimate of annual funds available in 1992: $2,100,000.

* Minority AIDS and Related Risk Factors Education/ Preservation Grants 93.160

Mrs. Williams
Grants Management Officer
Office of Minority Health
Office of Asst. Secretary for Health
Rockwall II Bldg., Suite 1102
5515 Security Lane
Rockville, MD 20852   301-227-8758

To demonstrate that minority community-based organizations and minority institutions can effectively develop and implement human HIV infection education and prevention strategies. Types of assistance: Grants. Estimate of annual funds available in 1992: $1,300,000.

* Human Genome Research 93.172

Dr. Mark Guyer
National Center for Human Genome Research
National Institutes of Health
Public Health Service
U.S. Department of Health and Human Services
Bethesda, MD 20892   301-496-0844

To obtain genetic maps, physical maps, and determine the DNA sequences of the genomes of humans and model organisms to be used as resources in biomedical research, medicine, and biotechnology, using Small Business Innovative Research (SBIR) Program objectives. Types of assistance: Grants. Estimate of annual funds available in 1992: $91,589,000.

* Research Related to Deafness and Communication Disorders 93.173

Dr. Naunton
National Institute on Deafness and Other Communication Disorders
National Institutes of Health
Public Health Service
U.S. Department of Health and Human Services
Executive Plaza South, Room 400-B
Bethesda, MD 20892   301-496-1804

To investigate solutions to problems directly relevant to patients with deafness or disorders of human communication, such as hearing, balance, smell, taste, voice, speech, and language. Types of assistance: Grants. Estimate of annual funds available in 1992: $127,244,000.

* Mental Health Research Grants 93.242

Mr. Ringler
Grants Management Officer

National Institute of Mental Health
Alcohol, Drug Abuse and Mental Health Administration
Public Health Service
U.S. Department of Health and Human Services
Room 7C-15, Parklawn Bldg.
5600 Fishers Lane
Rockville, MD 20857   301-443-3065

To increase knowledge and improve research methods on mental and behavioral disorders. Types of assistance: Grants. Estimate of annual funds available in 1992: $368,281,000.

* Occupational Safety and Health Research Grants 93.262

Mr. Cassell
Grants Management Officer
Procurement and Grants Office
Centers for Disease Control
Public Health Service
U.S. Department of Health and Human Services
255 E. Paces Ferry Road NE, MS-E14
Atlanta, GA 30333   404-842-6630

To understand occupational safety and health problems in industry and find effective solutions in dealing with them. Types of assistance: Grants. Estimate of annual funds available in 1992: $6,747,847.

* Drug Abuse Research Programs 93.279

Ms. Denney
Grants Management Officer
National Institute of Drug Abuse
Alcohol, Drug Abuse and Mental Health Administration
Public Health Service
U.S. Department of Health and Human Services
Room 8A-54, Parklawn Bldg.
5600 Fishers Lane
Rockville, MD 20857   301-443-6710

To develop new knowledge and approaches to diagnosis, treatment and prevention of drug abuse and intravenous(IV)-related AIDS. Types of assistance: Grants. Estimate of annual funds available in 1992: $276,704,000.

* Cancer Cause and Prevention Research 93.393

Leo Buscher, Jr.
Grants Management Officer
National Cancer Institute
National Institutes of Health
Public Health Service
U.S. Department of Health and Human Services, EPS-216
Bethesda, MD 20892   301-496-7753

To identify those factors which cause cancer and develop mechanisms for preventing cancer in people. Types of assistance: Grants. Estimate of annual funds available in 1992: $324,720,000.

* Cancer Detection and Diagnosis and Research 93.394

Leo Buscher, Jr.
Grants Management Officer
National Cancer Institute
National Institutes of Health
Public Health Service
U.S. Department of Health and Human Services, EPS-216
Bethesda, MD 20892   301-496-7753

To identify cancer in patients early and precisely enough to use the latest methods of treatment. Types of assistance: Grants. Estimate of annual funds available: $74,816,000.

* Cancer Treatment Research 93.395

Leo Buscher, Jr.
Grants Management Officer
National Cancer Institute
National Institutes of Health
Public Health Service
U.S. Department of Health and Human Services, EPS-216
Bethesda, MD 20892   301-496-7753

To develop the means to cure as many cancer patients as possible. Types of assistance: Grants. Estimate of annual funds available in 1992: $248,826,000.

* Cancer Biology Research 93.396

Leo Buscher, Jr.
Grants Management Officer
National Cancer Institute
National Institutes of Health
Public Health Service
U.S. Department of Health and Human Services, EPS-216
Bethesda, MD 20892   301-496-7753

To provide fundamental information on the cause and nature of cancer in humans to improve prevention, detection and diagnosis and treatment of neoplastic diseases. Types of assistance: Grants. Estimate of annual funds available in 1992: $216,223,000.

* Cancer Control 93.399

Leo Buscher
Grants Management Officer
National Cancer Institute
National Institutes of Health
Public Health Service
U.S. Department of Health and Human Services, EPS-216
Bethesda, MD 20892   301-496-7753

To reduce cancer incidence, morbidity and mortality. Types of assistance: Grants. Estimate of annual funds available in 1992: $32,159,000.

* Social Services Research and Demonstration 93.647

Division of Research and Demonstrations
Office of Policy, Planning and Legislation
Office of Human Development Service
U.S. Department of Health and Human Services
Room 684-C
370 L'Enfant Promenade, SW
Washington, DC 20201   202-472-3026

To promote effective social services for dependent and vulnerable populations such as the poor, the aged, children and youth, Native Americans, and the disabled. Types of assistance: Grants. Estimate of annual funds available in 1992: $10,379,000.

* Health Care Financing Research, Demonstrations and Evaluations 93.779

Joseph R. Antos, Director
Office of Research and Demonstrations (ORD)
HCFA, U.S. Department of Health and Human Services
6325 Security Blvd
Baltimore, MD 21207   301-966-6507

To support projects in efforts to resolve major health care financing issues. Types of assistance: Grants. Estimate of annual funds available in 1992: $78,380,000.

* Biophysics and Physiological Sciences 93.821

Ms. Tippery
Grants Management Officer
Office of Program Activities
National Institute of General Medical Sciences
National Institutes of Health
Public Health Service
U.S. Department of Health and Human Services
Bethesda, MD 20892   301-496-7746

To foster the application of physical and engineering principles in the study of biomedical problems. Types of assistance: Grants. Estimate of annual funds available in 1992: $164,076,000.

* Heart and Vascular Diseases Research 93.837

Thomas Turley
Grants Management Officer
Office of Program Policy and Procedures
National Heart, Lung and Blood Institute
National Institutes of Health

Public Health Service
U.S. Department of Health and Human Services
Bethesda, MD 20892   301-496-7255

To foster research and prevention, education and control of heart and vascular diseases. Types of assistance: Grants. Estimate of annual funds available in 1992: $530,543,000.

* Lung Diseases Research 93.838

Thomas Turley
Grants Management Officer
Office of Program Policy and Procedures
National Heart, Lung and Blood Institute
National Institutes of Health
Public Health Service
U.S. Department of Health and Human Services
Bethesda, MD 20892   301-496-7255

To use available knowledge and technology to solve specific diseases of the lungs and promote further studies of the lungs. Types of assistance: Grants. Estimate of annual funds available: $174,333,000.

* Blood Diseases and Resources Research 93.839

Thomas Turley
Grants Management Officer
Office of Program Policy and Procedures
National Heart, Lung and Blood Institute
National Institutes of Health
Public Health Service
U.S. Department of Health and Human Services
Bethesda, MD 20892   301-496-7255

To foster research for the prevention and improved diagnosis and treatment of blood diseases. Types of assistance: Grants. Estimate of annual funds available in 1992: $157,201,000.

* Arthritis, Musculoskeletal and Skin Diseases Research 93.846

Grants Management Officer
Division of Extramural Activities
National Institute of Arthritis, Musculoskeletal
    and Skin Diseases
National Institutes of Health
Public Health Service
U.S. Department of Health and Human Services
Room 732A, Westwood Bldg.
Bethesda, MD 20892   301-402-3352

To conduct research and train researchers in the above areas. Types of assistance: Grants. Estimate of annual funds available: $165,727,000.

* Diabetes, Endocrinology and Metabolism Research 93.847

John Garthune, Asst. Director
Division of Extramural Activities
National Institute of Diabetes, Digestive and Kidney Diseases
National Institutes of Health
U.S. Department of Health and Human Services
Room 637, Westwood Bldg.
Bethesda, MD 20892   301-496-7793

To support research and training for individuals interested in careers in these programs and stimulate technological innovation. Types of assistance: Grants. Estimate of annual funds available in 1992: $258,131,000.

* Digestive Diseases and Nutrition Research 93.848

John Garthune, Asst. Director
Division of Extramural Activities
National Institute of Diabetes, Digestive and Kidney Diseases
National Institutes of Health
Room 637, Westwood Bldg.
Bethesda, MD 20892   301-496-7793

To conduct research and train individuals in the above fields. Types of assistance: Grants. Estimate of annual funds available in 1992: $121,286,000.

* Kidney Diseases, Urology and Hematology Research 93.849

John Garthune, Asst. Director
Division of Extramural Activities
National Institute of Diabetes, Digestive and Kidney Diseases
National Institutes of Health
Room 637, Westwood Bldg.
Bethesda, MD 20892   301-496-7793

Types of assistance: Grants. Estimate of annual funds available in 1992: $167,727,000.

* Clinical Research Related to Neurological Disorders 93.853

Ms. Whitehead
Grants Management Officer
National Institute of Neurological Disorders and Stroke
National Institutes of Health
Public Health Service
U.S. Department of Health and Human Services
Federal Bldg., Room 1004A
Bethesda, MD 20892   301-496-9231

To investigate solutions to neurological disorders and stroke. Types of assistance: Grants. Estimate of annual funds available in 1992: $180,983,000.

* Biological Basis Research in the Neurosciences 93.854

Ms. Whitehead
Grants Management Officer
National Institute of Neurological Disorders and Stroke
National Institutes of Health
Public Health Service
U.S. Department of Health and Human Services
Federal Bldg., Room 1004A
Bethesda, MD 20892   301-496-9231

To support biological basis research of the brain and nervous system and their disorders. Types of assistance: Grants. Estimate of annual funds available in 1992: $281,074,000.

* Pharmacological Sciences 93.859

Ms. Tippery
Grants Management Officer
Office of Program Activities
National Institute of General Medical Sciences
National Institutes of Health
Public Health Service
U.S. Department of Health and Human Services
Bethesda, MD 20892   301-496-7746

To provide an improved understanding of the biological phenomena and related chemical and molecular processes involved in the action of therapeutic drugs and their metabolites and design new ones as well as research anesthetic agents. Types of assistance: Grants. Estimate of annual funds available in 1992: $122,066,000.

* Genetics Research 93.862

Ms. Tippery
Grants Management Officer
Office of Program Activities
National Institute of General Medical Sciences
National Institutes of Health
Public Health Service
U.S. Department of Health and Human Services
Bethesda, MD 20892   301-496-7746

To support research aimed at prevention, therapy, and control of genetic diseases, including multifactorial illnesses with a strong hereditary component. Types of assistance: Grants. Estimate of annual funds available in 1992: $229,530,000.

* Cellular and Molecular Basis of Disease Research 93.863

Ms. Tippery
Grants Management Officer
Office of Program Activities
National Institute of General Medical Sciences
National Institutes of Health
Public Health Service
U.S. Department of Health and Human Services
Bethesda, MD 20892   301-496-7746

To support research that seeks greater understanding of human cells and their environment in order to prevent, treat and cure diseases resulting from disturbed or abnormal cellular activities. Types of assistance: Grants. Estimate of annual funds available in 1992: $233,476,000.

* Population Research 93.864

Mr. Clark
Office of Grants and Contracts
National Institute of Child Health and Human Development
National Institutes of Health
Public Health Service
U.S. Department of Health and Human Services
Executive Plaza North
Rockville, MD 20892   301-496-5001

To seek solutions to the problems of reproductive processes; to develop safer and more effective contraceptives; to understand impact of population change and structure. Types of assistance: Grants. Estimate of annual funds available in 1992: $118,517,000.

* Research for Mothers and Children 93.865

Mr. Clark
Office of Grants and Contracts
National Institute of Child Health and Human Development
National Institutes of Health
Public Health Service
U.S. Department of Health and Human Services
Executive Plaza North
Rockville, MD 20892   301-496-5001

To stimulate, coordinate and support fundamental and clinical, biomedical and behavioral research of fetal and childhood development. Types of assistance: Grants. Estimate of annual funds available in 1992: $235,977,000.

* Aging Research 93.866

Mr. Ellis
Grants Management Officer
Office of Extramural Affairs
National Institute of Aging
National Institutes of Health
Public Health Service
U.S. Department of Health and Human Services
Bethesda, MD 20892   301-496-1472

To encourage biomedical, social, and behavioral research to understand the aging process and the needs, special problems, and diseases it produces. Types of assistance: Grants. Estimate of annual funds available in 1992: $291,003,000.

* Retinal and Choroidal Diseases Research 93.867

Ms. Carolyn Grimes
Extramural Services Branch
National Eye Institute
National Institutes of Health
Public Health Service
U.S. Department of Health and Human Services
Bethesda, MD 20892   301-496-5884

To support research on the structure and function of the retina in health and disease. Types of assistance: Grants. Estimate of annual funds available in 1992: $96,170,000.

* Anterior Segment Diseases Research 93.868

Ms. Carolyn Grimes
Extramural Services Branch
National Eye Institute
National Institutes of Health
Public Health Service
U.S. Department of Health and Human Services
Bethesda, MD 20892   301-496-5884

To support research on diseases of the cornea and external ocular structures. Types of assistance: Grants. Estimate of annual funds available in 1992: $72,109,000.

* Strabismus, Amblyopia and Visual Processing 93.871

Ms. Carolyn Grimes
Extramural Services Branch
National Eye Institute
National Institutes of Health
Public Health Service
U.S. Department of Health and Human Services
Bethesda, MD 20892   301-496-5884

To support studies of the structure and function of the central visual pathways, processing of visual information and the study of those structures in terms of their function, impairment and rehabilitation. Types of assistance: Grants. Estimate of annual funds available in 1992: $45,999,000.

* Special Loans for National Health Service Corps Members to Enter Private Practice 93.973

Director
National Health Service Corps
Health Resources and Services Administration
Public Health Service
U.S. Department of Health and Human Services
Parklawn Bldg., Room 7A-39
5600 Fishers Lane
Rockville, MD 20857   301-443-2900

To assist members of the National Health Service Corps in establishing their own private practice in a health manpower shortage area. Types of assistance: Loans. Estimate of annual funds available: Contact Office Above.

State Money and Help For Your Business

Who Can Use State Money?

All states require that funds be used solely by state residents. But that shouldn't limit you to exploring possibilities only in the state in which you currently reside. If you reside in Maine, but Massachusetts agrees to give you $100,000 to start your own business, it would be worth your while to consider moving to Massachusetts. Shop around for the best deal.

Types Of State Money And Help Available

Each state has different kinds and amounts of money and assistance programs available, but these sources of financial and counseling help are constantly being changed. What may not be available this year may very well be available next. Therefore, in the course of your exploration, you might want to check in with the people who operate the business "hotlines" to discover if anything new has been added to the states' offerings.

Described below are the major kinds of programs which are offered by most of the states.

Information

Hotlines or One-Stop Shops are available in many states through a toll-free number that hooks you up with someone who will either tell you what you need to know or refer you to someone who can. These hotlines are invaluable -- offering information on everything from business permit regulations to obscure financing programs. Most states also offer some kind of booklet that tells you to how to start-up a business in that state. Ask for it. It will probably be free.

Small Business Advocates operate in all fifty states and are part of a national organization (the National Association of State Small Business Advocates) devoted to helping small business people function efficiently with their state governments. They are a good source for help in cutting through bureaucratic red tape.

Funding Programs

Free Money can come in the form of grants, and works the same as free money from the federal government. You do not have to pay it back.

Loans from state governments work in the same way as those from the federal government -- they are given directly to entrepreneurs. Loans are usually at interest rates below the rates charged at commercial institutions and are also set aside for those companies which have trouble getting a loan elsewhere. This makes them an ideal source for riskier kinds of ventures.

Loan Guarantees are similar to those offered by the federal government. For this program, the state government will go to the bank with you and co-sign your loan. This, too, is ideal for high risk ventures which normally would not get a loan.

Interest Subsidies On Loans is a unique concept not used by the federal government. In this case, the state will subsidize the interest rate you are charged by a bank. For example, if the bank gives you a loan for $50,000 at 10 percent per year interest, your interest payments will be $5,000 per year. With an interest subsidy you might have to pay only $2,500 since the state will pay the other half. This is like getting the loan at 5 percent instead of 10 percent.

Industrial Revenue Bonds Or General Obligation Bonds are a type of financing that can be used to purchase only fixed assets, such as a factory or equipment. In the case of Industrial Revenue Bonds the state will raise money from the general public to buy your equipment. Because the state acts as the middleman, the people who lend you the money do not have to pay federal taxes on the interest they charge you. As a result, you get the money cheaper because they get a tax break. If the state issues General Obligation Bonds to buy your equipment, the arrangement will be similar to that for an Industrial Revenue Bond except that the state promises to repay the loan if you cannot.

Matching Grants supplement and abet federal grant programs. These kinds of grants could make an under-capitalized project go forward. Awards usually hinge on the usefulness of the project to its surrounding locality.

Loans To Agricultural Businesses are offered in states with large rural, farming populations. They are available solely to farmers and/or agribusiness entrepreneurs.

Loans To Exporters are available in some states as a kind of gap financing to cover the expenses involved in fulfilling a contract.

Energy Conservation Loans are made to small businesses to finance the installation of energy-saving equipment or devices.

Special Regional Loans are ear-marked for specific areas in a state that may have been hard hit economically or suffer from under-development. If you live in one of these regions, you may be eligible for special funds.

High Tech Loans help fledgling companies develop or introduce new products into the marketplace.

Loans To Inventors help the entrepreneur develop or market new products.

Local Government Loans are used for start-up and expansion of businesses within the designated locality.

Childcare Facilities Loans help businesses establish on-site daycare facilities.

Loans To Women And/Or Minorities are available in almost every state from funds specifically reserved for economically disadvantaged groups.

Many federally funded programs are administered by state governments. Among them are the following programs:

The SBA 7(A) Guaranteed and *Direct Loan* program can guarantee up to 90 percent of a loan made through a private lender (up to $750,000), or make direct loans of up to $150,000.

The SBA 504 establishes Certified Development Companies whose debentures are guaranteed by the SBA. Equity participation of the borrower must be at least 10 percent, private financing 60 percent and CDC participation at a maximum of 40 percent, up to $750,000.

Small Business Innovative Research Grants (SBIR) award between $20,000 to $50,000 to entrepreneurs to support six months of research on a technical innovation. They are then eligible for up to $500,000 to develop the innovation.

Small Business Investment Companies (SBIC) license, regulate and provide financial assistance in the form of equity financing, long-term loans, and management services.

Community Development Block Grants are available to cities and counties for the commercial rehabilitation of existing buildings or structures used for business, commercial, or industrial purposes. Grants of up to $500,000 can be made. Every $15,000 of grant funds invested must create at least one full-time job, and at least 51 percent of the jobs created must be for low and moderate income families.

Farmers Home Administration (FmHA) Emergency Disaster Loans are available in counties where natural disaster has substantially affected farming, ranching or aquaculture production.

FmHA Farm Loan Guarantees are made to family farmers and ranchers to enable them to obtain funds from private lenders. Funds must be used for farm ownership, improvements, and operating purposes.

FmHA Farm Operating Loans to meet operating expenses, finance recreational and nonagricultural enterprises, to add to family income, and to pay for mandated safety and pollution control changes are available at variable interest rates. Limits are $200,000 for an insured farm operating loan and $400,000 for a guaranteed loan.

FmHA Farm Ownership Loans can be used for a wide range of farm improvement projects. Limits are $200,000 for an insured loan and $300,000 for a guaranteed loan.

FmHA Soil And Water Loans must be used by individual farmers and ranchers to develop, conserve, and properly use their land and water resources and to help abate pollution. Interest rates are variable; each loan must be secured by real estate.

FmHA Youth Project Loans enable young people to borrow for income-producing projects sponsored by a school or 4H club.

Assistance Programs

Management Training is offered by many states in subjects ranging from bookkeeping to energy conservation.

Business Consulting is offered on almost any subject. Small Business Development Centers are the best source for this kind of assistance.

Market Studies to help you sell your goods or services within or outside the state are offered by many states. They all also have State Data Centers which not only collect demographic and other information about markets within the state, but also have access to federal data which can pinpoint national markets. Many states also provide the services of graduate business students at local universities to do the legwork and analysis for you.

Business Site Selection is done by specialists in every state who will identify the best place to locate a business.

Licensing, Regulation, And Permits information is available from most states through "one-stop shop" centers by calling a toll-free number. There you'll get help in finding your way through the confusion of registering a new business.

Employee Training Programs offer on-site training and continuing education opportunities.

Research And Development assistance for entrepreneurs is a form of assistance that is rapidly increasing as more and more states try to attract high technology-related companies. Many states are even setting up clearing houses so that small businesses can have one place to turn to find expertise throughout a statewide university system.

Procurement Programs have been established in some states to help you sell products to state, federal, and local governments.

Export Assistance is offered to identify overseas markets. Some states even have overseas offices to drum up business prospects for you.

Assistance In Finding Funding is offered in every state, particularly through regional Small Business Development Centers. They will not only identify funding sources in the state and federal governments but will also lead you through the complicated application process.

Special Help For Minorities And Women is available in almost every state to help boost the participation of women and minorities in small business ventures. They offer special funding programs and, often, one-on-one counseling to assure a start-up success.

Venture Capital Networking is achieved through computer databases that hook up entrepreneurs and venture capitalists. This service is usually free of charge. In fact, the demand for small business investment opportunities is so great that some states require the investor to pay to be listed.

Inventors Associations have been established to encourage and assist inventors in developing and patenting their products.

Annual Governors' Conferences give small business people the chance to air their problems with representatives from state agencies and the legislature.

Small Business Development Centers (SBDCs), funded jointly by the federal and state governments, are usually associated with the state university system. SBDCs are a god-send to small business people. They will not only help you figure out if your business project is feasible, but also help you draw up a sensible business plan, apply for funding, and check in with you frequency once your business is up and running to make sure it stays that way.

Tourism programs are prominent in states whose revenues are heavily dependent on the tourist trade. They are specifically aimed at businesses in the tourist industries.

Small Business Institutes at local colleges use senior level business students as consultants to help develop business plans or plan expansions.

Technology Assistance Centers help high tech companies and entrepreneurs establish new businesses and plan business expansions.

On-Site Energy Audits are offered free of charge by many states to help control energy costs and improve energy efficiency for small businesses. Some states also conduct workshops to encourage energy conservation measures.

Minority Business Development Centers offer a wide range of services from initial counseling on how to start a business to more complex issues of planning and growth.

Alabama

* General Information

Alabama Development Office
401 Adams Ave. #600
Montgomery, AL 36130

205-242-0400
FAX: 205-242-0486

Answers general inquiries about Alabama's programs. *Small Business is Big Business in Alabama* is a free packet with information on assistance programs, sources of financing, a licensing handbook, and tips on preparing business and financial plans.

Small Business Advocate: Assistance in cutting bureaucratic red tape. Information and expertise in dealing with state, federal and local agencies.

* Financing

Southern Development Council
401 Adams Ave. #680
Montgomery, AL 36130

205-264-5441

State of Alabama Economic Development Loan Fund: Favorable, long-term, fixed rates for land and building, construction, machinery and equipment, renovation/expansion, and working capital, for manufacturing only. $400,000 maximum, $35,000 minimum for any single project. Provides 40 percent of financing needs, 60 percent to be provided through private lender or owner equity. Can be used with Industrial Revenue Bonds.

Industrial Revenue Bonds: Long-term loans with interest rates below conventional rates for land and building acquisition, construction, and machinery and equipment for manufacturing facilities. $10 million maximum. Can finance 100 percent of project.

SBA 504: For any type of business. Provides loans using 50 percent conventional bank financing, 40 percent SBA involvement through Certified Development Companies, and 10 percent owner equity injection. A fixed asset loan, usually below market. Maximum amount $750,000, minimum $50,000. Loan can be used for land, building, construction, renovation/expansion, and machinery and equipment.

SBA 7(a) Loan Guarantee: Guarantees up to 90 percent of a loan made through a private lender, up to a maximum of $750,000. Can be used for working capital, inventory, machinery and equipment, and land and building. Can be used for debt refinancing if lender is changed to another bank. Available only to those unable to obtain a loan from conventional sources.

Float Program: Loans from $1-10 million for a 12 month term. Single pay. Usually carries a very low interest rate. Requires letter of credit as collateral.

Alabama Development Office
401 Adams Ave. #600
Montgomery, Alabama 36130

205-242-0400

Appalachian Regional Commission Grant: Provides supplemental funding for economic development projects under its Jobs and Private Investment Program. Funds, which supplement federal or state-administered federal funds, can be used to reduce the local matching requirement to a minimum of 20 percent of total project cost. Eligible activities include access roads, water and sewer system installation, rail spurs, and dock facilities. 205-242-5446.

State Industrial Development Authority Bonds: Interest free loans are available to qualified applicants to finance a portion of the cost of construction of speculative buildings intended for industrial use. Qualified applicants must be city or county industrial development boards. No loan may be greater than 25 percent of the anticipated total cost of the building. 205-242-0434.

State Industrial Site Preparation Grants: Grants can be made to counties, municipalities, local industrial development boards, airport authorities, and economic development councils organized as public corporations to pay a portion of the costs of site improvements on land to which they hold the title in order to attract new industry or to assist an existing industry in expansion. 205-242-0475.

EDA Funds: The Economic Development Administration (EDA) of the United States Department of Commerce may provide funds for industrial development in the form of grants and loans for technical assistance, public works, and business loan guarantees. 205-242-5488.

State Treasurer
204 Alabama State House
Montgomery, AL 36130

205-242-7517

The Wallace Plan For Linked Deposits/Small Business Loan: Lower (usually by 3 percent) than conventional rate loan. Can be used for land and buildings, equipment, repairs/renovations, rent, utilities, insurance, taxes, legal or accounting fees, wages, inventory. Any small business in Alabama with less that 150 employees is eligible and has debts equal to or greater than 35 percent of assets. One job must be created or sustained for each $15,000 of loan amount. Loans above $250,000 must create or sustain one job for every $10,000 of loan. 205-242-7535.

The Wallace Plan For Linked Deposits/Agricultural Loan: Lower (usually by 3%) than conventional rate loan can be used for feed, seed, fertilizer, chemicals, veterinary or legal/accounting fees, energy costs, crop insurance, equipment purchases, harvesting expense, labor, land rent, livestock, and repair costs. Any person, corporation, or partnership engaged in the production of agricultural products that derives at least 70 percent of their income from farming is eligible. Loans are up to $100,000 for a maximum term of one year. May apply every four years. Must have debts equal to or greater than 25 percent of assets, and have interest cost as a substantial portion of expenses. 205-242-7535.

Small Business Administration
2121 Eighth Avenue N, Suite 200   205-731-1344
Birmingham, AL 35203-2398   FAX: 205-731-1344

SBA 7(a) Guaranteed and Direct Loans: Guarantees up to 90 percent of a loan made through a private lender up to $750,000. Can be used for working capital, expand or convert facilities, purchase of machinery and equipment, and land and building. Available only to those unable to obtain a loan from conventional sources. Direct loans are made up to $150,000.

SBA 504: Provides loans using 50 percent conventional bank financing, 40 percent SBA involvement through Certified Development Companies, and 10 percent owner equity. Fixed-asset loans are available in amounts up to $750,000. The loan can be used for land and building, construction, machinery and equipment, and renovation/expansion.

Small Business Innovative Research Grants (SBIR): Phase I awards between $20,000 to $50,000 to entrepreneurs to support six months of research on a technical innovation. Phase II grants are an additional $500,000 for development. Private sector investment funds must follow.

International Trade Loans: Guaranteed long-term loans through private lenders to develop or expand export markets, or to recover from the effects of import competition. Maximum guaranteed loan is $1,000,000 for fixed assets and an additional $250,000 for working capital and/or export revolving line of credit.

Export Revolving Line of Credit Loan: Short term financing available to small businesses that are at least one year old. Loans provide working capital to finance the manufacturing or wholesaling of products for export and for export marketing. The SBA will guarantee up to 90 percent of a conventional loan in amounts up to $750,000.

Contract Loan: Short-term loans are available to small businesses to finance the costs of labor and materials on contracts for which the proceeds are assignable. Program guarantees up to 90 percent of loans not in excess of $750,000. Qualifying small businesses must be in business for at least 12 calendar months prior to the date of the loan application.

Seasonal Line of Credit Loan: Loans provide short-term working capital to finance seasonal increases in business activities. Program guarantees up to 90 percent of loans not in excess of $750,000. Qualifying business must be in operation for at least one year prior to application.

Pollution Control Loans: Long-term guaranteed loans can be made by conventional financing to small businesses for installation or required pollution control measures. Must be unable to adopt the pollution control measures without undue financial hardship. Maximum guaranteed loan is $1,000,000.

General Contractor Loans: Small general construction contractors may obtain short-term loans or loan guarantees for residential or commercial construction or rehabilitation of property to be sold. The SBA will guarantee up to 90 percent of qualifying loans made by private lenders up to a maximum of $750,000. Direct loans can be up to $150,000.

Energy Business Loan Guarantee: Small businesses that provide certain energy production and conservation services for others may qualify for long-term loans and loan guarantees for start-ups and expansions. Loans and guarantees are made for firms that develop, manufacture, sell, install, or service specific energy measures for others, or firms that provide engineering, architectural, consulting, or other professional services connected with specific energy measures. Guarantee is for up to 90 percent of a loan not in excess of $750,000. Direct loans up to $150,000.

Disaster Recovery Loans: Small businesses located in federally designated disaster areas and suffering property damage or economic losses from the disaster can obtain long-term recovery loans at low interest rates. Property damage loans are limited to 85 percent of the verified damage. Loans for economic losses are for operating capital to meet the business' obligations that could have been made had the disaster not occurred.

Handicapped Assistance Loans: Assists persons who have a physical, mental or emotional disability of a permanent nature which limits the selection of any type of employment for which the person would otherwise be qualified. Direct loans are available for up to $150,000. The interest rate is 3% on these loans.

Surety Bond Guaranty Program: Makes the bonding system more available to small contractors who may be denied access to the system. SBA can guarantee up to 80 percent of surety's loss on a bond that has a maximum in total contract value of up to $1,250,000.

Vietnam-era and Disabled Veterans Loan Program: Provides direct loans to veterans to establish or expand a small business. Funds may be used for working capital or fixed assets. Direct loans for amounts up to $150,000 are available. The interest rate may be fixed or variable.

First SBIC of Alabama
16 Midtown Park East
Mobile, AL 36606   205-476-0700

Hickory Venture Capital Corporation
200 W. Court Square
Suite 100
Huntsville, AL 35801   205-539-5130

Small Business Investment Companies (SBICs): The SBA licenses, regulates, and provides financial assistance to privately owned and operated Small Business Investment Companies. SBICs make venture or risk investments by supplying capital and extending unsecured loans and loans not fully collateralized to small enterprises which meet their investment criteria. Financing is made by direct loans and by equity investments.

* Women And Minority Business Assistance

Alabama State Office of Minority Business Enterprise
Alabama Development Office
401 Adams Ave. #660
Montgomery, AL 36130   205-242-0400

Acts as an advocate for minorities and women in their dealings with state, local, and federal agencies. Helps prepare business plans and applications for SBA loans.

Small Business Administration (SBA)
2121 Eighth Avenue N
Suite 200   205-731-1344
Birmingham, AL 35203-2398   FAX: 205-731-1404

SBA 8(a) Program - Business Procurement Assistance: Provides federal government contracting opportunities for small businesses owned by socially and economically disadvantaged persons, and assists these businesses to become independently competitive in the normal business environment. SBA monitors all government contracts to assure that a quota of contract work goes to 8(a) businesses. Also provides business management services to these businesses. Business must be approved for program participation prior to receipt of an 8(a) contract.

* Training

Division of Vocational Education Services
5106 Gordon Person Bldg.
50 North Ripley Street
Montgomery, AL 36130   205-242-9111

Job Training Partnership Act (JTPA): Provides employers with recruitment, screening, referral, training, 50 percent wage subsidy up to 3 months for on-the-job training. Available to any private employer.

* Management Consulting And Other Services

Technology Assistance Partnership
Science, Technology, and Energy Division
Alabama Department of Economic and Community Affairs
401 Adams Ave.
P.O. Box 5690
Montgomery, AL 36103-5690   205-242-5290

Technology Assistance Partnership: Assists existing and potential businesses with technology-oriented problems. Types of assistance include identifying and solving problems, referrals to appropriate technological resources, implementation of new technology, seminars and workshops, evaluation, protection, and development of innovations, guidance in the use of public and private funding, applying for Small Business Innovation Research contracts. Technology Representatives are located throughout the state.

Business Council of Alabama
468 South Perry Street
P.O. Box 7636101-0076
Montgomery, AL 36104   205-834-6000
    Lobbying group for business and industry.

Governor's Conference on Small Business
Alabama Development Office
401 Adams Ave.
Montgomery, AL 36130   205-242-0400
    Small Business Conference: An annual event held every January that gives small business people the chance to air their problems with representatives from state agencies and the legislature. A Source Fair features booths manned by government agencies, financial institutions, and computer companies to offer advice and help.

Alabama Inventors Association
Alabama Development Office
401 Adams Ave.
Montgomery, AL 36130   205-242-0400
    Dedicated to encouraging and assisting inventors in developing and patenting their products.

Small Business Administration
2121 Eighth Avenue N
Suite 200   205-731-1344
Birmingham, AL 35203-2398   FAX: 205-731-1404
    Small Business Institutes: This program provides personalized consulting services to the small business community. Consulting is provided by senior level business students, guided by a faculty advisor. Assistance in business plan preparation, marketing research, market planning, accounting, and seminars are provided.
    University Locations:
    Alabama A&M University
    Jacksonville State University
    Livingston University
    Troy State University
    University of Alabama
    University of Alabama - Birmingham
    University of Alabama - Huntsville
    University of North Alabama
    University of South Alabama

* Small Business Development Centers
The following offices offer free and fee-based services to new and expanding businesses:

Lead Center:
Alabama Small Business Development Center
University of Alabama at Birmingham
Medical Towers Building
1717 11th Avenue South, Suite 419   205-934-7260
Birmingham, AL 35294-7645   FAX: 205-934-7645

    Auburn: Auburn University, Small Business Development Center, College of Business, 226 Thach Hall, Auburn, AL 36849-5243, 205-844-4220, FAX: 205-844-4268.

    Birmingham: University of Alabama at Birmingham, Small Business Development Center, 901 South 15th Street, MCJ, Room 143, Birmingham, AL 35294-2060, 205-934-6760, FAX: 205-934-0534.

    Birmingham: Alabama Small Business Procurement System, University of Alabama at Birmingham, Small Business Development Center, 1717 11th Avenue South, Suite 419, Birmingham, AL 35294-4410, 205-934-7260.

    Florence: University of North Alabama, Small Business Development Center, P.O. Box 5017, Keller Hall, Florence, AL 35632-0001, 205-760-4629, FAX: 205-760-4813.

    Huntsville: North East Alabama Regional Small Business Development Center, P.O. Box 343, 225 Church Street, N.W., Huntsville, AL 35804-0343, 205-535-2061, FAX: 205-535-2050.

    Jacksonville: Jacksonville State University, Small Business Development Center, 113-B Merrill Hall, Jacksonville, AL 36265, 205-782-5271, FAX: 205-782-5124.

    Livingston: Livingston University, Small Business Development Center, Station 35, Livingston, AL 35470, 205-652-9661, ext. 439, FAX: 205-652-9318.

    Mobile: University of South Alabama, Small Business Development Center, College of Business & Management Studies, Building 101, Mobile, AL 36688, 205-460-6004, FAX: 205-460-6246.

    Montgomery: Alabama State University, Small Business Development Center, 915 South Jackson Street, Montgomery, AL 36195, 205-269-1102, FAX: 205-265-9144.

    Troy: Troy State University, Small Business Development Center, Sorrell College of Business, Troy, AL 36082-0001, 205-670-3771, FAX: 205-670-3636.

    Tuscaloosa: Alabama International Trade Center, University of Alabama, P.O. Box 870396 400-N, Martha Parham West, Tuscaloosa, AL 35487-0396, 205-348-7621, FAX: 205-348-6974.

    Tuscaloosa: University of Alabama, Small Business Development Center, P.O. Box 870397, 400-S Martha Parham West, Tuscaloosa, AL 35487-0397, 205-348-7011, FAX: 205-348-9644.

Alaska

* General Information

Division of Economic Development
Alaska Department of Commerce and
    Economic Development (DCED)
P.O. Box 110804
Juneau, AK 99811-0804   907-465-2018
    or
Division of Economic Development
Alaska Department of Commerce and
    Economic Development
3601 C St. #724
Anchorage, AK 99503   907-563-2165
    Answers general inquiries. A free booklet, *Establishing a Business in Alaska*, provides information on assistance programs, licensing requirements, taxation, labor laws, financial assistance programs, and state sources of information.

Small Business Advocate   907-465-2018 (Juneau)
Assistance in cutting bureaucratic red tape. Information and expertise in dealing with state, federal, and local agencies.

Business Development Information Network (BDIN)   907-465-2017
    Alaska Biz Link Computer: 907-272-7524
One-stop clearinghouse/marketing center for inter-state and intra-state businesses and corporations wishing to start, expand or relocate business operations into or within the state. Answer questions, provide information, technical assistance, referrals, and access to all state publications related to establishing, relocating, or expanding a business.

Department of Commerce and Economic Development (DCED)
Division of Economic Development
3601 C St.
Anchorage, AK 99503   907-563-2165
    Small Business Counseling Centers: Provide general assistance to small businesses such as business and finance plan development, marketing advice, etc.

* Financing

Department of Commerce and Economic Development (DCED)
P.O. Box 110804
Juneau, AK 99811-0804   907-465-2017
or
Yarmon Investments
5th Avenue
Suite 440
Anchorage, AK 99501   907-276-4466

The Polaris Fund, L.P.: Provides equity capital to young companies whose ideas and talents can lead to exceptional growth in sales and profits. They make their initial assessment based on a business plan which DCED, or a Small Business Development Center can assist you with.

Division of Investments   907-465-2510 Juneau
                                       907-562-3779 Anchorage

Small Business and Economic Development Revolving Loan Fund: Financing is available to small businesses that are located within rural areas for industrial or commercial ventures to support the start-up and expansion of businesses that will create significant long-term employment and help diversify the economy. Interest rates are below the prevailing market rates. Loan amounts from $10,000 to $150,000.

Small Business Loan Assumption Program: Assists purchasers in the assumption of an existing small business loan. Factors considered are ability to provide sufficient collateral and have knowledge of Alaska economic conditions, business potential for growth, ability to repay the loan, and potential to create more jobs and provide additional services to the community.

Commercial Fishing Loan Program

Permit, Vessel and Gear Loans: Direct loans to Individuals up to $100,000 at 10.5 percent interest for up to 15 years. Loans may be made to individuals who have been State residents for a continuous period of two years immediately preceding the date of application, do not have occupational opportunities available other than commercial fishing, or are economically dependent on commercial fishing for a livelihood, and for whom commercial fishing has been a traditional way of life in Alaska. Funds may be used to facilitate the repair, restoration or upgrade of exiting vessels and gear, for purchase of limited entry permits, gear and vessels.

Limited Entry Permits Loan Program: Loans up to $300,000 at 10.5 percent interest for up to 15 years are made to individual commercial fisherman who have been State residents for the two years immediately preceding the date of application and have held a limited entry permit, commercial fishing or crew member license for the year preceding the date of application. Applicants whose eligibility have been affected by the Exxon oil spill in 1989 should contact the division for further information.

SPAR Spill Prevention and Response   907-465-5250
Underground Storage Tank Assistance Fund: Assists owners of underground storage tanks to test, assess, clean up, and upgrade underground storage tanks. Grants and reimbursement programs are available. Reimbursement for tank testing is available for up to 50 percent of cost, not to exceed $300 per tank, maximum of $1,200 per facility. For site assessment, 50 percent of cost not to exceed $800 per tank, maximum of $2,300 per facility. For cleanup, grants of up to $1 million to cover 90 percent of cost, and no-interest loan for remaining 10 percent. For upgrade or closure, 60 percent of eligible costs up to a grant maximum of $60,000.

Alaska Industrial Development and Export Authority (AIDEA)
480 West Tudor Road
Anchorage, AK 99503-6690   907-561-8050

Umbrella Bond Program: AIDEA is a public corporation of the state that acts as an agent to put together an umbrella bond package to purchase a group of loans. Assists businesses in securing long-term financing for capital investments. AIDEA participates after a lender institution has approved a loan. Funds can be used for some tax-exempt project facilities, and many taxable facilities such as buildings, plants, property and equipment. Loan amount may not exceed 75 percent of project.

State Executive Director
Agricultural Stabilization and Conservation Service
800 W. Evergreen, Suite 216
Palmer, AK 99645   907-745-7982

Agricultural Conservation Grant Program: Established to solve soil, water, and related resource problems in farming. Persons eligible are those that have produced agricultural products in commercial quantities. Up to 75 percent of costs of implementing conservation practices (windbreaks, grass waterways, minimum tillage, slope management, grass seeding, tree planting, woodlot improvement, etc.) are eligible. Maximum of $3,500 per applicant per year. Not a "start-up" type of grant.

Farmers Home Administration
634 South Bailey
Suite 103   907-745-2176
Palmer, AK 99645   FAX: 907-745-5398

Farm Ownership Loans and Operating Loans: For established farms, generally inside the "railbelt" region. Guaranteed loans up to $300,000 for ownership; $400,000 for operating loans. Insured loans up to $200,000 for ownership as well as operating loans. Must be able to demonstrate ability to farm and to repay the loan, but unable to obtain sufficient credit elsewhere.

Business and Industrial Loans: Assistance to individuals, corporations, public or private organizations in a rural area or city of less than 50,000 population, to obtain quality loans for economic development. Nearly any purpose except recreational or tourist type projects are eligible. Loan guarantees of up to 90 percent. Loans may be up to $10 million. Projects which create or save jobs have the highest priority.

Alaska Department of Natural Resources
Division of Agriculture
P.O. Box 949
Palmer, AK 99645-0949   907-745-7200

Agricultural Revolving Loan Fund: Available to individual farmers, ranchers, homesteaders, partnerships or corporations who are Alaska residents and can demonstrate experience in the farming business. Provides direct short term loans (1-year) up to $200,000. Product processing and land clearing loans up to $250,000, farm development loans up to $1 million. Interest rates at 8 percent with varying pay back periods.

Department of Community and Regional Affairs
Rural Development Fund
333 W. 4th Ave. #220
Anchorage, AK 99501-2341

Anchorage:	907-269-4500, FAX: 907-269-4520
Bethel:	907-543-3475
Dilingham:	907-842-5135
Fairbanks:	907-452-7126
Juneau:	907-465-4814
Kotzebue:	907-442-3696
Kodiak:	907-486-5736
Nome:	907-443-5457

Entrepreneur Rural Development Fund: Available to small enterprises at least six months old or where the owner has considerable experience in the same business. A maximum of $25,000 may be borrowed for construction, purchase of equipment, inventory, and working capital.

Lender Participation Rural Development Fund: Matches other lenders in the financing of large projects than that of the Entrepreneur fund. Up to $100,000 may be borrowed as long as the business is able to raise an equal amount from bank financing or other sources and can explain why more private funds are not available.

Child Care Programs Coordinator:
Child Care Grant Program: Grants, and technical assistance in grant expenditures and recordkeeping are available. Must have a current Alaska child care license, participate in the Day Care Assistance Program (municipalities which have licensed child care facilities) and provide child care under an attendance payment policy. Funds can be used for staff wages, staff training, food for the children, toys and equipment for the children, and parent involvement activities.

Loan Officer
Alaska Energy Authority
P.O. Box 190869
701 East Tudor Road
Anchorage, AK 99519-0869   907-561-7877

Bulk Fuel Revolving Loan Fund: Assists communities in purchasing bulk fuel oil. A private individual who has a written endorsement from the government body of the community is eligible. Loan amount may not exceed 90 percent of the wholesale price of the fuel being purchased. Maximum loan amount is $50,000. Loan must be repaid within one year.

Community Enterprise Development Corporation (CEDC)
1577 C Street, Suite 304
Anchorage, AK 99501   907-274-5400

Fisheries Boat and Equipment Loan Program: Assists Western Alaska coastal residents to enter or remain in the area's commercial fishers. Boat and equipment loans of up to $25,000 at 12 percent interest. Applicants must reside in a western Alaska village from Cape Seppings to Port Heiden, and provide 10 percent equity and all program processing costs. Priority is given to those fishing under utilized fisheries and new entrants to commercial fisheries.

Rural Development Loan Fund: Direct loans ranging from $10,000 to $150,000 at 7 percent interest to rural individuals or organizations. Funds may be used for a wide variety of purposes including land, facility and equipment acquisition, construction and expansion, business acquisition, purchase of supplies, and working capital and start-up costs.

Direct Financing: Direct financing through equity investments and loans are made to business enterprises. To improve the economic well-being of communities, families and individuals in rural Alaska by promoting efficient, productive and self-sustaining business enterprises. Participation available to Native profit organizations serving communities with low incomes. Also provides information and technical assistance in business development and management.

Chief of Industry Services and Trade
National Oceanic and Atmospheric Administration
National Marine Fisheries Services
P.O. Box 21668
Juneau, AK 99802-1668   907-586-7224

Fisheries Development Grants and Cooperative Agreements Program: Emphasis is on the development of the groundfish resources off Alaska. Some work also underway on Alaska trade issues, aquaculture, product development and product quality assurance. A resource for serious fisheries development pilot projects, large and small. Good resource for fisheries development pilot project. Annual application period occurs in winter. Each year the agency publishes priorities for types of projects based on industry needs.

Railbelt Community Development Corporation
619-Warehouse Avenue, #256
Anchorage, AK 99501   907-277-5161

Small Business Administration (SBA) Business Expansion Loan Program - SBA 504 Program: Loan is provided by the Railbelt Community Development Corporation. Provides fixed-rate, long-term financing to small business when expansion will create or maintain job opportunities. Business must be an established, healthy small business unable to obtain private funds for the entire amount of a proposed expansion project. Fund up to 40 percent of a project's cost to a maximum of $750,000 at a fixed rate below market interest rate, 50 percent conventional financing, 10 percent owner equity. Funds may be used for land or building purchase, new building construction and/or building rehabilitation, machinery and equipment purchase, or leasehold improvements.

Alaska Commercial Fishing and Agriculture Bank (CFAB)
P.O. Box 92070
Anchorage, AK 99509   907-276-2007

Established by Alaska Statute, CFAB is a private lending cooperative in which borrowers become members. Loans may be made for harvesting, marketing, or processing of fish or agriculture products. Interest rates are determined by the periodic sale of Farm Credit bonds in the national market.

State Executive Director
Alaska State ASCS Office
800 W. Evergreen, #216
Palmer, AK 99645   907-745-7982

Forestry Incentive Program: Cost sharing eligible to non-industrial forest landowners with a minimum of 10 acres of forest land. Up to 65 percent of costs of implementing forest practices (tree planting, timber stand improvement, and site preparation for natural regeneration). Maximum of $10,000 per applicant per year.

Small Business Administration (SBA)
222 West 8th Avenue
P.O. Box 67   907-271-4022
Anchorage, AK 99513-7559   FAX: 907-271-4545

SBA 7(a) Guaranteed and Direct Loans: Guarantees up to 90 percent of a loan made through a private lender up to $750,000. Can be used for working capital, expand or convert facilities, purchase of machinery and equipment, and land and building. Available only to those unable to obtain a loan from conventional sources. Direct loans are made up to $150,000.

SBA 504: Provides loans using 50 percent conventional bank financing, 40 percent SBA involvement through Certified Development Companies, and 10 percent owner equity. A fixed-asset loan in amounts up to $750,000. Loan can be used for land and building, construction, machinery and equipment, and renovation/expansion.

Small Business Innovative Research Grants (SBIR): Phase I awards between $20,000 to $50,000 to entrepreneurs to support six months of research on a technical innovation. Phase II grants are an additional $500,000 for development. Private sector investment funds must follow.

International Trade Loans: Guaranteed long-term loans through private lenders to develop or expand export markets, or to recover from the effects of import competition. Maximum guaranteed loan is $1,000,000 for fixed assets and an additional $250,000 for working capital and/or export revolving line of credit.

Export Revolving Line of Credit Loan: Short term financing available to small businesses that are at least one year old. Loans provide working capital to finance the manufacturing or wholesaling of products for export and for export marketing. The SBA will guarantee up to 90 percent of a conventional loan in amounts up to $750,000.

Contract Loan: Short-term loans are available to small businesses to finance the costs of labor and materials on contracts for which the proceeds are assignable. Program guarantees up to 90 percent of loans not in excess of $750,000. Qualifying small businesses must be in business for at least 12 calendar months prior to the date of the loan application.

Seasonal Line of Credit Loan: Loans provide short-term working capital to finance seasonal increases in business activities. Program guarantees up to 90 percent of loans not in excess of $750,000. Qualifying business must be in operation for at least one year prior to application.

Pollution Control Loans: Long-term guaranteed loans can be made by conventional financing to small businesses for installation or required pollution control measures. Must be unable to adopt the pollution control measures without undue financial hardship. Maximum guaranteed loan is $1,000,000.

General Contractor Loans: Small general construction contractors may obtain short-term loans or loan guarantees for residential or commercial construction or rehabilitation of property to be sold. The SBA will guarantee up to 90 percent of qualifying loans made by private lenders up to a maximum of $750,000. Direct loans can be up to $150,000.

Energy Business Loan Guarantee: Small businesses that provide certain energy production and conservation services for others may qualify for long-term loans and loan guarantees for start-ups and expansions. Loans and guarantees are made for firms that develop, manufacture, sell, install, or service specific energy measures for others, or firms that provide engineering, architectural, consulting, or other professional services connected with specific energy measures. Guarantee is for up to 90 percent of a loan not in excess of $750,000. Direct loans up to $150,000.

Disaster Recovery Loans: Small businesses located in federally designated disaster areas and suffering property damage or economic losses from the disaster can obtain long-term recovery loans at low interest rates. Property damage loans are limited to 85 percent of the verified damage. Loans for economic losses are for operating capital to meet the business' obligations that could have been made had the disaster not occurred.

Handicapped Assistance Loans: Assists persons who have a physical, mental or emotional disability of a permanent nature which limits the selection of any type of employment for which the person would otherwise be qualified. Direct loans are available for up to $150,000. The interest rate is 3% on these loans.

Surety Bond Guaranty Program: Makes the bonding system more available to small contractors who may be denied access to the system. SBA can guarantee up to 80 percent of surety's loss on a bond that has a maximum in total contract value of up to $1,250,000.

Vietnam-era and Disabled Veterans Loan Program: Provides direct loans to veterans to establish or expand a small business. Funds may be used for working capital or fixed assets. Direct loans for amounts up to $150,000 are available. The interest rate may be fixed or variable.

* Women and Minority Business Assistance

Minority Business Development Center
1577 C Street, Suite 304
Anchorage, AK 99501   907-274-5400
   Provides management and financial consulting services including loan packaging development, marketing, investment decisions, accounting systems and other business advice.

Small Business Administration (SBA)
222 West 8th Avenue
P.O. Box 67   907-271-4022
Anchorage, AK 99513-7559   FAX: 907-271-4545
   SBA 8(a) Program - Business Procurement Assistance: Provides federal government contracting opportunities for small business owned by socially and economically disadvantaged persons, and assists these businesses to become independently competitive in the normal business environment. SBA monitors all government contracts to assure that a quota of contract work goes to 8(a) businesses. Also provides business management services to these businesses. Business must be approved for program participation prior to receipt of an 8(a) contract.

Alaska Federation of Natives
1577 C St., Suite 100
Anchorage, AK 99501   907-274-3611
   Offers Native land selection assistance and information and expertise on Native issues.

Bureau of Indian Affairs
Alaska Area Office
P.O. Box 25520
Juneau, AK 99802-5520   907-586-7103
   Indian Business Development Grants: Provides grants to assist in the development of Native-owned enterprise that will create jobs and other economic benefits for Alaska Native communities. Priority is given rural business development projects. For-profit businesses are eligible if at least 51 percent owned and operated by individual Natives. Grants to individual Natives up to $100,000 with a minimum 75 percent match from private and/or public sector. Must demonstrate that sufficient funding is not available from other sources.

   Indian Loans for Economic Development: Provides business management and technical, and financial assistance to individual Natives and Native organizations for starting, expanding, or purchasing a business enterprise whose enterprise will create jobs and have other economic benefits. Priority is given to rural business development projects. Financial assistance is in the form of guaranteed or direct loans. 20 percent equity is required on loans and business must demonstrate economic feasibility.

Indian Arts and Crafts Board
Department of the Interior, Room 4004
Main Interior Building
Washington, DC 20240   202-208-3773
   Indian Arts and Crafts Development: Advisory service and counseling available to Native Americans. Publish a national directory of Native art commercial enterprises which provides a nationwide marketplace for Native arts.

* Training

Child Care Programs Coordinator
Department of Community and Regional Affairs
Rural Development Fund
333 W. 4th, #220   907-269-4500
Anchorage, AK 99501-2341   FAX: 907-269-4520
   Child Care Education and Training Program: Grants for education and training of child care practitioners and administrators. Applicants must be facilities that are eligible to participate in the State's Child Care Grant Program (*See Finance Section*), or an organization which can provide education or training identified as needed by child care employees or administration who are eligible for the Child Care Grant Program.

Bureau of Indian Affairs
P.O. Box 25520
Juneau, AK 99802-5520   907-586-7600
   Employment Assistance Program: Financial assistance grants, career counseling, guidance, job development and job placement assistance are available to businesses.

Department of Community and Regional Affairs
Rural Development Division
333 W. 4th, #220   907-269-4500
Anchorage, AK 99508
   Job Training Partnership Act (JTPA): Provides employers with recruitment, screening, referral, training, 50 percent wage subsidy up to 3 months for on-the-job training. Available to any private employer.

* Management Consulting and Other Services

Office of Industrial Trade
Department of Commerce and Economic Development
3601 C Street, Suite 798   907-561-5585
Anchorage, AK 99503   FAX: 907-561-4577
   Office of International Trade: The office was created to encourage the development of new markets for Alaska resources, expand existing markets, locate sources of investment capital, increase the visibility of Alaska and its products in the international marketplace, and improve communication among members of the Alaskan and international business community. The Office makes referrals and provides technical assistance to Alaskans interested in developing business abroad. Maintain foreign offices in Tokyo, Seoul, and Taipei.

General Services Administration
Business Service Center
GSA Center, Room 2413
Auburn, WA 98001   206-931-7956
   Procurement Assistance: Advisory services and counseling in government procurement and services contracts. Especially interested in assisting small and disadvantages businesses. The federal government does a great deal of business in Alaska.

Community Development Program
2221 East Northern Lights Blvd.
Suite 132   907-276-2433
Anchorage, AK 99508-4143   FAX: 907-277-5242
   or
Cooperative Extension Service
University of Alaska Fairbanks   907-474-7246
Fairbanks, AK 99775-5200   FAX: 907-474-7439

Community and Rural Development Program: Workshops and technical assistance in community economic development, village tourism development, grant writing workshops, community gardening and small farm development, home based business assistance, energy conservation.

State Conservationist
Soil Conservation Service
949 E. 36th Ave., #400
Anchorage, AK 99508-4302   907-271-2424

    Provides advisory and counseling services for land use planning and application of conservation or development practices. Land/soils information upon request, based on Soil Conservation Service resource inventories.

Department of Natural Resources
Division of Agriculture
P.O. Box 949
Palmer, AK 99645-0949   907-745-7200
        or
4420 Airport Way
Fairbanks, AK 99709   907-451-2780

    Wholesale Agricultural Market Development: Technical advisory services and counseling in the area of efficient market development. Has a state-level clearinghouse service concerning agricultural development resources.

Department of Economic and Community Development
Division of Tourism
P.O. Box 110801   907-465-2012
Juneau, AK 99811-0801   FAX: 907-586-8399

    The division counsels tourist-related businesses regarding planning and implementing programs for the development and marketing of tourism attractions, services and facilities. Designs and implements an integrated marketing program directed to foreign markets in Asia and Western Europe.

Department of Environmental Conservation
Division of Environmental Quality
410 Willoughby Ave., #105
Juneau, AK 99801-1795   907-465-5260

    Pollution Prevention Program: Technical assistance to Alaska businesses on ways to reduce, recycle and prevent wastes, to include wastes that enter water and air as well as solid and hazardous wastes. Services include an information clearinghouse, pollution prevention resource library, and presentations.

Economic Development Administration
Old Federal Building
605 West Fourth Avenue, Room G-80
Anchorage, AK 99501   907-271-2272

    Economic Development Technical Assistance (EDA): Technical assistance is available to small private businesses on a paying basis.

Community Information Exchange
1029 Vermont Avenue Northwest, Suite 710
Washington, DC 20005   202-628-2981

    A nationwide computerized network for information sharing in the field of community economic development housing. A comprehensive database of information on exemplary projects, technical experts, funding sources, and bibliographic references, newsletter, funding opportunity alerts. Annual fee $50.

Small Business Administration
222 West 8th Avenue
Box 67   907-271-4022
Anchorage, AK 99513-7559   FAX: 907-271-4545

    Management Assistance: Assistance in the form of advisory services, video tapes, seminars and counseling, dissemination of technical information, training for both business owners and existing small businesses.

    Small Business Institutes: This program provides personalized consulting services to the small business community. Consulting is provided by senior level business students, guided by a faculty advisor. Assistance in business

plan preparation, marketing research, market planning, accounting, and seminars are provided.
University Locations:
University of Alaska - Anchorage
University of Alaska - Fairbanks

Alaska Business Assistance Centers

    The following are private companies which charge for services:
    Anchorage: Alaska Business Development Center, Inc., 821 N St., #103 Anchorage, AK 99501, 907-279-7427.

    Anchorage: Community Enterprise Development Corporation, Minority Business Development Center of Alaska, 1577 C St. Plaza #304, Anchorage, AK 99501, 907-274-5400.

    Fairbanks: Fairbanks Native Association, Manpower and Training, Native Business Center, 210 First Avenue, 2nd Floor, Fairbanks, AK 99701, 907-452-1648.

* Small Business Development Centers

The following offices offer free and fee-based services to new and expanding businesses:

Lead Center:
University of Alaska
Small Business Development Center
430 West 7th Avenue, Suite 110   907-274-7232
Anchorage, AK 99501   FAX: 907-274-9524

    Anchorage: University of Alaska-Anchorage, 430 West 7th Avenue, Suite 110, Anchorage, AK 99501, 907-274-7232; FAX: 907-274-9524.

    Fairbanks: University of Alaska-Fairbanks, Small Business Development Center, 510 Fifth Avenue, #421, Fairbanks, AK 99701, 907-456-1701, FAX: 907-456-1942.

    Juneau: University of Alaska-Southeast, Small Business Development Center, 124 West 5th Street, Juneau, AK 99801, 907-463-3789; FAX: 907-463-5670.

    Wasilla: University of Alaska-Anchorage/Matanuska-Susitna Borough, Small Business Development Center, 1801 Parks Highway, #C-18, Wasilla, AK 99654, 907-373-7232; FAX: 907-373-2560.

Arizona

* General Information

Arizona Office of Economic Development
Department of Commerce
3800 N. Central, #1500
Phoenix, AZ 85012   602-280-1300

    State Small Business Advocate: Assistance in cutting bureaucratic red tape. Information and expertise in dealing with state, federal, and local agencies.

Arizona Business Connection   602-280-1480
Business Development Division   1-800-528-8421
Small Business Ass. Center   1-800-524-5684

    This office provides information on licenses, applications, permits and any other requirements for small businesses. A customized packet containing the forms needed for starting a business, information on taxes and government regulations is available. Assistance with site selection, procurement of raw materials, financing sources, government agencies and programs referral is also provided. Speakers will be provided on request.

* Financing

Business Finance Unit
Arizona Office of Economic Development

Department of Commerce
3800 North Central, #1500
Phoenix, AZ 85012   602-280-1341

Community Development Block Grant: Regional grants are awarded to communities for development projects such as water, wastewater, community facilities, streets and curbs. Communities then loan the money to business for the projects. State Set-Aside Grants work the same way except they are for economic development in rural communities.

Eximbank Guarantees and Insurance: Conventional bank loan to finance production and shipment of goods for export guaranteed up to 90 percent of the bank loan by the U.S. Export-Import Bank. The Federal Credit Insurance Administration writes an insurance policy guaranteeing repayment if oversees buyer does not pay due to political risk.

Revolving Energy Loans: Companies with a minimum of two years of business operations, engaged in the manufacture of energy-conserving or energy-related products, or those installing renewable energy or energy conserving products in their own facilities. Funds may be used for fixed asset plant expansion for manufacturers of energy-related products, energy-conserving retrofits, or short term contract financing of production of energy-related products. Loan amounts range from $50,000 to $500,000. Interest rates are fixed.

Farmers Home Administration (FHA)   602-640-5086; 602-640-5088
Loan Guarantees: A commercial bank loan guaranteed up to 90 percent by the FHA. Minimum guarantee is $500,000.

Economic Development Administration   602-379-3750
Loan Guarantees: A commercial bank loan guaranteed up to 80 percent by the EDA.

Small Business Administration (SBA)
2828 N. Central Ave., #800   602-640-2316
Phoenix, AZ 85004-1025   FAX: 602-640-2360

SBA 7(a) Guaranteed and Direct Loans: Guarantees up to 90 percent of a loan made through a private lender up to $750,000. Can be used for working capital, expand or convert facilities, purchase of machinery and equipment, and land and building. Available only to those unable to obtain a loan from conventional sources. Direct loans are made up to $150,000.

SBA 504 Program: Arizona Enterprise Development Corporation: Long term fixed asset loans. Maximum loan guaranteed by SBA is 40 percent of the project cost up to a maximum of $750,000. One job must be created for every $35,000 of loan funds. The Arizona Enterprise Development Corporation is a private, non-profit corporation staffed by the Department of Commerce that provides loans to expanding businesses through the SBA 504 program.

SBA 502: Fixed asset loan. Maximum loan amount is $750,000. SBA guarantees up to 85-90 percent of the loan. Less restrictive job creation requirements than the SBA 504 program.

Small Business Innovative Research Grants (SBIR): Phase I awards between $20,000 to $50,000 to entrepreneurs to support six months of research on a technical innovation. Phase II grants are an additional $500,000 for development. Private sector investment funds must follow.

International Trade Loans: Guaranteed long-term loans through private lenders to develop or expand export markets, or to recover from the effects of import competition. Maximum guaranteed loan is $1,000,000 for fixed assets and an additional $250,000 for working capital and/or export revolving line of credit.

Export Revolving Line of Credit Loan: Short term financing available to small businesses that are at least one year old. Loans provide working capital to finance the manufacturing or wholesaling of products for export and for export marketing. The SBA will guarantee up to 90 percent of a conventional loan in amounts up to $750,000.

Contract Loan: Short-term loans are available to small businesses to finance the costs of labor and materials on contracts for which the proceeds are assignable. Program guarantees up to 90 percent of loans not in excess of $750,000. Qualifying small businesses must be in business for at least 12 calendar months prior to the date of the loan application.

Seasonal Line of Credit Loan: Loans provide short-term working capital to finance seasonal increases in business activities. Program guarantees up to 90 percent of loans not in excess of $750,000. Qualifying business must be in operation for at least one year prior to application.

Pollution Control Loans: Long-term guaranteed loans can be made by conventional financing to small businesses for installation or required pollution control measures. Must be unable to adopt the pollution control measures without undue financial hardship. Maximum guaranteed loan is $1,000,000.

General Contractor Loans: Small general construction contractors may obtain short-term loans or loan guarantees for residential or commercial construction or rehabilitation of property to be sold. The SBA will guarantee up to 90 percent of qualifying loans made by private lenders up to a maximum of $750,000. Direct loans can be up to $150,000.

Energy Business Loan Guarantee: Small businesses that provide certain energy production and conservation services for others may qualify for long-term loans and loan guarantees for start-ups and expansions. Loans and guarantees are made for firms that develop, manufacture, sell, install, or service specific energy measures for others, or firms that provide engineering, architectural, consulting, or other professional services connected with specific energy measures. Guarantee is for up to 90 percent of a loan not in excess of $750,000. Direct loans up to $150,000.

Disaster Recovery Loans: Small businesses located in federally designated disaster areas and suffering property damage or economic losses from the disaster can obtain long-term recovery loans at low interest rates. Property damage loans are limited to 85 percent of the verified damage. Loans for economic losses are for operating capital to meet the business' obligations that could have been made had the disaster not occurred.

Handicapped Assistance Loans: Assists persons who have a physical, mental or emotional disability of a permanent nature which limits the selection of any type of employment for which the person would otherwise be qualified. Direct loans are available for up to $150,000. The interest rate is 3% on these loans.

Surety Bond Guaranty Program: Makes the bonding system more available to small contractors who may be denied access to the system. SBA can guarantee up to 80 percent of surety's loss on a bond that has a maximum in total contract value of up to $1,250,000.

Vietnam-era and Disabled Veterans Loan Program: Provides direct loans to veterans to establish or expand a small business. Funds may be used for working capital or fixed assets. Direct loans for amounts up to $150,000 are available. The interest rate may be fixed or variable.

First Commerce & Loan LP
5620 N. Kolb, #260
Tucson, AZ 85715   602-298-2500

First Interstate Equity Corporation
100 West Washington Street
Phoenix, AZ 85003   602-528-6647

Rocky Mountain Equity Corporation
2525 East Camelback, Suite 275
Phoenix, AZ 85016   602-955-6100

Sundance Venture Partners, L.P.
(Main Office: Menlo Park, CA)
400 East Van Buren, Suite 650
Phoenix, AZ 85004   602-252-3441

Valley National Investors, Inc.
201 North Central Avenue, Suite 900
Phoenix, AZ 85004   602-261-1577

Wilbur Venture Capital Corporation
4575 South Palo Verde, Suite 305
Tucson, AZ 85714   602-747-5999

Small Business Investment Companies (SBICs): The SBA licenses, regulates, and provides financial assistance to privately owned and operated Small Business Investment Companies. SBICs make venture or risk investments by supplying capital and extending unsecured loans and loans not fully collateralized to small enterprises which meet their investment criteria. Financing is made by direct loans and by equity investments.

* Women and Minority Business Assistance

Arizona Business Connection
Arizona Department of Commerce
3800 N. Central, Suite 1400
Phoenix, AZ 85012   602-280-1480
> This office serves as a clearinghouse of information to assist small businesses. One on one counseling is available.

Small Business Administration (SBA)
2828 N. Central Ave., #800   602-640-2316
Phoenix, AZ 85004-1025   FAX: 602-640-2360
> **SBA 8(a) Program - Business Procurement Assistance:** Provides federal government contracting opportunities for small businesses owned by socially and economically disadvantaged persons, and assists these businesses to become independently competitive in the normal business environment. SBA monitors all government contracts to assure that a quota of contract work goes to 8(a) businesses. Also provides business management services to these businesses. Business must be approved for program participation prior to receipt of an 8(a) contract.

* Training

Arizona Office of Economic Development
Department of Commerce
3800 North Central
Phoenix, AZ 85012   602-280-1300
> **Economic Development:** Community colleges work with business and industry to recruit a work force, provide special training programs, provide technical assistance. Community colleges also provide advanced and technical training, retraining and upgrading the work force, in addition to on-the-job training.

> **Industry Training Services:** A Part of the Departments of Education and Economic Security that offers quick-start, short-term training for employees looking for entry-level positions or trying to upgrade their status. Matches cost of training through a 50-50 matching funds commitment up to $20,000 per project. State-of-the art instruction in the plant on actual operating equipment can be provided at little or no expense to the company with ITS monies are combined with additional funding sources. ITS funding is available to new and/or expanding Arizona companies. Assistance in recruiting and screening job candidates is also available.

> **Job Training Partnership Act (JTPA):** Provides employers with recruitment, screening, referral, training, 50 percent wage subsidy up to 3 months for on-the-job training. Available to any private employer.

* Management Consulting and Other Services

Arizona Business Connection
Arizona Department of Commerce
3800 N. Central, Suite 1400
Phoenix, AZ 85012   602-280-1480
> The Arizona Business Connection will refer small businesses to the appropriate government agencies for assistance. They also provide one on one counseling on marketing and management questions.

Small Business Administration
2828 N. Central Ave., #800   602-640-2316
Phoenix, AZ 85004-1025   FAX: 602-640-2360
> **Small Business Institutes:** This program provides personalized consulting services to the small business community. Consulting is provided by senior level business students, guided by a faculty advisor. Assistance in business plan preparation, marketing research, market planning, accounting, and seminars are provided.

University Locations:
Arizona State University - West Campus
Arizona State University
Northern Arizona University
Western International University

* Small Business Development Centers
The following offices offer free and fee-based services to new and expanding businesses:

Lead Center:
Arizona Small Business Development Center
9215 N. Black Canyon Highway   602-943-9818
Phoenix, AZ 85021   FAX: 602-943-3716

> **Coolidge:** Central Arizona College, Small Business Development Center, 141 N. Main, Coolidge, AZ 85222, 602-723-5522; FAX: 602-426-4234.

> **Flagstaff:** Coconino County Community College, Small Business Development Center, 3000 N. 4th Street, Suite 17, Flagstaff, AZ 86004, 602-526-5072; FAX: 602-526-8693; 1-800-266-5072.

> **Holbrook:** Northland Pioneer College, Small Business Development Center, P.O. Box 610, Holbrook, AZ 86025, 602-537-2976; FAX: 602-524-2227.

> **Lake Havasu City:** Mojave Community College, Small Business Development Center, 1977 W. Acoma Blvd., Lake Havasu City, AZ 86403, 602-453-1836; FAX: 602-453-8335.

> **Phoenix:** Rio Salado Community College, Small Business Development Center, 301 West Roosevelt, Suite D, Phoenix, AZ 85003, 602-238-9603; FAX: 602-340-1627.

> **Phoenix:** Gateway Community College, Small Business Development Center, 108 N. 40th Street, Phoenix, AZ 85008, 602-392-5220; FAX: 602-392-5329.

> **Prescott:** Yavapal College, Small Business Development Center, 1100 E. Sheldon Street, Prescott, AZ 86301, 602-776-2373; FAX: 602-776-2193.

> **Safford:** Eastern Arizona College, Small Business Development Center, 1111 Thatcher Boulevard, Safford, AZ 85546, 602-428-7603; FAX: 602-428-8462.

> **Sierra Vista:** Cochise College, Small Business Development Center, 901 N. Colombo, Room 411, Sierra Vista, AZ 85635, 602-459-9778; FAX: 602-459-9764; 1-800-966-7943, ext. 778.

> **Tucson:** Pima Community College, Small Business Development Center, 655 North Alvernon, #110, Tucson, AZ 85711, 602-884-6306; FAX: 602-884-6585.

> **Yuma:** Arizona Western College, Small Business Development Center, 281 W. 24th Street, #128 Century Plaza, Yuma, AZ 85364, 602-341-1650; FAX: 602-341-0234.

Arkansas

* General Information

Arkansas Industrial Development Commission
One State Capitol Mall   501-682-1121
Little Rock, AR 72201   FAX: 501-682-7341
> **Small Business Clearinghouse:** Counseling and referral service to serve small business and potential entrepreneurs, including invention assistance, reference catalog, printed materials, assistance programs evaluations.

Coordinator, Small Business Programs
Arkansas Industrial Development Commission
One State Capitol Mall, Room 4C300
Little Rock, AR 72201   501-682-5275
> **Small Business Advocate:** Assistance in cutting bureaucratic red tape. Information and expertise in dealing with state, federal, and local agencies.

* Financing

Arkansas Development Finance Authority (ADFA)
100 Main Street
Suite 200   501-682-5908
Little Rock, AR 72201-8023   FAX: 501-682-5859

Industrial Development Bond Guaranty Program: Offers taxable and tax exempt bond financing to both small and large businesses. Umbrella bonds, available to small businesses, spread the costs of the bond issue among all of the borrowers. ADFA also can provide interim financing for approved projects awaiting bond issuance. Available to manufacturing facilities.

Export Finance: Short-term loans to businesses based on export transactions. Financing is provided through the exporter's local bank which funds 10 percent of the loan value.

Tax Credit Program: Assists in the development of rental housing for owners of low income rental housing.

Arkansas Industrial Development Commission
Community Development Division
One State Capitol Mall   501-682-1211
Little Rock, AR 72291   FAX: 501-682-7341

Industrial Revenue Bonds: Provides guarantees for local governments which issue bonds for local industrial development such as infrastructure development, new or expanding industries, downtown revitalization of public works. Maximum guarantee is $2 million with a term of 10 to 15 years.

Enterprise Zone Program   501-682-7310
Established to stimulate growth and create jobs in areas with high poverty, unemployment, or other economic distress. Provides tax incentives designed to encourage new business locations and expansions in designated geographic areas where there are serious economic problems. Eligible firms are manufacturing, warehouse operations employing 100 or more (no retail sales), and computer firms.

Community Assistance Division   501-682-5193
Community Development Block Grants (CDBG)
State Economic Infrastructure Fund: CDBG Funds have been granted to communities for improving the quality of life for lower to moderate income families. Grant funds are used by the community which make locating and expansion of businesses by providing utility extensions and capacity expansions, building rehabilitation, airport expansions, etc.

Economic Development Set-Aside: 501-682-1151
Portions of the CDBG fund have enabled communities to take advantage of specific economic development including industrial locations and expansion. Projects include water and sewer systems, fire protection, and flood control. The community loans the funds they receive to businesses for development and finance job-creating activities.

Arkansas Science and Technology Authority
100 Main Street
Suite 450 (Technology Center)
Little Rock, AR 72201   501-324-9006

Promotes science and technology in both the public and private sectors and works to support scientific research and job creating technology development.

Applied Research Grant Programs: For companies in need of research and development and would welcome working with an Arkansas college or university to have this work completed on a cost-sharing basis.

Small Business Innovation Research Grants: Offers small business assistance in obtaining these grants for research and development. A federal program which insures that small businesses share in the expenditure of federal research dollars.

Seed Capital Investment Program: Program seeks to invest in innovative Arkansas companies that utilize new products or processes in their businesses. Does not fund entire projects, just the initial working capital portion of the financing package. *Also see Technology Section.*

Farmers Home Administration
700 West Capitol
Suite 5331
Little Rock, AR 72203   501-324-6281

Business and Industrial Loan Program: Works to improve economic conditions in rural areas. Guarantees up to 90 percent of a loan made by local lender. Loans can be made for capital improvements, machinery, real estate, and working capital. Limited to rural areas (towns of 50,000 population or less), no loans for actual agricultural production. General loan size from $500,000 to $10 million (less than $500,00 will refer to SBA).

Small Business Administration (SBA)
2120 Riverfront Dr., #100   501-324-5278
Little Rock, AR 72202   FAX: 501-324-5199

SBA 7(a) Guaranteed and Direct Loans: Guarantees up to 90 percent of a loan made through a private lender up to $750,000. Can be used for working capital, expand or convert facilities, purchase of machinery and equipment, and land and building. Available only to those unable to obtain a loan from conventional sources. Direct loans are made up to $150,000.

SBA 504: Provides loans using 50 percent conventional bank financing, 40 percent SBA involvement through Certified Development Companies, and 10 percent owner equity. A fixed-asset loan in amounts up to $750,000. Loan can be used for land and building, construction, machinery and equipment, and renovation/expansion.

Small Business Innovative Research Grants (SBIR): Phase I awards between $20,000 to $50,000 to entrepreneurs to support six months of research on a technical innovation. Phase II grants are an additional $500,000 for development. Private sector investment funds must follow.

International Trade Loans: Guaranteed long-term loans through private lenders to develop or expand export markets, or to recover from the effects of import competition. Maximum guaranteed loan is $1,000,000 for fixed assets and an additional $250,000 for working capital and/or export revolving line of credit.

Export Revolving Line of Credit Loan: Short term financing available to small businesses that are at least one year old. Loans provide working capital to finance the manufacturing or wholesaling of products for export and for export marketing. The SBA will guarantee up to 90 percent of a conventional loan in amounts up to $750,000.

Contract Loan: Short-term loans are available to small businesses to finance the costs of labor and materials on contracts for which the proceeds are assignable. Program guarantees up to 90 percent of loans not in excess of $750,000. Qualifying small businesses must be in business for at least 12 calendar months prior to the date of the loan application.

Seasonal Line of Credit Loan: Loans provide short-term working capital to finance seasonal increases in business activities. Program guarantees up to 90 percent of loans not in excess of $750,000. Qualifying business must be in operation for at least one year prior to application.

Pollution Control Loans: Long-term guaranteed loans can be made by conventional financing to small businesses for installation or required pollution control measures. Must be unable to adopt the pollution control measures without undue financial hardship. Maximum guaranteed loan is $1,000,000.

General Contractor Loans: Small general construction contractors may obtain short-term loans or loan guarantees for residential or commercial construction or rehabilitation of property to be sold. The SBA will guarantee up to 90 percent of qualifying loans made by private lenders up to a maximum of $750,000. Direct loans can be up to $150,000.

Energy Business Loan Guarantee: Small businesses that provide certain energy production and conservation services for others may qualify for long-term loans and loan guarantees for start-ups and expansions. Loans and guarantees are made for firms that develop, manufacture, sell, install, or service specific energy measures for others, or firms that provide engineering, architectural, consulting, or other professional services connected with specific energy measures. Guarantee is for up to 90 percent of a loan not in excess of $750,000. Direct loans up to $150,000.

Disaster Recovery Loans: Small businesses located in federally designated disaster areas and suffering property damage or economic losses from the disaster can obtain long-term recovery loans at low interest rates. Property damage loans are limited to 85 percent of the verified damage. Loans for economic losses are for operating capital to meet the business' obligations that could have been made had the disaster not occurred.

Handicapped Assistance Loans: Assists persons who have a physical, mental or emotional disability of a permanent nature which limits the selection of any type of employment for which the person would otherwise be qualified. Direct loans are available for up to $150,000. The interest rate is 3% on these loans.

Surety Bond Guaranty Program: Makes the bonding system more available to small contractors who may be denied access to the system. SBA can guarantee up to 80 percent of surety's loss on a bond that has a maximum in total contract value of up to $1,250,000.

Vietnam-era and Disabled Veterans Loan Program: Provides direct loans to veterans to establish or expand a small business. Funds may be used for working capital or fixed assets. Direct loans for amounts up to $150,000 are available. The interest rate may be fixed or variable.

Small Business Investment Capital, Inc.
10003 New Benton Hwy.
P.O. Box 3627
Little Rock, AR 72203   501-455-6599

Southern Ventures, Inc.
605 Main Street, Suite 202
Arkadelphia, AR 71923   501-246-9627
    Small Business Investment Companies (SBIC): The SBA licenses, regulates, and provides financial assistance to privately owned and operated Small Business Investment Companies. SBICs make venture or risk investments by supplying capital and extending unsecured loans and loans not fully collateralized to small enterprises which meet their investment criteria. Financing is made by direct loans and by equity investments.

Arkansas Capital Corporation
800 Pyramid Place
221 West Second Street
Little Rock, AR 72201   501-374-9247
    A private, non-profit corporation that provides fixed-rate financing for projects which do not meet the requirements for conventional bank loans. Most loans are in the $100,000 to $500,000 range and can be used for fixed assets or working capital. Projects must increase or maintain employment, and major portion of loan must be used for fixed assets.

* Women And Minority Business Assistance

Arkansas Industrial Development Commission
One State Capitol Mall
Little Rock, AR 72201
    Minority Business Development Division   501-682-1060
    Provides business loan packaging, contract procurement assistance, bonding information, general business counseling, seminars, workshops, and referrals to other agencies.

    Small Business Division   501-324-9043
    Will do limited business research, limited inventor/manufacturer matching, and limited energy efficiency counseling and information.

Small Business Administration (SBA)
2120 Riverfront Dr., Suite 100   501-324-5278
Little Rock, AR 72202   FAX: 501-324-5199
    SBA 8(a) Program - Business Procurement Assistance: Provides federal government contracting opportunities for small businesses owned by socially and economically disadvantaged persons, and assists these businesses to become independently competitive in the normal business environment. SBA monitors all government contracts to assure that a quota of contract work goes to 8(a) businesses. Also provides business management services to these businesses. Business must be approved for program participation prior to receipt of an 8(a) contract.

* Training

Office of Employment and Training Service
Employment Security Department
P.O. Box 2981
Little Rock, AR 72203   501-682-3105
    Job Training Partnership Act (JTPA): Provides employers with recruitment, screening, referral, training, 50 percent wage subsidy up to 3 months for on-the-job training. Available to any private employer.

* Management Consulting and Other Services

Arkansas Industrial Development Commission
One State Capital Mall
Little Rock, AR 72201
    Small Business Division   501-324-9043
    General counseling, business assistance referrals in the areas of agricultural and manufactured products, marketing-national and international.

    Marketing Division   501-682-7781
    This division provides counseling and hands-on assistance to Arkansas companies in selling agricultural and manufactured products both domestically and internationally. The division also promotes international investment in Arkansas. Some of its programs follow:

       Good Work, Arkansas: Point-of-purchase campaign promotes Arkansas-made products that consumers can buy in their local grocery stores.

       Taste of Arkansas: A show held out of the state to introduce and promote Arkansas food products to out-of-state markets.

       MatchMaker: Helps Arkansas companies locate other Arkansas companies that can offer competitive prices on parts or services currently being purchased out-of-state.

       Export Development: Helps develop or expand foreign markets for Arkansas products through its offices in Europe and Asia through international trade exhibitions. The three foreign offices are in Brussels, Belgium; Tokyo, Japan; and Taipei, Taiwan. These offices promote Arkansas products, both manufactured and agricultural, international business relations, and foreign in Arkansas.

    Motion Picture Development Office   501-682-7676
    This office works to attract motion picture and television commercial production companies to film in Arkansas. It promotes the state's diverse scenic and period locations and provides assistance to production companies during location filming. The vendors serving these activities are primarily small business and involve a wide variety of products and services.

    Research Section   501-682-2301
    Develops and maintains statistical data on available manpower, buildings, and sites in Arkansas communities. Provides each industrial prospect with a tailor-made package of information relevant to the prospect's criteria.

    Established Industries Division
    Quality/Productivity Program: Assists small businesses in competing through the use of task force which introduces innovative management and production techniques such as statistical process control, computer integrated manufacturing, etc.

    Energy Assistance Program: Helps firms find ways to lower their energy costs. Conduct on-site energy audits of plants, offices, and production methods.

    Resource Recovery Program: Promotes recycling or selling of industrial waste or by-products. Furnishes all manufacturers with copies of a waste exchange newsletter and the *Manufacturers Exchange Newsletter*.

Arkansas Inventors Congress
P.O. Box 411
Dardanelle, AR 72834   501-229-4515
    Provides inventor referrals, counseling, patent procedure and search information and contact with the National Congress of Inventor Organizations.

Arkansas Science and Technology Authority
100 Main Street, Suite 450, (Technology Center)
Little Rock, AR 72201   501-324-9006
>**Business Incubators:** There are six business incubators located in Arkansas. They offer start-up companies a variety of services ranging from shared office services to engineering support.

Small Business Administration
2120 Riverfront Dr., #100   501-324-5278
Little Rock, AR 72202   FAX: 501-324-5199
>**Small Business Institutes:** This program provides personalized consulting services to the small business community. Consulting is provided by senior level business students, guided by a faculty advisor. Assistance in business plan preparation, marketing research, market planning, accounting, and seminars are provided.
>**University Locations:**

Arkansas College, Batesville	501-753-9813
Arkansas State University, Jonesboro	501-972-3430
Arkansas Tech University, Russellville	501-968-0357
Harding University, Searcy	501-268-6161
Henderson State University, Arkadelphia	501-246-5511
Southern State University, Magnolia	501-234-5120
University of Arkansas, Fayetteville	501-575-3851
University of Arkansas, Little Rock	501-569-3353
University of Arkansas, Monticello	501-460-1041
University of Arkansas, Pine Bluff	501-541-6823
University of Central Arkansas, Conway	501-450-3190
University of the Ozarks, Clarksville	501-754-3839

Business and Industrial Institute
Westark Community College
P.O. Box 3649
Fort Smith, AR 72913   501-785-7311
>Sponsors seminars on management training, employee relations, small business marketing, and customer relations. Through their computer center and quality technology center offer classes available on and off campus.

Center of Economic Development
Economic Development Assistance Program
Arkansas State University
P.O. Box 2110
State University, AR 72467-2110   501-972-3850
>They work toward strengthening the relationship between the University and the business community and help foster regional and community development, solving problems of Arkansas business and industry, and communicate new developments to those who may be affected by applied research and development activities. Provide counseling, workshops, specialized training programs, general business courses. Most assistance is at no cost. More extensive assistance may be provided on a cost recovery basis. Primarily service twenty-six counties in northern and eastern Arkansas, but will consider requests from all over Arkansas.

Economic Development Districts (EDD)
Economic Development Administration
700 W. Capitol
Little Rock, AR 72201   501-324-5637
>Arkansas Economic Development Districts are private, non-profit organizations that serve eight different regions of the state to promote orderly, efficient growth in the economic sector. Typical services provided by the EDD offices are loan packaging, business plan preparation, grant application assistance, general business counseling, export/import information, and government procurement assistance. Contact a regional center below:

>**Batesville:** White River Planning and Development District, P.O. Box 2396, Batesville, AR 72501, 501-793-5233.

>**Fort Smith:** Western Arkansas Planning and Development District, 623 Garrison Avenue, P.O. Box 2067, Fort Smith, AR 72901, 501-785-2651.

>**Harrison:** Northwest Arkansas Economic Development District, P.O. Box 190, Harrison, AR 72601, 501-741-5404.

>**Hot Springs:** West Central Arkansas Planning and Development District, P.O. Box 1558, Hot Springs, AR 71901, 501-624-1036.

>**Jonesboro:** East Arkansas Planning and Development District, P.O. Box 1403, Jonesboro, AR 72401, 501-932-3957.

>**Lonoke:** Central Arkansas Planning and Development District, 112 N.E. Front Street, P.O. Box 187, Lonoke, AR 72086, 501-676-2721.

>**Pine Bluff:** Southeast Arkansas Economic Development District, P.O. Box 6806, Pine Bluff, AR 71601, 501-536-1971.

Entrepreneurial Service Center
College of Business Administration
University of Arkansas, BA 106
Fayetteville, AR 72701   501-575-6618
>Through field offices across the state, this agency offers the usual array of consulting services. The Investment Resource Network provides private sources of venture capital.

Tourism Development Section
Arkansas Department of Parks and Tourism
One State Capitol Mall
Little Rock, AR 72201   501-682-5240
>Offers festival planning workshops, hospitality training seminars, tourism development counseling, and other programs designed to increase awareness about the importance of tourism to the economy of Arkansas. Also maintains county profiles and statistical information.

* Small Business Development Centers
The following offices offer free and fee-based services to new and expanding businesses:

Lead Center:
Arkansas Small Business Development Center
University of Arkansas at Little Rock
Little Rock Technology Center Building
100 South Main, Suite 401   501-324-9043
Little Rock, AR 72201   FAX: 501-324-9049

>**Arkadelphia:** Henderson State University, Small Business Development Center, P.O. Box 7624, Arkadelphia, AR 71923, 501-246-5511, ext. 327.

>**Fayetteville:** University of Arkansas at Fayetteville, Small Business Development Center, College of Business - BA 117, Fayetteville, AR 72701, 501-575-5148.

>**Jonesboro:** Arkansas State University, Small Business Development Center, P.O. Drawer 2650, Jonesboro, AR 72467, 501-972-3517.

California

* General Information

California Department of Commerce
801 K Street, Suite 1700
Sacramento, CA 95814   916-322-1394
>**Office of Small Business**   916-324-1295
>Offers workshops, seminars, individual counseling, and publications.

>**Enterprise Zone**   916-324-8211
>**Main Street Development**   916-322-3520
>Provides case studies, handbooks, slide presentations, on-site training workshops, and seminars on a wide range of topics, including downtown revitalization, industrial development, streamlining the local permit process, and financing.
>**Field Offices:**
>**Los Angeles:** OBD Field Office, 200 East Del Mar Blvd., Suite 302, Los Angeles, CA 91105, 818-568-9856

>**San Jose:** OBD Field Office, 111 N. Market Street, Suite 815, San Jose, CA 95113, 408-277-9799

Small Business Advocate
801 K Street, #1700   916-322-6108
Sacramento, CA 95814   916-327-HELP

> **Small Business Advocate:** Provides assistance in cutting bureaucratic red tape and information and expertise in dealing with state, federal, and local agencies.

California Commission for Economic Development
Office of the Lieutenant Governor
State Capitol, Room 1028
Sacramento, CA 95814   916-445-8994

> Publishes *Doing Business in California: A Guide for Establishing Business.* Cost: $3.00.

* Financing

California Department of Commerce
801 K Street, Suite 1700
Sacramento, CA 95814

Office of Local Development   916-322-1394
Community Development Block Grant (CDBG) Program: Assists small business and developers in creating and/or retaining jobs in California. Conventional bank financing provides $2 for every $1 of CDBG. Fixed rate, no lower than 4 points below prime. Maximum loan amount $500,000. Maximum loan amount: $500,000. Loan can be used for purchase of land and improvements, purchase of existing building(s) and improvements, building construction, machinery/equipment, working capital, inventory, off-site improvements.

SBA 502: Provides loans at market rate using 50 percent conventional bank financing, SBA provides 40 percent, and 10-20 percent owner equity. Maximum loan 40 percent of project, not to exceed $750,000. Loan can be used for purchase of land and improvements, purchase of existing building(s) and improvements, building construction, machinery/ equipment, renovation and restoration.

SBA 7(a): Provides capital to meet short-and-long term needs. Conventional bank financing provides the loan, SBA guarantees up to 90 percent of the loan amount to $155,000, 85 percent over $155,000. 10-33 percent equity required. Maximum loan guarantee $750,000. Loans can be used for land and improvements, purchase of existing building(s) and improvements, building construction, machinery/equipment, working capital, inventory, business buy-outs.

Rural Economic Development Infrastructure Program: Assists financing rural public infrastructure projects which serve a specific business and result in the creation/retention of permanent, private sector jobs.

Office of Business Development   916-324-8211
Enterprise Zones: Designed to encourage job-producing business development in designated sections of cities or counties. State tax credits as well as incentives offered by cities and counties are available to firms that hire new employees or make new investments in these areas.

Main Street Development   916-322-3520

California Statewide Certified Development Corporation
129 C Street
Davis, CA 95616   916-756-9310

> **SBA 504:** Provides loans using 50 percent conventional bank financing, SBA provides 40 percent, and 10-20 percent owner equity. A fixed asset loan, below market. Maximum loan amount is 40 percent of project, not to exceed $750,000. Loan can be used for purchase of land and improvements, purchase of existing building(s) and improvements, building construction, machinery/equipment, renovation and restoration.

Small Business Administration (SBA)   (Los Angeles)
330 N. Brand   213-894-2956
Glendale, CA 91203   FAX: 213-894-5665

Small Business Administration (SBA)
211 Main Street   415-744-6820
San Francisco, CA 94105-1988   FAX: 415-744-6812

Local Offices
Fresno   209-487-5189
Los Angeles   213-894-2956
Sacramento   916-551-1426
San Diego   619-557-7252
San Francisco   415-744-6820
Santa Ana   714-836-2494
Ventura   805-642-1866

SBA 7(a) Guaranteed and Direct Loans: Guarantees up to 90 percent of a loan made through a private lender up to $750,000. Can be used for working capital, expand or convert facilities, purchase of machinery and equipment, and land and building. Available only to those unable to obtain a loan from conventional sources. Direct loans are made up to $150,000.

SBA 504: Provides loans using 50 percent conventional bank financing, 40 percent SBA involvement through Certified Development Companies, and 10 percent owner equity. A fixed-asset loan in amounts up to $750,000. Loan can be used for land and building, construction, machinery and equipment, and renovation/expansion.

Small Business Innovative Research Grants (SBIR): Phase I awards between $20,000 to $50,000 to entrepreneurs to support six months of research on a technical innovation. Phase II grants are an additional $500,000 for development. Private sector investment funds must follow.

International Trade Loans: Guaranteed long-term loans through private lenders to develop or expand export markets, or to recover from the effects of import competition. Maximum guaranteed loan is $1,000,000 for fixed assets and an additional $250,000 for working capital and/or export revolving line of credit.

Export Revolving Line of Credit Loan: Short term financing available to small businesses that are at least one year old. Loans provide working capital to finance the manufacturing or wholesaling of products for export and for export marketing. The SBA will guarantee up to 90 percent of a conventional loan in amounts up to $750,000.

Contract Loan: Short-term loans are available to small businesses to finance the costs of labor and materials on contracts for which the proceeds are assignable. Program guarantees up to 90 percent of loans not in excess of $750,000. Qualifying small businesses must be in business for at least 12 calendar months prior to the date of the loan application.

Seasonal Line of Credit Loan: Loans provide short-term working capital to finance seasonal increases in business activities. Program guarantees up to 90 percent of loans not in excess of $750,000. Qualifying business must be in operation for at least one year prior to application.

Pollution Control Loans: Long-term guaranteed loans can be made by conventional financing to small businesses for installation or required pollution control measures. Must be unable to adopt the pollution control measures without undue financial hardship. Maximum guaranteed loan is $1,000,000.

General Contractor Loans: Small general construction contractors may obtain short-term loans or loan guarantees for residential or commercial construction or rehabilitation of property to be sold. The SBA will guarantee up to 90 percent of qualifying loans made by private lenders up to a maximum of $750,000. Direct loans can be up to $150,000.

Energy Business Loan Guarantee: Small businesses that provide certain energy production and conservation services for others may qualify for long-term loans and loan guarantees for start-ups and expansions. Loans and guarantees are made for firms that develop, manufacture, sell, install, or service specific energy measures for others, or firms that provide engineering, architectural, consulting, or other professional services connected with specific energy measures. Guarantee is for up to 90 percent of a loan not in excess of $750,000. Direct loans up to $150,000.

Disaster Recovery Loans: Small businesses located in federally designated disaster areas and suffering property damage or economic losses from the disaster can obtain long-term recovery loans at low interest rates. Property damage loans are limited to 85 percent of the verified damage. Loans for economic losses are for operating capital to meet the business' obligations that could have been made had the disaster not occurred.

Handicapped Assistance Loans: Assists persons who have a physical, mental or emotional disability of a permanent nature which limits the selection of any type of employment for which the person would otherwise be qualified. Direct loans are available for up to $150,000. The interest rate is 3% on these loans.

Surety Bond Guaranty Program: Makes the bonding system more available to small contractors who may be denied access to the system. SBA can guarantee up to 80 percent of surety's loss on a bond that has a maximum in total contract value of up to $1,250,000.

Vietnam-era and Disabled Veterans Loan Program: Provides direct loans to veterans to establish or expand a small business. Funds may be used for working capital or fixed assets. Direct loans for amounts up to $150,000 are available. The interest rate may be fixed or variable.

AMF Financial, Inc.
4330 La Jolla Village Drive
Suite 110
San Diego, CA 92122   619-546-0167

BNP Venture Capital Corporation
3000 Sand Hill Road
Building 1, Suite 125
Menlo Park, CA 94025   415-854-1084

BankAmerica Ventures, Inc.
555 California Street, 12th Floor
c/o Department 3908
San Francisco, CA 94104   415-953-3001

City Ventures, Inc.
120 S. Spalding Drive, Suite 320
Beverly Hills, CA 90212   213-550-5686

DSC Ventures II, LP
20111 Stevens Creek Blvd., Suite 130
Cupertino, CA 95014   408-252-3800

Developers Equity Capital Corporation
1880 Century Park East, Suite 211
Los Angeles, CA 90067   213-277-0330

Draper Associates, a California LP
c/o Timothy C. Draper
3803 E. Bayshore Road, #125
Palo Alto, CA 94303   415-961-6669

First SBIC of California
650 Town Center Drive, 17th Floor
Costa Mesa, CA 92626   714-556-1964

First SBIC of California
(Main Office: Costa Mesa, CA)
2400 Sand Hill Road, Suite 101
Menlo Park, CA 94025   415-424-8011

First SBIC of California
(Main Office: Costa Mesa, CA)
2 North Lake Avenue, Suite 940
Pasadena, CA 91101   818-304-3451

G C & H Partners
One Maritime Plaza, 20th Floor
San Francisco, CA 94110   415-981-5252

Hall, Fullerton, Morris & Drufva II, LP
5000 Birch Street, Suite 10100
Newport Beach, CA 92660   714-253-4360

Imperial Ventures, Inc.
9920 South La Cienega Blvd.
Mail: P.O. Box 92991; L.A. 90009
Inglewood, CA 90301   213-417-5928

Jupiter Partners

600 Montgomery Street, 35th Floor
San Francisco, CA 94111   415-421-9990

Marwit Capital Corporation
180 Newport Center Drive, Suite 200
Newport Beach, CA 92660   714-640-6234

Merrill Pickard Anderson & Eyre I
Two Palo Alto Square, Suite 425
Palo Alto, CA 94306   415-856-8880

New West Partners II
4350 Executive Drive, Suite 206
San Diego, CA 92121   619-457-0723

New West Partners II
(Main Office: San Diego, CA)
4600 Campus Drive, Suite 103
Newport Beach, CA 92660   714-756-8940

Ritter Partners
150 Isabella Avenue
Atherton, CA 94025   415-854-1555

Ritter Partners
(Main Office: Atherton, CA)
3000 Sand Hill Road
Building 1, Suite 190
Menlo Park, CA 94025   415-854-1555

San Joaquin Capital Corporation
1415 18th Street, Suite 306
P.O. Box 2538
Bakersfield, CA 93301   805-323-7581

Seaport Ventures, Inc.
525 B Street, Suite 630
San Diego, CA 92101   619-232-4069

Sundance Venture Partners, L.P.
3000 Sand Hill Road
Building 4, #130
Menlo Park, CA 94025   415-854-8100

Union Venture Corporation
445 South Figueroa Street
Los Angeles, CA 90071   213-236-4092

VK Capital Company
50 California Street, Suite 2350
San Francisco, CA 94111   415-391-5600

Westamco Investment Company
8929 Wilshire Blvd., Suite 400
Beverly Hills, CA 90211   213-652-8288

Small Business Investment Companies (SBIC): The Small Business Administration (SBA) licenses, regulates, and provides financial assistance to privately owned and operated Small Business Investment Companies. SBICs make venture or risk investments by supplying capital and extending unsecured loans and loans not fully collateralized to small enterprises which meet their investment criteria. Financing is made by direct loans and by equity investments.

California World Trade Commission
Export Finance Office
107 South Broadway, Suite 8039
Los Angeles, CA 90012   213-897-3997

Export Financing Program: Small Business firms experienced in exporting may apply for financial assistance in their exporting business. Guarantees for short term loans and insurance to support export of California goods and commerce fees.

California Capital Small Business Development Corporation
926 J Street, Suite 1500
Sacramento, CA 95814   916-442-1729

California Coastal Rural Development Corporation
Five East Gabilan Street
Suite 218
Salinas, CA 93902 — 408-424-1099

California Regional Urban Development Corporation
3932 Harrison Street
Oakland, CA 94611 — 415-652-5262

CAL Southern Small Business Development Corporation
600 B Street, Suite 2200
San Diego, CA 92189 — 619-232-7771

Hancock Urban Development Corporation
3600 Wilshire Boulevard, Suite 926
Los Angeles, CA 90010 — 213-382-4300

Pacific Coast Regional Urban Development Corporation
3810 Wilshire Boulevard, Suite 1901
Los Angeles, CA 90010 — 213-739-2999

SAFE BIDCO
145 Wikiup Dr.
Santa Rosa, CA 95403 — 707-577-8621

Valley Small Business Development Corporation
2344 Tulare Street, Suite 302
Fresno, CA 93721 — 209-268-0166

Contact one of the above certified development corporations for application and inquiries on the following programs.

Underground Storage Tank Loan Program: Assists small businesses with underground storage tanks to upgrade, repair or remove underground storage tanks used to store petroleum. Low interest loans offered through Regional Development Corporations and Small Business Development Centers. Maximum loan $350,000.

Loan Guarantee Program: Permits Regional Development Corporations to use state funds to guarantee loans made by banks or financial institutions to small businesses. Funds can be used for working capital or short term credit needs. Maximum guarantee is 90 percent of the outstanding principal balance to a maximum of $350,000. Loans are guaranteed up to 90 percent of the outstanding principal balance.

Small Business Energy Conservation Program: Offers small businesses the opportunity to obtain low cost loan funds through the Regional Development Corporations to finance the installation of energy-saving equipment or devices. Interest rate will be 5 percent below the prime rate at the time of closing the loan. Loan amounts range from $15,000 to a maximum of $150,000. Term of loan not to exceed five years.

Hazardous Waste Reduction Loan Program: Low-cost loan funds are offered through the Regional Development Corporations for the acquisition and installation of hazardous waste reduction equipment or processes. Loan amounts range from $20,000 to a maximum of $150,000.

* Women and Minority Business Assistance

Office of Small and Minority Business
Department of General Services
1808 14th Street, Suite 100
Sacramento, CA 95814 — 916-322-5060

Offers assistance to businesses interested in participating in the State of California's purchasing/contracting system. Also, aid, counseling, assistance, and protection for the interests of small, minority and women-owned businesses.

Office of Civil Rights
Department of Transportation
1120 N Street, Room 2545
Sacramento, CA 95814 — 916-654-7048

Provides information for state certification for disadvantaged and women-owned businesses.

Small Business Administration (SBA) (Los Angeles)
330 N. Brand — 213-894-2956
Glendale, CA 91203 — FAX: 213-894-5665

Small Business Administration (SBA)
211 Main Street — 415-744-6820
San Francisco, CA 94105-1988 — FAX: 415-744-6812

SBA 8(a) Program - Business Procurement Assistance: Provides federal government contracting opportunities for small businesses owned by socially and economically disadvantaged persons, and assists these businesses to become independently competitive in the normal business environment. SBA monitors all government contracts to assure that a quota of contract work goes to 8(a) businesses. Also provides business management services to these businesses. Business must be approved for program participation prior to receipt of an 8(a) contract.

* Training

Manufacturing/Retention
California Department of Commerce
801 K Street, Suite 1700
Sacramento, CA 95814 — 916-322-1398

Job Training Partnership Act (JTPA): Provides employers with recruitment, screening, referral, training, 50 percent wage subsidy up to 3 months for on-the-job training. Available to any private employer.

Employment Training Panel (ETP): Assists small businesses in acquiring and retaining the skilled workers needed to increase competitiveness and productivity. Funds pay for costs associated with training new or current employees. Included is equipment, space (rent/lease) of facility, salaries of individuals conducting/administering training, supplies. Available to new business expansion/location in California, special opportunities for disabled, minorities, women and veterans, 30 percent of persons for whom training is proposed are unemployed at start of training.

Employer-Based Training (EBT) Set-Aside: Assists businesses with training needs to ensure a productive, quality workforce. EBT funds pay for costs associated with training new employees. Includes curriculum development education/training package, staff to screen, assess, counsel and refer applicants, equipment, space costs, salaries for instructors, books and supplies. Available to private businesses locating, expanding or starting up in California.

Job Service Program: Provides services and information to employers including recruitment, screening and referral for temporary or full-time employment, recruitment for permanent or seasonal agricultural employment, referral for working training and educational information. Available to private businesses locating, expanding or starting up in California.

* Management Consulting and Other Services

California Department of Commerce
801 K Street, Suite 1700
Sacramento, CA 95814

Office of Small Business — 916-324-1295

Small Business Development Board: Established to advise the Governor, Legislature and Office of Small Business on issues and programs important to the small business community. Holds public hearings and adopts regulations and policies to regulate and oversee the small business development corporations.

Office of Tourism: Activities geared to help increase tourism in the state include trade shows, sales missions, technical assistance, special promotions, and an annual Governor's Conference on Tourism.

Office of Business Development — 916-324-8211
This office works to encourage the expansion of existing companies and new facility locations by firms outside the state. Identifies available locations for business development in California and provides site-specific information on regional economic trends, labor supply, wage rates, real estate prices, infrastructure needs, transportation costs, regulations, taxes, tax-exempt bond financing, and government-sponsored job training.

Ombudsman: Represents the business interests to the administration and Legislature. This includes general issue advocacy, such as tax policy or environment issues, permit assistance with regulatory and licensing, company-specific problem solving such as permit assistance with regulatory and licensing authorities.

Site Selection: Offers free and confidential site selection assistance. They can canvas over 400 communities throughout the state to narrow the selection to these that meet each company's needs. Can also provide analysis of the cost and availability of the various site locations factors such as labor, utilities and land.

Office of Local Development   916-322-1394
Small Business Revitalization Program: Offers small and medium-sized businesses help in packaging financing using SBA, and HUD funded projects. Provides intensive financial structuring and packaging assistance to all parts of California, especially rural communities and distressed urban areas.

Economic Adjustment Unit: Assistance in preventing and responding to plant closures, re-employing dislocated workers, preparing economic development strategies for high unemployment areas and linking retraining programs with economic development.

Office of Economic Research   916-324-5853
Provide data, technical assistance, and research services to the Department of Commerce offices and programs. In many cases, the information prepared is available to the public in the form of reports and economic analyses. Research publications include tourism, foreign investment, small business, manufacturing, and a variety of special issues. Also prepare and distribute industry and geographic profiles and publishes a quarterly newsletter *The Economic Review* that summarizes recent economic trends and developments.

Office of Foreign Investment   916-323-8021
Information on exporting requirements, and schedule of workshops on starting an export business.

World Trade Commission
Office of Export Development
1 World Trade Center, Suite 990
Long Beach, CA 90831-0990   310-590-5965
     Information available on how to participate in a trade show.

CompTech
200 East Del Mar Blvd.
Suite 204
Pasadena, CA 91105   818-568-9660
     Competitive Technology Program: Program was initiated to create and maintain quality jobs by fostering technology transfer from the laboratory to the marketplace. The CompTech staff develops solicitations, manages the review process, negotiates grant agreements and manages the technology transfer projects. Projects may be in the areas of collaborate research, research and development consortia, technology transfer innovation, or entrepreneurial business development. Program contingent on new state budget.

California Film Commission
6922 Hollywood Boulevard
Suite 600
Hollywood, CA 90028   213-736-2465
     Works with communities to encourage film making in their area.

Western Association of Venture Capitalists
3000 Sand Hill Road
Building 1, Suite 190
Menlo Park, CA 94025   415-854-1322
     Venture Capital: You can request a directory of venture capital resources. The cost is $50.00.

Small Business Administration (SBA)   (Los Angeles)
330 N. Brand   213-894-2956
Glendale, CA 91203   FAX: 213-894-5665

Small Business Administration (SBA)
211 Main Street   415-744-6820
San Francisco, CA 94105-1988   FAX: 415-744-6812
     Small Business Institutes: This program provides personalized consulting services to the small business community. Consulting is provided by senior level business students, guided by a faculty advisor. Assistance in business plan preparation, marketing research, market planning, accounting, and seminars are provided.
     University Locations:
     Antelope Valley College
     California Poly. State University
     California State University - Fresno
     California State University - Fullerton
     California State University - Bakersfield
     California State University - Long Beach
     California State University - Northridge
     California State University - Hayward
     California State University - San Bernardino
     California State University - Pomona
     California State University - Sacramento
     California State University - Los Angeles
     California State University - Dominquez Hills
     California State University - Chico
     California Lutheran College
     DeAnza College
     Fresno Pacific College
     Golden Gate University
     Humboldt State University
     Loyola Marymount University
     Monterey Institute of International Studies
     Point Loma College
     San Diego State University
     San Francisco State University
     San Jose State University
     Sonoma State University
     University of California - LA
     University of Southern California - LA
     Westmont College

* Small Business Development Centers

The following offices offer free and fee-based services to new and expanding businesses:

Lead Center:
California Small Business Development Center
California Department of Commerce
Office of Small Business
801 K Street, Suite 1700   916-324-5068
Sacramento, CA 95814   FAX: 916-322-5084

     Aptos: Central Coast Small Business Assistance Center, 6500 Soquel Drive, Aptos, CA 95003, 408-479-6136; FAX: 408-479-5743.

     Auburn: Sierra College, Small Business Development Center, 560 Wall Street, Suite J, Auburn, CA 95603, 916-885-5488; FAX: 916-781-0455.

     Bakersfield: Weill Institute, Small Business Development Center, 2101 K Street Mall, Bakersfield, CA 93301, 805-395-4148; FAX: 805-395-4134.

     Chico: Butte College, Tri-County Small Business Development Center, 260 Cohasset Avenue, Chico, CA 95926, 916-895-9017; FAX: 916-895-9099.

     Chula Vista: Southwestern College, Small Business Development Center and International Trade Center, 900 Otay Lakes Road, Bldg. 1600, Chula Vista, CA 91910, 619-482-6393; FAX: 619-482-6402.

     Crescent City: North Coast Small Business Development Center, 882 H. Street, Crescent City, CA 95531, 707-464-2168; FAX: 707-465-3402.

     Eureka: North Coast Satellite Center, 408 7th Street, Suite "E", Eureka, CA 95501, 707-445-9720.

     Fresno: Cal-State University at Fresno, Central Valley Small Business Development Center, 2771 East Shaw Avenue, Fresno, CA 93740, 209-278-4946; FAX: 209-373-7740.

Gilroy: Gavilan College, Small Business Development Center, 5055 Santa Teresa Blvd., Gilroy, CA 95020, 408-847-0373; FAX: 408-847-0393.

La Jolla: Greater San Diego Chamber of Commerce, Small Business Development Center, 4275 Executive Square, Suite 290, La Jooa, CA 92037, 619-453-9388; FAX: 619-450-1997.

Lakeport: Business Development Center of Lake and Mendocino Counties, 341 North Main Street, Lakeport, CA 95453, 707-263-6180; FAX: 707-263-0920.

Los Angeles: Export Small Business Development Center of Southern California, 110 E. 9th, Suite A761, Los Angeles, CA 90079, 213-892-1111; FAX: 213-892-8232.

Merced: Merced Satellite Center, 1632 "N" Street, Merced, CA 95340, 209-385-7312; FAX: 209-383-4959.

Modesto: Valley Sierra Small Business Development Center, 1012 11th Street, Suite 300, Modesto, CA 95354, 209-521-6177; FAX: 209-521-9373.

Napa: Napa Valley College, Small Business Development Center, 1556 First Street, Suite 103, Napa, CA 94559, 707-253-3210; FAX: 707-255-0972.

Oakland: East Bay Small Business Development Center, 2201 Broadway, Suite 814, Oakland, CA 94612, 510-893-4114; FAX: 510-893-5532.

Oxnard: Export Satellite Center, 300 Explanade Drive, Suite 1010, Oxnard, CA 93030, 805-981-4633.

Pomona: Eastern Los Angeles County Small Business Development Center, 363 S. Park Avenue, #105, Pomona, CA 91766, 714-629-2247; FAX: 714-629-8310.

Riverside: Inland Empire Small Business Development Center, 1860 Chicago Avenue, Building 1, Suite 1, Riverside, CA 92507, 714-781-2345; FAX: 714-781-2353.

Sacramento: Greater Sacramento Small Business Development Center, 1787 Tribute Road, Suite A, Sacramento, CA 95815, 916-920-7949; FAX: 916-920-7940.

San Jose: Silicon Valley - San Mateo County, Small Business Development Center, 111 N. Market Street, #150, San Jose, CA 95113, 408-298-7694; FAX: 408-971-0680.

San Mateo: San Mateo County Satellite Center, Bayshore Corporate Center, 1730 S. Amphlett Blvd., Suite 208, San Mateo, CA 94402, 415-358-0271; FAX: 415-358-9450.

Santa Ana: Rancho Santiago Small Business Development Center, 901 East Santa Ana Boulevard, Suite 108, Santa Ana, CA 92701, 714-647-1172; FAX: 714-835-9008.

Stockton: San Joaquin Delta College, Small Business Development Center, 814 N. Hunter, Stockton, CA 95202, 209-474-5089; FAX: 209-474-5605.

Suisun: Solano County Small Business Development Center, 320 Campus Lane, Suisun, CA 94585, 707-864-3382; FAX: 707-864-3386.

Van Nuys: Northern Los Angeles Small Business Development Center, 14540 Victory Boulevard, Suite #206, Van Nuys, CA 91411, 818-373-7092; FAX: 818-373-7740.

Colorado

* General Information

Office of Business Development	303-892-3840
1625 Broadway, Suite 1710	FAX: 303-892-3848
Denver, CO 80202	HOTLINE: 1-800-592-5920 in Colorado

Provides information and assistance to local economic development organizations, assists in retaining and expanding existing businesses, and responds to out-of-state inquiries concerning expanding or relocating in Colorado. The booklet, *A Capital Venture*, lists sources and contacts for venture capital and is available from the above office.

Small Business Advocate: Provides assistance in cutting bureaucratic red tape and information and expertise in dealing with state, federal, and local agencies.

Colorado Office of Small Business: Offers information, assistance and referrals for Colorado's small business owners and operators. The Small Business Hotline provides access to the Colorado Business Clearinghouse, a computerized database that contains information on over 2,000 business resources.

* Financing

Office of Business Development	303-892-3840
1625 Broadway, Suite 1710	FAX: 303-892-3848
Denver, CO 80202	1-800-592-5920 in Colorado

Colorado Long Term Lending Program: Most for-profit businesses are eligible. Priority is given to primary dollar-importing businesses. Long-term loans of between $100,000 to $500,000 per project for the financing of machinery, equipment, or real estate purchases. Recipients have the choice of a fixed or variable rate loan. Priority will be given to dollar-importing businesses.

Revolving Loan Fund for Energy: For energy efficiency improvements in small businesses. Assists in financing the acquisition and installation or upgrading of equipment, materials and energy using devices that will result in a savings in the business' utility costs. Loans range from $20,000 to $40,000 and will generally not exceed $60,000.

Rural Development Financing Program: The Office of Economic Development allocates and administers federal community development funds which are set aside for business finance projects. Loans, loan guarantees, equity investments or, under special circumstances, grants are provided for projects which create or retain jobs principally for low or moderate income persons. Financing will not exceed $250,000 per project. State participation up to 35 percent of a project, 10 percent owner equity, at least 55 percent other sources. Funds may be used for working capital, fixed assets, real estate, and construction. Not all metropolitan areas are eligible as they have their own Community Development Block Grant programs.

Economic Development Commission Funds: Allocates appropriated general fund revenues for economic development. Incentives such as infrastructure improvements, site development costs and loans to businesses are possible. Requires that at least one job to be created for every $5,000 in state assistance, no more than 35 percent of the project be financed by the state, at least 10 percent in owner equity be provided. Terms are negotiated on a case-by-case basis.

Colorado Housing and Finance Authority (CHFA)	
1981 Blake Street	303-297-7329
Denver, CO 80202	1-800-877-2432 in Colorado

Quality Investment Capital Program: This loan program works in conjunction with the SBA 504 program (see Small Business Administration below). Provides fixed-rate financing for small business loans guaranteed by the SBA. The program stabilizes interest rates on the guaranteed portion of an SBA 7(a) loan. Maximum CHFA participation is $750,000 and a business may have no more than $750,000 outstanding on all SBA loans. Funds may be used for working capital, equipment purchase, business expansion, and real estate acquisition. See SBA 7(a) Loan Guarantee Program for terms.

Export Credit Insurance Program/Export Accounts Receivable Financing Program: Designed to help small exporters and those who have limited experience with exporting and extending credit to overseas customers. Provides credit insurance protection against commercial credit and political risks and can be used only to cover payments due for shipped exports. It covers 90 percent of commercial risk and 100 percent of political risk. Helps exporters finance their accounts receivable insured under this program by providing a financial bridge while those payments are outstanding. Financing is fully negotiable and depends on the individual needs and resources of the exporter as well as the contract that it covers. Financing will only cover the term of the export contract.

Colorado Department of Local Affairs
1313 Sherman Street
Suite 521
Denver, CO 80203   303-866-2156

Taxable Bond Financing for Fixed Assets: Industrial Development Revenue Bonds and Taxable Bonds are available for the purchase of land, building, equipment, and related soft costs for projects in the $500,000 to $20 million range. Interest rates are generally near the prime rate.

Enterprise Zones: These zones provide incentives for private enterprises to expand and for new businesses to locate in economically distressed areas of the state. A few of the tax incentives are a 3 percent investment tax credit for investments in equipment use exclusively in an enterprise zone, a job tax credit or refunds against state income taxes of $500 for each newly hired employee, hired in connection with a "new business" facility located in an enterprise zone for at least one year, an additional credit or refund of $500 per new business facility employee may be claimed by businesses which add value to agricultural commodities through manufacturing or processing, credit to rehabilitate vacant buildings.

Colorado FmHA State Office
655 Parfet Street
Room E100
Lakewood, CO 80215   303-236-2801

Business and Industrial Loan Program: Eligible projects must be located outside the boundary of a city of 50,000 or more. Development in adjacent urban areas is acceptable if the population density is less than 100 persons per square mile. Priority will be given to those projects located in open country, rural communities, and towns of 25,000 and smaller. Funds may be used for working capital or purchase of fixed assets. Guarantees of up to 90 percent for amounts up to $10 million. Alcohol fuel production facilities are eligible for up to $20 million. Loans are at market rates and may be fixed or variable.

Farm Operating Loans: Provides direct loans and loan guarantees to meet the operating expenses of family-size farms. Loans may be used for any purpose that facilitates successful operation of the farm. Loan guarantees up to 90 percent for amounts up to $400,000 at market rates that may be fixed or variable. Direct loans up to $200,000. Interest rates depend on the cost of money to the government at time of application. Applicants who have current FmHA farm ownership, soil and water, recreation, or operating loans are not eligible for this program.

Farm Ownership Loans: Direct and guaranteed loans to buy, improve, or enlarge family-size farms. Funds may be use to buy land, build or improve existing structures and facilities, and improve farm land and forests. Loan guarantees up to 90 percent for amounts up to $300,000 at market rates that may be fixed or variable. Direct loans up to $200,000. Interest rates depend on the cost of money to the government at time of application. Applicants who have current FmHA farm ownership, soil and water, recreation, or operating loans are not eligible for this program.

Limited Resource Farm Loans: Direct loans to low-income farmers and ranchers to buy, improve or enlarge family-size farms. Funds may be used to buy land, build or improve existing structures and facilities, and improve farm land and forests. Direct loans up to $200,000 at reduced interest rates that may be fixed or variable. Applicants who have current FmHA farm ownership, soil and water, recreation, or operating loans are not eligible for this program.

Colorado Agricultural Development Authority (CADA)
700 S. Kipling, #4000
Lakewood, CO 80215   303-239-4114

Agricultural Processing Feasibility Grant Program: May be used only for the development of a report or study that analyzes the feasibility of processing an agricultural commodity produced in Colorado. Maximum award s $15,000. Grants must be equally matched with a cash or in-kind contribution by applicant. Businesses need the approval of the local government where the proposed project is to be located.

Quality Agricultural Loan Program: The CADA works in conjunction with the Farmers Home Administration (FmHA) to provide fixed-rate financing on the guaranteed portion of a FmHa agricultural loan for farmers and ranchers. Funds can be used for working capital or purchase of fixed assets associated with the establishment or operation of the farm.

Small Business Administration (SBA)
Business Development Division
U.S. Customs House
999 18th Street, #701   303-294-7186
Denver, CO 80202   FAX: 303-294-7153

SBA 7(a) Guaranteed and Direct Loans: Guarantees up to 90 percent of a loan made through a private lender up to $750,000. Can be used for working capital, expand or convert facilities, purchase of machinery and equipment, and land and building. Available only to those unable to obtain a loan from conventional sources. Direct loans are made up to $150,000.

SBA 504: Provides loans using 50 percent conventional bank financing, 40 percent SBA involvement through Certified Development Companies, and 10 percent owner equity. A fixed-asset loan in amounts up to $750,000. Loan can be used for land and building, construction, machinery and equipment, and renovation/expansion.

Small Business Innovative Research Grants (SBIR): Phase I awards between $20,000 to $50,000 to entrepreneurs to support six months of research on a technical innovation. Phase II grants are an additional $500,000 for development. Private sector investment funds must follow.

International Trade Loans: Guaranteed long-term loans through private lenders to develop or expand export markets, or to recover from the effects of import competition. Maximum guaranteed loan is $1,000,000 for fixed assets and an additional $250,000 for working capital and/or export revolving line of credit.

Export Revolving Line of Credit Loan: Short term financing available to small businesses that are at least one year old. Loans provide working capital to finance the manufacturing or wholesaling of products for export and for export marketing. The SBA will guarantee up to 90 percent of a conventional loan in amounts up to $750,000.

Contract Loan: Short-term loans are available to small businesses to finance the costs of labor and materials on contracts for which the proceeds are assignable. Program guarantees up to 90 percent of loans not in excess of $750,000. Qualifying small businesses must be in business for at least 12 calendar months prior to the date of the loan application.

Seasonal Line of Credit Loan: Loans provide short-term working capital to finance seasonal increases in business activities. Program guarantees up to 90 percent of loans not in excess of $750,000. Qualifying business must be in operation for at least one year prior to application.

Pollution Control Loans: Long-term guaranteed loans can be made by conventional financing to small businesses for installation or required pollution control measures. Must be unable to adopt the pollution control measures without undue financial hardship. Maximum guaranteed loan is $1,000,000.

General Contractor Loans: Small general construction contractors may obtain short-term loans or loan guarantees for residential or commercial construction or rehabilitation of property to be sold. The SBA will guarantee up to 90 percent of qualifying loans made by private lenders up to a maximum of $750,000. Direct loans can be up to $150,000.

Energy Business Loan Guarantee: Small businesses that provide certain energy production and conservation services for others may qualify for long-term loans and loan guarantees for start-ups and expansions. Loans and guarantees are made for firms that develop, manufacture, sell, install, or service specific energy measures for others, or firms that provide engineering, architectural, consulting, or other professional services connected with specific energy measures. Guarantee is for up to 90 percent of a loan not in excess of $750,000. Direct loans up to $150,000.

Disaster Recovery Loans: Small businesses located in federally designated disaster areas and suffering property damage or economic losses from the disaster can obtain long-term recovery loans at low interest rates. Property damage loans are limited to 85 percent of the verified damage. Loans for economic losses are for operating capital to meet the business' obligations that could have been made had the disaster not occurred.

Handicapped Assistance Loans: Assists persons who have a physical, mental or emotional disability of a permanent nature which limits the selection of any type of employment for which the person would otherwise be qualified. Direct loans are available for up to $150,000. The interest rate is 3% on these loans.

Surety Bond Guaranty Program: Makes the bonding system more available to small contractors who may be denied access to the system. SBA can guarantee up to 80 percent of surety's loss on a bond that has a maximum in total contract value of up to $1,250,000.

Vietnam-era and Disabled Veterans Loan Program: Provides direct loans to veterans to establish or expand a small business. Funds may be used for working capital or fixed assets. Direct loans for amounts up to $150,000. Interest rate may be fixed or variable.

Solar Energy & Conservation Loan Program: Loan guarantees to small businesses engaged in engineering, manufacturing, distribution, marketing, installing or servicing of energy measures for conservation. Funds may be used for working capital or fixed assets. Loans are guaranteed up to 90 percent for amounts up to $155,000, and up to 85 percent for amounts up to $750,000. Winds energy conversion equipment, solar thermal energy equipment, equipment to produce energy from wood, biological waste, grain or other biomass sources, equipment for industrial cogeneration of energy, heating, or production of energy for industrial waste, products or services that improve the energy efficiency of existing equipment are a few of the eligible activities. Loans are guaranteed up to 90 percent for amounts up to $155,000, and up to 85 percent for amounts up to $750,000. Loans are at market rates that may be fixed or variable.

UBD Capital, Inc.
1700 Broadway
Denver, CO 80274   303-863-6329
Small Business Investment Companies (SBIC): The SBA licenses, regulates, and provides financial assistance to privately owned and operated Small Business Investment Companies. SBICs make venture or risk investments by supplying capital and extending unsecured loans and loans not fully collateralized to small enterprises which meet their investment criteria. Financing is made by direct loans and by equity investments.

Colorado Development Companies (CDC)
Four Colorado development companies lend to small and medium-sized businesses at fixed rates for terms of 10 to 20 years. Companies must create one job for every $15,000 they receive in financing. Contact your local CDC:

Colorado Springs: Pikes Peak Regional Development Corporation, 228 N. Cascade, #208, Colorado Springs, CO 80903, 719-471-2044. (El Paso County)

Denver: Community Economic Development of Colorado, 1111 Osage Street, Suite 110, Denver, CO 80204, 303-893-8989. (statewide focus)

Denver: Denver Urban Economic Development of Colorado, 303 West Colfax Avenue, Suite 1025, Denver, CO 80204, 303-296-5570. (City and County of Denver)

Pueblo: SCEDD Development Company, P.O. Box 1900, 212-West 13th, Pueblo, CO 81003, 719-545-8680. (19 counties)

SBA 504 Fixed Asset Loan Program: Provides long-term fixed rates for fixed asset purchases. At least one job must be created for every $15,000 in SBA assistance unless the project will produce a high community impact. Loans provided up to $750,000 or 40 percent of total project cost, whichever is less.

ACCESS Loan Program: ACCESS works in conjunction with the Small Business Administration's (SBA) 504 program. Together, they provide small businesses with long-term fixed rates on up to 95 percent of the financed portion of the fixed asset purchase (land & building, equipment, machinery). The ACCESS program cannot provide working capital. Loans are provided in amounts of $100,000 or more (no maximum). Industrial, manufacturing and wholesale distribution concerns located in enterprise zones are eligible for a lower rate. Through Access, businesses can borrow from local private lends which might not have been able to provide financing for total project needs.

Colorado Department of Local Affairs
1313 Sherman Street, #521
Denver, CO 80203   303-866-2205
Community Development Block Grant Funds: Available to cities and counties for the commercial rehabilitation of existing buildings or structures used for business, commercial, or industrial purposes. Funds are then loaned to businesses. Every $15,000 of funds invested must create at least one full-time job, and at least 51 percent of the jobs created must be for low- and moderate-income families. A number of rural areas have created local revolving loan funds which assist in financing new and expanded businesses in their communities.

Colorado Venture Management
4845 Pearl East Circle, Suite 300
Boulder, CO 80301   303-440-4055
CBM Equity Fund: Provides equity financing for start-up businesses in the state through private venture capital partnerships. CVM will run the seed capital fund. Focus is on start-up and early stage investments in service and technology-based businesses. Investments will be considered in the range of $25,000 to $300,000.

* Women and Minority Business Assistance

Minority Business Office
Office of Economic Development
1625 Broadway, Suite 1710   303-892-3840
Denver, CO 80202   FAX: 303-892-3848
Minority Business Office: The Minority Business Office promotes economic development for existing and new minority business enterprises. Programs establish networks between majority and minority businesses, promote minority participation in state and federal procurement, purchasing and contracting programs, and help address minority business issues.

Women's Business Office: Offers business information, management assistance, and referrals for the purpose of expanding economic and business opportunities for women.

Department of Transportation
Office of Small and Disadvantaged Business Utilization
Minority Business Resource Center
400 Seventh Street, N.W.
Washington, DC 20590   202-366-2852
Short Term Lending Program: Department of Transportation provides short-term loans for working capital to certified minority or women-owned businesses working on transportation related contracts.

Bonding Assistance Program: When required, Department of Transportation provides small business contractors who are certified as a disadvantaged business enterprise and are working on transportation related contracts, with guarantees on bid, performance or payment bonds to obtain a contract. Applicants must be working on a transportation related contract for any federal, state, or local transportation agency. 75 percent of the funds from Dept. of Transportation, minimum of 5 percent from Capital Bank N.A., and up to 20 percent local lender.

SBA Regional Office   303-294-7186
Section 8(a) Program: SBA acts as a prime contractor and enters into contracts with other government departments and agencies. SBA then negotiates subcontracts with small companies owned by socially and economically disadvantaged persons. Financial assistance is available utilizing this program and must be used to perform on a government procurement contract. SBA can make advance payment against the contract to help cover the cost of labor and materials as well as administrative overhead. Companies that cannot finance capital equipment essential to do the job under the contract may receive grant funds from the SBA.

National Minority Supplier Development
  Council, Inc. (NMSDC)
Business Consortium Fund   212-944-2430

NMSDC/Business Consortium Fund, Inc. is a not-for-profit minority business development program that provides working capital funds to certified minority businesses. Loans are to finance contracts with members of NMSDC. Contact the above telephone number, or your regional council, to find out if there is a Certified Bank Lender in your area.

* Training

Department of Business Development
1625 Broadway, Suite 1710   303-892-3840
Denver, CO 80202   FAX: 303-892-3848

Colorado FIRST Customized Training Program: Purpose is to encourage quality economic development by providing training assistance as an incentive for the location of new firms or the expansion of existing companies. Programs are coordinated through local community colleges or vocational/technical institutions. Payment of all direct training program costs are eligible for reimbursement including instructor wages, travel and per diem allowances; lease of training equipment and training space; purchase of expendable training supplies.

Existing Industry Training Program: Assists existing Colorado companies who are undergoing major technological change, and to train or retrain their workers for specific jobs where training is deemed crucial for the continued success of the company. Direct training program costs are eligible for payment and include trainee assessment and testing; instructor wages, per diem and travel; curriculum development and training materials; lease of training equipment and training space.

Colorado Community College and Occupational Education System
1391 North Speer Boulevard, Suite 600
Denver, CO 80204   303-620-4000

Colorado offers education and training programs throughout the state. They can train workers in virtually every occupation skill, upgrade job skills for current employees, meet specific training needs of company or organization. They also administer the Colorado FIRST program.

Governor's Job Training Office
720 S. Colorado Blvd., #550
Denver, CO 80222   303-758-5020

Job Training Partnership Act (JTPA): Provides employers with recruitment, screening, referral, training, 50 percent wage subsidy up to 3 months for on-the-job training. Available to any private employer.

Colorado Division of Employment and Training
600 Grant Street, Suite 900
Denver, CO 80203   303-837-3900

Job Service: Job Service has 23 offices around Colorado which can refer applicants to local training opportunities and provide placement services for job seekers and labor for employers. Employers may list job orders with any Job Service Center for statewide recruitment, screening and referral of skilled or unskilled workers. Some centers also offer training. If business provides training opportunities, they may be eligible for a tax credit for wages paid through the Targeted Jobs Tax Credit.

* Management Consulting and Other Services

CU Business Advancement Centers (BAC's)
4700 Walnut St., Suite 101   303-444-5723
Boulder, CO 80301   1-800-521-1243 in Colorado

Funded jointly by state, local, and federal agencies, Colorado's BAC's provide help to manufacturing and technology-based firms and to small businesses. BAC's diagnose and improve operations, expand domestic or foreign markets, determine the feasibility of a new venture, prepare business plans, obtain financing, and obtain business, technical, or market information. These firms have accessibility to the Business Research And Information Network (BRAIN), which transfers technologies from federal, university, and private laboratories to the private sector for commercialization. Pro-Bid provides one-on-one consulting to firms interested in developing sales in the federal marketplace. A consultant database of expertise at the University of Colorado at Boulder can also be utilized by small businesses.

Small Business Administration (SBA)
Business Development Division
U.S. Customs House
999 18th Street, #701   303-294-7186
Denver, CO 80202   FAX: 303-294-7153

Small Business Institutes: This program provides personalized consulting services to the small business community. Consulting is provided by senior level business students, guided by a faculty advisor. Assistance in business plan preparation, marketing research, market planning, accounting, and seminars are provided.
University Locations:
Adams State College
Colorado State University
Ft. Lewis College
Mesa College
University of Colorado - Colorado Springs
University of Denver
University of Northern Colorado
University of Southern Colorado
Western State College

* Small Business Development Centers

The following offices offer free and fee-based services to new and expanding businesses:

Lead Center:
Colorado Small Business Development Center
Office of Economic Development   303-892-3809
1625 Broadway, Suite 1710   303-892-3840
Denver, CO 80202   FAX: 303-892-3848

Alamosa: Adams State College, Small Business Development Center, Alamosa, CO 81102, 719-589-7372, 719-589-7199; FAX: 719-589-7522.

Aurora: Community College of Aurora, Small Business Development Center, 16000 E. Centretech Parkway, #A201, Aurora, CO 80011-9036, 303-360-4745; FAX: 303-360-4761.

Canon City: Canon City (Satellite), 402 Valley Road, Canon City, CO 81212, 719-275-5335; FAX: 719-275-4400.

Colorado Springs: Pikes Peak Community College/Colorado Springs Chamber of Commerce, Small Business Development Center, P.O. Drawer B, Colorado Springs, CO 80901-3002, 719-635-1551, 719-471-4836; FAX: 719-635-1571.

Craig: Colorado Northwestern Community College, Small Business Development Center, 50 Spruce Drive, Craig, CO 81625, 303-824-7071; FAX: 303-824-3527.

Delta: Delta Montrose Vocational School, Small Business Development Center, 1765 U.S. Highway 50, Delta, CO 81416, 303-874-8772; FAX: 303-874-8796.

Denver: Community College of Denver/Denver Chamber of Commerce, Small Business Development Center, 1445 Market Street, Denver, CO 80202, 303-620-8076; FAX: 303-534-3200.

Durango: Fort Lewis College, Small Business Development Center, Miller Student Center, Room 108, Durango, CO 81301, 303-247-7188; FAX: 303-247-7620.

Fort Collins: Fort Collins (Satellite), P.O. Box 2397, Fort Collins, CO 80522, 303-226-2500, ext. 108; FAX: 303-825-6819.

Fort Morgan: Morgan Community College, Small Business Development Center, 300 Main Street, Fort Morgan, CO 80701, 303-867-3351; FAX: 303-867-7580.

Grand Junction: Mesa State College, Small Business Development Center, 304 W. Main Street, Grand Junction, CO 81505-1606, 303-248-7314; FAX: 303-241-0771.

Greeley: Aims Community College/Greeley & Weld Chamber of Commerce, Small Business Development Center, 1407 8th Avenue, Greeley, CO 80631, 303-352-3661; FAX: 303-352-3572.

Lakewood: Red Rocks Community College, Small Business Development Center, 13300 W. 6th Avenue, Lakewood, CO 80401-5398, 303-987-0710; FAX: 303-969-8039.

Lamar: Lamar Community College, Small Business Development Center, 2400 South Main, Lamar, CO 81052, 719-336-8141; FAX: 719-336-2448.

Littleton: Arapaho Community College/South Metro Chamber of Commerce, Small Business Development Center, 7901 South Park Plaza, Suite 110, Littleton, CO 80120, 303-795-5855; FAX: 303-795-7520.

Pueblo: Pueblo Community College, Small Business Development Center, 900 West Orman Avenue, Pueblo, CO 81004, 719-549-3224; FAX: 719-546-2413.

Stratton: Stratton (Satellite), P.O. Box 28, Stratton, CO 80836, 719-348-5596; FAX: 719-348-5887.

Trinidad: Trinidad State Junior College, Small Business Development Center, 600 Prospect Street, Davis Building, Trinidad, CO 81082, 719-846-5645; FAX: 719-846-5667.

Vail: Colorado Mountain College, Small Business Development Center, 1310 Westhaven Drive, Vail, CO 81657, 303-476-4040, 1-800-621-1647; FAX: 303-479-9212.

Westminister: Front Range Community College, Small Business Development Center, 3645 West 112th Avenue, Westminister, CO 80030, 303-460-1032; FAX: 303-466-1623.

Connecticut

* General Information

Office of Small Business Services
Department of Economic Development
865 Brooks Street
Rocky Hill, CT 06067   203-258-4270
Offers a One Stop Licensing Center for call-in or drop-in service. Publishes *Establishing a Business in Connecticut*, a free booklet for ready reference to state licensing laws.

Small Business Advocate: Provides assistance in cutting bureaucratic red tape, and information and expertise in dealing with state, federal, and local agencies.

* Financing

Connecticut Development Authority
Business Development Division
217 Washington Street
Hartford, CT 06106   203-522-3730
Growth Fund: Direct state loans to small businesses in amounts up to $1 million for building, equipment, and working capital from $50,000 to $500,000. Available to those unable to obtain sufficient conventional financing on satisfactory terms or amounts, or for whom such assistance is important to locate or continue operations in Connecticut, and have sales less than $10,000,000. Eligible economic development projects are those that create or retain jobs, facilitate the export of goods and services or involve new products or services with potential for significant future contribution to the state's economy.

Business Assistance Fund: Direct state loans to businesses unable to obtain conventional financing on satisfactory terms or amounts, or for whom such state assistance is important to locate or continue operations in Connecticut. Loans available up to $250,000 to small contractors, private water companies, minority business enterprises holding a state contract, a business in an enterprise zone. Loans up to $500,000 for any business adversely affected by either a natural disaster or economic emergency as determined by the Commissioner of Economic Development.

Naugatuck Valley Fund: Available to companies engaged in manufacturing, processing or assembling of raw materials or finished products, or the significant servicing, overhaul or rebuilding of products, together with wholesale distribution of manufactured products who are unable to obtain sufficient private financing. Must create or retain one new job for every $10,000 obtained from the Fund. State loans of up to $200,000 for companies in the Naugatuck Valley and certain other towns for real estate projects, machinery and equipment, and working capital.

Investment Financing: Provides direct state loans and investments in developing businesses that present the greatest potential future contribution to Connecticut's job growth and economic bases. Eligibility is the same as the Growth Fund with priority to firms that have high-tech jobs, high value added production techniques or services, strong export sales, high growth and high profitability potential and have achieved market penetration. Loans amounts range between $250,000 and $500,000.

Mortgage Insurance Fund: State guarantee of bank loan for land and building, machinery and equipment up to $15,000,000, and $5,000,000 for equipment. Economic development projects for manufacturing, research, office, warehouse hydroponic or aquaponic facility, energy conservation, pollution abatement.

CT Business Development Corp.:
SBA 504 Program: Sponsor for participation in the federal SBA 504 Program. Fixed rate loan up 40 percent of project cost to a maximum of $750,000. 50 percent conventional bank financing, minimum of 10 percent owner equity for the purchase of buildings and equipment.

Self-Sustaining Bond Program: Taxable and tax exempt bond financing for manufacturing, public water supply, solid waste disposal, local district heating & cooling, and state and local government projects. Amounts and terms subject to market conditions.

Manufacturing Assistance Act: 100 percent exemption from local property taxes for a period of four years on the purchase of new manufacturing equipment. Low interest loans and grants to manufacturers expanding productive capacity.

Urban Enterprise Zones Programs: Offers special investment incentives and financing programs to businesses located in any of 11 different zones.

Innovation, Inc.
845 Brook St.
Rocky Hill, CT 06067   203-258-4305
Risk Capital: Provided for the development phase of a new product or process. Neither a loan nor a grant, this fund reimburses up to 60 percent of expenses on a regular basis, with other financing making up the balance. Payback is derived from a royalty based on sale of the product.

Innovation Development Loan Fund: Provides working capital for companies with new products and processes ready for manufacture, promotion, and sale.

Small Business Administration (SBA)
330 Main Street   203-240-4700
Hartford, CT 06106   FAX: 203-240-4659
SBA 7(a) Guaranteed and Direct Loans: Guarantees up to 90 percent of a loan made through a private lender up to $750,000. Can be used for working capital, expand or convert facilities, purchase of machinery and equipment, and land and building. Available only to those unable to obtain a loan from conventional sources. Direct loans are made up to $150,000.

SBA 504: Provides loans using 50 percent conventional bank financing, 40 percent SBA involvement through Certified Development Companies, and 10 percent owner equity. A fixed-asset loan in amounts up to $750,000. Loan can be used for land and building, construction, machinery and equipment, and renovation/expansion.

Small Business Innovative Research Grants (SBIR): Phase I awards between $20,000 to $50,000 to entrepreneurs to support six months of research on a technical innovation. Phase II grants are an additional $500,000 for development. Private sector investment funds must follow.

International Trade Loans: Guaranteed long-term loans through private lenders to develop or expand export markets, or to recover from the effects of import competition. Maximum guaranteed loan is $1,000,000 for fixed assets and an additional $250,000 for working capital and/or export revolving line of credit.

Export Revolving Line of Credit Loan: Short term financing available to small businesses that are at least one year old. Loans provide working capital to finance the manufacturing or wholesaling of products for export and for export marketing. The SBA will guarantee up to 90 percent of a conventional loan in amounts up to $750,000.

Contract Loan: Short-term loans are available to small businesses to finance the costs of labor and materials on contracts for which the proceeds are assignable. Program guarantees up to 90 percent of loans not in excess of $750,000. Qualifying small businesses must be in business for at least 12 calendar months prior to the date of the loan application.

Seasonal Line of Credit Loan: Loans provide short-term working capital to finance seasonal increases in business activities. Program guarantees up to 90 percent of loans not in excess of $750,000. Qualifying business must be in operation for at least one year prior to application.

Pollution Control Loans: Long-term guaranteed loans can be made by conventional financing to small businesses for installation or required pollution control measures. Must be unable to adopt the pollution control measures without undue financial hardship. Maximum guaranteed loan is $1,000,000.

General Contractor Loans: Small general construction contractors may obtain short-term loans or loan guarantees for residential or commercial construction or rehabilitation of property to be sold. The SBA will guarantee up to 90 percent of qualifying loans made by private lenders up to a maximum of $750,000. Direct loans can be up to $150,000.

Energy Business Loan Guarantee: Small businesses that provide certain energy production and conservation services for others may qualify for long-term loans and loan guarantees for start-ups and expansions. Loans and guarantees are made for firms that develop, manufacture, sell, install, or service specific energy measures for others, or firms that provide engineering, architectural, consulting, or other professional services connected with specific energy measures. Guarantee is for up to 90 percent of a loan not in excess of $750,000. Direct loans up to $150,000.

Disaster Recovery Loans: Small businesses located in federally designated disaster areas and suffering property damage or economic losses from the disaster can obtain long-term recovery loans at low interest rates. Property damage loans are limited to 85 percent of the verified damage. Loans for economic losses are for operating capital to meet the business' obligations that could have been made had the disaster not occurred.

Handicapped Assistance Loans: Assists persons who have a physical, mental or emotional disability of a permanent nature which limits the selection of any type of employment for which the person would otherwise be qualified. Direct loans are available for up to $150,000. The interest rate is 3% on these loans.

Surety Bond Guaranty Program: Makes the bonding system more available to small contractors who may be denied access to the system. SBA can guarantee up to 80 percent of surety's loss on a bond that has a maximum in total contract value of up to $1,250,000.

Vietnam-era and Disabled Veterans Loan Program: Provides direct loans to veterans to establish or expand a small business. Funds may be used for working capital or fixed assets. Direct loans for amounts up to $150,000 are available. The interest rate may be fixed or variable.

AB SBIC, Inc.
275 School House Road
Cheshire, CT 06410   203-272-0203

All State Venture Capital Corporation
The Bishop House
32 Elm Street, P.O. Box 1629
New Haven, CT 06506   203-787-5029

Capital Resource Co. of Connecticut
2558 Albany Avenue
West Hartford, CT 06117   203-236-4336

Financial Opportunities, Inc.
174 South Road
Enfield, CT 06082   203-741-9727

First New England Capital, LP
255 Main Street
Hartford, CT 06106   203-728-5200

Marcon Capital Corporation
49 Riverside Avenue
Westport, CT 06880   203-226-6893

Northeastern Capital Corporation
209 Church Street
New Haven, CT 06510   203-865-4500

RFE Capital Partners, LP
36 Grove Street
New Canaan, CT 06840   203-966-2800

SBIC of Connecticut, Inc.
965 White Plains Road
Trumbull, CT 06611   203-261-0011
    Small Business Investment Companies (SBIC): The SBA licenses, regulates, and provides financial assistance to privately owned and operated Small Business Investment Companies. SBICs make venture or risk investments by supplying capital and extending unsecured loans and loans not fully collateralized to small enterprises which meet their investment criteria. Financing is made by direct loans and by equity investments.

* Women and Minority Business Assistance

Small Business Administration
330 Main Street   203-240-4700
Hartford, CT 06106   FAX: 203-240-4659
    SBA 8(a) Program - Business Procurement Assistance: Provides federal government contracting opportunities for small businesses owned by socially and economically disadvantaged persons, and assists these businesses to become independently competitive in the normal business environment. SBA monitors all government contracts to assure that a quota of contract work goes to 8(a) businesses. Also provides business management services to these businesses. Business must be approved for program participation prior to receipt of an 8(a) contract.

* Management Consulting and Other Services

Connecticut Small Business Development Center
University of Connecticut
School of Administration
368 Fairfield Road
Box U-41, Room 422
Storrs, CT 06269-2041   203-486-4135
    Day Care Program: Sponsors educational workshops for current and prospective day care providers. Annually, May and June.

    Accounting Services Center: Provides access to professional accounting and financial services, as well as training and education to small and medium-sized businesses. Services include installation of accounting systems and procedures, assistance in setting-up computerized record-keeping systems and spreadsheets, financial management advice, preparation of tax returns, financial statements and loan applications.

    Connecticut Small Business Export Center: Assists small businesses in their export activities.

    Teenage Minority Entrepreneurial Program: Sponsors conferences to encourage inner-city students to think about business as a career.

    The Business Law Research Clinic: Answers legal questions for small business owners.

Small Business Administration
330 Main Street   203-240-4700

Hartford, CT 06106   FAX: 203-240-4659

Small Business Institutes: This program provides personalized consulting services to the small business community. Consulting is provided by senior level business students, guided by a faculty advisor. Assistance in business plan preparation, marketing research, market planning, accounting, and seminars are provided.

University Locations:
Central Connecticut State University
University of Bridgeport
University of Connecticut

* Small Business Development Centers

The following offices offer free and fee-based services to new and expanding businesses:

Lead Center:
Connecticut Small Business Development Center
University of Connecticut
School of Business Administration
Box U-41, Room 422
368 Fairfield Road   203-486-4135
Storrs, CT 06268   FAX: 203-486-1576

Bridgeport: Business Regional B.C., Small Business Development Center, 10 Middle Street, 14th Floor, Bridgeport, CT 06604-4229, 203-335-3800; FAX: 203-366-9105.

Bridgeport: University of Bridgeport, Small Business Development Center, 141 Linden Avenue, Bridgeport, CT 06601, 203-576-4538.

Danielson: Quinebaug Valley Community College, Small Business Development Center, 742 Upper Maple Street, Danielson, CT 06239-1440, 203-774-1133; FAX: 203-774-7768.

Hartford: University of Connecticut/MBA, Small Business Development Center, 1800 Asylum Avenue, West Hartford, CT 06117, 203-241-4907; FAX: 203-241-4907.

Groton: University of Connecticut, Small Business Development Center, Administration Building, Room 313, 1084 Shennecossett Road, Groton, CT 06340-6097, 203-449-1188; FAX: 203-445-3415.

Middletown: Middlesex County Chamber of Commerce, Small Business Development Center, 393 Main Street, Middletown, CT 06457, 203-344-2158; FAX: 203-346-1043.

New Haven: Greater New Haven Chamber of Commerce, Small Business Development Center, 195 Church Street, New Haven, CT 06506, 203-773-0782; FAX: 203-787-6730.

Stamford: Southwestern Area Commerce and Industry Association (SACIA), Small Business Development Center, One Landmark Square, Stamford, CT 06901, 203-359-3220; FAX: 203-967-8294.

Waterbury: Greater Waterbury Chamber of Commerce, Small Business Development Center, 83 Bank Street, Waterbury, CT 06702, 203-757-0701; FAX: 203-756-3507.

Willmantic: Eastern Connecticut State University, Small Business Development Center, 83 Windham Street, Willmantic, CT 06226-2295, 203-456-5349; FAX: 203-456-5670.

Delaware

* General Information

Delaware Development Office
99 Kings Highway
P.O. Box 1401
Dover, DE 19903   302-739-4271

Offers referrals to appropriate state agencies and other organizations. Free tabloid, *Small Business Start-Up Guide*, is available.

Small Business Advocate: Provides assistance in cutting bureaucratic red tape, and information and expertise in dealing with state, federal, and local agencies.

* Financing

Delaware Development Office
99 Kings Highway
P.O. Box 1401
Dover, DE 19903   302-739-4271

Tax-Exempt Industrial Revenue Bonds (IRBs): Financial assistance is available to new or expanding manufacturers, first-time farmers, and firms that have Section 501-status from the Internal Revenue Service. The interest earned by bondholders is exempt from federal income tax and is tax-exempt for Delaware resident investors. Therefore, long-term, low-interest financing may be obtained. These bonds may be used to finance fixed assets. For manufacturing projects, financing is limited to a maximum of $10 million for each project. Special rules apply to Section 501 and first-time farmer projects.

Taxable Industrial Revenue Bonds: Taxable bonds may be used by new or expanding manufacturing, industrial, commercial, wholesaling and agricultural concerns to finance working capital or fixed assets. Interest rates are subject to market conditions. A direct lending program administered through state banks. Minimum loan: $1,000,000, Maximum Loan: $4,000,000.

Small Business Development Fund: Short term loans (5 years or less) to be used for working capital. Available to companies with 100 or less employees (does not include restaurants). Provides loans using 75% conventional bank financing. 25 percent provided by the Development Fund.

Small Business Revolving Loan and Credit Enhancement Fund: Established to aid small businesses with 100 or fewer employees attain financing for economic development-related projects. Loans from the fund are not to exceed 25% of the total required to finance an eligible project, up to $100,000. The interest rate will be approximately 80% of the prime lending rate at the time the loan is executed. Credit enhancements purchased by the Delaware Economic Development Authority are not to exceed $100,000. In determining eligibility of projects, consideration will be given to the economic impact on the state and local community.

Small Business Administration (SBA)
1 Rodney Square, Suite 412
920 N. King Street   302-573-6295
Wilmington, DE 19801   FAX: 302-573-6060

SBA 7(a) Guaranteed and Direct Loans: Guarantees up to 90 percent of a loan made through a private lender up to $750,000. Can be used for working capital, expand or convert facilities, purchase of machinery and equipment, and land and building. Available only to those unable to obtain a loan from conventional sources. Direct loans are made up to $150,000.

SBA 504: Provides loans using 50 percent conventional bank financing, 40 percent SBA involvement through Certified Development Companies, and 10 percent owner equity. A fixed-asset loan in amounts up to $750,000. Loan can be used for land and building, construction, machinery and equipment, and renovation/expansion.

Small Business Innovative Research Grants (SBIR): Phase I awards between $20,000 to $50,000 to entrepreneurs to support six months of research on a technical innovation. Phase II grants are an additional $500,000 for development. Private sector investment funds must follow.

International Trade Loans: Guaranteed long-term loans through private lenders to develop or expand export markets, or to recover from the effects of import competition. Maximum guaranteed loan is $1,000,000 for fixed assets and an additional $250,000 for working capital and/or export revolving line of credit.

Export Revolving Line of Credit Loan: Short term financing available to small businesses that are at least one year old. Loans provide working capital to finance the manufacturing or wholesaling of products for export and for export marketing. The SBA will guarantee up to 90 percent of a conventional loan in amounts up to $750,000.

Contract Loan: Short-term loans are available to small businesses to finance the costs of labor and materials on contracts for which the proceeds are assignable. Program guarantees up to 90 percent of loans not in excess of $750,000. Qualifying small businesses must be in business for at least 12 calendar months prior to the date of the loan application.

Seasonal Line of Credit Loan: Loans provide short-term working capital to finance seasonal increases in business activities. Program guarantees up to 90 percent of loans not in excess of $750,000. Qualifying business must be in operation for at least one year prior to application.

Pollution Control Loans: Long-term guaranteed loans can be made by conventional financing to small businesses for installation or required pollution control measures. Must be unable to adopt the pollution control measures without undue financial hardship. Maximum guaranteed loan is $1,000,000.

General Contractor Loans: Small general construction contractors may obtain short-term loans or loan guarantees for residential or commercial construction or rehabilitation of property to be sold. The SBA will guarantee up to 90 percent of qualifying loans made by private lenders up to a maximum of $750,000. Direct loans can be up to $150,000.

Energy Business Loan Guarantee: Small businesses that provide certain energy production and conservation services for others may qualify for long-term loans and loan guarantees for start-ups and expansions. Loans and guarantees are made for firms that develop, manufacture, sell, install, or service specific energy measures for others, or firms that provide engineering, architectural, consulting, or other professional services connected with specific energy measures. Guarantee is for up to 90 percent of a loan not in excess of $750,000. Direct loans up to $150,000.

Disaster Recovery Loans: Small businesses located in federally designated disaster areas and suffering property damage or economic losses from the disaster can obtain long-term recovery loans at low interest rates. Property damage loans are limited to 85 percent of the verified damage. Loans for economic losses are for operating capital to meet the business' obligations that could have been made had the disaster not occurred.

Handicapped Assistance Loans: Assists persons who have a physical, mental or emotional disability of a permanent nature which limits the selection of any type of employment for which the person would otherwise be qualified. Direct loans are available for up to $150,000. The interest rate is 3% on these loans.

Surety Bond Guaranty Program: Makes the bonding system more available to small contractors who may be denied access to the system. SBA can guarantee up to 80 percent of surety's loss on a bond that has a maximum in total contract value of up to $1,250,000.

Vietnam-era and Disabled Veterans Loan Program: Provides direct loans to veterans to establish or expand a small business. Funds may be used for working capital or fixed assets. Direct loans for amounts up to $150,000 are available. The interest rate may be fixed or variable.

Delaware Development Corporation
99 Kings Highway
P.O. Box 1401
Dover, DE 19903   302-739-4271
    SBA 504 Loans: Provides loans using 50 percent conventional bank financing, 40 percent Small Business Administration (SBA) involvement through Certified Development Companies, and 10 percent owner equity. A fixed-asset loan in amounts up to $750,000. Loan can be used for land and building, construction, machinery and equipment, and renovation/expansion. Interest rates are generally 1.1 percent above U.S. Treasury Bond rates.

Wilmington Department of Commerce
City County Building
800 French Street
Wilmington, DE 19801   302-571-4169
    The Wilmington Department of Commerce offers Industrial Revenue Bond financing and other programs. Additionally, it's developing the key Brandywine and Christina Gateways in Center-City Wilmington and assisting in development of other parts of the city. Staff members are also

available to reduce regulatory hold-ups. The Department of Commerce can also provide you with free publications.

New Castle County Economic Development Corporation
704 King Street
1st Federal Plaza, Suite 536
Wilmington, DE 19801   302-656-5050
    The New Castle County Economic Development Corporation (NCCEDCO) offers SBA 504 and Industrial Revenue Bonds. Additionally, NCCEDCO offers small business counseling and is active in the development of the New Castle County Airport.

Wilmington Economic Development Corporation
605A Market Street Mall
Wilmington, DE 19801   302-571-9088
    The Wilmington Economic Development Corporation (WEDCO) provides financing through its direct lending program, the SBA 504 program, and other governmental mechanisms. WEDCO is also involved in the Brandywine Industrial Complex and offers management assistance to small businesses in the City of Wilmington.

Sussex County Department of Economic Development
Sussex County Courthouse
P.O. Box 589
Georgetown, DE 19947   302-855-7770
    The Sussex County Department of Economic Development issues Industrial Revenue Bonds. In addition, it's developing the Sussex County Industrial Airpark and assisting in development of other parts of the County.

Central Delaware Chamber of Commerce
Treadway Towers, Suite 2A
P.O. Box 576   302-678-3028
Dover, DE 19903   FAX: 302-678-0189
    This is the economic development agency in Kent County providing assistance in site selection, demographics, and statistical information as well as support to new and expanding firms.

* Women and Minority Business Assistance

Minority Business Development Agency
6th Floor, City/County Building
800 French Street
Wilmington, DE 19801   302-571-4169
    Assists minority businesses in the city of Wilmington by providing technical assistance, certification of minority businesses, and workshops. Sponsors a Minority Business Trade Fair (the largest in the Northeast) once a year. Works with the Wilmington Economic Development Corporation to provide financing.

Small Business Administration
1 Rodney Square
Suite 412
920 N. King Street   302-573-6295
Wilmington, DE 19801   FAX: 302-573-6060
    SBA 8(a) Program - Business Procurement Assistance: Provides federal government contracting opportunities for small businesses owned by socially and economically disadvantaged persons, and assists these businesses to become independently competitive in the normal business environment. SBA monitors all government contracts to assure that a quota of contract work goes to 8(a) businesses. Also provides business management services to these businesses. Business must be approved for program participation prior to receipt of an 8(a) contract.

* Management Consulting and Other Services

Delaware State Chamber of Commerce
One Commerce Center, Suite 200
Wilmington, DE 19801   302-655-7221

Small Business Financing Traveling Road Show: A series of special programs on small business financing which include segments on dealing with local bankers.

Division of Facilities Management/Energy Office
Margaret M. O'Neill Building
P.O. Box 1401   302-739-5644
Dover, DE 19903   Energy Hotline: 1-800-282-8616 in Delaware
Conducts free on-site energy audits. Workshops and seminars are offered on controlling energy costs and energy conservation measures for small businesses.

Delaware Development Office
Carvel State Office Building
P.O. Box 8911
Wilmington, DE 19899   302-577-6262

Governor's International Trade Council
Carvel State Office Building
P.O. Box 8911
Wilmington, DE 19899   302-577-3160

Delaware Department of Agriculture
2320 South duPont Highway
Dover, DE 19901   302-739-4811

Container Port of Wilmington
P.O. Box 1191
Wilmington, DE 19899   302-571-4600
The Delaware Development Office and the Governor's International Trade Council have established programs and devoted resources to assist small businesspersons in expanding operations to take advantage of international exporting opportunities. The Delaware Development Office's international trade specialists can provide detailed assistance to exporters concerning federal export rules and regulations, including licensing and custom requirements, as well as assist in the discovering of marketing opportunities abroad. The Delaware Development Office has also established a Shared Foreign Sales Corporation program, pursuant to which an exporter may qualify for a 15% federal tax exemption on export profits. In addition, the Governor's International Trade Council sponsors a series of special programs on international trade topics, including foreign market opportunities.

The Delaware Department of Agriculture and the City of Wilmington's Port of Wilmington are also resources for assistance to Delaware small businesspersons.

Small Business Administration
1 Rodney Square
Suite 412
920 N. King Street   302-573-6295
Wilmington, DE 19801   FAX: 302-573-6060
Small Business Institutes: This program provides personalized consulting services to the small business community. Consulting is provided by senior level business students, guided by a faculty advisor. Assistance in business plan preparation, marketing research, market planning, accounting, and seminars are provided.
University Locations:
University of Delaware

* Small Business Development Centers
The following offices offer free and fee-based services to new and expanding businesses:

Lead Center:
Delaware Small Business Development Center
University of Delaware
Purnell Hall, Suite 005   302-831-2747
Newark, DE 19716   FAX: 302-831-1423

Dover: Delaware Small Business Development Ctr, University of Delaware, 4 The Green, Dover, DE 19901, 302-735-8200; FAX: 302-735-8203.

District Of Columbia

* General Information

Office of Business and Economic Development
717 14th Street, NW
10th Floor
Washington, DC 20005   202-727-6600
Offers a wide range of technical and financial assistance programs.

* Financing

Office of Business and Economic Development
Financial Services Division
717 14th Street, NW
10th Floor
Washington, DC 20005   202-727-6600
Revolving Loan Fund: Can be used for direct loans in conjunction with private funds. Funds will be used primarily to provide guarantees for bank loans.

Business Development Loan Program: Offers direct loans for gap financing, construction, equipment purchases, inventory, and working capital. Funds can also be used to provide financing for development projects.

Commercial Development Assistance Program: Designed to encourage investment in small neighborhood commercial businesses, CDAP offers direct loans in conjunction with private funds. Typical fund uses are bridge financing, gap financing, acquisition of equipment, fixtures and furniture, inventory, and limited working capital.

Facade Loan Program: Designed to help revitalize neighborhood commercial corridors, this loan program offers direct loans to commercial property owners and business owners for the renovation of their building facades. Loan amounts are up to $25,000 at interest rates of 3%.

Met Loan/Met Grant Program: Designed to mitigate the disruptive costs suffered by businesses as a result of the Metro System's construction of the *Green Line*, this program can provide loans of up to $30,000 and grants of up to $20,000 per year. Projects must be CDBG-eligible and are only open to firms that had been sited along the Green Line's construction route. Loans may be funded at interest rates of 4% and must be repaid within five years of the Green Line's completion. Highly flexible, the program may underwrite equipment, inventory and even working capital costs.

Development Zones Loan Program (DLZP): Seeking to encourage the revitalization of the Alabama Avenue, DC Village, and Anacostia Development Zones, this business development program offers firms locating in these areas up to $200,000 or 90% of a project's cost. Low interest gap financing, typically set between 3% to 6%, may be used to secure land, equipment, inventory, leasehold improvements and working capital. Projects meeting federal CDBG standards, and furthering a specific zone's development goals, may thus access loans amortized over a term of up to twenty years, depending on the particular use of funds.

Economic Development Finance Corporation (EDFC)
1660 L Street, NW, Suite 308
Washington, DC 20036   202-775-8815
The Economic Development Finance Corporation (EDFC) is a quasi-public venture capital organization capitalized with public and private funds that provides equity capital and loans to DC businesses that meet EDFC's established investment criteria. The EDFC can provide financial assistance in a number of creative ways ranging from direct business loans to equity investments.

Washington District Small Business Administration
1111 18th Street, N.W., 6th Floor
P.O. Box 1993   202-634-1500
Washington, DC 20036   FAX: 202-634-1803
SBA 7(a) Guaranteed and Direct Loans: Guarantees up to 90 percent of a loan made through a private lender up to $750,000. Can be used for working capital, expand or convert facilities, purchase of machinery and

equipment, and land and building. Available only to those unable to obtain a loan from conventional sources. Direct loans are made up to $150,000.

SBA 504: Provides loans using 50 percent conventional bank financing, 40 percent SBA involvement through Certified Development Companies, and 10 percent owner equity. A fixed-asset loan in amounts up to $750,000. Loan can be used for land and building, construction, machinery and equipment, and renovation/expansion.

Small Business Innovative Research Grants (SBIR): Phase I awards between $20,000 to $50,000 to entrepreneurs to support six months of research on a technical innovation. Phase II grants are an additional $500,000 for development. Private sector investment funds must follow.

International Trade Loans: Guaranteed long-term loans through private lenders to develop or expand export markets, or to recover from the effects of import competition. Maximum guaranteed loan is $1,000,000 for fixed assets and an additional $250,000 for working capital and/or export revolving line of credit.

Export Revolving Line of Credit Loan: Short term financing available to small businesses that are at least one year old. Loans provide working capital to finance the manufacturing or wholesaling of products for export and for export marketing. The SBA will guarantee up to 90 percent of a conventional loan in amounts up to $750,000.

Contract Loan: Short-term loans are available to small businesses to finance the costs of labor and materials on contracts for which the proceeds are assignable. Program guarantees up to 90 percent of loans not in excess of $750,000. Qualifying small businesses must be in business for at least 12 calendar months prior to the date of the loan application.

Seasonal Line of Credit Loan: Loans provide short-term working capital to finance seasonal increases in business activities. Program guarantees up to 90 percent of loans not in excess of $750,000. Qualifying business must be in operation for at least one year prior to application.

Pollution Control Loans: Long-term guaranteed loans can be made by conventional financing to small businesses for installation or required pollution control measures. Must be unable to adopt the pollution control measures without undue financial hardship. Maximum guaranteed loan is $1,000,000.

General Contractor Loans: Small general construction contractors may obtain short-term loans or loan guarantees for residential or commercial construction or rehabilitation of property to be sold. The SBA will guarantee up to 90 percent of qualifying loans made by private lenders up to a maximum of $750,000. Direct loans can be up to $150,000.

Energy Business Loan Guarantee: Small businesses that provide certain energy production and conservation services for others may qualify for long-term loans and loan guarantees for start-ups and expansions. Loans and guarantees are made for firms that develop, manufacture, sell, install, or service specific energy measures for others, or firms that provide engineering, architectural, consulting, or other professional services connected with specific energy measures. Guarantee is for up to 90 percent of a loan not in excess of $750,000. Direct loans up to $150,000.

Disaster Recovery Loans: Small businesses located in federally designated disaster areas and suffering property damage or economic losses from the disaster can obtain long-term recovery loans at low interest rates. Property damage loans are limited to 85 percent of the verified damage. Loans for economic losses are for operating capital to meet the business' obligations that could have been made had the disaster not occurred.

Handicapped Assistance Loans: Assists persons who have a physical, mental or emotional disability of a permanent nature which limits the selection of any type of employment for which the person would otherwise be qualified. Direct loans are available for up to $150,000. The interest rate is 3% on these loans.

Surety Bond Guaranty Program: Makes the bonding system more available to small contractors who may be denied access to the system. SBA can guarantee up to 80 percent of surety's loss on a bond that has a maximum in total contract value of up to $1,250,000.

Vietnam-era and Disabled Veterans Loan Program: Provides direct loans to veterans to establish or expand a small business. Funds may be used for working capital or fixed assets. Direct loans for amounts up to $150,000 are available. The interest rate may be fixed or variable.

Allied Investment Corporation
1666 K Street, NW, Suite 901
Washington, DC 20006   202-331-1112
     Small Business Investment Companies (SBIC): The SBA licenses, regulates, and provides financial assistance to privately owned and operated Small Business Investment Companies. SBICs make venture or risk investments by supplying capital and extending unsecured loans and loans not fully collateralized to small enterprises which meet their investment criteria. Financing is made by direct loans and by equity investments.

* Women and Minority Business Assistance

Washington DC Minority Business Development Center
1133 15th Street, NW, Suite 1120
Washington, DC 20005   202-785-2886
     Assistance in preparing business plans and loan proposals, management and technical assistance in the areas of finance, business planning and operations, marketing, construction procurement services, and bid preparation. Services provided at a subsidized rate.

Minority Business Opportunity Commission
2000 14th Street, N.W., Room 324
Washington, DC 20009   202-939-8780
     The Minority Business Opportunity Commission (MBOC) is the District of Columbia Government agency that certifies minority businesses eligible to participate in the Minority Business Sheltered Market Program and provides assistance in identifying procurement opportunities with the District Government. The MBOC conducts seminars and workshops on District government and private sector contracting and publishes *Doing Business with the District: A How-To-Guide for Minority Participation.*

The Greater Washington Ibero-American Chamber of Commerce
2100 M Street, N.W., Suite 607
Washington, DC 20037   202-546-0959
     Technical and management services include financial packaging, market analysis, financial and business planning, procurement evaluation and contracting.

Washington District Small Business Administration
1111 18th Street, N.W., 6th Floor
P.O. Box 1993   202-634-1500
Washington, DC 20036   FAX: 202-634-1803
     SBA 8(a) Program - Business Procurement Assistance: Provides federal government contracting opportunities for small businesses owned by socially and economically disadvantaged persons, and assists these businesses to become independently competitive in the normal business environment. SBA monitors all government contracts to assure that a quota of contract work goes to 8(a) businesses. Also provides business management services to these businesses. Business must be approved for program participation prior to receipt of an 8(a) contract.

* Training

Office of Job Services
Department of Employment Services
500 C Street, NW
Washington, DC 20001   202-639-1601
     Offers employers a broad range of free services including customized manpower training and recruitment programs. Financial incentives and tax credits are available to employers who hire eligible DC workers.

     Job Training Partnership Act (JTPA): Provides employers with recruitment, screening, referral, training, 50 percent wage subsidy up to 3 months for on-the-job training. Available to any private employer.

* Management Consulting and Other Services

Office of Business and Economic Development
717 14th Street, N.W., 10th floor
Washington, DC 20005   202-727-6600
Offers a range of technical assistance programs, including identifying sources of market data, site location assistance, referrals to other business assistance sources, and loan programs.

Business and Permit Center
Department of Consumer and Regulatory Affairs
614 H Street, N.W., Room 100
Washington, DC 20001   202-727-7100
One-stop location for obtaining business licenses and construction permits. Permit and registration information, project counselling, and technical assistance is available.

George Washington University Small Business Legal Clinic
National Law Center
720 20th Street, NW, Suite SL-101
Washington, DC 20052   202-994-7463
The George Washington University Small Business Legal Clinic is part of the Small Business Administration-sponsored network of Small Business Development Centers. The clinic provides legal guidance and counseling to small businesses and handles a wide range of legal problems affecting small businesses such as filing appropriate forms for start-ups, incorporating a business, business tax requirements, lease and contract evaluation, and dispute resolution.

Washington District Small Business Administration
1111 18th Street, N.W., 6th Floor
P.O. Box 1993   202-634-1500
Washington, DC 20036   FAX: 202-634-1803
Small Business Institutes: This program provides personalized consulting services to the small business community. Consulting is provided by senior level business students, guided by a faculty advisor. Assistance in business plan preparation, marketing research, market planning, accounting, and seminars are provided.
University Locations:
Howard University

* Small Business Development Centers

The following offices offer free and fee-based services to new and expanding businesses:

Lead Center:
District of Columbia Small Business Development Center
Howard University
6th & Fairmont Street, N.W., Room 128   202-806-1550
Washington, DC 20059   FAX: 202-806-1777

Arlington: Marymount University, Small Business Development Center, Office of Continuing Education, 2807 North Glebe Road, Arlington, VA 22207-4299, 703-522-5600.

College Park: University of Maryland (UMCP), Small Business Development Center, College of Business and Management, Tydings Hall, College Park, MD 20742, 301-454-5072.

Landover: National Business League of Southern Maryland, Inc., Small Business Development Center, 9200 Basic Court, Suite 210, Landover, MD 20785, 301-794-4400.

Washington: Galludet University, Small Business Development Center, Management Institute, 800 Florida Avenue, N.E., Washington, DC 20002-3625, 202-651-5312.

Washington: George Washington University, Small Business Development Center, National Law Center, 720 20th Street, N.W., Suite SL-101B, Washington, DC 20052, 202-994-7463.

Florida

* General Information

Bureau of Business Assistance
Department of Commerce
107 W. Gains St.
Collins Building, Room 443
Tallahassee, FL 32399-2000   904-488-9357
Business Services Section   1-800-342-0771 in FL
Offers information and referral services for current and potential small business owners. Also serves as ombudsman to small businesses to help resolve problems being experienced with state agencies. They also sponsor workshops and business forums and an annual Small Business Development Workshop that brings together local, state, and federal agency representatives. Distributes and publishes the *Florida New Business Guide Checklist* for small businesses.

Bureau of Industry Development   904-488-9360
Provides assistance in obtaining labor, financing, zoning permits, and licenses, meeting regulations, and coordinating between state and local government. Assists businesses in locating hard-to-find suppliers of products or services. In addition, assists in several areas to manufacturing companies experiencing problems in staying in business.

Small Business Administration
7825 Baymeadows Way, Suite 100B   904-443-1900
Jacksonville, FL 32256   FAX: 904-443-1980
Small Business Advocate: Assistance in cutting bureaucratic red tape. Information and expertise in dealing with state, federal, and local agencies.

* Financing

Bureau of Economic Assistance
Florida Department of Community Affairs
2740 Centerview Drive
Rhyne Building
Tallahassee, FL 32399-2100   904-488-3581
Florida Enterprise Zone Program: Designed to benefit the most distressed areas of Florida. Benefits for businesses that locate within these zones or hire workers living within these zones include property tax credits and community tax credits, sales tax exemptions, corporate income tax credits, and credits against sales and corporate taxes for job creation.

Florida First Capital Finance Company
c/o Florida Department of Commerce
Bureau of Business Assistance
107 W. Gains St.
Collins Building
Tallahassee, FL 32399-2000
Business Finance Section   904-487-0466
SBA 504 Loan Program: Provides loans using 50 percent conventional bank financing, 40 percent SBA involvement through Certified Development Companies, and 10 percent owner equity. A fixed asset loan in amounts up to $700,000. Funds can be used for land and building, construction, machinery and equipment, and renovation/expansion.

SBA 7(a) Loan Guarantee Program: Guarantees up to 90 percent of a loan made through a private lender, up to $750,000. Can be used for start-up capital, working capital, inventory, machinery and equipment, and land and building. Available only to those unable to obtain a loan from conventional sources. Direct loans are made up to $150,000.

Florida Department of Commerce
Bureau of Business Assistance
Business Finance Section
107 W. Gains St.
Collins Building
Tallahassee, FL 32399-2000   904-487-0463
Small Business Innovation Research Grants (SBIR)   904-488-9357
The SBIR program stimulates innovate research among small technology-based business. They provide for financing of the very early research and

development phase of innovation that meet the needs of the participating agencies. Assists in registering potential proposers with the agencies. Provides small businesses with information on proposal writing and with the names and addresses of the participating agencies to contact.

Phase I: Awards between $20,000 to $50,000 to support six months of effort to demonstrate the scientific and technical merit and feasibility of the innovation.

Phase II: Awards are an additional $500,000 for two years to further development the innovation through the prototype stage. Projects with potential will receive special consideration for a Phase II award.

Phase III: Private sector investment is required to support a project to commercialization.

Economic Development Transportation Fund (EDTF): The EDTF fund is available to local governments in need of financial assistance for transportation projects which will facilitate economic development. The local governmental body must apply on behalf of a company that is considering an expansion or location of new facilities and that has an existing or anticipated transportation problem.

Economic Development and Commercial Revitalization
Bureau of Community Assistance
2740 Centerview Drive
Rhyne Building, Tallahassee, FL 32399-2100   904-488-3581

Small City Community Development Block Grant (CDBG): Available to cities populations of 50,000 or less or counties with populations of less than 200,000. Designed to address and resolve specific community and economic development needs for low and moderate income families. The state sets aside CDBG funds to assist private entities for the purpose of creating or retaining jobs for low and moderate income persons. Funds can be used for the acquisition, construction, rehabilitation, or installation of commercial or industrial buildings, structures and other real property and for public and private improvements.

Small Business Administration (SBA)
501 E. Polk Street, #104   813-228-2594
Tampa, FL 33602-3945   FAX: 813-228-2111

Small Business Administration (SBA)
7825 Baymeadows Way, Suite 100B   904-443-1900
Jacksonville, FL 32256   FAX: 904-443-1980

Small Business Administration (SBA)
Palm Beach Executive Plaza
5601 Corporate Way, Suite 402
West Palm Beach, FL 33407-2044   407-689-3922

Small Business Administration (SBA)
1320 South Dixie Highway, Suite 501   305-536-5521
Coral Gables, FL 33146-2911   FAX: 305-536-5058

SBA 7(a) Guaranteed and Direct Loans: Guarantees up to 90 percent of a loan made through a private lender up to $750,000. Can be used for working capital, expand or convert facilities, purchase of machinery and equipment, and land and building. Available only to those unable to obtain a loan from conventional sources. Direct loans are made up to $150,000.

SBA 504: Provides loans using 50 percent conventional bank financing, 40 percent SBA involvement through Certified Development Companies, and 10 percent owner equity. A fixed-asset loan in amounts up to $750,000. Loan can be used for land and building, construction, machinery and equipment, and renovation/expansion.

Small Business Innovative Research Grants (SBIR): Phase I awards between $20,000 to $50,000 to entrepreneurs to support six months of research on a technical innovation. Phase II grants are an additional $500,000 for development. Private sector investment funds must follow.

International Trade Loans: Guaranteed long-term loans through private lenders to develop or expand export markets, or to recover from the effects of import competition. Maximum guaranteed loan is $1,000,000 for fixed assets and an additional $250,000 for working capital and/or export revolving line of credit.

Export Revolving Line of Credit Loan: Short term financing available to small businesses that are at least one year old. Loans provide working capital to finance the manufacturing or wholesaling of products for export and for export marketing. The SBA will guarantee up to 90 percent of a conventional loan in amounts up to $750,000.

Contract Loan: Short-term loans are available to small businesses to finance the costs of labor and materials on contracts for which the proceeds are assignable. Program guarantees up to 90 percent of loans not in excess of $750,000. Qualifying small businesses must be in business for at least 12 calendar months prior to the date of the loan application.

Seasonal Line of Credit Loan: Loans provide short-term working capital to finance seasonal increases in business activities. Program guarantees up to 90 percent of loans not in excess of $750,000. Qualifying business must be in operation for at least one year prior to application.

Pollution Control Loans: Long-term guaranteed loans can be made by conventional financing to small businesses for installation or required pollution control measures. Must be unable to adopt the pollution control measures without undue financial hardship. Maximum guaranteed loan is $1,000,000.

General Contractor Loans: Small general construction contractors may obtain short-term loans or loan guarantees for residential or commercial construction or rehabilitation of property to be sold. The SBA will guarantee up to 90 percent of qualifying loans made by private lenders up to a maximum of $750,000. Direct loans can be up to $150,000.

Energy Business Loan Guarantee: Small businesses that provide certain energy production and conservation services for others may qualify for long-term loans and loan guarantees for start-ups and expansions. Loans and guarantees are made for firms that develop, manufacture, sell, install, or service specific energy measures for others, or firms that provide engineering, architectural, consulting, or other professional services connected with specific energy measures. Guarantee is for up to 90 percent of a loan not in excess of $750,000. Direct loans up to $150,000.

Disaster Recovery Loans: Small businesses located in federally designated disaster areas and suffering property damage or economic losses from the disaster can obtain long-term recovery loans at low interest rates. Property damage loans are limited to 85 percent of the verified damage. Loans for economic losses are for operating capital to meet the business' obligations that could have been made had the disaster not occurred.

Handicapped Assistance Loans: Assists persons who have a physical, mental or emotional disability of a permanent nature which limits the selection of any type of employment for which the person would otherwise be qualified. Direct loans are available for up to $150,000. The interest rate is 3% on these loans.

Surety Bond Guaranty Program: Makes the bonding system more available to small contractors who may be denied access to the system. SBA can guarantee up to 80 percent of surety's loss on a bond that has a maximum in total contract value of up to $1,250,000.

Vietnam-era and Disabled Veterans Loan Program: Provides direct loans to veterans to establish or expand a small business. Funds may be used for working capital or fixed assets. Direct loans for amounts up to $150,000 are available. The interest rate may be fixed or variable.

Allied Investment Corporation
(Main Office: Washington, DC)
Executive Office Center
Suite 305
2770 N. Indian River Blvd.
Vero Beach, FL 32960   407-778-5556

Florida Capital Venture, Ltd.
111 Madison Street, 26th Floor
Tampa, FL 33602   813-229-2294

J & D Capital Corporation
12747 Biscayne Blvd.
North Miami, FL 33181   305-893-0303

Mariner Venture Capital Corporation
2300 W. Glades Road
Suite 440 West Tower
Boca Raton, FL 33431   407-394-3066

Market Capital Corporation
1102 North 28th Street
P.O. Box 31667
Tampa, FL 33631   813-247-1357

Quantum Capital Partners, Ltd.
Main Office: New York, NY)
600 Fairway Drive, Suite 101
Deerfield Beach, FL 33441   305-570-6231

Southeast SBIC, Inc.
One Southeast Financial Center
Miami, FL 33131   305-375-6962

Western Financial Capital Corporation
(Main Office: Dallas, TX)
AmeriFirst Bank Building, 2nd Floor S
18301 Biscayne Boulevard
N. Miami Beach, FL 33160   305-933-5858
   Small Business Investment Companies (SBIC): The SBA licenses, regulates, and provides financial assistance to privately owned and operated Small Business Investment Companies. SBICs make venture or risk investments by supplying capital and extending unsecured loans and loans not fully collateralized to small enterprises which meet their investment criteria. Financing is made by direct loans and by equity investments.

Community and Business Loan Program
4440 NW 25th Place
Gainesville, FL 32606   904-338-3425
   The Farmers Home Administration (FmHA), an agency of the U.S. Department of Agriculture, makes loans and grants in rural areas, including towns, for housing, farming, community facilities, and business and industry. A firm wishing to establish itself in a rural area, population of 50,000 or less, or an existing firm that needs to expand may be eligible for a loan guarantee through a commercial lender. Loans may be used for land, building, and equipment, working capital, and in certain cases for refinancing debt. Loans in amounts in excess of $500,000. The FmHA has established goals for business and industry loans to businesses operated by women and/or minorities, job producing enterprises in deeply distressed areas and modernizing and upgrading run-down business centers in rural areas.

Certified Development Corporations (CDC's)
   Certified Development Corporations are non-profit organizations licensed by the Small Business Administration to administer small business loan programs for new or expanding businesses for the purpose of promoting economic growth in a particular area. Contact one in your area:

   Bartow: Central Florida Areawide Development Corporation, 490 East Davidson Street, Bartow, FL 33830, 813-533-6190. Operating Area: Desoto, Hardee, Highlands, Okeechobe, Polk Counties

   Gainesville: North Central Florida Areawide Development Company, Inc., 235 South Main Street, Suite 205, Gainesville, FL 32601, 904-336-2199. Operating Area: Alachua, Bradford, Columbia, Dixie, Gilchrist, Hamilton, Lafayette, Madison, Suwannee, Taylor and Union Counties

   Jacksonville: Jacksonville Local Development Company, Inc., 128 East Forsyth Street, Florida Theatre Building, Suite 600, Jacksonville, FL 32202, 904-630-1914. Operating Area: Duval County

   Miami: Miami Citywide Development, Inc., Dupont Plaza Center, 300 Biscayne Blvd. Way, Suite 614, Miami, FL 33131, 305-358-1025. Operating Area: City of Miami

   Miami: Miami-Date Business Development Corporation, 300 Southwest 12th Avenue, Suite A, Miami, FL 33130, 305-541-0457. Operating Area: Date County

Orlando: Orlando Neighborhood Improvement Corporation, Inc., 455 South Orange Avenue, Orlando, FL 32801, 305-849-2522. Operating Area: Orange County

St. Petersburg: St. Petersburg Certified Development Corporation, 475 Central Avenue, St. Petersburg, FL 33701, 813-892-5108. Operating Area: City of St. Petersburg

Tallahassee: Florida First Capital Finance Corporation, Inc., Florida Department of Commerce, 426 Collins Building, 107 West Gaines Street, Tallahassee, FL 32399-2000, 904-487-0466. Operating Area: Statewide

Tampa: Tampa Bay Economic Development Corporation, Office of Urban Development, 306 East Jackson Street, 7th Floor East, P. O. Box 3330, Tampa, FL 33601-3330, 813-223-8418. Operating Area: City of Tampa

* Women and Minority Business Assistance

Community Development Corporations (CDCs)
   Non-profit organizations designed to assist disadvantaged persons in starting or expanding a business. The program, which is administered by the Department of Community Affairs, provides low interest loans to or invests in existing or start-up businesses located in economically distressed communities. Other services provided may include technical assistance to potential entrepreneurs, job training programs, leadership development, and assistance in securing government contracts. Contact one of the following CDCs for further information.

   Coconut Grove: Coconut Grove Local Development Corporation, Inc., 3582 Grand Avenue, P.O. Box 75, Coconut Grove, FL 33133, 305-446-3095. Target Area Coconut Grove

   Dania: Liberia Economic and Social Development Corporation, Inc., 1190 Sheridan Street, Dania, FL 33004, 305-921-2371. Target Area: Cities of Hollywood and Dania

   Daytona Beach: Central Florida Community Development Corporation, Inc., 520 North Ridgewood Avenue, Suite B, Daytona Beach, FL 32014, 904-258-7520. Target Area: Daytona Beach

   Deerfield Beach: Deerfield Beach Community Development Corporation, Inc., 13 Southwest Tenth Street, Deerfield Beach, FL 33441, 305-427-3670. Target Area: Deerfield Beach

   Gainesville: United Gainesville Community Development Corporation, Inc. P.O. Box 2518, Gainesville, FL 32602, 904-376-8891. Target Area: Alachua County

   Jacksonville: Community Economic Development Council, Inc., 8911 Devenshire Blvd., Jacksonville, FL 32208, 904-764-1728. Target Area: Northside Section of Duval County

   Miami: New Washington Heights Community Development Conference, Inc. 1600 Northwest Third Avenue, Miami, FL 33136, 305-573-8217. Target Area: Culmer/Overtown Section of Miami

   Miami: Northeast Miami Chamber of Commerce, Inc., 8281 Northeast Second Avenue, Miami, FL 33138, 305-754-1444. Target Area: Little River Community of Miami.

   Miami: Martin Luther King Community Development Operation, Inc. 6116 Northwest Seventh Avenue, Miami, FL 33127, 305-757-7652. Target Area: Liberty City and Model City Areas of Miami

   Miami: Miami Beach Development Corporation, Inc., 1205-Drexel Avenue, 2nd Floor, Miami Beach, FL 33139, 305-538-1010. Target Area: The Art Deck District of Miami Beach

   Pensacola: Community Equity Investments, Inc., 302 North Barcelona Street, Pensacola, FL 32501, 904-433-5619, 904-433-5619. Target Area: Escambia County

   Quincy: Community and economic Development Organization of Gadsden County, Inc., 215 West Jefferson Street, Suite 2, Quincy, FL 32351, 904-627-7565. Target Area: Gadsden County

Sanford: Seminole Employment Economic Development Corporation, Inc. 1011 South Sanford Avenue, P.O. Box 2076, Sanford, FL 32771, 407-323-4360. Target Area: Seminole County

Additional information on Procurement - See Management Section

Black Business Investment Board (BBIC)

The Florida Black Business Investment Board (BBIC) has been allocated a $5 million Investment Incentive Trust Fund. The fund was established to assist new and expanding black-owned businesses. The board does not make direct loans to black businesses. Funds from the Investment Incentive Trust are matched dollar for dollar by the BBICs for eligible new and expanding businesses.

Broward County: Metro-Broward Capital Corp., 1100 W. St. Road 84, 2nd Floor, First Union Bank Building, Ft. Lauderdale, FL 33315, 305-463-3153

Duval County: First Coast Black Business Investment Corporation, 218 W. Adams Street, #504, Jacksonville, FL 32202, 904-634-0543

Dade County: Business Assistance Center, 6600 Northwest 27th Avenue, Miami, FL 33147, 305-693-3550

Orange, Seminole, Osceola Counties: Black Business Investment Fund of Central Florida, Landmark Building #655, 315 Robinson Street, Orlando, FL 32801, 407-649-4780

Palm Beach: Palm Beach County Black Business, Investment Corporation, Barnett Bank Building, Suite 301, 2001 Broadway, Riviera Beach, FL 33404, 407-845-8055

Hillsborough, Pinellas Counties: Tampa Bay Black Business Investment Corporation, 315 East Kennedy Blvd., Tampa, FL 32602, 813-223-8381

Florida Department of Transportation
Minority Programs Office
Hayden Burns Building, Room 260
Tallahassee, FL 32399-0450   904-488-3145

Develops outreach programs to recruit and inform disadvantaged business enterprises about contracting opportunities with the Department of Transportation. Also has a business support component which assesses business needs for training and technical assistance. Specific programs include classroom training, on-the-job training, conferences, seminars, workshops, and proficiency standards attainment.

Minority Construction Program
Florida Board of Regents
Florida Education Center, Room 1601
Tallahassee, FL 32399-1950   904-488-5251

A program to enhance minority participation in the State University System construction program. The goals of the Board of Regents are to achieve minority participation, to increase participation by minority architects and engineers, and to eliminate existing deterrents for the participation of socially and economically disadvantaged individuals and businesses. It long range goal is to achieve equitable distribution of contracts among all participants in the State University System.

Minority Business Office
Department of General Services
Knight Building
Koger Executive Center, Suite 201
2737 Centerview Drive
Tallahassee, FL 32399-0100   904-487-0915

The Office is responsible for certifying minority businesses to do business with the state and for maintaining a directory of the certified businesses. The directory is available to all state agencies.

Minority Business Development Centers

Minority Business Development Centers offer existing and potential minority entrepreneurs a wide range of services from initial counseling on how to start a business to more complex issues of planning and growth. General business counseling, information, and referral services are free of

charge. Assistance beyond this is provided at a fee according to client's ability to pay.

Ft. Lauderdale : Ft. Lauderdale MBDC, 3500 North State Road 7, Suite 407, Ft. Lauderdale, FL 33319, 305-485-5333.

Jacksonville: Jacksonville MBDC, 333 North Laura Street, Suite 465, Jacksonville, FL 32202-3508, 904-353-3826.

Miami: MBDC District Office, 51 Southwest 1st Avenue, Room 1314 Box 25, Miami, FL 33130, 305-536-5054.

Miami: Miami MBDC, 100 Northwest 78 Avenue, Suite 301, Miami, FL 33126, 305-591-7355.

Orlando: Orlando MBDC, 132 East Colonial Drive, Suite 211, Orlando, FL 32801, 305-422-6234.

Tampa: Tampa/St. Petersburg MBDC, 5020 West Cypress Street, Suite 217, Tampa, FL 33607, 813-228-7555.

Florida Regional Minority Purchasing Council, Inc.
7900 Northeast Second Avenue
Suite 501
Miami, FL 33138   305-757-9690

National Minority Supplier Development Council of Florida, Inc.
120 University Park Drive
Suite 170
Winter Park, FL 32792-4419   407-679-4147

Minority Purchasing Councils provide opportunities and business environments conducive to the development and participation of minority vendors. Encourage firms to procure goods and services from minority business enterprises and assist minority businesses a variety of certification, technical assistance, and referral activities.

Small Business Administration (SBA)
501 E. Polk St., #104   813-228-2594
Tampa, FL 33602-3945   FAX: 813-228-2111

Small Business Administration (SBA)
7825 Baymeadows Way, Suite 100B   904-443-1900
Jacksonville, FL 32256   FAX: 904-443-1980

Small Business Administration (SBA)
Palm Beach Executive Plaza
5601 Corporate Way, Suite 402
West Palm Beach, FL 33407-2044   407-689-3922

Small Business Administration (SBA)
1320 South Dixie Highway, Suite 501   305-536-5521
Coral Gables, FL 33146-2911   FAX: 305-536-5058

Office of Minority Small Business and Capital Ownership Development: Explain to potential minority entrepreneurs how SBA's services and programs can help them become successful owners.

SBA 8(a) Program - Business Procurement Assistance: Provides federal government contracting opportunities for small businesses owned by socially and economically disadvantaged persons, and assists these businesses to become independently competitive in the normal business environment. SBA monitors all government contracts to assure that a quota of contract work goes to 8(a) businesses. Also provides business management services to these businesses. Business must be approved for program participation prior to receipt of an 8(a) contract.

Small and Minority Business Advocate
Florida Department of Commerce
501-C Collins Building
Tallahassee, FL 32399-2000   904-487-4698

Small and Minority Business Advisory Council: Identifies the concerns and unique needs of small and minority-owned businesses in Florida. Serves as a liaison between the business community, state agencies, and the Legislature. Also serves as a review board for policies, procedures and regulations as they relate to key issues of concern.

* Training

Industry Services Training Program
Division of Vocational Education
Florida Department of Education
Florida Education Center, Room 1154
Tallahassee, FL 32399 904-487-1040
Provides customized training of employees for new, expanding, and diversifying industries in the state. Training is available at vocational-technical center, community colleges, or departments of comprehensive high schools, and on-site.

Economic Development and Industry Programs
State Board of Community Colleges
Florida Department of Education
Florida Education Center, Room 1314
Tallahassee, FL 32399-0400 904-487-4943
Provides grants to establish training partnerships between community colleges and employers who have specific training needs for employees in new, expanding, or diversifying businesses. The state has appropriate funds for training grants to be matched by industry with cash, equipment or facility use. Training programs include mechanical assembly, computer training, secretarial/clerical/word processing, basic electricity, critical-care nursing, marketing, and managerial skills.

State Job Training Coordinating Council
204 Atkins Building
1320 Executive Center Drive
Tallahassee, FL 32399-0667 904-488-9250
Job Training Partnership Act (JTPA): Provides employers with recruitment, screening, referral, training, 50 percent wage subsidy up to 3 months for on-the-job training. Available to any private employer.

* Management Consulting and Other Services

Florida Department of Commerce
Bureau of Business Assistance
107 W. Gains St., #443
Collins Building
Tallahassee, FL 32399-2000
Business Finance Section:
Venture Capital Clubs 904-488-9357
Venture capital clubs are located throughout the state and seek to invest in new businesses. The clubs are informally networked and supported by the Florida entrepreneurship program. Objective of the program is increased interaction among everyone needs for successful business start-ups.

Community Development Section 904-488-9357
Concerned with encourage business and economic development in small communities by providing technical assistance for industrial recruitment and assisting in business incubator development. Also, helps organize local venture capital pools and encourages support of an entrepreneurship club network.

Business Finance Section 904-487-9357
Assists businesses in locating financing alternatives to meet their needs. Also assists established Florida firms interested in exporting their products and services, loan packaging for the SBA 504 program.

Bureau of International Trade and Development
Florida Department of Commerce
107 W. Gains St.
366 Collins Building
Tallahassee, FL 32399-2000 904-487-1399
International Trade: Assist firms interested in exporting. The major responsibilities of the bureau include increasing Florida's domestic trade and exports and aiding foreign companies interested in identifying Florida business locations and opportunities.

Bureau of Economic Analysis
Florida Department of Commerce
107 W. Gains St.
315 Collins Building
Tallahassee, FL 32399-2000 904-487-2568
An Economic Data Base provides support information, research, and planning for community and economic development. The bureau maintains a comprehensive computer data bank and local economic information.

Small Business Administration
501 E. Polk Street
Suite 104
Tampa, FL 33602-3945 813-228-2594
FAX: 813-228-2111

Small Business Administration
7825 Baymeadows Way
Suite 100B
Jacksonville, FL 32256 904-443-1900
FAX: 904-443-1980

Small Business Administration
Palm Beach Executive Plaza
5601 Corporate Way, Suite 402
West Palm Beach, FL 33407-2044 407-689-3922

Small Business Administration
1320 South Dixie Highway, Suite 501
Coral Gables, FL 33146-2911 305-536-5521
FAX: 305-536-5058
Assists, counsels, and provides support for small business people. Provides new and established small businesses with management counseling and training as well as financial and procurement contracts assistance. Special efforts are made in assisting women and minorities, the handicapped, and veterans to get into business and stay in business.

Small Business Institutes: This program provides personalized consulting services to the small business community. Consulting is provided by senior level business students, guided by a faculty advisor. Assistance in business plan preparation, marketing research, market planning, accounting, and seminars are provided.
University Locations:
Florida Atlantic University
Florida International University
Florida State University
Nova University
Stetson University
University of Central Florida
University of Miami
University of North Florida
University of South Florida
University of Tampa
University of West Florida

STAC
University of Florida
Progress Center
One Progress Blvd., Box 24
Alachua, FL 32615 904-462-3913

Florida Atlantic University
NASA/STAC
1515 West Commercial Blvd.
Ft. Lauderdale, FL 33309 305-776-1257

University of North Florida
STAC/College of Business
Building 11, Room 2179
4567 St. Johns Bluff South
Jacksonville, FL 32216-6699 904-646-2487

Florida International University
STAC/College of Engineering
FIU University Park, ECS 445
Miami, FL 33199 305-348-3476

University of Central Florida
STAC/College of Engineering
Box 25000, CEBA 319
Orlando, FL 32816 407-823-5826

University of South Florida
STAC/College of Engineering
ENG-118, Trailer #3
Tampa, FL 33620-5350   813-974-4222

Southern Technology Application Center (STAC) was created by NASA and the State University System of Florida to assist the private sector in commercializing technology. It is a full service information research organization with information on almost any subject area from state-of-the art development in laser technology to the latest medical devices to business management information. Provides a variety of assistance to entrepreneurs such as marketing, technical assistance, and proposal development consulting. *Also see Technology section.*

Florida Atlantic University
Small Business Development Center
Office of International Trade
P.O. Box 3091
Boca Raton, FL 33431   305-367-2271

Offers individual assistance and training programs to businesses entering the world marketplace. Assists in generating dollars in exporting contracts for small businesses. Works closely with the Department of Commerce, World Trade Councils, and other groups involved in developing international trade opportunities.

Department of General Services
Division of Purchasing
2737 Centerview Drive
Knight Building, Room 220
Tallahassee, FL 32399-0950   904-488-8440

Coordinates and regulates the purchase of commodities and contractual services use by state agencies. Publishes *Doing Business With the State of Florida* designed to provide help to small and minority-owned companies interested in doing business with the state. Efforts should also be directed to each state agency's purchasing office as not all goods and services use by each state agency are purchase by this Department.

Bidders List: All companies doing business with the state on a repetitive basis for the sale of goods and contractual services, in excess of $3000 per purchase, should register with the purchasing office in each agency. After approval of the application, bid solicitations will be sent to the company by the agency.

Florida Small Business Development Center
University of West Florida
11000 University Parkway
Building 8
Pensacola, FL 32514   904-474-2908

Info-Bid: A statewide data bank program offered to help small and minority business locate bid opportunity to sell to federal, state, and local governments and participating commercial firms.

Statewide Contracts Register   904-474-3016
State agencies submit all bids to the Small Business Development Centers for inclusion in the statewide contracts register. The information on bids is distributed to interested small and minority businesses to assist them in identifying their markets.

* Small Business Development Centers

These centers provide assistance with Department of Defense procurement who continuously search for suppliers for its vast array of needs and offer many business opportunities for competent suppliers.

The following offices offer free and fee-based services to new and expanding businesses:

Lead Center:
Florida Small Business Development Center Network
University of West Florida
1100 University Parkway   904-474-3016
Pensacola, FL 32514   FAX: 904-474-2092

AltaMonte Springs: Seminole Community College, Small Business Development Center, Seminole Chamber of Commerce, P.O. Box 150784, AltaMonte Springs, FL 32715-0784, 407-834-4404.

Boca Raton: Florida Atlantic University, Small Business Development Center, Building T-9, P.O. Box 3091, Boca Raton, FL 33431, 407-367-2273.

Cocoa: Brevard Community College, Small Business Development Center, 1519 Clearlake Road, Cocoa, FL 32922, 407-951-1060, ext. 2045.

Dania: Small Business Development Center, 46 SW 1st Avenue, Dania, FL 33304, 305-987-0100.

Deland: Stetson University, Small Business Development Center, School of Business Administration, P.O. Box 8417, Deland, FL 32720, 904-822-7326.

Fort Lauderdale: Small Business Development Center, Florida Atlantic University, Commercial Campus, 1515 West Commercial Blvd., Room 11, Fort Lauderdale, FL 33309, 305-771-6520.

Fort Pierce: Indian River Community College, Small Business Development Center, 3209 Virginia Avenue, Room 114, Fort Pierce, FL 34981-5599, 407-468-4756.

Fort Myers: University of South Florida, Small Business Development Center, Sabal Hall, Rooms 219 and 220, 8111 College Parkway, Fort Myers, FL 33919, 813-489-4140.

Fort Walton Beach: University of West Florida, Fort Walton Beach Center, Small Business Development Center, 414 Mary Esther Cutoff, Fort Walton Beach, FL 32548, 904-244-1036.

Gainesville: Small Business Development Center, 214 W. University Avenue, P.O. Box 2518, Gainesville, FL 32601, 904-377-5621.

Gainesville: FSBDC Product Innovation Program, Florida Product Innovation Center, 2622 NW 43rd Street, Suite B-3, Gainesville, FL 32606, 904-334-1680.

Jacksonville: University of North Florida, Small Business Development Center, College of Business, 4567 St. John's Bluff Road, South, Building 11, Room 2163, Jacksonville, FL 32216, 904-646-2476.

Miami: Florida International University, Small Business Development Center, Trailer MO1, Tamiami Campus, Miami, FL 33199, 305-348-2272.

Miami: Florida International Univeristy, Small Business Development Center, North Miami Campus, N.E. 151 Street & Biscayne Boulevard, Academic Building #1, Room 350, Miami, FL 33181, 305-940-5790.

Ocala: Small Business Development Center, 110 East Silver Springs Blvd., P.O. Box 1210, Ocala, FL 32670, 904-629-8051.

Orlando: University of Central Florida, Small Business Development Center, Building CEBA II, P.O. Box 25000, Orlando, FL 32816, 407-823-5554.

Pensacola: University of West Florida, Small Business Development Center, Building 8, 11000 University Parkway, Pensacola, FL 32514, 904-474-2908.

St. Petersburg: University of South Florida, St. Petersburg Campus, Small Business Development Center, 830 First Street South, Room 113, St. Petersburg, FL 33701, 813-893-9529.

Sarasota: Small Business Development Center, 5700 North Tamiami Trail, Sarasota, FL 33580, 813-359-4292.

Tallahassee: Florida A & M University, Small Business Development Center, 1715-B South Gadsden Street, Tallahassee, FL 32301, 904-599-3407.

Tampa: University of South Florida, Small Business Development Center, College of Business Administration, 4202 E. Fowler Avenue, BSN 3403, Tampa, FL 33620, 813-974-4274.

West Palm Beach: Small Business Development Center, Prospect Place, Suite 123, 3111 South Dixie Highway, West Palm Beach, FL 33405, 407-837-5311.

Georgia

* General Information

Georgia Department of Community Affairs
1200 Equitable Building
100 Peachtree Street
Atlanta, GA 30303   404-656-6200
   Provides information on financing programs and other services offered by
   the state government.

Georgia Chamber of Commerce
233 Peachtree Street, #200
Atlanta, GA 30303   404-223-2271
   Information and referral for federal and state labor laws, publications,
   seminars, workshops, state legislation. The Business Council is a
   clearinghouse for information and makes referrals to the Georgia
   Department of Labor, the Georgia Department of Industry and Trade, and
   other agencies. The council often acts as a liaison between businesses and
   local chambers of commerce.

Department of Administrative Services
West Tower, Room 1620
200 Piedmont Avenue Southeast
Atlanta, GA 30334   404-656-6315
   Minority and Small Business Affairs: Assistance in cutting bureaucratic
   red tape. Information and expertise in dealing with state, federal, and local
   agencies.

* Financing

Georgia Department of Community Affairs
1200 Equitable Building
100 Peachtree Street, N.W.   404-656-6200
Atlanta, GA 30303   404-656-3872
   Community Development Block Grant (CDBG): Regular Round Economic
   Development Program and CDBG Employment Incentive Program. The
   purpose of these two programs is to expand economic opportunities in
   cities and counties, principally for persons of low and moderate income.
   Only projects which cannot be funded through private lenders are eligible.
   Projects must create or retain jobs for low and moderate income persons.
   Loans are usually made at below-market rates with favorable terms. The
   maximum loan amount for the CDBG Regular Round is $400,000, for the
   EIP program, $200,000.

   Revolving Loan Fund Programs   404-656-6200
   Revolving loan funds are administered by Regional Development Centers
   to help business expand and create jobs. There are other similar programs
   in Georgia cities and counties - see Community Development Block
   Grants above.

   Downtown Development Revolving Loan Fund: Below market rate loans
   to businesses for projects that support downtown development, create and
   save jobs, and/or preserve and enhance historic downtown buildings. Must
   be located within one of the 35 "Appalachian Region" counties in North
   Georgia. One job is to be created or saved for every $20,000 loaned. 50
   percent of total project cost must be provided by loan or equity injection.
   Maximum loan amount is $75,000.

   Tax Exempt Industrial Bond Financing: Industrial Development Bonds
   are a type of long-term, low-interest rate financing available for manufacturing facilities. Private financial services firms issue the bonds.

   Taxable Composite Bond Financing: Projects are pooled into a single
   bond issue of $15 million or more. Private financial services firms issue the
   bonds.

   Job Tax Credit: A tax credit on Georgia income taxes for eligible business
   in certain less-developed counties for each new full-time employee.

   Industrial Revenue Bonds (IRB): Local Industrial Development
   Authorities issue IRB's to small and minority businesses.

Small Business Administration (SBA)
1720 Peachtree Rd NW, 6th Floor   404-347-4749
Atlanta, GA 30309   FAX: 404-347-4745
   SBA 7(a) Guaranteed and Direct Loans: Guarantees up to 90 percent of
   a loan made through a private lender up to $750,000. Can be used for
   working capital, expand or convert facilities, purchase of machinery and
   equipment, and land and building. Available only to those unable to
   obtain a loan from conventional sources. Direct loans are made up to
   $150,000.

   SBA 504: Provides loans using 50 percent conventional bank financing, 40
   percent SBA involvement through Certified Development Companies, and
   10 percent owner equity. A fixed-asset loan in amounts up to $750,000.
   Loan can be used for land and building, construction, machinery and
   equipment, and renovation/expansion.

   Small Business Research Grants (SBIR): Phase I awards between $20,000
   to $50,000 to entrepreneurs to support six months of research on a
   technical innovation. Phase II grants are an additional $500,000 for
   development. Private sector investment funds must follow.

   International Trade Loans: Guaranteed long-term loans through private
   lenders to develop or expand export markets, or to recover from the
   effects of import competition. Maximum guaranteed loan is $1,000,000 for
   fixed assets and an additional $250,000 for working capital and/or export
   revolving line of credit.

   Export Revolving Line of Credit Loan: Short term financing available to
   small businesses that are at least one year old. Loans provide working
   capital to finance the manufacturing or wholesaling of products for export
   and for export marketing. The SBA will guarantee up to 90 percent of a
   conventional loan in amounts up to $750,000.

   Contract Loan: Short-term loans are available to small businesses to
   finance the costs of labor and materials on contracts for which the
   proceeds are assignable. Program guarantees up to 90 percent of loans not
   in excess of $750,000. Qualifying small businesses must be in business for
   at least 12 calendar months prior to the date of the loan application.

   Seasonal Line of Credit Loan: Loans provide short-term working capital
   to finance seasonal increases in business activities. Program guarantees up
   to 90 percent of loans not in excess of $750,000. Qualifying business must
   be in operation for at least one year prior to application.

   Pollution Control Loans: Long-term guaranteed loans can be made by
   conventional financing to small businesses for installation or required
   pollution control measures. Must be unable to adopt the pollution control
   measures without undue financial hardship. Maximum guaranteed loan is
   $1,000,000.

   General Contractor Loans: Small general construction contractors may
   obtain short-term loans or loan guarantees for residential or commercial
   construction or rehabilitation of property to be sold. The SBA will
   guarantee up to 90 percent of qualifying loans made by private lenders up
   to a maximum of $750,000. Direct loans can be up to $150,000.

   Energy Business Loan Guarantee: Small businesses that provide certain
   energy production and conservation services for others may qualify for
   long-term loans and loan guarantees for start-ups and expansions. Loans
   and guarantees are made for firms that develop, manufacture, sell, install,
   or service specific energy measures for others, or firms that provide
   engineering, architectural, consulting, or other professional services
   connected with specific energy measures. Guarantee is for up to 90 percent
   of a loan not in excess of $750,000. Direct loans up to $150,000.

   Disaster Recovery Loans: Small businesses located in federally designated
   disaster areas and suffering property damage or economic losses from the
   disaster can obtain long-term recovery loans at low interest rates. Property
   damage loans are limited to 85 percent of the verified damage. Loans for
   economic losses are for operating capital to meet the business' obligations
   that could have been made had the disaster not occurred.

   Handicapped Assistance Loans: Assists persons who have a physical,
   mental or emotional disability of a permanent nature which limits the
   selection of any type of employment for which the person would otherwise
   be qualified. Direct loans are available for up to $150,000. The interest rate
   is 3% on these loans.

Surety Bond Guaranty Program: Makes the bonding system more available to small contractors who may be denied access to the system. SBA can guarantee up to 80 percent of surety's loss on a bond that has a maximum in total contract value of up to $1,250,000.

Vietnam-era and Disabled Veterans Loan Program: Provides direct loans to veterans to establish or expand a small business. Funds may be used for working capital or fixed assets. Direct loans for amounts up to $150,000 are available. The interest rate may be fixed or variable.

Investor's Equity, Inc.
945 E. Paces Ferry Road, Suite 1735
Atlanta, GA 30326   404-266-8300

North Riverside Capital Corporation
50 Technology Park/Atlanta
Norcross, GA 30092   404-446-5556

Small Business Investment Companies (SBIC): The SBA licenses, regulates, and provides financial assistance to privately owned and operated Small Business Investment Companies. SBICs make venture or risk investment by supplying capital and extending unsecured loans and loans not fully collateralized to small enterprises which meet their investment criteria. Financing is made by direct loans and by equity investments.

Business Development Corporation of Georgia
4000 Cumberland Parkway, Suite 1200-A
Atlanta, GA 30339   404-434-0273

The BDC provides loans of $100,000 to $1,250,000 for up to 20 years to qualified businesses (no grants).

Georgia Development Authority
Agricultural Loan Division
2082 E. Exchange Pl, #102
Tucker, GA 30084   404-493-5700

Agribusiness Start-up Assistance: This program allows local commercial banks to offer agribusiness enterprises tax-exempt interest rates. Businesses that deal directly with food or forestry are eligible. Borrowers must have no more than 100 employees and gross sales of existing business must be under $2 million during the preceding year. Loans may go up to $1 million.

Georgia Department of Natural Resources
Historic Preservation Section
205 Butler Street, S.E., #1462
Atlanta, GA 30334   404-656-2840

Twenty Percent Investment Tax Credit: The ITC is an economic incentive that encourages the rehabilitation and re-use of historic buildings for business purposes. The rehab tax credit provides a dollar for dollar reduction of Federal income taxes for equity investors. Buildings must be certified historic through the Historic Preservation Section.

Georgia Residential Finance Authority
60 Executive Parkway South, Suite 250   404-679-0662
Atlanta, GA 30329   1-800-350-HOME Outside Metro Atlanta

Georgia Housing Trust Fund for the Homeless: Low-interest loans and grants for affordable housing activities. Primary criteria is impact on homelessness. Available to public-private partnerships.

Low Income Housing Tax Credits: Tax credit against annual tax liability for 10 years for development of rental housing. At least 20 percent of project's units must be occupied by tenants earning no more than 60 percent of an area's median income. Projects must have zoning in place, utilities to site, and site control.

Rental Rehabilitation Program: "Forgivable" loans to investors and property owners for 50 percent of eligible costs to rehabilitate substandard rental housing. Applicant must own property which must be located in a locally designated target area, and be substandard or failing HUD standards.

Economic Development Administration
Atlanta Regional Office
401 W. Peachtree Street, N.E., Suite 1820

Atlanta, GA 30308-3510   404-730-3002

Business Loan Guarantee Program: Guarantees up to 80 percent of the principal and interest of loans to be made to private borrowers for the purchase of fixed assets and/or working capital purposes for projects located in areas eligible for EDA assistance. Equity investment is 15 to 25 percent of total loan. Minimum loan amount is $600,000.

Farmers Home Administration (FmHA)
Georgia State Office
355 East Hancock Avenue
Athens, GA 30610   706-546-2165

Business and Industrial Loan Program: Assistance is provided in the form of loan guarantees. FmHA contracts to reimburse the lender for a maximum of 90 percent of principal and interest. Loans are limited to areas outside the boundaries of cities of 50,000 or more. Basic uses for loans include developing or financing business or industry, increasing employment, and controlling or abating pollution. Funds can be used for land, buildings, machinery and equipment, working capital and pollution control facilities.

Certified Development Company of Northeast Georgia
305 Research Drive
Athens, GA 30610   404-542-7064

Atlanta Local Development Corporation
230 Peachtree Street, N.W.
Suite 1810
Atlanta, GA 30303   404-658-7000

The Business Growth Corporation of Georgia
400 Cumberland Parkway, Suite 1200-A
Atlanta, GA 30339   404-434-0273

CSRA Local Development Corporation
2123 Wrightsboro Road
P.O. Box 2800
Augusta, GA 30904   404-737-1823

Fulton County Certified Development Corporation
10 Park Place South, Suite 305
Atlanta, GA 30303   404-572-2429

McIntosh Trail Area Development Corporation
P.O. Drawer A
Barnesville, GA 30204   404-358-3647

Coastal Area District Development Authority
P.O. Box 1917
127 F Street
Brunswick, GA 31521   912-264-7315

Sowega Economic Development Corporation
30 East Broad Street
P.O. Box 346
Camilla, GA 31730   912-336-5617

Columbus Local Development Corporation
P.O. Box 1340
Columbus, GA 31993   404-571-4886

Lower Chattachoochee Development Corporation
P.O. Box 1908
Columbus, GA 31994   404-322-5571

North Georgia Certified Development Corporation
503 West Waugh Street
Dalton, GA 30720   404-571-4886

Middle Flint Area Development Corporation
P.O. Box 6
Ellaville, GA 31806   912-937-2561

Heart of Georgia Area Development Corporation
501 Oak Street
Eastman, GA 31023   912-374-4771

Georgia Mountains Regional Economic Development Corporation
1010 Ridge Road
Gainsville, GA 30501   404-536-3431

Troup County Local Development Corporation
900 Dallis Street
LaGrange, GA 30240   404-883-1658

Development Corporation of Middle Georgia
600 Grand Building
Mulberry Street
Macon, GA 31201   912-751-6160

Oconee Area Development Corporation
P.O. Box 707
Milledgeville, GA 31061   912-453-4328

Savannah Certified Development Corporation
P.O. Box 1027
Savannah, GA 31402   912-235-4156

Southeast Georgia Development Corporation
3243 Harris Road
Waycross, GA 31501   912-285-6097

South Georgia Area Development Corporation
327 West Savannah Avenue
P.O. Box 1223
Valdosta, GA 31601   912-333-5277

Local or Certified Development Corporations: These corporations offer some local or SBA Section 502/503/7(a) loan funding for qualified small businesses in Georgia. Contact one of the above for further information:

Venture Capital Network of Atlanta (VCN)
230 Peachtree Street, N.W., Suite 1650
Atlanta, GA 30303   404-658-7000

VCN of Atlanta matches entrepreneurs and individual investors through a confidential computerized database. Entrepreneurs most likely to benefit are those that require from $25,000 to $750,000 in equity financing. A fee is charged for registration.

Georgia Capital Network
Georgia Tech Advanced Technology Development Center
430 10th Street NW, Suite N-116
Atlanta, GA 30318   404-894-5344

A confidential computerized matching service introducing entrepreneurs with new promising businesses that are too small for other equity sources to investors interested in early-state financing.

* Women and Minority Business Assistance

Small and Minority Business Affairs
Georgia Department of Administrative Services
200 Piedmont Avenue Southeast
West Tower #1620
Atlanta, GA 30334   404-656-6315

Assists with conducting business with state government, identification of coordinating offices in state agencies and prerequisites.

Minority Subcontractors Tax Credit: Available to any company which subcontracts with a minority-owned firm to furnish goods, property, or services to the State of Georgia. The credit is for 10 percent of the total amount of qualified payments to minority subcontractors during the tax year, but not to exceed $100,000 per year.

Office of Minority Business Development
Small Business Development Center
University of Georgia
Chicopee Complex
1180 East Broad Street
Athens, GA 30602   706-542-5760

Advocacy of minority entrepreneurship, consulting, and business training.

Small Business Administration (SBA)
1720 Peachtree Road, N.W.   404-347-4745
Atlanta, GA 30309   FAX: 404-347-4749

SBA 8(a) Program - Business Procurement Assistance: Provides federal government contracting opportunities for small businesses owned by socially and economically disadvantaged persons, and assists these businesses to become independently competitive in the normal business environment. SBA monitors all government contracts to assure that a quota of contract work goes to 8(a) businesses. Also provides business management services to these businesses. Business must be approved for program participation prior to receipt of an 8(a) contract.

Minority Enterprise Small Business Investment Companies (MESBICs): MESBICs are privately capitalized and invest in minority-owned ventures. They receive $3 for every $1 of private money invested. Contact your local office.
Atlanta MESBIC: Renaissance Capital Corp. (MESBIC), 161 Spring Street, NW, Suite 815, Atlanta, GA 30303, 404-658-9061

Minority Business Development Agency
401 W. Peachtree, Suite 1715
Atlanta, GA 30308   404-730-3300

Regional offices of the Minority Business Development Agency (of the U.S. Department of Commerce) manage a network of 25 local business assistance centers. At any of these centers a minority owner can get help with preparing a business loan package, securing sales, or solving a management problem. The centers maintain networks of local business development organizations, assist business people in the commercialization of technologies and coordinate other federal agency activities which assist minority entrepreneurs. Contact your local office:
Atlanta: Atlanta Minority Business Development Center, 75 Piedmont Avenue, Suite 256, Atlanta, GA 30303, 404-586-0973.

Augusta: Augusta Minority Business Development Center, 1394 Laney-Walker Boulevard, Augusta, GA 30901, 404-722-0994.

Columbus: Columbus Minority Business Development Center, 1214 First Avenue, Suite 430, Columbus, GA 30901, 404-324-4253.

Savannah: Savannah Minority Business Development Center, 31 West Congress Street, Savannah, GA 31401, 912-236-6708.

* Training

Georgia Department of Labor
Job Training Division
Suite 650, Sussex Place
148 International Boulevard
Atlanta, GA 30303   404-656-7392

Job Training Partnership Act (JTPA): Provides employers with recruitment, screening, referral, training, 50 percent wage subsidy up to 3 months for on-the-job training. Available to any private employer.

* Management Consulting and Other Services

Georgia Chamber of Commerce
1280 South CNN Center
233 Peachtree St., #200
Atlanta, GA 30303   404-223-2285

This is a statewide membership organization that promotes the interests of all businesses. It keeps members informed of pending legislation, changes in law/regulations, provides management assistance and advice, provides information, makes referrals, and provides a variety of other services for all businesses.

Georgia Department of Community Affairs
1200 Equitable Building
100 Peachtree Street
Atlanta, GA 30303   404-656-6200

Small Business Revitalization Program: Offers advice to businesses with less than 500 employees on securing long-term financing for expansions.

Downtown Development Technical Assistance: Provides technical assistance and a central information source for the redevelopment of central business districts and older commercial areas. Presents conferences and seminars in coordination with member communities.

Agricultural Affairs Department
Georgia Power Company
270 Peachtree, 5th Floor
Atlanta, GA 30303   404-526-6526
Assistance in recognizing and enhancing the agribusiness economy.

Georgia Tech Research Institute (GTRI) Economic Development Laboratory
Regional Offices:
Albany: GTRI Regional Office, 1117 Whispering Pines Road, Albany, GA 31707, 912-430-4188, FAX: 912-430-4200.

Augusta: GTRI Regional Office, Suite 307, 1054 Claussen Road, Augusta, GA 30907, 404-737-1414, FAX: 404-737-1420.

Brunswick: GTRI Regional Office, P.O. Box 1196 31521), 127 "F" Street, Brunswick, GA 31520, 912-262-2346, FAX: 912-262-2372.

Carrollton: GTRI Regional Office, P.O. Box 676, 201 Tanner Street, Carrollton, GA 30117, 404-836-6675, FAX: 404-836-6675.

Columbus: GTRI Regional Office, P.O. Box 8965 (31908), 3575 Macon Road, Suite 23, Governor's Place, Columbus, GA 31907, 404-568-2482, FAX: 404-568-2486.

Douglas: GTRI Regional Office, P.O. Box 1244, 405 N. Peterson Ave., Douglas, GA 31533, 912-384-1121, FAX: 912-384-4151.

Dublin: GTRI Regional Office, P.O. Box 4620 (31040-4620), 1205 Bellevue Ave., Bellevue Place, Suite B, Dublin, GA 31021, 912-275-6543, FAX: 912-275-6544.

Gainesville: GTRI Regional Office, P.O. Box 3015 (30503), 200 Main Street, Suite 108, Hunt Tower, Gainesville, GA 30501, 404-535-5728, FAX: 404-535-5847.

Macon: GTRI Regional Office, P.O. Box 5105 (31208), 990-B Riverside Drive, Macon, GA 31201, 912-751-6190, FAX: 912-751-6363.

Madison: GTRI Regional Office, 216 North Main Street, Madison, GA 30650, 404-342-4205, FAX: 404-353-9932.

Rome: GTRI Regional Office, 1 Reservation Street, Rome, GA 30161, 404-295-6008, FAX: 404-295-6049.

Savannah: GTRI Regional Office, 7395 Hodgson Memorial Drive, Savannah, GA 31406, 912-921-5510, FAX: 912-921-5512.

Economic and Marketing Services Branch   404-894-3851
Feasibility studies, cost-benefit analyses, industrial market research, business plans and other efforts.

Georgia Productivity and Quality Center   404-894-6091
Quality improvement, employee involvement and technology utilization to strengthen competitiveness.

Industrial Extension Service   404-894-3830
Technical and economic development assistance to communities, manufacturers and processors through 12 regional offices and campus-based experts.

Southeastern Trade Adjustment Assistance Center   404-894-3858
Technical and management assistance to regional firms adversely affected by competition with imported products.

Energy Resources Branch   404-894-3636
Audits, workshops and publications to help manufacturers, institutions, agribusiness and commercial operations conserve energy and reduce costs.

Agricultural Technology Research Program:
Environmental Science and Technology Laboratory   404-894-3412

Assistance for the poultry industry to maintain productivity and competitiveness by adopting new methods and technologies.

Georgia Procurement Assistance Center   404-894-6121
Bid information/preparation and marketing for firms seeking to sell goods or services to the federal government. Also contact the **Business Service Center**, U.S. General Services Administration, 404-331-5103 for information about contracts with the Federal Government.

Georgia Department of Industry, Trade, and Tourism
P.O. Box 1776
Atlanta, GA 30301   404-656-3545
Provides assistance such as site location and community analysis to businesses wishing to locate or expand their operations to Georgia. Publications are available on Georgia industries, companies involved in foreign trade and wage structures in industry.

Trade Division   404-656-2861
Documentation and administrative support, marketing, consultation, foreign networks to sell American Product. Available to Georgia manufacturers are matchmaking programs, research and educational programs, international database, international trade lead network, trade shows and missions, incoming buying missions, international advertising and speakers bureau.

Additional contacts for Georgia manufacturers interested in exporting are the Small Business Development Centers in Atlanta - 404-542-5760 and 404-980-2000.

Advanced Technology Development Center
430 Tenth Street, N.W., Suite N-116
Atlanta, GA 30318   404-894-3575
Offers assistance to high technology businesses by providing start-up space and research assistance. It also maintains a directory of high tech operations in Georgia. *Also see Technology Section.*

Director of Economic Development
Technical and Adult Education
Suite 660, South Tower, 1 CNN Center
Atlanta, GA 30303-2705   404-656-7826
Quick Start: Quick Start helps industries start-up and expand their operations by developing and implementing customized training programs to provide companies with a trained work force in the shortest time possible.

Vietnam Veterans Leadership Program
825 Fairfield Drive
Marietta, GA 30068   404-565-8444
Provides training and consulting programs to show veterans how to apply for SBA loans. Since 1983, 420 businesses have been successfully started.

Small Business Administration (SBA)
1720 Peachtree Rd NW, 6th Floor   404-347-4749
Atlanta, GA 30309   FAX: 404-347-4745
Small Business Institutes: This program provides personalized consulting services to the small business community. Consulting is provided by senior level business students, guided by a faculty advisor. Assistance in business plan preparation, marketing research, market planning, accounting, and seminars are provided.
University Locations:
Augusta College
Clayton College
Emory University
Georgia College
Georgia Southern College
Georgia Southwestern College
Georgia State University
Kennesaw College
Macon College
Mercer University - Atlanta
University of Georgia
West Georgia College

* Small Business Development Centers

The following offices offer free and fee-based services to new and expanding businesses:

Lead Center:
Georgia Small Business Development Center
University of Georgia
Chicopee Complex
1180 East Broad Street   404-542-6785
Athens, GA 30602   FAX: 404-542-6776

Albany: Small Business Development Center, Southwest Georgia District, Business & Technology Center, 230 S. Jackson Street, 3rd Floor, Suite 333, Albany, GA 31701, 912-430-4303; FAX: 912-430-3933.

Athens: Small Business Development Center, University of Georgia, Chicopee Complex, 1180 East Broad Street, Athens, GA 30602, 404-542-7436; FAX: 404-542-6825.

Atlanta: Georgia State University, Small Business Development Center, Box 874, University Plaza, Atlanta, GA 30303-3083, 404-651-3550.

Augusta: Small Business Development Center, 1061 Katherine Street, Augusta, GA 30910, 404-737-1790; FAX: 404-731-7937.

Brunswick: Small Business Development Center, 1107 Fountain Lake Drive, Brunswick, GA 31520, 912-264-7343; FAX: 912-262-3095.

Columbus: Small Business Development Center, P.O. Box 2441, Columbus, GA 31902, 404-649-7433; FAX: 404-649-1928.

Decatur: DeKalb Chamber of Commerce, Small Business Development Center, 750 Commerce Drive, Decatur, GA 30030, 404-378-8000; FAX: 404-378-3397.

Gainesville: Small Business Development Center, 455 Jesse Jewel Parkway, Suite 302, Gainesville, GA 30501, 404-531-5681; 404-531-5684.

Lawrenceville: Gwinnett Technical Institute, Small Business Development Center, P.O. Box 1505, 1230 Atkinson Road, Lawrenceville, GA 30246, 404-963-4902; FAX: 404-962-7985.

Macon: Small Business Development Center, Baconsfield Park, 640-K North Avenue, P.O. Box 13212, Macon, GA 31208-3212, 912-751-3592.

Marietta: Kennesaw State College, Small Business Development Center, P.O. Box 444, Marietta, GA 30061, 404-423-6450; FAX: 404-423-6564.

Morrow: Clayton State College, Small Business Development Center, P.O. Box 285, Morrow, GA 30260, 404-961-3440; FAX: 404-961-3428.

Rome: Floyd College, Small Business Development Center, P.O. Box 1864, Rome, GA 30163, 404-295-6326; FAX: 404-295-6732.

Savannah: Small Business Development Center, 6555 Abercorn Street, Suite 224, Savannah, GA 31405, 912-356-2755; FAX: 912-353-3033.

Statesboro: Small Business Development Center, Landrum Center, Box 8156, Statesboro, GA 30460, 912-681-5194; FAX: 912-681-0648.

Valdosta: Small Business Development Center, Valdosta Area Office, Baytree Office Park, Suite 9, Baytree Road, Valdosta, GA 31601, 912-245-3738; FAX: 912-245-3741.

Warner Robins: Middle Georgia Technical Institute, Small Business Development Center, 151 Asigian Blvd., Warner Robins, GA 31088, 912-953-9376; FAX: 912-953-9376.

Hawaii

* General Information

Small Business Information Service
Department of Business and Economic Development
P.O. Box 2359
Honolulu, HI 96804   808-586-2600

Assists both new and existing businesses with information on government permit and license requirements, government procurement, sources of alternative financing, marketing, preparing a business plan, and available entrepreneurship training programs.

Small Business Advocate: Assistance in cutting bureaucratic red tape. Information and expertise in dealing with state, federal, and local agencies.

* Financing

Director of Finance
State of Hawaii
P.O. Box 150
Honolulu, HI 96810   808-586-1518

Local Bond Issues: The State of Hawaii has enacted legislation enabling the State to issue special purpose revenue bonds for manufacturing, processing or industrial enterprises, utilities serving the general public, and qualified health care facilities. The maximum interest rate for general obligation bonds is 8 percent. No limit is specified for revenue bonds.

Hawaii Capital Loan Program
P.O. Box 2359
Honolulu, HI 96804   808-586-2576

Hawaii Capital Loan Program: Provides direct loans, or loans in participation with financial institutions, or the Small Business Administration to small businesses who are unable to obtain private financing. Funds can be used for plant construction, conversion or expansion, land acquisition for expansions, and purchase of equipment, machinery, supplies or materials, or for working capital. Maximum loan amount is $1 million. Current interest rate is 7 1/2 percent. Preference is given to businesses with job creating potential; use local resources or by-products; displace imports; create export opportunities, in the commercial or service sector; in research or development; in Pacific basin activities.

Hawaii Innovation Development Program: Loans are available to inventors to develop any early stage invention or new product which has not been exploited commercially. Loans are for the purpose of financing acquisitions of equipment, machinery, materials or supplies, or for working capital. Funds must be unavailable elsewhere.

State Department of Agriculture
1428 South King Street
Honolulu, HI 96814   808-948-0145

Farmers unable to secure financing from conventional or other governmental sources may qualify for a Department of Agriculture loan.

Small Business Administration (SBA)
Prince Kuhio Federal Building
Room 2213, Box 50207
300 Ala Moana Boulevard   808-541-2990
Honolulu, HI 96850-4981   FAX: 808-541-2976

SBA 7(a) Guaranteed and Direct Loans: Guarantees up to 90 percent of a loan made through a private lender up to $750,000. Can be used for working capital, expand or convert facilities, purchase of machinery and equipment, and land and building. Available only to those unable to obtain a loan from conventional sources. Direct loans are made up to $150,000.

SBA 504: Provides loans using 50 percent conventional bank financing, 40 percent SBA involvement through Certified Development Companies, and 10 percent owner equity. A fixed-asset loan in amounts up to $750,000. Loan can be used for land and building, construction, machinery and equipment, and renovation/expansion.

Small Business Research Grants (SBIR): Phase I awards between $20,000 to $50,000 to entrepreneurs to support six months of research on a technical innovation. Phase II grants are an additional $500,000 for development. Private sector investment funds must follow.

International Trade Loans: Guaranteed long-term loans through private lenders to develop or expand export markets, or to recover from the effects of import competition. Maximum guaranteed loan is $1,000,000 for fixed assets and an additional $250,000 for working capital and/or export revolving line of credit.

Export Revolving Line of Credit Loan: Short term financing available to small businesses that are at least one year old. Loans provide working capital to finance the manufacturing or wholesaling of products for export and for export marketing. The SBA will guarantee up to 90 percent of a conventional loan in amounts up to $750,000.

Contract Loan: Short-term loans are available to small businesses to finance the costs of labor and materials on contracts for which the proceeds are assignable. Program guarantees up to 90 percent of loans not in excess of $750,000. Qualifying small businesses must be in business for at least 12 calendar months prior to the date of the loan application.

Seasonal Line of Credit Loan: Loans provide short-term working capital to finance seasonal increases in business activities. Program guarantees up to 90 percent of loans not in excess of $750,000. Qualifying business must be in operation for at least one year prior to application.

Pollution Control Loans: Long-term guaranteed loans can be made by conventional financing to small businesses for installation or required pollution control measures. Must be unable to adopt the pollution control measures without undue financial hardship. Maximum guaranteed loan is $1,000,000.

General Contractor Loans: Small general construction contractors may obtain short-term loans or loan guarantees for residential or commercial construction or rehabilitation of property to be sold. The SBA will guarantee up to 90 percent of qualifying loans made by private lenders up to a maximum of $750,000. Direct loans can be up to $150,000.

Energy Business Loan Guarantee: Small businesses that provide certain energy production and conservation services for others may qualify for long-term loans and loan guarantees for start-ups and expansions. Loans and guarantees are made for firms that develop, manufacture, sell, install, or service specific energy measures for others, or firms that provide engineering, architectural, consulting, or other professional services connected with specific energy measures. Guarantee is for up to 90 percent of a loan not in excess of $750,000. Direct loans up to $150,000.

Disaster Recovery Loans: Small businesses located in federally designated disaster areas and suffering property damage or economic losses from the disaster can obtain long-term recovery loans at low interest rates. Property damage loans are limited to 85 percent of the verified damage. Loans for economic losses are for operating capital to meet the business' obligations that could have been made had the disaster not occurred.

Handicapped Assistance Loans: Assists persons who have a physical, mental or emotional disability of a permanent nature which limits the selection of any type of employment for which the person would otherwise be qualified. Direct loans are available for up to $150,000. The interest rate is 3% on these loans.

Surety Bond Guaranty Program: Makes the bonding system more available to small contractors who may be denied access to the system. SBA can guarantee up to 80 percent of surety's loss on a bond that has a maximum in total contract value of up to $1,250,000.

Vietnam-era and Disabled Veterans Loan Program: Provides direct loans to veterans to establish or expand a small business. Funds may be used for working capital or fixed assets. Direct loans for amounts up to $150,000 are available. The interest rate may be fixed or variable.

Bancorp Hawaii SBIC
111 South King Street, Suite 1060
Honolulu, HI 96813
808-521-6411
Small Business Investment Companies (SBICs): The SBA licenses, regulates, and provides financial assistance to privately owned and operated Small Business Investment Companies. SBICs make venture or risk investments by supplying capital and extending unsecured loans and loans not fully collateralized to small enterprises which meet their investment criteria. Financing is made by direct loans and by equity investments.

* Women and Minority Business Assistance

Honolulu Minority Business Development Center
1132 Bishop Street
1st Hawaiian Tower #1000
Honolulu, HI 96813
808-531-6232
Provides management and technical assistance to qualified ethnic minority individuals and firms in the areas of business and financial planning, contract procurement, marketing analyses, 8(a) certification application, general management, bonding, office systems and procedures.

Alu Like Business Development Center — Oahu
1120 Maunakea Street, #273
Honolulu, HI 96817
808-524-1225

Alu Like Molokai Island Center — Molokai, Maui
P.O. Box 392
Kaunakakai, HI 96748
808-533-5393

Alu Like Hawaii Island Center — Hawaii
P.O. Box 606
Hilo, HI 96720
808-961-2625
Offers classroom training, individualized assistance and research facilities to potential, new and expanding businesses to native Hawaiian-owned businesses. An Entrepreneurship Training Project is available which includes an introduction to small business ownership, marketing and financing a small business, and comprehensive planning courses. Also available is a Management and Technical Assistance Project which offers one-to-one assistance on completion of business plans, loan packaging, and start-up business management.

Small Business Administration
Prince Kuhio Federal Building
Room 2213, Box 50207
300 Ala Moana Boulevard
808-541-2990
Honolulu, HI 96850-4981
FAX: 808-541-2976
SBA 8(a) Program - Business Procurement Assistance: Provides federal government contracting opportunities for small businesses owned by socially and economically disadvantaged persons, and assists these businesses to become independently competitive in the normal business environment. SBA monitors all government contracts to assure that a quota of contract work goes to 8(a) businesses. Also provides business management services to these businesses. Business must be approved for program participation prior to receipt of an 8(a) contract.

* Training

Office of Employment and Training — Honolulu
Department of Labor and Industrial Relations
830 Punchbowl Street, Room 316
Honolulu, HI 96813
808-586-9060

WorkHawaii — Oahu
715 South King Street
Suite 500
Honolulu, HI 96813
808-523-4102

Kauai Community College — Kauai
3-1902 Kaumualii Highway
Lihue, HI 96766
808-245-8210

Hawaii State Employment Service — Maui
2064 Wells Street, Suite 108
Wailuku, HI 96793
808-243-5232

Hawaii State Employment Service — Hawaii Island
777 Kilavea Ave.
Kaiko'o Mall
Hilo, HI 96720
808-933-4481
Job Training Partnership Act (JTPA): Provides employers with recruitment, screening, referral, training, 50 percent wage subsidy up to 3 months for on-the-job training. Available to any private employer.

Apprenticeship Division: Works with employers, labor unions, and schools to produce skilled workers through on-the-job training programs. Apprentices are trained in many occupations including construction, welding, auto mechanics and body repair, and the culinary arts.

State Employment Service: Offers job-ready applicants in almost every occupation. Matches workers with jobs and jobs with workers, screens and refers qualified jobseekers, processes job orders through the computerized Job Bank.

Targeted Job Tax Credit (TJTC): A tax break is available to employers hiring people from any of nine targeted categories. A tax credit up to 40 percent may be earned for the first $6,000 in wages during the first year of employment for each qualified employee working 90 days or 120 hours (whichever comes first).

ASSET (Aloha State Specialized Employment Training) Program: Will custom train workers for specialized skills, to meet the needs of businesses, especially high tech companies, that move to Hawaii or expand existing operations.

* Management Consulting and Other Services

Department of Business, Economic Development & Tourism
Grosvenor Center
Mauka Tower, Suite 1900
Honolulu, HI 96813   808-586-2406

Government Marketing Assistance Program: Identifies federal, state and county government activities which purchase goods and services from the private sector. Assists in searching for additional selling opportunities. Explains the procurement policies and procedures of the federal, state and county procurement activities. Two publications are available: *How to Market and Sell to the Federal Government in Hawaii*, and *How to Market and Sell to the State and Counties of Hawaii*.

Small Business Center
The Chamber of Commerce of Hawaii
735 Bishop Street
Honolulu, HI 96813   808-522-8800

Business Service Center: A one-stop source for information on starting a business, business licensing, preparing a business plan, city, state, and federal regulations, plus others. Services include seminars, conferences, and workshops on a wide range of business needs. Assistance in loan package preparation, financial analysis, and profit-loss and financial statements, marketing, business, and procurement consulting.

Entrepreneurship Training Program: The training program is offered quarterly, twice a week for twelve weeks. It covers everything you need to know to start and run your own business, from start-up steps to the actual day-to-day management. There is a cost for this program.

Economic Development Corporation of Honolulu (EDCH)
1001 Bishop Street
Pacific Tower, Suite 735
Honolulu, HI 96813   808-545-4533

EDCH is a private non-profit corporation that actively recruits new business to Honolulu and assists existing businesses to develop import-export markets or expand and diversify.

Hawaii Island Economic Development Board (HIEDB)
First Federal Building
75-5737 Kuakini Highway, #206
Kailua-Kona, HI 96740   808-329-4713
or
1999 Ainaola Drive
Hilo, HI 96724   808-959-0108

HIEDB supports both start-up and established businesses in locating operations on the Island of Hawaii. HIEDB also assists businesses in developing plans, coordinates fixed-asset financing with local financial institutions and the SBA, provides information on permitting, zoning, and other governmental rules and regulations, and provides site selection information.

Kauai Economic Development Board (KEDB)
P.O. Box 1702
Lihue, HI 96766   808-245-6692

A resource center of information. Local entrepreneurs can receive assistance in securing financing, site selection, and state and county permits and regulations for business.

Maui Economic Development Board, Inc. (MEDB)
300 Ohukai Rd., #301
Kihkihei, HI 96753   808-875-2300

Develops programs to enhance Maui's economic diversification and vitality. A Research and Technology Park for new and small businesses is under development. MEDB also conducts conferences on topics of interest to small business owners.

Small Business Hawaii
770 Kapiolani Blvd., #111
Honolulu, HI 96813   808-533-2183

Offers advisory and counseling service for its members. Members have access to a choice of several comprehensive group medical plans. An Annual Small Business Conference is held each year. Also provides a Speakers Bureau, hosts radio and television series. Publishes monthly newsletter and an annual referral director.

Pacific Business Center Program (PBCP)
College of Business Administration
University of Hawaii
2404 Maile Way, A413   808-956-6286
Honolulu, HI 96822   FAX: 808-956-6278

The PBCP makes the resources of the University of Hawaii accessible to small businesses in Hawaii, the Territories of American Samoa and Guam, the Federated States of Micronesia, the Commonwealth of the Northern Mariana Island, the Republic of the Marshall Islands, and the Republic of Palau. Management and technical assistance includes business plans, feasibility studies, facilitating joint ventures, identifying sources of equipment and suppliers, loan packaging, market research, and management advice. Counseling and referral services are free to program clients and faculty consultants are available at reasonable rates.

Small Business Administration
Prince Kuhio Federal Building
Room 2213, Box 50207
300 Ala Moana Boulevard   808-541-2990
Honolulu, HI 96850-4981   FAX: 808-541-2976

Small Business Institutes: This program provides personalized consulting services to the small business community. Consulting is provided by senior level business students, guided by a faculty advisor. Assistance in business plan preparation, marketing research, market planning, accounting, and seminars are provided.
University Locations:
Hawaii Pacific University
Maui Community College
University of Hawaii - Hilo
University of Hawaii - Manoa

* Small Business Development Centers
The following offices offer free and fee-based services to new and expanding businesses:

Lead Center:
Hawaii Small Business Development Center
University of Hawaii at Hilo
523 West Lanikaula Street   808-933-3515
Hilo, HI 96720-4091   FAX: 808-933-3683

Hilo: Small Business Development Center - Big Island, University of Hawaii at Hilo, 523 W. Lanikaula Street, Hilo, HI 96720-4091, 808-933-3515.

Lihue: Small Business Development Center - Kauai, Kauai Community College, 3-1901 Kaumualii Highway, Lihue, HI 96766-9591, 808-246-1748.

Kihei: Small Business Development Center - Maui, Maui Research and Technology Center, 590 Lipoa Parkway, Kihei, HI 96753, 808-875-2402.

Honolulu: Small Business Development Center - Oahu, Business Action Center, 1130 N. Nimitz Highway, Suite A-254, Honolulu, HI 96817, 808-545-7726.

Idaho

* General Information

Idaho Department of Commerce
Economic Development Division
700 West State Street
State House Mail   208-334-2470
Boise, ID 83720-2700   FAX: 208-334-2631
  Small Business Advocate: Assistance in cutting bureaucratic red tape. Information and expertise in dealing with state, federal, and local agencies.

* Financing

Idaho Department of Commerce
Economic Development Division
700 West State Street, Room 108
Boise, ID 83720   208-334-2470
  Industrial Revenue Bonds (IRBs): Industrial Revenue Bonds allow Idaho businesses to borrow money at tax-exempt interest rates, up to $10 million, which are significantly lower than conventional rates. Fixed asset financing of land, buildings, machinery and equipment used in manufacturing, production, processing or assembly. A local public corporation issues bonds to finance the project. IRB's for small project's, $200,000 to $1 million, can be done similar to a commercial loan. Bonds over $1 million may find lower cost financing in the bond market (with letter of credit).

  Community Development Block Grants: Available to cities and counties for the commercial rehabilitation of existing buildings or structures used for business, commercial or industrial purposes. Grants of up to $500,000 can be made. Every $10,000 of grant funds invested must create at least one full-time job and at least 51 percent of the jobs created must be for low and moderate-income families. Industrial site development such as site preparation, construction of water and sewer facilities, access roads, railroad spurs, etc.

Small Business Administration (SBA)
1020 Main Street
Suite 290   208-334-1696
Boise, ID 83702-5745   FAX: 208-334-9353
  SBA 7(a) Guaranteed and Direct Loans: Guarantees up to 90 percent of a loan made through a private lender up to $750,000. Can be used for working capital, expand or convert facilities, purchase of machinery and equipment, and land and building. Available only to those unable to obtain a loan from conventional sources. Direct loans are made up to $150,000.

  SBA 504: Provides loans using 50 percent conventional bank financing, 40 percent SBA involvement through Certified Development Companies, and 10 percent owner equity. A fixed-asset loan in amounts up to $750,000. Loan can be used for land and building, construction, machinery and equipment, and renovation/expansion.

  Small Business Research Grants (SBIR): Phase I awards between $20,000 to $50,000 to entrepreneurs to support six months of research on a technical innovation. Phase II grants are an additional $500,000 for development. Private sector investment funds must follow.

  International Trade Loans: Guaranteed long-term loans through private lenders to develop or expand export markets, or to recover from the effects of import competition. Maximum guaranteed loan is $1,000,000 for fixed assets and an additional $250,000 for working capital and/or export revolving line of credit.

  Export Revolving Line of Credit Loan: Short term financing available to small businesses that are at least one year old. Loans provide working capital to finance the manufacturing or wholesaling of products for export and for export marketing. The SBA will guarantee up to 90 percent of a conventional loan in amounts up to $750,000.

  Contract Loan: Short-term loans are available to small businesses to finance the costs of labor and materials on contracts for which the proceeds are assignable. Program guarantees up to 90 percent of loans not in excess of $750,000. Qualifying small businesses must be in business for at least 12 calendar months prior to the date of the loan application.

  Seasonal Line of Credit Loan: Loans provide short-term working capital to finance seasonal increases in business activities. Program guarantees up to 90 percent of loans not in excess of $750,000. Qualifying business must be in operation for at least one year prior to application.

  Pollution Control Loans: Long-term guaranteed loans can be made by conventional financing to small businesses for installation or required pollution control measures. Must be unable to adopt the pollution control measures without undue financial hardship. Maximum guaranteed loan is $1,000,000.

  General Contractor Loans: Small general construction contractors may obtain short-term loans or loan guarantees for residential or commercial construction or rehabilitation of property to be sold. The SBA will guarantee up to 90 percent of qualifying loans made by private lenders up to a maximum of $750,000. Direct loans can be up to $150,000.

  Energy Business Loan Guarantee: Small businesses that provide certain energy production and conservation services for others may qualify for long-term loans and loan guarantees for start-ups and expansions. Loans and guarantees are made for firms that develop, manufacture, sell, install, or service specific energy measures for others, or firms that provide engineering, architectural, consulting, or other professional services connected with specific energy measures. Guarantee is for up to 90 percent of a loan not in excess of $750,000. Direct loans up to $150,000.

  Disaster Recovery Loans: Small businesses located in federally designated disaster areas and suffering property damage or economic losses from the disaster can obtain long-term recovery loans at low interest rates. Property damage loans are limited to 85 percent of the verified damage. Loans for economic losses are for operating capital to meet the business' obligations that could have been made had the disaster not occurred.

  Handicapped Assistance Loans: Assists persons who have a physical, mental or emotional disability of a permanent nature which limits the selection of any type of employment for which the person would otherwise be qualified. Direct loans are available for up to $150,000. The interest rate is 3% on these loans.

  Surety Bond Guaranty Program: Makes the bonding system more available to small contractors who may be denied access to the system. SBA can guarantee up to 80 percent of surety's loss on a bond that has a maximum in total contract value of up to $1,250,000.

  Vietnam-era and Disabled Veterans Loan Program: Provides direct loans to veterans to establish or expand a small business. Funds may be used for working capital or fixed assets. Direct loans for amounts up to $150,000 are available. The interest rate may be fixed or variable.

Panhandle Area Council, Inc.
11100 Airport Drive
Hayden, ID 83835   208-772-0584

Clearwater Economic Development Association
1626 B Sixth Avenue North
Lewiston, ID 83501   208-746-0015

Treasure Valley Certified Development Corporation/
Ida-Ore Planning and Development Association
10624 W. Executive
Boise, ID 83704   208-322-7033

Region IV Development Corporation/
Region IV Development Association
P.O. Box 1844
Twin Falls, ID 83303   208-736-3064

Eastern Idaho Development Corporation
Southeast Idaho Council of Governments
ISU Business & Technology Center
1651 Alvin Ricken Drive
Pocatello, ID 83201   208-233-4032

East Central Idaho Development Company/
East Central Idaho Planning & Development Association
P.O. Box 330
310 N. 2nd E
Rexburg, ID 83440   208-356-4524
    Certified Development Corporations: Contact one of the following six Certified Development Corporation's/Economic Development Districts for information on the SBA 504 Program and Revolving Loan Fund.

    SBA 504 Program: Provides loans using 50 percent conventional bank financing, 40 percent SBA involvement through Certified Development Companies and 10 percent owner equity. A fixed asset loan in amounts up to $750,000. Loan can be used for land and building, construction, machinery and equipment and renovation/expansion.

    Revolving Loan Fund: For business seeking to start up or expand. Loans must have job creation criteria. Some have fixed dollar requirements for each job created. Funding is not available in all counties. Interest rates are generally below prime interest rate. Used most often for loans under $100,000. Can be combined with SBA 7(a) Program.

Community and Business Programs
Farmers Home Administration (FmHA)
3232 Elder
Boise, ID 83705   208-334-1836
    FmHA Business and Industrial Loans: Assistance is provided in the form of loan guarantees. FmHA contracts to reimburse the lender for a maximum of 90 percent loan, but 60-70 percent is typical. Loans are limited to areas outside the boundaries of cities of 50,000 or less. Loans include development or improvement of land, buildings, machinery and equipment. May provide some working capital. Minimum guarantee is $500,000, maximum loan amount is $10 million. Interest rate may be fixed or variable. Hotels, restaurants and recreational business are not eligible. Public facility loans and grants also available for infrastructure development.

Energy Resources Division
Idaho Department of Water Resources
1301 North Orchard
Boise, ID 83720   1-800-334-SAVE (7283) in ID
    Energy Conservation Loans: Loans to businesses for energy conservation improvements to existing buildings, or new construction. Energy savings must have simple payback of less than 10 years. Interest rate of 6 percent term of 5 years. Maximum loan of $50,000.

Economic Development Districts or
Economic Development Administration
304 N. 8th, #441
Boise, ID 83702   208-334-1521
    EDA Loans and Grants: Grants to communities for industrial site development and 80 percent loan guarantees for loans equal to or greater than $600,000 for individual enterprises. One job must be created for every $10,000. Available only to those unable to obtain a loan from conventional sources. Grants to communities for site preparation and construction of water and sewer facilities, access roads, railroad spurs, etc. Frequently combined with other funding sources such as the Community Development Block Grant. Matching funds of varying proportions are required.

Local City Council or Mayor or
Association of Idaho Cities
3314 Grace
Boise, ID 83703   208-344-8594
    Revenue Allocation Financing: (Also known as increment financing) Tax exempt bonds for community development in designated areas. Amount of funding dependent upon increased property values within revenue allocation area. Only available within incorporated cities.

In addition to the government sponsored programs, there are many other financial loan and grant programs available through private institutions and private investors that you may wish to consider. You can obtain details on individual private assistance programs currently being offered by contacting the institutions directly.

* Women and Minority Business Assistance

Disadvantaged Business Enterprise
110 North 27th   208-344-0150
Boise, ID 83702   FAX: 208-343-5321
    This organization is funded by a federal grant. Its purpose is to assist women, minority, and disadvantaged business owners with the application process of becoming certified for federal government contracts.

Small Business Administration (SBA)
1020 Main Street
Suite 290   208-334-1696
Boise, ID 83702-5745   FAX: 208-334-9353
    SBA 8(a) Program - Business Procurement Assistance: Provides federal government contracting opportunities for small businesses owned by socially and economically disadvantaged persons, and assists these businesses to become independently competitive in the normal business environment. SBA monitors all government contracts to assure that a quota of contract work goes to 8(a) businesses. Also provides business management services to these businesses. Business must be approved for program participation prior to receipt of an 8(a) contract.

* Training

State Division of Vocational Education
LBJ Building
650 W. State Street
Suite 324
Boise, ID 83720   208-334-3213
    New Industry Training Program: Provides customized job training for new and expanding industries in the state. Training specialists design, develop and coordinate total training programs at minimal cost to the company. The program has been used to assist primarily manufacturing firms, but no business is discouraged from inquiring about training assistance.

State of Idaho
Department of Employment
317 Main Street
Boise, ID 83735   208-334-6100
    Job Training Partnership Act (JTPA): Provides employers with recruitment, screening, referral, training, 50 percent wage subsidy up to 3 months for on-the-job training. Available to any private employer.

* Management Consulting and Other Services

Idaho Department of Commerce
Economic Development Division
700 West State Street
State House Mail   208-334-2470
Boise, ID 83720-2700   FAX: 208-334-2631
    International Business Development Division: Assists local firms in exporting their manufactured, agricultural and service goods. Provides export firms with information on foreign market opportunities.

    Idaho Business Network: Assists small businesses through the process to obtain procurement contracts from federal, state and large private business.

    Division of Tourism Development: Provides training for Idaho hospitality service workers. This office also provides marketing and promotion assistance for businesses involved in tourism.

    Idaho Film Bureau: Promotes Idaho as a location for filming.

State Money – Illinois

Small Business Administration
1020 Main Street
Suite 290
Boise, ID 83702-5745

208-334-1696
FAX: 208-334-9353

Small Business Institutes: This program provides personalized consulting services to the small business community. Consulting is provided by senior level business students, guided by a faculty advisor. Assistance in business plan preparation, marketing research, market planning, accounting, and seminars are provided.
University Locations:
Boise State University
College of Southern Idaho
Idaho State University
Lewis Clark State College
University of Idaho

* Small Business Development Centers

The following offices offer free and fee-based services to new and expanding businesses:

Lead Center:
Idaho Small Business Development Center
Boise State University
College of Business
1910 University Drive
Boise, ID 83725

208-385-1640
FAX: 208-385-3877

Hayden: Small Business Development Center, Panhandle Area Council, 11100 Airport Drive, Hayden, ID 83835, 208-772-0587; FAX: 208-772-6196.

Idaho Falls: Idaho State University, Small Business Development Center, 2300 North Yellowstone, Idaho Falls, ID 83401, 208-523-1087; FAX: 208-523-1049.

Lewiston: Lewis-Clark State College, Small Business Development Center, 8th Avenue and 6th Street, Lewiston, ID 83501, 208-799-2465; FAX: 208-799-2831.

Pocatello: Idaho State University, Small Business Development Center, 1651 Alvin Ricken Drive, Pocatello, ID 83201, 208-232-4921; FAX: 208-233-0268; 1-800-232-4921.

Sandpoint: Panhandle Area Council, Small Business Development Center, Box 724, Sandpoint, ID 83864, 208-263-4073; FAX: 208-263-1911.

Twin Falls: College of Southern Idaho, Small Business Development Center, Region IV, P.O. Box 1844, Twin Falls, ID 83303, 208-733-9554, ext. 477; FAX: 208-734-6592.

Illinois

* General Information

Illinois Department of Commerce and Community Affairs
State of Illinois Center
100 West Randolph Street
Suite 3-400
Chicago, IL 60601

312-814-7179

One-Stop Permit Center: The Small Business Hotline is a "one-stop shop" for small business information. It offers quick, personalized answers to business owners' questions. Provides assistance in complying with government regulations by offering one-stop access to state permits and licenses, business assistance programs. Will provide you with a start-up packet which is specifically tailored to the business, and includes state tax forms and licensing information.

Small Business Advocate: 312-814-6648
Assistance in cutting bureaucratic red tape. Information and expertise in dealing with state, federal, and local agencies. Targets business populations such as minorities, women, start-ups and home based enterprises, providing, or referring to the appropriate technical, management and/or financial assistance program.

* Financing

Illinois Department of Commerce and Community Affairs
State of Illinois Center
100 West Randolph Street, Suite 3-400
Chicago, IL 60601

312-814-7179

In addition to programs listed below, *The Economic Development Resource Catalog* is available which provides financing programs that are available to Illinois communities and local governments.

Specific telephone numbers are located next to the program where applicable. If not noted, contact the above number.

Build Illinois Small Business Micro Loan Program: Provides direct financing at below-market interest rates in cooperation with private sector lenders. Money can be used for the same purposes as the SBD Loan Program above. Maximum amount to be loaned is $100,000.

Farmers Home Administration Business and Industrial Loan Program: Loan Guarantees in order to create or retain jobs in rural areas. Funds can be used for land and buildings, machinery and equipment, working capital. Guarantees from $500,000 to $10 million. Eligible business are those operating in areas where population density is less than 100 persons per square mile, and not in cities of 40,000 persons or more. Encourages loans which would not otherwise be made.

Equity Investment Fund: Provides financing to technology-based companies with significant potential for job creation. Funds can be used for real estate, machinery, equipment, working capital, organizational expenses, research and development costs. Can finance up to one-third of the total project cost with a maximum of $250,000.

Business Innovation Fund: Provides financing for technology-driven projects which might not attract traditional lenders or venture capitalists. Provides financial aid to start-up ventures which are in early to middle stage development and have a proprietary product or service. Aid up to $100,000 is offered for projects matched with private resources. Repayment is on a royalty basis when product is developed and sold in the marketplace.

Energy Conservation Interest Write-Down Grant Program: Provides direct grants to pre-pay loan interest for the purpose of reducing borrowing costs in cooperation with private sector lenders. Provides 100 percent of the total loan interest costs or a maximum of $10,000. Grant is based on the term of the loan, or the first five years of the loan, whichever is less. Purpose of the program is to help small businesses retrofit existing buildings and/or equipment with new energy efficient items. Money can be used for upgrading existing structures or equipment; insulation; meter improvement; efficient windows and lighting fixtures, HVAC systems, heat pumps, and use of hot water. The business must get an approved loan from an Illinois lending institution before applying for the grant.

Small Business Innovation and Research Grant Program (SBIR): SBIR federal grants finance research and development of small companies desiring to participate in government research. Money can be used for research and analytical efforts of the firm and costs for consultants and subcontractors. SBIR can help build scientific and technical leadership, attract other sources of funding, and augment research and development.

Illinois Fixed-Rate Financing Fund: Links federal, state, and private financing by using public finds in combination with the Small Business Administration SBA 7(a) Guaranteed Loan Program, bank funds, and equity.

Revolving Loan Program: Administered jointly by community action agencies and DCCA links private and public financing. Money can be used for fixed assets, and working capital. Average loan is $50,000. A minimum of one job must be created for and filled for each $3,000-$5,000 of CSBG investment.

Cook County Economic Development Revolving Loan Fund:
Provides financing to businesses located within Cook County, outside the City of Chicago and several other large cities. Funds can be used for real property acquisition; acquisition, construction, or rehabilitation of commercial or industrial buildings and other improvements; machinery and equipment acquisition and installation; and working capital. Loan amounts between $25,000 and $300,000 are available at an interest rate of

one-half of the prime rate. Must create and retain jobs for low and moderate-income persons. At least one new job must be created for every $10,000 in funds, or one job must be retained for every $5,000.

Illinois Export Development Authority (IEDA): IEDA was created to provide export financing to small and medium-sized business. They have the authority to issue $1 million in bonds to fund export loans through commercial banks, including loans for pre-export activities. Financing is available in the form of short term loans which can be arranged through the IEDA and a local bank or other financial institution. Money can be used for pre-shipment financing -- working capital to produce goods or services, post-shipment financing -- to allow the exporter to sell the goods or services at competitive prices and terms. At least 25 percent of the final value of the goods or services must be produced in Illinois.

Export Import Bank Credit Insurance: Insurance program available through ExIm Bank for exports who grant short-term credit to foreign buyers. The insurance protects exporters who grant credit for up to 90 percent of commercial losses and 100 percent of political losses.

ExIm Working Capital Guarantee: Designated banks may apply for delegated authority under this program. This allows the banks to guarantee up to $300,000 without prior Eximbank approval. The guarantees cover working capital loans for export activity.

Technology Challenge Grant Program: Program is intended to find new ways to keep businesses competitive in the world marketplace. Grants may be used to respond to unique opportunities for which no other source of funding is available or as awards for exemplary and outstanding research. The Governor's Science Advisor and a private sector coalition of scientists will provide guidance on the types of projects to be financed.

Technology Investment Program: Provides a source of funding for new and existing firms which need to research and develop new products, processes or technologies to improve their productivity. Program will provide equity type investments, in qualified securities, or up to $500,000 or 50 percent of a project, whichever is less.

Marketing Staff   312-814-6649
Build Illinois Small Business Development Loan Program: Provides direct financing for small businesses at below-market interest rates in cooperation with private sector lenders for expansion and subsequent job creation or retention. Purpose of the program is to help small businesses create or retain jobs and assist in providing businesses with the opportunity to expand. Money can be used for acquisition of land and buildings, construction, renovation or leasehold improvements, purchase of machinery and equipment, and inventory and working capital. Loans do not exceed 25 percent of a project. Maximum amount for any one business project is $750,000. One job must be created or retained for every $3,000 loaned. 55 percent-80 percent conventional financing, 10-25 percent Small Business Development Loan Program, 10-20 percent owner equity.

Community Services Block Grant Business Loan Programs
(CSBG)   312-917-6649
CSBG funding is to make affordable, long term , fixed-rate financing available to small businesses which are starting or expanding in Illinois and creating employment opportunity for low-income workers.

International Business Division   312-814-7164
International Finance Assistance Programs:
Office of Export Development Finance: Assists exporters to secure financing sources and to expedite such financing. Provides counseling on state and federal resources and helps match exports with financiers and credit insurance organizations. Also assists in assembly of loan packages and issues related to export financing.

Enterprise Zone Program   312-785-6148
Purpose of the program is to stimulate economic growth and neighborhood revitalization at the local level. Numerous state incentives are offered to encourage companies to locate or expand in enterprise zones. Local units of government typically offer additional incentives to further encourage economic growth and investment in the local enterprise zone.

Illinois Development Finance Authority IDFA)
2 North LaSalle Street, Suite 980
Chicago, IL 60602   312-793-5586

Industrial Revenue Bonds: Provide tax exempt low interest loans for manufacturers and first time farmers. Funds can be used for purchase of land, manufacturing machinery and equipment, facility construction, construction-related charges, and purchase of used buildings. Minimum loan amount $500,000, maximum is $10 million.

Illinois Venture Capital Fund: Provides seed capital for enterprises seeking to develop and test new products, processes, technologies and inventions.

Direct Loan Program: IDFA provides supplemental financing for small and medium-sized businesses undertaking a fixed-asset project which will result in increase employment opportunities. Can finance up to 30 percent of a fixed asset project, not to exceed $200,000.

Employee Ownership Assistance Act: Designed to encourage employees of plants which are about to be closed to acquire the facility and operate it as an employee-owned business. The program can provide small grants to fund feasibility studies and direct loans for up to 50 percent of the acquisition cost.

Small Business Administration (SBA)
500 West Madison, Suite 1250   312-353-4528
Chicago, IL 60661-2511   FAX: 312-886-5108
SBA (7a) Guaranteed and Direct Loans: Guarantees up to 90 percent of a loan made through a private lender up to $750,000. Can be used for working capital, expand or convert facilities, purchase of machinery and equipment, and land and building. Available only to those unable to obtain a loan from conventional sources. Direct loans are made up to $150,000.

SBA 504: Provides loans using 50 percent conventional bank financing, 40 percent SBA involvement through Certified Development Companies, and 10 percent owner equity. A fixed-asset loan in amounts up to $750,000. Loan can be used for land and building, construction, machinery and equipment, and renovation/expansion.

Small Business Research Grants (SBIR): Phase I awards between $20,000 to $50,000 to entrepreneurs to support six months of research on a technical innovation. Phase II grants are an additional $500,000 for development. Private sector investment funds must follow.

International Trade Loans: Guaranteed long-term loans through private lenders to develop or expand export markets, or to recover from the effects of import competition. Maximum guaranteed loan is $1,000,000 for fixed assets and an additional $250,000 for working capital and/or export revolving line of credit.

Export Revolving Line of Credit Loan: Short term financing available to small businesses that are at least one year old. Loans provide working capital to finance the manufacturing or wholesaling of products for export and for export marketing. The SBA will guarantee up to 90 percent of a conventional loan in amounts up to $750,000.

Contract Loan: Short-term loans are available to small businesses to finance the costs of labor and materials on contracts for which the proceeds are assignable. Program guarantees up to 90 percent of loans not in excess of $750,000. Qualifying small businesses must be in business for at least 12 calendar months prior to the date of the loan application.

Seasonal Line of Credit Loan: Loans provide short-term working capital to finance seasonal increases in business activities. Program guarantees up to 90 percent of loans not in excess of $750,000. Qualifying business must be in operation for at least one year prior to application.

Pollution Control Loans: Long-term guaranteed loans can be made by conventional financing to small businesses for installation or required pollution control measures. Must be unable to adopt the pollution control measures without undue financial hardship. Maximum guaranteed loan is $1,000,000.

General Contractor Loans: Small general construction contractors may obtain short-term loans or loan guarantees for residential or commercial construction or rehabilitation of property to be sold. The SBA will guarantee up to 90 percent of qualifying loans made by private lenders up to a maximum of $750,000. Direct loans can be up to $150,000.

Energy Business Loan Guarantee: Small businesses that provide certain energy production and conservation services for others may qualify for long-term loans and loan guarantees for start-ups and expansions. Loans and guarantees are made for firms that develop, manufacture, sell, install, or service specific energy measures for others, or firms that provide engineering, architectural, consulting, or other professional services connected with specific energy measures. Guarantee is for up to 90 percent of a loan not in excess of $750,000. Direct loans up to $150,000.

Disaster Recovery Loans: Small businesses located in federally designated disaster areas and suffering property damage or economic losses from the disaster can obtain long-term recovery loans at low interest rates. Property damage loans are limited to 85 percent of the verified damage. Loans for economic losses are for operating capital to meet the business' obligations that could have been made had the disaster not occurred.

Handicapped Assistance Loans: Assists persons who have a physical, mental or emotional disability of a permanent nature which limits the selection of any type of employment for which the person would otherwise be qualified. Direct loans are available for up to $150,000. The interest rate is 3% on these loans.

Surety Bond Guaranty Program: Makes the bonding system more available to small contractors who may be denied access to the system. SBA can guarantee up to 80 percent of surety's loss on a bond that has a maximum in total contract value of up to $1,250,000.

Vietnam-era and Disabled Veterans Loan Program: Provides direct loans to veterans to establish or expand a small business. Funds may be used for working capital or fixed assets. Direct loans for amounts up to $150,000 are available. The interest rate may be fixed or variable.

ANB Venture Corporation
33 North LaSalle Street
Chicago, IL 60690   312-855-1554

Alpha Capital Venture Partners, LP
Three First National Plaza, 14th Floor
Chicago, IL 60602   312-372-1556

Business Ventures, Inc.
20 North Wacker Drive, Suite 1741
Chicago, IL 60606   312-346-1580

Continental Illinois Venture Corporation
209 South LaSalle Street
Mail: 231 South LaSalle Street
Chicago, IL 60693   312-828-8023

First Capital Corporation of Chicago
Three First National Plaza, Suite 1330
Chicago, IL 60670   312-732-5400

Heller Equity Capital Corporation
500 West Monroe Street
Chicago, IL 60661   312-441-7200

Walnut Capital Corporation
Two North LaSalle Street, Suite 2410
Chicago, IL 60602   312-346-2033

Small Business Investment Companies (SBICs): The SBA licenses, regulates, and provides financial assistance to privately owned and operated Small Business Investment Companies. SBICs make venture or risk investments by supplying capital and extending unsecured loans and loans not fully collateralized to small enterprises which meet their investment criteria. Financing is made by direct loans and by equity investments.

Tax Credits

Illinois Department of Revenue   217-782-3128
State Investment Credit: Investment tax credit against Illinois' Personal Property Replacement Income Tax for purchases of property, including buildings, used in manufacturing, mining, or retail businesses.

State Investment and Jobs Credits: Tax credits against Illinois' Personal Property Replacement Income Tax for purchases of property, including buildings, used in manufacturing, mining or retail businesses if the base employment of the firm has increased at least one percent over the preceding year. This ta.. credit benefits those employers who place new property in service and also increases their employment.

Training Expenses Credit: An income tax credit of 1.6 percent of qualified educational or vocational training costs accrued or paid for employee training in semi-technical, technical, semi-skilled or skilled fields.

* Women and Minority Business Assistance

Illinois Department of Commerce and Community Affairs
State of Illinois Center
100 West Randolph Street, Suite 3-400
Chicago, IL 60601   312-814-7179
Minority Business Assistance: Provides assistance in the areas of management, operations, finance and procurement opportunities in the government and private sector. Conferences, workshops, networking and referral to other appropriate and available resources. Will assist in reviewing business plans, Small Business Administration 8(a) applications, and with federal and state loan information.

Women's Business Advocate: The Women's Business Advocate acts as a liaison between business owners and government agencies to serve as an advocate on the behalf of women entrepreneurs. Programs included are a business calendar of events, an extensive mailing list of women entrepreneurs, conferences. The Women's Business Development Center and The Neighborhood Institute (see Small Business Development Centers-Chicago below) offer women business owners assistance in all phases of business development.

Minority Business Advocate:
Minority Business Development Program: Acts as an advocate for minority businesses with the state government. Encourages government procurement efforts. Can assist in identifying both public and private capital funding sources and bonding assistance for minority businesses.

Minority and Women Business Loan Program: Provides long term, fixed rate direct financing to small business at below-market rates for loans from $5,000 to $50,000. One job must be created or retained for each $5,000 of the Minority and Women Business Loan funds utilized. Funds can be used for lease or purchase of land and building, construction or renovation of fixed assets, purchase and installation of machinery and equipment,and working capital.

Minority and Female Business Enterprise Centers: Located in Chicago and Springfield, these centers offer hands-on assistance and information regarding current or future state bid contracts.

Illinois Minority and Female Business Enterprise Program: Conducts Matchmaker Conferences to connect vendors with state and local purchasing agents.

Small Business Administration (SBA)
500 West Madison, Suite 1250   312-353-4528
Chicago, IL 60661-2511   FAX: 312-886-5108
SBA (8a) Program - Business Procurement Assistance: Provides federal government contracting opportunities for small businesses owned by socially and economically disadvantaged persons, and assists these businesses to become independently competitive in the normal business environment. SBA monitors all government contracts to assure that a quota of contract work goes to 8a) businesses. Also provides business management services to these businesses. Business must be approved for program participation prior to receipt of an 8a) contract.

* Training

Division of Job Training Programs
Illinois Department of Commerce and Community Affairs
620 E. Adams Street
Springfield, IL 62701
Industrial Training Program   217-785-6284
Designed to assist new and expanding industries and increases the skills of

new or existing employees. Assistance in the firm of direct reimbursement from state government for a percentage of costs incurred while training new or existing employees can be awarded to any manufacturing firm or other major employer that is locating, expanding or retooling in Illinois. Reimbursable costs may include training wages and benefits, training materials, instructor wages and benefits and instruction materials. Some administrative expenses may also qualify for reimbursement.

Job Training Partnership Act 217-785-6005
Provides employers with recruitment, screening, referral, training, 50 percent wage subsidy up to 3 months for on-the-job training. Available to any private employer.

* Management Consulting and Other Services

Illinois Department of Commerce and Community Affairs
State of Illinois Center
100 West Randolph Street, Suite 3-400
Chicago, IL 60601 312-814-7179
Illinois Product and Services Exchange Program (IPSE): Builds awareness on the part of small businesses of large business procurement opportunities and encourages large business purchasers to buy from smaller companies. The program connects large firms with smaller local suppliers of goods and services.

Small Business Energy Management Program: Offers a free, on-site energy conservation inspection, computerized energy analysis, and low-cost or no-cost recommendations to help reduce energy waste.

Procurement Assistance Program: Provides hands-on assistance to individual firms seeking state and federal government contracts. Services available through the Procurement Assistance Centers include identifying appropriate federal buying agencies, locating bid opportunities, providing information such as specifications and standards, and explaining the procurement process.

International Trade Assistance Program: Helps small businesses identify specific foreign markets for their goods and services, offers guidance in meeting U.S. government export criteria, and provides linkage with potential foreign investors and joint venture partners. Small businesses will be notified of the annual trade shows and missions organized by the Dept. of Commerce and Community Affairs' International Business Division.

International Business Division 312-814-7166
International Business Services: Trade specialists help develop the productive and efficient overseas network on behalf of Illinois companies. Services provided are International Trade Shows and Missions, Catalog Shows, Individual Technical Assistance, Trade Lead Program, plus others.

Technology Commercialization Centers (TCC): Located across the state at both public and private universities, TCC's provide technical assistance to help small businesses, entrepreneurs and inventors take their ideas from the laboratory to the marketplace. Call the Department of Commerce and Community Affairs for your local TCC.

Small Business Incubator Facilities: Used to nurture fledgling small businesses. Can keep potentially large overhead costs manageable by providing affordable rent and services on a shared basis or on a fee-for-service basis.

Office of Urban Assistance 312-814-6107
Small Business Utility Advocate: The Advocate has the statutory authority to intervene in the rate setting process for electric, gas or telephone prices. Acts as an ombudsman for small business regarding billing or deposit disputes with a public utility. Can also assist small business with energy conservation financing matters.

Industrial Development Support Services:
Springfield 217-785-6167
Industrial Site Assistance: Sites, Buildings and Community Database: Using the computer based inventory, suitable industrial locations can be identified. The Department can quickly search up to 95 factors such as building and site size, ceiling heights, utility and transportation. One page reports can be produced for each site or building selected, together with maps, site plans and photographs.

Bureau of Marketing:
Springfield 217-785-6317
Chicago 312-814-2811
Community Industrial Preparedness Manual: The manual is a detailed guide communities can use in whatever stage of industrial preparedness they are, and it lists the steps communities should take, beginning with the formation of an organization to conduct industrial development programs and ending with suggested ways to prospect for industry. The manual is available to any person, community, or business.

TEL-DCCA Information System 1-800-835-3222
A service which provides a 3-5 minute pre-recorded message on business, local government and community-related topics.

Small Business Administration
500 West Madison
Suite 1250 312-353-4528
Chicago, IL 60661-2511 FAX: 312-886-5108
Small Business Institutes: This program provides personalized consulting services to the small business community. Consulting is provided by senior level business students, guided by a faculty advisor. Assistance in business plan preparation, marketing research, market planning, accounting, and seminars are provided.
University Locations:
Auburn University
Bradley University
Chicago State University
DePaul University
Eastern Illinois University
Elmhurst College
Governors State University
Illinois College
Illinois State University
Lewis University
Millikin University
Monmouth College
National-Louis University
Northeastern Illinois University
Northern Illinois University
Northwestern University
Rockford College
Roosevelt University
Sangamon State University
Southern Illinois University - Edwardsville
Southern Illinois University - Carbondale
Trinity Christian College
University of Illinois - Chicago
University of Illinois - Urbana
Western Illinois University

* Small Business Development Centers
The following offices offer free and fee-based services to new and expanding businesses.

Lead Center:
Illinois Small Business Development Center Network
Dept. of Commerce & Community Affairs
620 East Adams Street, 6th floor 217-524-5856
Springfield, IL 62701 FAX: 217-785-6328

Aurora: Waubonsee Community College/Aurora Campus, SBDC, 5 East Galena Blvd., Aurora, IL 60506, 708-892-3334, Ext. 141.

Carbondale: Southern Illinois University/Carbondale, SBDC, Carbondale, IL 62901, 618-536-2424; FAX: 618-453-5040.

Centralia: Kaskaskia College (Satellite), SBDC, Shattuc Road, Centralia, IL 62801, 618-532-2049.

Chicago: Back of the Yards Neighborhood Council (Sub-Center), SBDC, 1751 West 47th Street, Chicago, IL 60609, 312-523-4419.

Chicago: Greater North Pulaski Economic Development Corp., SBDC, 4054 West North Avenue, Chicago, IL 60639, 312-384-2262.

Chicago: Women's Business Development Center, SBDC, 8 South Michigan, Suite 400, Chicago, IL 60603, 312-853-3477; FAX: 312-853-0145.

Chicago: Olive-Harvey College, SBDC, 10001 South Woodlawn Drive, Chicago, IL 60628, 312-660-4839.

Chicago: Industrial Council of NW Chicago, SBDC, 2023 West Carroll, Chicago, IL 60612, 312-421-3941.

Chicago: Latin American Chamber of Commerce, SBDC, 539 North Kedzie, Suite 11, Chicago, IL 60647, 312-252-5211; FAX: 312-252-7065.

Chicago: Eighteenth Street Development Corp., SBDC, 1839 South Carpenter, Chicago, IL 60608, 312-733-2287.

Chicago: Loop SBDC, DCCA, State of Illinois Ctr, 100 West Randolph, Suite 3-400, Chicago, IL 60601, 312-814-2829; FAX: 312-814-1749.

Crystal Lake: McHenry County College, SBDC, 8900 U.S. Highway 14, Crystal Lake, IL 60012-2761, 815-455-6098; FAX: 815-455-3999.

Danville: Danville Area Community College, SBDC, 28 West North Street, Danville, IL 61832, 217-442-7232.

Decatur: Richland Community College, SBDC, One College Park, Decatur, IL 62521, 217-875-7200, ext. 556.

DeKalb: Northern Illinois University, SBDC, Department of Management, 305 East Locust, DeKalb, IL 60115, 815-753-1403.

Dixon: Sauk Valley College, SBDC, 173 Illinois Route #2, Dixon, IL 61021-9110, 815-288-5605.

Edwardsville: Southern Illinois University/Edwardsville, SBDC, Campus Box 1107, Edwardsville, IL 62026, 618-692-2929; FAX: 618-692-2647.

Elgin: Elgin Community College, SBDC, 1700 Spartan Drive, Elgin, IL 60115, 708-697-1000, ext. 7923.

Evanston: Evanston Business & Technology Center, SBDC, 1840 Oak Ave., Evanston, IL 60201, 708-866-1841; FAX: 708-866-1808.

Freeport: Highland Community College (Satellite), SBDC, 2998 West Pearl City, Freeport, IL 61032-9341, 815-232-1362; FAX: 815-235-6130.

Glen Ellyn: College of DuPage, SBDC, 22nd and Lambert Road, Glen Ellyn, IL 60137, 708-858-2800, ext. 2771.

Grayslake: College of Lake County, SBDC, 19351 West Washington Street, Grayslake, IL 60030, 708-223-3633.

Harrisburg: Southeastern Illinois College (Satellite), SBDC, R.R. #4, College Drive, Harrisburg, IL 62946, 618-252-4411.

Ina: Rend Lake College, SBDC, Route #1, Ina, IL 62846, 618-437-5321, ext. 267.

Joliet: Joliet Junior College, SBDC, Renaissance Center, Room 319, 214 North Ottawa Street, Joliet, IL 60431, 815-727-6544, Ext. 1313.

Kankakee: Kankakee Community College, SBDC, Box 888, River Road, Kankakee, IL 60901, 815-933-0374; FAX: 815-933-0370.

Macomb: Western Illinois University, SBDC, 216 Seal Hall, Macomb, IL 61455, 309-298-1128.

Mattoon: Lake Land College, SBDC, South Route #45, Mattoon, IL 61938-9366, 217-235-3131.

East Moline: Black Hawk College, SBDC, 301 42nd Ave, East Moline, IL 61244, 309-752-9759.

Monmouth: Maple City Business and Technology (Satellite), SBDC, 620 South Main Street, Monmouth, IL 61462, 309-734-4664.

Oglesby: Illinois Valley Community College, SBDC, Building 11, Route 1, Oglesby, IL 61348, 815-223-1740.

Olney: Illinois Eastern Community College, SBDC, 233 East Chestnut, Olney, IL 62450, 618-395-3011.

Palos Hills: Moraine Valley College, SBDC, 10900 South 88th Avenue, Palos Hills, IL 60465, 708-974-5468; FAX: 708-974-0078.

Peoria: Bradley University, SBDC, 141 North Jobst Hall, 1st Floor, Peoria, IL 61625, 309-677-2992; FAX: 309-677-3386.

Rockford: Rock Valley College, SBDC, 1220 Rock Street, Rockford, IL 61102, 815-968-4087; FAX: 815-968-4157.

Springfield: Lincoln Land Community College, SBDC, 200 West Washington, Springfield, IL 62701, 217-524-3060.

East St. Louis: East St. Louis, DCCA, State Office Building, 10 Collinsville, East St. Louis, IL 62201, 618-583-2272; FAX: 618-588-2274.

Ullin: Shawnee College (Satellite), SBDC, Shawnee College Road, Ullin, IL 62992, 618-634-9618.

University Park: Governor's State University, SBDC, University Park, IL 60466, 708-534-3713.

Indiana

* General Information

Small Business Administration
429 N. Pennsylvania #100   317-226-7272
Indianapolis, IN 46204-1873   FAX: 317-226-7259

Small Business Advocate: Assistance in cutting bureaucratic red tape. Information and expertise in dealing with state, federal, and local agencies.

* Financing

Indiana Department of Commerce
One North Capitol
Suite 700
Indianapolis, IN 46204-2288   317-232-8888

Agricultural Development Corporation: Issues tax-exempt revenue bonds for financing agricultural enterprises. May finance farm land, equipment, buildings, improvements and additions, and breeding stock. For some projects being a first-time farmer is required.

Indiana Capital Assistance for Small Enterprises Program: Provides working capital in the form of grants and loans to small business owners.

Industrial Revenue Bonds: Issues tax-exempt bonds for financing industrial development projects. Bonds are payable from project revenues. Projects are generally manufacturing enterprises.

Investment Incentive Program: Provides loans for low-interest loans to expanding to re-locating businesses. Grants or loans are made to eligible cities, towns, and counties which then make the loan to the firm to finance land, or buildings and equipment.

Strategic Development Fund: Program attempts to team up two or more Indiana businesses by offering grant or loan money in the form of matching dollars. Program is designed to foster creativity and cooperation between industrial sectors or regions of the state. Some project ideas include marketing programs, technology deployment, cooperative research, export development programs, apprentice programs.

Dinosaur Building Program Industrial Recovery Site: Designed to rejuvenate large, vacant buildings, usually 20 years or older with at least 300,0000 square feet. Two tax incentives are offer to businesses interested in locating its facility here. One is an inventory tax credit, the other an investment tax credit.

Enterprise Zones: Designed to help revitalize specific distressed areas and to create jobs for zone residents. There are currently fourteen enterprise zones. Through this program there are prime business sites available to meet a wide variety of facility requirements. Some of the tax and financial incentives offered to businesses locating in an enterprise zone are as follows:

Gross Income Tax Exemption: Businesses new to an enterprise zone are exempt from the gross income tax, and all enterprise zone income exceeding the income earned in the zone prior to its designation is exempt from the gross income tax.

Employment Expense Call: Income tax credit for the lesser of 10 percent of resident employee wages or $1,500 per employee.

Inventory Tax Credit: Property tax credit in the amount of depreciable personal tax liability on inventory in an enterprize zone.

Equity Investment Credit: Individual investors receive up to a 30 percent income tax credit for the purpose of equity in start-up or expanding enterprise zone firms.

There are also other tax incentives available for businesses not located in an Enterprise Zone such as **Inventory/Interstate Inventory Tax Exemption,** and **Property Tax Abatement.**

International Trade Development Office:

Foreign Trade Zones (FTZ): An FTZ is a secured area legally outside of U.S. Customs territory. Foreign and domestic goods may enter a zone to be stored, distributed, exhibited, combined with other foreign and domestic products, or used in other manufacturing operations. While the goods are in the FTZ, no U.S. duties are paid on them. FTZ's are located in Indianapolis, South Bend, and Burns International Harbor.

Export Finance Program: Provides short-terms loans for export orders up to a maximum of $500,000. This enables Indiana companies to offer more advantageous terms on letters of credit to foreign companies.

Trade Show Assistance Program: Provides financial assistance to companies planning to attend trade shows overseas. It is designed to help small and medium-sized companies realize their export potential through participation in international trade fair and exhibitions. Companies can be reimbursed for up to $5,000 of the cost directly attributable to the trade show.

International Business Education Program: Provides financial assistance to Indiana businesses seeking marketing analyses, technical information for competitive and marketing assistance or education programs on international issues. Funding is provided to Indiana firms to work with a state university on these programs.

Indiana Statewide Certified Development Corp.
8440 Woodfield Crossing, Suite 315
Indianapolis, IN 46240   317-469-6166
Provides long-term fixed asset financing up to $500,000 in low-interest subordinated mortgages for small businesses.

Corporation for Innovation Development
201 North Illinois Street, Suite 1950
Indianapolis, IN 46204   317-237-2350
Encourages the entrepreneurial spirit through increased access to venture capital. Activities include providing venture capital as well as equity and financing to established industries.

Department of Economic Development
City of Fort Wayne
840 City-County Building
Fort Wayne, IN 46802   219-427-1127
Community Corporation - Ft. Wayne Community Development: Provides financial assistance at low interest rates. Designed to work in conjunction with private financing.

Small Business Administration (SBA)
Finance Division
429 N. Pennsylvania, #100   317-226-7272
Indianapolis, IN 46204-1873   FAX: 317-226-7259
SBA (7a) Guaranteed and Direct Loans: Guarantees up to 90 percent of a loan made through a private lender up to $750,000. Can be used for working capital, expand or convert facilities, purchase of machinery and equipment, and land and building. Available only to those unable to obtain a loan from conventional sources. Direct loans are made up to $150,000.

SBA 504: Provides loans using 50 percent conventional bank financing, 40 percent SBA involvement through Certified Development Companies, and 10 percent owner equity. Fixed-asset loans are available in amounts up to $750,000. The loan can be used for land and building, construction, machinery and equipment, and renovation/expansion.

Small Business Research Grants (SBIR): Phase I awards between $20,000 to $50,000 to entrepreneurs to support six months of research on a technical innovation. Phase II grants are an additional $500,000 for development. Private sector investment funds must follow.

International Trade Loans: Guaranteed long-term loans through private lenders to develop or expand export markets, or to recover from the effects of import competition. Maximum guaranteed loan is $1,000,000 for fixed assets and an additional $250,000 for working capital and/or export revolving line of credit.

Export Revolving Line of Credit Loan: Short term financing available to small businesses that are at least one year old. Loans provide working capital to finance the manufacturing or wholesaling of products for export and for export marketing. The SBA will guarantee up to 90 percent of a conventional loan in amounts up to $750,000.

Contract Loan: Short-term loans are available to small businesses to finance the costs of labor and materials on contracts for which the proceeds are assignable. Program guarantees up to 90 percent of loans not in excess of $750,000. Qualifying small businesses must be in business for at least 12 calendar months prior to the date of the loan application.

Seasonal Line of Credit Loan: Loans provide short-term working capital to finance seasonal increases in business activities. Program guarantees up to 90 percent of loans not in excess of $750,000. Qualifying business must be in operation for at least one year prior to application.

Pollution Control Loans: Long-term guaranteed loans can be made by conventional financing to small businesses for installation or required pollution control measures. Must be unable to adopt the pollution control measures without undue financial hardship. Maximum guaranteed loan is $1,000,000.

General Contractor Loans: Small general construction contractors may obtain short-term loans or loan guarantees for residential or commercial construction or rehabilitation of property to be sold. The SBA will guarantee up to 90 percent of qualifying loans made by private lenders up to a maximum of $750,000. Direct loans can be up to $150,000.

Energy Business Loan Guarantee: Small businesses that provide certain energy production and conservation services for others may qualify for long-term loans and loan guarantees for start-ups and expansions. Loans and guarantees are made for firms that develop, manufacture, sell, install, or service specific energy measures for others, or firms that provide engineering, architectural, consulting, or other professional services connected with specific energy measures. Guarantee is for up to 90 percent of a loan not in excess of $750,000. Direct loans up to $150,000.

Disaster Recovery Loans: Small businesses located in federally designated disaster areas and suffering property damage or economic losses from the disaster can obtain long-term recovery loans at low interest rates. Property damage loans are limited to 85 percent of the verified damage. Loans for economic losses are for operating capital to meet the business' obligations that could have been made had the disaster not occurred.

Handicapped Assistance Loans: Assists persons who have a physical, mental or emotional disability of a permanent nature which limits the selection of any type of employment for which the person would otherwise be qualified. Direct loans are available for up to $150,000. The interest rate is 3% on these loans.

Surety Bond Guaranty Program: Makes the bonding system more available to small contractors who may be denied access to the system. SBA can guarantee up to 80 percent of surety's loss on a bond that has a maximum in total contract value of up to $1,250,000.

Vietnam-era and Disabled Veterans Loan Program: Provides direct loans to veterans to establish or expand a small business. Funds may be used for working capital or fixed assets. Direct loans for amounts up to $150,000 are available. The interest rate may be fixed or variable.

1st Source Capital Corporation
100 North Michigan Street
Mail: P.O. Box 1602, South Bend 46634
South Bend, IN 46601   219-236-2180

Circle Ventures, Inc.
26 N. Arsenal Avenue
Indianapolis, IN 46201   317-636-7242
Small Business Investment Companies (SBIC): The SBA licenses, regulates, and provides financial assistance to privately owned and operated Small Business Investment Companies. SBICs make venture or risk investments by supplying capital and extending unsecured loans and loans not fully collateralized to small enterprises which meet their investment criteria. Financing is made by direct loans and by equity investments.

Metro Small Business Assistance Corporation
306 Civic Center Complex
1 N.W. Martin Luther King Blvd.
Evansville, IN 47708   812-426-5857
SBA Loan Guarantees and Direct Loans: Provides technical assistance to implement SBA finance programs.

Indiana Small Business Development Corporation
One North Capital, Suite 1275   317-264-2820
Indianapolis, IN 46204-2026   FAX: 317-264-2806
Enterprise Development Fund: Purpose of the Fund is to make loans to develop local investment pools for seed capital and local opportunity pools to help disadvantaged business and "non-traditional" entrepreneurs with financing.

Small Business Incubator Program: Provides grants available only in economically disadvantages areas, loans, or loan guarantees to community organizations for the purpose of establishing incubators. Funds can be used for the acquisition and renovation of existing facilities, acquisition of equipment, and operating expenses for the first 12 months. Both for-profit and not-for-profit corporations are eligible to participate in the program. Must match any funds provided, demonstrate a market-driven need for an incubator, and agree to provide assistance to incubator tenants. Loans or guarantees may not exceed the lessor of 50 percent of the total eligible project costs or $500,000. Grants may not exceed the lesser of 50 percent of the project costs or $250,000.

Metro Small Business Assistance Corporation
306 Civic Center Complex
1 N.W. Martin Luther King Blvd.
Evansville, IN 47708   812-426-5857
Working Capital Loan Pool: Provides short-term, working capital financing for small businesses in the city of Evansville and unincorporated areas of Vanderburg county.

Greater Bloomington Chamber of Commerce
116 West 6th Street, Suite 100
P.O. Box 1302
Bloomington, IN 47402   812-336-6381
Venture Capital Club of South-Central Indiana: Provides a forum for new and existing businesses to present their case for funding before potential investors at monthly lunch meetings.

Mount Vernon Venture Capital Company
P.O. Box 40177
Indianapolis, IN 46240   317-469-5888
Makes equity-type investments -- normally loans with warrants. Investments are in the $100,000 to $400,000 range. Mainly invest in enterprises that are past start-up.

Heritage Venture Partners II. Ltd.
135 N. Pennsylvania, #2380
Indianapolis, IN 46204   317-635-5696
Makes equity-type investments for a minimum of $400,000. In joint, ventures can make investments of up to $1 million.

CID Venture Partners
201 N. Illinois Street, #1950
Indianapolis, IN 46204   317-237-2350
Makes equity-oriented, direct investments in a wide range of industries and firms in various development stages.

* Women and Minority Business Assistance

Indiana Department of Commerce
Office of Minority and Women Business Development Division
402 W. Washington, #W461
Indianapolis, IN 46204   317-232-3061
Assists small businesses with all phases of development: management and technical assistance, contract bidding and procurement, advocacy, education and training, and financial alternatives.

Business Education Program: Offers information on specific types of businesses and technical aspects of management. Arranges seminars for minority business owners in conjunction with educational institutions.

Financial Information Program: Helps potential businesses prepare financial proposals, performs marketing, site analysis studies, and investigates franchising opportunities.

Procurement Program: Assists minority- and women-owned businesses in seeking government services contracts.

Department of Economic Development
City of Fort Wayne
840 City-County Building
Fort Wayne, IN 46802   219-427-1127
Minority Business Investment Program: Provides financial and management assistance to minority-owned businesses in the Fort Wayne area.

Small Business Administration (SBA)
Finance Division
429 North Pennsylvania, #100   217-226-7272
Indianapolis, IN 46204-1873   FAX: 317-226-7259
SBA 8(a) Program - Business Procurement Assistance: Provides federal government contracting opportunities for small businesses owned by socially and economically disadvantaged persons, and assists these businesses to become independently competitive in the normal business environment. SBA monitors all government contracts to assure that a quota of contract work goes to 8(a) businesses. Also provides business management services to these businesses. Business must be approved for program participation prior to receipt of an 8(a) contract.

* Training

Indiana Department of Commerce
One North Capitol, Suite 700
Indianapolis, IN 46204-2288   317-232-8888
Training for Profit Program: Provides assistance in meeting the upfront costs associated with the training of newly hired employees. Available to existing companies that are expanding and companies in the process of locating in Indiana.

Basic Industry Retraining Programs: Provides essential retraining assistance for the existing manufacturing sector in the utilization of new technology and/or the creation of a new product mix.

Department of Employment and Training Services
10 North Senate

Indianapolis, IN 46204   317-232-7670

Job Training Partnership Act (JTPA): Provides employers with recruitment, screening, referral, training, 50 percent wage subsidy up to 3 months for on-the-job training. Available to any private employer.

Job Service Matching System: A statewide computerized employment network that can put an employer immediately in touch with qualified applicants. Also assists in the screening, testing and selection of employees, using an employer's criteria.

* Management Consulting and Other Services

Inventors and Entrepreneurs Society of Indiana
Purdue University Calumet
P.O. Box 2224
Hammond, IN 46323   219-989-2354

Provides educational support and guidance for inventors and entrepreneurs through monthly seminars.

Indiana Department of Commerce
One North Capitol
Suite 700
Indianapolis, IN 46204-2288   317-232-8888

Energy Policy Office: A consulting service is provided to the industrial sector, at no charge, to help identify problem areas in energy efficiency. The Energy Policy Committee also offers seminars and energy resource development programs.

Small Business Program: Helps small businesses reduce energy costs by providing free Class-A energy audits and energy information.

Federal Marketing Development Division   317-232-8843
Government Marketing Assistance: Provides marketing and technical procurement assistance to Indiana businesses wishing to sell products and services to the federal government or increase their ongoing business in that market. Can identify new markets, obtain specification information, provide a complete list of government contracts available for bidding, assist in the process of bidding and acquiring governmental contracts.

Office of Business Ombudsman   317-232-7304
The Business Ombudsman: Assists businesses in complying with government regulations and in working through a permitting process and helps businesses understand regulatory agency requirements. Serves as a liaison between the small business sector and state agencies.

Business Development Marketing Division   317-232-8888
Serves as the center for information and assistance on expansion of Indiana companies, emerging growth companies, and export assistance.

International Trade Development Office   317-232-3527
Indiana has overseas offices in Canada, China, Japan, Korea, The Netherlands, and Taiwan. These offices can help foreign buyers source Indiana products or identify Indiana companies interested in representation overseas. The Hoosier Hospitality Days is sponsored once a year in which foreign investors and buyers are introduced to communities and products. The *Indiana International* newsletter regularly publishes foreign buyer requests, trade show information, trade leads and features about assistance programs.

Match Maker Program: Developed by the U.S. Department of Commerce to help U.S. firms explore new overseas markets for their products and services. Overseas commercial officers work to identify the best possible "match" for the marketing interest of participating companies.

Agriculture Division   317-232-8770
Rural Development Program: Promotes and assists development of the direct farmer-to-consumer sale of produce by assisting communities in organizing farm markets.

Business Development Division   317-232-8888
Provides assistance and information to firms planning to expand or relocate in Indiana. Tax and site and building selection information, and aid in lining up financial resources is also offered.

Partners in Contracting Corporation
8149 Kennedy Avenue
Highland, IN 46322   219-923-8181

Government Contract Assistance Program: Provides assistance to small firms interested in obtaining federal government contracts.

Small Business Administration
429 N. Pennsylvania, #100   317-226-7272
Indianapolis, IN 46204-1873   FAX: 317-226-7259

Procurement Division: Provides assistance and information on U.S. Government procurement.

Small Business Institutes: This program provides personalized consulting services to the small business community. Consulting is provided by senior level business students, guided by a faculty advisor. Assistance in business plan preparation, marketing research, market planning, accounting, and seminars are provided.
University Locations:
Ball State University
Butler University
Indiana State University
Indiana University - Northwest
Indiana University - Southeast
Indiana University - South Bend
Indiana University - Kokomo
Indiana University - Bloomington
Purdue University - North Central
Purdue University - Anderson
Purdue University - Calumet
Purdue University
Taylor University
University of Evansville
University of Southern Indiana
Valparaiso University

Indiana Small Business Development Corp.
One North Capitol, Suite 1275
Indianapolis, IN 46204-2026   317-264-2820

Encourages and supports the development of enterprises throughout the state by serving as a catalyst for linking prospective entrepreneurs and business owners with the managerial, technical and financial resources necessary to start and successfully operate a new enterprise. Assistance to minority and women in business, government marketing assistance, and an enterprise advisory service which helps entrepreneurs critically examine business concepts and development strategies.

Conferences, seminars, workshops, and forums on various topics are held throughout the year in areas such as Business Planning and Sources of Financing Workshops, an Emerging Business Forum, a Software Entrepreneurs Forum, an Entrepreneurs Day Conference, and the Great Midwest Venture Capital Conference.

Small Business Incubators: There are business incubators available in approximately five cities. Contact the above number if you are interested in becoming a tenant.

Entrepreneurs Alliance
P.O. Box 40609
Indianapolis, IN 46240-0609   317-843-1655

Holds monthly meetings where topics of interest to entrepreneurs are addressed. For further information write to the address given above.

School of Business, Room 510
Indiana State University
Terre Haute, IN 47809   812-237-3232

Center for Research and Management Services: Offers aid for proposal preparation, organizational assessment research in marketing and manufacturing and consultation services through the faculty, Small Business Development Centers, and Small Business Institute Program.

Technology Services Center: Arranges University-business research projects with emphasis on aerospace, manufacturing and construction technology, industrial technology education, electronics and computer technology.

1 City Center #200
Bloomington, IN 47404   1-800-624-8315

Industrial Research Liaison Program: Provides a variety of services to individuals and small businesses. Major programs include:

Grants Program: Special assistance to apply for grants such as advice on proposal writing and pricing. Specializes in Small Business Innovation Research (SBIR) Grant Program.

Partners in Applied Research (PAR): Designed to match your need for information to the expertise of an Indiana University faculty researcher.

Indiana Infonet: A statewide database service available to all Indiana businesses and individuals to provide names of manufacturers, expert consultants, and government procurement opportunities.

1284 Civil Engineering Building G-175
Purdue University
West Lafayette, IN 47907   317-494-6258

Technical Assistance Program (TAP): Provides assistance in implementing new, advanced technologies.

Technical Information Services
Krannert Graduate School of Management
Krannert Bldg., #209
Purdue University
West Lafayette, IN 47907   317-494-9876

Technical Information Services (TIS): Dial-up access into the Engineering Information System, a computerized catalog for the Engineering Library; documents can be ordered online. Dial-up access into the computerized catalog for the entire library system; documents available for photocopy or on a loan basis. In addition, a full information service providing literature searches.

Indiana Business Modernization and Technology Corporation (IBMT)
One North Capital, Suite 925
Indianapolis, IN 46294   317-635-3058

Works with businesses that are developing technologies or products for production purposes. It draws together resources from the public, private and education sectors to foster the development of technology-based research and industry.

* Small Business Development Centers

The following offer free and fee-based services to new and expanding businesses:

Lead Center:
Indiana Small Business Development Center
Economic Development Council
One North Capitol, Suite 420   317-264-6871
Indianapolis, IN 46204   FAX: 317-264-3102

Bloomington: Greater Bloomington Chamber of Commerce, Small Business Development Center, 116 W. 3rd Street, Bloomington, IN 47404, 812-339-8937.

Columbus: Columbus Enterprise Development Center, Inc., Small Business Development Center, 4920 North Warren Drive, Columbus, IN 47203, 812-372-6480; FAX: 812-372-0228.

Evansville: Evansville Chamber of Commerce, Small Business Development Center, 100 N.W. Second Street, Suite 200, Evansville, IN 47708, 812-425-7232.

Fort Wayne: Northeast Indiana Business Assistance Corporation, Small Business Development Center, 1830 West Third Street, Fort Wayne, IN 46803, 219-426-0040.

Jeffersonville: Hoosier Valley Economic Opportunity Corporation, Small Business Development Center, 1613 E. 8th Street, Jeffersonville, IN 47130, 812-288-6451.

Indianapolis: Indiana University, Small Business Development Center, 1317 West Michriver, Indianapolis, IN 46202, 317-274-8200.

Kokomo: Kokomo-Howard County Chamber of Commerce, Small Business Development Center, P.O. Box 731, Kokomo, IN 46903, 317-457-5301.

Lafayette: Greater Lafayette Progress, Inc., Small Business Development Center, 122 N. Third, Lafayette, IN 47901, 317-0457-5301.

Madison: Madison Area Chamber of Commerce, Small Business Development Center, 301 East Main Street, Madison, IN 47250, 812-265-3127.

Merrillville: Northwest Indiana Forum, Inc., Small Business Development Center, 8002 Utah Street, Merrillville, IN 46410, 219-942-3496; FAX: 219-942-5806.

Muncie: Muncie-Delaware County Chamber, Small Business Development Center, 401 South High Street, Muncie, IN 47308, 317-284-8144; FAX: 317-741-5489.

Richmond: Richmond Area Chamber of Commerce, Small Business Development Center, 33 South 7th Street, Richmond, IN 47374, 317-962-2887.

South Bend: South Bend Chamber of Commerce, Small Business Development Center, 300 North Michigan Street, South Bend, IN 46601, 219-282-4350.

Terre Haute: Indiana State University, Small Business Development Center, School of Business, Terre Haute, IN 47809, 812-237-3232.

Iowa

* General Information

Iowa Department of Economic Development
200 East Grand Avenue
Des Moines, IA 50309   515-242-4700

Small Business Division
Iowa Department of Economic Development
200 East Grand Avenue
Des Moines, IA 50309   515-242-4899

Small Business Advocate: Assistance in cutting bureaucratic red tape. Information and expertise in dealing with state, federal, and local agencies.

* Financing

Department of Economic Development
200 East Grand Avenue
Des Moines, IA 50309

Bureau of State Programs:
Division of Job Training   515-242-4819
Self Employment Loan Program (SELP): SELP offers low-interest loans up to $5,000 to low-income Iowans for self-employment ventures.

Small Business Loan Program: Provides limited financing to help new and expanding businesses through the sale of tax-exempt bonds and notes. Rates vary with the level of risk. Maximum loan amount is $10 million.

Bureau of Business Grants and Loans   515-242-4819
Division of Financial Assistance:
Community Economic Betterment Account (CEBA): Cities, counties or community colleges are eligible to apply on behalf of businesses that are expanding or are new business ventures in Iowa that increase the number of quality jobs in the state. Funds may be used to acquire and/or improve land and buildings, purchase machinery and equipment, working capital, and related projects costs. Loans are generally between $50,00 and $250,000.

Venture Capital Resources Fund: Provides an additional source in the way of equity financing of capital for small businesses that cannot get the full amount of financing needed from conventional sources for either a new or existing business. Loans range between $100,000 to $1 million.

Capital Access Program: Emphasis of this program is the revitalization of the livestock industry in Iowa. Assistance is provided in the form of loan guarantees and will vary from 4-1/2 percent to 10-1/2 percent depending on the characteristics of each loan.

Natural Rural Development Loan Program: Program is designed to assist in the revitalization and diversification of Iowa's rural economy. Available to any small business that locates or expands operations in a community with a population less than 20,000. Preference is given to light manufacturing, value added process projects, and/or projects that diversify the rural economy to emphasize development in areas other than agriculture. Loans are generally between $50,000 and $300,000. A Business Plan is necessary.

Community Development Block Grant:
Economic Development Set-Aside   515-242-4831
Any city under 50,000 population and all counties are eligible to apply on behalf of businesses that are expanding or are new business ventures in Iowa and who will increase the number of employment opportunities and increase the opportunity for low and moderate income individuals to find employment. Funds may be used to acquire and/or improve land and buildings, purchase machinery and equipment, working capital, and related project costs. Loans are generally between $25,000 and $200,000.

Community Development Block Grants:
Public Facilities Set-Aside   515-242-4825
Public Facilities Set-Aside funds assist with local infrastructure improvements such as sewer, water, street, and rail construction that support economic development. Priority given to projects creating the most jobs, those involving funds from local and private sources. Project must show benefit to low and moderate income persons usually in job creation. Cities under 50,000 population and all counties may apply. Project must support a specific identified development opportunity.

Bureau of Housing and Community Development   515-242-4825
Division of Financial Assistance:
Community Development Block Grants: Available to cities and counties for the commercial rehabilitation of existing buildings or structures used for business, commercial, or industrial purposes principally for low and moderate income families.

Export Trade Assistance Program   515-242-4742
International Bureau:
Export Trade Assistance Program: Promotes the development of international trade activities and opportunities for exporters in the state through encouraging increased participation in overseas trade shows and trade missions. Eligibility includes being a resident or an entity with corporate offices in Iowa employing fewer than 500 individuals, exhibit products or services or samples of Iowa manufactured, processed or value-added products in conjunction with a foreign trade show or trade mission. Up to 75 percent of expenses directly attributed to cost of participating in a trade show or trade mission may be reimbursed, not to exceed $5,000 per event with a limit of three events in state's fiscal year.

President, Iowa Product Development Corp. (IPDC)
200 East Grand Avenue
Des Moines, IA 50309   515-242-4860
IPDC was created to stimulate and encourage business development based on new products by the infusion of financial aid for invention and innovation where such aid is not reasonably available from commercial sources. Applicant may be either a new or existing business and must represent a venture that will maintain an Iowa presence, with the manufacturing of the product conducted in Iowa. Eligible projects should be advanced beyond the theoretic state and be readily capable of commercialization. A business plan will be necessary.

Small Business Administration (SBA)
210 Walnut, Room 749   515-284-4422
Des Moines, IA 50309   FAX: 515-284-4572
SBA 7(a) Guaranteed and Direct Loans: Guarantees up to 90 percent of a loan made through a private lender up to $750,000. Can be used for working capital, expand or convert facilities, purchase of machinery and equipment, and land and building. Available only to those unable to obtain a loan from conventional sources. Direct loans are made up to $150,000.

SBA 504: Provides loans using 50 percent conventional bank financing, 40 percent SBA involvement through Certified Development Companies, and 10 percent owner equity. Fixed-asset loans are available in amounts up to $750,000. The loan can be used for land and building, construction, machinery and equipment, and renovation/expansion.

Small Business Research Grants (SBIR): Phase I awards between $20,000 to $50,000 to entrepreneurs to support six months of research on a technical innovation. Phase II grants are an additional $500,000 for development. Private sector investment funds must follow.

International Trade Loans: Guaranteed long-term loans through private lenders to develop or expand export markets, or to recover from the effects of import competition. Maximum guaranteed loan is $1,000,000 for fixed assets and an additional $250,000 for working capital and/or export revolving line of credit.

Export Revolving Line of Credit Loan: Short term financing available to small businesses that are at least one year old. Loans provide working capital to finance the manufacturing or wholesaling of products for export and for export marketing. The SBA will guarantee up to 90 percent of a conventional loan in amounts up to $750,000.

Contract Loan: Short-term loans are available to small businesses to finance the costs of labor and materials on contracts for which the proceeds are assignable. Program guarantees up to 90 percent of loans not in excess of $750,000. Qualifying small businesses must be in business for at least 12 calendar months prior to the date of the loan application.

Seasonal Line of Credit Loan: Loans provide short-term working capital to finance seasonal increases in business activities. Program guarantees up to 90 percent of loans not in excess of $750,000. Qualifying business must be in operation for at least one year prior to application.

Pollution Control Loans: Long-term guaranteed loans can be made by conventional financing to small businesses for installation or required pollution control measures. Must be unable to adopt the pollution control measures without undue financial hardship. Maximum guaranteed loan is $1,000,000.

General Contractor Loans: Small general construction contractors may obtain short-term loans or loan guarantees for residential or commercial construction or rehabilitation of property to be sold. The SBA will guarantee up to 90 percent of qualifying loans made by private lenders up to a maximum of $750,000. Direct loans can be up to $150,000.

Energy Business Loan Guarantee: Small businesses that provide certain energy production and conservation services for others may qualify for long-term loans and loan guarantees for start-ups and expansions. Loans and guarantees are made for firms that develop, manufacture, sell, install, or service specific energy measures for others, or firms that provide engineering, architectural, consulting, or other professional services connected with specific energy measures. Guarantee is for up to 90 percent of a loan not in excess of $750,000. Direct loans up to $150,000.

Disaster Recovery Loans: Small businesses located in federally designated disaster areas and suffering property damage or economic losses from the disaster can obtain long-term recovery loans at low interest rates. Property damage loans are limited to 85 percent of the verified damage. Loans for economic losses are for operating capital to meet the business' obligations that could have been made had the disaster not occurred.

Handicapped Assistance Loans: Assists persons who have a physical, mental or emotional disability of a permanent nature which limits the selection of any type of employment for which the person would otherwise be qualified. Direct loans are available for up to $150,000. The interest rate is 3% on these loans.

Surety Bond Guaranty Program: Makes the bonding system more available to small contractors who may be denied access to the system. SBA can guarantee up to 80 percent of surety's loss on a bond that has a maximum in total contract value of up to $1,250,000.

Vietnam-era and Disabled Veterans Loan Program: Provides direct loans to veterans to establish or expand a small business. Funds may be used for working capital or fixed assets. Direct loans for amounts up to $150,000 are available. The interest rate may be fixed or variable.

MorAmerica Capital Corporation
101 2nd Street, SE, #800
Cedar Rapids, IA 52401   319-363-8249

Small Business Investment Companies (SBIC): The SBA licenses, regulates, and provides financial assistance to privately owned and operated Small Business Investment Companies. SBICs make venture or risk investments by supplying capital and extending unsecured loans and loans not fully collateralized to small enterprises which meet their investment criteria. Financing is made by direct loans and by equity investments.

* Women and Minority Business Assistance

Targeted Small Business
Bureau of Business
Division of Financial Assistance
Iowa Department of Economic Development
200 East Grand
Des Moines, IA 50309   515-242-4813

Targeted Small Business Financial Assistance Program: Assists in the creation and expansion of minority-and women-owned small businesses within Iowa by providing direct loans, loan subsidies, or grants up to a maximum of $25,000, and loan guarantees up 75 percent of project not to exceed $40,000.

Bureau of Business   515-242-4721

Targeted Small Business Program: Helps in the process of certification by the Iowa Department of Inspections and Appeals as a targeted small business (any business which is 51 percent or more owned by a woman or minority). Once certified, a targeted small business is eligible for set-aside procurement programs of the state government.

Iowa Procurement Outreach Center
c/o Kirkwood Community College
Building 12
P.O. Box 2068   319-398-5665
Cedar Rapids, IA 52406   1-800-458-4465 in Iowa

The Iowa Procurement Outreach Center helps Iowa businesses successfully compete for government contracts. Centers are located at 15 area community colleges, SBDC's, the Center for Industrial Research and Service Offices, and the Iowa Department of Economic Development. Call the above number for a center in your locality.

Small Business Administration (SBA)
210 Walnut, Room 749   515-284-4422
Des Moines, IA 50309   FAX: 515-284-4572

SBA 8(a) Program - Business Procurement Assistance: Provides federal government contracting opportunities for small businesses owned by socially and economically disadvantaged persons, and assists these businesses to become independently competitive in the normal business environment. SBA monitors all government contracts to assure that a quota of contract work goes to 8(a) businesses. Also provides business management services to these businesses. Business must be approved for program participation prior to receipt of an 8(a) contract.

* Training

Bureau of State Programs
Division of Job Training
Department of Economic Development
200 East Grand Avenue
Des Moines, IA 50309   515-242-4774

Job Training Partnership Act (JTPA): Provides employers with recruitment, screening, referral, training, 50 percent wage subsidy up to 3 months for on-the-job training. Available to any private employer.

Industrial New Jobs Training Program: Eligible to any new or expanding business or industry that produce products or provide services in interstate commerce. Provides on-the-job training funds and other education and training necessary for employees in newly created jobs. Training includes skill assessment, orientation, instructional salaries, seminar fees, travel expenses, pre-employment training, and on-the-job training.

Small Business New Jobs Training Program: Provides low interest loans of up to $50,000 to design specialized training programs for small businesses whose projects are not refundable under the Industrial New Jobs Training Program. Funds may be used for skills assessment, orientation, pre-employment training, instructional salaries, seminar fees, and on-the-job training. On-the-job training component can cover up to 50 percent of wages and fringe benefits for a period time determined by the skills to be acquired.

Retraining Program   515-242-4797

Created to assist Iowa businesses to retrain their currently employed workers, thereby helping firms remain competitive and retain their existing employees. Any business involved in interstate or intrastate commerce that is undertaking a retooling process that could displace its current workforce in the following ten years is eligible. Business can receive up to $50,000 in funding but must invest at least as much in retraining costs as it is requesting.

* Management Consulting and Other Services

Department of Economic Development
200 East Grand Avenue
Des Moines, IA 50309   515-242-4735

Existing Business and Industry Program: Provides assistance to firms with expansion plans, concerns about doing business in Iowa, and information needs. The staff acts as a resource center for Iowa businesses for tax credits, financing, job training programs, and more.

Small Business Vendor Application Program: Streamlines the vendor application process to help small businesses compete for state purchasing contracts. Conferences and vendor fairs are held throughout the year.

Business License Information Center/CALL ONE: Quick and accurate answers to business questions and referrals to other agencies. Serves as a working link between businesses and license-issuing agencies within the state government. Call: 1-800-532-1216.

Small Business Administration
210 Walnut, Room 749   515-284-4422
Des Moines, IA 50309   FAX: 515-284-4572

Small Business Institutes: This program provides personalized consulting services to the small business community. Consulting is provided by senior level business students, guided by a faculty advisor. Assistance in business plan preparation, marketing research, market planning, accounting, and seminars are provided.
University Locations:
Briar Cliff College
Buena Vista College
Central College
Coe College
Drake University
Grand View College
Iowa State University
Maharishi International University
St. Ambrose University
University of Dubuque
University of Iowa

* Small Business Development Centers
The following offer free and fee-based services to new and expanding businesses:

Lead Center:
Iowa Small Business Development Center
Iowa State University
College of Business Administration
Chamblynn Building, 137 Lynn Avenue   515-292-6351
Ames, IA 50010   FAX: 515-292-0020

Ames: Iowa State University, ISU Small Business Development Center, 137 Lynn Avenue, Ames, IA 50010, 515-292-6351; FAX: 515-292-0020.

Ames: ISU Small Business Development Center, ISU Ames Branch, 111 Lynn Avenue, Ames, IA 50010, 515-292-6355; FAX: 515-292-0020.

Audubon: ISU Small Business Development Center, ISU Audubon Branch, Circle West Incubator, P.O. Box 204, Audubon, IA 50025, 712-563-2623; FAX: 712-563-2301.

Cedar Falls: University of Northern Iowa, Small Business Development Center, Suite 5, Business Building, Cedar Falls, IA 50614-0120, 319-273-2696; FAX: 319-273-6830.

Council Bluffs: Iowa Western Community College, Small Business Development Center, 2700 College Road, Box 4C, Council Bluffs, IA 51502, 712-325-3260; FAX: 712-325-3424.

Creston: Southwestern Community College, Small Business Development Center, 1501 West Townline, Creston, IA 50801, 515-782-4161; FAX: 515-782-4164.

Davenport: Eastern Iowa Community College District, Small Business Development Center, 304 West Second Street, Davenport, IA 52801, 319-322-4499; FAX: 319-322-3956.

Des Moines: Drake University, Small Business Development Center, Drake Business Center, Des Moines, IA 50311-4505, 515-271-2655; FAX: 515-271-4540.

Dubuque: Dubuque Area Chamber of Commerce, Northeast Iowa Small Business Development Center, 770 Town Clock Plaza, Dubuque, IA 52001, 319-588-3350; FAX: 319-557-1591.

Iowa City: University of Iowa, Oakdale Campus, Small Business Development Center, 106 Technology Innovation Center, Iowa City, IA 52242, 319-335-4057; FAX: 319-335-4489.

Marion: Kirkwood Community College, Small Business Development Center, 2901 Tenth Avenue, Marion, IA 53302, 319-377-8256; FAX: 319-377-5667.

Mason City: North Iowa Area Community College, Small Business Development Center, 500 College Drive, Mason City, IA 50401, 515-421-4342; FAX: 515-424-2011.

Ottumwa: Indian Hills Community College, Small Business Development Center, 525 Grandview Avenue, Ottumwa, IA 52501, 515-683-5127; FAX: 515-683-5263.

Sioux City: Western Iowa Tech Community College, Small Business Development Center, 5001 East Gordon Drive, Box 265, Sioux City, IA 51102, 712-274-6302; FAX: 712-274-6238.

Spencer: Iowa Lakes Community College, Small Business Development Center, Gateway North Shopping Center, Highway 71 North, Spencer, IA 51301, 712-262-4213; FAX: 712-262-4047.

West Burlington: Southeastern Community College, Small Business Development Center, Drawer F, West Burlington, IA 52655, 319-752-2731, ext. 103; FAX: 319-752-4957.

Kansas

* General Information

First-Stop Clearinghouse
Existing Industry Development Division
Kansas Department of Commerce and Housing
700 SW Harrison Street, #1300
Topeka, KS 66603-3712   913-296-5298
A One-Stop Clearinghouse for general information. Also provides necessary state applications required by agencies which license, regulate and tax business, and furnishes information about starting or expanding a business.

Regional Advocates
SBA - Region VII Office
911 Walnut, Suite 1300
Kansas City, MO 64106   816-426-2803

Small Business Advocate: Assistance in cutting bureaucratic red tape. Information and expertise in dealing with state, federal, and local agencies.

* Financing

Kansas Department of Commerce and Housing
700 SW Harrison Street, #1300
Topeka, KS 66603-3712
Existing Industry Development Division   913-296-5298
Industrial Development Bonds (IDB's): Kansas cities and counties are authorized to issue IDB's for financing or construction of manufacturing facilities. They can be used to purchase or construct, or equip buildings, acquire sites, and enlarge or remodel buildings. The Existing Industry Division maintains records of bond activity within the state.

Venture Capital and Seed Capital: Privately run corporations were designed to create private risk capital for investment in smaller Kansas businesses. They seek projects that provide good, technically feasible ideas, the ability to generate a big profit, excellent management capability, and widespread market potential. Emphasis is placed on for development of a prototype product or process, a marketing study to determine the feasibility of a new product or process, or a business plan for the development and production of a new product or process.

Seed Capital - funds to a new business for such things as business and marketing planning, product development, and building prototypes.

Start-Up Capital - provided to a business which has generally been in business for less than one year and has some level of sales. Funds to be used for staffing and equipping the business.

Growth or Expansion Capital (Second Stage) - provided usually two to three years after start-up which allows the business to broaden its product line, expand geographically, and increase production.

Acquisition Capital (Third Stage) -- investments in a mature business which may be in a position to be acquired. Financing may be used to restructure the business to make it more attractive for acquisition.

Small Cities CDBG Program:
Community Development Division   913-296-3485
Small Cities Community Development Block Grant (CDBG): Awarded to cities and counties with populations less than 50,000 for projects which stimulate or support local economic activity, principally for persons of low and moderate income. Funds may be used for public facilities, housing rehabilitation, and economic development projects.

Rental Rehabilitation Program: Designed to ensure an adequate supply of standard rental housing is available to lower-income tenants. Funds are offered through local government units, with an emphasis on rehabilitation of family housing.

Enterprise Zones   913-296-3485
Designed to "expand and renew the local economy and improve the social and economic welfare of residents in economically distress zone areas located within the cities of Kansas." Allows qualified business and industry located in an approved enterprises zone to take enhanced job expansion and investment income tax credits and sales tax exemptions on specific capital improvements.

Low Income Housing Tax Credits   913-296-2686
Designed to encourage investment in the supply of low and moderate income rental housing. Tax credits are available to qualified applicants for new construction, acquisition and rehabilitation.

Business Tax Bureau
Kansas Department of Revenue
Docking State Office Building, 3rd Floor
P.O. Box 12001
Topeka, KS 66612-2001   913-296-2461
Job Expansion and Investment Credits: Designed to encourage businesses to expand employment and capital investment. It allows a qualifying business to receive $100 income tax credits for creating new jobs and investing capital in the state. Assists both new business and existing

businesses to expand. A higher level of tax credits are available if located in an enterprise zone.

Kansas Technology Enterprise Corporation (KTEC)
112 West 6th Street, Suite 400
Topeka, KS 66603   913-296-5272

Through the following programs, KTEC serves inventors, researchers, corporations, investors and entrepreneurs. In addition, they conduct an annual high tech expo.

Applied Research Matching Grants: KTEC funds 40 percent of the cost of industry R&D projects which lead to job creation in Kansas. Industrially-focused Centers of Excellence are operated at several major universities.

Seed Capital Fund: Provides equity financing for high tech product development. Matching funds are provided for the Small Business Innovation Research Program.

Pooled Money Investment Board
Landon State Office Building
900 SW Jackson, #304 N
Topeka, KS 66612-1220   913-296-3372

Kansas Small Business Fund: Assists businesses to start up or expand in the state. Primary focus is to create or retain employment opportunities. Provides a favorable financial incentive to those small businesses which may not be able to afford conventional financing rates. Maximum loan is $200,000. Must create or retain at least one job for every $20,000 of funds loaned, and must employ 100 employees in Kansas at time of application.

Kansas Development Finance Authority
Jayhawk Tower #1000
700 S.W. Jackson Street
Topeka, KS 66603-3758   913-296-6747

The Authority is authorized to issue bonds for the purpose of financing capital improvements facilities, industrial enterprises, agricultural business enterprises, educational facilities, health care facilities, and housing developments. Several small projects can be combined into one large bond issue.

Kansas Association of Certified Development Companies
Box 46, Emporia State University
1200 Commercial Street
Emporia, KS 66801-5057   316-342-7041

SBA 504 Program: Provides loans using 50 percent conventional bank financing, 40 percent SBA involvement through Certified Development Companies, and 10 percent owner equity. A fixed asset loan in amounts up to $750,000. Loan can be used for land and building, construction, machinery and equipment, and renovation/expansion.

Small Business Administration (SBA)
Wichita District Office
100 E. English Street, #510   316-269-6273
Wichita, KS 67202   FAX: 316-269-6499

Small Business Administration (SBA)
Kansas City District Office
323 W. 8th, #501   816-374-5557
Kansas City, MO 64105   FAX: 816-374-6759

SBA 7(a) Guaranteed and Direct Loans: Guarantees up to 90 percent of a loan made through a private lender up to $750,000. Can be used for working capital, expand or convert facilities, purchase of machinery and equipment, and land and building. Available only to those unable to obtain a loan from conventional sources. Direct loans are made up to $150,000.

SBA 504: Provides loans using 50 percent conventional bank financing, 40 percent SBA involvement through Certified Development Companies, and 10 percent owner equity. Fixed-asset loans are available in amounts up to $750,000. The loan can be used for land and building, construction, machinery and equipment, and renovation/expansion.

Small Business Research Grants (SBIR): Phase I awards between $20,000 to $50,000 to entrepreneurs to support six months of research on a technical innovation. Phase II grants are an additional $500,000 for development. Private sector investment funds must follow.

International Trade Loans: Guaranteed long-term loans through private lenders to develop or expand export markets, or to recover from the effects of import competition. Maximum guaranteed loan is $1,000,000 for fixed assets and an additional $250,000 for working capital and/or export revolving line of credit.

Export Revolving Line of Credit Loan: Short term financing available to small businesses that are at least one year old. Loans provide working capital to finance the manufacturing or wholesaling of products for export and for export marketing. The SBA will guarantee up to 90 percent of a conventional loan in amounts up to $750,000.

Contract Loan: Short-term loans are available to small businesses to finance the costs of labor and materials on contracts for which the proceeds are assignable. Program guarantees up to 90 percent of loans not in excess of $750,000. Qualifying small businesses must be in business for at least 12 calendar months prior to the date of the loan application.

Seasonal Line of Credit Loan: Loans provide short-term working capital to finance seasonal increases in business activities. Program guarantees up to 90 percent of loans not in excess of $750,000. Qualifying business must be in operation for at least one year prior to application.

Pollution Control Loans: Long-term guaranteed loans can be made by conventional financing to small businesses for installation or required pollution control measures. Must be unable to adopt the pollution control measures without undue financial hardship. Maximum guaranteed loan is $1,000,000.

General Contractor Loans: Small general construction contractors may obtain short-term loans or loan guarantees for residential or commercial construction or rehabilitation of property to be sold. The SBA will guarantee up to 90 percent of qualifying loans made by private lenders up to a maximum of $750,000. Direct loans can be up to $150,000.

Energy Business Loan Guarantee: Small businesses that provide certain energy production and conservation services for others may qualify for long-term loans and loan guarantees for start-ups and expansions. Loans and guarantees are made for firms that develop, manufacture, sell, install, or service specific energy measures for others, or firms that provide engineering, architectural, consulting, or other professional services connected with specific energy measures. Guarantee is for up to 90 percent of a loan not in excess of $750,000. Direct loans up to $150,000.

Disaster Recovery Loans: Small businesses located in federally designated disaster areas and suffering property damage or economic losses from the disaster can obtain long-term recovery loans at low interest rates. Property damage loans are limited to 85 percent of the verified damage. Loans for economic losses are for operating capital to meet the business' obligations that could have been made had the disaster not occurred.

Handicapped Assistance Loans: Assists persons who have a physical, mental or emotional disability of a permanent nature which limits the selection of any type of employment for which the person would otherwise be qualified. Direct loans are available for up to $150,000. The interest rate is 3% on these loans.

Surety Bond Guaranty Program: Makes the bonding system more available to small contractors who may be denied access to the system. SBA can guarantee up to 80 percent of surety's loss on a bond that has a maximum in total contract value of up to $1,250,000.

Vietnam-era and Disabled Veterans Loan Program: Provides direct loans to veterans to establish or expand a small business. Funds may be used for working capital or fixed assets. Direct loans for amounts up to $150,000 are available. The interest rate may be fixed or variable.

Kansas Venture Capital, Inc.
6700 Antioch Plaza, Suite 460
Overland Park, KS 66204   913-262-7117

Kansas Venture Capital, Inc.
(Main Office: Overland Park, KS)
One Main Place
Suite 806
Wichita, KS 67202 316-262-1221

Kansas Venture Capital, Inc.
(Main Office: Overland Park, KS)
500 S. Kansas Avenue
Suite J
Topeka, KS 66603 913-233-1368
Small Business Investment Companies (SBIC): The SBA licenses, regulates, and provides financial assistance to privately owned and operated Small Business Investment Companies. SBICs make venture or risk investments by supplying capital and extending unsecured loans and loans not fully collateralized to small enterprises which meet their investment criteria. Financing is made by direct loans and by equity investments.

Farmers Home Administration
1200 SW Executive Drive
P.O. Box 4653
Topeka, KS 66604 913-271-2700
Business and Industrial Loan Program: Provides loan guarantees to businesses and industries to benefit rural areas. Loans are made in any area outside the boundary of a city of 50,000 or more and its adjacent urbanized areas with population density of no more than 100 persons per square mile. Any legal entity, including individuals, public and private organizations, and federally recognized Indian tribes may borrow under its program. Priority is given to applications for projects in open country, rural communities and towns of 25,000 and smaller. Primary purpose is to create and maintain employment and improve the economic and environmental climate in rural communities. Guarantees of up to 90 percent of the principal and interest.

* Women and Minority Business Assistance

Office of Minority Business
Existing Industry Development Division
Kansas Department of Commerce and Housing
700 SW Harrison Street
Topeka, KS 66603-3712 913-296-3805
Provides assistance to minority-owned and women-owned businesses. The office educates businesses regarding bidding procedures for public and private procurement opportunities. Also provides management assistance, identifies financial resources, and serves as an advocate for minority and women-owned businesses.

Assistant Regional Administration for MSB-COD
Small Business Administration (SBA) - Region VII Office
911 Walnut, 13th Floor 816-426-3608
Kansas City, MO 64106 FAX: 816-426-5559
The Office of Minority Small Business has a number of programs specifically designed to assist socially and economically disadvantaged business, especially those small business persons who traditionally have faced unusual difficulties in gaining access to the private marketplace. Maintains a management counseling service for small firms. *Also see Management Consulting & Other Services Section.*

SBA 8(a) Program - Business Procurement Assistance: Provides federal government contracting opportunities for small businesses owned by socially and economically disadvantaged persons, and assists these businesses to become independently competitive in the normal business environment. SBA monitors all government contracts to assure that a quota of contract work goes to 8(a) businesses. Also provides business management services to these businesses. Business must be approved for program participation prior to receipt of an 8(a) contract.

* Training

Department of Human Resources
Job Service Administration
401 Topeka Boulevard
Topeka, KS 66603

Job Service Office:
Targeted Job Tax Credit: A federal tax credit is available for employers who hire disadvantaged persons.

Job Service 913-296-5317
Businesses can contract with Job Service to do all their hiring including testing and screening services. Maintains a potential work file from which employers may draw.

Program and Support Services 913-296-5317
Operate 35 Employment and Training Offices throughout Kansas to assist in matching potential employees with employers and to provide training to economically disable and displaced workers.

Older Workers Programs Administrator
Kansas Department of Aging
Docking State Office Building
Room 122S
915 SW Harrison Street
Topeka, KS 66612-1500 913-296-4986
Older Worker Programs: Employers who need experienced, reliable part-time or full-time workers can find resources though this program. Job candidates are pre-screened to meet job specifications prior to employer referral. Most programs are free of charge to the employer and the job candidate. Program expenses are paid with federal and state job development grants.

Job Training Coordinator
Industrial Development Division
Kansas Department of Commerce and Housing
700 SW Harrison Street
Topeka, KS 66603-3712 913-296-3483
Industrial Retraining Program: Provides customized training for employees of restructuring industries who are likely to be displaced because of obsolete or inadequate job skills and knowledge.

Industrial Training Program: Provides customized training to new or prospective employees of new or expanding industries.

Job Training Partnership Act (JTPA) 913-296-3588
Provides employers with recruitment, screening, referral, training, 50 percent wage subsidy up to 3 months for on-the-job training. Available to any private employer. Can also contact: Industrial Development Division of the Dept. of Commerce.

Business and Industry Institute
Johnson County Community College
12345 College Blvd.
Overland Park, KS 66210-1299 913-469-3845
Offers consulting services and develops specialized educational and training programs to match the needs of employers in the metropolitan Kansas City area with the skills and talents of the available work force.

* Management Consulting and Other Services

Wichita State University
Small Business Development Center
1845 N. Fairmount
Wichita, KS 67260-0148 316-689-3193
Procurement Technical Assistance Program: Provides both one-on-one counseling assistance and procurement training seminars to encourage Kansas businesses to compete for government contracts.

Kansas Department of Commerce and Housing
700 SW Harrison Street
Topeka, KS 66603-3712
Industrial Development Division 913-296-3483
Developing Kansas: A quarterly newsletter that focuses on announcements of new and expanding industries, industrial prospecting trips, industrial development conferences and other business recruitment activities.

Travel & Tourism Development Division 913-296-7091
1-800-2-KANSAS in Kansas
Film Production Services: Filmmakers and documentary and commercial producers are provided information on-location sites in Kansas. Publishes a film services directory for Kansas.

Trade Development Division 913-296-4027
Trade Promotion: Assists business with both international and domestic trade promotion. Trade shows, trade delegations, seminars, media events and public relations are used to develop promotional events and activities that will enhance consumer awareness and demand.

Trade Services: Provides communications between buyer and seller. Publishes and distributes general trade services information as well as catalogues and directories listing manufacturers of leading Kansas industries and export products.

International Product Marketing: Conduct trade shows, solicits and disseminates trade inquiries, hosts foreign trade delegations, conduct seminars and maintains and improves international relationships. Works through various overseas offices. Also assists with identifying, researching and accessing international markets for all types of manufactured goods, processed food products, and industry services, through trade lead development, communications assistance, and a series of product directories.

Small Business Administration
Kansas City District Office
323 W. 8th, #501
Kansas City, MO 64105 816-374-5557
FAX: 816-374-6759

Small Business Administration
Wichita District Office
100 E. English Street, #510 316-269-6273
Wichita, KS 67202 FAX: 316-269-6499
Small Business Institutes: This program provides personalized consulting services to the small business community. Consulting is provided by senior level business students, guided by a faculty advisor. Assistance in business plan preparation, marketing research, market planning, accounting, and seminars are provided.
University Locations:
Bethany College
Emporia State University
Fort Hays State University
Kansas Newman College
Kansas State University
Mid-America Nazarene
Pittsburg State University
Southwestern College
St. Mary College
University of Kansas
Washburn University
Wichita State University

Division of Purchases
Department of Administration
Landon State Office Building, Room 102
Topeka, KS 66612 913-296-2376
Small Business Procurement Program: The Small Business Set-Aside Program ensures a fair proportion of the contracts for property and services for the state be placed with qualified small business contractors. Counsels small businesses on how to prepare bids, obtain contracts and subcontracts, help to get listed on bidders' lists and assists in obtaining drawings and specifications for proposed purchases.

FACTS
State Board of Agriculture
9 Leasure Hall, Kansas State University 913-532-6958
Manhattan, KS 66506 1-800-321-FARM in Kansas
Farmer's Assistance, Counseling and Training Services (FACTS): Assists farmers, ranchers, and agribusiness persons with information and referrals during times of crises. The toll free hotline is staffed to provide free, confidential information. Also presents workshops, seminars, and regional meetings throughout the state.

Center for Economic Development and Business Research
Wichita State University, Box 48
Wichita, KS 67208 316-689-3225
Maintains a comprehensive data base for the state which includes economic information for South Central Kansas and all counties of the state. Also provides economic analysis for local government agencies and private businesses.

Center for Entrepreneurship
Devlin Hall
Wichita State University, Box 147
Wichita, KS 67208 316-689-3000
The Center is involved in developing and conducting seminars for special interest groups and practicing entrepreneurs and small business managers. An information bank, library and publication service are available for practitioners, academicians and students.

BETA
Space Technology Center
University of Kansas
2291 Irving Hill Drive, West Campus
Lawrence, KS 66045 913-864-7751
Business and Engineering Technical Applications Program: Purpose is to obtain technical information and relating it to a specific need. It is designed to assist business and industry on science and engineering, and administrative problems by providing specific technical information relevant to a company's needs.

Engineering Extension Program
133 Ward Hall, Kansas State University
Manhattan, KS 66506 913-532-6026
Technical assistance in energy management to energy consumers. Specialists are available to respond to individual questions, make site visits to commercial, and industrial facilities and provide educational programs.

Institute for Economic Development
Pittsburg State University
1501 S. Joplin
Pittsburg, KS 66762 316-231-7000, Ext. 4920
A one-stop center for financial, managerial, and technical assistance for entrepreneurs and businesses. Services include financial packaging, business plan development small business counseling, training and skill development, and research on business operations and markets.

Kansas State University Cooperative Extension Service
Kansas State University
Umberger Hall, Room 311
Manhattan, KS 66506 913-532-7987
Offers assistance to business start-ups and expansions. The DIRECT Line program provides a point of contact for information and referrals to other sources of assistance.

Kansas State Board of Agriculture
Marketing Division
901 S. Kansas Ave.
Topeka, KS 66612-1282 913-296-3736
Food Product Marketing Program: Assistance in marketing Kansas agricultural products and processed foods. Marketing programs include retail merchandising, food shows, training seminars, and media promotions.

* Small Business Development Centers
The following offer free and fee-based services to new and expanding businesses:

Lead Center:
Kansas Small Business Development Center
Wichita State University
1845 Fairmount 316-689-3193
Wichita, KS 67260-0148 FAX: 316-689-3647

Augusta: Butler County Community College, Small Business Development

Center, 600 Walnut, Augusta, KS 67010, 316-775-1124; FAX: 316-775-1370.

Arkansas City: Cowley County Community College, Small Business Development Center, 125 S. 2nd, Strother Field Training Facility, Arkansas City, KS 67005, 316-442-8142; FAX: 316-442-0713.

Colby: Colby Community College, Small Business Development Center, 1255 South Range, Colby, KS 67701, 913-462-3984, ext. 239; FAX: 913-462-8315.

Concordia: Cloud County Community College, Small Business Development Center, 2221 Campus Drive, P.O. Box 1002, Concordia, KS 66901, 913-243-1435; FAX: 913-243-1459.

Dodge City: Dodge City Community College, Small Business Development Center, 2501 North 14th Avenue, Dodge City, KS 67801, 316-225-1321, ext. 247; FAX: 316-225-0918.

Emporia: Emporia State University, Small Business Development Center, 207 Cremer Hall, Emporia, KS 66801, 316-343-5308; FAX: 316-341-5418.

Garden City: Garden City Community College, Small Business Development Center, 801 Campus Drive, Garden City, KS 67846, 316-276-9632; FAX: 316-276-9630.

Great Bend: Barton County Community College, Small Business Development Center, 3709 N. Main, P.O. Box 136Z, Great Bend, KS 67530, 316-792-1242; FAX: 316-792-8035.

Hays: Fort Hays State University, Small Business Development Center, 1301 Pine, Hays, KS 67601, 913-628-5340; FAX: 913-628-1471.

Hutchinson: Hutchinson Community College, Small Business Development Center, 815 N. Walnut, #225, Hutchinson, KS 67501, 316-665-4950; FAX: 316-665-7619.

Kansas City: Kansas City Community College, Small Business Development Center, 7250 State Avenue, Kansas City, KS 66112, 913-334-1100, ext. 228; FAX: 913-596-9606.

Lawrence: University of Kansas, Small Business Development Center, 734 Vermont, Suite 104, Lawrence, KS 66044, 913-843-8844; FAX: 913-865-4400.

Liberal: Seward County Community College, Small Business Development Center, 1801 North Kansas, Liberal, KS 67901, 316-624-1951, ext. 148; FAX: 316-624-0637.

Manhattan: Kansas State University, Small Business Development Center, 2323 Anderson Ave., Suite 100, Manhattan, KS 66502-2947, 913-532-5529; FAX: 913-532-7800.

Ottawa: Ottawa University, Small Business Development Center, College Avenue, Box 70, Ottawa, KS 66067, 913-242-5200, ext. 5457; FAX: 913-242-7429.

Overland Park: Johnson County Community College, Small Business Development Center, CEC Building, Room 3051, Overland Park, KS 66210-1299, 913-469-3878; FAX: 913-469-4415.

Pittsburg: Pittsburg State University, Small Business Development Center, Shirk Hall, Pittsburg, KS 66762, 316-231-8267; FAX: 316-232-6440.

Pratt: Pratt Community College, Small Business Development Center, Highway 61, Pratt, KS 67124, 316-672-5641; FAX: 316-672-5288.

Salina: KSU-Salina College of Technology, Small Business Development Center, 2409 Scanlan Avenue, Salina, KS 67401, 913-825-0275, ext. 445; FAX: 913-825-8475.

Topeka: Washburn University, Small Business Development Center, 101 Henderson Learning Center, Topeka, KS 66621, 913-231-1010, ext. 1305; FAX: 913-231-1063.

Wichita: Wichita State University, Small Business Development Center, Brennan Hall, 2nd Floor, 1845 Fairmount, Campus Box 148, Wichita, KS 67208, 316-689-3193; FAX: 316-689-3647.

Kentucky

* General Information

Business Information Clearinghouse
Cabinet of Economic Development
Department of Existing Business and Industry
2200 Capital Plaza Tower   502-564-4252
Frankfort, KY 40601   1-800-242-1545 in Kentucky

Kentucky Business Information Clearinghouse: Provides a centralized information source. Handles requests for business licensing and permit information, assembles customized application and information packets for business proposals, referrals to other state, federal and local government agencies, and problems with government red tape.

Small Business Division:
Small Business Advocate: Assistance in cutting bureaucratic red tape. Information and expertise in dealing with state, federal, and local agencies.

Division of Research & Planning   502-564-4886
A list of business development publications are available through this office. There is a charge for some.

* Financing

Kentucky Development Finance Authority (KDFA)
Capital Plaza Tower
24th Floor
Frankfort, KY 40601   502-564-4554

Small Business Loans: KDFA is a state government agency and makes loans for fixed asset financing for business start-ups and expansions. Loans are available to small businesses with fewer than 100 employees for fixed asset project costs of less than $100,000. KDFA loans up to 45 percent of project costs. Loans supplement other financing. Loans can be used for most types of business activities except retail or commercial development projects. Interest rate is at or below market rate.

Tax-Exempt Industrial Revenue Bonds: Issued by state and local governments, IRB's offer low-cost financing for manufacturing projects costing less that $10 million.

Industrial Bonds in Distressed Counties: Private companies placing new manufacturing plants in certain economically distressed Kentucky counties can recoup the cost of the facilities through tax incentives. These state bond financed projects can include the land and buildings used for manufacturing, along with storage warehousing, and related office facilities.

Commonwealth Small Business Development
  Corporation (CSBDC)
Capital Plaza Tower, 24th Floor
Frankfort, KY 40601   502-564-4320

State Loans for Small Businesses: Long term fixed interest rate financing loans for up to 40 percent of the costs of expansions by qualifying Kentucky small businesses are available, 50 percent conventional financing, and 10 percent owner equity. Maximum loan per single small business project is $750,000 or $35,000 per job created. Fixed assets eligible for financing include land and/or building purchases, new building construction and/or building rehabilitation, and machinery and equipment purchases. Funds are disbursed at the completion of the project. Business must obtain interim financing and the CSBDC loan commitment will assist in securing the interim financing.

Cabinet for Economic Development
Office of Business and Technology
Capital Plaza Tower, 500 Mero Street
Frankfort, KY 40601   **502-564-7670**

State Bridge Grants for Innovative Research (SBIR): Kentucky businesses participating in Small Business Innovative Research contracts with federal agencies are eligible for state bridge grants. Grants bridge the period between the completion of a company's award for the first phase of a federal research project and the second phase award to help eliminate interruptions in the firm's development and growth in highly competitive technologies. *Also see Technology Section.*

Cabinet for Economic Development
2300 Capital Plaza Tower
Frankfort, KY 40601   502-564-7140

Enterprise Zone Program: Enterprise zones were initiated to bring new or renewed development to targeted areas, and to make businesses and industry in those areas more competitive. Special tax incentives and eased regulations are available to businesses located in special zones. There are ten enterprise zones.

Small Business Division
Kentucky Department of Existing Business and Industry
Capital Plaza Tower, 22nd Floor
Frankfort, KY 40601   502-564-4252

Crafts Loan Guarantee Program: Small businesses producing crafts items can obtain state guaranteed loans ranging from $2,000 to $20,000 from local banks. Loans can be used to finance inventory, and for the purchase, repair or renovation of equipment. To qualify, product must be juried and a thorough business plan must be submitted along with application.

Small Business Administration (SBA)
Federal Building, Room 188
600 Dr. Martin Luther King, Jr. Place   502-582-5971
Louisville, KY 40202   FAX: 502-582-5009

SBA 7(a) Guaranteed and Direct Loans: Guarantees up to 90 percent of a loan made through a private lender up to $750,000. Can be used for working capital, expand or convert facilities, purchase of machinery and equipment, and land and building. Available only to those unable to obtain a loan from conventional sources. Direct loans are made up to $150,000.

SBA 504: Provides loans using 50 percent conventional bank financing, 40 percent SBA involvement through Certified Development Companies, and 10 percent owner equity. Fixed-asset loans are available in amounts up to $750,000. The loan can be used for land and building, construction, machinery and equipment, and renovation/expansion.

Small Business Innovative Research Grants (SBIR): Phase I awards between $20,000 to $50,000 to entrepreneurs to support six months of research on a technical innovation. Phase II grants are an additional $500,000 for development. Private sector investment funds must follow.

International Trade Loans: Guaranteed long-term loans through private lenders to develop or expand export markets, or to recover from the effects of import competition. Maximum guaranteed loan is $1,000,000 for fixed assets and an additional $250,000 for working capital and/or export revolving line of credit.

Export Revolving Line of Credit Loan: Short term financing available to small businesses that are at least one year old. Loans provide working capital to finance the manufacturing or wholesaling of products for export and for export marketing. The SBA will guarantee up to 90 percent of a conventional loan in amounts up to $750,000.

Contract Loan: Short-term loans are available to small businesses to finance the costs of labor and materials on contracts for which the proceeds are assignable. Program guarantees up to 90 percent of loans not in excess of $750,000. Qualifying small businesses must be in business for at least 12 calendar months prior to the date of the loan application.

Seasonal Line of Credit Loan: Loans provide short-term working capital to finance seasonal increases in business activities. Program guarantees up to 90 percent of loans not in excess of $750,000. Qualifying business must be in operation for at least one year prior to application.

Pollution Control Loans: Long-term guaranteed loans can be made by conventional financing to small businesses for installation or required pollution control measures. Must be unable to adopt the pollution control measures without undue financial hardship. Maximum guaranteed loan is $1,000,000.

General Contractor Loans: Small general construction contractors may obtain short-term loans or loan guarantees for residential or commercial construction or rehabilitation of property to be sold. The SBA will guarantee up to 90 percent of qualifying loans made by private lenders up to a maximum of $750,000. Direct loans can be up to $150,000.

Energy Business Loan Guarantee: Small businesses that provide certain energy production and conservation services for others may qualify for long-term loans and loan guarantees for start-ups and expansions. Loans and guarantees are made for firms that develop, manufacture, sell, install, or service specific energy measures for others, or firms that provide engineering, architectural, consulting, or other professional services connected with specific energy measures. Guarantee is for up to 90 percent of a loan not in excess of $750,000. Direct loans up to $150,000.

Disaster Recovery Loans: Small businesses located in federally designated disaster areas and suffering property damage or economic losses from the disaster can obtain long-term recovery loans at low interest rates. Property damage loans are limited to 85 percent of the verified damage. Loans for economic losses are for operating capital to meet the business' obligations that could have been made had the disaster not occurred.

Handicapped Assistance Loans: Assists persons who have a physical, mental or emotional disability of a permanent nature which limits the selection of any type of employment for which the person would otherwise be qualified. Direct loans are available for up to $150,000. The interest rate is 3% on these loans.

Surety Bond Guaranty Program: Makes the bonding system more available to small contractors who may be denied access to the system. SBA can guarantee up to 80 percent of surety's loss on a bond that has a maximum in total contract value of up to $1,250,000.

Vietnam-era and Disabled Veterans Loan Program: Provides direct loans to veterans to establish or expand a small business. Funds may be used for working capital or fixed assets. Direct loans for amounts up to $150,000 are available. The interest rate may be fixed or variable.

Mountain Ventures, Inc.
London Bank & Trust Building
400 S. Main Street, Fourth Floor
London, KY 40741   606-864-5175

Wilbur Venture Capital Corporation
(Main Office: Tucson, AZ)
400 Fincastle Building
3rd & Broadway
Louisville, KY 40202   502-585-1214

Small Business Investment Companies (SBIC): The SBA licenses, regulates, and provides financial assistance to privately owned and operated Small Business Investment Companies. SBICs make venture or risk investments by supplying capital and extending unsecured loans and loans not fully collateralized to small enterprises which meet their investment criteria. Financing is made by direct loans and by equity investments.

Kentucky Department of Local Government
Division of Community Programs
1024 Capital Center Drive
Frankfort, KY 40601   502-564-2382

Community Development Block Grant Loan (CDBG): Available to cities and counties for the commercial rehabilitation of existing buildings or structures used for business, commercial, or industrial purposes. The cities and counties loan the grant funds to business to be used for fixed assets and for the creation or retention of jobs. At least 51 percent of the jobs created must be for low-and moderate-income families.

Farmers Home Administration
771 Corporate Drive, Suite 200
Lexington, KY 40503   606-224-7300

FmHA Business and Industrial Guarantee Loan Program: Offers loan guarantees of up to 90 percent of principal and interest on conventional loans to businesses and industries in rural areas of Kentucky. The FmHA designates the eligible rural areas and are in areas with populations of less than 50,000. Priority is given where areas are in open country, rural communities, and cities of 25,000 or fewer. Funds can be used to purchase land, buildings, machinery, equipment, furniture, and fixtures; to finance construction, expansion, or modernization of buildings; and to provide start-up and working capital.

Economic Development Administration (EDA)
771 Corporate Plaza, Suite 200
Lexington, KY 40503 606-233-2596

EDA Loan Guarantee: The EDA can guarantee up to 80 percent of a loan made by a private lender. Guaranteed loans can be used to finance both fixed assets and working capital for businesses in eligible counties. EDA loans are generally for larger firms and range from about $500,000 to $10,000,000. Priority is given to projects that are labor intensive, with assistance usually limited to no more than $20,000 per permanent job created or saved.

Bowling Green:	Barren River Area Development District	502-781-2381
Catlettsburg:	FIVCO Area Development District	606-739-5191
Maysville:	Buffalo Trace Area Development District	606-546-6874
Elizabethtown:	Lincoln Trail Area Development District	502-769-2393
Florence:	Northern Kentucky Area Development	606-283-1885
Hazard:	Kentucky River Area Development District	606-436-3158
Hopkinsville:	Pennyrile Area Development District	502-886-9484
Lexington:	Urban County Economic Development Office	606-258-3131
London:	Cumberland Valley Area Development District	606-864-7391
Louisville:	Louisville and Jefferson County Economic Development Office	502-625-3051
Mayfield:	Purchase Area Development District	502-247-7171
Owensboro:	Green River Area Development District	502-926-4433
Owingsville:	Gateway Area Development District	502-674-6355
Russell Springs:	Lake Cumberland Area Development District	502-866-4200

Business Loans by Local Governments: Loans for local business start-ups and expansions are available through several Kentucky city and county governments and area development districts. Loans are generally restricted to $500,000 or less, or to a specified amount per job created or saved. Interest rates are typically at or below-market rates.

Commonwealth Venture Capital Fund
Office of Financial Management and Economic Analysis
261 Capital Annex
Frankfort, KY 40601 502-564-2924

State Venture Capital Funds Loans and Investments: Small businesses showing a potential for long-term growth may obtain start-up and early stage financing assistance at competitive rates from a state venture capital fund. Loans, loan guarantees or equity investments of up to $500,000 can be obtained by a qualifying small business which must be Kentucky based and employ fewer than 100 people.

Kentucky Highlands Investment Corporation (KHIC)
P.O. Box 1738
London, KY 40743 606-864-5175

A small business investment company licensed by the SBA, provide both short term and long term financing assistance to small businesses in Southeastern Kentucky. Venture capital loans and equity capital investments for higher-risk projects are available for start-ups, expansions, and relocations of manufacturing and services firms. Participation usually ranges from $50,000 to $750,000. Terms and interest rates are negotiated.

The Cumberland Fund
433 Chestnut Street
Berea, KY 40403 606-986-2373

Private Loans: Appalachian Counties: Loans and financial planning assistance are available to qualifying new and expanding manufacturing businesses in the 49 Appalachian counties of Kentucky. Loans range from $10,000 to $150,000. Funds can be used for working capital or to finance fixed assets.

* Women and Minority Business Assistance

Small Business Administration
Room 188
600 Dr. Martin Luther King, Jr. Place 502-582-5971
Louisville, KY 40202 FAX: 502-582-5009

SBA 8(a) Program - Business Procurement Assistance: Provides federal government contracting opportunities for small businesses owned by socially and economically disadvantaged persons, and assists these businesses to become independently competitive in the normal business environment. SBA monitors all government contracts to assure that a quota of contract work goes to 8(a) businesses. Also provides business management services to these businesses. Business must be approved for program participation prior to receipt of an 8(a) contract.

Louisville and Jefferson County Economic Development Office
401 South Fourth Avenue
Suite 200
Louisville, KY 40202 502-625-3051

Small businesses located within the City of Louisville and controlled by minority individuals or women may qualify for loans from the Metropolitan Business Development Corporation (METCO). Loans are made to qualifying businesses for real estate, equipment and working capital. Priority is given to projects with maximum job creation and to those that hire individuals from low to moderate income families. Loans are made up to 50 percent of the project cost with a maximum loan of $100,000 and a minimum of $5,000. Qualifying borrowers must have a minimum net worth of $100,000.

Equal Opportunity Finance, Inc.
420 S. Hurstbourne Pkwy, #201
Louisville, KY 40222-8002 502-423-1943

Kentucky businesses owned by minorities, the economically disadvantaged, the physically handicapped, or Vietnam war veterans may qualify for equity investments or long-term loans. Loans can be used for start-ups, buy-outs, or expansion projects for most types of businesses. Maximum loan is $300,000.

Kentucky Cabinet for Economic Development
Capital Plaza Tower
Frankfort, KY 40601

Minority Business Division: 502-564-2064
A resource center for minority business owners/managers. Identifies construction contracts, procurement opportunities, and offers training programs that address the business needs of the minority enterprises. Focuses on new job creation and job retention by serving existing minority businesses in the roles of ombudsman and expediter for business growth and retention.

Kentuckiana Minority Supplier Development Council (KMSDC)
Louisville Chamber of Commerce
One Riverfront Plaza, #804
Louisville, KY 40202 502-625-0135

Assists minority-owned businesses in identifying and successfully competing for business opportunities with majority-owned firms, government agencies, and suppliers. Business Opportunity Trade Fairs are held annually to link minority firms with potential buyers.

Louisville Minority Business Development Center (LMBDC)
611 W. Main
Louisville, KY 40202 502-589-6232

A one-stop business assistance and information center for qualified minority firms and individuals. Acts as an advocate for minority firms and creates linkages between these firms and market opportunities. Specializes in business planning and financial packaging.

* Training

Kentucky Cabinet for Economic Development
Capital Plaza Tower, 21st Floor
500 Mero Street
Frankfort, KY 40601

Bluegrass State Skills Corporation 502-564-2021
Created for the purpose of skills training for business and industry, from entry-level to advanced training, and from upgrading present employees to retraining experienced workers. Awards grants to educational institutions

which work with one or more private companies to train people for jobs. Also works in partnership with other employment and/or training resources and programs, as well as economic development activities to package a program customized to meet the specific needs of a company.

Job Training Partnership Act (JTPA): Provides employers with recruitment, screening, referral, training, 50 percent wage subsidy up to 3 months for on-the-job training. Available to any private employer.

* Management Consulting and Other Services

Kentucky Cabinet for Economic Development
Capital Plaza Tower, 21st Floor
500 Mero Street
Frankfort, KY 40601

Office of International Marketing:
Trade Section   502-564-2170
Promotes the exportation of Kentucky manufactured products in international markets by participating in overseas trade missions, locates Kentucky sources of raw materials or manufactured products for foreign customers, counsels and educates Kentucky firms on foreign trade opportunities and requirements, and matches Kentucky manufacturers with potential international importers. Maintains a Far East office in Tokyo, Japan, and a European office.

Department of Existing Business and Industry   502-564-5891
Existing Industries Division   1-800-633-2007 in Kentucky
Focuses on new job creating and job retention by serving existing businesses in the roles of ombudsman and expeditor for business growth and retention. Makes personal calls to the manufacturing community, alerts manufacturers about changes in programs and regulations, serves as liaison between businesses and state government agencies in alleviating problems, and acts as an advocate for policies and interests in the business community.

Small Business Division   502-564-2064
                                                1-800-633-2007
                                              FAX: 502-564-3256
Provides information on start-ups, training, financing, procurement, and business planning, programs, workshops, and seminars. Maintains a schedule of informative meetings or conferences related to women business owners, and assistance to individuals interested in operating businesses from their homes.

Kentucky Procurement Assistance Program: Assists Kentucky businesses in selling their products and/or services to the Federal Government. A computerized service that can match government purchasing needs with potential Kentucky suppliers. Other services offered are assistance in putting together a Federal bid package, training on how to do business with the Federal Government, and marketing to a federal agency.

Craft Marketing Branch   502-564-8076
Assists craftspeople to expand their regional and national markets by providing resource information, business training, technical assistance, and opportunities to participate in an annual craft market, national trade shows and other special activities.

Research and Planning Division   502-564-4886
Information and analytical services to support economic development in the state. Included within this Division is the General Research Branch that compiles data on financing, taxes, transportation, industrial services, manufacturers, and economic statistics. The Community Publications Branch compiles and publishes economic development resources booklets on communities throughout the state. The Economic Resources Library contains volumes and periodicals pertaining to and/or providing supportive data for economic development.

Site and Building Evaluation Branch   502-564-7140
Maintains current data on available industrial sites and buildings in the state, assists communities in evaluating potential industrial sites, and publishes and distributes site maps and site information.

Office of Business Technology   502-564-7670
Serves as a link between businesses and the technological resources and research capabilities of both the private and public sectors, and provides and manages incentive grants to facilitate technology development.

Kentucky Small Business Development Center
College of Business and Economics
University of Kentucky
225 Business & Economics Bldg.
Lexington, KY 40506-0034   606-257-1751
Porter Building, Room 23:
Center for Small Business Development: Provides assistance to small and medium-sized manufacturing and services businesses to enter international trade for the first time or expand their present international trade position.

Porter Building, Room 18:
Center for Business Development: The Kentucky Economic Expansion Program (KEEP) provides management specialists and college professors provide consulting services to small manufacturers that cannot afford to hire a consultant.

Kentucky Society of CPAs
310 West Liberty Street, #604   502-589-9239
Louisville, KY 40202   1-800-292-1754 in Kentucky
Provides a free CPA referral service to assist small businesses in locating an accountant proficient in the type of work needed. Sponsors seminars for small businesses on financing, income taxes, computers, cash flow analysis, working with an accounting, and simple accounting systems.

Louisville Bar Association
707 West Main Street
Louisville, KY 40202   502-583-5314
Provides a referral service to assist small businesses in identifying an attorney. The fee is $15.00 and entitles the client to a one-half hour consultation with an attorney.

Division of Purchases
Department of Administration
Capitol Annex Building, Room 354
Frankfort, KY 40601   502-564-4510
Procurement: The majority of the State Government purchases, non-construction, for commodities and serves are bid and contracted through this agency.

Commodities relating to highway maintenance and traffic requirements are bid and contracted by Division of Purchases, Department of Administrative Services, Transportation Cabinet, State Office Building, Frankfort, KY 40601, 502-564-4630.

Secretary of State
Capitol Building
P.O. Box 718
Frankfort, KY 40601   502-564-2848
Will provide information on obtaining a state trademark.

Center for Entrepreneurship and Technology
School of Business
University of Louisville, Shelby Campus
Louisville, KY 40292   502-588-7854
Provides counseling services to entrepreneurs and companies that have technology-dependent enterprises. Also will direct and assist you in the development of a patent, copyright or trademark idea.

Center for Small Business
Louisville Chamber of Commerce
One Riverfront Plaza
Louisville, KY 40202   502-625-0000
Acts as an information clearinghouse and referral service for local small business owners. Brings suppliers and purchasers together.

Jefferson Community College
Community Education Division

109 East Broadway
Louisville, KY 40202   502-584-0181
> Coordinates and sponsors the Affiliated Small Business Teams (ABST), made up of 20 small business owners who assist each other in problem solving.

Small Business Administration
Federal Building, Room 188
600 Dr. Martin Luther King, Jr. Place   502-582-5971
Louisville, KY 40202   FAX: 502-582-5009
> **Small Business Institutes:** This program provides personalized consulting services to the small business community. Consulting is provided by senior level business students, guided by a faculty advisor. Assistance in business plan preparation, marketing research, market planning, accounting, and seminars are provided.
> **University Locations:**
> Bellermine College
> Eastern Kentucky University
> Morehead State University
> Thomas More College
> University of Kentucky - Lexington
> University of Louisville
> Western Kentucky University

* Small Business Development Centers

The following offer free and fee-based services to new and expanding businesses:

Lead Center:
Kentucky Small Business Development Center
University of Kentucky
Center for Business Development
College of Business & Economics
225 Business & Economics Building   606-257-7668
Lexington, KY 40506-0034   FAX: 606-258-1907

Ashland: Ashland Small Business Development Center, Boyd-Greenup County Chamber of Commerce Building, P.O. Box 830, 207 15th Street, Ashland, KY 41105-0830, 606-329-8011; FAX: 606-325-4607.

Bowling Green: Western Kentucky University, Bowling Green Small Business Development Center, 245 Grise Hall, Bowling Green, KY 42101, 502-745-2901; FAX: 502-745-2902.

Cumberland: Southeast Community College, Small Business Development Center, Room 113, Chrisman Hall, Cumberland, KY 40823, 606-589-4514; FAX: 606-589-4941.

Elizabethtown: Elizabethtown Small Business Development Center, 238 West Dixie Avenue, Elizabethtown, KY 42701, 502-765-6737; FAX: 502-765-6737.

Highland Heights: Northern Kentucky University, North Kentucky Small Business Development Center, BEP Center, Room 463, Highland Heights, KY 41099-0506, 606-572-6524; FAX: 606-572-5566.

Hopkinsville: Hopkinsville Small Business Development Center, 300 Hammond Drive, Hopkinsville, KY 42240, 502-886-8666; FAX: 502-886-3211.

Lexington: University of Kentucky, Small Business Development Center, College of Business & Economics, 227 Business & Economics Building, Lexington, KY 40506-0034, 606-257-7666; FAX: 606-258-1907.

Louisville: Bellarmine College, Small Business Development Center, School of Business, 2001 Newburg Road, Louisville, KY 40205-0671, 502-452-8282; FAX: 502-452-8288.

Louisville: University of Louisville, Small Business Development Center, Center for Entrepreneurship & Technology, Room 122, Burhans Hall, Louisville, KY 40292, 502-588-7854; FAX: 502-588-8573.

Morehead: Morehead State University, Small Business Development Center, 207 Downing Hall, Morehead, KY 40351, 606-783-2895; FAX: 606-783-2678.

Murray: Murray State University, West Kentucky Small Business Development Center, College of Business and Public Affairs, Murray, KY 42071, 502-762-2856; FAX: 502-762-3049.

Owensboro: Owensboro Small Business Development Center, 3860 U.S. Highway 60 West, Owensboro, KY 42301, 502-926-8085; FAX: 502-684-0714.

Pikeville: Pikeville Small Business Development Center, 222 Hatcher Court, Pikeville, KY 41501, 606-432-5848.

Somerset: Eastern Kentucky University, Small Business Development Center, 107 West Mt. Vernon Street, Somerset, KY 42501, 606-678-5520; FAX: 606-678-8349.

Louisiana

* General Information

Louisiana Department of Economic Development
101 France Street, Suite 115
P.O. Box 94185
Baton Rouge, LA 70804-9185   504-342-3000

Community Development Division
Louisiana Department of Commerce & Industry
P.O. Box 94185
Baton Rouge, LA 70804-9184   504-342-3000
> **Small Business Advocate:** Assistance in cutting bureaucratic red tape. Information and expertise in dealing with state, federal, and local agencies.

* Financing

Louisiana Department of Economic Development
101 France Street, Suite 115
P.O. Box 94185
Baton Rouge, LA 70804-9185
> **Finance Division:**
> **Industrial Development Bonds**   504-342-3000
> Can be used to finance industrial sites and buildings, equipment, storage facilities and pollution abatement and control projects. The facilities are then leased to the participating company at a rental sufficient to retire the bonds. When bonds are use for pollution abatement projects, they may be issued in unlimited amounts.

> **Enterprise Zones:** Companies locating in specially-designated Enterprise Zones are eligible for a package of tax incentives in addition to those available elsewhere in the state. Incentives include a one-time tax credit of $2,500 for each new job created at start-up or added to the payroll during the five years of the program. There is also an exemption from most state and local sales taxes on building materials and operating equipment.

> **10-Year Industrial Tax Exemption:** New manufacturing operations and expansions can receive an exemption from property taxes on industrial buildings, machinery and equipment for 10 years. Improvements to industrial land are also exempt.

> **Jobs Tax Credit:** Companies may take a one-time tax credit ranging from $100 to $250 for each net new job created as the result of the start-up of new business or expansion of an existing one. Credits can be used to satisfy state corporate income tax obligations. Manufacturing companies can elect to take this credit in lieu of the industrial property tax exemption or the benefits of the Enterprise Zone program.

Louisiana Economic Development Corporation
Department of Economic Development
P.O. Box 94185
Baton Rouge, LA 70804-9185   504-342-3000
> **Small Business Innovative Research Matching Grant Program:** Issues grants to Louisiana small businesses that have received Small Business Innovative Research (SBIR) Phase 1 grant funds. Any out-of-state firm which agrees to relocate headquarters and research and development operations to Louisiana and has received a Federal SBIR Phase 1 research

award. Matches SBIR grant on a one-to-one basis not exceeding $50,000. Funds to be used for research and related costs not covered by the federal SBIR grant or contract. It acts as gap funding between Phase I and Phase II awards.

Venture Capital Incentive Program: Stimulates availability of venture capital and encourages formation of seed and venture capital funds through three different programs.

The Louisiana Venture Capital Co-Investment Program works with venture capital funds to invest in Louisiana businesses. Matches up to 1/4 of a venture capital investment round with a qualified Venture Capital Fund.

The Louisiana Venture Capital Match Program matches $1 for every $2 of private investment in a Venture Capital Fund.

Small Business Equity Program: Participation loans and loan guarantees up to $2,000,000 per project. Guaranty funds can be used for purchase of fixed assets, equipment or machinery, line of credit for accounts receivable or inventory. Uses of funds from participation loans can be used to purchase fixed assets, equipment or machinery, working capital.

Small Business Linked Deposit: Eligible to small business with less than 150 employees to create new jobs or saving present jobs. Maximum per project is $200,000.

SBA 504: Loan guaranty available to small businesses. Conventional bank financing 50 percent, SBA participation 40 percent, owner equity 10 percent. Maximum loan $750,000.

Small Business Administration
1661 Canal Street
Suite 2000
New Orleans, LA 70112   504-589-6685
                               FAX: 504-589-2339

SBA 7(a) Guaranteed and Direct Loans: Guarantees up to 90 percent of a loan made through a private lender up to $750,000. Can be used for working capital, expand or convert facilities, purchase of machinery and equipment, and land and building. Available only to those unable to obtain a loan from conventional sources. Direct loans are made up to $150,000.

SBA 504: Provides loans using 50 percent conventional bank financing, 40 percent SBA involvement through Certified Development Companies, and 10 percent owner equity. Fixed-asset loans are available in amounts up to $750,000. The loan can be used for land and building, construction, machinery and equipment, and renovation/expansion.

Small Business Innovative Research Grants (SBIR): Phase I awards between $20,000 to $50,000 to entrepreneurs to support six months of research on a technical innovation. Phase II grants are an additional $500,000 for development. Private sector investment funds must follow.

International Trade Loans: Guaranteed long-term loans through private lenders to develop or expand export markets, or to recover from the effects of import competition. Maximum guaranteed loan is $1,000,000 for fixed assets and an additional $250,000 for working capital and/or export revolving line of credit.

Export Revolving Line of Credit Loan: Short term financing available to small businesses that are at least one year old. Loans provide working capital to finance the manufacturing or wholesaling of products for export and for export marketing. The SBA will guarantee up to 90 percent of a conventional loan in amounts up to $750,000.

Contract Loan: Short-term loans are available to small businesses to finance the costs of labor and materials on contracts for which the proceeds are assignable. Program guarantees up to 90 percent of loans not in excess of $750,000. Qualifying small businesses must be in business for at least 12 calendar months prior to the date of the loan application.

Seasonal Line of Credit Loan: Loans provide short-term working capital to finance seasonal increases in business activities. Program guarantees up to 90 percent of loans not in excess of $750,000. Qualifying business must be in operation for at least one year prior to application.

Pollution Control Loans: Long-term guaranteed loans can be made by conventional financing to small businesses for installation or required pollution control measures. Must be unable to adopt the pollution control measures without undue financial hardship. Maximum guaranteed loan is $1,000,000.

General Contractor Loans: Small general construction contractors may obtain short-term loans or loan guarantees for residential or commercial construction or rehabilitation of property to be sold. The SBA will guarantee up to 90 percent of qualifying loans made by private lenders up to a maximum of $750,000. Direct loans can be up to $150,000.

Energy Business Loan Guarantee: Small businesses that provide certain energy production and conservation services for others may qualify for long-term loans and loan guarantees for start-ups and expansions. Loans and guarantees are made for firms that develop, manufacture, sell, install, or service specific energy measures for others, or firms that provide engineering, architectural, consulting, or other professional services connected with specific energy measures. Guarantee is for up to 90 percent of a loan not in excess of $750,000. Direct loans up to $150,000.

Disaster Recovery Loans: Small businesses located in federally designated disaster areas and suffering property damage or economic losses from the disaster can obtain long-term recovery loans at low interest rates. Property damage loans are limited to 85 percent of the verified damage. Loans for economic losses are for operating capital to meet the business' obligations that could have been made had the disaster not occurred.

Handicapped Assistance Loans: Assists persons who have a physical, mental or emotional disability of a permanent nature which limits the selection of any type of employment for which the person would otherwise be qualified. Direct loans are available for up to $150,000. The interest rate is 3% on these loans.

Surety Bond Guaranty Program: Makes the bonding system more available to small contractors who may be denied access to the system. SBA can guarantee up to 80 percent of surety's loss on a bond that has a maximum in total contract value of up to $1,250,000.

Vietnam-era and Disabled Veterans Loan Program: Provides direct loans to veterans to establish or expand a small business. Funds may be used for working capital or fixed assets. Direct loans for amounts up to $150,000 are available. The interest rate may be fixed or variable.

Premier Venture Capital Corporation
451 Florida Street
Baton Rouge, LA 70821   504-389-4421

Small Business Investment Companies (SBIC): The SBA licenses, regulates, and provides financial assistance to privately owned and operated Small Business Investment Companies. SBICs make venture or risk investments by supplying capital and extending unsecured loans and loans not fully collateralized to small enterprises which meet their investment criteria. Financing is made by direct loans and by equity investments.

* Women and Minority Business Assistance

Louisiana Economic Development Corporation
Department of Economic Development
P.O. Box 94185
Baton Rouge, LA 70804-9185   504-342-3000

Louisiana Minority and Women's Business Development Program: Issues loans or loan guarantees to qualified minority- and women-owned businesses in amounts up to $250,000. Funds to be used to finance construction, conversion, or expansions of business facilities, finance machinery, supplies, materials or working capital line of credit. Direct loan is available when applicant is turned down by at least two financial institutions for a guaranty. Applicants must submit a detailed business plan.

Division of Minority and Women's Business Enterprise
Department of Economic Development
Post Office Box 94185

Baton Rouge, LA 70804-9185   504-342-5373

Provides one-on-one assistance with information and counseling on the state procurement and bidding process; sources of management, technical, and financial assistance from state and federal government sources as well as the private sector; private sector industries which have incentive programs to obtain goods and services from businesses owned by minorities and women, or which have franchise opportunities target for these group members. Works as an advocate for the minority and women's business community, recommending new laws and regulations to improve the business climate.

Small Business Administration (SBA)
1661 Canal Street, Suite 2000   504-589-6685
New Orleans, LA 70112   FAX: 504-589-2339

SBA 8(a) Program - Business Procurement Assistance: Provides federal government contracting opportunities for small businesses owned by socially and economically disadvantaged persons, and assists these businesses to become independently competitive in the normal business environment. SBA monitors all government contracts to assure that a quota of contract work goes to 8(a) businesses. Also provides business management services to these businesses. Business must be approved for program participation prior to receipt of an 8(a) contract.

* Training

Development Division
Office of Commerce and Industry
Department of Economic Development
Post Office Box 94185
Baton Rouge, LA 70804-9185   504-342-5893

Industrial Training:
Start-Up Training Program: Direct service to new or expanding manufacturing plans. Program is designed to fit the company's particular needs. Commerce and Industry funds and plans the program with the advice and approval of the client firm, aids in recruiting the trainees and conducts the training to company specifications.

There are two training phases in the program: Pre-Employment is usually conducted before the plant opens and Post-Employment Training is training on the production line conducted by the supervisor under regular production requirements.

Job Training Partnership Act (JTPA): Provides employers with recruitment, screening, referral, training, 50 percent wage subsidy up to 3 months for on-the-job training. Available to any private employer.

* Management Consulting and Other Services

Office of Commerce and Industry
Department of Economic Development
Post Office Box 94185
Baton Rouge, LA 70804-9185

Market Analysis and Planning   504-342-3000
Maintains an up-to-date computerized listing of available industrial properties in the state, along with data on wages, utilities, transportation and other advantages to new and expanding businesses. Profiles on more than 100 communities and all 64 parishes are also maintained.

Directory of Louisiana Manufacturers   504-342-3000
Lists Louisiana sources and supplies.

Office of International Trade, Finance & Development   504-342-5361
Responsible for the Department of Economic Development's efforts to increase Louisiana exports and to attract foreign business investment and other commercial enterprises. There are field representatives in Asia, and business contacts on the continents of Europe and Africa. Have formed business information referral networks with several financial institutions and private industry trade groups in Japan, the Peoples Republic of China, Korea and Taiwan.

Services provided are export counseling, matching exporters to foreign markets, sponsoring foreign trade shows and exhibits, promoting foreign investment, assisting with export financing, identifying international trade opportunities, organizing export seminars, providing information on export programs.

Small Business Administration
1661 Canal Street
Suite 2000   504-589-6685
New Orleans, LA 70112   FAX: 504-589-2339

Small Business Institutes: This program provides personalized consulting services to the small business community. Consulting is provided by senior level business students, guided by a faculty advisor. Assistance in business plan preparation, marketing research, market planning, accounting, and seminars are provided.

University Locations:
Louisiana State University - Shreveport
Louisiana State University - Baton Rouge
Louisiana Tech University
Loyola University
McNeese State University
Northeast Louisiana University
Northwestern State University
Southeastern Louisiana University
Southern University - New Orleans
University of New Orleans
University of Southwestern Louisiana
Xavier University

* Small Business Development Centers

The following offices offer free and fee-based services to new and expanding businesses:

Lead Center:
Louisiana Small Business Development Center
Northeast Louisiana University
Adm. 2-57   318-342-5506
Monroe, LA 71209   FAX: 318-342-5510

Alexandria: Small Business Development Center, 5212 Rue Verdun, Alexandria, LA 71306, 318-487-5454; FAX: 318-487-5451.

Baton Rouge: Capital Small Business Development Center, 9613 Interline Avenue, Baton Rouge, LA 70809, 504-922-0998.

Hammond: Southeastern Louisiana University, Small Business Development Center, Box 522, SLU Station, Hammond, LA 70402, 504-549-3831; FAX: 504-549-2127.

Lafayette: University of Southwestern Louisiana, Arcadiana Small Business Development Center, Box 43732, Lafayette, LA 70504, 318-262-5344; FAX: 318-262-5296.

Lake Charles: McNeese State University, Small Business Development Center, College of Business Administration, Lake Charles, LA 70609, 318-475-5529; FAX: 318-475-5122.

Monroe: Northeast Louisiana University, College of Business Administration, Monroe, LA 71209, 318-342-1224; FAX: 318-352-5506.

Monroe: Northeast Louisiana University, Small Business Development Center, LA Electronic Assistance Program, College of Business Administration, Monroe, LA 71209, 318-342-1215; FAX: 318-342-1209.

Monroe: Northeast Louisiana University, Small Business Development Center, Adm. 2-57, Monroe, LA 71209, 318-342-5506; FAX: 318-342-5510.

Natchitoches: Northwestern State University, Small Business Development Center, College of Business Administration, Natchitoches, LA 71497, 318-357-5611; FAX: 318-357-6810.

New Orleans: University of New Orleans, Small Business Development Center, LA International Trade, 368 Business Administration, New Orleans, LA 70148, 504-286-6978; FAX: 504-286-7197.

New Orleans: Loyola University, Small Business Development Center, Box 134, New Orleans, LA 70118, 504-865-3474; FAX: 504-865-3347.

New Orleans: Southern University, Small Business Development Center, College of Business Administration, New Orleans, LA 70126, 504-286-5308; FAX: 504-286-5306 (call first).

New Orleans: University of New Orleans, Small Business Development Center, Lakefront Campus, College of Business Administration, New Orleans, LA 70148, 504-286-6978; FAX: 505-286-7197.

Ruston: Louisiana Tech University, Small Business Development Center, Box 10318, Tech Station, Ruston, LA 71271-0046, 318-257-3537; FAX: 318-257-3356.

Shreveport: Louisiana State University at Shreveport, Small Business Development Center, College of Business Administration, 1 University Place, Shreveport, LA 71115, 318-797-5144; FAX: 318-797-5156.

Thibodaux: Nicholls State University, Small Business Development Center, P.O. Box 2015, Thibodaux, LA 70310, 504-448-4242; FAX: 504-448-4922.

Maine

* General Information

Department of Economic and Community Development   207-287-2656
193 State Street   1-800-872-3838 in Maine
State House Station #59   1-800-541-5872 outside Maine
Augusta, ME 04333   FAX: 207-287-2861

Business Answers/Small Business Advocate: Serves as a central clearinghouse of information regarding business assistance programs and services available to state businesses.

* Financing

Department of Economic and Community Development
State House Station #59   207-624-6800
Augusta, ME 04333   1-800-872-3838 in Maine

Community Development Block Grant Program (CDBG): Available to cities and counties for the commercial rehabilitation of existing buildings or structures used for business, commercial, or industrial purposes, which are then loans to businesses. Grants of up to $500,000 can be made. Every $15,000 of grant funds invested must create at least one full-time job, and at least 51 percent of the jobs created must be for low- and moderate-income families. The following programs originate from the CDBG.

Development Fund: Flexible interest rate, repayment period, and qualifying requirements. It is limited to 40 percent of a project with a maximum of $100,000. Can finance working capital as well as fixed assets.

Interim Finance Program: Primarily a source of affordable working capital or construction financing based on need. A minimum of $500,000 must be requested.

Community Revitalization Grant Program: Funds are used for housing rehabilitation, downtown revitalization or public infrastructure. In some cases, portions of the grants can be loaned to private entities for commercial or industrial projects.

Finance Authority of Maine (FAME)
83 Western Avenue
P.O. Box 949
Augusta, ME 04332-0949   207-623-3263

Commercial Loan Insurance Program: Designed to promote economic development by providing business borrowers access to capital that would otherwise be denied by lender due to unacceptable level of credit risk. Must be exhibit responsible ability to repay loan. Insures up to 90 percent of a commercial loan. Loan proceeds may be used for purchase of, and improvements to real estate, fishing vessels, and machinery and equipment.

Small Business and Veterans Loan Insurance Program: Helps small businesses that cannot obtain conventional financing. Will insure up to 85 percent of a loan to a maximum of $500,000. For eligible Maine veterans, the amount is increased to $600,000. Must employ 20 or fewer employees or gross sales less than $25 million.

SMART-E Bond Program: Tax-exempt, fixed-asset financing for manufacturing facilities. SMART-E will finance up to 90 percent of a loan by grouping it with other similar loans and selling tax-exempt bonds to finance them. Maximum loan is $7 million. Assets that can be financed with loan proceeds include land and depreciable assets.

SMART Bond Program: Similar to the SMART-E Program, but available to businesses which are not eligible for tax-exempt financing. Lending institution provides a loan commitment for acquisition of real estate, equipment or other fixed assets.

Municipal Securities Approval Program: Issues Industrial Revenue Bonds. Proceeds may be used for land, land improvements, buildings, machinery and equipment, financing and interest charges, engineering, legal services, surveys, cost estimates and studies.

Maine Job Start Program: A revolving direct loan program designed to provide eligible small business people with necessary capital to start, expand, or strengthen a business operation. Targeted to business that cannot obtain financing through conventional sources (even with loan insurance). Maximum available loan is $10,000. Interest rate is 2 percent below the prime interest rate. Applicant must have annual gross household income at or below 80 percent of the federal median income.

Potato Marketing Improvement Fund: Provides direct loans to potato growers and packers to construct modern storages, packing lines, and sprout inhibitor facilities. Long-term, fixed-rate loans at below market interest rates are available to help finance construction or improvements to storage and packing facilities. Participating loans can finance between 45 and 55 percent of the costs of eligible construction and improvements.

Linked Investment Program for Agriculture and Small Business: State funds are invested in financial institutions which then lend out funds at reduced interest rates to Maine farmers and small business people.

Occupational and Safety Loan Fund Program: Targeted direct loans to Maine businesses seeking to make workplace safety improvements. A business may borrow up to $50,000 for up to 10 years. Interest rate is 3 percent fixed. Funds can be used to purchase, improve, or erect equipment which reduces workplace hazards or promotes health and safety of employees.

Export Financing Services:
Working Capital Insurance provides additional security to bankers.

Export Credit Umbrella Insurance reduces international credit risks, allows an exporter to offer credit terms to foreign buyers in a competitive market, and offers the opportunity to obtain current cash flow against foreign receivables. Provided by the Export-Import bank of the United States (Eximbank).

Either FAME or Eximbank is responsible for up to 100 percent of a loan made by a financial institution to the exporter.

Underground Oil Storage Facility Program: A replacement program that provides 100 percent loan insurance to lenders, or direct loans to borrowers for the removal, replacement and disposal of underground marketing and distribution tanks for oil, petroleum products or petroleum by-products. Must be an owner of an underground oil storage facility and may be either an individual or business engaged in the marketing o distribution of oil, petroleum products or petroleum by-products to persons or entities other than the owner. Funds must be used for the removal, replacement and/or disposal of marketing or distribution tanks for oil, petroleum products or by-products.

Small Business Administration (SBA)
Federal Building
40 Western Avenue, Room 512   207-622-8378
Augusta, ME 04330   FAX: 207-622-8277

SBA 7(a) Guaranteed and Direct Loans: Guarantees up to 90 percent of a loan made through a private lender up to $750,000. Can be used for working capital, expand or convert facilities, purchase of machinery and equipment, and land and building. Available only to those unable to obtain a loan from conventional sources. Direct loans are made up to $150,000.

SBA 504: Provides loans using 50 percent conventional bank financing, 40 percent SBA involvement through Certified Development Companies, and 10 percent owner equity. Fixed-asset loans are available in amounts up to $750,000. The loan can be used for land and building, construction, machinery and equipment, and renovation/expansion.

Small Business Innovative Research Grants (SBIR): Phase I awards between $20,000 to $50,000 to entrepreneurs to support six months of research on a technical innovation. Phase II grants are an additional $500,000 for development. Private sector investment funds must follow.

International Trade Loans: Guaranteed long-term loans through private lenders to develop or expand export markets, or to recover from the effects of import competition. Maximum guaranteed loan is $1,000,000 for fixed assets and an additional $250,000 for working capital and/or export revolving line of credit.

Export Revolving Line of Credit Loan: Short term financing available to small businesses that are at least one year old. Loans provide working capital to finance the manufacturing or wholesaling of products for export and for export marketing. The SBA will guarantee up to 90 percent of a conventional loan in amounts up to $750,000.

Contract Loan: Short-term loans are available to small businesses to finance the costs of labor and materials on contracts for which the proceeds are assignable. Program guarantees up to 90 percent of loans not in excess of $750,000. Qualifying small businesses must be in business for at least 12 calendar months prior to the date of the loan application.

Seasonal Line of Credit Loan: Loans provide short-term working capital to finance seasonal increases in business activities. Program guarantees up to 90 percent of loans not in excess of $750,000. Qualifying business must be in operation for at least one year prior to application.

Pollution Control Loans: Long-term guaranteed loans can be made by conventional financing to small businesses for installation or required pollution control measures. Must be unable to adopt the pollution control measures without undue financial hardship. Maximum guaranteed loan is $1,000,000.

General Contractor Loans: Small general construction contractors may obtain short-term loans or loan guarantees for residential or commercial construction or rehabilitation of property to be sold. The SBA will guarantee up to 90 percent of qualifying loans made by private lenders up to a maximum of $750,000. Direct loans can be up to $150,000.

Energy Business Loan Guarantee: Small businesses that provide certain energy production and conservation services for others may qualify for long-term loans and loan guarantees for start-ups and expansions. Loans and guarantees are made for firms that develop, manufacture, sell, install, or service specific energy measures for others, or firms that provide engineering, architectural, consulting, or other professional services connected with specific energy measures. Guarantee is for up to 90 percent of a loan not in excess of $750,000. Direct loans up to $150,000.

Disaster Recovery Loans: Small businesses located in federally designated disaster areas and suffering property damage or economic losses from the disaster can obtain long-term recovery loans at low interest rates. Property damage loans are limited to 85 percent of the verified damage. Loans for economic losses are for operating capital to meet the business' obligations that could have been made had the disaster not occurred.

Handicapped Assistance Loans: Assists persons who have a physical, mental or emotional disability of a permanent nature which limits the selection of any type of employment for which the person would otherwise be qualified. Direct loans are available for up to $150,000. The interest rate is 3% on these loans.

Surety Bond Guaranty Program: Makes the bonding system more available to small contractors who may be denied access to the system. SBA can guarantee up to 80 percent of surety's loss on a bond that has a maximum in total contract value of up to $1,250,000.

Vietnam-era and Disabled Veterans Loan Program: Provides direct loans to veterans to establish or expand a small business. Funds may be used for working capital or fixed assets. Direct loans for amounts up to $150,000 are available. The interest rate may be fixed or variable.

Trade Missions: The SBA participates by underwriting private firms and assisting them to enter trade missions with other Federal Agencies. SBA promotes and assists in cost share monies to a limited degree. Trade Shows have been sponsored in Europe, Asia, Mid East, Africa and North America.

Farmers Home Administration (FmHA)
444 Stillwater Ave., Suite 2
P.O. Box 405
Bangor, ME 04402-0405   207-990-9160
   FmHA Business and Industry Program: Assistance is provided in the form of loan guarantees. FmHA contracts to reimburse the lender for a maximum of 80 percent of on loans up to $10,000,000. Loans are limited to areas outside the boundaries of cities of 50,000 or more. Priority is given to communities with less than $25,000, as well as to job creation and retention. Basic uses for loans include developing or financing business or industry, and increasing employment. Maximum term for fixed-asset or working capital loans is 30 years, for machinery and equipment 15 years, for working capital 7 years. Interest rate may be fixed or variable.

Economic Development Administration
Department of Commerce
40 Western Avenue
Augusta, ME 04330   207-622-8271
   EDA Loans and Grants: Low-interest loans or grants to communities may be used to develop land or to make improvements to public facilities in order to promote development and business expansions.

Androscoggin Valley Council of Governments
70 Court Street
Auburn, ME 04210   207-783-9186

Coastal Enterprises, Inc. *
P.O. Box 268
Wiscasset, ME 04578   207-882-7552

Eastern Maine Development Corporation
1 Cumberland Place, #300
Bangor, ME 04401   207-942-6389

Northern Kennebec Regional Planning Commission
7 Benton Avenue
Winslow, ME 04902   207-873-0711

Northern Maine Regional Planning Commission
P.O. Box 779
Caribou, ME 04736   207-498-8736

Lewiston/Auburn Economic Growth Council
P.O. Box 1188
Lewiston, ME 04243   207-784-0161
   Certified Development Companies (CDC): CDCs are SBA certified and intended to assist communities, both urban and rural, by stimulating the growth and expansion of small businesses primarily through financial assistance. Financial assistance may be provided through the Development Company loan programs.

   Certified Development Corporations also package applications for other programs. Each administering organization sets its own policies regarding the targeting of particular industries.

   Regional Revolving Loan Funds: Capitalized with either public or private grants. These pools of money are loaned to expanding companies in order to fill financing gaps that will allow viable projects to proceed.

   SBA 504 Program: Provides loans using 50 percent conventional bank financing, 40 percent SBA involvement through Certified Development Companies, and 10 percent owner equity. Maximum loan amount is $750,000. Loan can be used for fixed assets (land and building, construction, machinery and equipment, and renovation/expansion).

   * Child Care Loans: Coastal Enterprises, Inc. is able to make loans to child care providers to expand or improve a child care business and to prospective child care providers to start-up a business.

* Women and Minority Business Assistance

Maine Department of Transportation
Division of Equal Opportunity/Employee Relations
State Station House #16   207-287-3576
Augusta, ME 04333   FAX: 207-287-2896
**Disadvantaged/Minority/Women Business Enterprise Program
(D/WBE):** Assists in obtaining certification as a D/WBE. Assists with
procurement procedures to obtain government contracts. Provides
technical assistance to contractors, consultants and subcontractors.

Small Business Administration (SBA)
Federal Building
40 Western Avenue, Room 512   207-622-8378
Augusta, ME 04330   FAX: 207-622-8277
SBA 8(a) Program - Business Procurement Assistance: Provides federal
government contracting opportunities for small businesses owned by
socially and economically disadvantaged persons, and assists these
businesses to become independently competitive in the normal business
environment. SBA monitors all government contracts to assure that a
quota of contract work goes to 8(a) businesses. Also provides business
management services to these businesses. Business must be approved for
program participation prior to receipt of an 8(a) contract.

* Training

Maine State Department of Labor
Job Training Administration Office
100 Hospital Street
State House Station #55
Augusta, ME 04333   207-287-3377
Job Training Partnership Act (JTPA): Provides employers with
recruitment, screening, referral, training, 50 percent wage subsidy up to 3
months for on-the-job training. Available to any private employer.

* Management Consulting and Other Services

Maine State Department of Agriculture
Food and Rural Resources
State House Station #28
Augusta, ME 04333   207-287-3871
Assists farmers in the formation of farmers' markets, provides information
related to agricultural production and marketing, and promotes Maine-
produced products.

State Department of Marine Resources
Bureau of Marine Development
State House Station #21
Augusta, ME 04333   207-624-6550
The Marketing Division assists Maine's commercial fishing industry in
marketing seafood and other marine-related products.

Maine Department of Economic and
Community Development   207-287-2656
State House Station #59   1-800-872-3838 in Maine
Augusta, ME 04333   1-800-541-5872 outside Maine
Maine Supplier Network Program: Links vendors and suppliers with the
Maine Procurement Assistance Center in Bangor.

Maine Products Marketing Program: Provides trade show assistance to
Maine producers and suppliers and develops catalogue-marketing
opportunities for Maine consumer and industrial products.

Maine Procurement Assistance Center
1 Cumberland Place, #300
Bangor, ME 04401   207-942-6389
Provides technical procurement assistance through one-on-one counseling
to help Maine businesses compete for and win state and federal contracts.

Finance Authority of Maine (FAME)
83 Western Avenue
P.O. Box 949
Augusta, ME 04332-0949   207-623-3263
Maine Capital Network (MCN): Matches potential investors with Maine
businesses. They maintain a confidential database of investors and business
investment opportunities, and matches them based on stated interests and
requirements. FAME acts as an information service for the investors and
businesses.

International Trade Assistance: The Small Business Administration offers
aid to current and potential small or minority exports through two major
programs, financial assistance and business development assistance.

Maine Procurement Assistance Center
1 Cumberland Place, #300
Bangor, ME 04401   207-942-6389
This center provides individual counseling to Maine businesses according
to their specific markets, and assists businesses in marketing their products
and services to the Federal government. This office helps obtain bid
packages and prepare bid proposals and quotes. It also supplies current
military and Federal government specifications and standards. It assists
businesses with all phases of government contracting. The service is free.

Small Business Administration
Federal Building
40 Western Avenue
Room 512   207-622-8378
Augusta, ME 04330   FAX: 207-622-8277
Small Business Institutes: This program provides personalized consulting
services to the small business community. Consulting is provided by senior
level business students, guided by a faculty advisor. Assistance in business
plan preparation, marketing research, market planning, accounting, and
seminars are provided.
University Locations:
Husson College
Thomas College
University of Maine - Augusta
University of Maine - Presque Isle
University of Maine - Orono
University of Southern Maine

* Small Business Development Centers
The following offices offer free and fee-based services to new and expanding
businesses:

Lead Center:
Maine Small Business Development Center
University of Southern Maine
99 Falmouth Street   207-780-4420
Portland, ME 04103   FAX: 207-780-4810

Auburn: Androscoggin Valley Council of Governments (AVCOG), Small
Business Development Center, 70 Court Street, Auburn, ME 04210, 207-
783-9186.

Bangor: Eastern Maine Development Corporation, Small Business
Development Center, 10 Franklin Street, Bangor, ME 04401, 207-942-6389.

Caribou: Northern Maine Regional Planning Commission, Small Business
Development Center, McElwain House, P.O. Box 779, 2 Main Street,
Caribou, ME 04736, 207-498-8736.

Machias: University of Maine at Machias, Small Business Development
Center, Math and Science Building, Machias, ME 04654, 207-255-3313.

Sanford: Southern Maine Regional Planning Commission, Small Business
Development Center, Box Q, 2 School Street, Sanford, ME 04073, 207-324-
2952.

Winslow: North Kennebec Regional Planning Commission, Small Business
Development Center, 7 Benton Avenue, Winslow, ME 04902, 207-873-0711.

Wiscasset: Coastal Enterprises, Inc., Small Business Development Center, Middle Street, Box 268, Wiscasset, ME 04578, 207-882-7552.

Maryland

* General Information

Maryland Business Assistance Center
217 East Redwood Street, 10th Floor
Baltimore, MD 21202   301-333-6975
    A direct link to state services including public financing, facility location, state-funded employee training, government procurement assistance, help with licensing and permit processing, and information on starting a business.

Department of Economic and Employment Development
30 Hudson Street
Annapolis, MD 21401   301-974-7942
    Small Business Advocate: Assistance in cutting bureaucratic red tape. Information and expertise in dealing with state, federal, and local agencies.

* Financing

Maryland Industrial Division of Finance Authority (MIDFA)
217 East Redwood Street, Suite 2244
Baltimore, MD 21202   301-333-6975
    Export Financing Program: For industrial/commercial businesses engaged in the export of Maryland products or services, this program insures up to 90 percent of a conventional loan of from $10,000 to $5 million. Proceeds may be used to finance pre-and/or post-shipment working capital needs and standby letters of credit required by the foreign buyer.

    Supplementary Export Financing Assistance: The Maryland International Division and MIDFA can arrange specialized financing for exports through the Export-Import Bank of the U.S. MIDFA can package and coordinate applications. In addition, MIDFA serves as administrator for the Foreign Credit Association, which provides insurance against commercial and political risks associated with foreign receivables. Can be used in conjunction if the Export Financing Program.

    Conventional Program: For industrial/commercial businesses except certain retail establishments. Insures up to 80 percent or $1 million, whichever is lower, of a conventional loan. Proceeds may be used to finance fixed assets such as land, building, machinery and equipment, working capital, government contracts, revolving credit lines. Projects normally range from $35,000 to $5 million. Interest rates of loan are determined by the lender.

    Enterprise Zone Program: For industrial/commercial business except certain retail establishes located in State Enterprise Zones. Insures up to 90 percent or $500,000, whichever is lower, of a conventional loan. Proceeds may be used to finance fixed assets such as land, building, machinery and equipment, working capital, and government contracts. Projects normally range from $35,000 to $500,000. Interest rates of loan are determined by the lender. Advantages of locating in an enterprise zone include property-tax reduction and income tax credits to eligible firms.

    Tax Exempt Program: Issues tax-exempt revenue bonds for manufacturers which may be totally or partially insured. Projects normally range from $200,000 to $10 million. Proceeds may be used for fixed assets such as land, new buildings, new machinery and equipment, existing buildings and use equipment. Interest rates are tax-exempt, floating, or fixed-rate as determined by bond purchaser or market conditions.

    Taxable Bond Program: For industrial/commercial businesses with certain exceptions. Insurance level varies with each project but is limited to $5 million. Can be used to finance fixed assets such as land, building-new or existing, permanent financing may be coupled with construction loan, new machinery and equipment.

Maryland Small Business Development Financing
Authority (MSBDFA)   301-333-6975
    Surety Bond Guarantee Assistance Program: Assists small contractors in obtaining bid, performance and payment bonds for government and public utility contracts. For small businesses employing fewer than 50 full-time employees or those with annual gross sales less than $10 million. Program guarantees up to 90 percent of the face value of issued bonds. Proceeds guarantee reimbursement of bid, payment, or performance bonds up to $1 million. Guarantee may not exceed term of the contract. Must have been denied bonding by a surety within 90 days of submitting an application, subcontract no more than 75 percent of the dollar value of the contract, and show that the contract will have substantial economic impact.

Development Credit Fund, Inc.
2530 N. Charles Street, Suite 200
Baltimore, MD 21218   301-467-7500
    Development Credit Fund Program: Loan guarantees for businesses owned by socially and economically disadvantaged persons. Must show experience in the trade. Projects range from $5,000 to $575,000. Proceeds may be used for working capital, acquisition of machinery and equipment acquisition, and business acquisitions, business real estate. Interest rates are variable, none more than 2 percent over prime rate.

Community Financing Group
Department of Economic and Employment Development
Redwood Tower, 217 East Redwood
Baltimore, MD 21202   301-333-4304
    Community Development Block Grant: Available to cities and counties for the commercial rehabilitation of existing buildings or structures used for business, commercial, or industrial purposes. Grants of up to $500,000 can be made. Every $15,000 of grant funds invested must create at least one full-time job, and at least 51 percent of the jobs created must be for low- and moderate-income families.

Maryland Business Assistance Center
217 East Redwood Street 10th floor
Baltimore, MD 21202   301-333-6975
    Maryland Industrial and Commercial Redevelopment Fund:
    Loan/Grant Program: The fund makes loans or grants to political subdivisions to cover part of the project costs of an industrial or commercial redevelopment project. Subdivisions then use proceeds to guarantee loans to redevelopers.

    **Maryland Department of Economic and
    Employment Development**   301-333-6975
    Maryland Industrial Land Act: Authorizes loans to counties and municipalities for options and acquisition of industrial land, development of industrial parks, construction of buildings, and purchase of options, access ways, utilities, and rail rights of way needed to serve industrial sites. Loans range from $750,00 to $1.5 million.

Department of Economic & Employment Development
217 East Redwood Street
Baltimore, MD 21202   301-333-6975
    Day Care Facilities Financing Programs (DCFP):
    Day Care Facilities Loan Guarantee Program   301-333-4308
    Loan guarantees insure up to 80 percent of loans. The project must create or expand day care facilities in the state and the applicant must demonstrate an inability to obtain adequate financing through normal lending channels. Must demonstrate the ability to manage the facility, or contract for management services. Funds can be used for construction, renovation, purchase of land and building, equipment, supplies and working capital. Funds can also assist in the financing of the purchase of an existing center, provided the center will be expanded to accommodate additional clients.

    Facilities for Elderly and Handicapped Adults: Guarantees of loans are made to individuals or businesses to finance the expansion or development of day care facilities for the elderly and for medically handicapped adults. Applicants who own or are acquiring a building for elderly or medically handicapped adult day care or wish to have an adult day care facility in the home may be eligible to apply to the **Maryland House Rehabilitation Program** to finance any required alterations or modifications to the structure. The two programs are working together.

    Loan guarantees are also available for Child Care.

Child Care Facilities Direct Loan Fund: Fund is designed to finance up to 50 percent of the "hard" costs for the expansion or development of a child care facility where care is provided for seven or more children. For those seeking to expand or develop day care facilities in the state, have demonstrated the ability to manage the facility, or contract for management services, and are unable to obtain necessary financing through normal lending channels. Funds may be used for construction, renovation, or acquisition of real property. $15,000 is the minimum that may be borrowed directly from the DCFP for a child care facility in the home.

Maryland Energy Financing Administration   301-333-4782
Maryland Energy Financing Program: Sale of revenue bonds are used to help businesses seeking to conserve energy, co-generate energy, and produce fuels and other energy sources. Projects range from $200,000 to $80 million. Proceeds may be used for land acquisition, building acquisition, construction or rehabilitation, machinery and equipment, and hydroelectric facilities.

Prince Georges County/Montgomery County
Small Business Administration
10 North Calvert   410-962-4392
Baltimore, MD 21202   FAX: 410-962-1805

Washington District Small Business Administration
1111 18th Street, N.W., 6th Floor
P.O. Box 1993   202-634-1500
Washington, DC 20036   FAX: 202-634-1803
SBA 7(a) Guaranteed and Direct Loans: Guarantees up to 90 percent of a loan made through a private lender up to $750,000. Can be used for working capital, expand or convert facilities, purchase of machinery and equipment, and land and building. Available only to those unable to obtain a loan from conventional sources. Direct loans are made up to $150,000.

SBA 504: Provides loans using 50 percent conventional bank financing, 40 percent SBA involvement through Certified Development Companies, and 10 percent owner equity. Fixed-asset loans are available in amounts up to $750,000. The loan can be used for land and building, construction, machinery and equipment, and renovation/expansion.

Small Business Innovative Research Grants (SBIR): Phase I awards between $20,000 to $50,000 to entrepreneurs to support six months of research on a technical innovation. Phase II grants are an additional $500,000 for development. Private sector investment funds must follow.

International Trade Loans: Guaranteed long-term loans through private lenders to develop or expand export markets, or to recover from the effects of import competition. Maximum guaranteed loan is $1,000,000 for fixed assets and an additional $250,000 for working capital and/or export revolving line of credit.

Export Revolving Line of Credit Loan: Short term financing available to small businesses that are at least one year old. Loans provide working capital to finance the manufacturing or wholesaling of products for export and for export marketing. The SBA will guarantee up to 90 percent of a conventional loan in amounts up to $750,000.

Contract Loan: Short-term loans are available to small businesses to finance the costs of labor and materials on contracts for which the proceeds are assignable. Program guarantees up to 90 percent of loans not in excess of $750,000. Qualifying small businesses must be in business for at least 12 calendar months prior to the date of the loan application.

Seasonal Line of Credit Loan: Loans provide short-term working capital to finance seasonal increases in business activities. Program guarantees up to 90 percent of loans not in excess of $750,000. Qualifying business must be in operation for at least one year prior to application.

Pollution Control Loans: Long-term guaranteed loans can be made by conventional financing to small businesses for installation or required pollution control measures. Must be unable to adopt the pollution control measures without undue financial hardship. Maximum guaranteed loan is $1,000,000.

General Contractor Loans: Small general construction contractors may obtain short-term loans or loan guarantees for residential or commercial construction or rehabilitation of property to be sold. The SBA will guarantee up to 90 percent of qualifying loans made by private lenders up to a maximum of $750,000. Direct loans can be up to $150,000.

Energy Business Loan Guarantee: Small businesses that provide certain energy production and conservation services for others may qualify for long-term loans and loan guarantees for start-ups and expansions. Loans and guarantees are made for firms that develop, manufacture, sell, install, or service specific energy measures for others, or firms that provide engineering, architectural, consulting, or other professional services connected with specific energy measures. Guarantee is for up to 90 percent of a loan not in excess of $750,000. Direct loans up to $150,000.

Disaster Recovery Loans: Small businesses located in federally designated disaster areas and suffering property damage or economic losses from the disaster can obtain long-term recovery loans at low interest rates. Property damage loans are limited to 85 percent of the verified damage. Loans for economic losses are for operating capital to meet the business' obligations that could have been made had the disaster not occurred.

Handicapped Assistance Loans: Assists persons who have a physical, mental or emotional disability of a permanent nature which limits the selection of any type of employment for which the person would otherwise be qualified. Direct loans are available for up to $150,000. The interest rate is 3% on these loans.

Surety Bond Guaranty Program: Makes the bonding system more available to small contractors who may be denied access to the system. SBA can guarantee up to 80 percent of surety's loss on a bond that has a maximum in total contract value of up to $1,250,000.

Vietnam-era and Disabled Veterans Loan Program: Provides direct loans to veterans to establish or expand a small business. Funds may be used for working capital or fixed assets. Direct loans for amounts up to $150,000 are available. The interest rate may be fixed or variable.

American Security Capital Corp., Inc.
100 S. Charles Street, 5th Floor
Baltimore, MD 21203   301-547-4523

First Maryland Capital, Inc.
107 West Jefferson Street
Rockville, MD 20850   301-251-6630

Greater Washington Investments, Inc.
5454 Wisconsin Avenue
Chevy Chase, MD 20815   301-656-0626
Small Business Investment Companies (SBIC): The SBA licenses, regulates, and provides financial assistance to privately owned and operated Small Business Investment Companies. SBICs make venture or risk investments by supplying capital and extending unsecured loans and loans not fully collateralized to small enterprises which meet their investment criteria. Financing is made by direct loans and by equity investments.

* Women and Minority Assistance

Maryland Small Business Development
Financing Authority   301-333-4270
Government Contract Program: Makes direct loans as well as loan guarantees to businesses owned 70 percent or more by socially or economically disadvantaged persons. Loans or guarantees are for up to $250,000. Maximum guarantee is 90 percent. Can be used for working capital, direct supplies and materials, purchase of equipment. required Funds can be acquired to begin, continue and complete government or public utility contracts, acquisition of machinery to perform government contracts. Loan term is for one year or duration of the contract. Cannot obtain adequate financing through other lending channels.

Long-Term Guaranty Program: Loan guarantees for amounts from $5,000 to $500,000 up to 80 percent of loan for business owned 70 percent or more by socially or other disadvantaged persons. Must have 18 successive months of experience in the trade or business for which financing is sought. Proceeds may be used for working capital, acquisition of machinery or equipment, and real property improvements if loan is owned by applicant. Interest rates are variable, none more that 1 percent over the prime rate.

Equity Participation Investment Program:
Franchise Component: Equity investment for franchises owned 70 percent or more by socially or economically disadvantaged persons. Projects range from $5,000 to $1 million. Proceeds may be used to finance land, buildings, franchise fees, training fees, equipment, leasehold improvements, working capital, and other franchise-related costs.

Business Acquisition Component: Can enhance business ownership potential of socially or economically disadvantaged persons by providing equity or debt financing for the acquisition of existing profitable business. Funds may be use for machinery and equipment, leasehold improvements, furniture and fixtures, inventory, working capital, purchase of existing franchise, real estate acquisition, sign package and supplies and franchise fees.

Applicants shall have a minimum net worth of at least $75,000 pledge as security, and shall have three or more years of successful experience with demonstrated achievements and management responsibilities. Financing shall not exceed the lessor of $500,000 for any enterprises acquiring an existing business or 25 percent of the total investment in the enterprises acquiring an existing business.

An existing business shall have been in existence for at least five years, been profitable for at least two of the previous three years, sufficient cash flow to service the debt, capacity for growth and job creation, a strong customer base.

Prince Georges County/Montgomery County
Small Business Administration
10 North Calvert   410-962-4392
Baltimore, MD 21202   FAX: 410-962-1805

Washington District Small Business Administration
1111 18th Street, N.W., 6th Floor
P.O. Box 1993   202-634-1500
Washington, DC 20036   FAX: 202-634-1803
    SBA 8(a) Program-Business Procurement Assistance: Provides federal government contracting opportunities for small businesses owned by socially and economically disadvantaged persons, and assists these businesses to become independently competitive in the normal business environment. SBA monitors all government contracts to assure that a quota of contract work goes to 8(a) businesses. Also provides business management services to these businesses. Business must be approved for program participation prior to receipt of an 8(a) contract.

* Training

Maryland Business Assistance Center
217 E. Redwood Street, 10th Floor
Baltimore, MD 21201   301-333-6975
    Partnership for Workforce Quality Training Program: Through the Partnership Program, training grants to businesses are provided where there is a need and commitment to upgrade the skills of the current workforce. To participate in the Partnership a company must be a Maryland Employer, request assistance in training for job-specific skills, request training for Maryland-based employees, and request training to upgrade or retrain existing employees. Priorities are given to employers with fewer than 100 employees. Helps assess employer's training needs, specific skill needs, human resource needs and training objectives. Also assists in designing and developing the skill training programs around these needs and goals. Training can be arranged in-house with the business or through specialized training vendors. The employer may be eligible for a state training grant for up to 50 percent of the direct training costs.

Maryland Business Assistance Center
217 East Redwood Street, 10th Floor
Baltimore, MD 21202   301-333-6975
    Employee Training Programs: The state's employee training programs are designed to provide Maryland business with the skilled manpower it needs to operate profitably. The programs offer performance-based, short-term training which is usually conducted during the pre-employment, start-up

phase of operations. Program design is flexible and tailored to meet the needs of the company.

Maryland Business Assistance Center
217 East Redwood
Baltimore, MD 21202   301-333-6975
    Job Training Partnership Act (JTPA): Provides employers with recruitment, screening, referral, training, 50 percent wage subsidy up to 3 months for on-the-job training. Available to any private employer.

* Management Consulting and Other Services

Department of Human Resource
Office of Child Care Licensing and Regulation
600 East Lombard Street, Suite 312
Baltimore, MD 21202   301-333-0988
    Day Care Licensing Programs: Provide technical assistance to employers and developers who want to sponsor day care services for their employees and offer assistance to day care entrepreneurs who are interested in becoming small business owners providing quality day care services.

    Procurement Board   410-333-0988
    The Board acts as a free telephone source of business procurement opportunities in Maryland.

Maryland Business Assistance Center
217 East Redwood Street 10th floor
Baltimore, MD 21202   301-333-6975
    Office of International Trade:
    Export Promotion Assistance: Provides assistance to existing and potential exporting companies. Provides informational and consulting services on the exporting process. Initiates and organizes trade missions in cooperation with the private sector. Assists in obtaining export-related financing, and services as a clearinghouse for seminars and conferences. Also aids Maryland business in barter, counter trade and joint venture transactions.

    Foreign Trade Zones: Three foreign trade zones provide economic incentives to companies doing business in international markets. Manufacturers, exports, importers and distributors can realize significant operating and financial advantages. Reduced customs duties and improved cash flow are two of the many benefits of operating in a foreign trade zone.

Prince Georges County/Montgomery County
Small Business Administration
10 North Calvert   410-962-4392
Baltimore, MD 21202   FAX: 410-962-1805

Washington District Small Business Administration
1111 18th Street, N.W., 6th Floor
P.O. Box 1993   202-634-1500
Washington, DC 20036   FAX: 202-634-1803
    Small Business Institutes: This program provides personalized consulting services to the small business community. Consulting is provided by senior level business students, guided by a faculty advisor. Assistance in business plan preparation, marketing research, market planning, accounting, and seminars are provided.
    University Locations:
    Frostburg State University
    Loyola College
    Salisbury State University
    University of Baltimore
    University of Maryland

* Small Business Development Centers
The following offer free and fee-based services to new and expanding businesses:

Lead Center:
Maryland Small Business Development Center
Department of Economic and Employment Development
217 East Redwood Street, 10th Floor   410-333-6995
Baltimore, MD 21202   FAX: 410-333-6609

Baltimore: Small Business Development Center, 1414 Key Highway, Suite 310, Baltimore, MD 21230, 301-234-0505.

Bethesda: Montgomery College, Small Business Development Center, 7815 Woodmount Avenue, Bethesda, MD 20814, 301-656-7482.

Cumberland: Western Region Small Business Development Center, 3 Commerce Drive, Cumberland, MD 21502, 301-724-6716.

Elkton: Cecil Community College, Eastern Region Small Business Development Center, 107 Railroad Avenue, Elkton, MD 21921, 301-392-3366.

Fredrick: Fredrick Community College, Small Business Development Center, 5340 Spectrum Drive, Suite K, Fredrick, MD 21701, 301-694-4647; FAX: 301-695-7332.

Hagerstown: Hagerstown Junior College, Small Business Development Center, Advanced Technology Center, 751 Robin Hood Drive, Hagerstown, MD 21740, 301-790-2800, ext. 388.

Landover: Suburban Washington Small Business Development Center, 9201 Basil Court, Suite 403, Landover, MD 20785, 301-925-5460; FAX: 301-925-5359.

Waldorf: Charles Community College, Southern Region Small Business Development Center, 235 Smallwood Village Center, Waldorf, MD 20601, 301-932-4155.

Massachusetts

* General Information

Massachusetts Office of Business Development
1 Ashburton Place, 21st Floor
Boston, MA 02108   617-727-3221
Operates the *SPIRIT* Business Line, a toll-free, direct hot-line service to answer business-related questions.

* Financing

Community Development Finance Corporation
10 P.O. Square
Suite 1090
Boston, MA 02109   617-482-9141
Venture Capital Program: Provides debt and equity financing to small, viable businesses for working capital. Preferred investment range is $75,000 to $300,000. Program provides up to one-third of the total financing required.

Small Loan Guarantee Program: Financing for businesses needing smaller amounts of capital (less that $50,000). Program guarantees up to 50 percent of a loan, or up to $25,000.

Community Development Program: Flexible, short-term financing for residential, commercial or industrial real-estate projects. May provide 20 percent or up to $250,000 for projects that will construct affordable housing or develop commercial property.

Massachusetts Economic Stabilization Trust Fund
100 Cambridge Street, #1302
Boston, MA 02202   617-727-8158
Industrial Services Program: Provides funding for companies in mature industries which face permanent layoffs or plant closings. Funds are in the form of conventional loans at favorable rates of interest with flexible terms.

Massachusetts Business Development Corporation
One Liberty Square
2nd Floor
Boston, MA 02109   617-350-8877
Business Loans: Provides loans to firms which are unable to obtain financing through conventional sources. Loans may be used for purchase

or construction of fixed business assets (land, plant, equipment) and for working capital. Can provide up to 100 percent of financing.

Massachusetts Capital Resource Company
420 Boylston Street
Boston, MA 02116   617-536-3900
Provides unsecured loans in the form of debt and equity financing to small and medium-sized firms that are unable to obtain financing through conventional sources. Maximum loan amount is $5 million.

Massachusetts Industrial Finance Agency
75 Federal Street
Boston, MA 02110   617-451-2477
Taxable Industrial Development Bond: Bonds are available for a wide range of industrial and commercial capital expansions, including manufacturing, warehouse and distribution, and research and development projects. Proceeds can be used for the acquisition, construction, or renovation of buildings and land, or for the purchase of equipment.

Tax-Exempt Industrial Development Bond Program: Bonds can be used by manufacturers planning to construct new facilities, expand or renovate existing facilities, or purchase new equipment.

Guaranteed Loan Program: Pools either tax-exempt or taxable IDB's into one large bond issue to enable smaller companies access to the public credit market.

Mortgage Insurance Program: Insures portions of loans from 10% to 40% with a ceiling of $500,000 for real estate and $250,000 for equipment.

Seafood Loan Fund: Provides low-rate, fixed-rate financing for companies engaged in the seafood processing industry. Direct loans of up to $200,000 are available.

Childcare Facilities Loan Fund: Provides direct loans of up to $250,000 to companies, developers, and non-profit organizations to be used for acquisition, renovation, construction, and permanent installed equipment for on-site day care facilities.

Thrift Fund: Direct loans are available for projects that create significant numbers of new jobs in areas of high unemployment and are unable to obtain conventional financing.

Massachusetts Government Land Bank
One Court Street
Suite 200
Boston, MA 02108   617-727-8257
Mortgage Financing: Below-market rates for mortgages in the $200,000 to $2 million range for industrial projects that increase jobs in areas of high unemployment and projects that provide lower-income housing.

CDAG Program Director
Division of Communities Development
Executive Office of Communities and Development
100 Cambridge Street
Boston, MA 02202   617-727-7180
Community Development Action Grant: Grants are made to cities and towns for public actions in support of private investments. Projects should create or retain long-term employment and/or housing opportunities and revitalize distressed areas.

Economic Development Set Aside Program   617-727-7180
Loans at low interest rates and favorable terms for businesses locating, expanding, or starting-up in communities that are eligible for HUD Small Cities Community Development Block Grants.

Farmers Home Administration
451 West Street
Amherst, MA 01002   413-253-4300
Business and Industry Loans: Loan guarantees for funds for business and industrial acquisition, construction, repair, modernization, purchase of land, machinery and equipment, furniture and fixtures, start up and

working capital, processing and marketing facilities, and pollution control. Minimum loan size is $500,00. Maximum loan size is $10 million.

Farm Loan Guarantees: Made to family farmers and ranchers to enable them to obtain funds from private lenders. Funds must be used for farm ownership, improvements, and operating purposes.

Farm Operating Loans: Loans to help meet operating expenses, finance recreational and nonagricultural enterprises to add to family income, and pay for mandated safety and pollution control changes. Available at variable interest rates. Limits are $200,000 for an insured farm operating loan and $400,000 for a guaranteed loan.

Farm Ownership Loans: Can be used to for a wide range of farm improvement projects. Limits are $200,000 for an insured loan and $300,000 for a guaranteed loan.

Soil and Water Loans: Must be used by individual farmers and ranchers to develop, conserve, and properly use their land and water resources and to help abate pollution. Interest rates are variable; each loan must be secured by real estate.

Youth Project Loans: Enable young people to borrow for income producing projects sponsored by a school or 4H club.

Economic Development Administration
545 Boylston Street, Suite 601
Boston, MA 02116   617-727-7001
Business Development Loans: Provides direct loans to be used for the acquisition of fixed assets, land preparation, building rehabilitation, and working capital for industrial or commercial enterprises. Loans are available for up to 65 percent of project cost.

Small Business Administration (SBA)
Boston District Office
10 Causeway Street
2nd Floor, Room 265   617-565-5590
Boston, MA 02222-1093   FAX: 617-565-5598
SBA 7(a) Guaranteed and Direct Loans: Guarantees up to 90 percent of a loan made through a private lender up to $750,000. Can be used for working capital, expand or convert facilities, purchase of machinery and equipment, and land and building. Available only to those unable to obtain a loan from conventional sources. Direct loans are made up to $150,000.

SBA 504: Provides loans using 50 percent conventional bank financing, 40 percent SBA involvement through Certified Development Companies, and 10 percent owner equity. Fixed-asset loans are available in amounts up to $750,000. The loan can be used for land and building, construction, machinery and equipment, and renovation/expansion.

Small Business Innovative Research Grants (SBIR): Phase I awards between $20,000 to $50,000 to entrepreneurs to support six months of research on a technical innovation. Phase II grants are an additional $500,000 for development. Private sector investment funds must follow.

International Trade Loans: Guaranteed long-term loans through private lenders to develop or expand export markets, or to recover from the effects of import competition. Maximum guaranteed loan is $1,000,000 for fixed assets and an additional $250,000 for working capital and/or export revolving line of credit.

Export Revolving Line of Credit Loan: Short term financing available to small businesses that are at least one year old. Loans provide working capital to finance the manufacturing or wholesaling of products for export and for export marketing. The SBA will guarantee up to 90 percent of a conventional loan in amounts up to $750,000.

Contract Loan: Short-term loans are available to small businesses to finance the costs of labor and materials on contracts for which the proceeds are assignable. Program guarantees up to 90 percent of loans not in excess of $750,000. Qualifying small businesses must be in business for at least 12 calendar months prior to the date of the loan application.

Seasonal Line of Credit Loan: Loans provide short-term working capital to finance seasonal increases in business activities. Program guarantees up to 90 percent of loans not in excess of $750,000. Qualifying business must be in operation for at least one year prior to application.

Pollution Control Loans: Long-term guaranteed loans can be made by conventional financing to small businesses for installation or required pollution control measures. Must be unable to adopt the pollution control measures without undue financial hardship. Maximum guaranteed loan is $1,000,000.

General Contractor Loans: Small general construction contractors may obtain short-term loans or loan guarantees for residential or commercial construction or rehabilitation of property to be sold. The SBA will guarantee up to 90 percent of qualifying loans made by private lenders up to a maximum of $750,000. Direct loans can be up to $150,000.

Energy Business Loan Guarantee: Small businesses that provide certain energy production and conservation services for others may qualify for long-term loans and loan guarantees for start-ups and expansions. Loans and guarantees are made for firms that develop, manufacture, sell, install, or service specific energy measures for others, or firms that provide engineering, architectural, consulting, or other professional services connected with specific energy measures. Guarantee is for up to 90 percent of a loan not in excess of $750,000. Direct loans up to $150,000.

Disaster Recovery Loans: Small businesses located in federally designated disaster areas and suffering property damage or economic losses from the disaster can obtain long-term recovery loans at low interest rates. Property damage loans are limited to 85 percent of the verified damage. Loans for economic losses are for operating capital to meet the business' obligations that could have been made had the disaster not occurred.

Handicapped Assistance Loans: Assists persons who have a physical, mental or emotional disability of a permanent nature which limits the selection of any type of employment for which the person would otherwise be qualified. Direct loans are available for up to $150,000. The interest rate is 3% on these loans.

Surety Bond Guaranty Program: Makes the bonding system more available to small contractors who may be denied access to the system. SBA can guarantee up to 80 percent of surety's loss on a bond that has a maximum in total contract value of up to $1,250,000.

Vietnam-era and Disabled Veterans Loan Program: Provides direct loans to veterans to establish or expand a small business. Funds may be used for working capital or fixed assets. Direct loans for amounts up to $150,000 are available. The interest rate may be fixed or variable.

Advent Atlantic Capital Company, LP
75 State Street, Suite 2500
Boston, MA 02109   617-345-7200

Advent Industrial Capital Company, LP
75 State Street, Suite 2500
Boston, MA 02109   617-345-7200

Advent V Capital Company
75 State Street, Suite 2500
Boston, MA 02109   617-345-7200

BancBoston Ventures, Inc.
100 Federal Street
Mail: P.O. Box 2016 Stop 01-31-08
Boston, MA 02110   617-434-2442

Business Achievement Corporation
1172 Beacon Street, Suite 202
Newton, MA 02161   617-965-0550

Chestnut Capital International II LP
75 State Street, Suite 2500
Boston, MA 02109   617-345-7200

Chestnut Street Partners, Inc.
75 State Street, Suite 2500
Boston, MA 02109   617-345-7220

First Capital Corporation of Chicago
(Main Office: Chicago IL)
One Financial Center, 27th Floor
Boston, MA 02111   617-542-9185

First SBIC of California
(Main Office: Costa Mesa, CA)
101 Federal Street, 19th Floor
Boston, MA 02110   617-542-7601

First United SBIC, Inc.
135 Will Drive
Canton, MA 02021   617-828-6150

Fleet Venture Resources, Inc.
(Main Office: Providence, RI)
1740 Massachusetts Avenue
Boxborough, MA 01719   508-263-0177

LRF Capital, LP
189 Wells Avenue, Suite 4
Newton, MA 02159   617-964-0049

Mezzanine Capital Corporation
75 State Street, Suite 2500
Boston, MA 02109   617-345-7200

Northeast SBI Corporation
16 Cumberland Street
Boston, MA 02115   617-267-3983

Northwest Venture Partners
(Main Office: Minneapolis, MN)
50 Milk Street, 20th Floor
Boston, MA 02109   617-426-1416

Norwest Equity Partners IV
(Main Office: Minneapolis, MN)
50 Milk Street, 20th Floor
Boston, MA 02109   617-426-1416

Norwest Growth Fund, Inc.
(Main Office: Minneapolis, MN)
50 Milk Street, 20th Floor
Boston, MA 02109   617-426-1416

Orange Nassau Capital Corporation
One International Place, 23rd Floor
Boston, MA 02110   617-951-9920

Pioneer Ventures LP
60 State Street
Boston, MA 02109   617-742-7825

Southern Berkshire Investment Corporation
P.O. Box 669
Sheffield, MA 01257   413-229-3106

TBM II Capital Corporation
One International Place, 23rd Floor
Boston, MA 02110   617-951-9920

UST Capital Corporation
40 Court Street
Boston, MA 02108   617-726-7137

Vadus Capital Corporation
One International Place, 23rd Floor
Boston, MA 02110   617-951-9920
> **Small Business Investment Companies (SBIC):** The SBA licenses, regulates, and provides financial assistance to privately owned and operated Small Business Investment Companies. SBICs make venture or risk investments by supplying capital and extending unsecured loans and loans not fully collateralized to small enterprises which meet their investment criteria. Financing is made by direct loans and by equity investments.

Office of Community Planning and Development Division
Department of Housing and Urban Development
10 Causeway Street, 3rd Floor
Boston, MA 02222   617-565-5345
> **Community Development Block Grant:** Available to cities and counties for the commercial rehabilitation of existing buildings or structures used for business, commercial, or industrial purposes. Grants of up to $500,000 can be made. Every $15,000 of grant funds invested must create at least one full-time job, and at least 51 percent of the jobs created must be for low- and moderate-income families.

> **Urban Development Action Grant:** Awarded to communities which then lend the proceeds at flexible rates to eligible businesses. Projects whose total costs are less than $100,000 are not eligible. UDAG funds should leverage at least three to four times their amount in private sector investment.

Executive Office of Communities and Development
14th Floor, 100 Cambridge Street
Boston, MA 02202   617-727-8690
> **Community Development Block Grant -- Small Cities:** Available to cities and counties for the commercial rehabilitation of existing buildings or structures used for business, commercial, or industrial purposes. Grants of up to $500,000 can be made. Every $15,000 of grant funds invested must create at least one full-time job, and at least 51 percent of the jobs created must be for low- and moderate-income families.

Massachusetts Technology Development Corporation
148 State Street, 9th Floor
Boston, MA 02109   617-723-4920
> Makes both debt and equity investments to provide working capital to new and expanding high technology companies which have the capacity to generate significant employment growth in the state.

The Thrift Fund
50 Congress Street, Suite 515
Boston, MA 02109   617-227-0404
> A loan pool established to fund job-intensive projects in areas of higher-than-average unemployment, supporting mature industries, and assisting small businesses.

* Women and Minorities Business Assistance

State Office of Minority and Women Business Assistance
Department of Commerce
100 Cambridge Street
Boston, MA 02202   617-727-8692
> Provides special assistance to women and minority-owned businesses.

Small Business Administration (SBA)
Boston District Office
10 Causeway Street
2nd Floor, Room 265   617-565-5590
Boston, MA 02222-1093   FAX: 617-565-5598
> **SBA 8(a) Program -Business Procurement Assistance:** Provides federal government contracting opportunities for small businesses owned by socially and economically disadvantaged persons, and assists these businesses to become independently competitive in the normal business environment. SBA monitors all government contracts to assure that a quota of contract work goes to 8(a) businesses. Also provides business management services to these businesses. Business must be approved for program participation prior to receipt of an 8(a) contract.

* Management Consulting and Other Services

New England Trade Adjustment Assistance Center
120 Boylston Street
Boston, MA 02116   617-542-2395
> Provides technical assistance to help Massachusetts manufacturers compete more effectively with imports.

Community Economic Development Assistance Corporation
19 Temple Pl., #200
Boston, MA 02111 617-727-0506
Offers technical assistance to community development corporations and other non-profit, community-based organizations in economically depressed areas of the state.

Small Business Administration
Boston District Office
10 Causeway Street
2nd Floor, Room 265 617-565-5590
Boston, MA 02222-1093 FAX: 617-565-5598
Small Business Institutes: This program provides personalized consulting services to the small business community. Consulting is provided by senior level business students, guided by a faculty advisor. Assistance in business plan preparation, marketing research, market planning, accounting, and seminars are provided.
University Locations:
American International College
Babson College
Bentley College
Boston College
Boston University
Clark University
Fitchburg State College
North Adams State College
Northeastern University
Southeastern Massachusetts University
Suffolk University
University of Lowell
University of Massachusetts -Amherst
University of Massachusetts -Boston
Western New England College
Westfield State College

* Small Business Development Centers
The following offices offer free and fee-based services to new and expanding businesses.

Lead Center:
Massachusetts Small Business Development Center
University of Massachusetts
205 School of Management 413-545-6301
Amherst, MA 01003 FAX: 413-545-1273

Boston: University of Massachusetts at Amherst, Minority Business Assistance Center, 250 Stuart Street, 12th Floor, Boston, MA 02116, 617-287-7016; FAX: 617-426-7854.

Chestnut Hill: Boston College, Metropolitan Regional Small Business Development Center, 96 College Road - Rahner House, Chestnut Hill, MA 02167, 617-552-4091; FAX: 617-552-2730.

Chestnut Hill: Boston College, Capital Formation Service/East, Small Business Development Center, 96 College Road - Rahner House, Chestnut Hill, MA 02167, 617-552-4091; FAX: 617-552-2730.

Fall River: University of Massachusetts at Dartmouth, Southeastern Massachusetts Regional Small Business Development Center, 200 Pocasset Street, P.O. Box 2785, Fall River, MA 02722, 508-673-9783; FAX: 508-674-1929.

Salem: Salem State College, North Shore Regional Small Business Development Center, 197 Essex Street, Salem, MA 01970, 508-741-6343; FAX: 508-741-6345.

Springfield: University of Massachusetts, Western Massachusetts Regional Small Business Development Center, 101 State Street, Suite #424, Springfield, MA 01103, 413-737-6712; FAX: 413-737-2312.

Worcester: Clark University, Central Massachusetts Regional Small Business Development Center, 950 Main Street, Worcester, MA 01610, 617-793-7615; FAX: 508-793-8890.

Michigan

* General Information

Michigan Business Ombudsman
P.O. Box 30107
525 W. Ottawa
5th Floor Law Bldg. 517-373-6241
Lansing, MI 48909 1-800-232-2727 in Michigan
Acts as a mediator in resolving regulatory disputes between business and the various state departments and also provides consultation and referral services. The ombudsman also serves as a "one-stop" center for business permits.

Michigan Department of Commerce
P.O. Box 30004
Lansing, MI 48909 517-373-1820
Small Business Advocate: Assistance in cutting bureaucratic red tape. Information and expertise in dealing with state, federal and local agencies.

* Financing

Michigan Strategic Fund
P.O. Box 30234
525 W. Ottawa
3rd Floor Law Bldg.
Lansing, MI 48933
State Research Fund 517-335-2139
Grants of $20,000 to $50,000 for prototype development and to support successful Phase I federal Small Business Innovation Research projects while awaiting Phase II funding. A minimum 25 percent cash match is required of applicants.

BIDCO Program 517-373-7551
Provides different types of financing including subordinate loans with equity features, royalty financing for product development, straight equity investments and guaranteed loans under the SBA 7(a) program.

Tax-Exempt Bonds 517-373-6213
Tax-exempt bonds are issued for up to $10 million per company to finance up to 100 percent of the cost of acquiring and/or rehabilitating fixed assets.

Capital Access Program 517-373-7551
Allows banks to make business loans that are riskier than conventional bank loans by providing a type of portfolio insurance to guarantee loan payments.

Seed Capital Funds 517-373-7551
Enterprise Development Fund: Invests in industrial technology, biomedical and biotechnology, computer, consumer and communications businesses.

Onset Seed Fund: Specializes in industrial technology, with a special emphasis on creating companies which will provide products to the major automotive companies, as well as to suppliers for use in their manufacturing processes.

Diamond Venture Associates: Focuses on manufacturing or product-oriented businesses and service-oriented businesses. Feasibility prototypes, marketing strategies and test marketing are some of the projects that can be funded.

Demery Seed Capital Fund: Specializes in product-oriented businesses and service organizations with a more intensive focus on food processing industries.

Alternative Investments Division:
Michigan Venture Capital Fund Program 517-373-4330
Invests in high growth, high margin companies with a potential return on investment of 35 percent or more.

MERRA
1050 Sixth Street, Second Floor
Detroit, MI 48226   313-964-5030
Small Business Innovation Research Grants: Award between $20,000 to $50,000 to entrepreneurs to support six months of research on a technical innovation. Second phase grants are an additional $500,000 for development. Private sector investment funds must follow.

Michigan Certified Development Corporation
525 W. Ottawa
Lansing, MI 48909   517-373-6378
SBA 504: Provides loans using 50 percent conventional bank financing, 40 percent SBA involvement through Certified Development Companies and 10 percent owner equity. A fixed asset loan in amounts up to $500,000. Loan can be used for land and building, construction, machinery and equipment and renovation/expansion.

Michigan Department of Commerce
525 W. Ottawa
Lansing, MI 48909   517-373-1820
Community Development Block Grants: Available to cities and counties for the commercial rehabilitation of existing buildings or structures used for businesses, commercial or industrial purposes. Grants of up to $500,000 can be made. Every $15,000 of grant funds invested must create at least one full-time job and at least 51 percent of the jobs created must be for low and moderate income families.

Small Business Administration
515 MacNamara Bldg.
477 Michigan Avenue   313-226-6075
Detroit, MI 48226   FAX: 313-226-4769
SBA 7(a) Guaranteed and Direct Loans: Guarantees up to 90 percent of a loan made through a private lender up to $750,000. Can be used for working capital, expand or convert facilities, purchase of machinery and equipment, and land and building. Available only to those unable to obtain a loan from conventional sources. Direct loans are made up to $150,000.

SBA 504: Provides loans using 50 percent conventional bank financing, 40 percent SBA involvement through Certified Development Companies, and 10 percent owner equity. Fixed-asset loans are available in amounts up to $750,000. The loan can be used for land and building, construction, machinery and equipment, and renovation/expansion.

Small Business Innovative Research Grants (SBIR): Phase I awards between $20,000 to $50,000 to entrepreneurs to support six months of research on a technical innovation. Phase II grants are an additional $500,000 for development. Private sector investment funds must follow.

International Trade Loans: Guaranteed long-term loans through private lenders to develop or expand export markets, or to recover from the effects of import competition. Maximum guaranteed loan is $1,000,000 for fixed assets and an additional $250,000 for working capital and/or export revolving line of credit.

Export Revolving Line of Credit Loan: Short term financing available to small businesses that are at least one year old. Loans provide working capital to finance the manufacturing or wholesaling of products for export and for export marketing. The SBA will guarantee up to 90 percent of a conventional loan in amounts up to $750,000.

Contract Loan: Short-term loans are available to small businesses to finance the costs of labor and materials on contracts for which the proceeds are assignable. Program guarantees up to 90 percent of loans not in excess of $750,000. Qualifying small businesses must be in business for at least 12 calendar months prior to the date of the loan application.

Seasonal Line of Credit Loan: Loans provide short-term working capital to finance seasonal increases in business activities. Program guarantees up to 90 percent of loans not in excess of $750,000. Qualifying business must be in operation for at least one year prior to application.

Pollution Control Loans: Long-term guaranteed loans can be made by conventional financing to small businesses for installation or required pollution control measures. Must be unable to adopt the pollution control measures without undue financial hardship. Maximum guaranteed loan is $1,000,000.

General Contractor Loans: Small general construction contractors may obtain short-term loans or loan guarantees for residential or commercial construction or rehabilitation of property to be sold. The SBA will guarantee up to 90 percent of qualifying loans made by private lenders up to a maximum of $750,000. Direct loans can be up to $150,000.

Energy Business Loan Guarantee: Small businesses that provide certain energy production and conservation services for others may qualify for long-term loans and loan guarantees for start-ups and expansions. Loans and guarantees are made for firms that develop, manufacture, sell, install, or service specific energy measures for others, or firms that provide engineering, architectural, consulting, or other professional services connected with specific energy measures. Guarantee is for up to 90 percent of a loan not in excess of $750,000. Direct loans up to $150,000.

Disaster Recovery Loans: Small businesses located in federally designated disaster areas and suffering property damage or economic losses from the disaster can obtain long-term recovery loans at low interest rates. Property damage loans are limited to 85 percent of the verified damage. Loans for economic losses are for operating capital to meet the business' obligations that could have been made had the disaster not occurred.

Handicapped Assistance Loans: Assists persons who have a physical, mental or emotional disability of a permanent nature which limits the selection of any type of employment for which the person would otherwise be qualified. Direct loans are available for up to $150,000. The interest rate is 3% on these loans.

Surety Bond Guaranty Program: Makes the bonding system more available to small contractors who may be denied access to the system. SBA can guarantee up to 80 percent of surety's loss on a bond that has a maximum in total contract value of up to $1,250,000.

Vietnam-era and Disabled Veterans Loan Program: Provides direct loans to veterans to establish or expand a small business. Funds may be used for working capital or fixed assets. Direct loans for amounts up to $150,000 are available. The interest rate may be fixed or variable.

* Women and Minorities Business Assistance

Michigan Department of Commerce
525 W. Ottawa
P.O. Box 30225
Lansing, MI 48909   HOTLINE: 1-800-831-9090 in Michigan
Women Business Owners Services   517-335-4720
Business guidance and problem solving, technical assistance, financial counseling and assistance in developing a business plan. Access to special entrepreneurial education programs and procurement programs. Also acts as an advocate for women-owned businesses.

Michigan Department of Commerce
Minority Business Enterprise
525 W. Ottawa
P.O. Box 30225   517-335-4720
Lansing, MI 48909   313-256-1972 in Detroit
Assistance in the form of education, training, information, advocacy and referral services. Workshops and seminars are held on a regular basis. Assistance in procuring state contracts and an annual Minority Procurement Conference which features workshops, a trade fair and contract procurement opportunities.

Small Business Administration
515 MacNamara Bldg.
477 Michigan Avenue
Detroit, MI 48226   313-226-4769
SBA 8(a) Program -Business Procurement Assistance: Provides federal government contracting opportunities for small businesses owned by socially and economically disadvantaged persons, and assists these businesses to become independently competitive in the normal business

environment. SBA monitors all government contracts to assure that a quota of contract work goes to 8(a) businesses. Also provides business management services to these businesses. Business must be approved for program participation prior to receipt of an 8(a) contract.

* Training

Bureau of Employment Training & Community Services
Michigan Department of Labor
P.O. Box 30015
Lansing, MI 48909   517-335-5853
   Job Training Partnership Act (JTPA): Provides employers with recruitment, screening, referral, training, 50 percent wage subsidy up to 3 months for on-the-job training. Available to any private employer.

* Management Consulting and Other Services

Technical Business Services Office
Department of Commerce
Law Building, 5th Floor
Lansing, MI 48909   517-373-7230
   This office administers the Technology Transfer program, which identifies leading edge technology for small businesses. Assistance is provided in the form of workshops and seminars.

Small Business Administration
515 MacNamara Bldg.
477 Michigan Avenue
Detroit, MI 48226   313-226-4769
   Small Business Institutes: This program provides personalized consulting services to the small business community. Consulting is provided by senior level business students, guided by a faculty advisor. Assistance in business plan preparation, marketing research, market planning, accounting, and seminars are provided.
   University Locations:
   Calvin College
   Central Michigan University
   Eastern Michigan University
   Ferris State College
   Kalamazoo College
   Lawrence Technological University
   Michigan Technological University
   Northern Michigan University
   Spring Arbor College
   University of Michigan -Dearborn
   Wayne State University
   Western Michigan University

* Small Business Development Centers
The following offices offer free and fee based services to new and expanding businesses.

Lead Center:
Michigan Small Business Development Center
2727 Second Avenue   313-577-4848
Detroit, MI 48201   FAX: 313-577-4222

   Allendale: Ottawa County Economic Development Office, Inc., Small Business Development Center, 6676 Lake Michigan Drive, Allendale, MI 49401, 616-892-4120; FAX: 616-895-6670.

   Ann Arbor: Merra Specialty Business Development Center, Small Business Development Center, 2200 Commonwealth, Suite 230, Ann Arbor, MI 48105, 313-930-0034; FAX: 313-663-6622.

   Bad Axe: Huron County Economic Development Corporation (Satellite), Small Business Development Center, Huron County building, Room 303, Bad Axe, MI 48413, 517-269-6431; FAX: 517-269-7221.

   Battle Creek: Kellogg Community College, Small Business Development Center, 450 North Avenue, Battle Creek, MI 49017-3397, 616-965-3023; 1-800-955-4KCC; FAX: 616-965-4133.

Benton Harbor: Lake Michigan College, Small Business Development Center, Corporate and Community Services, 2755 E. Napier, Benton Harbor, MI 49022-1899, 616-927-3571, ext. 247; FAX: 616-927-4491.

Big Rapids: Ferris State University, Small Business Development Center, Alumni 226, 901 S. State Street, Big Rapids, MI 49307, 616-592-3553; FAX: 616-592-3539.

Cadillac: Wexfor-Missaukee Business Development Center (Satellite), 117 W. Cass Street, Suite 1, Cadillac, MI 49601-0026, 616-775-9776; FAX: 616-775-1440.

Caro: Tuscola County Economic Development Corporation, Small Business Development Center, 1184 Cleaver Road, Suite 800, Caro, MI 48723, 517-673-2849; FAX: 517-673-2517.

Detroit: NILAC-Marygrove College, Small Business Development Center, 8425 West McNichols, Detroit, MI 48221, 313-945-2159; FAX: 313-864-6670.

Detroit: Wayne State University, Small Business Development Center, School of Business Administration, 2727 Second Avenue, Detroit, MI 48201, 313-577-4850; FAX: 313-577-8933.

Detroit: Comerica Small Business Development Center, 8300 Van Dyke, Detroit, MI 48213, 313-571-1040.

East Lansing: Michigan State University, International Business Development Center, 6 Kellogg Center, East Lansing, MI 48824-1022, 517-353-4336; FAX: 517-336-1009; 1-800-852-5727.

Escanaba: 1st Step, Inc., Small Business Development Center, 2415 14th Avenue, South, Escanaba, MI 49829, 906-786-9234; FAX: 906-786-4442.

Flint: Genesee Economic Area Revitalization, Inc. (Satellite), Small Business Development Center, 412 S. Saginaw Street, Flint, MI 48502, 313-238-7803; FAX: 313-238-7866.

Grand Rapids: Grand Rapids Community College, Small Business Development Center, Applied Technology Center, 151 Fountain N.E., Grand Rapids, MI 49503, 616-771-3600; FAX: 616-771-3605.

Hart: Oceana Economic Development Corporation (Satellite), Small Business Development Center, P.O. Box 168, Hart, MI 49420-0168, 616-873-7141; FAX: 616-873-3710.

Houghton: Michigan Technological University, Small Business Development Center, Bureau of Industrial Development, 1400 Townsend Drive, Houghton, MI 49931, 906-487-2470; FAX: 906-487-2858.

Howell: Livingston County Business Development Center, 404 E. Grand River, Howell, MI 48843, 517-546-4020; FAX: 517-546-4115.

Kalamazoo: Kalamazoo College, Small Business Development Center, Stryker Center for Management Studies, 1327 Academy Street, Kalamazoo, MI 49007, 616-383-8602; FAX: 616-383-5663.

Lansing: Lansing Community College, Small Business Development Center, P.O. Box 40010, Lansing, MI 48901, 517-483-1921; FAX: 517-483-9616.

Lapeer: Lapeer Development Corporation (Satellite), 449 McCormick Drive, Lapeer, MI 48446, 313-667-0080; FAX: 313-667-3541.

Marlette: Thumb Area Community Growth Alliance, Small Business Development Center, 3270 Wilson Street, Marlette, MI 48453, 517-635-3561; FAX: 517-635-2230.

Marquette: Northern Economic Initiative Corporation, Small Business Development Center, 1009 West Ridge Street, Marquette, MI 49855, 906-228-5571; FAX: 906-228-5572.

Mt. Clemens: Macomb County Business Assistance Network, 115 South Groesbeck Highway, Mt. Clemens, MI 48043, 313-469-5118; FAX: 313-469-6787,

Mt. Pleasant: Central Michigan University, Small Business Development

Center, 256 Applied Business Studies Complex, Mt. Pleasant, MI 48859, 517-774-3270; FAX: 517-774-2372.

Muskegon: Muskegon Economic Growth Alliance, Small Business Development Center, 349 West Webster Avenue, Suite 104, P.O. Box 1087, Muskegon, MI 49443-1087, 616-722-3751; FAX: 616-728-7251.

Peck: Sanilac County Economic Growth (Satellite), 175 East Aitken Road, Peck, MI 48466, 313-648-4311; FAX: 313-648-4617.

Port Huron: St. Claire County Community College, Small Business Development Center, 323 Erie Street, P.O. Box 5015, Port Huron, MI 48061-5015, 313-984-3881, ext. 457; FAX: 313-984-2852.

Saginaw: Saginaw Future, Inc., Small Business Development Center, 301 East Genesee, Fourth Floor, Saginaw, MI 48607, 517-754-8222; FAX: 517-754-1715.

Scottville: West Shore Community College (Satellite), Business and Industrial Development, 3000 North Stiles Road, Scottville, MI 49454-0277, 616-845-6211; FAX: 616-845-0207.

Sidney: Montcalm Community College (Satellite), 2800 College Drive SW, Sidney, MI 48885, 517-328-2111; FAX: 517-328-2950.

Sterling Heights: Sterling Heights Area Chamber of Commerce (Satellite), 12900 Paul, Suite 110, Sterling Heights, MI 48313, 313-731-5400.

Traverse City: Northwestern Michigan College, Center for Business and Industry, 1701 East Front Street, Traverse City, MI 49684, 616-922-1105.

Traverse City: Travers Bay Economic Development Corporation, Traverse City Small Business Development Center, 202 E. Grandview Parkway, P.O. Box 387, Traverse City, MI 49685-0387, 616-946-1596; FAX: 616-946-2565.

Traverse City: Greater Northwest Regional CDC, 2200 Dendrinos Drive, Traverse City, MI 49685-0506, 616-929-5000.

Traverse City: Traverse City Area Chamber of Commerce BDC, 202 E. Grandview Parkway, P.O. Box 387, Traverse City, MI 49685-0387, 616-947-5075.

Troy: Walsh/O.C.C. Business Enterprise Development Center, 340 E. Big Beaver, Suite 100, Troy, MI 48083, 313-689-4094; FAX: 313-689-4398.

University Center: Saginaw Valley State University (Satellite), Business and Industrial Development Institute, 2250 Pierce Road, University Center, MI 48710, 517-790-4000; FAX: 517-790-1314.

Minnesota

* General Information

Minnesota Small Business Assistance Office
900 American Center Building
150 East Kellogg Boulevard   612-296-3871
St. Paul, MN 55101   HOTLINE: 1-800-657-3858

Small Business and Business Licensing Assistance: Provides accurate, timely and comprehensive information and assistance to businesses in all areas of start up, operation, and expansion. Referrals to other state agencies.

Small Business Advocate: Assistance in cutting bureaucratic red tape. Information and expertise in dealing with state, federal and local agencies.

* Financing

Minnesota Department of Trade and Economic Development
900 American Center Building
150 East Kellogg Boulevard
St. Paul, MN 55101

Opportunities Minnesota Incorporated (OMNI)   612-296-5005
Administers SBA 504 loans. Provides subordinated financing through the issuance of debentures for businesses that are purchasing buildings or capital assets with useful lives greater than 15 years. Loans may not exceed 40 percent of the project cost or $750,000, whichever is less. A local lending institution is required to provide 50 percent of the project financing, and the borrower is required to put in 10 percent equity.

Economic Development Program: 612-296-5005
Contact Economic Development Director, Local Unit of Government. Local communities may use grant funds to make a loan to a specific businesses for expansion or start up purposes. A community may receive only one grant per year, with a maximum award of $500,000.

Rural Development Program   612-296-9090
Challenge grants are awarded to regional, non-profit, Initiative Fund organizations to encourage private investment. The regional organizations establish revolving loan funds to provide loans to new and expanding businesses in rural Minnesota. Minimum loan is $5,000, maximum is $100,000 and may not exceed 50 percent of the total cost of the project.

Minnesota Public Facilities Authority   612-296-4704
Provides loans and grants to qualified governmental units for the acquisition and betterment of public land, buildings, facilities and improvements of a capital nature.

Capital Access Program   612-297-1391
Provides credit enhancement to encourage financial institutions to make loans which may be more risky than traditional bank loans to small and medium-sized businesses. A reserve fund, funded by premium charges and state matching funds, covers losses on enrolled loans sustained by a lender.

Tourism Loan Program   612-296-6858
Low-interest revolving loan fund for resorts, campgrounds and other tourism related businesses.

Recycling Financial Assistance   612-649-5750
Grants to counties and loans to private entities to establish new markets for recyclable materials. Research and Development grants are also available.

Minnesota Technology, Inc.
111 Third Avenue South
Suite 400
Minneapolis, MN 55401   612-338-7722

Promotes jobs and economic growth through technology assistance services, and technology information. An early stage seed capital fund is expected to be available in 1992.

Indian Affairs Council
1819 Bemidji Avenue
Bemidji, MN 56601   218-755-3825

Provides resources for management and technical assistance for businesses owned by Minnesota-based Indians. A special revolving loan fund disburses funds on a case-by-case basis.

Small Business Administration (SBA)
610-C Butler Square Building
100 North Sixth Street
Minneapolis, MN 55403   612-370-2303

SBA 7(a) Guaranteed and Direct Loans: Guarantees up to 90 percent of a loan made through a private lender up to $750,000. Can be used for working capital, expand or convert facilities, purchase of machinery and equipment, and land and building. Available only to those unable to obtain a loan from conventional sources. Direct loans are made up to $150,000.

SBA 504: Provides loans using 50 percent conventional bank financing, 40 percent SBA involvement through Certified Development Companies, and 10 percent owner equity. Fixed-asset loans are available in amounts up to $750,000. The loan can be used for land and building, construction, machinery and equipment, and renovation/expansion.

Small Business Innovative Research Grants (SBIR): Phase I awards between $20,000 to $50,000 to entrepreneurs to support six months of research on a technical innovation. Phase II grants are an additional $500,000 for development. Private sector investment funds must follow.

International Trade Loans: Guaranteed long-term loans through private lenders to develop or expand export markets, or to recover from the effects of import competition. Maximum guaranteed loan is $1,000,000 for fixed assets and an additional $250,000 for working capital and/or export revolving line of credit.

Export Revolving Line of Credit Loan: Short term financing available to small businesses that are at least one year old. Loans provide working capital to finance the manufacturing or wholesaling of products for export and for export marketing. The SBA will guarantee up to 90 percent of a conventional loan in amounts up to $750,000.

Contract Loan: Short-term loans are available to small businesses to finance the costs of labor and materials on contracts for which the proceeds are assignable. Program guarantees up to 90 percent of loans not in excess of $750,000. Qualifying small businesses must be in business for at least 12 calendar months prior to the date of the loan application.

Seasonal Line of Credit Loan: Loans provide short-term working capital to finance seasonal increases in business activities. Program guarantees up to 90 percent of loans not in excess of $750,000. Qualifying business must be in operation for at least one year prior to application.

Pollution Control Loans: Long-term guaranteed loans can be made by conventional financing to small businesses for installation or required pollution control measures. Must be unable to adopt the pollution control measures without undue financial hardship. Maximum guaranteed loan is $1,000,000.

General Contractor Loans: Small general construction contractors may obtain short-term loans or loan guarantees for residential or commercial construction or rehabilitation of property to be sold. The SBA will guarantee up to 90 percent of qualifying loans made by private lenders up to a maximum of $750,000. Direct loans can be up to $150,000.

Energy Business Loan Guarantee: Small businesses that provide certain energy production and conservation services for others may qualify for long-term loans and loan guarantees for start-ups and expansions. Loans and guarantees are made for firms that develop, manufacture, sell, install, or service specific energy measures for others, or firms that provide engineering, architectural, consulting, or other professional services connected with specific energy measures. Guarantee is for up to 90 percent of a loan not in excess of $750,000. Direct loans up to $150,000.

Disaster Recovery Loans: Small businesses located in federally designated disaster areas and suffering property damage or economic losses from the disaster can obtain long-term recovery loans at low interest rates. Property damage loans are limited to 85 percent of the verified damage. Loans for economic losses are for operating capital to meet the business' obligations that could have been made had the disaster not occurred.

Handicapped Assistance Loans: Assists persons who have a physical, mental or emotional disability of a permanent nature which limits the selection of any type of employment for which the person would otherwise be qualified. Direct loans are available for up to $150,000. The interest rate is 3% on these loans.

Surety Bond Guaranty Program: Makes the bonding system more available to small contractors who may be denied access to the system. SBA can guarantee up to 80 percent of surety's loss on a bond that has a maximum in total contract value of up to $1,250,000.

Vietnam-era and Disabled Veterans Loan Program: Provides direct loans to veterans to establish or expand a small business. Funds may be used for working capital or fixed assets. Direct loans for amounts up to $150,000 are available. The interest rate may be fixed or variable.

FBS SBIC, LP
1100 First Bank Place East
Minneapolis, MN 55480   612-370-4764

Northland Capital Venture Partnership
613 Missabe Building
Duluth, MN 55802   218-722-0545

Northwest Venture Partners
2800 Piper Jaffray Tower
222 South Ninth Street
Minneapolis, MN 55402   612-667-1650

Norwest Equity Partners IV
2800 Piper Jaffray Tower
222 South Ninth Street
Minneapolis, MN 55402   612-667-1650

Norwest Growth Fund, Inc.
2800 Piper Jaffray Tower
222 South Ninth Street
Minneapolis, MN 55402   612-667-1650

Shared Ventures, Inc.
6550 York Avenue, South
Suite 419
Edina, MN 55435   612-925-3411

Small Business Investment Companies (SBIC): The SBA licenses, regulates, and provides financial assistance to privately owned and operated Small Business Investment Companies. SBICs make venture or risk investments by supplying capital and extending unsecured loans and loans not fully collateralized to small enterprises which meet their investment criteria. Financing is made by direct loans and by equity investments.

Department of Housing and Urban Development
220 Second Street South
Minneapolis, MN 55401   612-370-3000

Urban Development Action Grant: Awarded to communities which then lend the proceeds at flexible rates to eligible businesses. Projects whose total costs are less than $100,000 are not eligible. UDAG funds should leverage at least three to four times their amount in private sector investment.

Agri-Bank
375 Jackson Street
St. Paul, MN 55101   612-282-8800

Federal Land Bank Association: Provides long-term credit for land and other purchases to farmers and farm-related businesses.

Production Credit Association: Provides short- and intermediate-term credit to cover seasonal operating expenses, land improvements, and purchases of farm equipment, livestock, storage facilities and buildings.

Bank for Cooperatives: Credit services for agricultural and rural utility cooperatives.

Farmer's Home Administration
375 North Jackson
Suite 410
St. Paul, MN 55101   612-290-3866

Business and Industrial Loans: Assistance is provided in the form of a loan guarantee of up to 90 percent of the principal and interest. Funds can be used for financing construction, conversion, acquisition, equipment and machinery, supplies of materials, and working capital.

Northwest Minnesota Initiative Fund
4 West Office Building, #310
P.O. Box 975
Bemidji, MN 56601   218-759-2057

Midwest Minnesota Community Development Corp. (MMCDC)
803 Roosevelt Avenue
P.O. Box 623
Detroit Lakes, MN 56501   218-847-3191

Northeast Minnesota Initiative Fund
204 Ordean Building
424 West Superior Street
Duluth, MN 55802   218-726-4740

West Central Minnesota Initiative Fund
Norwest Bank
220 West Washington, Suite 205
Fergus Falls, MN 56537   218-739-2239

Southwest Minnesota Initiative Fund
163 Ninth Avenue
Granite Falls, MN 56241   612-564-3060

Central Minnesota Initiative Fund
58 1/2 East Broadway
P.O. Box 59
Little Falls, MN 56345   612-632-9255

Southeast Minnesota Initiative Fund
540 West Hill Circle
P.O. Box 570
Owatonna, MN 55060   507-455-3215

Initiative Funds: Private, non-profit organizations supplemented with funds from various public and private sources. Funds are distributed in grants and loans. The six initiative funds listed above are separate entities, and each has its own programs, funding levels, and guidelines. Call your regional Initiative Fund.

MMCDC receives grants and loans from public and private sources and re-lends these funds to businesses in the form of secured loans. The interest rate charged is normally at or near bank loan rates. The Revolving Loan Fund serves a five county area of Minnesota (Hubbard, Mahnomen, Beltrami, Clearwater, and Lake of the Woods). The Non-Profit National Corporations Loan Program serves rural communities with a population of 20,000 or less.

* Women and Minorities Business Assistance

Listed below are a number of organizations which offer business planning and business management assistance specifically targeted to businesses owned and operated by racial minorities, women, handicapped individuals, and other socially or economically disadvantaged persons.

Minneapolis: Metropolitan Economic Development Association, 2021 East Hennepin Avenue, Suite 370, Minneapolis, MN 55413, 612-378-0361.

Minneapolis: Emerging Small Business Clearing House, 1121 Glenwood Avenue North, Minneapolis, MN 55405, 612-374-5129.

Minneapolis: Minneapolis/St. Paul Minority Business Development Center, 2021 East Hennepin, #LL35, Minneapolis, MN 55413, 612-331-5576.

Minneapolis: Minnesota Chippewa Tribe, Indian Business Development Center, P.O. Box 217, Cass Lake, MN 56633, 218-335-8583.

Minneapolis: Minnesota Minority Purchasing Council (MMPC), 2021 East Hennepin Ave., Suite 370, Minneapolis, MN 55413, 612-378-0361.

St. Paul: Women's Venture, 2324 University Avenue, #200, St. Paul, MN 55114, 612-646-3808.

St. Paul: Minnesota Small Business Assistance Office, 900 American Center Building, 150 East Kellogg Boulevard, St. Paul, MN 55101, 612-296-3871.

Small Business Administration (SBA)
610-C Butler Square Building
100 North Sixth Street
Minneapolis, MN 55403   612-370-2324

SBA 8(a) Program -Business Procurement Assistance: Provides federal government contracting opportunities for small businesses owned by socially and economically disadvantaged persons, and assists these businesses to become independently competitive in the normal business environment. SBA monitors all government contracts to assure that a quota of contract work goes to 8(a) businesses. Also provides business management services to these businesses. Business must be approved for program participation prior to receipt of an 8(a) contract.

* Training

Minnesota Department of Labor and Industry
Division of Voluntary Apprenticeship
443 Lafayette Road
St. Paul, MN 55155   612-296-2371

Apprenticeship and Training Programs: Voluntary apprenticeship programs are operated by employers, employer associations, and/or unions to provide occupational training in industry and trade areas.

Job Training Partnership Act (JTPA): Provides employers with recruitment, screening, referral, training, 50 percent wage subsidy up to 3 months for on-the-job training. Available to any private employer.

* Management Consulting and Other Services

Minnesota Technical Assistance Program
1313 5th Street, SE
Suite 207   612-627-4646
Minneapolis, MN 55414   1-800-247-0015

Minnesota Waste Management Technical Assistance Program: Provides technical assistance to small and medium-sized companies that may generate hazardous waste.

Minnesota Trade Office
1000 World Trade Center
30 East 7th Street
St. Paul, MN 55101-4902   612-297-4222

International Trade Program: Assists small and medium-sized companies in developing international trade and export possibilities.

Small Business Management Programs:
Available at Technical Institutes located statewide. Instruction is provided in individualized sessions at the business site and in scheduled group sessions. Business planning, record systems, financial analysis, marketing, inventory management, payroll, negotiating for money, computer applications, and many other areas are covered.

Minnesota Small Business Assistance Office
900 American Center Building
150 East Kellogg Boulevard   612-296-3871
St. Paul, MN 55101   1-800-652-9747

State and Local Procurement Contacts: The Small Business Assistance Office publishes a free booklet to assist businesses in procurement efforts: *Public Procurement in Minnesota.*

Minnesota Project Innovation
The Mill Place
111 Third Avenue South, #410
Minneapolis, MN 55401-2554   612-338-3280

Promotes participation in the Small Business Innovation Research program by offering technical assistance to small businesses and individuals interested in submitting research and development proposals.

Minnesota Inventors Congress Inc.
Redwood Falls Inventors Resource Center
P.O. Box 71
1030 E. Bridge Street   507-637-2344
Redwood Falls, MN 56283   1-800-INVENT-1 in Minnesota

Provides information and assistance to inventors. An annual Inventors Congress provides an opportunity for inventors to display their inventions and receive public reaction and exposure. Provides answers to questions about idea development, patents, trademarks and copyrights, marketing inventions, and general invention support.

Small Business Administration
610-C Butler Square Building
100 North Sixth Street
Minneapolis, MN 55403   612-370-2324

Small Business Institutes: This program provides counseling services to small businesses using students under faculty supervision. The SBI technical assistance program is available on request and is free. Regional centers are listed below:

Bemidji: Bemidji State University, Small Business Institute, 1500 Birchmont Drive NE, Bemidji, MN 56601, 218-755-2750.

St. Paul: Bethel College, Small Business Institute, P.O. Box 77, 3900 Bethel Drive, St. Paul, MN 44112, 612-638-6318.

Mankato: Mankato State University, Small Business Institute, Mankato, MN 56001, 507-389-5401.

Moorhead: Moorhead State University, Small Business Institute, 1104 Seventh Avenue South, Moorhead, MN 56560, 218-236-2289.

St. Paul: St. Cloud State University, Small Business Institute, First Avenue South and Seventh Street, St. Cloud, MN 56301, 612-255-3215.

Winona: St. Mary's College, Dept. of Business Administration, Small Business Institute, 700 Terrace Heights, Winona, MN 55987, 507-452-4430.

Northfield: St. Olaf College, Small Business Institute, Department of Economics, Northfield, MN 55057, 507-663-3152.

St. Paul: University of St. Thomas, Small Business Institute, 2115 Summit Avenue, St. Paul, MN 55105, 612-647-5621.

Duluth: University of Minnesota-Duluth, Small Business Institute, 150 School of Business and Economics, Duluth, MN 55812, 218-726-8761.

Winona: Winona State University, Small Business Institute, Somsen Hall, Eighth and Jackson, Winona, MN 55987, 507-457-5176.

* Small Business Development Centers

The following offices offer free and fee-based services to new and expanding businesses

Lead Center:
Minnesota Small Business Development Center
Department of Trade and Economic Development
900 American Center Building
150 East Kellogg Blvd.   612-297-5770
St. Paul, MN 55101   FAX: 612-296-1290

Bemidji: Customized Training Center, Small Business Development Center, Bemidji Technical College, 905 Grant Avenue, SE, Bemidji, MN 56601, 218-751-0979.

Bloomington: Normandale Community College, Small Business Development Center, 9700 France Avenue South, Bloomington, MN 55431, 612-832-6395.

Brainerd: Brainerd Technical College, Small Business Development Center, 300 Quince Street, Brainerd, MN 56401, 218-828-5302.

Duluth: University of Minnesota at Duluth, Small Business Development Center, 10 University Drive, 150 SBE, Duluth, MN 55811, 218-726-8761.

Grand Rapids: Itasca Development Corporation, Grand Rapids Small Business Development Center, 19 NE Third Street, Grand Rapids, MN 55744, 218-327-2241; FAX: 218-681-5519.

Hibbing: Hibbing Community College, Small Business Development Center, 1515 East 25th Street, Hibbing, MN 55746, 218-262-6700.

Mankato: Mankato State University, Small Business Development Center, Box 145, Mankato, MN 56001, 507-389-1648.

Marshall: Southwest State University, Small Business Development Center, ST #105, Marshall, MN 56258, 507-537-7386.

Minneapolis: Minnesota Project Innovation, Small Business Development Center, Suite 410, 111 Third Avenue South, Minneapolis, MN 55401, 612-338-3280.

Moorhead: Moorhead State University, Small Business Development Center, P.O. Box 303, Moorhead, MN 56560, 218-236-2289.

Pine City: Pine Technical College, Small Business Development Center, Pine City, MN 55063, 612-629-7340.

Red Wing: Red Wing Technical Institute, Small Business Development Center, Highway 58 at Pioneer Road, Red Wing, MN 55066, 612-388-4079.

Rochester: Rochester Community College, Small Business Development Center, Highway 14 East, 851 30th Avenue, S.E., Rochester, MN 55904-4999, 507-285-7536.

Rosemount: Dakota County Technical Institute, Small Business Development Center, 1300 145th Street East, Rosemount, MN 55068, 612-423-8262.

St. Cloud: St. Cloud State University, Small Business Development Center, Business Resource Center, 1840 E. Hwy 23, St. Cloud, MN 56301, 612-255-4842.

St. Paul: University of St. Thomas, Small Business Development Center, 23 Empire Drive, St. Paul, MN 55103, 612-223-8663.

Thief River Falls: Thief River Falls Technical Institute, Small Business Development Center, Highway One East, Thief River Falls, MN 56701, 218-681-5424; FAX: 218-681-5519.

Virginia: Mesabi Community College, Small Business Development Center, 9th Avenue & W. Chestnut Street, Virginia, MN 55792, 218-749-7729.

Wadena: Wadena Technical College, Small Business Development Center, 222 Second Street, SE, Wadena, MN 56482, 218-631-1502.

White Bear Lake: North/East Metro Technical College, Small Business Development Center, 3554 White Bear Avenue, White Bear Lake, MN 55110, 612-779-5764.

Winona: Winona State University, Small Business Development Center, Winona, MN 55987, 507-457-5088.

Willmar: Willmar Small Business Development Center, Mid-Minnesota Development Commission, 333 West 6th Street, Willmar, MN 56201, 612-235-8504.

Mississippi

* General Information

Mississippi Department of Economic and Community Development
P.O. Box 849
1200 Walter Sillers Building   601-359-3449
Jackson, MS 39205   FAX: 601-359-2832
    Communications and Advertising Division   601-359-3593
    Current developments

    Small Business Advocate: 601-359-3552
Assistance in cutting bureaucratic red tape. Information and expertise in dealing with state, federal and local agencies. Assistance also available from Small Business Development Centers.

* Financing

Mississippi Department of Economic and Community Development
P.O. Box 849
1200 Walter Sillers Building   601-359-3449
Jackson, MS 39205   FAX: 601-359-2832
    Mississippi Business Investment Act: This program matches $1 of State money for each $2 of private funds generated for a project. Each project must create at least 10 new jobs within two years and create at least one new full-time job per $15,000 loaned. Applicants must be sponsored by their locality -- city, town, or county.

Industrial Revenue Bonds: Designed for companies interested in financing land, building, machinery and equipment, the bonds are issued by political subdivisions and backed by corporate guaranty.

Loan Guaranty Program: Guarantees private loans made to small businesses for development and expansion of commercial and industrial enterprises. Maximum loan is $200,000, and maximum guaranty is 74 percent of the loan, not to exceed $150,000.

SBA 504: Provides loans using 50 percent conventional bank financing, 40 percent SBA involvement through Certified Development Companies, and 10 percent owner equity. A fixed-asset loan in amounts up to $750,000. Loans can be used for land and building, construction, machinery and equipment, and renovation/expansion.

Small Enterprise Development Finance Act: Provides loans for small projects that will increase employment and investment in small communities Loans are through the Mississippi Small Enterprise Development Corp.

Farm Reform Act (MFRA):
Emerging Crop Loan Programs: Aids farmers with the production of emerging crops. Provides for the payment of interest on the farmer's original bank loan through MFRA funds until the initial crop is harvested. Offers long-term repayment of the interest loan to the State.

Tax Credits:
    Job Tax Credit: Five-year tax credit to the company's state income tax credit for each new job created by a new or expanding business.

    Research & Development Jobs Tax Credit: Provides an additional five-year tax credit of $500 per year for each new R&D job created by new or expanding businesses.

    Headquarters Jobs Tax Credit: Provides an additional five-year tax credit of $500 per year for each new job created by the transfer of a national or regional headquarters to Mississippi, provided that at least 35 jobs are created.

    Child Care Tax Credit: Tax credit of 25 percent of the unreimbursed expenses of a child's care to new or existing businesses that provide or contract for child care for employees during the employees' work hours.

CDBG Program: Available to cities and counties for the commercial rehabilitation of existing buildings or structures used for business, commercial, or industrial purposes. Grants of up to $500,000 can be made. Every $15,000 of grant funds invested must create at least one full-time job, and at least 51 percent of the jobs created must be for low- and moderate-income families.

EDA Grant Program: Funds to be used by communities for site preparation and construction of water and sewer facilities, access roads, and rail spurs for new or relocating businesses. Communities are required to provide 20-50 percent matching funds.

EDA Guaranty Loan: Proceeds of the loan can be used to acquire land, buildings, and equipment. Guarantee is for 80-90 percent of a conventional loan. Loan guaranties are restricted to a maximum of $10,000 per job to be created.

Small Business Investment Companies (SBIC): Provides equity capital and long-term funds to small businesses.

FmHA Business and Industrial Loans: Available to anyone engaged in the improvement of the economic and environmental climate in rural areas. Loans usually start at $500,000 with no top limit. Applicant must provide a minimum of 25 percent equity.

Small Business Administration (SBA)
101 W. Capital
Suite 400
First Jackson Century
Jackson, MS 39201

601-965-4378
FAX: 601-965-4294

    SBA 7(a) Guaranteed and Direct Loans: Guarantees up to 90 percent of a loan made through a private lender up to $750,000. Can be used for working capital, expand or convert facilities, purchase of machinery and equipment, and land and building. Available only to those unable to obtain a loan from conventional sources. Direct loans are made up to $150,000.

SBA 504: Provides loans using 50 percent conventional bank financing, 40 percent SBA involvement through Certified Development Companies, and 10 percent owner equity. Fixed-asset loans are available in amounts up to $750,000. The loan can be used for land and building, construction, machinery and equipment, and renovation/expansion.

Small Business Innovative Research Grants (SBIR): Phase I awards between $20,000 to $50,000 to entrepreneurs to support six months of research on a technical innovation. Phase II grants are an additional $500,000 for development. Private sector investment funds must follow.

International Trade Loans: Guaranteed long-term loans through private lenders to develop or expand export markets, or to recover from the effects of import competition. Maximum guaranteed loan is $1,000,000 for fixed assets and an additional $250,000 for working capital and/or export revolving line of credit.

Export Revolving Line of Credit Loan: Short term financing available to small businesses that are at least one year old. Loans provide working capital to finance the manufacturing or wholesaling of products for export and for export marketing. The SBA will guarantee up to 90 percent of a conventional loan in amounts up to $750,000.

Contract Loan: Short-term loans are available to small businesses to finance the costs of labor and materials on contracts for which the proceeds are assignable. Program guarantees up to 90 percent of loans not in excess of $750,000. Qualifying small businesses must be in business for at least 12 calendar months prior to the date of the loan application.

Seasonal Line of Credit Loan: Loans provide short-term working capital to finance seasonal increases in business activities. Program guarantees up to 90 percent of loans not in excess of $750,000. Qualifying business must be in operation for at least one year prior to application.

Pollution Control Loans: Long-term guaranteed loans can be made by conventional financing to small businesses for installation or required pollution control measures. Must be unable to adopt the pollution control measures without undue financial hardship. Maximum guaranteed loan is $1,000,000.

General Contractor Loans: Small general construction contractors may obtain short-term loans or loan guarantees for residential or commercial construction or rehabilitation of property to be sold. The SBA will guarantee up to 90 percent of qualifying loans made by private lenders up to a maximum of $750,000. Direct loans can be up to $150,000.

Energy Business Loan Guarantee: Small businesses that provide certain energy production and conservation services for others may qualify for long-term loans and loan guarantees for start-ups and expansions. Loans and guarantees are made for firms that develop, manufacture, sell, install, or service specific energy measures for others, or firms that provide engineering, architectural, consulting, or other professional services connected with specific energy measures. Guarantee is for up to 90 percent of a loan not in excess of $750,000. Direct loans up to $150,000.

Disaster Recovery Loans: Small businesses located in federally designated disaster areas and suffering property damage or economic losses from the disaster can obtain long-term recovery loans at low interest rates. Property damage loans are limited to 85 percent of the verified damage. Loans for economic losses are for operating capital to meet the business' obligations that could have been made had the disaster not occurred.

Handicapped Assistance Loans: Assists persons who have a physical, mental or emotional disability of a permanent nature which limits the selection of any type of employment for which the person would otherwise be qualified. Direct loans are available for up to $150,000. The interest rate is 3% on these loans.

Surety Bond Guaranty Program: Makes the bonding system more available to small contractors who may be denied access to the system. SBA can guarantee up to 80 percent of surety's loss on a bond that has a maximum in total contract value of up to $1,250,000.

Vietnam-era and Disabled Veterans Loan Program: Provides direct loans to veterans to establish or expand a small business. Funds may be used for working capital or fixed assets. Direct loans for amounts up to $150,000 are available. The interest rate may be fixed or variable.

* Women and Minority Business Assistance

Mississippi Department of Economic and Community Development
P.O. Box 849
1200 Walter Sillers Building — 601-359-3449
Jackson, MS 39205 — FAX: 601-359-2832
    Minority Business Enterprise Loan Program: Revolving loan funds for minority economic development.

Small Business Administration
101 W. Capital, Suite 400
First Jackson Century — 601-965-4378
Jackson, MS 39201 — FAX: 601-965-4294
    SBA 8(a) Program-Business Procurement Assistance: Provides federal government contracting opportunities for small businesses owned by socially and economically disadvantaged persons, and assists these businesses to become independently competitive in the normal business environment. SBA monitors all government contracts to assure that a quota of contract work goes to 8(a) businesses. Also provides business management services to these businesses. Business must be approved for program participation prior to receipt of an 8(a) contract.

* Training

Mississippi Department of Economic and Community Development
P.O. Box 849
1200 Walter Sillers Building — 601-359-3449
Jackson, MS 39205 — FAX: 601-359-2832
    Basic Skills Training Tax Credit: Available to new or existing businesses that pay for certain basic skills training or re-training for their employees. Credit equal to 25 percent of the unreimbursed expenses of training.

Mississippi State Department of Education
Office of Vocational Technical Education
Special Federal Program -JTPA
P.O. Box 771
Jackson, MS 39205-0771 — 601-359-3084
    Job Training Partnership Act (JTPA): Provides employers with recruitment, screening, referral, training, 50 percent wage subsidy up to 3 months for on-the-job training. Available to any private employer.

* Management Consulting and Other Services

Mississippi Department of Economic and Community Development
P.O. Box 849
1200 Walter Sillers Building — 601-359-3449
Jackson, MS 32905 — FAX: 601-359-2832
    This office provides information on the following programs: **Statewide Business Incubator Network, Workshops for Entrepreneurial Women,** and **Programs for High School Entrepreneurs.**

    Technology Transfer Office: Located at Stennis Space Center, this office helps transfer technology to Mississippi businesses. *Also see Technology Section.*

Small Business Administration
101 W. Capital
Suite 400
First Jackson Century — 601-965-4378
Jackson, MS 39201 — FAX: 601-965-4294
    Small Business Institutes: This program provides personalized consulting services to the small business community. Consulting is provided by senior level business students, guided by a faculty advisor. Assistance in business plan preparation, marketing research, market planning, accounting, and seminars are provided.

University Locations:
Delta State University
Millsaps College
Mississippi State University
University of Mississippi
University of Southern Mississippi

* Small Business Development Centers
These offices offer free and fee-based services to new and expanding businesses:

Lead Center:
Mississippi Small Business Development Center
University of Mississippi
Old Chemistry Building, Suite 216 — 601-232-5001
University, MS 38677 — FAX: 601-232-5650

Booneville: Northeast Mississippi Community College, Small Business Development Center, Cunningham Blvd., Stringer Hall, 2nd Floor, Booneville, MS 38829, 601-728-7751, ext. 317; FAX: 601-728-1165.

Cleveland: Delta State University, Small Business Development Ctr, P.O. Box 3235 DSU, Cleveland, MS 38733, 601-846-4236; FAX: 601-846-4443.

Greenville: Delta Community College, Small Business Development Center, P.O. Box 5607, Greenville, MS 38704-5607, 601-378-8183; FAX: 601-378-5349.

Hattiesburg: Pearl River Community College, Small Business Development Center, Route 9, Box 1325, 5448 U.S. Highway 49 South, Hattiesburg, MS 39401, 601-544-0030; FAX: 601-544-0032.

Jackson: Jackson State University, Small Business Development Center, Suite A1, Jackson Enterprise Center, 931 Highway 80 West, Jackson, MS 39204, 601-968-2795; FAX: 601-968-2358.

Jackson: Mississippi Department of Economic & Community Development, Small Business Development Center, P.O. Box 849, Jackson, MS 39205, 601-359-3179; FAX: 601-359-2832.

Long Beach: University of Southern Mississippi, Small Business Development Center, USM Gulf Park Campus, Long Beach, MS 39560, 601-865-4578; FAX: 601-865-4544.

Meridian: Meridian Community College, Small Business Development Center, 5500 Highway 19 North, Meridian, MS 39307, 601-482-7445; FAX: 601-482-5803.

Mississippi State: Mississippi State University, Small Business Development Center, P.O. Drawer 5288, Mississippi State, MS 39762, 601-325-8684; FAX: 601-325-8686.

Natchez: Copiah-Lincoln Community College, Small Business Development Center, Natchez Campus, Natchez, MS 39120, 601-445-5254; FAX: 601-446-9967.

Raymond: Hinds Community College, Small Business Development Center, International Trade Center, P.O. Box 1170, Raymond, MS 39154, 601-857-3536; FAX: 601-857-3535.

Tupelo: Itawamba Community College, Small Business Development Ctr, 653 Eason Blvd., Tupelo, MS 38801, 601-680-8515; FAX: 601-680-8423.

University: University of Mississippi, Small Business Development Center, Old Chemistry Building, Suite 216, University, MS 38677, 601-234-2120; FAX: 601-232-5650.

Missouri

* General Information

Missouri Business Assistance Center
Department of Economic Development
P.O. Box 118 — 314-751-4241
Jefferson City, MO 65102 — First-Stop Shop: 1-800-523-1434

The First-Stop Shop number for Missouri residents serves to link business owners and state government and provides information on state rules, regulations, licenses, and permits. The Business Assistance Center provides information and technical assistance to start-up and existing businesses on available state and federal programs.

Federal Information Center
Federal Building
601 East 12th Street
Kansas City, MO 64106   1-800-392-7711 in Missouri
Offers information regarding Missouri programs for business people.

Department of Economic Development
P.O. Box 118
Jefferson City, MO 65102   1-800-523-1434
Small Business Advocate: Assistance in cutting bureaucratic red tape. Information and expertise in dealing with state, federal, and local agencies.

* Financing

Missouri Department of Economic Development
P.O. Box 118
Jefferson City, MO 65102   314-751-0717
Missouri Economic Development Infrastructure Board Loan Guarantee: Works in the same way as an SBA 7(a) loan. Guarantees up to 85 percent of a maximum loan of $400,000. (see below)

Action Fund (MoDag) Program: Direct loans of up to $400,000 to be used as gap financing to supplement Community Development Block Grants.

Mo Bucks: Offers expanding companies low-interest, short-term loans based on creation of new jobs. Companies can get up to $25,000 for each new job created. Funds can be used for any costs involved in the expansion.

Tax Exempt Revenue Bonds: Can finance 100 percent of a project costing not more than $10 million in capital expenditures. Funds to be used for fixed assets only such as real property improvements, machinery, and equipment for manufacturing purposes.

Community Development Block Grant: Funds up to $500,000 are available to cities and counties. Every $10,000-$25,000 of funds invested must create at least one full time job,, and at least 51 percent of the jobs created must be for low-and-moderate income families.

Small Business Administration (SBA)
911 Walnut Street, 13th Floor
Kansas City, MO 64016   816-426-3608
                                                 FAX: 816-426-5559
SBA 7(a) Guaranteed and Direct Loans: Guarantees up to 90 percent of a loan made through a private lender up to $750,000. Can be used for working capital, expand or convert facilities, purchase of machinery and equipment, and land and building. Available only to those unable to obtain a loan from conventional sources. Direct loans are made up to $150,000.

SBA 504: Provides loans using 50 percent conventional bank financing, 40 percent SBA involvement through Certified Development Companies, and 10 percent owner equity. Fixed-asset loans are available in amounts up to $750,000. The loan can be used for land and building, construction, machinery and equipment, and renovation/expansion.

Small Business Innovative Research Grants (SBIR): Phase I awards between $20,000 to $50,000 to entrepreneurs to support six months of research on a technical innovation. Phase II grants are an additional $500,000 for development. Private sector investment funds must follow.

International Trade Loans: Guaranteed long-term loans through private lenders to develop or expand export markets, or to recover from the effects of import competition. Maximum guaranteed loan is $1,000,000 for fixed assets and an additional $250,000 for working capital and/or export revolving line of credit.

Export Revolving Line of Credit Loan: Short term financing available to small businesses that are at least one year old. Loans provide working capital to finance the manufacturing or wholesaling of products for export and for export marketing. The SBA will guarantee up to 90 percent of a conventional loan in amounts up to $750,000.

Contract Loan: Short-term loans are available to small businesses to finance the costs of labor and materials on contracts for which the proceeds are assignable. Program guarantees up to 90 percent of loans not in excess of $750,000. Qualifying small businesses must be in business for at least 12 calendar months prior to the date of the loan application.

Seasonal Line of Credit Loan: Loans provide short-term working capital to finance seasonal increases in business activities. Program guarantees up to 90 percent of loans not in excess of $750,000. Qualifying business must be in operation for at least one year prior to application.

Pollution Control Loans: Long-term guaranteed loans can be made by conventional financing to small businesses for installation or required pollution control measures. Must be unable to adopt the pollution control measures without undue financial hardship. Maximum guaranteed loan is $1,000,000.

General Contractor Loans: Small general construction contractors may obtain short-term loans or loan guarantees for residential or commercial construction or rehabilitation of property to be sold. The SBA will guarantee up to 90 percent of qualifying loans made by private lenders up to a maximum of $750,000. Direct loans can be up to $150,000.

Energy Business Loan Guarantee: Small businesses that provide certain energy production and conservation services for others may qualify for long-term loans and loan guarantees for start-ups and expansions. Loans and guarantees are made for firms that develop, manufacture, sell, install, or service specific energy measures for others, or firms that provide engineering, architectural, consulting, or other professional services connected with specific energy measures. Guarantee is for up to 90 percent of a loan not in excess of $750,000. Direct loans up to $150,000.

Disaster Recovery Loans: Small businesses located in federally designated disaster areas and suffering property damage or economic losses from the disaster can obtain long-term recovery loans at low interest rates. Property damage loans are limited to 85 percent of the verified damage. Loans for economic losses are for operating capital to meet the business' obligations that could have been made had the disaster not occurred.

Handicapped Assistance Loans: Assists persons who have a physical, mental or emotional disability of a permanent nature which limits the selection of any type of employment for which the person would otherwise be qualified. Direct loans are available for up to $150,000. The interest rate is 3% on these loans.

Surety Bond Guaranty Program: Makes the bonding system more available to small contractors who may be denied access to the system. SBA can guarantee up to 80 percent of surety's loss on a bond that has a maximum in total contract value of up to $1,250,000.

Vietnam-era and Disabled Veterans Loan Program: Provides direct loans to veterans to establish or expand a small business. Funds may be used for working capital or fixed assets. Direct loans for amounts up to $150,000 are available. The interest rate may be fixed or variable.

Bankers Capital Corporation
3100 Gilham Road
Kansas City, MO 64109   816-531-1600

Capital for Business, Inc.
11 South Meramec, Suite 800
St. Louis, MO 63105   314-854-7427

MBI Venture Capital Investors, Inc.
850 Main Street
Kansas City, MO 64105   816-471-1700

Midland Capital Corporation
One Petticoat Lane
Suite 110

1020 Walnut Street
Kansas City, MO 64106   816-471-8000

MorAmerica Capital Corporation
(Main Office: Cedar Rapids, IA)
911 Main Street
Suite 2724A
Commerce Tower Building
Kansas City, MO 64105   816-842-0114

United Missouri Capital Corporation
1010 Grand Avenue
Mail: P.O. Box 419226; Kansas City, MO 64141
Kansas City, MO 64106   816-556-7333

Small Business Investment Companies (SBIC): The SBA licenses, regulates, and provides financial assistance to privately owned and operated Small Business Investment Companies. SBICs make venture or risk investments by supplying capital and extending unsecured loans and loans not fully collateralized to small enterprises which meet their investment criteria. Financing is made by direct loans and by equity investments.

* Women and Minorities Business Assistance

Missouri Department of Economic Development
P.O. Box 118   314-751-3237
Jefferson City, MO 65102   1-800-523-1434 in Missouri

Minority Business Assistance Program: Designed to promote and encourage the development of minority-owned businesses in Missouri, the program provides assistance in obtaining technical and financial assistance, education programs, minority business advocacy, and networking with other programs and agencies.

Missouri Council on Women's Economic Development & Training: Assists women in small business enterprises. Conducts programs, studies, seminars and conferences. Promotes increased economic and employment opportunities through education, training, and greater participation in the labor force.

Small Business Administration
911 Walnut Street, 13th Floor   816-426-5502
Kansas City, MO 64016   FAX: 816-426-5559

SBA 8(a) Program -Business Procurement Assistance: Provides federal government contracting opportunities for small businesses owned by socially and economically disadvantaged persons, and assists these businesses to become independently competitive in the normal business environment. SBA monitors all government contracts to assure that a quota of contract work goes to 8(a) businesses. Also provides business management services to these businesses. Business must be approved for program participation prior to receipt of an 8(a) contract.

* Training

Division of Job Development and Training
221 Metro Drive
Jefferson City, MO 65109   314-751-4750

Job Training Partnership Act (JTPA): Provides employers with recruitment, screening, referral, training, 50 percent wage subsidy up to 3 months for on-the-job training. Available to any private employer.

* Management Consulting and Other Services

Missouri Department of Economic Development
P.O. Box 118   314-751-4982
Jefferson City, MO 65102   1-800-523-1434 in Missouri

Procurement Assistance Program: Helps Missouri businesses participate in the federal and state market place at both the primary and subcontracting levels.

Business Retention Program: Serves as an avenue to state programs assisting communities and their existing businesses in job retention and expansion needs, local concerns, layoffs and plant closings.

Missouri Economic Development Information System (MEDIS): A computerized program that provides timely and accurate information on sites, labor, taxes, utility costs, transportation costs, and other data essential to the business planning process.

Small Business Administration
911 Walnut Street, 13th Floor   816-426-5502
Kansas City, MO 64016   FAX: 816-426-5559

Small Business Institutes: This program provides personalized consulting services to the small business community. Consulting is provided by senior level business students, guided by a faculty advisor. Assistance in business plan preparation, marketing research, market planning, accounting, and seminars are provided.

University Locations:
Avila College
Central Missouri State University
Columbia College
Drury College
Fontbonne College
Lincoln University of Missouri
Lindenwood College
Missouri Southern State
Missouri Western State College
Northeast Missouri State
Northwest Missouri State
Rockhurst College
Southeast Missouri State University
Southwest Baptist University
Southwest Missouri State University
St. Louis University
University of Missouri -Kansas City
University of Missouri -St. Louis

* Small Business Development Centers
The following offices offer free and fee-based services to new and expanding businesses:

Lead Center:
Missouri Small Business Development Center
University of Missouri
Suite 300, University Place   314-882-0344
Columbia, MO 65211   FAX: 314-884-4297

Cape Girardeau: Southwest Missouri State University, Small Business Development Center, 222 N. Pacific, Cape Girardeau, MO 63701, 314-290-5965; FAX: 314-651-5005 (call first).

Columbia: University of Missouri at Columbia, Small Business Development Center, 1800 University Place, Columbia, MO 65211, 314-882-7096; FAX: 314-882-6156.

Flat River: Mineral Area College, Small Business Development Center, P.O. Box 1000, Flat River, MO 63601, 314-431-4593, ext. 283; FAX: 314-431-6807.

Joplin: Missouri Southern State College, Small Business Development Center, 107 Mathews Hall, 3950 Newman Road, Joplin, MO 64801-1595, 417-625-9313; FAX: 417-625-3121.

Kansas City: Rockhurst College, Small Business Development Center, 1100 Rockhurst Road, Kansas City, MO 64110-2599, 816-926-4572; FAX: 816-926-4588.

Kirksville: Northeast Missouri State University, Small Business Development Center, 207 East Patterson, Kirksville, MO 63501, 816-785-4307; FAX: 816-785-4181.

Maryville: Northwest Missouri State University, Small Business Development Center, 127 South Buchanan, Maryville, MO 64468, 816-562-1701; FAX: 816-582-8469.

Poplar Bluff: Three Rivers Community College, Small Business Development Center, Business Incubator Building, 3019 Fair Street, Poplar Bluff, MO 63901, 314-686-3499; FAX: 314-686-5467 (call first).

Rolla: Center for Technology Transfer and Economic Development, University of Missouri at Rolla, Room 104, Building 1, Nagogami Terrace, Rolla, MO 65401-0249, 314-341-4992; FAX: 314-341-4559.

Rolla: University of Missouri at Rolla, Small Business Development Center, 223 Engineering Management Building, Rolla, MO 65401-0249, 314-341-4561; FAX: 314-341-2071.

St. Louis: St. Louis University, Small Business Development Center, 3642 Lindell Boulevard, St. Louis, MO 63108, 314-534-7232; FAX: 314-658-3897.

Springfield: Southwest Missouri State University, Small Business Development Center, Center for Business Research, 901 S. National, Box 88, Springfield, MO 65804-0089, 417-836-5685; FAX: 417-836-6337.

Warrensburg: Central Missouri State University, Center for Technology, Grinstead #75, Warrensburg, MO 64093-5037, 816-543-4402; FAX: 816-747-1653.

Warrensburg: Central Missouri State, Small Business Development Center, Grinstead #75, Warrensburg, MO 64093-5037, 816-543-4402; FAX: 816-747-1653.

Montana

* General Information

Department of Commerce
1424 Ninth Avenue
Helena, MT 59620
> **Business Assistance Division** 406-444-3923
> *A Guide to Montana's Economic Development Assistance Program*, which lists state and federal agencies and other sources of business assistance is available at no charge.

> **Business Development Division** 406-444-4780
> Publications printed and on disk are available at a fee. Available are *Montana Exporters Guide, Montana Consumer Products Buyers Director, Montana Manufacturers Director, Business Planning Guide.*

> **Business Information System (BIS):**
> **On Line Electronic Bulletin Board** 404-444-4780
> The electronic bulletin board is accessible free of charge to anyone with a personal computer communications software and modem. The BIS posts a variety of economic, demographic and business data, including state government bid solicitations, export trade opportunity leads from U.S. Dept. of Commerce, and population, income and employment statistics for Montana cities and counties.

> **Small Business Advocacy and Licensing** 1-800-221-8015 in Montana
> Assistance in cutting bureaucratic red tape. Information and expertise in dealing with state, federal, and local agencies, licensing and permit questions.

* Financing

Board of Investments
Office of Development Finance
Capitol Station
Helena, MT 59620 406-442-1970
> **Coal Tax Loan Programs:** Trust funds are established each year with proceeds from state coal taxes. Loans are made to Montana businesses that will create long-term benefits to the state's economy. Long-term, fixed-rate direct loans are available through approved financial institutions. The maximum loan can not exceed 10 percent of the prior year's deposits into the funds.

> **Federally Guaranteed Loan Programs:** Financial institutions that have secured a federal guarantee on a fixed-rate loan to a business that is eligible for Board investment may sell the federally guaranteed portion of the loan to the Board at a pre-established rate. This program provides fixed-rate financing at lower-than-average interest rates. Proceeds may be used for the purchase of land, buildings, equipment, machinery, building expansion or repair, inventory, or funds for working capital.

> **Economic Development Linked Deposit Program:** State funds are placed in long-term deposit with approved financial institutions to back-up loans to specific borrowers. The proceeds from this fixed-rate loan can be used for working capital, interim construction, inventory, site development, and acquisition of machinery, equipment and buildings, among other uses.

> **Business Loan Participation Program:** May be used to finance commercial, multi-family or SBA 504 loans, it allows approved Montana financial institutions the opportunity to "sell" up to 80 percent of an eligible business loan to the Board of Investments. The Board then owns a participation interest in both the financing and the security for an approved commercial loan that is serviced by the originating financial institution. Funds are targeted to long-term fixed-rate loans that have the potential to positively benefit economic development within the State.

> **SBA 504 Loan Participation Program:** Essentially the same as the Business Loan Participation Program but in this case the Board funds a portion of a project financed under the SBA 504 Program.

> **Stand Alone Industrial Development Bond Program:** Borrowers able to assume responsibility for funding their own projects can have the Board of Investments issue industrial development bonds. Projects must be in the public interest.

Montana Capital Companies
> **Billings:** Renaissance Capital Ltd. Partnership, 115 N. Broadway, Billings, MT 59101, 406-248-6771.

> **Billings:** Treasure State Capital Ltd. Partnership, 512 N. 29th, Billings, MT 59101, 406-245-6102.

> **Billings:** KBK Venture Capital Co. of Montana, 722 Third Avenue North, Billings, MT 59101, 406-256-2355.

> **Black Eagle:** The Glacier Springs Company, P.O. Box 399, Black Eagle, MT 59414, 406-727-7500.

> **Butte:** Southwest Montana Development Corp., 305 West Mercury, Butte, MT 59701, 406-723-4349.

> **Great Falls:** Great Falls Capital Corporation, 9 Third Street North, Suite 305, Great Falls, MT 59401, 406-761-7978.

> **Missoula:** First Montana Capital Corporation, 310 West Spruce Street, Missoula, MT 59802, 406-721-4466.

> **Venture, Equity or Risk Capital:** The Montana legislature adopted an act to encourage the private sector in Montana to create organized pools of equity or venture capital that could be invested in Montana businesses. Through these companies, Montana Capital Companies invest funds in small business engaged in one of the following:
> > Manufacturing
> > Agricultural, fishery, or forestry production and processing
> > Mineral production and processing, except for conventional oil and gas exploration.
> > Nonfossil forms of energy generation
> > Transportation
> > Research and development of products or processes associated with any of the activities listed above
> > Wholesale or retail distribution activities for which products produced in Montana comprise 50% or more of gross sale receipts
> > Any activity conducted in the state for which 50% or more of the gross receipts are derived from the sale of products or services outside Montana
> > Tourism

Local Government Assistance Division
Department of Commerce
1424 9th Avenue
Helena, MT 59620 406-444-3757
> **Community Development Block Grant Program:** Available to cities and counties, and towns for the commercial rehabilitation of existing buildings or structures used for business, commercial, or industrial purposes. Grants of up to $500,000 can be made. Every $15,000 of grant funds invested must create at least one full-time job, and at least 51 percent of the jobs created must be for low- and moderate-income families.

County Land Planning Grant Program: County governments receive a percentage of the coal severance tax collected by the state, which may then be distributed by the counties to local planning boards. Funds are used for local land use planning, including downtown redevelopment, economic development, and capital improvements planning.

Local Impact Assistance Program: Funding is derived from the Montana coal severance tax. Loans and grants are awarded to local governments which have been required to expand the provision of public services as the result of large-scale development of coal mines and coal-using energy complexes.

Department of Agriculture
Agriculture/Livestock Building
Capitol Station
Helena, MT 59620-0201   406-444-2402

Junior Agriculture Loan Program: Direct, lower-interest rate financing to active members of rural youth organizations for junior livestock and other agricultural business loans. May also make direct loans to youths unable to participate as members of such organizations. Projects can involve crop and livestock production, custom farming, marketing and distribution processing. Loans shall not exceed $7,000.

Rural Assistance Loan Program: Provides loans to farmers and ranchers with modes financial investments in agriculture. Available to those who are unable to qualify for financing from commercial lenders. Maximum loan amount is $25,000, not to exceed 80 percent of the loan value. Funds can be used to finance agricultural property such as livestock and farm machinery, improvements such as barns and irrigation systems, annual operating expenses, and agricultural land.

Montana Growth Through Agriculture Act (MGTA): Intent of the MGTA is to create jobs and expand small agricultural business opportunities. The Programs receives a level of coal severance tax revenues for the purpose of funding seed capital loans, market enhancement and research grants, agricultural business incubators and foreign trade office activities.

Seed Capital Loans: Funds are specifically intended for the commercialization and marketing of new and innovative agricultural products or processes. Maximum loan amount in any one round of financing is $50,000.

Market Development Grant Program: Program is intended to benefit Montana's agricultural community by upgrading existing agricultural research capabilities, providing financial support to individual research projects, supporting organization improvements and marketing, facilitating the process of transferring research from the laboratory to the commercial marketplace. The project must demonstrate potential for commercial application by other prospective producers or processors, and the primary beneficiary of market development grants results must be the general public.

Agricultural Business Incubators: Funds for agricultural business incubators established in rural communities with a population of 15,000 or less is available. Maximum funding is $100,000.

Water Development Bureau
Department of Natural Resources and Conservation
1520 East 6th Avenue
Helena, MT 59620-2301   406-444-6668

Water Development Loan and Grant Programs: The state's coal severance tax provides grants, and two bonding authorities fund loans. Loans and grants available for such diverse water development projects as dam and reservoir construction, streambank stabilization and erosion control, development of water conservation measures, and water and sewer projects.

Reclamation and Development Grant Program: Funds projects that protect and restore the environment from damages resulting from mineral development and projects that meet other crucial state needs. Other projects may qualify if they enhance Montana's economy or develop, promote, protect, or otherwise further Montana's total environment and public interest.

Small Business Administration (SBA)
301 S. Park, Room 528   406-449-5381
Helena, MT 59626   FAX: 406-449-5474

SBA 7(a) Guaranteed and Direct Loans: Guarantees up to 90 percent of a loan made through a private lender up to $750,000. Can be used for working capital, expand or convert facilities, purchase of machinery and equipment, and land and building. Available only to those unable to obtain a loan from conventional sources. Direct loans are made up to $150,000.

SBA 504: Provides loans using 50 percent conventional bank financing, 40 percent SBA involvement through Certified Development Companies, and 10 percent owner equity. Fixed-asset loans are available in amounts up to $750,000. The loan can be used for land and building, construction, machinery and equipment, and renovation/expansion.

Small Business Innovative Research Grants (SBIR): Phase I awards between $20,000 to $50,000 to entrepreneurs to support six months of research on a technical innovation. Phase II grants are an additional $500,000 for development. Private sector investment funds must follow.

International Trade Loans: Guaranteed long-term loans through private lenders to develop or expand export markets, or to recover from the effects of import competition. Maximum guaranteed loan is $1,000,000 for fixed assets and an additional $250,000 for working capital and/or export revolving line of credit.

Export Revolving Line of Credit Loan: Short term financing available to small businesses that are at least one year old. Loans provide working capital to finance the manufacturing or wholesaling of products for export and for export marketing. The SBA will guarantee up to 90 percent of a conventional loan in amounts up to $750,000.

Contract Loan: Short-term loans are available to small businesses to finance the costs of labor and materials on contracts for which the proceeds are assignable. Program guarantees up to 90 percent of loans not in excess of $750,000. Qualifying small businesses must be in business for at least 12 calendar months prior to the date of the loan application.

Seasonal Line of Credit Loan: Loans provide short-term working capital to finance seasonal increases in business activities. Program guarantees up to 90 percent of loans not in excess of $750,000. Qualifying business must be in operation for at least one year prior to application.

Pollution Control Loans: Long-term guaranteed loans can be made by conventional financing to small businesses for installation or required pollution control measures. Must be unable to adopt the pollution control measures without undue financial hardship. Maximum guaranteed loan is $1,000,000.

General Contractor Loans: Small general construction contractors may obtain short-term loans or loan guarantees for residential or commercial construction or rehabilitation of property to be sold. The SBA will guarantee up to 90 percent of qualifying loans made by private lenders up to a maximum of $750,000. Direct loans can be up to $150,000.

Energy Business Loan Guarantee: Small businesses that provide certain energy production and conservation services for others may qualify for long-term loans and loan guarantees for start-ups and expansions. Loans and guarantees are made for firms that develop, manufacture, sell, install, or service specific energy measures for others, or firms that provide engineering, architectural, consulting, or other professional services connected with specific energy measures. Guarantee is for up to 90 percent of a loan not in excess of $750,000. Direct loans up to $150,000.

Disaster Recovery Loans: Small businesses located in federally designated disaster areas and suffering property damage or economic losses from the disaster can obtain long-term recovery loans at low interest rates. Property damage loans are limited to 85 percent of the verified damage. Loans for economic losses are for operating capital to meet the business' obligations that could have been made had the disaster not occurred.

Handicapped Assistance Loans: Assists persons who have a physical, mental or emotional disability of a permanent nature which limits the selection of any type of employment for which the person would otherwise be qualified. Direct loans are available for up to $150,000. The interest rate is 3% on these loans.

Surety Bond Guaranty Program: Makes the bonding system more available to small contractors who may be denied access to the system. SBA can guarantee up to 80 percent of surety's loss on a bond that has a maximum in total contract value of up to $1,250,000.

Vietnam-era and Disabled Veterans Loan Program: Provides direct loans to veterans to establish or expand a small business. Funds may be used for working capital or fixed assets. Direct loans for amounts up to $150,000 are available. The interest rate may be fixed or variable.

Montana Science and Technology Alliance
46 North Last Chance Gulch
Suite 2B
Helena, MT 59620   406-449-2778

The purpose of the Alliance is to provide a source of financing for technology-based, entrepreneurial development to revitalize Montana industries and encourage new ones. They operate two financing programs:

Seed Capital Financing Program: Give priority to companies which incorporate advanced or innovative technologies, include plans for full commercialization and address one or more the Alliance's target technologies. Available to companies which cannot be financed through conventional financing do to the need for working capital and the lack of collaterizable assets but which hold realistic promise for rapid and significant growth. Maximum amount of loan is $350,000 for a single round of financing and up to a total of $750,000 over multiple financing rounds. Program loans require a 100 percent co-investment from private sources.

Research and Development Financing Program:
Centers for Excellence Program: Assists in the accelerated development of technology in the state by providing a source of funds to research organizations for projects which have outstanding technological and commercial potential for development in the state.

* Women and Minority Business Assistance

DBE Program Specialist
Civil Rights Bureau
2701 Prospect Avenue
Helena, MT 59620   406-444-6331

Disadvantaged Business Enterprise and Women Business Enterprise: Identifies, certifies, and monitories DBE/WBE contractors in competitive budding and in obtaining federal-aid highway construction contracts. Also serves as an advocate for DBE/WBE businesses with other state agencies.

Small Business Administration (SBA)
301 S. Park
Room 528   406-449-5381
Helena, MT 59626   FAX: 406-449-5474

SBA 8(a) Program -Business Procurement Assistance: Provides federal government contracting opportunities for small businesses owned by socially and economically disadvantaged persons, and assists these businesses to become independently competitive in the normal business environment. SBA monitors all government contracts to assure that a quota of contract work goes to 8(a) businesses. Also provides business management services to these businesses. Business must be approved for program participation prior to receipt of an 8(a) contract.

* Training

Research, Safety and Training Division
Department of Labor and Industry
P.O. Box 1728
Helena, MT 59624   406-444-4525

Job Training Partnership Act (JTPA): Provides employers with recruitment, screening, referral, training, 50 percent wage subsidy up to 3 months for on-the-job training. Available to any private employer.

* Management Consulting and Other Services

Department of Commerce
1424 Ninth Avenue
Helena, MT 59620

**Marketing Assistance and Montana Product
Promotion**   406-444-4392, 406-444-4127
Marketing staff members work with individual small businesses and trade associations to develop and expand outlets for products manufactured or processed in Montana. Products of Montana manufacturers are represented at selected trade shows both in the United States and foreign countries.

Product Promotion Program is designed to elevate the status of Montana-made products in the marketplace. Also serves to educate Montanans about the diversity of products manufactured in their state.

Promotion Division   406-444-2654
Responsible for promoting the State of Montana as a travel destination. Divisions promotes group travel and markets Montana as a location for the film and television industries. Other programs are Group Travel Promotion, Motion Picture and Television Promotion, Consumer Travel Promotion.

Business Development Division   406-444-3923
Consulting and training are available to business in the areas of financial analysis, financial planning, loan packaging, industrial revenue bonding, state and private capital sources, and business tax incentives.

Procurement Assistance   406-444-3923
Disseminates current government procurement information to small businesses interested in contracting to provide goods or services to state and federal government agencies. Provides technical assistance to help businesses in market identification, production management, quality control, cost accounting, and payment procedures for government procurement contracting.

International Trade   406-444-3923
Designed to increase the international sales of Montana manufacturers and service providers. Tourism promotion and reverse investment opportunities are pursued by the international trade staff. One-stop technical assistance to business wishing to enter foreign markets. Trade shows and foreign buyers are matched to exporters, and special training programs are conducted throughout the year. The division maintains a product showroom in the Taipei World Trade Center on Taiwan and a Pacific Rim Trade Office in Japan.

Small Business Administration
301 S. Park, Room 528   406-449-5381
Helena, MT 59626   FAX: 406-449-5474

International Trade Counseling and Training: Helps develop programs to aid small firms in doing business abroad. Emphasis is placed on the practical application of successful exporting and importing procedures to small businesses.

Small Business Institutes: This program provides personalized consulting services to the small business community. Consulting is provided by senior level business students, guided by a faculty advisor. Assistance in business plan preparation, marketing research, market planning, accounting, and seminars are provided.
University Locations:
Carroll College
Eastern Montana College
Montana State University
University of Montana

Department of Agriculture
Agricultural Development Division
Agricultural/Livestock Building
Capitol Station
Helena, MT 59620   406-444-2402

Marketing Assistance: Provides market enhancement and development assistance to agricultural producers, agribusiness, and value added processors. Program seeks to develop and enhance domestic and foreign markets for agricultural products, transportation and product movement through the state are also areas of focus and research assistance.

Cooperative Extension Service
Montana State University

101 Taylor Hall
Bozeman, MT 59717   406-994-5608

Provides current and reliable information pertaining to agriculture, home economics, 4-H in Youth and community development. The economic development education programs includes educational programs and materials on community economic analysis, goal setting, program planning, small and home-based business management aimed at the needs of small and declining communities. They coordinate a 6-part series of workshops on starting or expanding a business. Also have video tapes available on community economic development strategies and small business management. Call the number above to find your local office.

University Technical Assistance Program
Montana State University
402 Roberts Hall
Bozeman, MT 59717   406-994-3812

Provides technical engineering and managerial assistance to those manufacturing companies that are not in a position to hire professional consultants. Services include technical training, publications, production improvement, cost analysis and control, feasibility and inventory analyses, among others.

Assistance in applying for Small Business Innovative Research Grants. Computerized data search programs to help find the latest published information on technical problems. *Also see Technology Section.*

National Center for Appropriate Technology
P.O. Box 3838
Butte, MT 59702   406-494-4572

Operates the National Appropriate Technology Assistance Service under contract with the U.S. Department of Energy. Can assist with identifying sources of financing, licensing, marketing, business planning, and business organization development. Can also answer technical questions and help solve problems related to energy-conservation and renewable energy uses. Rural development services and an agricultural service called Appropriate Technology Transfer for Rural Areas are also available.

Procurement & Printing Division
Division of Administration
Room 165, Mitchell Building
Helena, MT 59620   406-444-2575

Small Business Procurement Set Asides: State agency designates specific commodities, equipment or services as small business "set asides" when there is a reasonable expectation that bids will be obtained from at least three small businesses capable of furnishing the desired property or service at a fair and reasonable price.

Bidding Preferences: Provides for a three percent bidding preference for "resident" Montana bidders when they bid on state contracts. This preference is awarded to vendors who meet the residency requirements. Also provides for a five percent preference for vendors submitting bids for goods manufactured in Montana.

Research Bureau
Department of Revenue
Sam Mitchell Building, Room 418
Helena, MT 59620   406-444-2981

Tax Incentives:

Property Tax: Property assessment reductions for new or expanding industries and for certain remodeling projects; Property tax rate reductions for pollution control equipment and for qualified new industries and research and development firms; Property tax exemptions for business inventories and freeport merchandise (merchandise produced outside Montana, which while in transit through the state is temporarily consigned to a Montana storage facility.)

Individual Income and Corporation License Tax Incentives: Wage credit for new or expanding manufacturing corporations producing a product new to Montana; A five-year exemption from taxation for research and development firms organized to engage in business in Montana for the first time; A credit for investing in a Montana capital company; Exemptions for domestic international sales corporations (DISCs) and for investments in small business investment companies (SBICs).

Natural Resource Related Tax Incentives: Phase-down of coal severance tax rates; Reduced severance tax rate on new coal production for buyers of coal who have not previously purchased from Montana producers or who purchase more, on average, than they did from 1983-1984 or during 1986; 12 month net proceeds tax exemption and a 24 month severance tax exemption for new oil and gas production.

Other Incentives: Individual income or corporation license tax credit for investing in wind powered electrical generating equipment; Exemption for sellers of land to beginning farmers at less than 9 percent interest.

* Small Business Development Centers

The following offices offer free and fee-based services to new and expanding businesses:

Lead Center:
Montana Small Business Development Center
Department of Commerce
1424 Ninth Avenue   406-444-4780
Helena, MT 59620   FAX: 406-444-2808

Billings: Billings Area Business Incubator, Small Business Development Center, 115 N. Broadway, 2nd Floor, Billings, MT 59101, 406-256-6875; FAX: 406-255-7175.

Bozeman: Bozeman Human Resources Development Council, Small Business Development Center, 321 East Main, Suite 413, Bozeman, MT 59715, 406-587-3113; FAX: 406-587-9565.

Butte: Butte REDI, Small Business Development Center, 305 W. Mercury Street, Suite 211, Butte, MT 59701, 406-782-7333; FAX: 406-782-9675.

Haver: Haver Small Business Development Center, Bear Paw Development Corporation, P.O. Box 1549, Haver, MT 59501, 406-265-9226; FAX: 406-265-3777.

Kalispell: Flathead Valley Community College, Small Business Development Center, 777 Grandview Drive, Kalispell, MT 59901, 406-756-3835; FAX: 406-786-3815.

Missoula: Missoula Incubator, Small Business Development Center, 127 N. Higgins, 3rd Floor, Missoula, MT 59802, 406-278-9234; FAX: 406-721-4584.

Sidney: Sidney Small Business Development Center, 123 W. Main, Sidney, MT 59270, 406-482-5024; FAX: 406-482-5306.

Nebraska

* General Information

Department of Economic Development
P.O. Box 94666   402-471-3782
301 Centennial Mall South   1-800-426-6505 in Nebraska
Lincoln, NE 68509-4666   FAX: 402-471-3778

One-Stop Business Assistance Program: Provides assistance on identifying marketing and finance information; business information and research, regulations, licenses, fees, and other state requirements for business operation. searches, and business counseling.

Existing Business Division: Offers technical assistance to small businesses and acts as a clearinghouse for information on other state services. Activities include acting as a link between business and government contracts, promoting exports of Nebraska products to foreign markets, maintaining a job training liaison to coordinate labor training with industrial location and expansion, maintaining business finance consultants in outreach offices, and providing information on federal programs such as Community Development Block Grants, SBA loans, and FmHA Business and Industry loans.

Small Business Advocate: Assistance in cutting bureaucratic red tape. Information and expertise in dealing with state, federal, and local agencies.

* Financing

Nebraska Investment Finance Authority
1033 O Street, Suite 218
Lincoln, NE 68508   402-434-3900

Provides lower-cost financing for manufacturing facilities, certain farm property, healthcare, and residential development. Funds can be used for land, buildings or equipment. All types of manufacturing and industrial projects including assembling, processing, warehousing, distributing, and transporting are eligible for funding. Minimum loan is $700,000.

Industrial Development Revenue Bonds (IDRB): Lower-cost financing through tax-exempt bonds for manufacturing projects only. Proceeds can be used to buy land, plants, equipment and on-site utilities. Maximum loan is $10,000,000.

Department of Economic Development
P.O. Box 94666
301 Centennial Mall South   402-471-3119
Lincoln, NE 68509   1-800-426-6505 in Nebraska

Community and Rural Development Division:
Community Improvement Financing: Encourages private investment in economically depressed areas for public improvements. Loans are available for land purchase, clearance, and sale, construction of streets, sidewalks, utilities, and parks.

Existing Business Assistance Division   402-471-4167
Economic Development Finance Program/Community Development Block Grants: Direct loans or loan guarantees for fixed assets, real estate and working capital, grants for job training, and deferred loans to help meet equity requirements of commercial lender are available to businesses for job-creation business development in towns under 2,500 population. Maximum loan is up to 50 percent of the project costs. The remaining portion to come from conventional financing. At least one jew job must be created for every $20,000, and a majority of the jobs created/retained must be for made available to low-and moderate-income people.

Small Business Administration
11145 Mill Valley Road
Omaha, NE   402-221-4691
       FAX: 402-221-3680

SBA 7(a) Guaranteed and Direct Loans: Guarantees up to 90 percent of a loan made through a private lender up to $750,000. Can be used for working capital, expand or convert facilities, purchase of machinery and equipment, and land and building. Available only to those unable to obtain a loan from conventional sources. Direct loans are made up to $150,000.

SBA 504: Provides loans using 50 percent conventional bank financing, 40 percent SBA involvement through Certified Development Companies, and 10 percent owner equity. Fixed-asset loans are available in amounts up to $750,000. The loan can be used for land and building, construction, machinery and equipment, and renovation/expansion.

International Trade Loans: Guaranteed long-term loans through private lenders to develop or expand export markets, or to recover from the effects of import competition. Maximum guaranteed loan is $1,000,000 for fixed assets and an additional $250,000 for working capital and/or export revolving line of credit.

Export Revolving Line of Credit Loan: Short term financing available to small businesses that are at least one year old. Loans provide working capital to finance the manufacturing or wholesaling of products for export and for export marketing. The SBA will guarantee up to 90 percent of a conventional loan in amounts up to $750,000.

Contract Loan: Short-term loans are available to small businesses to finance the costs of labor and materials on contracts for which the proceeds are assignable. Program guarantees up to 90 percent of loans not in excess of $750,000. Qualifying small businesses must be in business for at least 12 calendar months prior to the date of the loan application.

Seasonal Line of Credit Loan: Loans provide short-term working capital to finance seasonal increases in business activities. Program guarantees up to 90 percent of loans not in excess of $750,000. Qualifying business must be in operation for at least one year prior to application.

Pollution Control Loans: Long-term guaranteed loans can be made by conventional financing to small businesses for installation or required pollution control measures. Must be unable to adopt the pollution control measures without undue financial hardship. Maximum guaranteed loan is $1,000,000.

General Contractor Loans: Small general construction contractors may obtain short-term loans or loan guarantees for residential or commercial construction or rehabilitation of property to be sold. The SBA will guarantee up to 90 percent of qualifying loans made by private lenders up to a maximum of $750,000. Direct loans can be up to $150,000.

Energy Business Loan Guarantee: Small businesses that provide certain energy production and conservation services for others may qualify for long-term loans and loan guarantees for start-ups and expansions. Loans and guarantees are made for firms that develop, manufacture, sell, install, or service specific energy measures for others, or firms that provide engineering, architectural, consulting, or other professional services connected with specific energy measures. Guarantee is for up to 90 percent of a loan not in excess of $750,000. Direct loans up to $150,000.

Disaster Recovery Loans: Small businesses located in federally designated disaster areas and suffering property damage or economic losses from the disaster can obtain long-term recovery loans at low interest rates. Property damage loans are limited to 85 percent of the verified damage. Loans for economic losses are for operating capital to meet the business' obligations that could have been made had the disaster not occurred.

Handicapped Assistance Loans: Assists persons who have a physical, mental or emotional disability of a permanent nature which limits the selection of any type of employment for which the person would otherwise be qualified. Direct loans are available for up to $150,000. The interest rate is 3% on these loans.

Surety Bond Guaranty Program: Makes the bonding system more available to small contractors who may be denied access to the system. SBA can guarantee up to 80 percent of surety's loss on a bond that has a maximum in total contract value of up to $1,250,000.

Vietnam-era and Disabled Veterans Loan Program: Provides direct loans to veterans to establish or expand a small business. Funds may be used for working capital or fixed assets. Direct loans for amounts up to $150,000 are available. The interest rate may be fixed or variable.

Small Business Assistance   402-471-3782
Small Business Innovation Research Program (SBIR): Provides small business concerns with an opportunity to propose innovation ideas that meet specific research and development needs of one or more of the eleven participating federal agencies and has the potential for future commercialization. Phase I awards are between $20,000 to $50,000 to entrepreneurs to support six months of research on a technical innovation. Phase II grants are an additional $500,000 to pursue further development. Phase III is for the commercialization of the results of Phase II and requires the use of private sector investment funds.
Businesses can be added to a list of firms that are sent copies of the SBIR Pre-Solicitation Announcement.

First of Nebraska Investment Corporation
One First National Center
Suite 701
Omaha, NE 68102   402-633-3585

United Financial Resources Corporation
6211 L Street
P.O. Box 1131
Omaha, NE 68101   402-734-1250

Small Business Investment Companies (SBIC): The SBA licenses, regulates, and provides financial assistance to privately owned and operated Small Business Investment Companies. SBICs make venture or risk investments by supplying capital and extending unsecured loans and loans not fully collateralized to small enterprises which meet their investment criteria. Financing is made by direct loans and by equity investments.

Nebraska Economic Development Corporation (NEDC)
2631 O Street
Lincoln, NE 68510   402-475-2795
    SBA 504: Provides loans using 50 percent conventional bank financing, 40 percent Small Business Administration involvement, and 10 percent owner equity. Loan-term fixed-asset financing in amounts up to $750,000. Loan can be used for land and building, construction, machinery and equipment, and renovation/expansion.

Farmers Home Administration
Federal Building, Room 308
100 Centennial Mall North
Lincoln, NE 68508   402-437-5556
    Business and Industrial Loan Program: The programs are to create and maintain employment, and improve the economic and environmental climate in rural areas with a population of 25,000 or less. Loan guarantees are available for business and industrial acquisitions, construction conversion, enlargement, repair and modernization, purchase of land, machinery and equipment, processing and marketing facilities, start-up and working capital, and pollution control. Guarantees up to 90 percent of project up to a maximum of $10 to $20 million dollars.

Nebraska Research and Development Authority
NBC Center, Suite 660   402-475-5109
Lincoln, NE 68508   FAX: 402-475-5170
    The Authority supports business development and technology transfer. Invests in "seed" capital in new businesses that export a substantial amount of their product or service outside of Nebraska. They take an equity position in the business created.

Northeast Nebraska Venture Capital Network
405 Madison Avenue
Norfolk, NE 68702   402-371-4862
    Encourages the development and expansion of home-grown enterprises. Private investors may provide seed capital for inventors, early stage financing for start-up firms, or expansion capital for established firms. Companies receiving funds must locate in a 20-county area in northeast Nebraska. Loan structure or equity position will vary with investors.

* Women and Minority Business Assistance

Office of Operations
Minority Business Development Agency
Department of Commerce
14th and Constitution Avenue, N.W.
Washington, DC 20230   202-377-8015
    American Indian Program: Provides management and technical assistance to American Indians and individuals interested in entering, expanding or improving their efforts in the marketplace.

Office of Women's Business Ownership
Small Business Administration (SBA)
11145 Mill Valley Road   402-221-4691
Omaha, NE 68154   FAX: 402-221-3680
    Directs SBA programs to women business owners through special women's groups, seminars, networks, and other activities for women in the private sector.

    SBA 8(a) Program -Business Procurement Assistance: Provides federal government contracting opportunities for small businesses owned by socially and economically disadvantaged persons, and assists these businesses to become independently competitive in the normal business environment. SBA monitors all government contracts to assure that a quota of contract work goes to 8(a) businesses. Also provides business management services to these businesses. Business must be approved for program participation prior to receipt of an 8(a) contract.

Minority Business Development Agency
Department of Commerce
Communications Division, Room 6708

Washington, DC 20230   202-377-2414
    Monitors and coordinates minority business activity in the public and private sectors, and sponsors a nation-wide network of Minority Business Development Centers that offer management counseling in areas such as accounting, marketing, personnel, and training.

Hispanic Chamber of Commerce
106 W. 11th
Suite 1137
Kansas City, MO 64105   816-221-5772
    Serves as the central link in a national network of Hispanic businesses and business associations that are working to expand business opportunities in the nation and around the world. Provides technical assistance to Hispanic business associations and entrepreneurs through seminars, workshops and conferences. Also publishes the *National Hispanic Business Directory*.

* Training

Division of Vocational Education
Nebraska Department of Education
P.O. Box 94987
301 Centennial Mall South
Lincoln, NE 68509-4987   402-471-2432
    Training to fulfill a diverse number of occupational needs is offered in the traditional classroom setting, and through cooperative arrangements with local business. Special programs can be designed to meet specific training needs. Some funding may be available.

Nebraska Department of Labor
P.O. Box 95004
550 South 16th Street
Lincoln, NE 68509-5004   402-471-2127
    Job Service Division: Has available a statewide labor pool and works with employers to provide a full range of qualified employees for blue collar and professional positions. Screen and refer applicants for consideration. Job Service is the only agency authorized to certify Targeted Jobs Tax Credit employees. Businesses may be qualify for tax credits when they hire these certified applicants for specific job categories.

    Job Training Partnership Act (JTPA): Provides employers with recruitment, screening, referral, training, 50 percent wage subsidy up to 3 months for on-the-job training. Available to any private employer.

Nebraska Association of Farmworkers (NAF)
Offices in:
Lincoln   402-476-6341
Grand Island   308-382-3956
North Platte   308-534-2630, 1-800-662-2904
Omaha   402-734-4100
Scottsbluff   308-632-5831

    NAF is instrumental in advancing farm workers toward self-sufficiency by upgrading their skills, enhancing employment opportunities, and providing supportive services essential for a successful transition from agricultural to business and industrial employment.

    NAF offers businesses willing to hire eligible employees services such as applicant pre-screening/counseling, reimbursement of a percentage of employee training costs; assistance with getting tax benefits through participation in the Targeted Jobs Tax Credit option, customized training.

Operation Able of Southeast Nebraska
129 North 10th Street, Room 332
Lincoln, NE 68508-3548
    Operation ABLE (Ability Based on Long Experience) specializes in job search and job training assistance for workers 50 years of age or better in southeast Nebraska. It is a source of mature, experienced applicants who offer stability, low turnover rates, reliability, high job morale, and low needs for supervision. Helps local businesses located experienced, skilled workers, recommend work-ready applicants, and participate in employer workshops.

Existing Business Assistance Division
Nebraska Department of Economic Development
P.O. Box 94666
301 Centennial Mall South 402-471-3780
Lincoln, NE 68509 1-800-426-6505 in Nebraska
Industrial Training Programs: Offers assistance in the design and implementation of industrial training programs. Aimed at providing new and expanding industry with a skilled labor force, programs can be developed at little or no cost to industry. Services include developing customized curriculum, providing qualified instructors, and locating training materials. If business utilizes specialized equipment, programs can be designed to train on-site.

* Management Consulting and Other Services

Department of Economic Development
P.O. Box 94666
301 Centennial Mall South 402-471-3111
Lincoln, NE 68509 1-800-426-6505 in Nebraska
Existing Business Assistance Division 402-471-3769
Procurement Assistance: Provides assistance to businesses to identify markets within the federal government. Local businesses can learn how the procurement process works and receive leads on bid opportunities. A new electronic bulletin board contains selected lists of current federal procurement bid opportunities.

International Commerce 402-471-4668
Provides literature that will assist in the development of successful export strategies, training sessions are offered through the year, participation in trade missions and trade shows throughout the world, consultation visits to help companies organize an export program.

Agriculture Promotion and Development Division 402-471-4876
Acts as a clearinghouse of information for buyers and sellers of agricultural products and their value-added derivatives. Can help a business develop international markets.

Small Business Administration
11145 Mill Valley Road 402-221-4691
Omaha, NE 68154 FAX: 402-221-3680
Small Business Institutes: This program provides personalized consulting services to the small business community. Consulting is provided by senior level business students, guided by a faculty advisor. Assistance in business plan preparation, marketing research, market planning, accounting, and seminars are provided.
University Locations:
Chadron State College
Creighton University
Doane College
Hastings College
Nebraska Business Development Center
Peru State College
University of Nebraska -Omaha
University of Nebraska -Kearney
University of Nebraska -Lincoln
Wayne State College

Material Division
Nebraska Department of Administrative Services
P.O. Box 94847
301 Centennial Mall South
Lincoln, NE 68509-4847 402-471-2401
State Procurement: Assistance in filling out bid applications and will receive vendor booklets.

Agriculture Promotion and Development Division
Nebraska Department of Agriculture
P.O. Box 94947
301 Centennial Mall South 402-471-4876
Lincoln, NE 68509-4947 1-800-442-6692
Works closely with other agencies, commodity groups, and public and private institutions to seek new and expanding markets for Nebraska

Products. All the resources, buyers, producers, processors, and contacts can be accessed through the division's extensive database. Also provide information and direction for new agricultural products, assists in channeling resources from federal agencies and national marketing associations, and securing federal funds to develop new agricultural enterprises, promote existing agricultural products and to encourage development of alternative products and uses, and securing booth space at international and domestic agricultural food trade shows. Publishes the *Nebraska Agricultural Trade Direction.*

Division of Safety & Labor Standards
Nebraska Department of Labor
P.O. Box 95024
Lincoln, NE 68509-5024 402-471-2239
Nebraska On-Site Safety and Health Consultation Program: Helps employers identify and correct potential safety and/or health hazards. Service is provide and no cost to the business. A state consultant will inspect your workplace and note any violations of the federal Occupational Safety and Health Act (OSHA) standards. No penalties, fines, citations are issued. Only obligation is that the employer eliminate any serious or imminent hazards identified by the consultant.

Nebraska Energy Office
Atrium Bldg., Suite 110
1200 N. Street
Lincoln, NE 68508 402-471-2867
Information and referral on energy related topics including conservation, energy sources, and price history. Also offer limited technical assistance on conservation measures.

Nebraska Gasohol Committee
P.O. Box 94922
301 Centennial Mall South
Lincoln, NE 68509-4922 402-471-2941
Assists private businesses market products containing ethanol (retail operations or producers), sponsors research into the industrial uses of ethanol, develops means to produce fuel, and promotes the use of fuels containing ethanol or its derivatives.

University of Nebraska
200 CBA
Lincoln, NE 68588-0406
Bureau of Business Research 402-472-2334
Compiles statistical information on business conditions, produces economic forecasts, and reports economic and demographics information. The Site Evaluation and Location System (SELS) offers a database containing more than 80 key market characteristics that can be used in the site selection process.

Extension Service:
Panhandle Center, Scottsbluff 308-632-1254
West Central Center, North Platte 308-532-3611
Northeast Center, Concord 402-584-2261
South Central Center, Clay Center 402-762-3535
Southeast Center, Lincoln 402-472-3674
Extension Administration, Lincoln 402-472-2966
For information about the business management and technical assistance available, call one of the offices above.

Food Processing Center:
Food Technical Assistance 402-472-5833
Assists the food processing industry by providing help in various product research and product improvement areas. The Center offers the use of its pilot plant facility and equipment for various product and process testing. Technical education programs are also sponsored.

Food Marketing Assistance 402-472-5791
Provides sales and marketing leads through a market network referral system. Links processors, brokers, distributors, and specific product growers to allow for specific business transactions. Also has an entrepreneurial and business development program for food processors, and holds state-wide seminars.

International Center for Franchise Studies 402-472-3353
Sponsors seminars and workshops for franchisers and franchisees. Also
provides consultations for individuals or business contemplating franchise
operations. A franchise resource library, and quarterly newsletter are also
available.

Nebraska Technical Assistance Center 402-472-5600
1-800-332-0265 in Nebraska
An engineering and technical outreach service that provides assistance for
new and existing businesses in product design or modification,
productivity, quality control, manufacturing processes, patents, and other
vital issues. Using local experts, computerized information services, and a
matching service for aid from other state agencies.

Nebraska Center for Entrepreneurship
1237 R Street
Suite 203
Lincoln, NE 68588-0226 402-472-3353
Provides general consultation and planning assistance for people wishing
to start new businesses. Seminars, workshops, and an annual Productivity
and Entrepreneurship Conference are sponsored.

A Nebraska Entrepreneurs Association has been formed through the
center for business persons who wish to network with other entrepreneurs.

* Small Business Development Centers
The following offices offer free and fee-based services to new and expanding
businesses:

Lead Center:
Nebraska Small Business Development Center
University of Nebraska
60th & Dodge Street
CBA, Room 407
Omaha, NE 68182 FAX: 402-554-3747
402-554-2521

Chadron: Chadron State College, Small Business Development Center,
Administration Building, Chadron, NE 69337, 308-432-6282.

Kearney: University of Nebraska at Kearney, Small Business Development
Center, Welch Hall, 19th and College Drive, Kearney, NE 68849, 308-234-
8344.

Lincoln: University of Nebraska at Lincoln, Small Business Development
Center, Cornhusker Bank Bldg., 11th & Cornhusker Hwy., Suite 302,
Lincoln, NE 68521, 402-472-3358.

North Platte: Mid-Plains Community College, Small Business
Development Center, 416 North Jeffers, Room 26, North Platte, NE 69101,
308-534-5115.

Omaha: University of Nebraska at Omaha, Small Business Development
Center, Peter Kiewit Conference Center, 1313 Farnam, Suite 132, Omaha,
NE 68182, 402-595-2381.

Peru: Peru State College, Small Business Development Center, T.J. Majors
Building, Room 248, Peru, NE 68421, 402-872-2274.

Scottsbluff: Small Business Development Center, Nebraska Public Power
Building, 1721 Broadway, Room 408, Scottsbluff, NE 69361, 308-635-7513.

Wayne: Wayne State College, Small Business Development Center,
Connell Hall, Wayne, NE 68787, 402-375-7575.

Nevada

* General Information

State of Nevada Commission on Economic Development
Capitol Complex 702-687-4325
Carson City, NV 89710 FAX: 702-687-4450
Publishes a pamphlet, *Business Assistance*. Acts as a clearinghouse for
information and technical assistance. Operates several business assistance

programs and performs advertising and public relations activities on behalf
of Nevada business. Maintains a computerized inventory of available
manufacturing and warehousing buildings, land and corporate office space,
customized site selection.

Small Business Advocate
Nevada Office of Community Services
400 W. King, Suite 400
Carson City, NV 89710 702-687-4990
Assistance in cutting bureaucratic red tape. Information and expertise in
dealing with state, federal, and local agencies.

* Financing

Nevada Commission of Economic Development
Capital Complex 702-687-4325
Carson City, NV 89710 FAX: 702-687-4450
Regional Development Grants: Provides matching grants to regional
development organizations to encourage cooperative economic diversi-
fication.

Nevada Department of Commerce
1665 Hot Springs Rd
Carson City, NV 89710 702-687-4250
Industrial Development Revenue Bonds (IDRBs): Tax-exempt industrial
revenue bonds are available to manufacturing facilities for a maximum of
40 years and can provide up to 100 percent financing for land, building,
improvements, and capital equipment for businesses incurring between $
1-10 million in development costs.

Department Commission of Economic Development
Capital Complex 702-687-4325
Carson City, NV 89710 FAX: 702-687-4450
Enterprise Zones: Offers incentives to businesses to encourage
development in designated zones. Las Vegas and North Las Vegas are
currently Enterprise zones.

Small Business Revitalization Program: Office specializes in creating loan
packages for businesses and reviews and assesses expansion projects. The
staff can also recommend the most efficient financing for a specific project
and acts as an advocate for small businesses with commercial lenders. The
program uses loans available from the public sector, such as the Small
Business Administration 504 loan guarantees and the Nevada Revolving
Loan Fund in order to encourage private sector investment in small
business expansion projects.

Nevada Revolving Loan Fund Program: Funded through the Small Cities
Community Development Block Grant, this program provides loans for
small business expansion if low- and moderate-income jobs are created.
Financing must not be available from conventional lenders. Loans of up
to $100,000 are available for "gap financing". Rates are variable.

SBA 7(a) Loan Guarantee Program: Guarantees up to 90 percent of a
loan, up to $750,000, made through conventional bank financing. Funds
can be used for working capital, fixed asset acquisition, and leasehold
improvements.

Nevada State Development Corporation
350 S. Center Street, Suite 310
Reno, NV 89501 702-323-3625
SBA 504: Provides loans using 50 percent conventional bank financing, 40
percent SBA involvement through Certified Development Companies, and
10 percent owner equity. A fixed-asset loan in amounts up to $750,000.
Loan can be used for land and building, construction, machinery and
equipment, and renovation/expansion.

Farmers Home Administration
Nevada State Development Corp.
350 South Center Street, Suite 310
Reno, NV 89501 702-323-3625

Business and Industry Loan Guarantee Program: Provides loan guarantees to improve, develop, or finance business, industry and employment in rural areas.

Working Capital Guarantee Program: Assists small and medium size exports obtain financing needed to produce goods and services for sales abroad by guaranteeing private lend loans.

Small Business Administration (SBA) District Office
301 East Stewart Street, Room 301   702-388-6611
Las Vegas NV 89125   FAX: 702-388-6469

SBA 7(a) Guaranteed and Direct Loans: Guarantees up to 90 percent of a loan made through a private lender up to $750,000. Can be used for working capital, expand or convert facilities, purchase of machinery and equipment, and land and building. Available only to those unable to obtain a loan from conventional sources. Direct loans are made up to $150,000.

SBA 504: Provides loans using 50 percent conventional bank financing, 40 percent SBA involvement through Certified Development Companies, and 10 percent owner equity. Fixed-asset loans are available in amounts up to $750,000. The loan can be used for land and building, construction, machinery and equipment, and renovation/expansion.

Small Business Innovative Research Grants (SBIR): Phase I awards between $20,000 to $50,000 to entrepreneurs to support six months of research on a technical innovation. Phase II grants are an additional $500,000 for development. Private sector investment funds must follow.

International Trade Loans: Guaranteed long-term loans through private lenders to develop or expand export markets, or to recover from the effects of import competition. Maximum guaranteed loan is $1,000,000 for fixed assets and an additional $250,000 for working capital and/or export revolving line of credit.

Export Revolving Line of Credit Loan: Short term financing available to small businesses that are at least one year old. Loans provide working capital to finance the manufacturing or wholesaling of products for export and for export marketing. The SBA will guarantee up to 90 percent of a conventional loan in amounts up to $750,000.

Contract Loan: Short-term loans are available to small businesses to finance the costs of labor and materials on contracts for which the proceeds are assignable. Program guarantees up to 90 percent of loans not in excess of $750,000. Qualifying small businesses must be in business for at least 12 calendar months prior to the date of the loan application.

Seasonal Line of Credit Loan: Loans provide short-term working capital to finance seasonal increases in business activities. Program guarantees up to 90 percent of loans not in excess of $750,000. Qualifying business must be in operation for at least one year prior to application.

Pollution Control Loans: Long-term guaranteed loans can be made by conventional financing to small businesses for installation or required pollution control measures. Must be unable to adopt the pollution control measures without undue financial hardship. Maximum guaranteed loan is $1,000,000.

General Contractor Loans: Small general construction contractors may obtain short-term loans or loan guarantees for residential or commercial construction or rehabilitation of property to be sold. The SBA will guarantee up to 90 percent of qualifying loans made by private lenders up to a maximum of $750,000. Direct loans can be up to $150,000.

Energy Business Loan Guarantee: Small businesses that provide certain energy production and conservation services for others may qualify for long-term loans and loan guarantees for start-ups and expansions. Loans and guarantees are made for firms that develop, manufacture, sell, install, or service specific energy measures for others, or firms that provide engineering, architectural, consulting, or other professional services connected with specific energy measures. Guarantee is for up to 90 percent of a loan not in excess of $750,000. Direct loans up to $150,000.

Disaster Recovery Loans: Small businesses located in federally designated disaster areas and suffering property damage or economic losses from the disaster can obtain long-term recovery loans at low interest rates. Property

damage loans are limited to 85 percent of the verified damage. Loans for economic losses are for operating capital to meet the business' obligations that could have been made had the disaster not occurred.

Handicapped Assistance Loans: Assists persons who have a physical, mental or emotional disability of a permanent nature which limits the selection of any type of employment for which the person would otherwise be qualified. Direct loans are available for up to $150,000. The interest rate is 3% on these loans.

Surety Bond Guaranty Program: Makes the bonding system more available to small contractors who may be denied access to the system. SBA can guarantee up to 80 percent of surety's loss on a bond that has a maximum in total contract value of up to $1,250,000.

Vietnam-era and Disabled Veterans Loan Program: Provides direct loans to veterans to establish or expand a small business. Funds may be used for working capital or fixed assets. Direct loans for amounts up to $150,000 are available. The interest rate may be fixed or variable.

* Women and Minority Business Assistance

Nevada Commission on Economic Development
3770 Howard Hughes Parkway #295
Las Vegas, NV 89158   702-486-7282

This office provides assistance to women and minority business owners. Business opening kits are also available. Links with financial services are also identified.

Small Business Administration District Office
301 East Stewart Street
Room 301   702-388-6611
Las Vegas NV 89125   FAX: 702-388-6469

SBA 8(a) Program -Business Procurement Assistance: Provides federal government contracting opportunities for small businesses owned by socially and economically disadvantaged persons, and assists these businesses to become independently competitive in the normal business environment. SBA monitors all government contracts to assure that a quota of contract work goes to 8(a) businesses. Also provides business management services to these businesses. Business must be approved for program participation prior to receipt of an 8(a) contract.

* Training

Nevada Commission of Economic Development
Capital Complex   702-687-4325
Carson City, NV 89710   FAX: 702-687-4450

Quick Start Job Training: State-supported program for new or expanding manufacturers that need employees to quickly learn new skills. Funds are provided for instructional personnel, and materials, and up to 30 days of on-the-job training. The state pays up to 75 percent of the total training costs.

Job Training Partnership Act   702-687-4310
Provides employers with recruitment, screening, referral, training, 50 percent wage subsidy up to 3 months for on-the-job training. Available to any private employer.

* Management Consulting and Other Services

Western Nevada Community College
Adult Basic Education
2201 West Nye Lane
Carson City, NV 89703   702-887-3000

Northern Nevada Community College
Adult Basic Education/Occupational Education
901 Elm St
Elko, NV 89801   702-738-8493

Community College of Southern Nevada
Center for Business and Industry Training

3200 East Cheyenne Avenue
N. Las Vegas, NV 89030   702-643-6060

Truckee Meadows Community College
Institute for Business and Industry Services
Old Town Mall
4001 S. Virginia
Reno, NV 89502   702-829-9000
   The community colleges cooperate with private businesses in providing
   various resources to Nevada firms. Areas of expertise include customized
   job training, commercialization of advanced technology, international
   trade, and advanced computer instruction.

Nevada Development Authority
3900 Paradise Road, Suite 155   702-791-0000
Las Vegas, NV 89109   1-800-634-6858 in Nevada

Economic Development Authority of Western Nevada
5190 Neil Road, Suite 111
Reno, NV 89502   702-829-3700
   Regional Development Authorities: Provide client services, help organize
   local resources and link statewide efforts in a single program geared to
   each region's economy. Funded by private donations and local governments, the Authorities provide new businesses with data on their localities,
   arrange site studies, and conduct all client service work at the local level.

Nevada Commission of Economic Development
Northern Nevada Regional Manager
Capital Complex   702-687-4325
5151 South Carson Street   1-800-336-1600
Carson City, NV 89710   FAX: 702-687-4450
            or
Southern Nevada Regional Manager
Tempe Plaza
3017 West Charleston Blvd., Suite 20
Las Vegas, NV 89102   702-486-6174
   Procurement Outreach Program: Helps Nevada-based companies
   interested in selling goods or services to the federal government. Advises
   on bid process and provides technical support services, conducts seminars,
   sponsors federal marketing fairs.

Commission on Economic Development
Nevada World Trade Council
Capital Complex   702-687-4235
Carson City, NV 89710   FAX: 702-687-4450

Nevada Commission on Economic Development
Nevada World Trade Council
3770 Howard Hughes Parkway, Suite 295   702-486-7282
Las Vegas, NV 89158   FAX: 702-486-7284
   International Trade: Services as a center for information on foreign
   business import and export promotion to attract foreign investment that
   will create jobs in Nevada, increase exports, and help Nevada's economic
   base. Provides customized client assistance to foreign companies seeking
   expansion or relocation to the U.S. Complete inventory of prospective site
   locations. Coordinates all international activity for the state. Provides
   assistance through export counseling, information distribution,
   development of an overseas network, and trade shows. Helps increase both
   the total number of exports and the number of products exported from
   Nevada. Maintain overseas offices in Tokyo, Korea, and Taiwan.

Department of Commerce
1665 Hot Springs Road
Carson City, NV 89710   702-885-4250
   Export Finance Program: Works to facilitate foreign investment in the
   state as well as exports in the areas of banking, finance, and insurance
   services. Provides loan guarantees.

Nevada Commission on Tourism
Capital Complex
Carson City, NV 89710   702-687-4322
   Provides grant and technical assistance to support the local tourist industry

which is a larger business than exports in Nevada. Conducts extensive
advertising and runs a tourism promotion office in Tokyo.

Small Business Administration District Office
301 East Stewart Street
Room 301
Las Vegas NV 89125   702-388-6611
   Small Business Institutes: This program provides personalized consulting
   services to the small business community. Consulting is provided by senior
   level business students, guided by a faculty advisor. Assistance in business
   plan preparation, marketing research, market planning, accounting, and
   seminars are provided.
   University Locations:
   University of Nevada -Las Vegas
   University of Nevada -Reno

* Small Business Development Centers
The following offer free and fee-based services to new and expanding businesses:

Lead Center:
Nevada Small Business Development Center
University of Nevada at Reno
College of Business Administration, Room 411   702-784-1717
Reno, NV 89577-0100   FAX: 702-784-4305

   Elko: Northern Nevada Community College, Small Business Development
   Center, 901 Elm Street, Elko, NV 89801, 702-738-8493.

   Las Vegas: University of Nevada at Las Vegas, Small Business
   Development Center, College of Business and Economics, 4505 Maryland
   Parkway, Las Vegas, NV 89154, 702-739-0852.

New Hampshire

* General Information

Small Business Advocate
Office of Business and Industrial Development
Director, Division of Economic Development
172 Pembroke Road
P.O. Box 856
Concord, NH 03302-0856   603-271-2591
   Assistance in cutting bureaucratic red tape. Information and expertise in
   dealing with state, federal, and local agencies.

Office of Business and Industrial Development
Division of Economic Development
P.O. Box 856   603-271-2591
Concord, NH 03302-0856   FAX: 603-271-2629
   Provides assistance and publications designed to support and promote
   business and industry in the state. Information in areas such as licensing
   and permits, financial counseling, marketing, and exporting, labor markets,
   economic and demographic statistics, and site location information.

* Financing

Industrial Development Authority
4 Park Street, Room 302
Concord, NH 03301-6313   603-271-2391
   Industrial Revenue Bonds: Tax exempt revenue bonds available to
   manufacturing facilities for purchase of land, buildings, machinery and
   equipment.

   Guaranteed Loans:
   Real Estate: May guarantee up to 50 percent of first mortgage loans made
   by financial institutions to manufacturing industries that acquire, construct
   or reconstruct facilities. 100 percent financing is available to out-of-state
   companies seeking to relocate to New Hampshire, as well as to New
   Hampshire companies wishing to establish or expand operations in the
   state. Guarantee limit of $5 million for any single project.

Machinery and Equipment: Guarantees up to 35 percent of the cost of new industrial machinery and equipment Maximum guarantee for any single project is $600,000.

Small Business Administration (SBA) District Office
143 N. Main
Suite 202   603-225-1400
Concord, NH 03302-1257   FAX: 603-225-1409

SBA 7(a) Guaranteed and Direct Loans: Guarantees up to 90 percent of a loan made through a private lender up to $750,000. Can be used for working capital, expand or convert facilities, purchase of machinery and equipment, and land and building. Available only to those unable to obtain a loan from conventional sources. Direct loans are made up to $150,000.

SBA 504: Provides loans using 50 percent conventional bank financing, 40 percent SBA involvement through Certified Development Companies, and 10 percent owner equity. Fixed-asset loans are available in amounts up to $750,000. The loan can be used for land and building, construction, machinery and equipment, and renovation/expansion.

Small Business Innovative Research Grants (SBIR): Phase I awards between $20,000 to $50,000 to entrepreneurs to support six months of research on a technical innovation. Phase II grants are an additional $500,000 for development. Private sector investment funds must follow.

International Trade Loans: Guaranteed long-term loans through private lenders to develop or expand export markets, or to recover from the effects of import competition. Maximum guaranteed loan is $1,000,000 for fixed assets and an additional $250,000 for working capital and/or export revolving line of credit.

Export Revolving Line of Credit Loan: Short term financing available to small businesses that are at least one year old. Loans provide working capital to finance the manufacturing or wholesaling of products for export and for export marketing. The SBA will guarantee up to 90 percent of a conventional loan in amounts up to $750,000.

Contract Loan: Short-term loans are available to small businesses to finance the costs of labor and materials on contracts for which the proceeds are assignable. Program guarantees up to 90 percent of loans not in excess of $750,000. Qualifying small businesses must be in business for at least 12 calendar months prior to the date of the loan application.

Seasonal Line of Credit Loan: Loans provide short-term working capital to finance seasonal increases in business activities. Program guarantees up to 90 percent of loans not in excess of $750,000. Qualifying business must be in operation for at least one year prior to application.

Pollution Control Loans: Long-term guaranteed loans can be made by conventional financing to small businesses for installation or required pollution control measures. Must be unable to adopt the pollution control measures without undue financial hardship. Maximum guaranteed loan is $1,000,000.

General Contractor Loans: Small general construction contractors may obtain short-term loans or loan guarantees for residential or commercial construction or rehabilitation of property to be sold. The SBA will guarantee up to 90 percent of qualifying loans made by private lenders up to a maximum of $750,000. Direct loans can be up to $150,000.

Energy Business Loan Guarantee: Small businesses that provide certain energy production and conservation services for others may qualify for long-term loans and loan guarantees for start-ups and expansions. Loans and guarantees are made for firms that develop, manufacture, sell, install, or service specific energy measures for others, or firms that provide engineering, architectural, consulting, or other professional services connected with specific energy measures. Guarantee is for up to 90 percent of a loan not in excess of $750,000. Direct loans up to $150,000.

Disaster Recovery Loans: Small businesses located in federally designated disaster areas and suffering property damage or economic losses from the disaster can obtain long-term recovery loans at low interest rates. Property damage loans are limited to 85 percent of the verified damage. Loans for economic losses are for operating capital to meet the business' obligations that could have been made had the disaster not occurred.

Handicapped Assistance Loans: Assists persons who have a physical, mental or emotional disability of a permanent nature which limits the selection of any type of employment for which the person would otherwise be qualified. Direct loans are available for up to $150,000. The interest rate is 3% on these loans.

Surety Bond Guaranty Program: Makes the bonding system more available to small contractors who may be denied access to the system. SBA can guarantee up to 80 percent of surety's loss on a bond that has a maximum in total contract value of up to $1,250,000.

Vietnam-era and Disabled Veterans Loan Program: Provides direct loans to veterans to establish or expand a small business. Funds may be used for working capital or fixed assets. Direct loans for amounts up to $150,000 are available. The interest rate may be fixed or variable.

Concord Community Development Corporation   (Merrimack County)
45 Airport Road
P.O. Box 664
Concord, NH 03301

Granite State Economic   (Belknap, Chesire,
Development Corporation   Hillsborough, Strafford, Sullivan,
P.O. Box 1491   Rockingham Counties)
Portsmouth, NH 03802   603-436-0009

Farmers Home Administration (FmHA)
3rd Floor, City Center
89 Main Street
Montpelier, VT 05602   802-828-4472

FMHA Business and Industrial Development Loan Program: Guarantees loans to all types of businesses and industries to benefit rural areas. Available for projects in all municipalities in New Hampshire except Manchester and Nashua and communities immediately contiguous to these two cities. Loans can be used for business; construction, conversion, enlargement, repair and modernization; purchase and development of land and facilities, easements, leases, machinery and equipment, supplies or materials; certain housing development sites; processing and marketing facilities; working capital; pollution control.

New Hampshire Office of State Planning
2-1/2 Beacon Street
Concord, NH 03301   603-271-2155

Community Development Block Grants (CDBG): Grants are awarded to municipalities who in turn loan the funds to help municipalities meet housing and community development needs by alleviating some form of physical or economical distress.

Economic Development Administration
Federal Building
55 Pleasant Street
Concord, NH 03301   603-225-1624

Loan Guarantee Program: Available to business unable to obtain conventional financing. Guarantees up to 80 percent of project. Funds can be used for land and machinery, new construction or rehabilitation of commercial or industrial buildings, and working capital. For each $20,000 of loan guarantee, a job must be created or saved.

New Hampshire Port Authority
555 Market Street
Box 506
Portsmouth, NH 03801   603-436-8500

Foreign Enterprise Zone: Foreign traders can store, mix, blend, repack and assemble various commodities with an exemption from normal custom duties and federal excise taxes. Four areas in New Hampshire have been designated as Foreign Trade Zone 81. They are the Port Authority Terminal, Portsmouth; Portsmouth Industrial Park; Crosby Road Industrial Park, Dover; Manchester Airport (formerly Grenier Air Base, Manchester).

Industrial Development Manager
Public Service of New Hampshire (PSNH)

1000 Elm Street
Manchester, NH 03105   603-669-4000

Development Incentive Rate Contract: PSNH offers an incentive rate to its new or expanding commercial and industrial customers that will provide benefits to all PSNH customers. PSNH negotiates special rate contracts with existing or new customers having incremental load requirements of more than 300 kilowatts.

NETAAC (New England Trade Adjustment Assistance Center)
120 Boylston Street
Boston, MA 02116   617-542-2395

Direct Loan Guarantees: Available to manufacturing firms for the purchase of equipment or plant expansions. Maximum available is $1 million.

Trade Adjustment Assistance: Manufacturing company must have experienced a decline in production or sales and an actual or threatened decrease in employment, attributable to increased imports of competitive products.

* Women and Minority Business Assistance

Office of Business and Industrial Development
Division of Economic Development
172 Pembroke Road
P.O. Box 856
Concord, NH 03302-0856   603-271-2591

This office serves as a clearinghouse and referral center of programs for women and minority-owned businesses.

Small Business Administration (SBA) District Office
143 N. Main
Suite 202   603-225-1400
Concord, NH 03302-1257   FAX: 603-225-1409

SBA 8(a) Program -Business Procurement Assistance: Provides federal government contracting opportunities for small businesses owned by socially and economically disadvantaged persons, and assists these businesses to become independently competitive in the normal business environment. SBA monitors all government contracts to assure that a quota of contract work goes to 8(a) businesses. Also provides business management services to these businesses. Business must be approved for program participation prior to receipt of an 8(a) contract.

* Training

New Hampshire Job Training Councils
64B Old Suncook Road
Concord, NH 03301   603-228-9500

Job Training Partnership Act (JTPA): Provides employers with recruitment, screening, referral, training, 50 percent wage subsidy up to 3 months for on-the-job training. Available to any private employer.

New Hampshire Department of Employment Security
32 South Main Street
Concord, NH 03301   603-224-3311

The 13 local offices provide a free labor market exchange by matching job applicants with the labor needs of local employers. Interview, test and screen applicants. Applicants skills and employer needs are placed in the Job Bank and are available throughout the state.

Other programs provided by the Department include veteran training and placement, Targeted Jobs Tax Credit, Summer Youth Employment, Older Workers, job training programs, and a national network to place workers anywhere in the country.

Bureau of Vocational-Technical Education
New Hampshire Department of Education
State Office Park South
101 Pleasant Street
Concord, NH 03301   603-271-3186

Apprenticeship Programs: Conducts a wide range of apprenticeship programs in a electrical, plumbing, masonry, culinary arts and sheet metal fabrication.

* Management Consulting and Other Services

Office of Industrial Development
Division of Economic Development
P.O. Box 856   603-271-2591
Concord, NH 03302   FAX: 603-271-2629

Export Assistance: Assistance to industries in the process of developing export markets and in the design of an export plan. Assistance is tailored to fit the demands of each company and situation. Also, works with the U.S. Department of Commerce and the New Hampshire International Trade Association to promote increased export of New Hampshire products.

NEDDS Program (New Hampshire Economic Development Data System): A one-stop information source of data on the state's communities, industrial and office buildings, sites and parks, labor markets, population and other demographic data.

Wiggin and Nourie
P.O. Box 808
Manchester, NH 03105   603-669-2211

The New Hampshire High Technology Council is a non-profit association designed to bring together representatives from the private sector, universities and the public sector to establish and maintain financial, technical, management, legislative, and education support programs that encourage innovative research and technology-based industrial development in the state.

New Hampshire International Trade Association
500 Market Street
P.O. Box 239
Portsmouth, NH 03802   603-431-6128

Provides members with consulting services and counseling, an international database with trade opportunities information, workshops, trade shows, and more.

New Hampshire Small Business Development Center
University of New Hampshire
108 McConnell Hall   603-862-2200
Durham, NH 03824   FAX: 603-862-4468

New Hampshire Small Business Program (NHSBP): A statewide small business support system based at the University of New Hampshire. In addition to the three components of the program listed, there are the Small Business Development Centers which follow this section.

Venture Capital Network: A formal market where entrepreneurs and other growing concerns needing financing can be linked with individuals of means and other sources of venture capital.

SBIR Data Match: Assists technology-based companies and individuals make the most of R&D opportunities presented by the Small Business Innovation Research (SBIR) Program by matching interests and skills with federal agency needs and helping develop sound proposals for funding.

Small Business Resource System: A database of skilled individuals, specialized machinery, resource groups, public and private organizations, and other resources of value to entrepreneurs and small business, cross-indexed by application and type of assistance provided.

Office of Sponsored Research
Room 111, Service Bldg.
University of New Hampshire (UNH)
Durham, NH 03824-3585   603-862-3750

The Center matches university resources with business and industry needs by utilizing over 600 faculty advisors and associates. Services provided include product development, process development, long range research and planning, modeling, software development, technical trouble shooting, feasibility studies, development of laboratory testing procedures, market analysis, risk analysis planning and educational programs. It also Patents inventions developed at UNH and licenses such technology to the private sector. The Center also invites business and individual inventors to submit proposals for joint participation in the development of inventions.

NETAAC (New England Trade Adjustment Assistance Center)
120 Boylston Street
Boston, MA 02116   617-542-2395
   Provides technical and financial assistance (*see Financing*) to manufacturing firms that have been hurt by import competition. Provides both specialized consulting services and financial assistance aimed at helping import-impacted companies achieve a competitive market position. The federal government assumes up to 75 percent of the cost of the services, with the client firm cost-sharing the remaining 25 percent.

Waste Management Division
NH Department of Environmental Services
6 Hazen Drive
Concord, NH 03301   603-271-2900
   Sponsors seminars for business and industry within the state to explain hazardous waste regulations, conducting public awareness activities, managing the hazardous waste transporters, cooperating with person's requesting information for preparing environmental site assessments, and managing the state's hazardous waste clean-up fund.

Small Business Administration District Office
143 N. Main
Suite 202   603-225-1400
Concord, NH 03302-1257   FAX: 603-225-1409
   Small Business Institutes: This program provides personalized consulting services to the small business community. Consulting is provided by senior level business students, guided by a faculty advisor. Assistance in business plan preparation, marketing research, market planning, accounting, and seminars are provided.
   University Locations:
   Keene State College
   New Hampshire College
   Plymouth State College
   Rivier College
   University of New Hampshire

* Small Business Development Centers
The following offices offer free consulting and information referral services. Nominal fees are charged for most training programs.

Lead Center:
New Hampshire Small Business Development Center
University of New Hampshire
108 McConnell Hall   603-862-2200
Durham, NH 03824   FAX: 603-862-4468

   Durham: Office of Economic Initiatives, Heidelberg Harris Building, Technology Drive, Durham, NH 03824, 603-862-0710.

   Durham: Small Business Development Center, Heidelberg Harris Building, Technology Drive, Durham, NH 03824, 603-862-0700.

   Keene: Keene State College, Small Business Development Center, Blake House, Keene, NH 03431, 603-358-2602.

   Littleton: Small Business Development Center, P.O. Box 786, Littleton, NH 03561, 603-444-1053.

   Manchester: Small Business Development Center, 1001 Elm Street, Manchester, NH 03101, 603-624-2000.

   Plymouth: Plymouth State College, Small Business Development Center, Hyde Hall, Plymouth, NH 03264, 603-535-2523.

   Nashua: Center for Economic Development, Small Business Development Center, 188 Main Street, Nashua, NH 03062, 603-881-8333.

New Jersey

* General Information

Office of Small Business Assistance
Department of Commerce and Economic Development
20 West State, CN 835
Trenton, NJ 08625   609-292-3860
   Advice on expansion and business start-ups, and marketing and procurement assistance are some of the services available to small businesses. The office also offers seminars throughout the state as part of its outreach program.

Office of Business Advocacy
Department of Commerce and Economic Development
20 West State Street, CN 823
Trenton, NJ 08625   609-292-0700
   Small Business Advocate: Assistance in cutting bureaucratic red tape. Information and expertise in dealing with state, federal, and local agencies.

* Financing

New Jersey Economic Development Authority
Capital Place One
200 S. Warren Street, CN 990
Trenton, NJ 08625   609-292-1800
   Direct Loans: Provides up to $500,000 in direct loans for qualified businesses unable to obtain conventional loans. Loans of up to $250,000 are available for working capital. Aimed at businesses in manufacturing, processing, or distributing that will either create jobs or are located in economically distressed areas. The interest rate is on par with the current federal discount rate.

   Urban Centers Small Loan Program: Loans up to $30,000 to encourage merchants to remain in downtown urban areas. These loans have set interest rates of 1 percent below the federal discount rate.

   Revolving Line of Credit: A one year revolving line of credit of up to $100,000 for companies interested in exporting.

   Fixed Asset Loans/Local Development Financing Fund: Loans are made for commercial and industrial projects in designated communities, for fixed assets only. Loans are for up to 25 years and range from $25,000 to $2 millions. Funds must be matched 1:1 from the public and private sector.

   Loan Guarantees: Aids businesses needing additional security to receive a conventional loan or bond financing. The Authority can guarantee a portion of a loan for fixed assets or for working capital needs up to $1 million. These guarantees are aimed at businesses involved in manufacturing, processing, or distribution that will create a significant number of jobs or are located in economically distressed areas. The guarantees cover up to 90 percent of the loan, for a maximum of 10 years.

   Industrial Revenue Bonds: Tax-exempt bonds for manufacturing needs, first-time farmers and certain non-profit organizations. The tax relief enjoyed by purchasers enables applicants to borrow money at more favorable interest rates. The Authority can also issue taxable bonds, as well as composite bonds when financing for smaller individual projects is grouped into a larger issue.

   Real Estate Development Program: Develops business parks and other commercial facilities, acquiring and improving vacant or existing sites, and subdividing the sites for sale to businesses. Newly constructed facilities may qualify for a 15 year property tax abatement.

New Jersey Urban Development Corp.
Capital Place One
200 S. Warren Street
CN 990
Trenton, NJ 08625   609-633-1100
   Provides financial and other assistance for development projects in qualified communities. Working as a complement to other urban development programs, the UDC tries to give impetus to joint

government/private sector development programs. The UDC can buy, sell, and lease property, make loans, construct projects, enter into joint ventures, and buy and sell stock in subsidiaries it creates.

Office of Urban Enterprise Zones
New Jersey Department of Commerce and Economic Development
20 W. State St., CN 829
Trenton, NJ 08625-0829   609-292-1912

Urban Enterprize Zones Program: Provides incentives for urban development projects through tax credits and tax exemptions. In certain areas, businesses receive a 50 percent reduction in the 6 percent state sales tax on goods sold. The tax collected in those locations goes into a special State Treasury account, to be released later for use in development projects in amounts equal to the proportion of taxes paid by each participating city.

Small Business Administration (SBA)
60 Park Place, 4th Floor   201-645-2434
Newark, NJ 07102   FAX: 201-645-6265

SBA 7(a) Guaranteed and Direct Loans: Guarantees up to 90 percent of a loan made through a private lender up to $750,000. Can be used for working capital, expand or convert facilities, purchase of machinery and equipment, and land and building. Available only to those unable to obtain a loan from conventional sources. Direct loans are made up to $150,000.

SBA 504: Provides loans using 50 percent conventional bank financing, 40 percent SBA involvement through Certified Development Companies, and 10 percent owner equity. Fixed-asset loans are available in amounts up to $750,000. The loan can be used for land and building, construction, machinery and equipment, and renovation/expansion.

Small Business Innovative Research Grants (SBIR): Phase I awards between $20,000 to $50,000 to entrepreneurs to support six months of research on a technical innovation. Phase II grants are an additional $500,000 for development. Private sector investment funds must follow.

International Trade Loans: Guaranteed long-term loans through private lenders to develop or expand export markets, or to recover from the effects of import competition. Maximum guaranteed loan is $1,000,000 for fixed assets and an additional $250,000 for working capital and/or export revolving line of credit.

Export Revolving Line of Credit Loan: Short term financing available to small businesses that are at least one year old. Loans provide working capital to finance the manufacturing or wholesaling of products for export and for export marketing. The SBA will guarantee up to 90 percent of a conventional loan in amounts up to $750,000.

Contract Loan: Short-term loans are available to small businesses to finance the costs of labor and materials on contracts for which the proceeds are assignable. Program guarantees up to 90 percent of loans not in excess of $750,000. Qualifying small businesses must be in business for at least 12 calendar months prior to the date of the loan application.

Seasonal Line of Credit Loan: Loans provide short-term working capital to finance seasonal increases in business activities. Program guarantees up to 90 percent of loans not in excess of $750,000. Qualifying business must be in operation for at least one year prior to application.

Pollution Control Loans: Long-term guaranteed loans can be made by conventional financing to small businesses for installation or required pollution control measures. Must be unable to adopt the pollution control measures without undue financial hardship. Maximum guaranteed loan is $1,000,000.

General Contractor Loans: Small general construction contractors may obtain short-term loans or loan guarantees for residential or commercial construction or rehabilitation of property to be sold. The SBA will guarantee up to 90 percent of qualifying loans made by private lenders up to a maximum of $750,000. Direct loans can be up to $150,000.

Energy Business Loan Guarantee: Small businesses that provide certain energy production and conservation services for others may qualify for long-term loans and loan guarantees for start-ups and expansions. Loans

and guarantees are made for firms that develop, manufacture, sell, install, or service specific energy measures for others, or firms that provide engineering, architectural, consulting, or other professional services connected with specific energy measures. Guarantee is for up to 90 percent of a loan not in excess of $750,000. Direct loans up to $150,000.

Disaster Recovery Loans: Small businesses located in federally designated disaster areas and suffering property damage or economic losses from the disaster can obtain long-term recovery loans at low interest rates. Property damage loans are limited to 85 percent of the verified damage. Loans for economic losses are for operating capital to meet the business' obligations that could have been made had the disaster not occurred.

Handicapped Assistance Loans: Assists persons who have a physical, mental or emotional disability of a permanent nature which limits the selection of any type of employment for which the person would otherwise be qualified. Direct loans are available for up to $150,000. The interest rate is 3% on these loans.

Surety Bond Guaranty Program: Makes the bonding system more available to small contractors who may be denied access to the system. SBA can guarantee up to 80 percent of surety's loss on a bond that has a maximum in total contract value of up to $1,250,000.

Vietnam-era and Disabled Veterans Loan Program: Provides direct loans to veterans to establish or expand a small business. Funds may be used for working capital or fixed assets. Direct loans for amounts up to $150,000 are available. The interest rate may be fixed or variable.

Amev Capital Corp.
333 Thornall Street, 2nd Floor
Edison, NJ 08837   903-603-8500

Bishop Capital, LP
500 Morris Avenue
Springfield, NJ 07081   201-376-0495

ESLO Capital Corporation
212 Wright Street
Newark, NJ 07114   201-242-4488

First Princeton Capital Corporation
Five Garret Mountain Plaza
West Paterson, NJ 07424   201-278-8111

Monmouth Capital Corporation
125 Wycoff Road
Midland National Bank Bldg.
P.O. Box 335
Eatontown, NJ 07724   201-542-4927

Tappan Zee Capital Corporation
201 Lower Notch Road
Little Falls, NJ 07424   201-256-8280

Small Business Investment Companies (SBIC): The SBA licenses, regulates, and provides financial assistance to privately owned and operated Small Business Investment Companies. SBICs make venture or risk investments by supplying capital and extending unsecured loans and loans not fully collateralized to small enterprises which meet their investment criteria. Financing is made by direct loans and by equity investments.

New Jersey Commission on Science & Technology
20 West State Street, CN 832
Trenton, NJ 08625-0832   609-984-1671

Small Business Innovative Research Grants (SBIR): Award between $20,000 to $50,000 to entrepreneurs to support six months of research on a technical innovation. Second phase grants are an additional $500,000 for development. Private sector investment funds must follow. *Also see Technology Section.*

Local Municipality

Small Cities Block Grant Program: Funding is available to businesses located in small cities and non-urban counties designated by the federal

Department of Housing and Urban Development. Funds are awarded competitively for use on fixed assets only. 51 percent of jobs created by the project must go to low- and moderate-income workers, and the business must be unable to obtain financing from other sources.

New Jersey Commission on Science and Technology
20 West State Street, CN 832
Trenton, NJ 08625-0832   609-984-1671

Helps small, technology-based companies in their formative years. Services include bridge grants for while they are waiting for the next installment of their SBIR funds; the Washington Technical Liaison, who helps companies obtain the SBIR grants; and Innovation Partnership Grants, which provide funds to assist academic researchers involved in projects of use to industry. The state's major scientific research centers at Princeton University, the New Jersey Institute of Technology, Rutgers State University, the University of Medicine and Dentistry of New Jersey, and the Stevens Institute of Technology are linked to the program. The New Jersey Entrepreneur's Forum, supported by the Commission, gives new companies the benefit of advice and assistance from experienced business people. *Also see Technology Section.*

Casino Reinvestment Development Authority (CRDA)
1301 Atlantic Ave, 2nd Floor
Atlantic City, NJ 08401   609-347-0500

Funnels a portion of casino revenues into state development projects, by mandatory investment in CRDA taxable or tax-free bonds (1.25 percent of casino gross receipts). CRDA pays interest at 2/3rds of market rate, freeing funds for development use. The CRDA then makes loans to designated municipalities at below-market rate financing.

* Women and Minority Business Assistance

Office of Technology Assistance
Department of Commerce and Economic Development
Division of Development for Small Businesses and
  Women and Minority Businesses
20 West State Street, CN 835
Trenton, NJ 08625-0835   609-292-3860

Provides financial, marketing, procurement, technical, and managerial assistance for women- and minority-owned small businesses. The Division is a centralized source for these businesses, combining all the small and minority business offices of the state.

Minority Business Enterprise
20 West State Street, CN 835
Trenton, NJ 08625-0835   609-292-3860

Assists minority businesses in financing, procurement, and management training. Issues Early Alert bulletins to inform owners of new bidding opportunities, conducts seminars, and offers consulting and problem-solving services.

Women Business Enterprise
20 West State Street, CN 835
Trenton, NJ 08625-0835   609-292-3860

Aids businesswomen in opening, expanding, or buying a company. The office also acts as an advocate for women entrepreneurs among state departments, other governmental offices and private enterprise.

Set-Aside and Certification Office
CN 835
Trenton, NJ 08625   609-984-9834

Helps increase the number of minority-and woman-owned businesses competing for government contracts by administering the New Jersey Unified Certification Program for Women and Minorities, the New Jersey Set-Aside Program and a grant program aimed at increasing local set-aside programs.

Bureau of Hispanic Enterprise
CN 835
Trenton, NJ 08625   609-292-3860

Provides bi-lingual financial, training, managerial, and consulting services for Spanish-speaking entrepreneurs. Helps them identify the various useful government programs.

Small Business Administration
60 Park Place, 4th Floor   201-645-2434
Newark, NJ 07102   FAX: 201-645-6265

SBA 8(a) Program - Business Procurement Assistance: Provides federal government contracting opportunities for small businesses owned by socially and economically disadvantaged persons, and assists these businesses to become independently competitive in the normal business environment. SBA monitors all government contracts to assure that a quota of contract work goes to 8(a) businesses. Also provides business management services to these businesses. Business must be approved for program participation prior to receipt of an 8(a) contract.

* Training

Employment and Training Service
New Jersey Department of Labor
Labor Building, Room 703
CN 055
Trenton, NJ 08625-0055   609-292-5005

Job Training Partnership Act (JTPA): Provides employers with recruitment, screening, referral, training, 50 percent wage subsidy up to 3 months for on-the-job training. Available to any private employer.

* Management Consulting and Other Services

Division of International Trade
153 Halsey Street, 5th Floor
P.O. Box 47024
Newark, NJ 07101   201-648-3518

Foreign Trade Assistance: Aids local companies in exporting their products and encourages foreign investment in the state. This office also runs overseas trade shows, how-to seminars, and a *Sister States Initiatives Program* with similar cities in other countries that encourages economic, educational, and cultural relationships.

Foreign Trade Zones: Companies can improve their cash flow and their return on investments by locating in a Foreign Trade Zone, which are areas within the state where customs duties can be deferred, reduced, or eliminated. The zones are designated by the U.S. Department of Commerce. New Jersey has three such areas.

Trade Adjustment Assistance Center (TAAC)
Economic Development Authority
Capital Place One
200 S. Warren Street, CN 990
Trenton, NJ 08625   609-292-0360

Operating under the U.S. Trade Act, TAAC offers consulting aid to businesses which have been hurt by foreign competition. The office works with companies to develop a recovery plan, offering planning, engineering, marketing, sales, and accounting advice.

Small Business Administration
60 Park Place, 4th Floor   201-645-2434
Newark, NJ 07102   FAX: 201-645-6265

Small Business Institutes: This program provides personalized consulting services to the small business community. Consulting is provided by senior level business students, guided by a faculty advisor. Assistance in business plan preparation, marketing research, market planning, accounting, and seminars are provided.
University Locations:
Brookdale Community College
Fairleigh Dickinson University
Glassboro State College
Montclair State College
New Jersey Institute of Technology
Stockton State College

* Small Business Development Centers

The following offices offer free and fee-based services to new and expanding businesses:

Lead Center:
New Jersey Small Business Development Center
Rutgers Graduate School of Management
University Heights
180 University Avenue   201-648-5950
Newark, NJ 07102   FAX: 201-648-1110

   Atlantic City: Small Business Development Center, Greater Atlantic City Chamber of Commerce, 1301 Atlantic Avenue, Atlantic City, NJ 08401, 609-345-5600; FAXL 609-345-4524.

   Camden: Rutgers - The State University Of New Jersey at Camden, Small Business Development Center, Business & Science Building, 2nd Floor, Camden, NJ 08102, 609-757-6221; FAX: 609-757-6231.

   Lincroft: Brookdale Community College, Small Business Development Center, Newman Springs Road, Lincroft, NJ 07738, 908-842-8685; FAX: 908-842-0203.

   Newark: Rutgers - The State University of New Jersey at Camden, Small Business Development Center, University Heights, 180 University Ave., 3rd Floor, Newark, NJ 07102, 201-648-5950; FAX: 201-648-1110.

   Trenton: Mercer County Community College, Small Business Development Center, P.O. Box B, Trenton, NJ 08690, 609-586-4800; FAX: 609-890-6338.

   Trenton: Mercer County Community College, Small Business Development Center, James Kerney Campus, North Broad & Academy Streets, Trenton, NJ 08608, 609-586-4800, ext. 633.

   Union: Kean College of New Jersey, Small Business Development Center, East Campus, Room 242, Union, NJ 07083, 908-527-2946; FAX: 908-527-2960.

   Washington: Warren County Community College, Small Business Development Center, Route 57 West, Box 55A, Washington, NJ 07882-9605, 201-689-7613; FAX: 908-689-7488.

New Mexico

* General Information

Department of Economic Development and Tourism
Joseph Montoya Building
1100 St. Francis Drive
P.O. Box 20003   505-827-0300
Santa Fe, NM 87503   FAX: 505-827-0407
   Office of Enterprise Development   MODEM: 1-800-827-0285
   One-Stop Shop: Provides business with a computer system that displays New Mexico's regulatory framework for firms considering relocation or expansion of their manufacturing operations. It consists of the following on-line computer data: Regulatory Environment Bulletin Board (REBB), financial resources, county profiles, site and building locations, directory of New Mexico manufacturers as well as licensing, permitting and taxation procedures.

   Small Business Advocate: Assistance in cutting bureaucratic red tape. Information and expertise in dealing with state, federal, and local agencies.

* Financing

Department of Economic Development and Tourism
Joseph Montoya Building
1100 St. Francis Drive
P.O. Box 20003
Santa Fe, NM 87503   505-827-0300
   Revolving Loan Fund: Assists communities with loan funds that are then disbursed to local businesses to encourage development in designated areas. Funds may be used for acquisition of real property, construction, rehabilitation or installation of public facilities, improve community's infrastructure, and other activities that encourage economic development. Maximum loan amount is $250,000 per project.

   Economic Development Department:
   Community Development Block Grant (CDBG) Set-A-Side Loan Program: Grants are awarded to communities in non-metropolitan areas for community development projects in a defined geographic area to create new jobs for low-to-moderate-income persons. In turn, the communities provide low interest gap financing for business start up and expansion.

State Investment Council
Ark Plaza, Suite 203
2025 South Pacheco Street
Santa Fe, NM 87505   505-827-4788
   Severance Tax Permanent Fund:
   Oil and Gas Loan Participations: New Mexico will purchase financial instruments such as certificates of deposit (using funds from its Severance Tax Permanent Fund) from private banks to support oil and gas production loans to qualified gas and oil producers. The aim is to encourage new oil and gas development in the state.

   Real Property-Related Business Loans: Available to start or expand operations. Loan amounts from $500,000 to $2,000,000.

   Venture Capital Investment Program: New Mexico has three venture capital programs, including one that targets high technology projects. Outside experts assess the feasibility of proposals before loans are granted. Recipients need not repay the state for unsuccessful projects, but if the project does succeed, the state receives royalty fees.

Securities Division
Regulation and Licensing Department
725 St. Michaels Drive
Santa Fe, NM 87501   505-827-7140
   "27 K" Exemption Program: A regulatory relief program for small businesses trying to raise capital. The exemption allows a corporation or limited partnership to make an offering of $1.5 million to an unlimited number of purchasers under certain circumstances (mostly related to requirements of doing business within the State of New Mexico), thus allowing them to sell shares of stock without adhering to a minimum price per share.

State Board of Finance, DFM
131 S. Capitol Street
Batan Memorial Bldg., Room 203
Santa Fe, NM 87503   505-827-4980
   Industrial Revenue Bonds: Bonds may be issued by counties or municipalities for use by manufacturing businesses only for capital development. Interest received by bondholders is exempt from federal and state taxes. 95 percent of proceeds must be used for hard costs (expenses subject to the allowance of depreciation).

New Mexico Taxation and Revenue Department
Revenue Division
Returns Processing Bureau
P.O. Box 630
Santa Fe, NM 87504   505-827-0700
   Investment Tax Credit: Available to manufacturing operations. For each $100,000 of equipment purchased (used directly and exclusively in a manufacturing process and subject to depreciation) by a company that simultaneously hires one employee, that company may receive credit against its gross receipts taxes or withholding tax due. A business must apply for the credit.

Small Business Administration (SBA)
625 Silver SW
Suite 320   505-766-1870
Albuquerque, NM 87102   FAX: 505-766-1057
   SBA 7(a) Guaranteed and Direct Loans: Guarantees up to 90 percent of a loan made through a private lender up to $750,000. Can be used for working capital, expand or convert facilities, purchase of machinery and

equipment, and land and building. Available only to those unable to obtain a loan from conventional sources. Direct loans are made up to $150,000.

SBA 504: Provides loans using 50 percent conventional bank financing, 40 percent SBA involvement through Certified Development Companies, and 10 percent owner equity. Fixed-asset loans are available in amounts up to $750,000. The loan can be used for land and building, construction, machinery and equipment, and renovation/expansion.

Small Business Innovative Research Grants (SBIR): Phase I awards between $20,000 to $50,000 to entrepreneurs to support six months of research on a technical innovation. Phase II grants are an additional $500,000 for development. Private sector investment funds must follow.

International Trade Loans: Guaranteed long-term loans through private lenders to develop or expand export markets, or to recover from the effects of import competition. Maximum guaranteed loan is $1,000,000 for fixed assets and an additional $250,000 for working capital and/or export revolving line of credit.

Export Revolving Line of Credit Loan: Short term financing available to small businesses that are at least one year old. Loans provide working capital to finance the manufacturing or wholesaling of products for export and for export marketing. The SBA will guarantee up to 90 percent of a conventional loan in amounts up to $750,000.

Contract Loan: Short-term loans are available to small businesses to finance the costs of labor and materials on contracts for which the proceeds are assignable. Program guarantees up to 90 percent of loans not in excess of $750,000. Qualifying small businesses must be in business for at least 12 calendar months prior to the date of the loan application.

Seasonal Line of Credit Loan: Loans provide short-term working capital to finance seasonal increases in business activities. Program guarantees up to 90 percent of loans not in excess of $750,000. Qualifying business must be in operation for at least one year prior to application.

Pollution Control Loans: Long-term guaranteed loans can be made by conventional financing to small businesses for installation or required pollution control measures. Must be unable to adopt the pollution control measures without undue financial hardship. Maximum guaranteed loan is $1,000,000.

General Contractor Loans: Small general construction contractors may obtain short-term loans or loan guarantees for residential or commercial construction or rehabilitation of property to be sold. The SBA will guarantee up to 90 percent of qualifying loans made by private lenders up to a maximum of $750,000. Direct loans can be up to $150,000.

Energy Business Loan Guarantee: Small businesses that provide certain energy production and conservation services for others may qualify for long-term loans and loan guarantees for start-ups and expansions. Loans and guarantees are made for firms that develop, manufacture, sell, install, or service specific energy measures for others, or firms that provide engineering, architectural, consulting, or other professional services connected with specific energy measures. Guarantee is for up to 90 percent of a loan not in excess of $750,000. Direct loans up to $150,000.

Disaster Recovery Loans: Small businesses located in federally designated disaster areas and suffering property damage or economic losses from the disaster can obtain long-term recovery loans at low interest rates. Property damage loans are limited to 85 percent of the verified damage. Loans for economic losses are for operating capital to meet the business' obligations that could have been made had the disaster not occurred.

Handicapped Assistance Loans: Assists persons who have a physical, mental or emotional disability of a permanent nature which limits the selection of any type of employment for which the person would otherwise be qualified. Direct loans are available for up to $150,000. The interest rate is 3% on these loans.

Surety Bond Guaranty Program: Makes the bonding system more available to small contractors who may be denied access to the system. SBA can guarantee up to 80 percent of surety's loss on a bond that has a maximum in total contract value of up to $1,250,000.

Vietnam-era and Disabled Veterans Loan Program: Provides direct loans to veterans to establish or expand a small business. Funds may be used for working capital or fixed assets. Direct loans for amounts up to $150,000 are available. The interest rate may be fixed or variable.

Albuquerque SBIC
501 Tijeras Avenue, NW
P.O. Box 487
Albuquerque, NM 87103   505-247-0145
   Small Business Investment Companies (SBIC): The SBA licenses, regulates, and provides financial assistance to privately owned and operated Small Business Investment Companies. SBICs make venture or risk investments by supplying capital and extending unsecured loans and loans not fully collateralized to small enterprises which meet their investment criteria. Financing is made by direct loans and by equity investments.

New Mexico Industry Development Corporation
1009 Bradbury Drive, SE
Albuquerque, NM 87106   505-246-6000
   New Mexico Industry Development Corporation Revolving Loan: Using grants from the U.S. Economic Development Administration (EDA) and the Community Development Block Grant Program (CDBG), New Mexico makes these loans available to small businesses in counties declared to be in a state of long-term economic deterioration. Funds are for fixed assets (land, buildings, machinery, equipment) with priority given to those who also have other sources of financing. Fixed-asset loans are for up to 15 years, and working capital loans are for up to 7 years. Rates under market level are possible.

FmHA Business and Industrial Loan Program
Farmers Home Administration
Room 3414, Federal Building
517 Gold Ave. S.W.
Albuquerque, NM 87102   505-766-2463
   To foster economic development in rural areas, this program offers guarantees to private lenders for projects by healthy, reliable companies that will benefit the community. Loans are for a wide range of rural and industrial purposes, including pollution control and transportation services. Projects should create jobs in areas with populations under 25,000.

New Mexico Housing Authority
Joseph Montoya Building
1100 St. Francis Drive
Santa Fe, NM 87503   505-827-0258
   Internal Revenue Service Low Income Housing Tax Credit Program: Private investors receive tax credits for use over a 10 year period. Housing units developed must meet low-income qualifications. Investors may receive credit if their project consists of new construction (9 percent), rehabilitation (9 percent), acquisition (4 percent), and uses federal subsidies. Portions of properties must be set aside for low-income residents.

   Housing And Urban Development Rental Rehabilitation Program: Serves the twin purposes of offering grants to developers to rehabilitate existing housing and subsidies to tenants who live in them. This is a 50/50 matching program, where the Housing Authority provides 50 percent of the costs, as a grant, and the investor provides 50 percent from other funds. Allowable funds range from $5000 to rehabilitate an efficiency apartment, to $8500 for a single-family home with 3 or 4 bedrooms. Other restrictions apply.

* Women and Minority Business Assistance

Department of Economic Development & Tourism
Joseph Montoya Building
1100 St. Francis Drive, Room 2006
Santa Fe, NM 87503
   Procurement Assistant Program   505-827-0425
   Educates business owners in all phases of government contracting, and provides comprehensive technical procurement counseling for obtaining defense, federal, state and local government contracts. Offers training seminars (hands-on workshops). Offers small, minority and women-owned

businesses the opportunity to be entered into the annual *New Mexico MSBPAP Business Director.*

Associated Southwest Investors Corporation
6400 Uptown Blvd. NE, Suite 580 W.
Albuquerque, NM 87110   505-881-0066
Specializes in financial aid to minority-owned businesses.

Small Business Administration (SBA)
625 Silver SW, Suite 320   505-766-1870
Albuquerque, NM 87102   FAX: 505-766-1057
SBA 8(a) Program - Business Procurement Assistance: Provides federal government contracting opportunities for small businesses owned by socially and economically disadvantaged persons, and assists these businesses to become independently competitive in the normal business environment. SBA monitors all government contracts to assure that a quota of contract work goes to 8(a) businesses. Also provides business management services to these businesses. Business must be approved for program participation prior to receipt of an 8(a) contract.

* Training

Department of Economic Development & Tourism
Joseph Montoya Building
1100 St. Francis Drive, Room 2150
Santa Fe, NM   505-827-0300
Industrial Development Training Program: Employee training for new or expanding businesses. Program places an emphasis on industries which manufacture or produce a product. Financial assistance is available, depending on the number of trainees and amount of training needed. Customized training is available and can be carried out in classroom or on-the-job sites. 50 percent of training cost is reimbursed to the company. Trainees must be guaranteed full-time employment upon successful completion.

Job Training Partnership Act (JTPA): Provides employers with recruitment, screening, referral, training, 50 percent wage subsidy up to 3 months for on-the-job training. Available to any private employer.

* Management Consulting and Other Services

Department of Economic Development and Tourism
Joseph Montoya Building
P.O. Box 20003
1100 St. Francis Drive
Santa Fe, NM 87503   505-827-0300
          505-827-0272
Business Plan Development
Provides assistance in developing a business plan and has a brochure available, *Developing A Business Plan.*

Trade Division:
Foreign Trade Assistance: Assists businesses with marketing and advertising strategies, develops promotional materials and campaigns, gives export counseling, and sends advisories to businesses about trade events or buyer inquiries. Also matches up possible sellers and buyers, and provides export training. Will brief local businessmen prior to overseas travel, and actively recruits New Mexico companies to participate in trade shows around the world.

Tourism Division: Strengthens tourism, the state's largest private sector employer, through contacts with travel agents and tour operators, as well as participating in domestic and foreign trade shows. This division also promotes the state through travel brochure and information distribution, public relations campaigns, and maintains welcome centers throughout the state aimed at travellers.

Science and Technology Commercialization Commission: Analyzes, designs, and delivers financial mechanisms in support of economic development and commercialization of technology with the help of the New Mexico Research and Development Institute and the Venture Capital Fund.

Business Development Section:
Industrial Recruitment Program: Assesses the compatibility of out-of-state firms interested in locating in New Mexico, as well as assisting New Mexico communities with recruitment of new businesses. Services include financial incentives and packaging, promotion and prospect development, and employee training.

Research and Statistics Division: Provides technical assistance through business-related statistical and economic information. The State Data Center--a federal/state joint program--provides Census information. The Business Industry Data Center is a pilot program that uses a data base on census information and the economic data of several federal agencies.

New Mexico Technet
4100 Osuna N.E., Suite 103
Albuquerque, NM 87109   505-345-6555

Rio Grande Technology Foundation
851 University Blvd., SE, Suite 100
Albuquerque, NM 87106   505-246-6400
Technet, a communications network linking public and private sector research organizations along the Rio Grande Research Corridor, allows subscribers to access a wide range of data for research, including an electronic mail system, an electronic bulletin board, technical and economic development databases, and access to outside databases. Rio Grande Technology Foundation (RIOTECH) assists university research efforts and encourages cooperation among universities, federal labs, and the private industry along the Rio Grande Research Corridor.

Small Business Administration
625 Silver SW, Suite 320   505-766-1870
Albuquerque, NM 87102   FAX: 505-766-1057
Small Business Institutes: This program provides personalized consulting services to the small business community. Consulting is provided by senior level business students, guided by a faculty advisor. Assistance in business plan preparation, marketing research, market planning, accounting, and seminars are provided.
University Locations:
Eastern New Mexico University
New Mexico Highland University
New Mexico State University
University of New Mexico

* Small Business Development Centers
The following offices offer free and fee-based services to new and expanding businesses:

Lead Center:
New Mexico Small Business Development Center
Santa Fe Community College
P.O. Box 4187   505-438-1362
Santa Fe, NM 87502-4187   FAX: 505-438-1237

Alamogordo: New Mexico State University at Alamogordo, Small Business Development Center, 1000 Madison, Alamogordo, NM 87310, 505-434-5272.

Albuquerque: Albuquerque Technical Vocational Institute, Small Business Development Center, 525 Buena Vista SE, Albuquerque, NM 87106, 505-224-4246.

Carlsbad: New Mexico State University at Carlsbad, Small Business Development Center, 301 South Canal, P.O. Box 1090, Carlsbad, NM 88220, 505-887-6562.

Clovis: Clovis Community College, Small Business Development Center, 417 Schepps Blvd., Clovis, NM 88101, 505-769-4136.

Espanola: Northern New Mexico Community College, Small Business Development Center, 1002 N. Onate Street, Espanola, NM 87532, 505-753-7141.

Farmington: San Juan College, Small Business Development Center, 203 West Main, Suite 201, Farmington, NM 87401, 505-326-4321.

Gallup: University of New Mexico at Gallup, Small Business Development Center, 103 W. Highway 66, P.O. Box 1395, Gallup, NM 87305, 505-722-2220.

Grants: New Mexico State University at Grants, Small Business Development Center, 709 E. Roosevelt Ave., Grants, NM 87020, 505-287-8821.

Hobbs: New Mexico Junior College, Small Business Development Center, 5317 Lovington Highway, Hobbs, NM 88240, 505-392-4510.

Las Cruces: Dona Ana Branch Community College, Small Business Development Center, 3400 S. Espina Street, Box 30001, Department 3DA, Las Cruces, NM 88003-0001, 505-527-7566.

Las Vegas: Luna Vocational Technical Institute, Small Business Development Center, Luna Camp, P.O. Drawer K. Las Vegas, NM 88701, 505-454-2595.

Los Alamos: University of New Mexico at Los Alamos, Small Business Development Center, 901 18th Street, #18, P.O. Box 715, Los Alamos, NM 87544, 505-662-0001.

Los Lunas: University of New Mexico at Valencia, Small Business Development Center, 280 La Entrada, Los Lunas, NM 87031, 505-865-9596, ext. 317.

Roswell: Eastern New Mexico University at Roswell, Small Business Development Center, #57 University Ave., P.O. Box 6000, Roswell, NM 88201-6000, 505-624-7133.

Santa Fe: Santa Fe Community College, Small Business Development Center, South Richards Avenue, P.O. Box 4187, Santa Fe, NM 87502-4187, 505-438-1343.

Silver City: Western New Mexico University, Southwest Small Business Development Center, Glazer Hall, Continuing Education Department, P.O. Box 2672, Silver City, NM 88062, 505-538-6320.

Tucumcari: Tucumcari Area Vocational School, Small Business Development Center, 824 W. Hines, P.O. Box 1143, Tucumcari, NM 88401, 505-461-4413.

New York

* General Information

Small Business Division
Department of Economic Development
One Commerce Plaza
Albany, NY 12245   518-474-7756

Small Business Division
Department of Economic Development
1515 Broadway
New York, NY 10036   212-827-6150
Business Opportunity Center   1-800-STATE NY, 1-800-782-8369
A special service that offers fast, up-to-date information on the State's economic development programs and can help in make contact with appropriate agencies in such areas as financing, job training, technical assistance, etc.

Small Business Advocate: Information and expertise in dealing with state, federal, and local agencies.

* Financing

New York State Urban Development Corporation
1515 Broadway
New York, NY 10036
Small and Medium-Sized Business Assistance Program   212-930-0356
Industrial Loans: A public finance and development authority that aims to create and retain jobs in economically distressed areas. It can provide low-interest financing for retooling and modernization to industrial

businesses. Maximum loan is 50 percent of total project costs, or $15,000 per job created to a maximum of $750,000. Minimum loan amount is $75,000. Funds may be used for acquisition of land and/or buildings, construction renovation and leasehold improvements, machinery and equipment, working capital.

Targeted Investment Program   212-930-0320
Provides low-cost financing to construct or renovate industrial, commercial, or mixed-use facilities and create substantial private sector jobs in economically distressed areas marked by high unemployment and physical blight. Funds may be used for construction, renovation and leasehold improvements, machinery and equipment. Financing generally does not exceed 33 percent of total project cost of $15,000 per job created and/or retained. Maximum loan amount is $1,000,000.

Regional Economic Development Partnership
Program (REDPP)   212-930-0297
Low-cost financing is available which will directly and quickly crete and/or retain permanent jobs in New York State. Projects must not be financially feasible without REDPP participation. Program available to projects that involve either distressed areas, minority-and women-owned businesses, productivity improvement, dislocated workers, public assistance recipients or long-term unemployed persons.

Loans are limited to the lesser of $500,000 or 1/3 of project cost. Interest subsidies limited to lesser of $250,000 or 1/3 project cost feasibility studies capped at $40,000.

Business Development Loans: Available to industrial, manufacturing, commercial, research and development, tourism, agricultural and service companies for working capital, equipment and machinery, land acquisition, and acquisition, renovation or construction of facilities.

Tourism Destination Loans: Available for projects that involve the development of a recreational, educational, cultural or historical facility and will attract visitors from outside its region.

Business Development Grants: Available for feasibility studies to examine local takeover efforts, and to reduce financing costs through interest subsidies.

Expansion, Retention and Attraction Assistance Program 212-930-0320
Provides low-cost loans to industrial firms involved in manufacturing, warehousing, distribution, or research and development and operating or proposing to move to New York State. Funds can be used for acquisition of land and/or buildings, construction, renovation, and leasehold improvements, machinery and equipment, and working capital. Maximum loan is 33 percent of total project cost, or $15,000 per job created and/or retained. Minimum loan amount is $100,000.

Commercial Revitalization Program: 212-930-0269
Commercial revitalization for neighborhoods or major cities, or for the main streets of small cities and communities. Flexible, low-cost financing to owners of commercial properties in distressed commercial districts, to improve their appearance. Loans are available for exterior property improvements, and technical assistance (TA) grants for design and architectural supervision. Funds may be used for selected masonry repair, cleaning and repainting, new awnings and signs, street facade lighting, and miscellaneous building features. Maximum funding is $300,000 per project, of which 25 percent is available as a TA grant for design and supervision.

New York State Department of
Economic Development
One Commerce Plaza
Albany, NY 12245
Industrial Effectiveness Program   518-474-1131
Technical and financial assistance for manufacturing firms to preserve and create permanent private sector jobs. Encourages firms to undertake productivity and other operational improvements to remain competitive, profitable, and viable, and by aiding local buyouts.

Grants: Available to share the cost of a consultant to conduct productivity assessment of an industrial firm or group of firms; feasibility study for corporate restructuring or turnaround; feasibility study for local buyout.

Loans: Working capital loans to improve productivity and for corporate restructuring or turnaround plans.

Loans to support a local buyout.

Secondary Materials Program: Designed to encourage and foster the implementation of waste reduction techniques by industrial or commercial firms and the expansion of markets for secondary materials (materials destined for the wastestream that can be recovered for recycling).

Grants: Made to companies, with less than 500 employees or less than $10 million in gross annual sales, to evaluate specific technologies or processes. Grants can fund 80 percent of total cost to a maximum of $100,000.

Financial Assistance: Loans up to $250,000, principal reductions up to $125,000, loan guarantees, or interest subsidies up to 75 percent of the prime rate. interest subsidies up to 75 percent of the prime rate. Available to businesses for construction, alternation, repair or improvement of buildings or equipment to utilize secondary materials.

Agricultural Wastewater Loan Program   518-486-6291
Financial assistance to food processing and farm production enterprises for the construction of wastewater treatment facilities that will enable the firm to meet current environmental standards and reduce energy consumption. Financial assistance available are direct, low interest loans up to $250,000, principal reductions up to 50 percent of eligible loan, not to exceed $125,000, loan guarantees, and interest subsidies up to 75 percent of the prime rate. Made to applicants with less than 500 workers or less than $10 million in gross annual sales.

Economic Development Zones   518-473-6930
Offers incentives, and financial and other targeted assistance programs to businesses expanding or relocating to one of the 19 enterprise zones. Businesses may receive an investment tax credit, real property tax exemption, tax credit related to wages, reduction on utility bills, among other incentives.

New York Job Development Authority (JDA)
605 Third Avenue
New York, NY 10158   212-818-1700
Direct Loan Program: Assist with financing needs of companies expanding or building new facilities or starting a new business. Provides low interest loans for construction, acquisition or rehabilitation of plant facilities, and for machinery and equipment. Loans may not exceed 40 percent of total project cost. Most kinds of businesses are eligible except for retail establishments,hotels, or apartment buildings.

Loan Guarantee Program: Provides guarantees of up to 80 percent of project cost for loans made by banking organizations. May be used for machinery and equipment and/or construction, acquisition, or rehabilitation of plant facilities for new or expanding companies. Most kinds of businesses are eligible except for retail establishments,hotels, or apartment buildings.

Bonding Assistance Program: Provides a limited guarantee on construction contracts of not more than $1,000,000 to small and/or minority-and women-owned contractors and subcontractors seeking to obtain construction contracts awarded by any governmental agency or authority.

Rural Development Loan Fund: Aimed at providing low-cost financing to small businesses in distressed rural areas and communities with less than 25,000 population. Loans range from $20,000 to $50,000 and are up to 20 percent of a project's total cost. Funds can be used for projects involving plant expansion, construction, acquisition or rehabilitation, purchase of machinery and equipment, and working capital.

Rural Areas Development Fund: Provides low-cost financing to businesses, individuals, and local public entities for economic and community development projects that provide jobs to displaced farm families, farm families needing additional income to supplement their farming operations, long-term unemployed, or persons on public assistance in rural areas.

Loans to businesses may be made to develop new businesses or expanding existing ones in manufacturing, service industries, and agribusiness. Proceeds may be used for infrastructure projects related to economic development, industrial parks and business incubators, child care centers, pollution control facilities and transportation facilities. Loans are available for real estate. machinery and equipment and working capital. Maximum loan is 90 percent of total project cost or $90,000, whichever is less.

XPORT Program: Joint program between the Job Development Authority and the Port Authority of New York and New Jersey. Offers payment in advance on accounts receivable from overseas customers through a revolving fund of $1.7 million. Has loaned $5.7 million in export financing to small businesses.

New York State Science & Technology Foundation
99 Washington Avenue, Suite 1730
Albany, NY 12210
Corporation for Innovation Development
Venture Capital Program   518-473-9741
Provides debt and equity capital to technology-based start-ups and young, growing business ventures in New York. Applicants must have innovative, technology-based products or services with significant potential for job creation. Investments normally range from $50,000 to $150,000 and is to be used primarily for working capital. Must be matched by loans or investments from other sources.

Research and Development Grants Program   518-473-9744
Grants are made for projects that can contribute to economic development by advancing technological innovation. Grants of up to $50,000 are made to competitively selected, peer-reviewed research projects and are selected by the industrial and economic relevance of the project. *Also see Technology Section.*

Small Business Innovation Research Promotion
Program (SBIR)   518-473-9746
Assists small research firms gain a larger share of research funds available under the federal SBIR program.

Small Business Innovation Research Grants: A federal program that awards between $20,000 to $50,000 to entrepreneurs to support six months of research on a technical innovation. Phase II grants are an additional $500,000 for development. Private sector investment funds must follow.

Small Business Innovation Research (SBIR) Matching Grants: Designed to increase participation in the Federal SBIR Program by small, technology-based New York businesses. Matching contracts up to $50,000 awarded to successful Federal SBIR Phase I award winners. Awards are made at conclusion of Phase I research and upon application for Federal Phase II funds, bridging a "gap" for small firms. Technical assistance is also provided.

Also see Technology Section.

Productivity Development Program: Provides financial support, on a cost-sharing basis, to help traditional manufacturing firms evaluate new technologies which can lead to improved productivity and profitability. Grants up to $35,000 to manufacturers to conduct selected technology feasibility analysis projects and must be matched by funds from the firm.

Technology and Disabilities Program: Funds development of marketable products originally researched and developed at an academic institution or non-profit organization to service the needs of disable clientele. Awards of up to $30,000 are made on a competitive bases twice annually to further product development or refinement which address physical, sensory, mental and other health-related disabilities.

New York State Department of Agriculture & Markets
Division of Agricultural Protection & Development Service
One Winners Circle, Capital Plaza
Albany, NY 12235   518-457-7076
Agricultural Research and Development Grants: Grants are offered annual to farmers, agri-businesses, institutions and individuals with original ideas in production, processing and marketing of farm products. Maximum amount of loan is $50,000. Proceeds are focused on creation of jobs in the food and agriculture industry, new capital investment and expansion in the food and agriculture industry, market development and expansion, among others.

New York State Energy Research Development Authority
Two Rockefeller Plaza
Albany, NY 12223   518-465-6251

Economic Development Through Greater Energy-Efficiency (EDGE) Program: Provides technical and financial assistance to firms interested in reducing their energy use and related costs. Technical and financial support available for detailed engineering feasibility studies of innovative and energy-efficient process modifications. Financial assistance available for the demonstration of innovation energy-efficient process technology. Eligibility requirements include firms not using current, available technology; there are energy conservation measures that can be implemented; limited capital prevents a firm's expansion or modernization. Funding for Engineering Studies is up to $25,000 but not to exceed 50 percent, and up to $500,000 for Demonstrations not to exceed 50 percent.

New York State Environment Facilities Corporation (EFC)
50 Wolf Road
Albany, NY 12205   518-457-4114

Industrial Pollution Control Financing Program: The EFC issues special obligation revenue bonds with provide low-cost loans to companies assisting industry in meeting its environmental responsibilities without incurring high financing costs. Eligible facilities include sewage treatment, solid waste disposal, resource recovery, water management, water supply, hazardous waste disposal. Bond interest is generally exempt from State and Federal income taxes. Several company projects at more than one location can be financed under one bond issue.

New York Business Development Corporation (NYBDC)
P.O. Box 738
Albany, NY 12201   518-463-2268

Corporation Loan Program: Provides long-term loans available to small businesses in industrial, commercial and service-oriented businesses, that might otherwise have problems obtaining financing. The loans are a complement to or in participation with conventional lenders. NYBDC share of the loan ranges from $50,000 to $1,000,000. Funds may be used for working capital, machinery and equipment, real estate construction, acquisition and renovations.

Small Business Administration (SBA)
Regional Office
26 Federal Plaza, Room 3100   212-264-2454
New York, NY 10278   FAX: 212-264-4963

SBA 7(a) Guaranteed and Direct Loans: Guarantees up to 90 percent of a loan made through a private lender up to $750,000. Can be used for working capital, expand or convert facilities, purchase of machinery and equipment, and land and building. Available only to those unable to obtain a loan from conventional sources. Direct loans are made up to $150,000.

SBA 504: Provides loans using 50 percent conventional bank financing, 40 percent SBA involvement through Certified Development Companies, and 10 percent owner equity. Fixed-asset loans are available in amounts up to $750,000. The loan can be used for land and building, construction, machinery and equipment, and renovation/expansion.

International Trade Loans: Guaranteed long-term loans through private lenders to develop or expand export markets, or to recover from the effects of import competition. Maximum guaranteed loan is $1,000,000 for fixed assets and an additional $250,000 for working capital and/or export revolving line of credit.

Export Revolving Line of Credit Loan: Short term financing available to small businesses that are at least one year old. Loans provide working capital to finance the manufacturing or wholesaling of products for export and for export marketing. The SBA will guarantee up to 90 percent of a conventional loan in amounts up to $750,000.

Contract Loan: Short-term loans are available to small businesses to finance the costs of labor and materials on contracts for which the proceeds are assignable. Program guarantees up to 90 percent of loans not in excess of $750,000. Qualifying small businesses must be in business for at least 12 calendar months prior to the date of the loan application.

Seasonal Line of Credit Loan: Loans provide short-term working capital to finance seasonal increases in business activities. Program guarantees up to 90 percent of loans not in excess of $750,000. Qualifying business must be in operation for at least one year prior to application.

Pollution Control Loans: Long-term guaranteed loans can be made by conventional financing to small businesses for installation or required pollution control measures. Must be unable to adopt the pollution control measures without undue financial hardship. Maximum guaranteed loan is $1,000,000.

General Contractor Loans: Small general construction contractors may obtain short-term loans or loan guarantees for residential or commercial construction or rehabilitation of property to be sold. The SBA will guarantee up to 90 percent of qualifying loans made by private lenders up to a maximum of $750,000. Direct loans can be up to $150,000.

Energy Business Loan Guarantee: Small businesses that provide certain energy production and conservation services for others may qualify for long-term loans and loan guarantees for start-ups and expansions. Loans and guarantees are made for firms that develop, manufacture, sell, install, or service specific energy measures for others, or firms that provide engineering, architectural, consulting, or other professional services connected with specific energy measures. Guarantee is for up to 90 percent of a loan not in excess of $750,000. Direct loans up to $150,000.

Disaster Recovery Loans: Small businesses located in federally designated disaster areas and suffering property damage or economic losses from the disaster can obtain long-term recovery loans at low interest rates. Property damage loans are limited to 85 percent of the verified damage. Loans for economic losses are for operating capital to meet the business' obligations that could have been made had the disaster not occurred.

Handicapped Assistance Loans: Assists persons who have a physical, mental or emotional disability of a permanent nature which limits the selection of any type of employment for which the person would otherwise be qualified. Direct loans are available for up to $150,000. The interest rate is 3% on these loans.

Surety Bond Guaranty Program: Makes the bonding system more available to small contractors who may be denied access to the system. SBA can guarantee up to 80 percent of surety's loss on a bond that has a maximum in total contract value of up to $1,250,000.

Vietnam-era and Disabled Veterans Loan Program: Provides direct loans to veterans to establish or expand a small business. Funds may be used for working capital or fixed assets. Direct loans for amounts up to $150,000 are available. The interest rate may be fixed or variable.

767 Limited Partnership
767 Third Avenue
c/o Harvey Wertheim
New York, NY 10017   212-838-7776

ASEA-Harvest Partners II
767 Third Avenue
New York, NY 10017   212-838-7776

American Commercial Capital Corporation
310 Madison Avenue
Suite 1304
New York, NY 10017   212-986-3305

Argentum Capital Partners, LP
405 Lexington Avenue
New York, NY 10174   212-949-8272

Atalanta Investment Company, Inc.
650 5th Avenue, 15th Floor
New York, NY 10019   212-956-9100

BT Capital Corporation
280 Park Avenue--10 West
New York, NY 10017   212-850-1916

Barclays Capital Investors Corp.
222 Broadway, 7th Floor
New York, NY 10038   212-412-6784

CIBC Wood Gundy Ventures, Inc.
425 Lexington Avenue, 9th Floor
New York, NY 10017
212-856-3713

CMNY Capital II, LP
135 East 57th Street
26th Floor
New York, NY 10022
212-909-8432

CMNY Capital, LP
135 East 57th Street
26th Floor
New York, NY 10022
212-909-8432

Chase Manhattan Capital Corporation
1 Chase Plaza--7th Floor
New York, NY 10081
212-552-6275

Chemical Venture Capital Associates
885 Third Avenue, Suite 810
New York, NY 10022
212-230-2255

Citicorp Venture Capital, Ltd.
399 Park Avenue, 6th Floor
New York, NY 10043
212-559-1127

Creditanstait Capital Corporation
245 Park Avenue
New York, NY 10167
212-856-1050

Edwards Capital Company
Two Park Avenue, 20th Floor
New York, NY 10016
212-686-5449

Fifty-Third Street Ventures, LP
155 Main Street
Cold Spring, NY 10516
914-265-4244

First Wall Street SBIC, LP
44 Wall Street
New York, NY 10005
212-495-4890

Fundex Capital Corporation
525 Northern Blvd.
Great Neck, NY 11021
516-466-8551

Genesee Funding, Inc.
100 Corporate Woods
Rochester, NY 14623
716-272-2332

Hanover Capital Corporation
315 East 62nd Street, 6th Floor
New York, NY 10021
212-980-9670

IBJS Capital Corporation
One State Street, 8th Floor
New York, NY 10004
212-858-2000

InterEquity Capital Corporation
220 Fifth Avenue, 10th Floor
New York, NY 10001
212-779-2022

J.P. Morgan Investment Corporation
60 Wall Street
New York, NY 10260
212-483-2323

Kwiat Capital Corporation
576 Fifth Avenue
New York, NY 10036
212-391-2461

M & T Capital Corporation
One M & T Plaza
Buffalo, NY 14240
716-842-5881

MH Capital Investors, Inc.
270 Park Avenue
New York, NY 10017
212-286-3222

NYBDC Capital Corporation
41 State Street
P.O. Box 738
Albany, NY 12201
518-463-2268

NatWest USA Capital Corporation
175 Water Street
New York, NY 10038
212-602-1200

Norwood Venture Corporation
145 West 45th Street
Suite 1211
New York, NY 10036
212-869-5075

Paribas Principal Incorporated
787 Seventh Avenue, 33rd Floor
New York, NY 10019
212-841-2000

Pyramid Ventures, Inc.
280 Park Avenue--29 West
New York, NY 10017
212-850-1702

Quantum Capital Partners, Ltd.
575 Fifth Avenue, 18th Floor
New York, NY 10017
212-661-5290

R & R Financial Corporation
1451 Broadway
New York, NY 10036
212-790-1441

Rand SBIC, Inc.
1300 Rand Building
Buffalo, NY 14203
716-853-0802

Small Business Electronics Investment Corporation
1220 Peninsula Blvd.
Hewlett, NY 11557
516-374-0743

Sterling Commercial Capital, Inc.
175 Great Neck Road
Suite 404
Great Neck, NY 11021
516-482-7374

TLC Funding Corporation
660 White Plains Road
Tarrytown, NY 10591
914-683-1144

Tappan Zee Capital Corporation
(Main Office: Little Falls, NJ)
120 North Main Street
New City, NY 10956
914-634-8890

Vega Capital Corporation
720 White Plains Road
Scarsdale, NY 10583
914-472-8550

Winfield Capital Corporation
237 Mamaroneck Avenue
White Plains, NY 10605
914-949-2600

Small Business Investment Companies (SBIC): The SBA licenses, regulates, and provides financial assistance to privately owned and operated Small Business Investment Companies. SBICs make venture or risk investments by supplying capital and extending unsecured loans and loans not fully collateralized to small enterprises which meet their investment criteria. Financing is made by direct loans and by equity investments.

Housing and Urban Development (HUD) Regional Office
26 Federal Plaza
New York, NY 10278-0068
212-264-8068

Community Development Block Grants: Available to cities and counties for the commercial rehabilitation of existing buildings or structures used for business, commercial or industrial purposes. Grants of up to $500,000 can be made. Every $15,000 of grant funds invested must create at least one full-time job, and at least 51 percent of the jobs created must be for low- and moderate-income families.

* Women and Minority Business Assistance

New York State Urban Development Corporation
Director
Minority and Women Revolving Loan Fund
1515 Broadway, 52nd Floor
New York, NY 10036   212-930-0452
> **Minority Revolving Loan Fund:** Provides low-interest financing to industrial, commercial, service-oriented, and start-up businesses; retail businesses evaluated case-by-cases; special programs for franchises. Loans range from $20,000 to $500,000 and may be used for construction, renovation, leasehold improvements, acquisition of land and buildings, acquisition of an ongoing business, establishment of a nationally recognized franchises outlet, machinery and equipment, and working capital.

> **Bonding Assistance Program:** *See Financing*

Division of Minority and Women's Business
Department of Economic Development
1 Commerce Plaza
Albany, NY 12245   518-474-6346
  or
1515 Broadway, 52nd Floor
New York, NY 1036   212-930-9000
> Provides consulting, and technical assistance in obtaining benefits from State programs, with a focus on business financing. Assists in attaining state certification as minority enterprises. Helps minority firms obtain federal government contracts.

> **Entrepreneurial Assistance Program:** Administered by the Department of Economic Development which funds nine programs throughout the State, that provide entrepreneurial training and business counseling to women, minorities, and dislocated workers.

Small Business Administration (SBA)
Regional Office
26 Federal Plaza
Room 3100   212-264-2454
New York, NY 10278   FAX: 212-264-4963
> **SBA 8(a) Program - Business Procurement Assistance:** Provides federal government contracting opportunities for small businesses owned by socially and economically disadvantaged persons, and assists these businesses to become independently competitive in the normal business environment. SBA monitors all government contracts to assure that a quota of contract work goes to 8(a) businesses. Also provides business management services to these businesses. Business must be approved for program participation prior to receipt of an 8(a) contract.

* Training

Job Training Partnership Council
Alfred E. Smith State Office
17th Floor
Albany, NY 12225   518-474-6014
> **Job Training Partnership Act (JTPA):** Provides employers with recruitment, screening, referral, training, 50 percent wage subsidy up to 3 months for on-the-job training. Available to any private employer. The JTPA sponsors an annual Job Training Policy Conference and maintains a statewide JTPA Management Information System, which provides standardized data on job training information to the 34 Service Delivery Areas in New York.

Department of Economic Development Regional Offices

Albany	518-432-2697
Binghamton	607-773-7813
Brooklyn	718-596-4120
Buffalo	718-847-3622
Jericho	516-325-1944
Kingston	914-331-6415
Ogdensburg	315-393-3980
Plattsburgh	518-561-5642
Rochester	716-325-1944
Syracuse	315-428-4097
White Plains	914-428-8000
Utica	315-793-2366

> **New Employee Training Assistance:** Customized Classroom Training Programs can be established at the employees' facility or at an educational institution, with the costs absorbed on a matching basis by the program. One-the-job Training Programs can be established which reimburse the wages of a newly hired worker during a specific training period for one or more new employees. Job-ready individuals who have completed vocational skills training can be referred to a company. Trainees can be tested and screen by employment counselors to ensure they meet specific basic requirements of employers.

> **Productivity Improvement Program:** Custom-designed training available to retrain and upgrade skills of employees to meet the demands of changing markets and technologies, and to improve the productivity of involved companies.

> **Skills Training Program:** Operates on a cost-sharing basis, this program helps business create or retain jobs,by providing funding to enhance the skill level of employees.

New York State Urban Development Corporation
1515 Broadway
New York, NY 10036   212-930-0297
> **REDPP Training Program (Regional Economic Development Partnership Program):** Grants available to eligible companies for employee training projects which result in the upgrading or retraining of current employees, or the creation of substantial new permanent, private sector jobs. Limited to the lesser of $200,000 or 49 percent of total project cost. Funds may be provided to construct or equip a training facility at the site to be used solely for training purposes. Not available to trainees of retail businesses.

New York State Department of Labor
Harriman State Office Campus
Building 12
Albany, NY 12240
Apprentice Training Office, Room 223   518-457-6820
> **Apprentice Training Assistance:** The program produces fully skilled workers in over 250 skilled occupations by blending structured, supervised, on-the-job training with at least 144 hours of related classroom instruction during each year of training. Occupations concentration is placed on are machinists, electricians, too and die maker,s, electronic technicians, etc.

Principal Occupational Analyst, Room 171   518-457-1988
> **Personnel Services:** Assists an employer in obtaining maximum utilization of its work force through better personnel selection techniques, workforce stabilization by reducing absenteeism and turnover, effective use of employee skills, and effective personnel practices and policies. Provides job analysis studies, development of training programs, determination of equitable wages, development of performance appraisal programs and job restructuring.

TJTC Unit, Room 238   518-457-6823
> **Targeted Groups Jobs Tax Credits:** A federal tax credit may be claimed by an employer for each certified target group member hired. The credit is 40 percent of the first $6,000 in wages paid during the first year of employment. Target groups include of people from economically disadvantaged families, handicapped individuals, including disabled veterans, undergoing vocational rehabilitation. Contact the TJTC Unit for information on recruiting potential employees who are JTC eligible.

Liability and Determination Section
Unemployment Insurance Division   518-457-5807
> **Alternatives to Layoffs/Shared Work:** A voluntary program providing an alternative to layoffs to employers with ten or more employees faced with a temporary decline in business. An employer can reduce the hours and wages of all or a particular group of employees. (Approval of affected unions is required).

New York State Education Department
Bureau of Economic Development Coordination

One Commerce Plaza
Albany, NY 12234   518-474-3852
  Workplace Literacy Program: At the request of an employer or group of
  employers, the State invests in basic skills education, alone or in
  conjunction with job skills training, for employees without a high school
  diploma to increase reading, communication and computation skills.

* Management Consulting and Other Services

New York State Office of Business Permits & Regulatory Assistance
Permit Coordinator
Alfred E. Smith Office Building
17th Floor   518-474-8275
Albany, NY 12225   1-800-342-3464 in New York
  Permit Assistance: Identifies State permits and licenses required for
  specific business ventures and assists clients in the application process.
  Provide individualized assistance, including a Permit Assistance Kit.

Department of Economic Development
One Commerce Plaza
Albany, NY 12224
or
1515 Broadway, 51st Floor
New York, NY 10036
  Business Services:
  Ombudsman Program   New York: 212-827-6150
  Assists businesses in resolving red tape difficulties they may encounter in
  their dealings with all levels of government.

  Domestic Attraction Group   Albany: 518-473-1325
  Site and Building Selection Assistance: Provides firms seeking a new
  location with a comprehensive, "one-stop" listing of available properties
  meeting their specifications, as well as coordination of inspection trips and
  follow-up assistance with developers and realtors.

  Division for Small Business   Albany: 518-474-7756
                                           New York: 212-827-6150
  Procurement Assistance Program: Provides marketing and technical
  assistance to New York State businesses interested in securing contracts
  and subcontracts from federal agencies and large federal contractors. Also
  helps business secure contracts from State agencies, departments and
  authorities. Can obtain bid packages and contract specifications, and learn
  about new bids through a computer matchmaking service. Sponsors
  training seminars and trade shows. Offers one-on-one counseling sessions.
  Publishes the *New York State Contract Reporter*, a weekly procurement
  opportunities newsletter through which all state agencies and public
  authorities announce their contract opportunities.

  International Division   New York: 212-827-6200
  Provides assistance and direct support to manufacturers, suppliers, and
  service sector firms in developing markets abroad. Publishes the Export
  Opportunities Bulletin which contains leads obtained from foreign buyers
  around the world for a variety of products, seeking new sources of supply.
  Operates foreign offices in Toronto, Montreal, Tokyo, Hong Kong,
  London, Frankfurt. Sponsors trade shows, and offers workshops and
  conferences.

  Foreign Marketing/Export Assistance: Assists New York companies
  interested in entering the field of exporting their products and to increase
  sales. Seminars and one-to-one counseling which provide practical
  information on export techniques, terminology and methods to obtain
  leads. Provides information on foreign trade opportunities, conducts trade
  shows, and participates in informational seminars.

  Foreign Direct Investment Program: Promotes investment in New York
  State by overseas investors either through joint venture, acquisition or
  licensing agreements. The programs goal is to create and retain jobs,
  diversity the industrial economy of the State, assist the expansion of
  foreign firms already located in New York State and attract New York's
  fair share of new foreign investment in the U.S.

  Governor's Hasidic and Orthodox Task Force New York: 212-827-6100
  Formed to overcome problems in receiving access to State and federal
  programs administered by the State due to religious and cultural practices.

The Task Force focuses on economic outreach into the Jewish community,
and assists in housing, job training,a nd business formation.

New York State Environment Facilities Corporation
50 Wolf Road
Albany, New York 12205   518-457-4138
  Industrial Materials Recycling Program: Provides assistance to industries
  whose activities generate hazardous waste and industrial sold waste.

New York State Science and Technology Foundation
99 Washington Avenue, Suite 1730
Albany, NY 12210
  Industrial Innovation Extension Service Program   518-473-9746
  Assists established, small and minimum-sized manufacturing firms to
  address issues of technology-based productivity improvements in order to
  remain viable and competitive. Short-term consultation services available
  at no charge.

Small Business Administration
Regional Office
26 Federal Plaza, Room 3100   212-264-2454
New York, NY 10278   FAX: 212-264-4963
  Small Business Institutes: This program provides personalized consulting
  services to the small business community. Consulting is provided by senior
  level business students, guided by a faculty advisor. Assistance in business
  plan preparation, marketing research, market planning, accounting, and
  seminars are provided.
  University Locations:
  Alfred University
  Baruch College
  C.W. Post
  Canisius College
  Cornell University
  Hofstra University
  Long Island University
  Manhattan College
  Niagara University
  Pace University
  Rochester Institute of Technology
  Sienna College
  Skidmore College
  St. John Fisher College
  St. Johns University
  State University College - Buffalo
  SUNY College - Albany
  SUNY College - Binghamton
  SUNY College - Buffalo
  SUNY College - Fredonia
  SUNY College - Geneseo
  SUNY College - Utica/Rome
  Syracuse University

* Small Business Development Centers
The following offices offer free and fee-based services to new and expanding
businesses:

Lead Center:
New York Small Business Development Center
State University of New York   518-443-5398
State University Plaza, S-523   FAX: 518-465-4992
Albany, NJ 12246   1-800-732-7232

  Albany: State University of New York at Albany (SUNY), Small Business
  Development Center, Draper Hall, 107, 135 Western Ave., Albany, NY
  12222, 518-442-5577; FAX: 518-442-5582.

  Binghamton: SUNY at Binghamton, Small Business Development Center,
  P.O. Box 6000, Vestal Parkway East, Binghamton, NY 13902-6000, 607-
  777-4024; FAX: 607-777-4029.

  Brooklyn: Long Island University, Small Business Development Center,
  School of Business, One University Plaza, Humanities Building, 7th Floor,
  Brooklyn, NY 11201, 718-852-1197; FAX: 718-852-3447.

Buffalo: State University College at Buffalo, Small Business Development Center, 1300 Elmwood Avenue, BA 117, Buffalo, NY 14222, 716-878-4030; FAX: 716-878-4067.

Corning: Corning Community College, Small Business Development Center, 24-28 Denison Parkway West, Corning, NY 14830, 607-962-9461; FAX: 607-936-6642.

Dobbs Ferry: Rockland Community College at Suffern, Small Business Development Center, Westchester Outreach Center, Mercy College, 555 Broadway, Dobbs Ferry, NY 10522, 914-693-4500, ext. 485; FAX: 914-693-4996.

Farmingdale: SUNY College of Technology at Farmingdale, Small Business Development Center, Laffin Administration Building, Farmingdale, NY 11735, 516-420-2765; FAX: 516-293-5343.

Jamaica: York College, Small Business Development Center, Science Building, Room 107, The City University of New York, Jamaica, NY 11451, 718-262-2880; FAX: 718-262-2881.

Jamestown: Jamestown Community College, Small Business Development Center, P.O. Box 20, Jamestown, NY 14702-0020, 716-665-5220, 1-800-522-7232; FAX: 716-665-6733.

New York: Pace University, Small Business Development Center, Pace Plaza, New York, NY 10038, 212-346-1899; FAX: 212-346-1613.

Plattsburgh: Clinton Community College, Small Business Development Center, Alpert Bldg., Route 9, Plattsburgh, NY 12901, 518-562-4260; FAX: 518-563-9759.

Riverdale: Manhattan College, Small Business Development Center, School of Business, Farrell Hall, Riverdale, NY 10471, 212-884-1880; FAX: 212-549-0089.

Rochester: Monroe Community College at Rochester, Small Business Development Center, 1000 East Henrietta Road, Rochester, NY 14623, 706-292-2000, ext. 303D.

Sanborn: Niagara County Community College at Sanborn, Small Business Development Center, 3111 Saunders Settlement Road, Sanborn, NY 14132, 716-693-1910; FAX: 716-731-3595.

Stone Ridge: Ulter County Community College at Stone Ridge, Small Business Development Center, Stone Ridge, NY 12484, 914-687-5272; FAX: 914-687-5271.

Stony Brook: SUNY at Stony Brook, Small Business Development Center, Harriman Hall, Room 109, Stony Brook, NY 11794, 516-632-9070; FAX: 516-632-7176.

Suffern: Rockland Community College at Suffern, Small Business Development Center, 145 College Road, Suffern, NY 10901, 914-356-0370; FAX: 914-356-0381.

Syracuse: Onondaga Community College at Syracuse, Small Business Development Center, Greater Syracuse Incubator Center, 1201 East Fayette Street, Syracuse, NY 13210, 315-475-0083; FAX: 315-475-8460.

Utica: SUNY College of Technology at Utica/Rome, Small Business Development Center, P.O. Box 3050, Utica, NY 13504-3050, 315-792-7546; FAX: 315-792-7554.

Watertown: Jefferson Community College at Watertown, Small Business Development Center, Watertown, NY 13601, 315-782-9262; FAX: 315-782-0901.

North Carolina

* General Information

North Carolina Department of Economic and Community Development
Business Industrial Development

430 North Salisbury Street
Raleigh, NC 27603   919-733-4151

Coordinates state small business assistance programs and financing. Includes pooled industrial revenue bonds, a certified SBA Development Company, and a long-term, fixed-rate financing program. Also provides information and referral services to small firms and prospective entrepreneurs and acts as advocate for the state's small business community.

Small Business Advocate   919-571-4154
Assistance in cutting bureaucratic red tape. Information and expertise in dealing with state, federal, and local agencies.

Business License Information Office
N.C. Department of the Secretary of State
301 West Jones Street   919-733-0641
Raleigh, NC 27603   1-800-228-8443 in NC

A central information source offering prompt, individualized assistance to new and existing businesses to secure the necessary State issued licenses, permits, and/or authorizations in order to operate a business in the State. Acts as an advocate for regulatory reform.

* Financing

North Carolina Department of Economic and Community Development
430 North Salisbury Street
Raleigh, NC 27611   919-733-4151

Small Business Development Division:
Long-term, Fixed Rate Financing Program: Allows North Carolina banks to win long-term fixed rate certificates of deposit from the State Treasurer and then re-lend the same money on a long-term, fixed rate basis to small businesses.

Industrial Revenue Bonds: Tax-exempt long-term, low interest financing available to manufacturing companies that will have a measurable economic impact on the community. Industrial firms may finance projects related to product manufacturing, distribution centers, or research and development facilities necessary to the manufacturing process. Generally, capital projects with investments under $10 million can be financed in full.

Industrial Development Bonds: For manufacturing companies that cannot qualify for financing that is exempt from federal taxes, North Carolina bond authorities can issue Industrial Development Bonds with interest income exempt from state income tax.

TIPP: Tarheel IRB Pool Program: Pooled industrial revenue bonds designed to allow small firms access to the IRB program. This enables borrowers in the $500,000 to $3,000,000 to use the bond vehicle cost effectively. Companies need a letter of credit from their bank. These bonds can have variable or fixed rates.

Job Creation Tax Credit: Companies creating full-time jobs in a designated economically-distressed counties may be eligible for a tax credit of $2,800 per job created and can be applied against state corporate or individual income taxes. The amount can offset up to 50 percent of a firm's state income tax. Companies can agree to hire a minimum of 20 new employees over two years, allowing them to still receive credits even if the county loses its distressed classification.

Industrial Building Renovation Fund: In certain economically distressed counties, companies may be eligible for funds to repair or renovate existing buildings for use as manufacturing and industrial operations. A firm can receive $1,200 per job created, up to a maximum of $250,000, for repair, renovation, or equipping a structure for industrial use. Funds used to benefit a private business, such as air-conditioning or equipment, are repayable at 2 percent interest. No repayment of funds is required where funds are used to provide a utility service to the building. The improvement is then loaned by the local government.

Manufacturer's Incentive Tax Formula: Can cut taxable income for businesses by up to 25 percent. This is an allocation formula that gives tax breaks to corporations that are located within North Carolina, even if they conduct a large volume of sales outside the state.

Finance Center 919-733-5297
Farmers Home Administration Loan Guarantees: Guarantees private lenders up to 90 percent of the principal and interest on a loan. Borrowers must have up to 25 percent equity in the project to qualify. Maturities can be up to 30 years for real estate, 15 years for machinery, and 7 years for working capital. This is a program for communities with populations under 50,000.

Pollution Control Tax Breaks: Facilities for pollution control, recycling and recovery qualify for rapid depreciation on state income tax returns. North Carolina counties offer additional tax advantages for costs of this type of equipment.

North Carolina Technological Development Authority
2 Davis Drive
Durham, NC 27709 919-990-8558
Seed and Incubator Capital: Through the Innovation Research Fund, up to $50,000 in seed money is available for development of new products or services. The Authority funds incubator facilities through its Incubator Facilities Program. It also conducts workshops across the state for those small business interested in the IRF and the Small Business Innovation Research program.

Small Business Administration (SBA) District Office
200 N. College St., Suite A-2015 704-344-6563
Charlotte, NC 28202-2173 FAX: 704-344-6769
SBA 7(a) Guaranteed and Direct Loans: Guarantees up to 90 percent of a loan made through a private lender up to $750,000. Can be used for working capital, expand or convert facilities, purchase of machinery and equipment, and land and building. Available only to those unable to obtain a loan from conventional sources. Direct loans are made up to $150,000.

SBA 504: Provides loans using 50 percent conventional bank financing, 40 percent SBA involvement through Certified Development Companies, and 10 percent owner equity. Fixed-asset loans are available in amounts up to $750,000. The loan can be used for land and building, construction, machinery and equipment, and renovation/expansion.

Small Business Innovative Research Grants (SBIR): Phase I awards between $20,000 to $50,000 to entrepreneurs to support six months of research on a technical innovation. Phase II grants are an additional $500,000 for development. Private sector investment funds must follow.

International Trade Loans: Guaranteed long-term loans through private lenders to develop or expand export markets, or to recover from the effects of import competition. Maximum guaranteed loan is $1,000,000 for fixed assets and an additional $250,000 for working capital and/or export revolving line of credit.

Export Revolving Line of Credit Loan: Short term financing available to small businesses that are at least one year old. Loans provide working capital to finance the manufacturing or wholesaling of products for export and for export marketing. The SBA will guarantee up to 90 percent of a conventional loan in amounts up to $750,000.

Contract Loan: Short-term loans are available to small businesses to finance the costs of labor and materials on contracts for which the proceeds are assignable. Program guarantees up to 90 percent of loans not in excess of $750,000. Qualifying small businesses must be in business for at least 12 calendar months prior to the date of the loan application.

Seasonal Line of Credit Loan: Loans provide short-term working capital to finance seasonal increases in business activities. Program guarantees up to 90 percent of loans not in excess of $750,000. Qualifying business must be in operation for at least one year prior to application.

Pollution Control Loans: Long-term guaranteed loans can be made by conventional financing to small businesses for installation or required pollution control measures. Must be unable to adopt the pollution control measures without undue financial hardship. Maximum guaranteed loan is $1,000,000.

General Contractor Loans: Small general construction contractors may obtain short-term loans or loan guarantees for residential or commercial construction or rehabilitation of property to be sold. The SBA will guarantee up to 90 percent of qualifying loans made by private lenders up to a maximum of $750,000. Direct loans can be up to $150,000.

Energy Business Loan Guarantee: Small businesses that provide certain energy production and conservation services for others may qualify for long-term loans and loan guarantees for start-ups and expansions. Loans and guarantees are made for firms that develop, manufacture, sell, install, or service specific energy measures for others, or firms that provide engineering, architectural, consulting, or other professional services connected with specific energy measures. Guarantee is for up to 90 percent of a loan not in excess of $750,000. Direct loans up to $150,000.

Disaster Recovery Loans: Small businesses located in federally designated disaster areas and suffering property damage or economic losses from the disaster can obtain long-term recovery loans at low interest rates. Property damage loans are limited to 85 percent of the verified damage. Loans for economic losses are for operating capital to meet the business' obligations that could have been made had the disaster not occurred.

Handicapped Assistance Loans: Assists persons who have a physical, mental or emotional disability of a permanent nature which limits the selection of any type of employment for which the person would otherwise be qualified. Direct loans are available for up to $150,000. The interest rate is 3% on these loans.

Surety Bond Guaranty Program: Makes the bonding system more available to small contractors who may be denied access to the system. SBA can guarantee up to 80 percent of surety's loss on a bond that has a maximum in total contract value of up to $1,250,000.

Vietnam-era and Disabled Veterans Loan Program: Provides direct loans to veterans to establish or expand a small business. Funds may be used for working capital or fixed assets. Direct loans for amounts up to $150,000 are available. The interest rate may be fixed or variable.

Heritage Capital Corporation
2095 Two First Union Center
Charlotte, NC 28282 704-372-5404

NCNB SBIC Corporation
One NCNB Plaza, T05-2
Charlotte, NC 28255 704-374-5583

NCNB Venture Company, LP
One NCNB Plaza, T-39
Charlotte, NC 28255 704-374-5723
Small Business Investment Companies (SBIC): The SBA licenses, regulates, and provides financial assistance to privately owned and operated Small Business Investment Companies. SBICs make venture or risk investments by supplying capital and extending unsecured loans and loans not fully collateralized to small enterprises which meet their investment criteria. Financing is made by direct loans and by equity investments.

North Carolina Department of Economic and Community Development
Division of Community Assistance
1307 Glenwood Ave., Suite 250
Raleigh, NC 27605 919-733-2850
Community Development Block Grants: Available to cities and counties, who in turn, loan the money to businesses for the commercial rehabilitation of existing buildings or structures used for business, commercial, or industrial purposes. Funds can be used for fixed assets and to partially finance working capital. Every $15,000 of funds invested must create at least one full-time job, and at least 51 percent of the jobs created must be for low- and moderate-income families.

North Carolina Enterprise Corporation
P.O. Box 20429
Raleigh, NC 27619 919-781-2691
A private, for-profit corporation with a board of directors representing private and public interests that is financed by both sectors. The corporation provides equity-type financing to small and medium-sized business, principally for manufacturing. Provides long-term capital for long-term investment. It is aimed at expanding the rural economic base in the state.

North Carolina Biotechnology Center
15 Alexander Drive
P.O. Box 13547
Research Triangle Park, NC 27709-3547   919-541-9366

Supports biotechnology research as a means of improving the state's economy. The center does not actually perform research itself, but supports, coordinates, and educates in the field of biotechnology. Grants are available for academic research, large-scale projects at universities and non-profit institutions, economic development, and for groups wishing to organize conferences and workshops. These grants total several million dollars per year.

Institute of Private Enterprise
University of North Carolina
The Kenan Center
CB 3440
Chapel Hill, NC 27599-3440   919-962-8201

Investment Contacts Network: A computerized matching service organized by the University of North Carolina's Institute of Private Enterprise. It matches investors with promising entrepreneurs. Entrepreneurs pay $100 for a six month listing, and investors pay $200 per year.

* Women and Minority Business Assistance

North Carolina Minority Business Development Agency
430 North Salisbury Street
Raleigh, NC 27603   919-571-4154

Provides information, referral, and support assistance to minority businesses. Offers technical referral assistance, procurement opportunities referral, management workshops and seminars, and coordination with other state and federal agencies.

Small Business Administration (SBA) District Office
200 N. College Street
Suite A-2015   704-344-6563
Charlotte, NC 28202-2173   FAX: 704-344-6769

SBA 8(a) Program - Business Procurement Assistance: Provides federal government contracting opportunities for small businesses owned by socially and economically disadvantaged persons, and assists these businesses to become independently competitive in the normal business environment. SBA monitors all government contracts to assure that a quota of contract work goes to 8(a) businesses. Also provides business management services to these businesses. Business must be approved for program participation prior to receipt of an 8(a) contract.

* Training

North Carolina Department of Economic and Community Development
Division of Employment and Training
111 Seaboard
Raleigh, NC 27604   919-733-6383

Job Training Partnership Act (JTPA): Provides employers with recruitment, screening, referral, training, 50 percent wage subsidy up to 3 months for on-the-job training. Available to any private employer.

North Carolina Department of Commerce
Finance Center
430 North Salisbury Street
Raleigh, NC 27611   919-733-5297

Job Training: Within North Carolina's Community College system, a free customized skills program is available to new or expanding industries. Using resources from government, industry, and academia, the program offers whatever specialists a company needs to train or re-train employees. The state will sponsor and assist companies in applying for federal Job Training Partnership Act money.

North Carolina Employment Security Commission (ESC)
700 Wade Ave.
P.O. Box 25903
Raleigh, NC 27611   919-733-3098

Job Screening and Tax Credit: Will screen, test and recommend job applicants for a company locating in the State. The firm provides the agency with a list of job openings and the requirements for each position, and the ESC matches its applicants with job positions and refer these people to the company. A 40 percent tax credit is available on the first $6,000 in wages paid in the first year of employment for hiring people in any of several hard-to-employ categories, such as economically disadvantaged youth or vocational rehabilitation clients.

* Management Consulting and Other Services

North Carolina Rural Economic Development Center
4 N. Blount Street, 2nd Floor
Raleigh, NC 27601   919-821-1154

A private, non-profit corporation aimed at stimulating economic growth in the states rural areas. It is funded through private and public sources and provides services and information in a variety of subjects. It coordinates various agencies that deal in rural economic issues, acts as advocate for rural interests, serves as a clearinghouse of information and programs dealing with rural interests, and conducts research on topics ranging from aquaculture, business development, and infrastructure to leadership development and strategic planning.

North Carolina Department of Commerce
430 North Salisbury Street
Raleigh, NC 27611   919-733-4151

International Development Division:
Foreign Trade Assistance: Provides counseling and assistance to firms involved in foreign trade. Works with outside agencies to improve export services to local businesses. Has targeted assistance programs for furniture and textile manufacturers. Also maintains offices in West Germany and Japan.

Science and Technology Research Center: Provides research and information services, including literature searches and document location. Serves business and industry on a wide variety of informational topics.

Small Business Division:
The Business Clearinghouse: Helps sellers and buyers of manufactured goods learn of mutually beneficial opportunities.

Buyer/Supplier Exchange   919-733-4151
North Carolina manufacturers and suppliers of goods are brought together in one place to meet and conduct business. This "reverse trade show" has been operating for several years, with notable success in helping buyers locate new sources of goods and services and providing suppliers with specific information on the procurement needs of the state's industries. Where there are special needs, the agency will research potential suppliers for a manufacturer.

Division of Small Business Development:
Business Information Referral Center (BIRC): Provides a database of state government programs and regulations affecting state businesses. Helps entrepreneurs more easily access specific services and resources available in the state.

Site Assistance: A site-by-site analysis of industrial locations will be provided, detailing the various services and incentives provided by local leadership and governmental units.

A and T State University
Agriculture Extension Program
P.O. Box 21928
Greensboro, NC 27420   919-334-7915

Agriculture Extension Program: Helps small farmers who have limited resources to develop farm plans, conduct financial analyses of their businesses, and formulate alternative marketing strategies.

Small Business Centers
North Carolina Department of Community Colleges
200 West Jones Street
Raleigh, NC 27603-1337   919-733-7051

Offers "how-to" information to small businesses throughout the state on topics such as how to start a business, tax reforms, employment procedures, marketing and advertising, among others. Also included are programs for minorities and firms involved in rural development. More recent offerings include a seminar series on trade and access to legal information. There are 40 centers in North Carolina, located in community colleges. Contact the address above for the center nearest you.

Small Business Administration District Office
200 N. College Street
Suite A-2015   704-344-6563
Charlotte, NC 28202-2173   FAX: 704-344-6769

Small Business Institutes: This program provides personalized consulting services to the small business community. Consulting is provided by senior level business students, guided by a faculty advisor. Assistance in business plan preparation, marketing research, market planning, accounting, and seminars are provided.
University Locations:
Appalachian State University
Duke University
East Carolina University
Pembroke State University
University of North Carolina - Charlotte
University of North Carolina - Chapel Hill
University of North Carolina - Greensboro
University of North Carolina - Wilmington
Western Carolina University

* Small Business Development Centers

The following offices offer free and fee-based services to new and expanding businesses:

Lead Center:
North Carolina Small Business Development Center
University of North Carolina
4509 Creedmoor Road, Suite 201   919-571-4154
Raleigh, NC 27612   FAX: 919-571-4161

Boone: Appalachian State University, Small Business Development Center, Northwestern Region, Walker College of Business, Boone, NC, 28608, 704-262-2095; FAX: 704-262-2027.

Chapel Hill: Small Business Development Center, Central Carolina Region, 608 Airport Road, Suite B, Chapel Hill, NC 27514, 919-962-0389.

Charlotte: Small Business Development Center, Southern Piedmont Region, The Ben Craig Center, 8701 Mallard Creek Road, Charlotte, NC 28262, 704-548-1090; FAX: 704-548-9050.

Cullowhee: Small Business Development Center, Center for Improving Mountain Living, Western Carolina University, Cullowhee, NC 28723, 704-227-7494; FAX: 704-227-7422.

Elizabeth City: Elizabeth City State University, Small Business Development Center, Northeastern Region, P.O. Box 874, Elizabeth City, NC 27909, 919-335-3247; FAX: 919-335-3648.

Fayetteville: Fayetteville State University, Small Business Development Center, Cape Fear Region, Continuing Education Center, P.O. Box 1334, Fayetteville, NC 28302, 919-486-1727; FAX: 919-486-1949.

Greenville: East Carolina University, Small Business Development Center, Eastern Region, Corner of First and Reade Street, Greenville, NC, 27858-4353, 919-757-6157; FAX: 919-757-6992.

Wilmington: University of North Carolina at Wilmington, Small Business Development Center, Southeastern Region, Room 131, Cameron Hall, 601 South College Road, Wilmington, NC 28403, 919-395-3744; FAX: 919-395-3815.

Winston-Salem: Winston-Salem University, Small Business Development Center, Northern Piedmont Region, P.O. Box 13025, Winston-Salem, NC 27110, 919-750-2030; FAX: 919-750-2031.

North Dakota

* General Information

Center for Innovation and Business Development
Box 8103
University Station
University of North Dakota
Grand Forks, ND 58202   701-777-3132

The *Business Plan* and *Marketing Plan* workbooks are step-by-step guides, with optional software, to writing your own business and marketing plans. They are targeted to new manufacturing ventures producing new products or technology, but the guides can also be relevant to many entrepreneurs, academics, and business professionals. The workbooks are $80 each; with software $99.

North Dakota Economic Finance Corp.
1833 E. Bismarck Expressway   701-221-5300
Bismarck, ND 58504   FAX: 701-221-5320

Small Business Advocate: Assistance in cutting bureaucratic red tape. Information and expertise in dealing with state, federal, and local agencies.

* Financing

Bank of North Dakota (BND)
700 East Main Avenue, Box 5509   701-224-5685
Bismarck, ND 58502-5509   1-800-472-2166

Micro Business Loans: Available to all small business activities including home-based businesses, retail, services, and manufacturing.

TRIP Loans (Tourism and Recreation Investment Program): Available to all tourism related businesses and activities including recreation, historical sites, festival and cultural events, unique lodging and food services, and guide services.

Both types of loans will require a local financing institution to act as lead lender for the loan. The Bank of North Dakota will take up to 50 percent of the total loan, to a maximum of $10,000. Funds may be used to establish or purchase a new or existing business, finance the acquisition of real property, remodel or expand an existing business, purchase equipment, working capital, purchase inventory.

PACE (Partnership in Assisting Community Expansion): Available to manufacturing, processing, value-added processing and targeted service industries such as data processing, data communications and tele-communications. Funds can be used for working capital, equipment and real property. BND will fund up to $300,000 for interest rate buydown to a maximum of 5 percent below prime. BND will fund 70 percent to 85 percent of interest buydown. Community must fund remainder.

Small Business Loan Program: Loans of up to $250,000 to any business, through a local lender, for working capital, equipment and real property. Terms are 3-5 years for working capital, 5-7 years for equipment, and 12-15 years for real estate. Equity requirement is 25 percent for new businesses. Local lender is required for 30-40 percent of loan.

Business Development Loans: Available to any business. Local lender is required for up 30 to 40 percent of total loan. BND share is up to $500,000 per project. Fund can be used for working capital, equipment and real property.

Match Program: Available to manufacturing and processing companies with a credit rate of "A" or better. BND's shall will be limited to $25 million. Funds can be used for real estate and for purchase and lease of machinery and equipment.

Export-Import Bank Working Capital Guarantee   701-224-5674
Provides repayment guarantees of up to 90 percent to eligible lenders on secured loans.

Export-Import Bank Medium and Long Term Loans   701-224-5674
Covers up to 85 percent of the export value. Support export sales facing foreign competition backed with subsidized official financing.

Export Credit Insurance   701-224-5674
Offers insurance policies protecting U.S. exporters against the risk of nonpayment by a foreign debtor.

Office of Urban Development
122 South 5th Street, Room 233
Grand Forks, ND 58201-1518   701-746-2545

Grand Forks Growth Fund: The fund is intended to provide gap and incentive financing for new or expanding businesses which have capacity to create new primary sector jobs and contribute to the local tax base. Funds can be used to provide temporary or permanent financing for capital costs (land, buildings, and infrastructure), equipment, working capital, seed capital, or other miscellaneous feasibility costs. A minimum 10 percent equity contribution is required. For requests in excess of $25,000, the applicant must obtain some levels of bank participation.

Office of Intergovernmental Assistance
600 E. Boulevard Avenue
Bismarck, ND 58505   701-224-2094

Community Development Revolving Loan Fund: Borrow to be user or develop through loan to eligible local government. Loans amounts up to $300,000 per project for primary sector, $50,000 per project for retail sector. Funds can be used for fixed assets related to business and infrastructure. A dollar for dollar non-public match, and 10 percent minimum equity requirement. Job creation criteria for low to moderate income people.

Community Development Block Grants: Available to cities and counties for the commercial rehabilitation of existing buildings or structures used for business, commercial, or industrial purposes. Grants of up to $300,000 can be made. Every $15,000 of grant funds invested must create at least one full-time job, and at least 51 percent of the jobs created must be for low- and moderate-income families.

Governor's Office
600 E. Boulevard Avenue
Bismarck, ND 58505   701-224-2200

Industrial Revenue Bonds: For developers, commercial or industrial users - sold through political subdivision. Up to 100 percent of cost of project for fixed assets and equipment. Market interest rates for 7-20 years. No equity requirements. For funding under $1 million on a first-come, first-served basis.

Agricultural Products Utilization Commission
600 East Boulevard, 6th floor
Bismarck, ND 58505-0020   701-224-4760

Provides funding and assistance to private industry in the establishment of agricultural processing plants for the manufacturing and marketing of agricultural derived fuels, chemicals and other processed products.

North Dakota Tax Commissioner
600 E. Boulevard Avenue
Bismarck, ND 58505-0599   701-224-2770

Special Tax Incentives for Businesses: Incentives include:
Five year property and corporation income tax exemptions for new business projects
Wage and salary income tax credits
Income tax credit for research expenditures and for investment in a North Dakota venture capital corporation
Deductions for selling or renting a business to a beginning business person or farmland to a beginning farmer

Fargo-Cass County Economic Development Corporation
417 Main Avenue
Suite 401
Fargo, ND 58103   701-237-6132

SBA 504: Provides loans using 50 percent conventional bank financing, 40 percent SBA involvement through Certified Development Companies, and 10 percent owner equity. A fixed asset loan in amounts up to $750,000. Loan can be used for land and building, construction, machinery and equipment, and renovation/expansion.

Small Business Administration (SBA)
657 2nd Avenue N., Room 218   701-239-5131
Fargo, ND 58108-3086   FAX: 701-239-5645

SBA 7(a) Guaranteed and Direct Loans: Guarantees up to 90 percent of a loan made through a private lender up to $750,000. Can be used for working capital, expand or convert facilities, purchase of machinery and equipment, and land and building. Available only to those unable to obtain a loan from conventional sources. Direct loans are made up to $150,000.

SBA 504: Provides loans using 50 percent conventional bank financing, 40 percent SBA involvement through Certified Development Companies, and 10 percent owner equity. Fixed-asset loans are available in amounts up to $750,000. The loan can be used for land and building, construction, machinery and equipment, and renovation/expansion.

Small Business Innovative Research Grants (SBIR): Phase I awards between $20,000 to $50,000 to entrepreneurs to support six months of research on a technical innovation. Phase II grants are an additional $500,000 for development. Private sector investment funds must follow.

International Trade Loans: Guaranteed long-term loans through private lenders to develop or expand export markets, or to recover from the effects of import competition. Maximum guaranteed loan is $1,000,000 for fixed assets and an additional $250,000 for working capital and/or export revolving line of credit.

Export Revolving Line of Credit Loan: Short term financing available to small businesses that are at least one year old. Loans provide working capital to finance the manufacturing or wholesaling of products for export and for export marketing. The SBA will guarantee up to 90 percent of a conventional loan in amounts up to $750,000.

Contract Loan: Short-term loans are available to small businesses to finance the costs of labor and materials on contracts for which the proceeds are assignable. Program guarantees up to 90 percent of loans not in excess of $750,000. Qualifying small businesses must be in business for at least 12 calendar months prior to the date of the loan application.

Seasonal Line of Credit Loan: Loans provide short-term working capital to finance seasonal increases in business activities. Program guarantees up to 90 percent of loans not in excess of $750,000. Qualifying business must be in operation for at least one year prior to application.

Pollution Control Loans: Long-term guaranteed loans can be made by conventional financing to small businesses for installation or required pollution control measures. Must be unable to adopt the pollution control measures without undue financial hardship. Maximum guaranteed loan is $1,000,000.

General Contractor Loans: Small general construction contractors may obtain short-term loans or loan guarantees for residential or commercial construction or rehabilitation of property to be sold. The SBA will guarantee up to 90 percent of qualifying loans made by private lenders up to a maximum of $750,000. Direct loans can be up to $150,000.

Energy Business Loan Guarantee: Small businesses that provide certain energy production and conservation services for others may qualify for long-term loans and loan guarantees for start-ups and expansions. Loans and guarantees are made for firms that develop, manufacture, sell, install, or service specific energy measures for others, or firms that provide engineering, architectural, consulting, or other professional services connected with specific energy measures. Guarantee is for up to 90 percent of a loan not in excess of $750,000. Direct loans up to $150,000.

Disaster Recovery Loans: Small businesses located in federally designated disaster areas and suffering property damage or economic losses from the disaster can obtain long-term recovery loans at low interest rates. Property damage loans are limited to 85 percent of the verified damage. Loans for economic losses are for operating capital to meet the business' obligations that could have been made had the disaster not occurred.

Handicapped Assistance Loans: Assists persons who have a physical, mental or emotional disability of a permanent nature which limits the selection of any type of employment for which the person would otherwise be qualified. Direct loans are available for up to $150,000. The interest rate is 3% on these loans.

Surety Bond Guaranty Program: Makes the bonding system more available to small contractors who may be denied access to the system. SBA can guarantee up to 80 percent of surety's loss on a bond that has a maximum in total contract value of up to $1,250,000.

Vietnam-era and Disabled Veterans Loan Program: Provides direct loans to veterans to establish or expand a small business. Funds may be used for working capital or fixed assets. Direct loans for amounts up to $150,000 are available. The interest rate may be fixed or variable.

Export Financing - SBA Revolving Line of Credit: Provides financial assistance through loans and loan guarantees for equipment, facilities, materials, working capital, and specified export market development activities.

Center for Innovation and Business Development
Box 8103
University Station
University of North Dakota
Grand Forks, ND 58202   701-777-3132

Small Business Innovation Research Grant: Awards between $20,000 to $50,000 to entrepreneurs to support six months of research on a technical innovation. Phase II grants are an additional $500,000 for development. Private sector investment funds must follow.

First Seed Capital Group: Brings together investors and businesses. Focuses on business start-ups and equity capital investment for businesses with needs of less than $150,000.

State Director
Farmers Home Administration
Third and Rosser Avenues
P.O. Box 1737
Bismarck, ND 58502-1737   701-250-4781

Business and Industrial Loan Programs: Provides loan guarantees to lenders. Proceeds can be used for working capital, equipment, and real property. Interest rates are negotiated between lender and borrower. Maximum terms: 7 years for working capital, 10 years for equipment, and 25 years for real property. Requires 10 percent equity for existing businesses and 20 percent-25 percent for new businesses. Additional funding allowed from any source. Only rural areas and areas with populations under 25,000 are eligible.

Economic Development Administration (EDA)
P.O. Box 1911
Bismarck, ND 58502   701-250-4321

EDA Loan Guarantee: Guarantees up to 80 percent of the principal and interest on loans to businesses in designated areas of high unemployment or low income. Funding limits are determined by project need. Uses are for working capital, equipment, and real property. The guarantee is made to private lending institutions in designated EDA eligible areas. Projects must be of direct benefit to local residents and demonstrate long-term employment opportunities in the area.

Capital Dimensions Inc.
400 East Broadway, Suite 420
Bismarck, ND 58501   701-222-0995

Myron G. Nelson Venture Capital Fund, Inc.: Established by legislation, this corporation provides a source of investment capital for the establishment, expansion, and rehabilitation of North Dakota businesses.

Roughrider Equity Corporation: A statewide development corporate designed to promote the development and expansion of new and existing primary sector businesses through the investment of equity funds.

* Women and Minority Business Assistance

Women Business Development Administration
Native American Business Development Administration
Department for Economic Development and Finance
1833 East Bismarck Expressway
Bismarck, ND 58504   701-221-5300

These offices provide technical assistance to try to get businesses started. Location of funding and preparation of business plans are some of the services provided.

Small Business Administration (SBA)
657 2nd Avenue North
Room 218   701-239-5131
Fargo, ND 58108-3086   FAX: 701-239-5645

SBA 8(a) Program - Business Procurement Assistance: Provides federal government contracting opportunities for small businesses owned by socially and economically disadvantaged persons, and assists these businesses to become independently competitive in the normal business environment. SBA monitors all government contracts to assure that a quota of contract work goes to 8(a) businesses. Also provides business management services to these businesses. Business must be approved for program participation prior to receipt of an 8(a) contract.

* Training

Governors Employment Training Forum
P.O. Box 1537
Bismarck, ND 58502-1537   701-224-2836

Job Training Partnership Act (JTPA): Provides employers with recruitment, screening, referral, training, 50 percent wage subsidy up to 3 months for on-the-job training. Available to any private employer.

Targeted Jobs Tax Credit Program: Provides employers a tax credit up to $2,400 per trainee when hiring a certified trainee.

* Management Consulting and Other Services

North Dakota Economic Development Commission
1833 E. Bismarck Expressway   701-221-5300
Bismarck, ND 58504   FAX: 701-221-5320

Procurement Technical Assistance Program: Conducts conferences, workshops, and seminars in the state to inform people about federal contract opportunities. Has a computer link between companies with bid opportunities and businesses wishing to do business with the government. A computerized Commerce Business Daily provides bid leads to your business. The PartsMaster database provides access to Department of Defense and federal agency purchasing data.

Foreign Trade Assistance: Helps companies find foreign markets for their products and promotes export sales, licensing agreements, and joint ventures between foreign firms and North Dakota companies. Sponsors trade missions, export seminars, and educational services.

World Trade, Inc.: Attracts foreign investment in North Dakota and helps export of North Dakota products abroad. Through World Trade, Inc., the state maintains an office in Japan to further North Dakota trade interests.

Retention and Expansion Program: Encourages maintenance through a joint effort between community groups and existing businesses. Community volunteers visit small and large businesses in the area to collect up-to-date, confidential data on their needs, problems, concerns and future plans. Provides counseling and business training to help these small entrepreneurs enter the wholesale market.

Regional Development Corporations: Eight multi-county entities that provide technical and grant-writing assistance and other help in applying for available federal and state funds.

Center for Innovation and Business Development
Box 8103
University Station
University of North Dakota
Grand Forks, ND 58202   701-777-3132

Aids small businesses in technology transfer and innovation and provides invention assistance. It is the major referral point for inventors and entrepreneurs needing technological help in areas such as invention evaluation, patent research and development, and feasibility analysis.

NDSE Extension Center for Rural Revitalization
North Dakota State University
P.O. Box 5437
Fargo, ND 58105   701-237-7394

The major aim of the Center is to develop a broad range of educational programs to enhance North Dakota's human and economic capital. A newsletter, *Business Sense*, is published bi-monthly and provides marketing and management information. In addition, the following are programs available.

Business Retention and Expansion Program: Helps retain or maintain existing businesses and to identify potential for expanding them. Emphasis is on maintaining or increasing jobs.

Home-Based Business Program: Workshops are offered to help people operate a business more effectively and improve their chances of success. Subjects such as marketing and advertising, recordkeeping, taxes, regulations, and insurance are covered in the workshops.

Main-Street Business Assistance: Educational programs in customer relations, marketing, promotion and merchandising are offered to business owners, managers and employees available to main street businesses in rural areas.

Farm and Ranch Management: Computer-based educational programs are provided to aid farmers who have limited resources and in combining existing resources to maximize net income.

Grand Forks Development Foundation
202 North 3rd Street, Suite 300
Grand Forks, ND 58203   701-780-9915

Foreign Trade Zone: The Zone may be used to store, sell,exhibit, break up, repack, assemble, distribute, sort, grade, clean and manufacturing goods without being subject to the custom law of the U.S.

North Dakota Micro Business Marketing Alliance
400 E. Broadway, Suite 420   701-244-9869
Bismarck, ND 58501   FAX: 701-222-3840

The goals of the Alliance are to create a marketing network to bring products to the urban marketplace, provide technical and project development assistance to create products which will sell in the urban marketplace, use existing skills, talents and resources--rural home-based individuals and rural worksites--to create products for the urban marketplace, develop a revolving loan pool for small rural enterprises.

Small Business Administration
657 2nd Avenue North, Room 218   701-239-5131
Fargo, ND 58108-3086   701-239-5645

Small Business Institutes: This program provides personalized consulting services to the small business community. Consulting is provided by senior level business students, guided by a faculty advisor. Assistance in business plan preparation, marketing research, market planning, accounting, and seminars are provided.
University Locations:
Jamestown College
North Dakota State University
University of Mary
University of North Dakota - Minot
University of North Dakota - Grand Forks

* Small Business Development Centers

The following offices offer free and fee-based services to new and expanding businesses:

Lead Center:
North Dakota Small Business Development Center
University of North Dakota
118 Gamble Hall, Box 7308
Grand Forks, ND 58202   701-777-3700
                                              FAX: 701-777-5099

Bismarck: Small Business Development Center, Bismarck Regional Center, 400 East Broadway, Suite 421, Bismarck, ND 58501, 701-223-8583; FAX: 701-222-3843.

Dickinson: Small Business Development Center, Dickinson Regional Center, 314 3rd Avenue West, Drawer L, Dickinson, ND 58602, 701-227-2096; FAX: 701-225-5116.

Fargo: Small Business Development Center, Fargo Regional Center, 417 Main Avenue, Fargo, ND 58103, 701-237-0986; FAX: 701-235-6706.

Grand Forks: Small Business Development Center, Grand Forks Regional Center, The Hemmp Center, 1407 24th Avenue S., Suite 201, Grand Forks, ND 58201, 701-772-8502; FAX: 701-775-2772.

Minot: Small Business Development Center, Minot Regional Center, 1020 20th Avenue Southwest, P.O. Box 940, Minot, ND 58702, 701-852-8861; FAX: 701-838-2488.

Ohio

* General Information

Ohio Department of Development
P.O. Box 1001
Columbus, OH 43266-0101

One-Stop Business Permit Center   614-644-8748
                                              1-800-848-1300
Provides new entrepreneurs with licensing and permit information, and acts as an advocate for licensing and permit problems. Directs you to proper area for technical, financial and management resources.

Small And Developing Business Division
Ohio Department of Development
77 S. High Street
P.O. Box 1001
Columbus, OH 43266-0101   614-466-2718

Small Business Advocate: Assistance in cutting bureaucratic red tape. Information and expertise in dealing with state, federal, and local agencies.

* Financing

Ohio Department of Development
P.O. Box 1001
Columbus, OH 43266-0101   1-800-848-1300
Economic Development Financing Division   614-466-5420
Direct Loans: Loans are available for land and building acquisition, expansion or renovation, and equipment purchase. Industrial projects are preferred. The state can fund up to 30 percent of the total fixed cost of a project, up to $1 million. Interest is at a 5 percent fixed rate for 10-15 years. Equity must be at least 10 percent from the borrower and 25 percent conventional financing. Must create one job for every $10,000 received.

Industrial Revenue Bonds: For fixed assets and equipment for manufacturing projects. Provides up to 100 percent of eligible fixed assets at 75 percent of prime, at a floating or fixed rate for up to 20 years.

Ohio Enterprise Bond Fund: For building and land acquisition, construction, expansion or renovation, and equipment purchase for commercial or industrial projects between $1 million and $15 million. Long-term, fixed-rate for up to 25 years at treasury bond rates, plus 1-1/2 percent for up to 90 percent of project amount.

Pooled Bond Program   614-644-5645
Available to manufacturing projects between $400,000 and $10 million in size. Funds can be used for building acquisition, construction, expansion, or renovation and new equipment purchase. Can finance up to 100 percent of eligible fixed assets at 3-4 percent below current market rates, for up to 30 years. Borrower must submit letter of credit from lender and project must create or retain jobs. Projects are pooled in one issue for companies too small for traditional Industrial Revenue Bonds.

Office of Local Government Services   614-466-2285
Revolving Loan Funds: Targeted at projects that will create or retain jobs for low-to-moderate income households, and help develop, rehabilitate or revitalize a participating "small city" community. Must be used for fixed

assets related to commercial, industrial, or infrastructure use. Loans available for users or developers, at 5-9 percent with flexible terms.

Community Development Block Grants: Available to cities and counties for the commercial rehabilitation of existing buildings or structures used for business, commercial, or industrial purposes. Grants of up to $350,000 can be awarded to cities or counties, who in turn, loan the money to user or developer. Projects must create or retain at least 5 jobs. At least 51% of the jobs created must be for low- and moderate-income families.

Office of Industrial Development   614-466-4551
Enterprise Zone Program: Offers up to 100 percent abatement of real estate or personal property taxes for up to 10 years. Business must retain or create jobs and establish, expand, renovate, or occupy a facility in an Enterprise Zone.

International Trade Division   614-466-5017
Export Credit Insurance: One year policy is backed by the Export-Import Bank of the United States for export sales made under short-term credit plans. Insurance covers 100 percent for political risks and 90 percent for commercial risks, for exporters with under $2 million sales who have not used Foreign Credit Insurance Agency policies in the past 2 years.

Ohio Thomas Edison Program   614-466-3887
                                                   1-800-848-1300
Edison Technology Incubators: Low-cost space for technology-based businesses that reduces operating costs during start-up phase. Access to business, technical, and professional services. Rents and fees are at below market rates. Some incubators provide access to separate seed capital funds.

Edison Seed Development Fund: Links business and university research facilities and provides matching funds for development of product ideas to help turn new ideas into marketable products. Matching funds up to $50,000 for early stage research, and up to $250,000 in matching funds for advanced state research.

Small Business Innovation Research Program   614-466-5967
                                                                  1-800-848-1300
Small Business Innovative Research Grants (SBIR): Phase I Awards between $20,000 to $50,00 to entrepreneurs to support six months of research on a technical innovation. Phase II grants are an additional $500,000 for development. Private sector funds must follow.

SBIR Bridge Grants: Helps companies maintain continuity on SBIR Phase I projects during the federal funding gap between Phases I and II. Awards up to the amount of Phase I SBIR award, not to exceed $50,000.

Ohio Coal Development Program   614-466-3465
Financial assistance for clean coal research and development projects. Up to $75,000 or two-thirds of total project cost for research. Pilot and demonstration scale project up to $5 million or one-half of total project cost for a pilot project, one-third total project cost for a demonstration product. Funds can be issued in the form of a grant, loan,or loan guarantee.

Ohio Statewide Development Corporation   614-466-5043
SBA 504: Provides loans using 50 percent conventional bank financing, 40 percent SBA involvement through Certified Development Companies, and 10 percent owner equity. A fixed-asset loan in amounts up to $750,000. Loan can be used for land and building, construction, machinery and equipment, and renovation/expansion. Must create one Ohio job for every $35,000 received.

Minority Development Financing Commission   614-644-7708
                                                                 1-800-848-1300
Ohio Mini-Loan Program: Fixed asset and equipment loans for small business with less than 25 employees for projects of $100,000 or less. Targeted 50 percent allocation to businesses owned by minorities and women. Available for start-up or existing business expansion. Up to 45 percent guarantee of an eligible bank loan.

Public Affairs Office
Treasurer of the State
Ohio State House
First Floor   614-466-8855
Columbus, OH 43215   1-800-228-1102 in Ohio

Withrow Linked Deposit Program: Funds are available for fixed assets, working capital, and refinancing for small businesses, creating or retaining jobs. Rates are 3 percent below current lending rate fixed for two years.

Agricultural Linked Deposit Program: Provides funds for Ohio full-time farmers to help meet planning deadlines. Provides up to $100,000 per farm at reduced rate, approximately 4 percent below borrower's current rate.

Both categories must have bank loans from eligible state depositories.

Small Business Administration (SBA)
2 Nationwide Plaza
Suite 1400   614-469-6860
Columbus, OH 43215-2592   FAX: 614-469-2391
SBA 7(a) Guaranteed and Direct Loans: Guarantees up to 90 percent of a loan made through a private lender up to $750,000. Can be used for working capital, expand or convert facilities, purchase of machinery and equipment, and land and building. Available only to those unable to obtain a loan from conventional sources. Direct loans are made up to $150,000.

SBA 504: Provides loans using 50 percent conventional bank financing, 40 percent SBA involvement through Certified Development Companies, and 10 percent owner equity. Fixed-asset loans are available in amounts up to $750,000. The loan can be used for land and building, construction, machinery and equipment, and renovation/expansion.

Small Business Innovative Research Grants (SBIR): Phase I awards between $20,000 to $50,000 to entrepreneurs to support six months of research on a technical innovation. Phase II grants are an additional $500,000 for development. Private sector investment funds must follow.

International Trade Loans: Guaranteed long-term loans through private lenders to develop or expand export markets, or to recover from the effects of import competition. Maximum guaranteed loan is $1,000,000 for fixed assets and an additional $250,000 for working capital and/or export revolving line of credit.

Export Revolving Line of Credit Loan: Short term financing available to small businesses that are at least one year old. Loans provide working capital to finance the manufacturing or wholesaling of products for export and for export marketing. The SBA will guarantee up to 90 percent of a conventional loan in amounts up to $750,000.

Contract Loan: Short-term loans are available to small businesses to finance the costs of labor and materials on contracts for which the proceeds are assignable. Program guarantees up to 90 percent of loans not in excess of $750,000. Qualifying small businesses must be in business for at least 12 calendar months prior to the date of the loan application.

Seasonal Line of Credit Loan: Loans provide short-term working capital to finance seasonal increases in business activities. Program guarantees up to 90 percent of loans not in excess of $750,000. Qualifying business must be in operation for at least one year prior to application.

Pollution Control Loans: Long-term guaranteed loans can be made by conventional financing to small businesses for installation or required pollution control measures. Must be unable to adopt the pollution control measures without undue financial hardship. Maximum guaranteed loan is $1,000,000.

General Contractor Loans: Small general construction contractors may obtain short-term loans or loan guarantees for residential or commercial construction or rehabilitation of property to be sold. The SBA will guarantee up to 90 percent of qualifying loans made by private lenders up to a maximum of $750,000. Direct loans can be up to $150,000.

Energy Business Loan Guarantee: Small businesses that provide certain energy production and conservation services for others may qualify for long-term loans and loan guarantees for start-ups and expansions. Loans and guarantees are made for firms that develop, manufacture, sell, install, or service specific energy measures for others, or firms that provide engineering, architectural, consulting, or other professional services connected with specific energy measures. Guarantee is for up to 90 percent of a loan not in excess of $750,000. Direct loans up to $150,000.

Disaster Recovery Loans: Small businesses located in federally designated disaster areas and suffering property damage or economic losses from the disaster can obtain long-term recovery loans at low interest rates. Property damage loans are limited to 85 percent of the verified damage. Loans for economic losses are for operating capital to meet the business' obligations that could have been made had the disaster not occurred.

Handicapped Assistance Loans: Assists persons who have a physical, mental or emotional disability of a permanent nature which limits the selection of any type of employment for which the person would otherwise be qualified. Direct loans are available for up to $150,000. The interest rate is 3% on these loans.

Surety Bond Guaranty Program: Makes the bonding system more available to small contractors who may be denied access to the system. SBA can guarantee up to 80 percent of surety's loss on a bond that has a maximum in total contract value of up to $1,250,000.

Vietnam-era and Disabled Veterans Loan Program: Provides direct loans to veterans to establish or expand a small business. Funds may be used for working capital or fixed assets. Direct loans for amounts up to $150,000 are available. The interest rate may be fixed or variable.

A.T. Capital Corporation
900 Euclid Avenue, 11th Floor
P.O. Box 5937
Cleveland, OH 44101   216-737-4090

Clarion Capital Corporation
Ohio Savings Plaza, Suite 1520
1801 E. 9th Street
Cleveland, OH 44114   216-687-1096

National City Capital Corporation
1965 East Sixth Street, Suite 400
Cleveland, OH 44114   216-575-2491

Society Venture Capital Corporation
800 Superior Avenue
Cleveland, OH 44114   216-689-5776

Small Business Investment Companies (SBIC): The SBA licenses, regulates, and provides financial assistance to privately owned and operated Small Business Investment Companies. SBICs make venture or risk investments by supplying capital and extending unsecured loans and loans not fully collateralized to small enterprises which meet their investment criteria. Financing is made by direct loans and by equity investments.

* Women and Minority Business Assistance

Minority Development Financing Commission
Ohio Department of Development
P.O. Box 1001   614-644-7708
Columbus, OH 43266-0101   1-800-848-1300

Minority Business Development Financing: Loans are available for the purchase or improvement of fixed assets. Can finance up to 40 percent of total project cost to a maximum of $700,000 at 4.5 percent fixed rate for up to 10 years. Equity may be required. Company must be a state-certified minority-owned business and must be 51 percent minority-owned and controlled. One job must be created for every $10,000 of loan.

Minority Contractor Bonding Program: Surety bonding assistance for state-certified minority contractors who have been denied a bond by two surety companies within its current fiscal year. Maximum bond pre-qualification of $1 million per contractor.

Minority Contractor and Business Assistance Program   614-466-5700
Offers management, technical, financial, and contract procurement assistance, as well as with loan, grant, bond packaging services. Counseling is provided at no charge. Fees may be charged for some programs using federal funding. Also the advocate for minority business.

Minority Management and Technical Services   614-466-5700
Provides assistance in management analysis, technical assistance,

educational services and financial counseling. Links minority firms with public and private sector funding sources.

Minority Contract Procurement Services   614-466-5700
Assists minority firms in procuring public and private sector contracts. Staff serves as a liaison between minority firms and prospective public and private sector contracting entities.

Women's Business Resource Program   614-466-4945
Assistance for start-up, expansion and management of women-owned businesses. Assures equal access to assistance and lending programs, and aids in locating government procurement opportunities. Services are free. Publishes *Ohio Women Business Leaders*, a directory of women-owned businesses in Ohio, provides free publications, statewide center of workshops, conferences, and Women's Business Owners (WBO) statistics.

Also see Ohio Financing Section - Ohio Mini-Loan Program

Small Business Administration (SBA)
2 Nationwide Plaza
Suite 1400   614-469-6860
Columbus, OH 43215-2592   FAX: 614-469-2391

SBA 8(a) Program - Business Procurement Assistance: Provides federal government contracting opportunities for small businesses owned by socially and economically disadvantaged persons, and assists these businesses to become independently competitive in the normal business environment. SBA monitors all government contracts to assure that a quota of contract work goes to 8(a) businesses. Also provides business management services to these businesses. Business must be approved for program participation prior to receipt of an 8(a) contract.

* Training

Ohio Department of Development
P.O. Box 1001
Columbus, OH 43266-0101   1-800-848-1300

Industrial Training Program: Available to manufacturing business. To receive aid, must create or retain jobs. Provides up to 50 percent for orientation, training, management programs, instructional materials, and instructor training.

Ohio Bureau of Employment Services
899 E. Broad
Columbus, OH 43215   614-644-7138

Job Placement: Screens, interviews, tests, and recruits individuals and groups of job applicants. Provides access to national pool of qualified workers, administers job training programs including JTP Ohio, the Work Incentive Program and the Veterans Job Training Act.

Veterans' Job Training Act   614-644-7301
Available to businesses hiring Korean Conflict and Vietnam-era veterans. Federal funding, up to 50 percent reimbursement for training period wages, and up to 410,000 per veteran.

Job Training Partnership/Ohio Division
Ohio Bureau of Employment Services
145 South Front St.
Columbus, OH 43215   614-466-3817

Job Training Partnership Act (JTPA): Provides employers with recruitment, screening, referral, training, 50 percent wage subsidy up to 3 months for on-the-job training. Available to any private employer.

Ohio Board of Regents
30 E. Broad Street
3600 State Office Tower
Columbus, OH 43266-0417   614-466-5810

Ohio Training Exchange: Trains companies that supply Ohio's major manufacturing firms in technologies, particularly those relating to quality control, time-cycle management and continuous cost reductions. Training is available through 37 two-year college campuses throughout Ohio.

Enterprise Ohio: Links business and industry to the training resources of Ohio's two-year community and technical colleges. Encourages training to upgrade individuals' skills, fosters job retention and increased productivity. Training is available through 53 two-year college campuses throughout Ohio.

* Management Consulting and Other Services

Ohio Department of Development
P.O.Box 1001
Columbus, OH 43266-0101   1-800-848-1300
    Ohio Procurement Technical Assistance Program   614-466-5111
Provides in-depth counseling, technical resources, and financial guidance for Ohio businesses. Advocate for small firms doing business with the federal government. Maintains a federal contracts bid-matching service for a fee.

    International Trade Division   614-466-5017
International Trade Assistance: Helps Ohio firms export their products, matches Ohio businesses with potential foreign buyers, represents businesses at international trade shows and conducts trade missions, sponsors export seminars, arranges business meetings between visiting foreign delegations and Ohio companies. No charge for counseling. Costs are incurred by firms for trade show and trade mission involvement, and for participation in export seminars.

    Ohio Technology Transfer Organization   614-466-3887
Provides access research and technology and colleges and universities, Wright Patterson Air Force Base, Federal Research Labs, and 700 federal and private research facilities. Offers on-site technical assistance and manufacturing consulting. Available to any Ohio business or potential business. Locations at 28 colleges and universities around the state.

    Ohio Data User Center   614-466-2115
Possesses an extensive database of current information on census and statistical, demographic, economic, specific trade, industry and labor analyses. Available to anyone at no charge. Offices are in Columbus and 42 affiliate centers.

    Small Business Innovation Research Program (SBIR)   614-466-5867
SBIR Winners Support System: Offers SBIR winners a wide range of services including funding between Phase I and Phase II awards (see Financing Section - Bridge Grant Program), assistance in identifying potential partners or customers, securing funding for commercialization through Phase III Funding conferences, and access to a network of public and private experts through a Mentor Network.

SBIR Research Technical Assistance Center: Provides small businesses with direct, hands-on assistance in identifying research topics, guides businesses through the proposal writing process from design to review, and offers educational and technical services. There are seven Technical Assistance Centers throughout the state.

    Buy Ohio Program   614-752-7393
Provides marketing consultation for Ohio-made products, assists with promotions, special events, and media coverage, develops buyer/seller relationships. Available to all Ohio retailers and manufacturers of Ohio-made products.

    Division of Travel and Tourism   614-466-8844
                                           1-800-BUCKEYE
Promotes Ohio as a "Getaway" travel destination. Assists the travel industry through a series of innovative programs, cooperative advertising, public relations, familiarization tours, special promotions and educational seminars. Available to all travel-related businesses and organizations.

Division of Technological Innovation
775 High Street, 25th Floor
State of Ohio
Department of Development   614-466-3086
Columbus, OH 43215   1-800-848-1300
    Technology Information Exchange and Innovation Network (TIE-IN):
TIE-IN combines information on research and development, resources, and funding in Ohio. Links entrepreneurs, investors, government, and

business resources. Available to business people, educational institutions, and government agencies, with access at 35 different sites. It also performs searches on the Small Business Innovative Research Grants.

Small Business Administration
2 Nationwide Plaza
Suite 1400   614-469-6860
Columbus, OH 43215-2592   FAX: 614-469-2391
    Small Business Institutes: This program provides personalized consulting services to the small business community. Consulting is provided by senior level business students, guided by a faculty advisor. Assistance in business plan preparation, marketing research, market planning, accounting, and seminars are provided.
    University Locations:
    Ashland University
    Baldwin-Wallace College
    Bluffton College
    Bowling Green State University
    Capital University
    Cleveland State University
    Defiance College
    Franciscan University - Steubenville
    Kent State University
    Lake Erie College
    Marietta College
    Miami University
    Mt. Union College
    Ohio Northern University
    Ohio University
    University of Akron
    University of Cincinnati
    University of Dayton
    University of Rio Grande
    University of Toledo
    Walsh College
    Wittenberg University
    Wright State University
    Xavier University
    Youngstown State University

* Small Business Development Centers
The following offices offer free and fee-based services to new and expanding businesses:

Lead Center:
Ohio Small Business Development Center
Department of Development
State Office Tower
P.O. Box 1001   614-466-2480
Columbus, OH 43226-0101   FAX: 614-466-0829

    Akron: Small Business Development Center, Akron Regional Development Board, One Cascade Plaza, 8th Floor, Akron, OH 44308, 216-379-3170; FAX: 216-379-3164.

    Archbold: Northwest Technical College, Small Business Development Center, Star Route 34, Box 246-A, Archbold, OH 43502, 419-267-5511; FAX: 419-267-5233.

    Athens: Ohio University, Small Business Development Center, Innovation Center, One President Drive, Suite 104, Athens, OH 45701, 614-593-1797; FAX: 614-593-1795.

    Athens: Athens Small Business Center, Inc., 900 East State Street, Athens OH 45701, 614-582-1188; FAX: 614-593-7744.

    Bowling Green: Wood County Small Business Development Center, WSOS Community Action Commission, Inc., P.O. Box 48, 118 E. Oak Street, bowling Green, OH 43402, 419-352-7469; FAX: 419-353-3291.

    Canton: Small Business Development Center, Greater Stark Development Board, 800 Savannah Avenue, N.E., Canton, OH 44704, 216-453-5900; FAX: 216-453-1793.

    Celina: Wright State University, Lake Campus, Small Business

Development Center, 7600 State Route 703, Celina, OH 45882, 419-586-2365; FAX: 419-586-4048.

Chillicothe: Chillicothe-Ross Chamber of Commerce, Small Business Development Center, 165 S. Paint Street, Chillicothe, OH 45601, 614-772-4530; FAX: 614-772-5335.

Cincinnati: Cincinnati Small Business Development Center, IAMS Research Park, MC189, 1111 Edison Avenue, Cincinnati, OH 45216-2265, 513-753-7141; FAX: 513-948-2109.

Cincinnati: Clemont County Chamber of Commerce, Small Business Development Center, 4440 Glen Este-Withamsville Road, Cincinnati, OH, 513-753-7141; FAX: 513-753-7146.

Cleveland: Greater Cleveland Growth Association, Small Business Development Center, 200 Tower City Center, 50 Public Square, Cleveland, OH 44113-2291, 216-621-3300; FAX: 216-621-6013.

Columbus: Columbus Small Business Development Center, Columbus Area Chamber of Commerce, 37 North High Street, Columbus, OH 43216, 614-221-1321; FAX: 614-469-8250.

Coshocton: Coshocton Area Chamber of Commerce, Small Business Development Center, 124 Chestnut Street, Coshocton, OH 43812, 614-622-5411; FAX: 614-622-9902.

Dayton: Dayton Area Chamber of Commerce, Small Business Development Center, Chamber Plaza, 5th and Main Streets, Dayton, OH 45402-2400, 513-226-8230; FAX: 513-226-8294.

Fremont: North Central Small Business Development Center, Fremond Office, Terra Technical College, 1220 Cedar Street, Freemont, OH 43420, 419-332-1002; FAX: 419-334-2300.

Jefferson: Ashtabula County Economic Development Council, Inc., Small Business Development Center, 36 West Walnut Street, Jefferson, OH 44047, 216-576-9134; FAX: 216-576-5003.

Lima: Lima Technical College, Small Business Development Center, 545 West Market Street, Suite 305, Lima, OH 45801-5320, 419-229-5320; FAX: 419-229-5424.

Logan: Logan-Hocking Chamber of Commerce, Small Business Development Center, 11 1/2 West Main Street, Box 838, Logan, OH 43138, 614-385-7259; FAX: 614-385-8999.

Lorain: Lorain County Chamber of Commerce, Small Business Development Center, 6001 S. Broadway, Lorain, OH 44053, 216-246-2833; FAX: 216-246-4050.

Mansfield: Mid-Ohio Small Business Development Center, 193 N. Main Street, Mansfield, OH 44902, 419-332-1002; FAX: 419-522-4198.

Marietta: Marietta College, Small Business Development Center, Marietta, OH 45750, 614-374-4649; FAX: 614-374-4763.

Marion: Marion Small Business Development Center, Marion Area Chamber of Commerce, 206 S. Prospect Street, Marion, OH 43302, 614-382-2181; FAX: 614-387-7722.

Mentor: Lakeland Community College, Lake County Economic Development Center, Small Business Development Center, Mentor, OH 44080, 216-951-1290; FAX: 216-953-4413.

New Philadelphia: Tuscarawas Chamber of Commerce, Small Business Development Center, 1323 Fourth Street, NW, P.O. Box 232, New Philadelphia, OH 44663, 216-343-4474; FAX: 216-343-6526.

Piqua: Upper Valley Joint Vocational School, Small Business Development Center, 8811 Career Drive, North County Road 25A, Piqua, OH 45356, 513-778-8419; FAX: 513-778-9237.

Portsmouth: Portsmouth Area Chamber of Commerce, Small Business Development Center, P.O. Box 509, 729 Sixth Street, Portsmouth, OH 45662, 614-353-1116; FAX: 614-353-5824.

St. Clairsville: Department of Development of the CIC of Belmont County, Small Business Development Center, St. Clairsville Office, 100 East Main Street, St. Clairsville, OH 43950, 614-695-9678; FAX: 614-695-4921.

Sandusky: North Central Small Business Development Center, Sandusky Office, 407 Decatur Street, Sandusky, OH 44870, 1-800-548-6507; FAX: 419-626-9176.

Southport: Lawrence County Chamber of Commerce, Small Business Development Center, U.S. Route 52 and Solida Road, P.O. Box 488, Southport, OH 45680, 614-894-3838; FAX: 614-894-3836.

Steubenville: Greater Steubenville Chamber of Commerce, Small Business Development Center, 630 Market Street, P.O. Box 278, Steubenville, OH 43952, 614-282-6226; FAX: 614-282-6285.

Youngstown: Youngstown State University, Cushwa Center for Industrial Development, Small Business Development Center, Youngstown, OH 44555, 216-742-3495; FAX: 216-742-3784.

Zanesville: Zanesville Area Chamber of Commerce, Small Business Development Center, 217 North Fifth Street, Zanesville, OH 43701, 614-452-4868; FAX: 614-454-2963.

Oklahoma

* General Information

Teamwork Oklahoma 405-843-9770
P.O. Box 26980 FAX: 405-841-5199
Oklahoma City, OK 73126-0980 1-800-879-6552
   A business referral service that acquaints business persons or potential business person with the many financial and consulting services available in Oklahoma.

Oklahoma Department of Commerce
P.O. Box 26980 405-841-5236
Oklahoma City, OK 73126-0980 FAX: 405-841-5199
   Small Business Advocate: Assistance in cutting bureaucratic red tape. Information and expertise in dealing with state, federal, and local agencies.

* Financing

Oklahoma Development Finance Authority
301 NW 63rd, Suite 225
Oklahoma City, OK 73116-7904 405-848-9687
   Loans: Provides funding in loan packages for manufacturing and industrial parks. May loan up to 33 1/3 percent of a project's cost of land, buildings, and stationary manufacturing equipment with a first mortgage on the assets up to a maximum loan of $1 million. It may also loan up to 66 percent of a project's cost for land, buildings, and stationary manufacturing equipment secured with a first mortgage on the assets. Maximum loan is $2 million.

Oklahoma Industrial Finance Authority
301 NW 63rd
Suite 225
Oklahoma City, OK 73116-7904 405-842-1145
   Loans: Available to manufacturers plus recreational, agriculture processing, livestock processing and conditioning, and mine resource processors. Can loan up to 66-2/3 percent of the cost of land, buildings and fixed equipment on a secured first mortgage and 33-1/3 percent on a second mortgage. Maximum loan amount is $1.25 million per project on a first mortgage, $750,000 on a second mortgage.

Office of the State Treasurer
Room 217, State Capitol Building
Oklahoma City, OK 73105 405-521-3191
   Oklahoma Small Business Linked Deposit Program: Loans are available of up to $1 million for small businesses and $5 million for industrial parks.

Loan must create new jobs or preserve existing ones. Terms not to exceed two years, but may be renewed up to 2 additional years.

Agricultural Linked Deposit Program: Available for farmers who meet certain criteria. The linked deposit commitment cannot exceed 2 years, but may be renewed. The interest rates are fixed and are calculated based on the current T-note auction rate minus 3 percent.

Small Business Administration (SBA) District Office
200 N.W. 5th St.
Oklahoma City, OK 73102   405-231-4301
                                        FAX: 405-231-4876

SBA 7(a) Guaranteed and Direct Loans: Guarantees up to 90 percent of a loan made through a private lender up to $750,000. Can be used for working capital, expand or convert facilities, purchase of machinery and equipment, and land and building. Available only to those unable to obtain a loan from conventional sources. Direct loans are made up to $150,000.

SBA 504: Provides loans using 50 percent conventional bank financing, 40 percent SBA involvement through Certified Development Companies, and 10 percent owner equity. Fixed-asset loans are available in amounts up to $750,000. The loan can be used for land and building, construction, machinery and equipment, and renovation/expansion.

Small Business Innovative Research Grants (SBIR): Phase I awards between $20,000 to $50,000 to entrepreneurs to support six months of research on a technical innovation. Phase II grants are an additional $500,000 for development. Private sector investment funds must follow.

International Trade Loans: Guaranteed long-term loans through private lenders to develop or expand export markets, or to recover from the effects of import competition. Maximum guaranteed loan is $1,000,000 for fixed assets and an additional $250,000 for working capital and/or export revolving line of credit.

Export Revolving Line of Credit Loan: Short term financing available to small businesses that are at least one year old. Loans provide working capital to finance the manufacturing or wholesaling of products for export and for export marketing. The SBA will guarantee up to 90 percent of a conventional loan in amounts up to $750,000.

Contract Loan: Short-term loans are available to small businesses to finance the costs of labor and materials on contracts for which the proceeds are assignable. Program guarantees up to 90 percent of loans not in excess of $750,000. Qualifying small businesses must be in business for at least 12 calendar months prior to the date of the loan application.

Seasonal Line of Credit Loan: Loans provide short-term working capital to finance seasonal increases in business activities. Program guarantees up to 90 percent of loans not in excess of $750,000. Qualifying business must be in operation for at least one year prior to application.

Pollution Control Loans: Long-term guaranteed loans can be made by conventional financing to small businesses for installation or required pollution control measures. Must be unable to adopt the pollution control measures without undue financial hardship. Maximum guaranteed loan is $1,000,000.

General Contractor Loans: Small general construction contractors may obtain short-term loans or loan guarantees for residential or commercial construction or rehabilitation of property to be sold. The SBA will guarantee up to 90 percent of qualifying loans made by private lenders up to a maximum of $750,000. Direct loans can be up to $150,000.

Energy Business Loan Guarantee: Small businesses that provide certain energy production and conservation services for others may qualify for long-term loans and loan guarantees for start-ups and expansions. Loans and guarantees are made for firms that develop, manufacture, sell, install, or service specific energy measures for others, or firms that provide engineering, architectural, consulting, or other professional services connected with specific energy measures. Guarantee is for up to 90 percent of a loan not in excess of $750,000. Direct loans up to $150,000.

Disaster Recovery Loans: Small businesses located in federally designated disaster areas and suffering property damage or economic losses from the disaster can obtain long-term recovery loans at low interest rates. Property damage loans are limited to 85 percent of the verified damage. Loans for economic losses are for operating capital to meet the business' obligations that could have been made had the disaster not occurred.

Handicapped Assistance Loans: Assists persons who have a physical, mental or emotional disability of a permanent nature which limits the selection of any type of employment for which the person would otherwise be qualified. Direct loans are available for up to $150,000. The interest rate is 3% on these loans.

Surety Bond Guaranty Program: Makes the bonding system more available to small contractors who may be denied access to the system. SBA can guarantee up to 80 percent of surety's loss on a bond that has a maximum in total contract value of up to $1,250,000.

Vietnam-era and Disabled Veterans Loan Program: Provides direct loans to veterans to establish or expand a small business. Funds may be used for working capital or fixed assets. Direct loans for amounts up to $150,000 are available. The interest rate may be fixed or variable.

Alliance Business Investment Company
17 East Second Street
One Williams Center
Suite 2000
Tulsa, OK 74172   918-584-3581

Small Business Investment Companies (SBIC): The SBA licenses, regulates, and provides financial assistance to privately owned and operated Small Business Investment Companies. SBICs make venture or risk investments by supplying capital and extending unsecured loans and loans not fully collateralized to small enterprises which meet their investment criteria. Financing is made by direct loans and by equity investments.

HUD Regional Office
Murrah Federal Building
200 N.W. Fifth St.
Oklahoma City, OK 73102-3202   405-231-4181

Urban Development Action Grants (UDAG): Awarded to communities which then lend the proceeds at flexible rates to eligible businesses. Projects whose total costs are less than $100,000 are not eligible. UDAG funds should leverage at least three to four times their amount in private sector investment.

Oklahoma Department of Commerce
P.O. Box 26980
Oklahoma City, OK 73126-0980   1-800-879-6552
Community Affairs and Development Division   405-841-9326
Community Development Block Grants - Economic Development Financing: Grants are awarded to cities and counties, who in turn provide gap financing to start-up and expanding businesses, for the commercial rehabilitation of existing buildings or structures used for business, commercial, or industrial purposes. Financing of up to $500,000 can be made per project. Purpose of the program is to create new jobs for low and moderate income persons in non-metropolitan areas of the state.

Small Business Demonstration Energy Conservation Grant Program: Provides grants to small businesses to provide practical demonstrations of energy conservation measures which have potential for widespread use.

Research and Planning Division   405-841-5156
Enterprise Zone Program: There are 27 cities, 9 counties and 35 Labor Surplus Areas that are designated enterprise zones. Incentives for qualified businesses locating in an enterprise zone includes double investment/new jobs tax credits, general obligation bond financing.

Capital Resources Division   405-841-5150
Export Finance Program: Helps to increase export opportunities and enhance the internal competitiveness of business by providing both export insurance coverage and access to working capital (based on insured accounts receivable).

Farmers Home Administration
USDA Agriculture Building
Stillwater, OK 74074   405-624-4294

Business and Industrial Loan Program: Encourages the retention of jobs in rural areas. FmHA will guarantee up to 90 percent of a loan from a commercial institution.

Venture Capital Exchange
Enterprise Development Center
University of Tulsa
600 South College Ave.
Tulsa, OK 74104   918-631-2684, ext. 3152 or 2684

A not-for-profit corporation geared toward linking entrepreneurs and investors, Venture Capital Exchange (VCE) helps fill the gaps in equity financing options available in the $20,000--$500,000 range. It operates a database available only to designated investors and entrepreneurs. Matches are made anonymously, until an investor finds a business he is interested in. Then the two parties are introduced and VCE ends its role. The service costs $100 for both investors and entrepreneurs. Following are some of the Venture Capital Companies in Oklahoma:

Oklahoma City: Energy Seed Fund, Oklahoma Department of Commerce, Capital Resources Division, P.O. Box 26980, Oklahoma City, OK 73126-0980, 405-843-9770, ext. 161.

Oklahoma City: McGowan Investment Company, P.O. Box 270008, 4341 Will Rogers Parkway, Oklahoma City, OK 73137, 405-946-9706.

Oklahoma City: OKC Innovation Center, 101 Park Ave., Suite 500, Oklahoma City, OK 73102, 405-235-3127.

Tulsa: ML Oklahoma Venture Partners, L.P., 6100 S. Yale Avenue, Suite 2019, Tulsa, OK 74136, 918-491-6700.

Tulsa: Davis Venture Partners, L.P., One Williams Center, Suite 2000, Tulsa, OK 74172, 918-584-7272.

Tulsa: TSF Capital Corporation, 2407 East Skelly Dr., Suite 102, Tulsa, OK 74105, 918-747-2600.

Tulsa: Tulsa Innovation Center, 1216 Lansing, Tulsa, OK 74106.

The three **Venture Capital Clubs** in Oklahoma offer forums where entrepreneurs can publicly present their ventures to potential investors:

Bartlesville: Venture Capital Club, Tri-County Business Assistance Center, 6105 S. Nowata Road, Bartlesville, OK 74006-6010, 918-333-3422.

Oklahoma City: The Oklahoma Venture Forum, P.O. Box 2176, Oklahoma City, OK 73101-2176, 405-636-9736.

Tulsa: Oklahoma Private Enterprise Forum, Metropolitan Tulsa Chamber of Commerce, 616 South Boston, Tulsa, OK 74119, 918-585-1201, ext. 242.

* Women and Minority Business Assistance

Oklahoma Department of Commerce
Small Business Division
P.O. Box 26980
Oklahoma City, OK 73126-0980   405-841-5227

Minority Business Development Program: Provides support and assistance in the establishment, growth and expansion of viable business enterprises. Counseling in the preparation of business plans and marketing strategies available. Provides assistance for loan packaging, bid preparation, feasibility studies and certification requirements.

Women-Owned Business Assistance Program   405-841-5242
A variety of technical assistance including business planning, marketing assistance, financial information and government procurement.

Small Business Administration (SBA) District Office
200 N.W. 5th St.   405-231-4301
Oklahoma City, OK 73102   FAX: 405-231-4876

SBA 8(a) Program - Business Procurement Assistance: Provides federal government contracting opportunities for small businesses owned by socially and economically disadvantaged persons, and assists these businesses to become independently competitive in the normal business environment. SBA monitors all government contracts to assure that a quota of contract work goes to 8(a) businesses. Also provides business management services to these businesses. Business must be approved for program participation prior to receipt of an 8(a) contract.

See Management Consulting and Other Services, Small Business Division

* Training

Oklahoma Department of Commerce
Employment and Training Division
P.O. Box 26980   405-843-9770
Oklahoma City, OK 73126-0980   1-800-879-6552

Job Training Partnership Act (JTPA): Provides employers with recruitment, screening, referral, training, 50 percent wage subsidy up to 3 months for on-the-job training. Available to any private employer.

Training for Industry Program (TIP): Provides tailor-made training free of charge for companies establishing new business ventures. Also meets continued training requirements for those companies expanding within the state. Includes planning, training facilities, training aid, supplies and materials and supervisor training.

* Management Consulting and Other Services

Oklahoma Business Assistance Network
1500 W. 7th
Stillwater, OK 74074   405-377-2000

Bid Assistance Network: For Oklahoma firms interested in obtaining federal government contracts. Provides federal bid research, notification and preparation assistance at 21 centers throughout the state. Services are free of charge.

Oklahoma Department of Commerce   405-843-9770
P.O. Box 26908   FAX: 405-851-5199
Oklahoma City, OK 73126-0980   1-800-879-6552

Community Affairs and Development Division   405-841-9326
Self Employment Entrepreneurial Development Program System (SEEDS): Provides start-up financing, business training, business plan development of viable micro-businesses initiated by low-income and unemployed persons. Intent of this program is to develop entrepreneurs and offer an alternative of self-employment.

Small Business Division   405-841-5255
Technical assistance programs available are General Small Business Assistance, Minority/Individual Indiana/Women Owned Business Assistance, Tribal Government Assistance and the Main Street Program. Provides a wide range of business assistance publications including *A Guide for Small Business* and *Teamwork Oklahoma Guide to Business Assistance.* Sponsors workshops and how-to seminars.

Capital Resources Division   405-841-5139
Tax Estimator Program: Assists the private sector with comprehensive Oklahoma business tax and incentive information. A specially designed computer tax program enables a business person planning an expansion in Oklahoma or planning relocation into Oklahoma to determine the tax costs and benefits. The program can project up to 10 years the next tax effect of various state tax laws and benefits programs. Available on diskette at a nominal cost.

International Division   405-841-5217
Assists small and medium size manufacturers by providing export marketing information, consultation and promotion of products in foreign markets. Offices are located in Japan, India, People's Republic of China and Singapore.

Foreign Trade Zones: Permit businesses engaged in international trade to benefit from special customs procedures while engaged in warehousing, manufacturing or assembling goods within the designated areas. Foreign trade zones have been designated in Oklahoma City, Tulsa and Muskogee.

International Recruitment Programs: Coordinates a network of foreign trade offices. Provide personalized assistance to foreign investors considering the state. Coordinate trade missions to various countries.

Export Council   405-841-5151
An organization of management leadership from companies and organizations whose international business knowledge and experience provide a source of advice, assistance, and program development to firms and persons seeking to develop or expand their export sales and operations.

U.S. Department of Commerce: 405-841-5221
Oklahoma International Export Services Program: A joint program of the state and federal Departments of Commerce and the International Trade Administration. Provides information and details of export marketing, financing, shipping, documentation, insurance, U.S. regulatory controls, foreign trade laws, overseas investment, marketing, licensing, patents and trademarks.

Capital Resources Division   505-841-5139
Capital Resources Network: Provides finance specialists to help businesses analyze their financing needs and options. Review business plans, recommend finance structures and offer guidance during the planning process.

Inventors Assistance Program: The program is designed to advance the techniques of new product development throughout the state. Works with individual inventors, with companies that have licensed technology, and with manufacturers seeking new product concepts. Coordinate the analysis of individual inventions for technical and market feasibility. Inventions that have commercial potential are linked with sources of marketing and manufacturing assistance.

Research and Planning Division   405-841-5170
Oklahoma State Data Center: Offers population, census and statistical information to governments, academic, private business clients, and others involved in development. Maintains a complete inventory of all Census products for the state and can provide these products on computer tapes and diskettes or in written form.

Business Development Division:
Small Business Incubator Incentives Program   405-841-5255
Tenants in an approved incubator are eligible to receive state income tax exemption for two years from the date of incubator occupancy.

Film Office   405-841-5136 Oklahoma City
918-581-2806 Tulsa
1-800-766-3456
Supports all aspects of the industry from pre-production to actual shooting days. Services provided include immediate response to initial inquiry, same day mailing of photos and information, free location scouting, acting as liaison with state, county, and local government, production directory updates, and on set assistance.

Community Affairs and Development Division   405-841-9326
Rural/Small Business Energy Audits: Provides professional industry-level energy audits at no charge to firms within the local electric co-op and annexed areas of less than 100 persons per square mile in larger communities.

Energy Public Information: Provides current information to the general public on a variety of energy conservation practices and commercially available technologies.

Interest Subsidy Program: Assists the small business owner/operator to obtain capital improvement loans for energy conservation.

Oklahoma Center for The Advancement of Science and Technology (OCAST)
205 N.W. 63rd, Suite 305
Oklahoma City, OK 73116   405-848-2633
Stimulates technological innovation in state businesses by funding basic and applied research, development, and technology transfer at academic institutions, non-profit research centers and the private sector. The Center provides funds for acquiring scientists and equipment, matching funds for applied research, funds for health research, and incentive funds for small business innovation research. It also provides matching funds to Centers of Excellence, which are collaborations between institutions of higher education and business. In addition, OCAST has begun a Seed Capital

Funding program, under which it will be able to issue grants, loans, and investment with promising business ventures.

Rural Enterprises
422 Cessena Drive
Durant, OK 74701   405-924-5094
Assists with business planning and finance packages in rural areas.

Center for Business and Economic Development
University of Oklahoma 1700 Asp
Norman, OK 73037   405-325-5627
Provides comprehensive business assistance.

Small Business Administration District Office
200 N.W. 5th St.   405-231-4301
Oklahoma City, OK 73102   FAX: 405-231-4876
Small Business Institutes: This program provides personalized consulting services to the small business community. Consulting is provided by senior level business students, guided by a faculty advisor. Assistance in business plan preparation, marketing research, market planning, accounting, and seminars are provided.
University Locations:
Cameron University
Central State University
East Central University
Langston University
Northeastern Oklahoma State University
Northwestern Oklahoma State University
Oklahoma Christian College
Oklahoma City University
Oklahoma State University
Oral Roberts University
Phillips University
Southeastern Oklahoma State University
Southern Nazarene University
Southwestern Oklahoma State University
University of Oklahoma
University of Tulsa

* Small Business Development Centers
The following offices offer free and fee-based services to new and expanding businesses:

Lead Center:
Oklahoma Small Business Development Center Network
Southeastern Oklahoma State University   405-924-0277
Station A, Box 2584   1-800-522-6154
Durant, OK 74701   FAX: 405-924-8531

Ada: East Central State University, Small Business Development Center, 1036 East 10th, Ada, OK 74820, 405-436-3190; FAX: 405-521-6516.

Alva: Northwestern State University, Small Business Development Center, Alva, OK 73717, 405-327-5883; FAX: 405-327-1881.

Durant: Southeastern State University, Small Business Development Center, 517 University, Durant, OK 74701, 405-924-0277; FAX: 405-924-7071.

Edmond: University of Central Oklahoma, Small Business Development Center, 100 North University Boulevard, Edmond, OK 73034, 405-359-1968; FAX: 405-341-4946.

Enid: Phillips University, Enid Satellite Center, 100 South University Avenue, Enid, OK 73701, 405-242-7989; FAX: 405-237-1607.

Langston: Langston University, Minority Assistance Center, P.O. Box 667, Langston, OK 73050, 405-466-3256; FAX: 405-466-3381.

Lawton: Lawton Satellite Center, Small Business Development Center, American National Bank Building, 601 SW "D", Suite 209, Lawton, OK 73501, 405-248-4946; FAX: 405-355-3560.

Midwest City: Rose State College, Procurement Specialty Center, 6420 Southeast 15th Street, Midwest City, OK 73110, 405-733-7348; FAX: 405-733-7495.

Oklahoma City: Oklahoma Department of Commerce, Small Business Development Center, 6601 Broadway Extension, Oklahoma City, OK 73116, 405-841-5236; FAX: 405-841-5199.

Poteau: Carl Albert Junior College, Poteau Satellite Center, Small Business Development Center, 1507 South McKenna, Poteau, OK 74953, 918-647-4019; FAX: 918-647-2980.

Tahlequah: Northeastern State University, Small Business Development Center, Tahlequah, OK 74464, 918-458-0802; FAX: 918-458-2193.

Tulsa: Tulsa Satellite Center, State Office Building, 440 South Houston, Suite 206, Tulsa, OK 74107, 918-581-2502; FAX: 918-581-2844.

Weatherford: Southwestern State University, Small Business Development Center, 100 Campus Drive, Weatherford, OK 73096, 405-774-1040; FAX: 405-772-5447.

Oregon

* General Information

Department of Economic Development
775 Summer Street N.E.
Salem, OR 97310

Business Development Division   503-373-1225
Provides information to business investors on land, buildings, financing, and other relevant issues. Provides consulting services for manufacturing and processing companies with problems. Supports local economic development organizations in expansion efforts. Manages the Oregon Enterprize Zone program which offers property tax relief incentives in 30 specified regions, and a computer-based inventory of available industrial sites and buildings in the state. The Division maintains regional offices in six locations around the state.

Small Business Program   503-373-1241
HOTLINE: 1-800-442-8275 in Oregon
Assistance in cutting bureaucratic red tape. Information and expertise in dealing with state, federal, and local agencies.

* Financing

Oregon Economic Development Department
775 Summer Street N.E.
Salem, OR 97310
Business Finance Section   503-373-1240
Oregon Business Development Fund Loans (OBDF): Structures and issues loans to small businesses. Manufacturing, processing, and tourism related projects are eligible. Emphasis on rural areas, enterprise zones, and businesses with 50 employees or less. Offers long-term fixed-rate financing land, buildings, machinery and equipment, permanent working capital. Preference given to projects which will create a minimum of one job every $15,000 of OBDF investment. 17 percent of OBDF money is set aside for OBDF loans of $50,000 or less. 15 percent of available money is set aside for emerging small business in economically depressed areas. Maximum loan is 40 percent of eligible project costs and may not exceed $250,000 per project. 10 percent owner equity required in most cases.

Industrial Development Revenue Bonds (IDRBs): Industrial revenue bonds are issued by the Economic Development Commission to qualified manufacturing, processing and tourism related facilities. Only manufacturing projects are exempt from federal taxes. Major program goal is job creation. Eligible companies may borrow from $500,000 to $10,000,000.

Composite Revenue Bond Program: Allows the state to combine several Industrial Development Revenue Bond projects into one bond issue. The composite" issue will be large enough to achieve an average issuance cost lower than individual borrowers within the issue could obtain alone. Each individual loan is secured by a letter of credit from borrower's bank. Tax exempt rates are typically 75-80 percent of conventional rates. Funds can be used to finance fixed assets.

Local Revolving Loan Funds: There are many revolving loan funds for small business financing administered by Oregon's local government, and development groups. These funds frequently come from sources such as Dept. of Housing and Urban Development (HUD) through the State of Oregon, and the Federal Economic Development Administration (EDA).

Community Development Section   503-378-3732
Community Development Block Grant Program (CDBG): Through grants to eligible cities and counties, individual businesses may apply for direct loans for expansion or relocation. Grants are to be used for businesses which will create or retain permanent jobs, the majority of which will be made available to low and moderate income people. Money can be used for either a loan from the city or county to a business or to pay for construction of public infrastructure required to serve a business project. Must create or retain at least one job per $12,000 of CDBG funds. For public infrastructure projects, one job must be created or retain for every $20,000 of CDBG funds. Loans are for a maximum of $500,000 per project.

Special Public Works Fund (SPWF): Provides Lottery funds for construction of public infrastructure necessary to support business development projects that result in creation or retention of permanent jobs. Eligible to Oregon cities, counties, port districts, water districts, metropolitan service districts, and federally recognized Indian tribes. Funding is provided by loans or combination of loans and grants. Maximum award per project is $1 million, and at lease one permanent, full-time job must be created or retained for every $20,000 of SPWF assistance. Technical assistance grants up to $10,000 available for municipalities with populations of less than 5,000.

Business Development Division   503-373-1225
Enterprise Zone Program: There are 30 enterprise zones established to stimulate business investment. Firms locating or expanding on an enterprise zone is eligible for property tax relief. In addition, state and local government land within an enterprise zone not already designated for some public use is available for sale or lease at fair market value. Individual enterprise zones may offer other incentives.

Oregon Economic Development Department
Ports Division/International Trade Division
1 World Trade Center
121 S.W. Salmon Street, Suite 300
Portland, OR 97204   503-229-5625
Oregon Port Revolving Loan Fund: Long-term loans to the 23 legally formed Port Districts are offered through this fund at lower than market interest rates. Individual loans may be made to a maximum of $500,000 per project. Money may be used for port development projects (infrastructure) or assist private business development projects. A wide variety of projects qualify such as water-oriented facilities, industrial parks, airports, and eligible commercial or industrial developments. Revolving fund loans may also be used for matching funds for grants from federal, state and local agencies.

In addition, port districts are authorized to issue **Tax Exempt Industrial Development Bonds** either for their own operations or for companies locating or expanding within the port districts.

Portland Development Commission
1120 SW Fifth, Suite 1100
Portland, OR 97204   503-796-5300
The City of Portland has authority to issue **Industrial Development Revenue Bonds.** The city also administers several **Revolving Loan Funds** targeted to serve business within specific areas of the City.

Oregon Department of Energy
625 Marion Street N.E.   503-373-1033
Salem, OR 97310   1-800-221-8035 in Oregon
Small-Scale Energy Loan Program (SELP): Finances energy conservation and renewable energy projects in Oregon. Projects may be sponsored by individuals, businesses, non-profit organizations, and municipal corporations. Eligible projects are those which conserve conventional energy such as electricity and natural gas; or produce renewable energy from geothermal or solar sources, or from water, wind, biomass, and some waste

materials. Can be used for equipment costs, construction, certain design and consultant fees, some reserves, construction interest, and most loan closing costs. Interest rates are fixed and typically lower than market. Can finance eligible equipment costs, construction, certain design and consultant fees, some reserves, construction interest, and most closing costs.

Business Energy Tax Credit: Designed to encourage businesses to invest in energy conservation, use renewable energy resources and recycle. Examples of qualifying projects are weatherization, energy-efficient lighting, and equipment to process and haul recyclable materials. Maximum allowable credit is 35 percent of the certified cost.

Oregon State Treasury
159 State Capitol
Salem, OR 97310 503-378-4111

Commercial Mortgage Program: Provides financing for large real estate development projects. Allows financial institutions to sell real estate mortgages to state of Oregon which enables lenders to provide financing for large projects that they might not otherwise be able to finance. Usually the program consists of ten-year, fixed-rate loan with a 25 year amortization for Oregon properties with multi-purpose use. Maximum loan to value is 75 percent.

Small Business Administration (SBA)
222 S.W. Columbia
Suite 500 503-326-2682
Portland, OR 97201-6605 FAX: 503-326-2808

SBA 7(a) Guaranteed and Direct Loans: Guarantees up to 90 percent of a loan made through a private lender up to $750,000. Can be used for working capital, expand or convert facilities, purchase of machinery and equipment, and land and building. Available only to those unable to obtain a loan from conventional sources. Direct loans are made up to $150,000.

SBA 504: Provides loans using 50 percent conventional bank financing, 40 percent SBA involvement through Certified Development Companies, and 10 percent owner equity. Fixed-asset loans are available in amounts up to $750,000. The loan can be used for land and building, construction, machinery and equipment, and renovation/expansion.

Small Business Innovative Research Grants (SBIR): Phase I awards between $20,000 to $50,000 to entrepreneurs to support six months of research on a technical innovation. Phase II grants are an additional $500,000 for development. Private sector investment funds must follow.

International Trade Loans: Guaranteed long-term loans through private lenders to develop or expand export markets, or to recover from the effects of import competition. Maximum guaranteed loan is $1,000,000 for fixed assets and an additional $250,000 for working capital and/or export revolving line of credit.

Export Revolving Line of Credit Loan: Short term financing available to small businesses that are at least one year old. Loans provide working capital to finance the manufacturing or wholesaling of products for export and for export marketing. The SBA will guarantee up to 90 percent of a conventional loan in amounts up to $750,000.

Contract Loan: Short-term loans are available to small businesses to finance the costs of labor and materials on contracts for which the proceeds are assignable. Program guarantees up to 90 percent of loans not in excess of $750,000. Qualifying small businesses must be in business for at least 12 calendar months prior to the date of the loan application.

Seasonal Line of Credit Loan: Loans provide short-term working capital to finance seasonal increases in business activities. Program guarantees up to 90 percent of loans not in excess of $750,000. Qualifying business must be in operation for at least one year prior to application.

Pollution Control Loans: Long-term guaranteed loans can be made by conventional financing to small businesses for installation or required pollution control measures. Must be unable to adopt the pollution control measures without undue financial hardship. Maximum guaranteed loan is $1,000,000.

General Contractor Loans: Small general construction contractors may obtain short-term loans or loan guarantees for residential or commercial construction or rehabilitation of property to be sold. The SBA will guarantee up to 90 percent of qualifying loans made by private lenders up to a maximum of $750,000. Direct loans can be up to $150,000.

Energy Business Loan Guarantee: Small businesses that provide certain energy production and conservation services for others may qualify for long-term loans and loan guarantees for start-ups and expansions. Loans and guarantees are made for firms that develop, manufacture, sell, install, or service specific energy measures for others, or firms that provide engineering, architectural, consulting, or other professional services connected with specific energy measures. Guarantee is for up to 90 percent of a loan not in excess of $750,000. Direct loans up to $150,000.

Disaster Recovery Loans: Small businesses located in federally designated disaster areas and suffering property damage or economic losses from the disaster can obtain long-term recovery loans at low interest rates. Property damage loans are limited to 85 percent of the verified damage. Loans for economic losses are for operating capital to meet the business' obligations that could have been made had the disaster not occurred.

Handicapped Assistance Loans: Assists persons who have a physical, mental or emotional disability of a permanent nature which limits the selection of any type of employment for which the person would otherwise be qualified. Direct loans are available for up to $150,000. The interest rate is 3% on these loans.

Surety Bond Guaranty Program: Makes the bonding system more available to small contractors who may be denied access to the system. SBA can guarantee up to 80 percent of surety's loss on a bond that has a maximum in total contract value of up to $1,250,000.

Vietnam-era and Disabled Veterans Loan Program: Provides direct loans to veterans to establish or expand a small business. Funds may be used for working capital or fixed assets. Direct loans for amounts up to $150,000 are available. The interest rate may be fixed or variable.

Northern Pacific Capital Corporation
937 SW 14th Street, Suite 200
Mail: P.O. Box 1658
Portland, OR 97207 503-241-1255

U.S. Bancorp Capital Corporation
111 SW Fifth Avenue, Suite 1570
Portland, OR 97204 503-275-5860

Small Business Investment Companies (SBIC): The SBA licenses, regulates, and provides financial assistance to privately owned and operated Small Business Investment Companies. SBICs make venture or risk investments by supplying capital and extending unsecured loans and loans not fully collateralized to small enterprises which meet their investment criteria. Financing is made by direct loans and by equity investments.

Oregon Department of Agriculture
635 Capitol Street, NE
Salem, OR 97310 503-378-3775

Agricultural Opportunity Fund: Provides grants to private, non-profit organizations and to public agencies for agricultural promotion and marketing projects. Encourages expansion of existing agribusiness and to locate in Oregon.

Oregon Resource and Technology Development Corporation (ORTDC)
1934 N.E. Broadway
Portland OR 97232 503-282-4462

Provides early-state capital to move products into commercial markets or to prove technical feasibility. Eligible to basic sector business and applied research and development projects likely to be successful commercially. Provides management assistance and technical referral services and sponsors a computer-based network to bring entrepreneurs and potential investors together.

Seed Capital Fund: Early found financing for new product development. Investment list is $500,000.

Applied Research: For research leading to commercially viable applications. Limit is $100,000 with a one-to-one match requirement.

Department of Environmental Quality
Management Services Division
811 S.W. Sixth Avenue   503-229-6022
Portland, OR 97204-1390   1-800-452-4011 in Oregon
Pollution Control Tax Credit: Tax credits are provided to encourage the use of pollution control facilities that prevent, control or reduce air, water, noise, hazardous waste, or solid waste pollution, or recycle or dispose of used oil. An income tax or excise tax credit of 50 percent of the cost of the facility that is allocable to pollution control is available.

* Women and Minority Business Assistance

Office of Minority, Women & Emerging Small Businesses (OMWESB)
155 Cottage Street NE, 3rd Floor
Salem, OR 97310   503-378-5651
Certifies disadvantaged and emerging small businesses, allowing their participation in the state's targeted purchasing programs. Also identifies and seeks to remove barriers that prevent these businesses from entering the mainstream of commercial activity.

Small Business Administration
222 S.W. Columbia, Suite 500   503-326-2682
Portland, OR 97201-6605   FAX: 503-326-2808
SBA 8(a) Program - Business Procurement Assistance: Provides federal government contracting opportunities for small businesses owned by socially and economically disadvantaged persons, and assists these businesses to become independently competitive in the normal business environment. SBA monitors all government contracts to assure that a quota of contract work goes to 8(a) businesses. Also provides business management services to these businesses. Business must be approved for program participation prior to receipt of an 8(a) contract.

* Training

Oregon Economic Development Department
775 Summer St. N.E.
Salem, OR 97310
Work Force Development Section:
Partnership Division   503-373-1995, ext. 227
Targeted Training Program: Provides grants to community colleges for targeted training projects to train new employees in order to aid business development and/or job retention in the community. Employers must provide matching funds of at least 50 percent of the grant. Matching funds can be cash or in-kind services.

Job Training Partnership Administration   503-373-1995
Job Training Partnership Act (JTPA): Provides employers with recruitment, screening, referral, training, 50 percent wage subsidy up to 3 months for on-the-job training. Available to any private employer.

Workplace Training for Key Industries
Department of Economic Development
775 Summer St. N.E.
Salem, OR 97310   503-373-1200
Provides grants to community colleges for development and implementation of training programs for multiple firms within an industry. Employers must provide matching funds or in-kind services.

Oregon Department of Education
Job Development and Training Section
700 Pringle Parkway S.E.
Salem, OR 97310-0290   503-378-3584
Oregon's 16 community colleges provide employee training and development programs tailored to each community's needs. Contracts can be negotiated directly with firms and training can be provided at the firm itself or on campus. Course content can be developed jointly by firms and colleges.

Bureau of Labor and Industries
Apprenticeship and Training Division
1400 S.W. Fifth, 4th Floor
Portland, OR 97201   503-731-4072
Apprenticeship: A system of training designed by employers and skilled workers for a particular industry or occupation. A structured program that combines progressively challenging work tasks with thorough classroom training. Programs are designed for one to five years of training.

Oregon Office of Educational Policy and Planning
225 Winter Street, N.E.
Salem, OR 97310   503-378-3921
Oregon Ed-Net: A statewide video, audio, and data network that will furnish job training, education, teleconference, and information services.

Employment Division
875 Union Street, N.E.   503-378-8420
Salem, OR 97311   1-800-237-3710 in Oregon
Employment, Training and Continuing Education Services: Offers employers job placement services in 32 locations throughout Oregon. A computerized job-matching system is used to select the best qualified applicants. Emphasis is placed on placing individuals receiving unemployment benefits. A Targeted Jobs Tax Credit may be available based on wages paid to workers from certain targeted groups.

* Management Consulting and Other Services

Small Business International Trade Program
One World Trade Center
121 S.W. Salmon St.
Suite 210
Portland, OR 97204   503-229-5625
International Trade Program: Assists small businesses to become active in international trade. Offers workshops, seminars, classes, and counseling. It works closely with the Small Business Development Center Network located at community colleges throughout Oregon.

Ports Division: Collects and analyzes data on port activities and researches economic objectives and strategies for port development. The Division also provides technical assistance to port districts for development projects.

Economic Development Department
775 Summer Street, N.E.
Salem, OR 97310
International Trade Division   503-373-1995
Assists wood products and manufacturing firms in approaching international markets. Primarily serves as a matchmaker between Oregon suppliers and potential overseas customers by hosting international delegations and organizing trade shows, trade missions, and technical symposia. Maintains three overseas offices in Japan, Taipei, and Korea.

Forest Products Marketing Program: Marketing program available for forest products which develops contacts and coordinate with other states, federal agencies and private organizations. Program assesses marketing obstacles and opportunities, develops marketing information and establishes trade contacts to improve sales of Oregon forest products.

Community Initiatives Section   503-373-1200
Industrial Retention Service: Provides technical help to companies involved in manufacturing and processing that are having problems that may result in closures or layoffs. Companies meeting certain qualifications may receive technical assistance from professional, private-sector consultants who will analyze all aspects of the company's operation and make recommendations for improvements. Fees are paid by the State from lottery proceeds.

International Trade Institute
One World Trade Center
121 SW Salmon, Suite 230
Portland, OR 97204   503-229-5625
Provides access to the international trade research, information and

advisory capabilities of the State's higher education system. Operates a trade information service that provides computer access to over 300 data sources. The **Business Assistance Program** helps business develop strategies by which they can successfully enter the internal marketplace.

Port of Portland
P.O. Box 3529
Portland, OR 97208   503-231-5000

Oregon International Port of Coos Bay
326 N. Front Street
Coos Bay, OR 97420   503-267-7678
   Foreign Trade Zones: Portland and Coos Bays are designated as Foreign Trade Zones--areas under U.S. Customs supervision into which foreign products may be brought into the country and have duty payments deferred until the goods have left the zone and enter the U.S. stream of commerce. Imports may be stored, exhibited, processed, or assembled without duties being paid until the goods are physically moved out of the zone.

International Trade Administration
Dept. of Commerce/Foreign Commercial Service
121 S.W. Salmon, Suite 242
Portland, OR 97204   503-326-3001
   Provides exporters with marketing information such as trade lists and leads, reports by country on economic conditions abroad, and background reports with historical and geographical information. An international library is maintained with information on marketing in foreign countries, trade statistics, trade regulations, U.S. export control regulations. Also provides individual counseling.

Department of Agriculture
Agricultural Development Division
121 S.W. Salmon, Suite 240
Portland, OR 97204   503-229-6734
   Agricultural Products Marketing Program: Promotes, develops and expands worldwide markets for agricultural products. Members work with cooperatives and processors, organize overseas trade missions and hose income foreign business delegates. Dept. of Agriculture also publishes supplier and trade directories.

Advanced Science and Technology Institute (ASTI)
University of Oregon
318 Hendricks Hall
Eugene, OR 97403   503-346-3189
            or
Advanced Science and Technology Institute
Oregon State University, ADS A312
Corvallis, OR 97331   503-737-0671
   Links research performed at universities with Oregon business. ASTI offers programs linking research to business through research colloquia, executive conferences, and newsletters.

Small Business Administration
222 S.W. Columbia, Suite 500   503-326-2682
Portland, OR 97201-6605   FAX: 503-326-2808
   Small Business Institutes: This program provides personalized consulting services to the small business community. Consulting is provided by senior level business students, guided by a faculty advisor. Assistance in business plan preparation, marketing research, market planning, accounting, and seminars are provided.
   University Locations:
   Cinfield College
   Eastern Oregon State College
   Oregon State College
   Portland State University
   Southern Oregon State College
   University of Oregon
   University of Portland
   Western Oregon State University
   Willamette University

Oregon Marketplace
618 Lincoln
Eugene, OR 97401   503-343-7712
   Oregon Marketplace: Matches product needs of business with production capabilities of other Oregon companies. Service helps manufacturers by providing information on the products of other firms looking for such products. Buyers may benefit by obtaining product services locally at a lower cost with greater convenience.

   Business Opportunities Program: Identifies products or services not currently produce in Oregon for which Oregon business can effectively compete.

Child Care Coordinator
Department of Human Resources
320 Public Service Building
Salem, OR 97310   503-373-7282
   Child Care Technical Assistance: Technical assistance is provided to employers interested in child care-related benefits programs.

Policy and Research Section
Partnership Division
Oregon Economic Development Department
775 Summer St., NE   503-378-2286
Salem, OR 97310   FAX: 503-581-5115
   Strategic Reserve Funds, Key Industries Development Program grants, Flexible Manufacturing Network Program grants, and High Performance Manufacturing Awards (non-monetary awards): Implements key industry strategies. Encourages flexible manufacturing networks within key industries. Promotes high performance manufacturing practices. Prepares policy analyses on major issues affecting the economy. Undertakes special projects. Develops and distributes publications with information on the Oregon economy.

* Small Business Development Centers
The following offices offer free and fee-based services to new and expanding businesses:

Lead Center:
Oregon Small Business Development Center
Lane Community College
99 West 10th, Suite 216   503-726-2250
Eugene, OR 97401   FAX: 503-345-6006

   Albany: Linn-Benton Community College, Small Business Development Center, 6500 S.W. Pacific Boulevard, Albany, OR 97321, 503-967-6112; FAX: 503-967-6550.

   Ashland: Southern Oregon State College, Small Business Development Center, Regional Service Institute, Ashland, OR 97520, 503-482-5838, FAX: 503-482-1115.

   Bend: Central Oregon Community College, Small Business Development Center, 2600 N.W. College Way, Bend, OR 97701, 503-385-5524; FAX: 503-385-5497; 1-800-422-3041, ext. 524.

   Coos Bay: Southwestern Oregon Community College, Small Business Development Center, 340 Central, Coos Bay, OR 97420, 503-267-2300; FAX: 503-269-0323.

   Eugene: Lane Community College, Small Business Development Center, 1059 Willamette Street, Eugene, OR 97401, 503-726-2255; FAX: 503-686-0096.

   Grants Pass: Rogue Community College, Small Business Development Center, 290 N.E. "C" Street, Grants Pass, OR 97526, 503-471-3515.

   Gresham: Mount Hood Community College, Small Business Development Center, 323 NE Roberts Street, Gresham, OR 97030, 503-667-7658, FAX: 503-666-1140.

   Klamath Falls: Oregon Institute of Technology, Small Business Development Center, 3201 Campus Drive, South 314, Klamath Falls, OR 97601, 503-885-1760; FAX: 503-885-1115.

Lincoln City: Oregon Coast Community College Service District, Small Business Development Center, P.O. Box 419, 4157 N.W. Highway 101, Suite 123, Lincoln City, OR 97367, 503-994-4166; FAX: 503-996-4958.

Medford: Small Business Development Center, 229 N. Bartlett, Medford, OR 97501, 503-772-3478; FAX: 503-776-2224.

Milwaukie: Clackamas Community College, Small Business Development Center, 7616 S.E. Harmony Road, Milwaukie, OR 97222, 503-656-4447; FAX: 503-652-0389.

Ontario: Treasure Valley Community College, Small Business Development Center, 88 S.W. Third Avenue, Ontario, OR 97914, 503-889-2617, FAX: 503-889-8331.

Pendleton: Blue Mountain Community College, Small Business Development Center, 37 S.E. Dorion, Pendleton, OR 97801, 503-276-6233.

Portland: Portland Community College, Small Business Development Center, 123 N.W. 2nd Avenue, Suite 321, Portland, OR 97209, 503-273-2828; FAX: 503-294-0725.

Portland: Small Business International Trade Program, 121 S.W. Salmon Street, Suite 210, Portland, OR 97204, 503-274-7482, FAX: 503-228-6350.

Rosenburg: Umpqua Community College, Small Business Development Center, 744 S.E. Rose, Rosenburg, OR 97470, 503-672-2535; FAX: 503-672-3679.

Salem: Chemeketa Community College, Small Business Development Center, 365 Ferry Street S.E., Salem, OR 97301, 503-399-5181; FAX: 503-581-6017.

Seaside: Clatsop Community College, Small Business Development Center, 1240 South Holladay, Seaside, OR 97138, 503-738-3347.

The Dalles: Columbia Gorge Community College, Small Business Development Center, 212 Washington, The Dalles, OR 97058, 503-296-1173, FAX: 503-296-2107.

Tillamook: Tillamook Bay Community College Service District, Small Business Development Center, 401 B Main Street, Tillamook, OR 97141, 503-842-2551; FAX: 503-842-2555.

Pennsylvania

* General Information

Bureau of Small Business Appalachian Development
461 Forum Building
Harrisburg, PA 17120   717-783-5700
    Acts as a clearinghouse to assist small business in finding resources and services available in the state.

Office Of Enterprise Development
461 Forum Building
Harrisburg, PA 17120   717-783-5700
    Business Resource Network: Assists with coordinating and expediting the necessary permits for start-up, expansion, or relocation of job creating opportunities. Publishes and distributed booklets on how to plan and start a business and on resources available to small business. Interacts with other state agencies to insure a timely response to the small business person.

    Small Business Advocate: Assistance in cutting bureaucratic red tape. Information and expertise in dealing with state, federal, and local agencies.

* Financing

Government Response Team
Commonwealth of Pennsylvania
Department of Commerce   717-787-8199
439 Forum Building   717-787-6500
Harrisburg, PA 17120   FAX: 717-234-4560

Machinery and Equipment Loan Fund (MELF): Available to manufacturing, industrial, agricultural processors, and mining operations. Uses of funds are for machinery and equipment, acquisition and upgrading, and related engineering and installation costs. Loans up to L$500,000, or 50 percent of the total eligible projects costs, whichever is less. One job must be created or retained for each $25,00 of loan funds. Interest rate between 3-9 percent depending upon local unemployment rate.

Environmental Technology Loan Fund (ETLF): Financing available to recyclers of municipal waste and manufacturers using recycled municipal waste materials. Funds can be used for acquisition or upgrade of machinery and equipment. Loans amounts up to $100,000, or 50 percent of the total eligible projects costs, whichever is less. Interest rate is 3%.

Business Infrastructure Development Program (BID): Funds for specific infrastructure projects such as access roads, water and sewer treatment and distribution, energy facilities, parking lots, storm sewer distribution, bridges, rail facilities, port facilities, and land acquisition and clearance. Available to manufacturing, industrial, research and development, agricultural processors, or firms establishing a national or regional headquarters. Both grants and loans are awarded to local sponsors. Loans to private businesses at 3 to 9 percent interest rate depending upon the unemployment rate. For every $1 of state BID assistance at least $2 in private sector matching funds are required. One job for every $15,000 must be created.

Site Development Program (SDP): Grants are available for construction and rehabilitation projects, such as water and sewer facilities, access roads, and channel realignment. Usually the limit for each grant is $50,000, or 50 percent of the total cost. Projects in certain economically distressed areas may receive up to $100,000 in grant money. Funds are available to manufacturing, industrial, and travel-related firms.

Community Facilities Program   717-787-7120
Grants are provided to communities with less than 12,000 population for water and sewer repair and construction, and access roads for these facilities. Grants can be up to $50,000 or 50 percent of the project cost. Projects in economically distressed areas may receive up to $75,000, or 75 percent of the project cost.

Pennsylvania Economic Development Financing Authority (PEDFA):
Tax-Exempt Pooled Bond Program: Variable interest rate loans tied to market for tax-exempt bonds available to manufacturing, energy, solid waste disposal and transportation facilities. Funds can be used for land and building acquisition, building renovation and new construction, machinery and equipment acquisition and installation and tax-exempt bond refunding. Minimum loan amount $400,000 to a maximum of $10 million. 100 percent of the project can be financed.

Taxable Bond Program: Variable interest rate loans available to all types of businesses needing access to low-cost capital. These funds may be used to purchase land and buildings, building renovation and new construction, machinery and equipment acquisition and installation, and working capital. Loans in an amount no less than $400,000. 100 percent of the of the project cost can be financed.

Pennsylvania Industrial Development Authority (PIDA): Available to manufacturing, industrial, research and development, agricultural processors, or firms establishing a national or regional headquarters. Use of funds are for land and building acquisition, building construction and renovation, industrial park development, and multi-tenant spec building construction and renovation. Loans up to $2 million. No more than 40-60 percent of total eligible project costs depending upon firms size and area unemployment rate. Interest rates vary between 3-9 percent depending upon local unemployment rate. One job must be created for every $15,000 of loan funds. Interest rate is 5 percent.

Pennsylvania Capital Loan Fund (PCLF): Available to manufacturing, industrial, export services, advanced-technology firms, small business with fewer than 100 employees. Provides low-interest loans to firms for capital development projects that create new jobs. Funds can be used for land and building, building construction and renovation, machinery and equipment acquisition and installation, and working capital. Loans amounts up to $100,000, or 50 percent of the total eligible projects costs, whichever is less.

Two other Pennsylvania Capital Loan Fund programs are as follows:

PCLF - PennAg: Available to agricultural processors with fewer than 100 employees. Uses of funds are the same as **Pennsylvania Capital Loan Fund** above with exception of working capital. Loan amounts are the same as **PCLF.**

PCLF - Apparel: Available to apparel manufacturers for machinery and equipment acquisition and installation. Loans up to $200,000, or 50 percent of the total eligible project costs, whichever is less. Interest rate is 3 percent. One job must be created for every $15,000 of funds.

Pennsylvania Economic Development Partnership Fund (EDP Fund): Available to manufacturing, industrial, research and development, or firms establishing national and regional headquarters in distressed communities. Funds use are land and building acquisition, building construction and renovation, site preparation, and infrastructure. Loan and grant amounts vary depending upon the financial needs and type of project. For every $15,000 of funds, one job must be created. Interest rates range between 3-9 percent depending upon local unemployment rate.

Pennsylvania Treasury Department
Room 129, Finance Building
Harrisburg, PA 17120   717-787-2520
Linked Deposit Program: Established to create and retain jobs through the financing of economic development projects, the Pennsylvania Treasury Department offers up to $200 million in support. Deposits of state funds are made in commercial banks and S & L's, which then make funds available as loans to new or expanding small businesses. Funds available to firms engaged in expanding or establishing a business within the state, employing fewer than 150 people. At least one full-time job, or equivalent, should be created or saved for every $15,000 to $25,000 loaned.

Nursing Home Loan Agency
Room 460, Forum Building
Harrisburg, PA 17120   717-783-8523
Provides financing for the state's nursing homes, offering low-interest loans to those unable to find financing elsewhere. The loans enable these institutions to comply with required safety and fire codes. Financing is also available to convert unneeded hospital beds into nursing home beds.

Revenue Bond and Mortgage Program
Room 466, Forum Building
Harrisburg, PA 17120   717-783-1108
Funds for this program are borrowed through a local Industrial Development Authority, with financing secured from private sector sources. Lenders do not pay taxes on interest earned from the loan and borrowers obtain interest rates lower than conventional ones. Funds may be used for purchase of land, buildings, machinery, or equipment.

Office of Technology Development
Forum Building, #352
Harrisburg, PA 17120   717-787-4147
Technology Business Incubator Loan Program: Grants and loans are available to construct, acquire, renovate, equip and furnish buildings for use as small technology business incubator facilities. Funds are available for up to 50 percent of total project cost, or $650,000, whichever is less. Grants may be made for technology business incubators located in designated economically distressed communities. Must be occupied by for-profit firms engaged primarily in product and process development, product commercialization or manufacturing.

Incubators provide for space and business development services needed in the start-up phase. A list of current technology incubator facilities is available.

Research Grants Division:
Research Seed Grants: Provides grants of up to $35,000 to businesses that are developing or commercializing a new technology. Preference is given to firms with fewer than 50 employees.

Executive Director
North East Tier BFTC

125 Goodman Drive
Lehigh University
Bethlehem, PA 18015   215-758-5200

Executive Director
BFTC of Southeastern Pennsylvania
University City Science Center
3526 Market Street
Philadelphia, PA 19104   215-895-3105

President
BFTC of Western Pennsylvania
4516 Henry Street
Suite 103
Pittsburgh, PA 15213   412-681-2625

President
BFTC of Central/Northern Pennsylvania
105 Barbara II Building
University Park, PA 16802-1013   814-863-4558
Ben Franklin Partnership Program: Funds research and development projects that will benefit the state's economy through commercialization of high tech advances. The four Ben Franklin Technology Centers, listed above, provide assistance in evaluating your ideas, developing business plans and introducing you to funding sources as well as provide information on the programs listed below.

Challenge Grant Program for Technological Innovation: Support may be in the form of grant awards, equity positions or investments with royalty payback provisions. Requires matching funds. Eligible activities include joint research and development between private companies and university, research and development by small companies, entrepreneurial development, including support for incubators, education and training.

Seed Venture Capital Funds: Provide equity financing to new businesses during their early stages of growth, including eligible firms located in small business incubators. Types of business eligible to receive investments include manufacturing firms, firms involved in international export-related mercantile ventures, and advanced technology and computer-related ventures. A firm must have 50 or fewer employees.

Environmental Technology Fund: Available to companies developing recycling processes or markets for recycled materials. Uses are research and development, and technology transfer. Grants available up to $100,000.

Small Business Administration (SBA)
100 Chestnut Street
Suite 309   717-782-3840
Harrisburg, PA 17101   FAX: 717-782-4839
SBA 7(a) Guaranteed and Direct Loans: Guarantees up to 90 percent of a loan made through a private lender up to $750,000. Can be used for working capital, expand or convert facilities, purchase of machinery and equipment, and land and building. Available only to those unable to obtain a loan from conventional sources. Direct loans are made up to $150,000.

SBA 504: Provides loans using 50 percent conventional bank financing, 40 percent SBA involvement through Certified Development Companies, and 10 percent owner equity. Fixed-asset loans are available in amounts up to $750,000. The loan can be used for land and building, construction, machinery and equipment, and renovation/expansion.

Small Business Innovative Research Grants (SBIR): Phase I awards between $20,000 to $50,000 to entrepreneurs to support six months of research on a technical innovation. Phase II grants are an additional $500,000 for development. Private sector investment funds must follow.

International Trade Loans: Guaranteed long-term loans through private lenders to develop or expand export markets, or to recover from the effects of import competition. Maximum guaranteed loan is $1,000,000 for fixed assets and an additional $250,000 for working capital and/or export revolving line of credit.

Export Revolving Line of Credit Loan: Short term financing available to small businesses that are at least one year old. Loans provide working capital to finance the manufacturing or wholesaling of products for export and for export marketing. The SBA will guarantee up to 90 percent of a conventional loan in amounts up to $750,000.

Contract Loan: Short-term loans are available to small businesses to finance the costs of labor and materials on contracts for which the proceeds are assignable. Program guarantees up to 90 percent of loans not in excess of $750,000. Qualifying small businesses must be in business for at least 12 calendar months prior to the date of the loan application.

Seasonal Line of Credit Loan: Loans provide short-term working capital to finance seasonal increases in business activities. Program guarantees up to 90 percent of loans not in excess of $750,000. Qualifying business must be in operation for at least one year prior to application.

Pollution Control Loans: Long-term guaranteed loans can be made by conventional financing to small businesses for installation or required pollution control measures. Must be unable to adopt the pollution control measures without undue financial hardship. Maximum guaranteed loan is $1,000,000.

General Contractor Loans: Small general construction contractors may obtain short-term loans or loan guarantees for residential or commercial construction or rehabilitation of property to be sold. The SBA will guarantee up to 90 percent of qualifying loans made by private lenders up to a maximum of $750,000. Direct loans can be up to $150,000.

Energy Business Loan Guarantee: Small businesses that provide certain energy production and conservation services for others may qualify for long-term loans and loan guarantees for start-ups and expansions. Loans and guarantees are made for firms that develop, manufacture, sell, install, or service specific energy measures for others, or firms that provide engineering, architectural, consulting, or other professional services connected with specific energy measures. Guarantee is for up to 90 percent of a loan not in excess of $750,000. Direct loans up to $150,000.

Disaster Recovery Loans: Small businesses located in federally designated disaster areas and suffering property damage or economic losses from the disaster can obtain long-term recovery loans at low interest rates. Property damage loans are limited to 85 percent of the verified damage. Loans for economic losses are for operating capital to meet the business' obligations that could have been made had the disaster not occurred.

Handicapped Assistance Loans: Assists persons who have a physical, mental or emotional disability of a permanent nature which limits the selection of any type of employment for which the person would otherwise be qualified. Direct loans are available for up to $150,000. The interest rate is 3% on these loans.

Surety Bond Guaranty Program: Makes the bonding system more available to small contractors who may be denied access to the system. SBA can guarantee up to 80 percent of surety's loss on a bond that has a maximum in total contract value of up to $1,250,000.

Vietnam-era and Disabled Veterans Loan Program: Provides direct loans to veterans to establish or expand a small business. Funds may be used for working capital or fixed assets. Direct loans for amounts up to $150,000 are available. The interest rate may be fixed or variable.

CIP Capital, Inc.
300 Chester Field Parkway
Malvern, PA 19355 — 215-251-5075

Enterprise Venture Cap Corp. of Pennsylvania
551 Main Street
Suite 303
Johnstown, PA 15901 — 814-535-7597

Erie SBIC
32 West 8th Street
Suite 615
Erie, PA 16501 — 814-453-7964

Fidelcor Capital Corporation
Fidelity Building, 7th Floor
123 South Broad Street
Philadelphia, PA 19109 — 215-985-3722

First SBIC of California
(Main Office: Costa Mesa, CA)
P.O. Box 512
Washington, PA 15301 — 412-223-0707

Meridian Capital Corporation
Horsham Business Center
Suite 200
455 Business Center Drive
Horsham, PA 19044 — 215-957-7520

Meridian Venture Partners
The Fidelity Court Building
259 Radnor-Chester Road
Radnor, PA 19087 — 215-293-0210

PNC Capital Corporation
Pittsburgh National Building
Fifth Avenue and Wood Street
Pittsburgh, PA 15222 — 412-762-2248

Small Business Investment Companies (SBIC): The SBA licenses, regulates, and provides financial assistance to privately owned and operated Small Business Investment Companies. SBICs make venture or risk investments by supplying capital and extending unsecured loans and loans not fully collateralized to small enterprises which meet their investment criteria. Financing is made by direct loans and by equity investments.

* Women and Minority Business Assistance

Pennsylvania Minority Business Authority
1704 State Office Building
1400 Spring Garden Street
Philadelphia, PA 19130 — 215-560-3236

Pennsylvania Minority Business Authority
404 Forum Building
Harrisburg, PA 17120 — 717-783-1127 / 717-783-1128 / FAX: 717-234-4560

Minority Economic Development Program: Provides procurement assistance for minority contractors. Assistance is provided in the form of working capital loans, surety bond guarantees, or other assistance and is available to applicants meeting eligibility requirements. Maximum loan is $100,000. A maximum of $200,000 providing that at least one full-time job or its equivalent in part-time jobs are created for each $15,000 over $100,000 is available if the project is located within an Enterprise Zone, is determined to be advanced technology, or is located within a redevelopment area and is a manufacturing or industrial enterprises.

Pennsylvania Minority Business Development Authority (PMBDA)
Room 461
Forum Building
Harrisburg, PA 17120 — 717-783-1127

Provides technical, managerial, and financial assistance for minority-owned businesses. The PMBDA offers low-interest, long-term loans and equity investment guarantees to assist these firms in start-up or expansion endeavors. It offers a Surety Bond Guaranty Program that guarantees up to 90 percent of bid and performance bonds that minority firms need in order to obtain contracts with state agencies. In addition, the Authority has a Working Capitol Loan Program which provides short-term loans for minority contractors.

Small Business Administration (SBA)
100 Chestnut Street
Suite 309
Harrisburg, PA 17101 — 717-782-3840 / FAX: 717-782-4839

SBA 8(a) Program - Business Procurement Assistance: Provides federal government contracting opportunities for small businesses owned by socially and economically disadvantaged persons, and assists these businesses to become independently competitive in the normal business environment. SBA monitors all government contracts to assure that a quota of contract work goes to 8(a) businesses. Also provides business management services to these businesses. Business must be approved for program participation prior to receipt of an 8(a) contract.

* Training

Economic Development Partnership
Bureau of Job Training Partnership
Labor and Industry Building, Room 1115
7th and Foster
Harrisburg, PA 17120   717-783-8944

 Training Plus: Helps businesses cut costs of hiring and training employees by offering federal and state tax credits to those who hire designated, pre-trained workers currently unemployed. Tax credits are worth up to $6000 per employee. Workers are recruited, trained and screened by the state, but final hiring decisions are up to the employers. The training can be customized to fit the types of workers needed.

Government Response Team
Pennsylvania Department of Commerce
439 Forum Building   717-787-8199
Harrisburg, PA 17120   FAX: 717-234-4560

 Customized Job Training Program: Available to manufacturing, industrial, research and development, advanced technology, and business service firms. Assistance is available in the form of grants up to 100 percent of the eligible costs for new job creating, up to 50 percent of the costs for job retention, up to 25 percent of the eligible costs for upgrade training which is to be used for instructional costs, supplies, equipment leasing, and relevant travel costs for instructors. Training should not exceed six months.

 Job Training Partnership Act (JTPA): Provides employers with recruitment, screening, referral, training, 50 percent wage subsidy up to 3 months for on-the-job training. Available to any private employer.

* Management Consulting and Other Services

Office of International Development
Room 464, Forum Building
Harrisburg, PA 17120   717-787-7190

 Foreign Trade Assistance: Works to attract foreign investment into the state and helps promote Pennsylvania products abroad, providing counseling and marketing information to firms engaged in exporting. The Office supports foreign bureaus in Belgium, West Germany, and Japan to promote Pennsylvania products and attract foreign investment.

PENNTAP
Pennsylvania Department of Commerce
110 Barbara II Building
University Park, PA 16802   814-865-0427

 The Pennsylvania Department of Commerce, in conjunction with Pennsylvania State University, helps businesses, especially small ones, compete in technological fields. PENNTAP provides specialists to work with businesses on production, computer systems, product development, and related issues.

Director, Governor's Response Team
Room 439, Forum Building   717-787-8199
Harrisburg, PA 17120   FAX: 717-234-4560

 Reacts quickly to shut-downs, move-outs, expansions, or recruitment problems. It recruits new industry to the state, assists existing firms to expand, and provides information about state economic development programs.

Office of Technology Development
Pennsylvania Department of Commerce
352 Forum Building   717-787-4147
Harrisburg, PA 17120   FAX: 717-234-4560

 Industrial Resource Center Network (IRCs): The Network was created to help manufacturers complete more effectively in the international marketplace. There are nine IRCs in the state that provide timely and cost-effective services to help manufacturers meet their quality, production, profit, and market goals. Some services provided are manufacturing and/or management advice, adoption of a new technique or technology, development of manufacturing strategies. The state subsidizes the cost to small manufacturers.

Small Business Administration
100 Chestnut Street, Suite 309
Harrisburg, PA 17101   717-782-3840

 Small Business Institutes: This program provides personalized consulting services to the small business community. Consulting is provided by senior level business students, guided by a faculty advisor. Assistance in business plan preparation, marketing research, market planning, accounting, and seminars are provided.

 University Locations:
Bloomsburg University
Bucknell University
California University of PA
Carnegie Mellon University
Clarion University - PA
Drexel University
Duquesne University
Gannon University
Gettysburg College
Indiana University of PA
Juniata College
Kings College
LaSalle University
Lehigh University
Marywood College
Mercyhurst College
Millersville University
Penn State University
Point Park College
Shippensburg University
Slippery Rock University
St. Francis College
St. Vincent College
Susquehanna University
University of Pennsylvania
University of Pittsburgh - Bradford
University of Pittsburgh
University of Scranton
Villanova University
Washington & Jefferson College
West Chester University
Westminster College
Widener College
Wilkes College

* Small Business Development Centers

The following offices offer free and fee-based services to new and expanding businesses:

Lead Center:
Pennsylvania Small Business Development Center
University of Pennsylvania
The Wharton School
444 Vance Hall   215-898-1219
Philadelphia, PA 19104-6374   FAX: 215-573-2135

 Bethlehem: Lehigh University, Small Business Development Center, Rauch Business Center #37, Bethlehem, PA 18015, 215-758-3980; FAX: 215-758-5205.

 Clarion: Clarion University of Pennsylvania, Small Business Development Center, Dana Still Building, Clarion, PA 16214, 814-226-2060; FAX: 814-226-2636.

 Erie: Gannon University, Small Business Development Center, 824 Peach Street, Carlisle Building, 3rd Floor, Erie, PA 16541, 814-871-7714; FAX: 814-871-7383.

 Latrobe: St. Vincent College, Small Business Development Center, Alfred Hall, 4th Floor, Latrobe, PA 15650-2690, 412-537-4572; FAX: 412-537-0919.

 Lewisburg: Bucknell University, Small Business Development Center, Dana Engineering Building, Lewisburg, PA 17837, 717-524-1249; FAX: 717-524-1768.

 Loretto: Small Business Development Center, Business Resource Center, Loretto, PA 15940, 814-472-3200; FAX: 814-472-3202.

Middletown: Pennsylvania State University, Small Business Development Center, 777 W. Harrisburg Pike, Middletown, PA 17057-4898, 717-948-6069; FAX: 717-948-6031.

Philadelphia: Temple University, Small Business Development Center, Room 6, Speakman Hall, 006-00, Philadelphia, PA 19122, 215-787-7282; FAX: 215-787-5698.

Philadelphia: LaSalle University, Small Business Development Center, 1900 West Olney Avenue, Box 365, Philadelphia, PA 19141, 215-951-1416; FAX: 215-951-1547.

Philadelphia: University of Pennsylvania, Small Business Development Center, The Wharton School, 409 Vance Hall, Philadelphia, PA 19104-6357, 215-898-4861; FAX: 215-898-1299.

Pittsburgh: Duquesne University, Small Business Development Center, Rockwell Hall-Room 10 Concourse, 600 Forbes Avenue, Pittsburgh, PA 15282, 412-434-6233; FAX: 412-434-5072.

Pittsburgh: University of Pittsburgh, Small Business Development Center, Room 343 Mervis Hall, Pittsburgh, PA 15260, 412-648-1544; FAX: 412-648-1693.

Scranton: University of Scranton, Small Business Development Center, St. Thomas Hall, Room 588, Scranton, PA 18503, 717-941-7588; FAX: 717-941-4053.

Wilkes-Barre: Wilkes College, Small Business Development Center, Hollenback Hall, 192 South Franklin Street, Wilkes-Barre, PA 18766, 717-824-4651, ext. 4340; FAX: 717-824-2245.

Rhode Island

* General Information

Good Neighbor Alliance Corp.
15 Messenger Drive   401-467-2880
Warwick, RI 02888   1-800-462-1910 in RI
Small Business Advocate: Assistance in cutting bureaucratic red tape. Information and expertise in dealing with state, federal, and local agencies.

Rhode Island Department of Economic Development (RIDED)
7 Jackson Walkway
Providence, RI 02903   401-277-2601
Business Action Center: One-stop problem-solving center which provides assistance and information businesses throughout the state. Guarantees an answer to each caller within two working days.

* Financing

Rhode Island Department of Economic Development (RIDED)
7 Jackson Walkway
Providence, RI 02903   401-277-2601
Small Business Loan Fund: Provides fixed rate loans at lower rates to manufacturing, processing, and selected services. Funds can be used for fixed assets (acquisition and improvement of land, buildings and equipment, including new construction), job creation criteria. Loans range from $25,000 to $150,000 for fixed assets and up to $30,000 for working capital. Program funds should average 25 percent of total project cost. Terms are for up to 15 years for land and buildings, machinery and equipment 10 years, and loans for working capital are for a maximum of 5 years.

Tax-Exempt Industrial Revenue Bonds: Tax-exempt Industrial Revenue Bonds, issued through R.I. Industrial Facilities Corp., (RIIFC) may be used to finance fixed assets (land, building, new machinery and equipment and certain other "soft" costs) for a manufacturing project. Financing may cover the entire project up to $10 million.

Taxable Industrial Revenue Bonds: Taxable bonds are also issued through RIIFC) for manufacturing and certain selected commercial facilities, including travel-tourist facilities. Financing may cover the entire project.

Interest rates are usually floating. Terms of the loan and interest rates are established by the lender. Funds may be used for fixed assets (land, building, machinery and equipment, and related "soft" costs).

Rhode Island Industrial-Recreational Building Authority (IRBA) Insured Bond and Mortgage: Debt insurance on tax-free bonds, taxable bonds and conventional mortgages. Insurance premiums are based on average annual outstanding principal balance for manufacturing, processing, office, wholesale, retail, and travel-tourist facilities. Funds can be used for new building acquisition, or additions/rehabilitation of existing buildings, new or used machinery and equipment. Limits on loans are 90 percent for real estate, 80 percent for machinery and equipment, 40 percent for second mortgages, and 75 percent for travel-tourist projects. IRBA can insure a minimum of $100,000 per project cost and maximum of $5 million.

Community Development Block Grants: The U.S. Department of Housing and Urban Development (HUD) program provides funds to cities and towns which may be used to furnish below-market interest loans for the expansion of business and the creation of new job opportunities. The larger cities receive this money directly. The small communities compete for funds administered by the state. $15,000 of grant funds invested must create at least one full-time job, and at least 51 percent of the jobs created must be for low- and moderate-income families.

Small Business Innovation Research Grants (SBIR): A federal program that provides Phase I awards for up to $50,000 for a feasibility study of a project's scientific and technical merit. Phase II awards up to $500,000 are available to qualified firms with viable innovative projects for more extended research and development.

Rhode Island Partnership for Science and Technology State Support SBIR: Program provides four categories of support to qualified SBIR applicants. The partnership pays for consulting that is provided by the RI Small Business Development Center in order to help applicants develop quality proposals. A Rhode Island company that submits a valid Phase I SBIR proposal to the federal government will receive a $1,000 grant to help defray the cost of preparing an application. A matching grant of 50 percent (up to a maximum of $2,500) is available to a Phase I recipient that uses a consultant who is a faculty member from any Rhode Island university or college. A Rhode Island Phase I SBIR grant recipient who submits a Phase II proposal is eligible to receive a matching state grant of 50 percent of the Phase I award up to a maximum of $25,000.

Applied Research Grants: Through the Rhode Island Partnership for Science and Technology, research grants are offered to business that can do research work with Rhode Island university, colleges or hospitals. For major, innovative projects with a minimum research budget of $200,000. Projects should offer the potential for commercialization with high profit. The Partnership will fund up to 60 percent of the research project.

Small Business Tax Incentives: Provides tax incentives for investments in qualified small companies less than four years old with annual gross revenue less than $2.5 million. Incentives are available to entrepreneurs or venture capital partnerships which meet the requirements of the program.

Ocean State Business Development Authority (OSBDA)
SBA 504 Loan Guarantee: Provides loans for healthy expanding companies having profits less than $2 million, net worth less than $6 million. A "blended rate" below conventional bank financing. 50 percent conventional bank financing, 40 percent SBA involvement through Certified Development Companies, and 10 percent owner equity. A fixed-asset loan in amounts up to $750,000 per project. Loan can be used for fixed assets (land acquisitions, buildings, machinery and equipment), and some leasehold improvements. There is job creation criteria.

Two other certified development companies serve specific areas:
Newport   401-277-2601
Bristol County   401-245-0750

Small Business Administration (SBA)
380 Westminster Street   401-528-4561
Providence, RI 02903   FAX: 401-528-4539
SBA 7(a) Guaranteed and Direct Loans: Guarantees up to 90 percent of a loan made through a private lender up to $750,000. Can be used for working capital, expand or convert facilities, purchase of machinery and equipment, and land and building. Available only to those unable to

obtain a loan from conventional sources. Direct loans are made up to $150,000.

SBA 504: Provides loans using 50 percent conventional bank financing, 40 percent SBA involvement through Certified Development Companies, and 10 percent owner equity. Fixed-asset loans are available in amounts up to $750,000. The loan can be used for land and building, construction, machinery and equipment, and renovation/expansion.

Small Business Innovative Research Grants (SBIR): Phase I awards between $20,000 to $50,000 to entrepreneurs to support six months of research on a technical innovation. Phase II grants are an additional $500,000 for development. Private sector investment funds must follow.

International Trade Loans: Guaranteed long-term loans through private lenders to develop or expand export markets, or to recover from the effects of import competition. Maximum guaranteed loan is $1,000,000 for fixed assets and an additional $250,000 for working capital and/or export revolving line of credit.

Export Revolving Line of Credit Loan: Short term financing available to small businesses that are at least one year old. Loans provide working capital to finance the manufacturing or wholesaling of products for export and for export marketing. The SBA will guarantee up to 90 percent of a conventional loan in amounts up to $750,000.

Contract Loan: Short-term loans are available to small businesses to finance the costs of labor and materials on contracts for which the proceeds are assignable. Program guarantees up to 90 percent of loans not in excess of $750,000. Qualifying small businesses must be in business for at least 12 calendar months prior to the date of the loan application.

Seasonal Line of Credit Loan: Loans provide short-term working capital to finance seasonal increases in business activities. Program guarantees up to 90 percent of loans not in excess of $750,000. Qualifying business must be in operation for at least one year prior to application.

Pollution Control Loans: Long-term guaranteed loans can be made by conventional financing to small businesses for installation or required pollution control measures. Must be unable to adopt the pollution control measures without undue financial hardship. Maximum guaranteed loan is $1,000,000.

General Contractor Loans: Small general construction contractors may obtain short-term loans or loan guarantees for residential or commercial construction or rehabilitation of property to be sold. The SBA will guarantee up to 90 percent of qualifying loans made by private lenders up to a maximum of $750,000. Direct loans can be up to $150,000.

Energy Business Loan Guarantee: Small businesses that provide certain energy production and conservation services for others may qualify for long-term loans and loan guarantees for start-ups and expansions. Loans and guarantees are made for firms that develop, manufacture, sell, install, or service specific energy measures for others, or firms that provide engineering, architectural, consulting, or other professional services connected with specific energy measures. Guarantee is for up to 90 percent of a loan not in excess of $750,000. Direct loans up to $150,000.

Disaster Recovery Loans: Small businesses located in federally designated disaster areas and suffering property damage or economic losses from the disaster can obtain long-term recovery loans at low interest rates. Property damage loans are limited to 85 percent of the verified damage. Loans for economic losses are for operating capital to meet the business' obligations that could have been made had the disaster not occurred.

Handicapped Assistance Loans: Assists persons who have a physical, mental or emotional disability of a permanent nature which limits the selection of any type of employment for which the person would otherwise be qualified. Direct loans are available for up to $150,000. The interest rate is 3% on these loans.

Surety Bond Guaranty Program: Makes the bonding system more available to small contractors who may be denied access to the system. SBA can guarantee up to 80 percent of surety's loss on a bond that has a maximum in total contract value of up to $1,250,000.

Vietnam-era and Disabled Veterans Loan Program: Provides direct loans to veterans to establish or expand a small business. Funds may be used for working capital or fixed assets. Direct loans for amounts up to $150,000 are available. The interest rate may be fixed or variable.

Domestic Capital Corporation
815 Reservoir Avenue
Cranston, RI 02910   401-946-3310

Fairway Capital Corporation
99 Wayland Avenue
Providence, RI 02906   401-454-7500

Fleet Venture Resources, Inc.
111 Westminster Street, 4th Floor
Providence, RI 02903   401-278-6770

Moneta Capital Corporation
99 Wayland Avenue
Providence, RI 02906   401-454-7500

NYSTRS/NV Capital, LP
111 Westminster Street
Providence, RI 02903   401-276-5597

New England Capital Corporation
111 Westminster Street
Providence, RI 02903   401-278-6770

Old Stone Capital Corporation
One Old Stone Square, 11th Floor
Providence, RI 02903   401-278-2559

Richmond Square Capital Corporation
1 Richmond Square
Providence, RI 02906   401-521-3000

Wallace Capital Corporation
170 Westminster Street, Suite 300
Providence, RI 02903   401-273-9191
> **Small Business Investment Companies (SBIC):** The SBA licenses, regulates, and provides financial assistance to privately owned and operated Small Business Investment Companies. SBICs make venture or risk investments by supplying capital and extending unsecured loans and loans not fully collateralized to small enterprises which meet their investment criteria. Financing is made by direct loans and by equity investments.

Business Development Company Financing   401-351-3036
BDC offers direct revolving and terms loans and SBA guarantee and term loans to healthy Rhode Island Businesses. Loans up to 90 percent of project cost to a maximum of $600,000. Minimum is $100,000. Funds can be used for any business purpose.

Governor's Office of Energy Assistance   401-277-3370
RISE Energy Conservation Program: Commercial and industrial firms can apply for an energy audit at subsidized cost. Based on the results of the study, the company may be eligible for a bank loan of $5,000 to $25,000 at rates up to 5 percent below market rate. Firms with $50,000 or more annual energy cost should contact the Governor's office, Smaller firms should contact RISE as above.

Department of Administration
Rhode Island Division of Taxation
1 Capital Hill
Providence, RI 02908   401-277-3050
> **Child Daycare Tax Credits:** Credits are available against the business corporation tax and other business taxes at 30 percent of amount of day care purchase and of the cost to establish and/or operate a licensed day care facility. Maximum annual credit is $30,000. Certain restrictions apply.

RI Department of Environmental Management (RIDEM)
83 Park Street
Providence, RI 02903   401-277-3434

Hazardous Waste Reduction, Recycling and Treatment Program: Grants are available to companies in four categories for development of hazardous waste reduction, recycling or treatment facilities. The categories are: feasibility study - 90 percent up to $140,000; project design - 70 percent to 90 percent up to $75,000; construction - 50 percent to 90 percent up to $250,000; evaluation - 90 percent to 100 percent up to $50,000.

Technical Assistance:

Cities and Towns: The following communities have revolving loan funds or other economic incentives for businesses. They also provide site location and technical services to resident companies or other companies looking to expand/start a business.

Bristol	401-253-7010
Central Falls	401-728-3270
Cranston	401-461-1000
Cumberland	401-728-2400
East Providence	401-434-3311
Newport	401-846-9600
North Providence	401-232-0900
Pawtuckett	401-725-5200
Providence	401-351-4300
Warwick	401-738-2000
West Warwick	401-822-9215
Westerly	401-596-7355
Woonsocket	401-762-6400

* Women and Minority Business Assistance

Department of Economic Development
7 Jackson Walkway
Providence, RI 02903   401-277-2601

Certifies minority and woman-owned businesses under federal and state set-aside and goal programs and provides counseling assistance to these companies.

Small Business Administration (SBA)
380 Westminster Street   401-528-4561
Providence, RI 02903   FAX: 401-528-4539

SBA 8(a) Program - Business Procurement Assistance: Provides federal government contracting opportunities for small businesses owned by socially and economically disadvantaged persons, and assists these businesses to become independently competitive in the normal business environment. SBA monitors all government contracts to assure that a quota of contract work goes to 8(a) businesses. Also provides business management services to these businesses. Business must be approved for program participation prior to receipt of an 8(a) contract.

* Training

Rhode Island Department of Employment & Training
101 Friendship Street
Providence, RI 02903   401-277-2090

Job Training Partnership Act (JTPA): Provides employers with recruitment, screening, referral, training, 50 percent wage subsidy up to 3 months for on-the-job training. Available to any private employer.

Workforce 2000
101 Friendship Street, 4th Floor
Providence, RI 02903   401-277-6700

Workforce 2000 Industry Training Support: Offers three training programs:

Customized Upgrade Training allows an employer to upgrade the skills of existing employees required because of changing technology.

Customized Training for New Hires allows training in occupational skills by either the employer or by an outside trainer.

On-the-Job Training allows small business to participate in Workforce 200 programs. A minimum entry wage of $8.00 per hour is required.

* Management Consulting and Other Services

Rhode Island Department of Economic Development
7 Jackson Walkway
Providence, RI 02903   401-277-2601

Business Counseling: Assists new businesses and proposed start-ups on requirements and procedures.

Export: Provides counseling on all phases of exporting. Represents Rhode Island companies at international trade fairs. Maintains Rhode Island trade offices in Europe, Hong Kong and Taiwan.

Department of Commerce (ITA):

U.S. and Foreign Commercial Services: Located at the Department of Economic Development, this office provides services to export businesses and is the federal government's only international trade agency with a global field organization and delivery system. It operates export information programs to help businesses evaluate and enter foreign markets and has access to 125 foreign commercial service posts in 68 countries. It also furnishes information on export licensing and requirements and shipping documents.

Federal Procurement: Provides individualized counseling, a bid matching service, a specifications library and establishes a network of assistance for companies who want to sell to federal agencies or to federal prime contractors. Government publications and information on contract and sub-contract opportunities are available. Bid preparation assistance referral is available.

Research: Provides socio-economic data on Rhode Island. Published descriptive monographs on Rhode Island's 39 communities. Maintains Directory of RI Manufacturers and their products as well as other business lists.

Marketing: Maintains an inventory of available buildings and sites for new and expanding companies throughout the state. Operates four industrial parks. Provides technical assistance for Rhode Island and out-of-state companies.

Small Business Administration (SBA)
380 Westminster Street   401-528-4561
Providence, RI 02903   FAX: 401-528-4539

Small Business Institutes: This program provides personalized consulting services to the small business community. Consulting is provided by senior level business students, guided by a faculty advisor. Assistance in business plan preparation, marketing research, market planning, accounting, and seminars are provided.

University Locations:
Bryant College
Johnson & Wales University
Roger Williams College
Salve Regina
University of Rhode Island

Brown University Venture Forum
Box 1949
Providence, RI 02912   401-863-3528

Brings together entrepreneurs, potential investors, and others to help expand and create business in the state. The Forum holds meetings in which a promising company presents itself for comments and advice by panelists and Forum members. The Forum also sponsors start-up clinics, and workshops.

University of Rhode Island
Ballentine Hall
Kingston, RI 02881   Switchboard: 401-792-1000
Sea Grant Advisory Services   401-792-6842
Technical information for marine-related businesses.

Business and Economic Research Center   401-792-2549
Conducts various marketing or empirical research projects on a grant basis.

Labor Research Center 401-792-2239
This center provides labor research and other union management information on a clearinghouse-basis to unions, corporate individuals and organizations.

Institute for International Business 401-792-4374
The Institute conducts teaching and training, summer internship programs, executive guest lecture series, and collaboration with foreign universities.

Center for Pacific-Basin Capital Markets Research 401-729-5105
This center maintains capital markets data bases, promotes research and teaching programs, and provides an international forum about the Pacific-Basin region.

MBA Job Bank 401-792-2337
The Job Bank provides job listings for MBA job applicants.

Research Institute for Telecommunications and Information Marketing 401-792-5065
The Research Institute initiates and implements research programs on telecommunications and information marketing Brown University Research Foundation.

Telemarketing Study Project: This project conducts a comprehensive, teaching research and development program for the study and practice of telemarketing.

* Small Business Development Centers
The following offices offer free and fee-based services to new and expanding businesses:

Lead Center:
Rhode Island Small Business Development Center
Bryant College
1150 Douglas Pike
Smithfield, RI 02917 401-232-6111
FAX: 401-232-6416

Kingston: University of Rhode Island, Small Business Development Center, 24 Woodward Hall, Kingston, RI 02881, 401-792-2451; FAX: 401-792-4017.

Middletown: Aquidneck Island, Small Business Development Center, 28 Jacome Way, Middletown, RI 02840, 401-849-6900; FAX: 401-849-0815.

Providence: Bryant College, Small Business Development Center, 7 Jackson Walkway, Providence, RI 02903, 401-831-1330; FAX: 401-454-2819.

Providence: Community College of Rhode Island, Small Business Development Center, Providence Campus, One Hilton Street, Providence, RI 02905, 401-455-6042; FAX: 401-455-6047.

Smithfield: Bryant College, Export Assistance Center, 1150 Douglas Pike, Smithfield, RI 02917, 401-232-6407; FAX: 401-232-6416/6319.

South Carolina

* General Information

South Carolina State Development Board
P.O. Box 927
Columbia, SC 29202 803-737-0400
Enterprise Development Department: This department stimulates the formation and growth of new businesses. It provides a network of services for development of business plans, offers assistance to small businesses on individual problems, and establishes a regional network for women-owned businesses. Technical assessments are available as well as educational and training programs and financial and marketing assistance.

Industry-Business and Community Services 803-734-1400
Small Business Advocate: Provides assistance in cutting bureaucratic red tape, as well as information and expertise in dealing with state, federal, and local agencies.

* Financing

South Carolina State Development Board
P.O. Box 927
Columbia, SC 29202 803-737-0400
Industrial Revenue Bonds (IRB): Cities and counties are all authorized to issue taxable or nontaxable IRB's. Bonds are issued for terms of 40 years maximum, but terms of 10-25 years are common. Interest rates are generally lower than conventional rates, since they are negotiated between the purchaser and the company using the facility. They are usually secured by the real estate or tangible property of the project.

Loan Program: For business and industry construction. Grantee must employ 51 percent low- and moderate-income personnel. Interest rates are negotiable, and payback is required within 12 months.

South Carolina Jobs/Economic Development Authority
1201 Main Street, Suite 1750
Columbia, SC 29201 803-737-0079
Export Trade and Finance Program: Financial and credit services are offered to South Carolina's export businesses, as well as counseling and information services. A state delivery system helps small businesses access and package pre- and post-shipment loans funded through the EximBank and the SBA.

Tax-Exempt Industrial Revenue Bond Program (IRB): This program is designed to provide accessibility to the public finance market for small manufacturing and non-profit firms. This market allows for variable and/or fixed rate funds at low rates. Individual company funding requirements (for land and depreciable assets) should range between $500,000 and $10 million. The program offers the small borrowers reduced up front closing costs making IRB's more economical than ever. IRB's may be done on a pooled or stand-alone basis as individual applications warrant.

Taxable Bond Business Loan Program: This program is designed to assist in fulfilling the financing needs of those firms that do not qualify for tax-exempt industrial revenue bonds. The program offers variable and/or fixed rate financing. Bonds may be issued on a stand-alone basis or through a pooled mechanism, as determined by an individual firm's needs.

Community Development Block Grant: Available to cities and counties for the commercial rehabilitation of existing buildings or structures used for business, commercial, or industrial purposes. Grants of up to $500,000 can be made. Every $15,000 of grant funds invested must create at least one full-time job, and at least 51 percent of the jobs created must be for low- and moderate-income families.

Urban Development Block Grant (UDBG): Awarded to communities which then lend the proceeds at flexible rates to eligible businesses. Projects with total costs less than $100,000 are not eligible. UDAG funds should leverage three to four times their amount in private sector investment.

Carolina Capital Investment Corporation:
Venture Capital Funding Program: Loans or equity funds are available directly to businesses for product and process innovations which will create employment and aid economic development. Eligibility is limited to private, for-profit businesses with a net worth of under $1 million--mostly in the manufacturing, industrial, or service sectors. Loans may be for capital expenditures and the purchase of new equipment, as well as for working capital needs. Maximum allowable funding is $75,000. Can be in the form of straight debt financing, straight equity financing, or a combination of the two.

Business Development Corporation
Suite 225, Enoree Building, Koger Center
111 Executive Center Drive
Columbia, SC 29210 803-798-4064
Business Development Board (BDB): A source of funds for business development and expansion. The BDB operates as a widely-held stock company made up of bank and savings and loan members. The BDB provides loans for companies which cannot obtain them elsewhere. Terms may range to 10 years or longer, and interest rates are usually comparable to the market rate. The BDB also makes loans under SBA guarantees.

Funds are available for any sound business purpose, excluding debt financing or speculative purposes.

Small Business Administration (SBA)
Strom Thurman Federal Bldg.
1835 Assembly Street, Room 358   803-765-5376
Columbia, SC 29201   FAX: 803-765-5962

SBA 7(a) Guaranteed and Direct Loans: Guarantees up to 90 percent of a loan made through a private lender up to $750,000. Can be used for working capital, expand or convert facilities, purchase of machinery and equipment, and land and building. Available only to those unable to obtain a loan from conventional sources. Direct loans are made up to $150,000.

SBA 504: Provides loans using 50 percent conventional bank financing, 40 percent SBA involvement through Certified Development Companies, and 10 percent owner equity. Fixed-asset loans are available in amounts up to $750,000. The loan can be used for land and building, construction, machinery and equipment, and renovation/expansion.

Small Business Innovative Research Grants (SBIR): Phase I awards between $20,000 to $50,000 to entrepreneurs to support six months of research on a technical innovation. Phase II grants are an additional $500,000 for development. Private sector investment funds must follow.

International Trade Loans: Guaranteed long-term loans through private lenders to develop or expand export markets, or to recover from the effects of import competition. Maximum guaranteed loan is $1,000,000 for fixed assets and an additional $250,000 for working capital and/or export revolving line of credit.

Export Revolving Line of Credit Loan: Short term financing available to small businesses that are at least one year old. Loans provide working capital to finance the manufacturing or wholesaling of products for export and for export marketing. The SBA will guarantee up to 90 percent of a conventional loan in amounts up to $750,000.

Contract Loan: Short-term loans are available to small businesses to finance the costs of labor and materials on contracts for which the proceeds are assignable. Program guarantees up to 90 percent of loans not in excess of $750,000. Qualifying small businesses must be in business for at least 12 calendar months prior to the date of the loan application.

Seasonal Line of Credit Loan: Loans provide short-term working capital to finance seasonal increases in business activities. Program guarantees up to 90 percent of loans not in excess of $750,000. Qualifying business must be in operation for at least one year prior to application.

Pollution Control Loans: Long-term guaranteed loans can be made by conventional financing to small businesses for installation or required pollution control measures. Must be unable to adopt the pollution control measures without undue financial hardship. Maximum guaranteed loan is $1,000,000.

General Contractor Loans: Small general construction contractors may obtain short-term loans or loan guarantees for residential or commercial construction or rehabilitation of property to be sold. The SBA will guarantee up to 90 percent of qualifying loans made by private lenders up to a maximum of $750,000. Direct loans can be up to $150,000.

Energy Business Loan Guarantee: Small businesses that provide certain energy production and conservation services for others may qualify for long-term loans and loan guarantees for start-ups and expansions. Loans and guarantees are made for firms that develop, manufacture, sell, install, or service specific energy measures for others, or firms that provide engineering, architectural, consulting, or other professional services connected with specific energy measures. Guarantee is for up to 90 percent of a loan not in excess of $750,000. Direct loans up to $150,000.

Disaster Recovery Loans: Small businesses located in federally designated disaster areas and suffering property damage or economic losses from the disaster can obtain long-term recovery loans at low interest rates. Property damage loans are limited to 85 percent of the verified damage. Loans for economic losses are for operating capital to meet the business' obligations that could have been made had the disaster not occurred.

Handicapped Assistance Loans: Assists persons who have a physical, mental or emotional nature which limits the selection of any type of employment for which the person would otherwise be qualified. Direct loans are available for up to $150,000. The interest rate is 3% on these loans.

Surety Bond Guaranty Program: Makes the bonding system more available to small contractors who may be denied access to the system. SBA can guarantee up to 80 percent of surety's loss on a bond that has a maximum in total contract value of up to $1,250,000.

Vietnam-era and Disabled Veterans Loan Program: Provides direct loans to veterans to establish or expand a small business. Funds may be used for working capital or fixed assets. Direct loans for amounts up to $150,000 are available. The interest rate may be fixed or variable.

Charleston Capital Corporation
111 Church Street
P.O. Box 328
Charleston, SC 29402   803-723-6464

Floco Investment Company, Inc.
Highway 52 North
Mail: P.O. Box 919; Lake City, SC 29560
Scranton, SC 29561   803-389-2731

Lowcountry Investment Corporation
4444 Daley Street
P.O. Box 10447
Charleston, SC 29411   803-554-9880

Reedy River Ventures
233 N. Main Street, Suite 350
P.O. Box 17526
Greenville, SC 29606   803-232-6198

Small Business Investment Companies (SBIC): The SBA licenses, regulates, and provides financial assistance to privately owned and operated Small Business Investment Companies. SBICs make venture or risk investments by supplying capital and extending unsecured loans and loans not fully collateralized to small enterprises which meet their investment criteria. Financing is made by direct loans and by equity investments.

* Women and Minority Business Assistance

Governor's Office of Small and Minority Business Assistance
1205 Pendleton Street, Room 437
Columbia, SC 29201   803-734-0564

This office assists minority businesses to become certified and placed on the state bidder's list for federal and state government contracts.

Small Business Administration (SBA)
Strom Thurman Federal Bldg.
1835 Assembly Street, Room 358   803-765-5376
Columbia, SC 29201   FAX: 803-765-4539

SBA 8(a) Program - Business Procurement Assistance: Provides federal government contracting opportunities for small businesses owned by socially and economically disadvantaged persons, and assists these businesses to become independently competitive in the normal business environment. SBA monitors all government contracts to assure that a quota of contract work goes to 8(a) businesses. Also provides business management services to these businesses. Business must be approved for program participation prior to receipt of an 8(a) contract.

* Training

South Carolina Jobs/Economic Development Authority
1201 Main Street, Suite 1750
Columbia, SC 29201   803-737-0079

Job Training Partnership Act (JTPA): Provides employers with recruitment, screening, referral, training, 50 percent wage subsidy up to 3 months for on-the-job training. Available to any private employer.

* Management Consulting and Other Services

South Carolina State Development Board
P.O. Box 927
Columbia, SC 29202   803-737-0400
    Foreign Trade Zones: Located in Summerville (near Charleston) and Columbia, these zones allow businesses to import goods or raw materials and store them without paying duty until they are shipped out of the zone.

    Export Assistance Programs: Export finance officers can aid exporters in locating, applying for, and arranging export financing, as well as export credit insurance. Tax incentives defer state income taxes on increases in export sales for companies with less than $5 million in export sales for the past three years. Workshops are available that target several companies with potential in the field and match them with experts who supply counseling. The State Development Board is also responsible for organizing trade missions, trade shows, and operating overseas offices in Belgium and Japan.

Small Business Administration
Strom Thurman Federal Bldg.
1835 Assembly Street, Room 358   803-765-5376
Columbia, SC 29201   FAX: 803-765-4539
    Small Business Institutes: This program provides personalized consulting services to the small business community. Consulting is provided by senior level business students, guided by a faculty advisor. Assistance in business plan preparation, marketing research, market planning, accounting, and seminars are provided.
    University Locations:
    Clemson University
    College of Charleston
    Francis Marion College
    University of South Carolina
    Winthrop College

* Small Business Development Centers

The following office offers free and fee-based services to new and expanding businesses:

Lead Center:
South Carolina Small Business Development Center
University of South Carolina
College of Business Administration   803-777-5118
Columbia, SC 29208   FAX: 803-777-4403

    Beaufort: University of South Carolina at Beaufort, Small Business Development Center, 800 Carterat Street, Beaufort, SC 29902, 803-521-4143; FAX: 803-521-4198.

    Charleston: Trident Technical College, Charleston Small Business Development Center, 66 Columbus Street, P.O. Box 20339, Charleston, SC 29413-0339, 803-727-2020; FAX: 803-727-2013.

    Clemson: Clemson University, Small Business Development Center, 425 Sirrine Hall, Clemson, SC 29634-1392, 803-656-3227; FAX: 803-656-4889.

    Columbia: University of South Carolina, USC Regional Small Business Development Center, College of Business Administration, Columbia, SC 29208, 803-777-5118; FAX: 803-777-4403.

    Conway: Coastal Carolina, Small Business Development Center, School of Business Administration, Conway, SC 29526, 803-349-2169; FAX: 803-349-2990.

    Florence: Florence Darlington Tech, Small Business Development Center, P.O. Box 100648, Florence, SC 29501-0548, 803-661-8324; FAX: 803-661-8041.

    Greenville: Greenville Technical College, Small Business Development Center, Box 5616, Station B-GHEC, Greenville, SC 29606, 803-271-4259; FAX: 803-250-8514.

    Greenwood: Upper Savannah Council of Governments, Small Business Development Center, SBDC Exchange Building, 222 Phoenix Street, Suite 200, P.O. Box 1366, Greenwood, SC 29648, 803-227-61100; FAX: 803-229-1869.

    Hilton Head Island: University of South Carolina at Hilton Head, Small Business Development Center, Suite 300, Kiawah Bldg., 10 Office Park Road, Hilton Head Island, SC 29928, 803-785-3995; FAX: 803-777-0333.

    North Augusta: Aiken/North Augusta Small Business Development Center, Triangle Plaza, Highway 25, 215-B Edgefield Road, North Augusta, SC 29481, 803-442-3670; FAX: 803-641-3445.

    Orangeburg: South Carolina State College, Small Business Development Center, School of Business Administration, Orangeburg, SC 29117, 803-536-8445; FAX: 803-536-8066.

    Rock Hill: Winthrop College, Small Business Development Center, 119 Thurmond Building, Rock Hill SC 29733, 803-323-2283, FAX: 803-323-3960.

    Spartanburg: Spartanburg Chamber of Commerce, Small Business Development Center, P.O. Box 1636, Spartanburg, SC 29304, 803-594-5080; FAX: 803-594-5055.

South Dakota

* General Information

Governor's Office of Economic Development
711 East Wells Avenue   1-800-872-6190
Pierre, SD 57501-3369   605-773-5032
    Small Business Advocate: Assistance in cutting bureaucratic red tape. Information and expertise in dealing with state, federal, and local agencies.

* Financing

Governor's Office of Economic Development
711 East Wells Avenue   605-773-5032
Pierre, SD 57501-3369   1-800-872-6190
    Community Development Block Grant: An anti-poverty block grant program whose funds are channeled towards those services and activities that will have an impact on the causes of poverty. About 90 percent of the funding goes to Community Action Agencies which can use the funds in various ways, such as revolving loan funds. Some of the types of activities funds are used for are to assist low-income people to secure and retain employment, obtain and maintain housing, obtain emergency assistance to meet immediate needs such as health services, nutritious food, housing, or employment assistance.

    Revolving Economic Development and Initiative Fund (REDI): Funded by a one year, 1 percent sales tax, the REDI funds are used for a low-interest revolving loan fund for economic development and job creation. Loans are available to any for-profit business or non-profit business cooperative, whether business start-ups, business expansions, or business relocation. Funds can be used for purchase of land and site improvements; construction, acquisition, or renovation of buildings; fees, services and other costs associated with construction; machinery and equipment, trade receivables; inventory; and other working capital needs. The fund may provide up to 45 percent of the total project cost and requires applicants to have matching funds available beforehand, including a 10 percent equity contribution. Interest rates begin at 3 percent, but will later be determined semi-annually. Terms are amortized up to 20 years.

    Economic Development Finance Authority:
    Pooled Development Bonds Program: Allows businesses to pool tax-exempt or taxable development bonds for the construction of any site, structure, facility, or service or utility for storage, distribution or manufacturing of industrial agricultural or nonagricultural products related to manufacturing, including the purchase of machinery and equipment. The Authority considers loan requests of $300,000. Pooled volume must be $1 million or more. Pooled bonds allow smaller projects to become part of the tax exempt issue and may lower interest rates.

    Industrial Revenue Bonds (IRB): May be issued by any municipality, county, or sanitary district and may be used to finance industrial, commercial, manufacturing, agricultural, natural resources, educational, and other facilities. IRB's are limited obligation bonds of the issuing municipality, and once issued, they are to be repaid exclusively from the revenue produced by the project being financed.

SBA 7(a) Guaranteed and Direct Loans: Guarantees up to 90 percent of a loan made through a private lender, up to $750,000. Can be used for working capital, inventory, machinery and equipment, and land and building. Available only to those unable to obtain a loan from conventional sources. Direct loans are made up to $150,000.

SBA 504: Provides loans using 50 percent conventional bank financing, 40 percent SBA involvement through Certified Development Companies, and 10 percent owner equity. A fixed-asset loan (land, building, and equipment with a useful life of 10 years or more) in amounts up to $750,000. Administered through the South Dakota Development Corporation, eligible businesses may borrow up to $500,000 with a minimum of $50,000. One job is to be created for each $35,000 of loan amount.

Community Development Block Grants Special Projects Account: Allows the state to provide grants to local government, who in turn, loan funds to businesses which will locate in the community to create jobs which benefit low and moderate income persons.

Fastrack Loan Guarantee Program: Enables students who have an idea for a new business to obtain back financing guaranteed through the Fastrack Foundation. High school students in grades 9-12 are eligible to participate. A business plan should be prepared which should include market, competition, promotion ideas, costs and financing needs.

Agricultural Processing and Export Loan Program (APEX): Eligible to businesses that will use and add value to one or more of South Dakota's agricultural products; locate in a community with a population of less than 2,000; employ low income persons, farm families or displaced farm families. Funds may be used for purchase of land and associated site improvements; construction, acquisition or renovation of building; fees, services and other costs associated with construction; trade receivables; inventory; other working capital needs; refinancing of existing debt; and crop and livestock production. Can provide up to 70 percent of the total project cost. Maximum loan amount is $150,000. Interest rates are between five and seven percent.

Department of Agriculture
Office of Rural Development
Anderson Building
445 East Capitol
Pierre, SD 57501   605-773-3375

Agricultural Loan Participation Program: A vehicle for supplementing existing credit, this program is administered through local lenders, with the state Department of Agriculture providing up to 80 percent of the funding. Interest can be up to 10 percent, with a maximum loan length of 10 years. Applicants must have lived in South Dakota for the past two years, be at least 21 years old, and have derived at least 60 percent of their income in the past tax year from farming. Projects funded are those which show they will add value to, or create innovative uses for South Dakota agricultural products, especially those of which there is a surplus. Can also be used in developing viable new agricultural products and subsequent markets or enhancing the economic viability of the applicant or the rural community.

Farmers Home Administration
200 4th Street, S.W.
Huron, SD 57350   605-353-1430

Guaranteed Business and Industrial Loans: Loans aimed at creating and maintaining employment and improving the economies of rural areas. Local lenders initiate and service the loans, while the FmHA guarantees up to 90 percent of the loan. Potential borrowers who want loans of $500,000 or less should apply to the Small Business Administration. Guarantees are limited to $10 million. Interest rates are determined between the borrower and the lender and can be fixed or variable. Eligible projects and costs are business and industrial acquisitions, construction, conversion, enlargement, repair or modernization; purchase of land, machinery and equipment, furniture and fixtures, and certain housing development sites; processing and marketing facilities, start-up and working capital; pollution control; feasibility studies.

Rural Rental Housing Loans: Loans are available to create, improve, or purchase modest but adequate housing units for people with low to moderate incomes and for those age 62 or older. Loans may be made for housing in open country and in communities with populations of up to $20,000. The borrowers must be unable to finance the housing with personal resources, and be unable to obtain credit from other sources. Funds can be used to build, purchase or repair apartment-style housing, buy and improve the land on which the buildings are to be located, provide streets and water and waste disposal systems, supply appropriate recreation and service facilities, install laundry facilities and equipment, landscaping.

Bureau of Indian Affairs
Area Credit Office
Federal Building
115 4th Avenue, S.E.
Aberdeen, SD 57401   605-226-7343

Economic Development Grant Program: Provides seed money to Indian entrepreneurs to establish and increase profit-making business ventures and employment on or near federal Indian reservations. Grants are awarded for up to 25 percent of the total project and may not exceed $100,000 for individuals. Applicants must be able to raise matching funds of at least 75 percent of the total project costs.

Indian Loan Guaranty Fund: Guarantees loans made by private lenders to individual Indians for up to 90 percent of the unpaid principal. Funds must be used for projects that will benefit the reservation economy, with a $350,000 limit on loans to individuals. A 20 percent equity contribution is required. Thirty years is the maximum maturity term for these loans. Interest rates may not exceed 2 3/4 percent of the New York prime.

Revolving Loan Fund: Makes direct loans to individual Indians for economic enterprises which will contribute to the economy of an Indian reservation. Applicants must be unable to obtain financing from other sources, and must use the Indian loan guaranty program before applying to the Revolving Loan Fund. Loans to individuals are limited to $500,000 with a 20 percent equity contribution required from the borrower. The duration of the loans is flexible (a maximum of 30 years), and interest rates are determined by the Secretary of the Treasury.

State Investment Council
4009 West 49th
Suite 300
Sioux Falls, SD 57106-3784   605-335-5023

Deals solely with venture capital funds that invest in equity or equity-participating instruments of businesses. The fund can invest only in businesses which have headquarters and the majority of their employees located within the state. The Investment Council's participation in a venture capital fund may not be greater than one-third of the total equity funds invested in the fund.

Small Business Administration (SBA)
101 S. Main Street
Suite 101   605-330-4231
Sioux Falls, SD 57102-0572   FAX: 605-330-4215

SBA 7(a) Guaranteed and Direct Loans: Guarantees up to 90 percent of a loan made through a private lender up to $750,000. Can be used for working capital, expand or convert facilities, purchase of machinery and equipment, and land and building. Available only to those unable to obtain a loan from conventional sources. Direct loans are made up to $150,000.

SBA 504: Provides loans using 50 percent conventional bank financing, 40 percent SBA involvement through Certified Development Companies, and 10 percent owner equity. Fixed-asset loans are available in amounts up to $750,000. The loan can be used for land and building, construction, machinery and equipment, and renovation/expansion.

Small Business Innovative Research Grants (SBIR): Phase I awards between $20,000 to $50,000 to entrepreneurs to support six months of research on a technical innovation. Phase II grants are an additional $500,000 for development. Private sector investment funds must follow.

International Trade Loans: Guaranteed long-term loans through private lenders to develop or expand export markets, or to recover from the effects of import competition. Maximum guaranteed loan is $1,000,000 for fixed assets and an additional $250,000 for working capital and/or export revolving line of credit.

Export Revolving Line of Credit Loan: Short term financing available to small businesses that are at least one year old. Loans provide working capital to finance the manufacturing or wholesaling of products for export and for export marketing. The SBA will guarantee up to 90 percent of a conventional loan in amounts up to $750,000.

Contract Loan: Short-term loans are available to small businesses to finance the costs of labor and materials on contracts for which the proceeds are assignable. Program guarantees up to 90 percent of loans not in excess of $750,000. Qualifying small businesses must be in business for at least 12 calendar months prior to the date of the loan application.

Seasonal Line of Credit Loan: Loans provide short-term working capital to finance seasonal increases in business activities. Program guarantees up to 90 percent of loans not in excess of $750,000. Qualifying business must be in operation for at least one year prior to application.

Pollution Control Loans: Long-term guaranteed loans can be made by conventional financing to small businesses for installation or required pollution control measures. Must be unable to adopt the pollution control measures without undue financial hardship. Maximum guaranteed loan is $1,000,000.

General Contractor Loans: Small general construction contractors may obtain short-term loans or loan guarantees for residential or commercial construction or rehabilitation of property to be sold. The SBA will guarantee up to 90 percent of qualifying loans made by private lenders up to a maximum of $750,000. Direct loans can be up to $150,000.

Energy Business Loan Guarantee: Small businesses that provide certain energy production and conservation services for others may qualify for long-term loans and loan guarantees for start-ups and expansions. Loans and guarantees are made for firms that develop, manufacture, sell, install, or service specific energy measures for others, or firms that provide engineering, architectural, consulting, or other professional services connected with specific energy measures. Guarantee is for up to 90 percent of a loan not in excess of $750,000. Direct loans up to $150,000.

Disaster Recovery Loans: Small businesses located in federally designated disaster areas and suffering property damage or economic losses from the disaster can obtain long-term recovery loans at low interest rates. Property damage loans are limited to 85 percent of the verified damage. Loans for economic losses are for operating capital to meet the business' obligations that could have been made had the disaster not occurred.

Handicapped Assistance Loans: Assists persons who have a physical, mental or emotional disability of a permanent nature which limits the selection of any type of employment for which the person would otherwise be qualified. Direct loans are available for up to $150,000. The interest rate is 3% on these loans.

Surety Bond Guaranty Program: Makes the bonding system more available to small contractors who may be denied access to the system. SBA can guarantee up to 80 percent of surety's loss on a bond that has a maximum in total contract value of up to $1,250,000.

Vietnam-era and Disabled Veterans Loan Program: Provides direct loans to veterans to establish or expand a small business. Funds may be used for working capital or fixed assets. Direct loans for amounts up to $150,000 are available. The interest rate may be fixed or variable.

* Women and Minority Business Assistance

Office of Indian Affairs
Governor's Office of Economic Development
118 W. Capitol Avenue, Public Safety Bldg.
Pierre, SD 57501   605-773-3415
Works to increase minority participation in all facets of business both within and beyond the state. The MBO works with civic and professional groups and state, tribal, and federal government agencies to act as a communications link for the minority business community. It provides

workshops and seminars, publishes a Minority Business Directory (which includes minority businesses, as well as related federal, state and tribal agencies and private groups) and tries to match a client's needs with the services available throughout the state.

Small Business Administration (SBA)
101 S. Main Street, Suite 101   605-330-4231
Sioux Falls, SD 57102-0572   FAX: 605-330-4215
SBA 8(a) Program - Business Procurement Assistance: Provides federal government contracting opportunities for small businesses owned by socially and economically disadvantaged persons, and assists these businesses to become independently competitive in the normal business environment. SBA monitors all government contracts to assure that a quota of contract work goes to 8(a) businesses. Also provides business management services to these businesses. Business must be approved for program participation prior to receipt of an 8(a) contract.

* Training

South Dakota Department of Labor
420 South Roosevelt
P.O. Box 4730
Aberdeen, SD 57402-4730   605-622-2302
On-The-Job Training: The employer agrees to hire an eligible individual or permanent employment before training begins and is responsible for all the employee's salary and fringe benefits during the training period. A written training agreement between the Department of Labor and the employer. Payment made to the employer under an on-the-job training agreement does not exceed 50 percent of the wages paid by the employer to the participant during the period of the agreement and is considered as compensation for extraordinary training costs and for the costs associated with the lower productivity of the participant.

Job Training Partnership Act (JTPA): Provides employers with recruitment, screening, referral, training, 50 percent wage subsidy up to 3 months for on-the-job training. The South Dakota Department of Labor can tailor job training programs to meet employers' needs. Available to any private employer.

Department of Education and Cultural Affairs:
Office of Vocational-Technical Education   605-773-3423
Business and Industry Training: Offered statewide and is coordinated through the state's four vocational-technical schools. The state has been divided into four multi-county areas. Each area has a vocational administrator who is responsible for designing the training programs for each client and are developed to enhance the productivity of the employees. Programs are designed to be cost effective and responsive to the needs of business and industry.

Department of Labor
Private Industry Council
700 Governor's Drive, Kneip Building
Pierre, SD 57501   605-773-5017
Job Service of South Dakota: There are 19 Job Service offices throughout the state. Each office can provide employers with "One Stop Shopping" in recruiting, testing, training and hiring a productive work force.

Targeted Jobs Tax Credit (TJTC): A federal income tax credit which private employers can claim when they hire employees in targeted groups.

Labor Market Information Center
P.O. Box 4730
420 South Roosevelt
Aberdeen, SD 57402-4730   605-622-2314
Staffed by labor economists who can provide information on such subjects as statistics, agricultural economics and labor economics. Publications available are the *South Dakota Labor Bulletin*, a monthly publication that contains information on employment and unemployment; *Labor Bulletin* contains articles on such markets as tourism-related employment, women in the work force and growth within the manufacturing industry.; *South Dakota Occupational Outlook Handbook* contains more than 300 occupations specific to South Dakota industries, plus others.

* Management Consulting and Other Services

Procurement Technical Assistance Program
Business Research Bureau
414 East Clark Street
Vermillion, SD 57069   605-677-5287

> **Procurement Assistance:** One-on-one counseling is provided to firms interested in selling their products to the federal government as well as seminars that are conducted statewide. Locates, screens and matches federal procurement requirements to the capabilities of individual businesses.

Governor's Office of Economic Development
Capitol Lake Plaza   1-800-872-6190
Pierre, SD 57501   605-773-5032

> **Financial Packaging:** Customize financial packages for individual companies. Review a project and confer with key company people to determine best combination of sources with the most appropriate rates and terms.

> **Export, Trade and Marketing Division**   605-773-5735
> Services offered are *South Dakota Made* decals available to manufacturers and processors to increase visibility and awareness of their products. *Taste of South Dakota* annual trade show held to increase awareness of South Dakota made products and to assist small to medium size firms with marketing their products. Assistance to manufacturers and processors who want to participate in regional, national and international trade shows, and also target trade shows for processors. Export services such as graining product and label clearances, assisting with customs documentation, research tariffs and subsidies, and determining best means of shipping. Exporters can register to receive computerized international trade leads. At the request of supplies, the Division with organize and lead firms on trade missions and industry specific trade shows.

> **Promotion of Agricultural Products**   1-800-872-6190
> Special services are offered for food processors, livestock owners, commodity groups, and domestic market development. Some of these services include one-on-one counseling, seminars and conferences, information on genetics and nutrition, and public information efforts aimed at increasing awareness of local products.

> **Site Location Assistance:** The state works with businesses interested in locating or expanding within South Dakota to help them find the best possible location by providing a prospective firm with information on available buildings, available labor force, tax advantages, utility rates, zoning requirements, etc.

Small Business Administration
101 S. Main Street
Suite 101
Sioux Falls, SD 57102-0572   605-330-4231
    FAX: 605-330-4215

> **Small Business Institutes:** This program provides personalized consulting services to the small business community. Consulting is provided by senior level business students, guided by a faculty advisor. Assistance in business plan preparation, marketing research, market planning, accounting, and seminars are provided.
> **University Locations:**
> Augustana College
> Black Hills State College
> Dakota State University
> Huron College
> Minot State College
> Northern State University
> Sioux Falls College
> South Dakota State University
> University of South Dakota

* Small Business Development Centers

The following offices offer free and fee-based services to new and expanding businesses:

Lead Center:
South Dakota Small Business Development Center

University of South Dakota
414 East Clark   605-677-5272
Vermillion, SD 57069   FAX: 605-677-5427

> **Aberdeen:** Small Business Development Center, 226 Citizens Building, Aberdeen, SD 57401, 605-225-2252.

> **Pierre:** Small Business Development Center, 105 South Euclid, Suite C, Pierre, SD 57501, 605-773-5941.

> **Rapid City:** Small Business Development Center, 444 Mount Rushmore Road, #208, P.O. Box 7715, Rapid City, SD 57709, 605-394-5311.

> **Sioux Falls:** Small Business Development Center, 200 North Phillips, L103, Sioux Falls, SD 57102, 605-339-3366.

Tennessee

* General Information

Office of Small Business
Department of Economic and Community Development
Rachel Jackson State Office Building
320 Sixth Avenue North
Nashville, TN 37243-0405   615-741-2626

> Serves as an advocate for the small business community. Acts as a clearinghouse on programs and projects in both the public and private sectors that assist small business.

> **Small Business Advocate**   615-741-2626
> Assistance in cutting bureaucratic red tape. Information and expertise in dealing with state, federal, and local agencies.

* Financing

Department of Economic and Community Development
Rachel Jackson State Office Building
320 Sixth Avenue North   615-741-6671
Nashville, TN 37243-0405   1-800-342-1340 in Tennessee

> **Energy Division, 8th Floor:**
> **Small Business Energy Loan Program:** Small businesses with under 500 employees, local governments or not-for-profit companies in good financial shape can qualify for loans at 5 percent annual interest with varying repayment periods. Maximum amount is $100,000 for installing energy efficiency measures in an existing structure at least one year old. Energy improvements include: insulation, storm doors and windows, specially coated glass, energy control devices, furnace systems, solar heating, and energy efficient lighting.

> **Program Management Section**   615-741-6201
> **Tennessee Industrial Infrastructure Program:** Available to manufacturing and other types of economic activities which export more than half of their product or services outside of Tennessee, businesses where more than half of their product or services enters into the production of exported products, and uses which primarily result in import substitution or the replacement of imported products or services with those produced in Tennessee. Provides grants and loans to local governments and businesses for job creation activities, including infrastructure improvements. Activities include those involved in water and wastewater systems, transportation, site improvements, and electrical and natural gas systems, among others.

> **Tennessee Small Cities Community Development Block Grants (CDBG) Industrial Grant/Loan Program:** The state allocates a significant amount of its available CDBG money for this program. Funds are awarded for grants and loans to assist industries in locating or expanding in Tennessee and providing jobs. Jobs must be for low and moderate income persons. Grants are made for public infrastructure, and loans are made for industrial buildings and equipment. Maximum loan generally is $500,000. Up to $750,000 to businesses locating or expanding in a community designated as a distressed area.

> **Venture Capital:** Works with private investors to inject seed capital into promising or expanding firms. Up to $500,000 is available for working capital or fixed assets in manufacturing, warehousing, distribution, and

other non-retail firms. The Corporation is limited to 50 percent of the total investment in a project.

Bond Reservation Section   615-741-2373
Industrial Development Bonds: These are mostly taxable bonds issued by local governments on behalf of businesses. Often used to finance manufacturing, multi-family housing, and single- family housing, these bonds may provide 100 percent financing, with interest rates lower than for conventional bonds.

Small Business Administration (SBA)
50 Vantage Way
Suite 201   615-736-5881
Nashville, TN 37228-1500   FAX: 615-736-7232
  SBA 7(a) Guaranteed and Direct Loans: Guarantees up to 90 percent of a loan made through a private lender up to $750,000. Can be used for working capital, expand or convert facilities, purchase of machinery and equipment, and land and building. Available only to those unable to obtain a loan from conventional sources. Direct loans are made up to $150,000.

  SBA 504: Provides loans using 50 percent conventional bank financing, 40 percent SBA involvement through Certified Development Companies, and 10 percent owner equity. Fixed-asset loans are available in amounts up to $750,000. The loan can be used for land and building, construction, machinery and equipment, and renovation/expansion.

  Small Business Innovative Research Grants (SBIR): Phase I awards between $20,000 to $50,000 to entrepreneurs to support six months of research on a technical innovation. Phase II grants are an additional $500,000 for development. Private sector investment funds must follow.

  International Trade Loans: Guaranteed long-term loans through private lenders to develop or expand export markets, or to recover from the effects of import competition. Maximum guaranteed loan is $1,000,000 for fixed assets and an additional $250,000 for working capital and/or export revolving line of credit.

  Export Revolving Line of Credit Loan: Short term financing available to small businesses that are at least one year old. Loans provide working capital to finance the manufacturing or wholesaling of products for export and for export marketing. The SBA will guarantee up to 90 percent of a conventional loan in amounts up to $750,000.

  Contract Loan: Short-term loans are available to small businesses to finance the costs of labor and materials on contracts for which the proceeds are assignable. Program guarantees up to 90 percent of loans not in excess of $750,000. Qualifying small businesses must be in business for at least 12 calendar months prior to the date of the loan application.

  Seasonal Line of Credit Loan: Loans provide short-term working capital to finance seasonal increases in business activities. Program guarantees up to 90 percent of loans not in excess of $750,000. Qualifying business must be in operation for at least one year prior to application.

  Pollution Control Loans: Long-term guaranteed loans can be made by conventional financing to small businesses for installation or required pollution control measures. Must be unable to adopt the pollution control measures without undue financial hardship. Maximum guaranteed loan is $1,000,000.

  General Contractor Loans: Small general construction contractors may obtain short-term loans or loan guarantees for residential or commercial construction or rehabilitation of property to be sold. The SBA will guarantee up to 90 percent of qualifying loans made by private lenders up to a maximum of $750,000. Direct loans can be up to $150,000.

  Energy Business Loan Guarantee: Small businesses that provide certain energy production and conservation services for others may qualify for long-term loans and loan guarantees for start-ups and expansions. Loans and guarantees are made for firms that develop, manufacture, sell, install, or service specific energy measures for others, or firms that provide engineering, architectural, consulting, or other professional services connected with specific energy measures. Guarantee is for up to 90 percent of a loan not in excess of $750,000. Direct loans up to $150,000.

  Disaster Recovery Loans: Small businesses located in federally designated disaster areas and suffering property damage or economic losses from the disaster can obtain long-term recovery loans at low interest rates. Property damage loans are limited to 85 percent of the verified damage. Loans for economic losses are for operating capital to meet the business' obligations that could have been made had the disaster not occurred.

  Handicapped Assistance Loans: Assists persons who have a physical, mental or emotional disability of a permanent nature which limits the selection of any type of employment for which the person would otherwise be qualified. Direct loans are available for up to $150,000. The interest rate is 3% on these loans.

  Surety Bond Guaranty Program: Makes the bonding system more available to small contractors who may be denied access to the system. SBA can guarantee up to 80 percent of surety's loss on a bond that has a maximum in total contract value of up to $1,250,000.

  Vietnam-era and Disabled Veterans Loan Program: Provides direct loans to veterans to establish or expand a small business. Funds may be used for working capital or fixed assets. Direct loans for amounts up to $150,000 are available. The interest rate may be fixed or variable.

Financial Resources, Inc.
200 Jefferson Avenue, Suite 750
Memphis, TN 38103   901-527-9411
  Small Business Investment Companies (SBIC): The SBA licenses, re-gulates, and provides financial assistance to privately owned and operated Small Business Investment Companies. SBICs make venture or risk invest-ments by supplying capital and extending unsecured loans and loans not fully collateralized to small enterprises which meet their investment criteria. Financing is made by direct loans and by equity investments.

Tennessee Valley Authority (TVA)
400 W. Summit Hill Drive, O.C.H. 1E
Knoxville, TN 37902   615-632-3148
  Special Opportunities Counties Program: There are approximately 24 Tennessee counties eligible for this program, the objective of which is to assist the Valley's poorest counties to create new private sector job opportunities and enable them to utilize local resources for economic development. TVA contributes no more than 50 percent of the project costs, and is based on a ration of $3,000 to $5,000 per job created. Investments may range from $2,000 for low-skilled jobs to $6,000 for high-skilled high-wage positions. TVA funds may go in combination with other federal or private funds to municipalities, industrial development authorities,or other non-profit organizations devoted to economic development. These entities may in turn lend the funds at TVA long-term borrowing rates.

Farmers Home Administration (FmHA)
Department of Agriculture
3322 W. End Ave., Suite 300
Nashville, TN 37203   615-736-7341
  FmHA Business and Industrial Loans: For rural areas outside cities of 50,000 or more with priority to areas of 25,000 or less population. This aid is in the form of loan guarantees in which the FmHA guarantees private lenders up to 90 percent reimbursement of losses. Applicants deal directly with private lenders. Maximum loan is $10 million, with an alcohol fuel loan limit of $20 million. (For loans under $500,000, borrowers are advised to contact the Small Business Administration.) Terms are 30 years for land, building and fixtures, 15 years for machinery or equipment, and 7 years for working capital. Interest rates may be fixed or varied.

Tennessee Technology Foundation (TTF)
P.O. Box 23184
Knoxville, TN 37933-1184   615-694-6772
  A private, non-profit corporation created to stimulate growth in technology-based businesses in Tennessee, TTF targets the "Technology Corridor" in the eastern part of the state where the Oak Ridge National Laboratory, the Tennessee Valley Authority, and the University of Tennessee are located. It provides services such as linking state, federal, and private sector resources, siting new facilities, identifying sources of capital and manpower for new or existing businesses, and helping with

business plans for new companies. It also maintains a computerized inventory of real estate including both raw and improved land. The Foundation works to assist high technology businesses in technical areas and to help with the commercialization of R&D products.

* Women and Minority Business Assistance

Office of Minority Business Enterprise (OMBE)
Department of Economic and Community Development
Rachel Jackson Building, 7th Floor
320 Sixth Avenue North   615-741-2545
Nashville, TN 37243-0405   1-800-251-8594 in Tennessee
    Provides information, advocacy, referral, procurement, and other services to minority businesses in the state. The office publishes a directory of minority businesses, offers conferences and seminars on topics useful to business owners, and serves as a clearinghouse of important information to minorities. OMBE also matches minority vendors with potential clients and helps minorities identify and obtain procurement opportunities.

Small Business Administration (SBA)
50 Vantage Way, #201   615-736-5881
Nashville, TN 37228-1500   FAX: 615-736-7232
    SBA 8(a) Program - Business Procurement Assistance: Provides federal government contracting opportunities for small businesses owned by socially and economically disadvantaged persons, and assists these businesses to become independently competitive in the normal business environment. SBA monitors all government contracts to assure that a quota of contract work goes to 8(a) businesses. Also provides business management services to these businesses. Business must be approved for program participation prior to receipt of an 8(a) contract.

* Training

Department of Economic and Community Development
Industrial Training Service
Suite 660, Volunteer Plaza   615-741-1746
500 James Robertson Parkway   1-800-342-8470 in Tennessee
Nashville, TN 37243-0406   1-800-251-8594 out-of-state
    Industrial Training Service Assistance: Assistance to companies training new employees or expanding or locating in Tennessee to provide them with a custom-trained workforce. The different types of training programs include Pre-employment Training, On-the-Job Training, Systems Support Training, First- and Second-line Supervisory Training, Train the Trainer, Training for Unique Equipment and Processes, Training Materials, New Technology Training for Existing Industries.

Private Industry Council
100 North Main Street
Memphis, TN 38103   901-576-6536
    Job Training Partnership Act (JTPA): Provides employers with recruitment, screening, referral, training, 50 percent wage subsidy up to 3 months for on-the-job training. Available to any private employer.

* Management Consulting and Other Services

Department of Economic and Community Development
Rachel Jackson State Office Building
320 Sixth Avenue North   1-800-342-1340 in Tennessee
Nashville, TN 37243   615-741-6671
    International Marketing Division: Recruits new foreign industry to the state, especially from countries of the Pacific Rim, Canada, and Europe. Organizes and conducts recruitment trips abroad and works with executives of foreign companies in site selection and other business needs.

    Export Trade Promotion Office: Assists local firms in exporting their manufactured, agricultural and service goods. Provides export firms with information on foreign market opportunities, holds seminars, provides logistical support, and conducts foreign trade missions, catalogue shows, and other marketing programs.

    High Technology Development Division: Coordinates delivery of technical assistance to high technology firms, especially with start-ups and small

business expansions. It also maintains a liaison with the Tennessee Technology Foundation, a private, non-profit organization involved in development.

    Existing Industries Services: Helps state manufacturers stay healthy and expand through promotion of manufacturing and services within Tennessee. Programs include an Existing Industry Visitation program which tries to reduce unnecessary obstacles to growth by government regulations, an Industry Image program which promotes Tennessee's business climate, and a Product Match program which encourages state manufacturers to buy supplies, materials, and equipment from other Tennessee businesses.

    National Marketing Division: Recruits new industry from outside Tennessee, with site selection assistance. Locates potential industries that could aid Tennessee communities.

    Industrial Training Service: Assists new and expanding businesses by providing a trained labor force, while helping residents acquire job skills necessary to compete in the labor market. The Service conducts the initial contact with industrial prospects, coordinates and contracts with vocational-technical institutions, and monitors and evaluates training programs.

    Industrial Research Section: Provides statistical information to assist sales and marketing efforts, as well as for community development and services to existing industry. Information includes prospect feasibility studies regarding potential industrial locations within Tennessee and a manufacturers database of 6,000 companies listed. State business cost comparisons are also on file.

Office of the Security of State
James K. Polk Building, 18th Floor
Nashville, TN 37243-0306   615-741-0531
    Trademarks and Service Marks: Trademarks and service marks used in business are registered here. Registration is effective for ten years and may be renewed six months prior to expiration for an additional ten years.

Small Business Administration
50 Vantage Way, #201   615-736-5881
Nashville, TN 37228-1500   FAX: 615-736-7232
    Small Business Institutes: This program provides personalized consulting services to the small business community. Consulting is provided by senior level business students, guided by a faculty advisor. Assistance in business plan preparation, marketing research, market planning, accounting, and seminars are provided.
    University Locations:
    Austin Peay State University
    Bethel College
    East Tennessee State University
    Memphis State University
    Middle Tennessee State University
    Tennessee State University
    Tennessee Technological University
    Tusculum College
    University of Tennessee - Chattanooga
    University of Tennessee - Knoxville
    Vanderbilt University

* Small Business Development Centers
The following offer free and fee-based services to new and expanding businesses:

Lead Center:
Tennessee Small Business Development Center
Memphis State University
South Campus (Getwell Road)
Building #1   901-678-2500
Memphis, TN 38152   FAX: 901-678-4072

    Chattanooga: Chattanooga State Technical Community College, Small Business Development Center, 4501 Amnicola Highway, Chattanooga, TN 37406-1097, 615-697-4410; FAX: 615-698-5653.

    Chattanooga: Southeast Tennessee Development District, Small Business

Development Center, 25 Cherokee Blvd., Chattanooga, TN 37405, 615-266-5781; FAX: 615-267-7705.

Clarksville: Austin Peay State University, Small Business Development Center, College of Business, Clarksville, TN 37044-0001, 615-648-7764; FAX: 615-648-7475.

Cleveland: Cleveland State Community College, Small Business Development Center, Business & Technology, P.O. Box 3570, Cleveland, TN 37320-3570, 615-478-6247; FAX: 615-478-6251.

Columbia: Small Business Development Center, Memorial Building, Room 205, 308 West 7th Street, Columbia, TN 38401, 615-388-5674.

Cookeville: Tennessee Technological University, Small Business Development Center, College of Business Administration, P.O. Box 5023, Cookeville, TN 38505-0001, 615-372-3648; FAX: 615-372-6112.

Dyersburg: Dyersburg Community College, Small Business Development Center, P.O. Box 648, Dyersburg, TN 38024, 901-286-3200; FAX: 901-286-3201.

Hartsville: Four Lakes Regional Industrial Development Authority, Small Business Development Center, P.O. Box 63, Hartsville, TN 37074-0063, 615-374-9521; FAX: 615-374-4608.

Jackson: Jackson State Community College, Small Business Development Center, 2046 North Parkway Street, Jackson, TN 38310-3797, 901-424-5389; FAX: 901-425-2647.

Johnson City: East Tennessee State University, Small Business Development Center, College of Business, P.O. Box 70, 698A, Johnson City, TN 37614-0698, 615-929-5630; FAX: 615-929-5274.

Knoxville: Pellissippi State Technical Community College, Small Business Development Center, P.O. Box 22990, Knoxville, TN 37933-0990, 615-694-6660; FAX: 615-694-6583.

Knoxville: International Trade Center, 301 E. Church Avenue, Knoxville, TN 37915, 615-637-4283.

Memphis: Memphis State University, Small Business Development Center, 320 South Dudley Street, Memphis, TN 38104-3206, 901-527-1041; FAX: 901-527-1047.

Memphis: Memphis State University, Small Business Development Center, International Trade Center, Memphis, TN 38152, 901-678-4174; FAX: 901-678-4072.

Morristown: Walters State Community College, Small Business Development Center, Business/Industrial Services, 500 S. Davy Crockett Parkway, Morristown, TN 37813-688, 615-587-9722; FAX: 615-586-1918.

Murfreesboro: Middle Tennessee State University, Small Business Development Center, School of Business, P.O. Box 487, Murfreesboro, TN 37132, 615-898-2745; FAX: 615-898-5538.

Nashville: Tennessee State University, Small Business Development Center, School of Business, 330 10th Avenue North, Nashville, TN 37203-3401, 615-251-1178; FAX: 615-251-1178 (call first).

Texas

* General Information

Texas Department of Commerce
Small Business Division
P.O. Box 12728   512-472-5059
Austin, TX 78711   1-800-888-0511

Provides business counseling for both new and established firms. Helps firms locate capital, state procurement opportunities, state certification program for minority and women-owned businesses, and resources for management and technical assistance. An Office of Business Permit Assistance serves as a clearinghouse for permit-related information throughout the state and refers applicants to appropriate agencies for

permit and regulatory needs. Publications available containing information and resources for start-up and existing businesses.

Small Business Advocate: Assistance in cutting bureaucratic red tape. Information and expertise in dealing with state, federal, and local agencies.

* Financing

Texas Department of Commerce
P.O. Box 12728
Austin, TX 78711

Texas Capital Fund
Community Development Block Grant   512-320-9649
Awards are made to a city or county that in turn provides a loan to a specific business for "gap financing". Project must be located in a rural area generally with a population of 50,000 or less. Funds can be used for land, building, machinery and equipment, working capital, and infrastructure to businesses creating jobs of which 51 percent benefit low and moderate income persons. Minimum loan is $50,000, and maximum loan up to $500,000. Up to $2.5 million for infrastructure projects.

Industrial Revenue Bonds/Tax-Exempt Bond Program: May be issued by political subdivisions, the state Department of Commerce or conservation districts through the formation of industrial development corporations. Eligible projects are mostly manufacturing, but also include student loans. Proceeds may be used for land and depreciable property with limitations. Up to $10 million in tax exempt bonds may be issued. Also, in most cases, a letter of credit is needed for each project.

Taxable Bond Program: Taxable bonds may be issued for manufacturing, industrial, or commercial projects. There is no limit to the maximum size. Applicants must provide either a buyer for the bond or a letter of credit indicating the credit enhancement needed to rate the bonds.

Texas Enterprise Zone Program   512-320-9579
Provides incentives and regulatory relief to stimulate job creation and investment in economically distressed areas. Types of incentives include tax abatement to encourage business retention, expansion and start-ups, sales tax rebates available for businesses in the zone which are designated Enterprise Zone Projects.

Texas Rural Economic Development Fund   512-320-9649
Eligible to a manufacturing or industrial enterprise located in a rural city with a population of 50,000 or less or a county with a population of 200,000 or less and predominantly rural in character. Preference is given to food and fiber processing industries. Up to 85 percent of loan made by a commercial lender is guaranteed to the State. Funds can be used for land, buildings, equipment, facilities, working capital. Minimum loan is $50,000. Maximum loan is $350,000. Must create at least one job for every $35,000 of guarantee.

Texas Exporters Loan Guarantee Program   512-320-9662
A manufactured product with at least 25 percent Texas source components, labor or intellectual property is eligible as well as the export preparation of agricultural product or livestock. Up to 85 percent of loan made by commercial lender is guaranteed by the State. Funds can be used for raw materials, inventory, other manufacturing costs, marketing and equipment. Minimum loan is $10,000. Maximum loan is $350,000. Term of loan is 1 year or less.

Eximbank Working Capital Guarantee   512-320-9662
Export working capital loans are made through a commercial lender. Exporters may apply for preliminary commitments and then "shop" for a lender. Up to 90 percent of loan is guaranteed. Funds can be used for inventory and working capital. Minimum loan is $10,000 with no maximum. Loans are generally up to 12 months.

Texas Export Credit Umbrella Insurance Program   512-320-9662
An insurance policy is underwritten by the Eximbank and is designed to stimulate the expansion of Texas exports to foreign countries by insuring a company's eligible export credit sales against loss due to political and commercial reasons.

Contract Loan Program: Guarantees available to contractors and subcontractors engaged in the construction, manufacturing and service industries. Business must provide a specific product or service under an assignable contract. Finance estimated cost of labor and material needed to perform on a specific contract.

Loans to Small General Contractors: Loan guarantees available to construction contractors and homebuilders. Funds can be used for construction, rehabilitation for property for resale. Maximum loan guarantee is $750,000.

Handicapped Assistance Loan: Available to 100 percent owned by one or more handicapped individuals who are actively involved in the management of the company. Funds can be used for working capital, fixed assets, improvements, some debt refinancing. Direct loans up to $150,000 and $750,000 on guarantee.

Farmers Home Administration
District Office
101 S. Main, Suite 102
Temple, TX 76501   817-774-1307

Business and Industry Loan Program: Loan guarantees available for projects located in cities with a population of less than 50,000. Funds can be used for working capital, acquisition of fixed assets (can include land and building), improvements, and in some cases debt refinancing. Recommend projects over $50,000. Maximum loan is $10 million. Up to $20 million for alcohol fuel production facilities.

Agriculture Finance Office
Department of Agriculture
P.O. Box 12847
Austin, TX 78711

Linked Deposit Program   512-463-7686
Available for non-traditional alternative crops, processing facilities for agricultural products, and direct marketing initiatives. Funds can be used to purchase or least land, buildings, equipment, seed, fertilizer, etc. Maximum loan is $100,000 for production, $250,000 for processing and marketing.

Rural Microenterprise Loan Program   512-463-7686
Loans or loan guarantees available to family owned and operated enterprises in rural Texas. Funds can be used for fixed assets and working capital. Maximum loan or guarantee is $15,000 for start-ups and $30,000 for existing businesses.

Texas Agricultural Finance Authority (TAFA)   512-463-7686
Loans, loan guarantees or revenue bonds available to small and medium size enterprises that contribute to the diversification of Texas agriculture. Funds can be used for fixed assets and working capital.

Tyler Seed/Venture Growth Fund
P.O. Box 2004
Tyler, TX 75710   903-593-2004

Seed Capital Funds: Tyler and Smith counties have established seed capital funds which in invest in local companies. The funds are typically used to leverage other sources of funding.

Small Business Administration (SBA)
8625 King George Drive   214-767-7633
Dallas, TX 75235-3391   FAX: 214-767-7870

SBA 7(a) Guaranteed and Direct Loans: Guarantees up to 90 percent of a loan made through a private lender up to $750,000. Can be used for working capital, expand or convert facilities, purchase of machinery and equipment, and land and building. Available only to those unable to obtain a loan from conventional sources. Direct loans are made up to $150,000.

SBA 504: Provides loans using 50 percent conventional bank financing, 40 percent SBA involvement through Certified Development Companies, and 10 percent owner equity. Fixed-asset loans are available in amounts up to $750,000. The loan can be used for land and building, construction, machinery and equipment, and renovation/expansion.

Small Business Innovative Research Grants (SBIR): Phase I awards between $20,000 to $50,000 to entrepreneurs to support six months of

research on a technical innovation. Phase II grants are an additional $500,000 for development. Private sector investment funds must follow.

International Trade Loans: Guaranteed long-term loans through private lenders to develop or expand export markets, or to recover from the effects of import competition. Maximum guaranteed loan is $1,000,000 for fixed assets and an additional $250,000 for working capital and/or export revolving line of credit.

Export Revolving Line of Credit Loan: Short term financing available to small businesses that are at least one year old. Loans provide working capital to finance the manufacturing or wholesaling of products for export and for export marketing. The SBA will guarantee up to 90 percent of a conventional loan in amounts up to $750,000.

Contract Loan: Short-term loans are available to small businesses to finance the costs of labor and materials on contracts for which the proceeds are assignable. Program guarantees up to 90 percent of loans not in excess of $750,000. Qualifying small businesses must be in business for at least 12 calendar months prior to the date of the loan application.

Seasonal Line of Credit Loan: Loans provide short-term working capital to finance seasonal increases in business activities. Program guarantees up to 90 percent of loans not in excess of $750,000. Qualifying business must be in operation for at least one year prior to application.

Pollution Control Loans: Long-term guaranteed loans can be made by conventional financing to small businesses for installation or required pollution control measures. Must be unable to adopt the pollution control measures without undue financial hardship. Maximum guaranteed loan is $1,000,000.

General Contractor Loans: Small general construction contractors may obtain short-term loans or loan guarantees for residential or commercial construction or rehabilitation of property to be sold. The SBA will guarantee up to 90 percent of qualifying loans made by private lenders up to a maximum of $750,000. Direct loans can be up to $150,000.

Energy Business Loan Guarantee: Small businesses that provide certain energy production and conservation services for others may qualify for long-term loans and loan guarantees for start-ups and expansions. Loans and guarantees are made for firms that develop, manufacture, sell, install, or service specific energy measures for others, or firms that provide engineering, architectural, consulting, or other professional services connected with specific energy measures. Guarantee is for up to 90 percent of a loan not in excess of $750,000. Direct loans up to $150,000.

Disaster Recovery Loans: Small businesses located in federally designated disaster areas and suffering property damage or economic losses from the disaster can obtain long-term recovery loans at low interest rates. Property damage loans are limited to 85 percent of the verified damage. Loans for economic losses are for operating capital to meet the business' obligations that could have been made had the disaster not occurred.

Handicapped Assistance Loans: Assists persons who have a physical, mental or emotional disability of a permanent nature which limits the selection of any type of employment for which the person would otherwise be qualified. Direct loans are available for up to $150,000. The interest rate is 3% on these loans.

Surety Bond Guaranty Program: Makes the bonding system more available to small contractors who may be denied access to the system. SBA can guarantee up to 80 percent of surety's loss on a bond that has a maximum in total contract value of up to $1,250,000.

Vietnam-era and Disabled Veterans Loan Program: Provides direct loans to veterans to establish or expand a small business. Funds may be used for working capital or fixed assets. Direct loans for amounts up to $150,000 are available. The interest rate may be fixed or variable.

AMT Capital, Ltd.
5910 North Central Expressway, Suite 920
Dallas, TX 75206   214-987-8110

Alliance Business Investment Company
(Main Office: Tulsa, OK)

911 Louisiana
One Shell Plaza, Suite 3990
Houston, TX 77002   713-224-8224

Banc One Capital Partners Corporation
300 Crescent Court, Suite 1600
Dallas, TX 75201   214-979-4360

Capital Southwest Venture Corporation
12900 Preston Road, Suite 700
Dallas, TX 75230   214-233-8242

Catalyst Fund, Ltd.
Three Riverway, Suite 770
Houston, TX 77056   713-623-8133

Central Texas SBI Corporation
1401 Elm Street, Suite 4764
Dallas, TX 75202   214-508-5050

Charter Venture Group, Inc.
2600 Citadel Plaza Drive, Suite 600
Houston, TX 77008   713-863-0704

Citicorp Venture Capital, Ltd.
(Main Office: New York, NY)
717 North Harwood
Suite 2920-LB87
Dallas, TX 75201   214-880-9670

Energy Assets, Inc.
4900 Republic Bank Center
700 Louisiana
Houston, TX 77002   713-236-9999

Enterprise Capital Corporation
515 Post Oak Boulevard
Suite 310
Houston, TX 77027   713-621-9444

FCA Investment Company
San Felipe Plaza, Suite 850
5847 San Felipe
Houston, TX 77057   713-781-2857

First City, Texas Ventures, Inc.
1001 Main Street, 15th Floor
Houston, TX 77002   713-658-5421

Ford Capital, Ltd.
1525 Elm Street
Mail: P.O. Box 2140; Dallas 75221
Dallas, TX 75201   214-954-0688

HCT Capital Corp.
3715 Camp Bowie Boulevard
Fort Worth, TX 76107   817-335-4417

Houston Partners, SBIP
Capital Center Penthouse, 8th Floor
401 Louisiana
Houston, TX 77002   713-222-8600

Jiffy Lube Capital Corporation
700 Milam Street
P.O. Box 2967
Houston, TX 77252   713-546-8910

Mapleleaf Capital Ltd.
55 Waugh, Suite 710
Houston, TX 77007   713-880-4494

NCNB Texas Venture Group, Inc.
1401 Elm Street, Suite 4764
P.O. Box 831000
Dallas, TX 75283   214-508-5050

Neptune Capital Corporation
5956 Sherry Lane, Suite 800
Dallas, TX 75225   214-739-1414

SBI Capital Corporation
6305 Beverly Hill Lane
Mail: P.O. Box 570368; Houston 77257
Houston, TX 77057   713-975-1188

San Antonio Venture Group, Inc.
2300 West Commerce Street
San Antonio, TX 78207   512-978-0513

South Texas SBIC
120 South Main Street
P.O. Box 1698
Victoria, TX 77902   512-573-5151

Sunwestern Capital, Ltd.
3 Forest Plaza
12221 Merit Drive
Suite 1300
Dallas, TX 75251   214-239-5650

Sunwestern Ventures, Ltd.
3 Forest Plaza
12221 Merit Drive
Suite 1300
Dallas, TX 75251   214-239-5650

UNCO Ventures, Inc.
520 Post Oak Blvd., Suite 130
Houston, TX 77027   713-622-9595

United Mercantile Capital Corp.
2237 Ridge Road, Suite 201
Rockwall, TX 75087   214-771-8977

Ventex Partners, Ltd.
1000 Louisiana, 7th Floor
Mail: P.O. Box 3326, Houston 77253
Houston, TX 77002   713-224-6611

Western Financial Capital Corporation
17772 Preston Road, Suite 101
Dallas, TX 75252   214-380-0044

Small Business Investment Companies (SBIC): The SBA licenses, regulates, and provides financial assistance to privately owned and operated Small Business Investment Companies. SBICs make venture or risk investments by supplying capital and extending unsecured loans and loans not fully collateralized to small enterprises which meet their investment criteria. Financing is made by direct loans and by equity investments.

* Women and Minority Business Assistance

Austin Business Development Center
Grant Thornton
301 Congress, Suite 1000
Austin, TX 78701   512-476-9700

Tri-Plex Minority Business Development Center
c/o Boutte Elmore & Company
Petroleum Building
550 Fannin Street, Suite 106A
Beaumont, TX 77701   409-835-6651

Brownsville Minority Business Development Center
2100 Boca Chica, Suite 301
Brownsville, TX 78520   512-546-3400

Corpus Christi Minority Business Development Center
Cara, Inc.
3649 Leopard Street, Suite 514
Corpus Christi, TX 78469   512-887-7961

Dallas/Ft. Worth Minority Business Development Center
Grant Thornton
1445 Ross Avenue
Dallas, TX 75202   214-855-7373

Department of Commerce
Minority Business Development Agency
1100 Commerce, Room 6b23
Dallas, TX 75242   214-767-8001

Houston Minority Business Development Center
Grant Thornton
2800 CitiCorp Center
1200 Smith Street
Houston, TX 77002   713-650-3831

Laredo Minority Business Development Center
777 Caye del North
Suite 2
Laredo, TX 78041   512-725-5177

Lubbock, Midland, Odessa Minority
  Business Development Center
1220 Broadway, #509
Lubbock, TX 79401   806-762-6232

McAllen Minority Business Development Center
Cara, Inc.
7701 West Bus. Highway 83, #1108
McAllen, TX 78501   512-687-5224

San Antonio Minority Business Development Center
University of Texas at San Antonio
Economic Development Center
San Antonio, TX 78285   512-224-1945

Center for Entrepreneurial Development
Minority Business Development Center
301 South Frio
San Antonio, TX 78207   512-270-4676

> Minority Business Development Centers provide management and technical assistance to minority business persons. These centers specifically provide loan packaging assistance, procurement identification assistance, and other related services applicable to the business needs. The centers are familiar with the different types of loan programs and procurement opportunities available to minority entrepreneurs.

Small Business Administration (SBA)
8625 King George Drive
Dallas, TX 75235-3391   214-767-7633
    FAX: 214-767-7870

> **SBA 8(a) Program - Business Procurement Assistance:** Provides federal government contracting opportunities for small businesses owned by socially and economically disadvantaged persons, and assists these businesses to become independently competitive in the normal business environment. SBA monitors all government contracts to assure that a quota of contract work goes to 8(a) businesses. Also provides business management services to these businesses. Business must be approved for program participation prior to receipt of an 8(a) contract.

* Training

Texas Department of Commerce
Work Force Development Division
P.O. Box 12728   512-472-5059
Austin, TX 78711   1-800-888-0511

> **Work Force Incentive Program:** Provides state-subsidized, industry-specific job training for new and expanding industries that create jobs in Texas. Customized training aimed at the specific needs of the industry and conduct either on-site or at local educational institutions.

> **Job Training Partnership Act (JTPA):** Provides employers with recruitment, screening, referral, training, 50 percent wage subsidy up to 3 months for on-the-job training. Available to any private employer.

* Management Consulting and Other Services

Texas Capital Network
8920 Business Park
Suite 160
Austin, TX 78759   512-794-9398

Texas Capital Network
Greater Houston Partnership
1100 Milam
25th Floor
Houston, TX 77002   713-651-7222

Southwest Venture Forum
Southern Methodist University
Box 333
Dallas, TX 75275-0333   214-692-3326

MIT Enterprises Forum of Dallas-Fort Worth, Inc.
625 Digital Drive
Suite 107
Plano, TX 75075   214-741-8700

Longview Venture Club
Longview Chamber of Commerce
P.O. Box 472
Longview, TX 75606   214-237-4000

Venture Forum of Lubbock
Northwest Texas Small Business Development Center
2579 South Loop 289
Suite 114
Lubbock, TX 79423   806-745-3973

South Texas Venture Capital Association
14785 Omicron Drive
San Antonio, TX 78245   512-677-6000

Central Texas Venture Capital Group
Greater Waco Chamber of Commerce
P.O. Drawer 1220
Waco, TX 76703   817-752-6551

MIT Enterprise Forum
P.O. Box 61385   713-237-2590
Houston, TX 77208-1385   713-237-5112

> **Venture Capital Clubs:** Provide a forum for entrepreneurs to present their companies to potential financing sources and related professionals. Some clubs meet regularly while others meet on an as-needed basis.

Texas Department of Commerce
P.O. Box 12728   1-800-888-0511
Austin, TX 78711   512-472-5059
    Office of Business Finance   512-320-9514

> Provides technical assistance and loan packaging to businesses preparing to expand operations and to start-up business through financial analysis and recommendations on appropriate private and public-sector funding programs.

> **Foreign Trade Zones (FTZ):** Designated areas within the state where U.S. Customs duties do not apply. Foreign or domestic goods may be brought into an FTZ, modified, then re-exported without paying any U.S. Customs fees. The zones are ideal for manufacturing products for export. There are sixteen FTZ's in Texas, including seven on the Texas/Mexican border.

Business Development Division   512-320-9699

> **Office of National/International Business Development:** Promotes Texas nationally and internationally to encourage businesses to locate, relocate or expand in Texas. Assists new business and industry with site selection and information on incentives for investing in Texas.

> **Office of International Trade:** Services such as counseling, educational activities, and an electronic bulletin board with up-to-date export information are available. New or existing businesses can obtain export

assistance, attend seminars and meetings, and have access to foreign trade leads at Export Assistance Centers. The state also maintains overseas offices in Mexico Japan, Taiwan, Republic of China, Korea, and Germany to promote trade between the two countries.

Office of International Business Development: Works with foreign investors to attract outside income into the state. The office targets investors from the Pacific Rim, Europe, Canada, and Mexico as having good investment potential.

Office of Advanced Technology: Networks public and private research needs/capabilities with federal, state and industry resources. Also administers the Product Commercialization and Development funds, established to aid in the financing of new or improved products or processes for which financing is not reasonably available from private sources.

Texas Film Commission: Assists film companies with location scouting and serves as a liaison for local production resources and information.

Texas Music Office: Assists in coordination of the Texas-based music community through information exchange and promotion of the industry.

Tourism Division   512-462-9191
Travel trade program works with tour operators, travel agents and other travel trade specialists to encourage packaged marketing of Texas as a travel destination. Represents Taxes at national and international travel and trade shows, publishes a monthly newsletter and conducts site inspection tours for qualified trade representatives. There is also marketing program and media relations program.

Research and Planning: Provides economic, demographic, and marketing information and analysis to other Commerce divisions, businesses, as well as to local economic development organizations and state agencies in both hard copy and electronic media. The division also compiles reports on Texas' population estimates and projections, business climate and domestic and international travel patterns.

Small Business Administration
8625 King George Drive   214-767-7633
Dallas, TX 75235-3391   FAX: 214-767-7870
Small Business Institutes: This program provides personalized consulting services to the small business community. Consulting is provided by senior level business students, guided by a faculty advisor. Assistance in business plan preparation, marketing research, market planning, accounting, and seminars are provided.
University Locations:
Abilene Christian University
Amber University
Angelo State University
Baylor University
Corpus Christi State University
East Texas State University - Commerce
East Texas State University - Texarkana
Houston Baptist University
Incarnate Word College
Jarvis Christian College
Lamar University
Midland College
Midwestern State University
Pan American University
Rice University
Southwest Texas State University
St. Edwards University
St. Mary's University
Stephen F. Austin State University
Sul Ross State University - Apine
Tarleton State University
Texas A & I University
Texas Tech University
Texas Woman's University
University of Houston - Clear Lake
University of Houston - Victoria
University of Houston - Downtown
University of Houston
University of North Texas

University of St. Thomas
University of Texas - El Paso
University of Texas - Austin
University of Texas - Pan American
University of Texas - San Antonio
University of Texas - Arlington
University of Texas - Permian Basin
University of Texas - Tyler
Wayland Baptist University
West Texas State University

* Small Business Development Centers
The following offices offer free and fee-based services to new and expanding businesses:

Lead Centers:
North Texas Small Business Development Center
Dallas County Community College
1402 Corinth Street   214-565-5837
Dallas, TX 75215   FAX: 214-565-5857

Houston Small Business Development Center
University of Houston
601 Jefferson
Suite 2330   713-752-8444
Houston, TX 77002   FAX: 713-752-8484

Northwest Texas Small Business Development Center
Center for Innovation
2579 South Loop 289, Suite 114   806-745-3973
Lubbock, TX 79423   FAX: 806-745-6207

South Texas Border Small Business Development Center
University of Texas at San Antonio
801 S. Bowie   512-224-0791
San Antonio, TX 78205   FAX: 512-222-9834

Abilene: Abilene Christian University, Caruth Small Business Development Center, College of Business Administration, ACU Station, Box 8307, Abilene, TX 79699, 915-674-2776; FAX: 915-674-2507.

Alvin: Alvin Community College, Small Business Development Center, 3110 Mustang Road, Alvin, TX 77511-4898, 713-338-4686; FAX: 713-388-4903.

Amarillo: West Texas State University, Panhandle Small Business Development Center, T. Boone Pickens School of Business, 1800 South Washington, Suite 110, Amarillo, TX 79102, 806-372-5151.

Athens: Trinity Valley Small Business Development Center, 500 South Prairieville, Athens, TX 75751, 903-675-7403; FAX: 903-675-6316.

Austin: Austin Small Business Development Center, 221 South IH 35, Suite 103, Austin, TX 78741, 512-326-2256; FAX: 512-447-9825.

Baytown: Lee College, Small Business Development Center, Rundell Hall, 511 South Whiting Street, Baytown, TX 77520-4703, 713-425-6309; FAX: 713-425-6307.

Beaumont: John Gray Institute/Lamar University, Small Business Development Center, 855 Florida Avenue, Beaumont, TX 77705, 409-880-2367; FAX: 409-880-2201; 1-800-722-3443.

Bonham: Bonham Small Business Development Center (Satellite), Sam Raybourn Center, Bonham, TX 75418, 903-583-4811.

Brenham: Blinn College, Small Business Development Center, 902 College Avenue, Brenham, TX 77833, 409-830-4137; FAX: 409-830-4116.

Bryan: Bryan/College Station Chamber of Commerce, Small Business Development Center, 401 South Washington, Bryan, TX 77806, 409-823-3034; FAX: 409-822-4818.

Corpus Christi: Corpus Christi Chamber of Commerce, Small Business Development Center, 1201 North Shoreline, Corpus Christi, TX 78403, 512-882-6161; FAX: 512-888-5627.

Corsicana: Navarro Small Business Development Center, 120 North 12th Street, Corsicana, TX 75110, 903-874-0658; FAX: 903-874-4187.

Dallas: International Business Center, 2050 Stemmons Freeway, World Trade Center, Suite #150, P.O. Box 58299, Dallas, TX 75258, 214-653-1777; FAX: 214-748-5774.

Denison: Grayson Small Business Development Center, 6101 Grayson Drive, Denison, TX 75020, 903-786-3551; FAX: 903-463-5284.

Denton: Denton Small Business Development Center (Satellite), P.O. Drawer P, Denton, TX 76202, 817-382-7151; FAX: 817-382-0040.

DeSoto: Best Southwest Small Business Development Center, 1001 N. Beckley, Suite 606D, DeSoto, TX 75115, 214-228-3783.

Edinburg: University of Texas/Pan American, Small Business Development Center, 1201 West University Drive, Edinburg, TX 78539-2999, 512-381-3361; FAX: 512-381-2322.

El Paso: El Paso Community College, Small Business Development Center, 103 Montana Avenue, Room 202, El Paso, TX 79902-3929, 915-534-3410; FAX: 915-534-3420.

Fort Worth: Tarrant Small Business Development Center, 1500 Houston Street, Room 163, 7917 Highway 80 West, Fort Worth, TX 76102, 817-244-7158; FAX: 817-877-9295.

Gainesville: Cooke Small Business Development Center, 1525 West California, Gainesville, TX 76240, 817-665-4785; FAX: 817-668-6049.

Galveston: Galveston College, Small Business Development Center, 4015 Avenue Q, Galveston, TX 77550, 409-740-7380; FAX: 409-740-7381.

Hillsboro: Hillsboro Small Business Development Center (Satellite), SOS Building, P.O. Box 619, Hillsboro, TX 76645, 817-582-2555, ext. 282.

Houston: North Harris Community College District, Small Business Development Center, 350 N. Sam Houston Parkway, Houston, TX 77060, 713-591-9320; FAX: 713-591-3513; 1-800-443-SBDC.

Huntsville: Sam Houston State University, Small Business Development Center, College of Business Administration, P.O. Box 2056, Huntsville, TX 77341, 409-294-3737; FAX: 409-294-3612.

Kingsville: Kingsville Chamber of Commerce, Small Business Development Center, 635 East King, Kingsville, TX 78363, 512-595-5088; FAX: 512-592-0866.

Lake Jackson: Brazosport College, Small Business Development Center, 500 College Drive, Lake Jackson, TX 77566, 409-265-6131, ext. 380; FAX: 409-265-7208.

Laredo: Laredo Development Foundation, Small Business Development Center, 616 Leal Street, Laredo, TX 78041, 512-722-0563.

Longview: Kilgore College, Small Business Development Center, 300 South High, Longview, TX 75601, 903-757-5857; FAX: 903-753-7920.

Lubbock: Texas Tech University, Small Business Development Center, Center for Innovation, 2579 South Loop 289, Suite 114, Lubbock, TX 79423, 806-745-1637; FAX: 806-745-6207.

Lufkin: Angelina Community College, Small Business Development Center, P.O. Box 1768, Lufkin, TX 75902, 409-639-1887; FAX: 409-639-4299.

Mt. Pleasant: Northeast Texarkana Small Business Development Center, P.O. Box 1307, Mt. Pleasant, TX 75455, 214-572-1911; FAX: 903-572-6712.

Odessa: University of Texas/Permian Basin, Small Business Development Center, 4901 East University, Odessa, TX 79762, 915-563-0400; FAX: 915-561-5534.

Paris: Paris Small Business Development Center, 2400 Clarksville Street, Paris, TX 75460, 214-784-1802; FAX: 903-784-1801.

Plano: Collin County Small Business Development Center, Plano Market Square, 1717 East Spring Creek Parkway, #109, Plano, TX 75074, 214-881-0506; FAX: 214-423-3956.

San Angelo: Angelo State University, Small Business Development Center, 2610 West Avenue N, Campus Box 10910, San Angelo, TX 76909, 915-942-2119; FAX: 915-942-2038.

San Antonio: UTSA, International Small Business Development Center, 801 S. Bowie, San Antonio, TX 78205, 512-227-2997; FAX: 512-222-9834.

Stafford: Houston Community College System, Small Business Development Center, 13600 Murphy Road, Stafford, TX 77477, 713-499-4870; FAX: 713-499-8194.

Stephenville: Tarleton State University, Small Business Development Center, Box T-158, Stephenville, TX 76402, 817-968-9330; FAX: 817-968-9329.

Texas City: College of the Mainland, Small Business Development Center, 8419 Emmett F. Lowry Expressway, Texas City, TX 77591, 409-938-7578; FAX: 409-935-5816.

Tyler: Tyler Small Business Development Center, 1530 South SW Loop 323, Suite 100, Tyler, TX 75701, 903-510-2975; FAX: 903-510-2978.

Victoria: University of Houston-Victoria, Small Business Development Center, 700 Main Center, Suite 102, Victoria, TX 77901, 512-575-8944; FAX: 512-575-8852.

Waco: McLennan Small Business Development Center, 4601 North 19th Street, Waco, TX 76708, 817-750-3600; FAX: 817-756-0776.

Wharton: Wharton County Junior College, Small Business Development Center, Administration Building, Room 102, 911 Boling Highway, Wharton, TX 77488-0080, 409-532-0604; FAX: 409-532-2201.

Wichita Fall: Midwestern State University, Small Business Development Center, Division of Business, 3400 Taft Boulevard, Wichita Falls, TX 76308, 817-696-6738; FAX: 817-689-4374.

Utah

* General Information

State Tax Commission
Heber M. Wells Building, First Floor
160 East 300 South
Salt Lake City, UT 84134　　　　　　801-530-4848 (recording)
    One-Stop Service Center: You can register a business name, file Articles of Incorporation, obtain application for State Sales Tax License and State and Federal Tax Identification Numbers, file a Status Report with the Department of Employment Security, and apply for State Workers' Compensation Insurance. A *Going Into Business Workbook* is also available which includes all the forms and instructions necessary to do any of these activities.

Utah Small Business Development Center
102 W. 500 South
Suite 315
Salt Lake City, UT 84101-2315　　　　　　801-581-7905
    Small Business Advocate: Assistance in cutting bureaucratic red tape. Information and expertise in dealing with state, federal, and local agencies.

* Financing

Small Business Administration (SBA)
Salt Lake District Office
125 South State Street　　　　　　801-524-5800
Salt Lake City, UT 84138-1195　　　　　　FAX: 801-524-4160
    SBA 7(a) Guaranteed and Direct Loans: Guarantees up to 90 percent of a loan made through a private lender up to $750,000. Can be used for working capital, expand or convert facilities, purchase of machinery and

equipment, and land and building. Available only to those unable to obtain a loan from conventional sources. Direct loans are made up to $150,000.

SBA 504: Provides loans using 50 percent conventional bank financing, 40 percent SBA involvement through Certified Development Companies, and 10 percent owner equity. Fixed-asset loans are available in amounts up to $750,000. The loan can be used for land and building, construction, machinery and equipment, and renovation/expansion.

Small Business Innovative Research Grants (SBIR): Phase I awards between $20,000 to $50,000 to entrepreneurs to support six months of research on a technical innovation. Phase II grants are an additional $500,000 for development. Private sector investment funds must follow.

International Trade Loans: Guaranteed long-term loans through private lenders to develop or expand export markets, or to recover from the effects of import competition. Maximum guaranteed loan is $1,000,000 for fixed assets and an additional $250,000 for working capital and/or export revolving line of credit.

Export Revolving Line of Credit Loan: Short term financing available to small businesses that are at least one year old. Loans provide working capital to finance the manufacturing or wholesaling of products for export and for export marketing. The SBA will guarantee up to 90 percent of a conventional loan in amounts up to $750,000.

Contract Loan: Short-term loans are available to small businesses to finance the costs of labor and materials on contracts for which the proceeds are assignable. Program guarantees up to 90 percent of loans not in excess of $750,000. Qualifying small businesses must be in business for at least 12 calendar months prior to the date of the loan application.

Seasonal Line of Credit Loan: Loans provide short-term working capital to finance seasonal increases in business activities. Program guarantees up to 90 percent of loans not in excess of $750,000. Qualifying business must be in operation for at least one year prior to application.

Pollution Control Loans: Long-term guaranteed loans can be made by conventional financing to small businesses for installation or required pollution control measures. Must be unable to adopt the pollution control measures without undue financial hardship. Maximum guaranteed loan is $1,000,000.

General Contractor Loans: Small general construction contractors may obtain short-term loans or loan guarantees for residential or commercial construction or rehabilitation of property to be sold. The SBA will guarantee up to 90 percent of qualifying loans made by private lenders up to a maximum of $750,000. Direct loans can be up to $150,000.

Energy Business Loan Guarantee: Small businesses that provide certain energy production and conservation services for others may qualify for long-term loans and loan guarantees for start-ups and expansions. Loans and guarantees are made for firms that develop, manufacture, sell, install, or service specific energy measures for others, or firms that provide engineering, architectural, consulting, or other professional services connected with specific energy measures. Guarantee is for up to 90 percent of a loan not in excess of $750,000. Direct loans up to $150,000.

Disaster Recovery Loans: Small businesses located in federally designated disaster areas and suffering property damage or economic losses from the disaster can obtain long-term recovery loans at low interest rates. Property damage loans are limited to 85 percent of the verified damage. Loans for economic losses are for operating capital to meet the business' obligations that could have been made had the disaster not occurred.

Handicapped Assistance Loans: Assists persons who have a physical, mental or emotional disability of a permanent nature which limits the selection of any type of employment for which the person would otherwise be qualified. Direct loans are available for up to $150,000. The interest rate is 3% on these loans.

Surety Bond Guaranty Program: Makes the bonding system more available to small contractors who may be denied access to the system. SBA can guarantee up to 80 percent of surety's loss on a bond that has a maximum in total contract value of up to $1,250,000.

Vietnam-era and Disabled Veterans Loan Program: Provides direct loans to veterans to establish or expand a small business. Funds may be used for working capital or fixed assets. Direct loans for amounts up to $150,000 are available. The interest rate may be fixed or variable.

Statewide
Deseret Certified Development Company
7050 Union Park Center, Suite 570
Midvale, UT 84047　　　801-566-1163

Utah Technology Finance Corporation
419 Wakara Way
Salt Lake City, UT 84108　　　801-364-4346
Assists the incubation and growth of new and emerging high technology businesses, especially small businesses. Provides funds for research contracts, program grants, equity investments, convertible loans, and venture financing.

* Women and Minority Business Assistance

Department of Commerce
350 East 500 South, Suite 101
Salt Lake City, UT 84111　　　801-328-8181
IMPACT Program: Provides assistance to minority businesses by through programs that provide information, referrals, planning and loan packaging assistance expertise.

Small Business Administration (SBA)
Salt Lake District Office
125 South State Street　　　801-524-5800
Salt Lake City, UT 84138　　　FAX: 801-524-4160
Section 8(a) Program - Business Procurement Assistance: Provides federal government contracting opportunities for small businesses owned by socially and economically disadvantaged persons, and assists these businesses to become independently competitive in the normal business environment. SBA monitors all government contracts to assure that a quota of contract work goes to 8(a) businesses. Also provides business management services to these businesses. Business must be approved for program participation prior to receipt of an 8(a) contract.

Available to Americans who are members of minority groups. The SBA works with procurement officials in other agencies, and serves as the prime contractor for federal goods and service purchases, and then subcontracts this federal work to small firms owned by socially and economically disadvantaged persons.

Management and Technical Assistance Program　　801-524-3208
Provided to small businesses in areas of high unemployment who meet the program's eligibility requirements. Eligible recipients include SBA certified 8(a) firms, socially and economically disadvantaged individuals and/or firms located in areas of high unemployment.

Women's Business Ownership Programs　　801-524-3203
Offers a series of business training seminars and workshops for women business owners and for women who want to start their own small firms with a focus on business planning and development, credit and procurement.

Also see Financing - Small Business Administration

* Training

Office of Job Training for Economic Development
Department of Community and Economic Development
324 S. State
Suite 200
Salt Lake City, UT 84111　　　801-538-8700
Job Training Partnership Act (JTPA): Provides employers with recruitment, screening, referral, training, 50 percent wage subsidy up to 3 months for on-the-job training. Available to any private employer.

* Management Consulting and Other Services

Small Business Administration
Salt Lake District Office
125 South State Street   801-524-5800
Salt Lake City, UT 84138-1195   FAX: 801-524-4160
  Small Business Institutes: This program provides personalized consulting services to the small business community. Consulting is provided by senior level business students, guided by a faculty advisor. Assistance in business plan preparation, marketing research, market planning, accounting, and seminars are provided.
  University Locations:
  Brigham Young University
  Southern Utah State College
  University of Utah
  Utah State University
  Weber State College

  Procurement Assistance: Distributes bid opportunities from its computerized network and through its regional offices. Assists with the procedure of obtaining federal contracts.

Business and Economic Specialist
USU Cooperative Extension
Logan, UT 84322-3505   801-750-2362
  Workbooks for homebased business are available in areas such as getting started; developing a business plan; financial record keeping; setting a price; acquiring capital; copyrights, patents and trademarks, selling your product plus others.

Utah Association of Certified Public Accountants
455 East 400 South, Suite 202
Salt Lake City, UT 84111   801-359-3533

Utah Society of Public Accountants
144 S. 500 E.
Salt Lake City, UT 84102   801-363-1776

Lawyer Referral Service
645 South 200 East
Salt Lake City, UT 84111-3834   801-531-9075
  in conjunction with
Utah State Bar
645 South 200 East
Salt Lake City, UT 84111-3834   801-531-9077

Attorney Referral Service
141 West Haven Avenue
Salt Lake City, UT 84115   801-363-9819
  in conjunction with
Utah Trial Lawyers Association
141 West Haven Avenue
Salt Lake City, UT 84115   801-531-7514
  The above organizations will make a referral for the professional services of an accountant or attorney.

Mountain West Venture Group
P.O. Box 210
Salt Lake City, UT 84144   801-531-8900
  A venture capital club which provides a public forum for business development. Investors, entrepreneurs, and others meet to exchange information. It does not lend funds itself. The Club holds monthly meetings and publishes a newsletter.

Utah Innovation Foundation
295 Chipeta Way
Salt Lake City, UT 84108   801-584-7610
  Provides training seminars and sponsors promotional activities to increase public awareness of opportunities in emerging technologies. Has a tie-in to Utah Innovation Center, a for-profit company providing various equity related services to small/emerging companies.

Metro Utah, Inc.
6150 State Office Building
Salt Lake City, UT 84114   801-538-3055
  Aids in the recruitment and expansion of businesses in the metropolitan areas of Utah. Responds to requests for information and distributes a quarterly newsletter, the *Metro Utah News*.

Utah Supplier Development Council
151 Annex Building
University of Utah   801-581-8169
Salt Lake City, UT 84112   801-581-8477
  The council is made up of major Utah firms that specifically look for small, minority and women-owned business to be suppliers for the Council. Also prints a directory of these business.

Department of Community and Economic Development
324 S. State, Suite 500
Salt Lake City, UT 84114   801-538-8700
  Procurement Outreach Program   801-538-8790
  Assists firms in preparation and solicitation for federal contracts. Matches Utah firms with requirements of specific federal and other procurement contracts.

  International Marketing Program   801-538-8737
  Sponsors seminars on basic export procedures and target markets, conducts trade missions, disseminates information on international trade, and publishes *Utah Export Directory*.

  Rural Marketing Program   801-538-8780
  Identifies and markets economic strengths of rural Utah. Works to attract companies to match those resources.

  Urban Marketing Program   801-538-8780
  Aids in the recruitment and expansion of businesses in the metropolitan areas of Utah.

  Business Expansion & Retention Program   801-538-8775
  Aids in the expansion and retention of existing businesses.

Bureau of Economic and Business Research
401 Kendall D. Garff Building
University of Utah
Salt Lake City, UT 84112   801-581-6333
  This office maintains the state's largest and most timely information base on the Utah and Rocky Mountain economies and uses computer models for data analysis. Periodicals include *Utah Economic and Business Review, Utah Construction Report, Utah Statistical Abstract, Utah Facts!. Labor Market Area Profiles* has the most comprehensive information base on the economy of Utah and surrounding states. It publishes the *Utah Economic and Business Review*, the *Utah Construction Report*, the *Utah Statistical Abstract*, and *Utah Facts*.

* Small Business Development Centers

The following offices offer free and fee-based service to new and expanding businesses:

Lead Center:
Utah Small Business Development Center
University of Utah
102 West 500 South, Suite 315   801-581-7905
Salt Lake City, UT 84101   FAX: 801-581-7814

  Cedar City: Southern Utah University, Small Business Development Center, 351 West Center, Cedar City, UT 84720, 801-586-5400; FAX: 801-586-5493.

  Ephraim: Snow College, Small Business Development Center, 345 West 1st North, Ephraim, UT 84627, 801-283-4021; 801-283-6890; FAX: 801-283-6913.

  Logan: Utah State University, Small Business Development Center, East Campus Building, Logan, UT 84322-8330, 801-750-2277; FAX: 801-750-3317.

Ogden: Weber State University, Small Business Development Center, College of Business and Economics, Ogden, UT 84408-3806, 801-626-7232; FAX: 801-626-7423.

Price: College of Eastern Utah, Small Business Development Center, 451 East 400 North, Price, UT 84501, 801-637-1995; FAX: 801-637-4102.

Provo: Brigham Young University, Small Business Development Center, School of Management, 790 Tanner Building, Provo, UT 84602, 801-378-4022; FAX: 801-378-4501.

Roosevelt: Uintah Basin Applied Technology Center, Small Business Development Center, 1100 East Lagoon, P.O. Box 124-5, Roosevelt, UT 84066, 801-722-4523; FAX: 801-722-5804.

St. George: Dixie College, Small Business Development Center, 225 South 700 East, St. George, UT 84770, 801-673-4811 ext 353; FAX: 801-673-8552.

Vermont

* General Information

Vermont Economic Development Department
109 State Street   802-828-3221
Montpelier, VT 05609   1-800-622-4553 in Vermont

Vermont Agency of Development and Community Affairs
109 State Street
Montpelier, VT 05609   802-828-3211
   Small Business Advocate: Assistance in cutting bureaucratic red tape. Information and expertise in dealing with state, federal, and local agencies.

* Financing

Vermont Industrial Development Authority
56 East State Street
Montpelier, VT 05602   802-223-7226
   Industrial Loan Programs: Makes direct loans to eligible companies in amounts up to 40 percent of the cost of acquiring land, buildings, machinery, or equipment to be used in an industrial facility. Participation may not exceed $300,000 for real estate and $200,000 for machinery and equipment projects.

   Industrial Revenue Bonds: Issues tax-exempt and taxable industrial revenue bonds to provide qualified borrowers with low interest funds for acquisition of land, machinery, buildings, or equipment for use in manufacturing facilities.

   SBA 504: Provides loans using 50 percent conventional bank financing, 40 percent SBA involvement through Certified Development Companies, and 10 percent owner equity. A fixed-asset loan in amounts up to $750,000. Loan can be used for land and building, construction, machinery and equipment, and renovation/expansion.

   Agricultural Finance Program: The Authority makes low interest loans to family farmers and agricultural facility operators for real estate and machinery and equipment acquisition. Maximum loan amount is $50,000.

   Debt Stabilization Program: The Authority re-lends funds borrowed from a Vermont bank consortium to refinance, at lower interest rates, operating debts of family farmers. The maximum loan amount is $150,000.

Agency of Development and Community Affairs
109 State Street
Pavilion Office Building
Montpelier, VT 05602   802-828-3211
Economic Development Department:
Job Development Zones   802-828-3221
   Job Development Zones are areas created for incentives such as tax credits, for communities to get new and existing business to locate in the area.

   Department of Housing and Community Affairs   802-828-3217
   Vermont Community Development Program: Provides grant funds to communities to improve housing, create and retain employment opportunities, and improve public facilities in support of housing and economic development activities to benefit persons of lower income. These funds are then loans to businesses for economic development.

Public Facilities Division   802-244-8744
Administers constructions grants and loans for engineering planning for municipal pollution control and water supply projects. Administers construction grand awards for pollution control projects, construction loans for municipal water supply and pollution control facilities through state and federal programs.

Vermont Housing Finance Agency
230 St. Paul Street   1-800-864-0538
Burlington, VT 05401   1-800-222-VHFA in Vermont
   Multi-Family Development: Issues tax-exempt bonds and loans the proceeds to developers of affordable housing. Issues low income housing tax credits to developers of low income rental housing.

Northern Community Investment Corporation (NCIC)
P.O. Box 904
St. Johnsbury, VT 05819   802-748-5101
   A private, non-profit, community-based corporation that assists development in Vermont and northern New Hampshire. The NCIC provides capital and professional assistance to both small and large businesses and community development projects. Some of its services include: personalized technical assistance, direct financing of $500,000 or more, attracting outside capital to supplement its own resources in order to expand its investments, developing industrial space for new or expanding businesses, and investment in residential and commercial development.

Small Business Administration (SBA)
Room 205
87 State Street   802-828-4422
Montpelier, VT 05602   FAX: 802-828-4485
   SBA 7(a) Guaranteed and Direct Loans: Guarantees up to 90 percent of a loan made through a private lender up to $750,000. Can be used for working capital, expand or convert facilities, purchase of machinery and equipment, and land and building. Available only to those unable to obtain a loan from conventional sources. Direct loans are made up to $150,000.

   SBA 504: Provides loans using 50 percent conventional bank financing, 40 percent SBA involvement through Certified Development Companies, and 10 percent owner equity. Fixed-asset loans are available in amounts up to $750,000. The loan can be used for land and building, construction, machinery and equipment, and renovation/expansion.

   Small Business Innovative Research Grants (SBIR): Phase I awards between $20,000 to $50,000 to entrepreneurs to support six months of research on a technical innovation. Phase II grants are an additional $500,000 for development. Private sector investment funds must follow.

   International Trade Loans: Guaranteed long-term loans through private lenders to develop or expand export markets, or to recover from the effects of import competition. Maximum guaranteed loan is $1,000,000 for fixed assets and an additional $250,000 for working capital and/or export revolving line of credit.

   Export Revolving Line of Credit Loan: Short term financing available to small businesses that are at least one year old. Loans provide working capital to finance the manufacturing or wholesaling of products for export and for export marketing. The SBA will guarantee up to 90 percent of a conventional loan in amounts up to $750,000.

   Contract Loan: Short-term loans are available to small businesses to finance the costs of labor and materials on contracts for which the proceeds are assignable. Program guarantees up to 90 percent of loans not in excess of $750,000. Qualifying small businesses must be in business for at least 12 calendar months prior to the date of the loan application.

   Seasonal Line of Credit Loan: Loans provide short-term working capital to finance seasonal increases in business activities. Program guarantees up to 90 percent of loans not in excess of $750,000. Qualifying business must be in operation for at least one year prior to application.

Pollution Control Loans: Long-term guaranteed loans can be made by conventional financing to small businesses for installation or required pollution control measures. Must be unable to adopt the pollution control measures without undue financial hardship. Maximum guaranteed loan is $1,000,000.

General Contractor Loans: Small general construction contractors may obtain short-term loans or loan guarantees for residential or commercial construction or rehabilitation of property to be sold. The SBA will guarantee up to 90 percent of qualifying loans made by private lenders up to a maximum of $750,000. Direct loans can be up to $150,000.

Energy Business Loan Guarantee: Small businesses that provide certain energy production and conservation services for others may qualify for long-term loans and loan guarantees for start-ups and expansions. Loans and guarantees are made for firms that develop, manufacture, sell, install, or service specific energy measures for others, or firms that provide engineering, architectural, consulting, or other professional services connected with specific energy measures. Guarantee is for up to 90 percent of a loan not in excess of $750,000. Direct loans up to $150,000.

Disaster Recovery Loans: Small businesses located in federally designated disaster areas and suffering property damage or economic losses from the disaster can obtain long-term recovery loans at low interest rates. Property damage loans are limited to 85 percent of the verified damage. Loans for economic losses are for operating capital to meet the business' obligations that could have been made had the disaster not occurred.

Handicapped Assistance Loans: Assists persons who have a physical, mental or emotional disability of a permanent nature which limits the selection of any type of employment for which the person would otherwise be qualified. Direct loans are available for up to $150,000. The interest rate is 3% on these loans.

Surety Bond Guaranty Program: Makes the bonding system more available to small contractors who may be denied access to the system. SBA can guarantee up to 80 percent of surety's loss on a bond that has a maximum in total contract value of up to $1,250,000.

Vietnam-era and Disabled Veterans Loan Program: Provides direct loans to veterans to establish or expand a small business. Funds may be used for working capital or fixed assets. Direct loans for amounts up to $150,000 are available. The interest rate may be fixed or variable.

Queneska Capital Corporation
123 Church Street
Burlington, VT 05401   802-865-1806

Small Business Investment Companies (SBIC): The SBA licenses, regulates, and provides financial assistance to privately owned and operated Small Business Investment Companies. SBICs make venture or risk investments by supplying capital and extending unsecured loans and loans not fully collateralized to small enterprises which meet their investment criteria. Financing is made by direct loans and by equity investments.

* Women and Minority Business Assistance

Minority Assistance Program
City Hall, Room 32
Burlington, VT 05401   802-865-7177

This office also provides technical assistance to women and minority business owners. Assistance is available in preparing business and marketing plans and with tax preparation. A resource library is maintained. Also a Minority Forum meeting is held monthly. The staff publishes a monthly newsletter covering topics of interest to minority business owners. Available on request is the *Vermont Entrepreneur Resource Guide*.

Women Small Business Project
City Hall, Room 32
Burlington, VT 05041   802-865-7177

This office offers a 15 week intensive course on how to start a small business.

Small Business Administration
Room 205, 87 State Street   802-828-4422
Montpelier, VT 05602   FAX: 802-828-4485

SBA 8(a) Program - Business Procurement Assistance: Provides federal government contracting opportunities for small businesses owned by socially and economically disadvantaged persons, and assists these businesses to become independently competitive in the normal business environment. SBA monitors all government contracts to assure that a quota of contract work goes to 8(a) businesses. Also provides business management services to these businesses. Business must be approved for program participation prior to receipt of an 8(a) contract.

* Training

Agency of Development and Community Affairs
Economic Development Department
109 State Street
Pavilion Office Building
Montpelier, VT 05609

Vermont Training Program   802-828-3221
Provides training programs for manufacturing businesses to upgrade and increase their workforce, working closely with the Department of Employment and Training, Department of Education, and the Department of Labor and Industry.

Department of Employment and Training Administration
5 Green Mountain Drive
Montpelier, VT 05602   802-229-0311

Jobs and Training Division: Assists Vermont employers in the selection of qualified applicants to fill their job openings. Provides access to the Employment Service National Labor Exchange System. The National Job Bank System assists employers in recruiting applicants outside the state for hard-to-fill openings. Assists employers applying for foreign workers when they are unable to obtain United States workers for a specific occupation.

Department of Labor and Industry
120 State Street
Montpelier, VT 05620

Division of Apprenticeship   802-828-2157
Registers skilled trades workers in state-approved, supervised and structured training programs through on-the-job training, and related classroom instruction.

Vermont Occupational Safety and Health Act   802-828-2765
Provides safety training programs to employers and provides voluntary safety inspection of work plans.

Vermont Department of Employment and Training Administration
5 Green Mountain Drive
Montpelier, VT 05602   802-229-0311

Job Training Partnership Act (JTPA): Provides employers with recruitment, screening, referral, training, 50 percent wage subsidy up to 3 months for on-the-job training. Available to any private employer.

* Management Consulting and Other Services

State Small Business Development Center
Suite 13, 1 Blair Park   802-878-0181
Williston, VT 05495-9404   FAX: 802-878-0145

Procurement Assistance: Small Business Development Centers work with businesses both individually and through periodic conferences, seminars and special training sessions to provide advice and assistance in procuring government contracts.

Foreign Trade Assistance: Small Business Development Centers offer individual help to businesses in doing business overseas, as well as periodic conferences, seminars, and training sessions on foreign trade.

Agency of Economic and Community Affairs
109 State Street
Pavilion Office Building
Montpelier, VT 05609

Economic Development Department   802-828-3221
Works with other state agencies to provide marketing services to promote Vermont-made products to foreign consumers. Organizes and develops international markets through seminars, trade missions, and referral to specialists. Provides financial packaging to meet the needs of business. Provides permit process assistance, and export product assistance.

Industrial Recruitment: Develops sites, attracts desirable businesses, and provides incentives to potential businesses for expansion or relocation in the state.

Small Business/Entrepreneurship Development: Provides counseling, training, and financial assistance for businesses working with the Small Business Development Centers and Regional Development Corporations.

Vermont Travel Division   802-828-3236
Provides technical, marketing, and promotional assistance to the travel industry and to communities.

Market Vermont: A cooperative marketing program aimed at helping state businesses in marketing their goods. Some of the services include research and assessment of state goods within their respective markets, promotional activities for state-made items, and free consulting services. This program uses information and resources from 11 state agencies and over 600 private companies to help Vermont companies market their goods.

Regional Economic Development Program: This program divides the state into 12 non-profit development corporations that assist new and existing businesses interested in locating in that area. The corporations maintain lists of available sites and buildings and work with municipalities and service providers to help set up businesses.

Department of Forest, Parks and Recreation
Forestry Division
103 South Main Street
Building 10 South
Waterbury, VT 05671-0602   802-244-8716
Provides technical assistance to private woodland owners on forest resource management, and in protecting forest land from fire, insects, disease, and pests. Assists forest-based industry in the utilization and marketing of wood products. Provides nursery stock for the reforestation of open lands.

Department of Agriculture
120 State Street
Montpelier, VT 05620-2901

Agriculture Development Division   802-828-2416
Provides for the promotion of various agricultural products and works with the commodity groups to improve market opportunities. Organizes evens such as the Farm Show and the Vermont Building at Easter States Exposition for purposes of improving markets for agricultural commodities.

Animal and Dairy Industries Division   802-828-2433
Provides counseling and training in proper handling of products and equipment. Provides publications and other materials on updated techniques as well as counseling and training. Grant/Loan Programs available.

Small Business Administration
Room 205
87 State Street   802-828-4422
Montpelier, VT 05602   FAX: 802-828-4485
Small Business Institutes: This program provides personalized consulting services to the small business community. Consulting is provided by senior level business students, guided by a faculty advisor. Assistance in business plan preparation, marketing research, market planning, accounting, and seminars are provided.
University Locations:
Green Mountain College
Johnson State College
Lyndon State College

Southern Vermont College
University of Vermont

* Small Business Development Centers
The following offices offer free and fee-based service to new and expanding businesses:

Lead Center:
Vermont Small Business Development Center
Suite 13
One Blair Park   802-878-0181
Williston, VT 05495-9404   FAX: 802-878-0245

Morrisville: UVM Extension System, Central Small Business Development Center, RFD 1 Box 2280, Morrisville, VT 05661, 802-888-4972; FAX: 802-888-2432.

Rutland: UVM Extension System, Southwest Small Business Development Center, Box 489, Rutland, VT 05701, 802-773-3349; FAX: 802-775-4840.

St. Johnsbury: UVM Extension System, Northeast Small Business Development Center, HCR 31, Box 436, Johnsbury, VT 05819, 802-748-5512.

West Brattleboro: UVM Extension System, Southeast Small Business Development Center Resource Center, Box 2430, 411 Western Ave., West Brattleboro, VT 05301, 802-257-7967; FAX: 802-257-0112.

Virginia

* General Information

Department of Economic Development
Office of Small Business
P.O. Box 798
Richmond, VA 23206-0798   804-371-8252
Helps new or expanding business by answering questions about licensing, taxes, regulations, assistance programs, etc. The office can also locate sources of information in other state agencies, and it also can identify sources of help for business planning, management, exporting, and financing.

Small Business Advocate: Assistance in cutting bureaucratic red tape. Information and expertise in dealing with state, federal, and local agencies.

Virginia Employment Commission Economic Information Services Division
703 East Main Street
P.O. Box 1358
Richmond, VA 23211   804-786-3047
Publishes the *Virginia Business Resource Directory*, a comprehensive source of information on every aspect of doing business in the state, from business planning, management and personnel issues to sources of finance, marketing assistance, and regulations and licenses.

* Financing

Virginia Small Business Financing Authority (VSBFA)
P.O. Box 798
Richmond VA 23206-0798   804-371-8254
Loan Guaranty Program: Assists small businesses in obtaining short-term capital to improve and expand their operations. Provides a maximum guaranty to private lenders of 50 percent of a bank loan, or $150,000 whichever is less, with terms of up to 36 months. Maximum interest rate is 2 percent over the lender's current prime. This is a program that can be used by businesses which have already taken advantage of the SBA guaranty program for fixed assets and are now in need of short-term capital to finance current operations.

Industrial Development Bonds (IDBs): VSBFA issues tax-exempt IDBs to provide a low-interest source of capital to creditworthy small manufacturing firms for their land, building and capital equipment needs.

Minimum project size is $250,000 and the total effective annual financing costs average 80-90 percent of the Prime interest rate. They are primarily interested in assisting businesses which are providers of goods or services and which are owned or directly managed by the applicant. Number of jobs created, fiscal impact of the project on the locality, and opinion of the local governing body regarding the project are all considered. An outside investor's interest in a project should not exceed 49 percent.

Umbrella IDB Program: Tax exempt revenue bonds are issued to small businesses for use in manufacturing projects. Funds can be used for land, buildings and new capital equipment. Through an Umbrella Program, the Authority provides small businesses access to the public capital market's rates and terms for tax exempt bonds, by pooling projects together in a single "umbrella" bond. Applicants must present a letter of credit from a financial institution guaranteeing the amount of the bond.

Taxable Commercial Paper Program: Provides long-term financing at reasonable interest rates for land, building, and capital equipment for small businesses. Requirements are similar to those for the Umbrella IDB program. Applicants need a letter of credit from a bank or other lending institution as a guaranty for the financing. Then a triple A-rated bank provides a master letter of credit and the Small Business Finance Authority issues the commercial paper in the national market to fund the project. This allows small businesses access to the low, short-term rates available in the commercial paper market to finance long-term projects.

Enterprize Zone Program: Virginia has 15 zones that offer business incentives to develop economically distressed areas of the state. Some incentives include a 5 year decreasing credit on the state corporate income tax (from 80 percent to 20 percent), a 5 year decreasing credit on the state corporate tax equal to the amount of state unemployment tax liability (80 percent to 20 percent), and a 5 year exemption from state sales and use taxes.

Virginia Department of Housing
and Community Development
205 N. Fourth Street
Richmond, VA 23219-1747   804-786-4474

Revolving Loan Funds: Administers two revolving loan funds which provide below market rate loans to manufacturing and related industries in eligible communities to finance land, buildings and equipment. One or two dollars of private investment is required for each dollar from the funds, and the maximum loan amount is limited by the number of permanent jobs created or maintained as a result of the financing.

Community Development Block Grants   804-786-4474
Available to cities and counties for projects which create or maintain jobs or which address the problems of community decline. The funds received by the city/county are, in turn, loaned to businesses. Eligible projects include the commercial rehabilitation of existing buildings or structures used for business, commercial, or industrial purposes, site development, access roads, railroad spans, water and sewer facilities. Every $15,000 of grant funds invested must create at least one full-time job, and at least 51 percent of the jobs created must be for low- and moderate-income families.

Virginia Coalfield Economic Development Authority
P.O. Box 1060
Lebanon, VA 24266   703-889-0381
Provides financial assistance to new or expanding industries in far southwestern Virginia through a revolving loan program. Businesses which will bring new income to the area may use the loans for real estate purchases, construction or expansion of buildings, and purchase of machinery and equipment. Job creation and average minimum hourly wage requirement apply.

Venture Capital Networks: There are various private venture capital firms and clubs in the state. The Department of Economic Development will refer inquirers to private investment firms for up to date information.

Small Business Administration (SBA)
Richmond District Office
400 N 8th Street, Room 3015   804-771-2400
Richmond, VA 23240   FAX: 804-771-8018

Small Business Administration (SBA)   Loudoun, Arlington, Fairfax Counties
District of Columbia Office   Alexandria and Fairfax City
1111 18th Street, N.W.
P.O. Box 19993   202-634-1500
Washington, DC 20036   FAX: 202-634-1803

SBA 7(a) Guaranteed and Direct Loans: Guarantees up to 90 percent of a loan made through a private lender up to $750,000. Can be used for working capital, expand or convert facilities, purchase of machinery and equipment, and land and building. Available only to those unable to obtain a loan from conventional sources. Direct loans are made up to $150,000.

SBA 504: Provides loans using 50 percent conventional bank financing, 40 percent SBA involvement through Certified Development Companies, and 10 percent owner equity. Fixed-asset loans are available in amounts up to $750,000. The loan can be used for land and building, construction, machinery and equipment, and renovation/expansion.

Small Business Innovative Research Grants (SBIR): Phase I awards between $20,000 to $50,000 to entrepreneurs to support six months of research on a technical innovation. Phase II grants are an additional $500,000 for development. Private sector investment funds must follow.

International Trade Loans: Guaranteed long-term loans through private lenders to develop or expand export markets, or to recover from the effects of import competition. Maximum guaranteed loan is $1,000,000 for fixed assets and an additional $250,000 for working capital and/or export revolving line of credit.

Export Revolving Line of Credit Loan: Short term financing available to small businesses that are at least one year old. Loans provide working capital to finance the manufacturing or wholesaling of products for export and for export marketing. The SBA will guarantee up to 90 percent of a conventional loan in amounts up to $750,000.

Contract Loan: Short-term loans are available to small businesses to finance the costs of labor and materials on contracts for which the proceeds are assignable. Program guarantees up to 90 percent of loans not in excess of $750,000. Qualifying small businesses must be in business for at least 12 calendar months prior to the date of the loan application.

Seasonal Line of Credit Loan: Loans provide short-term working capital to finance seasonal increases in business activities. Program guarantees up to 90 percent of loans not in excess of $750,000. Qualifying business must be in operation for at least one year prior to application.

Pollution Control Loans: Long-term guaranteed loans can be made by conventional financing to small businesses for installation or required pollution control measures. Must be unable to adopt the pollution control measures without undue financial hardship. Maximum guaranteed loan is $1,000,000.

General Contractor Loans: Small general construction contractors may obtain short-term loans or loan guarantees for residential or commercial construction or rehabilitation of property to be sold. The SBA will guarantee up to 90 percent of qualifying loans made by private lenders up to a maximum of $750,000. Direct loans can be up to $150,000.

Energy Business Loan Guarantee: Small businesses that provide certain energy production and conservation services for others may qualify for long-term loans and loan guarantees for start-ups and expansions. Loans and guarantees are made for firms that develop, manufacture, sell, install, or service specific energy measures for others, or firms that provide engineering, architectural, consulting, or other professional services connected with specific energy measures. Guarantee is for up to 90 percent of a loan not in excess of $750,000. Direct loans up to $150,000.

Disaster Recovery Loans: Small businesses located in federally designated disaster areas and suffering property damage or economic losses from the disaster can obtain long-term recovery loans at low interest rates. Property damage loans are limited to 85 percent of the verified damage. Loans for economic losses are for operating capital to meet the business' obligations that could have been made had the disaster not occurred.

Handicapped Assistance Loans: Assists persons who have a physical, mental or emotional disability of a permanent nature which limits the selection of any type of employment for which the person would otherwise be qualified. Direct loans are available for up to $150,000. The interest rate is 3% on these loans.

Surety Bond Guaranty Program: Makes the bonding system more available to small contractors who may be denied access to the system. SBA can guarantee up to 80 percent of surety's loss on a bond that has a maximum in total contract value of up to $1,250,000.

Vietnam-era and Disabled Veterans Loan Program: Provides direct loans to veterans to establish or expand a small business. Funds may be used for working capital or fixed assets. Direct loans for amounts up to $150,000 are available. The interest rate may be fixed or variable.

Crestar Capital, LP
9 South 12th Street, Third Floor
Richmond, VA 23219   804-643-7358

DC Bancorp Venture Capital Company
One Commercial Place, 3rd Floor
Norfolk, VA 23510   804-441-4041

Dominion Capital Markets Corporation
213 South Jefferson Street
Mail: P.O. Box 13327, Roanoke 24040
Roanoke, VA 24011   703-563-6110

Hampton Roads SBIC
420 Bank Street, P.O. Box 327
Norfolk, VA 23510   804-622-2312

Metropolitan Capital Corporation
2550 Huntington Avenue
Alexandria, VA 22303   703-960-4698

Rural America Fund, Inc.
2201 Cooperative Way
Herndon, VA 22071   703-709-6722

Sovran Funding Corporation
Sovran Center, 6th Floor
One Commercial Plaza
P.O. Box 600
Norfolk, VA 23510   804-441-4041

Walnut Capital Corporation
(Main Office: Chicago, IL)
8300 Boone Boulevard, Suite 780
Vienna, VA 22180   703-448-3771

Small Business Investment Companies (SBIC): The SBA licenses, regulates, and provides financial assistance to privately owned and operated Small Business Investment Companies. SBICs make venture or risk investments by supplying capital and extending unsecured loans and loans not fully collateralized to small enterprises which meet their investment criteria. Financing is made by direct loans and by equity investments.

Farmer's Home Administration (FmHA)
400 North Eighth Street, Room 8213   804-771-2451
Richmond, VA 23240   804-771-2453 (program info)

Farm Loan Program: Provides loans and loan guarantees to farm families, rural communities, and rural non-farm citizens. Loans are available to finance homes, community facilities such as water or sewer systems, and non-farm businesses.

Business and Industrial Loan Program: Encourages the creation and retention of jobs in rural areas. FmHA will guarantee loans by commercial institutions up to 90 percent.

Federal Land Bank: A nationwide cooperative credit system making long-term loans available to eligible farmers and other rural residents. These loans are for agriculture-related purposes only, including: farm real estate, livestock, farm operating expenses, housing related to farm operations, and to refinance debts or remove a lien from farm land. Loans are also available for farm-related sites, capital structures, equipment, and working capital. Federal Land Bank offices are located in counties throughout the state.

VEDCORP, Inc.
951 East Byrd Street, Suite 940   804-648-4802
Richmond, VA 23219   FAX: 804-648-4809

VEDCORP is a private, for-profit entity that makes investments in small businesses located in targeted areas of Virginia to encourages economic development and employment growth in these areas. Provides capital to businesses and entrepreneurs in support of their long term growth objectives. Investments range from $100,000 to $700,000 for five to eight years, repayments scheduled to match the cash flow expectations of the business, and an appropriate interest rate combined with an equity participation in the business.

* Women and Minority Business Assistance

Small Business Administration (SBA)
Richmond District Office
400 N. 8th Street, Room 3015   804-771-2400
Richmond, VA 23240   FAX: 804-771-8018

Small Business Administration   Loudoun, Arlington, Fairfax Counties
District of Columbia Office   Alexandria and Fairfax City
1111 18th Street, N.W.
P.O. Box 19993   202-634-1500
Washington, DC 20036   FAX: 202-634-1803

SBA 8(a) Program - Business Procurement Assistance: Provides federal government contracting opportunities for small businesses owned by socially and economically disadvantaged persons, and assists these businesses to become independently competitive in the normal business environment. SBA monitors all government contracts to assure that a quota of contract work goes to 8(a) businesses. Also provides business management services to these businesses. Business must be approved for program participation prior to receipt of an 8(a) contract.

Norfolk Business Development Center
355 Crawford Pkwy, Suite 608
Portsmouth, VA 23704   804-399-0888

Stimulates economic growth in distressed areas by assisting minorities in business. The Center provides management and technical assistance at low cost. Initial consultations are free of charge. Some of the services available include assistance in preparing business plans, loan packages, and market research; help in locating financial aid; and aid in contract procurement in both the public and private sectors.

* Training

Governor's Employment and Training Department
4615 W. Broad Street, 3rd Floor
Commonwealth Building
Richmond, VA 23230   804-367-9800

Job Training Partnership Act (JTPA): Provides employers with recruitment, screening, referral, training, 50 percent wage subsidy up to 3 months for on-the-job training. Available to any private employer.

Department of Economic Development
Workforce Services
James Center, 11th Floor
1021 E. Cary
Richmond, VA 23219   804-371-8120

This office provides free training programs for new and expanding industries, customizing each program to the company's individual needs. It also offers aid in recruitment, analysis of an industry's needs and schedules, and design and implement training programs, including the provision of training facilities.

* Management Consulting and Other Services

Center for Innovative Technology (CIT)
2214 Rock Hill Road, Suite 600
Herndon, VA 22070   703-689-3000

The Center works with business and universities in technology development, technology transfer, and commercialization. A business participating in CIT's co-sponsored cooperative research can gain access to CIT technology development resources. CIT can match a business's needs with available university resources can also co-sponsor specific university research to meet that business's needs. Through the Commonwealth Technology Information Service, a business can tap into databases containing technological information from around the state. CIT also runs a network of entrepreneurial centers and incubators associated with various colleges and universities. The centers provide outreach services on business-related topics, and the incubators offer shared physical space and support services to help reduce start-up costs.

Department of General Services
Division of Purchases and Supply
P.O. Box 267
Richmond, VA 23202-0267   804-786-5494

Procurement Assistance: *Virginia Business Opportunities* is a weekly newsletter that lists procurement opportunities within the state for all types of businesses. There is a fee to subscribe.

Department of Economic Development
P.O. Box 798
Richmond, VA 23206-0798   804-371-8100

Export Development Programs and Services: Offers help to cut through bureaucracy and assist export businesses to trade overseas. Provides one-on-one export development counseling, offers foreign market research studies, assists and represents Virginia businesses at overseas trade shows, sponsors and promotes seminars on exporting, arranges and sponsors foreign buying missions, provides businesses with trade leads, publishes a bi-monthly newsletter. Has offices in Belgium and Japan.

Virginia Site Location Assistance Program: Provides personalized analysis for prospective businesses on locations where their company might benefit the most, including information on specific communities, available labor, transportation, utilities, etc. The office maintains computerized site and building files which aid in providing a firm with an overview of business in Virginia.

Film Office: Provides location and production assistance to companies interested in filming in Virginia. Promotes the state in the Hollywood trade media. Annually publishes the *Virginia Production Services Directory* which lists the various services, companies, free-lance personnel and accommodations available for film production.

Division of Tourism: Produces quarterly trends and monthly marketing newsletters to keep industry leaders up to date on industry trends and cooperative marketing opportunities. Assists Virginia owners/managers of travel attractions and lodging properties in selling their attractions/destinations to major wholesalers and retailers of tour packages across the United States and Canada. Produces *The Virginia Group Tour and Travel Directory* and *The Package Plan Directory*.

Office of Small Business   804-371-8252
Ombudsman Program: Assists a business person who is having a specific problem with state government find the proper person in the proper agency to get a fair hearing and appropriate assistance.

Virginia Port Authority
600 World Trade Center
Norfolk, VA 23510   804-683-8000

Assists businesses in exporting through overseas promotion of Virginia products. Provides assistance in importing and exporting raw materials and exporting finished goods. The Authority also offers aid in locating foreign markets for Virginia goods; and has a special program, VEXTRAC, that aids small businesses in overseas trading. Manufacturing firms, export businesses, and any person or firm interested in overseas trade can benefit from the Authority's assistance.

Small Business Administration (SBA)
Richmond District Office
400 N. 8th Street
Room 3015
Richmond, VA 23240   804-771-2400
    FAX: 804-771-8018

Small Business Administration   Loudoun, Arlington, Fairfax Counties
District of Columbia Office   Alexandria and Fairfax City
1111 18th Street, N.W.
P.O. Box 19993   202-634-1500
Washington, DC 20036   FAX: 202-634-1803

Small Business Resource Centers: Sponsored jointly by the U.S. Small Business Administration and various Chambers of Commerce and business associations, these Centers offer counseling and training programs to small businesses. The Centers contain resource libraries and act as clearinghouses on SBA programs, as well as conduct seminars and meetings on business-related topics. Retired and active business executives volunteer their time to provide customized counseling to prospective and existing small businesses. There are currently 45 such centers in Virginia. The Small Business Administration can provide you with the address and phone number for the center nearest you.

Secondary Road Division of the Department of Transportation
State Secondary Roads Engineer
1401 East Broad Street
Richmond VA 23219   804-786-2746

Industrial Access Roads: This program assists development by constructing industrial access roads to serve new or expanding manufacturing industries. Road improvement, construction, and maintenance are all included in the program, which times road completion to completion of plant start-up operations.

Small Business Administration (SBA)
Richmond District Office
400 N. 8th Street, Room 3015   804-771-2400
Richmond, VA 23240   FAX: 804-771-8018

Small Business Administration   Loudoun, Arlington, Fairfax Counties
District of Columbia Office   Alexandria and Fairfax City
1111 18th Street, N.W.
P.O. Box 19993   202-634-1500
Washington, DC 20036   FAX: 202-634-1803

Small Business Institutes: This program provides personalized consulting services to the small business community. Consulting is provided by senior level business students, guided by a faculty advisor. Assistance in business plan preparation, marketing research, market planning, accounting, and seminars are provided.
University Locations:
Christopher Newport College
Clinch Valley College
College of William & Mary
George Mason University
Hampton University
James Madison University
Longwood College
Lynchburg College
Marymount University
Norfolk State College
Old Dominion University
Radford University
University of Virginia
Virginia Commonwealth University
Virginia Polytechnic Institute
Virginia State University

* Small Business Development Centers

The following offices offer free and fee-based services to new and expanding businesses:

Lead Center:
Virginia Small Business Development Center
P.O. Box 798   804-371-8258
Richmond, VA 23206-0798   FAX: 804-371-8185

Arlington: George Mason University/Arlington Campus, Small Business Development Center, 3401 N. Fairfax Drive, Arlington, VA 22201, 703-993-8129; FAX: 703-993-8130.

Big Stone Gap: Mt. Empire Community College, Southwest Small Business Development Center, Drawer 700, Route 23, Big Stone Gap, VA 24219, 703-523-6529; FAX: 703-523-4130.

Blacksburg: Western Virginia Small Business Development Center Consortium, VPI & SU, Economic Development Assistance Center, 404 Clay Street, Blacksburg, VA 24061-0539, 703-231-5278; FAX: 703-953-2307.

Charlottesville: Central Virginia Small Business Development Center, 700 Harris Street, Suite 207, Charlottesville, VA 22901-4553, 804-295-8198, FAX: 804-979-3749.

Fairfax: Northern Virginia Small Business Development Center, 4260 Chainbridge Road, Suite B-1, Fairfax, VA 22030, 703-993-2131; FAX: 703-993-2126.

Farmville: Longwood College, Small Business Development Center, Farmville, VA 23901, 804-395-2086, FAX: 804-395-2359.

Harrisonburg: James Madison University, Small Business Development Center, College of Business Building, Room 523, Harrisonburg, VA 22807, 703-568-3227; FAX: 703-568-3399.

Lynchburg: Lynchburg Regional Small Business Development Center, 147 Mill Ridge Road, Lynchburg, VA 24502, 804-582-6100; FAX: 804-582-6106.

Manassas: Small Business Development Center, Dr. William E.S. Flory, 10311 Sudley Manor Drive, Manassas, VA 22110, 703-335-2500; FAX: 703-335-1700.

Norfolk: Hampton Roads Inc., Small Business Development Center, P.O. Box 327, 420 Bank Street, Norfolk, VA 23501, 804-622-6414; FAX: 804-622-5563.

Radford: New River Valley Small Business Development Center, New River Valley Planning District Commission Office, P.O. Box 3726, 1612 Wadsworth Street, Radford, VA 24143, 703-731-9546; FAX: 703-831-6093.

Richlands: Southwest Virginia Community College, Small Business Development Center, P.O. Box SVCC, Richlands, VA 24641, 703-964-7345; FAX: 703-964-9307.

Richmond: Capital Area Small Business Development Center, 403 East Grace Street, Richmond, VA 23219, 804-648-7838; FAX: 804-648-7849.

Roanoke: The Blue Ridge Small Business Development Center, 310 First Street, S.W. Mezzanine, Roanoke, VA 24011, 703-983-0717; FAX: 703-983-0723.

South Boston: South Boston Small Business Development Center, P.O. Box 1116, South Boston, VA 24596, 804-575-0044, FAX: 804-572-4087.

Sterling: Loudoun County Small Business Development Center, One Steeplechase at Dulles, 21736 Atlantic Boulevard, Suite 100, Sterling, VA 22170, 703-430-7222; FAX: 703-430-9562.

Wytheville: Wytheville Community College, Small Business Development Center, 1000 E. Main Street, Wytheville, VA 24382, 703-228-5541, ext 314; FAX: 703-228-2542.

Washington

* General Information

Business Assistance Center
Department of Trade and Economic Development
2001 6th Avenue
Suite 2600
Seattle, WA 98121   206-464-7350
                          1-800-237-1233 in Washington
Services available are a Business Assistance Hotline, an Ombudsperson to assist with business/government dilemmas, a variety of publications, and an Electronic Bulletin Board, 206-441-5472, for quick computer access to business information.

Washington State Business Assistance Center
919 Lakeridge Way, Southwest
Suite A
Olympia, WA 98502   206-753-5632

Small Business Advocates: Assistance in cutting bureaucratic red tape. Information and expertise in dealing with state, federal, and local agencies.

* Financing

Department of Community Development
P.O. Box 48300   206-586-8974
Olympia, WA 98504-8300   1-800-562-5677 in Washington
Community Development Block Grant: Provides grants of federal funds to competitively selected small cities and counties for economic development, housing, and public facilities activities. Projects must benefit low-and moderate-income households, prevent or eliminate slums or blight, resolve urgent public health and safety needs. Assistance to businesses in the form of grants, loans, loans guarantees, interest supplements, technical assistance, and other forms of support for activities necessary to carry out an economic development project.

Community Development Finance Program: Helps businesses obtain long-term start-up or expansion loans at reasonable interest rates and low down payments. Funds are available for real estate, new construction, renovation, major leasehold improvements, machinery and equipment, and working capital.

Development Loan Fund: Offers loans to businesses in economically distressed areas where jobs will be increased, especially for low- and moderate-income residents. The Fund provides the difference between the total amount of the project cost and the private financing available. Loans are usually at interest rates below market levels.

Local Development Matching Fund Program   206-586-8979
Funds are available to economic development organizations on a public/private matching basis. The money is for use in technical assistance. May be used for strategic planning, technical analysis, aid to businesses in using certain state/federal programs, assistance in land use, transportation, site location, or employee training.

Coastal Revolving Loan Fund: Provides below-market rate loans to businesses in the five coastal counties of Clallam, Jefferson, Grays Harbor, Pacific and Wahkiakum for projects that will create permanent job opportunities for dislocated workers, the unemployed and lower-income persons.

Coastal Revolving Technical Assistance Loan Fund: Provides below-market rate loans to businesses or communities. Loans will purchase consulting assistance including accounting, engineering, architecture, design, market studies, feasibility analyses, tourism studies, land use planning, revitalization planning and strategic planning for community development.

Department of Trade and Economic Development
2001 Sixth Avenue, Suite 2600   206-464-7350
Seattle, WA 98121   1-800-237-1233
Industrial Revenue Bonds: For acquisition, construction or improvement of manufacturing facilities. Bonds are tax-exempt, with interest paid to the buyer not subject to federal income tax. The result is lower interest rates. Bonds may be issued by cities, counties, or port districts on behalf of a private business project proposal.

Umbrella Bond Program: For small businesses with borrowing needs too small for Industrial Revenue Bonds. This program pools several requests for industrial financing into one umbrella bond issue.

Washington State Business Assistance Center
Department of Trade and Economic Development
919 Lakeridge Way S.W., Suite A
Olympia, WA 98502   206-464-5832
Washington Economic Development Finance Authority: Provides financing for small export transactions, gives farmers who participate in federal, long-term land conservation programs an option to obtain lump-sum funds for machinery purchases, modernization, debt reduction or new business investment.

Washington State Energy Office
809 Legion Way S.E.

State Money – Washington

P.O. Box 43165
Olympia, WA 98504-3165   206-956-2000

Industrial Program: Low-interest loans provided to fund energy efficiency measures. Provides technical assistance in the form of industrial energy efficiency studies for small-and medium-size manufacturing facilities.

Export Assistance Center of Washington (EACW)
2001 Sixth Avenue, Suite 2100
Seattle, WA 98121   206-464-7123

Export Financing: Assists with the placement of a federal guarantee against commercial and political risks. EACW is a designated City/State Cooperative entity for the Export-Import Bank of the U.S. (Exim), a federal agency in this field. The Foreign Credit Insurance Agency offers insurance against foreign receivables may be assigned to a commercial lender so that the exporter can receive payment prior to collection on the foreign invoice. EACW also can help businesses secure private sector financing, including equity capital, and works with several federal and state agencies that offer various financing and other assistance.

Department of Revenue
Audit Section
1101 S. Eastside Street
Olympia, WA 98504-7470   206-753-3171

Distressed Area Tax Deferral Program: Sales or use tax deferral may be available for buildings, equipment, or machinery used in manufacturing, research, or development in distressed areas. Another provision is that one new job must be created for every $300,000 of investment. Repayment begin three years after completion of the project, with total repayment to be complete over the following five years.

Small Business Administration
Seattle Regional Office
915 2nd Avenue, Room 1792   206-553-1420
Seattle, WA 98174-1088   FAX: 206-553-8635

SBA 7(a) Guaranteed and Direct Loans: Guarantees up to 90 percent of a loan made through a private lender up to $750,000. Can be used for working capital, expand or convert facilities, purchase of machinery and equipment, and land and building. Available only to those unable to obtain a loan from conventional sources. Direct loans are made up to $150,000.

SBA 504: Provides loans using 50 percent conventional bank financing, 40 percent SBA involvement through Certified Development Companies, and 10 percent owner equity. Fixed-asset loans are available in amounts up to $750,000. The loan can be used for land and building, construction, machinery and equipment, and renovation/expansion.

Small Business Innovative Research Grants (SBIR): Phase I awards between $20,000 to $50,000 to entrepreneurs to support six months of research on a technical innovation. Phase II grants are an additional $500,000 for development. Private sector investment funds must follow.

International Trade Loans: Guaranteed long-term loans through private lenders to develop or expand export markets, or to recover from the effects of import competition. Maximum guaranteed loan is $1,000,000 for fixed assets and an additional $250,000 for working capital and/or export revolving line of credit.

Export Revolving Line of Credit Loan: Short term financing available to small businesses that are at least one year old. Loans provide working capital to finance the manufacturing or wholesaling of products for export and for export marketing. The SBA will guarantee up to 90 percent of a conventional loan in amounts up to $750,000.

Contract Loan: Short-term loans are available to small businesses to finance the costs of labor and materials on contracts for which the proceeds are assignable. Program guarantees up to 90 percent of loans not in excess of $750,000. Qualifying small businesses must be in business for at least 12 calendar months prior to the date of the loan application.

Seasonal Line of Credit Loan: Loans provide short-term working capital to finance seasonal increases in business activities. Program guarantees up to 90 percent of loans not in excess of $750,000. Qualifying business must be in operation for at least one year prior to application.

Pollution Control Loans: Long-term guaranteed loans can be made by conventional financing to small businesses for installation or required pollution control measures. Must be unable to adopt the pollution control measures without undue financial hardship. Maximum guaranteed loan is $1,000,000.

General Contractor Loans: Small general construction contractors may obtain short-term loans or loan guarantees for residential or commercial construction or rehabilitation of property to be sold. The SBA will guarantee up to 90 percent of qualifying loans made by private lenders up to to a maximum of $750,000. Direct loans can be up to $150,000.

Energy Business Loan Guarantee: Small businesses that provide certain energy production and conservation services for others may qualify for long-term loans and loan guarantees for start-ups and expansions. Loans and guarantees are made for firms that develop, manufacture, sell, install, or service specific energy measures for others, or firms that provide engineering, architectural, consulting, or other professional services connected with specific energy measures. Guarantee is for up to 90 percent of a loan not in excess of $750,000. Direct loans up to $150,000.

Disaster Recovery Loans: Small businesses located in federally designated disaster areas and suffering property damage or economic losses from the disaster can obtain long-term recovery loans at low interest rates. Property damage loans are limited to 85 percent of the verified damage. Loans for economic losses are for operating capital to meet the business' obligations that could have been made had the disaster not occurred.

Handicapped Assistance Loans: Assists persons who have a physical, mental or emotional disability of a permanent nature which limits the selection of any type of employment for which the person would otherwise be qualified. Direct loans are available for up to $150,000. The interest rate is 3% on these loans.

Surety Bond Guaranty Program: Makes the bonding system more available to small contractors who may be denied access to the system. SBA can guarantee up to 80 percent of surety's loss on a bond that has a maximum in total contract value of up to $1,250,000.

Vietnam-era and Disabled Veterans Loan Program: Provides direct loans to veterans to establish or expand a small business. Funds may be used for working capital or fixed assets. Direct loans for amounts up to $150,000 are available. The interest rate may be fixed or variable.

Norwest Growth Fund, Inc.
(Main Office: Minneapolis, MN)
777 108th Avenue, NE, Suite 2460
Bellevue, WA 98004   503-223-6622

Seafirst Capital Corporation
Columbia Seafirst Center
701 Fifth Avenue, P.O. Box 34662
Seattle, WA 98124   206-358-7441

U.S. Bancorp Capital Corporation
(Main Office: Portland, OR)
1415 Fifth Avenue
Seattle, WA 98171   206-344-8105

Small Business Investment Companies (SBIC): The SBA licenses, regulates, and provides financial assistance to privately owned and operated Small Business Investment Companies. SBICs make venture or risk investments by supplying capital and extending unsecured loans and loans not fully collateralized to small enterprises which meet their investment criteria. Financing is made by direct loans and by equity investments.

Department of Agriculture
Farmers Home Administration
P.O. Box 2427
Wenatchee, WA 98807   509-662-4358

Business and Industry Loan Guarantee Program: The FmHa grants loan guarantees for up to 90 percent of a lender's losses on loans used for business or industry development. Individuals, as well as public and private organizations and Indian tribal groups in rural areas with under 50,000 population, are eligible. Priority is given to towns under 25,000 population. Funds can be used for buy-outs, construction, conversion, modernization and repair of buildings, purchase of land, equipment, furniture and fixtures, processing and marketing facilities, and pollution control, feasibility studies.

Economic Development Administration
Jackson Federal Building
915 Second Avenue, Room 1856
Seattle, WA 98174   206-553-4740
Revolving Loan Funds: Grants are made to designated redevelopment areas, economic development districts, states, political subdivisions and Indian tribes to establish or expand revolving loan funds in depressed areas. These funds are loaned to businesses for fixed assets or working capital.

Washington State Business Assistance Center
Department of Trade and Economic Development
919 Lakeridge Way S.W., Suite A
Olympia, WA 98502   206-753-5632
Child Care Facility Fund: Makes direct loans at a fixed interest rate, guaranteed loans up to 80 percent of the loan, and matching grants on a dollar-for dollar basis with cash, goods, or services. Maximum loan amount is $25,000 to employers starting or expanding child care services. Funds can be used to make capital improvements in an existing licensed child care facility, start a licensed child care facility, including family child care homes, purchase equipment, and operations costs during the first three months of a new program.

* Women and Minority Business Assistance

Office of Minority and Women's Business Enterprises (OWMBE)
P.O. Box 41160
Olympia, WA 98504-1160   206-753-9693
Assists minority and women's business enterprises in state contracting. Business must be certified. Applications for certification are available from OWMBE. Maintains a central certification list for state agencies, education institutions and other jurisdictions. Once certified, you are eligible to receive a 5 percent preference when bidding competitively on purchased goods and services. Upon request, you can be placed on bid lists maintained by individual agencies, education institutions, or contractors by contacting them directly.

Small Business Administration
Seattle Regional Office
915 2nd Avenue, Room 1792   206-553-1420
Seattle, WA 98174-1088   FAX: 206-553-1420
SBA 8(a) Program - Business Procurement Assistance: Provides federal government contracting opportunities for small businesses owned by socially and economically disadvantaged persons, and assists these businesses to become independently competitive in the normal business environment. SBA monitors all government contracts to assure that a quota of contract work goes to 8(a) businesses. Also provides business management services to these businesses. Business must be approved for program participation prior to receipt of an 8(a) contract.

* Training

State Board for Community and Technical Colleges
P.O. Box 42495
Olympia, WA 98504-2495   206-753-0878
or Nearest Community College
Community colleges assist employers by providing education and training for new and current workers. Community colleges and cooperating employers can apply for special funding to provide customized job training to suite the requirements of new or expanding businesses.

Employment Security Department
212 Maple Park
Olympia, WA 98502   206-753-5211
Business Resource Network: A single service information and program brokerage service for new and expanding businesses. Ensures ease of access and optimum benefits from all hiring incentives and training programs.

Employment Security Department
605 Woodview Drive SE, MS: KG-11
Olympia, WA 98504-5311   206-438-4615
Employers can gain access to a large pool of experience, qualified workers, and receive financial assistance for training new employees through on-the-job or customized training. Provides assistance with outplacement or retraining of employees during a partial or complete closure.

Employment Security Department
212 Maple Park
MS: KG-11
Olympia, WA 98504-5311   206-753-5211
Job Training Partnership Act (JTPA): Provides employers with recruitment, screening, referral, training, 50 percent wage subsidy up to 3 months for on-the-job training. Available to any private employer.

Veterans Job Training Act: The Veterans Administration will pay an employer half of a veteran's entry wages up to 9 months, or up to 15 months for veterans with a disability. Maximum payment is $10,000.

Targeted Jobs Tax Credit   206-438-4119
Offers employers a credit against their tax liability for hiring individuals from nine target groups. Tax credit is 40 percent of the first year wages up to $6,000 earned. Maximum credit is $2,400.

State Board for Vocational Education
Building 17
Airdustrial Park
P.O. Box 43105
Olympia, WA 98504   206-586-8680
Job Skills Program: Matching grants program that supports short-term job-specific training for local business and industry. Eligible for funding are prospective employees before a new plant opens or when existing industry expands, upgrading existing employees to create new vacancies for unemployed applicants, and retraining current employees when retraining is vital to keep their jobs.

* Management Consulting and Other Services

Department of General Administration
Office of State Procurement
216 G.A. Building
P.O. Box 41017
Olympia, WA 98504-1017   206-753-0900
Procurement Assistance: The Department of General Administration, Office of State Procurement (OSP) is responsible for procuring goods and services to support state operations. Businesses and individuals wishing to sell to OSP can register on the state bidders' list through the *Supplier Information and Registration* packet. Additional information is provided in *A Guide to Purchasing Policies.* Both are available upon request.

Department of Trade and Economic Development
919 Lakeridge Way SW, Suite A
Olympia, WA 98502   206-753-5632
Tourism Development Program: Facilitates development of the tourism industry in Washington State through market development. product development. Produces statewide advertising and publicity campaigns, provides consumer travel planning information and referral services. Product development programs include marketing of resort investment sites, tour product development, and technical assistance coordination program to help local tourism development groups and communities plan and develop their local tourism industry.

Department of Labor and Industry
Office of Information and Assistance   1-800-LISTENS
Offers a single point of contact for help regarding industrial insurance, contractor registration, and other L&I services. There are 18 offices located statewide.

Business License Service
Department of Licensing

405 Black Lake Boulevard   206-586-2786
Olympia, WA 98504   1-800-562-8203 in Washington

License Information Service: A centralized source of information concerning licenses, permits and registrations administered by state agencies and the federal government.

Trade Name Registration: A centralized location for the registration, discovery, and disclosure of the ownership of businesses operating under an assumed name.

Corporations Division
Office of the Secretary of State
505 East Union Avenue
Olympia, WA 98504   206-753-7115

Trademarks: Provides registration for trademarks and service marks in use in Washington state.

Washington Public Ports Association
P.O. Box 1518
Olympia, WA 98507   206-943-0760

Port Districts: In Washington, Port Districts lease land, buildings and facilities to private companies, and they also develop various public projects that help with local development. The districts have wide authority to encourage economic development in port areas. The Washington Public Ports Association, a public trade association, conducts important port studies, exchanges operations information and acts as an intermediary between ports and the state government.

Washington Business Assistance Center
919 Lakeridge Way S.W.
Suite A
Olympia, WA 98502

Washington Investment Network   206-753-5632
Matches Washington entrepreneurs in need of seed, start-up or expansion capital with the resources of private investors, institutional investors and venture capital firms via a computer program. The program provides maximum exposure of entrepreneurial needs to investor resources.

Recycling Market Development Program   206-753-5632
Develops markets for recycled materials, attracts new businesses who use secondary materials to the state and help existing ones to expand, promotes business and consumer use of products made from recycled materials, provides technical market assistance to businesses. Special emphasis is placed on developing markets for mixed waste papers, yard waste, plastics and used tires.

Department of Trade and Economic Development
2001 Sixth Avenue
Suite 2600
Seattle, WA 98121   1-800-237-1233 in Washington

Site Selection   206-464-6282
Provides management assistance and consulting services to businesses considering expansion or relocation in Washington. Identifies potential locations and facilities based on business requirements and community resources.

Business Retention   206-464-6282
Provides direct technical assistance and turnaround consulting services to businesses threatened with closure, failure, layoffs or bankruptcy. Provides state and federal funding for feasibility studies of at-risk businesses.

Film and Video Office   206-464-7350
Markets statewide locations, business facilities and production personnel to out-of-state filmmakers, and encourages growth of in-state film and video production. Provides assistance to producers of feature films, TV movies, national and regional TV and print commercials, industrials, documentaries and music videos.

Export Information   206-464-7143
     FAX: 206-464-7222
Offices in both Seattle, Tokyo, London, and Taipei. This group develops new markets and expands existing ones for value-added products and services. It targets geographies regions, and industry sectors including biotechnology, software, food processing, forest products and air cargo. Counsels on the opportunities and problems of international trade, participates in international trade exhibitions, and trade shows, publishes a bimonthly trade leads newsletter.

CINTRAFOR
College of Forest Resources
AR-10
University of Washington
Seattle, WA 98195   206-543-8684

Responds to opportunities and problems of the export and import of wood and fiber products. Disseminates information on world trade in forest products by means of a symposia, conferences, workshops, outreach and publications. A database, INTRADATA, maintains a publicly accessible management service for forest products and international trade statistics.

Department of Community Development
906 Columbia Street SW
P.O. Box 48300
Olympia, WA 98504-8300   206-586-8984

Employee Ownership Program: Provides assistance, consultation, information and referrals to individuals and companies interested in possible employee ownership structure. Arranges for presentations and training workshops on employee ownership.

Washington State Energy Office
809 Legion Way S.E.
P.O. Box 43165
Olympia, WA 98504-3165   206-956-2000

Bioenergy Technical Information: Provides technical assistance to manufacturing and commercial facilities interested in using biomass (wood, municipal waste and agricultural residues) fuels. Helps identify biomass sources and in selecting appropriate technologies and/or consultants.

Washington Technology Center
University of Washington Campus Office
FJ-15, Fluke Hall
Seattle, WA 98195   206-685-1920

Combines technological skills and innovations of the academic, public, and private sectors through fellowship programs, research and development activities, and a Technology Assistance Program (TAP). TAP makes technical expertise available to small and medium-sized businesses and aids in the transfer of successful technological innovations. Also available is the portfolio of new inventions that have been sponsored by WTC research with industry and the federal government. Those inventions that are not tied up by previous corporate commitments are available for marketing and licensing to companies in Washington State.

Small Business Administration
Seattle Regional Office
915 2nd Avenue, Room 1792   206-553-1420
Seattle, WA 98174-1088   FAX: 206-553-8635

Small Business Institutes: This program provides personalized consulting services to the small business community. Consulting is provided by senior level business students, guided by a faculty advisor. Assistance in business plan preparation, marketing research, market planning, accounting, and seminars are provided.
University Locations:
Central Washington University
Eastern Washington University
Gonzaga University
Pacific Lutheran University
Seattle University
University of Puget Sound
University of Washington
Washington State University
Western Washington University

* Small Business Development Centers

The following offices offer free and fee-based services to new and expanding businesses:

Lead Center:
Washington Small Business Development Center
Washington State University
245 Todd Hall
Pullman, WA 99164-4727
509-355-1576
FAX: 509-335-0949

Aberdeen: Grays Harbor College, Small Business Development Center, 1602 Edward P. Smith Drive, Aberdeen, WA 98520, 206-532-9020.

Bellevue: Bellevue Community College, Small Business Development Center, 3000 Landerholm Circle, Bellevue, WA 98009, 206-641-2265; FAX: 206-453-3032.

Bellingham: Western Washington University, Small Business Development Center, College of Business and Economics, 415 Park Hall, Bellingham, WA 98225, 206-676-3899; FAX: 509-647-4844.

Centralia: Centralia Community College, Small Business Development Center, 600 West Locust Street, Centralia, WA 98531, 206-736-9391; FAX: 206-753-3404.

Everett: Edmonds Community College, Small Business Development Center, 917 134th Street, S.W., Everett, WA 98204, 206-745-0430; FAX: 206-745-5563.

Moses Lake: Big Bend Community College, Small Business Development Center, 7662 Chanute Street, Bldg. 1500, Moses Lake, WA 98837-3299, 509-762-6239; FAX: 509-762-6329.

Mt. Vernon: Skagit Valley College, Small Business Development Center, 2405 College Way, Mt. Vernon, WA 98273, 206-428-1282; FAX: 206-428-1186.

Olympia: South Puget Sound Community College, Small Business Development Center, 2011 Mottman Road SW, Olympia, WA 98501, 206-754-7711; FAX: 206-586-6054.

Omak: Wenatchee Valley College, Small Business Development Center, P.O. Box 1042, Omak, WA 98841, 509-826-5107; FAX: 509-826-4604.

Pasco: Columbia Basin College, Small Business Development Center, 2600 North 20th, Pasco, WA 99301, 509-547-0511; FAX: 509-546-0401.

Seattle: South Seattle Community College, Small Business Development Center, 6000 16th Avenue, SW, Seattle, WA 98106, 206-764-5339; FAX: 206-764-5393.

Seattle: Washington State University at Seattle, Small Business Development Center, 2001 Sixth Avenue, Suite 2608, Seattle, WA 98121-2518, 206-464-5450.

Seattle: North Seattle Community College, Small Business Development Center, International Trade Institute, 9600 College Way North, Seattle, WA 98103, 206-527-3732; FAX: 206-527-3734.

Spokane: Community College of Spokane, Small Business Development Center, West 601 First, Spokane, WA 99204, 509-459-3741; FAX: 509-459-3433.

Tacoma: Washington State University at Tacoma, Small Business Development Center, 950 Pacific Avenue, Suite 300, Box 1933, Tacoma, WA 98401-1933, 206-272-7232; FAX: 206-597-7305.

Tacoma: Pierce College, Small Business Development Center, 9401 Farwest Drive, SW, Tacoma, WA 98498, 206-964-6776; FAX: 206-964-6746.

Vancouver: Columbia River Economic Development Council, Small Business Development Center, 100 East Columbia Way, Vancouver, WA 98660-3156, 206-693-2555; FAX: 206-694-9927.

Wenatchee: Wenatchee Valley College, Small Business Development Center, 1300 Fifth Street, Wenatchee, WA 98801, 509-662-1651; FAX: 206-764-5393.

Yakima: Yakima Valley Community College, Small Business Development Center, P.O. Box 1647, Yakima, WA 98907, 509-575-2284; FAX: 509-575-2461.

West Virginia

* General Information

Small Business Development Center
1115 Virginia Street E
Charleston, WV 25301
304-558-2960

Acts as a one-stop resource center for information and assistance in filing state and federal forms and coordinates assistance programs with other agencies.

Small Business Advocate: Assistance in cutting bureaucratic red tape. Information and expertise in dealing with state, federal, and local agencies.

* Financing

Governor's Office of Community and Industrial Development
Community Development Division, Room B 553
State Capitol Complex, Bldg. 6
Charleston, WV 25305
304-558-4010

Grants In Aid Programs: Provides money for infrastructure construction or improvement to provide planned, orderly development of communities and to lay the basis for economic growth. Funds go for such projects as public utilities, access roads, public buildings, streets, and sidewalks.

Community Development Block Grant Program: Available to cities and counties, who in turn, loan the money to businesses for the commercial rehabilitation of existing buildings or structures used for business, commercial, or industrial purposes. Every $15,000 of funds invested must create at least one full-time job, and at least 51 percent of the jobs created must be for low and moderate-income families.

Appalachian Regional Commission: This Federal Commission provides discretionary funds to governor's for regional improvement in the areas of water quality, waste disposal, planning, access roads, and highways. The Department of Community Development has preliminary review jurisdiction over proposals.

West Virginia Economic Development Authority (WVEDA)
Building 6, Room 525
State Capitol Complex
Charleston, WV 25305
304-558-3650

Direct Loans: The WVEDA is a public corporation charged with promoting economic development through financial assistance to state industries for expansion or construction purposes. The Authority works in conjunction with other state industrial development agencies and lending institutions. It offers below market rates. Funds can be used for acquisition, construction and/or renovation of land, buildings, and equipment. Loans are mostly for manufacturing businesses. Can provide up to 45 percent of the total project cost, with a $500,000 limit per project.

State Industrial Development Pool Funds: A $50 million investment fund set up by the State Board of Investments, this money is available through the WVEDA to larger industrial development projects. Loan terms are similar to the revolving fund, but letters of credit are required. Rates are based on U.S. Treasury bill rates.

SBA 504: Provides long-term fixed-rate loans for small and medium-sized firms. SBA participation is 40 percent through the West Virginia Certified Development Corporation, 50 percent conventional bank financing, and 10 percent owner equity. A fixed-asset loan in amounts up to $750,000. Loan can be used for land and building, construction, machinery and equipment, and renovation/expansion.

Capital Access Program: A loan loss reserve fund created to expand the availability of commercial bank loans to businesses in West Virginia.

Farmer's Home Administration Business and Industry Guaranteed Loan Program: This program covers up to 90 percent of the principal of a loan in order to protect investors.

West Virginia State Tax Department
State Capitol, Room 417 West

Building 1
1800 Washington Street E
Charleston, WV 23505   304-348-2500

Small Business Tax Credit: To qualify, businesses must have an annual payroll of at most $1,700,000 and annual sales not exceeding $5,500,0000, and the median salary of the company's employees must be at least $12,000 per year. Must create at least 10 new jobs. Firm is then allowed 30 percent of its qualified investment as credit.

Warehouse "Freeport" Tax Exemption: Allows goods in transit to an out-of-state destination to be exempt from local ad valorem property tax when "warehoused" in West Virginia. Exemption is applicable for "property in the form of inventory in the flow of interstate commerce or while in transit is consigned to a warehouse, public or private, within the state for final destination outside the state".

Investment Tax Credits: Credit against **Business Franchise Taxes** for industrial expansion or revitalization is available to manufacturers and persons providing manufacturing services. Also available for utilities paying the Business & Occupational Tax and natural resource producers who pay Severance Taxes.

Credit against franchise taxes for investment in a qualified research and development project is available to producers of natural resources, manufacturers, generators of electric power and persons providing manufacturing services.

Small Business Development Center
1115 Virginia Street E
Charleston, WV 25301   304-558-2960

SBA 7(a) Guaranteed and Direct Loans: Guarantees up to 90 percent of a loan made through a private lender up to $750,000. Can be used for working capital, expand or convert facilities, purchase of machinery and equipment, and land and building. Available only to those unable to obtain a loan from conventional sources. Direct loans are made up to $150,000.

SBA 504: Provides loans using 50 percent conventional bank financing, 40 percent SBA involvement through Certified Development Companies, and 10 percent owner equity. Fixed-asset loans are available in amounts up to $750,000. The loan can be used for land and building, construction, machinery and equipment, and renovation/expansion.

Small Business Innovative Research Grants (SBIR): Phase I awards between $20,000 to $50,000 to entrepreneurs to support six months of research on a technical innovation. Phase II grants are an additional $500,000 for development. Private sector investment funds must follow.

International Trade Loans: Guaranteed long-term loans through private lenders to develop or expand export markets, or to recover from the effects of import competition. Maximum guaranteed loan is $1,000,000 for fixed assets and an additional $250,000 for working capital and/or export revolving line of credit.

Export Revolving Line of Credit Loan: Short term financing available to small businesses that are at least one year old. Loans provide working capital to finance the manufacturing or wholesaling of products for export and for export marketing. The SBA will guarantee up to 90 percent of a conventional loan in amounts up to $750,000.

Contract Loan: Short-term loans are available to small businesses to finance the costs of labor and materials on contracts for which the proceeds are assignable. Program guarantees up to 90 percent of loans not in excess of $750,000. Qualifying small businesses must be in business for at least 12 calendar months prior to the date of the loan application.

Seasonal Line of Credit Loan: Loans provide short-term working capital to finance seasonal increases in business activities. Program guarantees up to 90 percent of loans not in excess of $750,000. Qualifying business must be in operation for at least one year prior to application.

Pollution Control Loans: Long-term guaranteed loans can be made by conventional financing to small businesses for installation or required pollution control measures. Must be unable to adopt the pollution control measures without undue financial hardship. Maximum guaranteed loan is $1,000,000.

General Contractor Loans: Small general construction contractors may obtain short-term loans or loan guarantees for residential or commercial construction or rehabilitation of property to be sold. The SBA will guarantee up to 90 percent of qualifying loans made by private lenders up to a maximum of $750,000. Direct loans can be up to $150,000.

Energy Business Loan Guarantee: Small businesses that provide certain energy production and conservation services for others may qualify for long-term loans and loan guarantees for start-ups and expansions. Loans and guarantees are made for firms that develop, manufacture, sell, install, or service specific energy measures for others, or firms that provide engineering, architectural, consulting, or other professional services connected with specific energy measures. Guarantee is for up to 90 percent of a loan not in excess of $750,000. Direct loans up to $150,000.

Disaster Recovery Loans: Small businesses located in federally designated disaster areas and suffering property damage or economic losses from the disaster can obtain long-term recovery loans at low interest rates. Property damage loans are limited to 85 percent of the verified damage. Loans for economic losses are for operating capital to meet the business' obligations that could have been made had the disaster not occurred.

Handicapped Assistance Loans: Assists persons who have a physical, mental or emotional disability of a permanent nature which limits the selection of any type of employment for which the person would otherwise be qualified. Direct loans are available for up to $150,000. The interest rate is 3% on these loans.

Surety Bond Guaranty Program: Makes the bonding system more available to small contractors who may be denied access to the system. SBA can guarantee up to 80 percent of surety's loss on a bond that has a maximum in total contract value of up to $1,250,000.

Vietnam-era and Disabled Veterans Loan Program: Provides direct loans to veterans to establish or expand a small business. Funds may be used for working capital or fixed assets. Direct loans for amounts up to $150,000 are available. The interest rate may be fixed or variable.

* Women and Minorities Business Assistance

Small Business Development Center
1115 Virginia Street E
Charleston, WV 25301   304-558-2960

SBA 8(a) Program - Business Procurement Assistance: Provides federal government contracting opportunities for small businesses owned by socially and economically disadvantaged persons, and assists these businesses to become independently competitive in the normal business environment. SBA monitors all government contracts to assure that a quota of contract work goes to 8(a) businesses. Also provides business management services to these businesses. Business must be approved for program participation prior to receipt of an 8(a) contract.

* Training

Guaranteed Work Force Program
Governor's Office of Community and Industrial Development
State Capitol, M-146
Charleston, WV 25305-0311   304-558-0400

One-Stop Shopping: Provides one-stop shopping for all economic development related job training needs. By coordinating state job training programs for new or expanding businesses, the program helps cut the red tape and meets needs for training, retraining, skills upgrading. All training information, application forms, funding guidelines and program design assistance is available. Matches an employer's needs with the best possible training solution, customized training programs can be developed. Programs are coordinated through the following:

Governor's Office of Community and Industrial Development:
Guaranteed Work Force Funding: Customized job training.

West Virginia Bureau of Employment Programs/Division of Employment:
Job Training Partnership Act (JTPA): Provides employers with recruitment, screening, referral, training, 50 percent wage subsidy up to 3 months for on-the-job training. Available to any private employer.

West Virginia Department of Education/Bureau of Vocational, Technical and Adult Education:

New and Expanding Industry Training (NEIT): Supervisory training and specialized programs; Job Training Partnership Act; Classroom/vestibule training

* Management Consulting and Other Services

Small Business Development Center
1115 Virginia Street E
Charleston, WV 25301   304-558-2960

Procurement Assistance Program: Receives requests for bids from the state Department of Finance and Administration and from the Federal government. The Center then mails a list of bid opportunities to any small business requesting it. The center will also counsel firms on doing business with the government, using representatives of the General Services Administration and the Defense Department.

Small Business Institutes: This program provides personalized consulting services to the small business community. Consulting is provided by senior level business students, guided by a faculty advisor. Assistance in business plan preparation, marketing research, market planning, accounting, and seminars are provided.
University Locations:
Concord College
Fairmont State College
Marshall University
West Liberty State College
West Virginia State College
West Virginia University

Business and Industrial Development Division
Governor's Office of Community and Industrial Development
Room 517, Building 6
Capitol Complex
Charleston, WV 25305   304-348-2234

Site Selection Assistance: Helps businesses identify suitable locations that meet the requirements of a particular project. The divisions maintains a computerized inventory of buildings, industrial properties and industrial parks. In the process of establishing a computerized inventory of available office space. The office prepares brochures on available properties which include photographs, location maps and specifications fact sheets.

* Small Business Development Centers
The following offices offer free and fee-based services to new and expanding businesses:

Lead Center:
West Virginia Small Business Development Center
West Virginia Development Office
1115 Virginia Street, East
Capitol Complex   304-558-2960
Charleston, WV 25310-2406   FAX: 304-558-0127

Athens: Concord College, Small Business Development Center, Center for Economic Action, Box D-125, Athens, WV 24712, 304-384-5103.

Bluefield: Bluefield State College, Small Business Development Center, 219 Rock Street, Bluefield, WV 24701, 304-327-4107; FAX: 304-325-7747.

Fairmount: Fairmount State College, Small Business Development Center, Fairmount, WV 26554, 304-367-4125.

Huntington: Marshall University, Small Business Development Center, 1050 Fourth Avenue, Huntington, WV 25701, 304-696-6789.

Keyser: Potomac State College, Rural and Small Business Development Center, 75 Arnold Street, Keyser, WV 26726, 304-788-3011.

Montgomery: West Virginia Institute of Technology, Small Business Development Center, Room 102, Engineering Building, Montgomery, WV 25136, 304-442-5501.

Morgantown: West Virginia University, Small Business Development Center, P.O. Box 6025, Morgantown, WV 26506, 304-293-5839.

Parkersburg: West Virginia University at Parkersburg, Small Business Development Center, Route 5, Box 167-A, Parkersburg, WV 26101, 304-424-8277.

Shepherdstown: Shepherd College, Small Business Development Center, 120 North Princess Street, Shepherdstown, WV 25443, 1-800-344-5251, ext 261.

Wheeling: West Virginia Northern Community College, Small Business Development Center, College Square, Wheeling, WV 26003, 304-233-5900; ext. 206.

Wisconsin

* General Information

Department of Development
P.O. Box 7970   608-266-1018
Madison, WI 53707   FAX: 608-267-2829

One-Stop Business Hotline
Permit Information Center   1-800-HELP-BUS
Coordinates state regulatory and business development needs by providing information on permit requirements, expedition of permit issuance, monitoring of a permit's progress in the bureaucracy, and recommending improvements in the permit process.

Small Business Ombudsman Program: Provides information and referral to new businesses regarding government regulations, management assistance and financing.

Bureau of Advocacy:
Small Business Advocate   608-266-1018
Assistance in cutting bureaucratic red tape. Information and expertise in dealing with state, federal, and local agencies.

* Financing

Wisconsin Housing and Economic
  Development Authority
P.O. Box 1728   608-266-0976
Madison, WI 53701-1728   FAX: 608-267-1099

Business Development Bonds: These are essentially industrial revenue bonds issued by the Wisconsin Housing and Economic Development Authority (WHEDA) on behalf of small businesses. Eligible projects qualify for low-cost, fixed-rate financing. Businesses need to supply lenders with a letter of credit from WHEDA to guarantee these bonds. Available to manufacturers and first-time farmers with gross sales of $35 million or less. Project funded must create or retain employment. Proceeds can be used for land, building, or equipment purchase or improvement. Other restrictions apply. BDB's are generally range from $500,000 to $1 million with $10 million maximum.

Venture Capital Fund: Available to business that have fewer than 25 employees and gross sales of less than 2.5 million. Financing type is an equity investment. Investments are made to very early stage business ventures with potential for significant growth.

Wisconsin Community Capital   608-256-3441
Business must be located in a distressed community and must expect to create or retain 10 to 15 jobs for unemployed or underemployed residents within 2 years. Loans range between $30,000 to $200,000. Funds can be used for land, buildings, equipment, inventory, working capital.

Department of Development
P.O. Box 7970   608-266-1018
Madison, WI 53707   FAX: 608-267-2829

Industrial Revenue Bonds: Available to manufacturing businesses for land, buildings, equipment, new or expanded facilities/equipment. Maximum loan amount is $10,000,000.

Wisconsin Development Fund:

Technology Development Program: Eligible are Wisconsin-based businesses applying in conjunction with a school in the University of Wisconsin System or another post-baccalaureate institution in Wisconsin. Preference is given to proposals with strong market potential, contributing to state economy and to research aims of education institution, and be completed within 2 years. Provides loans or repayable grants up to 25 percent of total research costs, to fund product or process development research. Amounts range from $50,000 to $200,000.

Major Economic Development Projects: Projects are evaluated on the potential contribution to job creation or retention, new capital investment, infrastructure needs and local unemployment among others. Businesses may apply directly, or local government may apply on their behalf. Grants or loans up to 75 percent of the cost of the project.

Small Cities Community Development Block Grant Program: Federally funded. The Department administers the Small Cities portion of the Program. Available to cities with populations under 50,000 (populations over 50,000 apply directly to the federal government.) For economic development projects. Focuses on job creation and retention with a requirement that a portion of the jobs be made available to persons of low- and moderate-income. The applicant must be a local government acting on behalf of a business. The assistance to the business is in the form of a loan with terms that vary based on the firm's need.

Employee Ownership Fund: Makes loans to employee groups to study the feasibility of converting an operating or recently-closed business to employee ownership. Loans are awarded on a competitive basis to those groups with greatest management ability and promise for success and where economic impact and affected employment is largest. Requires 25 percent match by borrowing group, unless hardship can be shown.

Small Business Innovation Research (SBIR) Program 608-267-9383
A federal Research & Development Program available to small businesses for projects at the earliest stage of research that have commercial potential. Phase I awards up to $50,000 over six months to evaluate the scientific and technical merit and feasibility of an idea. Phase II awards are up to $500,000 over two years to pursue the technological development of the innovation. Phase III is for commercialization with private or non-SBIR government funding. Each federal agency issues a solicitation bulletin, generally once a year, describing the areas of research it will fund.

SBIR Bridge Gap Financing 608-267-9383
Business that submit a Phase II proposal will be guaranteed up to $40,000 in state funding to "bridge the gap" in federal funding between the end of Phase I and the start of Phase II.

Bureau of International Development 608-266-1480
Export Development Loan Program 608-266-1480
Offers loans of up to $30,000 for small Wisconsin businesses wishing to enter exporting or to expand into new markets. Business must match a minimum of 60 percent of the loan funds.

Development Zone Program 608-267-2045
Businesses who expand, start or relocate in one of the 8 development zones in the state, and meet certain requirements may be eligible for tax benefits. Tax credit include a refundable jobs credit for hiring members of certain targeted groups, refundable sales tax credit for the amount of sales tax paid on building materials and equipment used in a trade or business, plus a non-refundable 2.5 percent location credit, non-refundable 2.5 percent investment credit, and a non-refundable 5 percent additional research credit.

Recycling Loan Program 608-266-2742/2766
Designed to encourage new or expanding businesses to make products from recycled materials. Funds will be awarded to those recycling activities that best contribute to the state's goals.

Recycling Rebate Program 608-267-2742/2766
Designed to offset the increased costs of making products from recycled materials. Also encourages the start-up and expansion of recycling firms, and the promotion of new markets for waste products. Firms may apply for a one-time rebate on qualified equipment, or up to five annual rebates, to offset the cost of a recycling process.

Export-Import Bank of the United States
811 Vermont Avenue, N.W.
Washington, DC 20571   202-566-8990
Working Capital Guarantee: Loan guarantees to assist small to medium-sized companies having the potential to export but inability to access working capital lines of credit from their banks to finance operations. Funds can be used for inventory, working capital, materials, labor, marketing activities. Other export credit programs available include medium and long term credit, and various types of export/import insurance.

Small Business Administration (SBA)
310 West Wisconsin Avenue, #400   414-297-3941
Milwaukee, WI 53203   FAX: 414-297-4267

Small Business Administration
212 East Washington Avenue   608-264-5261
Madison, WI 53703   FAX: 608-264-5541
SBA 7(a) Guaranteed and Direct Loans: Guarantees up to 90 percent of a loan made through a private lender up to $750,000. Can be used for working capital, expand or convert facilities, purchase of machinery and equipment, and land and building. Available only to those unable to obtain a loan from conventional sources. Direct loans are made up to $150,000.

SBA 504: Provides loans using 50 percent conventional bank financing, 40 percent SBA involvement through Certified Development Companies, and 10 percent owner equity. Fixed-asset loans are available in amounts up to $750,000. The loan can be used for land and building, construction, machinery and equipment, and renovation/expansion.

Small Business Innovative Research Grants (SBIR): Phase I awards between $20,000 to $50,000 to entrepreneurs to support six months of research on a technical innovation. Phase II grants are an additional $500,000 for development. Private sector investment funds must follow.

International Trade Loans: Guaranteed long-term loans through private lenders to develop or expand export markets, or to recover from the effects of import competition. Maximum guaranteed loan is $1,000,000 for fixed assets and an additional $250,000 for working capital and/or export revolving line of credit.

Export Revolving Line of Credit Loan: Short term financing available to small businesses that are at least one year old. Loans provide working capital to finance the manufacturing or wholesaling of products for export and for export marketing. The SBA will guarantee up to 90 percent of a conventional loan in amounts up to $750,000.

Contract Loan: Short-term loans are available to small businesses to finance the costs of labor and materials on contracts for which the proceeds are assignable. Program guarantees up to 90 percent of loans not in excess of $750,000. Qualifying small businesses must be in business for at least 12 calendar months prior to the date of the loan application.

Seasonal Line of Credit Loan: Loans provide short-term working capital to finance seasonal increases in business activities. Program guarantees up to 90 percent of loans not in excess of $750,000. Qualifying business must be in operation for at least one year prior to application.

Pollution Control Loans: Long-term guaranteed loans can be made by conventional financing to small businesses for installation or required pollution control measures. Must be unable to adopt the pollution control measures without undue financial hardship. Maximum guaranteed loan is $1,000,000.

General Contractor Loans: Small general construction contractors may obtain short-term loans or loan guarantees for residential or commercial construction or rehabilitation of property to be sold. The SBA will guarantee up to 90 percent of qualifying loans made by private lenders up to a maximum of $750,000. Direct loans can be up to $150,000.

Energy Business Loan Guarantee: Small businesses that provide certain energy production and conservation services for others may qualify for long-term loans and loan guarantees for start-ups and expansions. Loans and guarantees are made for firms that develop, manufacture, sell, install, or service specific energy measures for others, or firms that provide engineering, architectural, consulting, or other professional services connected with specific energy measures. Guarantee is for up to 90 percent of a loan not in excess of $750,000. Direct loans up to $150,000.

Disaster Recovery Loans: Small businesses located in federally designated disaster areas and suffering property damage or economic losses from the disaster can obtain long-term recovery loans at low interest rates. Property damage loans are limited to 85 percent of the verified damage. Loans for economic losses are for operating capital to meet the business' obligations that could have been made had the disaster not occurred.

Handicapped Assistance Loans: Assists persons who have a physical, mental or emotional disability of a permanent nature which limits the selection of any type of employment for which the person would otherwise be qualified. Direct loans are available for up to $150,000. The interest rate is 3% on these loans.

Surety Bond Guaranty Program: Makes the bonding system more available to small contractors who may be denied access to the system. SBA can guarantee up to 80 percent of surety's loss on a bond that has a maximum in total contract value of up to $1,250,000.

Vietnam-era and Disabled Veterans Loan Program: Provides direct loans to veterans to establish or expand a small business. Funds may be used for working capital or fixed assets. Direct loans for amounts up to $150,000 are available. The interest rate may be fixed or variable.

Banc One Venture Corporation
111 East Wisconsin Avenue
Milwaukee, WI 53202   414-765-2274

Bando-McGlocklin Capital Corporation
13555 Bishops Court
Suite 205
Brookfield, WI 53005   414-784-9010

Capital Investments, Inc.
Commerce Building, Suite 540
744 North Fourth Street
Milwaukee, WI 53203   414-273-6560

M & I Ventures Corporation
770 North Water Street
Milwaukee, WI 53202   414-765-7910

MorAmerica Capital Corporation
(Main Office: Cedar Rapids, IA)
600 East Mason Street
Milwaukee, WI 53202   414-276-3839

Polaris Capital Corporation
One Park Plaza
11270 W. Park Place, Suite 320
Milwaukee, WI 53224   414-359-3040

Small Business Investment Companies (SBIC): The SBA licenses, regulates, and provides financial assistance to privately owned and operated Small Business Investment Companies. SBICs make venture or risk investments by supplying capital and extending unsecured loans and loans not fully collateralized to small enterprises which meet their investment criteria. Financing is made by direct loans and by equity investments.

Wisconsin Business Development Finance Corporation
P.O. Box 2717
Madison, WI 53701   608-258-8830

Wisconsin Business Development (WBD): Offers long-term financing at below conventional rates. Fund can be used for land, building, equipment, and certain soft costs such as architect, accounting, legal fees are also eligible. WBD participation may not exceed 40 percent or a maximum of $750,000 of the project cost.

Farmers Home Administration (FmHA)
4949 Kirschling Court
Stevens Point, WI 54481   715-345-7600

Business & Industrial Loans: Loan guarantees up to 90 percent of project cost. Businesses must be located in an area outside the boundary of a city of 50,000 or more. Priority will be given to projects in rural communities and communities of 25,000 or less. Funds can be used for land, buildings, equipment, inventory, and working capital. Special loans also available for alcohol fuel projects.

Northwest Planning Commission
302 Walnut Street
Spooner, WI 54801   715-635-2197

Program services businesses primarily in timer, and wood, manufacturing and tourism industries in Northwestern Wisconsin. Must create 1 job for every $5,000 loans to business. A subordinated loan covering 10 to 20 percent of project. Funds can be used for land, buildings, and equipment.

Impact Seven
320 Industrial Avenue
Turtle Lake, WI 54889-9109   715-986-4171

Rural Development Loan Fund: Loans available with a preference to Northwest Wisconsin. Loans generally range between $40,000 to $150,000. One job must be created for each $20,000 of loan funds. Funds can be used for land, buildings, equipment, and inventory.

Venture Capital: Financing type is equity investment. Prefer businesses in Northwest Wisconsin but will consider anywhere in the state, any industry. Job creation is a criterion. Available from start-up to mature business buyout or expansion. No restrictions on use of funds.

First Commercial Financial Corporation
330 South Executive Drive, #204
Brookfield, WI 53005   414-786-0699

Venture Capital: Financing type is equity investment. Most investments are for second state or later, and start-up funds are also available. Prefer biotech, high-tech, medical, communications, computers, electronics and other manufacturing. Will consider service or distribution businesses and businesses in other industry areas. Prefer investments in the midwest.

Venture Investor of Wisconsin, Inc.
University Research Park
565 Science Drive
Suite A
Madison, WI 53711   414-272-4400

Venture Capital: Financing type is equity investment. Works with Wisconsin companies or those willing to be to start and develop their business. Preference is given to those having products or services with national market potential. Deals with early state companies as well as special situations such as new product launches or significantly changed corporate strategies.

* Women and Minorities Business Assistance

Bureau of Minority Business Development
Department of Development
P.O. Box 7970
Madison, WI 53707   608-267-9550

This office works to help create and expand minority businesses in the state through consultation and other services. Some of its activities include financial consulting and technical assistance, marketing and certification assistance, business development and employment assistance, special help for the disabled, and coordinating the Wisconsin Marketplace, a marketing brokerage service for minority firms. It publishes a Directory of Minority-Owned Firms listing certified minority businesses on a computerized database for state-wide access. It also serves as a clearinghouse for information for firms, government and corporate buyers, and other agencies.

Business Development Initiative: Utilizes a competitive proposal process to identify the entrepreneurs and business venture opportunities which are most likely to succeed. Designed to provide professional technical assistance to eligible applicants who are interested in starting or expanding a business venture which would enhance the employment opportunities for persons with severe disabilities.

Eligible Applicants:
Entrepreneurs with a Disability, Rehabilitation Facilities
> Maximum $15,000 grant with 25 percent match required.
> Maximum $25,000 equity financing

Business Ventures Integrating Employees with Severe Disability
> Maximum $15,000 grant with 25 percent match

Grant dollars are to be used to hire professional consultants for marketing plans and services, business plans, financial plans and services, and other professional business development services such as engineering and legal.

Minority Business Development Fund   608-266-8380
Provides financial support for early business planning or stimulate acquisition or expansion of an existing business. Projects may require matching funds. Project must retain or increase employment.

Minority Business Recycling Development Program   608-266-8380
Awards grants and loans to minority businesses. Funds can be used to make products, acquire equipment, or operate plants to recycle waste.

Wisconsin Housing and Economic
    Development Authority (WHEDA)   608-266-0976
P.O. Box 1728   608-266-7884
Madison, WI 53701-1728   FAX: 608-267-1099
> **Linked Deposit Loan Program:** A low-rate loan fund for small, minority, or women-owned businesses with gross annual sales less than $500,000. Loans are available at under prime rate for purchase or improvement of buildings, equipment, or land, but not for working capital. Business must be in manufacturing, retail trade, tourism or agricultural packaging or processing. Also permitted are R&D and/or headquarters facilities, railroads, solid waste recycling. Loans range from $10,000 to $99,000. A qualified small or minority business makes its application at a commercial bank, which must get WHEDA's approval.

Future Value Ventures, Inc.
622 North Water Street, #500
Milwaukee, WI 53202   414-278-0377
> A Small Business Investment Company that provides equity financing to minorities, Vietnam Era veterans or others with cultural and historical barriers to business ownership, as well as women who can demonstrate economic handicap. Prefer businesses with potential to create jobs. Funds can be used for equipment, inventory, working capital.

Small Business Administration (SBA)
310 West Wisconsin Avenue   414-297-3941
Milwaukee, WI 53203   FAX: 414-297-4267

Small Business Administration (SBA)
212 East Washington Avenue   608-264-5261
Madison, WI 53703   FAX: 608-264-5541
> **SBA 8(a) Program - Business Procurement Assistance:** Provides federal government contracting opportunities for small businesses owned by socially and economically disadvantaged persons, and assists these businesses to become independently competitive in the normal business environment. SBA monitors all government contracts to assure that a quota of contract work goes to 8(a) businesses. Also provides business management services to these businesses. Business must be approved for program participation prior to receipt of an 8(a) contract.

> **Handicapped Assistance Loans:** Must be a business 100 percent owned by a handicapped person and other funding is not available. Funds can be used for land, buildings, equipment, inventory, working capital. Maximum amount available is $150,000.

Bureau of Indian Affairs
Great Lakes Agency, P.O. Box 273
Ashland, WI 54806   715-682-4527
> Business must be on or within 25 miles of reservation and 51 percent owned by Indians. Must also employ Indians and have a direct tie to reservation. Guarantees and direct loans for financing of projects. Grants are available for larger projects. Loan guarantees up to 90 percent and 25 percent project grants up to $100,000 for individuals.

Milwaukee County Department of Public Works & Transportation
907 North 10th Street
Suite 311
Milwaukee, WI 53233   414-278-5248
> **Milwaukee County Revolving Loan Program:** Available to a minority or woman or disadvantaged owned businesses acting as contractors, subcontractors or suppliers on county contracts. Funds can be used for equipment, inventory, working capital. Use must directly relate to meeting county contract.

City of Milwaukee-Minority Business Enterprise Program
200 East Wells Street
Suite 101
Milwaukee, WI 53202   414-278-5553
> **Minority Business Enterprise Revolving Loan Program:** Available to any minority or woman-owned business that receives a City of Milwaukee contract. Loans for up to 25 percent of contract with a maximum of $35,000. Funds can be used for equipment, inventory, working capital.

Milwaukee Economic Development Corporation
P.O. Box 324
Milwaukee, WI 53201   414-223-5812
> **Minority/Women's Business Loans:** Any minority or women-owned business or business start-up located in the City of Milwaukee is eligible. Provides financing to fill the gap between ownership funds and bank financing. Funds can be used for land, buildings, equipment, inventory, working capital. Loans range between $10,000 and $40,000. Minimum 10 percent of project must be contributed by borrower.

Wisconsin Department of Transportation
Disadvantaged Business Program
4802 Sheboygan Avenue, Room 936
Madison, WI 53707   608-266-6961
> Certification program for contracts with the State of Wisconsin Department of Transportation.

Wisconsin Women Entrepreneurs
1126 South 70th Street
Suite 106
Milwaukee, WI 53214   414-475-2436
> Provides monthly programs, training seminars, mentor committees, membership directory.

* Training

Department of Industry, Labor and Human Relations
201 E. Washington Avenue
Madison, WI 53701   608-266-3131
> **Job Training Partnership Act (JTPA):** Provides employers with recruitment, screening, referral, training, 50 percent wage subsidy up to 3 months for on-the-job training. Available to any private employer.

> **Dislocated Workers Program:** Trainees must be unemployed due to major plant closing or permanent lay-off, be long-term unemployed and unlikely to return to previous job or be displaced due to farm failure. Offers trained employees and/or customized training programs, on-the-job training with wage reimbursement to employers, and assistance in dealing with anticipated layoffs.

> **Targeted Jobs Tax Credit:** IRS offers a 40 percent employer tax credit on first $6,000 of wages paid to employees certified eligible by Job Service.

Department of Development
P.O. Box 7970   608-266-1018
Madison, WI 53707   FAX: 608-267-2829
> **Customized Labor Training Program:** This program is for businesses locating or expanding within the state that need training in new technological skills or new industrial skills. Grants are awarded for retraining. Requires a 100 percent matching requirement. Businesses must show that they cannot receive training help from any other source.

Board of Vocational, Technical and Adult Education
P.O. Box 7874
Madison, WI 53707-7874   608-266-1207
    Grants are available to support training designed to create or retain jobs.
    Type of programs available to businesses include employee assessment,
    seminars, technology programs, associate degree programs, quality and
    productivity training, management training.

Bureau of Apprenticeship Standards
DILHR
P.O. Box 7972
Madison, WI 53707   608-266-3331
    Employers must have employees in occupations considered to be
    apprenticeable, with persons currently on the job able to give training.

* Management Consulting and Other Services

Department of Development   608-266-1018
P.O. Box 7970   FAX: 608-267-2829
Madison, WI 53707
    SBIR Coordinator   608-267-9383
    SBIR Support Program: An annual statewide conference and regional
    proposal writing workshops provide businesses with the information and
    strategies they need to submit competitive SBIR proposals. In addition, a
    network of resources is available to assist firms in preparing a proposal
    which include editorial review of proposals, samples of past winning
    proposals, and identification of university faculty interested in collaborating
    on an SBIR project.

    Bureau of International Development   608-266-1480
    Helps Wisconsin businesses in exploring international sales opportunities,
    joint ventures and licensing, and encourages foreign firms and individuals
    to invest in productive Wisconsin activities. Arranges participation in trade
    missions, and sponsors several seminars and other information-sharing
    events. Foreign offices are located in Germany, Hong Kong, Japan, and
    Korea. Various publications are, some of which are at no cost. In addition,
    the bureau library offers hundreds of books and periodicals on
    international business.

    Entrepreneurial Networking Program   608-267-9384
    Provides coordination of state entrepreneurial assistance programs and
    assists in arrangements of meetings for industry, trade and professional
    organizations to introduce entrepreneurs and assistance providers to
    procedures by which venture capital is invested. Offers a resource series
    of entrepreneurial assistance publications. Also offers workshops and
    seminars.

    Bureau of Business Development:
    Technology Transfer and Commercialization Program: Provides develop-
    mental assistance such as one-on-one technical aid on marketing, business
    structure, site and building locations, financial management, productivity
    improvements, technology transfer, capital formation, and others.

    Division of Research and Planning:
    Strategic Planning and Research: Prepares and distributes information on
    the state economy and related policy issues. Recommends long-term eco-
    nomic development plans and coordinates with other agencies and the pri-
    vate sector in strategic planning. The office prepares research reports and
    studies on economic issues, staffs various planning and advisory councils,
    and conducts seminars on economic development issues. It also prepares
    educational materials to encourage economic development in all sectors.

    Wisconsin Film Office   608-267-3686
    Assists in-state and out-of-state producers by obtaining permits and coope-
    ration with local and state governmental agencies. Provides information on
    private-sector businesses that serve the film and television industry.

    The Photo/Video Resource Centers holds more than 40,00 photos, many
    hours of video images, and several slide programs which are used in
    tourism publications and programs and are made accessible to media,
    writers, publishers, and are available for free loan to those promoting
    travel to Wisconsin.

Department of Defense DCASMA, Milwaukee
310 West Wisconsin Avenue, #340
Milwaukee, WI 53203-2282   414-297-4329
    Counsels and assists small and small, disadvantaged businesses interested
    in entering the Department of Defense marketplace. Offers seminars to
    acquaint company with government business, assists in understanding con-
    tracting process, brochures on buying activities, referrals to other agencies,
    and general information on the Department of Defense marketplace.

Department of Commerce
517 East Wisconsin Ave, #596
Milwaukee, WI 53202   414-291-3473
    Assists business with import/export of products and services. Offers in-
    plant consultation to help determine export potential, documentation
    assistance on exports shipment. Offers export sales leads, maintains export
    mailing lists, foreign market studies, new products information service,
    trade statistics, and background information on foreign firms. Also offers
    export seminars.

    Assistance also in franchise opportunities, patents and trademarks and
    government procurement. Publishes the *Commerce Business Daily*.

Wisconsin Rural Development Center
P.O. Box 504
1406 Highway 18-151 E
Mt. Horeb, WI 53572   608-437-5971
    Offers Farm and Home Business workshop that provides business training
    for rural people who have businesses at home or on the farm. Has a small
    business development consultant available and offers networking between
    established and start-up rural businesses.

Center for Innovation and Development
School of Industry and Technology   715-232-2565
UW-Stout   715-232-5026
    Offers technical assistance in manufacturing, materials and processing;
    graphic communications automation; CAD/CAM; robotics and assembly;
    industrial safety, financial planning, market research, and limited patent
    assistance.

Wisconsin Innovation Service Center
402 McCutchan Hall
Whitewater, WI 53190   414-472-1365
    Helps businesses identify strengths and weaknesses of new products at an
    early stage through review by a network of technical consultants.

Technology Assistance:
Marquette University
    - College of Engineering   414-288-6720
Medical College of Wisconsin
    - MCW Research Foundation   414-257-8219
Milwaukee School of Engineering
    - Applied Technology Center   414-277-7324
UW-Madison
    - Biotechnology Transfer Office   608-262-8606
    - Engineering Industrial Relations   608-263-1600
    - Office of Industrial Research & Technology Transfer   608-229-5000
Wisconsin Center of Manufacturing and Productivity   608-262-0921
    For those without existing contacts to obtain technology assistance, the
    above should be a starting point.

Council of Small Business Executives (COSBE)
756 North Milwaukee Street
Milwaukee, WI 53202   414-273-3000
    Assistance provided by COSBE are those directly relating to operating a
    businesses and those that related to businesses working together to affect
    government decisions. Must be a member of the Metropolitan Milwaukee
    Association of Commerce for most services.

Small Business Administration
310 West Wisconsin Avenue, #400   414-297-3941
Milwaukee, WI 53203   FAX: 414-297-4267

Small Business Administration
212 East Washington Avenue   608-264-5261
Madison, WI 53703   FAX: 608-264-5541

Small Business Institutes: This program provides personalized consulting services to the small business community. Consulting is provided by senior level business students, guided by a faculty advisor. Assistance in business plan preparation, marketing research, market planning, accounting, and seminars are provided.

University Locations:
Cardinal Stritch College
Marquette University
University of Wisconsin - Madison
University of Wisconsin - Milwaukee
University of Wisconsin - Eau Claire
University of Wisconsin - LaCrosse
University of Wisconsin - Oshkosh
University of Wisconsin - Whitewater
University of Wisconsin - Green Bay
University of Wisconsin - Parkside
University of Wisconsin - Stevens Point
University of Wisconsin - Superior

* Small Business Development Centers

The following offices offer free and fee-based services to new and expanding businesses:

Lead Center:
Wisconsin Small Business Development Center
University of Wisconsin
432 N. Lake Street, Room 423   608-263-7794
Madison, WI 53706   FAX: 608-262-3878

Eau Claire: University of Wisconsin at Eau Claire, Small Business Development Center, Schneider Hall, #113, Eau Claire, WI 54701, 715-836-5637.

Green Bay: University of Wisconsin at Green Bay, Small Business Development Center, Library Learning Center, Room 710, Green Bay, WI 54302, 414-465-2089.

Kenosha: University of Wisconsin at Parkside, Small Business Development Center, 234 Tallent Hall, Kenosha, WI 53141, 414-595-2620.

La Crosse: University of Wisconsin at LaCrosse, Small Business Development Center, School of Business, La Crosse, WI 54601, 608-785-8782.

Madison: University of Wisconsin at Madison, Small Business Development Center, 905 University Avenue, Madison, WI 53715, 608-263-2221.

Milwaukee: University of Wisconsin at Milwaukee, Small Business Development Center, 929 North Sixth Street, Milwaukee, WI 53203, 414-227-3241.

Oshkosh: University of Wisconsin at Oshkosh, Small Business Development Center, Clow Faculty Building, Room 157, Oshkosh, WI 54901, 414-424-1453.

Stevens Point: University of Wisconsin at Stevens Point, Small Business Development Center, 012 Main Building, Stevens Point, WI 54481, 715-346-2004.

Superior: University of Wisconsin at Superior, Small Business Development Center, 29 Sundquist Hall, Superior, WI 54880, 715-394-8352.

Whitewater: University of Wisconsin at Whitewater, Small Business Development Center, 1000 Carlson, Whitewater, WI 53190, 414-472-3217.

Wyoming

* General Information

Division of Economic & Community Development
Department of Commerce
Barrett Building   307-777-7284

4th Floor North   FAX: 307-777-5840
Cheyenne, WY 82002   1-800-262-3425

Provides information on Wyoming's favorable tax structure and corporation laws.

Business Permit Coordinator (Small Business Advocate):
Business Permit Officer: Assistance in cutting bureaucratic red tape. Information and expertise in dealing with state, federal, and local agencies. Publishes a comprehensive guide to permits and licensing.

Business Development Officer:
Small Business Reports: Designed to help small businesses deal with basic business issues.

* Financing

Division of Economic & Community Development
Department of Commerce
Barrett Building   307-777-7284
4th Floor N   FAX: 307-777-5840
Cheyenne, WY 82002   1-800-262-3425 out of state

Planning & Marketing Grants: Local governments may apply for grants under this program on behalf of for-profit businesses. Funds may be used to defray cost of feasibility studies, business plan preparation, marketing studies and test marketing. The for-profit business may be either a start-up or existing business planning to expand. Up to $25,000 available per applicant.

Main Street Program: Main Street communities have received funds from the Petroleum Violations Fund (PVF). PVF funds must be matched dollar for dollar with private funds and may be used for energy conservation related renovation projects in downtown areas.

Industrial Revenue Bonds: Private lenders purchase these bonds which provide low-interest loans for large business expansion. Maximum loan is $10 million, minimum loan is $500,000. Interest rates may be fixed or variable. A broker should be consulted for details. Division of Economic & Community Development can refer you to one.

Both of the following programs can be used for direct loans and loan guarantees, or in conjunction with other public or private financing sources.

Federally Funded Business Loan Program (Economic Development Block Grant): Offers low-interest loans to businesses creating jobs for low-to-moderate income citizens. Funds can be to buy or lease land, buildings, machinery and equipment, construction and renovation. The state grants money to participating cities, towns and counties, which then loan it to your business at below-market rates. Up to $250,000 is available, but should not exceed 25 percent of total project cost. One position must be created for each $10,000 of loan funds. 51 percent of jobs created must be filled by low-to-middle income citizens.

State Funded Business Loan Program: Offers loans and loan guarantees at flexible rates and terms. A business must use Wyoming resources and employees and contribute to the state's basic economy. Service companies are generally not eligible. Applicants need equity equal to at least 20 percent of the total project cost and loans are usually limited to $750,000, or 60 percent of the total cost. 10 year maximum.

Office of the State Treasurer
State Capitol
Cheyenne, WY 82002   307-777-7408

Small Business Assistance Act: Provides fixed-asset financing and 5-year interest rate subsidies of loans to be used for creating jobs. Wyoming residents who own and operate medium-sized industrial or manufacturing firms are eligible. Funds may be used to acquire land and buildings, purchase machinery and equipment, and build or renovate facilities.

State Linked Deposit Program: Offers a 5-year, fixed-rate interest subsidy at below market rate on loans used for creation and retention of jobs. Businesses may use funds for construction of plants, expansions of existing structures, equipment, machinery, land, livestock, and capital. Maximum amount of loan is $750,000. Must certify creation of jobs. Loans cannot give the business an unfair advantage over its competitors. Farm and ranch operations are not considered to be in competition with each other.

Wyoming Industrial Development Corporation
P.O. Box 3599
Casper, WY 82602 307-234-5351
Provides non-bank lending through various Small Business Administration programs and other public finance sources for companies with moderately strong credit risks. Funds may be used for acquiring fixed assets, renovation and construction of facilities, financing costs, or working capital. These loans range from $25,000 to $3 million, but most do not exceed $750,000. Some size restrictions and employment requirements apply. Depending on which program is used, the SBA will guarantee between 40 percent-90 percent of a loan. Terms run from between 7 to 10 years, with maturity in 25 years.

SBA 504 Program: Provides loans using 50 percent conventional bank financing, 40 percent SBA involvement through Certified Development Companies, and 10 percent owner equity. A fixed-asset loan in amounts up to $750,000. Loan can be used for land and building, construction, machinery and equipment, and renovation/expansion.

SBA 7(a) Guaranteed and Direct Loan: Guarantees up to 90 percent of a loan made through a private lender, up to 750,000. Can be used for working capital, inventory, machinery and equipment, and land and building. Available only to those unable to obtain a loan from conventional sources. Direct loans are made up to $150,000.

Western Research Institute
Box 3395
Laramie, WY 82071 307-721-2327
Science, Technology & Energy Authority Program (STEA): Designed to assist business involved with advanced technology move from research & development to the marketplace. STEA leverages state funds with private and federal dollars to provide financing.

Farmers Home Administration
P.O. Box 820
Casper, WY 82602 307-261-5144
Provides loan guarantees to help local industry in rural communities of less than 50,000. Program allows financial institutions to make loans beyond their capital limitations.

Small Business Administration
100 E. B Street
Room 4001 307-261-5761
Casper, WY 82602-2839 FAX: 307-261-5499
SBA 7(a) Guaranteed and Direct Loans: Guarantees up to 90 percent of a loan made through a private lender up to $750,000. Can be used for working capital, expand or convert facilities, purchase of machinery and equipment, and land and building. Available only to those unable to obtain a loan from conventional sources. Direct loans are made up to $150,000.

SBA 504: Provides loans using 50 percent conventional bank financing, 40 percent SBA involvement through Certified Development Companies, and 10 percent owner equity. Fixed-asset loans are available in amounts up to $750,000. The loan can be used for land and building, construction, machinery and equipment, and renovation/expansion.

Small Business Innovative Research Grants (SBIR): Phase I awards between $20,000 to $50,000 to entrepreneurs to support six months of research on a technical innovation. Phase II grants are an additional $500,000 for development. Private sector investment funds must follow.

International Trade Loans: Guaranteed long-term loans through private lenders to develop or expand export markets, or to recover from the effects of import competition. Maximum guaranteed loan is $1,000,000 for fixed assets and an additional $250,000 for working capital and/or export revolving line of credit.

Export Revolving Line of Credit Loan: Short term financing available to small businesses that are at least one year old. Loans provide working capital to finance the manufacturing or wholesaling of products for export and for export marketing. The SBA will guarantee up to 90 percent of a conventional loan in amounts up to $750,000.

Contract Loan: Short-term loans are available to small businesses to finance the costs of labor and materials on contracts for which the proceeds are assignable. Program guarantees up to 90 percent of loans not in excess of $750,000. Qualifying small businesses must be in business for at least 12 calendar months prior to the date of the loan application.

Seasonal Line of Credit Loan: Loans provide short-term working capital to finance seasonal increases in business activities. Program guarantees up to 90 percent of loans not in excess of $750,000. Qualifying business must be in operation for at least one year prior to application.

Pollution Control Loans: Long-term guaranteed loans can be made by conventional financing to small businesses for installation or required pollution control measures. Must be unable to adopt the pollution control measures without undue financial hardship. Maximum guaranteed loan is $1,000,000.

General Contractor Loans: Small general construction contractors may obtain short-term loans or loan guarantees for residential or commercial construction or rehabilitation of property to be sold. The SBA will guarantee up to 90 percent of qualifying loans made by private lenders up to a maximum of $750,000. Direct loans can be up to $150,000.

Energy Business Loan Guarantee: Small businesses that provide certain energy production and conservation services for others may qualify for long-term loans and loan guarantees for start-ups and expansions. Loans and guarantees are made for firms that develop, manufacture, sell, install, or service specific energy measures for others, or firms that provide engineering, architectural, consulting, or other professional services connected with specific energy measures. Guarantee is for up to 90 percent of a loan not in excess of $750,000. Direct loans up to $150,000.

Disaster Recovery Loans: Small businesses located in federally designated disaster areas and suffering property damage or economic losses from the disaster can obtain long-term recovery loans at low interest rates. Property damage loans are limited to 85 percent of the verified damage. Loans for economic losses are for operating capital to meet the business' obligations that could have been made had the disaster not occurred.

Handicapped Assistance Loans: Assists persons who have a physical, mental or emotional disability of a permanent nature which limits the selection of any type of employment for which the person would otherwise be qualified. Direct loans are available for up to $150,000. The interest rate is 3% on these loans.

Surety Bond Guaranty Program: Makes the bonding system more available to small contractors who may be denied access to the system. SBA can guarantee up to 80 percent of surety's loss on a bond that has a maximum in total contract value of up to $1,250,000.

Vietnam-era and Disabled Veterans Loan Program: Provides direct loans to veterans to establish or expand a small business. Funds may be used for working capital or fixed assets. Direct loans for amounts up to $150,000 are available. The interest rate may be fixed or variable.

* Women and Minority Business Assistance

Small Business Administration (SBA)
100 E. B Street
Room 4001 307-261-5761
Casper, WY 82602-2839 FAX: 307-261-5499
SBA 8(a) Program - Business Procurement Assistance: Provides federal government contracting opportunities for small businesses owned by socially and economically disadvantaged persons, and assists these businesses to become independently competitive in the normal business environment. SBA monitors all government contracts to assure that a quota of contract work goes to 8(a) businesses. Also provides business management services to these businesses. Business must be approved for program participation prior to receipt of an 8(a) contract.

* Training

Job Training Program
Employment Service Division
Department of Employment
P.O. Box 2760
Casper, WY 82602   307-235-3280

Job Training Partnership Act (JTPA): Provides employers with recruitment, screening, referral, training, 50 percent wage subsidy up to 3 months for on-the-job training. Available to any private employer.

* Management Consulting and Other Services

Division of Economic & Community Development
Department of Commerce
Barrett Building   307-777-7284
4th Floor N   FAX: 307-777-5840
Cheyenne, WY 82002   1-800-262-3425

Customized Training Program: Packages training resources to provide maximum assistance for employers. Design curriculum specifically for individual companies in conjunction with the Job Training Partnership Act and other state programs.

Wyoming First: Provides marketing assistance to Wyoming businesses to help increase sales.

Government Marketing Assistance Program (GMAP): Provides group or one-on-one counseling to businesses interested in selling to the government.

Buy American Program: Private initiative sponsored by one of the country's biggest retailers. Objective is to encourage American manufacturers to compete with foreign firms for retailer business.

Small Business Administration
100 E. B Street, Room 4001   307-261-5761
Casper, WY 82602-2839   FAX: 307-261-5499

Small Business Institutes: This program provides personalized consulting services to the small business community. Consulting is provided by senior level business students, guided by a faculty advisor. Assistance in business plan preparation, marketing research, market planning, accounting, and seminars are provided.
University Locations:
University of Wyoming

Community College Resources
Community College Commission
Herschler Building, 1st Floor W
Cheyenne, Wy 82002   307-777-7763

The state's eight community college offer educational seminars and other resources to business people. Will work with you to provide classroom training for new employees. Training can be subsidized under the Job Training Partnership Act.

Job Training Administration
P.O. Box 2760
Casper, WY 82602   307-235-3601

Offers a cost-effective way for a business to find and train new employees. With qualified employees you may opt for subsidized on-the-job training, classroom training, or a combination of the two.

Business Assistance Center
Box 3275
Laramie, WY 82071   307-766-2363

Part of the University of Wyoming, the Institute offers two programs and serves as one of the state's SBDC offices. The Student Intern Program helps students gain practical work experience and help businesses solve pressing problems. The Small Business Institute Practician matches students and business for semester long projects such as market studies and computerization of businesses.

Office of International Trade
Barrett Building, 4th Floor N
Cheyenne, WY 82002   307-777-6412

Links Wyoming firms with new markets overseas. Encourages companies to begin exporting to international trade markets through counseling, educational programs and direct export promotion assistance including market research, financial grants, and overseas events such as trade shows.

Marketing Division
Department of Agriculture
2219 Carey Avenue
Cheyenne, WY 82002   307-777-7577

Provides marketing assistance with food and agricultural products made or grown in Wyoming.

Department of Employment
Labor Standards/Fair Employment
Herschler Building, 2nd Floor E
Cheyenne, WY 82002   307-777-7261

Provides information on Wyoming's labor laws and how to comply with them. Subjects include hours of work, minimum wage, and other laws and regulations.

* Small Business Development Centers
The following offices offer free and fee-based services to new and expanding businesses:

Lead Center:
Wyoming Small Business Development Center
111 West 2nd Street, Suite 416   307-235-4825
Casper, WY 82601   FAX: 307-473-7243

Casper: Small Business Development Center, 350 West A, Suite 200, Casper, WY 82601, 307-235-4827.

Cheyenne: Laramie County Community College, Small Business Development Center, 1400 East College Drive, Cheyenne, WY 82007, 307-778-1222.

Douglas: Eastern Wyoming Community College, Small Business Development Center, Douglas Branch, 203 North Sixth Street, Douglas, WY 82633, 307-358-4090.

Gillette: Sheridan College, Small Business Development Center, 720 West 8th, Gillette, WY 82716, 307-686-0297.

Lander: Central Wyoming College, Small Business Development Center, 360 Main Street, Lander, WY 82520, 307-332-3394; 1-800-338-1864.

Laramie: University of Wyoming, Small Business Development Center, P.O. Box 3275, University Station, Laramie, WY 82070, 307-766-2363.

Powell: Northwest Community College, Small Business Development Center, 146 South Bent #103, Powell, WY 82435, 307-754-3745.

Rock Springs: Western Wyoming Community College, Small Business Development Center, P.O. Box 428, Rock Springs, WY 82902, 307-382-1830.

Real Estate Ventures:
Federal Money for Housing and Real Estate

The following is a description of the federal funds available to renters, homeowners, developers, and real estate investors for housing in urban and rural areas. This information is derived from the *Catalog of Federal Domestic Assistance* which is published by the U.S. Government Printing Office in Washington, D.C. The number next to the title description is the official reference for this federal program. Contact the office listed below the caption for further details. The following is a description of the terms used for the types of assistance available:

Loans: money lent by a federal agency for a specific period of time and with a reasonable expectation of repayment. Loans may or may not require payment of interest.

Loan Guarantees: programs in which federal agencies agree to pay back part or all of a loan to a private lender if the borrower defaults.

Grants: money given by federal agencies for a fixed period of time and which does not have to be repaid.

Direct Payments: funds provided by federal agencies to individuals, private firms, and institutions. The use of direct payments may be "specified" to perform a particular service or for "unrestricted" use.

Insurance: coverage under specific programs to assure reimbursement for losses sustained. Insurance may be provided by federal agencies or through insurance companies and may or may not require the payment of premiums.

* Water Bank Program 10.062
Agricultural Stabilization and Conservation Service
U.S. Department of Agriculture
P.O. 2415
Washington, DC 20013   202-720-6221
To conserve surface waters; preserve and improve the nation's wetlands; increase migratory waterfowl habitat in nesting, breeding, and feeding areas in the U.S.; and secure environmental benefits for the nation. Types of assistance: direct payment. Estimate of annual funds available: $ 11,395,000.

* Rural Clean Water Program (RWCP) 10.068
Conservation and Environmental Protection Division
Agricultural Stabilization and Conservation Service
U.S. Department of Agriculture
P.O. Box 2415
Washington, DC 20013   202-720-6221
To achieve improved water quality in the most cost-effective manner possible in keeping with the provisions of adequate supplies of food, fiber, and a quality environment. Types of assistance: direct payment. Estimate of annual funds available: $ 0.

* Emergency Loans 10.404
Administrator, Farmers Home Administration
U.S. Department of Agriculture
Washington, DC   202-690-1533
To assist family farmers, ranchers and aquaculture operators with loans to cover losses resulting from major and/or natural disasters. Types of assistance: loan guarantee. Estimate of annual funds available: $ 100,000,000.

* Farm Operating Loans 10.406
Director, Farmer Programs Loan Making Division
Farmers Home Administration
U.S. Department of Agriculture
Washington, DC 20250   202-720-1632
To enable operators of not larger than family farms through the extension of credit and supervisory assistance, to make efficient use of their land, labor, and other resources. Types of assistance: loan guarantee. Estimate of annual funds available: $ 1,250,000,000.

* Farm Ownership Loans 10.407
Administrator, Farmers Home Administration
U.S. Department of Agriculture
Washington, DC 20250   202-382-1632
To assist eligible farmers, ranchers, and aquaculture operators, including farming cooperatives, corporations, partnerships, and joint operations through the extension of credit to become owner-operators of not larger than family farms. Types of assistance: loan guarantee. Estimate of annual funds available: $ 300,000,000.

* Very Low and Low Income Housing Loans (Section 502 Rural Housing Loans) 10.410
Administrator
Farmers Home Administration (FmHA)
U.S. Department of Agriculture
Washington, DC 20250   202-447-7967
To assist lower-income rural families to obtain decent, safe, and sanitary dwellings and related facilities. Subsidized funds are available only for low- and very low-income applicants. The funds are loans for new or existing construction not currently financed or owned by FMHA. Types of assistance: direct loans. Estimate of annual funds available: $ 650,000,000.

* Rural Housing Site Loans (Section 523 and 524 Site Loans) 10.411
Administrator
Farmers Home Administration
U.S. Department of Agriculture
Washington, DC 20250   202-720-1474
To assist public or private nonprofit organizations interested in providing sites for housing, to acquire and develop land in rural areas to be subdivided as adequate building sites. Types of assistance: direct loans. Estimate of annual funds available: $ 0.

* Rural Rental Housing Loans 10.415
Administrator, Farmers Home Administration
U.S. Department of Agriculture
Washington, DC 20250   202-382-1604

Real Estate Ventures

To provide economically designed and constructed rental and cooperative housing and related facilities suited for independent living for rural residents. Types of assistance: loan guarantee. Estimate of annual funds available: $ 341,000,000.

* Very Low-Income Housing Repair Loans and Grants (Section 504 Rural Housing Loans and Grants) 10.417

Administrator
Farmers Home Administration
U.S. Department of Agriculture
Washington, DC 20250   202-720-1474

To give very low-income rural homeowners an opportunity to make essential repairs to their homes to make them safe and to remove health hazards to the family or community. Types of assistance: loans, grants. Estimate of annual funds available: loans - $ 11,100,000. Grants - $5,000,000.

* Rural Rental Assistance Payments (Rental Assistance) 10.427

Administrator
Farmers Home Administration
U.S. Department of Agriculture
Washington, DC 20250   202-720-1599

To reduce the rents paid by low-income families occupying eligible Rural Rental Housing (RRH) Rural Cooperative Housing (RCH), and Farm Labor Housing (LH) projects financed by the Farmers Home Administration through its Sections 515, 514, and 516 loans and grants. Types of assistance: direct payment. Estimate of annual funds available: $ 342,000,000.

* Rural Housing Preservation Grants 10.433

Multiple Family Housing Loan Division
Farmers Home Administration
U.S. Department of Agriculture
Washington, DC 20250   202-720-1606

To assist very low and low-income rural homeowners in obtaining adequate housing to meet their needs by providing the necessary assistance to repair or rehabilitate their housing. Types of assistance: grants. Estimate of annual funds available: $ 10,000,000.

* Interest Reduction Payments-Rental and Cooperative Housing for Lower Income Families (236) 14.103

Director, Office of Multifamily Housing Management
U.S. Department of Housing and Urban Development
Washington, DC 20410   202-708-3730

To provide good quality rental and cooperative housing for persons of low- and moderate-income by providing interest reduction payments in order to lower their housing costs. Types of assistance: direct payments. Estimate of annual funds available: $ 634,159,000.

* Rehabilitation Mortgage Insurance 203(k) 14.108

Director, Single Family Development Division
U.S. Department of Housing and Urban Development
Washington, DC 20410   202-708-2720

To help families repair or improve, purchase and improve, or refinance and improve existing residential structures more than one year old. Types of assistance: loan guarantee. Estimate of annual funds available: $ 98,507,000.

* Manufactured Home Loan Insurance-Financing Purchase of Manufactured Homes as Principal Residences of Borrowers (Title I) 14.110

Director, Title I Insurance Division
U.S. Department of Housing and Urban Development   1-800-733-4663
Washington, DC 20410   202-708-2880

To make possible reasonable financing of manufactured home purchases. Types of assistance: loan guarantee. Estimate of annual funds available: (loan insured including funding for programs 14.142 and 14.162) $1,358,812,000.

* Mortgage Insurance-Construction or Substantial Rehabilitation of Condominium Projects 234 (d) 14.112

Insurance Division
Office of Insured Multifamily Housing Development
U.S. Department of Housing and Urban Development
Washington, DC 20410   202-708-2556

To enable sponsors to develop condominium projects in which individual units will be sold to home buyers. Types of assistance: loan guarantee. Estimate of annual funds available: $ 10,254,000.

* Mortgage Insurance - Homes 203(b) 14.117

Director
Insured Family Development Division
Office of Single Family Housing, HUD
Washington, DC 20410   202-708-2700

To help families undertake home ownership. Types of assistance: loan guarantee. Estimate of annual funds available: (Mortgage Insured-including funding for 14.119, 14.121, 14.163, 14.175) $47,411,931,000.

* Mortgage Insurance 203(h): Homes for Disaster Victims 14.119

Director, Single Family Development Division
Office of Insured Single Family Housing, HUD
Washington, DC 20410   202-708-2700

To help victims of a major disaster undertake home ownership on a sound basis. Types of assistance: loan guarantee. Estimate of annual funds available: Funding included in 14.117.

* Mortgage Insurance-Homes for Low and Moderate Income Families 221(d)(2) 14.120

Director, Single Family Development Division
Office of Insured Family Housing, HUD
Washington, DC 20410   202-708-2700

To make homeownership more readily available to families displaced by a natural disaster, urban renewal, or other government actions and to increase homeownership opportunities for low-income and moderate-income families. Types of assistance: loan guarantee. Estimate of annual funds available: $ 87,551,000.

* Mortgage Insurance: Homes in Outlying Areas 203(i) 14.121

Director, Insured Single Family Development Division
Office of Single Family Housing
U.S. Department of Housing and Urban Development
Washington, DC 20410   202-708-2700

To help families purchase homes in outlying areas. Types of assistance: loan guarantee. Estimate of annual funds available: Funding included in 14.117.

* Mortgage Insurance: Homes in Urban Renewal Areas (22 Homes) 14.122

Director, Insured Single Family Development Division
Office of Single Family Housing
U.S. Department of Housing and Urban Development
Washington, DC 20410   202-708-2700

To help families purchase or rehabilitate homes in urban renewal areas. Types of assistance: loan guarantee. Estimate of annual funds available: $ 393,000.

* Mortgage Insurance-Housing in Older, Declining Areas 223(e) 14.123

Single Family Development Division
Office of Insured Single Family Housing
Washington, DC 20410   202-708-2700

To assist in the purchase or rehabilitation of housing in older, declining urban areas. Types of assistance: loan guarantee. Estimate of annual funds available: $ 19,881,000.

* Mortgage Insurance-Cooperative Projects (213 Cooperatives) 14.126

Insurance Division
Office of Insured Multifamily Housing Development
U.S. Department of Housing and Urban Development
Washington, DC 20410   202-708-2556

To make it possible for nonprofit cooperative ownership housing corporations or trusts to develop or sponsor the development of housing projects to be operated as cooperatives. Types of assistance: loan guarantee. Estimate of annual funds available: $ 0.

* Mortgage Insurance-Manufactured Home Parks (207(m) Manufactured Home Parks) 14.127

Insurance Division
Office of Insured Multifamily Housing Development
U.S. Department of Housing and Urban Development
Washington, DC 20410   202-708-2556

To make possible the financing of construction or rehabilitation of manufactured home parks. Types of assistance: loan guarantee. Estimate of annual funds available: $ 0.

* Mortgage Insurance - Purchase by Homeowners of Fee Simple Title from Lessors (240) 14.130

Director, Single Family Development Division
Office of Insured Single Family Housing
U.S. Department of Housing and Urban Development
Washington, DC 20410   202-708-2700

To help homeowners obtain fee-simple title to the property which they hold under long-term leases and on which their homes are located. Types of assistance: loan guarantee. Estimate of annual funds available: $ 0.

* Mortgage Insurance: Purchase of Sales-Type Cooperative Housing Units (213 Sales) 14.132

Director, Single Family Development Division
Office of Insured Family Housing
U.S. Department of Housing and Urban Development
Washington, DC 20410   202-708-2700

To make available good quality, new housing for purchase by individual members of a housing cooperative. Types of assistance: loan guarantee. Estimate of annual funds available: $ 0.

* Mortgage Insurance: Purchase of Units in Condominiums (234(c)) 14.133

Director, Single Family Development Division
Office of Insured Single Family Housing
U.S. Department of Housing and Urban Development
Washington, DC 20410   202-708-2700

To enable families to purchase units in condominium projects. Types of assistance: loan guarantee. Estimate of annual funds available: $ 2,856,274,000.

* Mortgage Insurance: Rental Housing (207) 14.134

Insurance Division
Office of Insured Multifamily Housing Development
U.S. Department of Housing and Urban Development
Washington, DC 20410   202-708-2556

To provide good quality rental housing for middle income families. Types of assistance: loan guarantee. Estimate of annual funds available: $ 0.

* Mortgage Insurance: Rental Housing for Moderate Income Families and Elderly Market Interest Rate 221(d)(3) and (4) Multifamily 14.135

Insurance Division
Office of Insured Multifamily Housing Development
U.S. Department of Housing and Urban Development
Washington, DC 20410   202-708-2556

To provide good quality rental or cooperative housing for moderate income families and the elderly. Types of assistance: loan guarantee. Estimate of annual funds available: $ 890,238,000.

* Mortgage Insurance-Rental Housing for the Elderly (231) 14.138

Insurance Division
Office of Insured Multifamily Housing Development
U.S. Department of Housing and Urban Development
Washington, DC 20410   202-708-2556

To provide good quality rental housing for the elderly. Types of assistance: loan guarantee. Estimate of annual funds available: $ 0.

* Mortgage Insurance-Rental Housing in Urban Renewal Areas (220 Multifamily) 14.139

Insurance Division
Office of Insured Multifamily Housing Development
U.S. Department of Housing and Urban Development
Washington, DC 20410   202-708-2556

To provide good quality rental housing in urban renewal areas, code enforcement areas, and other areas designated for overall revitalization. Types of assistance: loan guarantee. Estimate of annual funds available: $ 7,576,000.

* Section 106(b) Nonprofit Sponsor Assistance Program (Nonprofit Sponsor Loan Fund) 14.141

Director
Assisted Elderly and Handicapped Housing Division
Office of Elderly and Assisted Housing
U.S. Department of Housing and Urban Development
Washington, DC 20410   202-708-2730

To assist and stimulate prospective private nonprofit sponsors/borrowers of Section 202 housing to develop sound housing projects for the elderly or handicapped. Types of assistance: loan. Estimate of annual funds available: $ 0.

* Property Improvement Loan Insurance for Improving All Existing Structures and Building of New Nonresidential Structures (Title I) 14.142

Director, Title I Insurance Division
U.S. Department of Housing and Urban Development   1-800-733-4663
Washington, DC 20410   202-708-2880

To facilitate the financing of improvements to homes and other existing structures and the building of new nonresidential structures. Types of assistance: loan guarantee. Estimate of annual funds available: $ 1,358,812,000.

* Supplemental Loan Insurance-Multifamily Rental Housing 14.151

Insurance Division
Office of Insured Multifamily Housing Development
U.S. Department of Housing and Urban Development (HUD)
Washington, DC 20411   202-708-2556

To finance repairs, additions and improvements to multifamily projects, group practice facilities, hospitals, or nursing homes already insured by HUD or held by HUD. Types of assistance: loan guarantee. Estimate of annual funds available: $ 246,206,000.

* Mortgage Insurance for the Purchase or Refinancing of Existing Multifamily Housing Projects (Section 223(f) Insured Under Section 207) 14.155

Office of Insured Multifamily Housing Development
Insurance Division, HUD
Washington, DC 20410   202-708-2556

To provide mortgage insurance to lenders for the purchase or refinancing of existing multifamily housing projects, whether conventionally financed or subject to federally insured mortgages. Types of assistance: loan guarantee. Estimate of annual funds available: $ 558,295,000.

* Housing for the Elderly or Handicapped (202) 14.157 Assisted Elderly and Handicapped Housing Division

Office of Elderly and Assisted Housing, HUD
Washington, DC 20410   202-708-2730

To provide for rental or cooperative housing and related facilities (such as central dining) for the elderly or handicapped. Types of assistance: loan. Estimate of annual funds available: $ 0.

* Section 245 Graduated Payment Mortgage Program 14.159

Director, Single Family Development Division
Office of Insured Single Family Housing
U.S. Department of Housing and Urban Development
Washington, DC 20410   202-708-2700

To facilitate early home ownership for households that expect their incomes to rise. Types of assistance: loan guarantee. Estimate of annual funds available: $ 548,027,000.

* Mortgage Insurance-Combination and Manufactured Home Lot Loans (Title I) 14.162

Director, Title I Insurance Division
U.S. Department of Housing and Urban Development   1-800-733-4663
Washington, DC 20410   202-708-2880

To make possible reasonable financing of manufactured home purchases and lot to place it on. Types of assistance: loan guarantee. Estimate of annual funds available: Funding including in 14.110.

* Mortgage Insurance-Cooperative Financing (203(n)) 14.163

Director, Single Family Development Division
Office of Insured Single Family Housing
U.S. Department of Housing and Urban Development
Washington, DC 20410   202-708-2700

To provide insured financing for the purchase of the Corporate Certificate and Occupancy Certificate. Types of assistance: loan guarantee. Estimate of annual funds available: Funding included in 14.117.

* Operating Assistance for Troubled Multifamily Housing Projects (Flexible Subsidy Fund) (Troubled Projects) 14.164

Chief, Program Support Branch
Management Operations Division
Office of Multifamily Housing Management
U.S. Department of Housing and Urban Development
Washington, DC 20410   202-708-3730

To provide assistance to restore or maintain the physical and financial soundness of certain projects assisted or approved for assistance under the National Housing Act or under the Housing and Urban Development Act of 1965. Types of assistance: grants, direct payments. Estimate of annual funds available: $ 0.

* Mortgage Insurance-Homes-Military Impacted Areas (238(c)) 14.165

Director, Single Family Development Division
Office of Insured Single Family Housing, HUD
Washington, DC 20410   202-708-2700

To help families undertake home ownership in military impacted areas. Types of assistance: loan guarantee. Estimate of annual funds available: $ 13,425,000.

* Mortgage Insurance-Homes for Members of the Armed Services (Section 222) 14.166

Director, Single Family Development Division
Office of Insured Single Family Housing, HUD
Washington, DC 20410   202-708-2700

To help members of the armed services on active duty to purchase a home. Types of assistance: loan guarantee. Estimate of annual funds available: $ 4,588,000.

* Mortgage Insurance-Two Year Operating Loss Loans, Section 223(d) 14.167

Office of Insured Multifamily Housing Development
Insurance Division Housing, HUD
Washington, DC 20410   202-755-2556

To insure a separate loan covering operating losses incurred during the first two years following the date of completion of a multifamily project with a HUD insured first mortgage. Types of assistance: loan guarantee. Estimate of annual funds available: $ 10,890,000.

* Mortgage Insurance-Growing Equity Mortgages (GEMs) 14.172

Director, Single Family Development Division
Office of Insured Single Family Housing, HUD
Washington, DC 20410   202-708-2700

To provide a rapid principal reduction and shorter mortgage term by increasing payments over a 10 year period, thereby expanding housing opportunities to the homebuying public. Types of assistance: loan guarantee. Estimate of annual funds available: Funding included in 14.159.

* Multifamily Coinsurance (Section 223(f); Section 221(d); Section 232) 14.173

Office of Insured Multifamily Housing Development
Coinsurance Division
U.S. Department of Housing and Urban Development (HUD)
Washington, DC 20410   202-708-3730

Under the coinsurance programs, HUD authorizes approved lenders to coinsure mortgage loans. In exchange for the authority to perform the required underwriting, servicing, management and property disposition functions, approved lenders assume responsibility for a portion of any insurance loss on the coinsured mortgage. Types of assistance: loan guarantee. Estimate of annual funds available: $ 0.

* Housing Development Grants 14.174

Director, Development Grants Division
Rm. 6110, Office of Elderly and Assisted Housing
U.S. Department of Housing and Urban Development
451 7th St., SW
Washington, DC 20410   202-755-4961

To support the construction or substantial rehabilitation of rental housing in areas experiencing severe shortages of decent rental housing opportunities for families and individuals without other reasonable and affordable housing alternatives in the private market. Types of assistance: grants. Estimate of annual funds available: $ 0.

* Adjustable Rate Mortgages (ARMS) 14.175

Director, Single Family Development Division
Office of Insured Single Family Housing, HUD
Washington, DC 20410   202-708-2700

To provide mortgage insurance for an adjustable rate mortgage which offers lenders more assurance of long term profitability than a fixed rate mortgage, while offering consumer protection. Types of assistance: loan guarantee. Estimate of annual funds available: Funding included in 14.117.

* Nehemiah Housing Opportunity Grant Program (Nehemiah Housing) 14.179

Morris E. Carter, Director
Single Family Housing Development Division, HUD
451 7th St, SW
Washington, DC 20410   202-708-2700

To provide an opportunity for those families who otherwise would not be financially able to realize their dream of owning a home. Types of assistance: grant. Estimate of annual funds available: $ 18,834,000.

* Community Development Block Grants/Entitlement Grants 14.218

Entitlement Cities Division
Office of Block Grant Assistance
Community Planning and Development
451 7th St., SW
Washington, DC 20410   202-708-1577

To develop viable urban communities, by providing decent housing and a suitable living environment. Types of assistance: grants. Estimate of annual funds available: $ 1,958,529,000.

* Community Development Block Grants/Small Cities Program (Small Cities) 14.219

State and Small Cities Division
Office of Block Grant Assistance
Community Planning and Development
U.S. Department of Housing and Urban Development
451 7th St., SW
Washington, DC 20410   202-708-1322

The primary objective of this program is the development of viable urban communities by providing decent housing, a suitable living environment, and expanding economic opportunities. Types of assistance: grants. Estimate of annual funds available: $ 36,539,000.

* Specially Adapted Housing for Disabled Veterans (Paraplegic Housing) 64.106

U.S. Department of Veterans Affairs
Washington, DC 20420

To assist certain severely disabled veterans in acquiring suitable housing units, with special fixtures and facilities made necessary by the nature of the veterans disabilities. Types of assistance: direct payment. Estimate of annual funds available: $ 14,815,000.

* Veterans Housing-Guaranteed and Insured Loans (VA Home Loans) 64.114

U.S. Department of Veterans Affairs
Washington, DC 20420

To assist veterans, certain service personnel, and certain unmarried surviving spouses of veterans, in obtaining credit for the purchase, construction or improvement of homes on more liberal terms than are generally available to non-veterans. Types of assistance: loan guarantee. Estimate of annual funds available: $ 121,594,141,000.

* Veterans Housing-Direct Loans for Disabled Veterans 64.118

U.S. Department of Veterans Affairs
Washington, DC 20420

To provide certain severely disabled veterans with direct housing credit in connection with grants for specially adaptable housing with special features or movable facilities made necessary by the nature of their disabilities. Types of assistance: direct loans. Estimate of annual funds available: $ 33,000.

* Veterans Housing-Manufactured Home Loans 64.119

U.S. Department of Veterans Affairs
Washington, DC 20420

To assist veterans, servicepersons, and certain unmarried surviving spouses of veterans in obtaining credit for the purchase of a manufactured home on more liberal terms than are available to non-veterans. Types of assistance: loan guarantee. Estimate of annual funds available: $ 9,633,000.

* Weatherization Assistance for Low-Income Persons 81.042

Mary E. Fowler, Chief
Weatherization Assistance Programs, Branch 232
Conservation and Renewable Energy, DOE
Forrestal Bldg.
Washington, DC 20585   202-586-2204

To insulate the dwellings of low income persons particularly the elderly and handicapped low income in order to conserve needed energy and to aid those persons least able to afford higher utility costs. Types of assistance: grants. Estimate of annual funds available: $ 80,000,000.

* Flood Insurance 83.100

David L. Cobb, Federal Insurance Administration
FEMA
Washington, DC 20472   202-646-2780

To enable persons to purchase insurance against losses from physical damage to or loss of buildings and or contents therein caused by floods, mudflow, or flood related erosion in the U.S. Types of assistance: Insurance. Estimate of annual funds available: $ 764,687,000.

State Money For Housing and Real Estate

State Initiatives

While affordable housing has long held an important place on the federal government's policy agenda, budget cutbacks in recent years have forced the government to turn over many housing responsibilities to the states. Housing finance agencies (HFAs) have been created by states to issue tax-exempt bonds to finance mortgages for lower-income first-time home buyers and to build multi-family housing.

States are involved in a host of initiatives throughout the broad spectrum of housing finance and development. Interim construction financing programs which can reduce the basic costs of lower-income housing projects have been initiated in a number of states, together with innovative home ownership programs and programs directed toward rehabilitation and improved energy conservation.

States are also venturing into areas which have not received as much public sector attention until recently. By encouraging non-traditional types of housing, such as accessory units, shelters, and single room occupancy housing, states are addressing important elements of the housing market.

In Colorado, the state Housing and Finance Authority (CHFA) has issued more than $2 billions of bonds and notes since its establishment in 1973, providing housing for more than 33,000 families and individuals of low and moderate income; 19,000 first-time home buyers and over 14,500 rental housing units. In recent years the state has broadened CHFA's authority to allow it to develop finance programs to assist the growth of small business, help exports with insurance on goods sold overseas, and similar projects.

Colorado has done more than simply help its citizens find housing: the programs have resulted in construction employment of more than 20,000 jobs, with wages estimated at almost $20 million in new local real estate taxes and an indirect gain of $1.6 billion for the state.

Wisconsin, Maine and New York each have 20 programs including special ones for women and minorities, for disabled persons, and for environmental hazard removal.

Maryland operates 25 programs, including those to help people with closing costs and settlement expenses. It also has special funds available for the elderly and is developing an emergency mortgage fund to help people who have fallen behind in their payments. Non-profit developers can also tap the state for money to build low-cost rental units.

Among Michigan's 29 programs and Minnesota's 25 are several for neighborhood revitalization. Minnesota also offers programs targeting the needs of urban Indians and migrant farm workers. Alaska, Oregon and Vermont offer financing for tenant acquisition of mobile home parks.

Funds are also available for persons who take steps to make their homes more energy efficient, for home owners and landlords who remove lead paint from dwelling units, for houses without plumbing or those with plumbing that is dysfunctional, for handicapped persons, and to help landlords defray the costs of bringing low-income housing into compliance with state and local housing codes. There are also funds for non-profit organizations to acquire or renovate existing houses and apartments for use as group homes for special needs such as mentally retarded.

In many states, elderly home owners can look to the HFA to obtain financing and/or support services they need to remain in their homes and avoid institutionalization. Some of the states have more than one agency dedicated to housing and we have attempted to list them all here. Also, many cities and counties have quasi-federal/quasi-local "housing authorities" with additional programs. Check your local government listings for these.

The following is a complete listing of state housing programs.

Housing Offices

Alabama
Alabama Housing Finance Authority, P.O. Box 230909, Montgomery, AL 36123-0909; 205-242-4310.
1) Mortgage Revenue Bond Program: low-rate loans for income-eligible first-time home buyers.
2) Downpayment Assistance Program: matching funds for lower-income home buyers.
3) Mortgage Credit Certificate Program: provides a 20% federal tax credit on mortgage loan interest for lower-income home buyers.
4) Low-Income Housing Tax Credit Program: federal tax credits for owners of low-income rental housing.
5) Multi-Family Bond Program: tax-exempt bonds for financing multi-family projects with units affordable to low-income tenants.

Alaska
Alaska Housing Finance Corp., P.O. Box 101020, 235 East 8th Avenue, Anchorage, AK 99510; 907-561-1900.
1) Home Ownership Assistance Program: interest subsidy to as low as 6%.
2) Mobile Home Loan Program: low downpayment.
3) Taxable Mortgage Program: for others than first time home buyers and veterans.
4) Triplex/Fourplex Mortgage Program: up to $384,000 with 20% down.
5) Tax Exempt Mortgage Program: loans up to $157,190 for single family and $176,996 for duplexes.
6) Second Mortgage Program: up to $99,900 for single family homes and $127,800 for duplexes can be used for home purchase or home improvement.
7) Veterans Mortgage Program: low interest loans to veterans and members of the reserve and National Guard.
8) Refinance Program: reduce monthly payments on existing loans.
9) Non-Conforming Property Program: homes which cannot be financed through traditional financing.
10) Condominium Projects: loans for condominium owners.
11) Mobile Home Park Loans:
12) Home Owners' Assistance Program: lowers mortgage payments and assists home owners in financial difficulty.
13) Refinance Program of a Non-AHFC Loan: refinancing for a loan not held by AHFC.
14) Second Mortgage Program for Health and Safety Repairs: for AHFC loan borrowers to bring property up to safety and health requirements.
15) Condo Association Loan Program: loans to home owners' associations for

common area improvements necessary to health and safety.

16) Mortgage Guaranty Insurance Corporation: special financing for borrowers purchasing certain foreclosed condo and Planned Unit Development units.

Arizona

Arizona Department of Commerce, Office of Housing Development, 1700 West Washington, Phoenix, AZ 85007; 602-280-1365.

1) Low-Income Housing Tax Credits: federal income tax credits for owners of low-income housing units.

2) Low Interest Mortgage Programs: typically below 9% interest loans for eligible Arizonans to purchase homes.

3) Arizona Housing Trust Fund: construction, housing rehabilitation, down payment, and closing cost assistance for low/moderate income home buyers.

4) Rental Rehabilitation Program: assists owners in rehabilitating rental housing for low/moderate income households.

Arkansas

Arkansas Development Finance Authority, P.O. Box 8023, 100 Main St., Suite 200, Little Rock, AR 72203; 501-682-5900.

1) Affordable Housing Program: loans to developers to build houses in designated areas.

2) Single-Family: below market rate loans to first time home buyers for the purchase of a single-family home.

3) Low-Income Housing Tax Credit Program: federal tax credits for owners of low-income rental housing.

4) Home Energy Loan Program: low-rate loans for home owners making energy conservation repairs and improvements.

California

California Housing Finance Agency, 1121 L Street, 7th Floor, Sacramento, CA 95815; 916-322-3991.

1) Multi-Family Program: permanent financing for builders and developers of multi-family unit, elderly and congregate rental housing.

2) Development Loan Program: 7% loans to small and minority developers.

3) Self-Help Housing Program: funds to non-profit developers in order to produce self-help housing.

4) Home Purchase Assistance Program: low interest loans for low/moderate income first-time home buyers.

5) Matching Downpayment Program: deferred payment second mortgage loans to assist with closing costs or reduce monthly payments on first mortgages of limited-income home buyers.

6) CHFA Resale Program: below market-rate loans to first-time home buyers who meet income limits and are purchasing previously-owned property within CHFA sales price limits.

7) Compensating Balance Program: construction financing to minority/women-owned business enterprises and self-help program developers.

8) Self-Help Builder Assistance Program: construction financing for self-help builders.

9) Self-Help Housing Program: finances self-help homes under supervision of non-profit organizations.

California Department of Housing and Community Development, P.O. Box 952050, Sacramento, CA 94252-2050; 916-322-1560.

1) California Home Ownership Assistance Program (CHAP): loans for up to 49% of purchase price for low/moderate-income home buyers.

2) California Housing Rehabilitation Program-Owner Component: low-rate loans to bring homes up to code, make general improvements, or to make adaptations for handicapped.

3) Natural Disaster Assistance Program: rehabilitation loans for property damaged by natural disaster.

4) Self-Help Housing Program: technical assistance for low/moderate income households building or rehabilitating their own homes.

5) Mobile Home Park Assistance Program: loans and technical assistance to mobile home park resident organizations that are purchasing their park.

6) Rental Housing Construction Program: very low-rate loans for development and construction costs associated with new rental housing units for low-income households.

7) Family Housing Demonstration Program: very low-rate loans to develop new, or rehabilitate existing, rental or co-op housing that provides on-site support programs for low-income households.

8) Permanent Housing for the Handicapped Homeless Program: partial funding to acquire, rehabilitate, and operate housing for the disabled homeless.

9) State Rental Rehabilitation Program: partial funding to rehabilitate low/moderate-income rental housing in small rural communities.

10) California Energy Conservation Rehabilitation Program: grants of up to $5,000 per unit to assist energy conservation rehabilitation of low-income owner

and renter farmworker housing, residential hotels, and rental housing for the elderly and handicapped.

11) Pre-Development Loan Program: low-rate, 3-year loans for pre-development costs of low-income housing projects.

12) PLP Natural Disaster Component: low-rate, 3-year loans for pre-development costs of reconstruction or rehabilitation of subsidized housing damaged by natural disaster.

13) Emergency Shelter Program: grants to provide emergency shelter for homeless households.

14) Farmworker Housing Grant Program: grants to provide owner-occupied and rental units for year-round, low-income agricultural workers and to rehabilitate those damaged by natural disaster.

15) Federal Emergency Shelter Grant Program: grants to provide emergency shelter to homeless households.

16) Section 8 Housing Assistance Program: rental assistance payments for very low-income households.

17) Office of Migrant Services: grants to provide housing and support services for migrant families during peak season.

18) Rental Security Deposit Guarantee Demonstration Program: provides landlords with rental deposit guarantees for homeless families transitioning to permanent rental housing.

19) Rural Communities Facilities Technical Assistance Program: grants and technical assistance to rural communities seeking federal and state water and wastewater project loans and grants.

20) Senior Citizen Shared Housing Program: grants to assist seniors in obtaining shared housing or for development of group residences.

Colorado

Colorado Housing & Finance Authority, 1981 Blake Street, Denver, CO 80202; 303-297-7427.

1) Single-Family Program: lower-than-market interest rates available to first-time home owners.

2) Commercial Division Programs: financial assistance provided to assist small businesses with expansion of their facilities.

3) Rental Acquisition Program: offers affordable multi-family housing for low-income households.

4) Section 8 Moderate Rehabilitation Program: incentives to property owners who rehabilitate substandard rental housing for low-income tenants qualifying for rent subsidies.

5) Low-Income Housing Tax Credit Program: federal tax credits for owners of low-income rental housing.

6) Mortgage Credit Certificates: reduction of federal income tax for home buyers.

7) Tax-Exempt Bond Program: financing for acquisition and/or rehabilitation of low-income rental housing.

8) Special Needs Housing Fund: financing for housing for frail elderly, mentally ill, battered persons, runaways, etc.

9) Shelter Housing Assistance Program: financing for emergency or transitional housing.

10) Construction Loan Fund: Short-term loans to non-profits for acquisition, rehab, construction and development costs of low-income housing to be sold.

11) Housing Development Loan Fund: short-term loans to non-profits for pre-development costs or acquisition of property for low-income multi-family housing projects.

12) Special Projects Program: short-term loans to non-profits for acquisition, rehab, or construction of projects such as group homes, shelters, co-ops, mobile home parks.

13) Deferred-5 (D-5) Program: assistance with downpayment, repairs, and other costs associated with home purchase for participants in Colorado Single-Family Mortgage Program.

14) Rural Development Loan Program: loans for businesses in rural areas of Colorado.

Connecticut

Connecticut Housing Finance Authority, 40 Cold Spring Road, Rocky Hill, CT 06067; 203-721-9501.

1) Home Mortgage Program: low-interest mortgages for low-and moderate-income persons and families.

2) Rehabilitation Mortgages: loans to protect or improve livability or energy efficiency of a home.

3) Reverse Annuity Mortgages (RAM): allows senior citizens to convert their home's equity into monthly tax-free cash payments.

4) Market Rate Multi-Family Program: below conventional-rate financing to develop or rehabilitate multi-family housing with units affordable to low-income households.

5) Low-Income Housing Tax Credit Program: federal tax credits for owners of

low-income rental housing.

6) Private Rental Investment Mortgage and Equity Program: financing for mixed-income rental developments.

7) Apartment Conversion for the Elderly: loans to home owners 62 years of age or older for additions or conversions to their homes to create income-producing rental units.

Delaware

Delaware State Housing Authority, Division of Housing and Community Development, 18 the Green, P.O. Box 1401, Dover, DE 19901; 302-739-4263.

1) Single-Family Mortgage Program: low-interest loans to first-time home buyers.

2) Housing Development Funds: loans to developers of housing for low- and moderate-income persons and families.

3) Housing Rehabilitation Loan Program: $15,000 for ten years at 3% to fix up single-family homes.

4) Rent Subsidy Programs: money to provide subsidies for low- and moderate-income rental housing.

5) Public Housing Home Ownership Program: provides public housing tenants and families on the waiting list the opportunity to purchase affordable homes in residential neighborhoods.

6) Rental Rehabilitation Program: loans to cover up to 50% of rehab costs for low/moderate income housing.

7) Emergency Shelter Grants Program: to assist emergency housing shelters for the homeless.

8) Community Development Block Grants: funding to maintain or improve housing of low/moderate-income households.

9) Multi-Family Mortgage Revenue Bonds: financing for profit and non-profit developers of low-income housing.

10) Low-Income Housing Tax Credit Program: federal tax credits for owners of low-income rental housing.

District of Columbia

DC Housing Finance Agency, 1401 New York Avenue, NW, Suite 540, Washington, DC 20005; 202-408-0415.

1) Single-Family Purchase Program: loans to first-time home buyers with 5% down and 8.5% interest.

2) Multi-Family Program: construction and permanent financing for developers of multi-family housing with at least 20% of the units designated for low-income households.

District of Columbia Department of Housing and Community Development, 51 N Street, NE, Washington, DC 20002; 202-535-1353.

1) Home Purchase Assistance Program: low or no interest loans for low- and moderate-income home buyers.

2) First Right Purchase Assistance Program: low-cost loans for low- and moderate-income individuals and tenant groups to exercise their right to purchase their rental housing that is being offered for sale.

3) Homestead Housing Preservation Program: repossessed properties are sold to eligible District residents at low cost and with deferred payment loans.

4) Multi-Family Housing Rehabilitation Loan Program: low-rate financing for construction and rehabilitation of multi-family housing.

5) Direct Loan Rehabilitation Program: below-market financing (as low as 3%) for rehabilitation of single- and multi-family residential, mixed use, and commercial property.

6) Rental Rehabilitation Program: low or no interest deferred loans for rehabilitation and rent subsidies for property owners and tenants of low-income housing.

7) Distressed Properties Program: tax incentives to encourage the development of new rental housing or for the rehabilitation of vacant rental housing; similar benefits for occupied properties in economic difficulty.

8) Section 8 Moderate Rehabilitation Program: incentives for property owners to rehabilitate rental apartments for low-income households; rental income guaranteed via rent subsidies.

9) Low-Income Housing Tax Credit Program: tax credits for owners of low-income rental housing.

10) Single-Family Housing Rehabilitation Program: low-cost financing for the rehabilitation of one to four unit low-income housing in designated areas.

11) Home Improvements for the Handicapped: grants to remove barriers and improve accessibility; for home owners or landlords on behalf of handicapped tenants.

12) Weatherization Assistance Program: grants to low-income home owners and renters for weatherization of properties as determined by an energy audit.

13) Delinquent Home Mortgage Payments Program: low-cost, three-month loans to avoid foreclosure due to loss of employment or other crisis.

14) Housing Finance for Elderly, Dependent, and Disabled: loans for development of housing for special needs households.

Florida

Florida Housing Finance Agency, 2571 Executive Center Circle East, Tallahassee, FL 32399; 904-488-4197.

1) First-Time Homebuyer Mortgage Revenue Bond Program: below-market rate financing for first-time home buyers with low/moderate income.

2) Home Ownership Assistance Program: $1700 zero interest, due-on-sale loan to defer closing costs.

3) Affordable Housing Loan Program: below market financing for developers/home buyers of rental and for-sale housing.

4) State Apartment Incentive Loan Program: low-rate financing for developers who build or rehabilitate rental housing with 20% of units for low-income households and to eligible non-profit sponsors of housing projects.

5) Low-Income Housing Tax Credit Program: federal tax credits for owners of low-income rental housing.

6) Market-Rate Multi-Family Bond Loan Program: below-market financing to developers of rental housing with 20% for low-income households.

7) Section 8 Program: federal rent subsidies for low-income tenants.

Georgia

Georgia Residential Finance Authority, 60 Executive Parkway South, Suite 250, Atlanta, GA 30329; 404-679-4840.

1) Single-Family Home Ownership Loan Program: 1.5% below prevailing interest rates for first-time home owners.

2) Mortgage Credit Certificate Program: 20% of mortgage interest can be used as a federal tax credit.

3) Payment of some or all of rental costs for low-income families or singles who are elderly, handicapped or disabled.

4) Multi-family Bond Program: below-market interest rate loans to develop or rehabilitate multi-family rental housing.

5) Low-Income Housing Credit Program: federal income tax credits to construct or rehabilitate low-income rental housing.

6) Section 8 Existing Housing Assistance: rental assistance subsidy payments to landlords of low-income individuals or families.

7) Rental Rehabilitation Program: loans and grants up to $5,000 per unit to rehabilitate rental housing.

8) Appalachian: grants and loans for site development, technical assistance and others for low-and moderate-income housing projects.

9) Development Advances for Non-Profit Sponsors: financial and technical assistance to qualified non-profit organizations engaged in the development of low- and moderate-income rental housing.

10) Georgia Energy Fund: loans and grants up to $3,00 for energy saving home improvements.

11) Homeless Shelter Programs: grants to shelter facilities for building improvements and renovation.

Hawaii

Hawaii Housing Authority, 1002 North School Street, P.O. Box 17907, Honolulu, HI 96817; 808-848-3277.

1) Hula Mae Single-Family Program: low-interest loans to first-time home buyers.

2) State Rent Supplement Program: rent subsidies to tenants in approved projects.

3) Tax Reform: Multi-Family Program: tax credits to investors in qualified low-income rental housing projects.

4) Modernization and Maintenance: funds for the preservation and maintenance of existing housing.

5) Housing Finance Revolving Fund: long-term mortgage financing in geographic areas or for projects where private mortgage insurers will not insure.

6) Section 8 Certificate/Voucher Programs: rental housing subsidies.

7) Public Housing Projects: low rent housing for eligible families, elderly or disabled.

Idaho

Idaho Housing Agency, 760 W. Myrtle, Boise, ID 83702; 208-336-0161.

1) Mortgage Credit Certificates: home buyers who have not owned a home in the last three years can claim 20% of their mortgage interest as a tax credit.

2) Single Family Mortgage Purchase Program: below-market rate loans for first-time and limited-income home buyers.

3) Section 8 New Construction/Substantial Rehab Program: financing of multi-family housing affordable to very low-income households via rent subsidies.

4) Section 8 Moderate Rehab Program: incentives for property owners to upgrade substandard rental units to be occupied by low-income tenants qualifying for rent subsidies.

5) Section 8 Existing Certificate and Voucher Program: assistance for low-income households to meet costs of rental housing.

6) Rental Rehabilitation Program: funding for private property owners to make

improvements to rental units in eligible locations.

7) Low-Income Housing Tax Credit Program: tax credit for owners/developers of housing for low-income households.

8) Stewart B. McKinney Permanent Housing Program for Handicapped Homeless: grant funds for private non-profit project sponsors.

9) Multi-Family Housing Financing: loans for new construction or substantial rehab of multi-family housing with a percentage rented to low-income tenants.

Illinois

Illinois Housing Development Authority, 401 N. Michigan Ave., Suite 900, Chicago, IL 60611; 312-836-5200 or 1-800-942-8439.

1) Moderate Rehabilitation Program: low-interest loans to rehabilitate low-income housing.

2) Congregate Housing Finance Program: loans for congregate housing for the elderly.

3) Illinois Homebuyer Program: low-interest mortgages for first-time income-eligible home buyers.

4) Affordable Housing Trust Fund: grants and loans to profit and non-profit developers of low-income housing projects.

Indiana

Indiana Housing Finance Authority, One North Capitol, Suite 515, Indianapolis, IN 46204; 317-232-7777.

1) Single-Family Program: loans to home buyers at 1 to 2 percentage points below the market rate.

2) Multi-Family Program: loans for developers of low- and moderate- income housing.

3) Mortgage Credit Certificate Program: tax credits to families purchasing mobile homes.

4) Low-Income Housing Tax Credit: federal tax credit to owners of low-income rental housing.

5) Low-Income Housing Trust Fund: matching funds for development of low-income housing, permanent or transitional.

Iowa

Iowa Finance Authority, 100 East Grand Avenue, Suite 250, Des Moines, IA 50309; 515-281-4058.

1) Single-Family Mortgage Loans: low-interest loans to home buyers

2) Mortgage Credit Certificate Program: tax credits of up to 20% of the interest paid annually on home loans.

3) Small Business Loan Program: loans for small business.

4) Title Guaranty Program: to guaranty (insure) titles to Iowa real estate.

5) Economic Development Loan Program: for businesses exceeding the limitations of the Small Business Loan Program.

6) Targeted Area Assistance Program: assistance with origination fees and discount points.

7) Closing Cost Assistance: up to 3% or $1200 to help with closing costs of eligible buyers.

8) Low-Income Housing Tax Credit Program: federal tax credits for owners of low-income rental housing.

9) Housing Assistance Fund Program: funding for multi-family rehab and construction, rent subsidies, group homes, shelters, and other housing projects.

10) Homeless Shelter Assistance: funding for homeless shelters.

Kansas

Kansas Office of Housing, Department of Commerce, 400 S.W. 8th, 5th Floor, Topeka, KS 66603; 913-296-3481.

1) Tax Credits for Low-Income Housing: tax credits for developers who rent to low-income families.

2) Rental Rehabilitation Loan Program: loans up to $5,000 per rental unit to bring unit up to city code standard.

3) Emergency Shelter Grant Program: grants to local government agencies to provide emergency shelters for homeless households.

4) Permanent Housing for Handicapped Homeless: grants for acquisition, rehabilitation, and operation of multi-unit and group home projects for disabled homeless.

Kentucky

Kentucky Housing Corporation, 1231 Louisville Road, Frankfort, KY 40601; 502-564-7630 or 1-800-633-8896.

1) Single-Family Home Ownership: low-interest loans to home buyers who currently do not own property.

2) Elderly Rural Rehabilitation Program: grants to elderly in rural areas for the installment of indoor plumbing facilities.

3) Grants to the Elderly for Energy Repairs (GEER): grants to elderly for home energy repairs.

4) Housing Trust: single-family loans for eligible low-income families.

5) EPIC (Equity Partners Investing in the Commonwealth) Program: financing for eligible Kentuckians for downpayment and closing costs.

6) KHC Urban Program: initiatives to produce affordable housing in designated urban areas.

7) KHC Rural Program: loans and administrative assistance to non-profit organizations for construction or rehab of low-income housing.

8) Kentucky Appalachian Housing Program: site development grants and loans for housing developments in 49 eastern KY counties.

9) Country Home Program: low-rate construction financing for families in 63 counties.

10) Field Services/Special Population Needs Emergency Fund: loans for emergency repairs for low-income Kentuckians.

11) Permanent Housing for Homeless Handicapped Persons: funds for acquisition/rehabilitation of housing for homeless handicapped persons.

12) Section 8 Programs: rent subsidies and other assistance to low-income households.

13) Rental Housing Finance Program: below-market financing for low-income rental housing.

14) Rental Deposits Surety Program: assistance with utility and security deposits for low-income households.

15) Residential Investment Program: fixed-rate mortgages for non-profit sponsors of new rental units in rural counties.

16) Low-Income Housing Tax Credits: federal tax credits for owners of low-income rental housing.

Louisiana

Louisiana Housing Finance Agency, 5615 Corporate, Suite 6A, Baton Rouge, LA 70808-2515; 504-925-3675.

1) Single-Family: lower-interest rate 8.8%) 30 yr. FHA/VA financing for first-time home buyers.

2) Multi-Family: financing available for developers of low-moderate income housing development.

3) Tax Credit Programs: federal and state income tax credit provisions provided to developers of low-to-moderate multi-family development.

4) Housing Development Action Grants: financing for multi-family housing developments.

Maine

Maine State Housing Authority, P.O. Box 2669, 295 Water Street, Augusta, ME 04330; 207-626-4600, 1-800-452-4668.

1) Home Start Program: low-income loans for first-time home buyers.

2) Home Preservation Grant Program: grants for home improvements for very low-income home owners.

3) New Housing Initiatives Program: loans, grants, revolving funds, or administrative fees for developing non-traditional single family and rental housing initiatives to persons of low-income.

4) Home Purchase Program: low downpayment and low-rate financing for first-time income-eligible home buyers.

5) Purchase Plus Improvement: home improvement loans for borrowers in the Home Purchase or Home Start programs.

6) Underground Oil Storage Tank Removal Program: grants or interest-free loans to property owners for removal and disposal of environmentally hazardous underground oil storage tanks and pipes and installation of replacements.

7) Home Equity Conversion Mortgage: supplies elderly home owners with cash for some of the equity in their homes.

8) Home Improvement Program: low-rate home improvement loans.

9) Rental Loan Program: below market rate loans for new or rehabilitated rental housing affordable to low/moderate income households.

10) Rental Rehabilitation Program: low-interest deferred payment loans to repair substandard apartments.

11) Mental Health Facilities Fund: low-rate loans for housing the mentally ill.

12) MSHA 202 Start Program: up-front loans to non-profit developers of new rental housing for very low-income elderly or handicapped.

13) Land Acquisition Program: low-rate deferred payment loans to non-profit housing corporations to buy land for affordable housing.

14) Homeless Shelter Assistance: funding to operate or improve shelters.

15) Environmental Access Grants and Loans (EAGL): grants or 0% loans for disabled persons to make adaptations in their homes.

16) Supportive Housing Initiative Program (SHIP): low-rate, no/low down payment loans for non-profit organizations developing housing for special needs households.

17) Low-Income Housing Tax Credit: tax credits to developers of housing for low-income households.

18) Section 8 New Construction: rent subsidies for low-income households.

19) Section 8 Moderate Rehabilitation: rent subsidies for low-income households

in rehabilitated rental units.

20) Section 8 Certificates and Vouchers: rental assistance for low-income tenants.

Maryland

Department of Housing and Community Development, 45 Calvert St., Annapolis, MD 21401; 301-974-2176.

1) Rental Housing Production Program: loans to developers or non-profit organizations to cover the costs of construction, rehabilitation, acquisition or related development costs through interest rate writedowns or rent subsidies.

2) Mortgage Program: below-market interest rate mortgage financing for low- and moderate-income home buyers.

3) Home and Energy Loan Program: below-market interest rate loans for home and energy conservation improvements for single-family homes.

4) Multi-Family Home & Energy Loan Program: rehabilitation and energy conservation loans for multi-family rental projects and single scattered-site rental properties.

5) Housing Rehabilitation Program: loans to limited income home owners, owners of multi-unit residential buildings and owners of small nonresidential properties.

6) Group Home Financing Program: low-interest, no interest deferred payment loans to non-profit organizations to purchase and modify housing for use as group homes and shelters.

7) Residential Lead Paint Abatement Program: loans to finance the abatement of lead paint in rental properties.

8) Elderly Rental Housing Program: new construction financing for rental housing for elderly citizens.

9) Rental Housing Allowance Pilot Program: subsidies to very low-income individuals with emergency needs.

10) Emergency Mortgage Assistance: assists home owners in imminent danger of losing homes to foreclosure after loss of income due to critical circumstances.

11) Reverse Equity Program: enables low-income elderly to access home equity to pay housing and other expenses that facilitate continued occupancy.

12) Settlement Expense Loan Program: low-rate loans up to $5000 toward settlement expenses for low-moderate income home buyers.

13) Multi-Family Bond Program: below-market financing for low-income multi-family rental housing development.

14) Non-Profit Rehabilitation Program: low-rate loans to non-profit organizations to rehabilitate low-income rental housing.

15) Partnership Rental Housing Program: loans for local governments and housing authorities for development or acquisition of low-income rental housing.

16) Construction Loan Program: low-rate financing for development of affordable single-family or multi-family housing.

17) Shelter One: loans and technical assistance to non-profit organizations undertaking their first housing project.

18) Housing Rehabilitation Program-Single Family: low-rate financing for rehabilitation of small residential properties for low-income households.

19) Accessory, Shared and Sheltered Housing Program: low-rate loans to finance additions and improvements to create accessory, shared or sheltered housing for low-income households.

20) Indoor Plumbing Program: low-rate loans to provide indoor plumbing.

21) Energy Bank Program: matching funds to low-income home owners for energy conservation improvements.

22) Section 8 Existing Certificate/Voucher Program: rent subsidies for low-income households.

23) Section 8 Moderate Rehabilitation Program: incentives to property owners for improvements to deteriorating housing units to be rented to households eligible for rent subsidies.

24) Section 8 Rental Rehabilitation Program: rehab funds for property owners renting to low-income households.

25) Low-Income Housing Tax Credit Program: federal tax credits to owners of low-income rental housing.

Massachusetts

Massachusetts Housing Finance Agency, 50 Milk Street, Boston, MA 02190; 617-451-3480.

1) Home Ownership Opportunity Program: housing for purchase by first time low- and moderate-income home buyers at 30 to 40 percent below market rates.

2) General Lending: special loans for Vietnam Era Veterans, low-income and minority borrowers and physically handicapped.

3) Neighborhood Rehabilitation Programs: funds for people who buy and/or rehabilitate homes in locally designated neighborhoods.

4) New Construction Set-Aside: funds for purchasers of new homes and condominiums built by specific developers.

5) Home Improvement Program: loans for owner-occupied, one- to four-family homes.

6) State Housing Assistance for Rental Productions (SHARP): interest rate subsidies to developers for production of rental housing where at least 25% are available to low-income households.

7) Project TAP (Tenant Assistance Program): training for project residents for drug- and alcohol-related problems.

8) Low-Income Housing Tax Credit Program: federal tax credits for owners of low-income rental housing.

9) 80/20 Program: financing for developments with 20% of the units designated for low-income households.

10) Mortgage Credit Certificate Program: federal tax credits for eligible first-time home buyers.

11) Mortgage Insurance Program: lower premium private mortgage insurance available to HOP- and MHFA-assisted borrowers.

12) Rental Acquisition Development Initiative: low-rate financing for developers of rental properties with units affordable to low-income households.

13) Supportive Services in Elderly Housing: assists elderly residents in avoiding premature placement in nursing homes by delivering affordable homemaking, health care, and other services.

14) Acquisition Set-Aside Program: allows builders to offer lower interest mortgages to eligible home buyers as a sales incentive in return for reducing cost of units.

Executive Office of Communities and Development, Commonwealth of Massachusetts, 100 Cambridge Street, Room 1804, Boston, MA 02202; 617-727-7765.

1) Section 8 Certificate/Voucher Programs: rent subsidies for low-income households.

2) Chapter 707 Scattered Site Certificate Program: rent subsidies similar to Section 8 Certificate Program.

3) Chapter 707 Transitional Housing Program: for battered women, pregnant teenagers, and homeless women and children.

4) Chapter 707 Residential Services Programs: provide long-term housing opportunities for the chronically mentally ill.

Michigan

Michigan State Housing Development Authority, Plaza One, Fourth Floor, 401 South Washington Square, P.O. Box 30044, Lansing, MI 48909; 517-373-8370 or 1-800-327-9158.

1) Single-Family Home Mortgage: low-interest loans for single-family homes and condominiums.

2) Michigan Mortgage Credit Certificates: federal income tax credits that give home buyers more income to qualify for a mortgage.

3) Home and Neighborhood Improvement Loans: home improvement loans for homes over 20 years old at interest rates from 1 to 9 percent.

4) Section 8 Existing Rental Allowance Program: rent subsidies for low-income persons who find their own housing in private homes and apartment buildings.

5) Moderate Rehabilitation Loans to Landlords: loans to landlords for rehabilitation of units.

6) Housing for the Handicapped: financing for group homes for the handicapped.

7) Housing for the Homeless: grants to organizations to operate shelters for the homeless.

8) High Risk Home Improvement Program: interest-free home repair loans to high-risk and low-income households in the City of Grand Rapids and in Buena Vista.

9) Low-Income Housing Tax Credit Program: federal tax credits for owners/developers of low-income rental housing.

10) 70/30 Rental Housing Program: low interest loans to construct or rehabilitate low-income rental housing.

11) 80/20 Direct Lending Program: low interest financing for development or renovation of low-income rental housing.

12) Community Development Block Grant (Small Cities) Program: for neighborhood revitalization and improvements to infrastructure and rental housing.

13) Comprehensive Neighborhood Rehabilitation Competition: for neighborhood revitalization projects.

14) Emergency Housing Apartment Program (EHAP): pilot project; loans and grants for purchase and renovation of a homeless shelter.

15) Home Improvement Loan Program (HIP/CHIP): low cost home improvement loans.

16) Homeless Children's Fund: funds raised for shelters and transitional housing.

17) HOPE (Housing Opportunities Providing Equity): low rate loans to developers of housing for families receiving public assistance.

18) Housing Assistance Program: targeted technical and financial assistance to local governments.

19) Loans to Non-Profits: for neighborhood revitalization of single-family and rental housing.

20) Neighborhood Builders Alliance: targeted technical and financial assistance

to local governments and non-profits.

21) Neighborhood Housing Grant Program: assistance to non-profits for neighborhood revitalization of single-family and rental housing.

22) Neighborhood Preservation Program (NPP): targeted technical and financial assistance for local governments sponsoring neighborhood infrastructure improvements and building preservation.

23) Pass Through Program: loans for low-income rental housing development.

24) Set-Asides for Non-Profits: homebuyer assistance for low-income households participating in programs of non-profit organizations.

25) Special Housing Program: for handicapped group homes and other housing needs of the handicapped.

26) Supported Independent Living Program and Respite Program: for housing needs of the handicapped.

27) Taxable Bond Program: rental housing construction and renovation.

28) Urban Development Initiative: targeted technical assistance to local governments.

29) Freddie Mac/MSHDA Housing Initiative: low downpayment loans with liberal eligibility requirements; not restricted to first-time buyers.

Minnesota

Minnesota Housing Finance Agency, 400 Sibley Street, St. Paul, MN 55101; 612-296-9951, 612-296-7608, or 1-800-652-9747.

1) Indian Housing Programs: mortgage and home improvement financing for tribal housing as well as home ownership loans at below-market interest rates.

2) Innovative Housing Loan Program: no-interest and low-interest loans to develop housing that is innovative in design, construction, marketing and/or financing.

3) Accessibility Deferred Loan Program: interest-free loans to households with a disabled member.

4) Rental Rehabilitation Grant Program: dollar-for-dollar grants to rental property owners.

5) Rental Rehabilitation Loan Program: low-interest loans to rental property owners.

6) Section 8 Housing Assistance: rents subsidies for low-income renters.

7) Elderly Home Sharing Program: grants to non-profits who assist elderly in sharing homes.

8) Purchase Plus Program: financing for both purchase and rehabilitation of existing housing for median income or below.

9) Minnesota Mortgage Program: below-market rate loans for low/moderate income first-time home buyers.

10) Home Ownership Assistance Fund: downpayment and monthly payment assistance to lower income MHFA mortgage recipients.

11) Urban Indian Housing Program: below-market financing for Indians in Duluth, Minneapolis and St. Paul.

12) Urban and Rural Homesteading Program: grants to organizations to acquire and rehabilitate vacant and condemned properties for sale to first-time "at risk" home buyers.

13) Deferred Loan Program: deferred payment loans to assist low-income home owners making home improvements.

14) Great Minnesota Fix-Up Fund: below-market home-improvement loans for low/moderate income credit-worthy home owners.

15) Home Energy Loan Program: low-rate loans for increasing energy-efficiency of homes; no maximum income limits.

16) Neighborhood Preservation Loan Program: property improvement loans for low/moderate income households or owners of low/moderate income rental housing in designated areas.

17) Revolving Loan Program: rehabilitation financing for low/moderate income home owners who don't qualify for other programs.

18) Housing Trust Fund: zero-interest deferred loans for development of low-income rental and co-op housing.

19) $1.00 Home Set-Aside Program: HUD lease program for non-profit use of repossessed HUD homes to house the homeless.

20) Intermediate Care Facilities for the Developmentally Disabled: below-market financing for non-profit sponsors to develop residential facilities for the developmentally disabled.

21) Low-Income Housing Tax Credit Program: federal tax credit for owners of low-income rental housing.

22) Low-Income Individuals and Small Family Rental Housing Program: zero-interest deferred loans to rehabilitate small family low-income housing.

23) Low-Income Large Family Rental Housing Program: financing for construction of large rental units for low-income families.

24) Migrant Housing Program: matching funds to eligible sponsors developing housing for migrant farm workers and their families.

25) New Construction Tax Credit Mortgage/Bridge Loan Program: for construction/rehabilitation of rental units for low-income households.

Mississippi

Mississippi Home Corporation, 510 George Street, Suite 107 Dickson Building, Jackson, MS 39201; 601-359-6700.

1) Single-Family Home Ownership Program: low-rate financing for income-eligible first-time home buyers.

2) Low-Income Housing Tax Credit Program: tax credits for owners of low-income rental housing.

3) Downpayment Assistance Program: for buyers who can afford mortgage payments but not a downpayment.

4) Rental Rehabilitation Program: (under development).

5) Energy Conservation Revolving Loan Fund: (under development).

Missouri

Missouri Housing Development Commission, 3770 Broadway, Kansas City, MO 64111; 816-756-3790.

1) Multi-Family Program: low-interest rate mortgages to developers of multi-family developments.

2) Single-Family Housing: below-market interest rate mortgages for first-time home buyers.

3) Neighborhood Loan Program: loans to neighborhood organizations and/or developers for acquiring and rehabilitating residential properties.

4) Home Improvements/Weatherization Loan Program: low-interest loans to assist qualified home owners in home improvements that will increase energy efficiency.

5) Blended Multi-Family Program: low-interest rates to developers to stimulate production of housing for low-and moderate-income families and individuals.

6) RTC Home Purchase Program: low-rate financing to purchase reduced cost housing.

7) HUD Repo Properties: HUD-insured low-rate loans for low-income households to purchase HUD-foreclosed properties.

8) Low-Income Housing Tax Credit Program: tax credits for owners of low-income rental housing.

9) Section 8 Programs: subsidies and financial assistance for low-income tenants.

10) Operation Homeless: provides homeless households with Section 8 certificates or vouchers to secure affordable subsidized rental housing.

11) Housing Trust Fund Program: non-Section 8 rental assistance payments for low-income households.

12) Housing Inventory Recycling Program: funds to facilitate purchase of foreclosed homes by lower income households.

13) FmHA Supplemental Subsidy Program: rent subsidies for low-income elderly in FmHA housing projects.

14) Missouri Low-Income Housing Tax Credit Program: supplements the federal Low-Income Housing Tax Credit Program.

Montana

Montana Board of Housing, 2001 Eleventh Avenue, Helena, MT 59620; 406-444-3040.

1) Single-Family Programs: low-interest loans to low-income families.

2) Multi-Family Program: construction loans to developers of multi-family units for persons and families of lower income.

3) Mortgage Credit Certificate Program: federal tax credits for low/moderate income mortgage holders.

4) Low-Income Housing Tax Credit Program: federal tax credits for owners of low-income housing.

5) Reverse Annuity Mortgage Loans: home-equity loans for senior 68+) home owners.

6) Recycled Mortgage Purchase Program: assists lower income households who cannot purchase homes through the Single-Family Mortgage Program; grant funds help lower construction costs for developers, reduce home prices, create low-interest loans, and assist with downpayments and closing costs.

Nebraska

Nebraska Investment Finance Authority, 1033 O Street, Suite 218, Lincoln, NE 68508; 402-434-3900.

1) Single-Family Mortgage Program: low-cost loans for single family homes, townhomes, condominiums, mobile homes, and up to 4-unit dwellings.

2) Multi-Family Loan Program: attractive interest rates for developers of rental housing for low- and moderate-income households.

3) Home Improvement Loan Program: low-interest loans to home owners to make needed home improvements.

4) Agricultural Finance Programs:
First-Time Farmer Loan: loans to purchase agricultural real estate.
FmHA: loans to refinance existing agricultural loans.

5) Low-Income Housing Tax Credit Program: federal tax credits for owners of low-income housing.

Nevada

Department of Commerce, Housing Division, 1802 N. Carson St., Suite 154, Carson City, NV 89710; 702-687-4258.

1) Single Family Mortgage Purchase Program: loans to moderate-income families with no previous home ownership interest within the last 3 years.

2) Industrial Development Bonds: low financing costs for new construction or expansion manufacturing projects.

3) Rural Area Housing Program: low-interest mortgage loans to developers to develop affordable rental units outside metropolitan areas.

Nevada Rural Housing Authority, 2100 California Street, Carson City, NV 89701; 702-687-5797.

New Hampshire

Housing Finance Authority, P.O. Box 5087, Manchester, NH 03108; 603-472-8623.

1) Rental Assistance: rental subsidies to eligible families, elderly, disabled or handicapped.

2) Single-Family Mortgage Program: low-interest mortgage funds to qualifying individuals and households.

3) Multi-Family Housing Program: construction loans for small rental projects for private for profit developers and non-profit organizations.

4) Special Needs Fund: funding for housing for individuals with special needs.

5) Affordable Housing Fund: financing primarily for non-profit or co-op multi-family projects.

6) Downpayment/Closing Cost Assistance Program: for borrowers who can afford mortgage payments but lack downpayment and closing costs.

7) Home Equity Conversion Program: loans to help seniors meet living and medical expenses while retaining ownership and residence in their own homes.

8) Section 8 Housing Programs: rental assistance for low-income households.

9) Low-Income Housing Tax Credit Program: tax credits for owners of low-income rental housing.

10) Supportive Services Program: funding for seniors to receive services they need to remain independent.

11) Mortgage Credit Certificate Program: federal tax credits for low/moderate income home buyers.

12) Mixed Income Rental Programs: funding for housing developments with some units affordable to lower income households.

13) Energy Improvements Program: matching grants and loans for low-income households to make energy conservation improvements.

14) Affordable Home Ownership Program: financing for developers of single family homes to be sold at below market cost.

New Jersey

New Jersey Housing Agency, 3625 Quakerbridge Road, Trenton, NJ 08650-2085; 609-890-1300 or 1-800-NJ-HOUSE.

1) Home Buyers Program: low-interest loans to urban area first-time buyers with a 5% downpayment.

2) Rental Repair Loan Program: loans to finance the rehabilitation of occupied rental developments.

3) Continuing Care Retirement Communities: construction loans and lower-than-market mortgage interest rates for residential communities for senior citizens.

4) Home Buyers Program: low-rate financing and low downpayments for income-eligible first-time home buyers or home buyers in 41 targeted urban areas.

5) Home Buyers 100% Financing Program: for low/moderate-income first-time or urban buyers.

6) Home Ownership for Performing Employees (HOPE) Program: financial assistance from sponsoring employers to reduce downpayment, closing costs and monthly payments for their employees.

7) Development Set-Aside Program: mortgage funding for purchasers of housing units in Agency-approved housing developments.

8) Multi-Family Rental Housing Program: low-rate financing for developers of rental housing for low/moderate income households.

9) Low-Income Housing Tax Credit Program: federal tax credits for owners of low-income rental housing.

10) Revolving Loan Program: financing for the production of small and medium-sized rental housing projects with units affordable to low-income households.

11) Services for Independent Living Program: support services that enable senior citizens in Agency-financed housing to avoid institutionalization.

12) Boarding House Life Safety Improvement Loan Program: low-rate loans to finance safety improvements in boarding homes.

13) Transitional Housing Program: financing for the construction of transitional housing for the homeless.

14) Seed Money Loan Program: funding of pre-development costs for non-profits seeking to develop affordable housing.

New Mexico

Mortgage Finance Authority, P.O. Box 2047, Albuquerque, NM 87103; 505-843-6880 or 1-800-444-6880.

1) Single-Family Program: below-market loans to first-time home buyers.

2) Multi-Family Programs: financing of multi-family housing for low- and moderate-income tenants.

New Mexico State Housing Authority, 1100 St. Francis Drive, Santa Fe, NM 87503; 505-827-0258.

1) Low-Income Housing Tax Credit Program: federal tax credits for owners of low-income rental housing.

2) State Housing Rehabilitation Program: rehabilitation grants for low-income elderly, handicapped and disabled home owners.

3) Section 8 Housing Assistance Payments Program (Voucher): rent subsidies for low-income households who locate their own housing.

4) HUD Rental Rehabilitation Program: grants to rehabilitate sub-standard rental units for rental to low-income tenants qualifying for rent subsidies.

New York

State of New York, Executive Department, Division of Housing and Community Renewal, One Fordham Plaza, Bronx, NY 10458; 212-519-5700.

1) Special Needs Housing Program: grants to non-profit sponsors for single room occupancy dwellings units for low-income individuals.

2) Low-Income Housing Trust Fund: funds to non-profit sponsors to rehabilitate existing properties into affordable low-income housing.

3) Housing Development Fund: temporary financing to non-profit sponsors developing housing with private or government-aided mortgages

4) Rental Rehabilitation Program: up to $8,500 per unit to subsidize up to 50% of the cost of moderate rehabilitation of residential units in lower-income neighborhoods.

5) Rural Preservation Program: funds to local not-for-profit organizations engaging in a variety of activities for the benefit of low- and moderate-income persons.

6) Rural Rental Assistance Program: monthly rent subsidy payments to owners of multi-family projects on behalf of low-income tenants.

7) Turn Key/Enhanced Housing Trust Fund: financing for developers of low-income rental housing.

8) Infrastructure Development Demonstration Program: grant funds for infra-structure improvements (water lines, roads, sidewalks, utility lines) that serve affordable housing projects.

9) Urban Initiative Program: funding for community preservation and improvement in designated urban areas.

10) Rural Area Revitalization Program: funding for not-for-profit organizations to make housing improvements in designated areas.

11) Housing Opportunities Program for the Elderly-RESTORE: funds for not-for-profit organizations to make emergency home repairs for elderly home owners.

12) Shared Housing Development Program: funding for boarding houses, accessory apartments and "granny flats" in designated areas.

13) Clinton Preservation Program: financing to preserve and improve the Clinton neighborhood in NYC.

14) Low-Income Housing Tax Credit Program: federal tax credits for owners of low-income housing rental.

15) Neighborhood Preservation Program: funding to defray administrative costs of not-for-profit organizations performing neighborhood preservation activities.

16) Rural Home Ownership Assistance Program: funds to defray administrative costs of not-for-profit organizations assisting low-income households in the acquisition, financing, and rehabilitation of affordable housing.

17) Neighborhood Redevelopment Demonstration Program: funds for planning, administration and project costs for activities that promote affordable housing or improve neighborhoods.

18) Section 8 Moderate Rehabilitation Program: incentives for property owners to upgrade substandard rental housing for tenants qualifying for rent subsidies.

19) Section 8 Existing Housing Program: rent subsidies for low-income households.

20) Senior Citizen Rent Increase Exemption: exemption from rent increases for tenants 62 years of age or older who live in rent-controlled apartments in NYC and 15 other areas; landlords are compensated with certificates to pay real estate taxes or to convert to cash.

New York State Housing Authority, 250 Broadway, New York, NY 10007; 212-306-3000.

North Carolina

North Carolina Housing Finance Agency, 3300 Drake Circle, Suite 200, Raleigh, NC 27611; 919-781-6115.

1) Single-Family Mortgage Loan Program: below-market, fixed-rate loans for first-time home buyers with low/moderate income.
2) Home Improvement Loan Program: rehabilitation loans of up to $15,000 at rates as low as 1% to improve owner occupied housing.
3) Governor's NCHFA/FmHA Elderly Subsidy Program: rental subsidy of up to $100 per month based on occupant's income.
4) Mortgage Credit Certificate Program: tax-credit for first-time home buyers paying mortgage interest.
5) Home Ownership Challenge Fund: funding to non-profits that create home ownership opportunities for low-income households.
6) Maxwell/Fuller Self-Help Housing Program: zero-interest loans to nonprofits managing self-help or owner-built housing projects for low-income households.
7) Multi-Family Loan Program: below-market financing for developers of low/moderate-income rental housing.
8) Multi-Family subsidized Program: rent subsidies for low-income tenants.
9) Low-Income Housing Tax Credit Program: federal tax credits for owners of low-income housing.
10) Catalyst Loan Program: funding for non-profits for front-end costs in the development of low-income rental housing.
11) Rental Rehabilitation Program: rehabilitation funds for privately-owned rental housing for low-income households.
12) Energy Conservation and Housing Rehab Incentive Program: deferred payment loans and grants for energy conservation and housing rehab improvements on low-income housing.
13) Energy-Efficient Housing Production Program: financing for new or rehabilitated housing for low-income households.
14) Non-Profit Development Program: funds for non-profits for pre-development costs, construction financing and administrative expenses associated with development of affordable housing.
15) Resolution Trust Corporation Clearinghouse: property information for purchasers, allowing qualified purchasers right of first refusal for single family and multi-family properties affordable to low/moderate income households.

North Dakota

Housing Finance Agency, P.O. Box 1535, Bismarck, ND 58502; 701-224-3434.
1) Housing Assistance: rental assistance program for low-income renter households and mobile home space renters.
2) Single Family Program: low interest loans for low- to moderate-income first-time home buyers.
3) Housing Assistance Program: certificates and vouchers to assist low-income tenants with rent payments.
4) Moderate Rehabilitation Program: incentives for rehabilitation of substandard housing for rental to low-income tenants qualifying for rent-subsidies.
5) Low-Income Housing Tax Credit Program: federal tax credits for owners of low-income rental housing.

Ohio

Ohio Housing Finance Agency, 775 High St., 26th Floor, Columbus, OH 43266; 614-466-7970.
1) Seed Money Loan Program: no-interest loans to non-profit, public and limited profit entities to arrange financing for low- and moderate-income rental housing developments.
2) First-Time Homebuyer Program: below-market financing for first-time home buyers.
3) Home Ownership Incentive Programs: low interest rates and downpayments for non-profit developers of housing to meet special needs (single parents, minorities, disabled, rural, inner city).
4) Development Loan Program: financing for construction and development costs of low/moderate income housing by non-profit and limited profit sponsors.
5) Low-Income Housing Tax Credit Program: federal tax credits for owners of low-income rental housing.
6) 403 Rental Housing Gap Financing Program: financial assistance to non-profit organizations for development of low-income rental housing.
7) Rental Housing Energy Conservation Program: funds to non-profits for energy-efficient rehabilitation or new construction of low-income rental housing.
8) Multi-Family Rental Development Program: financing for purchase, construction, and rehabilitation of multi-family rental housing for the elderly.
9) Section 8 Rental Assistance Program: rent subsidies.

Oklahoma

Oklahoma Housing Finance Agency, P.O. Box 26720, Oklahoma City, OK 73126-0720; 405-848-1144 or 1-800-256-1489.
1) Single-Family Mortgage Revenue Bond Program: low-rate loans to first-time home buyers.
2) Multi-Family Mortgage Revenue Bond Program: funds for the purchase, construction or rehabilitation of housing for low/moderate income families.

3) Homeless Program: support for homeless families while they await funds for housing.
4) Section 8 Existing Housing Assistance Program: rent subsidies for low-income tenants.
5) Section 8 Rental Rehabilitation Program: matching funds for property owners who renovate rental units for low/moderate-income households.
6) Section 8 Voucher Assistance Program: rent subsidies for low-income households who locate their own housing.

Oregon

Oregon Housing Agency, Housing Division, 1600 State St., Suite 100, Salem, OR 97310; 503-378-4343.
1) Elderly and Disabled Housing Program: below-market interest rate mortgage loans for multi-family housing for elderly and disabled.
2) Family Rental Housing Program: financing for multi-unit rental housing for low-income families.
3) Seed Money Advance Program: no-interest advances to non-profits to cover pre-construction costs.
4) Low-Income Housing Tax Credit: federal income tax credits to developers who construct, rehabilitate, or acquire qualified low-income rental housing.
5) Single-Family Mortgage Program: below-market interest rate loans to low- and moderate-income Oregon home buyers.
6) Mortgage Credit Certificate Program: federal tax credit for low- and moderate-income Oregonians to purchase, improve or rehabilitate a single-family residence.
7) Oregon Lenders' Tax Credit Program: very low interest loans to non-profits from qualified Oregon financial institutions for low-income multi-family housing.
8) Low-Income Rental Housing Fund: rental assistance for low-income families.
9) Mobile Home Park Purchase Program: financial and technical assistance for tenants' associations to purchase their mobile home parks.
10) Partnership Housing Team: technical assistance to local governments and non-profits developing low-income housing.
11) Community Development Corporation Program: grants and technical assistance for local community development corporations to increase their skills in establishing low-income housing.

Pennsylvania

Pennsylvania Housing Finance Agency, 2101 North Front St. Harrisburg, PA 17105; 717-780-3800.
1) Home Owners Emergency Mortgage Assistance Program: loans to keep delinquent home owners from losing their homes to foreclosure.
2) Rental Housing Development Program: low-interest financing for developers of low-income multi-family rental housing.
3) Low-Income Housing Tax Credit Program: federal tax credit for owners of low-income rental housing.
4) Rental Rehabilitation Program: financing for property owners who rehabilitate low-income rental units.
5) Statewide Home Ownership Program: low-interest financing for first-time home buyers or buyers of property in targeted areas.
6) HomeStart Program: financing for middle-income first-time home buyers, single-parent families, and certain veterans.
7) Lower-Income Home Ownership Program: low-interest financing, reduced fees and closing cost assistance for low-income first-time home buyers and handicapped persons.
8) Non-Profit Seed Fund Program: pre-development loans for non-profits constructing or rehabilitating multi-family low-income housing.
9) Supportive Services Program: to help elderly residents of subsidized senior citizen rental apartments meet routine needs that enable them to remain in their own homes.

Rhode Island

Rhode Island Housing and Mortgage Finance Corporation, 60 Eddy St., Providence, RI 02903; 401-751-5566.
1) Home Repair: fixed rate-loans to make needed repairs on 1 to 6 unit dwellings owned or occupied by low- and moderate-income persons.
2) Rental Housing Production and Rehabilitation: tax-exempt and/or taxable bond financing for developers for projects where a minimum of 20% of the units are rented to low-income tenants.
3) First Homes Program: low-rate mortgages for income-eligible first-time home buyers.
4) Accessory Apartments: low-rate loans to create a separate apartment unit in the home.
5) Energy-Efficient Homes Program: additional assistance to FIRST HOMES mortgagees if their home receives a high energy-efficiency rating.
6) Buy-It/Fix-It Program: low-rate financing to buy or refinance an older home and make substantial repairs.

7) Home Equity Conversion Mortgage Program: reverse mortgages to enable older home owners to remain in and retain ownership of their homes.

8) Home Owner's Notes Program: helps first-time home buyers assemble funding from several sources.

9) Mortgage Credit Certificates: tax credit for first-time home buyers.

10) Construction Loan Program: below market rate loans to build/rehab affordable 1)4 family homes for low/moderate-income persons.

11) Cooperative Housing Demonstration Program: funding packages for non-profit organizations to develop cooperative housing.

12) Land Bank Program: below market rate loans for purchase or refinancing of undeveloped land to be used for low/moderate-income housing.

13) Lease-Purchase Program: financing for non-profit organizations to develop housing that will be leased to low/moderate-income households.

14) Low-Income Housing Tax Credit Program: tax credits for owners of rental housing for low-income households.

15) Pre-Development Loan Program: short-term loans to cover pre-development costs for non-profit developers.

16) Preservation Loan Fund: below-market rate loans to preserve affordability of existing subsidized rental housing.

17) Emergency Housing Assistance Program: assistance to qualified low-income households facing a temporary housing crisis.

18) Employer Assisted Housing: employer resources combine with existing programs to provide affordable housing for employees.

19) Supportive Services/Robert Wood Johnston Foundation: supportive services for residents of RI Housing-financed developments to enable them to remain independent.

South Carolina

South Carolina State Housing Financing and Development Authority, 1710 Gervais St., Suite 300, Columbia, SC 29201; 803-734-8836.

1) Multi-Family Development Programs: construction loans to construct houses for rental to low and moderate-to-low income persons.

2) Moderate Rehabilitation Program: mortgage financing for the upgrade of substandard rental housing.

3) Home Ownership Mortgage Purchase Program: below market rate financing for income-eligible home buyers.

4) Community Home Ownership Opportunity Partnership (CHOP): below market rate financing for purchase of affordable homes by qualified borrowers in conjunction with local communities' contributions.

5) Low-Income Housing Tax Credit Program: tax credits for developers of low-income rental housing.

6) Section 8 Certificates and Vouchers: rental assistance for low-income households.

7) Section 8 Moderate Rehabilitation Program: rent subsidies for low-income households.

South Dakota

South Dakota Housing Development Authority, P.O. Box 1237, Pierre, SD 57501; 605-773-3181.

1) Existing Housing Assistance Payments Program: money to assist lower-income families pay for modest rental housing.

2) Energy Efficiency Program - New Construction: new construction loans for homes complying with super-insulation standards.

3) Home Ownership Mortgage Program: low-rate financing for eligible single families to build, rehabilitate or buy homes.

4) Multi-Family Housing Trust Fund: permanent and temporary mortgage loans to finance the construction of multi-family housing.

5) Low-Income Housing Tax Credit Program: federal tax credits for developers/owners of low-income housing.

6) Emergency Shelter Grants Program: financing of shelters for homeless and special needs households.

7) Rental Rehab Program: financing for owners of rental properties occupied by low-income households.

Tennessee

Tennessee Housing Development Agency, 700 Landmark Center, 401 Church St., Nashville, TN 37219; 615-741-4979.

1) Home Ownership Program: reduced interest rate loans to low- and moderate-income families.

2) Veterans: permanent mortgage financing available for disabled Veterans who need specially designed homes.

3) Rental Rehabilitation: lower-than-market loans to owners of rental property to rehabilitate units. This program also offers a grant of up to $5000 per unit to keep the cost of rehabilitation down.

4) Owner-Built Homes: permanent financing for homes built by the owners. Sweat equity serves as the downpayment.

5) Turn Key III: subsidized rent to bring economically viable residents into personal home ownership.

6) Section 8 Rental Assistance Program: subsidy funds to low-income households.

7) Technical Assistance Program: technical assistance to public and private sponsors of low- and moderate-income housing.

8) Low-Income Housing Tax Credit: tax credits for owners of low-income housing.

9) Moderate Rehabilitation Program: incentives for property owners to upgrade substandard rental units to be occupied by low-income tenants qualifying for rent subsidies.

10) HOUSE Program: funding for special needs housing projects.

Texas

Texas Housing Agency, PO Box 13941 Capitol Station, Austin, TX 78711; 512-472-7500.

1) Mortgage Credit Certificate Program: up to $2,000 of federal tax credits for first-time home owners.

2) Low-Income Rental Housing Tax Credit: federal tax credits for those who wish to acquire, construct, or rehabilitate rental housing for low-income families.

3) Single-Family Bond Program: low-rate financing for low/moderate income first-time home buyers.

4) Section 8 Housing Assistance Program: rental assistance via subsidies for low-income households.

Utah

Utah Housing Finance Agency, 177 East 100 South, Salt Lake City, UT 84111; 801-521-6950.

1) Single-Family Mortgage Program: money to first-time home buyers or home buyers in targeted areas with required downpayment.

Vermont

Vermont Housing Finance Agency, One Burlington Sq., PO Box 408, Burlington, VT 05402; 802-864-5743, 1-800-222-VFHA.

1) Mortgage Plus: federal income tax credit for up to 20% of interest on a home loan.

2) Mortgages for Vermonters: low-interest mortgages for first-time buyers.

3) Energy-Rated Homes of Vermont Mortgage Program: money to modify homes to make them energy efficient.

4) New Home Financing: low-rate financing for qualified borrowers purchasing new homes.

5) Mobile Home Financing: mortgage financing for modular or permanently fixed mobile homes; financing for non-profit or tenant acquisition of mobile home parks.

6) Perpetually Affordable Housing Program: low-rate financing for non-profit housing developers providing home ownership opportunities that will remain affordable over the long term.

7) Rural Vermont Mortgage: low-rate financing for low-income households in rural areas.

8) Home Energy/Improvement Loan Program: low-rate loans for low/moderate-income home owners to make energy improvements.

9) Multi-Family Financing: financing to eligible housing sponsors who wish to build or renovate low/moderate-income rental or cooperative housing.

10) Low-Income Housing Tax Credit Program: tax credits for developers/owners of rental housing for low-income households.

11) Vermont Housing Ventures: low-rate financing to cover pre-development costs of locally based non-profit housing.

12) Housing Foundation, Inc.: purchases and preserves housing units threatened with conversion to unsubsidized stock; aids in tenant acquisition of mobile home parks.

13) Housing Vermont: develops affordable housing in partnership with non-profit organizations throughout the state.

14) Vermont Home Mortgage Guarantee Board (VHMGB): low-cost mortgage insurance for low/moderately-priced housing.

15) Vermont Housing and Conservation Board: grants and loans to projects which meet both affordable housing and conservation goals.

16) ENABLE Program: low-rate loans to finance modifications designed to make housing more accessible for the elderly and disabled.

Vermont State Housing Authority, P.O. Box 397, Montpelier, VT 05601-0397; 802-828-3295.

Virginia

Virginia Housing Development Authority, 601 S. Belvedere Street, Richmond, VA 23220; 804-782-1986.

1) Home Mortgage Loan Program: below-market loans to eligible home buyers

with required downpayment.

2) Virginia Housing Fund: flexible, below-market rate loans for lower-income people.

3) Home Rehabilitation Loan Program: loans at 8% interest for 6 months to 8-year terms.

4) Targeted Area Program: below-market loans with low downpayments for purchasers of homes in designated areas.

5) Multi-Family Loan Program: below-market loans to developers of low/moderate-price rental housing.

6) Low-Income Housing Tax Credit Program: federal tax credits for owners of low-income rental housing.

7) Rental Rehabilitation Program: grants for up to 50% of rehab costs for low-income rental housing.

8) Section 8 Rent Subsidy Programs: subsidies to assist low-income households in meeting rental housing costs.

9) Joint Program for Housing Persons with Mental Disabilities and Recovering Substance Abusers: below-market loans to assist non-profit sponsors in developing supportive housing facilities.

Washington

Washington State Housing Finance Commission, 111 Third Ave., Suite 2240, Seattle, WA 98101-3202; 206-464-7139.

1) Mortgage Credit Certificate Program: tax credits to prospective first-time home buyers purchasing manufactured, newly-constructed or existing homes.

2) Multi-Family Program: financing to developers of multi-family projects where at least 20% or more units will be rented to lower- to mid-income persons, the elderly or the handicapped.

3) Low-Income Housing Tax Credit Program: federal tax credits to developers/owners of low-income rental housing.

4) Single Family Mortgage Revenue Bond Program: below market rate loans for income-eligible first time home buyers and buyers of residences in targeted areas.

5) Non-Profit Owners Program: tax-exempt financing for group homes, congregate housing, and retirement housing (non-medical).

6) Multi-Family Tax Exempt Bond Financing Program: tax exempt financing for developers/owners of multi-family housing with a percentage set aside for low-income households; new construction, acquisition and rehabilitation.

West Virginia

West Virginia Housing Development Fund, 814 Virginia St., East, Charleston, WV 25301; 304-345-6475.

1) Mortgage Credit Certificate Program: federal tax credit for home buyers.

2) Single Family Mortgage Program: financing for single family homes with deferred payment loans to pay downpayment and closing costs.

3) Multi-Family Construction Loan Incentive Program: construction financing for sponsors of low-income multi-family housing.

4) Building Revitalization/Reutilization Program: funds for rehabilitation of existing downtown residential and commercial buildings.

5) Emergency Shelters Program: financing for construction, rehabilitation, and acquisition of shelters.

6) Housing Development Fund/Army Corps of Engineers Flood Mitigation: includes flood-proofing of individual homes.

7) Community Provider Financing Program: low-interest loans to non-profits for financing the acquisition or construction of health facilities.

8) Home Rehab Program: low-cost loans to repair flooded homes.

9) Low-Income Housing Tax Credit Program: federal tax credits for developers/owners of low-income multi-family housing.

10) Land Development Program: low-rate financing for developers of raw land to support housing developments.

11) Rental Rehab Program: grants for upgrading rental units for low-income households.

12) ARC Program: funding of site development costs in the Appalachian region.

Wisconsin

Wisconsin Housing and Economic Development Authority, PO Box 1728, Madison, WI 53701; 608-266-7884 or 1-800-362-2767.

1) HOME Program: low interest, fixed rate, 30-year loans.

2) Home Energy Loan Program: low-interest loans to make energy conserving improvements on homes.

3) DEER Program: money to non-profits to acquire and rehabilitate older single-family and two-family homes with special emphasis on energy conservation. Restored homes are then sold.

4) Rental Housing Programs: financing of rental housing for low-and moderate-income individuals and families, elderly and disabled.

5) Community Housing Alternatives Program: loans for construction, purchase or rehabilitation of projects to house those who are chronically disabled due to mental illness, development disability, physical disability, or alcohol- or other drug-related dependence, or those over 60 years of age.

6) Rental Rehabilitation Program: money for rehabilitation of rental units for low-income households.

7) Low-Income Housing Tax Credits: federal tax credits for low-income rental housing in Wisconsin.

8) WHEDA Foundation Grants: grants to non-profit housing project sponsors.

9) Business Development Bond Program: financing for small- and medium-sized businesses.

10) Linked Deposit Loan Program: loans to businesses that are more than 50% owned by women or minorities.

11) Business Energy Fund Program: low-cost financing to small businesses for energy conservation improvements.

12) Credit Relief Outreach Program: agricultural related families can receive interest rate reduction and loan guarantees of up to $20,000.

13) Home Improvement Loan Program: below-market financing for low/moderate income home owners to make eligible home improvements such as energy-conserving improvements.

14) Blueprint Loan Program: low cost, short-term financing for pre-development costs associated with creating multi-family housing under government programs.

15) Section 8 Rent Subsidy Program: rent subsidies for low/moderate income rental households.

16) Small Business Loan Guarantee Program: funding necessary to guarantee conventional loans needed by businesses to fulfill awarded contracts.

17) Neighborhood Housing Program Fund: supports development and improvement of low-income housing and urban and rural neighborhood revitalization.

18) Elderly Housing Program Fund: supports development and improvement of non-institutional housing facilities for frail or low-income elderly persons.

19) Persons-in-Crisis Housing Program Fund: supports development and improvement of emergency shelters and group/transitional housing.

20) Wisconsin Partnership for Housing Development: development financing and technical assistance to community-based organizations providing housing to low-income households.

21) Rental Property Energy Efficiency Loan Fund: financing for purchase and installation of energy-saving measures in rental properties.

Wyoming

Wyoming Community Development Authority, 123 S. Durbin St., P.O. Box 634, Casper, WY 82602; 307-265-0603.

Funding for single-family homes, multi-family projects, and economic development.

1) Single Family Mortgage Program: low-rate financing for first-time home buyers.

2) Section 8 Rental Assistance Program: certificates and vouchers to assist low-income rental households.

3) Rental Rehab Program: loans for owners of rental housing in targeted areas.

4) Urban Homesteading Program: sale of deteriorating government-owned residences to "urban homesteaders" who agree to restore and live in them.

5) WCDA CDBG Revolving Loan Fund: for housing rehabilitation that benefits low/moderate income households.

6) Low-Income Tax Credit Program: tax credits for owners of rental housing affordable to low-income households.

Venture Capital: Finding A Rich Angel

With federal and state money getting harder to come by, and banks experiencing serious problems, anyone interested in starting his own business or expanding a current one may do well to look into venture capital. Venture capitalists are willing to invest in a new or growing venture for a percentage of the equity. Below is a listing of some of the associations, government agencies and businesses that have information available on venture capital.

In addition, there are Venture Capital Clubs throughout the country where entrepreneurs have a chance to present their ideas to potential investors and learn about the process for finding funds.

Associations

The National Venture Capital Association (NVCA)
1655 North Fort Meyer Drive, Suite 700
Arlington, VA 22209　　　　703-528-4370
The association works to improve the government's knowledge and understanding of the venture capital process. Staff members can answer questions about federal legislation and regulations, and provide statistical information on venture capital. NVCA members include venture capital organizations, financiers and individuals investing in new companies.

The association publishes a membership directory that includes a listing of the members with addresses, phone numbers, tax numbers and contacts. There are now about 200 members. The directory is available for $10.

The Western Association of Venture Capitalists
3000 San Hill Road, Bldg. 1, Suite 190
Menlo Park, CA 94025　　　　415-854-1322
Publishes a directory of its 130 members.

National Association of Investment Companies
1111 14th Street NW, Suite 700
Washington, DC 20005　　　　202-289-4336
It is composed of specialized Small Business Investment Companies (SSBICs). The SSBIC Directory lists about 150 companies across the country including names, addresses and telephone numbers. It also describes each company's investment preferences and policies. The 23-page publication costs $5.

It also publishes *Perspective*, a monthly newsletter geared toward specialized small business investment companies. It includes articles about legislation and regulations affecting SSBICs. (Note: This association was formerly called the American Association of Minority Enterprise Small Business Investment Companies (AAMESBIC)).

National Association of Small Business Investment
　Companies (NASBIS)
1199 North Fairfax Street, Room 200
Alexandria, VA 22314　　　　703-683-1601
This association serves as an information clearing house on venture capital. Staff can direct you to venture capital sources, experts and literature.

The 1991 membership directory, *Venture Capital: Where to Find It*, has 120 pages listing about 300 small business investment companies and specialized small business investment companies. It gives names, addresses, phone numbers, investment policies, industry preferences, and preferred dollar limits on loans and investments. The directory is available for $10. To order, send a check or money order to NASBIS Directory, P.O. Box 2039, Merrifield, VA 22116.

Venture Capital Network
201 Vassar Street
Cambridge, MA 02139　　　　617-253-7163
This non-profit corporation tries to match entrepreneurs in need of capital with venture capital sources. Investors and entrepreneurs register for up to 12 months for $250.

Government Agencies

U.S. Small Business Administration
Investment Division
Washington, DC 20416
This office licenses, regulates, and funds some 350 Small Business Investment Companies (SBICs) nationwide. SBICs supply equity capital, long-term loans and management assistance to qualifying small businesses. They invest in a broad range of industries. Some seek out small businesses with new products or services, other in the field in which their management has special competency.

The office publishes the *Directory of Operating Small Business Investment Companies*, a listing by state of the names, addresses, telephone numbers and investment policies of SBICs. The directory will be sent free of charge by writing to the above address.

The U.S. Small Business Administration (SBA), Office of Business Development has videotapes and publications available on starting and managing a successful small business. For information on business development programs and services call the SBA Small Business Answer Desk at 1-800-827-5722.

Venture Capital Clubs

There are more than 150 Venture Capital Clubs worldwide where inventors can present their ideas to potential investors. At a typical monthly meeting, a couple of entrepreneurs may give short presentations of their ideas. It is a great way for entrepreneurs and potential investors to talk informally.

The International Venture Capital Institute (IVCI)
P.O. Box 1333
Stamford, CT   203-323-3143

The IVCI publishes an annual directory of domestic and international venture groups (venture capital clubs). The cost of the *1991 IVCI Directory of Domestic and International Venture Groups*, which includes contact information for all of the clubs, is $9.95.

Association of Venture Capital Clubs
265 East 100 South, Suite 300
P.O. Box 3358
Salt Lake City, UT 84110-3358   801-364-1100

The association was formed to facilitate and encourage creation and participation in growth-oriented businesses. The association publishes a directory of its members and will put you in touch with the club nearest you. If you are interested in starting a club, the association publishes a 15-chapter manual which sells for $50.

Below is a partial listing of clubs in the United States.

Alabama
Birmingham Venture Club, P.O. Box 10127, Birmingham, AL 35202; 205-323-5461. Attn: Patricia Tucker Fox.

Mobile Venture Club, c/o Mobile Area Chamber of Commerce, 451 Government Street, Mobile, AL 36652; 205-433-6951.

California
Sacramento Valley Venture Capital Forum, Univ. of California Graduate School of Management, Davis, CA 95616; 916-752-7395. Attn: Professor Richard Dorf.

Orange Coast Venture Group, P.O. Box 7282, Newport Beach, CA 92658; 714754-1191. Attn: Mike Reagan.

San Diego Venture Group, Girard Capital, 4320 La Jolla Village Dr., Suite 210, San Diego, CA 92122. Attn: Gregory Beck.

Connecticut
Connecticut Venture Group, 200 Fisher Drive, Avon, CT 06001; 203-677-0183. Attn: Sam McKay.

District of Columbia
Baltimore-Washington Venture Group, Michael Dingman Center for Entrepreneurship, College Park, MD 20742-7215; 301-405-2144. Attn: John C. VerSteeg.

Florida
Gold Coast Venture Capital Club, 110 E. Atlantic Ave., #208E, Delray Beach, FL 33444; 407-272-1040, 1-800-624-6009 (in state only). Attn: Oscar Ziemba, Sy Lubner.

Gulf Coast Venture Club, P.O. Box 5042, South Station, Fort Myers, FL 33901; 813-939-5714.

Idaho
Treasure Valley Venture Capital Forum, Idaho Small Business Development Center, Boise State University College of Business, 1910 University Drive, Boise, ID 83725; 208-385-1640.

Iowa
Venture Club of Iowa City, ICAD Group, P.O. Box 2567, Iowa City, IA 52244; 319-354-3939.

Minnesota
The Entrepreneur's Network, 1433 Utica Avenue S., Suite 70-3, Minneapolis, MN 55416; 612-542-0682.

Michigan
New Enterprise Forum, 211 E. Huron #1, Ann Arbor, MI 48174; 313-662-0550.

New York
Rochester Venture Capital Group, 100 Corporate Woods, Suite 300, Rochester, NY 14623; 716-232-4160.

Wisconsin
Wisconsin Venture Network, 823 N. Second Street, Suite 605, Milwaukee, WI 53203; 414-278-7070.

Other groups with information on venture capital include:

The CPA Firm Coopers & Lybrand
1251 Avenue of the Americas
New York, NY 10020   212-536-2000

The firm publishes several publications on venture capital including *Three Keys to Obtaining Venture Capital*, *The Economic Impact of Venture Capital*, *Venture Capital: The Price of Growth*, and *Charting a Course for Corporate Venture Capital*.

Venture Economics, Inc.
1180 Raymond Blvd.
Newark, NJ 07102   201-622-4500

The company provides information, research and consulting services for corporations, major institutions and government agencies on venture capital trends. Its database contains information on more than 6,000 companies that have received venture capital. Among its publications are:

Venture Capital Journal, a monthly periodical that cites new issues and trends in venture capital investments. Subscription rate is $695.

Pratt's Guide to Venture Capital Sources, an annual directory that lists 800 venture capital firms in the U.S. and Canada. It also includes articles recommending ways to raise venture capital. $175.

Venture Capital Journal Yearbook, an annual publication that summarizes investment activities of the previous year. It includes statistics and data about capital commitments and investment activities in specific industries. $175.

Additional Reading Material

A Venture Capital Primer for Small Business, a U.S. Small Business Administration publication that identifies what venture capital resources are available and explains how to develop a proposal for obtaining these funds. 50 cents. SBA Publications, P.O. Box 30, Denver, CO 80201-0030. Item number FM5.

Venture Capital Handbook. An entrepreneur's quick guide to obtaining capital to start a business, buy a business, or expand an existing business. David Gladstone. Prentice Hall, Englewood Cliffs, NJ 07632. 1988. Includes listing of venture capital companies listed state by state.

Venture Capital: Finding A Rich Angel

The MacMillan Small Business Handbook. Mark Stevens. MacMillan Publishing Co., 866 Third Ave., New York, NY 10022. 1988. $35. Provides information on finding venture capital and writing winning business plans. Includes listing of Small Business Investment Companies, types of venture capital firms and information on preparing a venture capital proposal.

Mancuso's Small Business Resource Guide. Joseph R. Mancuso. Prentice Hall Press, Gulf & Western Bldg., New York, NY 10023. 1988. $19.95. Lists Small Business Administration regional offices in the U.S., Small Business Development Centers and Small Business Investment Companies.

The Best of INC. Guide to Finding Capital. Editors of Inc. Magazine. Prentice Hall Press, New York. 1988.

Get Free Help With The New Law
Requiring Businesses To Accommodate The Disabled

A new federal law makes it illegal for businesses to discriminate against individuals with physical or mental disabilities (including AIDS). Employers are required to accommodate the disabled, and public places like restaurants, hotels, retail stores, and rental car agencies must accommodate the disabled as customers. All new construction must be made accessible, and alterations must be made to existing facilities to accommodate the disabled as long as the cost does not impose an undue hardship.

The law called, the *American with Disabilities Act*, required businesses with 25 or more employees to make changes by July 1992. And they must have done this whether they hire disabled workers or not. Companies with 15 to 24 employees have until July 1994 to make the necessary changes. Businesses that deal with the public, like restaurants, retails stores, etc., had to have been made accessible to the disabled by January 26, 1992.

How To Beat The New Crop Of Fear Consultants

New laws, like this one that affect so many businesses, will instantly spawn an entire new industry of high priced consultants, lawyers, architects and other specialists who live off a business's fear of the unknown.

You don't have to pay a high consultant to eliminate your fears. You can get the information better than most of these consultants, and you can get it free, by going directly to the source....the government. You can also get free architectural advice, consulting help, information on funding needed construction and most any other assistance you need to help determine if you have to make changes in you business. And you can also get free help in choosing the plans, construction materials, and contractors to implement them.

Why Was This Law Passed?

According to a 1988 study by the Bureau of the Census there are currently 13 million Americans aged 16 to 64 who do not live in an institution or have a disability that limits the kind or amount of work they can do. Only 5 million of these are currently employed. Studies show that up to 6 million more would be employed once the new rules go into effect. The White House estimates the cost to business for implementing these laws will be $1 to $2 billion. The current annual cost in federal benefits to the disabled is $60 billion. The law is designed not only to tap into the resources of those disabled who wish to work but also to substantially reduce the outlays in federal benefits. The U.S. Department of Labor and the General Accounting Office estimate that half of all workers with disabilities can be employed with changes that cost less than $50. Twenty percent of disabled workers require measures that cost $50 to $100, and another 20% would cost between $500 and $1,000 each to employ. The price of this new legislation will be paid for by business but there is help.

What Your Business Must Do
and How To Do It

The new law has financed 10 Regional Disability and Business Accommodation Centers to which businesses and individuals can turn to find out more the law. Businesses can learn exactly what changes have to be made to their facilities. In many cases free consultants will come out to your business and identify what will have to be changed and how it can be changed in the least expensive manner.

The objectives of these centers are to help the community by:
- disseminating information;
- providing direct technical assistance;
- providing referrals for specialized information and technical assistance; and
- training interested and affected parties.

Call 1-800-949-4232 or contact the office listed below which covers your state:

Region I (CT, ME, MA, NH, RI, VT)
Jennifer Eckel, Director
ADA Regional Disability and Business
   Accommodation Center
145 Newbury Street   Voice/TDD: 207-874-6535
Portland, ME 04101   FAX: 207-874-6529

Region II (NJ, NY, PR)
Richard Dodds, Director
ADA Regional Disability and Business
   Accommodation Center
United Cerebral Palsy Association   Voice: 609-392-4004
354 S. Broad Street   TDD: 609-392-7044
Trenton, NJ 08608   FAX: 609-392-3505

Region III (DE, DC, MD, PA, VA, WV)
Sharon Mistler, Director
ADA Regional Disability and Business
   Accommodation Center
Independence Center of Northern VA
2111 Wilson Blvd., #40   Voice/TDD: 703-525-3268
Arlington, VA 22201   FAX: 703-525-6835

Region IV (AL, FL, GA, KY, MS, NC, SC, TN)
Shelly Kaplan, Director
ADA Regional Disability and Business
   Accommodation Center
United Cerebral Palsy Association/
U.S. - National Alliance of Business   404-888-0022
1776 Peachtree Road, #310   TDD: 404-888-9098
Atlanta, GA 30309   FAX: 404-888-9091

Region V (IL, IN, MI, MN, OH, WI)
David Braddock, Director
ADA Regional Disability and Business

Accommodation Center
University of Illinois at Chicago
University Affiliated Program in
  Developmental Disabilities
1640 W. Roosevelt Road
Chicago, IL 60608　　　Voice/TDD: 312-413-7756

Region VI (AR, LA, NM, OK, TX)
Lex Frieden, Director
ADA Regional Disability and Business
  Accommodation Center
Independent Living Research Utilization
The Institute for Rehabilitation
  and Research　　　713-520-0232
2323 W. Shepherd Blvd., Suite 1000　FAX: 713-520-5785
Houston, TX 77019　　　TDD: 713-520-5136

Region VII (IA, KS, NE, MO)
Jim DeJong, Director
ADA Regional Disability and Business
  Accommodation Center
University of Missouri at Columbia
4816 Santoma Dr.
Columbia, MO 65203　　　Voice/TDD: 314-882-3600

Region VIII (CO, MT, ND, SD, UT, WY)
Randy W. Dipner, Director
ADA Regional Disability and Business
  Accommodation Center
Meeting the Challenge, Inc.
3630 Sinton Road, Suite 103　Voice/TDD: 719-444-0252
Colorado Springs, CO 80907-5072　FAX: 719-444-0269

Region IX (AZ, CA, HI, NV)
Erica Jones, Director
ADA Regional Disability and Business
  Accommodation Center
Berkeley Planning Associates
440 Grand Avenue, Suite 500　Voice: 510-465-7884
Oakland, CA 94610　　　TDD: 510-465-3172

Region X (AK, ID, OR, WA)
Toby Olson, Director
Washington State Governor's Committee
ADA Regional Disability and Business
  Accommodation Center　　206-438-3168
P.O. Box 9046　　　TDD: 206-438-3167
Olympia, WA 98507-9046　　FAX: 206-438-4014

More Info About Laws and Requirements

If one of the regional centers listed above does not satisfy your information needs, you can always get more detail about the law and its implications by contacting either of the following:

President's Committee on Employment of People with
  Disabilities
1331 F St, NW, 3rd Floor
Washington, DC 20004　　　202-376-6200

Civil Rights Division
U.S. Department of Justice
Coordination and Review Section　　202-514-0301
P.O. Box 66118　　　TDD: 202-514-0381
Washington, DC 20035　　　TDD: 202-514-0383

Franchising: How To Select The Best Opportunity

Franchising can be the way for you to launch a new business, but it is not risk free, and needs to be entered into with a degree of caution. According to the Federal Trade Commission (FTC), there is no accurate data available to prove that franchises have a lower failure rate than new businesses, so there are a few steps you need to take in order to protect yourself. The following organizations and publications will help you find the right franchise for you.

Organizations

Federal Trade Commission (FTC)
Bureau of Consumer Protection
Division of Enforcement
Pennsylvania Avenue at 6th Street, NW
Washington, DC 20580
Craig Tregillus   202-326-2970

Buying a franchise or a business opportunity may be appealing if you want to be your own boss, but have limited capital and business experience. However, without carefully investigating a business before you purchase, you may make a serious mistake. It is important to find out if a particular business is right for you and if it has the potential to yield the financial return you expect. A Federal Trade Commission rule requires that franchise and business opportunity sellers provide certain information to help you in your decision. Under the FTC rule, a franchise or business opportunity seller must give you a detailed disclosure document at least ten business days before you pay any money or legally commit yourself to a purchase. This document gives 20 important items of information about the business, including: the names, addresses, and telephone numbers of other purchasers; the fully-audited financial statement of the seller; the background and experience of the business's key executives; the cost required to start and maintain the business; and the responsibilities you and the seller will have to each other once you buy. The disclosure document is a valuable tool that not only helps you obtain information about a proposed business, but assists you in comparing it with other businesses. If you are not given a disclosure document, ask why you did not receive one. Some franchise or business opportunity sellers may not be required to give you a disclosure document. If any franchise or business opportunity says it is not covered by the rule, you may want to verify it with the FTC, an attorney, or a business advisor. Even if the business is not required to give the document, you still may want to ask for the data to help you make an informed investment decision.

Some Important Advice From The FTC:

1. Study the disclosure document and proposed contracts carefully.

2. Talk to current owners. Ask them how the information in the disclosure document matches their experiences with the company. Visit the franchises to be sure they really exist. One group you should interview is those who have been in business less than a year. Ask about the company's training program. Find out how long it took to break even and if the company's estimate of operating and working capital was accurate. The second group should be those in business for six years. Find out what kind of deal they got for the franchise and compare it to yours. There are strains in every franchise marriage. Find out what they are. Some franchises hire their own accountants to double check the franchises' accounting. When mistakes are made, it is often attributed to the franchise.

3. Investigate earnings claims. Earnings claims are only estimates. The FTC rule requires companies to have in writing the facts on which they base their earnings claims. Make sure you understand the basis for a seller's earnings claims.

4. Shop around: compare franchises with other available business opportunities. You may discover that other companies offer benefits not available from the first company you considered. The *Franchise Opportunities Handbook*, which is published annually by the Department of Commerce, describes more than 1,400 companies that offer franchises. Contact other companies and ask for their disclosure documents. Then you can compare offerings.

5. Listen carefully to the sales presentation. Some sales tactics should signal caution. A seller with a good offer does not have to use pressure.

6. Get the seller's promises in writing. Any important promises you get from a salesperson should be written into the contract you sign.

7. Consider getting professional advice. You may want to get a lawyer, an accountant, or a business advisor to read the disclosure document and proposed contract to counsel you and help you get the best deal.

Although the FTC cannot resolve individual disputes, information about your experiences and concerns is vital to the enforcement of the Franchise and Business Opportunities Rule. The time to protect yourself is before you buy rather than after. Only fifteen states give you private rights to sue, and there is often a limited ability to recover. A franchiser knows your financial situation, and can often outwait you. Many franchise owners have no money left to hire a lawyer to try to recoup their losses. The FTC has two phone numbers of places you can call to ask for assistance. The Franchise Complaint Line, 202-326-3128, is staffed by a duty attorney and takes complaints about franchisers or disclosure requirements. The second number is:

FTC Franchise Rule Information Hotline   202-326-3220
    Information on Federal Presale Disclosure Requirements
    for Franchise and Business Opportunity
    Ventures ext.2

Franchising

Information on Disclosure Statements for Specific Franchise and Business Opportunity Companies . . ext.3

Information on Complaints on File for a Particular Franchise or Business Opportunity Venture ext.4

For Filing a Complaint Against a Franchise or Business Opportunity Venture ext.5

List of States with Franchise Laws and their Telephone Numbers. ext.6

List of States with Business Opportunity Laws and their Telephone Numbers. ext.7

To Speak With an Attorney ext.1

Franchise and Business Opportunities -- a four-page guide about what to consider before buying a franchise.

The Franchise Rule: Questions and Answers -- a one-page summary of the disclosure rule and penalties for infractions by the franchiser.

Franchise Rule Summary -- a seven-page, detailed technical explanation of the federal disclosure rule, which requires franchisers to furnish a document (with information on twenty topics) to the potential franchisee before a sale. This includes an explanation and description of the Uniform Franchise Offering Circular (UFOC) required in fourteen states.

State Agencies Administering Franchise Disclosure Laws

California - filing required
Franchise Division
Department of Corporations
3700 Wilshire Blvd., Suite 600
Los Angeles, CA 90010   213-736-2741

Hawaii - filing required
Franchise and Securities Division
State Department of Commerce
1010 Richards Street
Honolulu, HI 96813   808-548-2021

Illinois - filing required
Franchise Division
Office of Attorney General
500 South Second Street
Springfield, IL 62706   217-782-1090

Indiana - filing required
Franchise Division
Office of Secretary of State
302 W. Washington Street, #E-111
Indianapolis, IN 46204   317-232-6681

Maryland - filing required
Franchise Office
Division of Securities
200 St. Paul Place, 20th Floor

Baltimore, MD 21202   301-576-6360

Michigan - filing required
Antitrust and Franchise Unit
Office of Attorney General
670 Law Building, P.O. Box 30215
Lansing, MI 48909   517-373-7117

Minnesota - filing required
Franchise Division
Department of Commerce
133 East Seventh St.
St. Paul, MN 55101   612-296-6328

New York - filing required
Franchise and Securities Division
State Department of Law
120 Broadway
New York, NY 10271   212-416-8211

North Dakota - filing required
Franchise Division
Office of Securities Commission
600 East Boulevard, 5th floor
Bismarck, ND 58505   701-224-4712

Oregon - no filing
Corporate and Securities Division
Department of Insurance and Finance
Labor and Industries Bldg.
Salem, OR 97310   503-378-4387

Rhode Island - filing required
Franchise Office
Division of Securities
233 Richmond St., Suite 232
Providence, RI 02903-4232   401-277-3048

South Dakota - filing required
Franchise Office
Division of Securities
118 W. Capitol Ave.
Pierre, SD 57501   605-773-4013

Virginia - filing required
Franchise Office
State Corporation Commission
1300 E. Main St., 9th Floor
Richmond, VA 23219   804-371-9051

Washington - filing required
Franchise Office
Business License Services
State Securities Division
P.O. Box 9033
Olympia, WA 98507-9033   206-753-6928

Wisconsin - filing required
Franchise Office
Wisconsin Securities Commission
P.O. Box 1768
Madison, WI 53701   608-266-8559

States With Business Opportunity Laws For Franchises

California	619-237-6553
Colorado	203-566-4560
Florida	904-488-9805; 1-800-342-2176
Georgia	404-651-8600
Indiana	317-232-6331
Iowa	515-281-4441
Kentucky	502-564-2200
Louisiana	504-342-7373
Maine	207-582-8760
Maryland	410-576-6360
Michigan	517-373-7117
Nebraska	402-471-2171
New Hampshire	603-271-3641
North Carolina	919-733-3924
Ohio	614-466-8831; 1-800-282-0515
Oklahoma	405-521-2451
South Carolina	803-734-2168
South Dakota	605-773-4823
Texas	512-475-1769
Utah	801-530-4849
Virginia	804-786-0594; 1-800-451-1525
Washington	206-753-6210

International Franchise Association (IFA)
1350 New York Avenue, NW
Washington, DC 20005
John Reynolds, Public Relations Officer   202-628-8000
Founded in 1960, the International Franchise Association (IFA) has more than 600 franchiser members, including thirty-five overseas. IFA members are accepted into the organization only after meeting stringent requirements regarding number of franchises, length of time in business, and financial stability. The IFA offers about twenty-five educational conferences and seminars yearly, including an annual convention and a legal symposium. There is a program on financing and venture capital designed to bring together franchisers and franchisees. Each year the association also sponsors several trade shows, open to the public, so that franchisers may attract potential franchisees. There is a library, but as yet no database, for members. Mr. Buzzy Gordon, Public Relations Officer, will answer inquiries from the public and make referrals for speakers, courses, and resources on franchising.

The International Franchise Association publishes the following publications, which you can order by phone (1-800-543-1038)

To Help You Buy a Franchise

Answers to the 21 Most Commonly Asked Questions - $2.25
Investigate Before Investing - $5.00
Is Franchising For You? - $5.00
Franchise Opportunities Guide - $15.00
Franchising: The Inside Story - $20.00

To Help You Franchise Your Business

Blueprint For Franchising A Business - $28.00
Financial Strategies For The Growing Franchisor - $25.00
The Franchise Advantage - $30.00
The Franchise Option - $26.00

Franchising: A Planning And Sales Compliance Guide - $48.00
Franchising & Licensing - $27.00
Franchising in the U.K. - $35.00
Franchising - The How-To Book - $20.00
How To Be A Franchisor - $8.00
How To Franchise Internationally - $30.00
How To Organize A Franchise Advisory Council - $10.00
McDonald's: Behind the Arches - $22.00
Multiple-Unit Franchising - $25.00
Public Relations For The Franchise - $21.00

Legal Information

Franchise Legal Digest - $195.00
Franchising: Business and the Law (VHS set) - $200.00
The Law of Franchising (VHS set) - $200.00
The IFA Compliance Kit - $225.00
International Franchising - $175.00
Legal Symposium binder - $250.00
Mock Trial (VHS set) - $195.00
Survey of Foreign Laws and Regulations Affecting International Franchising - $140.00

Reference Material

A Comparison of International vs. Domestic - $50.00
Conversion of Dealer Organizations - $395.00
Franchise Marketing & Sales Survey - $295.00
Franchising in the Economy - $25.00
Franchisor/Franchisee Relations Survey - $5.00
The Future of Franchising - $10.00
Glossary of Franchising Terms - $4.00

Audiocassettes, Videotapes, Computer Diskettes

Franchise Finder (IBM compatible) - $79.00
Franchise Finder (Macintosh compatible) - $79.00
Franchising: A World of Opportunity (VHS) - $145.00
Franchising: How To Be In Business For Yourself Not By Yourself (VHS) - $49.95
How to Select a Franchise (Audio) - $15.00
IFA: A World of Difference (VHS) - $20.00
Let's Talk: Bringing Your Franchise To Canada (VHS) - $95.00
Your Future in Franchising (VHS) - $75.00
Franchising World Magazine - $12.00

Minority Business Development Agency
Department of Commerce
14th and Constitution Ave, NW
Washington, DC 20230   202-377-3237
The Minority Business Development Agency (MBDA) can provide information to all business, not just minority-owned businesses, regarding franchising. They are the publishers of *Franchise Opportunities Handbook* -- a bible of franchising information, this 390 page directory includes detailed listings of 1,500 companies, facts about the franchising industry, guidance for investing in a franchise, resource listings of helpful agencies and organizations, and a bibliography. Cost is $15.00; U.S. Government Printing Office, Superintendent of Documents, Washington, DC 20420; 202-783-3238. MBDA has several other free publications to assist people who are interested in learning more about franchising. They can also answer

questions regarding FTC rules, major growth areas, how does a franchise chain start, where do franchise sales come from, and other general questions.

Experts

Michael Wood
Business Development Office
U.S. Small Business Administration (SBA)
1441 L Street, NW
Washington, DC 20005   202-205-6665

Mr. Wood is coordinator of a coalition between the International Franchising Association (IFA) and the Small Business Administration (SBA), and is available to answer questions and provide assistance to regional offices or the SBA. Mr. Wood leads training programs at various IFA exhibits and shows for people interested in buying a franchise. Your local SBA office also may run seminars on franchising. Some SBA District Offices, such as the one in Kansas City, hold large Franchise Expos, which deal with all aspects of the franchise business. The SBA has a free 4 page brochure titled, *Evaluating Franchise Opportunities*, for people considering franchises as a way to start a business. Contact your local SBA office for more information (1-800-827-5722 for the office nearest you).

Government Contracts:
How To Sell Your Goods And Services To The World's Largest Buyer

The Federal Government spends over $180 billion each year buying everything from toilet paper to bombs. They buy these goods and services from someone, and why can't that someone be you? All you need to do is learn to talk "governmentese", and get yourself into the purchasing loop. There are just a few easy steps you need to take to get you and your company into the government contracting business. Last year the government took action (either initiating or modifying) on 368,372 contracts.

Step 1

Each department within the federal government has a procurement office that buys whatever the department needs. Most of these offices have put together their own *Doing Business With the Department of ____* publication, which usually explains procurement policies, procedures, and programs. This booklet also contains a list of procurement offices, contact people, subcontracting opportunities, and a solicitation mailing list. Within each department is also an Office of Small and Disadvantaged Business Utilization, whose sole purpose is to push the interests of the small business, and to make sure these companies get their fair share of the government contracts. Another resource is your local Small Business Administration Office which should have a listing of U.S. Government Procurement Offices in your state.

Step 2

Once you have familiarized yourself with the overview, you need to find out who is buying what from whom and how much, as well as who wants what when. There are three ways to find out this information.

A. Daily Procurement News
Each weekday, the *Commerce Business Daily* (CBD) gives a complete listing of products and services (over $25,000) wanted by the U.S. government -- products and services that your business may be selling. Each listing includes the following: the product or service, along with a short description; name and address of the agency; deadline for proposals or bids; phone number to request specifications; and the solicitation number of the product or service needed. Many business concerns, including small businesses, incorporate CBD review into their government marketing activities. To obtain a $208/year subscription, contact Superintendent of Documents, U.S. Government Printing Office, Washington, DC 20402; 202-783-3238.

B. Federal Data Systems Division (FDSD)
This Center distributes consolidated information about federal purchases, including research and development. FDSD can tell you how much the federal government spent last quarter on products and services, which agencies made those purchases, and who the contractors were. FDSD summarizes this information through two types of reports: The FDSD standard report and the FDSD special report. The standard report is a free, quarterly compilation containing statistical procurement information in "snapshot" form for over 60 federal agencies, as well as several charts, graphs, and tables which compare procurement activities by state, major product and service codes, method of procurement, and contractors. The report further includes quarterly and year-to-year breakdowns of amounts and percentages spent on small, women-owned, and minority businesses. Special reports are prepared upon request for a fee, based on computer and labor costs. They are tailored to the specific categories, which can be cross-tabulated in numerous ways. A special report can help you analyze government procurement and data trends, identify competitors and locate federal markets for individual products or services. Your Congressman may have access to the Federal Procurement Database from his/her office in Washington, which you may be able to use for free. For more information, contact Federal Data Systems Division, General Services Administration, 7th and D Street, SW, Room 5652, Washington, DC 20407; 202-401-1529.

C. Other Contracts
For contracts under $25,000, you need to be placed on a department's list for solicitation bids on the contracts. The mailing list forms are available through the Procurement Office, the Office of Small and Disadvantaged Business Utilization, or your local Small Business Association office. Last year 18.7 billion dollars was spent on these "small" purchases, so these contracts are not to be overlooked.

Step 3: Subcontracting Opportunities

All of the federal procurement offices or Offices of Small and Disadvantaged Business Utilization (SBDU) can provide you with information regarding subcontracting. Many of the departments' prime contracts require that the prime contractor maximize small business subcontracting opportunities. Many prime contractors produce special publications which can be helpful to those interested in subcontracting. The SDBU Office can provide you with more information on the subcontracting process, along with a directory of prime contractors. Another good source for subcontract assistance is your local Small Business Administration (SBA) office, 1-800-827-5722. SBA develops subcontracting opportunities for small business by maintaining close contact with large business prime contractors and referring qualified small firms to them. The SBA has developed agreements and close working relationships with hundreds of prime contractors who cooperate by offering small firms opportunities to compete for their subcontracts. In addition, to complete SBA's compliance responsibilities, commercial market representatives monitor prime contractors in order to assess their compliance with laws governing subcontracting opportunities for small businesses.

Step 4: Small Business Administration's 8(a) Program

Are you a socially or economically disadvantaged person who has a business? This group includes, but is not limited to, Black Americans, Hispanic Americans, Native Americans, Asian Pacific Americans, and Subcontinent Asian Americans. Socially and economically disadvantaged individuals represent a significant percentage of U.S. citizens, yet account for a disproportionately small percentage of total U.S. business revenues. The 8(a) program assists firms to participate in the business sector and to become independently competitive in the marketplace. SBA may provide participating firms with procurement, marketing, financial, management or other technical assistance. A Business Opportunity Specialist will be assigned to each firm that participates, and is responsible for providing the firm with access to assistance that can help the firm fulfill its business goals. SBA undertakes an extensive effort to provide government contracting opportunities to participating businesses. SBA has the Procurement Automated Source System (PASS) which places your company's capabilities online so that they may be available to Government agencies and major corporations when they request potential bidders for contracts and subcontracts. To apply for the 8(a) program you must attend an interview session with an official in the SBA field office in your area. For more information, contact your local Small Business Administration Office, or you can call 1-800-827-5722 for the SBA office nearest you.

Step 5: Bond

A Surety bond is often a prerequisite for government and private sector contracts. This is particularly true when the contract involves construction. In order for the company to qualify for an SBA Guarantee Bond, they must make the bonding company aware of the capabilities based on past contract performance and meeting of financial obligations. SBA can assist firms to obtain surety bonding for contracts that do not exceed $1,250,000. SBA is authorized, when appropriate circumstances occur, to guarantee as much as 90 percent of losses suffered by a surety resulting from a breach of terms of a bond.

Step 6: Publications

The Government Printing Office has several publications for sale which explain the world of government contracts. For ordering information, contact Superintendent of Documents, Government Printing Office, Washington, DC 20402; 202-783-3238.

* *U.S. Government Purchasing and Sales Directory* ($5.50): The Directory is an alphabetical listing of the products and services bought by the military departments, and a separate listing of the civilian agencies. The Directory also includes an explanation of the ways in which the SBA can help a business obtain government prime contracts and subcontracts, data on government sales of surplus property, and comprehensive descriptions of the scope of the government market for research and development.

* *Guide to the Preparation of Offers for Selling to the Military* ($4.75)

* *Small Business Specialists* ($3.75)

* *Small Business Subcontracting Directory* ($7.00): designed to aid small businesses interested in subcontracting opportunities within the Department of Defense (DOD). The guide is arranged alphabetically by State and includes the name and address of each current DOD prime contractor as well as the product or service being provided to DOD.

* *Women Business Owners; Selling to the Federal Government* ($3.75)

* *Selling to the Military*, ($8.00)

Step 7: What is GSA?

General Services Administration (GSA) is the Government's business agent. On an annual budget of less than half a billion dollars, it directs and coordinates nearly $8 billion a year worth of purchases, sales, and services. Its source of supply is private enterprise, and its clients are all branches of the Federal Government. GSA plans and manages leasing, purchase, or construction of office buildings, laboratories, and warehouses; buys and delivers nearly $4 billion worth of goods and services; negotiates the prices and terms for an additional $2.3 billion worth of direct business between federal groups and private industry; sets and interprets the rules for federal travel and negotiates reduced fares and lodging rates for federal travelers; and manages a 92,000 vehicle fleet with a cumulative yearly mileage of over 1 billion. For a copy of *Doing Business With GSA, GSA's Annual Report*, or other information regarding GSA, contact Office of Publication, General Services Administration, 18th and F Streets, NW, Washington, DC 20405; 202-501-1235. For information on GSA's architect and engineer services, such as who is eligible for GSA professional services contracts, how to find out about potential GSA projects, what types of contracts are available, and where and how to apply, contact Office of Design and Construction, GSA, 18th and F Streets, NW, Washington, DC 20405; 202-501-1888. Information on specifications and standards of the Federal Government is contained in a booklet, *Guide to Specifications and Standards*, which is available free from Specifications Sections, General Services Administration, 470 E L'Enfant Plaza, SW, Suite 8100, Washington, DC 20407; 202-755-0325.

Step 8: Bid and Contract Protests

The General Accounting Office (GAO) resolves disputes between agencies and bidders for government contracts, including grantee award actions. The free publication, *Bid Protests at GAO; A Descriptive Guide*, contains information on GAO's procedures for determining legal questions arising from the awarding of government contracts. Contact Information Handling and Support Facilities, General Accounting Office, Gaithersburg, MD 20877; 202-275-6241. For Contract Appeals, the GSA Board of Contract Appeals works to resolve disputes arising out of contracts with GSA, the Departments of Treasury, Education, Commerce, and other independent government agencies. The Board also hears and decides bid protest arising out of government-wide automated data processing (ADP) procurements. A contractor may elect to use either the GSA

Board or the General Accounting Office for resolution of an ADP bid protest. Contractors may elect to have their appeals processed under the Board's accelerated procedures if the claim is $50,000 or less, or under the small claims procure if the claim is $10,000 or less. Contractors may also request that a hearing be held at a location convenient to them. With the exception of small claims decisions, contractors can appeal adverse Board decisions to the U.S. Court of Appeals for the Federal Circuit. For more information, contact Board of Contract Appeals, General Services Administration, 18th and F Streets, NW, Washington, DC 20405; 202-501-0720. There are other Contract Appeals Boards for the other Departments. One of the last paragraphs in your government contract should specify which Board you are to go to if a problem arises.

Free Local Help:
The Best Place To Start To Sell To The Government

Within each state there are places you can contact to receive help in getting started in the federal procurement process. As was stated previously, your local Small Business Administration (SBA) office is a good resource. In addition to their other services, the SBA can provide you with a list of Federal Procurement Offices based in your state, so you can visit them in person. Other places to turn are your local Small Business Development Center (look under Economic Development in your phone book). These offices are funded jointly by federal and state governments, and are usually associated with the state university system. They are aware of the federal procurement process, and can help you draw up a sensible business plan. Some states have established programs to assist businesses in the federal procurement process for all departments in the government. These programs are designed to help businesses learn about the bidding process, the resources available, and provide information on how the procurement system operates. They can match the product or service you are selling with the appropriate agency, and then help you market your wares. Several programs have online bid matching services, whereby if a solicitation appears in the *Commerce Business Daily* that matches what your company markets, then the program will contact you to start the bid process. They can then request the appropriate documents, and assist you to achieve your goal. These Procurement Assistance Offices (PAOs) are partially funded by the Department of Defense to assist businesses with Defense Procurement. For a current listing of PAOs contact:

Defense Logistics Agency
Office of Small and Disadvantaged Utilization
Bldg. 4, Cameron Station, Room 4B110
Alexandria, VA 22304-6100   703-274-6471

Let Your Congressman Help You

Are you trying to market a new product to a Department of the Federal Government? Need to know where to try to sell your wares? Is there some problem with your bid? Your Congressman can be of assistance. They want business in their state to boom, so they will make an effort to assist companies in obtaining federal contracts. Frequently, they will write a letter to accompany your bid, or if you are trying to market a new product, they will write a letter to the procurement office requesting that they review your product. Your congressman can also be your trouble-shooter. If there is some problem with your bid, your Congressman can assist you in determining and resolving the problem, and can provide you with information on the status of your bid. Look in the blue pages of your phone book for your Senators' or Representatives' phone numbers, or call them in Washington at 202-224-3121.

Small Business Set-Asides

The Small Business Administration (SBA) encourages government purchasing agencies to set-aside suitable government purchases for exclusive small business competition. A purchase which is restricted to small business bidders is identified by a set-aside clause in the invitation for bids or request for proposals. There is no overall listing of procurements which are, or have been, set-aside for small business. A small business learns which purchases are reserved for small business by getting listed on bidders' lists. It also can help keep itself informed of set-aside opportunities by referring to the *Commerce Business Daily*. Your local SBA office can provide you with more information on set-asides, as can the Procurement Assistance Offices listed below. You can locate your nearest SBA office by calling 1-800-827-5722.

Veterans Assistance

Each Small Business Administration District Office has a Veterans Affairs Officer which can assist veteran-owned businesses in obtaining government contracts. Although there is no such thing as veterans set-aside contracts, the Veterans Administration does make an effort to fill its contracts using veteran-owned businesses. Contact your local SBA office for more information.

Woman-Owned Business Assistance

There are over 3.7 million women-owned businesses in the United States, and the number is growing each year. Current government policy requires federal contracting officers to increase their purchases from women-owned businesses. Although the women-owned firms will receive more opportunities to bid, they still must be the lowest responsive and responsible bidder to win the contract. To assist these businesses, each SBA district office has a Women's Business Representative, who can provide you with information regarding government programs. Most of the offices hold a *Selling to the Federal Government* seminar, which is designed to educate the business owner on the ins and outs of government procurement. There is also a helpful publication, *Women Business Owners: Selling to the Federal Government*, which provides information on the procurement opportunities available. Contact your local SBA office or your Procurement Assistance Office for more information.

Minority and Labor Surplus Area Assistance

Are you a socially or economically disadvantaged person who has a business? This group includes, but is not limited to, Black Americans, Hispanic Americans, Native Americans, Asian Pacific Americans, and Subcontinent Asian Americans. Socially and economically disadvantaged individuals represent a significant percentage of U.S. citizens yet account for a disproportionately small percentage of total U.S. business revenues. The 8(a) program assists firms to participate in the business sector and to become independently competitive in the marketplace. SBA may provide participating firms with procurement, marketing, financial, management or other technical assistance. A Business Opportunity Specialist will be assigned to each firm that participates, and is responsible for providing the firm with access to assistance that can help the firm fulfill its business goals. SBA undertakes an extensive effort to provide government contracting opportunities to participating businesses. SBA has the Procurement Automated Source System (PASS) which places your company's capabilities online so that they may be available to government agencies and major corporations when they request potential bidders for contracts and subcontracts. To apply for the 8(a) program you must attend an interview session with an official in the SBA field office in your area. Some areas of the country have been determined to be labor surplus areas, which means there is a high rate of unemployment. Your local SBA office can tell you if you live in such an area, as some contracts are set-asides for labor surplus areas. For more information contact your local Small Business Administration office, or you can call 1-800-827-5722 for the SBA office nearest you.

Alabama

University of Alabama at Birmingham, School of Business, Ms. Patricia E. Thompson, UAB Station, Birmingham, AL 35294; 205-934-7260.

Alaska

University of Alaska at Anchorage, Small Business Development Center, Ms. Jan Fredericks, 430 W. Seventh Ave., Suite 110, Anchorage, AK 99501; 907-274-7232.

Arizona

Arizona Procurement Technical Assistance Network, Arizona Department of Commerce, 3800 N. Central Ave., Bldg. D, Phoenix, AZ 85012; 602-280-1348.

National Center for American Indians Enterprise Development, National Center Headquarters, Mr. Steve L.A. Stallings, 953 E. Juanita Ave., Mesa, AZ 85204; 602-831-7524.

Arkansas

Southern Arkansas University (SAU), Mr. Robert E. Graham, P.O. Box 1239, Hwy. 19 North, Magnolia, AR 71753; 501-235-4375.

California

c/o AMD, Procurement Assistance Center m/s 31, Dr. Murray P. Leavitt, 901 Thompson Place, Sunnyvale, CA 94088-3453; 408-739-6283.

Private Industry Council of Imperial County, Inc., 1411 State Street, El Centro, CA 92243; 619-353-5050.

Merced County Office of Economic and Strategic Development, Contract Procurement Center, Karen Prentiss, 1632 N. Street, Merced, CA 95340; 209-752-3891.

PIC of Solano County, Business Services Division, Terrye Miller-Davis, 320 Campus Lane, Suisun, CA 94585; 707-864-3370.

Delaware

Delaware State College, Dept. of Economics and Business, Dr. Winston Awadzi, 1200 N. Dupont Hwy., Dover, DE 19901; 302-739-3521.

Florida

University of West Florida, Florida Procurement Technical Assistance Program, Mr. Jerry Cartwright, 11000 University Parkway, Bldg. 38, Pensacola, FL 32514; 904-474-3016.

Georgia

Columbus College, Division of Continuing Education, Columbus, GA 31993-2399; 404-649-1092.

Georgia Tech Research Corporation, Georgia Institute of Technology, Mr. Charles P. Catlett, O'Keefe Building, Room 246, Atlanta, GA 30332; 404-894-6121.

Hawaii

State of Hawaii, Department of Business, Economic Development and Tourism, Mr. Larry Nelson, P.O. Box 2359, Honolulu, HI 96804; 808-586-2598.

Idaho

Business Network, Mr. Larry Demirelli, Department of Commerce, 700 W. State St., Boise, ID 83720; 208-334-2470.

Illinois

State of Illinois, Department of Commerce and Community Affairs, 620 East Adams, 6th Floor, Springfield, IL 62701; 217-524-5696.

Indiana

Indiana Institute for New Business Ventures, Government Marketing Assistance Group, Mr. A. David Schaff, One North Capitol, Suite 1240, Indianapolis, IN 46204-2026; 317-264-5600.

Iowa

State of Iowa, Iowa Department of Economic Development, Mr. Allen Williams, 200 East Grand Avenue, Des Moines, IA 50309; 319-398-5665.

Kentucky

Kentucky Cabinet for Economic Development, Department of Existing Business and Industry, Mr. Bernard L. Williams, 500 Mero Street, Capital Plaza Tower, 23rd Floor, Frankfort, KY 40601; 1-800-626-2930.

Louisiana

Jefferson Parish Economic Development Commission, The Bid Center, Ms. Phyllis McLaren, 1221 Elmwood Park Blvd., Suite 405, Harahan, LA 70123; 504-736-6550.

Louisiana Productivity Center/USL, Procurement Technical Assistance Network, Mr. Stephen A. Killingsworth, P.O. Box 44172, 241 E. Lewis Street, Lafayette, LA 70504-4172; 318-231-6767.

Northwest Louisiana Government Procurement Center, Greater Shreveport Economic Development, P.O. Box 20074, 400 Edwards Street, Shreveport, LA 71120-0074; 318-677-2530.

Maine

Eastern Maine Development Corporation, Acadia Development Corporation, Mr. Richard L. Allen, One Cumberland Place, Suite 300, Bangor, ME 04402-2579; 207-942-6389, 1-800-339-6389 (ME), 1-800-955-6549.

Maryland

Morgan State University, School of Business and Management, Dr. Otis Thomas, Cold Spring Lane and Hillen Road, Baltimore, MD 21239; 410-319-3160.

Tri-County Council for Western Maryland Inc., Michael J. Wagoner, 111 South George Street, Cumberland, MD 21502; 301-777-2158.

Michigan

Genesee County Metropolitan Planning Commission, Procurement Technical Assistance Program, 1101 Beach Street, Room 223, Flint, MI 48502; 313-257-3010.

Kalamazoo County CGA, Inc., Government Contracting Office, Ms. Sandra Ledbetter, 100 W. Michigan, Suite 294, Kalamazoo, MI 49007; 616-342-0000.

Downriver Community Conference, Economic Development Department, 15100 Northline, Southgate, MI 48195; 313-281-0700.

Northwest Michigan Council of Governments, Procurement Technical Assistance Center, Mr. James F. Haslinger, P.O. Box 506, Traverse City, MI 49685-0506; 616-929-5036.

Saginaw County, Contract Procurement Office, Ms. JoAnn Crary, 301 E. Genessee, 4th Floor, Saginaw, MI 48607; 517-754-8222.

Schoolcraft College, Ms. Judi Zima, 18600 Haggerty Road, Livonia, MI 48152-2696; 313-462-4438.

Thumb Area Consortium/Growth Alliance, Local Procurement Office, Mr. Marvin N. Pichla, 3270 Wilson Street, Marlette, MI 48453; 517-635-3561.

Warren, Center Line, Sterling Heights, Chamber of Commerce, Ms. Janet E. Masi, 30500 Van Dyke Ave., Suite 118, Warren, MI 48093-2178; 313-751-3939.

West Central Michigan Employment and Training Consortium, Procurement Technical Assistance, Mr. John Calabrese, 110 Elm Street, Big Rapids, MI 49307; 616-796-4891.

Minnesota

Minnesota Project Innovation, Procurement Assistance Center, 111 3rd Ave., S, Minneapolis, MN 55401-2554; 612-338-3280.

Mississippi

Mississippi Contract Procurement Center, Mr. Charles W. Ryland, P.O. Box 610, Gulfport, MS 39502; 601-864-2961.

Missouri

Curators of the University of Missouri, University Extension, Steve Wyatt, 215 University Hall, Columbia, MO 65211; 314-882-0344.

Montana

Billings Area Business Incubator, James F. Ouldhouse, 115 No. Broadway, Suite 200, Billings, MT 59101; 406-256-6876.

High Plains Development Authority Inc., Janet L. Seagrave, #2 Railroad Square, P.O. Box 2568, Great Falls, MT 59401; 406-454-1934.

Procurement Technical Institute, Butte PTA Center, Greg Depuydt, 305 West Mercury, Butte, MT 59701; 406-782-7333.

Nebraska

Nebraska Department of Economic Development, Existing Business Assistance Division, Mr. Jack Ruff, 301 Centennial Mall So., P.O. Box 94666, Lincoln, NE 68509-4666; 402-471-3769.

Nevada

State of Nevada, Commission on Economic Development, Mr. Ray Horner, Capitol Complex, Carson City, NV 89710; 702-687-4325.

New Hampshire

Small Business Development Center, University Center, Room 311, 400 Commercial Street, Manchester, NH 03101; 603-743-3995, 1-800-322-0390 (in NH).

New Jersey

Elizabeth Development Corporation of New Jersey, Elizabeth Procurement Assistance Center, Mr. Arthur Myers, 1045 East Jersey Street, P.O. Box 512, Elizabeth, NJ 07207-0512; 908-289-0262.

New Jersey Institute of Technology, Defense Procurement Technical Assistance Center, Mr. John McKenna, 240 Martin Luther King Blvd., Newark, NJ 07102; 201-596-3105.

New Mexico

State of New Mexico, Procurement Assistance program, 1100 St. Francis Drive, Room 2006, Santa Fe, NM 87503; 505-827-0423.

American Indian Business and Technologies Corporation, Richard A. Ailes, 2015 Wyoming Blvd. NE, Suite E, Albuquerque, NM 87112; 505-275-7484.

New York

Cattaraugus County, Department of Economic Development and Tourism, Mr. David K. Yarnes, 303 Court Street, Little Valley, NY 14755; 716-938-9111.

Long Island Development Corporation, Procurement Technical Assistance Program, Mr. Morris Breiman, 255 Glen Cove Road, Carle Place, NY 11514; 516-741-5690.

New York City Office of Business Development, Procurement Outreach Program, Mr. Martin Bass, 17 John Street, New York, NY 10038; 212-513-6356.

Rockland Economic Development Corporation, Procurement Division, Mr. Martin Penn, 1 Blue Hill Plaza, Room 812, Pearl River, NY 10965; 914-735-7040.

South Bronx Overall Economic Development Corporation, 370 East 149th Street, Bronx, NY 10455; 212-292-3113.

North Carolina

University of North Carolina, Small Business and Technology Development Center, Mr. Scott R. Daugherty, 4509 Creedmoor Road, Raleigh, NC 27612; 919-571-4154.

North Dakota

State Small Business Development Center Office, Economic Development Commission, Business Development Assistance Division, Liberty Memorial Building, Bismarck, ND 58505; 701-224-2810.

Ohio

Central State University, Developing Nations Center, Mr. James H. Sangster, Wilberforce, OH 45384; 513-376-6514.

Columbus Area Chamber of Commerce, Central Ohio Government Marketing Assistance Program, 37 N. High Street, Columbus, OH 43215; 614-225-6940.

Community Improvement Corporation of Lake County, Northeast Ohio Government Contract Assistance Center, 7750 Clocktower Drive, Mentor, OH 44060; 216-951-1290.

Greater Cleveland Government Business Program, 200 Tower City Center, 50 Public Square, Cleveland, OH 44113; 216-621-3300.

Lawrence Economic Development Corporation, Procurement Outreach Center, 101 Sand Road, P.O. Box 488, South Point, OH 45680; 614-894-3838.

Mahoning Valley Economic Development Corporation, Mahoning Valley Technical Procurement Center, Mr. Stephen J. Danyi, 4319 Belmont Ave., Youngstown, OH 44505; 216-759-3668.

Terra Technical College, North Central Ohio Procurement Technical Assistance Program, Ms. Ronda Gooden, 1220 Cedar St., Fremont, OH 43420; 419-332-1002.

University of Cincinnati, CECE-Extension Unit Small Business Center, Ms. Nancy Rogers, 1111 Edison Drive, IAMS Building, Cincinnati, OH 45216; 513-948-2082.

Oklahoma

Oklahoma Department of Vocational-Technical Education, Business Assistance and Development Division, Ms. Denise Agee, 1500 West Seventh Ave., Stillwater, OK 74074-4364; 405-743-5574.

Tribal Government Institute, 111 N. Peters, Suite 200, Norman, OK 73069; 405-329-5542.

Oregon

State of Oregon, Economic Development Department, Mr. J. Rick Evans, 775 Summer Street NE, Salme, OR 97310; 503-888-2595.

Pennsylvania

Economic Development Council of Northeastern Pennsylvania, Local Development District, Ms. Karen D. Ostroskie, 1151 Oak Street, Pittston, PA 18640; 717-655-5581.

Indiana University of Pennsylvania, Dr. Robert Camp, Robertshaw Building, Incubator Office, 650 South 13th Street, Suite 303, Indiana, PA 15705-1087; 412-357-2520.

Northern Tier Regional Planning and Development Commission, Economic-Community Development, Ms. Katherine A. Shatinsky, 507 Main Street, Towanda, PA 18848; 717-265-9103.

Northwest Pennsylvania Regional Planning and Development Commission, Mr. Richard A. Mihalic, 614 Eleventh Street, Franklin, PA 16323; 814-437-3024.

Private Industry Council of Westmoreland/Fayette, Inc., Procurement Assistance Center, Mr. Charles R. Burtyk, 531 South Main Street, Greensburg, PA 15601; 412-836-2600.

SEDA - Council of Governments, Mr. A. Lawrence Barletta, RD 1, Timberhaven, Lewisburg, PA 17837; 717-524-4491.

Southern Alleghenies Planning and Development Commission, Local Development District, Mr. Daniel R. Shade, 541 58th Street, Altoona, PA 16602; 814-949-6528.

University of Pennsylvania, PASBDC, Snider Entrepreneurial Center, Mr. Paul A Fickes, Philadelphia, PA 19104-6374; 215-898-1282.

Geneva College, Geneva College Government Procurement Assistance Center, Jeffrey Milroy, 3231 Fourth Ave., Beaver Falls, PA 15010; 412-847-4022.

Johnstown Area Regional Industries, Defense Procurement Assistance Center, Robert J. Murphy, 111 Market St., Johnstown, PA 15901; 814-539-4951.

Mon Valley Renaissance, Califoria University of Pennsylvania, Joseph E. Hopkins, California, PA 15419; 412-938-5881.

Puerto Rico

Commonwealth of Puerto Rico (FOMENTO), Economic Development Administration, Mr. Pedro J. Acevedo, 355 Roosevelt Avenue, Hato Rey, PR 00918; 809-752-6861.

Rhode Island

Rhode Island Department of Economic Development, Business Development Office, 7 Jackson Walkway, Providence, RI 02903; 401-277-2601.

South Carolina

University of South Carolina, College of Business Administration, Small Business Development Center, Mr. John Lenti, Columbia, SC 29208; 803-777-4907.

South Dakota

South Dakota Procurement Technical Assistance Center, School of Business, Mr. Stephen L. Tracy, 414 E. Clark, Vermillion, SD 57069; 605-677-5287.

Tennessee

University of Tennessee, Center for Industrial Services, Mr. T.C. Parsons, 226 Capitol Boulevard Bldg., Suite 606, Nashville, TN 37219-1804; 615-242-2456.

Texas

City of San Antonio Procurement Outreach Center, Department of Economic and Employment Development, Ms. Rosalie O. Manzano, P.O. Box 839966, San Antonio, TX 78283; 512-554-7133.

Northeast Texas Community College, East Texas Procurement Technical Assistance Program, P.O. Box 1307, Mt. Pleasant, TX 75455; 903-572-1911.

University of Houston/TIPS, Texas Information Procurement Service, 4800 Calhoun, Houston, TX 77204; 713-752-8477.

University of Texas at Arlington, Automaton and Robotics Research Institute, P.O. Box 19125, Arlington, TX 76019; 817-273-2105.

Angelina College, Defense PTA Center, Dr. Larry Phillips, P.O. Box 1768, Lufkin, TX 75902; 409-639-1301.

El Paso Greater Chamber of Commerce, Wes Jury, 10 Civic Center Plaza, El Paso, TX 79901; 915-534-0500.

Utah

Utah Department of Community and Economic Development, Utah Procurement Outreach Program, Mr. James F. Odle, 324 South State Street, Suite 235, Salt Lake City, UT 84111; 801-538-8791.

Vermont

State of Vermont, Agency of Development and Community Affairs, Mr. William P. McGrath, 109 State Street, Montpelier, VT 05609; 802-828-3221.

Virginia

Crater Planning District Commission, The Procurement Assistance Center, Mr. Dennis K. Morris, 1964 Wakefield Street, P.O. Box 1808, Petersburg, VA 23805; 804-861-1667.

George Mason University, Entrepreneurship Center, Dean John O'Malley, 4400 University Drive, Fairfax, VA 22030; 703-330-5091.

Southwest Virginia Community College, Ms. Maxine B. Rogers, P.O. Box SVCC, Richlands, VA 24641; 703-964-7334.

Washington

Economic Development Council of Snohomish County, Ms. C. Grace Brown, 913 134th Street SW, Everett, WA 98204; 206-743-4567.

Spokane Area Economic Development Council, Local Business Assistance, Mr. Ken Olson, 221 N. Wall, Suite 310, Spokane, WA 99210-0203; 509-624-9285.

Economic Development Council of Kitsap County, Earle Smith, 4841 Auto Center Way, Suite 204, Bremerton, WA 98312; 206-377-9499.

West Virginia

Mid-Ohio Valley Regional Council, Procurement Technical Assistance Center, P.O. Box 5528, Vienna, WV 26105; 304-295-8714.

Regional Contracting Assistance Center, Inc., Mr. Mick Walker, 1116 Smith Street, Suite 202, Charleston, WV 25301; 304-344-2546.

Wisconsin

Aspin Procurement Institute, Inc., Mr. Mark F. Wagner, 840 Lake Avenue, Racine, WI 53403; 414-632-6321.

Madison Area Technical College, Small Business Assistance Center, Ms. Wendy L. Lein, 211 North Carroll Street, Madison, WI 53703; 608-258-2330.

Government Buys Bright Ideas From Inventors:
Small Business Innovative Research Programs (SBIR)

The SBIR stimulates technological innovation, encourages small science and technology-based firms to participate in government-funded research, and provides incentives for converting research results into commercial applications. The program is designed to stimulate technological innovation in this country by providing qualified U.S. small business concerns with competitive opportunities to propose innovative concepts to meet the research and development needs of the Federal Government. Eleven federal agencies with research and development budgets greater than $100 million are required by law to participate: The Departments of Defense, Health and Human Services, Energy, Agriculture, Commerce, Transportation, and Education; the National Aeronautics and Space Administration; the National Science Foundation; the Nuclear Regulatory Commission; and the Environmental Protection Agency.

Businesses of 500 or fewer employees that are organized for profit are eligible to compete for SBIR funding. Nonprofit organizations and foreign-owned firms are not eligible to receive awards, and the research must be carried out in the U.S. All areas of research and development solicit for proposals, and the 1992 budget for SBIR is $475 million. There are three phases of the program. Phase I determines whether the research idea, often on high-risk advanced concepts, is technically feasible, whether the firm can do high quality research, and whether sufficient progress has been made to justify a larger Phase II effort. This phase is usually funded for 6 months with awards up to $50,000. Phase II is the principal research effort, and is usually limited to a maximum of $500,000 for up to two years. The third phase, which is to pursue potential commercial applications of the research funded under the first two phases, is supported solely by non-federal funding, usually from third party, venture capital or large industrial firms. SBIR is one of the most competitive research and development programs in government. About one proposal out of ten received is funded in Phase I. Generally, about half of these receive support in Phase II. Solicitations for proposals are released once a year (in a few cases twice a year). To assist the small business community in its SBIR efforts, the U.S. Small Business Administration publishes the Pre-Solicitation Announcement (PSA) in December, March, June and September of each year. Every issue of the PSA contains pertinent information on the SBIR Program along with details on SBIR solicitations that are about to be released. This publication eliminates the need for small business concerns to track the activities of all of the federal agencies participating in the SBIR Program. In recognition of the difficulties encountered by many small firms in their efforts to locate sources of funding essential to finalization of their innovative products, SBA has developed the Commercialization Matching System. This system contains information on all SBIR awardees as well as financing sources that have indicated an interest in investing in SBIR innovations. Firms interested in obtaining more information on the SBIR Program or receiving the PSA, should contact the Office of Innovation, Research and Technology, Small Business Association, 1441 L Street, NW, Washington, DC, 202-205-6450.

SBIR representatives listed below can answer questions and send you materials about their agency's SBIR plans and funding.

Department of Agriculture
Office of Grants and Program Systems, Department of Agriculture, Room 323, Aerospace Center, 901 D Street, SW, Washington, DC 20250; 202-401-4002.

Department of Defense
Small Business and Economic Utilization, Office of Secretary of Defense, Room 2A340, Pentagon, Washington, DC 20301; 1-800-225-DTIC.

Department of Education
Dr. Ed Esty, The Brown Building, 1900 M Street, NW, Room 722, Washington, DC 20208; 202-708-5366.

Department of Energy
SBIR Program, U.S. Department of Energy, ER-16, Washington, DC 20585; 301-903-5867.

Department of Health and Human Services
Mr. Richard Clinkscales, Director, Office of Small and Disadvantaged Business Utilization, Department of Health and Human Services, 200 Independence Ave., SW, Room 513D, Washington, DC 20201; 202-690-7300.

Department of Transportation
SBIR Program, Transportation System Center, Department of Transportation, Kendall Square, Cambridge, MA 01242; 617-494-2051.

Environmental Protection Agency
EPA Small Business Ombudsman, 401 M Street, SW, A149-C, Washington, DC 20460; 1-800-368-5888.

National Aeronautics and Space Administration
SBIR Program, National Aeronautics and Space Administration, 250 E Street, SW, Suite 380, Washington, DC 20024; 202-488-2931.

National Science Foundation
Mr. Ritchie Coryell, Mr. Roland Tibbetts, SBIR Program Managers, National Science Foundation, 1800 G Street, NW, Washington, DC 20550; 202-653-5002.

Nuclear Regulatory Commission
Ms. Mary Ann Riggs, SBIR Coordinator, Office of Nuclear Regulatory Research, Nuclear Regulatory Commission, Mail Stop NLS-007, Washington, DC 20555; 301-492-3625.

State Procurement Offices

The following offices are starting places for finding out who in the state government will purchase your products or services.

Alabama
Finance Department, Purchasing Division, 11 South Union, Room 200, Montgomery, AL 36130; 205-242-7250.

Alaska
State of Alaska, Department of Administration, Division of General Services and Supply, P.O. Box 110210, Juneau, AK 99811-0210; 907-465-2253.

Arizona
State Purchasing, Executive Tower, Suite 101, 1700 W. Washington, Phoenix, AZ 85007; 602-542-5511.

Arkansas
Office of State Purchasing, P.O. Box 2940, Little Rock, AR 72203; 501-324-9312.

California
Office of Procurement, Department of General Services, 1823 14th Street, Sacramento, CA 95814; 916-445-6942.

Colorado
Division of Purchasing, 225 E. 16th Ave., Suite 900, Denver, CO 80203; 303 866-6100.

Connecticut
State of Connecticut, Department of Administrative Services, Bureau of Purchases, 460 Silver Street, Middletown, CT 06457; 203-638-3280.

Delaware
Purchasing Division, Purchasing Bldg., P.O. Box 299, Delaware City, DE 19706; 302-577-3070.

District of Columbia
Department of Administrative Services, 441 4th Street NW, Room 7544, Washington, DC 20001; 202-727-0171.

Florida
General Service Department, Division of Purchasing, Knight Bldg., 2737 Centerview Drive, 2nd Floor, Tallahassee, FL 32399-0950; 904-488-1194.

Georgia
Administrative Services Department, 200 Piedmont Ave., Room 1308 SE, Atlanta, GA 30334; 404-656-3240.

Hawaii
Purchasing Branch, Purchasing and Supply Division, Department of Accounting and General Services, Room 416, 1151 Punch Bowl, Honolulu, HI 96813; 808-586-0575.

Idaho
Division of Purchasing, Administration Department, 5569 Kendall, State House Mail, Boise, ID 83720; 208-327-7465.

Illinois
Department of Central Management Services, Procurement Services, 801 Stratton Bldg., Springfield, IL 62706; 217-782-2301.

Indiana
Department of Administration, Procurement Division, 402 W. Washington Street, Room W-468, Indianapolis, IN 46204; 317-232-3032.

Iowa
State of Iowa, Department of General Services, Purchasing Division, Hoover State Office Building, Des Moines, IA 50319; 515-281-3089.

Kansas
Division of Purchasing, Room 102 North, Landon State Office Building, 900 SW Jackson Street, Topeka, KS 66612; 913-296-2376.

Kentucky
Purchases, Department of Finance, Room 354, Capital Annex, Frankfort, KY 40601; 502-564-4510.

Louisiana
State Purchasing Office, Division of Administration, P.O. Box 94095, Baton Rouge, LA 70804-9095; 504-342-8010.

Maine
Bureau of Purchases, State House Station #9, Augusta, ME 04333; 207-289-3521.

Maryland
Purchasing Bureau, 301 West Preston Street, Mezzanine, Room M2, Baltimore, MD 21201; 410-225-4620.

Massachusetts
Purchasing Agent Division, One Ashburton Place, Room 1017, Boston, MA 02108; 617-727-8081.

Michigan
Office of Purchasing, Mason Bldg., P.O. Box 30026, Lansing, MI 48909, or 530 West Ellegan, 48933; 517-373-0330.

Minnesota
State of Minnesota, 112 Administration Bldg., 50 Sherburne Ave., St. Paul, MN 55155; 612-296-6152.

Mississippi
Office of Purchasing and Travel, 1504 Sillers Bldg., Jackson, MS 39201; 601-359-3409.

Missouri
State of Missouri, Division of Purchasing, P.O. Box 809, Jefferson City, MO 65102; 314-751-3273.

Montana

Department of Administration, Procurement Printing Division, 165 Mitchell Bldg., Helena, MT 59620-0135; 406-444-2575.

Nebraska

State Purchasing, Material Division, 301 Centennial Mall S., P.O. Box 94847, Lincoln, NE 68509; 402-471-2401.

Nevada

Nevada State Purchasing Division, 505 E. King Street, Room 400, Kinkead Bldg., Carson City, NV 89710; 702-687-4070.

New Hampshire

Plant and Property Management, 25 Capitol Street, State House Annex, Room 102, Concord, NH 03301; 603-271-2201.

New Jersey

Purchase and Property, CN-230, Trenton, NJ 08625; 609-292-4700.

New Mexico

State Purchasing Division, 1100 St. Frances Dr., Joseph Montoya Bldg., Room 2016, Santa Fe, NM 87503; 505-827-0472.

New York

Division of Purchasing, Corning Tower, Empire State Plaza, 38th Floor, Albany, NY 12242; 518-474-3695.

North Carolina

Department of Administration, Division of Purchase and Contract, 116 W. Jones St., Raleigh, NC 27603-8002; 919-733-3581.

North Dakota

Office of Management and Budget, Purchasing, 600 E Blvd., Bismarck, ND 58505-0400; 701-224-2683.

Ohio

State Purchasing, 4200 Surface Road, Columbus, OH 43228-1395; 614-466-5090.

Oklahoma

Office of Public Affairs, Central Purchasing Division, Room B4, State Capital Bldg., Oklahoma City, OK 73105; 405-521-2110.

Oregon

General Services, Purchasing, 1225 Ferry Street, Salem, OR 97310; 503-378-4643.

Pennsylvania

Procurement Department Secretary, Room 414, Harrisburg, PA 17125; 717-787-5295.

Rhode Island

Department of Administration, Purchases Office, One Capital Hill, Providence, RI 02908-5855; 401-277-2317.

South Carolina

Materials Management Office, General Service Budget and Control Board, 1201 Main Street, Suite 600, Columbia, SC 29201; 803-737-0600.

South Dakota

Division of Purchasing, 523 East Capitol Ave., Pierre, SD 57501; 605-773-3405.

Tennessee

Purchasing Division, C2-211, Central Services Bldg., Nashville, TN 37219; 615-741-1035.

Texas

State Purchasing and General Services Commission, P.O. Box 18047, Austin, TX 78711; 512-463-3445.

Utah

Purchasing Division, Department of Administrative Services, State Office Bldg., Room 350, Salt Lake City, UT 84114; 801-538-3026.

Vermont

Purchasing Division, 128 State Street, Drawer 33, Montpelier, VT 05633-7501; 802-828-2211.

Virginia

Department of General Services, Purchasing Division, P.O. Box 1199, Richmond, VA 23209; 804-786-3172.

Washington

Office of State Procurement, 216 GA Building, P.O. Box 41017, Olympia, WA 98504-1017; 206-753-6461.

West Virginia

Department of Administration, Purchasing Section, Room E102, Building One, 1900 Kanawha Blvd. E, Charleston, WV 25305; 304-348-2309.

Wisconsin

Division of State Agency Services, Bureau of Procurement, 101 East Wilson, 6th Floor, P.O. Box 7867, Madison, WI 53707-7867; 608-266-2605.

Wyoming

Department of Administration, Procurement Services, 2001 Capitol Ave., Cheyenne, WY 82002; 307-777-7253.

Help For Inventors: Patents, Trademarks and Copyrights

Protecting your invention, copyrighting your work, and obtaining a patent or trademark are often necessary parts of doing business. Described below are the major sources you can consult when you need information about any of these procedures. For additional information on monitoring patents and copyrights, refer to the Section on Technology.

Patent and Trademark Office

United States patent and trademark laws are administered by the Patent and Trademark Office (PTO). States also have trade secret statutes, which generally state that if you guard your trade secret with a reasonable amount of care, you will have rights. The PTO examines patent and trademark applications, grants protection for qualified inventions, and registers trademarks. (It also collects, assembles, and disseminates the technological information patent grants). The PTO maintains a collection of more than 5 million United States patents issued to date, several million foreign patents, and 1.2 million trademarks, together with supporting documentation. Here's how to find what you need.

What a Great Idea

To help you get started with patenting your invention, the Patent and Trademark Offices will send you a free booklet upon request called *Summary of How the Patent Process Works*. (Address and phone number for the PTO are given below). There are three legal elements in the process of invention: the conception of the idea, diligence in working it out, and reducing it to practice -- i.e., getting a finished product that actually works. If you have a great idea you think might work, but you need time to develop it further before it is ready to be patented, what should you do?

Protect Your Idea for $6

You can file a Disclosure Statement with the Patent and Trademark Office. They will keep it in confidence as evidence of the date of conception.

```
Disclosure Statement
Commissioner of Patents and Trademarks
Patent and Trademark Office
Washington, DC 20231
Recorded Message            703-557-3158
Disclosure Office           703-308-HELP
Legal Counsel               703-308-HELP
```

Send an 8 1/2 x 13" drawing, a copy, signed disclosure, SASE, and a check or money order for $6 to file. Upon request, the above office will also send you a free brochure on Disclosure Statements.

This is a way to keep the idea you are working on completely secret and yet document the date you conceived the idea. You can file the Disclosure Statement at any time after the idea is conceived, but the value of it will depend on how much you put into it -- so put as much detail into it as you can.

Another way to document the date of conception is to have someone vouch for you. Explain your idea to another person who is able to understand it and have them acknowledge what you have said to them in a signed, dated, notarized affidavit. Keep the voucher statement in a safe place in case you should ever need to produce it as proof of conception.

Either of the above two methods produces documentation you can use as evidence if someone else later claims to have thought of your idea first and patents it before you do. The drawback to the voucher method is that it does not preserve absolute secrecy as does filing a disclosure statement. The person you told may tell someone else.

Telling the World

Another way to document the date of conception is to publish it in a journal. Suppose that while in your basement to see why your old furnace is not working, you trip over your stationary exercise bicycle, which you never use, and hit your head. You also hit upon a way to heat your home by hooking up the furnace to one of the bike wheels and pedalling for 15 minutes. You're not sure if this method will work with any other furnace except your own, but it might. If you publish the idea in a journal, your idea is protected for a year.

Publication acts as collateral evidence of the date of conception. If you are the first to conceive of an idea, and no one else has previously filed a Disclosure Statement on it or taken a Voucher Affidavit or published it, then for a year no one can patent your idea. Note that during the year you have to patent your invention you may not know whether someone else has documented an earlier conception date. The other catch to this method is that you have only a year to act. The heat is on because after a year **you** are barred from patenting your own invention! This is because the government wants you to use a reasonable amount of diligence in putting the idea to work.

The Purpose of Documenting the Date of Conception

If someone else should try to patent your idea, filing a Disclosure Statement shows that you thought of it first. Filing a Disclosure Statement does not legally protect your invention. Only being granted a patent does that. Documentation of the conception date gives you time to patent your invention, and is invaluable if you need to prove when you thought of your idea if a dispute should arise. (Note that filing a Disclosure

Statement gives you limited defensive legal protection only if you follow it up with a patent in two years. Unlike a patent, it cannot be used offensively, to stop someone else from patenting the same idea.) When you go to file for a patent, if you and a competitor get into a dispute as to who was the first to invent it, the PTO will hold an Interference Proceeding. If you thought of the idea first, your Disclosure Statement or Voucher Affidavit will go a long way towards establishing that you were the first inventor and should get the patent. (If you published your idea before anyone else documented a prior date of conception, no one but you will be granted a patent to the idea for a year.)

Research Resources That Can Help You Turn Your Idea Into Reality

While diligently working out the details of your invention you can use the very extensive resources of over 150,000 scientific and technical journals, articles and books at the Scientific Document Library at the PTO in Crystal City, VA.

Facilitating public access to the more than 25 million cross-referenced United States patents is the job of PTO's Office of Technology Assessment and Forecast (OTAF), 703-557-5652. It has a master database which covers all United States patents, and searches are available for a fee which depends on the size of the project. The minimum search fee is $150. No fee is charged if the information you need is already in a report they have on hand. This office can run a search for you based on classification, sub-class, country or company name, but not by work or topic. An OTAF search will not result in an in-depth patent search. (More on that, and how to find classifications in the *Conducting Your Own Patent Search* section below.) OTAF extracts information from its database and makes it available in a variety of formats, including publications, custom patent reports, and statistical reports. The purpose of most of the reports generated by an OTAF search is to reveal patent trends.

Copies of the specifications and drawings of all patents are available from PTO. Design patents and trademark copies are $1.50 each. Plant patents not in color are $10 each. Plant patents in color are $20 each. To request, you must have the patent number. For copies, contact:

> Commissioner of Patent and Trademarks
> U.S. Department of Commerce
> U.S. Patent and Trademark Office (PTO)
> P.O. Box 9
> Washington, DC 20231
> Public Information Line   703-308-HELP

Patenting Your Invention

To patent your invention, order the Patent Booklet called *General Information Concerning Patents*, and Application Form.

> Superintendent of Documents
> U.S. Government Printing Office
> Washington, DC 20402   202-783-3238

The cost is $2 and may be charged to Mastercard, VISA or Choice Card. The booklet must be ordered by stock number 003-004-00641-2.

The application will ask you for a written description, oath and drawing where possible. The cost to file for a patent to individuals or small businesses of under 15 employees (defined by SBA standards) is $315. It generally takes 18 months to two years for the PTO to grant a patent. Rights start the date the patent is granted. If you use your invention prior to being granted a patent, you can put "patent pending" on your product. This warns competitors that you have taken the necessary steps, but otherwise affords you no legal protection. Before embarking on the patenting process, you will want to conduct a patent search to make sure no one else has preceded you.

Conducting Your Own Patent Search

Before investing too much time and money on patenting your idea, you will want to see if anyone has already patented it. The PTO will only conduct searches on a specific inventors' name that you request. The fee is $10 and covers a 10-year time span. Call 703-308-0595. If you wish to hire a professional to do your patent search, consult the yellow pages or obtain a copy of *Patent Attorneys and Agents Registered to Practice Before the U.S. Patent and Trademark Office*. View this publication at the PTO Search Room, or obtain it from the U.S. Government Printing Office. Even if your search is not as in-depth as that of a patent attorney or a patent agent, you may still find out what you need to know. You may conduct your patent search at the Patent and Trademark Office Search Room located at:

> Patent and Trademark Office (PTO)
> Washington, DC 20231   703-308-0595

You may also conduct your patent search at any one of the 72 Patent Depository Libraries (PDLs) throughout the country. For information about the Patent Depository Library Program and the location of a library near you, call the toll-free number listed below.

> Office of Patent Depository Library Programs
> U.S. Patent and Trademark Office
> 1921 Jefferson Davis Highway
> Crystal Mall 2, Room 306   1-800-435-7735
> Arlington, VA 22202   703-557-9685

The mailing address is:

> Office of Patent Depository Libraries Office
> U.S. Patent and Trademark Office
> Crystal Mall 2, Room 306
> Washington, DC 20231

This office distributes the information to the 72 PDL's. The information is kept on CD-Rom discs, which are constantly updated. You or the library personnel can use them to do a patent search. CD-Rom discs have been combined to incorporate CASSIS (Classification and Search Support Information System). CD-Rom discs do not give you online access to the PTO database. Online access will be available through APS (Automated Patent Systems) within two years. APS is presently available only to patent examiners, public users of the PTO Search Room and to 14 of the 72 Patent Depository Libraries on a pilot program basis. Each PDL with the online APS has its own rules regarding its use. To use the online APS at the PTO Search Room, you must first sign up and take a class at the Search Room. Online access costs $40 for connect hour, and the charge for paper used for printouts is additional.

If you do not live near a PDL, the three CD-Rom discs are available through subscription. You may purchase the Classification disc, which dates back to 1790, for $210; the Bibliography disc, which dates back to 1969, for $210; and the ASIST disc, which contains a roster of patent attorneys, assignees, and other information for $151. You can also conduct your patent search and get a copy of it through commercial database services such as:

Mead Data Central, NEXIS Express, LEXPAT; 1-800-543-6862, FAX: 513-865-7418. Searches are done free of charge on patent topics. The charge for information found is $30 for a list of abstracts, plus print charges. Copies of patents (which you may decide to order after viewing the listing, or order directly if you already know which patent you want) cost $20. Copies include full text and detailed description of drawing, but no actual drawing because it is pulled from the electronic database.

If complete secrecy or doing your own search is your object, you may also subscribe to LEXPAT through the full library service. Cost is $28 per hour access charge plus 65 cents per minute connect time. To subscribe call 1-800-843-6476.

Derwent, 1313 Dolly Madison Blvd., Suite 401, McLean, VA 22101; 1-800-451-3451, 703-790-0400, FAX: 703-790-1426. Patent searches are $360 per hour plus 80 cents per record and $40 per hour for technical time. Copies of patents are $13-16 for the first 25 pages and 67 cents for each additional page thereafter.

Rapid Patent, 1921 Jefferson Davis Highway, Suite 1821D, Arlington, VA 22202; 1-800-336-5010, 703-920-5050, FAX: 703-685-3987. Minimum costs for patent searches are: $240 for Mechanical, $290 for Electrical or Chemical. They are done manually. Delivery time is 4 weeks. Copies of patents cost $3.25 for each 25 pages.

CompuServe, 1-800-848-8199. There is a $39.95 one-time fee. Search time is $12.50 per hour or 21 cents per minute. Searches are available for abstracts ($4), full listing ($4), or classification ($4).

If you are going to do your own patent search at your local Patent Depository Library, begin with the *Manual and Index to U.S. Patent Classifications* to identify the subject area where the patent is placed. Then use the CD-Rom discs to locate the patent. CD-Rom discs enable you to do a complete search of all registered patents but do not enable you to view the full patent, with all its specific details. Lastly, view the patent, which will be kept on microfilm, cartridge or paper. What is there to view varies by library, depending on what they have been able to purchase. If the library you are using does not have the patent you want, you may be able to obtain it through inter-library loan.

Copies of patents can be ordered from the PTO, 703-308-1200,

or more quickly, but for a price, from commercial services such as Derwent or Rapid Patent. Depending on which each individual PDL has available, copies of patents can be obtained for no fee.

To obtain a certified copy of a patent, call 703-308-1200 (Patent Search Library at the PTO). The fee is $5 and you must have the patent number. For a certified copy of an abstract of titles, the fee is $15. For a certified copy of patent assignments, with a record of ownership from the beginning until present, call 703-308-9700. The cost is $15 and to request you must have the reel and frame number.

Trademarks

Registering a trademark for your product or service is the way to protect the recognition quality of the name you are building. The PTO keeps records on more than 1.2 million trademarks and records. The over 500,000 active trademarks are kept on the floor of the library. "Dead" trademarks are kept on microfilm. Books contain every registered trademark ever issued, starting in 1870. You can visit the Patent and Trademark Office to research a trademark. There you can conduct your search manually for no charge or use their Trademark Search System (T-Search) for $40 per hour, plus ten cents per page and $25 per hour for office staff assistance time.

Trademark Search Library
2900 Crystal Drive
Second Floor, Room 2B30
Arlington, VA 22202   703-308-9800/9805

If that's not possible, you can hire someone to do the search for you. For an agent consult the yellow pages under "Trademark Agents/Consultants" or "Trademark Attorneys". You can also locate an agent by calling your local bar association for a list of recommendations.

To conduct your own search at a Patent Depository Library use the CD-Rom disc on trademarks. It is not presently available for purchase. The CD-Rom disc contains trademarks but not images. Images are in the *Official Gazette*, which contains most current and pending trademarks. Subscriptions to the *Gazette* for trademarks cost $312 per year. The *Gazette* for patents costs $583 per year. Both are issued every two weeks and can be ordered from the U.S. Government Printing Office. You can also purchase an image file which contains pending and registered trademarks and corresponding serial or registration numbers through Thomson and Thomson, 1-800-692-8833. It dates back to April 1, 1987 and is updated by approximately 500 images weekly. However, the PDL you use is likely to have an image of the trademark on microfilm or cartridge, and also have copies of the *Official Gazette*. If not, and you have the registration number, you may obtain a copy of the trademark you want for $1.50 from the PTO. Contact:

The Patent and Trademark Office
U.S. Department of Commerce
P.O. Box 9
Washington, DC 20231
Public Information Line   703-557-4357

Help for Inventors

There are also commercial services you can use to do trademark searches.

CompuServe, 1-800-848-8199. Fees are: $39.95 one time charge, plus $12.80 per hour or 21 cents per minute online time plus $4 per search and $4 for full entry call-up.

Trademark Scan (produced by Thomson and Thomson- can be purchased, 1-800-692-8833), or accessed directly via Dialog. Trademark Scan is updated three times per week, includes state and federal trademarks, foreign and domestic. To access Trademark Scan you must already have Dialog. Cost is $130 per hour. Call 703-524-8004 or 1-800-334-2564. FAX for Trademark Producer Scan (People who actually own the database): 617-786-8273.

Derwent, 1-800-451-3451, is a commercial service that will conduct the search for you. They will access the Trademark Scan database via Dialog. Cost is $60 per mark plus $1 per record. If required, 24 hour turnaround time is available.

Visual image of trademarks are not available on any of the electronic services above.

Online services and database discs for both patents and trademarks are constantly being expanded. For information on an extensive range of existing and projected products, call the PTO Office of Electronic Information at 703-557-5652 and ask for the U.S. Department of Commerce, PTO Office of Information Systems' *Electronic Products Brochure*. For example, there is a Weekly Text File, containing text data of pending and registered trademarks. Information can be called up by almost any term. It can be purchased from IMSMARQ, 215-834-5089, the Trademark Register through Bell Atlantic Gateway, 1-800-638-6363 Operator 2606, and Thomson & Thomson, 1-800-692-8833.

How to Register a Trademark

Get a copy of the booklet, *Basic Facts about Trademarks* from the U.S. Government Printing Office. It is free upon request from the Trademark Search Library. Call 703-308-9800/9805. The mark you intend to use needs to be in use before you apply. The fee to register your trademark is $175. The time to process it can take up to 14 months.

The Right Way to Get a Copyright

Copyrights are filed on intellectual property. A copyright protects your right to control the sale, use of distribution and royalties from a creation in thought, music, films, art or books. For information, contact:

Library of Congress
Copyright Office, Room 401
101 Independence Ave., SE
Washington, DC 20540   202-479-0700
Public Information Office   202-707-2100

If you know which copyright application you require, you can call the Forms Hotline, open 7 days per week, 24 hours per day at 202-707-9100. The fee is $20 for each registration.

The Library of Congress provides information on copyright registration procedures and copyright card catalogs which cover 28 million works that have been registered since 1870. The Copyright Office will research the copyright you need and send you the information by mail. Requests must be in writing and you must specify exactly what it is you need to know. Contact the Copyright Office, Reference & Bibliography, Library of Congress, 101 Independence Ave., SE, Washington, DC 20559; 202-707-6850, public information 479-0700. The fee for the search is $30 per hour. You can get a certificate stating the search was conducted by qualified researchers. There is no fee if you conduct the search yourself. Staff at the Library of Congress will show you how. You may then, if you wish, request a certificate. The Copyright Office will conduct its own search, but your work will probably reduce the time of the search and save you money.

Subscriptions to the following parts of the Library of Congress *Catalogue of Copyright Entries* are available from the Superintendent of Documents, U.S. Government Printing Office, Washington, DC 20402-9325. Each lists material registered since the last issue was published. Order by stock number using Mastercard, VISA, check or money order. To order, call the Government Printing Office Order Desk at 202-783-3238. FAX for delays in receiving orders: 202-275-7810. For help or complaints call the Superintendent of Documents Office at 202-275-3050.

Part 1: Nondramatic Literary Works - this quarterly costs $16 per year. Stock number 730-001-0000-2.

Part 2: Serials and Periodicals - this semiannual costs $5 per year. Stock number 730-002-0000-9.

Part 3: Performing Arts - this quarterly costs $16 per year. Stock number 730-003-0000-5.

Part 4: Motion Pictures and Filmstrips - this semiannual costs $5 per year. Stock number 730-004-0000-1.

Part 5: Visual Arts - this semiannual does not include maps and costs $5 per year. Stock number 730-005-00000-8.

Part 6: Maps - this semiannual costs $4 per year. Stock number 730-006-0000-4.

Part 7: Sound Recordings - this semiannual costs $7.50 per year. Stock number 730-007-0000-1.

Part 8: Renewal - this semiannual costs $5 per year. Stock number 730-008-0000-7.

Free Help For Inventors

If you have a great idea and want to turn it into reality, don't rush out and spend what could be thousands of dollars for a private invention company and a patent attorney. You can get a lot of this help for free of at a fraction of the cost. There is a lot of help out there; university-sponsored programs, not-for-profit groups, state affiliated programs, profit-making companies, etc. Depending on the assistance and the organization, some services are free, others have reasonable fees.

Many of the inventors organizations hold regular meetings where speakers share their expertise on topics such as licensing, financing and marketing. These groups are a good place for inventors to meet other inventors, patent attorneys, manufacturers, and others with whom they can talk and from whom they can get help.

Below is a listing of some of these groups, listed state by state. Some organizations listed under the state where they are located are regional or national in scope. In states where there is no specific program for inventors, the Small Business Development Centers (under the U.S. Small Business Administration) can often be of help. They are usually found at the colleges and universities. The Small Business Development Center office in Washington, DC is 202-205-6766.

Alabama

Office for the Advancement of Developing Industries
University of Alabama - Birmingham
1075 13th South
Birmingham, AL 35205   205-934-2190
Inventors can receive help on the commercialization and patent processes and critical reviews of inventions in this office. Assessments can be made on an invention's potential marketability and assistance is available for patent searches. There is a charge for services.

Small Business Development Center
University of Alabama at Birmingham
Medical Towers Building
1717 11th Ave. South, Suite 419   205-934-7260
Birmingham, AL 35294   FAX: 205-934-7645
The center offers counseling for a wide range of business issues and problems.

Alaska

Small Business Development Center
University of Alaska
430 W. 7th Ave., Suite 110   907-274-7232
Anchorage, AK 99501   FAX: 907-274-9524
The SBDC offers free counseling to inventors on commercialization and patent processes, arranges meetings between inventors, manufacturers, and others who can be of help.

Arizona

Arizona State Research Institute
Technology Transfer & Industry Liaison Office
Arizona State University   602-965-4795
Temple, AZ 85287   602-965-0922
This office offers free counseling to inventors on the commercialization and patent processes and arranges meetings between inventors, manufacturers and others. Arizona State University is a depository for the U.S. Patent and Trademark Office and has the PTO forms and publications available.

Arizona SBDC Network
108 N. 40th Street, Suite 148   602-392-5224
Phoenix, AZ 85034   FAX: 602-392-5300
The center offers counseling for a wide range of business issues and problems.

Arkansas

Arkansas Inventors Congress
P.O. Box 411
Dardanell, AR 72834   501-229-4515
Contact Person: Garland Bull

The Arkansas Inventors Congress counsels inventors on commercialization and patent processes, and provides communications among inventors, manufacturers and financial people. It will provide assessments of the market potential on inventions. U.S. Patent and Trademark Office forms and publications are available. Dues are required.

Small Business Development Center
University of Arkansas at Little Rock
100 S. Main, Suite 401   501-324-9043
Little Rock, AR 72201   FAX: 501-324-9049
The center offers counseling for a wide range of business issues and problems.

California

Inventors of California
P.O. Box 6158
Rheem Valley, CA 94570   510-376-7541
This group holds regular meetings with speakers, promotes communications between inventors and manufacturers, and for a fee, provides critical reviews of inventions. Dues are required.

Inventors Workshop International
Inventor Center, Suite 304
3201 Corte Malpaso
Camarillo, CA 93012   805-484-9786
This foundation has chapters nationwide. They hold meetings, conduct seminars, and counsel inventors on important issues, including product development and market research. The foundation publishes journals and a guidebook. There are dues and subscription fees.

Invent Magazine
8 West Janss Rd.
A Thousand Oaks, CA 91360-3325
This is a nationally distributed magazine for inventors. It is not affiliated with any single inventors group. It is published quarterly, and there is a subscription fee.

Small Business Development Center
801 K Street
17th Floor, Suite 1700   916-324-9234
Sacramento, CA 95814   916-322-3524
The center offers counseling for a wide range of business issues and problems.

Colorado

Affiliated Inventors Foundation, Inc.
2132 E. Bijou Street
Colorado Spring, CO 80909   719-635-1234
This foundation counsels inventors on commercialization and patent processes,

and provides detailed information on the steps needed to reach commercialization. Preliminary appraisals, evaluations and other services are available for a fee.

Small Business Development Center
Office of Business Development
1625 Broadway, Suite 1710   303-892-3809
Denver, CO 80202   FAX: 303-892-3848
The center offers counseling for a wide range of business issues and problems.

Connecticut

Inventors Association of Connecticut
P.O. Box 3325
Westport, CT 06880   203-226-9890
This association offers programs, speakers and seminars. A directory of members' inventions is available to interested companies and marketers. The annual dues are $35.

Small Business Development Center
University of Connecticut
Box U-41, Room 422
368 Fairfield Road   203-486-4135
Storrs, CT 06269-2041   FAX: 203-486-1576
The center offers counseling for a wide range of business issues and problems.

Delaware

Small Business Development Center
University of Delaware
Purnell Hall   302-451-2747
Newark, DE 19716   FAX: 302-451-6750
The office offers free management counseling and seminars on various topics, and can counsel inventors on areas such as the commercialization and patenting processes. Services are by appointment only.

District of Columbia

U.S. Department of Commerce
U.S. Patent and Trademark Office
Washington, DC   703-308-4357
Also see Maryland for National Institute of Standards and Technology.

District of Columbia SBDC
Howard University
6th & Fairmount Street NW
Room 128   202-806-1550
Washington, DC 20059   FAX: 202-797-6393
The center offers counseling for a wide range of business issues and problems.

Florida

Florida Product Innovation Center
2622 NW 43rd Street, #B3
Gainesville, FL 32606   904-734-1680
Developed by the Florida Small Business Development Center, the Innovation Center offers individual guidance and group training in: determining technical feasibility of an idea; facilitating technology transfer from the laboratories to product development; patent, copyright, trademark and licensing procedures, etc. Individual consultation and assistance are free. Technical evaluations conducted by qualified engineers are $100.

Tampa Bay Inventors Council
P.O. Box 2254
Largo, FL 34649   813-391-0315
This group counsels inventors on commercialization and patent processes, and provides critical reviews of inventions. It offers referrals and communications for inventors with manufacturers, venture capitalists, patent attorneys, etc. The annual dues are $30.

Small Business Development Center
University of West Florida
414 Marv Esther Cutoff
Fort Walton Beach, FL 32548   904-244-1036
The center offers counseling for a wide range of business issues and problems.

Georgia

Inventors Association of Georgia
525 Page Ave. NE
Atlanta, GA 30307   404-427-8024
This association holds regular meetings where members are encouraged to report on progress on inventions. Counseling is available. A newsletter is published. The annual dues are $50 for corporate members, $25 for individuals.

Small Business Development Center
University of Georgia
Chicopee Complex
1180 East Broad Street
Athens, GA 30602   404-542-5760
The center offers counseling for a wide range of business issues and problems.

Hawaii

Inventors Council of Hawaii
P.O. Box 27844
Honolulu, HI 96827   808-595-4296
The council holds monthly meetings with topical speakers and some workshops. It serves as a Patent Information Center for the state, and publishes a monthly newsletter. The annual dues are $25.

Small Business Development Center
University of Hawaii at Hilo
523 W. Lanikaula Street   808-933-3515
Hilo, HI 96720-4091   FAX: 808-933-3683
The center offers counseling for a wide range of business issues and problems.

Idaho

Idaho Research Foundation, Inc.
University of Idaho
121 Sweet Ave.
Moscow, ID 83843-2309   208-883-8366
This foundation counsels inventors on commercialization and patent processes, and provides critical reviews on inventions. Computerized data searching and marketing service is available. It takes a percentage of intellectual property royalties.

Small Business Development Center
Boise State University
1910 University Drive
Boise, ID 83725   208-385-1640
The center offers counseling for a wide range of business issues and problems.

Illinois

Illinois Business Innovation Fund
Illinois Department of Commerce and Community Affairs
100 W. Randolph Street, #3-400
Chicago, IL 60601   312-814-5246
This fund provides up to $100,000 for R&D, organizational fees, patenting costs and other charges to Illinois businesses for projects matched with private resources. The Department of Commerce also administers the Technology and Product Development Program which provides evaluations, prototype development and new product testing.

Argonne National Laboratory
Energy Systems Division
9700 S. Cass Ave.
Argonne, IL 60439   708-252-2000
This organization published *Catalog of Organizations That Assist Inventors: Activities and Services, Edition II*, January 1990. It summarizes activities and services of 145 national, state and local programs and organizations in the U.S. and Canada that assist independent inventors or inventors associated with small businesses. It is available for $26.

Inventor's Council
53 W. Jackson, Suite 1643
Chicago, IL 60604   312-939-3329
This group provides a liaison between inventors and industries. It holds meetings and workshops on commercialization, evaluation, marketing, financing, etc., for U.S. and Canadian inventors. Dues are required.

Small Business Development Center
Department of Commerce & Comm. Affairs
620 East Adams Street, 6th Floor 217-524-5856
Springfield, IL 62701 217-785-6328
The center offers counseling for a wide range of business issues and problems.

Indiana

The Inventors and Entrepreneurs Society of Indiana, Inc.
c/o Purdue University Calumet
Hammond, IN 46323 219-989-2354
Residents of Illinois, Michigan, and Kentucky are also served by this society. It holds monthly meetings, counsels inventors, and will assess market potential of specific inventions on request. It also publishes a newsletter. Annual dues are $30.

Small Business Development Center
Economic Development Council
One North Capitol, Suite 200 317-634-1690
Indianapolis, IN 46204 FAX: 317-264-6855
The center offers counseling for a wide range of business issues and problems.

Iowa

Drake Business Center
Drake University
2401 University Ave.
Des Moines, IA 50311-4505 515-271-2655
This center evaluates innovations for marketability, counsels inventors on commercialization, and helps match inventors with business persons. The fee for invention assessment is $100.

Small Business Development Center
Administrative Office
Iowa State University
Chamberlynn Building
137 Lynn Avenue 515-292-6351
Ames, IA 50010 FAX: 515-292-0020
The center offers counseling for a wide range of business issues and problems.

Kansas

Kansas Association of Inventors, Inc.
2015 Lakin
Great Bend, KS 67530 316-792-1375
This association primarily serves Kansas residents, but has members from other states and from Canada. It holds monthly chapter meetings, assesses market potential of inventions, and provides for communications between inventors and manufacturers, investors, etc. There is a quarterly newsletter. Annual dues are $35.

Small Business Development Center
Wichita State University
Campus Box 148 316-689-3193
Wichita, KS 67208 FAX: 316-689-3647
The center offers counseling for a wide range of business issues and problems.

Kentucky

Center for Entrepreneur and Technology
University of Louisville
Burhans Hall, Room 121
Shelby Campus
Louisville, KY 40292 502-588-7854
This center counsels inventors on commercialization and patent processes and provides critical reviews of inventions. It provides assistance in technically refining inventions. There are no fees.

Bluegrass Inventors Guild
917 Watterson Trail
Louisville, KY 40299 502-244-5626
This group has informal monthly meetings, speakers, networking and counseling. Dues are $30/year.

Office of Business and Technology
500 Mero Street

Cabinet of Economic Development
Capital Plaza Tower 1-800-626-2930
Frankfurt, KY 40601 1-800-633-2007 (in KY)
This office provides self-help assistance in the form of related articles, marketing ideas, and technical information. If you have a patent, they will try to match you with an investor through their Investment Capitol Network data base.

Small Business Development Center
Kentucky Small Business Development Center
Center for Business Development
College of Business & Economics Building
205 Business & Economics Bldg.
University of Kentucky 606-257-7668
Lexington, KY 40506-0034 FAX: 606-258-1907
The center offers counseling for a wide range of business issues and problems.

Louisiana

Technology Innovation Center
1720 Kaliste Saloom Road, Bldg. D3
Lafayette, LA 70508-6141 318-981-0842
The Technology Innovation Center counsels inventors on commercialization and patent processes, assists in prototype development, helps in selection of patent attorney, etc. The registration fee is $100; the center takes a percentage of future profits in exchange for certain consulting services, and requires reimbursement of costs.

Small Business Development Center
Northeast Louisiana University
College of Business Administration
700 University Avenue 318-342-5506
Monroe, LA 71209 FAX: 318-342-5510
The center offers counseling for a wide range of business issues and problems.

Maine

Center for Innovation and Entrepreneurship
University of Maine
Maine Tech Center
16 Godfrey Drive
Orono, ME 04473 207-581-1465
This center counsels inventors on the commercialization process, provides referrals for critical reviews of inventions and for financial and patent assistance, and conducts inventors' forums. It publishes a newsletter and bulletins. The communicative services are usually free; there are fees for educational services and materials.

Small Business Development Center
University of Maine at Machias
Math and Science Building
Machias, ME 04654 207-255-3313
The center offers counseling for a wide range of business issues and problems.

Maryland

Office of Energy-Related Inventions
National Institute of Standards and Technology
Gaithersburg, MD 20899 301-975-5500
The office evaluates all promising non-nuclear energy-related inventions, particularly those submitted by independent inventors and small companies for the purpose of obtaining direct grants for their development from the U.S. Department of Energy. Although individual grant or contract awards have exceeded $100,000, the average award is $70,000.

Small Business Development Center
Department of Economic & Employment Dev.
217 E. Redwood Street, 10th Floor 301-333-6995
Baltimore, MD 21202 FAX: 301-333-6608
The center offers counseling for a wide range of business issues and problems.

Massachusetts

Inventors Association of New England
P.O. Box 335
Lexington, MA 02173 617-862-5008
The association holds regular meetings with speakers, and counsels inventors on

the commercialization process. It assesses product marketability, and publishes a newsletter. Annual dues are $35. This association covers eastern New England.

Small Business Development Center
University of Lowell
450 Aiken Street
Lowell, MA 01854 — 508-458-7261
The center offers counseling for a wide range of business issues and problems.

Michigan

Inventors Council of Michigan
Metropolitan Center for High Technology
2727 Second Ave.
Detroit, MI 48201 — 313-963-0616
The Council holds regular meetings with topical speakers, counsels inventors on the commercialization and patent processes through the statewide Small Business Development Centers, and provides communications among inventors, manufacturers, patent attorneys, and venture capitalists. There are annual dues.

Small Business Development Center
2727 Second Avenue — 313-577-4848
Detroit, MI 48201 — FAX: 313-577-4222
The center offers counseling for a wide range of business issues and problems.

Minnesota

Minnesota Project Innovation, Inc.
111 3rd Ave. S., #410
Minneapolis, MN 55401-2554 — 612-338-3280
This project is affiliated with the Minnesota Department of Energy and Economic Development, U.S. Small Business Administration, and private companies. It provides referrals to inventors for sources of technical assistance in refining inventions.

Minnesota Inventors Congress (MIC)
P.O. Box 71 — 1-800-468-3681 (in MN)
Redwood Falls, MN 56283-0071 — 507-637-2344
Established in 1958, MIC assists and promotes inventors worldwide through directories, newsletters, seminars, etc. The Congress is held annually during the second full weekend in June. For a nominal fee, an inventor can display his invention and receive public exposure and reaction. The organization keeps inventors abreast of reputable resources available as well as "rip-offs". There are membership fees.

The Inventors Resource Center
P.O. Box 71 — 1-800-468-3681 (in MN)
Redwood Falls, MN 56283 — 507-637-2344
The Minnesota Inventors Congress established this center as a focal point for a statewide invention support system. It offers walk-in services, referrals, literature, and a toll-free hotline in the state, 1-800-INVENT 1.

Small Business Development Center
Department of Trade and Economic Development
900 American Center Bldg.
150 East Kellogg Blvd. — 612-297-5570
St. Paul, MN 55101 — FAX: 612-296-1290
The center offers counseling for a wide range of business issues and problems.

Mississippi

Confederacy of Mississippi Inventors
4759 Nailor Rd.
Vicksburg, MS 39180 — 601-636-6561
This group holds quarterly meetings, counsels inventors on patent processes, sponsors invention fairs at schools, and publishes a quarterly newsletter. Annual dues are $12.

Small Business Development Center
Old Chemistry Bldg.
Suite 216 — 601-232-5001
University, MS 38677 — FAX: 601-232-5650
The center offers counseling for a wide range of business issues and problems.

Missouri

Missouri Innovation Center
T-16 Research Park
Columbia, MO 65211 — 314-882-2822
This group provides communications among inventors, manufacturers, patent attorneys and venture capitalists, and provides general consultations. It is sponsored by the state, city of Columbia, and the University of Missouri. There are fees for some services.

Inventors Association of St. Louis
P.O. Box 16544
St. Louis, MO 63105 — 314-432-1291
The group holds monthly meetings, provides communications among inventors, manufacturers, patent attorneys, and venture capitalists. It publishes a newsletter. There are annual dues.

Missouri Small Business Development Center (State Office)
University of Missouri
300 University Place — 314-882-0344
Columbia, MO 56211 — FAX: 314-884-4297
The center offers counseling for a wide range of business issues and problems.

Montana

Montana Science and Technology Alliance
46 North Last Chance Gulch, Suite 2B
Helena, MT 59620 — 406-449-2778
The Alliance provides funds to early stage, technology based companies seeking to commercialize products or processes in the state.

Montana Inventors Association
RR #1, Box 31
Highwood, MT 59450 — 406-733-5031
Contact Fred Davison

Small Business Development Center
Montana Department of Commerce
1424 Ninth Avenue
Helena, MT 59620 — 406-444-4780
The center offers counseling for a wide range of business issues and problems.

Nebraska

Nebraska Technical Assistance Center
University of Nebraska - Lincoln
P.O. Box 880535
W 191 Nebraska Hall — 402-472-5600
Lincoln, NE 68588-0535 — 1-800-332-0265 (in NE)
Found within the College of Engineering and Technology, the center offers counseling services to inventors on patents and trademarks. The free assistance is for preliminary information. For more technical help, the office will refer inventors elsewhere.

Small Business Development Center
University of Nebraska at Omaha
60th & Dodge Street
CBA, Room 407 — 402-554-2521
Omaha, NE 68182 — FAX: 402-554-3747
The center offers counseling for a wide range of business issues and problems.

Nevada

Nevada Inventors Association
P.O. Box 9905
Reno, NV 89507
Contact: Don Costar
This association holds monthly meetings, workshops and publishes a monthly newsletter. It networks with other inventors associations to keep abreast of their activities. Annual dues are $25.

Small Business Development Center
University of Nevada Reno
College of Business Administration — 702-784-1717
Reno, NV 89557-0100 — FAX: 702-784-4337
The center offers counseling for a wide range of business issues and problems.

New Hampshire

Service Corps of Retired Executives (SCORE)
Stewart Nelson Bldg.
143 Main Street   603-226-7763
Concord, NH 03302   603-666-7561
SCORE offices offer counseling on a variety of questions and can help inventors with marketing, commercialization and related issues.

Small Business Development Center
University of New Hampshire
108 McConnell Hall   603-862-2200
Durham, NH 03824   FAX: 603-862-4468
The center offers counseling for a wide range of business issues and problems.

New Jersey

Corporation for the Application of Rutgers Research
Rutgers, The State University of New Jersey
P.O. Box 1179
Piscataway, NJ 08854   908-932-4038
This corporation counsels inventors on commercialization and patent processes, provides critical reviews of inventors, and assesses marketability. Equity for services.

National Society of Inventors
539 Laurel Place
South Orange, NJ 07079   201-596-3322
This society counsels inventors on the commercialization and patenting processes; provides critical reviews of inventions and provides communications among inventors, manufacturers, developers and venture capitalists. It holds monthly meetings and publishes a newsletter. There are annual dues.

Small Business Development Center
Rutgers University
180 University Avenue
3rd Floor - Ackerson Hall   201-648-5950
Newark, NJ 07102   FAX: 201-648-1110
The center offers counseling for a wide range of business issues and problems.

New Mexico

Thunderbird Technical Group
(Also known as the Albuquerque Invention Club)
P.O. Box 30062
Albuquerque, NM 87190   505-266-3541
The contact is Dr. Albert Goodman, president of the club. The club meets on a monthly basis for speakers and presentations by different inventors. Members include patent attorneys, investors, and manufacturers. Annual dues are $10.

Small Business Development Center
Santa Fe Community College
P.O. Box 4187   505-438-1362
Santa Fe, NM 87502-4187   FAX: 505-438-1237
The center offers counseling for a wide range of business issues and problems.

New York

Center for Technology Transfer
State University of New York College of Oswego
209 Park Hall
Oswego, NY 13126-3599   315-341-2128
The center counsels inventors on the commercialization and patent processes, provides critical reviews of inventions, and provides prototype fabrication and development. There are fees or royalties from sales, as well as laboratory and materials costs.

Inventors Society of Western N.Y.
P.O. Box 23654
Rochester, NY 14692   716-454-6899
This non-profit organization provides inventors with information and guidance so the inventor can decide what is the best course of action. There are some fees for services, $65/year.

Small Business Development Center
State University of New York
SUNY Central Plaza S-523   518-443-5398

Albany, NY 12246   FAX: 518-465-4992
The center offers counseling for a wide range of business issues and problems.

North Carolina

Innovation Research Fund
North Carolina Technology Development Authority
P.O. Box 13169
Research Triangle Park, NC 27709-3169   919-990-8558
This fund provides financial assistance to enable inventors to commercialize inventions or develop improvements. The authority receives a return on its investments through royalties from sales of the sponsored product.

Small Business Development Center
University of North Carolina
4509 Creedmoor Road, Suite 201   919-571-4154
Raleigh, NC 27612   FAX: 919-571-4161
The center offers counseling for a wide range of business issues and problems.

North Dakota

Center for Innovation and Business Development
University of North Dakota
University Station, Box 8103
Grand Forks, ND 58202   701-777-3132
This center conducts seminars and workshops with speakers; counsels on the commercialization and patenting process; provides communications among inventors, manufacturers, and patent attorneys. There are fees for services.

Small Business Development Center
118 Gamble Hall, UND
University Station, Box 7308   701-777-3700
Grand Forks, ND 58202-7308   FAX: 701-777-3650
The center offers counseling for a wide range of business issues and problems.

Ohio

Ohio Inventors Association
9855 Sand Ridge Rd.
Millfield, OH 45761   614-797-4434
This association is affiliated with the Inventors Connection of Greater Cleveland, Inventors Club of Greater Cincinnati, Inventors Network of Columbus, Inventors Council of Dayton, etc. The Ohio Association helps local clubs and works to solve problems common to all inventors. Ron Docie, the contact person, is knowledgeable about a wide range of inventors' issues and keeps abreast of inventors' organizations.

Numbers for other organizations:
Inventors Connection of Greater Cleveland   216-226-9681
Inventors Council of Dayton   513-294-7447
Inventors Club of Cincinnati   513-298-8423
Columbus Inventors Council   614-292-1993
Inventors Network of Columbus   614-291-7900
These associations all meet on a regular basis, provide communications among inventors, manufacturers, patent attorneys, etc., and often publish newsletters. There are annual dues.

Docie Marketing
9855 Sand Ridge Rd,
Millfield, OH 45761   614-797-4434
This profit-making company counsels inventors on the commercialization process, provides critical review of inventions and arranges meetings between inventors and manufacturers.

Small Business Development Center
Department of Development
30 East Broad Street
23rd Floor, P.O. Box 1001   614-466-2711
Columbus, OH 43226   FAX: 614-466-0829
The center offers counseling for a wide range of business issues and problems.

Oklahoma

Invention Development Center
8230 SW 8th Street
Oklahoma City, OK 73128   405-376-2362

The center holds regular meetings, often with speakers, publishes a newsletter, and offers counseling and technical assistance to inventors. Annual dues are $25.

Inventors' Assistance Act
P.O. Box 26980
Oklahoma City, OK 73126   405-841-5143
This Act provides counseling and market analysis for inventors accepted into the program. There is a filing fee.

Oklahoma Inventors Congress
P.O. Box 18797
Oklahoma City, OK 73154-0797   405-848-1991
The Congress holds regular meetings with topical speakers, counsels inventors on the patent process, and publishes a monthly newsletter. It is affiliated with the Office of the Governor, Department of Commerce, National Congress of Inventors Organizations. Annual dues are $10.

Small Business Development Center
Southeastern Oklahoma State University
Station A, Box 2584   405-924-0277
Durant, OK 74701   FAX: 405-924-7071
The center offers counseling for a wide range of business issues and problems.

Oregon

Small Business Development Centers (SBDCs) at three state colleges and the community colleges can counsel inventors and direct them where to go for patent process, etc. SBDCs at state colleges are: Southern Oregon State, 503-482-5838; Oregon Institute of Technology, 503-885-1760; and Eastern Oregon State, 1-800-452-8639.

Pennsylvania

American Society of Inventors
P.O. Box 58426
Philadelphia, PA 19102-8426   215-546-6601
Members are counseled on the commercialization and patent processes; critical reviews of inventions, and assessments of market potential are provided. The Society also offers technical assistance and referrals. There are dues.

Technology Commercialization
Lehigh University
Rauch Business Center #37
621 Taylor Street
Bethlehem, PA 18015   215-758-3446
The main focus is directed towards commercialization of university research although commercialization assistance is given to some private inventors each year. This group provides critical reviews of inventions and provides communication among inventors, manufacturers, patent attorneys, and venture capitalists. There are fees for services.

Small Business Development Center
Bucknell University
Dana Engineering Bldg., 1st Floor
Lewisburg, PA 17837   717-524-1249
The center offers counseling for a wide range of business issues and problems.

Rhode Island

Service Corps of Retired Executives (SCORE)
c/o U.S. Small Business Administration
380 Westinghouse, Room #511
Providence, RI 02903   401-528-4571
Volunteers in the SCORE office are experts in many areas of business management and can offer advice to inventors in areas including marketing and the commercialization process.

Small Business Development Center
7 Jackson Walkway
Providence, RI 02903   401-831-1330
The center offers counseling for a wide range of business issues and problems.

South Carolina

Center for Applied Technology (CAT)
Emerging Technology Center

Clemson University
511 Westinghouse Rd.
Pendleton, SC 29670
CAT Center   803-646-4000
Emerging Technology Center   803-646-4020
The center helps inventors on the commercialization and patent processes, assesses market potential of specific inventions and assists inventors in technically refining inventions. It works with the Small Business Development Center, South Carolina Research Authority, Battelle Institute and other organizations. Some of the services are free, others have nominal fees.

Small Business Development Center
South Carolina State College
School of Business Administration
Orangeburg, SC 29117   803-536-8445
The center offers counseling for a wide range of business issues and problems.

South Dakota

Dakota State University
SBIR PTAC Assistance Center
East Hall, Room 3
Madison, SD 57042   605-256-5555
This office can provide guidance to inventors on a wide range of issues: commercialization, patent process, marketability, etc. It has grant money available.

Small Business Development Center
University of South Dakota
School of Business
414 East Clark   605-677-5272
Vermillion, SD 57069   FAX: 605-677-5427
The center offers counseling for a wide range of business issues and problems.

Tennessee

Tennessee Inventors Association
P.O. Box 11225
Knoxville, TN 37939-1225   615-690-3109
Monthly meetings are held where a wide range of topical subjects are discussed: patenting, venture capital, marketing, etc. Workshops and invention exhibitions are held periodically. Annual dues are $30.

Venture Exchange Forum
P.O. Box 23184
Knoxville, TN 37933-1184   615-694-6772
The Forum holds monthly meetings, and arranges meetings between inventors and manufacturers. Annual dues are $25.

Small Business Development Center
Jackson State Community College
2046 North Parkway Street
Jackson, TN 38104   901-424-5389
The center offers counseling for a wide range of business issues and problems.

Texas

Technology Business Development
Texas Engineering Experiment Station
Texas A&M University
310 Wisenbaker Engineering Research Center
College Station, TX 77843-3369   409-845-0538
The organization conducts workshops, provides counseling on commercialization and patent processes, offers critical reviews of inventions on a selected basis, assesses invention's marketability, and assists with patent searches. State appropriations, federal grants and subscriptions to newsletter are available.

Texas Inventors Association
4000 Rock Creek Drive, #100
Dallas, TX 75204
The association holds meetings, and provides counseling for inventors on commercialization and patent processes. There are annual dues.

North Texas-Dallas SBDC
Dallas Community College District
1402 Corinth Street   214-565-5831

Dallas, TX 75215   FAX: 214-565-5815
The center offers counseling for a wide range of business issues and problems.

Utah

Utah Small Business Development Center
University of Utah
College of Business
Salt Lake City, UT 84101   801-581-7905
The center offers workshops, seminars and conferences, counsels inventors on the commercialization and patent processes, and supplies publications about patenting, licensing and financing. There are nominal fees for workshops, etc.

Vermont

Economic and Development Office
State of Vermont
109 State Street
Montpelier, VT 05609   802-828-3221
Staff member Curt Carter can counsel inventors on the commercialization and marketing processes as well as other areas, and refer them to other places as needed. There are no fees.

Small Business Development Center
University of Vermont
Extension Service, Morrill Hall   802-656-4479
Burlington, VT 05405   FAX: 802-656-8642
The center offers counseling for a wide range of business issues and problems.

Virginia

Technology Commercialization
Virginia's Center for Innovative Technology
2214 Rock Hill Rd., #600
Herndon, VA 22070   703-689-3043
The center provides seed money to colleges and universities to set up entrepreneurship or innovation centers. Such centers are at the College of William and Mary, George Mason University, James Madison University, Longwood College, Old Dominion University, University of Virginia, and Virginia Commonwealth. Inventors are counseled on the commercialization and patent processes at these centers and can have their inventions assessed for market potential.

Small Business Development Center
Department of Economic Development
1021 East Cary Street, 11th Floor   804-371-8258
Richmond, VA 23219   FAX: 804-371-8137
The center offers counseling for a wide range of business issues and problems.

Washington

Innovation Assessment Center
2001 6th Ave., Suite 2608
Seattle, WA 98121   206-464-5450
Part of the Small Business Development Center, it performs commercial evaluations of inventions, counseling and provides assistance with patentability searches. There are fees for services.

Small Business Development Center
Washington State University

245 Todd Hall   509-335-1576
Pullman, WA 99164   FAX: 509-335-0949
The center offers counseling for a wide range of business issues and problems.

West Virginia

Small Business Development Center
West Virginia Institute of Technology
Montgomery, WV 25136   304-442-5501
The center offers counseling for a wide range of business issues and problems.

Wisconsin

Center for Innovation and Development
University of Wisconsin - Stout
103 First Ave, W
Menomonie, WI 54751   715-232-5026
The center counsels inventors on the commercialization and patent processes; provides critical reviews of inventions; assists inventors on technically refining inventions; and provides prototype development. There are fees for services.

Wisconsin Innovation Service Center
402 McCutchan Hall
UW-Whitewater
Whitewater, WI 53190   414-472-1365
Provides early stage market research for inventors. There are fees for services.

Small Business Development Center
University of Wisconsin
432 North Lake Street, Room 423   608-263-7794
Madison, WI 53706   FAX: 608-262-3878
The center offers counseling for a wide range of business issues and problems.

Wyoming

Small Business Development Center
Casper College
350 West A, Suite 200
Casper, WY 82601   307-235-4827
Barbara Stuckert, who works in the office, is able to help inventors on a wide range of issues including patenting, commercialization and intellectual property rights. There are no fees for services.

Canada

Innovative Center
156 Columbia Street W.
Waterloo, Ontario NN26363   519-885-5870
Provides inventors with market research, idea testing, and helps guide inventors up to the patent stage.

Note: The U.S. Small Business Administration, Office of Business Development publishes *Ideas Into Dollars* which identifies the main challenges in product development and provides a list of resources to help inventors and innovators take their ideas into the marketplace. The price is $2. To order, send check or money order to SBA Publications, P.O. Box 30, Denver, CO 80201-0030. Order number PI1.

Home-Based Business Resources

If you're looking for a $10,000 loan to start a craft business out of your home, or you would love to get a $100,000 freelance writing contract you can operate from your kitchen table, call your favorite uncle, Uncle Sam. Did you know that government offices, like the National Park Service, routinely award contracts to artists and photographers for over $50,000?

The government is likely to have all the money, help and information you will ever need for running your home-based business and what's great about these resources is that they're free. All the Fortune 500 companies rely on government programs and information sources for succeeding in their business, and you can too.

Why spend hundred of dollars hiring a lawyer to explain the trade laws that might apply to your business when you can talk to a legal expert at the Federal Trade Commission about them for the price of a phone call? Why pay for expensive crime insurance from a private carrier to protect your home office, when you might be able to get the same coverage from the federal government for a fraction of the cost? Why hire a high-priced specialist who will promise to find you customers, when the government can help you do it for free? And just because you work out of your home doesn't mean that you can't compete for lucrative government contracts just like the big companies do.

Not only can the government help you start and run your home-based business, they can even help you furnish it at bargain basement prices. By attending government surplus property auctions, you can get all the office furniture, computer equipment, and filing cabinets you need for pennies on the dollar. The Department of Defense, for example, has auctioned off office chairs for $10 and desks for $25.

Home-based businesses are among the fastest growing kinds of business in the U.S. The Small Business Administration estimates that there are about 4 million home-based businesses in the U.S. today. That represents 25% of the total number of sole proprietorship businesses in the country. And according to the American Home-Based Business Association, about 63 million Americans do some kind of work out of their home. There are a lot of people who've decided against the morning commute and fighting over the Xerox and coffee machines at the office.

The big advantage of running a business out of your home is that it keeps overhead costs to a minimum. A big overhead can be fatal to any new business venture. You don't have to spend half-a-million dollars to find out that running a fumigation or TV repair service really isn't your dream business -- no big office space to rent, no extra employees sitting around, no big insurance bills.

One of the safest ways to start a business is by starting a home-based business. And even a safer way is to take advantage of all the free help available from your Uncle Sam.

* Free Videos on How To Start a Business In Your Home

Office of Business Development & Marketing
Small Business Administration (SBA)
409 3rd St., SW
Washington, DC 20416   202-205-6665
or
Oklahoma State University
Agricultural Communications
111 Public Information Building
Stillwater, OK 74078   405-744-3737

The SBA has produced a home video especially geared toward home-based business owners. *Home-Based Business: A Winning Blueprint* takes you through many of the steps necessary to a successful home-based business, from setting up your home office and networking strategies, to avoiding isolation and building the right kind of image for your company. You can purchase the video for $39 from the following address: SBA, "Successes", Dept. A, P.O. Box 30, Denver, CO 80202-0030. You can **review the video for free for 30 days** before you decide to purchase. Contact the office listed above in Washington, DC.

Home-Based Business Basics shows potential business owners how to do market research, handle finances, cope with legal problems, do promotions and juggle family relationships. The film is produced by a member of the County Cooperative Extension service and is available on a free loan basis at local county cooperative extension service offices throughout the country. Call your local operator for your nearest office. Or, you can purchase the film for $30 directly from the producer listed above.

* Is Your Advertising Legal?

Advertising Practices Division
Federal Trade Commission (FTC)
6th and Pennsylvania Ave., NW
Washington, DC 20580   202-326-3131

Attracting new customers through advertising is an important part of a successful business, but you'll want to do it fairly and honestly. This division of the FTC can provide you with information on ways to comply with the law and avoid making deceptive advertising claims.

* Is Your Office Asbestos and Radon Free?

Office of Information and Public Affairs
Consumer Product Safety Commission (CPSC)
Washington, DC 20207   1-800-638-2772
or
Radon Division (ANR-464)
Office of Radon Programs
U.S. Environmental Protection Agency (EPA)
401 M St., SW   1-800-SOS-RADON
Washington, DC 20460   202-233-9370

If you've set your office up in your basement, you might be exposing yourself to hazardous asbestos insulation. To find out more about home asbestos and eliminating its hazards, contact the CPSC for a free copy of *Asbestos in the Home*. Setting up an office in the basement may also make you vulnerable to the effects of radon gas, which often enters homes through cracks in the basement floors. To get more information on the radon risks in your area, how to test for radon, and how to protect your home, contact the EPA office above. They can send you free radon publications, along with the number of a radon expert in your state.

* Keep Up To Date On The Cheapest Way To Send Mail

Business Mailer Updates
P.O. Box 999
Springfield, VA 22150-0999
or
Marketing Department
Regular Mail Services Division
U.S. Postal Service
475 L'Enfant Plaza, SW
Washington, DC 20260-6336   1-800-238-3150

When you do business through the mail, you need to keep up on rate and classification changes when they occur. The U.S. Postal Service puts out *Memo To Mailers*, a free monthly publication to keep you posted of any of these changes, along with other relevant postal news. To be put on the mailing list, write to the above address, or for more information about the *Memo*, contact: Communications Department, U.S. Postal Service, 475 L'Enfant Plaza, SW, Washington, DC 20260; 1-800-238-3150.

Part of having a successful home-based business is knowing how to use the mail service effectively. To help you better prepare your mail for sending, the Marketing Department of the Postal Service has put together a free booklet, *A Guide To Business Mail Preparation*. This booklet gives you information on addressing for automation, postnet bar codes, and FIM patterns, all of which prepare your mail to be processed more efficiently, economically, and accurately, which makes for happier customers.

* How Business Reply Mail Can Bring You New Customers

Rates and Classification Department
U.S. Postal Service
475 L'Enfant Plaza
Washington, DC 20260   1-800-238-3150

If you often use the mail in your business to solicit customers, you might look into using business reply mail. Under this service, you guarantee to pay the postage for all replies returned to you at the regular first class rate plus a business reply fee. To use this service, you have to pay a small annual permit charge. Contact this office for more information on setting up this service for your business mailings.

* How to Write Off Your Car and Home, and Summer Vacation As a Business Expense

Taxpayer Services
Internal Revenue Service (IRS)
U.S. Department of the Treasury
1111 Constitution Ave., NW
Room 2422
Washington, DC 20224   1-800-829-3676

One advantage to owning a home-based business is being able to write off car expenses related to your job. For more information on guidelines for writing off your car, get a free copy of *Business Use Of A Car* (#917), which explains the expenses you may deduct for the use of your car in your home-based business. A copy of *Business Use Of Your Home* (#587) can help you decide if you qualify to deduct certain expenses for using part of your home for your business. Deductions for the business use of a home computer are also discussed. The IRS will also show you how to piggyback a vacation onto your business travel. *Travel, Entertainment, and Gift Expenses* (#463) explains what expenses you may deduct for business-related travel, meals, entertainment, and gifts for your business, along with the reporting and record-keeping requirements for these expenses.

* Free Tax Consulting By The Experts

Internal Revenue Service (IRS)
1111 Constitution Ave, NW
Washington, DC 20224   1-800-829-1040
          or
Your Local IRS Office

Why pay big money to a tax attorney or accountant when you can get better information for free? Many entrepreneurs believe that you will get a more favorable answer by hiring your own expert than you would if you call the IRS, but this has not shown to be the case. The law is the law, and private studies show that your chances of saving money on your tax bill is no greater whether you go to the IRS or to a high priced consultant for help. The problem is that most people don't know how to call the IRS to get the right answer. If the person at the IRS hotline seems a little unsure of their answer or if you just want another opinion, ask the IRS person to have a specialist call you back. Within a day or two you will get a call from an IRS expert who specializes in your question. They will take as much time as you need to make sure that you get all the deductions to which you are entitled.

* Free Help To Start a Home-Based Tax Preparation Business

Volunteer and Education Branch

Taxpayer Service Division
Internal Revenue Service (IRS)
U.S. Dept. of Treasury
1111 Constitution Ave, NW, Room 1315
Washington, DC 20224   202-829-1040

If you want to start your own tax preparation business you don't have to pay H&R Block or some other commercial organizations $200 to take a course. You can take a free course from the best experts in the world, the IRS. Many times these courses are given by IRS auditors and this is how you really learn the inside secrets on how to avoid the wrath of the IRS computer. Courses are available every year during the fall. In return for free training you are required to volunteer a few hours of your time during one tax season to help others prepare their returns. The rest of your time you can charge for preparing tax returns. The IRS also offers free small business workshops which assist entrepreneurs in understanding their tax obligations.

* Make Sure Your Computer Screen Isn't Hazardous To Your Health

Information & Consumer Affairs
Occupational Safety and Health Administration (OSHA)
U.S. Department of Labor
Washington, DC 20210   202-219-8148

People who run home-based businesses often spend many hours sitting in front of their computer screens doing work. If you're one of these people, you should be aware of what the U.S. Department of Labor has discovered about the hazardous of display terminals. The following two relevant publications are available from OSHA: *Display Terminals* and *Working Safely with Display Terminals*.

* Getting The Most Out Of Your Home Computer

Office of Business Development & Marketing
Small Business Administration (SBA)
409 3rd St., SW
Washington, DC 20416   202-205-6665

Setting up the right computer system is very important for many home-based businesses. The SBA has a couple of publications to help you out with computer problems:

How To Get Started With A Small Business Computer. Helps you forecast your computer needs, evaluate the alternatives and select the right computer system for your business. (MP14) $.50.

Focus on the Facts: Buying a Computer for a Small Business. Covers most common questions about whether and what to buy in terms of home computers. Also includes a list of common computer lingo to know when selecting a computer. Free.

* Free Help In Setting Up Your Own Complaint Handling System

Marketing Practices Division
Federal Trade Commission (FTC)
6th & Pennsylvania Ave., NW
Washington, DC 20580   202-326-3128

A successful business knows how to keep consumers coming back, even after they've complained about a product or service. The way they do this is by establishing a fair and effective system of resolving customer complaints quickly and inexpensively. The FTC works to promote such procedures among businesses, and they will provide you with information to help you develop an effective consumer complaint process for your business.

* How To Handle Salesmen Who Come To Your Home

Enforcement Division
Federal Trade Commission (FTC)
6th & Pennsylvania Ave., NW
Washington, DC 20580   202-326-3034

If your home based business gets sales people coming to your door trying to sell you items you can't really decide if you want, you should be aware of the FTC's *Cooling-Off Rule*, which requires sellers to give consumers notice of their three-day cancellation rights. For more information about the Cooling Off Rule, including a free pamphlet that describes the law, contact the FTC.

Home-Based Business Resources

* Free Seminars On Starting A Business At Home

Contact your County Cooperative Extension Service
listed under county government in your telephone book

Most counties in the U.S. have Cooperative Extension Services that can provide you with information on how to start up and run a home-based business. Many can provide you with free publications, while others may even run free workshops or seminars on home-based business--it all depends on what your county Extension Service is doing. Most of these Services put out free newsletters that describe upcoming events, such as workshops, along with articles that might be of interest to you as a home-based business owner. Contact your Cooperative Extension Service to be put on their mailing list and for more information about their home-based business resources.

* Does Your Business Have Good Credit? Get It Fixed For Free

Contact your County Cooperative Extension Service
listed under county government in your telephone book
or
Consumer Credit Counseling Service (CCCS)
8701 Georgia Ave   301-589-5600
Silver Spring, MD 20910   1-800-388-CCCS

Can't get a business loan because you have bad credit? Don't spend hundreds of dollars to a credit repair clinic to tell you how to do it -- contact your county's Cooperative Extension Service. These Services routinely run money and budgeting workshops at no charge that can show you how to fix your credit problems and pay off your bills more efficiently. If your county Cooperative Extension Service doesn't hold money workshops, you might consider contacting the Consumer Credit Counseling Service, which runs non-profit counseling services across the country, including in your state. Call them at 1-800-388-CCCS for the service nearest you.

* Cheap Crime Insurance for Your Business Equipment

Federal Crime Insurance
P.O. Box 6301   1-800-638-8780
Rockville, MD 20850   301-251-1660

If your home is burglarized, your home-based business could suffer large losses, such as expensive computer and telephone equipment. Residents in 13 states are eligible for a federal crime insurance program that actually subsidizes the cost of insurance to you. This means cheaper insurance premiums because the federal government is paying part of the bill for you. The following states and territories participate: AL, CA, CT, DE DC, FL, GA, IL, KS, MD, NJ, NY, PA, RI, TN, and Puerto Rico and the Virgin Islands. Contact this office for more information about the program and an application.

* The Best Way To Keep Your Customers

Office of Consumer Affairs
U.S. Department of Commerce
14th & Constitution Ave., NW
Room H5718
Washington, DC 20230   202-482-5001

Finding customers is only half the story of a successful business; you also need to know how to keep them once you have them. And to do that you need to know how to develop good customer relations through honest and effective advertising, warranties, product safety, and complaint handling procedures. Contact this office for more information on these subjects, along with getting free copies of the following publications from their series of *Consumer Affairs Guides For Business*:

Advertising, Packaging, and Labeling
Product Warranties and Servicing
Managing Consumer Complaints
Credit And Financial Issues
Consumer Product Safety

This office can also provide you with information about local small business conferences based on these consumer affairs issues.

* Choosing Day Care for Work-At-Home Families

County Cooperative Extension Service
6707 Groveton Dr.
Clinton, MD 20735   301-868-9410

If you're running your own small business or a business out of your home, you might need to consider finding good and reliable day care for your children to give you the time you need for your business. This office can send you a free copy of *How To Select Quality Day Care For Your Child*, which shows you what to look for in day care.

* How The Law Protects You If You Don't Pay Your Bills

Credit Practices Division
Federal Trade Commission (FTC)
6th & Pennsylvania Ave., NW
Washington, DC 20580   202-326-3758

If you're thinking of starting a debt collection agency, you'll need to know what the law says you can and cannot do to collect a debt for a client. The FTC can provide you with information on the *Fair Debt Collection Practices Act*, which prohibits debt collectors from engaging in unfair, deceptive, or abusive practices, such as overcharging, harassment, and disclosing consumers' debts to third parties. If you're being harassed by a debt collection agency, the FTC would like to hear about it.

* Free Legal Help On The Best Way To Treat Your Employees

Employment Standards Administration (ESA)
U.S. Department of Labor
Room C4325
Washington, DC 20210   202-219-8743

One of the reasons people want to run their own businesses is that they don't like working for unfair and abusive bosses. To make sure that you don't turn into one of them, you'll need to know the federal laws that protect your employees' rights. The following free publications from the ESA will give you a good introduction to those labor laws:

Employer's Guide to Compliance with Federal Wage-Hour Laws
Federal Minimum Wage and Overtime Pay Standards
Handy Reference Guide to the Fair Labor Standards Act
Highlights of Computing Overtime Pay Under the FLSA
How the Federal Wage and Hour Laws Applies to Holidays
Employment of Apprentices
Employment of Messengers
Making EEO and Affirmative Action Work

Also see *Labor Laws and Small Business* below for more information on this subject.

* How To Get People and Companies Who Owe You Money To Pay Up

Local Postmaster of the U.S. Postal Service
  Call the information operator for the city in question
State Division of Motor Vehicles
  Call your state government operator in your state capitol
State Attorney General Office
  Call your state government operator in your state capitol
State Office of Uniform Commercial Code
  Call your state government operator in your state capitol
State Office of Corporations
  Call your state government operator in your state capitol

Before you pay an attorney big money to help you collect a bad debt, there are a number of government offices you can turn to that will help you get your money for free or for just a few dollars.

If you are looking for an individual who moved, contact the U.S. Postal Service and the state Division of Motor Vehicles. The Post Office in the city of the last known address of your deadbeat friend will give you their forwarding address and charge you only $1.00. This information is kept at most Post Offices for 18 months. And for a few dollars, almost every state government will give you the address of anyone from their file of driver's licenses. Almost everyone has a driver's license.

If a business owes you money, a letter to the Attorney General in the state where the business is headquartered can easily shake loose your money. Most Attorney General offices will send the business an official letter of inquiry, and this is enough to scare any legitimate business person into paying their bills.

Another effective method is to use the information in government offices to shame a business into paying their bill. The Office of Corporations in every state capitol will give you the name and address of all the officers of any businesses in their state. And the state Office of Uniform Commercial Code will give you the names of all the other people that this business owes money. It is a law that anytime a business, or individual, borrows money and puts up an asset as collateral, the information is filed at the Office of Uniform Commercial Code. When you send a letter asking someone for payment, you can send copies of the letter to all these other people. And what is most effective, is that the people listed as officers of most small businesses are friends and relatives of the owner, and it can be very embarrassing for a business owner to have them know how unfairly they are treating you.

* Free Accounting Help

Contact your State Department of Economic Development Office for the Small Business Development Center (SBDC) near you

Accountants are expensive, especially if your small business, like most, doesn't have a lot of working capital to throw around. Instead of going out and hiring your own personal accountant, contact your local SBDC. Many of these centers have accounting experts who will sit down with you and help you develop your own accounting and record keeping systems. They can also help you work through any accounting problems that you might encounter. If you don't have an SBDC near you, contact your nearest Small Business Administration Office; they work with the Service Corps of Retired Executives (SCORE) whose members can also provide you with free accounting assistance and advice.

* Entrepreneur Quiz

Superintendent of Documents
Government Printing Office (GPO)
Washington, DC 20402   202-783-3238

For $2.00, GPO will send you a copy of *Starting and Managing a Business from Your Home*, which includes a questionnaire for you to answer to help you decide if you have the right kind of personality to be a successful entrepreneur and home-based business owner. Also included are descriptions of products and services to help you start your own home-based business, such as business planning, record keeping, taxes, and insurance.

* What You Need To Know When Selling Food and Medical Products

Small Business Coordinator
Food and Drug Administration (FDA)
5600 Fishers Lane
Room 15-61, HFC 50
Rockville, MD 20857   301-443-1583

If you are going to be selling any food or drug products as part of your business, you'll need to know how to comply with the FDA's packaging and labeling regulations for these products. This office can explain FDA procedures and help you comply with their rules. Contact them for a free copy of *A Small Business Guide to the FDA*, which will give you an overview of the small business compliance program.

* How To Pick A Work-At-Home Franchise

Bureau of Consumer Protection
Federal Trade Commission
6th and Pennsylvania Ave, NW
Washington, DC 20580   202-326-2970
or
International Franchising Association
1350 New York Ave, NW
Washington, DC 20005   202-628-8000
or
Your State Franchising Office

Just because you want to run a business out of your home, doesn't mean that you're not in a position to consider owning a franchise. Owning a franchise can mean you already have name recognition and advertising done for you. Of course, Pizza Hut isn't going to let you run a business out of your home, but others might, like lawn care companies, leak detection services, upholstery cleaners, commercial office cleaners, maid services, sewer and drain cleaning services, and many more.

The Federal Trade Commission will send you a number of free publications that will tell you what you need to know before buying a franchise. The International Franchise Association also has a number of publications on this topic, but they charge a small fee.

There are a number of state governments that require franchisors who are selling franchises in their state to file detailed background information on their company which is made available to the public. Call your state capitol operator to see if

your state has such requirements, or call the Federal Trade Commission and they will tell you which states you can contact to get this information.

* Work At Home On A $100,000 Government Contract

Contact your State Department of Economic Development Office for the Small Business Development Center near you
or
Your U.S. Congressman or Senator

Both the federal and state governments buy all kinds of products and services, regardless of whether the seller works out of their home or not. And you don't have to sell missile or tank parts to land a contract. They buy the services of freelance writers, artists, computer consultants, even janitors. Each U.S. Congressman's office has access to a computer database that keeps track of all the current government contract opportunities for businesses. By contacting your congressman, you can have them do a computer search to find out if the government is looking for products or services that your business provides. The same is true for the Small Business Development Centers and Procurement Assistance Offices in your state.

* Check If You And Your Employees Are Safe Working In Your Home

Publications Office
Occupational Safety and Health Administration (OSHA)
U.S. Department of Labor
200 Constitution Ave., NW
Room N-3101
Washington, DC 20210   202-219-4667

Depending on what your small business is, you might be faced with potential health and safety concerns, anything from indoor air quality to stiff joints from typing too much. OSHA has put out a series of free publications of interest to small businesses to help you remedy or avoid potential health and safety problems: *Handbook For Small Businesses, General Industry Digest, Construction Industry Digest*, and *Consultation Services For Employers*.

* Free Inspections of Your Home for Health And Safety Hazards

National Institute for Occupational Safety and Health
4676 Columbia Parkway
Cincinnati, OH 45226   1-800-356-4674

The National Institute for Occupational Safety and Health (NIOSH) is responsible for conducting research to make the nation's workplaces healthier and safer by responding to urgent requests for assistance from employers, employees, and their representatives where imminent hazards are suspected. They conduct inspections, laboratory and epidemiologic research, publish their findings, and make recommendations for improved working conditions. **They will also inspect any workplace for free if three employees sign a form alleging that the environment may be dangerous.** Employees have the option of keeping anonymous. If any of the following applies to you, NIOSH can provide you with more information:

Do you use a video display terminal most of the day?
Are you concerned abut the chemicals you are using in your dry cleaning?
Do you have tingling in your hands (carpal tunnel syndrome)?
Do you use a jackhammer most of the day and are now finding that your fingers are no longer sensitive to heat or cold?
Do you do the same motion again and again, such as on an assembly line?
Do you feel your job is causing you mental stress?
Are you having trouble hearing?

* How To Choose The Best Health Insurance Coverage

Office of Business Development & Marketing
Small Business Administration (SBA)
409 3rd St., SW
Washington, DC 20416
National Health Information Clearinghouse Hotline   1-800-827-5722

Owning your own business means that you no longer will have your health insurance taken care of the way it was when you worked for somebody else. To help you figure out the best way to find a health insurance plan best suited to your needs, the SBA has produced a free publication that's part of their *Focus on the Facts* series called *Small Business Health Insurance*. This publication covers such topics as indemnity, managed care, selecting a plan, and self insurance. Contact this office for your free copy.

Home-Based Business Resources

* How To Get Free Health Care If You Can't Afford Health Insurance

Public Health Service
Health Resource and Services Administration
5600 Fishers Lane, Room 11-25
Department of Health and Human Services   1-800-492-0359 (in MD)
Rockville, MD 20857   1-800-638-0742

If you can't afford health insurance and you meet certain income requirements, you may be eligible to receive free medical care under the Hill-Burton law. Under this law, hospitals and other health facilities that receive federal funding for construction and modernization must provide certain medical services at no charge to those who can't afford to pay. By calling the toll-free number above, you can find out which hospitals in your area are participating in this program, along with income eligibility requirements. If your home-based business is your only source of income, and it's making little or no profit, you may in fact be eligible for free health care.

* Free Home-Based Business Start Up Guide

Office of Business Development & Marketing
Small Business Administration (SBA)
Washington, DC 20416   1-800-827-5722

The SBA has put together a free pamphlet for those who are thinking about starting their own small business out of their homes: *How To Start A Home-Based Business*. This guide is part of the SBA's *Focus On The Facts* series of publications, which also includes information on raising capital, business planning, marketing, pricing, and exporting.

* $50,000 To Work On Your Invention

Office of Innovation, Research and Technology
U.S. Small Business Administration
409 3rd Street, SW
Washington, DC 20416   202-205-6450
or
Office of Technology Evaluation & Assessment
National Institute of Standards and Technology
Bldg. 411, Room A115
Gaithersburg, MD 20899   301-975-5500

Each year eleven government departments and agencies offer over $475 million in grant money to small businesses and individual entrepreneurs to work on new ideas under the Small Business Innovation Research program (SBIR). Recently a consultant working at home received $500,000 to develop a children's measuring board. A small business in Virginia received $50,000 to work on a new dental cream in his basement. There are three phases to the programs for those ideas that are accepted. Phase I is usually funded for 6 months with awards up to $50,000. This phase is used to investigate the feasibility of the researcher's idea. Phase II offers funding up to $500,000 and is offered if the feasibility phase is successful. Phase III is used for the pursuit of private funding from venture capitalist or other third parties in order to commercialize the product. These funds are granted on a competitive basis, but most state governments offer free assistance, and sometimes money, to entrepreneurs who want to apply for these grants. Contact the Small Business Administration office listed above for further information.

The National Institute of Standards and Technology in recent years made millionaires out of six people who submitted ideas to their Energy Related Inventions Assistance Program. This program will evaluate any energy related-invention and submit it to the U.S. Department of Energy for grant funding. Contact the office above to investigate the possibility of having your invention evaluated.

* How Labor Laws Affect Your Small Business

Office of Small and Disadvantaged
   Business Utilization
U.S. Department of Labor
200 Constitution Ave., NW, Room C-2318
Washington, DC 20210   202-523-9148

Just because you run a small or home-based business doesn't mean you don't have to obey federal labor laws like larger companies do. To find out what laws apply to your small business regarding such topics as wages, overtime, pensions, and health and safety, contact this office for a free copy of the booklet, *Major Laws Administered by the U.S. Department of Labor That Affect Small Business*. You should also contact your state's labor department to find out what state laws you should know.

* Should You Lease Or Buy A Car For Your Business

Consumer Information Center
Pueblo, CO 81009

As a small business owner, you might have to decide whether it's better for you to lease or buy a car for the business. Using plain English, the *Consumer Guide To Vehicle Leasing* will give you an explanation of the advantages and disadvantages of buying and leasing a car, and show you how to decide what's best for you. It's available for $.50 from the Consumer Information Center.

* Get Legal Help at Little or No Cost

Contact your State Department of Economic Development Office for the Small Business Development Center near you

Many Small Business Development Centers offer free or low-cost legal advice concerning laws that you might encounter in running your small business. And since most small businesses, especially home-based businesses, have very little working capital to throw around, the last thing you want to do is spend what you do have on an expensive lawyer. They can help you with legal question like:

When should you form a corporation?
Can my employer sue me if I take some of his business with me?

Before getting your own personal, and expensive, lawyer, contact a Small Business Development Center and see if they can give you the legal advice you need without having to spend a lot of money.

* Legal Advice On Trade Laws

Public Reference Branch
Federal Trade Commission (FTC)
Washington, DC 20580   202-326-2222

If you're not sure what business laws may apply to your new business, contact the FTC's Public Reference Branch. If you let them know what kind of business you're thinking of running, they'll be able to direct you to an expert at the FTC who specializes in the laws that you might need to know. They can send you copies of the regulations and help you comply with them. The following laws may apply to your small business. The FTC experts and their direct phone numbers are included:

Mail Order Rule, which requires companies to ship purchases made by mail when promised or give consumers the option to cancel an order for a refund. Elaine Kolish, 202-326-3042.
Care Labeling Rule, which requires manufacturers of textile clothing and fabrics to attach care label instructions. Steve Ecklund, 202-326-3034.
Unordered Merchandise Statute, which permits consumers to keep, as a free gift, unordered merchandise they receive through the U.S. mail. Vada Martin, 202-326-3034.
Cooling-Off Rule, which gives consumers three days to cancel sales for $25 or more made away from the seller's place of business. Brent Mickum, 202-326-3132.
Games of Chance in the Food Retailing and Gasoline Industries Rule, which requires disclosure of odds of winning prizes, the random distribution of winning prize pieces, and publication of winners' names. 216-522-4210.
Magnuson-Moss Act, which requires warranty information to be made available to consumers before making a purchase. 202-326-3128.
Holder-In-Due-Course Rule, which gives consumers certain protections when goods they buy on credit are not satisfactory. 202-326-3758.

* How Not To Pay For Cheap Products You Buy Through The Mail

Public Affairs Branch
Postal Inspection Service
U.S. Postal Service
475 L'Enfant Plaza, SW
Washington, DC 20260   202-268-4293
or
Enforcement Division
Federal Trade Commission
6th & Pennsylvania Ave., NW
Washington, DC 20580   202-326-3002

Since many home-based businesses do business through the mail, you should be aware of the ways some con artists use the mail to steal from you. To help you, the Postal Service publishes the free booklet, *Postal Crime Prevention: A Business Guide*, which shows business owners how to protect themselves. It includes information on different types of mail fraud, check cashing precautions, guidelines for mailroom security, bombs in the mail, and other problems with mail-related crime.

If you receive merchandise through the mail that you did not order, you can keep it as a gift. Find out your rights by contacting the Federal Trade Commission and obtaining a free copy of the *Unordered Merchandise Statute*.

* Have The Government Find Your Customers

Contact your State Office of Economic Development to locate a Small Business Development Center near you

or

State Government Offices

Contact your State Government Operator located in your state capitol

or

Federal Government Offices

Call your local U.S. Government Federal Information Center listed in your telephone directory or call the main Federal Information Center at 301-722-9000.

The government has what is indisputably the best marketing information in the world, and all the Fortune 500 companies use it to make their millions. If Citicorp uses government information to decide the best place to put up a new branch bank or for getting a list of rich people to sell trust services to, you can use the same sources to decide the best place to market a home improvement business or to get a mailing list of all the women in your neighborhood who are over 150 pounds to sell them a new diet product.

There are three basic starting places for tapping into all this huge marketing information. The best place to get free, or very-low-cost marketing consulting help is at your local Small Business Development Center (SBDC). These offices will sit down with you and help you work out the specifics on who your market is and how to reach them.

State governments offer a wide variety of market information. The Division of Motor Vehicles sells information from drivers licenses and motor vehicle registrations. With this you can identify all the rich single men over 6 feet tall in your zip code. You can also get listings of doctors, lawyers, real estate agents, and even delicatessens from state licensing and regulatory offices. Or, your state Census Data Center can identify those zip codes most likely to have young children who can afford orthodontist work. Your state government operator in your state capitol can help you locate the specific office that may be able to help you.

Federal government offices spend hundreds of millions of dollars on marketing information rarely used by entrepreneurs. The U.S. Dept. of Agriculture can give you information on the market for thousands of products, including house plants, diets, aquaculture, and even bull sperm. The U.S. Department of Commerce can give you the latest information on hundreds of products, including golf balls, computers, toys, or biotechnology. And the U.S. International Trade Administration provides marketing information on items like video games, mushrooms, and broom handles. Your local U.S. Government, Federal Information Center can help you locate the specific office that can help you.

* The Government Will Sell Your Service or Product In Other Countries

State Office of International Marketing

Contact your State Office of Economic Development located in your state capitol

Don't hire a high-priced international marketing consultant if you want to see if your product or service has any opportunity of being a success in another country. Both state and federal governments are very active in offering free and low cost assistance to small businesses who wish to take advantage of markets overseas. There are programs that will provide you with free market studies for your product in any country in the world. Other programs will have embassy officials who will locate local businesses who are willing to sell your product or service in that country. And other programs will provide you with financing to sell your products overseas.

* Find A Free Government Expert On Any Topic

Federal Government Offices

Call your local U.S. Government Federal Information Center listed in your telephone directory or call the main Federal Information Center at 301-722-9000

It is estimated that there are approximately 700,000 experts in the federal government, each spending their careers studying some aspect of business that entrepreneurs can use. If you are looking for expertise on how to sell a new t-shirt idea, you can call the government's underwear expert at the U.S.

International Trace Commission. This expert gets paid over $60,000 a year to study the t-shirt business, and if you treat her properly, she is available to you for the price of a telephone call. You are never going to find a private consultant who will know as much as this government expert. In fact, if you were to hire a private marketing consultant, they'd probably call a government expert to find the answer. They'd then turn around and charge you big bucks for the same information! You may be interested in the pasta expert at the Department of Commerce if you have a new pasta product. Or, the 900 number expert at the Federal Communication Commission if you're planning to start your own Love Line.

* What Are The Rules If You Sell Your Products Through The Mail?

Enforcement Division
Federal Trade Commission (FTC)
6th & Pennsylvania Ave., NW
Washington, DC 20580   202-326-3042

Since many home-based businesses do business through the mail, you'll need to be aware of the FTC's *Mail Order Rule*, which requires companies to ship purchases made by mail when promised or to give consumers the option to cancel their order for a refund. For more information on the rule and how it might apply to your business, contact the FTC.

* Free Marketing Help

Contact your State Office of Economic Development to locate a Small Business Development Center near you

Finding out if there's a market for your products or services is the most critical part of planning a successful business. This process includes having to analyze your competition, suppliers, and new customers. The SBA can hook you up with experts through the Service Corps of Retired Executives (SCORE) who can provide you with free advice on how to develop and execute an effective marketing plan. Don't spend a lot of money you don't have on a marketing "expert" you heard of or found in the telephone book. Get it done for free through an expert at your SBA office.

* $10,000 To Start a Craft Business In Your Home

Contact your State Office of Economic Development to locate a Small Business Development Center near you

Although there are no money programs especially targeted for home-based businesses, you can still apply for money that regular small businesses apply for through the SBA and state offices of economic development. There are, however, other sources of money aside from the SBA. The USDA's Farmers Home Administration, for example, provides grants and low-interest loans to businesses in rural areas with sagging economies and high unemployment.

* How To Set Up A Pension Plan For One Employee

Superintendent of Documents
Government Printing Office (GPO)
Washington, DC 20402   202-783-3238

If you hire permanent employees, you might be interested in finding out how to set up a pension plan for them. To do this, you'll need to know more about the pension laws. For $1.50, GPO will send you a copy of *Simplified Employee Pensions: What Small Businesses Need to Know*, a publication especially geared toward small business owners. For more general information about the pension laws, the following office will send you a list of their free pension publications: Division of Public Information, Pension and Welfare Benefits Administration, U.S. Department of Labor, Washington, DC 20210; 202-523-8921.

* 80% Discount on Office Equipment and Supplies

U.S. General Services Administration
18th & F Sts., NW
Washington, DC 20405   703-557-7786

If you need office furniture, typewriters, computers, wastebaskets, postage meters, paper clips -- practically anything you could possibly imagine -- for your home-based business, but don't have much money to spend on it, the federal government might be your best buy. The General Services Administration (GSA) is the federal government's housekeeper. They keep track of what supplies the government needs and doesn't need to run properly. And anything they don't need, such as overstock of office furniture and equipment, is auctioned off at rock-bottom prices. Auctions are held at GSA regional offices throughout the U.S. This office can put you on a mailing list to notify you of up-coming auctions, or you can contact the GSA office nearest you:

Atlanta
GSA, Surplus Sales Branch, 75 Spring St. SW, Atlanta, GA 30303; 404-331-0972.

Boston
GSA, Surplus Sales Branch, 10 Causeway St., 9th Floor, Boston, MA 02109; 617-565-7316.

Chicago
GSA, 230 S. Dearborn St., Chicago, IL 60604; 312-353-6061.

Denver
GSA, Surplus Supply Branch, Denver Federal Center, Building 41, Denver, CO 80225; 303-236-7705.

Fort Worth
GSA, Surplus Sales Branch, 819 Taylor St., Ft. Worth, TX 76102; 817-334-2351.

Kansas
GSA, Surplus Sales Branch, 6F BPS 4400, College Blvd., Suite 175, Overland, KS 66211; 913-236-2523.

New York
GSA, Surplus Sales Branch, 26 Federal Plaza, Room 20-2016, New York, NY 10278; 212-264-4824.

Philadelphia
GSA, Surplus Sales Branch, 9th & Market Sts., Philadelphia, PA 19107; 215-597-SALE.

San Francisco
GSA, Surplus Sales Branch, 525 Market St., 32nd Floor, San Francisco, CA 94105; 415-744-5242.

Washington State
GSA, Surplus Sales Branch, GSA Center, Auburn, WA 98002; 206-931-7566.

Washington, DC
GSA, 6808 Loisdale Rd., Bldg. A, Springfield, VA 22150; 703-557-7785.

What follows is a small list of other federal agencies that sell office furniture and supplies at auctions. Contact them for further information:

Internal Revenue Service	1-800-829-1040
U.S. Postal Service	202-268-2000
U.S. Customs Service	703-351-7887
Dept. of Defense	1-800-222-DRMS or 616-961-7331

* How To Protect Yourself From Office Supply Sale Schemes

Marketing Practices Division
Federal Trade Commission (FTC)
6th & Pennsylvania Ave., NW
Washington, DC 20580   202-326-3128

One of the ways small businesses can lose money is by becoming the victims of office supply sales schemes. This occurs when your company gets billed for supplies that you never ordered or received. You don't find out about the scheme until after your check is cashed. If you think you've been the victim of such a scheme or would like information about how con artists run them, contact the FTC.

* How To Package and Label Your Products According To The Law

Enforcement Division
Federal Trade Commission (FTC)
6th & Pennsylvania Ave., NW
Washington, DC 20580   202-326-3042

If you're producing and selling any consumer product, you need to be aware of the *Fair Packaging and Labeling Act*, which requires consumer commodities to be accurately labeled to describe the product's identity and net quantity. For more information on how this law might apply to your products, contact the FTC.

* How To Price Your Product So You Make The Most Money

Small Business Administration (SBA) Publications
409 3rd Street, SW
Washington, DC 20416   202-205-6670

You've got a good product or service but don't know how much you should charge. The SBA's publication, *Pricing Your Products And Services Profitably (FM13)*, tells you how to do it, and includes various pricing techniques and when to use them. Price: $1.00.

* How To Make Your Product Safe For Your Customers

Office of Information and Public Affairs
Consumer Product Safety Commission (CPSC)
Washington, DC 20207   1-800-638-2772

You might think that the product you're making or selling in your home-based business is great, but it needs to meet certain government safety standards before you can sell it. The CPSC publishes three free publications that will explain those standards to you:

Retailers Guide
Guide for Manufacturers, Distributors, and Retailers
Guide for Retailers

It's important that you know and follow their guidelines, because if a consumer is hurt from using your product, the CPSC has the authority to force you to recall it and correct the problem.

* Free Book On How To Raise Money for Your Small Business

Office of Business Development & Marketing
Small Business Administration (SBA)
409 3rd St., SW
Washington, DC 20416   202-205-6665

Raising money to run your business is as basic a task as there is to be successful. As part of its *Focus on the Facts* series, the SBA has put together a free publication titled *How to Raise Money for a Small Business*. This free fact sheet outlines the basics of raising money, where to find it, borrowing it, types of business loans, how to write a loan proposal, and SBA financial programs. Contact this office for a copy.

* How To Set Up A Self-Employed Retirement Plan

Taxpayer Services
Internal Revenue Service (IRS)
U.S. Department of the Treasury
1111 Constitution Ave., NW, Room 2422
Washington, DC 20224   1-800-829-1040

This IRS office can provide you with a free copy of *Self-Employed Retirement Plans (#560)*, which discusses retirement plans (Keogh plans) for self-employed individuals, such as those running home-based businesses, and certain partners in partnerships. These retirement plans allow the self-employed to put away a certain amount of their earnings each year into a tax free account retirement account.

* Free Consultants (SCORE)

Contact your local U.S. Small Business Administration (SBA) office
or
SBA Hotline   1-800-827-5722

SCORE members work with local SBA offices to provide small business owners with free advice and assistance on all kinds of problems that you might run into in your day-to-day work, such as problems in accounting, marketing, business planning, and so on. Contact your local Small Business Administration office for more information on how SCORE might help you out with you special business needs.

* Free Videos Show How To Start Or Expand A Small Business

Office of Business Development & Marketing
Small Business Administration
409 3rd St., SW
Washington, DC 20416   202-205-6665

The SBA has three VHS tapes that are helpful to business owners who are trying to develop marketing, promotional, and business plans. You can purchase these from the above address, or you can **request a copy to review for 30 days free of charge.**

Marketing: Winning Customers With A Workable Plan. Offers a step-by-step approach on how to write the best possible marketing plan for your business. Explains the best methods for determining customer needs, how to identify and develop a working profile for potential customers and much more. $30.00

The Business Plan: Your Roadmap To Success. Teaches the essentials of developing a business plan that will help lead you to capital, growth, and profitability. Tells what to include, what to omit, and how to get free help from qualified consultants. $30.00

Promotion: Solving The Puzzle. Shows you how to coordinate advertising, public relations, direct mail, and trade shows into a successful promotional strategy that targets new customers, increases sales, and saves you money. $30.00

* Hotline to Help Entrepreneurs Handle Small Business Stress

National Health Information Clearinghouse (NHIC)
P.O. Box 1133   1-800-336-4797
Washington, DC 20012   301-565-4167

Trying to run a business out of your home can put a lot of added stress on you, your family, and your marriage, especially when business isn't going very well. NHIC puts out a pamphlet titled *Healthfinder: Stress Information Resources,* which lists and describes several government agencies and private organizations that offer publications and resources on work-related stress and stress management. It's available for $1.00.

* Get A Tax Break For Hiring and Training New Employees

Employment Training Administration
Office of Public Affairs
U.S. Department of Labor, Room S-2322
Washington, DC 20210   202-219-8743

If your business employs certain types of people, such as dislocated workers or workers who have lost their jobs because of competition, your business may qualify for a federal tax credit. This Targeted Jobs Tax Credit allows businesses to write off a portion of the salaries they pay to these special workers from these taxes. This federal tax credit program is run on the state and local levels. To find out specific information on eligibility requirements, contact your state Department of Labor or local private industry council. If you are interested in participating in this program, these offices can locate workers for you and help you through the paperwork.

This Targeted Jobs Tax Credit program can be used in conjunction with another program under the Job Training Partnership Act. Under this program the government will pay part of your employee's salary if you meet certain eligibility requirements and provide on-the-job training, such as computer or carpentry skills to the employee. Under this program, you need to hire certain disadvantaged employees, such as the handicapped, the economically disadvantaged, minorities, and the like. The office above can send you free copies of fact sheets on the Job Training Partnership Act and the Targeted Jobs Tax Credit Program.

* Tax Information For Home-Based Businesses

Taxpayer Services
Internal Revenue Service (IRS)
U.S. Department of the Treasury
1111 Constitution Ave., NW, Room 2422
Washington, DC 20224   1-800-829-1040

Depending on the size and nature of your home-based business, there may be a lot of information you'll need to know about your federal tax responsibilities. The IRS puts out a whole series of free publications that explain the current tax laws to help you better understand them. The titles, along with brief descriptions and ordering numbers, are listed below.

Accounting Periods and Methods (#538) explains which accounting periods and methods can be used for figuring federal taxes, and how to apply for approval to change from one period or method to another.

Bankruptcy And Other Debt Cancellation (#908) explains the income tax aspects of bankruptcy and discharge of debt for individuals and small businesses.

Business Expenses (#535) discusses such expenses as fringe benefits, rent, interest, taxes, insurance, and employee benefit plans. It also explains the choice to capitalize certain business expenses; amortization and depletion; and the circumstances in which expenses are and are not deductible.

Business Use Of A Car (#917) explains the expenses you may deduct for the use of your car in your home-based business.

Business Use Of Your Home (#587) can help you decide if you qualify to deduct certain expenses for using part of your home for your business. Deductions for the business use of a home computer are also discussed.

Circular E, Employer's Tax Guide (#15) explains what you'll need to know if you employ others as part of your home-based business.

Condemnations and Business Casualties and Thefts (#549) explains how to deduct for casualties and thefts to your business property, such as when your business computer is stolen during a robbery.

Depreciation (#534) tells you how to calculate how to write off the depreciated value of property and equipment associated with your home-based business.

Earned Income Credit (#596) discusses who may receive the earned income credit, and how to figure and claim the credit.

Educational Expenses (#508) explains how, if you take educational courses related to your home-based business, you can deduct these expenses from your taxes.

Examination of Returns, Appeal Rights, and Claims for Refund (#556) is helpful if your tax return is examined by explaining the procedures for the examination of items of partnership income, deduction, gain, loss, and credit.

Interest Expense (#545) tells you how to deduct interest payments on loans you take out to run your home-based business.

Moving Expenses (#521) explains how you can deduct moving expenses when you relocate a home-based business as you move.

Sales and Other Dispositions of Assets (#544) explains how to figure gain and loss on such transactions as trading or selling an asset used in a business, along with the tax results of different types of gains and losses.

Self-Employed Retirement Plans (#560) discusses retirement plans (Keogh plans) for self-employed individuals, such as those running home-based businesses, and certain partners in partnerships.

Self-Employment Tax (#533) explains the self-employment tax (i.e., social security tax) that self-employed, home-based business owners must pay.

Tax Guide for Small Business (#334) explains the federal tax laws that apply to businesses, including the four major forms of business organizations -- sole proprietorships, partnerships, corporations, and S corporations -- along with the tax responsibilities for each.

Tax Information For Direct Sellers (#911) gives you helpful information if your home-based business involves "direct selling," that is, selling products to others on a person-to-person basis, such as door-to-door sales, sales parties, or by appointment in your home.

Tax Information on Corporations (#542) tells you what you need to know if you incorporate your home-based business.

Tax Information on Partnerships (#541) tells you what you'll need to know if you run your home-based business as a partnership.

Tax Information On S Corporations (#589) explains how corporations are taxed under subchapter S of the tax code.

Taxpayers Starting A Business (#583) shows sample records that a small business can use if it operates as a sole proprietorship. Records like these will help you prepare complete and accurate tax returns and make sure you pay only the tax you owe. It also discusses the taxpayer identification number that you must use, information returns you may have to file, and the kinds of business taxes you may have to pay.

Home-Based Business Resources

Travel, Entertainment, and Gift Expenses (#463) explains what expenses you may deduct for business-related travel, meals, entertainment, and gifts for your business, along with the reporting and record keeping requirements for these expenses.

* Is Your Name Legal?

Trademark Search Library
Patent and Trademark Office
U.S. Department of Commerce
Washington, DC 20231   703-308-HELP

Before you decide to name your new business something like Disneyland or Nutrisystem, it might be a good idea to find out if someone else already owns the trademark on the name. All registered trademarks, logos, and slogans are filed in the Trademark Search Library, and you can visit the library to research the name you want to use for your business. If you can't get to the library yourself, you can find a professional trademark specialist to hire do the search for you by looking in the telephone directory. The library staff will not do a search for you if you haven't formally applied for a trademark. However, if you do apply for a trademark, the library will tell you if the name is already taken, and if it isn't, they'll award you the trademark. Contact this office for more information on researching and applying for a trademark.

* Do A Patent Search Yourself and Save Money

Office of Patent Depository Library Programs
Patent and Trademark Office
U.S. Department of Commerce
Washington, DC 20231   703-308-HELP

Instead of going out and hiring an expensive lawyer or researcher to do your patent search for you, try doing it yourself first -- it's not that difficult. There are about 70 Patent Depository Libraries across the country that receive current issues of the U.S. patents and maintain backfile collections of earlier-issued patents. And about half of these libraries have complete patent collections that will allow you to do a complete search. The others have collections that will allow you to do at least a good preliminary search. All the libraries have their patent files available on computer to help cut down on the time you'll need to spend searching your patent. To find out where the nearest Patent Depository Library is to you, call the following toll-free number. An operator will provide you with both the address and telephone number: 1-800-435-7735, or 1-800-543-2313 in Virginia.

* Protect Your Idea For $6.00

Commissioner of Patents and Trademarks
Patent and Trademark Office
U.S. Department of Commerce
Washington, DC 20231   703-308-HELP

If you don't want to immediately invest the time or money in doing a patent search on an idea you have, you might consider applying for a *Disclosure Statement* instead. A *Disclosure Statement* will cost you only $6.00, and you can use it as evidence of the dates of conception of your invention. It is not a full patent and good for only two years, but many times this is long enough to see if your idea is sellable.

* How Much Should You Pay For A Typist With 2 Years Experience

Bureau of Labor Statistics
U.S. Department of Labor
#2 Massachusetts Ave., NE
Washington, DC 20212   202-606-7800

or   Your State Department of Labor

When you run a small business, you need to know how much to pay your employees and how much to charge for your services based on average wage rates in your area of the country. The Bureau of Labor Statistics has compiled *Area Wage Surveys* for major industries across the country. BLS also publishes an annual white-collar wage study, *Professional, Administrative, Technical, and Clerical Survey*. Contact this office or your Local Department of Labor Office located in your state capitol.

* What's The Law If Your Business Offers a Warranty

Marketing Practices Division
Federal Trade Commission (FTC)
6th & Pennsylvania Ave., NW
Washington, DC 20580   202-326-3128

If you're selling a product with a warranty, you should know about the *Magnuson-Moss Warranty Act*, which requires you to make warranty information available to consumers before making a purchase, and to honor your warranty obligations. To find out more about this law and how to comply with it, contact the FTC.

* Do You Need A Permit For Running A Business Out of Your Home?

Contact your local Business Council

Depending on what your home-based business is, you might need to get zoning permits to run your business at home. Local zoning laws exist so that residential neighborhoods aren't overrun by traffic created by having daily business going on in the area. This is especially true if a business has a steady flow of customers showing up to buy things. Your local business council will be able to tell you if your business will require a zoning permit.

* Home-Based Child Care Business

County Cooperative Extension Service
6707 Groveton Dr.
Clinton, MD 20735   301-868-9410

If you're interested in running a child care business out of your home, you'll need some background information before you start. This office, or the Cooperative Extension Service in your own county, can send you free copies of *A Home-Based Business: Child Care* and *Running A Child Care Business*, which include information on such topics as record keeping, registration and certification, rates to charge, advertising, and insurance. You'll also find a list of questions you should answer about how suitable you are for the job. Topics covered include: your feelings toward children, physical stamina, personal family life, and much more.

* Videos On Starting A Child Care Business

Contact your County Cooperative Extension Service
listed under county government in your telephone book
or
Distribution and Supply
Attn: Molly Byrd
Texas A & M University
System Bldg., Room 104
College Station, TX 77843   409-845-3850

A video program in day care training includes the following topics: Child Development, Nutrition, Health and Safety, and Business Management. It is produced by the Texas Agricultural Extension Service and is available through their office listed above for a modest fee. It is also available on a free loan basis through many County Cooperative Extension Service offices around the country.

Women Entrepreneurs: Special Money, Help And Programs
For Women Only

When someone mentions the word "entrepreneur," many people might conjure up an image of a man like Donald Trump smiling on the cover of some glossy business magazine. What these people don't realize is that women, *not men* like Donald Trump, are quickly becoming both the most common and the most successful entrepreneurs in the U.S. The new, successful entrepreneurs are actually more likely to be named Donna, not Donald. Just look at some of these incredible statistics that the U.S. Small Business Administration has gathered on women business owners:

- Over the last 15 years, the number of women-owned businesses has almost doubled.

- In that same amount of time, the percentage of women-owned businesses increased by 10%, while those owned by men decreased by as much.

- Over one-third of all businesses are now owned by women.

- Women-owned businesses were awarded over $2 billion in federal prime contracts last year, compared to only $180 million about ten years ago, an increase of over ten fold.

- 75% of new businesses started by women succeed, compared to only 25% of those started by men.

Since most people in the U.S. actually work for small businesses, the government has sat up and taken notice of these ever-increasing trends toward women-owned businesses. Chances are, your new boss or CEO is going to be a woman, not someone like Lee Iacocca. Why else would the SBA put a women's business ownership specialist at over 100 SBA offices across the country? You don't see the SBA bending over to help men out with special programs -- anyone who reads the statistics can see who's going to be the most powerful group of emerging business owners over the next couple of decades.

As you'll see in this chapter, both the federal and state governments have created special programs and information sources to help women business owners compete and succeed. As long as these agencies consider businesses "disadvantaged" simply because they're women-owned, you should take advantage of their free help, like preference when bidding on government contracts, or special low-interest loan guarantees. The statistics say women are competing just fine, but if the government wants to help you out anyway through these kinds of programs, why not use them? Just think of what someone who doesn't need an advantage can do with one.

* Fight Suppliers Who Won't Give You Credit
Public Reference Branch
Federal Trade Commission (FTC)

Washington, DC 20580   202-326-2222

Sometimes women, because they've been divorced, have trouble establishing credit. And you need credit if you're going to run a business. The FTC enforces the laws that prohibit creditors and credit bureaus from discriminating against women because of their sex or marital status, and they can send you the free publication, *Women and Credit Histories*. This pamphlet explains your credit rights under the law, how to get help in establishing your own credit, and what to do if you feel your credit application was unfairly denied.

* Grants, Loans and Loan Guarantees for Women Owned Businesses
Contact your state office of Economic Development located in your state capitol

All federal money programs aimed at small business do not discriminate between women and non-women owned businesses. However, at the state level there are a number of specific money programs that are set aside only for women owned businesses. The programs vary from state to state and are changing all the time so it is best to check with your state office of Economic Development in your state capital to insure you have the latest available information. Here is a listing for what a few states have specifically for women entrepreneurs:

- Illinois has low interest loans up to $50,000
- Iowa has grants up to $25,000 and loan guarantees up to $40,000
- Louisiana has loans and loan guarantee programs up to $250,000
- Minnesota offers low interest loans for up to 50% of your project
- New York offers low interest loans from $20,000 to $500,000
- Wisconsin offers low interest loans for women owned businesses under $500,000 in sales

* Federal Government Set-Asides For Women Entrepreneurs
Contact your state office of Economic Development located in your state capitol

or

Government Printing Office
Superintendent of Documents
Washington, DC 20402   202-783-3238

Many federal government contracting offices are trying to insure that a certain percentage of their contracts go to women entrepreneurs. Most even have special offices that will help women entrepreneurs sell to their agencies. For help in selling your product or service to the government contact your state Economic Development Office in your state capitol and obtain a copy of *Women Business Owners: Selling to the Federal Government*. It is available for $3.75 from the Government Printing Office.

* 15% Set-Aside for Women Entrepreneurs
Contact your state office of Economic Development located in your state capitol.

Not only is the federal government active in insuring that women get a fair share of government contracts, but many of the state governments are doing the same. Some states, like California for example, have passed laws that force their state agencies to give at least 15% of their contracts to women and minority owned firms. Other states like Illinois, Iowa, Maine, Minnesota, Montana, New Jersey, Oregon, and Washington are among those who are active in insuring that women obtain a fair share of state government contracts. Contact your state office of Economic Development to see how your business can take advantage of set-asides in your state.

* 28 States Offer Free Consulting To Women-Only
Contact your state office of Economic Development located in your state capitol.

Although every state offers free help to any person wishing to start or expand a business in their state, there are 28 states that have set up special offices just for

Women Entrepreneurs: Special Money, Help and Programs

women entrepreneurs. Colorado established a women's clearinghouse which provides hands-on assistance with business planning, marketing, financing and government contracts. They also hold seminars at 16 locations throughout the state. Ohio offers a wide range of free services including loan packaging and marketing research. Contact your state office of Economic Development to see what your state has to offer. If they don't have a "Women Only" office, don't let that stop you. It just means you'll have to share with the men in your state.

* What To Do If You Suspect Your Bank Denied You Credit Because You Are a Woman or Divorced

Credit Practices Division
Federal Trade Commission
Washington, DC 20580   202-326-3758

Women looking for money to start up and run their businesses might run into lenders that discriminate against them simply because they are women or divorced. The Federal Trade Commission (FTC) enforces the Equal Credit Opportunity Act, which prohibits any creditor from denying credit to a consumer on the basis of sex or marital status. If you think you've been discriminated against by a lender, contact the FTC. While the FTC won't act on individual complaints, if they get enough complaints against the same lender, they may decide to investigate. If necessary, they will take them to court to get them to stop their illegal practices. If you want your complaint investigated and action taken immediately, contact one of the following agencies, depending on the type of lending institution involved:

National Banks
Comptroller of the Currency, Compliance Management, U.S. Department of the Treasury, Washington, DC 20219, 202-874-5000

FDIC-Insured Banks
Office of Consumer Affairs. 550 17th Street, NW, Room F-130, Washington, DC 20429, 202-898-3535

Savings & Loans
Office of Thrift Supervision, U.S. Department of Treasury, 1700 G Street, NW, Washington, DC 20552, 202-906-6000

State Banks
Contact your State Banking Commissioner

* How To Select Quality Day Care For Your Child

County Cooperative Extension Service
6707 Groveton Dr.
Clinton, MD 20735   301-868-9410

If you're running your own small business or a business out of your home, you might need to consider finding good and reliable day care for your children to give you the time you need for your business. This office can send you a free copy of *How To Select Quality Day Care For Your Child*, which shows you what to look for in day care.

* How To Start a Child Care Business In Your Home

County Cooperative Extension Service
6707 Groveton Dr.
Clinton, MD 20735   301-868-9410

If you're interested in running a child care business out of your home, you'll need some background information before you start. This office can send you a free copy of *Homebased Business: Child Care and Running a Child Care Business*, which includes information on such topics as record-keeping, registration and certification, rates to charge, advertising, and insurance. You'll also find a list of questions you should answer such as how suitable you are for the job, your feelings toward children, your physical stamina, your personal family life and much more.

* Videos On Starting A Child Care Business

Contact your County Cooperative Extension Service
listed under county government in your telephone book
or
Video Production
Texas A & M University
107 Reed McDonald Bldg.
College Station, TX 77843   409-845-2840

Better Kid Care - Family Day Care Training is a 4 part video program in day care training. It includes the following topics: 1) Child Development, 2) Nutrition, 3) Health and Safety, and 4) Business Management. It is produced by the Texas Agricultural Extension Service and is available through their office (listed above) for a modest fee, or on a free loan basis through many County Cooperative Extension Service offices around the country. Call your local County Cooperative Extension Service for availability.

* How To Juggle The Stress of Your Business and Your Family

National Health Information Clearinghouse (NHIC)
P.O. Box 1133   301-565-4167
Washington, DC 20013-1133   1-800-336-4797

Trying to run a business can put a lot of added stress on you, your family, and marriage, especially when business isn't going very well. NHIC puts out a pamphlet titled *Healthfinder: Stress Information Resources*, which lists and describes several government agencies and private organizations that offer publications and resources on work-related stress and stress management. It is available for $1.00.

* Free Publications For Women Business Owners

Women's Bureau
Office of the Secretary
U.S. Department of Labor
200 Constitution Ave, NW
Washington, DC 20210   202-219-6652

Are you interested in how many other women business owners there are in the U.S? How about what your chances are climbing up through the management levels? If you're interested in finding out more about women in the workforce, including trends and future projections, you might find the following free publications informative:

Alternative Work Patterns
American Indian/Alaska Native Women Business Owners
Asian American Women Business Owners
Benefits to Employers Who Hire Women Veterans
Black Women Business Owners
Black Women in the Labor Force
Earning Differences Between Women and Men
Flexible Workstyles: A Look at Contingent Labor
Hispanic Origin Women Business Owners
State Maternity/Parental Leave Laws
Women Business Owners
Women in Management
Women in Skilled Trades
Women of Hispanic Origin in the Labor Force
Women on the Job: Careers in the Electronic Media
Women Who Maintain Families
Women With Work Disability
Women Workers: Outlook to 2005
Work and Family Resource Kit
Working Mothers and Their Children

* How To Get Start-Up Capital From Being Pregnant, Sexually Harassed, or From A Bad Shopping Experience

U.S. Customs Service
Fraud Division   1-800-BE-ALERT
Washington, DC 20229
or

U.S. Equal Employment Opportunity Commission (EEOC)
1801 L St., NW
Washington, DC 20570   1-800-669-3362

More people would quit what they're doing and start their own business if they had a small windfall of money to get them started. Well, there are two government programs that may turn a bad experience into the capital needed to start a business.

As a business owner, there are times you may come across unscrupulous wholesalers who try to sell you some counterfeit products at cut-rate prices. Instead of risking your business by buying and reselling the bogus products, report the fraud to the U.S. Customs Service. If your complaint, which will be kept completely anonymous, leads to the seizure of counterfeit goods, you could get a reward of up to $250,000, depending on the size of the case. And what small business couldn't use some extra operating capital like that to keep them going?

So you want to start your own business because you've just been fired because you were pregnant, or wouldn't sleep with your boss to get a promotion? Before you go taking out any business loan, contact the EEOC and report how you think your former boss discriminated against you. The EEOC will investigate your complaint, and if they think there are grounds for prosecuting your former boss, they'll proceed with the case. If they prove the case, you could end up with enough money in back pay and other remedies to finance your own company with you as the boss.

* Health Insurance for Divorcees Who Start Their Own Business

National Displaced Homemakers Network (NDHN)
1625 K St NW, #300
Washington, DC 20006   202-467-6346

Under the new law, divorced and separated women and their children can continue to receive the same health insurance coverage they had before they were divorced or separated from their husbands at the group rate. The only difference is that they have to pay the premium, not the employer. This law applies to all private businesses that employ more than 20 people and to federal, state and local government plans. And depending on the reason for displacement, you may be eligible to continue coverage for up to 36 months. You must contact the health plan within 60 days of the divorce or separation to indicate that you're electing to continue coverage. If the plan refuses to honor the law, contact your state's Insurance Commissioner, and they will investigate your complaint and get you the coverage to which you're entitled. For more information on this law, contact the NDHN at the above address.

* Meet Women Entrepreneurs In Your Neighborhood For Lunch

Office of Women's Business Ownership
U.S. Small Business Administration
409 3rd St., SW
Washington, DC 20416   202-205-6673

In almost every major city in the United States you can go to lunch with a group of women entrepreneurs by just asking. One of the biggest problems women entrepreneurs face is breaking into the "old boys" network of successful businessmen. Opportunities can be lost without access to the right connections. To help women interested in networking with other successful business people, the U.S. Small Business Administration has a new program that pairs up a woman who is just starting out with an experienced female Chief Executive Officer running the same kind of company. This business mentor can help the novice businesswoman make connections that might otherwise take her years to make on her own. Those interested in networking should also think about joining relevant professional associations, such as the National Association of Women Business Owners at 212-922-0465 or the National Association for Female Executives at 212-645-0770, and contacting their local Chambers of Commerce.

* Seminars On How Women Can Sell to the Government

Office of Women's Business
U.S. Small Business Administration
409 3rd St., SW

Washington, DC 20416   202-205-6673

If you're not sure how to get into doing business with the government, you might consider taking a seminar sponsored by the U.S. Small Business Administration on the procurement process. These seminars will give you a complete overview on what you'll need to know and do to get involved in bidding on and landing government business contracts. For information on when these seminars are scheduled in your area, contact the office above, or better yet, contact the Women's Business Ownership Representative nearest you listed elsewhere in this chapter.

* Creative Financing for Women Entrepreneurs

Office of Women's Business Ownership
U.S. Small Business Administration
409 3rd St., SW
Washington, DC 20416   202-205-6673

One of the toughest parts of running a business is finding the capital resources to do it: MONEY. The Women's Business Ownership Office runs seminars on how women can find creative ways to find financing if they've been turned down for loans by regular banks. For more information about these seminars, contact the office above or the Women's Business Ownership Representative nearest you listed elsewhere in this chapter.

* Free Mentors for New Women Entrepreneurs

Office of Women's Business Ownership
U.S. Small Business Administration
409 3rd St., SW
Washington, DC 20416   202-205-6673

How valuable would it be to your business to find a successful role model who's already gone through what's facing you as a female entrepreneur and who's willing to share her expertise at no charge? Through the SBA's Women's Network for Entrepreneurial Training (WNET) you can be paired up with a successful mentor who will meet with you at least once a week for an entire year, allowing you to learn from her experience and begin networking with other successful business people. If you've had your business going for at least a year and have gross receipts of at least $50,000, you can qualify for the WNET program. For more information, contact the office above or the Women's Business Ownership Representative nearest you listed elsewhere in this chapter.

* Changing Laws to Help Women Business Owners

Congressional Caucus for Women's Issues
2471 Rayburn Bldg.
Washington, DC 20515   202-225-6740

If you think that the climate for women business owners could be helped out by passing some new law, you might think of sending your ideas to the Congressional Caucus for Women's Issues. This group keeps track of the issues most important to women across the country and helps introduce new legislation that can help meet those needs, including those of the community of women entrepreneurs. Recently, for example, a new law was passed that allowed federal funding for U.S. Small Business Administration Demonstration Centers that specialize in offering counseling to women interested in starting and expanding businesses. Contact this office if you have any new ideas or would simply like them to send you information about the most recent legislation concerning women that is before Congress.

For Starters:
Call Your Local Women's Business Ownership Representative

Women entrepreneurs have special needs, and the U.S. Small Business Administration recognizes this. That why they've added staff members who specialize in promoting women-owned businesses in the U.S. These Women's Business Ownership Reps can help solve your unique business problems, such as how to network with other women business owners, where to find financial assistance on the state level, or how to get in on the lucrative government procurement programs, especially the ones that offer preferences to women-owned businesses. The WBO rep serving your area is your best starting place to help you cut through the red tape and direct you to free counseling and other information sources.

Alabama
Judy York
U.S. Small Business Administration
2121 8th Ave., North Suite 200
Birmingham, AL 35203-2398   205-731-1338.

Alaska
Joyce Jansen
U.S. Small Business Administration
Federal Bldg., #67, 222 West 8th Ave.
Anchorage, AK 99513-7559   907-271-4837.

Arizona
Gail Gesell
U.S. Small Business Administration
2828 North Center, Suite 800
Phoenix, AZ 85004-1025   602-640-2316.

Arkansas
Valerie Coleman
U.S. Small Business Administration
2120 Riverfront, Suite 100
Little Rock, AR 72202   501-324-5871

California
Gloria Minarik
U.S. Small Business Administration
71 Stevenson St., 20th Floor
San Francisco, CA 94105-2939   415-744-6432

Lisa Zuffi
U.S. Small Business Administration
211 Main St., 4th Floor
San Francisco, CA 94105-1988   415-744-6771

Bobby Connor
U.S. Small Business Administration
660 J St., Suite 215
Sacramento, CA 95814-2413   916-551-1445

Delores Braswell
U.S. Small Business Administration
800 Front St., Room 4-S-29
San Diego, CA 92188-0270   619-557-7252, ext. 46

Rachel Bavanick
U.S. Small Business Administration
901 W. Civic Center Dr., Suite 160
Santa Ana, CA 92703-2352   714-836-2494

Marie Teeple
U.S. Small Business Administration
330 N. Brand Blvd., Suite 1200
Glendale, CA 91203-2304   213-894-2956

Nancy Gilbertson
U.S. Small Business Administration
2719 N. Air Fresno Dr., 5th Floor
Fresno, CA 93727-1547   209-487-5189

Colorado
Nancy McCray
U.S. Small Business Administration
999 18th St., Suite 701
Denver, CO 80202   303-294-7067

Evelyn Gross
U.S. Small Business Administration
721 19th St.
Denver, CO 80202   303-844-6515

Connecticut
Kathleen Duncan
U.S. Small Business Administration
330 Main St., 2nd Floor
Hartford, CT 06106   FAX 203-240-4659
    203-240-4642

Delaware
Carlotta Catullo
U.S. Small Business Administration
One Rodney Square, Suite 412
920 N. King St.
Wilmington, DE 19801   302-573-6295

District of Columbia
Jeanne Alexander
U.S. Small Business Administration
1111 18th St., NW
Washington, DC 20036   202-634-1500, ext. 258

Florida
Kim Lucas
U.S. Small Business Administration
7825 Bay Meadows Way, Suite 100B
Jacksonville, FL 32256-7504   904-443-1912

U.S. Small Business Administration
1320 S. Dixie Hwy., Suite 501
Coral Gables, FL 33146   305-536-5521

Georgia
Paula Hill
U.S. Small Business Administration
1720 Peachtree St., NW, 6th Floor
Atlanta, GA 30309   404-347-2356

Edith Fuller
U.S. Small Business Administration
1375 Peachtree St., NE
Atlanta, GA 30367   404-347-2386

Hawaii
Donna Hopkins
U.S. Small Business Administration
30 Ala Moana, Room 2213
P.O. Box 50207
Honolulu, HI 96850-4981   808-541-2973

Idaho
Roger Horton
U.S. Small Business Administration
1020 Main St., Suite 290
Boise, ID 83702   208-334-9079

Illinois
Nancy Smith
U.S. Small Business Administration
300 S. Riverdale, Room 1975S
Chicago, IL 60606   312-353-5000 ext.764

Sam McGrier
U.S. Small Business Administration
500 W. Madison St., Suite 1250
Chicago, IL 60606   312-353-5429 ext.6243

Valerie Ross
U.S. Small Business Administration
511 W. Capitol St., Suite 302
Springfield, IL 62704   217-492-4416

Indiana
Don Owen
U.S. Small Business Administration
429 N. Pennsylvania St., Suite 100
Indianapolis, IN 46204   317-226-7272

Iowa
Diane Reinerston
U.S. Small Business Administration
373 Collins Rd., NE   FAX 319-393-7585
Cedar Rapids, IA 52402   319-393-8630

Sandy Jerde
U.S. Small Business Administration
210 Walnut St., Room 749   FAX 515-284-4572
Des Moines, IA 50309   515-284-4762

Kansas
Dennis Larkin
U.S. Small Business Administration
100 E. English, #510   FAX 316-269-6499
Wichita, KS 67202   316-269-6273

Kentucky
Carol Hatfield
U.S. Small Business Administration
Dr. Luther King, Jr. Pl., Room 188
Louisville, KY 40201   502-582-5971

Louisiana
Loretta Poree
U.S. Small Business Administration
1661 Canal St., 2nd Floor

New Orleans, LA 70112   504-589-2354

Maine
Bonnie Erickson
U.S. Small Business Administration
40 Western Ave., Room 512   FAX 207-622-8277
Augusta, ME 04330   207-622-8242

Maryland
Mindye Allentoff
U.S. Small Business Administration
10 N. Calvert St., 4th Floor
Baltimore, MD 21202   301-962-2235

Massachusetts
Barbara Manning
U.S. Small Business Administration
155 Federal St., 9th Floor
Boston, MA 02110   617-451-2040

Mildred Cooper
U.S. Small Business Administration
10 Causeway St., Room 265   FAX 617-565-5598
Boston, MA 02222-1093   617-565-5595

Harry Webb
U.S. Small Business Administration
1550 Main St., Room 212
Springfield, MA 01103   413-785-0268

Michigan
Cathy Gase
U.S. Small Business Administration
477 Michigan Ave.
Detroit, MI 48226   313-226-6075, ext. 23

Minnesota
Cynthia Collett
U.S. Small Business Administration
610 C Butler Square
Minneapolis, MN 55403   612-370-2312

Missouri
Patricia Ingram
U.S. Small Business Administration
911 Walnut St., 13th Floor
Kansas City, MO 64106   816-426-5311

Colene Watley
U.S. Small Business Administration
323 W 8th, 5th Floor   FAX 816-374-6795
Kansas City, MO 64106   816-374-6701

LaVerne Johnson
U.S. Small Business Administration
815 Olive St., Suite 242   FAX 314-539-3785
St. Louis, MO 63101   314-539-6600

LuAnn Wylie
U.S. Small Business Administration
620 S. Glenstone, Suite 110   FAX 417-864-4108
Springfield, MO 65802-3200   417-864-7670

Mississippi
Judith N. Adcock
U.S. Small Business Administration
One Hancock Plaza, Suite 1001
Gulfport, MS 39501   601-863-4449

Ora Rawls
U.S. Small Business Administration
101 W. Capitol St., Suite 400
Jackson, MS 39201   601-965-5323

Montana
Michelle Johnston
U.S. Small Business Administration
301 S. Park Ave., Room 528
Helena, MT 59626-0054   406-449-5381

Nebraska
Betty Gutheil
U.S. Small Business Administration
11145 Mill Valley Rd.   FAX 402-221-3680
Omaha, NB 68154   402-221-3604

Nevada
Marie Papile
U.S. Small Business Administration
301 E. Stewart, Box 7527, Downtown Station
Las Vegas, NV 89125-2527   702-388-6611

New Hampshire
Sandra Sullivan
U.S. Small Business Administration
P.O. Box 1257   FAX 603-225-1409
Concord, NH 03302-1257   603-225-1400

New Jersey
Mr. Frank Burke
U.S. Small Business Administration
Military Park Building
60 Park Place, 4th Floor
Newark, NJ 07102   201-645-3683

New Mexico
Susan Chavez
U.S. Small Business Administration
625 Silver SW, Room 320
Albuquerque, NM 87102   505-262-1879

New York
Sheila Thomas
U.S. Small Business Administration
26 Federal Plaza, Room 3108
New York, NY 10278   212-264-1046

Margie Donovan
U.S. Small Business Administration
26 Federal Plaza, Room 3100
New York, NY 10278   212-264-1762

Stephanie Ubowski
U.S. Small Business Administration
100 S. Clinton St., Room 1071
Syracuse, NY 13260   315-423-5375

Thomas Agon
U.S. Small Business Administration
333 E. Water St.
Elmira, NY 14901   607-734-8142

Carol Kruszona
U.S. Small Business Administration
111 W. Huron St., Room 1311
Buffalo, NY 14202   716-846-4517

Josephine Bermudez
U.S. Small Business Administration
35 Pinelawn Rd., Room 102E
Melville, NY 11747   516-454-0753

Sharon Kelleher
U.S. Small Business Administration
Leo O'Brien Bldg. #815
Albany, NY 12207   518-472-4300

Marcia Ketchum
U.S. Small Business Administration
Federal Bldg., 100 State St.
Rochester, NY 14614   716-263-6700

North Carolina
Eileen Joyce
U.S. Small Business Administration
200 N. College St., Suite A2015
Charlotte, NC 28202-2173   704-344-6587

North Dakota
Marelene Koenig
U.S. Small Business Administration
657 2nd Ave. North, Room 218
P.O. Box 3088
Fargo, ND 58102   701-239-5131

Ohio
Rosemary Darling
U.S. Small Business Administration
1240 E. 9th St., Room 317
Cleveland, OH 44199   216-522-8236

Janice Sonnenburg
U.S. Small Business Administration
2 Nationwide Plaza, Suite 1400
Columbus, OH 43215-2542   614-469-6860, ext. 274

Gene O'Connell
U.S. Small Business Administration
550 Main St., Room 5028
Cincinnati, OH 45202   513-684-6907

Oklahoma
Joyce Jones
U.S. Small Business Administration
200 NW 5th St., Suite 670
Federal Bldg.
Oklahoma City, OK 73102   405-231-4884

Oregon
Inge McNeese
U.S. Small Business Administration
222 SW Columbia Ave., Room 500
Portland, OR 97201-6605   503-326-5202

Pennsylvania
Daniel Sossaman
U.S. Small Business Administration
475 Allendale Square Rd., Suite 201
King of Prussia, PA 19406   215-962-3755

Doris Young
U.S. Small Business Administration
475 Allendale Square Rd., Suite 201
King of Prussia, PA 19406   215-962-3818

Mary Merman
U.S. Small Business Administration

960 Penn Ave., 5th Floor
Pittsburgh, PA 15222   412-644-2785

Rhode Island
Linda Smith
U.S. Small Business Administration
380 Westminister Mall   FAX 401-528-4539
Providence, RI 02903   401-528-4598

South Carolina
Kim Hite
U.S. Small Business Administration
1835 Assembly St., Room 358
Columbia, SC 29202   803-253-3360

South Dakota
Darlene Michael
U.S. Small Business Administration
101 S. Main Ave., Suite 101
Sioux Falls, SD 57102   605-330-4231

Tennessee
Saundra Jackson
U.S. Small Business Administration
50 Vantage Way, Suite 201
Nashville, TN 37228   615-736-7176

Texas
Gwen Syers
U.S. Small Business Administration
10737 Gateway West, Suite 320
El Paso, TX 79902   915-540-5564

Gail Goodloe
U.S. Small Business Administration
606 N. Caranchua
Corpus Christi, TX 78476   512-888-3301

Diane Cheshier
U.S. Small Business Administration
8625 King George Dr., Bldg. C
Dallas, TX 75235-3391   214-767-7615

Ken Jennings
U.S. Small Business Administration
1100 Commerce St., Suite 715
Dallas, TX 75241   214-767-0386

Gladys McKnight
U.S. Small Business Administration
9301 SW Freeway, Suite 550
Houston, TX 77074   713-953-6255

Gracie Guillen
U.S. Small Business Administration
222 E. Van Buren St., Suite 500
Harlingen, TX 78550   512-427-8533

Joanna Teeters
U.S. Small Business Administration
1611 10th St., Suite 200
Lubbock, TX 79401   804-743-7462

Geraldine Cook
U.S. Small Business Administration

7400 Blanco Rd., Suite 200
North Star Executive Center
San Antonio, TX 78216   512-229-4535

Utah
Suzan Yoshimura
U.S. Small Business Administration
Federal Bldg., 125 S. State St.
Salt City, UT 84138-1195   801-524-3203

Vermont
Brenda Foster
U.S. Small Business Administration
87 State St., Room 204
P.O. Box 605   FAX 802-828-4485
Montpelier, VT 05602   802-828-4422

Virginia
Fannie Gergoudis
U.S. Small Business Administration
400 N. 8th St., Room 3015
P.O. Box 10126
Richmond, VA 23240   804-771-2765

Washington
Gwen Elliott
U.S. Small Business Administration
2615 4th St., Room 440
Seattle, WA 98121-1233   206-553-2460

Connie Alvarado
U.S. Small Business Administration
915 2nd Ave., Room 1792
Seattle, WA 98174-1088   206-553-4438

Coralie Myers
U.S. Small Business Administration
West 601 First Ave., 10th Floor East
Spokane, WA 99204-0317   509-353-2815

West Virginia
Sharon Weaver
U.S. Small Business Administration
168 W. Main St., P.O. Box 1608
Clarksburg, WV 26302   304-623-5631

Wisconsin
Ms. Rebecca Jorgensen
U.S. Small Business Administration
212 E. Washington Ave., Room 213
Madison, WI 53703   608-264-5516

Mr. John Lonsdale
U.S. Small Business Administration
310 W. Wisconsin Ave.
Milwaukee, WI 53202   414-297-3941

Wyoming
Kay Stucker
U.S. Small Business Administration
100 E. B St., Room 4001
P.O. Box 2839
Casper, WY 82602   307-261-5761

Local Woman-To-Woman Entrepreneur Help Centers

The U.S. Small Business Administration (SBA) has co-funded 19 Demonstration Centers across the country to assist women interested in starting up and expanding small businesses. What is unique about most of these programs is that most offer woman-to-woman, one-on-one counseling in all aspects of business, from employee relations, budgeting, and dealing with lenders, to legal, marketing, and accounting assistance. Unlike the help you'd get at, say, an SBA office, these centers offer help by women only for women. These non-profit Centers are public/private-funded ventures, which means that they will charge nominal fees for their services, although much less than you'd expect to pay for your own private business advisor.

California

American Woman's Economic Development Corp.
301 E. Ocean Blvd., Suite 1010, Long Beach, CA 90802; 213-983-3747, FAX 213-983-3750.

West Co., A Women's Economic Self-Sufficiency Training Program
413 N. State St., Ukiah, CA 95482; 707-462-2348.

West Co., A Women's Economic Self-Sufficiency Training Program
333 C North Franklin St., Fort Bragg, CA 95437; 707-964-7571.

Colorado

Mi Casa, Business Center for Women
571 Galapago St., Denver, CO 80204; 303-573-1302, FAX 303-573-0422.

District of Columbia

American Woman's Economic Development Corp.
2445 M St., NW, Room 490, P.O. Box 65644, Washington, DC 20035; 202-857-0091, FAX 202-223-2775.

Georgia

YMCA of Greater Atlanta
957 N. Highland Ave., NE, Atlanta, GA 30306; 404-872-4747.

Illinois

Women's Business Development Center
8 S. Michigan Ave., Suite 400, Chicago, IL 60603; 312-853-3477, FAX 312-853-0145.

Women's Business Development Center
SBDC/Joliet Junior College, 214 N. Ottawa, 3rd Floor, Joliet, IL 60431; 815-727-6544, ext. 1312.

Women's Business Development Center
Kankakee Community College, 4 Dearborn Square, Kankakee, Il 60901; 815-933-0375.

Women Business Owners Advocacy Program
SBDC/Rock Valley College, 1220 Rock St., Rockford, IL 61101; 815-968-4087.

Women's Economic Venture Enterprise
229 16th St., Rock Island, IL 61201; 309-788-9793.

Indiana

Indiana Regional Minority Supplier Development Council, Inc.
300 E. Fall Creek Parkway, N.D., P.O. Box 44801, Indianapolis, IN 46244-0801; 317-923-2110.

Michigan

EXCEL! Women Business Owners Development Team
200 Renaissance Ctr., Suite 1600, Detroit, MI 48243-1274; 313-396-3576.

EXCEL! Women Business Owners Development Team
200 Ottawa NW, Suite 900, Grand Rapids, MI 49503-2465; 616-458-4783, FAX 616-774-9081.

Minnesota

BI-CAP, Inc., Women in New Development WIND-
P.O. Box 579, Bemidji, MN 56601; 218-751-4631, FAX 218-751-8452.

Missouri

NAWBO of St. Louis
911 Washington Avenue, Suite 140, St. Louis, MO 63101; 314-621-6162.

New Mexico

Women's Economic Self-Sufficiency Team WESST Corp.-
414 Silver Southwest, Albuquerque, NM 87102; 505-848-4760.

Women's Economic Self-Sufficiency Team WESST Corp.-
Taos County Economic Development Corp., P.O. Box 1389, Taos, NM 87571; 505-758-1161.

New York

American Woman's Economic Development Corp.
641 Lexington Ave., 9th Floor, New York, NY 10022; 212-688-1900, FAX 212-688-2718.

Ohio

Ohio Coordinator
Melody Borchers, 614-466-4945

Minority Female Entrepreneurship Program
Charles Christian, Director, 37 North High St., Columbus, OH 43215-3065; 614-225-6910, FAX 614-469-8250.

Women's Economic Assistance Ventures (WEAV)
Rosann Miller-Wethington, Executive Director, 105 West North College, P.O. Box 512, Yellow Springs, OH 45387; 513-767-2667, FAX 513-767-1354

Women's Entrepreneurial Growth Organization (WEGO)
Barbara Lange, Director, 58 W. Center St., P.O. Box 544, Akron, OH 44309; 216-535-9346, FAX 216-535-4523.

Women's Business Resource Program/Ohio University
Mary Ann McClure, Director, One President St., Athens, OH 45701; 614-593-0474, FAX 614-593-1795.

Women Entrepreneurs, Inc.
Joe-Ann Gibbons, Acting President/Director, 525 Vine St., 3rd Floor, Cincinnati, OH 45202; 513-684-0700.

Cleveland Women's Consortium
Michelle Spain, 1979 East 56th St., Cleveland, OH 44199; 216-881-8146.

Texas

Center for Women's Business Enterprise
1200 Smith St., 2800 Citicorp Building, Houston, TX 77002; 713-658-0300.

Center for Women's Business Enterprise
301 Congress Ave., Suite 1000, Austin, TX 78701; 512-476-7501, FAX 512-476-2738.

Center for Women's Business Enterprise
800 Interstate Bank Tower, Dallas, TX 75202; 214-855-7300, FAX 214-855-7370.

Southwest Resource Development
8700 Crownhill, Suite 700, San Antonio, TX 78209; 512-828-9034.

Center for Women's Business Enterprise
8023 Vantage Dr., Suite 600, San Antonio, TX 78230; 512-377-2100.

Wisconsin

Women's Business Initiative Corp.
1020 N. Broadway, Milwaukee, WI 53202; 414-277-7004.

State Women Business Assistance Programs

The feds aren't the only ones noticing the emerging importance of female entrepreneurship in the U.S. Many states now have special programs to help new and expanding women-owned businesses get the special assistance they need to succeed. So far, about half the states offer some kind of assistance to women business owners, from special set-aside programs to help women compete for lucrative government contracts, to nuts-and-bolts, one-on-one counseling, to special low-interest loan programs, such as the ones in Iowa and Louisiana.

It's important to keep in mind that just because your state doesn't currently have any special programs for women entrepreneurs doesn't mean that they won't in the near future. In fact, many states, like Florida and Utah, now have special women's business advocates in the state capital to help bring the needs of women business owners to the attention of their legislators. This could mean new business programs for women sometime down the road. So keep in touch with your state capital to find out the status of these issues.

Alabama

Office of Minority Business Enterprise (OMBE)
Alabama Development Office
401 Adams Ave. #600
Montgomery, AL 36130   1-800-248-0033

OMBE helps women and minority entrepreneurs interested in starting or expanding their businesses prepare business plans and applications for SBA loans, fill out applications for state and federal procurement opportunities, and certify women- and minority-owned businesses to participate in the state purchasing programs.

Arkansas

Arkansas Industrial Development Commission
One State Capitol Mall
Little Rock, AR 72201   501-682-1060

The Minority Business Development Division provides business loan packaging, contract procurement assistance, bonding information, general business counseling, seminars, workshops, and referrals to other agencies.

California

Office of Small and Minority Business
Department of General Services
1808 14th St., Suite 100
Sacramento, CA 95814   916-322-5060

This office helps women-owned businesses interested in participating in the State's purchasing/contracting system, along with counseling, assistance, and protection for their interests.

Office of Civil Rights
Department of Transportation
1120 N St., Room 3400
Sacramento, CA 95814-5690   916-445-2276

This office offers women-owned businesses information on the certification necessary to participate in the state procurement program.

Colorado

Minority Business Office
Office of Business Development
1625 Broadway, Suite 1710
Denver, CO 80202   303-892-3840

The Women's Business Program acts as a resource clearinghouse for women business owners. They refer callers to the appropriate state and local offices that can provide them with the hands-on assistance they need, on everything from business planning and marketing assistance to procurement programs and financing. They also hold business planning seminars at 16 locations throughout the state.

Illinois

Small Business Advocate
Illinois Department of Commerce and Community Affairs
State of Illinois Center

100 W. Randolph St., Suite 3-400
Chicago, IL 60601   312-814-3540

The Small Business Advocate specializes in helping women, minorities, start-ups, and home-based business owners cut through the bureaucratic red tape and get the answers they need by offering information and expertise in dealing with state, federal, and local agencies.

Small Business Assistance Bureau
Illinois Department of Commerce and Community Affairs
State of Illinois Center
620 E. Adams
Springfield, IL 62701   800-252-2923

The Women's Business Advocate offers programs to women entrepreneurs through a business calendar of events, which includes conferences at which business owners get an opportunity to network. The Advocate also maintains an extensive mailing list of women entrepreneurs. Through the Women's Business Development Center of The Neighborhood Institute, women business owners can get assistance in all phases of business development.

Under the Minority and Women Business Loan Program, women business owners can get long-term, fixed rate direct financing at below-market rates for loans from $5,000 to $50,000. One job must be created or retained for each $5,000 borrowed. Business owners can use the money for leasing or purchasing land and buildings, construction or renovation of fixed assets, purchase and installation of machinery and equipment, and working capital.

Under the Minority and Female Business Enterprise Program, Matchmaker Conferences are held to connect women business owners interested in landing government contracts with state and local purchasing agents.

Indiana

SBDC
Office of Minority and Women Business Development Division
One North Capitol, Suite 1275   317-264-2820
Indianapolis, IN 46204

This office helps women- and minority-owned small businesses with all phases of development, from management and technical assistance, to contract bidding, procurement, educational seminars and training, and financial alternatives. As part of their Procurement Program, women- and minority-owned businesses receive help in seeking government services contracts.

Iowa

Targeted Small Business Program Manager
Department of Economic Development
200 E. Grand Ave.
Des Moines, IA 50309   515-242-4813

Under the Targeted Small Business Financial Assistance Program, women-owned small businesses in Iowa can receive direct loans, loan subsidies, or grants of up to $25,000 and loan guarantees up to 75% of project not to exceed $40,000 for start up and expansion.

Targeted Small Business
Iowa Department of Inspections and Appeals
Lucas Building
2nd Floor
Des Moines, IA 50319-0083 515-281-7250

Under the Targeted Small Business Program, women- and minority-owned businesses can get help in getting certified as a targeted small business (any business 51% or more women- or minority-owned), and thereby become eligible for set-aside procurement programs of the state.

Kansas

Office of Minority Business
Existing Industry Development Division
Kansas Department of Commerce
700 SW Harrison, #1300
Topeka, KS 66603-3712 913-296-3805

This office helps out women- and minority-owned businesses with the bidding procedures for public and private procurement opportunities in Kansas. They also offer these businesses management assistance, and help identify financial resources for them.

Kentucky

Office of Minority Affairs
State Office Building
Room 904
501 High St.
Frankfort, KY 40622 502-564-3601

This office certifies women- and minority-owned businesses interested in participating in the procurement program for state highway-related contracts.

Louisiana

Louisiana Economic Development Corporation
Department of Economic Development
P.O. Box 94185
Baton Rouge, LA 70804-9185 504-342-5675

Under the Minority and Women's Business Development Program, qualified women-and minority-owned businesses can receive loans or loan guarantees in amounts up to $250,000. This money can be used to finance construction, conversion, or expansions of business facilities, finance machinery, supplies, materials or working capital line of credit. Direct loans are available when these businesses have been turned down by at least two financial institutions for a loan.

Division of Minority and Women's Business Enterprise
Department of Economic Development
P.O. Box 94185
Baton Rouge, LA 70804-9185 504-342-5373

This office offers women- and minority-owned businesses with one-on-one assistance and counseling on the state procurement and bidding process. They will direct these business owners to sources of management, technical, and financial assistance from state and federal government sources, as well as from the private sector. This office will also direct women and minority business owners to certain private sector industries in the state that have incentive programs to obtain goods and services from businesses owned by women or minorities, or which have franchise opportunities targeted for these group members.

Maine

Maine Department of Transportation
Division of Equal Opportunity/Employee Relations
State Station House #16
Augusta, ME 04333 207-289-3576

Under the Disadvantaged/Minority/Women Business Enterprise Program, women-owned businesses can get certification to obtain government contracts. This office helps business owners with the procurement procedures used to obtain government contracts.

Massachusetts

State Office of Minority and Women Business Assistance
Department of Commerce
100 Cambridge Street
Room 1305
Boston, MA 02202 617-727-8692

This office helps women- and minority-owned businesses get certified to participate in the state procurement programs.

Michigan

Targeted Services Division
Michigan Department of Commerce
4th Floor Law Building
P.O. Box 30225
Lansing, MI 48909 517-335-1835

This office runs Women Business Owners Services program which works largely as a referral service for women business owners. Business owners can also participate in special entrepreneurial education programs and procurement programs.

Minnesota

Department of Administration
Materials Management Division
112 Administrative Bldg.
St. Paul, MN 55155 612-296-2600

This office certifies women-owned businesses to participate in the Small Business Program for procurement opportunities with the state. Once certified, a business earns a 6% preference on government contract bids.

Mississippi

Department of Economic and Community Development
P.O. Box 849
Jackson, MS 39205 601-359-3449

Under the Minority Business Enterprise Loan Program, women-owned businesses that can show that they are economically disadvantaged are eligible to receive low-interest loans for up to 50% of a business project's cost.

Missouri

Council on Women's Economic Development & Training
1442 Aaron Court
Suite E
P.O. Box 1684
Jefferson City, MO 65102 314-751-0810

The Council helps women small business owners through different programs, seminars, and conferences.

Montana

DBE Program Specialist
Civil Rights Bureau
Montana Department of Highways
2701 Prospect Avenue
P.O. 201001
Helena, MT 59620-1001 406-444-6331

The Disadvantaged Business Enterprise and Women Business Enterprise program certifies women-owned businesses interested in bidding on and obtaining federal-aid highway construction contracts.

New Jersey

Office of Women Business Enterprise
CN 835
Trenton, NJ 08625-0835 609-292-3862

This office helps businesswomen interested in opening, expanding, or buying a company.

Set-Aside and Certification Office
CN 835
Trenton, NJ 08625-0835 609-984-9835

This office helps women- and minority-owned businesses compete for government contracts by administering the New Jersey Unified Certification Program for Women and Minorities and the Set-Aside Program. Under the Set Aside Program, women- and minority-owned businesses earn a preference on government contract bids.

Division of Development for Small Businesses
and Women and Minority Businesses
CN 835
Trenton, NJ 08625-0835   609-292-3860
This office offers women- and minority-owned small businesses financial, marketing, procurement, technical, and managerial assistance.

New York

Division of Minority and Women's Business
Department of Economic Development
1 Commerce Plaza
Albany, NY 12245   518-474-6346
or
1515 Broadway
52nd Floor
New York, NY 10036   212-827-6266
This office gives women- and minority-owned businesses consulting and technical assistance in obtaining benefits from State programs, with a focus on business financing. They also help these businesses get the proper certification to participate in the state procurement opportunities. This office can help these business owners obtain federal government contracts.

New York Urban Development Corp.
Minority and Women Revolving Loan Fund
1515 Broadway
New York, NY 10036   212-930-0452
Women- and minority-owned industrial, commercial, service-oriented, and start-up businesses can receive low-interest loans. Retail businesses are evaluated on a case-by-case basis before they qualify. These loans range from $20,000 to $500,000 and may be used for construction, renovation, leasehold improvements, acquisition of land and buildings, acquisition of an ongoing business, establishment of a nationally recognized franchise outlet, machinery and equipment, and working capital.

Ohio

Minority Development Financing Commission
Ohio Department of Development
P.O. Box 1001   1-800-848-1300
Columbus, OH 43266-0101   614-466-4945
Under the Women's Business Resource Program, women can get help for start-up, expansion and management of their businesses. They work to make sure that women have equal access to assistance and lending programs, and help businesswomen locate government procurement opportunities. This office also acts as a state-wide center of workshops, conferences, and Women's Business Owners statistics. All of the program's services are free. This office also publishes *Ohio Women Business Leaders*, a directory of women-owned businesses in Ohio, along with other free publications.

Oklahoma

Oklahoma Department of Commerce
Small Business Division
P.O. Box 26980
Oklahoma City, OK 73126-0980   405-841-5227
Under the Women-Owned Business Assistance Program, businesswomen can get a variety of technical assistance, from business planning and marketing assistance, to financial information and government procurement.

Oregon

Office of Minority, Women & Emerging Small Businesses
155 Cottage St., NE
Salem, OR 97310   503-378-5651
This office certifies women-owned, disadvantaged and emerging small businesses, allowing them to participate in the state's targeted purchasing programs.

Pennsylvania

Bureau of Women's Business Development
Forum Building, Room 462
Harrisburg, PA 17120   717-787-3339
This Bureau offers women business owners one-on-one counseling and helps them get the information they need to solve their problems and get them up and going. They also will refer women business owners to the appropriate state offices and agencies that can best help them with every kind of issue, from procurement assistance to developing business and financial strategies.

Rhode Island

Office of Minority Business Assistance
Department of Economic Development
7 Jackson Walkway
Providence, RI 02903   401-277-2601
This office certifies women- and minority-owned businesses under federal and state set-aside and goal programs and provides counseling assistance to these companies.

Tennessee

Office of Minority Business Enterprise
Department of Economic & Community Development
Rachel Jackson Building
7th Floor
320 6th Avenue North   (in state) 1-800-342-8470
Nashville, TN 37219-5308   615-741-2545
This office offers information, advocacy, referral, procurement, and other services to minority businesses in the state. They publish a directory of minority businesses, offer conferences and seminars on topics useful to business owners, and serve as a clearinghouse of important information to minorities. They also match minority vendors with potential clients and help minorities identify and obtain procurement opportunities.

Washington

Office of Minority and Women's Business Enterprises
P.O. Box 41160
Olympia, WA 98504-1160   206-753-9693
This office helps women- and minority-owned businesses interested in participating in state contracting opportunities by moving them through the certification process. Once certified, you are eligible to receive a 5% preference when bidding competitively on goods and services purchased by the state. Upon request, you can be placed on bid lists maintained by individual agencies, education institutions, or contractors by contacting them directly.

Wisconsin

Women's Business Services
Department of Development
P.O. Box 7970   (in state) 1-800-435-7287
Madison, WI 53707   608-266-1018
The Women's Business Services offers assistance in gaining information about the state's loan programs available to women business owners. The office keeps track of the top 50 fastest growing and top 10 women-owned business in Wisconsin. They also maintain a database of women-owned businesses in the state.

Wisconsin Housing and Economic Development Authority
One South Pinckney St., #500
P.O. Box 1728
Madison, WI 53701-1728   608-266-0976
Under the Linked Deposit Loan Program, women- or minority-owned businesses with gross annual sales of less than $500,000 can qualify for low-rate loans. Loans are available at under prime rate for purchase or improvement of buildings, equipment, or land, but not for working capital. Business must be in manufacturing, retail trade, tourism or agriculture packaging or processing.

State Women's Business Advocates

These state funded offices provide technical support and referral services for planning financing, training and women's business issues.

Ms. Hank Barnes
Director
Governor's Office of Women's Services
1700 West Washington, #420
Phoenix, AZ 85007   602-542-1755

Ms. Melody K. Borchers
Manager
Women's Business Resource Program
Ohio Department of Development
77 South High St., 28th Floor
Columbus, OH 43215   614-466-4945

Ms. Lenore Cameron, Exq.
Director
Bureau of Women's Business Development
462 Forum Building
Harrisburg, PA 17120   717-787-3339

Ms. Mary Ann Campbell, CFP
Money Magic, Inc.
2923 Imperial Valley Drive
Little Rock, AR 72212   501-277-6644

Ms. Mollie Cole
Women's Business Advocate
Department of Commerce and Community Affairs
100 West Randolph, Suite 3-400
Chicago, IL 60601   312-814-6111

Ms. Dora D'Amico
Assistant Regional Administrator for Public
 Affairs and Communications
U.S. Small Business Administration
999 18th St., Suite 701   303-292-7033
Denver, CO 80202   FTS-330-7033

Ms. Alice Flissinger
Office of Small and Minority Business
Department of General Services
1808 14th St., Room 100
Sacramento, CA 95814   916-322-5060

Ms. Anabel Gray
P.O. Box 3604
Lynchburg, VA 24503-0604   804-528-9424

Mr. James Guyer
District Director
U.S. Small Business Administration
2005 North Central Ave., 5th Floor   602-379-3737

Phoenix, AZ 85004   FTS-261-3737

Ms. Angelisa Harris
Executive Director
Louisiana Department of Economic Development
Division of Minority and Women's Business Enterprise
P.O. Box 94185
Baton Rouge, LA 70804-9185   405-841-5242

Ms. Marketia Head
Coordinator for Women-Owned Business
 Assistance Program
Department of Commerce
6601 Broadway Extension
Oklahoma City, OK 73116   405-841-5242

Ms. Saundra Herre
President, Herrewood Associates
4101 Pennington
Racine, WI 53403   414-554-8301

Kathleen Mechem
Director of Women Business Owner Services
Michigan Dept. of Commerce
4th Floor Law Bldg., Box 30225
Lansing, MI 48909   517-335-1835

Ms. Katy Klarnet
Director of Public Relations
Connecticut Mutual Life Insurance Co.
140 Garden St., MS-G-26
Hartford, Ct 06154   800-234-2865
                          access code 1086, ext. 5073

Ms. Lindsey Johnson
Director
Office of Women's Business Ownership
U.S. Small Business Administration
409 Third St., SW
Washington, DC 20416   202-205-6673

Ms. Rieva Lesonsky
Editor in Chief
Entrepreneurial Woman
2392 Morse Ave.
Irvine, CA 92714   714-261-2325

Ms. Diana McClelland
Co-Founder
The Foundation for Women Owned Businesses
5031 East Foothills Rd.
Lake Oswego, OR 97034   503-790-7672

Ms. Betty McDonald
Programs Manager
Government Marketing Assistance Group
Indiana Department of Commerce
1 North Capitol St., Suite 700
Indianapolis, IN 46204   317-232-3393

Ms. Helen Myers
Director
Office of Small Business
State of Nevada
2501 East Sahara, #304
Las Vegas, NV 89158   702-486-4506

Ms. Charlotte Redden
Coordinator
Women's Business Program
Office of Business Development
1625 Broadway, Suite 1710
Denver, Co 80202   303-892-3840

Ms. Nancy Smith
Women's Business Ownership Coordinator
U.S. Small Business Administration
230 South Dearborn St., Suite 510
Chicago, IL 60604   312-353-4252

Ms. Mary Strickland
Women's Business Services
Department of Development
123 West Washington Ave.
P.O. Box 7970
Madison, WI 53707   608-266-0593

Ms. Tracy Thompson
Director
U.S. Small Business Development Center
Winona State University
Somsen Hall
Winona, MN 55987   507-334-3965

Green Entrepreneuring:
Making Money While Protecting The Environment

The entrepreneur of the 1990s will not only worry about making money but will also worry about how her business operations may be affecting the environment or how the environment may be affecting her employees. Instead of hiring high priced engineers, therapists and other consultants, you can turn to the government for help and information by some of the best experts in the world. If your office is not ventilated well and is in a "sick building," the government will provide a free analysis and tell you how to solve the problem. If you have an employee worried about the effects of working in front of a computer screen, the government will send you a free study showing the latest results of research on this topic. The government will also show your business how to save money on your water, electric and commuting bills, as well as lend you money to make your business more energy efficient.

* Government Loans To Start Your Own Energy Conservation Business

Contact your state Economic Development Office
in your state capitol
or
Your Local Small Business Administration Office

The Small Business Administration has established a separate funding program to assist entrepreneurs who provide energy production and conservation services for others. This can include engineering, architectural, consulting or other professional services specializing in specific energy measures. The funding may be in the form of direct loans or loan guarantees and can be as high as $750,000. They can be used for start-up or expansion purposes. Ask about Energy Business Loan Guarantees.

* Free Government Study Shows That Plants Eliminate 90% of Office Pollution

National Aeronautic and Space Administration (NASA) Library
Bldg. 1100, Room 517A
Stennis Space Center, MS 39529   601-688-3244

A recent NASA study called, *Interior Landscape Plants for Indoor Air Pollution Abatement* shows that indoor plants are not only aesthetically pleasing but are also healthier. Most house plants are very effective at removing chemicals from the air and can clean up to 90% of your indoor air pollution. This report is free.

* Buying Fuel Efficient Company Cars

Public Information Center
Environmental Protection Agency (EPA)
401 M St, SW
Washington, DC 20460   202-260-7751

When purchasing company cars or vans, you can make sure that you are buying the best fuel efficient model for your needs by obtaining a free copy of EPA's annual Mileage Guide which contains fuel economy estimates for all new makes and models.

* Help Your Employees Carpool: It's The Law

Traffic Operations Division
Federal Highway Administration
U.S. Dept. of Transportation
400 7th St SW, TV-31
Washington, DC 20590   202-366-4069
or
Association for Commuter Transportation
808 17th St NW

Washington, DC 20006   301-656-0555

The Federal Highway Administration has several publications to get you started on what your company can do to cut down on the number of cars, fuel and pollutants used in commuting. The publications include: *Introduction to Ridesharing, Guidelines for Using Vanpools and Carpools*, and *The Employee Transportation Coordinator (ETC) Handbook*.

Passage of the Clean Air Act now requires companies "by law" to help their employees with carpooling. If your business is in any of the following metropolitan areas, and you have over 100 employees, then you have 2 years to increase the commuting vehicle occupancy rate by 25% for your employees. The two years begin ticking as of November 1994. After that each state will impose penalties for noncompliance. If a state does not meet their targets, they can lose federal money for highways and construction. In November 1992, the U.S. Environmental Protection Agency will send Clean Air Implementation Plans to each of the states involved. The areas affected are: Baltimore, MD; Chicago, IL; Houston, TX; Los Angeles, CA; Milwaukee, WI; New York City; Most of New Jersey; Delaware; Philadelphia, PA; San Diego, CA. The Association for Commuter Transportation can answer any further questions you may have on this topic.

* Low Interest Loans To Buy Energy Saving Equipment

Contact Your State Office of Economic Development
Located In Your State Capitol

Some state governments, like California, have established low interest loans for small businesses to purchase energy saving equipment or to use for building energy saving facilities. California offers up to $150,000 for 4 years at 5% interest.

* Encouraging Commuting By Bicycle

Bicycle-Pedestrian Program
Office of the Secretary
U.S. Dept. of Transportation
400 7th St., SW   202-366-5007
Washington, DC 20590   202-366-4812

It takes very little effort for a business to encourage its employees to commute by bicycle. You can: provide bike racks and lockers; provide showers; pass out bike maps with information on local bike commuter routes and other bike commuters; and, support bike paths and lanes in your community as well as upgrading the access roads to your business. Information is available from this office for those interested in bicycle commuting. Also contact your state bicycling and walking coordinator at your state capitol.

* Employees Get A Tax Break For Using Public Transportation

Taxpayer Services
Internal Revenue Service (IRS)
U.S. Department of the Treasury
1111 Constitution Ave., NW, Room 2422
Washington, DC 20224   1-800-829-3676
or
Your Local IRS Office

It's not much, but businesses can provide their employees with $15 per month to take public transportation, and no one has to pay taxes on it. At the time of this publication, there was legislation pending that would increase the amount available as a tax deduction. This tax benefit is explained in IRS Publication #535. It's free.

* Hotline Helps You Save On Your Trash Bill

Resource Conservation and Recovery Act (RCRA) Hotline
Environmental Protection Agency
401 M St, SW   703-920-9810
Washington, DC 20460   1-800-424-9346

Green Entrepreneuring

Recycling not only can reduce the amount of trash being sent to landfills, but can be cost-effective too. It is easy to start simple recycling programs and help is close by. Each state has a recycling office that can give you advice, direction, and information regarding the establishment of recycling efforts. Help varies from state to state but can include recycling literature to distribute to employees, lists of people who will haul away scrap paper, and speakers who will come to your business to educate your employees on recycling. The RCRA Hotline also has several free publications on recycling including: *Recycle* - provides basic information on recycling; and *Recycling Works* - explains the recycling process and takes you through examples of programs in various states.

* Save Money Recycling Office Paper

National Technical Information Service
5285 Port Royal Road
Springfield, VA 22161   703-487-4650

A handy guide has been published by the government titled *Office Paper Recycling: An Implementation Manual* (PB90199431) which is designed for those responsible for office paper recovery programs. It moves step-by-step through the process of setting up a high-grade paper recovery program, including assessing recycling potential, finding a market for paper and educating employees. The cost is $19.50.

* Local Help To Recycle Anything

If you are looking for specific information or answers to individual problems, like how to get rid of motor oil, or how to get your neighbor to recycle his plastic bottles, call your state recycling office listed below:

Alabama
Dept. of Environmental Management
Solid Waste Division
1715 Congressman Wm. Dickinson Drive
Montgomery, AL 36130   205-271-7700

Alaska
Department of Environmental Conservation
Solid Waste Program
P.O. Box O
Juneau, AK 99811-1800   907-465-5163

Arizona
Department of Environmental Quality - O.W.P.
Waste Planning Section, 4th Floor
Phoenix, AZ 85004   1-800-947-3873

Arkansas
Department of Pollution Control and Ecology
Solid Waste Division
8001 National Drive
Little Rock, AK 72219   501-562-7444

California
Recycling Division
Department of Conservation
819 19th Street
Sacramento, CA 95814   916-323-3743

Colorado
Department of Health
Hazardous Materials Division
4300 Cherry Creek Drive S
Denver, CO 80220-1530   303-692-3300

Delaware
Department of Natural Resources and Environmental Control
89 Kings Highway
P.O. Box 1401
Dover, DE 19903   302-739-4403

District of Columbia
Office of Recycling
65 K Street NE
Washington, DC 20002   202-727-5887

Florida
Department of Environmental Regulation
2600 Blairstone Road
Tallahassee, FL 32201   904-488-0300

Georgia
Department of Community Affairs
40 Marietta St., NW
8th Floor
Atlanta, GA 30303   404-656-3851

Hawaii
Litter Control Office
Department of Health
205 Koula Street
Honolulu, HI 96813   808-973-9700

Idaho
Department of Environmental Quality
Hazardous Materials Bureau
450 W. State Street
Boise, ID 83720   208-334-5860

Illinois
Illinois EPA
Land Pollution Control Division
2200 Churchill Road
P.O. Box 19276
Springfield, IL 62706   217-782-6761

Indiana
Office of Solid and Hazardous Waste Management
Department of Environmental Management
105 S. Meridian Street
Indianapolis, IN 46225   317-232-8600

Iowa
Department of Natural Resources
Waste Management Division
Wallace State Office Building
Des Moines, IA 50319   515-281-8176

Kansas
Department of Commerce
700 SW Harrison, Suite 1300
Topeka, KS 66603-3712   913-296-4225

Kentucky
Resources Management Branch
Division of Waste Management
18 Reilly Road
Frankfort, KY 40601   502-564-6716

Louisiana
Department of Environmental Quality
Solid Waste Division
P.O. Box 82178
Baton Rouge, LA 70884-2178   504-765-0249

Maine
Office of Waste Reduction and Recycling
Department of Economic and Community Development
State House Station #130
Augusta, ME 04333   207-287-5300

Maryland
Department of Environment
Hazardous and Solid Waste Administration
2500 Broening Highway, Building 40
Baltimore, MD 21224   410-631-3315

Massachusetts
Division of Solid Waste Management
D.E.Q.E.

1 Winter Street, 4th Floor
Boston, MA 02108   617-292-5960

Michigan
Waste Management Division
Department of Natural Resources
P.O. Box 30028   1-800-662-9278
Lansing, MI 48909   517-335-4789

Minnesota
Pollution Control and Waste Management
520 Lafayette Road
St. Paul, MN 55155   612-649-0824

Mississippi
Non-Hazardous Waste Section
Bureau of Pollution Control
Department of Natural Resources
P.O. Box 10385
Jackson, MS 39209   601-961-5171

Missouri
Department of Natural Resources
Solid Waste Management Program
P.O. Box 176
Jefferson City, MO 65102   314-751-5401

Montana
Solid Waste Program
Department of Health and Environmental Science
Cogswell Building, Room B201
Helena, MT 59620   406-444-2821

Nebraska
Litter Reduction and Recycling Programs
Department of Environmental Control
P.O. Box 98922
Lincoln, NE 68509   402-471-4210

Nevada
Energy Extension Service
Office of Community Service
1100 S. Williams Street
Carson City, NV 89710   702-687-4990

New Hampshire
Waste Management Division
Department of Environmental Services
6 Hazen Drive
Concord, NH 03301   603-271-2900

New Jersey
Office of Recycling
Department of Environmental Protection
CN 414, 401 E. State Street
Trenton, NJ 08625   609-530-8208

New Mexico
Solid Waste Section
Environmental Improvement Division
1190 St. Francis Drive
Santa Fe, NM 87503   505-827-2909

New York
Bureau of Waste Reduction and Recycling
Department of Environmental Conservation
50 Wolf Road, Room 208
Albany, NY 12233   518-457-7337

North Carolina
Waste Reduction Branch
Department of Human Resources
P.O. Box 2091
Raleigh, NC 27602   919-571-4100

North Dakota
Division of Waste Management
Department of Health
1200 Missouri Avenue
Room 302
Box 5520
Bismarck, ND 58502-5520   701-221-5166

Ohio
Division of Litter Prevention and Recycling
Ohio EPA
Fountain Square Building, E-1
Columbus, OH 43224   614-265-7061

Oklahoma
Solid Waste Division
Department of Health
1000 NE 10th Street
Oklahoma City, OK 73152   405-271-7159

Oregon
Department of Environmental Quality
811 SW Sixth
Portland, OR 97204   503-229-5913

Pennsylvania
Waste Reduction and Recycling Section
Division of Waste Minimization and Planning
Department of Environmental Resources
P.O. Box 2063
Harrisburg, PA 17120   717-787-7382

Rhode Island
Office of Environmental Coordination
Department of Environmental Management
83 Park Street
Providence, RI 02903   401-277-3434

South Carolina
Department of Health and Environmental Control
2600 Bull Street   1-800-768-7348
Columbia, SC 29201   803-734-5200

South Dakota
Department of the Environment and Natural Resources
Office of Waste Management
319 S. Coteau
c/o 500 E. Capitol Ave.
Pierre, SD 57501   605-773-3153

Tennessee
Department of Public Health
Division of Solid Waste Management
Customs House
4th Floor
701 Broadway
Nashville, TN 37219-5403   615-532-0074

Texas
Division of Solid Waste Management
Department of Health
1100 W. 49th Street
Austin, TX 78756   512-908-6750

Utah
Bureau of Solid and Hazardous Waste
Department of Environmental Health
P.O. Box 16690
Salt Lake City, UT 84116-0690   801-536-4480

Vermont
Agency of National Resources
103 S. Main Street, West Building   1-800-932-7100
Waterbury, VT 05676   802-224-7831

Green Entrepreneuring

Virginia

Department of Waste Management
Division of Litter Control and Recycling
11th Floor, Monroe Building
101 N. 14th Street
Richmond, VA 23219   1-800-KeepIt

West Virginia

Department of Natural Resources
Conservation, Education, and Litter Control
1800 Washington Street E.
Charleston, WV 25305   304-558-3370

Washington

Department of Ecology
Mail Stop PV-11
Olympia, WA 95804   1-800-Recycle

Wisconsin

Department of Natural Resources
P.O. Box 7921
Madison, WI 53707   608-266-2111

Wyoming

Solid Waste Management Program
Department of Environmental Quality
Herschler Building
122 W. 25th Street
Cheyenne, WY 82002   307-777-7752

* Help For Your Company To "Buy Green"

Resource Conservation and Recovery Act
Environmental Protection Agency
401 M St. SW
Washington, DC 20460   202-260-9327

Your company can support recycling by examining your purchase orders to determine what items can be substituted with recycled products. Is your paper made from recycled paper? Your state recycling office may be able to direct you to vendors in your area who carry recycled products. The Resource Conservation and Recovery Act office has a free publication titled *Procurement Guidelines for Buying Recycled Products*, which provides guidance in making the switch to green.

* Light Up Your Life and Business More Efficiently

Green Lights
Global Change Division
Environmental Protection Agency (EPA)
401 M St, SW
Washington, DC 20460   202-479-6936

About 20% of the electricity used annually in the U.S. is for lighting. Lighting for industry, stores, offices, and warehouses represent more than 80% of that total. But if energy-efficient lighting were used whenever profitable, the electricity required would be cut in half, thereby reducing sulfur dioxide, nitrogen oxide, and carbon dioxide emission. Green Lights is a voluntary, non-regulatory program sponsored by the EPA to help U.S. companies realize the profit of pollution prevention by installing energy-efficient lighting designs and technologies only where they are profitable and only where they maintain or improve lighting quality. EPA provides technical support, an analysis system that will allow corporations to assess their upgrade options quickly, compiles databases of products, contractors, etc., has an independent testing program, assists in securing financing sources for the upgrading, and will publicize successful Green Lights companies.

* Your Local Utility Will Help You Save Money On Your Energy Bill

Public Information
U.S. Department of Energy
Washington, DC 20585   202-586-5575
or
Your Local Utility Company

Your local gas, electric, and water utility can provide you with information regarding ways to make your systems work more efficiently. They will often conduct energy or water assessments, and will advise you concerning products on the market which will help your systems run more efficiently. They can also provide you with pamphlets and brochures. Some local utilities are getting into the recycling game by offering to haul away your old refrigerator for free. They make sure the freon is safely removed and the rest is sold for scrap metal. The Department of Energy is also a good source. They have a great deal of information on energy conservation, and how to get your appliances or heating/cooling system to work more efficiently.

* Is Your Business In A "Sick Building"?

Indoor Air Division
Environmental Protection Agency
P.O. Box 37133
ANR-445W
Washington, DC 20013   1-800-438-4318

Do you suffer from headaches and have difficulty concentrating only while you are at work? Do your eyes or nose burn? Are you dizzy or nauseous at work? You could be working in a Sick Building. The term Sick Building Syndrome (SBS) is used to describe situations where workers experience acute health or comfort effects when they are at work, but no specific illness can be identified. It can be when you are in a particular room or floor, or it may be the whole building. Symptoms of SBS can be headaches, eye, nose, or throat irritation, dizziness and nausea, difficulty in concentration, fatigue, and sensitivity to odors. The causes can be due to inadequate ventilation, chemical contaminants from indoor or outdoor sources or biological contaminants, such as molds or pollen. An indoor air quality investigation is needed to determine whether the pollutant can be removed or the ventilation rates increased. The Indoor Air Division can provide you with fact sheets on a wide variety of indoor air problems such as SBS, tobacco smoke, office ventilation, and air cleaners. They have a summary of Air Cleaning Devices, as well as a directory of State Indoor Air Contacts. *Building Air Quality: A Guide for Building Owners and Facility Managers* is a handbook for all air quality questions and remedies.

* How To Help Your Employees With Drug or Alcohol Problems

Division of Applied Research
National Institute on Drug Abuse
Room 10A53, 5600 Fishers Lane
Rockville, MD 20857   301-443-0802

Is there a problem with some of your employees' work habits? Are some coming in late or not at all? It could be that drugs or alcohol are involved. The National Institute of Drug Abuse is developing programs to eliminate illegal drug use in the workplace. Its programs include research, treatment, training and prevention activities, as well as projects related to the development of a comprehensive Drug-Free Workplace program. They will analyze and recommend Employee Assistance Programs and distribute a four-part videotape series on drugs at work. Other free loan videos include:

Drugs At Work (employee/employer versions) - presents information about the nature and scope of the alcohol and drug problem in the workplace and about the federal government's initiative to prevent and reduce the problem.

Getting Help (employee/employer versions) - highlights the benefits of an effective employee assistance program to employees and employers through comments by business, labor, and government leaders and EPA professionals.

Drug Testing: Handle With Care (employee/employer versions) - describes the options available for designing a drug testing component as part of a comprehensive drug-free workplace program.

Finding Solutions - drug abuse in the workplace is portrayed as a community-wide problem. The solutions offered through education and prevention are presented as personal, workplace, and community responsibilities.

* Free Help For Your Employees With Cholesterol, High Blood Pressure or Smoking Problems

National Heart, Lung, and Blood Institute
National Institutes of Health
Building 31, 4A-21
9000 Rockville Pike
Bethesda, MD 20892   301-496-4236

This office offers a free Workplace Information Pack dealing with high blood pressure, cholesterol, and smoking. The pack contains literature explaining how to educate your employees on these health risks, including handouts, bibliographies, and publications lists. This information is free for the asking.

* Free Speakers and Videos To Teach Your Employees Environmental and Safety Concerns

Consumer Product Safety Commission
5401 Westbard Ave.
Washington, DC 20207   202-492-6580
or
Office of Field Programs
U.S. Dept. of Labor
Occupational Safety and Health Administration (OSHA)
200 Constitution Ave, NW, Room N3606
Washington, DC 20210   202-523-7725
or
National Institute of Occupational Safety and Health (NIOSH)
4676 Columbia Parkway
Cincinnati, OH 45226   513-533-8287

These government offices are willing to provide free speakers on topics covering the environment, safety hazards and accident prevention.

NIOSH has a catalog of videos available for free loan. The tapes deal with a variety of industrial health and safety issues. Some of the titles include:

1) *Dual Protection (Spray Painting)* - highlights the technology available to control safety and health hazards in spray painting operations
2) *Behavior Based Safety Management* - safety engineers at Proctor and Gamble present their approach to safety management
3) *It's A New Day* - shows how The Drackett Company, a household products manufacturer, manages occupational safety and health
4) *The Finest Tools (Carpal Tunnel Syndrome)* - covers the nature of cumulative trauma disorders of the hand and wrist and describes how repetitive jobs can damage a worker's body
5) *Industrial Loss Control Through Behavior Management* - illustrates behavioral solutions to industrial safety problems
6) *Asbestos Screening Process* - examines an inexpensive and simple method for identifying asbestos
7) *Vibration Syndrome* - a brief introduction to the physics of vibration, and an examination of different assessment techniques
8) *Lifting and Analysis* - demonstrates how to calculate the parameters for safe lifting activity in specific example situations

Each of the regional OSHA offices offers free loan videos on worker safety topics. Some of the titles covered are:

1) *Basic Guide to Voluntary Compliance in Safety and Health* - develops a self inspection procedure for the correction of workplace deficiencies in accordance with Occupational Safety and Health Act Standards
2) *Facts About Vinyl Chloride* - identifies facts about working with this potentially hazardous substance
3) *I Never Had An Accident On The Job in My Life* - dramatizes accidents and potential hazards employees face in their everyday routines
4) *Eye Injuries and Eye Protection Equipment* - helps workers take steps to prevent the estimated 1,000 eye injuries that occur daily

Contact the office nearest you for further information on free videos:

Region I
(CT,MA,ME,NH,RI,VT)
133 Portland Street, 1st Floor
Boston, MA 02114   617-565-7164

Region II
(NJ, NY, Puerto Rico, Virgin Islands)
201 Varick Street
Room 670
New York, NY 10014   212-337-2378

Region III
(DC,DE,MD,PA,VA,WV)
Gateway Building, Suite 2100
3535 Market Street
Philadelphia, PA 19104   215-596-1201

Region IV
(AL,FL,GA,KY,MS,NC,SC,TN)
1375 Peachtree St., NE, Suite 587
Atlanta, GA 30367   404-347-3573

Region V
(IL,IN,MI,MN,OH,WI)
230 South Dearborn St.
32nd Floor, Room 3244
Chicago, IL 60604   312-353-2220

Region VI
(AR,LA,NM,OK,TX)
525 Griffin St. Building, Room 602
Dallas, TX 75202   214-767-4731

Region VII
(IA,KS,MO,NE)
911 Walnut Street, Room 406
Kansas City, MO 64106   816-426-5861

Region VII
(CO,MT,ND,SD,UT,WY)
Federal Building, Room 1576
1961 Stout Street
Denver, CO 80294   303-844-3061

Region IX
(American Samoa, AZ,CA,HI,NV, Pacific Trust Territories)
71 Stevenson Street
Room 415
San Francisco, CA 94105   415-744-6670

Region X
(AK,ID,OR,WA)
1111 Third Avenue, Suite 715
Seattle, WA 98101-3212   206-442-5930

* Free Hotline Helps You Save Your Energy Dollars

National Technology Assistance Service
U.S. Department of Energy
P.O. Box 2525
Butte, MT 59702   1-800-428-2525

The U.S. Dept. of Energy supports the National Appropriate Technology Assistance Service (NATAS), which can answer any question you have concerning energy conservation and renewable energy sources, such as solar energy. They try to get you to be as specific as possible with your questions, so they can better tailor the packets of information they send you. They can answer questions regarding the maintenance of your heating/cooling systems, adding insulation, or passive solar design (which is a good idea for people to consider when constructing a new building). They also have a staff of commercialization specialists who work with small energy business or inventors. They provide help in identifying funding sources, answer patent and licensing questions, assist with business plans, and offer marketing suggestions. There is a two to four week turnaround time, so plan ahead. Some of the help they provide includes helping a financial analyst determine if she should approve funding of a cogeneration project (where steam and electricity are simultaneously produced from a single source). NATAS provides information on cogeneration, how it works, and other instances of its use. NATAS also provided a wind energy company with marketing information for their product. They encouraged the company to write to energy related publications to get their product editorial coverage, and even provided the company with the names and addresses.

* Keeping Your Company Grounds Environmentally In-Tune

Executive Officer
U.S. Department of Agriculture
Administration Bldg. Room 340A
Washington, DC 20250   202-720-4111
(to locate your local County Cooperative Extension Service)
or
General Accounting Office
P.O. Box 6015

Gaithersburg, MD 20877   202-512-6000
or
National Pesticides Telecommunications   1-800-858-7378
Network Hotline   1-800-743-3091 (in Texas)
or
Public Information Center
U.S. Environmental Protection Agency
401 M St., SW
Washington, DC 20460   202-260-7751

Look at what your maintenance staff is using to clean your offices and other work areas. Are the products dangerous or could they harm the environment, such as high phosphorous detergents? Your local County Cooperative Extension Service Office can advise you on safer substitute products. They can also provide information regarding your landscape practices, such as composting your leaves and grass clippings. They can tell you which trees (and how to plant and maintain them) will grow well around your building, and which can lower your heating and cooling bills.

Pesticide use is also a big issue. There may be safer products or other things you can do to keep the pests away. The U.S. General Accounting Office has a free publication called *Lawn Care Pesticides: Risks Remain Uncertain While Prohibited Safety Claims Continue* which shows that safety claims from the lawn care pesticides industry are false and misleading.

The National Pesticides Telecommunication Network Hotline provides information on pesticide products, basic safety practices, health and environmental effects, and cleanup and disposal procedures. The Environmental Protection Agency's Public Information Center is also a good source of help on this topic.

* Don't Throw Out Old Paint, Batteries, Etc.

Resource Conservation and Recovery Act Hotline
U.S. Environmental Protection Agency
401 M St., SW   703-920-9810
Washington, DC 20460   1-800-424-9346

When your maintenance staff is cleaning out the storeroom, don't let them throw leftover paint in the trash. Paint, along with batteries, lawn care products and other products can emit chemicals harmful to you and your employees. Your state recycling office or the U.S. Environmental Protection Hotline can help you properly dispose of these materials.

* Government Money For Your Business Not To Pollute

Office of Advocacy
U.S. Small Business Administration
1725 Eye St, NW, Room 414
Washington, DC 20416   1-800-827-5722

The government has special funds set aside for companies who wish to cut down on their pollution. Your local Small Business Administration office can provide you with more information about what you need to do to qualify.

* Recycle With A Tax Break

Taxpayer Services
Internal Revenue Service
1111 Constitution Ave., NW Room 2422
Washington, DC 20224   1-800-829-3676

Before you throw away your old office furniture or equipment, give it away instead and get a tax break. Local non-profit organizations, churches and even schools could use a lending hand. And the IRS will let you have a tax deduction for "gifts in kind". Request a copy of *Determining the Value of Donated Property, Pub #561* from your local IRS office or the office listed above.

* Free Updated Reports On Any Aspect Of The Environment

Capitol Hill Switchboard
Washington, DC   202-224-3121

Your U.S. Representative and Senators have instantaneous access to over 10,000 reports on current events through a computerized online network. A phone call or letter to one of your legislators is all it takes for you to tap into this rich information resource. There is no charge for these concise reports which are unquestionably the best information value because the material contained in these studies are the highlights from materials prepared by other experts in federal government agencies as well as the private sector. You can contact all

legislators in Washington by calling the Capitol Hill Switchboard. The Congressional Research Service (CRS) writes these reports on a wide variety of environmental topics including:

- *Asbestos in Buildings: Current Issues*
- *Clean Air Act Issues: Motor Vehicle Emission Standards and Alternative Fuels*
- *Indoor Air Pollution*
- *Directory of Environmental and Conservation Organizations in Washington, DC*
- *Radon*
- *Hazardous Air Products*
- *Degradable Plastics*
- *Solid Waste Management*
- *Hotlines and Other Useful Government Telephone Numbers Info Pack*
- *Recycling Info Pack*
- *Acid Rain*
- *Global Climatic Changes*

* Free Health Inspection of Your Workplace

National Institute for Occupational Safety and Health
4676 Columbia Parkway
Cincinnati, OH 45226   1-800-356-4674

The National Institute for Occupational Safety and Health (NIOSH) is responsible for conducting research to make the nation's workplaces healthier and safer by responding to urgent requests for assistance from employers, employees, and their representatives where imminent hazards are suspected. They conduct inspections, laboratory and epidemiologic research, publish their findings, and make recommendations for improved working conditions. They will inspect any workplace for free, if three employees sign a form stating that the environment may be dangerous. Employees have the option of keeping anonymous. If any of the following applies to you, NIOSH can provide you with more information:

- Do you use a video display terminal most of the day?
- Are you concerned about the chemicals you are using in your dry cleaning?
- Do you have tingling in your hands (carpal tunnel syndrome)?
- Do you use a jackhammer most of the day and are now finding that your fingers are no longer sensitive to heat or cold?
- Do you do the same motion again and again, such as on an assembly line? You could be at risk for repetitive motion-associated trauma.
- Do you feel your job is causing you mental stress?
- Are you having trouble hearing?

* Free Consultants Make Your Company A Safe And Healthy Place To Work

Occupational Safety and Health Administration (OSHA)
U.S. Dept. of Labor
200 Constitution Ave, NW
Washington, DC 20210   202-219-7266

The Occupational Safety and Health Administration was created to encourage employers and employees to reduce workplace hazards and to implement new, or improve existing, safety and health programs. They provide research on innovative ways of dealing with these problems, maintain a record keeping system to monitor job related injuries and illnesses, and develop standards and enforce them, as well as establish training programs.

If you are concerned about the health and safety of your employees, and are having trouble establishing a safe workplace, OSHA will provide free and confidential consultation assistance.

If you have been working hard to clean up your employees' work space, and have reduced the number of injuries occurring on the job, you can be eligible for a Voluntary Protection Program award certificate.

If you are responsible for training your employees in ways they can work safely in a variety of situations, you can have access to over 65 high quality, low-cost, training videos.

If you are interested in the safety record of another company, OSHA can provide you with the entire range of inspection data, including who, what, when, where and why companies are inspected and the violations that were found (Contact: Office of Management Data Systems, 202-219-7008).

If you want to take a class to learn more about ways you can make your workplace safe and healthy for your employees, OSHA has courses covering areas such as electrical hazards, machine guarding, ventilation and ergonomics (Contact: Safety and Health Training Institute, 708-297-4810).

An extensive list of publications is available including:
- *Asbestos Standards for the Construction Industry*
- *Grain Handling*
- *Hearing Conservation*
- *Respiratory Protection*

* Manuals Show How Much Pollution Is In Your Business

Center for Environmental Research Information
U.S. Environmental Protection Agency
P.O. Box 19962
Cincinnati, OH 45219   513-569-7562

The Office of Research and Development has several publications on a wide variety of environmental topics. These manuals and guides are very technical in nature, but are an invaluable resource for your business or industry. Some of the publications include:
- *The Pesticide Formulating Industry*
- *The Paint Manufacturing Industry*
- *The Fabricate Metal Industry*
- *The Printed Circuit Board Manufacturing Industry*
- *The Commercial Printing Industry*
- *Selected Hospital Waste Streams*
- *Research and Educational Institutions*

* Free Research For Employee's Health Problems

National Health Information Center
ODPHP
P.O. Box 1133   301-565-4167
Washington, DC 20013   1-800-336-4797

U.S. businesses have begun implementing health education/promotion programs at worksites to help keep employees healthy and to help contain long-term health care costs. Simultaneously, groups of local businesses throughout the country have established coalitions for the purpose of implementing plans to reduce health care costs. Many of these groups view worksite health promotion programs, such as physical fitness, stress management, weight control, smoking cessation, nutrition, and drug and alcohol awareness, as an effective strategy that will contribute to achieving their goals. The National Health Information Center can provide you with publications and brochures on a wide variety of health topics, and can refer you to organizations which can help you set up programs at your place of business. This could be a one day event to test for high blood pressure, a blood donation program, free speakers, or more extensive health promotion programs.

* Save Water and Water Costs

National Small Flows Clearinghouse
West Virginia University
P.O. Box 6064
Morgantown, WV 26506   1-800-624-8301

One leaky faucet can use up to 4,000 gallons of water a month. By installing a faucet aerator you can reduce water use by 60 percent while maintaining a strong flow. Building fewer and smaller new water projects can help preserve wetlands, which naturally treat pollutants. Efficient water use means less power needed to pump and treat water and wastewater. The National Small Flows Clearinghouse or your local utility company can help you with these problems.

* Is Your Water At Work Safe To Drink Hotline

Safe Drinking Water Hotline
U.S. Environmental Protection Agency   1-800-426-4791

The chemicals and pesticides used every day eventually seep into our water table, thereby getting into your drinking water. Even the lead solder used to hold our pipes together becomes a hazard. The Safe Drinking Water Hotline can answer any question or concern you may have regarding your drinking water. They have an extensive list of publications, covering topics like water systems, lead, and volatile organic chemicals in your water. They can also provide you with information on ways to get your water tested as well as information on water purification techniques.

* Radon and Asbestos Can Be Silent Trouble In Your Office

Public Information Center
U.S. Environmental Protection Agency
401 M St, SW, PM-211B
Washington, DC 20460   202-260-7751

You can't feel it, taste it, or smell it, yet radon can be contaminating the air in your place of work. Asbestos was used for insulation many years ago, and now we know the danger it can cause. The Public Information Center at the U.S. Environmental Protection Agency has extensive literature on both of these topics including information on ways to remove radon and asbestos safely. They can also refer you to experts in the field that can provide you with up to the minute research.

* Video Shows What To Do About Radon

Contact your County Cooperative Extension Service
listed under county government in your telephone book
or
Cooperative Extension Service
University of Maryland System
Video Resource Center
0120 Symons Hall
College Park, MD 20742   301-405-4591

A video called *Radon: What Is It and What You Can Do About It*, explains the nature of radon and the dangers of high radon levels. It features steps toward determining radon levels as well as ways in which radon can be controlled. It is available for free from many of the local County Cooperative Extension Service Offices or for sale for $25 from the University of Maryland extension service at the address above.

* Will Your Employees Get Carpal Tunnel Syndrome?

National Institute for Occupational Safety and Health
4676 Columbia Parkway
Cincinnati, Ohio 45226   1-800-356-4674

Carpal Tunnel Syndrome is a tingling sensation in the hands and fingers and can be caused or aggravated by repeated twisting or awkward postures, particularly when combined with high force. The population at risk includes persons employed in such industries or occupations as construction, food preparation, clerical work, product fabrication and mining. The National Institute for Occupational Safety and Health provides free information on this syndrome including the latest developments in research, preventive recommendations, and bibliographies.

* Are Your Video Display Terminals Making Your Employees Sick?

National Institute for Occupational Safety and Health
4676 Columbia Parkway
Cincinnati, OH 45226   1-800-356-4674

Over one million people each day sit down to work in front of a computer terminal, imputing and outputing information. There have been concerns about its effect on people's eyesight, its effects on pregnant women, and its potential for causing carpal tunnel syndrome. The National Institute for Occupational Safety and Health offers a free booklet describing the latest research covering all these issues.

* State By State Listing of EPA Offices

Your State EPA office can be a gold mine of information for all your environmental needs. They have information on your state laws regarding hazardous waste, superfund sites, air pollution and drinking water. These offices also have pamphlets, brochures and fact sheets on a wide variety of topics, and can refer you to experts in your state for further information. Some examples of information the state offices provide include:

1)   A listing of superfund sites in your state as well as their current status

2)   The emergency planning and community right to know program requires anyone who stores, uses, generates or releases hazardous materials to identify the chemicals and report the locations and volume. Your state EPA office can supply you with this information.

3)   This office has publications and other information about pollution prevention for your home or office, as well as pollution prevention activities in your state.

Alabama
Environmental Management Department
Congressman Wm. Dickinson Dr.
Montgomery, AL 36130   205-271-7700

Alaska
Department of Environmental Conservation
P.O. Box O
Juneau, AK 99811   907-465-2600

Arizona
Department of Environmental Quality
2005 N. Central Avenue
Phoenix, AZ 85004   602-257-2300

Arkansas
Pollution Control and Ecology Department
8001 National Drive
Little Rock, AR 72209   501-562-7444

California
Environmental Protection Agency
555 Capitol Mall
Sacramento, CA 95814   916-445-3846

Colorado
Air Pollution Control Division
Department of Health
4210 E. 11th Avenue
Denver, CO 80220   303-331-8500

Connecticut
Environmental Protection Department
165 Capitol Avenue
Hartford, CT 06106   203-566-5599

Delaware
Natural Resources and Environmental Control Department
89 Kings Highway
Dover, DE 19901   302-739-4506

District of Columbia
Department of Consumer and Regulatory Affairs
614 H. Street, NW, Room 505
Washington, DC 20001   202-727-7395

Florida
Environmental Regulation Department
Twin Towers
2600 Blair Stone Road
Tallahassee, FL 32399   904-488-9334

Georgia
Department of Natural Resources
205 Butler St., SE
Floyd Towers, Suite 1252
Atlanta, GA 30334   404-656-0772

Hawaii
Environmental Health Services Division
Environmental Health Administration
1250 Punchbowl Street
Honolulu, HI 96813   808-548-6455

Idaho
Environmental Quality Division
Department of Health and Welfare
450 W. State Street
Boise, ID 83720   208-334-5839

Illinois
Environmental Protection Agency
P.O. Box 19276
Springfield, IL 62794   217-782-3397

Indiana
Department of Environmental Management
105 S. Meridian Street
Indianapolis, IN 46206   317-232-8162

Iowa
Environmental Protection Division
Department of Natural Resources
Wallace State Office Building
Des Moines, IA 50319   515-281-6284

Kansas
Environment Division
Department of Health and Environment
Forbes Field
Topeka, KS 66620   913-296-1535

Kentucky
Natural Resources and Environmental Protection
Capital Plaza, 5th Floor
Frankfort, KY 40601   502-564-3350

Louisiana
Department of Environmental Quality
P.O. Box 44066
Baton Rouge, LA 70804   504-765-0741

Maine
Environmental Protection Department
State House Station #17
Augusta, ME 04333   207-289-2812

Maryland
Maryland Environmental Service
2020 Industrial Drive
Annapolis, MD 21401   301-974-7281

Massachusetts
Executive Office of Environmental Affairs
100 Cambridge Street, 20th Floor
Boston, MA 02202   617-727-9800

Michigan
Environmental Protection Bureau
Department of Natural Resources
P.O. Box 30028
Lansing, MI 48909   517-373-7917

Minnesota
Pollution Control Agency
520 Lafayette Road
St. Paul, MN 55155   612-296-6300

Mississippi
Environmental Quality Department
P.O. Box 20305
Jackson, MS 39209   601-961-5100

Missouri
Department of Natural Resources
P.O. Box 176
Jefferson City, MO 65102   314-751-3443

Montana
Natural Resources and Conservation Department
1520 E. Sixth Avenue
Helena, MT 59620   406-444-6873

Nebraska
Department of Environmental Control
301 Centennial Mall S.
P.O. Box 98922
Lincoln, NE 68509   402-471-2186

Nevada
Environmental Protection Division
123 W. Nye Lane
Carson City, NV 89710 702-687-4670

New Hampshire
Department of Environmental Services
6 Hazen Drive
Concord, NH 03301 603-271-3503

New Jersey
Department of Environmental Protection
CN 402
Trenton, NJ 08625 609-292-3131

New Mexico
Environment Department
1190 St. Francis Drive
Santa Fe, NM 87503 505-827-2850

New York
Department of Environmental Conservation
50 Wolf Road
Albany, NY 12233 518-457-5400

North Carolina
Environment, Health and Natural
 Resources Department
P.O. Box 27687
Raleigh, NC 27611 919-733-4984

North Dakota
Environmental Health Section
Department of Health
1200 Missouri Avenue
Bismarck, ND 58501 701-221-5150

Ohio
Environmental Protection Agency
1800 Watermark Drive
Columbus, OH 43266 614-644-3020

Oklahoma
Department of Pollution Control
10000 NE 10th Street
P.O. Box 53504
Oklahoma City, OK 73152 405-271-4468

Oregon
Department of Environmental Quality
811 SW Sixth Avenue
Portland, OR 97204 503-229-5696

Pennsylvania
Department of Environmental Resources
P.O. Box 2063
Harrisburg, PA 17120 717-783-2300

Rhode Island
Department of Environmental Management
9 Hayes Street
Providence, RI 02908 401-277-2771

South Carolina
Division of Environmental Quality Control
Department of Health and
 Environmental Control
2600 Bull Street
Columbia, SC 29201 803-734-5360

South Dakota
Environment and Natural Resources Department
Foss Building
Pierre, SD 57501 605-773-3151

Tennessee
Environment and Conservation Department
701 Broadway
Nashville, TN 37243 615-742-6758

Texas
Environment and Consumer Health
Department of Health
1100 W. 49th Street
Austin, TX 78756 512-458-7542

Utah
Division of Environmental Health
Department of Health
288 N. 1460 W.
P.O. Box 16690
Salt Lake City, UT 84116 801-538-6121

Vermont
Environmental Conservation Department
103 S. Wissell
Waterbury, VT 05676 802-244-8755

Virginia
Environment Council
202 N. Ninth Street
Suite 900
Richmond, VA 23219 804-786-4500

Washington
Department of Ecology
M/S: PV-11
Olympia, WA 98504 206-459-6000

West Virginia
Division of Natural Resources
1800 Washington Street, E.
Building 3, Room 669
Charleston, WV 25305 304-348-2754

Wisconsin
Division of Environmental Equality
Department of Natural Resources
P.O. Box 7921
Madison, WI 53707 608-266-2621

Wyoming
Department of Environmental Quality
Herschler Building, 4W
Cheyenne, WY 82002 307-777-7937

* Regional Environmental Offices Offer Help

To insure that EPA is truly responsive to the American People it has established regional offices which cooperate with federal, state, inter-state and local agencies, industry and academic institutions, to insure that regional needs are considered and federal environmental laws implemented. They can answer your questions regarding EPA rules and regulations as well as questions on a wide variety of environmental topics.

EPA Region 1
(CT, MA, ME, NH, RI, VT)
JFK Federal Building
Boston, MA 02203 617-565-3420

EPA Region 2
(NJ, NY, Puerto Rico, Virgin Islands)
26 Federal Plaza
New York, NY 10278 212-264-2657

Field Component
Caribbean Field Office
P.O. Box 792
San Juan, PR 00909 809-725-7825

EPA Region 3

(DE, MD, PA, VA, WV, DC)
841 Chestnut Street
Philadelphia, PA 19107   215-597-9800

EPA Region 4

(AL, FL, GA, KY, MS, NC, SC, TN)
345 Courtland Street NE
Atlanta, GA 30365   404-347-4727

EPA Region 5

(IL, IN, MI, MN, OH, WI)
77 West Jackson Blvd.
Chicago, IL 60604   312-353-2000

Field Component
Eastern District Office
25089 Center Ridge Road
West Lake, OH 44145   216-835-5200

EPA Region 6

(AK, LA, NM, OK, TX)
1445 Ross Avenue
Dallas, TX 75202-2733   214-655-6444

EPA Region 7

(IA, KS, MO, NE)
726 Minnesota Avenue
Kansas City, KS 66101   913-236-2800

EPA Region 8

(CO, MT, ND, SD, UT, WY)
One Denver Place
999 18th Street
Denver, CO, 80202-2405   303-293-1603

EPA Region 9

(AZ, CA, HI, NV, American Samoa, Guam,
Trust Temtones of the Pacific)
75 Hawthorne Street
San Francisco, CA 94105   415-744-1305

Field Component
Pacific Islands Office
P.O. Box 50003
300 Ala Moana Boulevard, Room 1302
Honolulu, HI 96850   808-546-8910

EPA Region 10

(AK, ID, OR, WA)
1200 Sixth Avenue
Seattle, WA 98101   206-442-1200

Field Components
Alaska Operations Office
Room E556, Federal Building
701 C Street
Anchorage, AK 99513   907-271-5083

Alaska Operations Office
3200 Hospital Drive
Juneau, AK 99801   907-586-7619

Idaho Operations Office
422 West Washington Street
Boise, ID 83702   208-334-1450

Oregon Operations Office
811 SW Sixth Avenue
Portland, OR 97204   503-221-3250

Washington Operations Office
c/o Department of Ecology (PV-11)
Olympia, WA 98504   206-753-9437

Videos From Uncle Sam To Help Your Business

Titles like these you're not going to find in your local video store:

How To Protect The Information In Your Computer,
How To Market, Promote and Prepare a Business Plan,
How To Prepare a Balance Sheet,
How to Start a Home Based-Business, or
Getting Rid of Stinky Neighbors: Skunk Control.

But, you will find them in the government and thousands more like them, if you know where to look. The government is not like a private business, that will spend a few thousand dollars to produce a "how-to video" and then spend millions in advertising its availability. The government can easily spend millions in production costs for their videos and then not spend a nickel to let the public know about them.

Here's your chance to view some of these little-known videos. The list below is a sampling of some of the more interesting videos that should be relevant to entrepreneurs. Many of the videos are available on a free loan basis or can be borrowed for a small fee. Some of the videos are available on a free loan basis only to non-profit organizations, like a local women's group or professional society, and others may be seen for a small viewing charge.

* How High Technology Will Affect Your Business

Office of Public Information
National Institute of Standards and Technology (NIST)
Gaithersburg, MD 20899   301-975-2761
NIST, the nation's technology laboratory, produces all kinds of videos about their research and how it can be applied to solve current industry problems. Videos are available on a free loan basis.

High Tech Ceramics: Key to the Future (40m, free loan) - A National Institute of Standards and Technology lab report describes state of the art advanced ceramics research that characterizes different materials and provides an understanding of how advanced ceramics are formed and measured.

Near-Field Antenna Facility (40m, free loan) - This National Institute of Standards and Technology lab report describes near-field antenna measurement methods and how they can be used by business and industry.

Measurement: The Vital Link (14m, free loan) - Describes how the National Institute of Standards and Technology uses its measurement expertise to work cooperatively with industry, universities, and other government agencies to help improve productivity and increase industrial competitiveness.

Color Under Energy Efficient Lighting (22m, free loan) - Describes work done at the National Institute of Standards and Technology on how energy-efficient lighting systems can affect the way colors look, and provides suggestions for designing such lighting systems for commercial, industrial, and institutional buildings.

* Staying Competitive by Making Your Employees More Productive

Bureau of Labor-Management
U.S. Department of Labor, Room N5419,
FPB, 200 Constitution Ave., NW
Washington, DC 20210   202-219-7910
The Bureau of Labor-Management distributes all kinds of videos that deal with cooperative and employee involvement programs. These videos are available on a free loan basis.

Dr. Michael Maccoby: Resistance to Quality of Work Life (21m, free loan) - The director of Harvard's Project on Technology, Work, and Character, discusses the psychological reasons for managerial and worker resistance to quality of work life and focuses on traditional values people have toward work.

The Union and Quality of Work Life at General Motors (29m, free loan) - Describes the quality of work life program at General Motors through an interview with Irving Bluestone, then vice president of the UAW.

Employee Participation (27m, free loan) - Workers draw on the skills of a resource expert and take part in restructuring their work environment.

A Conversation with William G. Ouchi (30m, free loan) - Professor Ouchi of the UCLA Graduate School of Management contrasts the roles of Japanese and American government in fostering business applications of quality of work life.

Adapting to a Changing World (27m, free loan) - Explains how business, government, and universities use the National Institute of Standards and Technology's Manufacturing Research Facility to help them improve the manufacture of parts in small quantities.

The People Factor--Employee Involvement at Ford (21m, free loan) - Emphasizes the vital role blue- and white-collar employees play in large American corporations.

The Process of Organizational Change at General Motors (23m, free loan) - Emphasizes the idea that productivity and quality of work life are interdependent and shows different ways of measuring a program's effectiveness.

Profit and Equity Sharing and Ownership (27m, free loan) - Focuses on employee decision making, profit sharing, and ownership.

Labor-Management Relations (27m, free loan) - Describes cooperative programs at Labatt Breweries of Canada where a single team bargaining concept has evolved as an approach to collective bargaining negotiations.

QWL--A Union Perspective (50 m, free loan) - Addresses such issues as job pressures and work freedoms, flexibility between labor and management, measurement of results, impact of new technology, and the company and union role in promoting quality of work life.

QWL: The CWA Story (35m, free loan) - Features proceedings of the first quality of work life update by the National Committee on QWL, jointly established in 1980 by AT&T and the Communication Workers of America.

The Real Bottom Line (27m, free loan) - Gives an overview of the concept, purpose, and philosophy of quality of work life efforts focusing on two cooperative programs in Sacramento, California.

Self-Regulating Work Groups (27m, free loan) - Explores self-regulating work groups at a Canadian Government transportation bureau and Shell Canada LTD.

Videos From Uncle Sam To Help Your Business

* How To Find Customers For Your Products and Overseas

International Trade Administration (ITA)
U.S. Department of Commerce
14th and Constitution Ave., NW
Washington, DC 20230   202-482-2000

To help businesses expand their markets, the ITA has produced several videos that explain many different aspects of international trade, such as selling abroad and taking advantage of foreign trade shows. Videos are available on a free loan basis.

The $ and Sense of Exporting (You Can Sell Them) (18m, free loan) - Designed to show non-exporting companies how they can be successful in developing overseas markets for their products. Several U.S. companies explain how they became successful exporters.

Finding Buyers for Your Products (14m, free loan) - Describes the Commerce Department's trade promotion programs and how they assist businesses in selling abroad.

Bring the World to Your Fingertips (14m, free loan) - Demonstrates the Department of Commerce's worldwide Commercial Information Management System, an international marketing information retrieval system.

* Protecting Your Info On Computer, How To Make Money In The Futures Market, and Managing McDonalds

Modern Talking Picture Service
5000 Park St., North
St. Petersburg, FL 33709   1-800-243-MTPS

The Modern Talking Picture Service will loan you any of their videos free of charge, and they will even pay for the postage to send it to you and for you to return it. Any organization qualifies for this free video loan service, including your own club with only you as a member.

Futures in Your Life (10m, free loan) - Using the Chicago Board of Trade, this video shows how futures rates of farm commodities, precious metals, and financial instruments are determined.

Information...Handle with Care (10m, free loan) - Illustrates the importance of protecting information in today's computer environment.

What is a Mutual Fund? (14m, free loan) - Explains the basics of mutual fund investing and how they make billions of dollars of investments.

Inside Corporate America (28m, free loan) - An inside look at McDonalds Corporation and how it is managed.

Where the World's Market Forces Converge: The Chicago Board of Trade (14m, free loan) - Describes the functions of the Chicago Board of Trade, what futures are, the roles of the hedger and speculator/investor, price-risk transfer, and futures role in the world economy.

* Advertising Strategies, and Future Markets For Your Products and Services

Modern Talking Picture Service
5000 Park St., North
St. Petersburg, FL 33709   1-800-243-MTPS

The Modern Talking Picture Service will loan you any of their videos free of charge, and they will even pay for the postage to send it to you and for you to return it. Any organization qualifies for this free video loan service, including your own club with only you as a member.

The Many Faces of Marketing: Changing American Lifestyles and Social Trends (26m, free loan) - Documents a presentation to the Federal Trade Commission by Florence Skelly, a renowned marketing research expert.

The More Creative the Ad, The Harder It Works (in 2 parts) (21m & 27M, free loan) - Presented by leading advertising agency executives, these videos cover case histories and marketing strategies of individual product success stories.

The Need to Know (VT003, 23m, $15) - Outlines the history, significance, and contributions of agricultural statistics and USDA's National Agricultural

Statistics Service.

Today and Tomorrow (VT002, 23m, $15) - Analyzes the current situation for U.S. and world crops and forecasts supplies and prices.

* How You Can Use Government Research For Business Opportunities

Sales Desk
National Technical Information Service (NTIS)
U.S. Department of Commerce
5285 Port Royal Road
Springfield, VA 22161   703-487-4650

To find out how your business might benefit from the results of government-sponsored research and development projects, contact this office for a free video that will show you how to put their information to use.

NTIS--The Competitive Edge (#PR-858/827, 8m, free loan) - Provides an introduction to the National Technical Information Service, the clearinghouse for U.S. and foreign government-sponsored scientific and technical information.

* Success Story On The Quality of Working Life

Program on Third Party Studies
Department of Communication
205 Derby Hall
Ohio State University (OSU)
Columbus, OH 43210   614-292-3400

To receive a copy of OSU's videos, simply send them a blank 1/2" VHS tape and they will copy and return it to you at no charge. Make sure that the tape you send is long enough to fit the entire video.

The Quality of Working Life (27m, free copy) - Describes the history and the process of initiating and implementing the 1976 quality of working life program in Columbus, Ohio.

* Free Services To Expand Your Markets

Office of Public Affairs
U.S. Department of Commerce
14th St. & Constitution Ave., NW
Washington, DC 20230   202-482-2000

The U.S. Department of Commerce distributes videos that show businesses how they can use the Department resources to maintain their competitiveness. Videos are available on a free loan basis.

Show Business is Good Business: How U.S. Manufacturers Expand Their Markets Through Exports, (18m, free loan) - Shows you how the different agencies within the Commerce Department can help American businesses.

* Help In Selling Your Products Overseas

Office of Public Affairs
Bureau of Export Administration (BEA)
U.S. Department of Commerce
14th St. & Constitution Ave., NW
Washington, DC 20230   202-482-2000

The BEA is responsible for enforcing export laws and controls, and also helps businesses apply for export licenses. They also produce videos about the export licensing process that are available on a free loan basis.

Keep America Strong, Keep America Competitive (18m, free loan) - Provides a good introduction to the Bureau of Export Administration for businesses considering expansion into the export market.

* How To Help Your Employees With Drug or Alcohol Problems

Division of Applied Research
National Institute on Drug Abuse
Room 10A53, 5600 Fishers Lane
Rockville, MD 20857   301-443-6245

Is there a problem with some of your employees' work habits? Are some coming in late or not at all? It could be that drugs or alcohol are involved. The National Institute of Drug Abuse is developing programs to eliminate illegal drug use in the workplace. Its programs include research, treatment, training and prevention activities, as well as projects related to the development of a comprehensive Drug-Free Workplace programs. They will analyze and recommend Employee Assistance Programs (EAP) and distribute a four-part videotape series on drugs at work. Other free loan videos include:

Drugs At Work (employee/employer versions) - Presents information about the nature and scope of the alcohol and drug problem in the workplace and about the Federal government's initiative to prevent and reduce the problem.

Getting Help (employee/employer versions) - Highlights the benefits of an effective employee assistance program to employees and employers through comments by business, labor, and government leaders and EAP professionals.

Drug Testing: Handle With Care (employee/employer versions) - Describes the options available for designing a drug testing component as part of a comprehensive drug-free workplace program.

Finding Solutions - Drug abuse in the workplace is portrayed as a community-wide problem. The solutions offered through education and prevention are presented as personal, workplace, and community responsibilities.

* Safety Hazards, Back Injuries, Noise and AIDS

Office of Field Programs
U.S. Department of Labor
Occupational Safety and Health Administration (OSHA)
200 Constitution Ave, NW, Room N3606
Washington, DC 20210   202-523-7725

Each of the regional OSHA offices offer free loan videos on worker safety topics. The following titles are a sample of what is available from the Kansas City office:

Asbestos: Fighting a Killer
Back Injuries
Beyond Fear: AIDS
Camcorder, Introduction to the Use of
Drugs at Work and Testing
Manual Lifting and Handling/ Hand Tools
Motorcycle Safety (The Expert Rider)
Noise On People
To Catch a Killer - High Blood Pressure
Tools
Winter Hazards
Workplace Drug Abuse
AIDS, Part I & II
What You Should Know About AIDS
AIDS Prevention for Laboratory Professionals
AIDS Prevention for Nursing Professionals
AIDS Prevention for Support Services Employees

Contact the office nearest you for further information on free videos:

Region I
(CT,MA,ME,NH,RI,VT)
16-18 North St.
1 Dock Square Building, 4th Floor
Boston, MA 02109   617-223-6710

Region II
(NJ,NY,Puerto Rico, Virgin Islands)
1 Astor Plaza, Room 3445
1515 Broadway
New York, NY 10036

Region III
(DC,DE,MD,PA,VA,WV)
Gateway Building, Suite 2100
3535 Market Street
Philadelphia, PA 19104   215-596-1201

Region IV
(AL,FL,GA,KY,MS,NC,SC,TN)
1375 Peachtree St., NE
Suite 587
Atlanta, GA 30367   404-347-7482

Region V
(IL,IN,MI,MN,OH,WI)
230 South Dearborn St.
32nd Floor, Room 3244
Chicago, IL 60604   312-353-2220

Region VI
(AR,LA,NM,OK,TX)
535 Griffin Sq. Building, Room 602
Dallas, TX 75202   214-767-4731

Region VII
(IA,KS,MO,NE)
911 Walnut Street, Room 406
Kansas City, MO 64106   816-426-5861

Region VIII
(CO,MT,ND,SD,UT,WY)
Federal Building, Room 1554
1961 Stout Street
Denver, CO 80294   303-844-3061

Region IX
(American Samoa, AZ,CA,HI,NV, Pacific Trust Territories)
P.O. Box 36017
450 Golden Gate Avenue
San Francisco, CA 94102   415-556-7260

Region X
(AK,ID,OR,WA)
Federal Office Building
Room 6003, 909 First Avenue
Seattle, WA 98174   206-442-5930

* Asbestos, Vibration and Lifting Safety

National Institute of Occupational Safety and Health (NIOSH)
4676 Columbia Parkway
Cincinnati, OH 45226   513-533-8287

The following videos are available on a free loan basis from the office above. Copies are available upon written request only on a first come first served basis. Copies are also available for sale from The National Audiovisual Center, National Archives and Records Administration, 8700 Edgeworth Drive, Capitol Heights, MD 20543, 301-763-1896.

Alice Hamilton: Science Service and Compassion - The program summarizes the professional life of a woman widely credited as the mother of industrial medicine in America. From her education, through her public health work at Jane Adams' famous Hull House in Chicago, her work for state and federal government, and her academic career at Harvard University.

The Finest Tools - Covers the nature of Cumulative Trauma Disorders of the hand and wrist, e.g. carpal tunnel syndrome. Describes how to analyze a job to determine how stressful it is.

Case Study of an Assembly Line - By examining a study of telephone assembly line workers, the programs shows how important ergonomics and its sub-field, biomechanics, are to a successful operation.

Asbestos Screening Process - This program examines an inexpensive and simple method for identifying asbestos in bulk samples.

Vibration Syndrome - It covers etiology, symptomatology, assessment, and treatment of this condition. It includes a brief introduction to the physics of vibration, and an examination of different assessment techniques.

Lifting and Analysis - It demonstrates how to calculate the parameters for safe lifting activity in specific example situations.

Fire Prevention and Control - Discusses potential sources of fire and explosion in the school science laboratory and compares and contrasts different types of fire extinguishers.

Safety Program Planning - Discusses specific mechanisms for getting everyone actively involved in a comprehensive safety program: safety committees, safety contracts, safety and health research, and other techniques are covered.

Videos From Uncle Sam To Help Your Business

* How To Market, Promote and Prepare a Business Plan

Office of Business Development & Marketing
Small Business Administration (SBA)
409 3rd St., SW
Washington, DC 20416   202-205-6665

The SBA has three VHS tapes that are helpful to business owners who are trying to develop marketing, promotional, and business plans. You can purchase these from the above address, or you can **request a copy to review for 30 days free of charge.**

Marketing: Winning Customers With A Workable Plan - Offers a step-by-step approach on how to write the best possible marketing plan for your business. Explains the best methods for determining customer needs, how to identify and develop a working profile for potential customers and much more. $30

The Business Plan: Your Roadmap To Success - Teaches the essentials of developing a business plan that will help lead you to capital, growth, and profitability. Tells what to include, what to omit, and how to get free help from qualified consultants. $30

Promotion: Solving The Puzzle - Shows you how to coordinate advertising, public relations, direct mail, and trade shows into a successful promotional strategy that targets new customers, increases sales, and saves you money. $30

* Step-By-Step On How To Keep Records and Prepare Your Taxes

Audio/Visual Branch
Public Affairs Division
Internal Revenue Service (IRS)
U.S. Department of the Treasury
1111 Constitution Ave., NW
Washington, DC 20224   202-566-6860

The IRS provides audio cassettes and video cassettes for loan to the public on how to fill out Forms 1040EX, 1040A, 1040, and schedules A and B. These tax tapes contain simple step-by-step instructions to the forms and tax tips. Other titles include:

Hey, We're In Business - Explains record keeping, tax deadlines, and free IRS assistance to business persons (also in Spanish).

Line By Line - Takes you through every line of the 1040 and the 1040A and shows you how to fill them out.

Why Us, The Lakens? - Highlights taxpayer examination and appeal rights (also in Spanish).

?Por Que Los Impriestos? - Covers the history of taxation, how tax revenues are used, rights and responsibilities of taxpayers, and different kinds of IRS assistance.

Helping to Recover - Focuses on how to claim disaster, casualty, and theft losses.

A Vital Service - Aims at enlisting groups and organizations into the Volunteer Income Tax Assistance (VITA) Program in which IRS trains volunteers to assist low income and other needy people with their tax forms.

The IRS has distributed these tapes to many local libraries, as well as IRS district offices. Contact an IRS office near you for more information regarding these videos.

* Home Based Business Basics

Oklahoma State University
Home Based Business Office
135-HES
Stillwater, OK 74078   405-744-5776

Home Based Business Basics shows potential business owners how to do market research, handle finances, cope with legal problems, do promotions and juggle family relationships. The film is produced by a member of the County Cooperative Extension service and is available on a free loan basis at local county cooperative extension service offices throughout the country. Call your local operator for your nearest office. Or, you can purchase the film for $30 direct from the producer listed above.

* How To Inspect A Home Before You Invest

University of Illinois Film Center
1324 South Oak Street
Champagne, IL 61820   1-800-367-3456

From Roof to Foundation follows a building inspection expert on a home tour, and shows examples of what to look for when considering buying a home. The film is produced by a member of the County Cooperative Extension service and is available on a free loan basis at local county cooperative extension service offices throughout the country. Call your local operator for your nearest office. Or, you can purchase the film for $45, or rent it for 10 days for $10, directly from the producer listed above.

* Financial Planning Investments and Rattlesnakes

Contact Your Local County Cooperative Extension Service

Hundreds of helpful videos are available on a free loan basis through your local County Government Cooperative Extension Service. The available programs differ from state to state, and you should contact your local office to see what titles are available to you. The office listed above has oversight over video services in every state and may be helpful in locating a specific title. Listed below are some of the titles produced by various extension service offices:

- *Risk Management*
- *Types of Investments*
- *Investment Series: The Fundamentals (Part I)*
- *Investment Series: The Fundamentals (Part II)*
- *Family and Economic Well Being: 5 Critical Issues*
- *The Choice is Yours: Housing Options for Seniors Today*
- *Packing Your Home To Sell*
- *You're Accountable: How To Select and Use Financial Accounts*
- *Cake Decorating*
- *Bread Baking*
- *Microwave Cooking*
- *Removing Rattlesnakes from Human Dwellings*
- *Pruning Walnut Trees For Profit*
- *How To Calibrate a Manure Spreader*
- *Baby Pig and Sow Management*
- *Getting Rid of Stinky Neighbors - Skunk Control in Residential Areas*

* Job Discrimination, Sexual Harassment, Women's Work

National Audiovisual Center
8700 Edgeworth Drive
Capitol Heights, MD 20743   301-763-1896

The National Audiovisual Center is the U.S. Government's largest distributor of films, audio and videos. This office would be happy to send you free catalogues covering topics like health, history and foreign languages.

EEOC and The Laws It Enforces (150 min) - Contains comments by EEOC commissioners, a question and answer session, and three segments dealing with sex, race/national origin, and age discrimination. Each segment contains a brief explanation of the law and vignettes of different discriminatory acts. (free preview to non-profits, $12 preview to others, $150 sale)

There's No Such Thing As Women's Work (30 min) - Describes history of women in the workplace from the 1890's to the 1980's. Shows the effect of various legislation on women in the workplace and the role of the Department of Labor's Women's Bureau in the labor force. (free preview to non-profits, $12 preview to others, $45 sale)

The Harmonics of Conflict (25 min) - Indicates the nature of conflict: necessary, permanent, and universal. Presents different methods for managing conflict, and considers the similarities and differences between private and public sector collective bargaining negotiations. Accomplishes these objectives by combining a commentary with a series of scenes describing and explaining the major purposes. (free preview to non-profits, $12 preview to others, $45 sale)

Why Not A Woman? (26 min) - Shows women working successfully in non-traditional jobs such as welder, carpenter and mechanic. Explores the attitudes of their male co-workers. Demonstrates the wide range of job options and training available to girls and women. Presents a realistic and entertaining argument against the long-standing myths about women and work. Attempts to persuade audiences to reassess their deep-seated attitudes about working women. (free preview to non-profits, $12 preview to others, $45 sale)

* Free Video on How To Start a Business In Your Home

Office of Business Development and Marketing
Small Business Administration (SBA)
409 3rd St., SW
Washington, DC 20416 (202) 205-6665

The SBA has produced a home video especially geared toward home-based business owners. *Home-Based Business: A Winning Blueprint* takes you through many of the steps necessary to a successful home-based business, from setting up your home office and networking strategies, to avoiding isolation and building the right kind of image for your company. You can purchase it for $39 from the following address: SBA, "Success", Dept. A, P.O. Box 30, Denver, CO 80202-0030. You can **review the video for free for 30 days** before you decide to purchase. Contact the office listed above in Washington, DC.

* Home-Based Businesses, Stress, Kid Entrepreneurs, Weatherstripping, and Cockroaches

Oklahoma State University
Home Based Business Office, 135-HES
Stillwater, OK 74078 405-744-5776

The following videos are available on a free loan basis for residents of Oklahoma and may be available on a free loan basis in other states through the County Cooperative Extension Service system. Contact your local County Extension Office listed under your county government for availability. Copies are also available for sale at prices ranging from $15 to $30.

Home Based Business Basics - Shows potential business owners how to do market research, handle finances, cope with legal problems, do promotions and juggle family relationships. The film is produced by a member of the County Cooperative Extension service and is available on a free loan basis at local County Cooperative Extension Service offices throughout the country. Call your local operator for your nearest office. Or, you can purchase the film for $30 direct from the producer listed above.

Home-Based Businesses: Oklahoma Success Stories - Provides a broad overview of home-based businesses in Oklahoma. Includes four interviews; two businesses still in the home, two businesses that have grown out of the home. Discusses pros and cons of home-based businesses.

Stress: What Is It and How Do I Deal With It? - Provides an in-depth look at what various definitions of stress are, what stress does to people, and how people react to stress pile-up. Examples are given of families under various kinds of stress: psychological, interpersonal, physical and behavioral. Also gives examples of suicidal tendencies.

Balancing Work and Family - A conference consisting of two panels of researchers, professors, extension specialists, and business professionals as well as a live audience of people with various family situation and philosophies. Various topics discussed by these groups include time management, caring for children and elderly, delayed child-bearing, dual family incomes and models for balancing work and family.

Selecting and Working with Financial Advisors - This tape will help viewers learn to select professional financial advisors. A specialist in family management at the Ohio State University, tells you what to look for in a financial planner.

Youth Entrepreneurs: 4-H'ers with Home-Based Businesses - A group of Sunup news stories that feature 4-H'ers across the state who have their own home-based businesses.

The Cold Facts: Winter Protection for Older Adults - Hypothermia is a serious national health problem which affects the elderly. This training workshop stresses identification, prevention and treatment of this serious health hazard.

The How To's of Weatherstripping - One homeowner introduces you to weatherization specialist Don Lemonier who takes you through a sample home showing you places to weatherstrip, the tools you'll need to do the job, then how to actually do the work.

The How To's of Caulking - Covers how to weatherstrip double-hung windows, places to caulk, the tools needed to do the job, and how to actually do the work.

Energy Basics - A review of what we use energy for in the home and ideas on how to reduce costs including caulking, weatherstripping, storm windows, plastic sheeting, insulation, window coverings, turning down the hot water heater and changing living habits.

The Cooling of Summer Heat - A humorous approach to low-cost, no-cost ways of controlling summer heat in the home and controlling utility bills.

* Mortgage Rates, Bankruptcy and Credit

Satellite Programming
Virginia Cooperative Extension Service
217 Hutcheson Hall
Blacksburg, VA 24061 703-231-6941

The following videos are available on a free loan basis for residents of Virginia and may be available on a free loan basis in other states through the County Cooperative Extension Service system. Contact your local County Extension Office listed under your county government for availability. Copies are also available for sale from the office above at prices ranging from $20 to $30.

Choosing Adjustable Rate Mortgages
Avoiding Bankruptcy
Problems with Credit

* Sales Training, Management, Financial Planning, Leadership and Motivation

Video Resource Center
University of Maryland
Cooperative Extension Service
0120 Symons Hall
College Park, MD 20742 301-405-2902

The following videos are available on a free loan basis for residents of Maryland and may be available on a free loan basis in other states through the County Cooperative Extension Service system. Contact your local County Extension Office listed under your county government for availability. Copies are also available for sale from this office at prices up to $25. Program time ranges from 30 minutes to 2 hours.

Analyzing Financial Performance - With Freddie Barnard, Assistant Professor and Extension Economist at Purdue University.

Preparing a Balance Sheet - With Freddie Barnard, Assistant Professor and Extension Economist at Purdue University.

Preparing a Cash Flow Statement - With Freddie Barnard, Assistant Professor and Extension Economist at Purdue University.

Preparing an Income Statement - With Freddie Barnard, Assistant Professor and Extension Economist at Purdue University.

Strategic Planning for Financial Success - With A. Gene Nelson, Head of the Agriculture Resource Economic Department at Texas A & M University.

Financial Planning Before and During Retirement - Three part series featuring Maryland Extension Financial Management specialist Patricia Tengel.

Down the Home Stretch - Looks at factors that usually lead to decision to retire. Also explores retirement income and budgeting.

Financial Planning During Retirement - Explains how to improve financial worth during retirement. Covers making a budget, management assets, and how to increase income.

Sources of Retirement Income - Workshop style presentation of need for retirement planning and sources of income for retirees. Covers Social Security, pension benefits, tax deferred plans and savings.

Clear as Mud - Characters enact why clear communication is important to efficient and meaningful relations. Poor planning, jargon, improper listening, and subjective interpretation of messages are some of the pitfalls shown.

Communications: Getting in Touch - Explores the communications process applied to sales.

Creative Problem Solving - Offers managers specific tips for finding solutions to business, personal and management problems.

Group Productivity - A model group demonstrates the evolution of group development.

How to Influence Motivation - Demonstrates how to translate organization needs into individual worker's needs.

How to Lead Effectively - Teaches leaders to be more effective by demonstrating four models: consulting, delegating, participating and directing.

How To Solve Problems - Three-step plan teaches managers a way to turn problems into opportunities.

Working with Difficult People - Demonstrates four-step strategy for modifying and coping with the behavior of difficult people.

Cross Cultural Communication - Covers understanding communication differences between members of different races and cultures.

Money and Help To Companies Which Want To Use or Sell Technology

It is not uncommon today for many small technology-based businesses to fail simply because the owners aren't aware of the state programs that could significantly reduce their crucial, first year start-up costs. If a new company needs some kind of technical service assistance for which private consulting firms charge large amounts of money, chances are that an appropriate state program is available to do it for much less. Why pay consulting firms thousands of dollars of your hard-to-come-by start-up capital for financial planning and product refinement when free or low cost help is available? Many states have programs that will provide assistance at no cost or at reduced rates simply because your company is a technology-oriented small business.

It is no secret that successful businesses are run by people who either know all the right information themselves or know where to find it. So, before your company spends a dime on technical problem-solving in Maryland, for example, you should know to call the Technology Extension Service, which just may be able to solve the problem for free. Or, before you spend hundreds of dollars for preliminary patent searches in Wisconsin, you should know to call the University-Industry Research program, which can do it for about $15. But, to save the money, you need to know where to get this important information.

To keep up with the rapidly growing advanced technology-based industries in the U.S., over half of the states have developed program offices that cater to the special needs of these businesses. Aside from administering the individual programs, these offices often act as information clearinghouses and referral services for those interested in any of their state's technology-related services. Instead of having to go to ten different offices for information on such programs as technical assistance, business planning, and technology transfer, these central offices provide, in many cases, one-stop information shopping.

Since many of these offices are closely associated with their state's Department of Economic Development, you can get information on, let's say, technical assistance, venture capital, product marketing strategies, and managerial assistance all in the same place.

Unfortunately, many states do not yet have such umbrella organizations to oversee and coordinate their state technology initiatives, and your state may be one of them. If that's the case, don't automatically assume that there are no special programs for technology-oriented businesses in your state. Start at your state's Department of Economic Development or Commerce, or Small Business Association to find out what programs are offered to address your particular needs. You also might try your state universities, which may have technology-oriented and business assistance programs. Also, call the Department of Commerce, 202-377-8100, for information on a clearinghouse for state and local initiatives on productivity, technology, and innovation technology administration.

Following are some brief descriptions of the programs most often offered:

Seed Capital
Although its funding policies vary from state to state, Seed Capital is usually awarded in the form of a grant to especially promising new business ideas that demonstrate strong potential for creating jobs and broadening the state economic base. Through the program, companies can often use this capital to leverage financial support from other resources as well. On the other hand, some businesses may obtain seed capital on a dollar-for-dollar basis whereby the state program fund will match the capital that the business has raised through other resources. Note, however, that some state programs consider seed capital and venture capital one and the same.

Venture Capital
Venture Capital programs often provide financing specifically for technology-oriented businesses through networks which match entrepreneurs with investors. Some states, such as Michigan and Missouri, have developed computerized matching services whereby individuals with specific investment interests can be matched with the appropriate entrepreneurs. Other states have compiled venture capital directories and formal venture referral networks to accomplish a similar matching process. Also see the *State Money* and *Venture Capital* Sections.

Small Business Innovative Research Grants
Small Business Innovation Research (SBIR) programs provide assistance to companies of 500 employees or less that wish to tap into the lucrative federal research and development funding annually available for the development and commercialization of new products. Each year federal agencies publish a list of specific topics they would like researched, and small businesses submit proposals in response to these solicitations to obtain the SBIR funding. Since the composition of these proposals is highly technical and complex, many of these state SBIR programs will walk small businesses through the procurement process, showing them successful proposal strategies that have worked in the past. A Small Business Association pamphlet titled, *Proposal Preparation for Small Business Innovation Research*, is also available at your local Small Business Administration office. Also see the *State Money* Section.

Technology Transfer
Technology Transfer programs establish contacts between businesses and university researchers to facilitate the transfer of new technologies from the lab to industry. This collaboration can, in turn, help solve technical problems and create new economic opportunities. For example, a business will contact a tech transfer office, such as the Center for Innovative Technology in Virginia or the New Jersey Commission on Science and Technology, to discuss its problem. The office will then use its technology resource networks with universities, private industry, and federal agencies to locate potential

Money and Help To Companies Which Want To Use Or Sell Technology

solutions, which are then related back to the business. Tech transfer can also take other forms, such as gaining access to state-of-the art technical information through database searches, buying or leasing necessary technology- oriented equipment, or using technical consulting resources.

A detailed listing of the state technology transfer programs follows this listing of the state technology information offices.

Technical And Managerial Assistance

Many states' Technical and Managerial Assistance programs provide short-term assistance to businesses with specific technological problems. Much like technology transfer, technical assistance programs, such as PENNTAP in Pennsylvania, are designed to target and solve problems using the most up-to-date technology at little or no cost. Many of these technical consultants, for example, can redesign facilities, analyze manufacturing costs, refine computer systems, and much more.

Incubator Programs

Businesses often fail during their critical early stages. Incubator programs are geared toward avoiding this high failure rate by reducing start-up costs. Like the Center for the Advancement of Developing Industries in Alabama, these incubators provide office, laboratory, and manufacturing space at significantly reduced rates to qualifying start-up companies that exhibit a strong potential for growth. The incubator services to these companies often include technical and managerial assistance, access to university expertise and technology, financial backing, and business and finance planning.

If the following technology development offices do not have the specific information you need, they can most likely refer you to someone who does. And since many of these technology programs are new, it is not uncommon for one office to say no to your inquiry while another will say yes. Persistence is one of the greatest money savers.

State Offices Offering Technology-Oriented Assistance

Alabama
Office for the Advancement of Developing Industries (OADI), University of Alabama at Birmingham, UAB Station, Birmingham, AL 35294; 205-934-2190. OADI provides information on the following: seed and venture capital; technology transfer; incubator facilities; legal, financial, business, and technical assistance; and conferences and seminars.

Alaska
Alaska Science and Technology Foundation, (ASTF), 550 West 7th Avenue, Suite 360, Anchorage, AK 99501-3555; 907-272-4333. This Foundation assists in taking a good technical idea to application or commercialization. Grants are awarded on a competitive basis and grantees are expected to contribute time, effort and resources.

Arkansas
Arkansas Science and Technology Authority (ASTA), 100 Main Street, Suite 450, Little Rock, AR 72201; 501-324-9006. ASTA provides information on the following for young technology-based businesses: incubator facilities, research grants, seed capital investment, SBIR funding, and technology transfer.

Colorado
University of Colorado Business Advancement Centers (UCBAC), 4700 Walnut

Street, Suite 101, Boulder, CO 80301; 1-800-369-1243 or 303-444-5723. UCBAC can provide information on the following: SBIR funding, financial planning, marketing and feasibility studies, government contract procurement, technology transfer, and technical expertise.

Connecticut
Connecticut Technology Assistance Center (CONNTAC), Department of Economic Development, 210 Washington Street, Hartford, CT 06106; 203-241-0777. CONNTAC provides information on the following programs and services: business plan development; technical, managerial, and marketing assistance; new product funding; start-up, expansion, and research and development grants; private sector financing and venture capital funds; access to university technical expertise; state hi-tech business profiles; employee education and training; incubator facilities; and educational forums and conferences.

Florida
Southern Technology Applications Centers (STAC), One Progress Boulevard, Box 24, Allachua, FL 32615; 1-800-225-0308, 904-462-3913. STAC will provide information on their following programs: technology transfer, entrepreneurial assistance, SBIR funding, venture capital, incubator facilities, workshops and seminars, and extensive technical information.

Georgia
Advanced Technology Development Center (ATDC), 430 Tenth Street, N.W., Suite N-116, Atlanta, GA 30318; 404-894-3575. ATDC's assistance programs include the following services: business planning and management; financing, marketing, and manufacturing strategy development; accounting, financial, and legal services; access to Georgia Tech research and development equipment and services, including computing systems; on-campus space for labs, research and development, office, and light manufacturing uses; and access to university technical consultants.

Hawaii
Hawaii High Technology Development Corporation (HTDC), 300 Kahelu Avenue, Suite 35, Mililani, HI 96789; 808-625-5293. HTDC provides information on the following programs: business planning and assistance, technical assistance, and incubator facilities. HTDC also publishes the *Hawaii HiTech Journal*, and *Hawaii HiTech Business Directory*, which covers state technology-related economic growth.

Indiana
Indiana Business of Modernization and Technology Corporation, One North Capitol Avenue, Suite 925, Indianapolis, IN 46204; 317-635-3058. This corporation provides support to qualifying technology-based companies through three major programs: 1) technological counseling and assistance; 2) business and financial counseling development; and 3) funding support. Programs are also provided for small and medium size industries.

Iowa
Center for Industrial Research and Service (CIRAS), ISU Research Park, Suite 500, 2501 North Loop Drive, Ames, IA 50010-8286; 515-294-3420. CIRAS assists manufacturing and processing firms by providing information in technical and management areas which include manufacturing, engineering, management, marketing, and database access.

Kansas
Kansas Technology Enterprise Corporation (KTEC), 112 W. 6th, Suite 400, Topeka, KS 66603; 913-296-5272. KTEC provides information on its following programs: seed capital investment and SBIR funding; the Kansas Technology Resource Database, which will provide information on research objectives, facilities, equipment, consulting services, training programs, market sources; technology expositions and conferences; and technology transfer.

Kentucky
Kentucky Business & Technology Branch, Kentucky Cabinet for Economic Development, 500 Mero Street, 22nd Floor, Frankfort, KY 40601; 502-564-7670. This office provides information on the following: newly developing technologies, technology transfer, technical expertise, access of research and development

contracts, business development funds, and seminars and workshops on emerging technologies.

Louisiana

The Louisiana Business and Technology Center (LBTC), South Stadium Drive, Louisiana State University; Baton Rouge, LA 70803-6100; 504-334-5555. The LBTC is a high-tech incubator offering start-up assistance to new high-tech companies. It operates a Small Business Institute, a Management Assistance Office, and a Technology Utilization Office at NASA-Stennis Space Center. The LBTC offers technology transfer and utilization as well as technical and business expertise. It is linked with experts in engineering, agriculture, basic sciences, micromachining, and biomedics. Services include space, office support, grant writing, financial counseling, business planning and marketing planning.

Maine

Maine Science and Technology Commission (MSTC), State House Station #147, Augusta, ME 04333; 207-624-6350. The MSTC offers technology support and can refer companies to its three branches for electronics, bio-technology, and aquaculture for technical assistance and development.

Maryland

Office of Business Development, 217 E. Redwood St., 12th Floor, Baltimore, MD 21202; 410-333-6990. This office provides information on the following: venture capital, incubator facilities, SBIR funding, national and international technologies markets, and technical assistance. The Challenge Grant program is also provided.

Massachusetts

Massachusetts Technology Development Corporation (MTDC), 148 State Street, 9th Floor, Boston, MA 02109; 617-723-4920. MTDC directly provides some financing in the areas of equity, working capital, and product development. There are also high-tech task forces (one each for bio-tech, enviro-tech and medi-tech) which nurture high-tech companies as well as the Small Business Development Centers which provide free consulting and start-up advice to entrepreneurs.

Michigan

Business Resources Group (BRG), P.O. Box 30234, Lansing, MI 48909; 517-335-4720. BRG oversees the following technology programs: seed capital, research and development grants, technology transfer, technical consulting, product development and testing services, computer assistance, and technical training.

Minnesota

Minnesota Technology, Inc. (MTI), 920 Second Avenue S., Suite 1250, Minneapolis, MN 55402; 612-338-7722. MTI can provide information on the following: SBIR, economic development grants, technology transfer, product development, marketing assistance, incubator facilities, employee training, and much more. MTI also distributes a hi-tech company directory, a state technology economic impact report, the state software technology commission report, and others.

Mississippi

Mississippi Technology Transfer Office (MITTO), John C. Stennis Space Center, Bldg. 1103, Stennis Space Center, MS 39529-6000; 601-688-3144. MITTO provides access to technology developed by federal agencies housed at NASA's John C. Stennis Space Center and various federal laboratories. It also gives assistance in applying for Small Business Innovation Research (SBIR) grants.

Missouri

Missouri Corporation for Science and Technology (MCST), P.O. Box 118, Jefferson City, MO 65102, Attn: Thomas W. Barry; 314-751-5095. MCST oversees the SBIR/Hi-Tech programs, which distributes information on the following programs: business planning and financing, marketing assistance, venture capital network, technical and managerial assistance, product design, and employee training. MCST distributes directories of in-state hi-tech companies and venture capital firms. MCST also provides assistance to four innovation centers that deal with new product development and other aspects concerning start-up ventures. It also provides three centers in Advanced Technology in the areas of manufacturing, telecommunications, and plant bio-technology.

Montana

Montana Science and Technology Alliance (MSTA), 46 N. Last Chance Gulch, Helena, MT 59620; 406-449-2778. MSTA provides information on the following: seed and venture capital, SBIR funding, research project financial assistance, technology transfer, technical assistance, business development assistance, and incubator facilities.

Nebraska

Nebraska Technical Assistance Center (NTAC), W191 Nebraska Hall, University of Nebraska-Lincoln, Lincoln, NE 68588-0535; 402-472-5600, toll free in Nebraska 1-800-332-0265. NTAC provides the following services: provides consultants for short-term diagnostic assistance; helps in finding sources of technical and scientific information; assists in providing information about new technologies. Other services are also provided.

Nevada

The Center for Business and Economic Research at the University of Nevada Las Vegas, 4505 Maryland Pkwy, Las Vegas, 89154 NV; 702-739-3191. The center encourages technology transfer through the collection of data, analysis of issues, and dissemination of finds on the business and economic environment of Nevada. It also studies markets, economic and fiscal impacts, financial feasibility and specific management issues.

New Hampshire

The University of New Hampshire, Vice President for Research and Public Service, 108 Thompson Hall, Durham, NH 03824; 603-862-1234, has various programs and offices which assist high technology companies, some of which are the Biomedical Engineering Center, Biotechnology Resource Group, Computer-Aided Design Laboratory, and Partnership for Technology and Management Training.

New Jersey

New Jersey Commission on Science and Technology, 20 West State Street, CN 832, Trenton, NJ 08625; 609-984-0832. The commission oversees the following programs for hi-tech businesses: managerial and technical assistance, venture capital network, business planning, product design, incubator facilities, technology transfer, and entrepreneurial seminars.

New Mexico

Technology Enterprise Division, State of New Mexico Economic Development Department, 1009 Bradbury S.E., Albuquerque, NM 87106; 505-272-7576. TED provides support services to businesses through the State Technical Assistance Resource System (STARS) a reference service which can be accessed via touch-tone phone. The service can lead you to the best starting place to gain the assistance desired. It also provides a national database of specialty experts and industry organizations which can be called upon for specific problem solving assistance. Also included is a One-Stop Shop for information on all state and local licensing requirements, taxation, and regulations which may affect a business.

New York

New York State Science and Technology Foundation, 99 Washington Avenue, Albany, NY 12210; 518-474-4349. The Foundation administers the Regional Technology Development Organization Program, which encourages economic development through the following: technology transfer, product development, venture capital sources, technical and managerial assistance, incubator facilities, application assistance, and sponsored conferences and seminars on technology development.

North Carolina

North Carolina Technological Development Authority, Inc. (NCTDA), 2 Davis Drive, or P.O. Box 13169, Research Triangle Park, Raleigh, NC 27709; 919-990-8558. The NCTDA can provide information on the following: SBIR funding, incubator facilities, technical and managerial assistance, research and development funding, and technology transfer.

North Dakota

Wally Kerns, Center for Innovation and Business Development, University of

North Dakota, P.O. Box 7308, Grand Forks, ND 58202; 701-777-3700. This office administers program to assist technology based companies. They provide management assistance and facilitate technology transfer.

Ohio

Thomas Edison Program (TEP), 77 S. High Street, 26th Floor, Columbus, OH 43266; 614-466-3086. TEP oversees the following programs: matching seed capital funding, incubator facilities, technology transfer, technical training, venture capital, business assistance resources, technical expertise, research and development funding, and seminars.

Oklahoma

Oklahoma Center For The Advancement of Science and Technology (OCAST), 205 N.W. 63rd, Suite 305, Oklahoma City, OK 73116-8209; 405-848-2633. OCAST provides information on their following programs: seed capital, research and development funding, technical expertise, technology transfer, SBIR funding, and venture capital.

Oregon

Oregon Resource and Technology Development Corporation (ORTDC), 1934 NE Broadway, Portland, OR 97232; 503-282-4462. ORTDC acts as a clearinghouse for the following information: technological data, managerial assistance, venture capital networks, technology transfer, applied research grants for joint university-industry research, and seed capital funding working in the area of natural resources.

Pennsylvania

Office of Technology Development, Pennsylvania Department of Commerce, 352 Forum Building, Harrisburg, PA 17120; 717-787-4147. This office oversees the Ben Franklin Partnership, which provides information on the following programs: technology transfer and assistance, technical expertise, SBIR funding, incubator facilities, and financial planning.

Rhode Island

Rhode Island Partnership for Science and Technology, Rhode Island Department Economic Development, 7 Jackson Walkway, Providence, RI 02903; 401-277-2601. This agency has two programs it administers to aid technology based companies. The Applied Research Grant Program provides grants to businesses to do research with other institutions within the state. Only major research projects that have commercial potential and have a minimum combined business and research budget of $200,000 qualify. The State Support Small Business Innovation Research Program provides counseling and financial incentives for companies interested in submitting proposals to the Federal Small Business Innovation Program.

South Carolina

Enterprise Development, Inc. of South Carolina (EDI), P.O. Box 1149, Columbia, SC 29202; 803-737-0888 is a private, non-profit corporation which established the Center for Applied Technology. It serves as an incubator for the development and housing of university spin-off technology based companies. It also provides information to companies through the Technical Information Research Data Base, assists in locating funding, and works with a seed capital fund which assists new entrepreneurial companies.

Tennessee

Tennessee Technology Foundation (TTF), P.O. Box 23184, Knoxville, TN 37933-1184; 615-694-6772. TTF provides information on the following programs: venture capital, SBIR workshops, technology transfer, technical and managerial assistance, technical training, and networking services.

Texas

Technology Business Development (TBD), 310 Wisanbaker Engineering Research Center, College Station, TX 77843-3369; 409-845-0538. TBD provides information on the following: technology transfer and commercialization, patent licensing, venture capital, access to technological databases, prototype testing and evaluation, and business planning and assistance.

Utah

Weber State University, Community and Economic Partnerships (CEP), Ogden, UT 84408-4001; 801-626-6344 provides the business community with a variety of programs that have working relationships with business, industry, government, and other organizations such as the following: Center for Aerospace Technology, Center for Business and Economic Training and Research and the Center for Chemical Technology, Technology Assistance Center and Environmental Research.

Virginia

Center for Innovative Technology (CIT), CIT Tower, 2214 Rock Hill Road, Suite 600, Herndon, VA 22070-4005; 703-689-3000. CIT provides information on their following programs: technology development funding, technology transfer, technical problem assistance, business planning, financing and marketing assistance, incubator facilities, patent licensing, and conferences and seminars for entrepreneurs.

Washington

Washington Technology Center (WTC), University of Washington, Sluke Hall, FJ-15, Seattle, WA 98195; 206-685-1920. WTC provides information on its following programs: acquisition of federal research and development contracts and funding (SBIR), technical and managerial assistance, technology transfer, and technology seminars and workshops.

West Virginia

West Virginia Robert C. Byrd Institute for Advanced Flexible Manufacturing Systems, 1050 Fourth Ave., Huntington, WV 25755; 304-696-3092 provides computer facilities for training, networking and demonstration; it has an advanced telecommunications network to transfer data from computer to machine tools. It also facilitates research and development in the areas of computer engineering, design, and manufacturing, electronics, computer hardware and software, and engineering applications.

Wisconsin

University-Industry Research Program, University of Wisconsin-Madison, 1215 WARF Office Building, Room 215, 610 Walnut Street, Madison, WI 53705; 608-263-2840. This program provides information on the following: technology transfer, technical and scientific information services, seminars for business and industry, patent licensing, managerial and technical assistance, and SBIR funding.

Wyoming

State/Science, Technology and Energy Authority (STEA) Director, STEA University of Wyoming, P.O. Box 3985, UW Station, Laramie, WY 83071; 307-766-6797. STEA helps businesses involved with advanced technology move from research and development to the marketplace. Some financing is provided through state dollars for applied research.

Free Technology Help:
Futuristic Solutions To Today's Business Problems

The federal government is not the only one helping businesses solve their technology-oriented problems:

A $17,000 Savings on Software: A Pittsburgh company, having trouble gathering information on some computer software and hardware they needed to purchase, contacted the Pennsylvania Technical Assistance Program (PENNTAP) for help. As a result, the company ended up saving $17,000, and months of searching, on a computer system they chose based on the suggestions from one of PENNTAP's computer specialists who visited the firm and gathered the necessary information for them.

Laser Company Gets Market Study: Tigart Laser, a small laser machine shop in Indianapolis, asked the Technical Assistance Program at Purdue University for advice on improving its industrial marketing to new customers. TAP completed a study of the company's strengths and potential markets and made recommendations, all of which were implemented. Since then, sales have increased by 18%, three employees were added, and negotiations are under way for the purchase of a new $170,000 six-axis laser cutting machine.

These success stories are just two examples of how companies can benefit from the different state-level technology transfer programs across the country. The state level programs are similar to the federal government's technology transfer program which requires federal labs to conduct research that responds to industry and governmental problems. Many states with major research universities now have technology transfer programs. These programs help private businesses tap into the great economic potential of the technology being developed at their state research laboratories. By having a "window in" and "window out" of the research and technical expertise available at research institutions, these programs can seek out businesses that use the technologies they have developed. They are also able to locate technologies in their labs based on requests from private industry.

Using University Research Projects

The commercial application of university-generated research projects and expertise is a rapidly growing phenomenon. In the past, research projects developed at universities often sat on the shelf after completion. Many states have taken initiatives to get projects that are patentable intellectual properties into the market place where they can do the greatest good. After all, the states have poured a lot of their money into these university research programs, and they see no reason why they shouldn't try to convert some of that investment into tangible economic benefits for their businesses.

Helping Both Business and Research Communities

This transfer of technical innovations and expertise from the lab to private industry usually involves a two-sided process:

1) Helping university researchers identify companies that can use their technologies, and

2) Helping companies that need specific types of technologies identify the appropriate university expertise to develop and/or apply them.

The goal, then, of many of these state-based technology transfer programs is to maintain an active system of communication between the universities and industry. In this way industry knows what the university labs have to offer, and the university labs know what kinds of technology industry is interested in developing. It's through this back and forth dialogue, effective transfer of information can take place.

Definition of Technology Transfer

You will find that the definition of "technology transfer" changes from program to program, and from state to state. It is not as simple as the phrase suggests: the transfer of technology from one place to another, from the laboratory to industry. It can mean everything from research and development to data-base search services, depending on what state program you consult. But for the purposes of this survey, we will confine our definition of technology transfer to the following categories:

Technical Assistance
Modeled after the Department of Agriculture's Cooperative Extension Service, many states have created programs to help your company solve short-term, technology-related problems at no charge or substantial discount. Many of the states that have such programs provide the assistance through a network of offices that serve specific regional areas of the state. The Technical Extension Service in Maryland, for example, has field representatives who provide on-site technical assistance to companies within their six or so designated regional areas. Some states consider such services "technology transfer" because they involve transferring the expertise and knowledge of university-based faculty to private sector businesses. Usually, this type of technology assistance and application involves the use of already existing and proven technologies to solve particular problems. Also note that these services are usually limited to in-state companies. Here are some *examples*:

Honda Clone Discovers Better Plastic: In New Jersey, a small manufacturer had created a plastic clone part for Honda automobile carburetors that he could sell much cheaper than the ones produced by Honda. Unfortunately, the plastic part he designed corroded when exposed to petroleum products. He contacted the Technical Extension Program at the New Jersey Commission on Science and Technology, and they helped him choose a better plastic polymer that wouldn't corrode.

Free Technology Help

Free Chemist Helps Ticket Maker: In Montana, a woman who owned a ticket making business was having trouble with her inking process. She contacted the University Technical Assistance Program at Montana State University. They arranged for a chemist to consult with her and remedy the problem for no charge.

Candy Firm Gets New Plant Layout: A candy manufacturer in Georgia was concerned about the high rejection rate of its products that were coming out broken, so they contacted the Industrial Extension Program at Georgia Tech. After appraising the problem, an expert suggested a new layout for cooling and handling the candy which remedied the problem.

Technical Expertise Referral Services
Many of the states' technology transfer programs, such as Michigan's Technology Transfer Network and the Connecticut Technical Assistance Center, will act as referral services that match up companies that have technology-based problems with experts with the appropriate background to solve those problems. These services can differ slightly from the technical extension programs in that they often end up in a contractual arrangement for the necessary consultation between the two parties. Here are some *examples*:

Windmill Saves Electricity for Restauranteur: A Virginia restauranteur with a seaside location wanted to reduce his $34,000 annual electricity bill by installing a windmill to generate some of his power. He contacted the Center for Innovative Technology for a feasibility assessment for selection and installation of his windmill. The CIT member gathered the necessary information, demonstrated the feasibility and operating methods, and helped the owner secure the correct government permits. The windmill is expected to provide a 35% return on the initial $12,000 investment, and will supply 8% of the electricity for the restaurant.

Automated Printing System: A Michigan textile company that needed help in designing an innovative printing system using lasers contacted the Michigan Technology Transfer Network. TTN's staff found two university experts who, after meeting with the company, wrote a project design proposal which was then developed into a prototype model. The new automated printing system is expected to substantially lower the company's printing costs and raise its manufacturing efficiency.

Solves a Smelly Business Problem: In Wisconsin, a manufacturer of door panels for automobiles had received numerous complaints from the neighboring community about an unpleasant odor that his plant was emitting. Facing a major shutdown of operations, the owner contacted the University-Industry Research Program at the University of Wisconsin. They quickly located an expert who made recommendations to reduce the offensive odor and also helped the company undertake plans to relocate in an area further away from communities with families living in them.

University-Industry Joint Research and Development
Some states have programs which help link up companies having technical problems that cannot be solved with already existing technologies with capable university-based researchers. Together they conduct research and develop an answer to the problem. The resulting products are then transferred from the lab to industry under licensing agreements that are worked out between the companies and the university researchers. Here are some *examples*:

$80,000 Grant For Tool Company: Master Machine Tool Inc., a small company in Hutchinson, Kansas, received a $80,000 grant from the Kansas Technology Enterprise Corporation to undertake a joint research and development project with a university faculty member. Together they developed a high speed cutting device to be used in welding and painting. The company projects a $20 to $40 million increase in revenues over the next 2-3 years.

Food Company Lowers Cholesterol: A food manufacturer in Minnesota developed a food product that they believed has a cholesterol lowering quality to it. The Office of Research and Technology Transfer at the University of Minnesota helped the company locate a faculty member at the medical school who was interested in further researching the properties and commercial potential of this innovative product.

Airplane Manufacturer Makes Rivetting Rosy: A large airplane manufacturer in Washington State was having problems with their automated riveters. They were putting good rivets into poorly drilled holes, which was causing unwanted metal fatigue in the assembled parts. The company contacted the Washington Technology Center whose researchers designed and developed an automatic hole gate censor for the automatic riveters which wouldn't allow a riveter to put a rivet in a hole that wasn't perfectly drilled. WTC then negotiated a licensing agreement with the airplane manufacturer for its use.

Centers of Excellence
Some states, such as Utah, Colorado, and Ohio, have developed research centers that receive funding from state and private industry to undertake designated research and development projects that address the state's industrial needs and plans. The technologies developed at these centers are available to private companies that are either subscribers to the centers or that provide research and development matching funds. Each center has its own licensing and purchasing agreements with its industry sponsors. Here is an *example*:

Biotechnology in Colorado: The Colorado Institute For Research in Biotechnology, a partnership of three Colorado universities and 20 private biotechnology company sponsors, conducts research and development in response to the mutual needs of both partners, and transfers the resulting innovations to the private companies for commercial use.

Currently, about 35 states have offices, many of which are located at the state universities, that assist companies in identifying the appropriate kinds of technology they may need. If your state is not listed, it doesn't necessarily mean you cannot gain access to innovative technologies developed in the state universities. Many research universities have informal networks to get their innovative, patentable ideas into the private sector. Try contacting their research offices to see if they can help you. Also, most of the states that do have technology transfer programs, such as Minnesota, Wisconsin, and Ohio, are willing to allow companies from other states to license their new technologies as long as companies from their own state have had the opportunity to do so first.

Also, many universities have developed databases of their faculty members' professional profiles which can be searched, often times at no cost to you. You will find a listing of the offices that will conduct these searches for you in our new edition of the *State Data and Database Finder*. Of course, if you still can't get the technology you are looking for, you can always get involved in the federal technology transfer program through their regional offices. For the location of the NASA Applications Center nearest you, contact the Federal Laboratory Consortium (FLC), U.S. Department of Agriculture, 3865 South Building, Washington, DC 20250; 202-447-7185.

Alabama

Alabama Development Office, 135 S. Union St., Montgomery, AL 36130; 205-263-0048. The Alabama Development Office provides technical and management training as well as financing through industrial revenue bonds (IRBs). The Alabama Development Office's Research Division prepares cost and feasibility studies for clients as well as cost analyses of labor, transportation, utilities, and state and local taxes. The division prepares studies, reports, and promotional brochures containing information on natural resources, quality of life, demographics, economics, and technology. It also maintains a comprehensive industrial research library.

Alaska

Alaska Science and Technology Foundation, (ASTF), 550 West 7th Avenue, Suite 360, Anchorage, AK 99501-3555; 907-272-4333. This Foundation assists in taking a good technical idea to application or commercialization. Grants are awarded on a competitive basis and grantees are expected to contribute time, effort and resources.

Arkansas

Arkansas Science and Technology Authority (ASTA), 100 Main Street, Suite 450, Little Rock, AR 72201; 501-324-9006. By maintaining contacts with Arkansas' research universities, federal labs, and its business community, ASTA is able to coordinate the transfer of technologies available for technical problem solving as well as commercialization to the businesses that need them. After discussing its technology needs with ASTA, a business will be directed toward the appropriate university experts to solve the problem.

Arkansas Industrial Development Commission (AIDC), One State Capitol Mall, Little Rock, AR 72201; 501-682-5275. The AIDC was established in 1955 and is guided by an advisory board of 16 commissioners appointed by the governor. The agency publishes the *Manufacturers Exchange Bulletin*, which contains a "bulletin board" of information for small manufacturers.

Colorado

Business Research and Information Network (BRAIN), University of Colorado Business Advancement Center, 3333 Iris Ave., #101, Boulder, CO 80301; 303-444-5723 or (in state only) 1-800-369-1243. For CO companies needing technical problem solving assistance and access to state-of-the-art technologies, BRAIN will conduct searches of the NASA Industrial Application Center's (NIAC) databases. For technical information not available through computer searches, the BRAIN office will contact experts at NASA Field Centers, Federal Labs, and universities, and relay the answers to the problem back to the client.

Colorado Advanced Technology Institute (CATI), 1625 Broadway, Suite 700, Denver, CO 80202; 303-620-4777. CATI oversees the funding of five state research centers at which joint university-industry research and development projects are undertaken. Each of the centers, along with their corporate partners, determine the areas they wish to target for their research and development projects. Colorado businesses wishing access to the technologies developed at these centers must pay subscription or membership fees, along with any licensing or purchasing charges.

Connecticut

Connecticut Technology Assistance Center (CONNTAC), Department of Economic Development, 210 Washington Street, Hartford, CT 06106; 203-566-4587. CONNTAC acts as a referral agency to coordinate the linking up of industry and university technology. After a company contacts the office and discusses their technology needs, CONNTAC will then make the necessary connections with university experts that solve the problem. This program can also work the other way, by finding appropriate industries that can use technologies with commercial potential developed by university researchers.

Florida

Southern Technologies Applications Center (STAC), One Progress Boulevard, Box 24, Allachua, FL 32615; 1-800-225-0308. For a fee, STAC will conduct a database search of their Florida college and university faculty members to locate the appropriate expert to solve a particular technology-based problem.

Bureau of Industry Development, Florida Department of Commerce, G-34 Collins Building, Tallahassee, FL 32399-2000; 904-488-9360. The Business Supplier Program in the Bureau of Industry Development helps Florida companies locate other Florida-based companies that can be used as suppliers of goods and services.

Florida High Technology and Industrial Council, Room 501A, Collins Building, 107 West Gaines Street, Tallahassee, FL 32399-2000; 904-487-3136. The Florida High Technology and Industrial Council coordinates the needs of high technology businesses and industries with the resources of universities and vocational schools.

Georgia

Economic Development Laboratory (EDL), GTRI, Georgia Institute of Technology, Atlanta, GA 30332; 404-894-3830. Attn: Dr. David Swanson. EDL provides free on-site, short-term assistance to manufacturing companies with technology-based problems. They will also conduct free database searches and document retrievals for the most up-to-date information that can help companies solve their problems. Businesses can also contact the EDL office if they are looking for new, already existing technologies they would like implemented into their companies.

Advanced Technology Development Center (ATDC), 430 10th Street, NW, Suite N-116, Atlanta, GA 30318; 404-894-3575. The ATDC encourages high technology growth in the state by supporting technology-based entrepreneurs and small businesses, and by helping existing businesses with new product development.

Georgia Tech Research Institute, Centennial Research Building, 10th and Danley, Atlanta, GA 30332; 404-894-3400. The Engineering Extension Program provides technical services through its field offices throughout the state.

Idaho

Science and Technology Committee/SBIR Support Services State Advisory Council: c/o Karl Tueller, Chairman; Idaho Department of Commerce, 700 West State Street, Boise, ID 83720-2700; 208-334-2470. By maintaining contacts with both the university and business community, the Science and Technology committee helps to promote the transfer of technologies for commercialization to businesses that need them.

Illinois

Technology Commercialization Centers (I-TEC), Department of Commerce and Community Affairs, 100 Randolph Street, Suite 3-400, Chicago, IL 60601; 312-814-7179. Attn: John Straus. I-TEC promotes the commercialization of new ideas and products that will contribute to the state's economic growth. I-TEC does this by linking Illinois' businesses with the appropriate research expertise. Areas covered include feasibility studies, prototype development and testing, technical problem solving, identification of manufacturers to produce new products, and commercialization of new technologies.

Governor's Commission on Science and Technology, 100 West Randolph, Suite 3-400, Chicago, IL 60601; 312-917-2269. The Governor's Commission on Science and Technology was founded in 1983. The commission promotes public/private collaborative and cooperative research ventures and projects.

Free Technology Help

Indiana

Technical Assistance Program (TAP), Purdue University, 1284 Civil Building, Room G175, West Lafayette, IN 47907-1284; 317-494-6258. TAP offers free, limited technical assistance to Indiana companies in the following areas: product development, manufacturing processes, and management. TAP experts will use existing technologies already available to their staff to solve business problems involving product design, quality control, and operational cost strategies. Assistance is also provided for small and medium size industries.

Iowa

Center for Industrial Research and Service (CIRAS), ISU Research Park, Suite 500, 2501 North Loop Drive, Ames, IA 50010-8286; 515-294-3420. CIRAS provides businesses with technology transfer through linkage with faculty researchers, data base searches, and federal laboratories.

Iowa Department of Economic Development, Technology Transfer System, 200 East Grand Avenue, Des Moines, IA 50309; 515-281-3036. The Technology Transfer System responds to technical inquiries to discover, define, evaluate, and provide data, theory, method, practice, sources, resources and expertise that will allow technical solutions to a problem. The system relies on the transfer of information on research, technology, and other scientific endeavors among industry, laboratories, government, and the public.

Kansas

Kansas Technology Enterprise Corporation (KTEC), 112 West 6th Street, Suite 400, Topeka, KS 66603; 913-296-4490. KTEC offers manufacturing assistance for automation problems and provides subsidized technology audits and feasibility studies. If a business wishes to purchase existing technologies developed at the universities, they must pay for it themselves through a agreement with the licenser. If a company has a specific technology need which cannot be addressed by existing technologies, KTEC offers research matching grants to develop that technology.

Division of Existing Industry Development, Kansas Department of Commerce, 400 SW 8th Street, 5th Floor, Topeka, KS 66603-3957; 913-296-5298. The Division of Existing Industry Development promotes the growth, diversification, and retention of business and industry in Kansas, The division provides assistance both directly and through a statewide business assistance network, channeling appropriate resources for business technical help and other related problems.

Space Center Technology, University of Kansas, 2291 Irving Hill Dr., West Campus, Lawrence, KS 66045; 913-864-4775. The Business and Engineering Technical Applications Program was founded to assist business and industry by providing information on technical and administrative problems.

Kansas Technology Enterprise Corporation, 112 SW 6th Street, Suite 400, Topeka, KS 66603-3957; 913-296-5272. The Kansas Technology Enterprise Corporation (KTEC) is a non-profit public organization established in 1987 to foster innovation in existing and developing Kansas enterprises. KTEC programs have many functions, one of which is providing technical information and referral services to new, emerging, or mature business.

Kentucky

Kentucky Office of Business and Technology (OBT), Cabinet for Economic Development, Capital Plaza Tower, Frankfort, KY 40601; 502-564-7670. Attn: Debbi Kimbrough. OBT links businesses with sources of technology information, expertise, and opportunities by identifying newly developed technologies, technical problem solving experts, and research and development contracts. After discussing their technical needs with OBT's staff, a business will be directed toward the appropriate sources of innovative technologies to solve the problem.

Louisiana

Office of Technology Transfer, Louisiana State University Business and Technology Center, Room 146 A, South Stadium Drive, Baton Rouge, LA 70803; 504-388-6830; FAX 504-388-4925. OT helps take new ideas, inventions or discoveries and solicits commercial interest as well as negotiates contracts with prospective clients. The office also assists in determining the patentability of new products.

Maine

Maine Science and Technology Commission, State House Station #147, Augusta, ME 04333; 207-289-3703. The Commission helps industry introduce technical innovation by providing researchers in the fields of biomedical technology, metals electronics and aquaculture.

Maryland

Engineering Research Center (ERC), University of Maryland, Stadium Drive Bldg., Room 2120, College Park, MD 20742-3415; 301-405-3906. ERC oversees two programs which involve the transfer of technology from the university to industry: The Technology Extension Service (TES) provides Maryland-based businesses with free, short-term technical problem solving services, including problem identification, direct technical assistance, plant modernization planning, new product evaluation, and more. The other program, the Maryland Industrial Partnerships (MIPS), provides matching funds for joint industry-university research and development projects having commercialization potential that can produce economic benefits for the state. The company has to be involved in a Hi-Technology business or industry.

Massachusetts

Center for Applied Technology (CAT), 101 Summer Street, 2nd Floor, Boston, MA 02110; 617-292-5100. CAT is unique in its approach to the transfer of manufactory technology into new forms of work organization into industries. After a business contacts CAT with a technical problem, the Center brings together all the parties involved -- management, workers, and university-based technical experts -- to analyze and decide on the appropriate solution. CAT acts as a matching service by linking up the companies with the appropriate technical consultants. Small and medium sized industries and companies can save from 30% to 50% on consultation fees by using CAT's services.

Michigan

Michigan Department of Commerce, Technology Transfer Network (TTN), Tech Services, P.O. Box 30004, Lansing, MI 48909; 517-335-2139. Attn: Sharon Wollard. TTN helps link up businesses in need of problem solving expertise with the technical sources at Michigan research universities. A TTN staff member will evaluate the problem and then identify the appropriate technical expertise to solve it. This conferral part of the program is free. Although many problems can be solved at little or no cost, some may require consulting or research by an expert faculty member on a contractual basis paid for by the company. TTN assists companies in obtaining product evaluations, feasibility studies, cooperative university-industry research and development, technologies available for commercialization, technical information, and access to research universities facilities and equipment.

Michigan Modernization Service, Room 212, Hollister Bldg., 106 W. Allegan, Lansing, MI 48913; 517-373-7411. The Michigan Modernization Service (MMS) will help small to medium sized manufacturers (between 20 to 500 employees) that are considering adoption of new computer-based manufacturing tools and methods. The technology and training assessment recommendations provided by MMS are free to clients.

Metropolitan Center for High Technology, 2727 Second Ave., Detroit, MI 48201; 313-963-0616. The Metropolitan Center for High Technology operates a small business incubator for companies that produce technological products and services. The center also conducts applied research in such areas as use of robots in rehabilitation, hazardous materials, educational technology, and economic networks.

Industrial Development Division (IST), University of Michigan, 2200 Bonisteel Blvd., Ann Arbor, MI 48109; 313-764-5260. The Innovation Center uses resources at the University of Michigan to help Michigan firms develop new products using new technologies.

Michigan Technology Transfer Centers:
University of Michigan, 313-763-9000
Wayne State University, 313-577-2788
Michigan Technological University, 906-487-2470
Michigan State University, 517-355-1660
Western Michigan University, 616-387-2714

Minnesota

Office of Research and Technology Transfer Administration, University of Minnesota, 1100 Washington Ave. S, Minneapolis, MN 55415-1226; 612-624-1648. Attn: Tony Potami. This office seeks out companies that can use the patented innovations developed at the university. It also responds to requests from private businesses by locating appropriate technologies developed at their labs. The office will also help link up businesses with faculty expertise for technical problem solving arrangements and joint research and development projects.

Mississippi

Institute for Technology Development (ITD), 700 North State Street, Suite 500, Jackson, MS 39202; 601-960-3600. In the transfer of technology, ITD assists in two ways: it locates projects for interested companies at university research and development facilities with commercial potential and helps implement them. ITD also identifies key problem areas in industry needing innovative technology and initiates research and development projects to respond to those needs. Part of this communication between the lab and industry is accomplished through TechNet, a program which seeks out in-state manufacturers that can profit from existing technology, and then helps them apply it in a practical manner.

Mississippi Technology Transfer Office (MITTO), John C. Stennis Space Center, Bldg. 1103, Stennis Space Center, MS 39529; 601-688-3144. The office provides access to technology developed by various federal laboratories and the Stennis Space Center, and helps with identifying commercial applications for that technology. It also provides help to solve specific technical problems.

Missouri

Center for Technology Transfer and Economic Development (CTT), Nagogami Terrace, Building 1, University of Missouri -- Rolla Rolla, MO 65401; 314-341-4555. Attn: Harold Dean Keith. CTT provides companies that have technology-based problems with the following assistance: access to appropriate university and federal lab-based expertise and innovations, patentability analysis of new products, and technical document searches.

Missouri Technology Development Center, Grinstead Building, Room 80, Central Missouri State University, Warrensburg, MO 64093; 816-543-4402. The Center assists companies in solving their technology-based problems by providing the following: access to technical consultants, prototype analysis and improvement, new product development, plant layout assistance, access to published technical information, energy audits, and the transfer of university-researched technologies into the marketplace.

Montana

Montana Science and Technology Alliance (MSTA), Department of Commerce, 46 N. Last Change Gulch, Helena, MT 59620; 406-449-2778. MSTA oversees the Technology Review and Transfer Program which give university researchers who have developed technologies that they feel have commercial potential the opportunity to present those projects to a review board. The board then assesses commercial potential, need for further research, and appropriateness for venture financing.

University Technical Assistance Program (UTAP), 402 Roberts Hall, Montana State University, Bozeman, MT 59717; 406-994-3812. UTAP offers free, short-term technical assistance to Montana manufacturers. Examples are plant facility layout, reducing manufacturing costs, and computer aided design of product specifications.

Census and Economic Information Center, Department of Commerce, 1424 Ninth Avenue, Helena, MT 59620; 406-444-2896. The Census and Economic Information Center (CEIC) is the lead agency of the Montana State Data Center. The CEIC serves as a central location for businesses, government agencies, and the general public to obtain population and economic information for research, planning, and decision-making purposes.

Nebraska

Nebraska Technical Assistance Center (NTAC), W191 Nebraska Hall, University of Nebraska-Lincoln, Lincoln, NE 68588-0535; 402-472-5600, toll free in Nebraska 1-800-332-0265. NTAC provides engineering assistance to Nebraska manufacturing companies, and promotes technology transfer within the state from the university and various other sources to the manufacturing segment.

Nevada

The Center for Business and Economic Research at the University of Nevada Las Vegas, 4505 Maryland Pkwy, Las Vegas, NV 89154; 702-739-3191 encourages technology transfer through collection of data, analysis of issues, and dissemination of finds on the business and economic environment of Nevada. It also studies markets, economic and fiscal impacts, financial feasibility or specific management issues. The Office of Technology Liaison, University of Nevada-Reno, Mail Stop 326, Reno, NV 89557; 702-784-6869 serves as a focal point for strengthening the university/industry partnership by providing research funding and patent search.

New Hampshire

The University of New Hampshire, Vice President for Research and Technical Assistance, 105 Main Street, 108 Thompson Hall, Durham, NH 03824-3547; 603-862-1234 provides interfaces with business and industry to transfer technology through its various departments and programs.

New Jersey

New Jersey Commission on Science and Technology, 20 West State Street, CN 832, NJ 08625-0832; 609-984-1671. Companies that have developed technologies at the Advanced Technology Centers with state funding support must actively seek out small NJ businesses that can use the new technologies. Each Technology Center publishes "Capability Sheets," which describe what new technologies are available to small businesses. The Commission also oversees the Technology Extension Centers which provide free to low-cost short-term technical problem solving assistance to New Jersey companies.

New Mexico

Technology Enterprise Division (TED), State of New Mexico Economic Development Department, 1009 Bradbury S.E., Albuquerque, NM 87106; 505-272-7576. TED provides support to businesses in a variety of ways including technology transfer through its network with several national laboratories, U.S. installations with the state, colleges, and universities in the state and Centers of Technical Excellence. It also provides the State Technical Assistance Resource System (STARS), a reference service which can be accessed via touch-tone phone. The service answers inquiries such as which agency in the State is the best starting place to gain the assistance desired. It also includes a national database of specialty experts and industry organizations which can be called upon for specific problem solving assistance.

New York

New York State Science and Technology Foundation, Suite 1730, 99 Washington Avenue, Albany, NY 12210; 518-474-4348. The Foundation oversees the Industrial Technology Extension Service (ITES), which assists companies through its ten regional offices in implementing new technologies into their operations. ITES field representatives will assist a company in linking up with the appropriate expertise -- from universities, federal or State labs, and private consulting firms -- to best solve the company's technology needs. There is no charge for this matching up process. Companies can also contact these regional offices to inquire about available new technologies developed at the state universities and laboratories. Regional staff members act as liaisons between the labs and industry to help match specific needs with the appropriate technical solutions.

North Carolina

Industrial Extension Service (IES), College of Engineering, North Carolina State University, Box 7902, Raleigh, NC 27695-7902; 919-515-2358. IES uses the resources of NCSU to provide short-term assistance in the following areas free of charge or on a cost recovery basis: problem identification, quality assurance, metalworking production and inventory control, work simplification, energy audits, plant layout, computer aided design, and much more. Using the expertise of the university, IES also acts as a referral service for companies needing long-term consulting assistance.

North Carolina Technological Development Authority, Room 4216, 430 N. Salisbury St., Raleigh, NC 27611; 919-733-7022. The North Carolina Technological Development Authority was established by the New Technology Jobs Act of 1983. The authority makes grants to establish incubator facilities for small firms, and to oversee the North Carolina Innovative Research Fund, which provides equity financing for the research activities of new and existing small businesses.

Science and Technology Research Center, P.O. Box 12235, Research Triangle Park, NC 27709; 919-549-0671. The North Carolina Science and Technology Research Center began in 1964 to aid the National Aeronautics and Space Administration (NASA). Currently, it acts as a national information dissemination network allowing access to more than 100 million documents in hundreds of research fields.

North Carolina Biotechnology Center, P.O. Box 13547, Research Triangle Park, NC 27709; 919-541-9366. The North Carolina Biotechnology Center was established in 1981 to support biotechnology research and development statewide through research, programmatic activities, new facilities, meetings, and commercial ventures. It encourages technology transfer between universities, industry and small businesses.

Research Triangle Institute, P.O. Box 12194, Research Triangle Park, NC 27709; 919-541-6000. The Research Triangle Institute is a nonprofit consulting research and development firm of approximately 900 employees. The institute conducts contract research involving physical, life, and social sciences.

Center for Applied Technology, 134 Ragsdale Bldg., East Carolina University, Greenville, NC 27858; 919-757-6708. The Center for Applied Technology provides technical and scientific assistance through contract research for industries, businesses, and municipalities. Assistance includes feasibility studies, literature studies, and training programs.

North Dakota

Center for Innovation and Business Development, Box 8372, Grand Forks, ND 58202; 701-777-3132. Through the University of North Dakota School of Engineering and Mines and the Department of Industrial Technology, the Center can help companies identify and analyze technology-based problems and then provide solutions in the following areas: computer aided design, quality control, safety and energy evaluations, prototype development, and more.

Wally Kerns, Center for Innovation and Business Development, University of North Dakota, P.O. Box 7308, Grand Forks, ND 58202; 701-777-3700. This office administers programs to assist technology based companies. They provide management assistance and facilitate technology transfer.

Technology Transfer Center, North Dakota State University, Civil Engineering Bldg., Room 214, Fargo, ND 58105; 701-237-7051. The Technology Transfer Center was established at North Dakota State University, Fargo to enable North Dakota firms to use the most advanced technologies available. It provides to North Dakota businesses Control Data Corporation's access to worldwide computer software.

Ohio

Ohio Technology Transfer Organization (OTTO), Division of Technology Innovation, 77 S. High Street, 25th Floor, Columbus, OH 43266-0101; 614-466-3086, 1-800-848-1300. OTTO provides businesses with access to university-based research and technology, and helps in their application through hands-on assistance. Many of these services are without charge.

Thomas Edison Program, Division of Technological Innovation, Department of Development, State of Ohio, 77 S. High Street, 25th Floor, Columbus, OH 43266-0101; 614-466-3086, 1-800-848-1300. Businesses can gain access to technologies developed at the Edison Technology Centers by becoming a center partner through membership fees or jointly funding the research and development at the centers.

Oklahoma

Oklahoma Center for the Advancement of Science and Technology (OCAST), 301 NW 63rd St., Suite 110, Oklahoma City, OK 73116; 405-848-2633. OCAST oversees three programs that involve technology transfer. When state funding is approved, the Centers of Excellence will conduct joint university-industry research and development that must culminate in the transfer of the resulting innovations to private businesses. The Applied Research program also encourages university-industry collaboration that will result in commercially viable products. The Oklahoma Technical and Research Network is a database that will link up companies with the appropriate technical experts to conduct joint research and development and on-site consultation.

Central Industrial Applications Center, P.O. Box 1335, Durant, OK 74702; 405-924-6822 or 1-800-633-0720 (in OK). The Central Industrial Applications Center

(CIAC) provides technology data searches to Oklahoma businesses, utilizing over 400 data bases, and makes available a library of world technology information with assistance from NASA. Answers to technical questions are available from CIAC through use of computer banks holding over 50 million references.

Rural Enterprises, Inc., Durant, OK 74702; 405-924-5094, out of state toll free 800-658-2823. Rural Enterprises, Inc. (REI) is a nonprofit industrial development corporation and national demonstration model headquartered in Durant. It provides financial services, technology transfer, new product evaluation, and other resources to rural businesses.

Oregon

Advance Science and Technology Institute (ASTI), University of Oregon, 318 Hendricks Hall, University of Oregon, Eugene, Oregon 97403; 503-346-3189. Attn: Robert McQuate. ASTI matches technologies developed at the University of Oregon, Oregon State University, Portland State University, and Oregon Health Science University with appropriate companies in the private sector. This process also works from the opposite point of view by matching up companies which approach ASTI with particular technology needs with the appropriate university expertise. ASTI also matches up private companies wishing to do research and development on a particular project with university research faculty members.

Technology Transfer Services (TTS), 311 Hendricks Hall, University of Oregon, Eugene, OR 97403-1238; 503-346-3176. Attn: Martin Wybourne. TTS coordinates the funding and contractual aspects of the technology transfer program-- patent rights, licensing agreements, research and development contracts, and so on.

Pennsylvania

Pennsylvania Technical Assistance Program (PENNTAP), 110 Barbara Bldg 2, 810 N. University Dr., University Park, PA 16802; 814-865-0427. PENNTAP provides free, short-term technical problem solving assistance by linking up businesses with the appropriate expertise. PENNTAP staff members assemble the most up-to-date information concerning the problem and presents the most practical solutions to the company in easy to understand terminology.

Ben Franklin Partnership, Department of Commerce, 463 Forum Bldg., Harrisburg, PA 17120; 717-787-4147. The Ben Franklin Partnership (BFP) programs promote entrepreneurial assistance services, which include: linking research, financial, and human resources; assisting in the preparation of business plans and feasibility studies; and providing small business incubator and technology transfer services.

Rhode Island

Economic Innovation Center of Rhode Island, 28 Jacome Way, Middletown, RI 02840; 401-849-9889. This center provides a variety of programs for technology based companies. The key program, Enterprise Development Teams, assists in identifying, preparing, and developing markets for newly developed products. Technology transfer assistance is also provided.

South Carolina

The Southeast Manufacturing Technology Center (SMTC) Swearingen Engineering Center, USC, Columbia, SC 29208; 803-777-9595, works statewide to assist manufacturing companies in transferring known technology to their operations. The Emerging Technology Center, 511 Westinghouse Rd., Pendleton, SC 29670 assists inventors in the maturation and commercialization of newly developed products.

South Dakota

South Dakota Governor's Office of Economic Development, 711 E. Wells Ave., Pierre, SD 57501-3369; 605-773-5032 works with the Centers for Innovation, Technology and Enterprise (CITEs), located on each state-supported university campus to provide university-industry linkage.

Tennessee

Center for Industrial Services, Suite 606, 226 Capitol Boulevard Building, Nashville, TN 37219-1806; 615-242-2456. Attn: T.C. Parsons. By drawing on university resources, CIS provides TN manufacturers and industries with free, short- term technical problem solving services in the following areas: product design and refinement, environmental impact assessments, waste reduction, quality control, computer systems, and more. CIS also helps small companies identify and implement new technologies that would be useful to their operations.

Tennessee Technology Foundation, P.O. Box 23184, Knoxville, TN 37933; 615-694-6772. The Tennessee Technology Foundation, a not-for-profit, private-sector organization, was chartered in 1982 to assist entrepreneurs in finding answers to their technology questions.

Texas

Center For Technology Development and Transfer (CTDT), College of Engineering, Cockrell Hall, University of Texas -- Austin, Austin, TX 78712-1080; 512-471-4325. CTDT's main objective is the commercialization of university-based research and technologies through cooperation between the university and industry. The Center will find appropriate companies to license university-based research and find university-developed technology for companies looking for innovative solutions to their problems.

Technology Business Development (TBD), 310 Wisenbaker Engineering Research Center, College Station, TX 77843-3369; 409-845-0538. TBD coordinates a state-wide network of technical assistance centers which provide services on a cost recovery basis in the following areas: prototype testing, product design, automation evaluations, technology assessment, and much more. TBD also matches up researchers at Texas universities with the appropriate companies which can use their ideas. TBD will also assist companies in identifying university-developed technologies that are available for commercialization.

Utah

Centers of Excellence Program, 324 S. State, Suite 500, Salt Lake City, UT 84111-7380; 801-538-8770. The Centers receive state funding, which is matched by industry at least on a two to one basis, to develop technologies in targeted areas important to the state's industrial needs. To obtain access to technologies developed at the Centers, UT businesses must become program members, which involves offering matching research and development funds to the projects. Fees for transferred technologies depend on technology patents.

Utah has several offices which assist with technology transfer; Technology Transfer Office, University of Utah, 421 Wakara Way, Suite 170, Salt Lake City, Utah 84108; 801-581-7792 which manages and protects licensing of technology developed at the University of Utah; Technology Transfer Office, Utah State University, Research Technology Park, 1780 North Research Park Way, Suite 108, North Logan, Utah 84321; 801-750-6924 which evaluates protectability of inventions, assists in marketing and facilitates the formation of new business entities based on the invention; Technology Transfer Office, Brigham Young University, A-268 Abraham Smoot Bldg., Provo, UT 84602; 801-378-4866; Technology Transfer Administration, Weber State University, 3750 Harrison Blvd., Ogden, UT 84408-1001; 801-626-7313 provides administrative support for economic development activities involving the University.

Vermont

Governor's Advisory Council on Technology, Office of Technology Transfer, 428 Waterman Bldg., University of Vermont, Burlington, VT 05405; 805-656-1318. The Governor's Advisory Council on Technology reviews the technology and economic development in the state and aids businesses in solving their technology related problems.

Virginia

Center for Innovative Technology (CIT), 2214 Rock Hill Rd., Suite 600, Herndon, VA 22070; 703-689-3000. CIT, in conjunction with the Virginia Community College system, provides free, short-term technical assistance to VA businesses. A company contacts a regional technology assistance transfer office to discuss their problem. The office, in turn, finds potential solutions from existing technologies and then presents them to the company. CIT also coordinates active industry involvement in research and development conducted at universities that demonstrates practical, commercial potential.

Washington

Washington Technology Center, Fluke Hall, FJ-15, Seattle, WA 98195; 206-645-1920. Located at the state's major research universities, WTC's labs conduct research and development projects for companies with specific technology oriented needs, and works out licensing agreements for the use of the new innovations. Companies wanting use of technologies already developed from WTC labs can do so through licensing agreements.

Wisconsin

University-Industry Research Program (UIR), University of Wisconsin-Madison, 1215 WARF Building, 610 Walnut Street, Madison, WI 53705; 608-263-2840. Businesses with technical problems can contact UIR, which will search their faculty databases for the appropriate expert to solve the problem. The company and expert then work out any consulting contractual arrangements on their own. UIR's search services are done at no charge.

Office of Industrial Research and Technology Transfer, University of Wisconsin -- Milwaukee, P.O. Box 340, Milwaukee, WI 53201; 414-229-5000. This office offers a two-part program. Companies wishing to develop a certain new technology can contact the above office which will in turn arrange a collaborative research and development project between an appropriate faculty expert and that company, or the other way around. If a faculty member has a patentable product to be commercialized, the office will make the appropriate contacts with industry to set up a licensing agreement or sale. The services are not exclusive to WI companies, although they have the first opportunity to the available new technologies.

Company Intelligence:
How To Find Information On Any Company

When many researchers are doing investigations on companies they often rely only on two major information sources:

Public Companies =   U.S. Securities and Exchange
                               Commission Filings
Privately Held Companies =   Dun & Bradstreet Reports

Although many people still depend heavily on the Securities and Exchange Commission (SEC) and Dun & Bradstreet (D & B), these two resources have severe limitations. The Securities and Exchange Commission has information on approximately only 10,000 public companies in the United States. However, according to the IRS and the U.S. Bureau of the Census (both agencies count differently), there are between 5,000,000 and 12,000,000 companies in the country. So you can see that the SEC represents only a small fraction of the universe. Also, if you are interested in a division or a subsidiary of a public corporation and that division does not represent a substantial portion of the company's business, there will be no information on their activities on file at the SEC. This means that for thousands of corporate divisions and subsidiaries, it is necessary to look beyond the SEC.

D & B Won't Jail You For Not Telling The Truth
But The Government Will

The problems with Dun & Bradstreet (D & B) reports are more significant than the shortcomings of company filings at the SEC. The main drawback is that D & B reports have been established primarily for credit purposes and are supposed to indicate the company's ability to pay its bills. Therefore, you will find information from current creditors about whether a business is late in its payments, which may or may not be a useful barometer to evaluate the company.

If there is additional financial information in these reports, you should also be aware of who in the company provides D & B with information and their motives. The information contained in these reports does not carry the legal weight of the company information registered with the Securities and Exchange Commission. If a company lies about any information it turns over to the SEC, a corporate officer could wind up in jail. Dun & Bradstreet, however, collects information by telephoning a company and asking it to voluntarily provide information. The company is under no obligation to comply and, equally important, is under no obligation to D & B to be honest. Unlike the government, Dun & Bradstreet cannot prosecute.

If a competitor or someone was interested in acquiring Information USA, Inc., for example, probably the first step would be to obtain any financial data about this privately held company. In this hypothetical case, Information USA, Inc. might be interested in such a sale or perhaps want to impress the competition. Consequently, the information supplied to Dun & Bradstreet most likely would be the sanitized version which

I would want outsiders to see. My only dilemma would be in remembering what half truths we told D & B last year so that our track record would appear consistent. However, Information USA, Inc. would not and does not play such games with its financial information filed with the Maryland Secretary of State.

This is why resourceful researchers are starting to appreciate the value of the thousands of non-traditional information sources such as public documents and industry experts.

Starting At The Securities And Exchange Commission

The first question to resolve is whether the company you are gathering intelligence about is a public corporation. If it is, you should get your hands on copies of the company's SEC filings. The fastest way to make this determination is to call:

Disclosure Inc.
5161 River Road Building 60   301-951-1300
Bethesda, MD 20816   1-800-638-8241/231-3282

The price depends on which document you wish to have retrieved. The range is between $13 to $30 per document. If the company in question files with the Securities and Exchange Commission, the least you should do is to obtain a copy of the Annual Report, known as 10-K. This disclosure form will give you the most current description of the company's activities along with their annual financial statement.

Financial Statements In Addition To The Annual Report

In addition to the 10-K you may also want to see the company's most current financial statements by obtaining copies of all 10-Q's filed since their last 10-K. 10-Q's are basically quarterly financial statements which will bring you up-to-date since the last annual report.

The two other documents which may be of immediate interest are the 8-K's and the Annual Report to Stockholders. An 8-K will disclose any major developments that have occurred since the last annual report, such as information about a takeover or major lawsuit. The Annual Report to Stockholders, the glossy quasi-public relations tool that is sent to all those who own stock in the company, can provide another component in assembling a company's profile. The most interesting item in this report, which is not included in the 10-K Annual Report, is the message from the President. This message often provides insights about the company's future plans.

Obtaining Copies of SEC Documents

The fastest way to get SEC documents is through one of the many document retrieval companies which provide this service.

In addition to the firm mentioned above, other companies that specialize in quickly obtaining corporate SEC filings include:

1) FACS Info Service, Inc.
157 Fisher Avenue — 1-800-303-6901
Eastchester, NY 10709 — FAX: 914-779-7038

2) Federal Document Retrieval, Inc.
SEC Building, 450 5th St. NW
Washington, DC 20001 — 202-347-2824

3) Meredith Hurt & Associates
11526 Maple Ridge Road
Reston, VA 22090 — 202-628-9628

4) Research Information Services
717 D Street, NW — 202-737-7111
Washington, DC 20004 — FAX: 202-737-3324

5) Prentice Hall Legal and Financial Services
1090 Vermont Ave., NW, Suite 430 — 202-408-3120
Washington, DC 20005 — FAX: 202-408-3142

6) Washington Service Bureau
655 15th Street NW, Room 275 — 202-508-0600
Washington, DC 20005 — FAX: 202-508-0694

7) Washington Document Service
450 5th Street NW, Suite 1C45 — 202-628-5200
Washington, DC 20001 — FAX: 202-626-7628

8) Vickers Stock Research Corp.
600 S Street NW, Suite 504
Washington, DC 20004 — 202-626-4951

You can also go to one of the four major SEC Document Rooms to see any public filing. These reference rooms are located in Washington, DC, New York City, Chicago, and Los Angeles.

If the company headquarters or main office is located in the area served either by the Atlanta, Boston, Denver, Fort Worth, or Seattle regional offices, the 10-K and other documents can be examined at the appropriate SEC office. For the exact location of any of the regional offices mentioned contact:

Office of Public Affairs
U.S. Securities and Exchange Commission
450 5th Street NW, Stop 1-2
Washington, DC 20549 — 202-272-2650

One way to obtain free copies of these reports is to call the company directly and tell them you are a potential investor. Many public corporations are set up to respond to this sort of inquiry.

Before you order any of these SEC filings, it is wise to ask for the total number of pages contained in each of the documents you want to obtain. Most of these document retrieval firms charge by the page and, no doubt, you don't want to be surprised if a company's amendment to its 10-K happens to run 500 pages in length.

Once you have the SEC documents you can then explore the additional sources described below.

Guide To Securities And Exchange Filings

The following information references the most commonly requested corporate filings made with the SEC. There is a short description of each filing, the location of the filing in the Public Reference Room and the retention period for the filing. It also gives the Division of the SEC responsible for interpreting the rules, regulations and forms used in connection with the filing.

This information cannot take the place of the Commission's official rules and regulations. It is not to be used as a legal reference document. Please refer to the federal securities laws and the rules and regulations thereunder (Title 17 of the Code of Federal Regulations, Parts 200 to End) for the official description of the forms mentioned. These are available at most law libraries. They may also be ordered through:

Superintendent of Documents
Government Printing Office
Washington, DC 20402

SEC Rules and regulations are also available in the Appeals Handbook through subscription to:

Sorg, Inc.
Appeals Handbook Division
345 Hudson Street
New York, NY 10014 — 212-741-6600

Form ADV
This form is used to apply for registration as an investment adviser or to amend a registration. It consists of two parts. Part I contains general and personal information about the applicant. Part II contains information relating to the nature of the applicant's business, including basic operations, services offered, fees charged, types of clients advised, educational and business backgrounds of associates and other business activities of the applicant. Location: Filings are available on microfiche. No paper copy is maintained. Retention: For as long as the investment adviser is registered plus ten years. Interpretive Responsibility: Division of Investment Management.

Form ADV-S
This is an annual supplement required to be filed by persons registered as investment advisers with the Commission. It must be filed not later than 90 days after the end of the registrant's fiscal year. Location: Filings are available on microfiche within 30 days of receipt by the Commission. No paper copy is maintained. Retention: For as long as the investment adviser is registered plus ten years. Interpretive Responsibility: Division of Investment Management.

Annual Report to Shareholders
The Annual Report to Shareholders is the principal document used by most public companies to disclose corporate information to shareholders. The Report is not a required SEC filing. It is usually a state-of-the-company report including an opening letter from the Chief Executive Office, financial data, results of continuing operations, market segment information, new product plans, subsidiary activities and research and development activities on future programs. Location: Filings received within 60 days of the current date are available in paper form. Filings are available on microfiche. Retention: Ten years. Interpretive Responsibility: Division of Corporation Finance, Office of Chief Counsel.

Form BD
This form is used to apply for registration as a broker or dealer of securities, or as a government securities broker or dealer, and to amend a registration. It

provides background information on the applicant and the nature of its business. It includes lists of the executive officers and general partners of the company. It also contains information on any past securities violations. Location: Filings are available on microfiche. No paper copy is maintained. Retention: For as long as the broker or dealer is registered plus ten years. Interpretive Responsibility: Division of Market Regulation, Office of Chief Counsel.

Form D

Companies selling securities pursuant to a Regulation D exemption or a Section 46-exemption from the registration provisions of the '33 Act must file a Form D as notice of such a sale. The form must be filed no later than 15 days after the first sale of securities. For additional information on Regulation D and Section 46-offerings, ask for a copy of the Regulation and the pamphlet entitled *Q & A: Small Business and the SEC*. Location: Filings received within 30 days of the current date are available in paper copy. Earlier filings are available on microfiche. Retention: Six years. Interpretive Responsibility: Division of Corporation Finance, Office of Small Business Policy.

Form MSD

This report is used by a bank or a separately identifiable department or division of a bank to apply for registration as a municipal securities dealer with the SEC, or to amend such registration. Location: Filings are available on microfiche. No paper copy is maintained. Retention: For as long as the municipal securities dealer is registered plus ten years. Interpretive Responsibility: Division of Market Regulation, Office of Chief Counsel.

Form N-SAR

This is a semi-annual report filed by registered investment management companies. Unit investment trusts are required to file this form at the end of the calendar year. It shows names of various entities providing services to the investment company as well as information about sales of shares, 12b-1 plans, contracts, type of fund, portfolio turnover rate, financial information and fidelity bonds. This form replaces forms N-1Q, N-1R, N-30A-2, N-30A-3, and N-27D-1. Location: Filings received within 30 days of the current date are available in paper copy. Earlier filings are available on microfiche. Retention: Ten years. Interpretive Responsibility: Division of Investment Management.

Prospectus

The preliminary prospectus constitutes Part I of 1933 Act registration statements. It contains the basic business and financial information on an issuer with respect to a particular securities offering. Investors may use the prospectus to help appraise the merits of the offering and make educated investment decisions. A prospectus in its preliminary form is frequently called a "red herring" prospectus and is subject to completion or amendment before the registration statement becomes effective, after which a final prospectus is issued and sales can be consummated. Location: Filings received within 60 days of the current date are available in paper form. Filings are available on microfiche. Retention: Permanent. Interpretive Responsibility: Division or Corporation Finance or Division of Investment Management, Office of Chief Counsel.

Proxy Solicitation Materials

A proxy statement is a document which is intended to provide security holders with the information necessary to enable them to vote in an informed manner on matters intended to be acted upon at security holders' meetings, whether the traditional annual meeting or a special meeting. Typically, a security holder is also provided with a "proxy" to authorize designated persons to vote his or her securities in the event the holder does not attend the meeting. Definitive (final) copies of proxy statements and proxies are filed with the Commission at the time they are sent to security holders. Preliminary proxy filings are non-public upon filing, but may be obtained under FOIA once the definitive proxy has been filed and released. Location: Definitive filings received within 60 days of the current date are available in paper copy. Filings are also available on microfiche. Retention: Permanent. Interpretive Responsibility: Division of Corporation Finance, Office of the Chief Counsel.

1933 Act Registration Statements

One of the major roles of the SEC is to require companies making a public issuance of securities to disclose material business and financial information in order that investors may make informed investment decisions. The 1933 Act requires issuers to file registration statements with the Commission, setting forth

such information, before offering their securities to the public. (See Section 6 of the Securities Act of 1933 for information concerning the "Registration of Securities and Signing of Registration Statement"; Section 8 of the Securities Act of 1933 for information on "Taking Effect of Registration Statements and Amendments Thereto".

The registration statement is divided into two parts. Part I is the preliminary prospectus. It is distributed to interested investors and others. It contains data to assist in evaluating the securities and make informed investment decisions.

Part II of the registration statement contains information not required to be filed in the prospectus. This includes information concerning the registrants' expenses of issuance and distribution, indemnification of directors and officers, and recent sales of unregistered securities as well as undertakings, copies of material contracts, and financial statement schedules.

Location: Filings received within 30 days of the current date are available in paper copy. Earlier filings are available on microfiche. Retention: Permanent. Interpretive Responsibility: Division of Corporation Finance, Office of Chief Counsel. (Except for Forms F-1, F-2, F-3, F-4, and F-6, for which the Office of International Corporate Finance should be consulted).

The most widely used 1933 Act registration forms are as follows:

S-1   This is the basic registration form. It can be used to register securities for which no other form is authorized or prescribed; except, securities of foreign governments or political subdivisions thereof.

S-2   This is a simplified optional registration form that may be used by companies which have reported under the '34 Act for a minimum of three years and have timely filed all required reports during the 12 calendar months and any portion of the month immediately preceding the filing of the registration statement. Unlike Form S-1 because it permits incorporation by reference from and delivery to the company's annual report to stockholders.

S-3   This is usually the most simplified registration form and it may only be used by companies which have reported under the '34 Act for a minimum of three years and meet the timely filing requirements set forth under Form S-2. Also, the offering and issuer must meet the stringent qualitative tests prescribed by the form. The form maximizes incorporating by reference information from '34 Act filings.

S-4   This form is used to register securities in connection with business combinations and applies the principles of the integrated disclosure system to disclosure in the context of mergers and exchange offers.

S-6   This form is used to register securities issued by unit investment trusts registered under the Investment Company Act of 1940 on Form N-8B-2.

S-8   This form is used for the registration of securities to be offered solely to an issuer's employees pursuant to certain plans.

S-11 This form is used to register securities of certain real estate companies including real estate investment trusts.

S-18 This is an optional form to be used by certain "small insurers" for registration of securities to be sold for an aggregate cash price of $7.5 million or less. It requires somewhat less disclosure than Form S-1.

S-20 This form may be used to register standardized options where the issuer undertakes not to issue, clear, guarantee or accept an option registered on Form S-20 unless there is a definitive options disclosure document meeting the requirements of Rule 9b-1 of the '34 Act.

F-1   This is the basic registration form authorized for certain foreign private issuers. It is used to register the securities of those eligible foreign issuers for which no other more specialized form is authorized or prescribed.

F-2   This is an optional registration form that may be used by certain foreign private issuers which are world class issuers (i.e., they have an equity float of at least $300 million worldwide or are registering non-convertible investment grade debt securities) or have reported under the '34 Act for a minimum of three years. The form is somewhat shorter than Form F-1 because it utilizes filings made by the issuer under the '34 Act, particularly Form 20-F.

F-3 This form may only be used by certain foreign private issuers which are both world class issuers and have reported under the '34 Act for a minimum of three years. The form makes maximum use of '34 Act filings.

F-4 This form is used to register securities in connection with business combinations involving foreign private registrants and applies the principles of the integrated disclosure system to disclosure in the context of mergers and exchange orders.

F-6 This form is used to register depository shares represented by American Depository Receipts issued by a depositary against the deposit of the securities of a foreign issuer.

SR This form is used as a report by first time registrants under the Act of sales of registered securities and use of proceeds therefrom. They are required at specified periods of time throughout the offering period, and a final report is required after the termination of the offering.

Other Securities Act Forms:

Form 144

This form must be filed as notice of the proposed sale of restricted securities or securities held by an affiliate of the issuer in reliance on Rule 144 when the amount to be sold during any three month period exceeds 500 shares or units or has an aggregate sales price in excess of $10,000. Location: Filings received within 30 days of the current date are available in paper copy. However, they are filed by the date of receipt in the Public Reference Room as opposed to company name. If you are uncertain as to the date of receipt or are interested in viewing earlier filings, check with a Specialist at the Reference Desk. Retention: Six years. Interpretive Responsibility: Division of Corporation Finance, Office of Chief Counsel.

1934 Act Registration Statements

All companies whose securities are registered on a national securities exchange, and, in general, companies whose assets exceed $5,000,000 with a class of equity securities held by 500 or more persons, must register such securities under the 1934 Act.

This registration establishes a public file containing material financial and business information on the company for use by investors and others, and also creates an obligation on the part of the company to keep such public information current by filing periodic reports on Forms 10-Q and 10-K, and on current event Form 8-K, as applicable.

The periodic reports must be filed by a company for the year in which a public offering of its securities was made, and, in subsequent years if such securities are held by more than 300 persons.

Location: Filings received within 30 days of the current date are available in paper copy. Earlier filings are available on microfiche. Retention: 30 years. Interpretive Responsibility: Division of Corporation Finance, Office of Chief Counsel (Except for Form 20-F, as to which the Office of International Corporate Finance should be consulted.)

The most widely used 1934 Act registration forms are as follows:

10 This is the general form for registration of securities pursuant to Section 12(b) or (g) of the Securities Exchange Act of 1934 of classes of securities of issuers for which no other form is prescribed.

8-A This optional short form may be used by companies already required to file reports under the '34 Act to register securities under that Act.

8-B This specialized registration form may be used by an issuer with no securities registered under the '34 Act which is the successor to another issuer which had securities so registered at the time of succession.

20-F This is an integrated form used both as a registration statement for purposes of registering securities of qualified foreign registrants under Section 12, or as an annual report under Section 13(a) or 15(d) of the Exchange Act of 1934.

Other Exchange Act Forms
Form TA-1

This form is used to apply for registration as a transfer agent or to amend such registration. It provides information on the company's activities and operation. Location: Filings are available on microfiche. No paper copy is maintained. Retention: for the life of the indenture. Interpretive Responsibility: Division of Market Regulation, Branch of Stock Surveillance.

Form X-17A-5

Every broker or dealer registered pursuant to Section 15 of the Exchange Act must file annually, on a calendar or fiscal year basis, a report audited by an independent public accountant. Location: Reports are available on microfiche within 30 days of receipt by the Commission. No paper copy is maintained. Retention: Ten years. Interpretive Responsibility: Division of Market Regulation, Branch of Financial Reporting.

Forms 3, 4 and 5

Every director, officer or owner of more than ten percent of a class of equity securities registered under Section 12 of the '34 Act must file with the Commission a statement of ownership regarding such security. The initial filing is on Form 3 and changes are reported on Form 4. The Annual Statement of beneficial ownership of securities is on Form 5. The forms contain information on the reporting person's relationship to the company and on purchases and sales of such equity securities. Location: Filings received within 30 days of the current date are available in paper copy. However, they are filed by the date of receipt as opposed to company name. If you are uncertain as to the date of receipt or are interested in viewing earlier filings, check with a Specialist at the Reference Desk. Information contained in these reports is extracted, compiled and published monthly by the Government Printing Office as the Official Summary of Securities Transactions. Interested persons may subscribe through the GPO. Retention: Six years. Interpretive Responsibility: Division of Corporation Finance, Office of Chief Counsel.

Form 6-K

This report is used by certain foreign private issuers to furnish information: (1-required to be made public in the country of its domicile; 2-filed with and made public by a foreign stock exchange on which its securities are traded; or 3-distributed to security holders. The report must be furnished promptly after such material is made public. The form is not considered "filed" for Section 18 purposes. This is the only information furnished by Foreign private issuers between annual reports, since such issuers are not required to file on Forms 10-Q or 8-K. Location: Filings received within 30 days of the current date are available in paper coy. Earlier filings are available on microfiche. Retention: Ten years. Interpretive Responsibility: Division of Corporation Finance, Office of International Corporate Finance.

Form 8

This form is used to amend Exchange Act registration statements (Forms 10, 8A, etc.) and most Exchange Act reports (Forms 8-K, 10-Q, 10-K). Location: Filings received within 30 days of the current date are available in paper copy. Earlier filings are available on microfiche. Retention: Ten years. Interpretive Responsibility: Division of Corporation Finance, Office of Chief Counsel.

Form 8-K

This is the "current report" which is used to report the occurrence of any material events or corporate changes which are of importance to investors or security holders and previously have not been reported by the registrant. It provides more current information on certain specified events than would Forms 10-Q or 10-K. It must be filed within 15 days of any event specified in the form (Except for Item 5). Location: Filings received within 30 days of the current date are available in paper copy. Earlier filings are available in microfiche. Retention: Permanent. Interpretive Responsibility: Division of Corporation Finance, Office of Chief Counsel.

Form 10-C

This form must be filed by an issuer whose securities are quoted on the NASDAQ interdealer quotation system. Reported on the form is any change that exceeds five percent in the number of shares of the class outstanding and any change in the name of the issuer. The report must be filed within ten days of such change. Location: Filings received within 60 days of the current date are available in paper copy. Filings are also available on microfiche. Retention: Ten years. Interpretive Responsibility: Division of Corporation Finance, Office of Chief Counsel.

Form 10-K

This is the annual report which most reporting companies file with the Commission. It provides a comprehensive overview of the registrant's business. The report must be filed within 90 days after the end of the company's fiscal year. Location: Filings received within 60 days of the current date are available in paper copy. Filings are also available on microfiche. Retention: Permanent. Interpretive Responsibility: Division of Corporation Finance, Office of Chief Counsel.

Form 10-Q

The Form 10-Q is a report filed quarterly by most registered companies. It includes unaudited financial statements and provides a continuing view of the company's financial position during the year. The report must be filed for each of the first three fiscal quarters and is due within 45 days of the close of the quarter. Location: Filings received within 60 days of the current date are available in paper copy. Filings are also available on microfiche. Retention: Permanent. Interpretive Responsibility: Division of Corporation Finance, Office of Chief Counsel.

Form 13-F

This is a quarterly report of equity holdings by institutional investment managers having equity assets under management of $100 million or more. Included in this category are certain banks, insurance companies, investment advisers, investment companies, foundations and pension funds. Location: Filings for the current quarter are available in paper copy. Filings are also available on microfiche. Retention: Four years. Interpretive Responsibility: Division of Investment Management, Office of Chief Counsel.

Form 15

This form is filed by a company as notice of termination of registration under Section 12(g) of the '34 Act, or suspension of the duty to file periodic reports under Section 15(d) of the '34 Act. Location: Filings are available on microfiche within 30 days of receipt by the Commission. No paper copy is maintained. Retention: Ten years. Interpretive Responsibility: Division of Corporation Finance, Office of Chief Counsel.

Form 18

This form is used for the registration on a national securities exchange of securities of foreign governments and political subdivisions thereof. Location: Filings are available on microfiche within 30 days of receipt by the Commission. No paper copy is maintained. Retention: Ten years. Interpretive Responsibility: Division of Corporation Finance, Office of International Corporate Finance

Form 18-K

This form is used for the annual reports of foreign governments or political subdivisions thereof. Location: Filings are available on microfiche within 30 days of receipt by the Commission. No paper copy is maintained. Retention: Ten years. Interpretive Responsibility: Division of Corporation Finance, Office of International Corporate Finance

Schedule 13D

This schedule[*] discloses beneficial ownership of certain registered equity securities. Any person or group of persons who acquire a beneficial ownership of more than 5% of a class of registered equity securities of certain issuers must file a Schedule 13D reporting such acquisition together with certain other information within ten days after such acquisition. Moreover, any material changes in the facts set forth in the Schedule precipitates a duty to promptly file an amendment.

The Commission's rules define the term "beneficial owner" to be any person who directly or indirectly shares voting power or investment power (the power to sell the security). Location: Filings received within 30 days of the current date are available in paper copy. Earlier filings are also available on microfiche. Retention: Seven years. Interpretive Responsibility: Division of Corporation

Finance, Office of Tender Offers.

Schedule 13E-3

This schedule[*] must be filed by certain companies and their affiliates (such as companies with any equity securities registered under Section 12 of the '34 Act) whenever they engage in a transaction to "take the company private", for example, when the transaction would decrease the number of shareholders to such a point that the company would no longer be required to file reports with the SEC. The transaction could take the form of a merger, tender offer, sale of assets or a reverse stock split. Location: Filings received within 30 days of the current date are available in paper copy. Earlier filings are available on microfiche. Retention: Seven years. Interpretive Responsibility: Division of Corporation Finance, Office of Tender Offers.

Schedule 13E-4

This schedule[*] (called an Issuer Tender Offer Statement) must be filed by certain issuers (such as companies with securities registered under Section 12 of the '34 Act) when they are making a tender offer for their own securities. Location: Filings received within 30 days of the current date are available in paper copy. Earlier filings are available on microfiche. Retention: Seven years. Interpretive Responsibility: Division of Corporation Finance, Office of Tender Offers.

Schedule 13G

Schedule 13G is a much abbreviated version of Schedule 13D that is only available for use by a limited category of "persons" (such as banks, broker/dealers, and insurance companies) and even then only when the securities were acquired in the ordinary course of business and not with the purpose nor effect of changing or influencing the control of the issuer. Location: Filings received within 30 days of the current date are available in paper copy. Earlier filings are available on microfiche. Retention: Seven years. Interpretive Responsibility: Division of Corporation Finance, Office of Tender Offers.

Schedule 14B

In the event that there is a proxy contest with respect to the election or removal of a company's directors, any "participant" in such contest must file a Schedule 14B. As a general rule participants other than the issuer must file Schedule 14B's at least five business days prior to making any solicitation, whereas the issuer's participants, must file within five business days after the opposition solicitation has begun. Location: Filings received within 60 days of the current date are available in paper copy. Earlier filings are available on microfiche. Retention: Ten years. Interpretive Responsibility: Division of Corporation Finance, Office of Chief Counsel.

Schedule 14D-1

Any person, other than the issuer itself (see Schedule 13E-4), making a tender offer for certain equity securities (such as equity securities registered pursuant to Section 12 of the '34 Act), which offer, if accepted, would cause that person to own over 5 percent of that class of the securities, must at the time of the offer file a Schedule 14D-1. This schedule[*] must be filed with the Commission and sent to certain other parties, such as the issuer and any competing bidders. Location: Filings received within 30 days of the current date are available in paper copy. Earlier filings are available on microfiche. Retention: Seven years. Interpretive Responsibility: Division of Corporation Finance, Office of Tender Offers.

Schedule 14D-9

This schedule must be filed with the Commission when an interested party, such as an issuer, a beneficial owner of securities, or a representative of either, makes a solicitation or recommendation to the shareholders with respect to a particular tender offer (A tender offer which is, of course, subject to Regulation 14D). Location: Filings received within 30 days of the current date are available in paper copy. Earlier filings are available on microfiche. Retention: Seven years. Interpretive Responsibility: Division of Corporation Finance, Office of Tender Offers.

---

[*] There is an hourly display of the receipt of these filings shown on two electronic display boards in the Public Reference room. The display coincides with the hourly delivery of the asterisked filings for rotation. Plans are being made for a cumulative display at the end of the day.

Trust Indenture Act of 1939 Forms

T-1 This form is a statement of eligibility and qualification of a corporation to act as a trustee under the Trust Indenture Act of 1939.

T-2 This form is basically the same as Form T-1 except it is to be used for individual, rather than corporate trustees.

T-3 This form is used as an application for qualification of indentures pursuant to the Trust Indenture Act of 1939, but only when securities to be issued thereunder are not required to be registered under the Securities Act of 1933.

T-4 This form is used to apply for an exemption from certain provisions of the Trust Indenture Act.

Location: Filings received within 30 days of the current date are available in paper copy. Earlier filings are available on microfiche. Retention: For the life of the indenture. Interpretive Responsibility: Division of Corporation Finance, Office of Chief Counsel.

1940 Act Investment Company Registration Statements

Mutual funds, the most common type of registered investment company, make a continuous offering of their securities and register on simplified, three-part forms. The prospectus, or Part A, provides a concise description of the fundamental characteristics of the initial fund in a way that will assist investors in making informed decisions about whether to purchase the securities of the fund. The statement of additional information, Part B, contains additional information about the fund which may be of interest to some investors but need not be included in the prospectus. Part C contains other required information and exhibits. Unit investment trusts, insurance company separate accounts, business development companies and other registered investment companies register their shares and provide essential information about them on other registration forms. See the following:

N-1A This form is used to register open-end management investment companies ("mutual funds").

N-2 This form is used to register closed-end management investment companies.

N-3 This form is used to register insurance company separate accounts organized as management investment companies offering variable annuity contracts.

N-4 This form is used to register insurance company separate accounts organized as unit investment trusts offering variable annuity contracts.

Clues At The State Level About Privately Held Companies Plus Divisions And Subsidiaries Of Public Corporations

The following sources are designed primarily to help you gather information on privately held companies or those divisions and subsidiaries of public corporations which are not contained in documents filed with the U.S. Securities and Exchange Commission. However, the sources described here will enhance your work in collecting data on all types of companies. If the company in question is not publicly owned, the next step is to turn your attention to the appropriate state government offices. All companies doing business in any state leave a trail of documentation there. The number of documents and the amount of detail vary widely depending upon the state regulations and the type of company.

One of the main reasons you should begin your search with the state government is that it may take longer to retrieve the information from the state offices than from other checkpoints which are described in this Section.

Puzzling Together Bits of Information

Remember that only the U.S. Securities and Exchange Commission documents fulfill the purpose of providing you with information on your competitor or acquisition candidate. All other government documents are generated to comply with some law or policy, such as pollution control, consumer protection, or tax collection. Because of this, government bureaucrats who collect and analyze these documents have no idea just how valuable the information can be to you. Do not expect that the data contained in other government documents will be presented in a way that automatically will suit your particular needs. Furthermore, no single document will provide all the information about a corporate entity that you are after.

The strategy is to get any information whatever because each piece might contribute to your overall information mosaic. Although a full profit and loss statement will be out of reach, the office of uniform commercial code can tell you to whom the company owes money and a description of the corporation's assets. The state office of corporations may not give you the total sales figure, but if the company is headquartered out of state, it may tell you the corporation's total sales in that state and what percentage this is of its total. With a little bit of algebra you can estimate the total sales.

If it were as easy as making one phone call and getting complete financial information on any company, everyone would be doing it. Your competitive advantage lies in getting information that other people don't know about or are too lazy to get.

In the event you intend to dig around at the state level, the following three offices are a must. They offer the biggest potential for the least amount of effort:

1) Office of Corporations

Every corporation, whether it is headquartered or has an office in a state, must file some information with a state agency. The corporations division or office of corporations usually is part of the office of the Secretary of State. When a company incorporates or sets up an office in the state, it must file incorporation papers, or something similar, which provides--at a minimum -- the nature of the business, the names and addresses of officers and agents, and the amount of capital stock in the company. In addition to this registration, every company must file some kind of annual report. These annual reports may or may not contain financial data. Some states require sales figures, and others ask just for asset figures.

2) Office of Uniform Commercial Code

Any organization, and for that matter, any individual, which borrows money and offers an asset as collateral, must file within the state at the office of uniform commercial code. A filing is made for each loan and each of the documents is available to the public. To obtain these documents is a two step process. First, one must request a search to see if there are any filings for a certain company. The fee for a search is usually under $10. Such a search will identify the number of documents filed against the company. You then will have to request copies of each of these documents. The cost for each document averages only a few dollars. This office of uniform commercial code usually is located in or near to the same office of corporations.

3) State Securities Office

The U.S. Securities and Exchange Commission in Washington, DC regulates only those corporations which sell stock in their company across state lines. There is another universe of corporations which sells stock in their companies only within state lines. For such stock offerings, complete financial information is filed with the state securities regulator. These documents are similar to a those filed at the U.S. Securities and Exchange Commission. But remember that the documents vary from one state to the next and, equally important, the requirement of filing an annual report differs from state to state. Usually a telephone call to the office in charge can tell you whether a particular company has ever offered stock intrastate. If so, you are then in a position of getting copies of these filings. Usually the Secretary of State's office can refer you to the state's securities regulator.

Finding The Right State Office

Because of the multitude of differences between the 50 state governments, expect to make half a dozen calls before you locate the right office. Several starting places are described below with the simplest ones listed first.

1) State Government Operator

The AT&T information operator can give you the telephone number for the state government operator. Then, in turn, you can ask for the phone number of the specific government office.

2) State Department of Commerce

Now that every state is aggressively trying to get companies to expand or relocate to their state, these departments can serve as excellent starting points because they are familiar with other government offices which regulate business. Many times these departments have established a "one-stop office" with a separate staff on call to help business find whatever information it needs.

3) State Capital Library

By asking the state government operator to connect you to the state capital library, a reference librarian can identify the state agency which can best respond to your queries.

4) Directories

If you intend to dig around various state government offices on more than just an infrequent basis, you might consider purchasing a state government directory. Usually the state office of Administrative Services is the place that will sell you a directory, or you might want to contact the state bookstore. If you want to purchase a directory that covers all 50 states, consider:

State Executive Directory
Carroll Publishing Company
1058 Thomas Jefferson Street NW
Washington, DC 20007   202-333-8620
(Price is $135 per year plus shipping and handling.)

Tracking The Trail of Company Information
In Other State Offices

The three offices described earlier are only the starting places for information on companies. There are dozens of other state agencies that are brimming with valuable bits of data about individual corporations; however, these sources require a bit more care because they can be used only under certain circumstances or require extra resourcefulness.

1) Utility and Cable TV Regulators

Utility companies are heavily regulated by state agencies, and as a result there is a lot of financial and operational information that is accessible. Most people know that gas and electric companies fall into this category, but you may not be aware that this also applies to water companies, bus companies, rail systems, telephone companies, telecommunication companies, and cable TV operators.

2) Other State Regulators

State government is very similar to the federal government in that its function is to regulate many of the activities of the business community. In those states where state laws and enforcement are very effective, Uncle Sam relies on those states to enforce the federal laws. For example, the U.S. Food and Drug Administration will use the records from the state of New Jersey for information on pharmaceutical manufacturers instead of sending out its own team of federal data collectors. The U.S. Environmental Protection Administration will use state records in those states that have strict environmental statutes rather than using its own resources.

3) Financial Institutions

Banks, savings and loans, credit unions and other financial institutions all file information with the state bank regulator. Many of these organizations are also regulated by federal agencies so what you get from the state office often will be a copy of the form filed with the federal government.

4) Environment Regulators

Almost every state has an office which regulates pollutants in the air, water and ground. Such departments are similar to the U.S. Environmental Protection Agency in Washington, DC and monitor whether any new or old business is polluting the environment. If the company you are investigating has plans to build a new plant in the state, get ready to collect some valuable information. Before construction can begin, the company must file information with the state environmental protection agency. These documents will detail the size of the plant, what kind of equipment it will use, and how much this equipment will be used. With such information, other manufacturers in the same business can tell exactly what the capacity and estimated volume of the plant will be. Sometimes there will be three separate offices with authority over air, water or solid waste. Each will collect basically the same information, and they can be used, one against each other, to ensure that you get all the information you need.

5) Department of Commerce/Economic Development

As mentioned earlier, each state is now actively trying to attract and develop business development within the state. The state's office of economic development or department of commerce is normally charged with this responsibility. To attract business to the state, this agency has to know all about existing business throughout the state, which all translates into who is doing what, how successful they are, and how large the company is. At a minimum, the economic development office can probably provide you with information on the number of employees for a given company. They will also be aware what other government offices in the state keep records about the industry or company which interests you. The experts at this state agency are similar to the 100 industry analysts at the U.S. Department of Commerce and can serve as excellent resources for collecting government information on an industry.

6)   State Government Contractors

Although many states are not accustomed to sharing information with researchers, you should be able to obtain details about any purchase the state makes. If the company in question sells to the state, you should get copies of their contracts. Just like the federal government which makes all this procurement information available, the state which spends public funds guarantees that the public has a right to know how the money is being spent. You may have to enforce your rights under the state law which is equivalent to the federal Freedom of Information Act.

7)   Minority and Small Business

Many states maintain special offices which track minority firms and other small companies. These offices can be helpful not only in identifying these businesses but may also be able to tell you the size or products of a given business. The small business office and possibly a separate minority business division normally fall under the state department of commerce.

8)   Attorney General

The state Attorney General's office is the primary consumer advocate for the state against fraudulent practices by businesses operating within the state. So, if the company you are investigating is selling consumer services or products, it would be worth the effort to check with this office. In some states the attorney generals have begun to concentrate on certain areas. For example, the office in Denver specializes in gathering information on companies selling energy saving devices, and the one in New York investigates companies with computerized databases which provide scholarship information.

9)   Food and Drug Companies

Any company which produces, manufactures or imports either food or drug products is likely to come under the jurisdiction of the state food and drug agency. This office makes routine inspection of facilities and the reports are generally accessible; however, a Freedom of Information Act request is sometimes necessary.

County and Local Sources

County and local sources can prove to be the biggest bucket of worms as far as information sources go. Unlike state government where there are 50 varieties to choose from, there are over 5,000 different jurisdictions at the local level. Here are some basic checkpoints that can enhance your information gathering efforts.

Local Newspapers: Business Editors

The local newspaper can provide the best leads for anything you are investigating at the local level. It is perhaps the best source mentioned in this book. A well-placed telephone call to the business editor or the managing editor, if there is not a business section, can prove to be most useful. In smaller towns, and even in suburbs of larger cities where there are suburban newspapers, a local business generates a good deal of news. A local reporter often knows the company like no one else in the country. The company executives usually are more open with the local media because they like to show off about how big they are, how much the company is growing, etc. A reporter is also likely to know company employees who can corroborate or refute the executive's remarks.

Ask the local newspaper if you can get copies of all articles written about the company in question. After you review them, call the reporter to see what additional information may be stored in his or her head.

Other Checkpoints

It is worth fishing for information in a number of other places, including agencies and private organizations.

1)   Chamber of Commerce

Talking to someone on the research staff or the librarian can help you identify sources within the community about a company. A friendly conversation with Chamber executives can also provide insight into a company's financial position and strategies.

2)   Local Development Authority

Many local communities, counties, and regional areas have established development authorities to attract business and industry to their area. They operate pretty much the same as the state department of economic development described above, and as a result collect a lot of data about the businesses in their area.

3)   Local Courts

Civil and criminal court actions can provide excellent source material for company investigations. Perdue Chicken Company, a private corporation in Maryland, revealed its annual sales figures while fighting Virginia sales tax in the courts. A recent search revealed four financial-related suits filed against a large privately held political campaign fundraising firm in McLean, Virginia. If you are not in close proximity to the court, it may be worthwhile to hire a local freelance reporter or researcher. In most jurisdictions there are chronological indexes of both civil and criminal cases which are kept by the clerk of the court. These indexes record all charges or complaints made, the names of the defendants and plaintiffs in the event of civil cases, the date of the filing, the case number, and the disposition if one has been reached. Armed with the case number you can request to see the case files from the clerk.

Company Information At The Office Of
Federal Regulators

The federal offices identified in the preceding section on market studies also are excellent sources for information on companies. Industry specialists within the federal government are likely to have information on companies or can refer you to other sources which may have just the information you need.

Company Intelligence

The 26 government agencies listed here are those that are involved with regulating industries and/or the companies within those industries. The information held at each federal office varies from agency to agency; however, most of the offices maintain financial or other information that most researchers would consider sensitive.

Airlines, Air Freight Carriers, and Air Taxis
Office of Community and Consumer Affairs
U.S. Department of Transportation
400 7th Street SW, Room 10405
Washington, DC 20590   202-366-2220/5957

Airports
Airport Section
National Flight Data Center, Room 634
Federal Aviation Administration, ATM-612
800 Independence Avenue SW
Washington, DC 20591   202-267-9311

Bank Holding Companies and State Members of the Federal Reserve System
Freedom of Information Act Office
Board of Governors of the Federal Reserve System
20th Street & Constitution Avenue NW
Room B1122
Washington, DC 20551   202-452-3684

Banks, National
Communications Division
Comptroller of the Currency
250 E St., SW
Washington, DC 20219   202-874-4700

Barge and Vessel Operators
Financial Analysis, Tariffs
Federal Maritime Commission
1100 L Street NW
Washington, DC 20573   202-523-5876

Cable Television System Operators
Cable TV Branch
Federal Communications Commission
1919 M Street NW, Room 416
Washington, DC 20554   202-632-7480

Colleges, Universities, Vocational Schools, and Public Schools
Office of Educational Research & Improvement
U.S. Department of Education
555 New Jersey NW, Room 600
Washington, DC 20208-5530   202-219-2050

Commodity Trading Advisors
National Futures Association
200 W. Madison St., Suite 1600
Chicago, IL 60606-3447   1-800-621-3570
Attn: Compliance Dept.   FAX: 312-781-1467

Consumer Products
Corrective Actions Division
U.S. Consumer Product Safety Commission
5401 Westbard Avenue
Bethesda, MD 20816   301-492-6608

Electric and Gas Utilities and Gas Pipeline Companies
Federal Energy Regulatory Commission
825 North Capitol Street NE, Room 9204
Washington, DC 20426   202-208-0200

Exporting Companies
Office of Export Trading Companies Affairs
U.S. Department of Commerce
14th & Constitution Avenue, Room 1800
Washington, DC 20230   202-482-5131

Federal Land Bank and Production Credit Associations
Farm Credit Administration
1501 Farm Credit Drive
McLean, VA 22102-5090   703-883-4000

Foreign Corporations
World Traders Data Report
U.S. Department of Commerce
Washington, DC 20230   202-482-4204

Government Contractors
Federal Procurement Data Center
General Services Administration
7th and D Streets, SW, Room 5652
Washington, DC 20407   703-401-1529

Hospitals and Nursing Homes
National Center for Health Statistics
6525 Belcrest Rd.
Hyattsville, MD 20782   301-436-8500

Land Developers
Office of Interstate Land Registration
U.S. Department of Housing and Urban Development
451 7th Street SW, Room 6262
Washington, DC 20410   202-708-0502

Mining Companies
Mine Safety and Health Administration
U.S. Department of Labor
4015 Wilson Boulevard
Arlington, VA 22203   703-235-1452

Non-Profit Institutions
U.S. Internal Revenue Service
Freedom of Information Reading Room
1111 Constitution Avenue NW, Room 1563
P.O. Box 388, Ben Franklin Station
Washington, DC 20044   202-566-3770

Nuclear Power Plants
Director, Office of Nuclear Reactor Regulation
U.S. Nuclear Regulatory Commission
2120 L Street NW
Washington, DC 20037   301-492-7000/7758

Pension Plans
Division of Inquiries and Technical Assistance
Office of Pension and Welfare Benefits Programs
U.S. Department of Labor
200 Constitution Avenue NW, Room N5658
Washington, DC 20210   202-219-8233

Pharmaceutical, Cosmetic and Food Companies
Associate Commissioner for Regulatory Affairs
U.S. Food and Drug Administration
5600 Fishers Lane, Room 14-90
Rockville, MD 20857   301-443-1594

Pesticide and Chemical Manufacturers
U.S. Environmental Protection Agency
Office of Pesticides and Toxic Substances
401 M Street SW (TS-788)
Washington, DC 20460   202-260-2902

Radio and Television Stations
Mass Media Bureau
Federal Communications Commission
1919 M Street NW, Room 302
Washington, DC 20554   202-632-6485

Railroads, Trucking Companies, Bus Lines, Freight Forwarders, Water Carriers, Oil Pipelines, Transportation Brokers, Express Agencies

U.S. Interstate Commerce Commission
12th & Constitution Avenue NW, Room 4126
Washington, DC 20423   202-927-7119

Savings and Loan Associations

Office of Thrift Supervision
1700 G Street NW
Washington, DC 20552   202-906-6000

Telephone Companies, Overseas Telegraph Companies, Microwave Companies, Public Land and Mobile Service

Common Carrier Bureau
Federal Communications Commission
1919 M Street NW, Room 500
Washington, DC 20554   202-632-6910

Suppliers And Other Industry Sources

If all of the above sources fail to provide information you need on a given company, your last resort is to go directly into the industry and try to extract the information by talking with insiders.

Your telephone is an essential, and perhaps the best, research tool. Two other good reference sources are:

1) **Trade Associations** are identified in *Encyclopedia of Associations* - (Gale Research Inc., Book Tower, 835 Penobscot Building, Detroit, MI 48277, 313-961-2242, 1-800-877-4253. For prepaid order, mail check for $322 to P.O. Box 71701, Chicago, IL 60694-1701);

2) **100 Industry Analysts** at the U.S. Department of Commerce. These Government Industry Analysts cover industries such as athletic goods, dairy products or truck trailers.

Your first step is to begin casting around for someone in the industry who knows about the company in question. When hunting for an expert, it is essential that you remain determined and optimistic about eventually finding one or several individuals who will be "information jackpots."

People who know their industry will be able to give you the details you need about any company (i.e., its size, sales, profitability, market strategies). These sources probably will not be able to give you the precise figure that is on the balance sheet or profit and loss statement, but they will offer a very educated guess which is likely to be within 10 to 20% of the exact figure. And usually this estimate is good enough for anyone to work with.

The real trick is finding the right people -- the ones who know. Talk to them and get them to share their knowledge with you.

Where Else To Look For Industry Experts

Industry experts are not concentrated in Washington, DC but are located all over the world, so you need to exercise some common sense to figure out where to find them. Here are some general guidelines.

1) Industry Observers

These are specialists on staff at trade associations, think tanks, and at the U.S. Department of Commerce and other government agencies. Anyone who concentrates on an industry has familiarity with the companies that comprise that industry.

2) Trade Magazines

You will find that there is at least one magazine which reports on every industry. The editors and reporters of these trade publications also are well acquainted with individual companies.

3) Suppliers

Most industries have major suppliers which must know about the industry they service and the companies within that industry. For example, the tire manufacturers anticipate every move among auto makers well before any other outsiders. Suppliers also have to know the volume of every manufacturer to whom they sell or intend to sell to because of the obvious repercussions on the supplier's business. Every company is like this, even Information USA, Inc. We are basically a publisher, and if you talk to our printers, you would get a pretty good picture of exactly what we are doing.

Company Case Studies and Databases

1) Company Case Studies For As Little As $2.00 Each

Case studies of major and minor companies as well as subsidiaries of public companies can provide valuable competitive intelligence. Thousands of such cases are identified in an $8 publication titled *Directory of Harvard Business School Cases and Related Course Materials, 1991-92*. A supplement to the directory, covering the period between April 1987 and January 1988 is available for $5.

HBS Publications Division
Operations Department   617-495-6117/6006
Boston, MA 02163   FAX: 617-495-6985

2) Government and Commercial Databases

ABI/Inform, Disclosure, and Management Contents are just a few of the online databases which provide quick access to information about all types of companies. Additional leads for gathering intelligence about companies can be derived from diverse databases maintained by the U.S. government, many of which are identified in the *Federal Database Finder* (Information USA, Inc.).

Complete Financials On Franchising Companies

Franchising companies, whether public or privately held, must file detailed financial information in 14 different states. These state statutes create excellent opportunities for gathering competitive and marketing data as outlined below.

Inside Information

If the company of interest is a franchise organization, a great deal of financial information for their average franchisee is available in addition to their corporate profit and loss statements and balance sheets. A typical table of contents for a filing includes:

* biographical information on persons affiliated with the franchisor
* litigation
* bankruptcy
* franchisees' initial franchise fee or other initial payment
* other recurring or isolated fees and payments
* the franchisee's initial investment
* obligations of the franchisee to purchase or lease from designated sources
* obligations of the franchisee to purchase or lease in accordance with specifications or from approved suppliers
* financing arrangements
* obligations of the franchisor: other supervision, assistance or services
* territorial rights
* trademarks, service marks, trade names, logotypes and commercial symbols
* patents and copyrights
* obligation of the franchisee to participate in the actual operation of the franchise business
* restrictions on goods and services offered by the franchisee
* term, renewal, termination, repurchase, modification, assignment and related information
* agreements with public figures
* actual, average, projected or forecasted franchisee sales, profits and earnings
* information regarding franchises of the franchisor
* financial statements
* contracts
* standard operating statements
* list of operational franchisees
* estimate of additional franchised stores
* company-owned stores
* estimate of additional company-owned stores
* copies of contracts and agreements

Market Information and Franchising Trends

The franchise information packet often includes information on the results of their market studies which establish the need for their product or service. These can provide valuable market information as well as forecasts for potential markets. Is the ice cream boom over? A quick check into Ben and Jerry's forecast for future stores will give you a clue of what the experts think.

Franchise companies are often the first to jump current trends and fads in the U.S., for example, ice cream shops and diet centers. You can get an instant snapshot of such a trend by reviewing the marketing section of a franchise agreement.

Career Opportunities

If you ever wondered how much it would cost to open up your own bookstore, restaurant, video store, or most any other kind of venture, you can get all the facts and figures you need without paying a high-priced consultant or tipping your hand to your current employer. Just take a look at a franchise agreement from someone in a similar line of business. You can even discover the expected salary level.

New Business for Suppliers

If you are looking to sell napkins, Orange Julius or computer services to Snelling & Snelling, their franchise statements will disclose what kind of agreements they currently have with similar suppliers.

State Checkpoints for Franchising Intelligence

To obtain franchise agreements from the 14 states that require such disclosure, simply call one or more of the offices listed below and ask if a specific company has filed. Copies of the documentation are normally sent in the mail with a copying charge of $0.10 to $0.40 a page.

California
Department of Corporations, 1115 11th Street, Sacramento, 95814, 916-445-7205. Fee is 30 cents per page. Send blank check stating $25 limit. They will call with price for orders exceeding that amount.

Hawaii
Department of Commerce and Consumer Affairs, Business Registration Department, 1010 Richards Street, Honolulu, 96813, P.O. Box 40, Honolulu, 96810, 808-586-2730. Fee is 25 cents per page.

Illinois
Franchise Division, Office of Attorney General, 500 South Second Street, Springfield, 62704, 217-782-1090. Charge is a $40 flat fee per company franchise.

Indiana
Franchise Division, Secretary of State, 302 West Washington Street, Room E-111, Indianapolis, 46204, 317-232-0735. Fee is 10 cents per page plus handling charges.

Maryland
Assistant Attorney General, Maryland Division of Securities, 200 St. Paul Place, 21st Floor, Baltimore, 21202-2020, 301-576-6360. Maryland does not make copies. Suggests contacting Documents-To-Go, 1-800-879-4949.

Minnesota
Minnesota Department of Commerce, Enforcement Division, 133 East Seventh Street, St. Paul, 55101, 612-296-2594. Contact Ann Hagestad at 612-296-6328. Fee is 50 cents per page.

New York
Bureau of Investor and Protection Securities, New York State Department of Law, 120 Broadway, New York, 10271, 212-341-2200. Fee is 25 cents per page.

North Dakota
Franchise Examiner, North Dakota Securities Commission, 600 East Blvd., Fifth Floor, Bismarck, 58505, 701-224-2910. Documents are open for the public to inspect and copy, but this office does not provide copies as a service.

Oregon
Department of Insurance and Finance, Corporate Securities Section, Division of Finance and Corporate Securities, 21 Labor and Industries Bldg., Salem, 97310, 503-378-4387. Oregon does not keep franchise documents on file.

Rhode Island
Securities Section, Securities Division, 233 Richmond Street, Suite 232, Providence, 02903-4237, 401-277-3048. Special request form must be used. Fee is 15 cents per page copy and $15 an hour per search time.

South Dakota
Franchise Administrator, Division of Securities, State Capitol, Pierre, 57501, 605-773-4013. Fee is 50 cents per sheet.

Virginia
Franchise Section, Division of Securities and Retail Franchising, 1229 Bank Street, 4th Floor, Richmond, 23219, 804-786-7751. Fee is $1 per page.

Washington

Department of Licensing, Securities Division, 405 Black Lake Blvd., SW, Olympia, 98507-9033, 206-753-6928. No charge for orders under 30 pages, then 10 cents for each page thereafter, plus tax.

Wisconsin

Franchise Investment Division, Wisconsin Securities Commission, PO Box 1768, 111 West Wilson Street, Madison, 53701, 608-266-3414/3364. Wisconsin does not provide copies of franchise agreements. One must come in person or hire a private service.

Every Company Has To File With The State

State documents on 9,000,000 public and private companies have hit the computer age. Nine states already offer online access to their files and 15 states intend to follow suit within the next year. Computerized records are such a major issue with state officials who administer corporate division offices that they have placed online access on their annual convention agenda. Furthermore, 27 states will make their complete file available on magnetic tape, and, I should say, at bargain prices. And if you are not computerized, all but a few states offer free telephone research services. Here are a dozen ways to ferret out current information on companies:

- a list of companies by SIC code within a given state or county
- names and addresses of a company's officers and directors
- a list of all new companies incorporated in a given week or month
- the location of any company with a single phone call
- a mailing list of 300,000 companies for $100
- the availability of a given company name
- a complete list of non-profit organizations
- list of companies by city, zip, date of incorporation, or size of capital stock
- a mailing list of limited partnerships
- a listing of companies on which a given individual is an officer or board member
- a listing of trademarks for a given state
- what companies in a given state are subsidiaries of a given company

Financial Data and Other Documents on File

Although there are variations, most all states maintain the following documents for every company doing business in their state: Certificate of Good Standing; Articles of Incorporation; Reinstated Articles of Incorporation; Articles of Amendment; Articles of Merger; Articles of Correction; Articles of Dissolution; Certificate of Incorporation; Certificate of Authority; and Annual Report (which contains list of officers and directors).

All states require corporations to file the original Articles of Incorporation, a yearly annual report and amendments to the Articles of Incorporation. Clerks can provide you with certifications of good standing stating that the corporation has complied with the regulation to file a yearly annual report. A certificate of good standing does not assure financial stability, but is only a statement that the corporation has abided by the law. You may obtain a statement of name availability if you are searching for a name for your new corporation. Most states require prepayment for copies of documents. You can mail them a blank check stipulating the amount not to exceed a certain amount. You may want to call the phone information number for details before sending in your written request.

Only a few states require financial information in their annual

reports. However, every state requires companies to list the value of the capital stock in their Articles of Incorporation. Some states, such as Massachusetts used to require financial data in the past, so it may be useful to request annual reports of previous years.

Data on Six Different Types of Companies

The types of companies required to file documents with the state include: Domestic Companies (those incorporated within the state), Foreign Companies (those incorporated in another state, but doing business in the state), Partnerships, Limited Partnerships, Non-Profit Organizations, Business Names (incorporated and non-incorporated firms). It should be emphasized that all public and private companies as well as subsidiaries of public corporations are required to reveal this information.

Company Information Available in Numerous Formats

Each state provides information about corporations in some or all of the following formats:

1) Telephone, Mail and Walk-In Services:
Telephone information lines have been established in all but one state to respond to inquiries regarding the status of a specific corporation. New Jersey and North Dakota charge for phone service. The NJ Expedite Service allows you to receive information over the phone and charge the cost of the service to your credit card. Another option for New Jersey company information is to have it sent via Western Union's electronic mail service.

Telephone operators can verify corporate names, identify the resident agent and his address, the date of incorporation, the type of corporation (foreign, domestic, etc.), and the amount of capital stock. Often these operators can either take your request for documents on file pertaining to a corporation or they can refer you to the appropriate number. Names of officers and directors are never given over the phone. This information is usually contained in a company's annual report, copies of which can be requested by phone or letter.

These state telephone lines tend to be quite busy. It is not unusual for the larger offices of a corporation to answer over 1200 inquiries a day. Persistence and patience are essential on your part. Requests for copies of documents usually require prepayment. You can mail them a blank check stipulating the amount not to exceed a certain amount. You may want to call the phone information number for details before sending in your written request.

Walk-in service, with access to all documents, is an option in every state. However, if you do not want to do the research yourself, most every state can suggest private firms which will obtain the pertinent data for you.

2) Mailing Labels:

The following six states will print mailing labels of companies on file: Arizona, Idaho, Maine, New Mexico, Mississippi, and Nebraska. However, over half the states will sell you a computer tape of their files, from which mailing labels can be generated easily by a good mailhouse or service bureau.

3) Computer Tape Files:

Currently 27 states will provide you with magnetic tapes of their corporate files. The cost is very reasonable, and in many cases the state will require the user to supply blank tapes.

4) Custom Services:

Many of the states provide custom services with outputs ranging from computer printouts and magnetic tape files to statistical tables. Such services are a valuable way to obtain specific listings of corporations such all non-profit corporations or all companies within a given SIC code. Most states that offer this option compute cost by figuring time, programming time, and printing expense.

5) New Companies:

Most all of the states offer some type of periodic listing of newly formed companies. As a rule, these can be purchased on a daily, weekly, or monthly subscription basis.

6) Microfiche and Microfilm:

Eleven of the states will also sell you copies of their documents on microfiche or microfilm at a nominal fee.

7) Online Access:

As mentioned earlier, nine states now provide online access to their files, and 15 other states are in the active planning stages. The states currently with online systems include:

* Alaska - available through Motznik Computer Service
* Arizona - their only customer for this service is Dun and Bradstreet
* Florida - available through CompuServe
* Georgia - available through Information America
* Illinois - available through Mead Data Central
* Missouri - available through Mead Data Central
* New Mexico - available through New Mexico Technet
* Oklahoma - their only customer for this service is Dun and Bradstreet
* Texas - available through Information America

State Corporation Divisions

Alabama

Division of Corporation, Secretary of State, 4121 Carmichael Road, Montgomery, AL 36106 or P.O. Box 5616, Montgomery, AL 36103-5616, 205-242-5324; Selected Publications: *Guide to Incorporation*. Phone Information: 205-242-5324. Office is not completely computerized yet, but can do word search or partial name search by officer, incorporator, or serving agent. Copies of Documents on File: Available by written request for $1 per page plus $5 for certified copies. Mailing Labels: No. Magnetic Tape: No. Microfiche: No. New Corporate Listings: No. Custom Searches: Can do word search or partial name search. Online Access: Yes. Dial-up Program available. No fee for this pilot program. Contact Robina Jenkins, 205-242-5974. This office is in the process of being computerized. In 1992, when fully on computer access, fee for online service may be charged. Number of Active Corporations on File: Figures not available.

Alaska

State of Alaska, Division of Banking, Securities and Corporation, Corporation Section, P.O. Box 110808, Juneau, AK 99811-0808, 907-465-2530. Selected Publications: *Establishing Business in Alaska* ($3), from State of Alaska, Division of Economic Development, P.O. Box 110808, Juneau, AK 99811-0808. Phone Information: 907-465-2530. Copies of Documents on File: Complete corporate record (Articles of Incorporation, annual report, amendments, etc.). Certified copies cost $20, list of Officers and Directors cost $1, Certificate of Status cost $25. Mailing Labels: No. Magnetic Tape: IBM- compatible. Copy of complete master file, excluding Officers and Directors is priced at $100. Hard copy directory is $65. Weekly supplements are an additional $5. Requester must supply blank tape. Microfiche: Yes. Complete file for $6. New Corporate Listings: No. Custom Searches: Available directly from them soon. Online Access: Yes. Contact Mike Monagle, 907-465-2530. Other: Printouts are available by corporation, SIC code, and zip code for $25 per list. Number of Active Corporations on File: 23,000.

Arizona

Arizona Corporations Division, Records Division, Secretary of State, 1200 W. Washington, Phoenix, AZ 85007 or P.O. Box 6019, Phoenix, AZ 85005, 602-542-3026. Selected Publications: Sample packet with forms and statutes mailed for $4. Guideline booklets will be available soon. Phone Information: 602-542-3026. Copies of Documents on File: Cost 50 cents per page, $5 for certified copies. Mailing Labels: No. Magnetic Tape: Master File $400, issued monthly. Requester must supply blank tape. Microfiche: All corporations statewide $75. New Corporate Listing: Monthly Listing of New Domestic Companies for $200 plus $200 for new foreign listings. Custom Searches: No. Can search by title or cross-reference by statutory agent only. Online Access: Yes. Available through Information America (1-800-235-4008), Dunn and Bradstreet and other commercial services. Number of Corporations on File: 100,000.

Arkansas

Secretary of State, Corporations Division, State Capitol Building, Room 058, Little Rock, AR 72201, 501-682-5151. Selected Publications: *Corporate Guide*. Phone Information: 501-682-5151. Copies of Documents on File: Call 501-371-3431 for copies at 50 cents a page plus $5 for certified copies. Mailing Labels: No. Magnetic Tape: Master file 2 cents per name. Microfiche: No. New Corporate Listing: Statistics only. Custom Searches: Categories include foreign, domestic, profit, and non-profit corporations. Cost: 2 cents per name, 50 cents per page. Online Access: Contact Philip Hoots at 501-682-3411. Number of Active Corporations on File: 1000,000.

California

Corporations, Supervisor of Records, Secretary of State, 1230 J Street Sacramento, CA 95814, 916-324-1485. Selected Publications: *Corporations Checklist Booklet*. Request must be in writing and cost is $5. Phone Information: Name Availability at 916-322-2387, Forms and Samples at 916-445-0620. Copies of Documents on File: Cost is $1 for first page, 50 cents for each additional page plus $5 for certified copies (written requests only). You must pay in advance or send check stating limit. Mailing Labels: No. Magnetic Tape: Yes. You must supply the tapes or be charged $24 for tape. Charges for making 22 tapes is $300. Contact Kevin Tibown. Categories: Active $521; Active Stock $427; Active Non-Stock $150; Active Non-Stock by Classification $150 per tape. Microfiche: No. Custom Searches: Computer generated listing of Active Stock ($17,030), Active Non-Stock ($422), Active Non-Stock by Classification $150 per list. Contact: Patricia Gastelum, Management Services Division, Information Systems Section, 1230 J Street, Suite 242, Sacramento, CA 95814, 916-322-0418. All orders must be submitted in writing. Basic cost of magnetic tape copy is $1.02 per 1,000 names. Basic cost of same run, for custom search, printed on paper, is $4.13 per 1,000 names. $150 minimum is applied to both. Online Access: No. Number of Corporations on File: 1,050,000.

Colorado

Corporate Division, Secretary of State, 1560 Broadway, Suite 200, Denver, CO 80202, 303-894-2251. Selected Publications: *Corporate Guide*. Copies of Documents on File: Cost is $1 a page, plus $5 for certification. Mailing Labels: No. Magnetic Tape: Available for $500 for complete set of five. Tapes must be purchased individually. Categories: Foreign and Domestic. Microfiche: Available at $1 a sheet (includes Summary of Master Computer File, total of 60-75 sheets - must be purchased in its entirety). New Corporate Listings: Reporting Service costs $200 a year. Weekly List of New Corporations. Written requests only. Custom Searches: Yes. Categories: Foreign and Domestic available on a cost recovery basis. The minimum fee is $50. Online Access: Available. Contact Patty Webb, 303-894-2200, ext. 300. Fee is $300 for 3 months or $1,000 per year. Number of Corporations on File: 235,000.

Connecticut

Office of Secretary of State, Division of Corporations, 30 Trinity Street, Hartford, CT 06106, 203-566-2448. Selected Publications: None, but to get a copy of *The Connecticut Law Book*, call 203-458-8000 or 203-741-3027. Phone Information: 203-566-8570. Copies of Documents on File: Fees are $6 for plain copy, $12 for certified. Written requests only. Mailing Labels: No. Magnetic Tape: Copy of master file $110. Requester must provide tapes. Microfiche: No. New Corporate Listing: No. Custom Searches: No. Online Access: Not at this time, but Southern New England Telephone (SNET) is working on a pilot program which should be available soon. Number of Corporations on File: 325,000.

Delaware

Delaware Department of State, Division of Corporations, Secretary of State, P.O. Box 898, Dover, DE 19903, 302-739-3073. Selected Publications: *Incorporating in Delaware*. Phone Information: 302-739-3073. Copies of Documents on File: Available at $1 per page plus $20 for certification, $100 for long forms of good standing. Contains all documents on the corporation. Requests may be faxed to 302-739-3812, but written requests are preferred. Requests must be paid for in advance. Call for number of pages. Documents filed prior to 1983 are not on computer and must be requested in writing. They offer Corporate Expedited Services (same day or 24-hour service) to file or retrieve certified documents. Additional fee is $20. You can pay by MasterCard or Visa and it is sent by Federal Express. Mailing Labels: No. Magnetic Tape: No. Microfiche: No. New Corporate Listings: Monthly New Corporation Listing. Fees are $10 per month which can be paid in advance for 6 months or a year. Contact Karen Scaggs. Custom Searches: Yes. Categories include foreign and domestic which are available on cost recovery basis. For manual search of foreign corporations, the fee is $30. Online Access: Not available. Number of Active Corporations on File: 212,000.

District of Columbia

Corporations Division, Consumer and Regulatory Affairs, 614 H Street, N.W., Room 407, Washington, DC 20001, 202-727-7278. Selected Publications: *Guideline and Instruction Sheet for Profit, Non-Profit, Foreign, or Domestic*. Phone Information: 202-727-7283. Copies of Documents on File: Available for $5 each (all copies certified). Mailing Labels: Will be available in near future. Profit and non-profit lists updated quarterly. Magnetic Tape: No. Microfiche: No. New Corporate Listings No. Custom Searches: Computer searches on agents are available. Online Access: Possibly available in 1993. Number of Active Corporations on File: 40,000.

Florida

Division of Corporations, Secretary of State, PO Box 6327, Tallahassee, FL 32314, 904-487-6000. Selected Publications: *Copy of the Law Chapter 607* (corporate law). Forms included. (Publications on laws of non-profit corporations and limited partnerships also available.) Phone Information: 904-488-9000. Limit of up to 3 inquiries per call. No charge to receive hard copy of microfiche on the corporations. Copy of Documents on File: Available at $1 per page if you do it yourself. Written requests must be paid for advance: $1 for non-certified annual report; $10 for plain copy of complete file; $52.50 for any certified document including complete file. Microfiche: Yes. Contact Frank Reinhart or Ed Bagnell at Anacomp 813-289-1608. Categories: Officers and Directors, Registered Agents and Domestic Corporations $250; Foreign, Non-Profit $85, Limited Partnerships $50, Trademarks $75 (addresses are included). Magnetic Tape: No. New Corporate Listings: No. Custom Searches: No. Online Access: Available on CompuServe, 1-800-848-8199. Address written request to Attn: Public Access, Division of Corporations 904-487-6866. Ask for a CompuServe Intro-Pak. Charge for connect time is $24 per hour, plus $12.50 per hour additional corporate access fee. Both are prorated by time used. CompuServe can be contacted directly at South Eastern Information Systems, P.O. Box 6867, Tallahassee, FL 32314, Attn: Keith Meyer, 904-656-4500. As of February, 1992, Anacomp will handle. Contact Eileen Self, 904-487-6073 for service. Number of Active Corporations on File: 691,000.

Georgia

Division of Business Services and Regulation, Secretary of State, Suite 306, West Tower #2, Martin Luther King Drive, S.E., Atlanta, GA 30334, 404-656-2185.

Selected Publications: None, but information package sent upon request. Phone Information: 404-656-2817. Copies of Documents on File: Available for at least a minimum of $10 and all copies certified. Bills will be sent for orders over $10. Mailing Labels: No. Magnetic Tape: Master file available for $600 a month if you supply the tape. Add $18 if they supply tape. Microfiche: No. New Corporate Listings: Quarterly Listing of New Corporations on magnetic tape. There are three lists which include Fulton County, the remainder of the state and foreign. Cost is $25 each. Send written requests to James Gullion. Custom Searches: No. Online Access: Available by subscription through Information America at 404-892-1800. Connect fee is $50. Access time is 55 cents per minute. Monthly service charge is $25-$55 per month depending on size of the firm. Number of Active Corporations on File: 200,000.

Hawaii

Business Registration Division, Department of Commerce and Consumer Affairs, 1010 Richards Street, PO Box 40, Honolulu, HI 96810, 808-586-2727. Selected Publications: None. Phone Information: 808-586-2727. Copies of Documents on File: Available at 25 cents per page, plus 10 cents per page for certified copies. Expedited service available for $10 fee plus 25 cents per sheet, plus $1 per page. Mailing Labels: No. Magnetic Tape: No. Microfiche: No. New Corporate Listing: Weekly printout available but only for walk-ins. Custom Searches: No. Online Access: Available through FYI for no charge. Call 808-536-7133 (direct access number) or 808-586-1919. Number of Active Corporations on File: 45,000.

Idaho

Corporate Division, Secretary of State, Room 203, Statehouse, Boise, ID 83720, 208-334-2300. Selected Publications: *Idaho Corporation Law*. Phone Information: 208-334-2300. Copies of Documents on File: Available at 25 cents per page, $2 for certified copies. Mailing Labels: Very flexible and may be combined with custom search. Fee is $10 for computer base, 25 cents for first 100 pages, 10 cents for next 500 pages, and 5 cents per page thereafter. Magnetic Tape: Available for $20 per tape if you supply the tape. They will supply diskette for additional $10. Microfiche: Available for $10, 50 cents for each additional copy of same. Custom Searches: Available on basis of serving agent, profit, non-profit, type, status, state and jurisdiction. Very flexible. Same prices and categories apply to labels, microfiche and custom search. You supply the tapes or they will at cost. Contact Everett Wholers. New Corporate Listing: No, but published weekly in *The Idaho Business Review*. Online Access: Available through Data Share Program. Fee is $150 per year plus $18 per hour plus telephone line charges. Number of Active Corporations on File: 30,000.

Illinois

Corporations Division, Centennial Building, Room 328, Springfield, IL 62756, 217-782-6961. Selected Publications: *Guide for Organizing (Domestic, Non-profit, or Foreign)*. Phone Information: 217-782-7880. Copies of Documents on File: Available at $5 per page up to first 10 pages; 50 cents for each page thereafter. Fee is $10 for first 10 certified copies; 50 cents for each page thereafter. Mailing Labels: No. Magnetic Tape: Yes. Categories: Domestic and Foreign cost $1,500; Not-for-Profit cost $1,500. You must supply tape. Microfiche: Only condominiums list available for $150. New Corporate Listings: Daily list of newly formed corporations costs $318 per year; Monthly List priced at $180 per year. Custom Searches: No. Other: Certified List of Domestic and Foreign Corporations (Address of Resident Agent included) costs $38 for two volume set. Online Access: Available from Mead Data Central (LEXIS), 9393 Springboro Pike, P.O. Box 933, Dayton, OH 45401, Contact: Diane Fisher at 1-800-227-4908, ext. 6382. Cost is $500 per month. Number of Active Corporations on File: 240,000.

Indiana

Office of Corporation, Secretary of State, Room E018, 302 West Washington Street, Indianapolis, IN 46204, 317-232-6582. Selected Publications: *Indiana Corporation Guide*. Phone Information: 317-232-6576. Copies of Documents on File: Available at $1 per page and $15 to certify. May pay in advance or be billed. Mailing Labels: No. Magnetic Tape: No. Microfiche: No. New Corporate Listings: Daily Listing is published monthly for $20 a month. Custom Searches: No. Online Access: Available. Tapes made into computer database by Mead Data (LEXIS), 1-800-634-9738 and Information America, 1-800-235-4008. Contact Bob Gardner, 317-232-6691. Number of Active Corporations on File: 200,000.

Iowa

Corporate Division, Secretary of State, Hoover State Office Building, Des Moines, IA 50319, 515-281-5204. Selected Publications: *Iowa Profit Corporations*.

Phone Information: 515-281-5204. Copies of Documents on File: Available at $1 per page; certified copies cost $5. Mailing Labels: No. Magnetic Tape: Master file costs $165; detailed domestic profit $415; domestic non-profit $160 and requester must supply tape. Microfiche: No. New Corporate Listings: No. Custom Searches: Searches by Chapters of Incorporation (profit, non-profit, etc.) and or. Cost determined at time of request. Online Access: Available through Dial Up Program. Contact Allen Welsh at 515-281-8363. Cost is $150 per year, 30 cents per minute plus telephone charges. Number of Active Corporations on File: 97,000.

Kansas

Corporate Division, Secretary of State, Capitol Building, Second Floor, Topeka, KS 66612, 913-296-4564. Selected Publications: None. Will send out forms with instruction sheets. Phone Information: 913-296-4564. Copies of Documents on File: Available at 50 cents per page plus $7.50 for certified copies (written requests only). Must be paid for in advance. Mailing Labels: No. Magnetic Tape: Available. Master file costs $2,000. Microfiche: No. Other: Microfilm is available for $25 a roll plus $7.50 postage for up to 50 rolls. Master File on magnetic tape will be needed to use. Contact Cathy Martin. New Corporate Listings: No. Custom Searches: No. May be available in the future. Online Access: No. May be available in near future. Number of Active Corporations on File: 66,000.

Kentucky

Corporate Division, Secretary of State, Room 154, Capitol Building, Frankfort, KY 40601, 502-564-2848. Selected Publications: *Rules & Laws Manual* ($8). Phone Information: 502-564-7336. Copies of Documents on File: Mail in request with payment. Call 502-564-7330 to obtain number of copies in advance. Cost is 50 cents per page; $5 for certified copies. Mailing Label: No. Magnetic Tape: Available for $250. Tape contains all profit and non-profit corporations on file. Microfiche: No. New Corporate Listings: Available for $50 a month. Custom Searches: No. Online Access: No, but is being considered. Number of Active Corporations on File: 80,000.

Louisiana

Corporate Division, Secretary of State, 3851 Essen Lane, Baton Rouge, LA 70809, 504-925-4704. Selected Publications: *Corporate Law Book* ($6). Phone Information: 504-925-4704. Copies of Documents on File: Available starting at $10 for certified articles. Cost for total file is $20. Mailing Label: No. Magnetic Tape: Available in the future. Microfiche: No. New Corporate Listing: Weekly Newsletter at no charge. (Requester must supply large pre-addressed envelope). Custom Searches: No. Online Access: Dial Up Access, using a 900 number, will be available after January, 1992. Number of Active Corporations on File: 120,000.

Maine

Information and Report Section, Bureau of Corporations, Secretary of State, State House Station 101, Augusta, ME 04333, 207-289-4195. Selected Publications: *Guide to Completing Forms of Incorporation* (Blue Guide). Phone Information: 207-289-4195. Copies of Documents on File: Available for $1 per page, plus $5 for certified copies. Mailing Labels: No. Magnetic tape: No, but hope to have it in the near future. Contact Rebecca Wyke at 207-289-6308. Microfiche: No. New Corporate Listings: Monthly Corporations Listing costs $8. Contact Betsy at 207-289-4183. Custom Searches: No, but hope to have it in near future. Online Access: No. Number of Active Corporations on File: 40,000.

Maryland

Corporate Charter Division, Department of Assessments and Taxation, 301 W. Preston Street, Baltimore, Maryland 21201, 410-225-1330. Selected Publications: *Guide to Corporations*. Phone Information: 410-225-1330. Copies of Documents on File: Available for $1 per page, plus $6 for certified copies for walk-ins. If they make copy there is a $20 expediting fee. Mailing Labels: No. Magnetic Tape: Available for $250 weekly. Infrequent requests cost $425. Microfiche: No. New Corporate Listings: Monthly Corporate Computer Printout costs $25 a month. Custom Searches: Not at this time. Online Access: Hope to have in near future. Number of Active Corporations on File: 300,000.

Massachusetts

Corporate Division, Secretary of State, 1 Ashburton Place, Boston, MA 02108, 617-727-2850. Selected Publications: *Organizing a Business Corporation, Organizing a Non-Profit Corporation, When You Need Information About Corporations in Massachusetts, Choose a Name for Your Business, Compendium*

of Corporate Law ($15). Phone Information: 617-727-2850. Copies of Documents on File: Available for 20 cents per page (send a minimum of 80 cents), $12 for certified copies. Mailing Labels: No. Magnetic Tape: Cost is $300 for copy of master file and record layout. Requester must supply tapes. Microfiche: No. New Corporate Listings: Semi-monthly Filings cost $15; Quarterly Filings cost $50; bi-weekly printout cost $15. Custom Searches: Available on a cost recovery basis. Online Access: Direct Access program. Cost is $149 annually. Connect time is 40 cents per minute. Number of Corporations on File: 375,000.

Michigan

Corporation Division, Corporation and Securities Bureau, Michigan Department of Commerce, PO Box 30054, 6546 Mercantile, Lansing, MI, 48909, 517-334-6302. Selected Publications: None. Phone Information: 517-334-6311. Copies of Documents on File: Available at a minimum of $6 for 6 pages or less, $1 for each page thereafter. Certified copies cost $10. (Request a price list.) Mailing Labels: No. Magnetic Tape: No. Microfiche: Available for $145. New Corporate Listings: Monthly Listing costs $90 per month. Custom Searches: No. Online Access: Available through Information America, 1-800-235-4008 or Mead Data, 313-259-1156. Number of Corporations on File: 251,000.

Minnesota

Corporate Division, Secretary of State, 180 State Office building, St. Paul, MN 55155, 612-296-2803. Selected Publications: *Guide to Starting a Business in Minnesota*. Phone Information: 612-296-2803. Copies of Documents on File: Available for $3 per document, $8 for certified copies. Mailing Labels: Yes. Categories: Domestic, Limited Partnerships, Non-profits, Foreign, Foreign Limited, Foreign Non-profits, Trademarks, Business Trusts. Cost determined at time of request. Magnetic Tape: No. Microfiche: Available documents on file (Articles of Incorporation, annual reports, amendments) cost 21 cents sheet plus filing or retrieval fees. Paper copy of microfiche is $6 per corporation for complete file. $3 for articles of incorporation. New Corporate Listings: Daily Log costs 25 cents per page. Custom Searches: Available on a cost recovery basis. Categories same as for mailing labels. Online Access: Direct Access available for $50 annually plus transaction charge of $1 to $4. Number of Corporations on File: 194,500.

Mississippi

Office of Corporations, Secretary of State, PO Box 136, Jackson, MS 39205, 601-359-1350 or mailing address: 202 N. Congress, Suite 601, Jackson, MS 39201. Selected Publications: None. Phone Information: 601-359-1627. Copies of Documents on File: Available at $1 per page plus $10 for certified copies. Mailing Labels: No. Magnetic Tape: Available for $200 for set of 2. You are to supply tapes. Microfiche: No. New Corporate Listings: Monthly Listing costs $25. Custom Searches: Available to limited extent. Printout costs $2 per page. Online Access: Yes. $250 sign-up fee, plus flat monthly fee. $50 is monthly minimum for first 100 transactions. Contact Sheryl Crawford at 601-359-1548. Number of Active Corporations on File: 80,000. This office has converted to an automated system with advanced search capabilities.

Missouri

Corporate Division, Secretary of State, 301 High Street, PO Box 77, Jefferson City, MO 65102, 314-751-4194. Selected Publications: *Corporation Handbook*. Phone Information: 314-751-4153. Copies of Documents on File: Available at 50 cents per page plus $5 for certified copies. Send in written requests and they will bill. Mailing Labels: No. Magnetic Tape: Cost is between $100 and $200 for copy of master file. Contact Sara Welch at 314-751-5832. Microfiche: No. New Corporate Listings: Not usually, but can be set up on special request. Custom Searches: No. Online Access: Available through Mead Data Central (LEXIS), 9393 Springboro Pike, PO Box 933, Dayton, OH 45401, 513-865-6800; Prentice-Hall, Dunn and Bradstreet or Information America. Direct Dial Up access is available through the State Access Center. Contact John Bluma at 314-751-4780 or Sara Welch at 314-751-5832. Number of Active Corporations on File: 140,000.

Montana

Corporate Department, Secretary of State, Capitol Station, Helena, MT 59620, 406-444-3665. Selected Publications: None. Phone Information: 406-444-3665. Copies of Documents on File: Available for 50 cents per page; $2 for certification. Mailing Labels: No. Magnetic Tape: No. Microfiche: No. New Corporate Listings: No. Custom Searches: No, but can search by name of corporation only. Online Access: No. Number of Active Corporations on File: 33,000.

Company Intelligence

Nebraska

Corporate Division, Secretary of State, State Capitol, Lincoln, NE 68509, 402-471-4079. Selected Publications: None. Phone Information: 402-471-4079. Copies of Documents on File: Available for $1 per page, $10 for certified copies. Will bill for requests under $50. Mailing Labels: Available on a cost recovery basis. Can do for entire data base only. Contact Mr. Englert at 402-471-2554. Magnetic Tape: Available on a cost recovery basis. Also contact Mr. Englert. Microfiche: No. New Corporate Listings: Available upon request. Will set up for number of issues customer requests. $100 per issuance. Custom Searches: No. Online Access: No. Number of Active Corporations on File: 50,000.

Nevada

Office of Corporations, Secretary of State, Capitol Complex, Carson City, NV 89710, 702-687-5203. Selected Publications: *Guidelines*. Phone Information: Corporate Status call 702-687-5105. Copies of Documents on File: Available for $1 per page, $10 for certified copies. Written request only, prepayment required (send a blank check stating limit). Mailing Labels: No. Magnetic Tape: Copy of master file available. Corporations takes 2 tapes which requester supplies. Cost per tape is $25. Microfiche: No. New Corporate Listings: Monthly Listing of New Corporations costs $25 a month. Custom Searches: Yes. Searches may be done by location of resident agent and other ways. Cost determined at time of request. Other: A three volume listing of corporations on file, in the "Alpha Listing", is published twice a year which includes names of active and inactive corporations but not addresses. Cost for set is $25. Contact Cindy Woodgate. Online Access: Dial Up Direct Access through subscription service. Your computer needs a communication pack and you must set up trust account from which $24.50 per hour, prorated by actual minutes used, will be deducted. For ID number and password, contact Cindy Woodgate. Number of Active Corporations on File: 60,000.

New Hampshire

Corporate Division, Secretary of State, State House, Room 204, Concord, NH 03301, 603-271-3244. Selected Publications: *How to Start a Business*, *New Hampshire Corporate Law*. Phone Information: 603-271-3246. Copies of Documents on File: Available for $1 per page, plus $5 for certified copies. Mailing Labels: No. Magnetic Tape: No. Microfiche: Complete listing of all registrations. No breakdown by type of entity (updated monthly). Annual Subscription costs $200. New Corporate Listings: Monthly Subscriber List costs $15 plus postage. Custom Searches: No. Other: Booklet listing all non-profit corporations is available for $45. Online Access: No. Number of Active Corporations on File: 33,000.

New Jersey

Commercial Recording Division, Secretary of State, 820 Bear Tavern Road, West Trenton, NJ 08628, (Mailing address: CN 308), 609-530-6400. Selected Publications: *Corporate Filing Packet*. Phone Information: General Information call 609-530-6405; Forms call 609-292-0013; Expedite Service call 609-984-7107. There is a charge for standard information, $5 look-up fee for each request plus $10 expedite fee. User may use VISA or Master Charge for payment. Answers available by phone, mail or Western Union Electronic Mail. Requests and answering copies may be done through FAX at 609-530-6433. Copies of Documents on File: Available for $10 plus $15 for certified copies. Mailing Labels: No. Magnetic Tape: No. Microfiche: No. New Corporate Listings: Monthly List of Corporations costs $100 per month. Custom Searches: Numerous search capabilities are available. Each request is reviewed on individual basis. Requester is billed for computer time. Online Access: No. Number of Active Corporations on File: 436,314.

New Mexico

State Corporation Commission, PO Drawer 1269, Santa Fe, NM 87504-1269, 505-827-4502. Selected Publications: None. Phone Information: 505-827-4504. Copies of Documents on File: Available for 75 cents per page, plain copy; $1 per page for certified copy. Mailing Labels: No. Magnetic Tape: No. Microfiche: No. New Corporate Listings: Yes. Monthly listings available. Requester must send manilla self-addressed envelope. Online Access: Available through New Mexico Technet, 4100 Osuna N.E., Albuquerque, NM 87109, 505-345-6555. You may also pay the same charge as the State by purchasing it directly from the Corporation Division. They will bill you for usage monthly. Contact Mr. Salinas at 505-827-4502. Custom Searches: Yes. Categories: Corporate Name, Domestic or Foreign, Profit or Non-profit, Date of Incorporation, Active or Inactive, Identification Number, Amount of Capital Stock, Authorized Stock, Instrument file, Principal Office Address, Officers and Directors Names (includes addresses, Social Security

numbers and titles), Name of Incorporators, Registered Agent and Office, Good Standing Status, Parent/Subsidiary Information. Call or put request in writing. Only a limited number of custom searches can be performed each month. Number of Active Corporations on File: 50,000.

New York

New York State, Department of State, Division of Corporations, 162 Washington Avenue, Albany, NY 12231, 518-474-6200. Selected Publications: *Extract of Laws for Incorporating*. Phone Information: 518-474-6200. Copies of Documents on File: Available for $5 per document, $10 for certified copies. Mailing Labels: No. Magnetic Tape: No. Microfiche: No. New Corporate Listing: Report of Corporations is printed daily and mailed out every other day. It is available by subscription only for $125 per year, $75 for 6 months or $40 for 3 months. Online Access: Available in the near future. Number of Corporations on File: 1,200,000.

North Carolina

Division of Corporation, Secretary of State, 300 N. Salisbury Street, Raleigh, NC 27603-5909, 919-733-4201. Selected Publications: *North Carolina Business Corporation Guidelines*, *North Carolina's Non-profit Corporation Handbook*. Phone Information: 919-733-4201. Copies of Documents on File: Available for $1 per page, $5 for certified copies. Mailing Labels: No. Magnetic Tape: Available on cost recovery basis. To make a request, write Bonnie Elek. Categories: All active corporations, foreign, domestic, non-profit, and profit. Microfiche: No. New Corporate Listings: Available for $20 per month and issued in hard copy only. Custom Searches: Yes. Categories: Type of Corporation, Professional Corporations, Insurance Corporations, Banks, and Savings and Loans. Not available for the type of business a corporation conducts. This may be available in the future. Online Access: Available. Number of Active Corporations on File: 180,000.

North Dakota

Corporation Division, Secretary of State, Capitol Building, 600 East Boulevard Avenue, Bismarck, ND 58505, 701-224-2905. Selected Publications: *North Dakota Business Corporation Act Statute*, $3. Phone Information: 701-224-4284. Copies of Documents on File: Search of records cost $5, four pages for $1, $10 for certified copies. Written or phone requests accepted. Requester will be billed for phone orders. Mailing Labels: No. Magnetic Tape: No. Microfiche: No. New Corporate Listings: Monthly Corporation List costs $10 per month. Custom Searches: No. Online Access: No, but may be available in the future. Number of Active Corporations on File: 22,500.

Ohio

Corporation Division, Secretary of State, 30 East Broad Street, 14th Floor, Columbus, OH 43266-0418, 614-466-3910. Selected Publications: *Corporate Checklist*. Phone Information: Corporate Status call 614-466-3910; Name Availability call 614-466-0590. Copies of Documents on File: Contact 614-466-1776. Available for $1 per page, $5 for certified copies. Mailing Labels: No. Magnetic Tape: Available for $125 for 6,250 corporation names, thereafter the cost is 2 cents per corporate name with a maximum of 25,000 names. Microfiche: No. New Corporate Listing: Call 614-466-8464. Weekly County-Wide Listing costs 25 cents per page, Weekly Statewide Listing costs 10 cents per page ($45 a month). Custom Searches: Yes. Categories: location (county), Foreign, Domestic, Profit, Non-Profit. Price structure is same as for Magnetic tape. Online Access: No. Number of Active Corporations on File: 400,000.

Oklahoma

Corporations, Secretary of State, 101 State Capitol Building, Oklahoma City, OK 73105, 405-521-3911. Selected Publications: *Forms and Procedures to Incorporate*. Phone Information: 1-900-820-2424 for record search. Charge is $3 per call. Copies of Documents on File: Available for $1 per page, $5 for certified copies. Mailing Labels: No. Magnetic Tape: $5 per tape which is supplied by requester. Microfiche: No. New Corporate Listings: Monthly Charter List costs $150 a month, plus Amendments $250 a month plus postage. Custom Searches: No. Online Access: Contact Beverly Curry at Information Systems, 404-892-1800. They purchase magnetic tape of Division's master file weekly to make a database which is complete except for new names. Number of Corporations on File (Active and Inactive): 224,159.

Oregon

Corporation Division, Department of Commerce, 158 12th Street N.E., Salem, OR 97310, 503-378-4166. Selected Publications: *Business Organizations, Assumed Trademarks, and Securities (BOATS)*. Phone Information: 503-378-4166. Copies of Documents on File: Available for $5 for all documents in a corporation's file except annual report. Annual reports are an additional $5. Certification fee is $15. Mailing Labels: No. Magnetic Tape: Complete master file costs $190. Contact Joy Lorenz at 503-373-7920. Requester must provide tape or charge will be an additional $20 per tape. Microfiche: No. New Corporate Listings: Statistical Report of New Corporations is available for $17 per monthly issue. Custom Searches: Yes. Numerous categories with a minimum charge of $150. Address inquiries to Attn: Joy Lorenz. Online Access: Yes. Contact Joy Lorenz, 503-373-7920). Charges include $100 for hookup, $70 monthly fee, plus telephone charges and prorated computer time with a minimum $10 charge. Total minimum monthly cost is $80. Cost of average user is $100 per month. Mead Data, Information America and Dunn and Bradstreet also have database. Number of Active Corporations on File: 56,000.

Pennsylvania

Corporation Bureau, 308 N. Office Building, Harrisburg, PA 17120, 717-787-1997. Selected Publications: *Corporate Guide* (currently under revision). Phone Information: 717-787-1057. Copies of Documents on File: Available for $2 per page, $12 search fee, $28 for certified copies. Mailing Labels: No. Magnetic Tape: Copy of master file available for $900 per tape, Requester must supply 11 blank tapes. Microfiche: No. New Corporate Listings: County or area listing available for 25 cents per name. Custom Searches: Yes. Categories: Non-Profit, Domestic, Foreign, county location, Limited Partnerships, Fictitious name, Trademarks, Foreign Non-profits, Cooperatives, Professional Corporations 25 cents per name). Online Access: Available from Information America at 404-892-1800; Prentice-Hall, Legal and Financial Services at 518-458-8111; or Mead Data Central at 513-865-6800. Number of Corporations on File: 616,000.

Rhode Island

Corporations Division, Secretary of State, 100 North Main Street, Providence, RI 02903, 401-277-3040. Selected Publications: Instruction sheet, *The Rhode Island Law Book* ($10). Phone Information: 401-277-3040. Staff will look up two corporations per call. Copies of Documents on File: Available for 50 cents per page, $5 for certified sheet. Mailing Labels: No. Magnetic Tape: Available for $250 per tape. Requester supplies tape. They will put their database on disc. You supply 5 1/4 disc, MAG high density. Printouts cost 50 cents per page. There approximately 11 names per page. Microfiche: No. New Corporate Listings: Not usually provided. New corporate listings are published weekly in *The Providence Journal*, Sunday Business Section. Send a letter requesting weekly printouts. Custom Searches: No. Online Access: No. Number of Active Corporations on File: 90,000.

South Carolina

Division of Corporations, Secretary of State, PO Box 11350, Columbia, SC 29211, 803-734-2158. Selected Publications: None. Phone Information: 803-734-2158. Copies of Documents on File: Available for $1 for first page, 50 cents thereafter. $2 for plain charter and $4 for certified charter. Amendments are $1 per page thereafter and it costs $2 for certification. Mailing Labels: No. Magnetic Tape: No. Microfiche: No. New Corporate Listing: Special request only; contact Amy Hoskin at 803-734-2159. Custom Searches: No. Online Access: Yes. Available for $70 per month. Contact Bob Knight, Deputy Secretary. Number of Active Corporations on File: 250,000.

South Dakota

Corporate Division, Secretary of State, 500 East Capitol, Pierre, SD 57501, 605-773-4845. Selected Publications: None. Phone Information: 605-773-4845. Copies of Documents on File: Available for 50 cents per page plus $5 for certification. Mailing Labels: No. Magnetic Tape: No. Microfiche: No. New Corporate Listings: No. Custom Searches: No. Online Access: No. Number of Active Corporations on File: 30,000.

Tennessee

Office of Secretary of State, Services Division, Suite 1800, James K. Polk Building, Nashville, TN 37243-0306, 615-741-2286. Select Publications: None. Phone Information: 615-741-2286. Copies of Documents on File: Certified copies only are available for $10. Mailing Labels No. Magnetic Tape: Yes. Categories: All Corporations on file, Foreign, Domestic, Profit, Non-Profit, Banks, Credit Unions, Cooperative Associations. Charge of an additional $2 for each tape supplied. Cost, done on a cost recovery basis, is determined at time of request. Contact Mr. Thompson at 615-741-0584. Microfiche: No. New Corporate Listings: Monthly New Corporation Listing on a cost recovery basis of 25 cents per page, 8 names per page. Call 615-741-1111. Custom Searches: Yes. Categories: Same as for magnetic tape. Cost is same as for New Corporate Listing. Contact Mr. Thompson at 615-741-0584. Online Access: No. Number of Active Corporations on File: 100,000.

Texas

Corporation Section, Statute Filing Division, Secretary of State, PO Box 13697, Austin, TX 78711, 512-463-5586. Selected Publications: *Filing Guide to Corporations*. (Written requests only for a $15 fee.) Phone Information: 512-463-5555. Copies of Documents on File: Available for 85 cents for first page, 15 cents for each additional page. Certification is $5 plus $1 for each additional page. Invoices are sent for order not in excess of $100. Mailing Labels: No. Magnetic Tape: No. Microfiche: Names of officers and directors available. Cost determined at time of request. New Corporate Listings: Weekly Charter Update costs $27.50 per week. Custom Searches: Yes. Online Access: Available through Information America, 404-892-1800. Contact Linda Gordon at 713-751-7900. Number of Active Corporations on File: 400,000.

Utah

Corporations and UCC, Division of Business Regulations, P.O. Box 45801, 160 East 300 South Street, Second Floor, Salt Lake City, UT 84145-0801, 801-530-6012. Selected Publications: *Going into Business, Doing Business in Utah, A Guide to Business Information*. (Send $2 to cover mailing costs.) Phone Information: 801-530-4849. Copies of Documents on File: Available for 30 cents a page plus $10 for certified copies. Mailing Labels: No. Magnetic Tape: Yes. Categories: Profit, Non-Profit, Foreign, Domestic. Cost includes computer time and programming fee. Microfiche: No. New Corporate Listing: Weekly New Corporation List 30 cents per page, New Doing Business As (DBA) List 30 cents per page. Custom Searches: Yes. Categories: Same as for Magnetic tape. Cost includes printing charge of 30 cents per page plus computer time and programming fee. Online Access: Available for $10 per month, 10 cents per minute. Contact Ted Wiggin at 801-530-6643 about Data Share. Number of Active Corporations on File: 40,000.

Vermont

Corporate Division, Secretary of State, 109 State Street, Montpelier, VT 05602-2710, 802-828-2386. Selected Publications: *Doing Business in Vermont*. Phone Information: 802-828-2386. Copies of Documents on File: Available for $1 per page, $5 for certified copies. Send the $5 certification fee in advance. They will bill you for the copies. Mailing Labels: No. Magnetic Tape: Diskettes available for $6 - $10 plus 1 cent per name. Entire date base costs $250. Microfiche: No. New Corporate Listings: Yes. Monthly New Corporations and Trade names on diskette is $6 plus 1 cent per name. Total cost is never more than $15. Out-of-State Corporations, $50 for complete list. Custom Searches: Yes. Categories: Foreign, Domestic, Non-profits, by date of registration. Cost is 1 cent per name plus $6 to run list. Online Access: Will be available mid 1992. Contact: Betty Poulin. Number of Active Corporations on File: 24,000.

Virginia

Clerk of Commission, State Corporation Commission, Secretary of State, P.O. Box 1197, Richmond, VA 23209, street address: 1220 Bank Street, Richmond, VA 23219, 804-786-3672, FAX: 804-371-0118. Selected Publications: *Business Registration Guide*. Phone Information: 804-786-3733. Copies of Documents on File: Available for $1 per page, $3 for certified copies. Mailing Labels: No. Magnetic Tape: Possibly in the future. Microfiche: No. New Corporate Listings: No. Custom Searches: Yes. Categories: Foreign, Domestic, Non-profit, Professional corporation, Non-Stock, Public Service, Cooperatives. Available on cost recovery basis. Online Access: Available. Contact Betty Williams at 804-786-6703. Free while in pilot stage, then available on cost recovery basis. Number of Active Corporations on File: 160,000.

Washington

Corporate Division, Secretary of State, 2nd Floor Republic Bldg., 505 Union Ave, Mail Stop PM-21, Olympia, WA 98504, 206-753-7120. Selected Publications: *None*. Phone Information: 206-753-7115. Copies of Documents on File: Call 206-586-2061 to leave recorded message for document orders. Fees are $1 for the first page and 20 cents thereafter. Certification is $10. Mailing Labels: No.

Magnetic Tape: No. Microfiche: Cost is $10 a month per set. New Corporate Listings: No except for statistical sheet. Custom Searches: No. Online Access: No. Number of Active Corporations on File: 145,000. This office is not computerized.

West Virginia

Corporate Division, Secretary of State, Room 139 West, State Capitol, Charleston, WV 25305, 304-342-8000. Selected Publications: *The Corporate Filings Requirements*. Phone Information: 304-342-8000. Copies of Documents on File: Available for 50 cents per page, $10 for certified copies. Mailing Labels: No. Magnetic Tape: No. Microfiche: No. New Corporate Listing: Monthly Report costs $5 a month or $50 per year. Custom Searches: Yes. Cost is $1 for first hour and $5 for every hour thereafter, prorated. Online Access: No. Number of Active Corporations on File: 39,000.

Wisconsin

Corporate Division, Secretary of State, PO Box 7846, Madison, WI 53707; Street address: 30 W. Mifflin St., 9th Floor, Madison, WI 53703, 608-266-3590. Selected Publications: *Chapter 180 Statutes Book ($5)*. Phone Information: 608-266-3590, FAX: 608-267-6813. Copies of Documents on File: For simple copy request must be in writing. Fee is $2. Faxed copies are 50 cents per page. Requests for certified copies may be phoned in. Fee is $10. Mailing Labels: No. Magnetic Tape: Available for $175. Address inquiries to Molly O'Connell.

Microfiche: Yes. Monthly New Corporations costs $11 per month. New Corporate Listing: Yes (see microfiche entry). Minimum cost is $10 per week. Custom Searches: No. Online Access: No. Number of Active Corporations on File: 176,000.

Wyoming

Corporate Division, Secretary of State, State of Wyoming, Capitol Building, Cheyenne, WY 82002, 307-777-7311; FAX: 307-777-5339. Selected Publications: *Wyoming Business Corporation Act ($4)*. Phone Information: 307-777-7311. Copies of Documents on File: Available for 50 cents for first 10 pages then 15 cents per page, $3 for certified copies. Mailing Labels: No. Magnetic Tape: Yes. Categories: Trademarks, New Domestic, New Foreign all available on a cost recovery basis. Other categories may be possible for $200 plus monthly fees. Information cannot be used for solicitation. Submit written request with letter of purpose. Microfiche: Available for foreign and nonprofit corporations for $15. New Corporate Listings: Yes. (See magnetic tape entry). Also, you may be put on mailing list for weekly press release that appears in local journals, Business Section. Custom Searches: Yes. Categories: Trademarks 25 cents per name and address, New Domestic $120 or $80 if in-state request, New Foreign $120 or $80 if instate request. Limited capacity for other types of searches. Information cannot be used for solicitation. Submit written request with letter of purpose. Listing of all active profit corporation can be purchased for $25. Online Access: Will soon be available. Contact Jeanie Sawyer. Number of Active Corporations on File: 25,000.

Who Owes Money To Whom

Any public or private company, organization, and for that matter, any individual, who borrows money and offers an asset as collateral, must file with the state at the Office of Uniform Commercial Code (UCC). A filing is made for each loan and each of the documents is available to the public. To obtain these documents is a two-step process. The first step is to request a search to see if there are any filings for a certain company. The fee for such a search usually is under $10. Then you will want to request copies of each of these documents. The cost for each document averages only a few dollars. This Office of Uniform Commercial Code is part of the state government and usually is located near or in the same office as the Office of Corporations which falls under the Secretary of State.

The initial search of records will provide:
- the number of listings under one name;
- the file number for each of the listings;
- the date and time of filing; and
- the name and address of the debtor.

Each UCC filing will disclose:
- a description of the asset placed as collateral; and
- the name and address of the secured party.

This disclosure not only provides insight into the financial security of an individual or organization, but it can also give a picture of their assets. Remember, this information is available on any public or private company or individual. The next time your brother-in-law asks you for money for a new business venture, it probably is worth the investment of a few dollars for a UCC search to see whether your relative owes money to others.

Most states will ask if you would like certified or non-certified information. Certification means that they will stand by the accuracy of the information if it is used in a court or other legal proceeding. For most cases, business researchers will not need the extra procedure of certification.

Farm Loan Filings

A new law, the Food and Security Act of 1986, involves filings on crop and livestock loans. Not all states have adopted this law. However, those which have must set up an automated central filing system under the Office of Uniform Commercial Code. Many states have not adopted the law because of the expense involved in setting up the system. Under this system the office must be able to provide information on filings in 24 hours. The purpose of the system is to notify those who purchase crops from growers if the farmer has already offered that crop as collateral.

UCC Request Forms

Some states provide you with current information about recent filings over the telephone, but others will only accept your request if it is stated on a standard UCC Form. And still others will respond if you send your request in writing but will give you a discount if your query is on an official UCC Form. Almost all states use UCC Form 11 for requesting information. Copies of UCC Forms for all 50 states can be obtained by calling Forms, Inc. (1-800-854-1080). The cost for any amount under 100 is sixty cents a form.

Online Access

With online capabilities one can usually search by such categories as: personal or commercial debtor, type of amendments, name of secured party, name of assigned party, and type of collateral. The following states offer online access to their files: Alabama, Colorado, Florida, Illinois, Iowa, Kansas, Massachusetts, Mississippi, New Mexico, Oregon, South Dakota, Texas, Utah, Washington, and Wyoming.

Exceptions

Louisiana is the only state that has not adopted the Uniform Commercial Code. Some parishes (counties) require filings. In Georgia these filings are maintained by the Clerk of the Superior Court.

Uniform Commercial Code Offices

Alabama
Uniform Commercial Code Division, Secretary of State, 4121 Carmichael Rd. Suite 200, Montgomery, AL 36106; 205-242-5231 (mailing address: P.O. Box 5616, Montgomery, AL 36103). Searches: Requests must be submitted in writing. The charge is $5 for name searches submitted on Alabama Form UCC-11, $7 for searches submitted by letter and $1 for each additional listing. Copies of Documents: Available for $1 per page. Farm Filings: Call 205-242-5231. List of new farm filings published every month. Regular printed listing is $25 per year for each collateral code. Microfiche listing is $15 per year for each collateral code. Online Access: Pilot Dial Up Program. Free. Does not show collateral. Contact: Robina Jenkins, 205-242-5136.

Alaska
Uniform Commercial Code Division, Central Filing System, 3601 C Street, Suite 1140-A, Anchorage, AK 99503; 907-762-2104. Searches: Requests must be submitted in writing on an Alaska Form UCC-11. The charge is $15 per listing for copy search, $5 for information search. Information search only states whether any encumbrances exist and when it was filed. Copies of Documents: Available for $15 for all documents in a file (this charge includes search fee.). File does not include lapsed documents. Farm Filings: Maintained by the District Recorder's Office.

Arizona
Uniform Commercial Code Department, Secretary of State, 7th Floor, 1700 W. Washington, Phoenix, AZ 85007; 602-542-6178. Searches: Requests must be submitted in writing on Arizona Form UCC-3 or UCC-11. The charge is $8 per name plus 50 cents per listing for copying fee. Fees must be paid in advance. Send blank check with stated limit or $8 and they will call you with the additional amount. When they receive it they will release the documents. Copies of Documents: Available for 50 cents a page. Farm Filings: Maintained by the County Recorder.

Arkansas

Uniform Commercial Code, Secretary of State, State Capitol Building, Room 25, Little Rock, AR 72201; 501-682-5078. Searches: Requests must be submitted in writing in a letter or on a Arkansas Form UCC-11. The charge is $5 per debtor name. Copies of Documents: Available for $5 for the first three pages. Each additional page is $1. They will bill you for copies. Farm Filings: Maintained in this office. Same price and search request structure.

California

Uniform Commercial Code Division, Secretary of State, P.O. Box 1738, Sacramento, CA 95812 (street address: 1230 J Street, Sacramento, CA 95814); 916-445-8061. Searches: Request must be submitted in writing in a letter, on a California Form UCC-3 or Form UCC-11. Charge is $11 per name. One name per request only. For $30 a one name search will be conducted and all documents copied. Additional charges will be billed by invoice. Copies of Documents: Available for $1 for the first page and 50 cents for every additional page. All documents are certified. For additional gold seal certification, or to certify a file number, the fee is an additional $5. Farm Filings: If you do not find them at the state level, remember some are filed with the county government (there is no standard procedure in California).

Colorado

Uniform Commercial Code Division, Secretary of State, 1560 Broadway, Suite 200, Denver, CO 80202; 303-894-2200. Searches: A telephone information searches of two debtor's names (last four filings of each) is available at no cost. These searches are not certified. Written requests must be on a Form UCC-11 or it will not be processed. They prefer you send no money in and let them bill you. The charge is $25 for a search of one debtor name. A computer printout will be sent to verify the search if you do not want a copy search. Copies of Documents: Available for $1.25 per page. Farm Filings: Maintained at the County Court Recorder. Online Access: Call Patti Webb at 303-894-2200 ext. 300 for information on orientation classes for new accounts. They offer several subscription packages: 3 months for $300, or 1 year for $1000 with 15 minute access time each call; 1 year for $5000 with private telephone number, and 1 year for $10,000 with direct computer hookup, which allows user to connect as many as 8 computer terminals to the system.

Connecticut

Uniform Commercial Code Division, Secretary of State, 30 Trinity Street, Hartford, CT 06106; 203-566-4021. Searches: Request must be submitted in writing. The charge is $18 for request submitted on a Connecticut Form UCC-11. The charge for requests submitted by letter is $22. Copies of Documents: The charge for the first three pages is $5, each additional page is $3. Farm Filings: Maintained in this office. Use Connecticut Form UCC-a.

Delaware

Uniform Commercial Code Section, P.O. Box 793, John G. Townsend Building, Dover, DE 19903 (Street Address: Federal and Duke of York Street, Dover, DE 19901); 302-739-4279 (Choose 8 for UCC recorded message, choose 0 for a UCC service representative). Searches: Requests must be submitted in writing on UCC-11 Form. $10 per each debtor's name search. Copies of Documents: Available for $2 per page. They will bill you. Farm Filings: Maintained by this office. This office is in the middle of being computerized. List of new filings in a particular category can be provided upon special request.

District of Columbia

Recorder of Deeds, 515 D Street N.W., Washington, DC 20001; 202-727-5374. Searches: Requests must be submitted in writing. No special form required. The charge is $30 for each secured party. Must be paid in advance. Copies of Documents: Available for $2.25 per page, plus $2.25 for certification. Farm Filings: Maintained in this office. This office is computerized.

Florida

Uniform Commercial Code Division, Department of State, P.O. Box 5588, Tallahassee, FL 32314 (Street Address: 409 Gaines Street, Tallahassee, FL 32301); 904-487-6845. Searches: 904-487-6063. For printed verification a written request must be submitted on Florida Form UCC-11. Copies of Documents: Available for $2.75 per page. Farm Filings: Filings are maintained by the County Circuit Court. Online Access: UCC Division, 409 E. Gaines Street, Tallahassee, FL 32399; 904-487-6866. Write or call and they will send you an information booklet that describes the service they have available through CompuServe, 1-800-848-8199. The cost for online service is $24 per hour, plus $2 per month flat fee and other small fees charged by CompuServe.

Georgia

The State of Georgia does not maintain Uniform Commercial Code Filings. Contact the Clerk of Superior Court at the County level for these filings.

Hawaii

Uniform Commercial Code, Bureau of Conveyance, P.O. Box 2867, Honolulu, HI 96803; 808-548-3108. Searches: Requests must be submitted in writing on a Hawaii Form UCC-3 or any state's UCC-11. The search charge is $25 per debtor name, plus an additional 50 cents per listing. They will call you if there will be more charges for additional names found. Copies of Documents: Available for 50 cents per page. Farm Filings: Maintained by this office. Online Access: No.

Idaho

Secretary of State, Uniform Commercial Code Division, State House, Boise, ID 83720; 208-334-3191. Searches: Information may be requested by phone or in writing. The charge is $13 for phone requests and for written requests. An additional $1 is charged if the request is not submitted on an Idaho UCC-4 Form. Charge for written requests submitted on UCC Form is $12. Copies of Documents: The charge for copying all documents involved in a search is $1. Farm Filings: A 24-hour Expedite Service is available for these filings. The charge is $17 for info search and $23 for copies. Online Access: Hopefully will be available in the future.

Illinois

Uniform Commercial Code Division, Secretary of State, Centennial Building, Room 30, 2nd & Edwards Street, Springfield, IL 62756; 217-782-7518. Searches: All requests must be in writing. Requests on non-standard forms will not be processed. Requests submitted on a Illinois Form UCC-11.7 are $10. Copies of Documents: The charge is 50 cents per page. Farm Filings: If you do not find them at the state level, remember, some are filed with the county government. (There is no standard procedure in Illinois.) Payment for searches and copies may be charged to VISA or Master Charge. Microfilm: Copies of all documents filed within the month are available on a subscription basis for $250 per month. Daily Computer Printout Listing: Available for $250 per month. Online Access: For information write the above office, or contact: Louise Blakley, 217-785-2235. A brochure explaining the system will be sent to you.

Indiana

Uniform Commercial Code Division, Secretary of State, 302 West Washington Street, Room E 018, Indianapolis, IN 46204; 317-232-6393. Searches: All searches must be requested in writing. An Indiana Form UCC-11 is preferred. The charge is $1 per debtor's name and 50 cents for each filing, and 50 cents per statement on the listing. All requests for searches received by Federal Express or Express Mail with return envelope are given a priority. Copies of Documents: The charge is 50 cents per page and $1 for certification. Farm Filings: If incorporated they are filed both at this office and the county recorder where the land is located. If the farm is not incorporated the filing is placed at the county recorder's office only. Online Access: Not available. This office has one of the quickest turnaround times in the nation but is not computerized.

Iowa

Uniform Commercial Code Division, Secretary of State, Second Floor, Hoover Building, Des Moines, IA 50319; 515-281-5204. Searches: Information may be requested by phone if you already have an established account, or in writing. The cost of a phone search is $5, plus $1 for a printout. The charge for a non-standard request is $6 and $5 for a request submitted on an Iowa Form UCC-11. Copies of Documents: The fee is $1 for each copy requested. All copies of liens are certified. Farm Filings: Maintained by this office. (Monthly updating may be obtained from Iowa Public Record Service, 515-223-1153.) Online Access: Available. Contact Allen Welsh, 515-281-8363. Cost is $150 per year, 30 cents per minute, plus telephone charges for dialup program.

Kansas

Uniform Commercial Code Division, Secretary of State, Second Floor, State Capitol, Topeka, KS 66612; 913-296-3650. Searches: Phone requests are accepted with VISA or MC or from those holding a prepaid account with the UCC. The charge for phone requests is $15 per name for verbal information and $5 for an order. The charge for written requests is $5. If staffing permits, all requests are filled within 24 hours. Copies of Documents: The charge is $1 per page. There is no additional charge for certification of name searches. They are always sent out certified. For file number searches, certification must be requested. Fee is 50 cents. Farm Filings: This office has handled farm filings since 1984. Filings prior to that year are maintained by the County Register of Deeds. Online Access: Will be available in the future from Kansas Information Network with imaging capacity. Contact: Cathy. Other: Microfilm cost $25 per roll plus $7.50 for postage and handling, for up to 50 rolls. Total file has 42 rolls. New rolls, 4-5 monthly can be sent. Magnetic Tape: Master file costs $2,000. Updates are $15 weekly or $75 monthly.

Kentucky

Uniform Commercial Code Division, Office of Secretary of State, State Capitol Building, Capitol Avenue, Frankfort, KY 40601; 502-564-2848 Ext. 441. Searches: All searches of UCC filings must be conducted in person by requester or by outside agencies. Law firms or Kentucky Lender's Assistance, 606-278-6586 may do it for you. In addition to their fee, the UCC charges 10 cents per page for plain copies; $5 for certification and 50 cents for every page thereafter. Farm Filings: Filings are maintained by the County Circuit Court. Online Access: No.

Louisiana

The state of Louisiana has not adopted the Uniform Commercial Code. Filings may be maintained at the Parish (county) level.

Maine

Uniform Commercial Code Division, Secretary of State, State House Station 101, Augusta, ME 04333; 207-289-4177. Searches: All requests must be submitted in writing in a letter or on a Form UCC-11. State whether plain or certified copies are desired. Cost is $2 per page plus $10 for certification. Will bill. For expedited service an additional $5 fee guarantees a 24 hour turnaround time. Farm Filings: Maintained by this office. Online Access: No.

Maryland

Uniform Commercial Code Division, State Department of Assessments and Taxation, 301 West Preston Street, Baltimore, MD 21201; 301-225-1340. Searches: The State of Maryland does not conduct searches. They will provide a list of title companies that do provide that service. Some are: Hylinf Infoquest, 301-728-4990 and Harbor City Research, 301-539-0400. Copies cost $1 per page. Cost to certify a document is $6. Farm Filings: Maintained by this office. Online Access: No.

Massachusetts

Uniform Commercial Code Division, Secretary of State, Room 1711, 1 Ashburton Place, Boston, MA 02108; 617-727-2860. Searches: Requests must be submitted in writing on a Form UCC-11 (any state's form is acceptable). The charge is $5 for an information computer printout and $10 for computer printout with face page and up to 15 pages. They will call you if pages exceed this limit. All fees must be paid in advance. Requests sent by Federal Express or Express Mail will be sent out same way with Air Bill, but all requests are processed in order received. No expediting service available. Copies of Documents: Charge is $2 per page and $3 for certification. Farm Filings: Maintained in Town Clerk's Office. Online Access: Available for $149 per year plus 40 cents per minute. Also carried by commercial services. Contact Richard Shipley, 617-729-5412.

Michigan

Uniform Commercial Code Section, P.O. Box 30197, Lansing, MI 48909-7697 (Mailing Address: 7064 Crowner Dr., Lansing, MI 48909); 517-322-1495. Searches: Telephone requests are handled on an expedite basis for already established accounts. The charge is an additional $25. You must have an account number with the UCC Section to obtain this service. The charge for requests submitted on non-standard forms are $6. Requests submitted on a Michigan Form UCC-11 is $3. Requests sent out by Federal Express or Express Mail are given priority, but all requests are processed in the order received. Copies of Documents: The charge is $1 per page and $1 for certification. Farm Filings: Filings are maintained by the County Recorder of Deeds. Online Access: No. Other: Microfilm available in contract basis for $50 per month. Format is not computer indexed. Write above address for details and contract.

Minnesota

Uniform Commercial Code Division, Secretary of State, 180 State Office Building, St. Paul, MN 55155; 612-296-2434. Searches: Requests must be submitted in writing and include a SASE. The charge for a request submitted on a Minnesota Form UCC-11 is $11. The charge for a request submitted on a non-standard form is $14. These charges include information on 5 listings and/or 5 copies. You will be billed if there are additional copies in excess of five. The charge for additional listings is 50 cents/listing. Copies of Documents: Available for 50 cents/page. Charge for certified copies is a $5 plus 50 cents for each page. Farm Filings: Available from the County Recorder of Deeds unless the debtor is a non-resident or a corporation and then they are filed with the UCC Division.

Mississippi

Uniform Commercial Code Division, Secretary of State, 202 N. Congress St., #601, Jackson, MS 39201; 601-359-1614. Searches: Phone information is available

at no cost. Information available by phone is: approximate number of filings, secured party, file numbers, and date and time of filing. The charge for written requests submitted on Mississippi Form UCC-11 is $5. The charge for written requests submitted on non-standard forms is $10. Copies of Documents: Available for $2 a pages. Send initial $5 or $10 fee only. They will bill you for the exact amount of copies made. Farm Filings: Farm Filings are maintained by the above office. Other: Master list of all farm registrations available for $2040. Master list by type is $500 per crop. Online Access: Contact Cheryl Crawford, 601-359-1548. The cost is $250 per month plus 50 cents per transaction with minimum of 100 transactions. Service will be available as of 1/92. Will display name, address and collateral. Complete file microfilm available for $50 per roll.

Missouri

Uniform Commercial Code Division, Secretary of State, P.O. Box 1159, Jefferson City, MO 65102; 314-751-2360. Searches: Information searches will be given over the phone. These searches are not certified and are free of charge. (This service is not available on Mondays or the day after a holiday.) The charge for written requests is $8. Copies of Documents: Available for $8 per listing. The $8 fee covers the first 10 pages. Additional pages are 50 cents each. Farm Filings: Maintained by the County Recorder.

Montana

Uniform Commercial Code Bureau, Secretary of State, Capitol Station, Helena, MT 59620; 406-444-3665, FAX: 406-444-3926. Searches: Requests for searches will be accepted by phone. The charge if you have a prepaid account is $7, the same as for a written request. There are no restrictions on form in which you put written requests. Searches are conducted the day of the request for a $5 fee. Regular requests processed in 48 hours. Copies of Documents: Available for 50 cents a page. The charge for certification is $2. Farm Filings: Maintained in this office. For total listing of crop you are interested in, fill out a Buyer's Registration Form for crops you want on the list. Results can be done on paper or microfiche. Service is done on a cost recovery basis. Online Access: Contact Florence, 406-444-3665. She will send you an information brochure. The charge is $25 per month for unlimited use. Printed copies cost 50 cents each and are statutorily accepted documents.

Nebraska

Uniform Commercial Code Division, P.O. Box 95104, 301 Centennial Mall S., Lincoln, NE 68509; 402-471-4080. Searches: The charge for requests by phone is $1 per debtor's name. No verification is sent unless requested. If requested the charge for the printout is $3. The charge for written requests is $3. A computer printout containing a list of the filings is sent to the requester. Copies of Documents: Available for 50 cents per page. They will bill. Farm Filings: Maintained by the county government, but the above office is hooked up to all 93 countries and will do a search for you. The county will bill you directly for its service. Magnetic Tape: Available to large companies for $250 per month. Online Access: Available. Charge is $2 per inquiry. Contact Debbie Pester.

Nevada

Uniform Commercial Code Division, Secretary of State, Capitol Complex, Carson City, NV 89710; 702-687-5298. Searches: Only written requests for information will be accepted. The charge is $6 for a request submitted on a Nevada Form UCC-3, Form UCC-11 or any type of letter. For an additional $10 your request will be expedited. This fee must be paid with a separate check. Copies of Documents: Available for $1 per page and an additional $6 for certified copies. Farm Filings: Maintained at the office of the County Recorder. Online Access: No.

New Hampshire

Uniform Commercial Code Division, Secretary of State, State House, Room 204, Concord, NH 03301; 603-271-3276 or 271-3277. Searches: Requests must be submitted in writing by letter or on a Form UCC-11, and must contain a SASE in which requested documents will be mailed. Requests will not be processed without SASE enclosed. The charge for a request submitted on a New Hampshire Form UCC-11 is $5. The charge for a request submitted on a letter or non-standard form is $7. Copies of Documents: Available for 75 cents per file. Farm Filings: Maintained by this office. Microfiche: Available from New England Micrographics. Contact Nick Brattan, 603-625-1171. Online Access: No. This office is not computerized.

New Jersey

Uniform Commercial Code Division, State Department, State Capitol Building, CN303, Trenton, NJ 08625; 609-530-6426. Searches: Requests must be submitted in writing with exact name and address of debtor or on a New Jersey Form UCC-11 or a security agreement signed by the debtor. Payment must accompany request unless prepaid UCC account, Visa or MasterCard is used. Request may be Faxed, 609-530-0688. The charge is $25. Document is certified. Expedite Service is available for $5. The requester pays the express mail expense. Copies of Documents: Available for $1 per page. Farm Filings: Maintained by the county and the state. At the county level you will want to check with the County Recorder. Online Access: No.

New Mexico
Uniform Commercial Code Division, Bureau of Operations, Secretary of State, Executive Legislative Building, Room 400, Santa Fe, NM 87503; 505-827-3600. Searches: Certification is $8. Copies cost $1 per page. The State of New Mexico does not do searches, but they will provide you with a list of abstract companies that are authorized to do so. Call Bureau of Operations for list, 505-827-3608. Farm Filings: This office located at the same address with conduct a search for an Agricultural Eddective Financing Statement for $15. Contact Ben Vegil, 505-827-3609. They will follow-up the verbal report with a written statement. Online Access: Available through local services: Federal Abstracts, 505-982-5537, Lawyer's Title, 505-988-2333 and Capitol Documents, 505-984-2696. Also available from Dun and Bradstreet.

New York
Uniform Commercial Code Division, Secretary of State, P.O. Box 7021, Albany, NY 12225; 518-474-4763. Searches: Requests must be submitted in writing. For requests submitted on a New York Form UCC-11 the charge is $7. For requests submitted on non-standard forms the charge is $12. Copies of Documents: Available for $1.50 per page. Farm Filings: Maintained by both the state and the County Recorder. Online Access: No. Other: Microfiche available for $300 per month. Contact Virginia Cellery at 518-432-2733.

North Carolina
Uniform Commercial Code Division, Secretary of State, 300 N. Salisbury Street, Raleigh, NC 27611; 919-733-4205. Searches: Requests must be submitted in writing. Signature for the requester is required, therefore make request on Form UCC-11 or North Carolina Form UCC-11. The charge is $8 per name. Search fee must be sent with request. All requests are handled within 24 hours of receipt. Copies of Documents: Available for $1 per page. Will bill. Farm Filings: Maintained by this office and County Recorder. Online Access: No, but will be available in the future. Other: Microfilm can be purchased for $50 per roll. New monthly listings generate about 2 rolls per month. Contact Judy Chapman.

North Dakota
Uniform Commercial Code Division, Secretary of State, Main Capitol Building, 600 Boulevard Avenue East, Bismarck, ND 58505; 701-224-3662. Searches: Requests may be phoned in or be submitted in writing preferably on a North Dakota UCC-11. Letters and nonstandard forms also accepted. The charge is $5. Copies of Documents: Available for $5 for the first three pages and $1 a page for additional pages. Farm Filings: The Central Notice staff will take requests for searches over the phone for crop and livestock filings. The charge is the same as above. Written requests are the same as stated above. Farm equipment and real estate filings are optional and may be maintained by the state or the County Register of Deeds until 1/92. As of 1/92 the UCC and County Register of Deeds will be hooked up to the same system. Online Access: No, but will be available in the future.

Ohio
Uniform Commercial Code Division, Secretary of State, 30 E. Broad Street, 14th Floor, Columbus, OH 43266-0418; 614-466-9316. Searches: Phone requests for information are not certified and are free of charge. Call 614-466-3623/3126. Limit is 3 requests per phone call. Written requests may be submitted on a non-standard letter form, Form UCC-11 or on an Ohio Form UCC-11. The charge is $9. It takes 6 months for these searches to be conducted. Expedite service is available for an additional $9. These requests are processed in 5 working days. Copies of Documents: Available for $1 per page. Farm Filings: Maintained by the County Recorder. Online Access: No.

Oklahoma
Uniform Commercial Code Office, Oklahoma County Clerk, 320 Robert S. Kerr, Room 105, Oklahoma City, OK 73102; 405-278-1521. Searches: Requests must be submitted in writing. The charge is $5. Copies of Documents: Available for $1 per page. Send $5 search fee with request. They will bill you for copies and call if amount is over $25. The charge for certification is $1. Farm Filings: Maintained by Secretary of State's Office, 405-521-2474. Online Access: No.

Oregon
Uniform Commercial Code Division, Secretary of State, Room 41, State Capitol, Salem, OR 97310; 503-378-4146. Searches: Requests must be phoned in using

Visa or MasterCard, charged to an established prepaid UCC account or submitted in writing by letter, or on Form UCC-11 or preferably on a Oregon Form UCC-25R. The charge is $5 per debtor's name. Copies of Documents: Available for $1 per page. Farm Filings: Maintained by this office. The charge for a search is $5 per name. Monthly reports by agricultural product code are available on microfilm or paper copy. For microfilm contact Micelle. Cost is $10 per reel weekly. Online Access: Available for $25 per month, plus 20 cents a minute for online use. Contact Michelle. Commercially available from Prentice Hall, 1-800-452-7856.

Pennsylvania
Uniform Commercial Code Division, Corporation Bureau, State Department, 308 N. Office Building, Harrisburg, PA 17120; 717-787-8712. Searches: Requests for searches must be paid in advance by check or money order only and submitted in writing on a Pennsylvania Form UCC-11. The charge is $12 per name search. $28 to certify. Must may in advance by check or money order. Copies of Documents: Available for $2 per page. Farm Filings: Maintained by this office. Online Access: Information America, 404-892-1800.

Rhode Island
Uniform Commercial Code Division, Secretary of State, 100 North Main Street, Providence, RI 02903; 401-277-2521. Searches: Requests must be submitted in writing. Same charge for request in letter form or on Form UCC-11. Call for number of pages. Requests will not be processed without payment in full. The charge is $5. Copies of Documents: Available for 50 cents per copy. Farm Filings: Maintained by the City Recorder of Deeds. Online Access: No.

South Carolina
Uniform Commercial Code Division, Secretary of State, P.O. Box 11350, Columbia, SC 29211; 803-734-2175. Searches: Requests must be submitted in writing on Form UCC-11, or preferably South Carolina Form UCC-4. Letters are not accepted. The charge is $5 per debtor name. No priority or expediting service. All requests done in the order received. Copies of Documents: Available for $2 for the first page, $1 for each page thereafter. Farm Filings: Maintained by County Recorder. Online Access: No. Other: Microfilm from Archives is purchased by Dun and Bradstreet and may be purchased from the UCC division directly. Contact Thresha Southerland, 803-734-2176. One tape costs $50.

South Dakota
Central Filing System, Secretary of State, 500 E. Capitol, Pierre, SD 57501; 605-773-4422. Searches: Telephone information provided for no charge. Requests for searches are accepted from those with prepaid deposit accounts. Written requests are accepted on any UCC standard request form. The charge is $4. Fee for certification is $5. Copies of Documents: Available for 50 cents per page. They will bill you. Farm Filings: Maintained by this office. Online access at no charge is available. Online Access: Available by subscription. The system can be used by those with IBM compatible computers and Hayes compatible modems. Cost is $240 per year for 200 transactions and 10 cents per transaction thereafter.

Tennessee
Uniform Commercial Code Section, Secretary of State, J.K. Polk Building, 505 Deaderick St., Suite 1800, Nashville, TN 37219; 615-741-3276. Searches: Requests must be submitted in writing, preferably on a Tennessee Form UCC-11. Indicate if you want information or information plus copies. The charge is $10 even if the search shows no listing. Send the $10 fee with request. Copies of Documents: Available for $1 per copy. Do not send money with request. They will bill you. Requests sent with Express Mail envelopes will be sent the next day. All other requests take 3-4 days to process. Farm Filings: Maintained by this office and County Recorder. It is necessary to check with both offices. Online Access: No.

Texas
Uniform Commercial Code, Secretary of State, P.O. Box 13193, Austin, TX 78711-3193; 512-475-2705. Searches: The charge for a search requested by phone is $25. The charge for written requests submitted on Texas Form UCC-11 is $10. May be FAX: 512-475-2812. The charge for written requests submitted on a letterhead or non-standard form is $25. Copies of Documents: Available for $1.50 per page with a $5 minimum charge. The charge for certification is an additional $5. Farm Filings: Maintained by the above office. Online Access: Available by Dialup Service. Cost is $3 per search, deducted from prepaid account. Contact Tina Whiteley, 512-475-2700.

Utah
Uniform Commercial Code Division, Business Regulation Department, 300 South Street, Second Floor, Salt Lake City, UT 84110; 801-530-6020. Searches: Written request may be on letter, UCC-11 or Utah Form UCC-2. The charge is

$10 per debtor name. Copies of Documents: Available for 30 cents per page. Will bill. Certification: No additional charge. Document already certified. Farm Filings: Central Filings maintained these files. Phone requests are accepted. The charge is $10. Online Access: Available through Data-Share program on a subscription basis. The charge is $10 per month plus 10 cents per minute and telephone charges. Contact Mary Ann Saddler or Ted Wiggin at 801-530-6643.

Vermont

Uniform Commercial Code, Secretary of State, Montpelier, VT 05609 (Regular mail to: 109 State Street, Montpelier, VT 05609-1104; Fed Ex to: 94 Main Street, Montpelier, VT 05609); 802-828-2388. Searches: Requests for searches may be phoned in or submitted in writing. They will bill for phone requests. The charge is $5 per debtor name, plus 50 cents for an information sheet containing debtor's name, secured party, file number, and date and time filed. Copies of Documents: Available for $2 for 5" x 8" or $5 for 8 1/2" x 11" copies. Certification fee is $5. Farm Filings: Central Filings Section maintains these files. Contact the above address. The charges for searches is the same. Online Access: No.

Virginia

Uniform Commercial Code Division, State Corporation Commission, P.O. Box 1197, Richmond, VA 23209 (Street Address: 1220 Bank Street, Richmond, VA 23209); 804-786-3689. Searches: Requests for searches must be submitted in writing in a letter or Form UCC-11. The charge is $6 per debtor name. Copies of Documents: Available for $1 per page. There is an additional charge of $6 for certification. Farm Filings: Maintained by this office and the County Recorder. Online Access: No.

Washington

Uniform Commercial Code Division, Department of Licensing, 405 Black Lake Blvd., Olympia, WA 98502 (Mailing Address: PO Box 9660, Olympia, WA 98507); 206-753-2523. Searches: Requests must be submitted in writing. Indicate if you want information or information and copies. The charge is $7 for all the listings of one debtor. Copies of Documents: Available for $12. This includes search fee, plus copies of all documents for one debtor. Farm Filings: Maintained in this office. Microfilm: Copies of each days filings are available for $6.50 per day plus shipping and handling fees. Online Access: Contact Darla Gehrke at 206-752-2523 for information on how to set up a prepaid account. Monthly minimum deposit is $200 from which $1 per minute online time and other fees are deducted.

West Virginia

Uniform Commercial Code Division, Secretary of State, 1900 Kanawha, Bldg. 1, Room 131W, Charleston, WV 25305-0770; 304-345-4000. Searches: Phone requests for information are accepted. The charge is $5. They will bill you. Written requests are preferred. The charge is $3 if UCC-11 is used, $5 for all others. Copies of Documents: Available for 50 cents per page. The charge for certification is $5. Farm Filings: Maintained by this office. Online Access: No.

Wisconsin

Uniform Commercial Code Division, Secretary of State, 30 West Mifflin St., Madison, WI 53703 (Mailing Address: P.O. Box 7847, Madison, WI 53707); 608-266-3087. Searches: Phone requests for information are accepted. The charge is $5 per filing. The charge for written requests is $5 per debtor name. Copies of Documents: Available for $1 per document. Certification certificate must be requested in writing and is an additional 50 cents. Farm Filings: Maintained by the County Register of Deeds. Other: Microfiche is available on a monthly basis. Contact Bonnie Fredrick at 608-266-3087.

Wyoming

Uniform Commercial Code, Secretary of State, State Capitol Building, Cheyenne, WY 82002; 307-777-5372. Searches: Phone requests for information are accepted for 2 debtor names. Requests may be Faxed to 307-777-5339. The charge is $5 for each name. The charge for written requests is the same. Copies of Documents: Available for 50 cents per page. Farm Filings: Maintained by this office and the County Recorder. Check both. Online Access: Available for $50 per month, plus telephone charges and usage fee. Minimum usage fee is $26 per month. Contact Jeanie Sawyer.

Companies That Only Sell Stock In One State

State Securities Offices Offer Company Information, Mailing List of Brokers and More

The offices of state security regulators offer financial data on thousands of companies which are not required to file with the U.S. Securities and Exchange Commission as well as the names, addresses, financial data, and consumer information on thousands of stockbrokers and broker-dealers.

State regulation of the sale of securities in the United States began in 1911 when the Kansas legislature passed the first securities law. North Carolina enacted a law the same year; Arizona and Louisiana did so in 1912. By 1919, 32 states had followed suit. Now, all states and the federal government have laws regulating the sale of corporate securities, bonds, investment contracts and stocks.

The reason for these laws is simple enough: they protect the public, unfamiliar with the intricacies of investing, against deceitful promoters and their often worthless stocks. This is the same type of function that the U.S. Securities and Exchange Commission performs in Washington, DC. The United States covers companies trading stocks across state boundaries, and the states cover companies trading stocks within their state. The laws -- called Blue Sky laws -- prevent speculative schemes "which have no more basis than so many feet of blue sky," according to the Commerce Clearing House Blue Sky Law Reports.

The Blue Sky Law is usually administered by each state's Securities Commission or Securities Division. Securities to be sold within a state must register with this office. If the issuer is a corporation, for example, it must submit the following information:

- articles of incorporation
- purpose of proposed business
- names and addresses of officers and directors
- qualifications and business history of applicant - detailed financial data

Each state, however, has numerous exemptions. Securities issued by national banks, savings and loan associations, non-profit organizations, public utilities, and railroads are usually exempt from the Blue Sky laws, as are securities listed on the stock exchange, those issued by companies registered with the U.S. Securities and Exchange Commission, and those issued by foreign governments with which the U.S. has diplomatic relations.

Securities offices also require broker-dealer firms, the agents (or sales representatives), and investments advisers wanting to work in the state to file applications.

Agents wanting to work in one or more states now apply for registration by filing with National Association of Securities Dealers' Central Registration Depository (CRD). To keep the CRD current, agents must submit all pertinent employment and application changes. All state securities offices are hooked up to the CRD through computer terminals and use them to monitor agents registered or applying to register in their jurisdictions as well as any complaints filed against individuals.

Most states will also use the system for registration of broker-dealer firms. Information kept in the repository will include registration applications, amendments to applications, complaints on file, and so forth. The purpose is to reduce the amount of paperwork for the states and to promote more uniformity.

The system is not set to accept broker-dealers' audited financial statements or annual reports so applicants will have to continue to file in the states requiring them. The broker-dealer phase of the CRD is now in operation. Several states are now trying to determine what, if any, information they will require broker-dealers to file with their securities divisions. Most of those states that have made a decision said they will continue to require annual financial reports to be filed with their offices.

Below are the names, addresses and telephone numbers for the state securities offices. Most of these offices will routinely provide information over the phone on whether specific companies, agents, or broker-dealers are registered in their states. Requests for more detailed information may have to be submitted in writing.

Securities Offices

Alabama
Securities Commission, 770 Washington Ave., Suite 570, Montgomery, AL 36130; 205-242-2984.

Alaska
Division of Banking, Securities and Corporations, Department of Commerce and Economic Development, State Office Building #94, PO Box 110807, Juneau, AK 99811-0807; 907-465-2521.

Arizona
Securities Division, Arizona Corporation Commission, 1200 West Washington St., Suite 201, Phoenix, AZ 85007; 602-542-4242.

Arkansas
Securities Department, Heritage West Building, Third Floor, 201 East Markham, Little Rock, AR 72201; 501-324-9260.

California
Securities Regulation Division, Department of Corporations, 3700 Wilshire Blvd., 6th Floor, Los Angeles, CA 90010; 213-736-2741.

Colorado
Division of Securities, Department of Regulatory Agencies, 1580 Lincoln, Suite 420, Denver, CO 80203; 303-894-2320.

Connecticut
Securities and Business Investments Division, Department of Banking, Securities and Business, 44 Capitol Ave., Hartford, CT 06106; 203-566-4560.

Delaware
Division of Securities, Department of Justice, 8th Floor, Civil Division, 820 North French St., Wilmington, DE 19801; 302-577-2515.

District of Columbia
Division of Securities, DC Public Service Commission, 450 5th St., NW, Suite 821, Washington, DC 20001; 202-626-5105.

Florida
Division of Securities and Investor Protection, Department of Banking and Finance, Office of Comptroller, The Capitol, LL-22, Tallahassee, FL 32399-0350; 904-488-9805.

Georgia
Business Services and Regulations, Office of Secretary of State, Suite 315 West Tower, Two Martin Luther King Dr., Atlanta, GA 30334; 404-656-2894.

Hawaii
Business Registration Division, Department of Commerce and Consumer Affairs, 1010 Richards St., PO Box 40, Honolulu, HI 96810; 808-586-2737.

Idaho
Securities Bureau, Department of Finance, 700 West State St., Boise, ID 83720-2700; 208-334-3684.

Illinois
Securities Department, Office of Secretary of State, 900 South Spring St., Springfield, IL 62704; 217-782-2256.

Indiana
Securities Division, Office of Secretary of State, 302 W. Washington, Room E-111, Indianapolis, IN 46204; 317-232-6681.

Iowa
Securities Bureau, Office of Commissioner of Insurance, Lucas State Office Building, 2nd Floor, Des Moines, IA 50319; 515-281-4441.

Kansas
Office of Securities Commissioner, 618 S. Kansas, 2nd Floor, Topeka, KS 66603-3804; 913-296-3307.

Kentucky
Division of Securities, Department of Financial Institutions, 477 Versailles Rd., Frankfort, KY 40601; 502-564-3390.

Louisiana
Securities Commission, 1100 Poydras Street, Suite #2250, New Orleans, LA 70163; 504-568-5515.

Maine
Securities Division, Bureau of Banking, Department of Professional and Financial Regulation, State House Station 121, Augusta, ME 04333; 207-582-8760.

Maryland
Division of Securities, Office of Attorney General, 200 St. Paul Place, 21st Floor, Baltimore, MD 21202-2020; 410-576-6360.

Massachusetts
Securities Division, Department of Secretary of State, 1719 John W. McCormack Building, One Ashburton Place, Boston, MA 02108; 617-727-3548.

Michigan
Corporation and Securities Bureau, Department of Commerce, 6546 Merchantile Way, Lansing, MI 48909; 517-334-6200.

Minnesota
Registration and Licensing Division, Department of Commerce, 133 East 7th Street, St. Paul, MN 55101; 612-296-4026.

Mississippi
Securities Division, Office of Secretary of State, P.O. Box 136, Jackson, MS 39205; 601-359-1350.

Missouri
Office of Secretary of State, 600 West Main, Jefferson City, MO 65101; 314-751-4136.

Montana
Securities Department, State Auditor's Office, 126 North Sanders, Room 270, Helena, MT 59620; 406-444-2040.

Nebraska
Bureau of Securities, Department of Banking and Finance, 1200 N Street, The Atrium #311, Lincoln, NE 68508; 402-471-3445.

Nevada
Securities Division, Office of Secretary of State, 1771 E. Flamingo Rd., Suite 212-B, Las Vegas, NV 89158; 702-486-6440.

New Hampshire
Department of State, Bureau of Securities Regulation, State House, Room 204, Concord, NH 03301-4989; 603-271-1463.

New Jersey
Bureau of Securities, 153 Halsey Street, 6th Floor, Newark, NJ 07101; 201-648-2040.

New Mexico
Securities Division, Regulation and Licensing Department, 725 St. Michaels Dr., P.O. Box 25101, Santa Fe, NM 87501; 505-827-7140.

New York
Bureau of Investor Protection and Securities, Department of Law, 120 Broadway, 23rd Fl., New York, NY 10271; 212-416-8200.

North Carolina
Securities Division, Department of State, 300 N Salisbury St., Suite 1000, Raleigh, NC 27603; 919-733-3924.

North Dakota
Office of Securities Commissioner, 600 E. Boulevard, 5th Floor, Bismarck, ND 58505; 701-224-2910.

Ohio
Division of Securities, Department of Commerce, 77 South High St, 22nd Fl., Columbus, OH 43266-0548; 614-644-7381.

Oklahoma
Department of Securities, 2401 North Lincoln Blvd., 4th Fl., Oklahoma City, OK 73152; 405-521-2451.

Oregon
Division of Finance and Corporate Securities, Department of Insurance and Finance, 21 Labor & Industries Bldg., Salem, OR 97310; 503-378-4387.

Pennsylvania
Securities Commission, Division of Licensing and Compliance, 1010 North Seventh St., Second Floor, Harrisburg, PA 17102-1410; 717-787-8061.

Rhode Island
Securities Division, Department of Business Regulation, 233 Richmond St., #232, Providence, RI 02903-4232; 401-277-3048.

South Carolina
Securities Division, Department of State, 1205 Pendelton St., #501, Columbia, SC 29201; 803-734-1087.

South Dakota
Division of Securities, Department of Commerce and Regulation, 118 W. Capitol, Pierre, SD 57501-2017; 605-773-4823.

Tennessee
Division of Securities, Department of Commerce and Insurance, Volunteer Plaza, Suite 680, 500 James Robinson Pkwy., Nashville, TN 37243; 615-741-3187.

Texas

State Securities Board, 221 W. 6th Street, Suite 700, Austin, TX 78701; 512-474-2233.

Utah

Securities Division, Department of Business Regulation, P.O. Box 45808, Salt Lake City, UT 84145-0808; 801-530-6600.

Vermont

Securities Division, Department of Banking & Insurance, 89 Main Street, Drawer 20, Montpelier, VT 05620-3101; 802-828-3420.

Virginia

Division of Securities and Retail Franchising, State Corporation Commission, PO Box 1197, Richmond, VA 23209; 804-371-9051.

Washington

Securities Division, Department of Licensing, PO Box 9033, 405 Black Lake Blvd., SW, 2nd Floor, Olympia, WA 98507-9033; 206-753-6928.

West Virginia

Securities Division, State Auditor's Office, Room W-118, State Capitol, Charleston, WV 25305; 304-558-2257.

Wisconsin

Office of Commissioner of Securities, 101 East Wilson St., P.O. Box 1768, Madison, WI 53701; 608-266-3431.

Wyoming

Securities Division, Office of the Secretary of State, State Capitol Building, Cheyenne, WY 82002; 307-777-7370.

State Licensing Offices

Buried within each state government are several and sometimes dozens of offices where individuals as well as business establishments must register in order to perform certain types of services and commercial activities. State laws require accountants, architects, concert promoters, employment agencies, podiatrists and numerous other professionals to register. The data derived from these regulatory boards provide unique opportunities for researchers and marketing executives to obtain demographic data, mailing lists and even competitive information.

Mailing Lists

Mailing lists offer the biggest potential from these offices. The unusual as well as the mundane are available in a variety of formats. Not only are many of these lists not accessible commercially, if they are, you can get them from the states cheaper and usually without restrictions. In other words, you can purchase a state list once, and use it over and over again. Commercial list brokers will never let you do this. Here is a sampling of mailing lists:

- 1 cent per name for all dentists in Kentucky;
- Free directory of real estate agents in Arizona;
- $40 for a list of all nurses in Colorado;
- A mailing list of all contractors in Arkansas for $10;
- 2 cents per name for all swimming pool dealers in Florida;
- A listing of librarians in Georgia;
- 4 cents a name for all the psychologists in California;
- $100 for a computer tape of all accountants in Florida;
- $1.45 per 1,000 names for all medical practices in Illinois; or
- Free list of all attorneys in Maine.

Almost every state provides mailing labels in the form of cheshire or pressure sensitive labels. In many cases, the charge is nominal.

Common Lists and Specialized Rosters

Every state maintains a variety of standard rosters. Some states keep as few as 20 lists and others have over 100. Names of licensed professionals and business establishments available from most every state include:

- medical professionals
- accountants
- real estate agents and brokers
- veterinarians
- barbers
- insurance agents
- architects
- nursing homes
- cosmetologists
- hearing aid dealers
- social workers
- lawyers

After reviewing the rundown of all 50 states and District of Columbia licensing boards, you will be amazed at the variety of lists that are within easy reach. In most cases you can obtain printouts for such licensed services as:

- burglar alarm contractors in Maine
- tow truck operations in Minnesota
- hat cleaners in Ohio
- ski areas in Michigan
- day care centers in New York
- security guards in New Hampshire
- outfitters in Colorado

Computer Tapes and Diskettes: Selections and Sorting Options

Many states can provide the information on magnetic tape and some are beginning to offer data on IBM PC compatible diskettes. Almost every state will allow you to select names by zip code or county whether the licensee is active or inactive. Some states will allow you to select certain demographic characteristics, such as years of formal education.

Markets and Demographics

With a little creativity and resourcefulness, the information at licensing boards can provide pertinent clues in formulating a market profile. For example, you can determine:

- which counties have the highest concentration of psychologists;
- what is the average number of years of schooling for real estate agents in certain zip codes;
- which zip codes have experienced the fastest growth for accountants for the past 10 years;
- the number of out-of-state licensed paralegals;
- which counties have the most podiatrists or veterinarians per capita; or,
- how many insurance agents there are in a given county.

Some states have the capability of performing historical analysis, while others will supply you with the raw data.

Competitive Intelligence

Depending upon the type of business you are investigating, pertinent competitive information may be ferreted from state licensing boards. For example, if you are a dentist, mobile home dealer, nursing home administrator or real estate broker, you could plot how many competitors you are up against in a given zip code or county. Or, you may be able to determine how many opticians work for an eye care chain, or tax consultants for a given tax preparer.

Organization of Licensing Boards

Approximately half of the states have a central office which is responsible for all licensed professions. For such states it is a relatively easy process to obtain information because it is all generated from a single source. However, the other states make this task difficult. Typically, each separate independent board maintains information for one profession. The only connection these agencies have to the state government is that their board members are appointed by the governor.

States With Restrictions

Six states have laws that place certain stipulations on the use of their lists of licensed professionals. In these cases the data may not be used for commercial purposes. Iowa, Montana, New York, North Dakota, Rhode Island and Washington have such restrictions. The District of Columbia, Hawaii and Kansas do not release addresses but will provide names.

Licensing Boards

Besides issuing licenses to professionals so that they can do business, the following offices act as consumer watchdogs to make sure that those with licenses do business fairly and ethically. Not only will these offices investigate complaints against licensed professionals, they also have the ability to revoke or suspend the licenses if the professional repeatedly acts unprofessionally or unethically. Each state listing includes the professionals licensed in that state, including health professionals, along with their different licensing offices where noted.

Alabama

State Occupational Information Coordinating Community (SOICC), 401 Adams Ave., P.O. Box 5690, Montgomery, AL 36103-5690; 205-242-2990. Licensing boards & professions: accountants, aircraft personnel, architects, auctioneers, audiologists, speech pathologists, bar pilots, water transportation personnel, boxer and wrestler trainers, classroom teachers, coal mine foremen/mine electricians, cosmetologists, counselors, dentists, dental hygienists, chiropractors, doctors of medicine, physician's assistants, surgeon's assistants, school bus drivers, embalmer/funeral directors, engineer-in-training and professional engineers, land surveyors, fire fighters, foresters, general contractors, hearing aid specialists, heating and air conditioning contractors, insurance agents, interior designers, landscape architects, landscape horticulturist/planters, lawyers, pest control operators and fumigators, tree surgeons, law enforcement personnel, nurses, nursing home administrators, optometrists, pharmacists, physical therapists, physical therapist assistants, plumbers, podiatrists, polygraph examiners, psychologists, real estate brokers, security salespersons, social workers, veterinarians.

Alaska

Division of Occupational Licensing, Department of Commerce and Economic Development, State of Alaska, P.O. Box 110806, Juneau, AK 99811-0806; 907-465-2534. Licensing boards & professions: architects, engineers, land surveyors, audiologists, barbers and hairdressers, chiropractors, collection agencies, construction contractors, concert promoters, dental professionals, dispensing opticians, electrical administrators, geologists, guides, hearing aid dealers, marine pilots, physicians, morticians, naturopaths, nursing, nursing home administrators, optometrists, pharmacists, physical therapists, psychologists, public accountants, veterinarians.

Arizona

Arizona Department of Revenue, 1600 West Monroe, Phoenix, AZ 85007; 602-542-4576. Licensing boards & professions: pharmacists, physical therapists, podiatrists, psychologists, chiropractors, dentists, teachers, homeopathic specialists, veterinarians, medical examiners, radiologic technicians, naturopathic physicians, nurses, opticians, optometrists, osteopaths, barbers, cosmetologists, real estate brokers, contractors, technical registrars, insurance agents, physician assistants, nursing care administrators.

Arkansas

Governor's Office, State Capitol Building, Little Rock, AR 72201; 501-682-2345. Licensing boards & professions: architects, abstracters, accountants, barber examiners, funeral directors, contractors, cosmetologists, dental examiners, electricians, speech pathologists, audiologists, nurses, pharmacists, real estate brokers, veterinary engineers, land surveyors, athletic trainers, chiropractors, collection agencies, counselors, embalmers, foresters, landscape architects, manufactured home builders, physicians, opticians, optometrists, podiatrists, psychologists, sanitarians, social workers, soil classifiers, therapy technologists.

California

State of California, Department of Consumer Affairs, 400 R Street, Sacramento, CA 95814; 916-323-2191, or 1-800-344-9940 (toll-free in CA). Licensing boards professions: professional engineers, cosmetologists, fabric care technicians, physical therapists, medical quality assurance, physician's assistants, chiropractors, acupuncture specialists, accountants, psychologists, registered nurses, pharmacists, architects, funeral directors, embalmers, landscape architects, veterinarians, animal health technicians, home Furnishings decorators, collection and investigative agents, dentists, dental auxiliaries, barbers, behavioral scientists, optometrists, shorthand reporters, structural pest control operators, athletic trainers, vocational nurses, psychiatric technicians, osteopaths, electronic repair dealers, personnel services, geologists and geophysicists, dispensing opticians/contact lens examiners, respiratory care specialists, nursing home administrators, podiatrists, hearing aid dispensers, speech pathologists, audiologists, tax preparers.

Colorado

Department of Regulatory Agencies, State Services Building, 1560 Broadway, Suite 1550, Denver, CO 80202; 303-894-7855. Licensing Board/Professions: accountants, architects, barbers, cosmetologists, chiropractors, dentists, electricians, engineers, hearing aid dealers, insurance agents, land surveyors, mobile home dealers, nurses, nursing home administrators, optometrists, outfitters, pharmacists & pharmacies, physical therapists, physicians, plumbers, psychologists, realtors, ski lift operators, social workers, veterinarians.

Connecticut

Occupational Licensing Division, Department of Consumer Products, 165 Capitol Avenue, Hartford, CT 06106; 203-566-1107, or 1-800-842-2649 (toll-free in CT). Licensed Occupations: electricians, plumbers, heating and cooling specialists, well drillers, elevator installers, home improvement contractors, arborists, TV and radio repair specialists. Licensed Health Professions: Department of Health Services, 150 Washington St., Hartford, CT 06106; 203-566-7398. Physicians, dentists, optometrists, osteopaths, naturopaths, homeopaths, chiropractors, psychologists, registered nurses, licensed practical nurses, dental hygienists, registered physical therapists, hypertrichologists, audiologists, speech pathologists, podiatrists, hairdressers, barbers, embalmers, funeral directors, sewer installers/cleaners, registered sanitarians, nursing home administrators, hearing aid dealers, opticians, veterinarians, occupational therapists. Other Licensed Professions: Contact Professional Licensing Division, 165 Capitol Avenue, Room G1, Hartford, CT 06106, 203-566-1814: architects, landscape architects, engineers, engineers-in-training, land surveyors, pharmacists, patent medicine distributors, mobile manufactured home parks.

Delaware

Division of Professional Regulation, P.O. Box 1401, O'Neil Building, Dover, DE 19903; 302-739-4522. Complaints in writing only. Licensed Professionals: architects, accountants, landscape architects, cosmetologists, barbers, podiatrists, chiropractors, dentists, electricians, adult entertainment, physicians, nurses, real estate brokers, land surveyors, private employment agencies, athletic (wrestling and boxing), deadly weapons dealers, nursing home administrators, funeral directors, social workers, speech pathologists, hearing aid dealers, audiologists, psychologists, veterinarians, optometrists, occupational therapists, pharmacists, river boat pilots.

District of Columbia

Department of Consumer and Regulatory Affairs, 614 H Street NW, Room 108, Washington, DC 20001; 202-727-7080. Licensing Board/Professions: accountants, architects, barbers, cosmetologists, dentists, dieticians, electricians, funeral directors, physicians, nurses, nursing home administrators, occupational therapists, optometrists, pharmacists, physical therapists, plumbers, podiatrists, engineers, psychologists, real estate agents, refrigeration and air conditioning specialists, social workers, steam and other operating engineers, veterinarians.

Florida

Florida Department of Professional Regulation, 1940 N. Monroe St., Tallahassee, FL 32399-075; 904-488-6602. Licensing boards & professions: accountants, architects, barbers, chiropractors, cosmetologists, dentists, dispensing opticians, electrical contractors, professional engineers and land surveyors, landscape architects, funeral directors and embalmers, medical examiners, hearing aid dispensers, naturopathics, nursing home administrators, nurses, optometrists, osteopaths, pharmacists, pilot commissioners, podiatrists, psychologists, real estate brokers, veterinarians, acupuncture technicians, radiological health technicians, laboratory services, entomology specialists, emergency medical personnel.

Georgia

Examining Board Division, Secretary of State, 166 Pryor Street, SW, Atlanta, GA 30303; 404-656-3900. Licensing boards & professions: accountants, architects, athletic trainers, auctioneers, barbers, chiropractors, construction industry, cosmetologists, professional counselors, social workers, marriage and family therapists, dietitians, dentists, engineers, land surveyors, foresters, funeral directors/embalmers, geologists, hearing aid dealers and dispensers, landscape architects, librarians, physicians, nurses, nursing home administrators, occupational therapists, dispensing opticians, optometrists, pharmacists, physical therapists, podiatrists, polygraph testers, practical nurses, private detectives and security agencies, psychologists, recreation specialists, sanitarians, speech pathologists, audiologists, used car dealers, used motor vehicle dismantlers, rebuilders, and salvage dealers, veterinarians, water and wastewater treatment plant operators and laboratory analysts.

Hawaii

Office of the Director, Department of Commerce and Consumer Affairs, P.O. Box 3469, Honolulu, HI 96801; 808-548-7462. Licensing boards & professions: accountants, acupuncture specialists, barbers, boxers, chiropractors, contractors, cosmetologists, dental examiners, detectives and guards, electricians and plumbers, elevator mechanics, engineers, architects, land surveyors, landscape architects, hearing aid dealers and fitters, massage specialists, physicians, motor vehicle Industry, motor vehicle repair technicians, naturopaths, nurses, nursing home administrators, dispensing opticians, optometrists, osteopaths, pest control operators, pharmacists, physical therapists, psychologists, real estate brokers, speech pathologists, audiologists, veterinarians, embalmers/funeral directors, collection agencies, commercial employment agencies, mortgage and collection servicing agents, mortgage brokers and solicitors, port pilots, time sharing and travel agents.

Idaho

State of Idaho, Department of Self-Governing Agencies, Bureau of Occupational Licenses, Owyhee Plaza, 1109 Main, #220, Boise, ID 83702; 208-334-3233. Licensing boards & professions: accountants, athletic directors, bartenders, engineers, land surveyors, dentists, geologists, physicians, architects, barbers, chiropractors, cosmetologists, counselors, dentists, environmental health specialists, hearing aid dealers and fitters, landscape architects, morticians, nursing home administrators, optometrists, podiatrists, psychologists, social workers, outfitters and guides, pharmacists, public works contractors, real estate brokers.

Illinois

State of Illinois, Department of Professional Regulations, 320 W. Washington, Third Floor, Springfield, IL 62786; 217-785-0800. Licensed professions: athletic trainers, architects, barbers, cosmetologists, chiropractors, collection agencies, controlled substance specialists, dentists and dental auxiliaries, polygraph testers, detectives, embalmers, funeral directors, land sales, land surveyors, physicians, nurses, nursing home administrators, occupational therapists, optometrists, pharmacists, physical therapists, podiatrists, boxing and wrestling, engineers, psychologists, accountants, real estate brokers and salespersons, roofing contractors, shorthand reporters, social workers, structural engineers, veterinarians.

Indiana

Indiana Professional Licensing Agency, Indiana Government Center S., 302 W. Washington Street, Room E-034, Indianapolis, IN 46204; 317-232-3997. Licensing boards & professions: accountants, architects, auctioneers, barbers, beauticians, boxers, engineers and land surveyors, funeral directors, plumbers, real estate agents, TV-radio and watch repair technicians. Licensed health professionals: Indiana Health Professional Bureau, One America Square #1020, Indianapolis, IN 46282; 317-232-2960 for the following medical specialties: chiropractors, dentists, health facility administrators, nurses, optometrists, pharmacists, sanitarians, speech pathologists, audiologists, psychologists, veterinarians, hearing aid dealers, podiatrists, physical therapists.

Iowa

Bureau of Professional Licensing, Iowa Department of Health, Lucas State Office Building, Des Moines, IA 50319; 515-281-4401. Licensed professionals: dietitians, funeral directors and embalmers, hearing aid dealers, nursing home administrators, optometrists, ophthalmology dispensers, podiatrists, psychologists, physical and occupational therapists, occupational therapist assistants, social workers, speech pathologists and audiologists, respiratory care therapists, barbers, cosmetologists, chiropractors, nurses, physicians, dentists, pharmacists, veterinarians. Other licensed professionals: Professional Licensing Regulation Division, Department of Commerce, 1918 SE Hulsizer, Ankeny, IA 50021: accountants, engineers and land surveyors, landscape architects, architects, real estate agents.

Kansas

Secretary of State, State Capitol, 2nd Floor, Topeka, KS 66612; 913-296-3489. Licensing boards: abstracters, accountants, adult home administrators, operating engineers, plumbers and pipefitters, carpenters, electrical workers, attorneys, barbers, cosmetologists, court reporters, dentists and dental auxiliaries, educators, emergency medical services, healing arts specialists, hearing aid dispensers, insurance agents, land surveyors, embalmers/funeral directors, nurses, optometrists, pharmacists, physical therapists, podiatrists, private schools, real estate agents, engineers, architects, landscape architects, veterinarians.

Kentucky

Division of Occupations and Professions, P.O. Box 456, Frankfort, KY 40602-0456; 502-564-3296. Licensing boards & professions: hearing aid dealers, nurses, private schools, psychologists, social workers, speech and audiologists. Other licensed professionals: Kentucky Occupational Information Coordinating Committee, 275 E. Main St., Two Center, Frankfort, KY 40621; 502-564-4258: accountants, agriculture specialists, architects, auctioneers, bar examiners, barbers, chiropractors, dentists, hairdressers, cosmetologists, emergency medical technicians Services, radiation and product safety specialists, insurance agents, medical licensure supervisors, natural resources and environmental protection specialists, nursing home administrators, ophthalmic dispensers, optometric examiners, pharmacists, physical therapists, podiatrists, polygraph examiners, professional engineers and land surveyors, real estate agents, veterinarians.

Louisiana

Department of Economic Development, 101 France St., Baton Rouge, LA 70802; 504-342-5361. Licensing boards & professions: acupuncture assistants, adoption agencies, adult day care administrators, agricultural consultants, alcoholic beverages solicitors, ambulatory surgical centers, arborists, archaeological investigators, architects, auctioneers, barbers, beauticians, bedding and furniture upholsterers, beer distributors, blind business enterprise operators, blood alcohol analysts, embalmers/funeral directors, accountants, shorthand reporters, chiropractors, pesticide applicators, driving school instructors, sewage/construction contractors, cotton buyers, waste-salvage oil operators, cut flower dealers, dairy product retailers, day care centers, fuels dealers, dentists, drug manufacturers, egg marketers, electrolysis technicians, embalmers, emergency medical technicians, employment service agencies, family support counselors, grain dealers, hearing aid dealers, hemodialysis clinics, home health centers, horticulturists, independent laboratories, sewage system installers, insurance, landscape architects, nurses, lime manufacturers, liquefied gas distributors, livestock dealers, maternity homes, mental and substance abuse clinics, midwives, nursing home administrators, nursery stock dealers, occupational therapists, optometrists, pesticide dealers, pharmacists, physical therapists, physicians, physicians, plant breeders, plumbers, podiatrists, solid waste processors, seafood distributors, psychologists, radiation therapists, radio and television repair technicians, radiologic technologists, real estate brokers, sanitarians, social workers, speech pathologists and audiologists, veterinarians, voice stress analysts.

Company Intelligence

Maine

Department of Professional and Financial Regulation, State House Station 35, Augusta, ME 04333; 207-582-8700. Licensing boards & professions: veterinarians, itinerant vendors, consumer credit protection services, insurance agents, athletic trainers, real estate agents, geologists and soil scientists, solar energy auditors, hearing aid dealers and fitters, accountants, arborists, barbers, commercial drivers, education instructors, speech pathologists and audiologists, auctioneers, electricians, funeral directors, foresters, dietitians, nursing home administrators, oil and solid fuel installers, substance abuse counselors, mobile home parks, river pilots, physical therapists, plumbers, psychologists, social workers, radiological technicians, occupational therapists, respiratory care therapists, nurses, dentists, chiropractors, osteopaths, podiatrists, physicians, engineers, attorneys.

Maryland

Division of Maryland Occupational and Professional Licensing, 501 St. Paul Pl., 9th Floor, Baltimore, MD 21202; 410-333-6209. Licensed professionals: architects, master electricians, engineers, foresters, hearing aid dealers, landscape architects, pilots, plumbers, land surveyors, public accountants, second hand dealers, precious metal and gem dealers, pawnbrokers, real estate agents and brokers, home improvement contractors, barbers and cosmetologists. Referral to the licensing agency for collection agencies, mortgage brokers and insurance agents can be provided by the office listed above. Other licensed professions: Boards and Commissions, Department of Health and Dental Hygiene, 4201 Patterson Ave., Baltimore, MD 21215; 410-764-4747: audiologists, chiropractors, dentists, dietitians, electrologists, medical examiners, morticians, nurses, nursing home administrators, optometrists, occupational therapists, pharmacists, physical therapists, podiatrists, professional counselors, psychologists, environmental sanitarians, speech pathologists, social workers, well drillers, water work and waste system operators.

Massachusetts

Division of Registration, 100 Cambridge St., Boston, MA 02202; 617-727-3074. Licensing boards & professions: electrologists, gas fitters, hairdressers, health officers, landscape architects, licensed practical nurses, nursing home administrators, optometrists, physician's assistants, podiatrists, pharmacists, plumbers, psychologists, real estate brokers, registered nurses, sanitarians, speech pathologists, audiologists, social workers, tv-repair technicians, physical therapists, occupational therapists, athletic trainers, architects, barbers, barber shops, certified public accountants, chiropractors, dental hygienists, dentists, dispensing opticians, pharmacies, electricians, embalmers, engineers, veterinarians.

Michigan

Michigan Department of License and Regulation, P.O. Box 30018, Lansing, MI 48909; 517-373-1870. Licensing board & professions: accountants, architects, barbers, athletic control (wrestlers and boxers), builders, carnival amusement rides, cosmetologists.

Minnesota

Office of Consumer Services, Office of Attorney General, 1400 NCL Tower, 445 Minnesota Street, St. Paul, MN 55101; 612-296-2331. Licensing boards & professions: abstracters, accountants, adjusters, alarm and communications contractors, architects, assessors, attorneys, auctioneers, bailbondsmen, barbers, beauticians, boiler operators, boxing related occupations, brokers, building officials, burglar installers, chiropractors, clergy, cosmetologists, dentists, dental assistants, dental hygienists, private detectives, electricians, energy auditors, engineers, financial counselors/financial planners, funeral directors/embalmers/morticians, hearing aid dispensers, insurance agents, investment advisors, landscape architects, land surveyors, midwives, notary publics, nursing home administrators, optometrists, osteopathic physicians, pawnbrokers, peace officers, pharmacists, physical therapists, physicians, surgeons, physician's assistants, high pressure pipefitters, plumbers, podiatrists, practical nurses, precious metal dealers, process servers, psychologists, real estate brokers, registered nurses, rehabilitation consultants, sanitarians, securities brokers, tax preparers, teachers, tow truck operators, transient merchants, veterinarians, water conditioning contractors and installers, water and waste treatment operators, water well contractors/explorers/engineers.

Mississippi

Secretary of State, P.O. Box 136, Jackson, MS 39205; 601-359-3123. Licensing boards & professions: agricultural aviation pilots, architects, landscape architects, athletic trainers, funeral directors, chiropractors, dentists, physicians, nurses, nursing home administrators, optometrists, pharmacists, physical therapists, psychologists, veterinarians, barbers, cosmetologists, engineers and land surveyors, foresters, polygraph examiners, public accountants, public contractors, real estate agents.

Missouri

Division of Professional Registration, Department of Economic Development, 3605 Missouri Blvd., Jefferson City, MO 65109; 314-751-0293. Licensing boards and professions: accountants, architects/engineers/land surveyors, athletic trainers, barbers, chiropractors, cosmetologists, professional counselors, dentists, embalmers/funeral directors, healing arts specialists, employment agencies, hearing aid dealers/fitters, nurses, optometrists, podiatrists, pharmacists, real estate agents, veterinarians, insurance agents, nursing home administrators, lawyers, dental hygienists, physicians, physical therapists, speech pathologists and audiologists, psychologists.

Montana

Professional and Occupational Licensing, Business Regulation, Department of Commerce, 111 N. Jackson St., Helena, MT 59620; 406-444-3737. Licensing boards & professions: accountants, acupuncturists, architects, athletic trainers, barbers, beer distributors, chiropractors, cosmetologists, dental hygienists, dentists, denturists, electricians, electrologists, employment Agencies, engineers and land surveyors, hearing aid dispensers, insurance, landscape architects, lawyers, librarians, medical doctors, morticians, nurses, nursing home administrators, occupational therapists, operating engineers (boiler), optometrists, osteopathic physicians, pawnbrokers, physical therapists, plumbers, podiatrists, polygraph examiners, private investigators, psychologists, contractors, radiologic technologists, real estate brokers and salesmen, sanitarians, securities brokers and salesmen, social workers and counselors, speech pathologists and audiologists, taxidermists, tourist campground and trailer courts, veterinarians, water well drillers.

Nebraska

Bureau of Examining Boards, Nebraska Department of Health, P.O. Box 95007, Lincoln, NE 68509; 402-471-2115. Licensing boards & health professions: athletic trainers, advanced emergency medical technicians, audiologist/speech pathologists, cosmetologists, chiropractors, dentists/dental hygienists, embalmers/funeral directors, hearing aid dealers and fitters, pharmacists, podiatrists, optometrists, physical therapists, nurses, nursing home administrators, massage specialists, occupational therapists, professional counselors, psychologists, respiratory care specialists, social workers, sanitarians, veterinarians. For other licensing boards & professions, contact the NE state operator at 402-471-2311 to be connected with the board that licenses the following professions: accountants, engineers/architects, barbers, abstracters, appraisers, land surveyors, landscape architects.

Nevada

State of Nevada Executive Chamber, Capitol Complex, 1 E. Liberty Street, #311, Reno, NV 89501; 702-786-0231. Licensing boards & professions: accountants, architects, athletic trainers, audiologists and speech pathologists, barbers, chiropractors, contractors, cosmetologists, dentists, engineers and land surveyors, funeral directors and embalmers, hearing aid specialists, homeopaths, landscape architects, liquefied petroleum gas distributors, marriage and family counselors, physicians, naturopathic healing arts specialists, nurses, dispensing opticians, optometrists, oriental medicine, osteopaths, pharmacists, physical therapists, podiatrists, private investigators, psychologists, shorthand reporters, taxicab drivers, veterinarians.

New Hampshire

SOICC of New Hampshire, 64 B Old Sun Cook Rd., Concord, NH 03301; 603-228-9500. Licensing boards & professions: accountants, emergency medical technicians, engineers/architects/land surveyors, attorneys, auctioneers, insurance (bailbondsmen), barbers, cosmetologists, chiropractors, court reporters, dentists, drivers education Instructors, electricians, funeral directors/embalmers, engineers, physicians, private security guards, lobbyists, nurses, nursing home administrators, occupational therapists, optometrists, psychologists, pesticide control operators, pharmacists, plumbers, podiatrists, real estate agents, teacher agents, veterinarians, water supply and pollution control operators.

New Jersey

Director, Centralized Licensing for the Licensing Boards, Division of Consumer Affairs, 375 West State Street, Trenton, NJ 08625; 609-292-4670. Licensing boards and professions: accountants, architects, barbers, beauticians, dentists, electrical contractors, marriage counselors, plumbers, morticians, nurses, ophthalmic dispensing technicians, optometrists, pharmacists, physical therapists, professional engineers and landscape surveyors, professional planners, psychological examiners, shorthand reporters, veterinarians, public movers and warehousemen, acupuncture specialists, landscape architects, athletic trainers, hearing aid dispensers, chiropractors, opthomologists.

New Mexico
Regulation and Licensing Department, 725 St. Michael's Drive, P.O. Box 25101, Santa Fe, NM 87504; 505-827-7000. Licensing boards & professions: accountants, architects, athletic promoters, barbers, chiropractors, cosmetologists, dentists, engineers and land surveyors, landscape architects, physicians, nurses, nursing home administrators, occupational therapists, optometrists, osteopaths, pharmacists, physical therapists, podiatrists, polygraphers, private investigators, psychologists, realtors, thanatopractice, veterinarians.

New York
New York State Education Department, Division of Professional Licensing, Cultural Education Center, Empire State Plaza, Albany, NY 12230; 518-474-3852, or 1-800-342-3729 (toll-free in NY). Licensed professionals: acupuncturists, architects, audiologists, certified shorthand reporters, chiropractors, dentists, landscape architects, land surveyors, massage therapists, physicians, osteopaths, nurses, occupational therapists, ophthalmic dispensers, optometrists, pharmacists, physical therapists, podiatrists, engineers, psychologists, public accountants, social workers, speech pathologists, veterinarians.

North Carolina
North Carolina Center for Public Policy Research, P.O. Box 430, Raleigh, NC 27602; 919-832-2839. Licensing boards & professions: architects, auctioneers, barbers, boiler operators, accountants, chiropractors, cosmetologists, registered counselors, dental, electrical contractors, foresters, general contractors, hearing aid dealers and fitters, landscape architects, landscape contractors, marital and family therapists, physicians, navigators and pilots, morticians, nurses, nursing home administrators, opticians, optometrists, osteopaths, pesticide operators, pharmacists, physical therapists, plumbers and heating specialists, podiatrists, practicing psychologists, private protective services, professional engineers and land surveyors, public librarians, real estate, refrigeration technicians, sanitarians, social workers, speech and language pathologists, structural pest control operators, veterinarians, waste water treatment operators, water treatment facility operators.

North Dakota
North Dakota Legislative Council Library, 600 East Boulevard Avenue, Bismarck, ND 58505; 701-224-2916. Licensing boards & professions: abstracters, accountants, architects, athletic trainers, audiologists and speech pathologists, barbers, chiropractors, cosmetologists, dentists, dietitians, electricians, embalmers, emergency medical services, engineers and land surveyors, hearing aid dealers and fitters, massage therapists, physicians, nurses, nursing home administrators, occupational therapists, optometrists, pharmacists, physical therapists, plumbers, podiatrists, private investigators, private police security, psychologists, real estate agents, respiratory care specialists, social workers, soil classifiers, veterinarians, water well contractors.

Ohio
State of Ohio, Department of Administrative Services, Division of Computer Services, 30 East Broad St., 40th Floor, Columbus, OH 43215-0409; 614-466-8029. Licensed professionals: wholesale distributors of dangerous drugs, terminal distributors of dangerous drugs, pharmacists, accountants, barbers, barber shops, beauty shops, managing cosmetologists, cosmetologists, manicurists, architects, landscape architects, practical nurses, registered nurses, surveyors, engineers, surveyors, dentists, dental hygienists, osteopaths, physicians, podiatrists, chiropractors, midwives, embalmers, funeral directors, embalmer and funeral directors, hat cleaners, dry cleaners, public employment agencies, auctioneers, private investigators, auctioneers.

Oklahoma
Governor's Office, State Capitol, Oklahoma City, OK 73105; 405-521-2342 or State Information Operator 405-521-1601. Licensing board & professions: accountants, real estate agents, physicians, foresters, medico-legals, nursing homes, nurses, optometrists, osteopaths, physicians, pharmacists, polygraph examiners, psychologists, shorthand reporters, social workers, speech pathologists, veterinarians, landscape architects, architects, chiropractors, cosmetologists, dentists, embalmers and funeral directors. For other licensed professionals, contact Occupational Licensing, OK State Health Department, 1000 North East, 10th Street, Oklahoma City, OK 73117; 405-271-5217: barbers, hearing aid dealers, electricians, water and waste treatment plant operators.

Oregon
Department of Economic Development, Small Business Advocates, 595 Cottage St. NE, Salem, OR 97310; 1-800-547-7842 or 1-800-233-3306 (toll-free in OR). Licensing boards & professions: accountants, architects, barbers and hairdressers, builders, contractors, collection agencies, debt consolidators, geologists, landscape architects, landscape contractors, and TV/radio service dealers, engineering examiners, fire marshals, insurance agents, maritime pilots, real estate agents, tax practitioners.

Pennsylvania
Bureau of Professional and Occupational Affairs, 618 Transportation and Safety Building, Harrisburg, PA 17120-2649; 717-787-8503, or 1-800-822-2113 (toll-free in PA). Licensing boards & professions: accountants, architects, auctioneers, barbers, cosmetology, funeral directors, landscape architects, professional engineers, real estate agents. For licensed health professions, contact Bureau of Professional and Occupational Affairs, Secretary of State, 618 Transportation and Safety Building, Harrisburg, PA 17120; 717-783-1400: dentists, physicians, nurses, nursing home administrators, occupational therapists, optometrists, osteopaths, pharmacists, physical therapists, podiatrists, psychologists, speech-language and hearing specialists, veterinarians, navigators.

Rhode Island
Rhode Island Occupational Information Coordinating Commission, 22 Hayes Street, Providence, RI 02908; 401-272-0830. Licensing boards & professions: nurses aides, psychologists, respiratory therapists, sanitarians, speech pathologists, veterinarians, physical therapists, plumbers, podiatrists, prosthetists, nurses, nursing home administrators, occupational therapists, opticians, optometrists, osteopaths, physician assistants, embalmers/funeral directors, hairdressers, cosmetologists, manicurists, massage therapists, physicians, midwives, acupuncturists, athletic trainers, audiologists, barbers, barber shops, chiropractors, dentists, dental hygienists, electrologist, architects, coastal resource management, engineers and land surveyors.

South Carolina
South Carolina State Library, 1500 Senate St., Columbia, SC 29201; 803-734-8666. Licensing boards & professions: accountants, architects, auctioneers, barbers, morticians, chiropractors, contractors, cosmetologists, dentists, engineers, environmental systems (well diggers), foresters, funeral services, landscape architects, physicians, nurses, nursing home administrators, occupational therapists, opticians, optometrists, pharmacists, physical therapists, professional counselors, marriage and family therapists, psychologists, real estate agents, sanitarians, home builder, social workers, speech pathologist/audiologists, veterinarians, athletic trainers (boxing and wrestling), geologists.

South Dakota
Department of Commerce and Regulation, 500 E. Capitol Ave., Pierre, SD 57501-5070; 605-773-3178. South Dakota Medical and Osteopath Examiners, 1323 S. Minnesota Avenue, Sioux Falls, SD 57105; 605-336-1965. Licensing boards & professions: physicians, osteopaths, physician's assistants, physical therapists, medical corporations, emergency technicians, abstracters, accountants, barbers, chiropractors, cosmetologists, electricians, engineers/architects, funeral directors, hearing aid dispensers, medical/osteopaths, nurses, nursing home administrators, optometrists, pharmacists, plumbers, podiatrists, psychologists, real estate agents, social workers, veterinarians.

Tennessee
Division of Regulatory Boards, Department of Commerce & Insurance, 500 James Robertson Parkway, Nashville, TN 37243; 615-741-3449. Licensing boards & professions: accountants, architects and engineers, auctioneers, barbers, collection services, contractors, cosmetologists, funeral directors and embalmers, land surveyors, motor vehicle salesmen and dealers, personnel recruiters, pharmacists, polygraph examiners, real estate. For other licensed health

professionals, contact Division of Health Related Professions, Department of Health and Environment, 283 or 287 Plus Park Blvd Complex, Nashville, TN 37247-1010; 615-367-6220: dentists, dental hygienists, podiatrists, physicians, physician's assistants, osteopaths, optometrists, veterinarians, nursing home administrators, dispensing opticians, chiropractors, social workers, hearing aid dispensers, registered professional environmentalists, marital and family counselors, speech pathology/audiologists, occupational and physical therapists, x-ray technicians, registered nurses, licensed practical nurses.

Texas

Texas Department of Commerce, 410 E. 5th Street, P.O. Box 12047, Austin, TX 78711-2728; 512-320-0110, or 1-800-888-0511 (toll-free in TX). Licensing boards & professions: accountants, architects, barbers, cosmetologists, morticians, educators, public safety, chiropractors, psychologists, dentists, real estate agents, engineers, veterinarians, insurance agents, land surveyors, landscape architects, fitting and dispensing of hearing aids, private investigators and private security agencies, polygraph, Vocational nurses, nursing home administrators, physicians, optometrists, structural pest control operators, pharmacists, physical therapists, plumbers, podiatrists, professional counselors, dietitians, speech-language pathology and audiology.

Utah

Division of Occupational and Professional Licensing, Department of Business Regulation, Heber M. Wells Building, 160 East 300 South, P.O. Box 45805, Salt Lake City, UT 84145-0805; 801-530-6628. Licensing boards & professions: accountants, architects, barbers, cosmetologists, electrologists, chiropractors, podiatrists, dentists, dental hygienists, embalmers, funeral directors, pre-need sellers, engineers, land surveyors, physicians, surgeons, Naturopaths, registered nurses, licensed practical nurses, nurse midwives, nurse anesthetists, nurse specialists, prescriptive practice specialist, IV therapists, optometrists, osteopaths, pharmacists, pharmacies, manufacturing pharmacies, shorthand reporters, veterinarians, health facility administrators, sanitarians, morticians, physical therapists, psychologists, clinical social workers, conduct research on controlled substance, marriage and family therapists, master therapeutic recreational specialists, speech pathologists, audiologists, occupational therapists, hearing aid specialists, massage therapists, massage establishments, acupuncture practitioners, physician assistants, dieticians, contractors.

Vermont

Division of Licensing and Registration, Secretary of State, Pavilion Office Building, Montpelier, VT 05609; 802-828-2363. Licensing boards & professions: accountants, architects, barbers, boxing control, chiropractors, cosmetologists, dentists, engineers, funeral directors/embalmers, land surveyors, medical board (physicians, podiatrists, real estate brokers, veterinarians, physical therapists, social workers, physician assistants, motor vehicle racing, nurses, nursing home administrators, opticians, optometrists, osteopaths, pharmacies, pharmacist, psychologists, private detectives, security Guards, radiological technicians.

Virginia

Virginia Department of Commerce, 3600 W. Broad St., Richmond, VA 23230; 804-367-8500. Licensed professions: accountants, architects, auctioneers, audiologists, barbers, boxers, contractors, commercial driver training schools, employment agencies, professional engineers, geologists, hairdressers, harbor pilots, hearing aid dealers and fitters, landscape architects, nursing home administrators, librarians, opticians, polygraph examiners, private security services, real estate brokers, speech pathologists, land surveyors, water and wastewater works operators, wrestlers. For licensed health professions, contact receptionist, Health Professionals: 804-662-9900. The office listed above can pro

vide you with phone numbers for the following licensing boards: dentists, funeral directors/embalmers, physicians, medical/legal assistants, nurses, optometrists, pharmacists, psychologists, professional counselors, social workers, veterinarians.

Washington

Department of Health, P.O. Box 47860, Olympia, WA 98504-7860; 206-586-4561. Licensed professions: acupuncturists, auctioneers, architects, barbers, camp club registration/salespersons, chiropractors, cosmetology schools/instructors, cosmetologists, manicurists, collection agencies, debt adjusters/agencies, dentists, dental hygienists, drugless therapeutic-naturopaths, employment agencies/managers, professional engineers, engineers-in-training, land surveyors, engineering corporations/partnerships, escrow officers/agents, firearms dealers, embalmers, apprentice embalmers, funeral directors, funeral establishments, hearing aid dispensers/trainees, land development registration, landscape architects, massage operators, midwives, notary publics, nursing home administrators, occularists, occupational therapists, dispensing opticians, optometrists, osteopaths, osteopathic physician/ surgeon, osteopathic physician assistants, physicians, surgeons, physician's assistants, limited physician, podiatrists, practical nurses, psychologists, physical therapists, real estate (brokers, salespersons, corporations, partnerships, branch offices), land development representatives, registered nurses, timeshare registration & salespersons, veterinarians, animal technicians.

West Virginia

Administrative Law Division, Secretary of State, State Capitol, Charleston, WV 25305; 304-345-4000. Licensing boards & professions: accountants, architects, barbers, beauticians, chiropractors, dentists, and dental hygienists, embalmers and funeral directors, engineers, foresters, hearing-aid dealers, landscape architects, land surveyors, law examiners, physicians, practical nurses, registered nurses, nursing home administrators, occupational therapists, optometrists, osteopaths, pharmacists, physical therapists, psychologists, radiologic technicians, real estate agents, sanitarians, state water resources, veterinarians.

Wisconsin

Department of Regulation and Licensing, P.O. Box 8935, Madison, WI 53708; 608-266-7482. Licensed professions: accountants, animal technicians, architects, architects, engineers, barbers, bingo organizations, morticians, chiropractors, cosmetologists, distributors of dangerous drugs, dental hygienists, dentists, interior designers, private detectives, drug manufacturers, electrologists, professional engineers, funeral directors, hearing aid dealers/fitters, land surveyors, manicurists, physicians, surgeons, nurse midwives, registered nurses, licensed practical nurses, nursing home administrators, optometrists, pharmacists, physical therapists, physician's assistants, podiatrists, psychologists, raffle organizations, real estate brokers, beauty salons, electrolysis salons, veterinarians.

Wyoming

Governor's Office, State Capitol, Cheyenne, WY 82002; 307-777-7434. Licensing boards & professions: funeral directors and embalmers, health service administrators, buyers and purchasing agents, shorthand reporters, medical record technicians, accountants and auditors, claims adjusters, appraisers, engineers, architects, surveyors, interior designers and decorators, medical laboratory workers, dental laboratory technicians, opticians, radiological technicians, respiratory technicians, quality control inspectors, security salespeople, insurance agents, real estate agents, physicians, physician's assistants, chiropractors, pharmacists, occupational therapists, activity therapists, physical therapists, speech pathologist and audiologist, veterinarian, optometrist, dietitians, dentists, dental hygienists, registered nurses, licensed practical nurses, emergency medical technicians, nurse's aides, medical assistants, counselors, lawyers, legal assistants, cosmetologists and barbers.

State Company Directories

Market Info, Mailing Lists, Databases Available From State Company Directories

Would you like to know what kind of computing systems and software 24,000 manufacturing firms in California use? Or where to find out what materials 7,000 manufacturers in North Carolina need for their manufacturing processes? Or which of 2,700 manufacturers in Nevada have contracts with the federal government? You can get quick answers to these questions and more in the state directories of manufacturing companies.

These directories contain valuable information concerning what products are bought, sold, and distributed in each state. At the very least, each directory lists the companies' names, addresses, phone numbers, products, and Standard Industrial Codes (SIC), and is cross- referenced by company name, location, and SIC code/product. So, if you want to find out which companies in Tennessee manufacture a certain type of electronic component and where they are located, all you have to do is look it up in the product index. If you want to find out what manufacturing firms are operating in a certain town or county, the geographic index will tell you. These directories can be invaluable for targeting new market areas, monitoring industry trends, developing more effective mailing lists, and much more.

The majority of these directories are put out by the individual state's Chamber of Commerce or Department of Economic Development, while private publishing firms compile and distribute the rest. The price and sophistication of these directories vary widely from state to state. While some, like Montana's, may offer only the basic information mentioned above, others, like the Illinois directory, will also include key personnel, CEO, parent company, employment figures, import/ export market, computer system used, and more. Prices range from no charge for North Dakota's directory, all the way to $250 for Alabama's five volume set. Most of the prices listed below include shipping and handling, and state sales tax where applicable.

Many of these directories are also available in database formats and differ widely in cost. While there are some real bargains, such as Rhode Island's directory of 2,600 firms on diskette for $20, some, like Colorado's of 4,700 firms, will cost you $1,000. Before ordering any of these databases, make sure that the software is compatible with your own system. Mailing labels for many of the directories are also available, and many states allow you to chose the companies you want for your mailing list on a cost per label basis.

List of State Company Directories

Alabama

Alabama Development Office, Research Division, State Capitol, 135 S. Union Street, Montgomery, AL 36130; 205-263-1171. $275/5 volumes. Listing of 6,500 companies includes name, address, phone, CEO, year established, employee figures, product lines, parent company, import/export, and SIC code. Cross-referenced by company name, location, product, parent company, international trade, and SIC code. Available on diskette or tape database format for $42 plus 3 cents per entry plus cost of software.

Alaska

Alaska Center for International Business, University of Alaska, 3211 Providence, Suite 203, Anchorage, AK 99508; 907-786-4300. *The Alaska Trade Directory*, a listing of 150 Alaska companies and industries that import or export, includes name, address, phone, CEO, key personnel, market area, product/service, and SIC code. Cross-referenced by company name and product/SIC code. Prices available on request.

Arizona

Phoenix Chamber of Commerce, 34 West Monroe, Suite 900, Phoenix, AZ 85003; 602-254-5521. $65. Listing of 5,000 companies includes name, address, phone, CEO, employee figures, market area, products, and SIC code. Cross-referenced by company name, location, market area, and products/SIC code.

Arkansas

Arkansas Industrial Development Foundation, P.O. Box 1784, Little Rock, AR 72203; 501-682-1121. $50. Listing of 2,500 companies includes name, address, phone, contact person, parent company, products, and SIC code. Cross-referenced by company name, location, and product/SIC code.

California

Database Publishing Company, 523 Superior Avenue, Newport Beach, CA 92663; 1-800-888-8434. $160. Listing of 24,000 companies includes name, address, phone, CEO, key personnel, sales volume, year established, parent company, products, computer brand used, import/export, employee figures, and SIC code. Cross-referenced by company name, location, products, and SIC code. Available on diskette for $975, book included.

Colorado

Business Research Division, University of Colorado, Campus Box 420, Boulder, CO 80309; 303-492-8227. $75. Listing of 4,700 companies includes name, address, phone, employee figures, market area, CEO, products, and SIC code. Cross-referenced by company name, location, and SIC code. Available in database format for $1,250. Mailing labels: $275/set. Prices may vary.

Connecticut

Connecticut Labor Department, Employment Security Division, Attn: Business Management, 200 Folly Brook Boulevard, Weathersfield, CT 06109; 203-566-2120. $22. The 1984 directory of 4,000 companies includes name, address, products, and SIC code. Cross-referenced by company name, location, products, and SIC codes. A quarterly updated listing is available for $7/year.

MacRae's Industrial Directories, 817 Broadway, 3rd Floor, New York, NY 10003; 1-800-622-7237. $129.50. Listing of 8,200 CT and RI manufacturing firms includes name, address, phone, parent company, key personnel, employee figures, size, products, and SIC code. Cross-referenced by company name, location, and SIC code.

Delaware

Delaware State Chamber of Commerce, 1201 N. Orange Street, P.O. Box 671, Wilmington, DE 19899; 302-655-7221. $45 for state Chamber members; $55 for non-members. The directory of commerce and industry, listing over 5,600 companies, includes name, address, phone, CEO, employee figures, products/ services, and SIC code. Cross-referenced by company name, location, and SIC code. Mailing labels: 25 cents/company.

Florida

Florida Chamber of Commerce, P.O. Box 11309, Tallahassee, FL 32302; 904-425-1200. $65. Listing of over 10,000 companies includes name, address, phone, CEO, employee figures, products, import/export, and SIC code. Cross-referenced by company name, location, SIC code. Available in database format, diskette or tape, for 12 cents/company or about $1,903.67. Mailing labels: 10 cents per company, $150 per 1,000 names, 1,000 minimum.

Georgia

Georgia Department of Industry and Trade, Directory Section, P.O. Box 56706, Atlanta, GA 30343; 404-656-3619. $55. Listing of 8,000 companies includes name, address, phone, market area, parent company, key personnel, employee figures, year established, products, and SIC code. Cross-referenced by company name, location and SIC code.

Hawaii

Chamber of Commerce of Hawaii, 735 Bishop Street, Honolulu, HI 96813; 808-522-8800. $45. The current edition of over 150 companies includes name, address, phone, contact person, product, and SIC code. Cross-referenced by company name, location, and SIC code.

Idaho

Center for Business Development & Research, University of ID, Moscow, ID 83844-3227; 208-885-6611. The new directory of over 1,300 manufacturers will include name address, phone, CEO, product/service, contact person, import/export, employee figures, and SIC code. Cross-referenced by company name, location, and SIC code. Diskette: PC compatible, $200.

Illinois

Harris Publishing Company, 2057 Aurora Road, Twinsburg, OH 44087; 1-800-321-9136. $116.45. Listing of over 20,000 companies includes name, address, phone, CEO, employee figures, computer brand used, year established, sales volume, product, and SIC code. Cross-referenced by company name, location, product, and SIC code. Diskette format, containing 9,000 companies with 20 or more employees, available for $276.75.

Indiana

Harris Publishing Company, 2057 Aurora Road, Twinsburg OH 44087; 1-800-321-9136. $75.65. Listing of over 8,000 companies includes name, address, phone, CEO, employee figures, year established, annual sales, computer brand used, products, and SIC code. Cross-referenced by company name, location, product, and SIC code. Diskette format, containing 6,000 companies with 10 or more employees, available for $233.75.

Iowa

Iowa Department of Economic Development, Research Section, 200 East Grand Avenue, Des Moines, IA 50309; 515-281-3925. $55. Listing of over 5,000 companies includes name, address, phone, CEO, purchasing agent, parent company, employee figures, product, and SIC code. Cross-referenced by company name, location, product, and SIC code. Available on diskette, $125. Book and diskette, $150. Purchase address: Business Publishing Corporation, 100 4th Street, Des Moines, IA 50309; 1-800-626-6000.

Kansas

Kansas Department of Commerce, 700 SW Harrison Street, Suite 1300, Topeka, KS 66603-3712; 913-296-3481. $40. Listing of 4,000 companies includes name, address, phone, contact person, parent company, employee figures, product, and SIC code. Cross-referenced by company name, location, product, and SIC code. Diskettes will be available in 1992.

Kentucky

Department of Economic Development, Maps & Publications, 133 Holmes Street, Frankfort, KY 40601; 502-564-4715. $30. Listing of 3,600 companies includes name, address, phone, CEO, year established, employee figures, products, and SIC code. Cross-referenced by company name, location, and SIC code.

Louisiana

Department of Economic Development, Commerce & Industry, P.O. Box 94185, Baton Rouge, LA 70804-9185; 504-342-5361. $48. Listing of 3,000 companies includes name, address, phone, CEO, purchasing agent, marketing area,

import/export, products, and SIC code. Cross-referenced by company name, location, and SIC code. Database price available on request.

Maine

Maine Manufacturing Directory, Tower Publishing Company, 34 Diamond Street, P.O. Box 7220, Portland, ME 04112; 1-800-431-2665 in-state; 207-774-9813 out-of-state. $37.50. Listing of 2,200 companies includes name, address, phone, three contact persons, employee figures, gross sales, product, and SIC code. Cross-referenced by company name, location, and SIC code. Mailing labels: $55 for first 1,000, then 5 cents each.

Maryland

Harris Publishing Company, 2057 Aurora Rd., Twinsburg, OH 44087; 1-800-888-5900. $50.35. Listing of 2,500 companies includes name, address, phone, employee figures, year established, annual sales, products, key personnel, and SIC code. Divided into sections by company name, location, industry, import/export, products, and SIC code. Mailing labels: $75 per 1,000 names, minimum charge $150. Diskette available for $228.

Massachusetts

George D. Hall Publishing Company, 50 Congress Street, Boston, MA 02109; 617-523-3745. $67.95 in-state; $56.95 out-of-state. Listing of 7,400 companies includes name, address, phone, CEO, sales volume, employee figures, products, and SIC code. Cross-referenced by company name, location, and product. Database format on diskette for any 3,000 companies available for $400. Mailing labels $225 minimum per 3,000; 6 cents per name.

Michigan

Harris Publishing Company, 2057 Aurora Road, Twinsburg, OH 44087; 1-800-321-9136. $123.50. Listing of 14,000 companies includes name, address, phone, CEO, employee figures, computer brands used, year established, products, and SIC code. Cross-referenced by company name, location, product, and SIC code. Diskette format, containing 7,000 companies with 20 or more employees, available for $308.75.

Minnesota

National Information Systems, 4401 West 76th Street, Edina, MN 55435; 612-893-8308. $83.49. Listing of 9,000 companies includes name, address, phone, contact person, employee figures, sales volume, year established, products, and SIC code. Cross-referenced by company name, location, and product/SIC code.

Mississippi

Mississippi Department of Economic and Community Development, 1400 Walter Sillers Bldg., P.O. Box 849, Jackson, MS 39205; 601-359-3448. $50. Listing of 2,600 companies includes name, address, phone, CEO, key personnel, employee figures, parent company, products, international trade, and SIC code. Cross-referenced by company name, location, product, and SIC code. Available on diskette for $400, and $200 for yearly update.

Missouri

Harris Publishing Company, 2057 Aurora Road, Twinsburg, OH 44087; 1-800-321-9136. $89.30. Listing of 8,000 companies includes name, address, phone, CEO, employee figures, computer brand used, year established, product, and SIC code. Cross-referenced by company name, location, product, and SIC code. Diskette format, containing 4,800 companies with 10 or more employees, available for $261.25.

Montana

Department of Commerce, Business Assistance Division, 1424 9th Avenue, Helena, MT 59620; 406-444-3923. $20. Listing of 2,500 companies includes name, address, phone, owner, size classification, products, and SIC code. Cross-referenced by company name, location, product, and SIC code.

Nebraska

Nebraska Department of Economic Development, P.O. Box 94666, Lincoln, NE 68509; 402-471-3784. $40. Listing of 1,849 companies includes name, address, phone, CEO, parent company, employee figures, import/export, products, and SIC code. Cross-referenced by company name, location, and product/SIC code. Available on IBM compatible diskette for $150.

Nevada

Gold Hill Publishing Company, P.O. Drawer F, Virginia City, NV 89440; 702-847-0222. $75 out-of-state; $75 plus shipping and handling in-state. Listing of 6,530 companies includes name, address, phone, parent company, CEO, key personnel, FAX #, square footage occupied, sales volume, products, import/export, federal contracts, year established, years in NV, products, and SIC code. Cross-referenced by company name, location, and product/SIC code. Available on diskette for $400.

New Hampshire

Department of Research & Economic Development, Industrial Development Office, 172 Pembroke Road, P.O. Box 856, Concord NH 03302-0856; 603-271-2591. $34.75. Listing of 4,800 companies includes name, address, phone, CEO, ranking officers, year established, sales volume, import/export, products, and SIC code. Cross-referenced by company name, location, and product/SIC code. Available on IBM compatible diskette for $250/set of 4 + $4.74 postage & handling.

New Jersey

Commerce Register, Inc., 190 Godwin Avenue, Midland Park, NJ 07432; 1-800-221-2172. $92.50. Listing of 11,000 companies includes name, address, phone, key personnel, sales volume, products, employee figures, square footage and acreage occupied, year established, SIC code, and bank, accountants, and law firms used. Cross-referenced by company name, location, and product/SIC code. Available on diskette for $153 minimum charge, depending on number of listings ordered.

New Mexico

Department of Economic Development, Joseph M. Montoya Building, 1100 St. Francis Drive, Santa Fe, NM 87503; 505-827-0300. $25. Listing of 1,800 companies includes name, address, phone, CEO, employee figures, products/services, and SIC code. Cross-referenced by company name, location, and product/SIC code.

New York

MacRAE's Industrial Directories, 817 Broadway, 3rd Floor, New York, NY 10003; 1-800-622-7237. $135. Listing of 12,000 companies includes name, address, phone, key personnel, size classification, products, location, and SIC code.

North Carolina

North Carolina Business Industry, Department D, P.O. Box 25249, Raleigh, NC 27611; 919-733-4151. $52.50. The new edition of 7,000 companies includes name, address, phone, CEO, year established, employee figures, parent company, import/export, product, and purchasing and product SIC codes. Cross-referenced by company name, location, parent company, product, products purchased, and import/export capabilities. Available on IBM magnetic tape database format for $1,000.

North Dakota

North Dakota Department of Economic Development and Finance, 1833 E. Bismarck Express, Bismarck, ND 58504; 701-224-2810. $20. Listing of over 600 companies includes name, address, phone, contact person, employee figures, products, and SIC code. Cross-referenced by company name, location, and product/SIC code.

Ohio

Harris Publishing Company, 2057 Aurora Road, Twinsburg, OH 44087; 1-800-321-9136. $130.15. Listing of 18,000 companies includes name, address, phone, CEO, employee figures, year established, annual sales, computer brand used, products, and SIC code. Cross-referenced by company name, location, product, and SIC code. Diskette format, containing 8,700 companies with 20 or more employees, available for $308.75.

Oklahoma

Oklahoma Department of Commerce, P.O. Box 26980, Marketing Division, Oklahoma City, OK 73126-0980; 405-843-9770, ext. 207. $40. Listing of 4,500 companies includes name, address, phone, owner's name, employee figures, product, and SIC code. Cross-referenced by company name, location, product, and SIC code.

Oregon

Oregon Economic Development Department, 775 Summer Street, NE, Salem, OR 97310; 503-373-1200. $60. Listing of 7,500 companies includes name, address, phone, employee figures, parent company, CEO, import/export, products, and SIC code. Cross-referenced by company name, product, and SIC code. Available in database formats and mailing labels at variable cost.

Pennsylvania

Harris Publishing Company, 2057 Aurora Road, Twinsburg, OH 44087; 1-800-321-9136. $130.15. Listing of 18,000 companies includes name, address, phone, CEO, employee figures, computer brand used, year established, products, and SIC code. Cross-referenced by company name, location, product, and SIC code. IBM compatible diskette format, containing 8,800 companies with 20 or more employees, available for $308.75.

Rhode Island

Department of Economic Development, Research Division, 7 Jackson Walkway, Providence, RI 02903; 401-277-2601. $10 for RI residents; $30 for non-residents. Listing of 2,600 companies includes name, address, phone, CEO, employee figures, parent company, products, and SIC code. Cross-referenced by company name, location, and SIC code. Available on IBM or MacIntosh compatible diskette for $50. Mailing labels: 5 cents per name.

South Carolina

State Development Board, P.O. Box 927, Columbia, SC 29202; 803-737-0400. Attn: Industrial Directory sales. $60. Listing of 3,200 companies includes name, address, phone, CEO, geographical location, purchasing agent, employee figures, product line, parent company, and SIC code. Cross-referenced by company name, location, product, and SIC code. Available on IBM compatible diskette for $500. Mailing labels: $50 set up fee, 10 cents per label.

South Dakota

Governor's Office of State Economic Development, Capitol Lake Plaza, Pierre, SD 57501; 605-773-5032. $35. Listing of 1,000 companies includes name, address, phone, trade name, county, FAX number, marketing area, employee figures, CEO, purchasing agent, sales manager, products, and SIC code. Cross-referenced by company name, location, and SIC code. Mailing labels: $35/set.

Tennessee

M. Lee Smith Publishers & Printers, P.O. Box 198867, Arcade Station, Nashville, TN 37219; 615-242-7395. $68 in-state; $65 out-of-state. Listing of 5,300 companies includes name, address, phone, parent company, key personnel, employee figures, marketing area, computer brand used, products, and SIC code. Available in database format, magnetic tape or diskette: $100 conversion fee, then $250 per 1,000 chosen. Mailing labels: $90 per 1,000. Diskette is available for $395. Diskette and book available for $345.

Texas

University of Texas, Bureau of Business Research, P.O. Box 7459, Austin, TX 78713-7459; 512-471-1616. $120. Two volume directory of 17,000 companies includes name, address, phone, key personnel, year established, sales volume, employee figures, market area, import/export, products, and SIC code. Volume 1 lists companies by name; volume 2 lists companies by product/SIC code. Available on diskette for $400 per 2,000 companies.

Utah

Utah Department of Community and Economic Development, 324 S. State Street, Suite 500, Salt Lake City, UT 84111; 801-538-8700. $26. Listing of 2,600 companies includes name, address, phone, employee figures, products, and SIC code. Cross-referenced by company name and SIC code. Available in dBase 3

Company Intelligence

database format, high or low density diskettes. Prices may vary.

Vermont

Agency of Development & Community Affairs, Pavillion Office Building, Montpelier, VT 05609; 802-828-3221. $12. Listing of 1,300 companies includes name, address, phone, geographical listing, plant location, CEO, parent company products trade names, products exported, employee figures, retail/mailorder/or wholesale distribution, and SIC code. Cross-referenced by company name, location, and product/SIC code. Available on diskette for $300.

Virginia

Virginia Chamber of Commerce, 9 South 5th Street, Richmond, VA 23219; 804-644-1607. $78.38 in-state; $75 out-of-state. Listing of 4,000 companies includes name, address, phone, CEO, employee figures parent company, products, and SIC code. Cross-referenced by product, SIC code, county, and city. Available in ASCII and ABCDIC magnetic tape database formats for $225. Mailing labels vary in price.

Washington

Database Publishing Company, 523 Superior Avenue, Newport Beach, CA 92663; 1-800-888-8434. $99. Listing of 4,100 companies includes name, address, phone, CEO, key personnel, sales volume, year established, parent company, products, computer brand used, employee figures, import/export, product, and SIC code.

Cross-referenced by company name, location, products, and SIC code. Diskette available for $495. Mailing labels, $65/1,000.

West Virginia

Harris Publishing Company, 2057 Aurora Rd., Twinsburg, OH 44087; 1-800-321-9136. $42.75. Listing of 1,200 companies includes name, address, phone, CEO, employee figures, computer brand used, year established, products, and SIC code. Cross-referenced by company name, location, product, and SIC code.

Wisconsin

WMC Service Corporation, P.O. Box 352, 501 East Washington Street, Madison, WI 53701-0352; 608-258-3400. $89.68/member, $131.88/non-member. Listing of 9,000 companies includes name, address, phone, CEO, year established, computer brand used, employee figures, parent company, FAX #, import/export, out-of-state affiliates, products, and SIC code. Cross-referenced by company name, location, product, and SIC code. Available on IBM compatible diskette $300/member, $450/non-member.

Wyoming

Department of Commerce, Division of Economic and Community Development, Barrett Bldg. 4 North, Cheyenne, WY 82002; 307-777-7284. No charge. Listing of 250 companies includes name, address, phone, CEO, market area, employee figures, product, and SIC code. Cross-referenced by company name, location, and SIC code.

Company Background Reports Free From Better Business Bureaus

If you are looking for information on a private or public company, and the company sells goods and services to consumers, you would be wise to check with the local Better Business Bureau in the city closest to the company's headquarters. A recent investigation into a patent research firm by our staff turned up a comprehensive report which outlined the company's activities, officers, claims and problems. For example, it revealed that the state of Wisconsin had filed a suit against the company. Moreover, it also outlined the company's response to the lawsuit.

The Better Business Bureaus (BBB) around the country provide this service **free** to consumers who may be interested in dealing with any given company. Simply call, and the local BBB will search its files for any information about the company in question. If the report is brief and straightforward, they will read it over the telephone. If it is more complex, like the report on the patent research company, a copy of it will be sent to you free of charge.

Listed below are the telephone numbers for the Better Business Bureaus in the U.S. and Canada.

Better Business Bureau Directory

Alabama
Birmingham	205-558-2222
Dothan	205-792-3804
Huntsville	205-533-1640
Mobile	205-433-5494/95
Montgomery	205-262-5606

Alaska
Anchorage	907-562-0704

Arizona
Phoenix	602-264-1721
Tucson	Inq. 602-662-7651
	Comp. 602-662-7654

Arkansas
Little Rock	501-664-7274

California
Bakersfield	805-322-2074
Colton	714-825-7280
Cypress	714-527-0680
Fresno	209-222-8111
Los Angeles	213-251-9696
Monterey	408-372-3149
Oakland	415-839-5900
Sacramento	916-443-6843
San Diego	619-281-6422
San Francisco	415-243-9999
San Jose	408-978-8700
San Mateo	415-696-1240
Santa Barbara	805-963-8657
Santa Rosa	707-577-0300
Stockton	209-948-4880/81

Colorado
Colorado Springs	719-636-1155
Denver	Inq. 303-758-2100
	Comp. 303-758-2212
Fort Collins	303-484-1348
Pueblo	719-542-6464

Connecticut
Fairfield	203-374-6161
Rocky Hill	203-529-3575
Wallingford	Inq. 203-269-2700
	Comp. 203-269-4457

Delaware
Wilmington	302-996-9200

District Of Columbia
Washington	202-393-8000

Florida
Clearwater	813-535-5522
Fort Myers	813-334-7331/7152
Jacksonville	904-721-2288
Maitland	407-660-9500
Miami	Inq. 305-625-0307
	Comp. 305-624-1302
New Port Richey	813-842-5459
Pensacola	904-433-6111
Port St. Lucie	407-878-2010
Tampa	813-875-6200
West Palm Beach	407-686-2200

Georgia
Albany	912-883-0744
Atlanta	404-688-4910
Augusta	404-722-1574
Columbus	404-324-0712/13
Macon	912-742-7999
Savannah	912-354-7521

Hawaii
Honolulu	808-942-2355

Idaho
Boise	208-342-4649
Idaho Falls	208-523-9754
Twin Falls	208-736-3971

Illinois
Chicago	Inq. 312-444-1188
	Comp. 312-346-3313
Peoria	309-688-3741
Rockford	815-963-2222

Indiana
Elkhart	219-262-8996
Evansville	812-473-0202
Fort Wayne	219-423-4433
Gary	219-980-1511
Indianapolis	317-637-0197
South Bend	219-277-9121

Iowa
Bettendorf	319-355-6344
Des Moines	515-243-8137
Sioux City	712-252-4501

Kansas
Topeka	913-232-0455
Wichita	316-263-3146

Kentucky
Lexington	606-259-1008
Louisville	502-583-6546

Louisiana
Alexandria	318-473-4494
Baton Rouge	504-926-3010
Houma	504-868-3456
Lafayette	318-981-3497
Lake Charles	318-433-1633
Monroe	318-387-4600
New Orleans	504-581-6222
Shreveport	318-221-8352

Maine
Portland	207-878-2715

Maryland
Baltimore	301-347-3990

Massachusetts
Boston	Inq. 617-426-9000
Hyannis	508)771-3022
Springfield	413-734-3114
Worcester	508-755-2548

Michigan
Grand Rapids	616-774-8236
Southfield	Inq. 313-644-1012
	Comp. 313-644-9136

Minnesota
Minneapolis/St. Paul	612-699-1111

Mississippi
Jackson	601-956-8282

Company Intelligence

Missouri
Kansas City	816-421-7800
St. Louis	Inq. 314-531-3300
Springfield	417-862-9231

Nebraska
Lincoln	402-467-5261
Omaha	402-346-3033

Nevada
Las Vegas	702-735-6900/1969
Reno	702-322-0657

New Hampshire
Concord	603-224-1991

New Jersey
Newark	201-642-INFO
Paramus	201-845-4044
Parsippany	201-334-5990
Toms River	201-270-5577
Trenton	201-588-0808
Westmont	609-854-8467

New Mexico
Albuquerque	505-884-0500
Farmington	505-326-6501
Las Cruces	505-524-3130

New York
Buffalo	716-856-7180
Farmingdale (Long Island)	516-420-0500
New York	212-533-7500
Rochester	716-546-6776
Syracuse	315-479-6635
Wappinger Falls	914-297-6550
White Plains	914-428-1230/31

North Carolina
Asheville	704)-253-2392
Charlotte	704-332-7151
Greensboro	919-852-4240/41/42
Hickory	704-464-0372
Raleigh	919-872-9240
Winston-Salem	919-725-8348

Ohio
Akron	216-253-4590
Canton	216-454-9401
Cincinnati	513-421-3015
Cleveland	216-241-7678
Columbus	614-486-6336
Dayton	513-222-5825
Lima	419-223-7010
Mansfield	419-522-1700
Toledo	419-241-6276
Wooster	216-263-6444
Youngstown	216-744-3111

Oklahoma
Oklahoma City	Inq. 405-239-6081
	Inq. 405-239-6860
	Comp. 405-239-6083
Tulsa	918-492-1266

Oregon
Portland	503-226-3981

Pennsylvania
Bethlehem	215-866-8780
Lancaster	717-291-1151
Toll-Free York Co. Resident	846-2700
Philadelphia	215-496-1000
Pittsburgh	412-456-2700
Scranton	717-342-9129

Puerto Rico
San Juan	809-756-5400

Rhode Island
Warwick	Inq. 401-785-1212
	Comp. 401-785-1213

South Carolina
Columbia	803-254-2525
Greenville	803-242-5052
Myrtle Beach	803-497-8667

Tennessee
Blountville	615-323-6311
Chattanooga	615-266-6144
Knoxville	615-522-2552
Memphis	901-795-8771
Nashville	615-254-5872

Texas
Abilene	915-691-1533
Amarillo	806-358-6222
Austin	512-476-1616
Beaumont	409-835-5348
Bryan	409-823-8148/49
Corpus Christi	512-854-2892
Dallas	214-220-2000
El Paso	915-545-1212
Fort Worth	817-332-7585
Houston	713-868-9500
Lubbock	806-763-0459
Midland	915-563-1880
San Angelo	915-949-2989
San Antonio	512-828-9441
Tyler	214-581-5704
Waco	817-772-7530
Weslaco	512-968-3678
Wichita Falls	817-723-5526

Utah
Salt Lake City	801-487-4656

Virginia
Fredericksburg	703-786-8397
Norfolk	804-627-5651
(Peninsula area)	804-851-9101
Richmond	804-648-0016
Roanoke	703-342-3455

Washington
Kennewick	509-582-0222
Seattle	206-448-8888
Spokane	509-747-1155
Tacoma	206-383-5561
Yakima	509-248-1326

Wisconsin
Milwaukee	414-273-1600

Wyoming
None

International Bureaus

National Headquarters For Canadian Bureaus
Concord, Ontario	416-669-1248

Alberta
Calgary	403-258-2920
Edmonton	403-482-2341
Red Deer	403-343-3280

British Columbia
Vancouver	604-682-2711
Victoria	604-386-6348

Manitoba
Winnipeg	204-943-1486

New Brunswick
Saint John	709-658-1622

Newfoundland
St. John's	709-364-2222

Nova Scotia
Halifax	Inq. 902-422-6581
	Comp. 902-422-6582

Ontario
Hamilton	416-526-1111
Kitchener	519-579-3080
London	519-673-3222
Ottawa	613-237-4856
Toronto	416-766-5744
Windsor	519-258-7222

Quebec
Montreal	514-286-9281
Quebec	418-523-2555

Saskatchewan
Regina	306-352-7601

Israel
Tel Aviv	03-28-25-28

Market Studies, Demographics, And Statistics

Existing Market Studies

Finding information about a market, whether it is a comprehensive market study or a single fact or figure, seems to be one of the most common challenges for business researchers. And how one handles this problem can depend upon a number of variables, including time and money. Since it is virtually impossible to map out a research strategy for all possible circumstances, presented here is a collection of some obvious and not so obvious sources to help with such an effort. If you are under the gun to get the most information in the shortest amount of time, the good old telephone is the efficient method (refer to the section entitled *The Art of Getting A Bureaucrat To Help You*).

Traditional Published Sources

If you want to begin with traditional published sources, start with a local library that is oriented toward the business community. A nearby university with a business school or a large public library can be a good starting place. Many business libraries offer free or low-cost telephone research service. For example, the Brooklyn Public Library's Business Library (280 Cadman Plaza West, Brooklyn, NY 11201, 718-780-7800) will answer brief questions over the telephone and hold your hand in identifying information sources if you visit in person.

If you are not familiar with traditional published information sources, using the services of a research librarian can be an efficient way to get at exactly what is there that you need. If you are in a hurry, see what you can get over the telephone. If time is not critical, it will be worth visiting the library to become acquainted with local resources, because if these reference sources are not useful to you now, most likely they will be in the future. Many of the questions we answer for clients at a rate of $100 an hour can be answered for free by a local reference librarian.

Computerized Data Bases And Data Sources

Currently there are an estimated 3,000 to 5,000 computerized data bases available to the public. Some publications which identify online data bases include:

1) *Data Base Directory Service* by Knowledge Industry Publications ($395, includes one year of monthly newsletters, a Directory available separately for $195, and a supplement published mid-year, *Data Base Alert*, from Knowledge Industry Publications, Inc., 701 Westchester Avenue, White Plains, NY 10604, 914-328-9157);

2) *Directory of Online Data Bases* by Gale Research, Inc., 835 Penobscot Bldg., Detroit, MI 48226, 1-800-877-4253. ($199 for two issues per year.)

3) *Directory of Portable Data Bases*, by Gale Research, Inc., 835 Penobscot Bldg., Detroit, MI 48226, 1-800-877-4253. ($99 for biannually issued subscription.)

Almost all major vendors maintain data bases which contain marketing information. A review of any of the four books cited above will help you pinpoint data bases which may be helpful, or you can call BRS, Dialog and other data base vendors directly. Some of the more popular data bases which contain marketing information on a wide variety of industries are basically indexes and abstracts of current trade and business periodicals. Included in this category are:

- ABI/INFORM
- Management Contents
- Predicasts
- NewsNet
- HARFAX Industry Data Sources

If you are a first time user of data bases, it may be wise to have someone else do your searching. Companies called Information Brokers are in this line of business. The best way to find such brokers is to contact your local reference librarian. They are in a good position to tell you what retrieval services exist locally.

If you have trouble with this method, you may find help by calling Dialog Information Services, Customer Service at 1-800-334-2564. This major data base vendor maintains a list of those organizations which provide this service. Dialog can narrow down your options according to what city you are in and what subjects you want searched. There is no charge for these referrals.

Be sure to inquire whether a nearby public, academic or specialized library performs online retrieval services. If they do, it is probably going to be much cheaper. For example, the Brooklyn Business Library will do **data base searches and charge only for direct out-of-pocket costs**. An information broker is likely to cost you three to four times more.

If you have a PC with a modem but have been reluctant to access the more complicated business data bases, you may want to contact EASYNET. This service offers simple and uniform access to over 850 data bases from 13 hosts worldwide, including most of the major business data bases. Your search is automatically intermediated by the Easynet Knowledge Gateway computer. Easynet covers most of the major business data bases. They have a set fee of $10 per search for a successful search. Some data bases have a surcharge and Easynet will let you know about them before the searches are made.

EASYNET/Telebase Systems, Inc.
435 Devon Park Dr., Suite 600
Wayne, PA 19087
1-800-EASYNET (modem number)
1-800-220-7616
215-293-4700

Market Studies, Demographics and Statistics

Refer to the section entitled *What's Good And Bad About Using Computers In The Information Age* for a more detailed discussion of the pros and cons of commercial online data bases.

Existing Market Studies

In order to find relevant market studies which have already been published, several checkpoints should be covered:

1) The data bases described above are likely to cover the news of currently released market studies.

2) Many industries have market research firms which specialize only in that industry. To identify these firms contact one or all of the following:

- an industry analyst at the U.S. Department of Commerce, Office of the Assistant Secretary for Trade Development at 202-482-1461;

- a specialist at an industry trade association (see *Encyclopedia of Associations* published by Gale Research Inc., 835 Penobscot Bldg., Detroit, MI 48226, 1-800-877-4253, available in most libraries);

- relevant trade magazines which can be identified by either one of the first two choices.

3) Contact those organizations which publish market studies on many industries, for example:

- Predicasts, 362 Lakeside Dr., Foster City, CA 94404, 1-800-321-6388, 415-378-5200;

- Frost and Sullivan, Inc., 106 Fulton Street, New York, NY 10038, 212-233-1080;

- Arthur D. Little Decision Resources, Bay Colony Corporate Center, 1100 Winter Street, Waltham, MA 02154, 617-487-3700;

- International Resource Development Inc., P.O. Box 1716, New Canaan, CT 06840, 203-966-2525;

- Creative Strategies Research International, 4633 Old Ironsides Drive, Suite 133, Santa Clara, CA 95054, 408-748-3400; or

- BusinessCommunications Co. Inc., 25 Van Zant St., Norwalk, CT 06855, 203-853-4266;

4) Review the major data bases and publications which index available market studies for sale. These include:

- FINDEX: its data base or book identifies studies available from Wall Street investment firms and management consulting firms, contact: FIND/SVP, 625 Avenue of the Americas, 2nd Floor, New York, NY 10011, 212-645-4500. Call 1-800-346-3787 for a free catalogue or table of contents of Market Research Reports;

- INVESTEXT: its data base provides full text of research reports produced by Wall Street and regional investment banking companies. Contact: Thompson Financial Network, Investext, 11 Farnsworth Street, Boston, MA 02110, 617-345-2704, 1-800-662-7878; and

- Arthur D. Little/Online: provides access to the non-exclusive publications of Arthur D. Little Decision Resources and Arthur D. Little, Inc. Includes references and selected full-text items covering industry forecasts, strategic planning, company assessments, and emerging technologies. Contact: Arthur D. Little Decision Resources, Bay Colony Corporate Center, 1100 Winter Street, Waltham, MA 02154, 617-487-3700.

Market Studies From Associations

Many trade associations conduct market studies about their member organizations and/or industries. These reports may or may not be included in the data bases and other sources described above. It is worth contacting relevant associations directly to ensure that you have not missed an important report. To identify a relevant association use Gale's *Encyclopedia of Associations* (see reference above). This book is well indexed and available at most libraries. The proper association can normally be identified with a simple phone call to the reference desk or visit to a local library. If you cannot find what you need in this encyclopedia, the American Society of Association Executives may be of further help.

Information Central
American Society of Association Executives
1575 Eye Street, NW
Washington, DC 20005
202-626-2723

You should be aware that some associations will not sell their studies to non-members. However, there are some ways you can circumvent this problem.

1) Join the association; some memberships are relatively inexpensive.

2) Access thanks to antitrust laws; the association may be violating antitrust laws if it does not make the study available to non-members. This does not mean the organization cannot charge you a whole lot more than they do for its members. And, you must keep in mind that the ultimate action in pursuing this strategy is to take the association to court. But it is worth trying because many associations are very concerned about the antitrust laws, and simply mentioning that you are going to check with your legal counsel about possible antitrust violations may be enough to shake free the report.

If you want to investigate further about how an association may be violating antitrust laws, obtain a copy of *Association Law Handbook*, $65 for members, $80 for non-members, or *The Law of Associations*, $170 for members, $204 for non-members, or *Anti-Trust Procedures*, a compilation of anti-trust articles, $22 for members, $44 for non-members from American Society of Association Executives, plus $5.25 for regular UPS or first class postage and handling on all orders (see address above). This book explores association executives' worries and ways to avoid possible antitrust problems.

A $1,500 Market Study For Free

Many business researchers are unaware of the fact that if a high priced market study carries a copyright, like a Frost and Sullivan or Predicasts study, it may be **available for free** at the Library of Congress in Washington, DC. The Library receives two copies of all copyrighted material and usually adds these reports to its collection. The problem is that these companies are aware that people use the Library of Congress to see these studies and, as a result, they often wait for the last possible legal moment before filing their copyright. This can be 3 months or more after the study is published which means that it may take several more months before it gets into the collection.

Here are examples of how much money you can save by using this approach. Recently, we searched the Library of Congress catalog under "videotext" and found 39 reports, studies and publications, including the following:

- *Videotex & Teletex Markets* - a study published by Predicasts and for sale at $1,500; and

- *Advertising In The New Electronic Media* - a study available for $985 from International Resource Development.

Although both of these studies were about 10 years old, a recent review of the catalog showed that International Resource Development, Inc. alone, already had 20 new studies including:

- *Equipment Leasing in Europe*
- *Robot Vision Systems*
- *Speech Recognition and Voice Systems*
- *Microcomputer Educational Software for the Home*
- *Consumer Telephone Equipment*
- *High-Tech Drug Delivery Systems*
- *Uninterruptible Power Systems and Power Line Conditioning Equipment*

If you get to Washington, it will certainly be worth your time to visit the Library of Congress and discover market studies in your area of interest.

The Library is basically set up for visiting researchers, so it may be a bit more difficult, but not impossible, to see these studies if you do not come to Washington. However, you can arrange to obtain these studies through an interlibrary loan. The best way to do this is to identify the title of the study and then telephone the Reference Section at the Library of Congress to see if it is in their collection (telephone number noted below). If it is, then ask how to arrange an interlibrary loan. Any local library will also be happy to work with you on this matter.

If you do not know the title of a particular market study, it will be a bit harder to work remotely. The Library is not set up to do this sort of general reference work over the telephone. You can try calling the telephone reference number below to see what kind of assistance you can get to such an inquiry. If you do not get the help you need, call the office of your U.S.

Representative or Senator (simply phone the Capitol Hill switchboard at 202-224-3121). What you should request is a list of Library of Congress holdings covering a specific subject area of interest. Requesting the titles of all Frost and Sullivan reports would not be of value because the publisher's name is not always an index term. **How successful you are at getting the Library to help may depend a lot on when you call and on how good you are at working with people over the telephone** (refer to the section entitled *The Art Of Getting A Bureaucrat To Help You*). Keep in mind that the Library is open weekdays 8:30 am until 9:30 pm Eastern standard time, Saturdays from 8:30 am to 5 pm, and Sundays from 1:00 pm to 5 pm.

Telephone Reference Section
Library of Congress
Washington, DC 20540
202-707-5522 (general public)
202-707-2905 (news media queries)

The Library of Congress is not the only collection that contains copies of expensive market studies which can be viewed on sight or through an interlibrary loan. Practically every major federal agency has a library which collects studies in those fields within its mandate. The National Library of Medicine contains hundreds of market studies relating to health care; the U.S. Department of Energy has studies about the oil and gas industry; the U.S. Department of Defense maintains surveys of the aerospace industry, etc. If you cannot figure out which government agency is responsible for certain industries, either one of the following books can help:

1) *U.S. Government Manual*, ($21, Superintendent of Documents, U.S. Government Printing Office, Washington, DC 20402-9325, 202-783-3238); or

2) *Lesko's Info-Power*, by Matthew Lesko, ($39.95, 1994 Information USA), available at local bookstores and public libraries, or call 1-800-955-POWER.

If you don't have time to locate either of these books, the following free resources are designed to help you learn how the government can help you:

- The district or Washington office of your Member of Congress;

- Local Federal Information Center which is part of the General Services Administration, 410-722-9000; or

- Washington, DC Directory Assistance at 202-555-1212. These operators are equipped to identify phone numbers of major agencies.

Free Government Market Studies

The federal government serves as a major repository of market studies it generates. Not only are these reports likely to be available at very reasonable prices, such surveys also offer powerful information opportunities by virtue of the fact that most people are unaware of their availability. And, unlike market studies produced by commercial organizations which may invest 6 to 12 man-months on a project, a government sponsored effort is likely to represent several man-years worth of investment. The value for the money is unbeatable. The seven major government institutions which produce market studies are described below.

U.S. Congress

Each year the United States Congress conducts several thousand hearings which either analyze proposed legislation or oversee existing laws. In the same way that the government seems to affect every facet of our lives, the Congress seems to get involved in most every aspect of business. For instance, take the time when six franchise agreements from privately held companies became part of public testimony at hearings before the Senate Commerce Committee. Everyone in the industry said this information was proprietary and not available to anyone outside the companies in question.

In order to convince you of the broad range of areas probed by the Congress, listed below are a sampling of subject headings we recently found under the letter "M" in the index of bills for a recent session of Congress:

- Mail Order Business
- Major League Sports Community Protection
- Malpractice Insurance
- Malt Beverage Interbrand Competition
- Management Buyouts
- Management Consultants
- Management Information System
- Manganese
- Manufacturing Industries
- Marathon Running
- Marine Energy Resources
- Marketing of Farm Produce
- Materials Handling
- Meat Packing Industry
- Medical Corporations

An important aspect of a congressional hearing is that the committee in charge is usually very thorough in covering a subject. The best experts in the world normally present testimony or submit written comments. Committee staffers identify all available information sources and collect the latest research. Many times the committee will even commission a research study on the subject. Documentation from committee hearings normally exists in a number of formats which are described next.

1) **Published reports:** It often takes 6 months to one year after the date of the hearing before the report is published. Sometimes the printed committee or subcommittee hearings can be obtained free from the professional staffers or the full committee documents clerk. More popular transcripts on controversial subjects are frequently available for sale from the Government Printing Office (Superintendent of Documents, Washington, DC, 202-402-9325, 202-783-3238).

2) **Unedited transcripts:** Debates are published the following day in the *Congressional Record*. The Senate only has official reporters for debates. For unedited transcripts of Senate committee or subcommittee hearings, contact the committee to see what commercial transcription service they employed.

House committee transcripts, if available, are only available from the Office of Official Reporters to the House Committees, Room B-25, Cannon Building, Washington, DC 20515, 202-225-7187. Commercial reporting services are prohibited from transcribing and selling hearing transcripts. Transcripts are available from 1 to 10 working days after the hearing for $1.25 per page. The House Committees that allow transcripts of their hearings to be purchased are:
  Agriculture
  Budget
  Education & Labor
  Merchant Marines and Fisheries
  Science, Space and Technology

Committees that sometimes make transcripts available for public purchase are:
  Armed Services
  DC Committee
  Energy and Commerce
  Small Businesses
  Select Committee on Aging
  Select Committee on Hunger

The remaining House committees do not publicly release transcripts of their hearings.

3) **Prepared testimony presented by witnesses:** These formal statements sometimes are made available before the hearing date, but usually a limited number of copies are distributed at the hearings. If you are trying to get this documentation and cannot wait until the hearing is printed, contact the committee or subcommittee staffer responsible for the hearing or call the witness directly to request a copy. These statements sometimes are made available before the hearing date and usually only a limited number of copies are distributed at the hearings. Both oral and written statements will comprise the published hearing record.

4) **Studies commissioned by congressional committees:** Such studies are usually conducted by the Congressional Research Service (CRS) of the Library of Congress. If copies are available, they can be obtained only through a Member of Congress. (More details about CRS reports are provided later in this Section.)

5) **Formal comments about proposed legislation sent to the committee by interested parties, including government agencies:** Such comments often are included in the published hearing and also are contained in the committee report on the bill. Moreover, they became part of the committee files and usually can be viewed in the committee office.

There are a number of options for finding out if hearings have been held on a specific topic. However, since there is no centralized list of all congressional hearings, you should expect to make a dozen or so calls.

1) **Bill Status Office: 202-225-1772**
This can be the fastest source because by accessing the LEGIS computerized data base, congressional staffers can tell you over the phone if legislation has been introduced on a specific topic. In addition to telling you which committees are working on the legislation, they can give you the status of a bill, who sponsored

the measure, when it was introduced, and the status of similar bills. Although this congressional data base is limited because it does not cover investigative or "oversight" hearings, it is still quite inclusive since the information goes back to 1975. If a committee held a hearing on a subject because of proposed legislation, it is also likely to be responsible for oversight hearings on that subject. Telephone assistance is free and printouts are available for a $5 minimum, 20 cents per page. If you cannot easily arrange to have the printout picked up by messenger, you may want to ask your Representative or Senator's office to have it sent to you (and that way you can avoid the charge). Contact: Office of Legislative Information and Status, Ford House Office Building, 3rd & D Streets SW, Room 696, Washington, DC 20515.

2) Congressional Committees: 202-224-3121

Contacting a committee or subcommittee directly is another way to identify relevant hearings. However, the problem with this approach is that there are approximately 300 from which to choose. You must prepared to make a few calls before landing on target. The advantage to this method is that if the committee you call does not cover a particular subject area, it is usually very helpful in suggesting the appropriate committee. Keep in mind that the jurisdictions of many committees overlap, so it is necessary to check with all those committees when searching for valuable market information. If you do not get help, ask the Capitol Hill Switchboard at the number noted above to transfer you to the House or Senate Parliamentarian. These offices are very knowledgeable about the jurisdictions of all the committees. And, of course, you can also ask your Member of Congress to help identify the right committees.

3) Congressional Caucuses: 202-224-3121

The Steel Caucus, The Textile Caucus, and several dozen other "informal" study groups composed of House Members and Senators frequently produce reports on particular industries.

4) Congressional Information Service: 410-654-1550

This commercial firm indexes and provides copies of all published committee hearings. This service, *CIS Index*, has its limitations because some hearings are never published or are published a long time after the hearing has been held. Remember that copies of unpublished documentation can be obtained by using the methods described above. The complete service costs approximately $3,240 per year or $1,040 for the annual index. Most libraries are subscribers to this service. Contact: Congressional Information Service, Inc., 4520 East-West Highway, #800, Bethesda, MD 20814.

5) *The C.Q. Weekly Report*: 202-887-8500

Congressional Quarterly publishes *The C.Q. Weekly Report*, which lists all printed committee and subcommittee hearings. It contains an analysis of the week's current and pending legislative and political activity, including voting records and legislative, oversight and investigative activities released during the past week. Annual subscription is $1299 and it is also available online for $2,500 for 12 hours of online time. A hardbound *Almanac*, available for $295, is a compendium of a particular session's activity. To order, call 1-800-543-7793. Contact: Congressional Quarterly, Inc., 1414 22nd Street NW, Washington, DC 20037.

U.S. International Trade Commission

Part of the function of this agency is to study the volume of imports in comparison to domestic production and consumption. As a result, it produces close to 100 market studies each year on topics ranging from ice hockey sticks to clothespins. Some of the studies released recently include:

- Fresh Cut Flowers
- Malts and Starches
- Floor Coverings
- Body Supporting Garments
- Glass Mirrors
- Computers and Calculators
- Sewing Machines
- Loudspeakers
- Fork Lift Trucks
- Brooms and Brushes

If you are interested in publications produced prior to 1984, this office has the *Publications and Investigations of the United States Tariff Commission and the United States International Trade Commission* list. It is for in-house use only, but may be viewed at the Docket Room. This office will send you a free copy of *Lists of Selected Publications of the United States International Trade Commission*, which contains a list of reports that are now in print. You can also request to be placed on a list to be notified of future studies. Call 202-205-2000 to add your name to the mailing list. Free copies of any of the above publications can be ordered 24 hours a day, seven days a week by calling 202-205-1809 (recording), or contact:

Docket Room
Office of the Secretary
U.S. International Trade Commission
500 E Street SW, Room 112
Washington, DC 20436
202-252-1806/1807

Congressional Research Service: Reports

The Congressional Research Service (CRS) is an important research arm of the Library of Congress and conducts custom research for the Members of Congress on **any subject**. When a congressional committee plans hearings on a subject such as the insurance industry, often the Congressional Research Service will churn out a background report on the industry. Here are examples of some current studies which may be of interest to the business community:

- *Compensation in the Airline Industry*
- *Information Technology for Agriculture America*
- *Financial Innovations & Deregulation: Non-Bank Banks*
- *The Shrinking Market for Foreign Cars in Japan*
- *Wall Street Analysts' Reasons for the Decline in U.S.*
- *Production of Primary Petrochemicals*
- *Health Information Systems*
- *Attorney-Client Privilege*
- *Discount Brokerage of Securities: A Status Report*
- *Top Corporate Executive Compensation & Economic Performance*
- *Economic Statistics: Sources of Current Information*

- *Industrial Robots in the United States*
- *Domestic Crude Oil Production Projected to the Year 2000*

Free copies of these reports can be obtained only by contacting the Washington or district office of your Senator or Representative. The Congressional Research Service also publishes an index to all its reports. Although this *Index* is free, it can be difficult to obtain. If your legislator's office tells you they cannot get you an *Index*, ask to have a copy sent to the district office so you can review it at your Member's local office. Oddly enough, the reports are easier to get than the CRS Index. You can simply call your Member of Congress through the Capitol Hill Switchboard at 202-224-3121 or put your request in writing:

U.S. Senate
Washington, DC 20510

U.S. House of Representatives
Washington, DC 20515

Congressional Research Service: Current Issue Briefs

Each day the Congressional Research Service updates over 400 studies, called Current Issue Briefs. These reports are designed to keep Members of Congress informed on timely topics. Listed below is a sampling of subjects covered.

- *Advertising of Alcoholic Beverages in the Broadcast Media*
- *CBS Takeover Attempts*
- *Greenmail and the Market for Corporate Control*
- *Backyard Satellite Earth Stations*
- *Commercial Banking Competition*
- *Genetic Engineering*
- *U.S. Automobile Industry: Issues and Statistics*
- *Foreign Investment in the U.S.: Trends and Impact*
- *Why Some Corporations Don't Pay Taxes*
- *Biotechnology*
- *Problems Facing U.S. Petroleum Refiners*
- *The Fortune 500: Name, Address, and Officers of the 500 Largest Industrial Corporations in the U.S.*

To receive a complete list of all Current Issue Briefs, you must contact the office of your Representative or Senator.

Every month the Congressional Research Service publishes *Update* which includes a list of new and updated issue briefs of current interest. Briefs that are no longer of intense public or congressional interest are listed in the *Archived Issue Briefs List*. These publications, along with copies of the Issue Briefs listed above, are available only by making arrangements through your Member of Congress in the same manner as described above.

U.S. Commerce Department International Trade Administration

Each year the International Trade Administration (ITA) at the U.S. Department of Commerce investigates dozens of products from certain countries for possible violations of Anti-Dumping laws or the use of unfair subsidies under countervailing duty laws. These statutes have been established to protect domestic manufacturers from unfair foreign competition.

When the government conducts an investigation, the resulting file, that is open to public inspection, usually contains a complete report of the industry in question. The final determination of an investigation is published in *The Federal Register*. A few of the products the ITA has investigated since 1978 include:

- Butter Cookies
- Electric Golf Carts
- Iron Ore Pellets
- Ice Cream Sandwiches
- Moist Towelettes
- Motorcycle Batteries
- Photo Albums
- Electronic Tuners
- Ceramic Wall Tile
- Thin Sheet Glass

A complete listing of cases of industries studied by the ITA is available upon request. Copies of documentation from any of the above investigations are available for 10 cents per page if you make the copies yourself, 15 cents per page if they make the copies. However, this office is not set up to supply copies of files by mail and it is generally necessary to come in person or send someone on your behalf to get copies.

Central Records Unit
International Trade Administration
U.S. Department of Commerce
14th & Constitution Avenue NW, Room B-009
Washington, DC 20230
202-482-1248

General Accounting Office

The General Accounting Office (GAO) conducts special audits, surveys and investigations at the request of the U.S. Congress. It produces as many as 600 reports annually, many of which identify market opportunities. Below are just a few of their recent reports which have marketing potential.

- *Assessment of New Chemical Regulation Under the Toxic Substances Control Act*
- *Electronic Marketing of Agricultural Commodities*
- *SEC's Efforts to Find Lost and Stolen Securities*
- *Natural Gas Profit Data*
- *The U.S. Synthetic Fuels Corporation's Contracting With Individual Consultants*
- *Information on Historic Preservation Tax Incentives*
- *Licensing Data for Exports to Non-Communist Countries*
- *Disaster Assistance: Problems in Administering Payment for Nonprogram Crops*
- *Telecommunication Services: the 1991 Survey of Cable Television Rates and Services*
- *International Trade: Soviet Agricultural Reforms and the U.S. Government Response*
- *Foreign Assistance Aid: Energy Assistance and Global Warming*
- *Experience of Countries Using Alternative Motor Fuels*
- *Abandoned Mine Reclamation; Interior May Have Approved State Shift to Non-Coal Projects Prematurely*
- *Long Term Care Projected Needs of the Aging Baby Boom Generation*

- *Financial Markets: Computer Security at Five Stock Exchanges Need Strengthening*

The first copy of a report is available free of charge and additional copies can be obtained for $2 each. You can also receive a free annual index of available GAO reports, a free monthly catalog of current reports, and a free printout from a data base which contains all titles and document numbers. For further information or for any of the above contact the General Accounting Office. The pickup address is: Distribution Section, 700 4th Street NW, Room 1000, Washington, DC 20548; 202-512-6000. The mailing address is: General Accounting Office, Documents Center, P.O. Box 6015, East Gaithersburg, MD 20877. FAX requests to 301-258-4066.

Federal Trade Commission

Besides the antitrust activities of the U.S. Department of Justice, the Federal Trade Commission (FTC) also has the authority to investigate certain industries or companies for possible antitrust violations. Recent FTC investigations have targeted particular industries.

- Travel Industry
- Mail-Order Stamp Sales
- Motion Picture Industry
- Tuna Industry
- Bail Bond Industry

- Buying Clubs
- Business Opportunity Companies
- Hearing Aid Industry
- Dental Laboratories
- Fine Paper Industry

You can inquire to determine whether a specific company has been probed by the Commission. The investigation itself is confidential, but much results in documentation that is public record and available for 12 cents per page. Recent FTC reports and publications are:

- *The Business Guide to the Mail Order Rule*
- *The Impact of State Price and Entry Regulations on Intrastate Long Distance Telephone Rates*
- *How Should Health Claims for Food Be Regulated?*
- *Mergers in the U.S. Petroleum Industry*
- *General Equilibrium of the Analyses of the Welfare and Employment Effects on the U.S. Auto and Steel Industries*

The FTC will mail copies of reports they have on hand to you free of charge. Contact:

Public Reference Branch
Federal Trade Commission (FTC)
6th & Pennsylvania Avenue NW, Room 130
Washington, DC 20580
202-326-2222

Nine Federal Statistical Agencies

Everyone Is Selling Demographic Data That's Available Free

Almost everyone who sells demographic data is getting it from a public source and repackaging it for the convenience of the customer. A few years ago we were looking for demographic data on the use of health care facilities and were told by all the experts in the business that the Association of Blue Cross and Blue Shield Companies was the only place to obtain this data. After finally locating the office in the Association which produced this information, we were told it would cost us $50. At the time we were feeling a little poor, so we decided to check sources in the federal government. Soon we located an office at the Social Security Administration in Baltimore that actually collected the pertinent data which Blue Cross requested periodically. The statistician at the Social Security Administration said he would be happy to give us the data for free and, equally important, his information was more current than the data contained in the Blue Cross report because the Association had not yet asked him for the latest figures.

Many times it may be worth buying information from private firms, but there are times when it may not. In any case, you owe it to your organization to check on the availability of public demographic data from the primary non-commercial sources.

Nine Major Federal Statistical Agencies

The federal government is the place where you should definitely begin. Without a doubt it is the largest collector of demographic data in the world. Over $1 billion dollars are spent to amass the decennial census which counts all the noses and toilets in the country. Although budget cuts have reduced some federal data collection activities, more data still are generated by departments and agencies in Washington than you could imagine or could ever put to use. **Actually federal spending cutbacks have been more harmful to the dissemination of the information rather than the collection of demographic and statistical data.** Nowadays it is somewhat more difficult to determine what data are available and where to find it.

There are nine major federal statistical agencies which are listed below. Contact the ones you feel may be of some help in your data search. When you call, ask to speak to the data expert who concentrates on the specific issue you are investigating. If the expert tells you that his or her agency does not collect the exact data you require, remember that this government specialist probably can tell you who might have the information. These statisticians stay current by reading all pertinent journals and attending international conferences. Most likely they can tell you which organizations and individuals to contact.

Plotting The Baby Boom

Recently we were trying to obtain the forecast of births in the U.S., and in particular, first births (how many first born sons

and daughters). The Bureau of the Census and the National Center for Health Statistics were very cooperative in giving us this data quickly. Equally helpful was a statistician at the Census Bureau who recommended an expert at the Urban Institute in Washington, DC who studied how much money parents spend on their children. A call to this expert produced a free report just published by the Institute, which showed that the average family spends over 50% more on their first child than they do on their second or third. This report, together with federal data on the boom in first births, proved to our client that the outlook for the baby products industry was on a large upswing.

The federal agencies noted here can probably provide much of the demographic data you need and also suggest sources elsewhere in the government as well as experts in the private sector.

1) Agriculture and Food Statistics
   National Agriculture Statistics Service
   Director, Estimates Division
   U.S. Department of Agriculture
   14th & Independence Avenue SW
   Washington, DC 20250   202-720-3896

2) Economic and Demographic Statistics
   Bureau of the Census
   U.S. Department of Commerce
   Data User Service Division
   Customer Service
   Washington, DC 20233   301-763-4100

3) Crime Statistics
   Uniform Crime Reporting Section
   Federal Bureau of Investigations (FBI)
   U.S. Department of Justice-GRB
   7th & D Streets, NW
   Washington, DC 20535   202-324-5038

4) Economics-National, Regional and International
   Bureau of Economic Analysis
   U.S. Department of Commerce
   Washington, DC 20230   202-523-0777

5) Education Statistics
   Office of Educational Research & Improvement
   555 New Jersey Avenue NW, Room 300
   Washington, DC 20208-5641   1-800-424-1616

6) Health Statistics
   National Center for Health Statistics
   U.S. Department of Health & Human Resources
   6525 Belcrest Road
   Hyattsville, MD 20782   301-436-8500

7) Employment, Prices, Living Conditions, Productivity, and
   Occupational Safety and Health

Bureau of Labor Statistics
U.S. Department of Labor
441 G Street NW
Washington, DC 20212
Information   202-606-7828
Publications   202-606-7828, ext. 6

8)   Import and Export Statistics
      World Trade Reference Room
      U.S. Department of Commerce
      Room 2233
      Washington, DC 20230   202-482-2185

9)   World Import and Export Statistics
      World Trade Statistics
      U.S. Department of Commerce
      Washington, DC 20230   202-482-5242

Tips For Finding Federal Data

We have found that one of the best sources for identifying data in the federal government is a publication titled the *Statistical Abstract of the United States*. Do not expect to find the precise data you need in this book. What you will discover is an invaluable index to hundreds of data tables on literally thousands of subjects. Below each table is the name of the agency which produced the data. This means that if you are trying to locate how many left-handed monkeys there are in the United States, you can refer to the index under monkey and turn to the appropriate table. What you are likely to find is a table that contains data on all the monkeys in the country and not how many are left-handed. You can then look at the bottom of the table and see what office compiled the numbers. If you call the office directly, someone there can probably track down the information you need in their files (in this case of monkeys, it may be difficult). Remember this *Abstract* contains only a small fraction of data available from any government office, but it serves as an excellent starting point for identifying which federal office collects what kind of information. The latest edition can be purchased from the U.S. Government Printing Office (noted earlier).

Another way to uncover opportunities in the vast federal repository is to obtain a copy of the forms that are filled out in the data collection phase. For example, if you are selling toothpaste, you may see that those who completed the long census form in the last decennial census stated what kind of toothpaste they use. This may not be printed in any report offered by the Census Bureau, but that does not mean you cannot get this data. The Bureau can do a special search for you and charge you on a cost recovery basis. This is true with any federal agency. What you should do is request copies of the data collection forms for any survey you think may be of interest to you. If you are in a consumer-related business, you should at least get a copy of the long form used in the decennial census.

Hotlines For Monitoring The Economy And Your Markets: Listen To Tomorrow's News Today

Why wait for tomorrow's *Wall Street Journal* to find out the latest economic statistics that will affect your business? You can find out today by calling the U.S. Department of Commerce Hotline. This is the same message that the *Wall Street Journal* listens to before going to press. If you want to know when the best time is to convert your adjustable rate mortgage to a fixed rate mortgage, you don't have to wait until your mortgage banker gives you the information at the end of the month. You can plot the trends daily by calling the Mortgage Rate Hotline at the Federal National Mortgage Association. This is where your mortgage banker gets the information, and you can be a month ahead of him.

Banks and Savings and Loans, Information on Failed Banks
Federal Deposit Insurance Corporation
202-393-8400

Banks and Savings and Loans, Obtaining a Financial Statement on Your Bank
Federal Deposit Insurance Corporation
202-393-8400

Banks, Aggregate Reserves of Depository Institutions
Thursday, Federal Reserve Board
202-452-3206

Banks, Assets and Liabilities of Insured Domestically Chartered and Foreign Banks
Monday, Federal Reserve Board
202-452-3206

Benefits, Employment Costs
Middle of Month, Bureau of Labor Statistics
202-606-7828 ext. 4

Collective Bargaining Settlements in Private Industry
Middle of Month, Bureau of Labor Statistics
202-606-7828 ext. 5

Construction
Beginning of Month, Department of Commerce
202-393-4100

Consumer Price Index
Middle of Month, Bureau of Labor Statistics
202-606-7828 ext. 1

Credit, Consumer Installment
5th Working Day of Month; Federal Reserve Board
202-452-3206

Earnings, Hourly and Weekly
Beginning of Month; Bureau of Labor Statistics
202-606-7828 ext. 3

Earnings, Real
Middle of Month, Bureau of Labor Statistics
202-606-7828 ext. 5

Economic News
GNP, Trade Figures, Housing Starts, and Other Economic Figures, Department of Commerce
202-393-4100

Economic News Highlights
Department of Commerce
202-393-1847

Economic News Weekend Preview
Department of Commerce
202-393-4102

Employment Situation
Beginning of Month, Bureau of Labor Statistics
202-606-7828 ext. 3

Foreign Exchange Rates
Monday, and 1st of Month, Federal Reserve Board
202-452-3206

Foreign Trade
End of Month, Department of Commerce
202-393-4100

Gross National Product
End of Month, Department of Commerce
202-898-2451

Housing, New Home Sales
Beginning of Month, Department of Commerce
202-393-4100

Housing Starts
Middle of Month, Department of Commerce
202-393-4100

Hours Worked In A Week
Beginning of Month, Bureau of Labor Statistics
202-606-7828 ext. 3

Income, Personal
End of Month, Department of Commerce
202-898-2452

Industrial Production and Capacity Utilization
Middle of Month, Federal Reserve Board
202-452-3206

Interest Rates, Selected
Monday, Federal Reserve Board
202-452-3206

International Trade, Merchandise Trade
Middle of Month, Department of Commerce
202-898-2453

Inventories and Sales, Manufacturing and Trade
Middle of Month, Department of Commerce
202-393-4100

Leading Economic Indicators
Beginning of Month, Department of Commerce
202-898-2450

Loans and Securities at All Commercial Banks
3rd Week of Month, Federal Reserve Board
202-452-3206

Merchandise Trade
Middle of Month, Department of Commerce
202-898-2453

Hotlines For Monitoring The Economy And Your Markets

Money Stock, Liquid Assets, and Debt Measures
Thursday, Federal Reserve Board
202-452-3206

Mortgage Rates, Adjustable Rate Information
Middle of Month, Federal Housing Finance Board
202-408-2940

Mortgage Rates, National Average Contract Rate For Purchase of Previous Occupied Homes By Combined Lenders
Middle of Month, Federal Housing Finance Board
202-408-2940

Mortgage Rates, 30-Year Fixed Rate Yields
Continually Updated, Federal National Mortgage Association
1-800-752-7020, 202-752-0471 ext. 3

Mortgage Rates, Fixed Intermediate Term Yields
Continually Updated, Federal National Mortgage Association
1-800-752-7020, 202-752-0471 ext. 4

Mortgage Rates, Adjustable Yields
Continually Updated, Federal National Mortgage Association
1-800-752-7020, 202-752-0471 ext. 5

Payroll for Industry
Beginning of Month, Bureau of Labor Statistics
202-606-7828 ext. 3

Personal Income and Outlays
End of Month, Bureau of Labor Statistics
202-606-7828

Plant and Equipment Expenditures
Middle of Month, Department of Commerce
202-898-2453

Producer Price Index
Middle of Month, Bureau of Labor Statistics
202-606-7828 ext. 2

Production and Capacity Utilization, Industrial
Middle of Month, Federal Reserve Board
202-452-3206

Productivity and Cost
Beginning of Month, Bureau of Labor Statistics
202-606-7828 ext. 5

Retail Trade, Advance Report for Previous Month
Middle of Month, Department of Census
202-393-4100

Salaries and Wages Information
Middle of Month, Bureau of Labor Statistics
202-606-7828 ext. 4

Sales and Inventories, Manufacturing and Trade
Middle of Month, Department of Commerce
202-393-4100

Treasury Bill Auction Results
Department of the Treasury
202-874-4400 ext. 221

Treasury Bill, Notice of Next Auction
Department of the Treasury
202-874-4400 ext. 211

Treasury Note and Bond Auction Results
Department of the Treasury
202-874-4400 ext. 222

Treasury Note and Bond, Notice of Next Auction
Department of the Treasury
202-874-4400 ext. 212

Treasury Securities, How To Purchase Notes, Bonds and Bills
Continually Updated, Department of the Treasury
202-874-4400 ext. 251

Unemployment Rates
Beginning of Month, Department of Labor Statistics
202-606-7828 ext. 3

Wholesale Trade
Middle of Month, Department of Commerce
202-393-4100

Wages and Salaries Information
Beginning of Month, Department of Labor Statistics
202-606-7828 ext. 4

State Data Centers

Approximately 1,300 organizations nationwide receive data from the U.S. Bureau of the Census and in turn disseminate the information to the public free of charge or on a cost recovery basis. These organizations are called state data centers and serve as ideal information sources for both local and national markets. The centers listed in this report are the major offices for each state. If you are looking for national markets, start with a center in your state. If you are searching for local market data, contact the center located in the relevant area.

Demographics and Target Market Identification

State data center offices are most frequently used for obtaining information on target markets. For instance, the Army and Navy used such services to identify which areas are populated with large numbers of teenagers in order to open recruiting offices and focus their advertising campaign. Avon door-to-door sales reps used state data center generated demographic maps to identify homes with highest potential. L.L. Bean relied on a center to determine large Hispanic populations for a special promotion of outdoor recreational products. These offices could provide current data including:

- The age distribution within a given county;
- Moving patterns for particular geographical areas;
- The number of wells and mobile homes in 85 counties;
- How many gravel pits in the state of Montana;
- Counties with the highest rate of illegitimate children;
- Analysis of why certain stores in an auto parts chain are doing better than others;
- Demographic profile of a person in need of child care;
- The top 25 markets by zip code;
- The number of male secretaries in a dozen contiguous counties.

Forecasting Future Markets

The biggest opportunities often lie in knowing the future of a market. Many of the state data centers have developed specific software for analyzing Census and other data to project growth of specific markets. Here is a sampling of what some centers can do:

- Population projections for every three years to the year 2020 (done by California center);
- State population changes by the year 2000;
- What year the white population will not be in the majority;
- The number of teenagers by the next century;
- Series of economic indicators for plotting future economic health in state (Oklahoma center provides such data).

Site Location

Another major area of interest is in providing information to companies considering relocating into a state. Because most states are aggressively trying to attract business, numerous customized services receive a high priority. Local centers can provide information such as the number of fast food restaurants in the area and the best location for another one. And some states, like Arkansas, have special site evaluation software which can manipulate Census data to show the demographic characteristics for market radiuses which are 2, 5 or 10 miles from a given site. Oklahoma and other states have free data sheets covering every community in their state which are loaded with specifics for choosing a location. Their reports contain data on:

- Distance from major cities
- Population: past and future
- Climate
- Municipal services
- Utilities
- Labor market analysis
- List of major manufacturers
- List of major employers
- Transportation
- Commercial services
- Major freight lines and truck terminals
- Educational facilities
- Financial institutions
- Tax structure
- Housing and churches
- Medical facilities
- Retail business in city
- Industrial financial assistance
- Water analysis report
- Recreational facilities
- Wholesale business in city
- Items deserving special consideration

Professional and Personal Relocation

The same services that are intended to help businesses relocate also can be useful to individuals and professionals. For example, if you are looking for a place to start an orthodontics practice, a local data center could determine which counties and cities have the most affluent families with young people -- a prime market for braces. Also, if you get an offer for a new job in another city, obtaining a data sheet on the local community like the one described above provides insight into the types of housing, schools, churches, and recreational facilities available.

Business Proposals Plus Loan and Grant Applications

If you are looking for money for either a grant, a loan or even venture money, data centers can provide the information needed for proposal writing. Grantors must have information such as what percent of people live below poverty line, and banks want to know current business patterns for a new enterprise when seeking a loan. These sorts of data can be obtained easily from these centers.

Level of Detail

Because the data centers use information from other sources in addition to the Bureau of Census, the level of detail will vary according to subject area as well as the state and office contacted. Much of the Census data can be provided at the state, county, city, census tract and block group level (which is normally even smaller than a zip code). Data according to zip code are also available for many categories of information. All states also have the public use micro data sample, which do not contain aggregate data, but actual questionnaire information filled out by respondents. They can be manipulated into any kind of special detail required.

Custom Work, Workshops and Other Services

A lot of work performed by the data centers is customized in nature. The organizations collect data from other federal and state sources to enhance their Census information. Many have arrangements with other state data centers to send any computer file needed to do special analysis. This is how local centers can provide national information or inter-market comparisons. Some centers will even perform custom census projects for clients, which means raw data collection for market research.

Free and low cost workshops about services and information opportunities are sponsored in some areas for potential users. These workshops are important at the local level because in the past they were readily available from the Bureau of Census, but recent budget cuts have reduced their frequency and increased their price. Because of the centers' familiarity of census data, these offices are excellent starting places for almost any information search.

Formats

Data centers offer some of the most sophisticated formats you are likely to find from public organizations. They all provide computer tapes, off-the-shelf reports, custom reports from computer analysis, and quick answers over the telephone. Most are also set up to provide custom analysis and/or raw data on computer diskettes, and some -- like Ohio -- have developed a PC database from which they can generate standard reports and download onto diskettes. Colorado and other states are beginning to make data accessible online.

Prices

Although the U.S. government provides most of the data to these centers, the feds do not interfere with fee schedules. Most offices try to give out information free, but some charge on a cost recovery basis. Some states do not charge for the first so many pages of a report but charge a nominal fee for additional pages. Some say they have a minimum fee of $20 for customized computer runs. It is interesting that these centers sell you computerized data cheaper than the U.S. Bureau of the Census in Washington. In contrast to the Bureau's fee of $140, Illinois and Georgia only charge $50 for a data tape file, and in Florida, the cost is $15 for a file.

In the dozens of interviews we conducted with these centers about the complicated market research reports they have provided to clients, the highest figure we found they ever charged was $2,000. That amount of money would buy virtually nothing from most marketing consultants.

State Data Centers

Below is a roster of data centers in all 50 states as well as the District of Columbia, Puerto Rico and Virgin Islands. Some of these Census Bureau information providers are based in state departments and agencies, universities, business colleges, and libraries. Each center listed below includes the name and phone number of the data expert.

Alabama

Center for Business and Economic Research, University of Alabama, P.O. Box 870221, Tuscaloosa, AL 34587-0221, Ms. Annette Walters, 205-348-2953.

Alabama Department of Economic and Community Affairs, Office of State Planning, P.O. Box 250347, 3465 Norman Bridge Road, Montgomery, AL 36125-0347, Mr. Parker Collins, 205-284-8630.

Alabama Public Library Service, 6030 Monticello Drive, Montgomery, AL 36130, Ms. Hilda Dent, 205-277-7330.

Alaska

Alaska State Data Center, Research and Analysis, Department of Labor, P.O. Box 25504, Juneau, AK 99802-5504, Ms. Kathryn Lizik, 907-465-4500.

Office of Management and Budget, Division of Policy, Pouch AD, Juneau, AK 99811, Mr. Jack Kreinheder, 907-465-3568.

Department of Education, Division of Libraries and Museums, Alaska State Library, Pouch G, Juneau, AK 99811, Ms. Catherine Gruenberg, 907-465-2927.

Department of Community & Regional Affairs, Division of Municipal and Regional Assistance, P.O. Box BH, Juneau, AK 99811, Ms. Laura Walters, 907-465-4756.

Institute for Social & Economic Research, University of Alaska, 3211 Providence Drive, Anchorage, AK 99508, Mr. Jim Kerr, 907-786-7710.

Arizona

Arizona Department of Economic Security, Mail Code 045Z, 1789 West Jefferson Street, Phoenix, AZ 85007, Ms. Betty Jeffries, 602-255-5984.

Center for Business Research, College of Business Administration, Arizona State University, Tempe, AZ, 85287, Mr. Tom Rex, 602-965-3961.

College of Business Administration, Northern Arizona University, Box 15066, Flagstaff, AZ 86011, Dr. Joseph Walka, 602-523-3657.

Federal Documents Section, Department of Library, Archives, and Public Records, 1700 West Washington, 2nd Floor, Phoenix, AZ 85007, Ms. Janet Fisher, 602-621-4121.

Division of Economic & Business Research, College of Business & Public Administration, University of Arizona, Tucson, AZ 85721, Ms. Holly Penix, 602-621-2155.

Arkansas

State Data Center, University of Arkansas-Little Rock, 2801 South University, Little Rock, AR 72204, Ms. Sarah Breshears, 501-569-8530.

Arkansas State Library, 1 Capitol Mall, Little Rock, AR 72201, Ms. Mary Honeycutt, 501-682-2864.

Research & Analysis Section, Arkansas Employment Security Division, P.O. Box 2981, Little Rock, AR 72203, Mr. Coy Cozart, 501-682-3159.

Market Studies, Demographics and Statistics

California

State Census Data Center, Dept. of Finance, 915 L St., Sacramento, CA 95814, Ms. Linda Gage, Director, 916-322-4651, Mr. Richard Lovelady, 916-323-2201.

Sacramento Area COG, 106 K Street, Suite 200, Sacramento, CA 95814, Mr. Bob Faseler, 916-441-5930.

Association of Bay Area Governments, Metro Center, 8th and Oak Streets, P.O. Box 2050, Oakland, CA 94604-2050, Ms. Patricia Perry, 415-464-7937.

Southern California Association of Governments, 818 West 7th Street, 12th Floor, Los Angeles, CA 90017, Mr. Javier Minjares, 213-236-1800.

San Diego Association of Governments, First Federal Plaza, 401 B Street, Suite 800, San Diego, CA 92101, Ms. Karen Lamphere, 619-236-5353.

State Data Center Program, University of California-Berkeley, 2538 Channing Way, Berkeley, CA 94720, Ms. Ilona Einowski/Fred Gey, 415-642-6571.

Association of Monterey Bay Area Governments, 977B Pacific Street, P.O. Box 190, Monterey, CA 93942, Mr. Steve Williams, 408-373-6116.

Colorado

Division of Local Government, Colorado Department of Local Affairs, 1313 Sherman Street, Room 521, Denver, CO 80203, Mr. Reid Reynolds/Ms. Rebecca Picasso, 303-866-2156.

Business Research Division, Graduate School of Business Administration, University of Colorado-Boulder, Boulder, CO 80309 , Mr. Richard Wobbekind, 303-492-8227.

Natural Resources & Economics, Department of Agriculture, Colorado State University, Fort Collins, CO 80523, Ms. Sue Anderson, 303-491-5706.

Documents Department, The Libraries, Colorado State University, Fort Collins, CO 80523, Ms. Suzanne Taylor, 303-491-1880.

Connecticut

Comprehensive Planning Division, Connecticut Office of Policy and Management, 80 Washington Street, Hartford, CT 06106-4459, Mr. Theron Schnure, 203-566-8285.

Government Documents, Connecticut State Library, 231 Capitol Avenue, Hartford, CT 06106, Mr. Albert Palko, 203-566-4971.

Connecticut Department of Economic Development, 865 Brook Street, Rocky Hill, CT 06067-3405, Mr. Jeff Blodgett, 203-258-4239.

Employment Security Division, Connecticut Department of Labor, 200 Folly Brook Blvd., Wethersfield, CT 06109, Mr. Richard Vannuccini, 203-566-2120.

Delaware

Delaware Development Office, 99 Kings Highway, P.O. Box 1401, Dover, DE 19903, Ms. Judy McKinney-Cherry, 302-739-4271.

College of Urban Affairs and Public Policy, University of Delaware, Graham Hall, Room 286, Academy Street, Newark, DE 19716, Mr. Ed Ratledge, 302-451-8406.

District of Columbia

Data Services Division, Mayor's Office of Planning, Room 570, Presidential Bldg., 415 12th Street, N.W., Washington, DC 20004, Mr. Gan Ahuja, 202-727-6533.

Metropolitan Washington Council of Governments, 777 North Capitol Street, Suite 300, Washington, DC 20006, Mr. Robert Griffith/Ms. Jenean Johanningmeier, 202-962-3200.

Florida

Florida State Data Center, Executive Office of the Governor, Office of Planning & Budgeting, The Capitol, Tallahassee, FL 32399-0001, Mr. Steve Kimble, 904-487-2814.

Center for the Study of Population, Institute for Social Research, 654 Bellemy Building, Florida State University, Tallahassee, FL 32306-4063, Dr. Ike Eberstein, 904-644-1762.

State Library of Florida, R.A. Gray Building, Tallahassee, FL 32399-0250, Ms. Linda Close, 904-487-2651.

Bureau of Economic Analysis, Florida Department of Commerce, 107 East Gaines Street, 315 Collins Building, Tallahassee, FL 32399-2000, Ms. Sally Ramsey, 904-487-2568.

Georgia

Division of Demographic & Statistical Services, Georgia Office of Planning and Budget, 254 Washington Street, S.W., Room 640, Atlanta, GA 30334, Ms. Marty Sik, 404-656-0911.

Documents Librarian, Georgia State University, University Plaza, Atlanta, GA 30303, Ms. Gayle Christian, 404-651-2185.

Robert W. Woodruff Library for Advanced Studies, Emory University, Atlanta, GA 30322, Ms. Elizabeth McBride, 404-727-6880.

Main Library, University of Georgia, Athens, GA 30602, Ms. Susan C. Field, 404-542-0664.

Georgia Department of Community Affairs, Office of Coordinated Planning, 100 Peachtree Street, N.E. #1200, Atlanta, GA 30303, Mr. Phil Thiel, 404-656-5526.

Documents Librarian, State Data Center Program, Albany State College, 504 College Drive, Albany, GA 31705, Ms. Juanita Miller, 912-430-4799.

Documents Librarian, State Data Center Program, Georgia Southern College, Statesboro, GA 30460, Ms. Lynn Walshak, 912-681-5117.

State Data Center Program, Mercer University Law Library, Mercer University, Macon, GA 31207, Mr. Ismael Gullon, 912-752-2668.

Data Services, University of Georgia Libraries, 6th Floor, Athens, GA 30602, Ms. Hortense Bates, 404-542-0727.

Price Gilbert Memorial Library, Georgia Institute of Technology, Atlanta, GA 30332, Mr. Richard Leacy, 404-894-4519.

Guam

Guam Department of Commerce, 590 South Marine Drive, Suite 601, 6th Floor GITC Building, Tamuning, Guam 96911, Mr. Peter R. Barcinas, 671-646-5841.

Hawaii

Hawaii State Data Center, Department of Business & Economic Development, Kamamalau Building, Room 602A, 220 S. King Street, Suite 400, Honolulu, HI 96813, Mailing Address: P.O. Box 2359, Honolulu, HI 96804, Mr. Robert Schmitt, State Statistician/Ms. Emogene Estores, 808-586-2482.

Information and Communication Services Division, State Department of Budget and Finance, Kalanimoku Building, 1151 Punchbowl Street, Honolulu, HI 96813, Ms. Joy Toyama, 808-548-6180.

Idaho

Idaho Department of Commerce, 700 West State Street, Boise, ID 83720, Mr. Alan Porter, 208-334-2470.

Institutional Research, Room 319, Business Building, Boise State University, Boise, ID 83725, Mr. Don Canning, 208-385-1613.

The Idaho State Library, 325 West State Street, Boise, ID 83702, Ms. Stephanie Nichols, 208-334-2150.

Center for Business Research and Services, Campus Box 8450, Idaho State University, Pocatello, ID 83209, Dr. Paul Zelus, 208-236-2304.

Illinois

Division of Planning and Financial Analysis, Illinois Bureau of the Budget, William Stratton Building, Room 605, Springfield, IL 62706, Ms. Suzanne Ebetsch, 217-782-1381.

Census & Data Users Services, Department of Sociology, Anthropology & Social Work, Illinois State University, 604 South Main Street, Normal, IL 61761-6901, Dr. Roy Treadway, 309-438-5946.

Center for Governmental Studies, Northern Illinois University, Social Science

Research Bldg., DeKalb, IL 60115, Ms. Ruth Anne Tobias, 815-753-1901, ext 221.

Regional Research and Development Service, Southern Illinois University at Edwardsville, Box 1456, Edwardsville, IL 62026-1456, Mr. Charles Kofron, 618-692-3500.

Chicago Area Geographic Information Study, Room 2102, Building BSB, P.O. Box 4348, University of Illinois at Chicago, Chicago, IL 60680, Mr. Jim Bash, 312-996-6367.

Northeastern Illinois Planning Commission, 400 West Madison Street, Chicago, IL 60606-2642, Max Dieber/Mary Cele Smith, 312-454-0400.

Indiana

Indiana State Library, Indiana Data Center, 140 North Senat Avenue, Indianapolis, IN 46204, Mr. Ray Ewick, Director/Ms. Roberta Eads, 317-232-3733.

Indiana Business Research Center, Indiana University, 10th and Fee Lane, Bloomington, IN 47405, Dr. Morton Marcus, 812-335-5507.

Indiana Business Research Center, P.O. Box 647, 801 West Michigan, B.S. 4013, Indianapolis, IN 46202-5151, Ms. Carol Rogers, 317-274-2205.

Research Division, Indiana Department of Commerce, 1 North Capitol, Suite 700, Indianapolis, IN 46204, Mr. Robert Lain, 317-232-8959.

Iowa

Research Section, Iowa Department of Economic Development, 200 E. Grand Avenue, Des Moines, IA 50309, 515-281-3005.

State Library of Iowa, East 12th and Grand, Des Moines, IA 50319, Ms. Beth Henning, 515-281-4350.

Center for Social and Behavioral Research, University of Northern Iowa, Cedar Falls, IA 50614, Dr. Robert Kramer, 319-273-2105.

Census Services, Iowa State University, 320 East Hall, Ames, IA 50011, Dr. Willis Goudy, 515-294-8337.

Iowa Social Science Institute, University of Iowa, 345 Shaeffer Hall, Iowa City, IA 52242, Mr. Brian Dalziel, 319-335-2371.

Census Data Center, Department of Education, Grimes State Office Building, Des Moines, IA 50319, Mr. Steve Boal, 515-281-4730.

Kansas

State Library, Room 343-N, State Capitol Building, Topeka, KS 66612, Mr. Marc Galbraith, 913-296-3296.

Division of the Budget, Room 152-E, State Capitol Building, Topeka, KS 66612, Ms. Teresa Floerchinger, 913-296-2436.

Institute for Public Policy and Business Research, 607 Blake Hall, The University of Kansas, Lawrence, KS 66045-2960, Ms. Thelma Helyar, 913-864-3123.

Center for Economic Development & Business Research, Box 48, Wichita State University, Wichita, KS 67208, Ms. Janet Nickel, 316-689-3225.

Population and Resources Laboratory, Department of Sociology, Kansas State University, Manhattan, KS 66506, Dr. Jan L. Flora, 913-532-5984.

Kentucky

Urban Studies Center, College of Urban & Public Affairs, University of Louisville, Louisville, KY 40292, Mr. Ron Crouchs, 502-588-7990.

Office of Policy & Management, State of Kentucky, Capitol Annex, Frankfort, KY 40601, Mr. Steve Rowland, 502-564-7300.

State Library Division, Department for Libraries & Archives, 300 Coffeetree Road, P.O. Box 537, Frankfort, KY 40601, Ms. Brenda Fuller, 502-875-7000.

Louisiana

Office of Planning and Budget, Division of Administration, P.O. Box 94095, Baton Rouge, LA 70804, Ms. Karen Paterson, 504-342-7410.

Division of Business and Economic Research, University of New Orleans, Lake Front, New Orleans, LA 70122, Mr. Vincent Maruggi, 504-286-6248.

Division of Business Research, Louisiana Tech University, P.O. Box 10318, Ruston, LA 71272, Dr. Edward O'Boyle, 318-257-3701.

Reference Department, Louisiana State Library, P.O. Box 131, Baton Rouge, LA 70821, Mrs. Blanche Cretini, 504-342-4918.

Center for Life Cycle and Population Studies, Department of Sociology, Room 126, Stubbs Hall, Louisiana State University, Baton Rouge, LA 70803, Mr. Pete McCool, Director, 504-388-5359.

Center for Business and Economic Research, Northeast Louisiana University, Monroe, LA 71209, Dr. Jerry Wall, 318-342-1215.

Maine

Division of Economic Analysis and Research, Maine Department of Labor, 20 Union Street, Augusta, ME 04330, Mr. Raynold Fongemie, Director, Ms. Jean Martin, 207-289-2271.

Maine State Library, State House Station 64, Augusta, ME 04333, Mr. Gary Nichols, 207-289-5600.

Maryland

Maryland Department of State Planning, 301 West Preston Street, Baltimore, MD 21201, Mr. Michel Lettre/Mr. Robert Dadd, 301-225-4450.

Computer Science Center, University of Maryland, College Park, MD 20742, Mr. John McNary, 301-405-3037.

Government Reference Service, Pratt Library, 400 Cathedral Street, Baltimore, MD 21201, Mr. Wesley Wilson, 301-396-5468.

Small Business Development Center, 217 E. Redwood Street, 9th Floor, Baltimore, MD 21202, Mr. Eliot Rittenhouse, 301-333-6995.

Massachusetts

Massachusetts Institute for Social and Economic Research, 128 Thompson Hall, University of Massachusetts, Amherst, MA 01003, Dr. Steve Coelen, Director, 413-545-3460, Ms. Nora Groves, 413-545-0176.

Massachusetts Institute for Social and Economic Research, Box 219, The State House, Room 50, Boston, MA 02133, Mr. William Murray, 617-727-4537.

Michigan

Michigan Information Center, Department of Management & Budget, Office of Revenue and Tax Analysis, P.O. Box 30026, Lansing, MI 48909, Mr. Eric Swanson, 517-373-7910.

MIMIC/Center for Urban Studies, Wayne State University, Faculty/ Administration Bldg., 656 W. Kirby, Detroit, MI 48202, Dr. Mark Neithercut/ Kurt Metzger, 313-577-8350.

The Library of Michigan, Government Documents Service, P.O. Box 30007, Lansing, MI 48909, Ms. F. Anne Diamond, 517-373-1307.

Minnesota

State Demographer's Office, Minnesota State Planning Agency, 300 Centennial Office Building, 658 Cedar Street, St. Paul, MN 55155, Mr. David Birkholz, 612-297-2360, Mr. David Rademacher, 612-297-3255.

Interagency Resource & Information Center, Department of Education, 501 Capitol Square Building, St. Paul, MN 55101, Ms. Patricia Tupper, 612-296-6684.

Mississippi

Center for Population Studies, The University of Mississippi, Bondurant Bldg., Room 3W, University, MS 38677, Dr. Max Williams, Director/Ms. Pattie Byrd, Manager, 601-232-7288.

Governor's Office of Federal-State Programs, Dept. of Community Development, 301 West Pearl Street, Jackson, MS 39203-3096, Mr. Jim Catt, 601-949-2219.

Division of Research and Information Systems, Department of Economic and Community Development, 1200 Walter Sillas Building, P.O. Box 849, Jackson, MS 39205, Ms. Linda Penton, 601-359-3739.

Market Studies, Demographics and Statistics

Missouri

Missouri State Library, 2002 Missouri Boulevard, P.O. Box 387, Jefferson City, MO 65102, Ms. Marlys Davis, 314-751-3615.

Office of Administration, 124 Capitol Building, P.O. Box 809, Jefferson City, MO 65102, Mr. Ryan Burson, 314-751-2345.

Urban Information Center, University of Missouri-St. Louis, 8001 Natural Bridge Road, St. Louis, MO 63121, Dr. John Blodgett, 314-553-6014.

Office of Social & Economic Data Analysis, University Missouri-Columbia, 224 Lewis Hall, Columbia, MO 65211, Ms. Evelyn J. Cleveland, 314-882-7396.

Geographic Resources Center, University of Missouri-Columbia, 4 Stewart Hall, Columbia, MO 65211, Dr. Christopher Salter.

Montana

Census and Economic Information Center, Montana Department of Commerce, 1424 9th Avenue, Capitol Station, Helena, MT 59620-0401, Ms. Patricia Roberts, 406-444-4393.

Montana State Library, 1515 East 6th Avenue, Capitol Station, Helena, MT 59620, Ms. Kathy Brown, 406-444-3004.

Bureau of Business and Economic Research, University of Montana, Missoula, MT 59812, Mr. Jim Sylvester, 406-243-5113.

Survey Research Center, Wilson Hall, Room 1-108, Montana State University, Bozeman, MT 59717, Ms. Lee Faulkner, 406-994-4481.

Research & Analysis Bureau, Employment Policy Division, Montana Department of Labor & Industry, P.O. Box 1728, Helena, MT 59624, Ms. Cathy Shenkle, 406-444-2430.

Nebraska

Center for Applied Urban Research, The University of Nebraska-Omaha, Peter Kiewit Conference Center, 1313 Farnam-on-the-Mall, Omaha, NE 68182, Mr. Jerome Deichert/Mr. Tim Himberger, 402-595-2311.

Policy Research Office, P.O. Box 94601, State Capitol, Room 1319, Lincoln, NE 68509-4601, Ms. Prem L. Bansal, 402-471-2414.

Federal Documentation Librarian, Nebraska Library Commission, 1420 P Street, Lincoln, NE 68508-1683, 402-471-2045.

The Central Data Processing Division, Department of Administration Services, 1312 State Capitol, Lincoln, NE 68509-5045, Mr. Skip Miller, 402-471-4862.

Nebraska Department of Labor, 550 South 16th Street, P.O. Box 94600, Lincoln, NE 68509-4600, Mr. Robert H. Shanahan, 402-471-2518.

Natural Resources Commission, 301 Centennial Mall South, P.O. Box 94876, Lincoln, NE 68509-4876, Mr. Mahendra Bansal, 402-471-2081.

Nevada

Nevada State Library, Capitol Complex, 401 North Carson, Carson City, NV 89710, Ms. Joan Kerschner/Ms. Betty McNeal, 702-687-5160.

New Hampshire

Office of State Planning, 2-1/2 Beacon Street, Concord, NH 03301, Mr. Tom Duffy, 603-271-2155.

New Hampshire State Library, 20 Park Street, Concord, NH 03301-6303, Mr. John McCormick, 603-271-2239.

Office of Biometrics, University of New Hampshire, James Hall, 2nd Floor, Durham, NH 03824, Mr. Owen Durgin, 603-862-1700.

New Jersey

New Jersey Department of Labor, Division of Labor Market and Demographic Research, CN 388-John Fitch Plaza, Trenton, NJ 08625-0388, Ms. Connie O. Hughes, Asst. Director, 609-984-2593.

New Jersey State Library, 185 West State Street, CN 520, Trenton, NJ 08625-0520, Ms. Beverly Railsback, 609-292-6220.

CIT - Information Services, Princeton University, 87 Prospect Avenue, Princeton, NJ 08544, Ms. Judith S. Rowe, 609-258-6052.

Center for Computer & Information Services, Rutgers University, CCIS-Hill Center, Busch Campus, PO Box 879, Piscataway, NJ 08854, Ms. Mary Jane Face Cedar, 908-932-2889.

Rutgers University - The State University, Kilmer Campus, Lucy Stone Hall, B Wing, New Brunswick, NJ 08903, Dr. James Hughes, Chair and Graduate Director, 908-932-3822.

New Mexico

Economic Development and Tourism Department, 1100 St. Francis Drive, Santa Fe, NM 87503, Mr. John Beasley, 505-827-0272.

New Mexico State Library, 325 Don Gaspar Avenue, P.O. Box 1629, Santa Fe, NM 87503, Ms. Laura Chaney, 505-827-3826.

Bureau of Business and Economic Research, University of New Mexico, 1920 Lomas NE, Albuquerque, NM 87131, Mr. Kevin Kargacin, 505-277-6626, Ms. Julian Boyle, 505-277-2216.

Department of Economics, New Mexico State University, Box 30001, Las Cruces, NM 88003, Dr. Kathleen Brook, 505-646-4905.

New York

Division of Policy & Research, Department of Economic Development, 1 Commerce Plaza, Room 905, 99 Washington Avenue, Albany, NY 12245, Mr. Robert Scardamalia, 518-474-6005.

CISER Data Archive, Cornell University, 262 Caldwell Hall, Ithaca, NY 14853, Ms. Ann Gray, 607-255-4801.

Nelson A. Rockefeller Institute of Government, 411 State Street, Albany, NY 12203, 518-255-1300.

New York State Library, Cultural Education Center, Empire State Plaza, Albany, NY 12230, Ms. Mary Redmond, 518-474-3940.

Division of Equalization and Assessment, 16 Sheridan Avenue, Albany, NY 12210, Mr. Wilfred B. Pauquette, 518-474-6742.

North Carolina

North Carolina Office of State Budget and Management, 116 West Jones Street, Raleigh, NC 27603-8005, Ms. Francine Stephenson, Director of State Data Center, 919-733-7061.

State Library, North Carolina Department of Cultural Resources, 109 East Jones Street, Raleigh, NC 27611, Mr. Joel Sigmon, 919-733-3683.

Institute for Research in Social Science, University of North Carolina, Manning Hall CB 3355, Chapel Hill, NC 27599-3355, Mr. Glenn Deane, 919-966-3346.

Division of Land Resources, P.O. Box 27687, Raleigh, NC 27611, Ms. Karen Siderelis/Tim Johnson, 919-733-2090.

North Dakota

Department of Agricultural Economics, North Dakota State University, Morrill Hall, Room 224, P.O. Box 5636, Fargo, ND 58105, Dr. Richard Rathge, 701-237-8621.

Office of Intergovernment Assistance, State Capitol, 14th Floor, Bismarck, ND 58505, Mr. Jim Boyd, 701-224-2094.

Department of Geography, University of North Dakota, Grand Forks, ND 58202, Mohammad Hemmasi, 701-777-4246.

North Dakota State Library, Liberty Memorial Building, Capitol Grounds, Bismarck, ND 58505, Ms. Susan Pahlmeyer, 701-224-2490.

Ohio

Ohio Data Users Center, Ohio Department of Development, P.O. Box 1001, Columbus, OH 43266-0101, Mr. Barry Bennett, 614-466-2115.

State Library of Ohio, 65 South Front Street, Columbus, OH 43215, Mr. Clyde Hordusky, 614-644-7051.

Cleveland State University, Northern Ohio Data and Information Service, Euclid Ave. and East 24th St., Cleveland, OH 44115, Mr. Mark Salling, 216-687-2209.

Ohio State University Library/ Census Data Center, 126 Main Library, 1858 Neil Avenue Mall, Columbus, OH 43210, Ms. Marge Murfin, 614-292-6175.

Southwest Ohio Regional Data Center, Institute for Policy Research, Mail Loc. 132, Cincinnati, OH 45221, 513-556-5082.

Oklahoma

Oklahoma State Data Center, Oklahoma Department of Commerce, 6601 Broadway Extension, (Mailing address) P.O. Box 26980, Oklahoma City, OK 73126-0980, Ms. Karen Selland, 405-841-5184.

Oklahoma Department of Libraries, 200 N.E. 18th Street, Oklahoma City, OK 73105, Mr. Steve Beleu, 405-521-2502.

Oregon

Oregon State Library, State Library Building, Salem, OR 97310, Mr. Craig Smith, 503-378-4276.

Bureau of Governmental Research & Service, University of Oregon, Hendricks Hall, Room 340, P.O. Box 3177, Eugene, OR 97403, Ms. Karen Seidel, 503-346-5232.

Center for Population Research and Census, Portland State University, P.O. Box 751, Portland, OR 97207-0751, Mr. Ed Shafer/Ms. Maria Wilson-Figueroa, 503-725-3922.

Oregon State Housing Agency, 1600 State Street, Suite 100, Salem, OR 97310-0161, Mr. Mike Murphy, 503-373-1611.

Pennsylvania

Pennsylvania State Data Center, Institute of State and Regional Affairs, Pennsylvania State University at Harrisburg, Middletown, PA 17057-4898, Mr. Michael Behney, 717-948-6336.

Pennsylvania State Library, Forum Building, Harrisburg, PA 17120, Mr. John Gerswindt, 717-787-2327.

Penn State at Harrisburg, Acquisitions, Heindel Library, Middletown, PA 17057-4898, Ms. Grace M. Finn, 717-948-6074.

Puerto Rico

Puerto Rico Planning Board, Minillas Government Center, North Bldg., Avenida De Diego, P.O. Box 41119, San Juan, PR 00940-9985, Sra. Lillian Torres Aguirre, 809-728-4430.

Recinto Universitario de Mayaguez, Edificio Anexo Pineiro, Carretera Num 2, Mayaguez, PR 00708, Prfa. Grace Quinones Seda, 809-834-4040.

Biblioteca Carnegie, Ave. Ponce de Leon, Parada 1, San Juan, PR 00901, Sra. Carmen Martinez, 809-724-1046.

Rhode Island

United Way of Rhode Island, 229 Waterman Street, Providence, RI 02908, Ms. Jane Nugent, 401-521-9000.

Rhode Island Department of State Library Services, 300 Richmond Street, Providence, RI 02903, Mr. Frank Iacona, 401-277-2726.

Social Science Data Center, Brown University, P.O. Box 1916, Providence, RI 02912, Dr. Alden Speare, 401-863-2550.

Department of Administration, Office of Municipal Affairs, 1 Capitol Hill, Providence, RI 02908-5873, Mr. Paul Egan, 401-277-6493.

Office of Health Statistics, Rhode Island Department of Health, 3 Capitol Hill, Providence, RI 02908, Dr. Jay Buechner, 401-277-2550.

Rhode Island Department of Economic Development, 7 Jackson Walkway, Providence, RI 02903, Mr. Vincent Harrington, 401-277-2601.

South Carolina

Division of Research and Statistical Services, South Carolina Budget and Control Board, Rembert Dennis Bldg. Room 425, Columbia, SC 29201, Mr. Bobby Bowers/Mr. Mike Macfariane, 803-734-3780.

South Carolina State Library, P.O. Box 11469, Columbia, SC 29211, Ms. Mary Bostick, 803-734-8666.

South Dakota

Business Research Bureau, School of Business, University of South Dakota, 414 East Clark, Vermillion, SD 57069, Ms. DeVee Dykstra, 605-677-5287.

Documents Department, South Dakota State Library, Department of Education and Cultural Affairs, 800 Governors Drive, Pierre, SD 57501-2294, Ms. Margaret Bezpaletz, 605-773-3131.

Labor Market Information Center, South Dakota Department of Labor, 420 S. Roosevelt, Box 4730, Aberdeen, SD 57402-4730, Ms. Mary Susan Vickers, 605-622-2314.

Center for Health Policy & Statistics, South Dakota Department of Health, Foss Building, 523 E. Capitol, Pierre, SD 57501, Mr. Brian Williams, 605-773-3693.

Rural Sociology Department, South Dakota State University, Scobey Hall 226, Box 504, Brookings, SD 57007, Mr. Jim Satterlee, 605-688-4132.

Tennessee

Tennessee State Planning Office, John Sevier State Office Bldg., 500 Charlotte Ave., Suite 307, Nashville, TN 37243-0001, Mr. Charles Brown, 615-741-1676.

Center for Business and Economic Research, College of Business Administration, University of Tennessee, Room 100, Glocker Hall, Knoxville, TN 37996-4170, Ms. Betty Vickers, 615-974-5441.

Texas

State Data Center, Texas Department of Commerce, 9th and Congress Streets, (Mailing address) P.O. Box 12728, Capitol Station, Austin, TX 78711, Ms. Susan Tully, 512-472-9667.

Department of Rural Sociology, Texas A & M University System, Special Services Building, College Station, TX 77843-2125, Dr. Steve Murdock, 409-845-5115 or 5332.

Texas Natural Resources Information System (TNRIS), P.O. Box 13231, Austin, TX 78711, Mr. Charles Palmer, 512-463-8399.

Texas State Library and Archive Commission, P.O. Box 12927, Capitol Station, Austin, TX 78711, Ms. Diana Houston, 512-463-5455.

Utah

Office of Planning & Budget, State Capitol, Room.116, Salt Lake City, UT 84114, Mr. Brad Barber, Director/Ms. Linda Smith, 801-538-1036.

Bureau of Economic and Business Research, 401 Garff Building, University of Utah, Salt Lake City, UT 84112, Mr. Frank Hachman, 801-581-6333.

Population Research Laboratory, Utah State University, UMC 07, Logan, UT 84322, Mr. Yun Kim, 801-750-1231.

Department of Employment Security, 174 Social Hall Avenue, P.O. Box 11249, Salt Lake City, UT 84147, Mr. Ken Jensen, 801-533-2372.

Vermont

Office of Policy Research and Coordination, Pavilion Office Building, 109 State Street, Montpelier, VT 05602, Mr. Bernie Johnson, 802-828-3326.

Center for Rural Studies, University of Vermont, 207 Morrill Hall, Burlington, VT 05405-0106, Ms. Cathleen Gent, 802-656-3021.

Vermont Department of Libraries, 111 State Street, Montpelier, VT 05602, Ms. Patricia Klinck, State Librarian, 802-828-3265.

Vermont Agency of Development and Community Affairs, Pavilion Office Building, 109 State Street, Montpelier, VT 05602, Mr. Jed Guertin, 802-828-3211.

Virginia

Virginia Employment Commission, 703 East Main Street, Richmond, VA 23219, Mr. Dan Jones, 804-786-8308.

Center for Public Service, University of Virginia, Dynamics Building, 4th Floor, 2015 Ivy Road, Charlottesville, VA 22903-1795, Dr. Michael Spar, 804-924-7451.

Virginia State Library, Documents Section, 11th Street at Capitol Square, Richmond, VA 23219-3491, Mr. Robert Keeton, 804-786-2175.

Virgin Islands
University of the Virgin Islands, Caribbean Research Institute, Charlotte Amalie, St. Thomas, VI 00802, Dr. Frank Mills, 809-776-9200.

Virgin Islands Department of Economic Development, P.O. Box 6400, Charlotte Amalie, St. Thomas, VI 00801, Mr. Richard Moore, 809-774-8784.

Washington
Estimation & Forecasting Unit, Office of Financial Management, 450 Insurance Building, MS: AQ-44, Olympia, WA 98504-0202, Ms. Sharon Estee, 206-586-2504.

Documents Section, Washington State Library, AJ-11, Olympia, WA 98504, Ms. Ann Bregent, 206-753-4027.

Puget Sound Council of Govts., 215 1st Avenue South, Seattle, WA 98104, Ms. Elaine Murakami, 206-464-5355.

Social Research Center, Department of Rural Sociology, Washington State University, Pullman, WA 99164-4006, Dr. Annabel Kirschner Cook, 509-335-4519.

Department of Sociology, Demographic Research Laboratory, Western Washington University, Belligham, WA 98225, Mr. Lucky Tedrow, Director, 206-676-3167.

Applied Social Data Center, Department of Sociology, Central Washington University, Ellensburg, WA 98926, Dr. David Kaufman, 509-963-1305.

West Virginia
Community Development Division, Governor's Office of Community and Industrial Development, Capitol Complex, Building 6, Room 553, Charleston, WV 25305, Ms. Mary C. Harless, 304-348-4010.

Reference Library, West Virginia State Library Commission, Science and Cultural Center, Capitol Complex, Charleston, WV 25305, Ms. Karen Goff, 304-348-2045.

Office of Health Services Research, Health Science Center South, West Virginia University, Morgantown, WV 26506, Ms. Stephanie Pratt, 304-293-2601.

The Center for Economic Research, West Virginia University, 323 Business and Economic Building, Morgantown, WV 26506-6025, Dr. Tom Witt, Director/Ms. Linda Culp, 304-293-5837.

Wisconsin
Demographic Services Center, Department of Administration, 101 South Webster Street, 6th Floor, P.O. Box 7868, Madison, WI 53707-7868, Ms. Nadene Roenspies/Mr. Robert Naylor, 608-266-1927.

Applied Population Laboratory, Department of Rural Sociology, University of Wisconsin, 1450 Linden Drive, Room 316, Madison, WI 53706, Mr. Michael Knight, 608-262-3097.

Wyoming
Survey Research Center, University of Wyoming, P.O. Box 3925, Laramie, WY 82071, Mr. G. Fred Doll, 307-766-2931.

Dept. of Administration and Fiscal Control, Emerson Building 327E, Cheyenne, WY 82002-0060, Ms. Mary Byrnes, Director/Kreg McCollums, 307-777-7504.

Campbell County Library, 2101 Four J Road, Gillette, WY 82716, 307-682-3223.

State Labor Information Centers

Labor market information departments are an overlooked resource within state governments. These little-known offices can provide current, customized data such as:

- which cities have the highest concentration of restaurants or credit agencies;
- how many Hispanic males were living in Bridgeport, Connecticut in 1987;
- which zip codes have the fastest growing population of working women in managerial positions;
- the name, address and size of each new business or business expansion in a given state;
- which U.S. counties offer the highest entry level salaries for market research analysts.

Two reasons for tapping state government labor offices for market and demographic data are that in most cases the information is free and less than one year old.

Source of Data

The primary function of each state labor information office is to collect data in conjunction with the federal government in order to produce employment, unemployment, occupational and wage information. The most interesting data sources, are state unemployment contribution forms filled out by every employer in the state. This form is filed quarterly revealing total wages and number of employees for companies by Standard Industrial Code (SIC) in each city and county.

In addition, each state also compiles data showing future manpower needs within the state. By studying labor trends, economic conditions and school enrollments, these agencies project the future supply and demand for up to 1,000 different occupations. Many offices also supplement their information with data from the U.S. Bureau of Census as well as other state data collection agencies to provide additional studies and forecasts.

More Current Than Federal Data

If you are a user of the Census Bureau's *County Business Patterns*, you are aware that the latest information available is for 1984, and 1985 data was out around July 1987. But, are you aware that right now you can obtain basically the same information from most states that was collected in the second quarter of 1986? This information is 18 months more current than Census data. If you are looking for personal income figures by state, county or city, the latest available data from the federal government dates back to 1984. Moreover, the majority of personal income is made up of wage data which is available from most states for June 1986.

Also remember that all data, such as state unemployment information, are passed on to the federal government for publication, but are available from state governments several weeks before being released from Washington.

State Data More Detailed, Cheaper and More Accessible Than Federal Data

Unemployment rate data are released by the U.S. Bureau of Labor Statistics for approximately 150 major cities. However, the state of Connecticut alone can provide unemployment data for 169 cities. If you are looking for salary by type of occupation, the Bureau of the Census covers about 400 occupations in their data. But state governments will cover up to one thousand occupations based on data which can be up to three years more current.

Federal policies combined with the public's increased reliance on traditional federal data sources have caused many of major federal statistical agencies to increase prices and to decrease services. In contrast, using state labor information centers is like walking into virgin data territory. Almost everything is still free from these offices, and state employees are eager to do a lot of free research for those who call. In a conversation I had with the labor information office in Ohio, the director recounted how a local bank requested demographic data for a few dozen zip codes in a three state area. Not only did the state office assemble this information but also gave it to the bank on diskettes...all for free.

Multiple Uses of Labor Market Data

State labor data provide an endless array of uses, but here are some of the primary applications.

1) **Marketing:**
The marketing information available from the states is overwhelming. The data cover both the consumer and industrial markets. It can be used for determining your current market size as well as identifying new or emerging marketing opportunities. For example, you can find:

- monthly employment and average wages by SIC code, by county;
- annual employment for up to 1,000 occupations, by county, by SIC code;
- which counties have the highest concentration of hairdressers making over $20,000 per year;
- how many bartenders are working in a given city;
- how many hotels with fewer than 100 employees operate in a given city;
- what are the fastest growing jobs or industries in any county or city;
- one year projections (1987) of demographic data for each city and county; or
- five to ten year projections of industries and occupations by city and county.

Market Studies, Demographics and Statistics

Many labor market information centers also offer special market studies to cover specific industries which may be important within the state. You can get free studies covering the hospital industry, ski industry, finance industry and many high tech related industries.

2) Company Information:

These offices can tell you how many companies in a given SIC code are located in any county or city. States also can provide the median salary and average starting salary for up to 1,000 different jobs, and can even tell you how many people are employed in all these companies by type of job. Many states keep information on any company which is a newcomer to the state or undertaking major business expansion. And, almost every state can give you the number of employees for any manufacturer in the state.

3) Business Location:

Whether you are establishing a new plant, a real estate business or fast food franchise, these offices can help you locate the best location with regards to labor availability, customer availability and competition. The state labor experts can furnish specifics on how many college graduates, typists or computer programmers with 3 years of experience are looking for work in any given area; or how many are unemployed and looking for work, or how many are working for other companies in the area and their salaries. You can discover what wages are being paid by your competitors in the area for these jobs. Some states volunteer to provide information on union activity in any area. Some states can give you an indication of the work ethic of potential employees. Work ethic can be quantified by showing the number of days off taken by specific employees in certain industries. And if your customers are going to be consumers or businesses in the area, these labor market specialists can share estimates on your potential clientele.

4) Employee Development:

If you are worried about the availability of skilled employees for the future growth of your business, these offices can forecast for you the exact number of people who will be available from school training programs and other employers. This can help you determine if your business will have to move to another location or begin an in-house training program to ensure a plentiful supply of trained labor.

5) Labor Negotiations:

You can find out what the average entry wage for a typist is in your area or what the average fringe benefit package looks like for businesses in your industry. What is the maximum amount of days off allowed for sick leave in your industry? How many companies in your industry offer paid dental care? Answers to these and other employee benefit questions can be useful leverage in negotiating employee benefit packages.

6) Affirmative Action, EEOC and Government Contracts:

Organizations which have to comply with EEOC and affirmative action criteria can get all the data necessary from these offices. Labor force data for any area can pinpoint how many women, Hispanics, etc., are in the labor force for various occupations. Such data can be compared with a company's current employee demographics. This information can be useful when seeking government contracts. Also, remember that many government contracts are set aside for those companies in high

unemployment areas. This data, too, can be obtained from these offices to see if you qualify.

7) Economic Analysis:

If you are interested in any local area economic forecasting or economic monitoring, this is an ideal place to start. All of these offices have monthly and quarterly newsletters which plot economic health down to the city and county level. If your business is dependent on the economic conditions of a specific region, state, city or county, this approach is an easy way to keep your finger on the pulse of what is happening.

8) Careers and Job Search:

An important function of each of these offices is to provide career and job counseling information. If you are looking for a job, each office has access to a state database which identifies available job openings throughout the state. They project which jobs will in demand in the next 10 to 20 years. And more importantly, the future supply is projected for these positions so that you can more easily spot important opportunities. Moreover, you can obtain the starting salaries and median wages for approximately 1,000 occupations in hundreds of industries. Many states give out free books designed for job seekers, as well as information on how to participate in training programs and vocational education opportunities.

9) Computer Formats and Special Services:

You must remember that no two states operate in the same manner or generate identical data. Although many offer the same reports, some may break down the data into 2-digit SIC codes and others into 4-digit SIC codes. What you must never forget is that although one state may NOT provide the data in the format you need, this does not rule out the possibility when dealing with other states. A few states now have their data online and more are beginning to offer diskettes and computer tapes. But if a state labor office says it does not provide computer readable formats, you may be able to convince them to let you be the first. These offices all seem to be very flexible and not heavily encumbered in bureaucracy.

Be sure to investigate any special services which may be offered by the state. Some offer free sources on how to interpret and use labor data and others provide customized affirmative action reports.

State Labor Offices

Alabama

Department of Industrial Relations, Research & Statistics Division, 649 Monroe St., Montgomery, AL 36131, 205-242-8855; Selected Publications: *Monthly Labor Market, Annual Average Labor Force, Area Trends in Employment and Unemployment*; Computer Readable Formats: No; Custom Research: Limited amount available free.

Alaska

Department of Labor, Research and Analysis, P.O. Box 25501, Juneau, AK 99802-5501, 907-465-4500; Selected Publications: *Economic Trends, Akcens Quarterly Newsletter, Career Guide, Industry-Occupation Outlook to 1994, Micro-Computer Occupational Information System (Micro-OIS), Wage Rates, Occupational Supply and Demand Information, Occupational Injury and Illness Information, Population Overview, Special Demographic Reports, Directory of Licensed Occupations, Residency Analysis of Alaska's Workers by Firm, Employment Insurance, Actuarial Study and Financial Handbook, State Salary Survey*; Computer Readable Formats: Limited availability; Custom Research: Limited amount available free.

Arizona

Department of Economic Security West, Research Administration, 1789 West Jefferson, Site Code 733A, Phoenix, AZ 85007, 602-542-3871; Selected Publications: *Arizona Economic Trends, First Job, Staying in School, Job Searchers Guide, Job Leads; Where to Look, Metro, Non-Metro Affirmative Action Planning Information, Annual Planning Information, Applying for Government Jobs, Arizona Labor Market Newsletter, Arizona Licensed Occupation Requirements, Arizona Occupational Employment Forecasts, Arizona Occupational Profiles, Employer Wage Survey, Employment Interview Guide, Helpful Hints for Job Seekers, Map of Major Employers, The Resume, Summer Jobs For Students*; Computer Readable Formats: Forthcoming; Custom Research: Charge for special projects; all shelf publications are free.

Arkansas

Employment Security Department, Labor Market Information Section, P.O. Box 2981, Little Rock, AR 72203, 501-682-3197; Selected Publications: *Annual Planning Information, Annual Report, Annual Report of the Employment Security Division, Arkansas Labor Force Statistics, Covered Employment and Earnings, Interface Supply and Demand, Statistical Review, Current Employment Developments, Monthly Employment Trends, Monthly County Labor Market Information, Directory of Licensed Occupations, Job Hunters Guide to AR, Occupational Trends, Staffing Patterns*; Computer Readable Formats: Occupational trends on disk; Custom Research: Limited amount available free.

California

Employment Development Department, Labor Market Information Division, 7000 Franklin Blvd., #1100, Sacramento, CA 95823, 916-262-2162; Selected Publications: *Annual Planning Information, California Labor Market Bulletin, Labor Market Information for Affirmative Action Programs, Labor Market Conditions in California, California Occupational Guides, California Employment and Payrolls, Projections of Employment By Industry and Occupation*; Computer Readable Formats: Limited; Custom Research: Most everything is free.

Colorado

Department of Labor and Employment, Labor Market Information Section, 393 S. Harland Street, Lakewood, CO 80226; 303-937-4935; Selected Publications: *Affirmative Action Packets, Annual Planning Information Report, Colorado Springs Labor Force, Employment and Wages Quarterly, Occupational Employment Outlook Projection, Job Bank Wage Listing, Occupational Employment in Selected Industries, Quarterly Occupational Supply/Demand Outlook, Pueblo Labor Force, Occupational Supply and Demand, Denver, Boulder, Front Range, Western Slope, Occupational Employment Survey Publishing, Employment Projections*; Computer Readable Formats: No; Custom Research: Free on a limited basis.

Connecticut

Department of Labor, Office of Research and Information, 200 Folly Brook Blvd, Wethersfield, CT 06109-1114, 203-566-3472; Selected Publications: *Annual Report of the Commission of the Labor in Economy Work Force and Training Needs in Connecticut, Planning for the Future Publishing, Work Place 2000, Labor Situation, Labor Force Data, Annual Planning Information, The Occupational Outlook, New Manufacturing Firms* ($7 per year fee), *Occupations in Demand, Labor Market Review, Occupational Projections and Training Data*; Computer Readable Formats; No: Custom Research: Free.

Delaware

Labor Department, Occupational and Labor Market Information Office, University Office Plaza, Newark, DE 19714, 302-368-6962; Selected Publications: *Delaware Annual Brief, Delaware Monthly Digest, Delaware Jobs to 2005* $7.50, *Delaware Career Compass, Career Guidance-High School Information on Job Growth, ES202 Series, Occupational Wage Data-Government and Educational Services* (three year cycle), *Delaware Labor Supply and Demand: Occupational and Industrial Projections*; Computer Readable Formats: Inquire requested; Custom Research: Limited amount available free.

District of Columbia

Employment Services Department, Labor Market Information, Room 201, 500 C St., NW, Washington, DC 20001, 202-639-1175; Selected Publications: *Area Labor Summary, Labor Market Information for Affirmative Action Programs, Directory of 200 Major Employers, Occupational Employment in Selected Industries, Annual Population Estimates By Census Tract*; Computer Readable Formats: No; All shelf publications are free.

Florida

Department of Labor and Employment Security, Bureau of Labor Market Information, Suite 200, Hartman Building, 2012 Capital Circle, S.E., Tallahassee, FL 32399-2151, 904-488-1048; Selected Publications: *Affirmative Action Statistical Packets, Florida Employment Statistics, Florida Industry and Occupational Employment 1995, Florida Occupational Employment in Hospitals, Labor Force Summary, Labor Market Trends, Occupational Employment in Federal Government, Occupations Employment in the Finance, Insurance and Real Estate Industry, Occupational Employment in the Services Industry, Occupational Wage Surveys*; Computer Readable Formats: Bulletin board system for direct downloading.

Georgia

Department of Labor, Labor Information Systems, 148 International, Atlanta, GA 30303, 404-656-3177; Selected Publications: *Area Labor Profiles, Civilian Labor Force Estimates, GA Employment and Earnings, GA Employment and Wages, GA Labor Market Trends, GA Occupational Employment, Civilian Labor Force Estimates, Data on Occupational Supply and Demand, Earnings by Industry and Area*; Computer Readable Formats: No; Custom Research: Charge for Large projects, all others free.

Hawaii

Labor Market and Employment Services Branch, Labor & Industrial Relations Dept., 830 Punchbowl St., Room 302, Honolulu, HI 96813, 808-586-8711; Selected Publications: *Labor Shortages in Agriculture, Demand Occupations, Occupations in Communication Industry, Job Hunters's Guide, Selected Wage Information, Unemployment Insurance Fact Book, Licensed Occupations, Occupational Employment Statistics, Occupational Illness and Injuries, Wage Rate, Workers Compensation, Characteristics of the Insured Unemployed, Employment and Payrolls, Permanent Mass Layoffs and Plant Closings 1988, Labor Area News, Labor Force Information for Affirmative Action Programs*; Computer Readable Formats: No; Custom Research: Free.

Idaho

Department of Employment, Research and Analysis Bureau, 317 Main St., Boise, ID 83735, 208-334-6469; Selected Publications: *Economic Projects of Idaho Cities and Counties, LMI Directory, Idaho Monthly employment Newsletter, Labor Forces in idaho, Basic Economic Data, Annual Demographics Report, Affirmative Action Statistics, Area Employment Newsletter, Employment and Wages by Industry in Idaho*; Computer Readable Formats: Forthcoming; Custom Research: Most everything is free, Fee for larger projects.

Illinois

Employment Security Bureau, Research and Analysis, 401 South State St., Chicago, IL 60605, 312-793-2316; Selected Publications: *Country Labor Force Summary-2000, Labor Market Review, Illinois at Work, Affirmative Action Information, Occupational Employment Statistics, Occupational Projections, Wage Survey, Where Workers Work, Illinois Employment Industrial Summary*; Computer Readable Formats: No; Custom Research: Nominal fee.

Indiana

Employment Security Division, Labor Market Information, 10 N. Senate Ave., Indianapolis, IN 46204, 317-232-7701; Selected Publications: *Annual County Employment Patterns, Indiana Employment Review, Labor Force Estimates, Quarterly Covered Employment and Payrolls, Regional Economic Profiles, Occupational Employment Projections, Occupational Wage Surveys, Occupations In Demand, Hours and Earnings of Production Workers*; Computer Readable Formats: No; All shelf publications are free.

Iowa

Department of Employment Services, Labor Market Information Unit, 1000 E. Grand Ave., Des Moines, IA 50319, 515-281-8182; Selected Publications: *Condition of Employment Report/Analysis of the Iowa Market, Labor Force Employment and Unemployment Information, Labor Market Information for Service Delivery Areas, State-Wide Wage Surveys, Labor Market Information for Affirmative Action Programs, Industry/Occupational Projections, Job Insurance Benefits, Iowa Occupational Planning Guide, Licensed Occupations, Labor Market Information Directory, Wages and Employment Covered by Employment Security, Affirmative Action Data for Iowa, Condition of Employment*; Computer Readable Formats: Electronic bulletin board; Custom Research: Free, nominal fee for larger projects.

Kansas

Department of Human Resources, Division of Employment & Training, Research & Analysis Section, 401 S.W. Blvd., Topeka, KS 66603, 913-296-5058; Selected Publications: *Occupational Staffing Patterns, Kansas Unemployment Insurance Claims, Monthly Labor Market Summary, Kansas Wage Survey, Affirmative Action Packet, Labor Market Review, Report on Employment-Hours*

Market Studies, Demographics and Statistics

and Earnings, Labor Force Estimates, Employment by Area and Industry; Computer Readable Formats: Limited; Custom Research: Charge for large projects, all others free.

Kentucky

Department for Employment Services, Research & Statistics, CHR Bldg 2C, Frankfort, KY 40621, 502-564-7976; Selected Publications: *Non-Agricultural Wage and Salary Employment, Kentucky Labor Market Newsletter, Estimate of Production Workers and Average Hours and Earnings, Labor Force Estimates, Occupational Outlook, Occupational Career Brief, Occupational Profiles, Labor Area Summary, Labor Area Profile, Annual Planning Information, Affirmative Action, Labor Supply Estimates, Characteristics of Insured Unemployed, Average Covered Monthly Workers in Manufacturing by Industry Division and County, Total Wages by Industrial Division and County, Average Weekly Wages by Industrial Division and County;* Computer Readable Formats: No; Custom Research: Limited.

Louisiana

Department of Employment Security, Research and Statistics Unit, P.O. 94094, Baton Rouge, LA 70804-9094, 504-342-3141; Selected Publications: *Occupational Projections-1999-2000, Quarterly Employment and Wages, Annual Employment and Wages, Monthly Labor Market Information, Manpower for Affirmative Action, Annual Planning Report, Occupational Employment Statistics, Average Weekly Wage, LA Occupational Injuries and Illnesses;* Computer Readable Formats: Limited; Custom Research: Limited amount available free.

Maine

Bureau of Employment Security, Division of Economic Analysis and Research, 20 Union St., Augusta, ME 04330-6826, 207-289-2271; Selected Publications: *Labor Market Digest Monthly, Maine Occupational Staffing Patterns in Hospitals-Government-Manufacturing/Nonmanufacturing-Trade, Careers In Maine Woods;* Computer Readable Formats: Yes; Custom Research: Charge for larger projects, all others free.

Maryland

Department of Human Resources, Research and Analysis, Employment and Training, 1100 N. Eutaw St., Baltimore, MD 21201, 410-333-5007; .PA Selected Publications: *Affirmative Action Data, Maryland Occupational Industrial Outlook, Civilian Labor Force Employment and Unemployment by Place of Residence, Claims Processed for Unemployment Insurance Benefits, Occupations in Maryland, Current Employment Statistics, Labor Market Dimensions, Employment and Payrolls Covered by the Unemployment Insurance Law of Maryland, Zoned Employment and Unemployment Statistics, Industries in Maryland, Highlights of Maryland's Population Projections, Maryland Rural Manpower Report, Occupational Wage Information, Year in Review, Population and Labor Force in Maryland, A Profile: Services Industry in Maryland 1980-Present;* Computer Readable Formats: No. Customer Research: Limited amount available free.

Massachusetts

Division of Employment Security, Massachusetts Employment and Training Center, 19 Saniford Street, Charles F. Hurley Building, Boston, MA 02114, 617-727-6531; Selected Publications: *Planning Data: Massachusetts, Employment and Wages, Massachusetts Employment Review (monthly), Careers and Training in Allied Health, Occupational Profiles of Manufacturing Industries, Career Choices in a Changing Economy, New England Economic Indicators;* Computer Readable Formats: No; Publications free when available.

Michigan

Employment Security Commission, Bureau of Research and Statistics, 7310 Woodward Ave., Detroit, MI 48202, 313-876-5439; Selected Publications: *Affirmative Action Information Report, Annual Planning Information, Claims Counter, Covered Employment Statistics, Monthly Labor Market Review, Occupational Employment Statistics Survey Publications, Occupations in Education, Occupational Wage Information, Michigan Regulated and Trade Industries, Occupational Projections and Training Data, Michigan Occupation/Industry Outlook 2000, Michigan Metropolitan Areas Occupation/Industry Outlook 2000, Michigan Non-metropolitan Areas Occupation/Industry Outlook 2000, Michigan Occupational Supply/Demand Report, Occupational Projections and Training Information for Michigan-OPTIM, Civilian Labor Force, Employment and Unemployment Estimates, Employment Hours and Earnings Estimates, Unemployment Insurance Program Statistics, Employment Trends, Hours and Earnings Trends, Women Employment Trends 1982 to Present, Production Worker Employee Trends 1982 to Present;* Computer Readable Formats: Limited, electronic bulletin board forthcoming; Custom Research: Limited amount available free.

Minnesota

Department of Jobs and Training, Research Office, 390 North Robert Street, St. Paul MN 55101, 612-296-8716; Selected Publications: *Consumer Price Index, Career Bulletin, Minnesota Projections and Monthly Reports* (available on diskette), *Employment Outlook by Region, Minnesota Wage Data by Industry and Area, Minnesota Employment Outlook to 1996, Important MN Occupations by Industry by Area, Minnesota Careers, MN Wage Data By Industry and Size of Firm, Employment and Wage Data By County, Minnesota Labor Market Review;* Computer Readable Format: Some data available via electronic bulletin board; Custom Research: Charge for large projects, all others free.

Mississippi

Employment Security Commission, Labor Market Information Department, P.O. Box 1699, Jackson, MS 39215-1699, 601-961-7424; Selected Publications: *Guide to Labor Market Information, LMI Catalogue, Annual Labor Force Averages, Annual Report, Employment and Job Openings 2005, Farm Income and Expenditures, Affirmative Action Programs, Monthly Labor Market Data, Labor Market Trends for Jackson Metro Area, Mississippi's Business Population, Occupational Employment and Job Openings by Unit of Analysis, Personal Income by Major Sources, Quarterly Labor Market Summary, Transfer Payments by Major Sources;* Computer Readable Formats: Some publications available on diskettes; Customer Research: Limited amount available free.

Missouri

Division of Employment Security, Research and Analysis, P.O. Box 59, Jefferson City, MO 65104, 314-751-3602; Selected Publications: *Monthly Labor Area Trends, Labor Market Information for Affirmative Action Programs, Wages Paid in Selected Occupations, Employment Outlook;* Computer Readable Formats: Electronic bulletin board; Custom Research: Limited research available.

Montana

Department of Labor and Industry, Research and Analysis Bureau, P.O. Box 1728, Helena, MT 59624, 406-444-2430; Selected Publications: *Wage Surveys of the Private Sector, Wage Surveys of the Public Sector, Wage Surveys of Public Education, Quarterly Employment and Labor Force, Monthly Statistics in Brief, Annual Planning Information, Montana Supply and Demand Report, Montana Apprenticeable Occupations;* Computer Readable Formats: Forthcoming; Custom Research: Limited Amount available free.

Nebraska

Dept. of Labor, Labor Market Information, 550 S. 16th St., Lincoln, NE 68509, 402-471-2600; Selected Publications: *Prairie/Farm and Ranch Profile, NE Labor Market Information, Supply and Demand/Selected Occupations, Careers and Education in Nebraska, Monthly Labor Area Summary, Occupational Employment Statistics by Industry, Monthly Labor Force, Affirmative Action, Survey of Average Hourly Wage Rates, Occupational Newsletter, Nebraska Job Prospects;* Computer Readable Formats: No; Custom Research: Limited amount available free.

Nevada

Employment Security Department, Employment Security Research Section, 500 East Third Street, Carson City, NV 89713, 702-687-4550; Selected Publications: *Area Labor Review, Directory of Labor Market Information, Quarterly and Monthly Economic Update, Nevada Wage Survey, Occupational Projections, Job Finding Techniques;* Computer Readable Formats: Limited; Custom Research: Limited amount available free.

New Jersey

Labor Department, Labor Market Information Office, John Fitch Plaza CN056, Trenton, NJ 08625, 609-292-7376; Selected Publications: *Regional Labor Market Reviews, Regional Labor Market Newsletters, PA Compendium of New Jersey Wage Surveys, Employment and Economy Newsletter, Employment Trends, Economic Indicators Monthly;* Computer Readable Formats: Limited electronic bulletin board usage; Custom Research: Limited amount available free.

New Hampshire

Employment Security Department, Economic Analysis and Reports and Labor Market Information Bureau, 32 South Main Street, Concord, NH 03301, 603-224-3311; Selected Publications: *Wage Survey, Vital Signs, Staffing Patterns in NH, Annual Report, Annual Planning Information, Annual Planning Information MSA's, Community Patterns NH, Economic Conditions, Employment and Wages by County, Employment and Wages MSA's, Employment and Wages by Planning Region, Fact Book: Cities and Towns, Firms By Size, Local Area Unemployment Statistics, NH Affirmative Action Data, NH Occupational Outlook 2005, Users Guide to Labor Market Information;* Computer Readable Formats: Call for availability and cost; Custom Research: Free.

New Mexico

Department of Employment Security, Economic Research and Analysis, P.O. Box 1928, Albuquerque, NM 87103, 505-841-8645; Selected Publications: *Covered Employment and Wages, Basic Concepts, Monthly Labor Market Review, Nonagricultural Wage and Salary Employment, Facts and Figures about New Mexico, Hours and Earnings Estimates, Albuquerque Small Employer Wage Survey, Jobs to 2000, Area Job Market Flyers, Large Employers in New Mexico by County*; Computer Readable Formats: Limited; Customer Research: Limited amount available for free.

New York

Department of Labor, Division of Research & Statistics, State Office Bldg. Campus #12, Albany, NY 12240, 518-457-3800; Selected Publications: *Statistics on Operations, Characteristics of Job Openings, Civilian Labor Force by Occupation, Selected Demographic Groups, Regular and Extended Benefits, State Unemployment Insurance, Collective Bargaining Settlements, Directory of Labor Unions and Employee Organizations in New York State Employment Review, Current Population Survey Data, A Guide to Career Opportunities in New York State Government, Earnings and Hours in Selected Industries, The Job Seeker, Labor Area Summary Monthly Statistical Report, Labor Area Summary Quarterly Analytical Report, Labor Market Assessment: Occupational Supply and Demand, Occupational Brief, Occupational Projections, Occupational Employment Statistics, Occupational Guide, Occupational Needs, Occupation Licensed or Certified by New York State, Operations, Resident Employment Status of the Civilian Labor Force, Careers Exploration and Job Seeking, Total and Civilian Labor Force Summary, Selected Demographic Groups - NYS, Counties and SMSA's, Selected Labor Research Reports, Apprentice Training Hours and Earnings, Insured Employment and Payrolls, Local Area Unemployment Statistics, Non-Agricultural Wage and Salary Employment, Unemployment Insurance Operating Statistics*; Computer Readable Formats: Forthcoming; Custom Research: Charge for large projects, all others free.

North Carolina

Employment Security Commission, Labor Market Information Division, P.O. Box 25903, Raleigh, NC 27611, 919-733-2936; Selected Publications: *Employment and Wages in NC Quarterly, Market Areas Newsletter, Past High School Intentions of NC Graduates by County, Equal Employment Data Series, Occupational Trends: Year 2000: NC, NC Metro State Planning Regions A-F; G-L; M-R, Announced New and Expanding Manufacturing Firms, NC Preliminary Civilian Labor Force Estimates, Active Job Applicants by County, Registered Applicants and Job Openings, Follow-Up Survey of NC High School Graduates by County, Wage Rates in Selected Occupations*; Computer Readable Formats: Forthcoming; Custom Research: Free, charge for larger projects.

North Dakota

Job Service, Research and Statistics, P.O. Box 1537, Bismarck, ND 58502, 701-224-3048; Selected Publications: *Occupational Supply/Demand Report, Employment and Wages, Monthly Labor Market Advisor, Occupations Wage Surveys and Benefits for Major Cities, Occupational Projections to 2000, Employment Surveys by Major City, Annual Planning Report*; Computer Readable Formats: No; Custom Research: Charge for large amounts, all others free.

Ohio

Bureau of Employment Services, Labor Market Information Division, 145 South Front St., Columbus, OH 43216, 614-466-4636; Selected Publications: *Employment and Unemployment Estimates, Covered Employment and Payroll, Trend Tables, Monthly Labor Market Review, County Labor Force Reports, Labor Force Estimates, Metropolitan Profile, Occupational Projections, Composition of Job Placements, Summary of Ohio Worker Training Program Activities*; Computer Readable Formats: Yes; Custom Research: Charge for large projects, all others free.

Oklahoma

Oklahoma Employment Security Commission, Economic Analysis, 2401 N. Lincoln Blvd., Oklahoma City, OK 73105, 405-557-7104; Selected Publications: *Labor Market Information, Handicap Labor Force Data for Selected Areas, Manpower Information for Affirmative Action, Annual Report to the Governor, Handbook of Employment Statistics, County Employment and Wage Data, Occupational Wage Surveys, OK Monthly Economic Newsletter*; Computer Readable Formats: Yes; Custom Research: Charge for large projects, all other free.

Oregon

Employment Division, Research and Statistics, 875 Union NE, Salem, OR 97311, 503-378-8656; Selected Publications: *Oregon Work Force at Risk, Dislocated Workers, Oregon Works, Affirmative Action Programs, Agricultural Employment, Average Weekly Earnings-Hours, Business and Employment Outlook, Monthly Local Labor Trends, Occupational Program Planning System, Oregon Wage Information*; Computer Readable Formats: No; Custom Research: Charge for large projects, all others free.

Pennsylvania

Department of Labor & Industry, Research & Statistics Division, 7th & Forster Sts., Harrisburg, PA 17121, 717-787-2114; Selected Publications: *Work Force 2000, Civilian Work Force Data by Labor Market Area of Residence, Annual Average Labor Force Data, Civilian Labor Force Series by Labor Market Area, PA Labor Market Areas Ranked on Basis of Rate of Unemployment, PA Unemployment Fact Sheet, Directory of Occupational Wage Information, Occupational Trends and Outlook for Total Civilian Employment, Industry Trends and Outlook 2000, Employment and Wages of Workers Covered by the PA Unemployment Compensation Law, Occupations Employment in Hospital Occupational Staffing Patterns for Selected Non-Manufacturing Industries, Annual Planning Information, Affirmative Action Report, Labor Market Job Guides, Directory of Licensed Occupational Information Systems, Labor Demand-Supply Relationships, Career Guide, Labor Market Letters, PA Employment and Earnings, PA's Microcomputer Occupational Information System, Hours and Earnings, Current Trends in Employment and Wages in PA Industries, PA Labor Force, Annual Planning Information Report, Hours and Earnings in Manufacturing and Selected Non-manufacturing Industries, Industry Trends and Outlook Projected 1995*; Computer Readable Formats: Yes; Custom Research: Charge for large projects, all others free.

Rhode Island

Department of Employment Security, Research and Statistics, 101 Friendship St., Providence, RI 02903, 401-277-3706; Selected Publications: *Occupational Projections 2000, Monthly Labor Force Statistics, Characteristics of Insured Unemployed, RI Employment Newsletter, Quarterly Labor Supply and Demand Report, Employment and Wages by City and Industry, Annual Planning Information, Manpower Information for Affirmative Action Programs, Employment In RI Hospitals*; Computer Readable Format: No; Custom Research: Free.

South Carolina

Employment Security Commission, Labor Market Information Division, P.O. Box 995, Columbia, SC 29202, 803-737-2660; Selected Publications: *Industrial Monographs, Wage Survey, SC Job Search Assistance Guide, Labor Market Review, Employment Trends, Occupational Projections 2000, Labor Force in Industry, Employment and Wages in SC*; Computer Readable Formats: Limited; Custom Research: Charge for large projects, all others free.

South Dakota

Department of Labor, Labor Market Information Center, P.O. Box 4730, Aberdeen, SD 57402-4730, 605-622-2314; Selected Publications: *Labor Availability Studies, Labor Bulletin, Occupational Wage Information, Occupational Outlook Handbook, Employment and Earnings, Affirmative Action Package, Statewide Job Listings*; Computer Readable Formats: Yes; Custom Research: Limited amount available free.

Tennessee

Department of Employment Security, Research and Statistics Division, 11th Floor, James Robertson Parkway, Nashville, TN 37245-1040, 615-741-3639; Selected Publications: *Occupational Wage and Benefit Information, Minorities in Tennessee, Occupations in Demand, Licensed Occupations in Tennessee, Monthly Available Labor, Monthly Labor Force Summary, Commuting Patterns, Tennessee Employment Projections 2000, Tennessee Youth Report, Veterans in Tennessee, Women in the Labor Force, Tennessee High School Graduates*; Computer Readable Formats: Limited; Custom Research: Limited amount available free.

Texas

Texas Employment Commission, Economic Research & Analysis Dept., Room 208-T, TEC Building, Austin, TX 78778, 512-463-2616; Selected Publications: *Labor Force Estimates, Current Population Survey, Nonagricultural Wage and Salary Employment Estimates, Average Hours and Earnings Data, Employment and Wages by Industry and County, Affirmative Action Packets, Characteristics of the Insured Unemployed, Regional Reports, Labor Demand Projects by 2000, Occupational Employment Statistics*; Computer Readable Formats: Limited; Custom Research: Charge for large projects, all others free.

Utah

Utah Department of Employment Security, Labor Market Information Services, P.O. Box 11249, Salt Lake City, UT 84147, 801-536-7800; Selected Publications:

Market Studies, Demographics and Statistics

Annual Labor Market Research, Licensed Occupations in Utah, Monthly Utah Labor Market Report, Utah Directory of Business and Industry; Computer Readable Formats: On a limited basis. Custom Research: Free.

Vermont

Department of Employment and Training, Labor Market Information, P.O. Box 488, Montpelier, VT 05601, 802-229-0311; Selected Publications: *Occupation, Wage and Employment Survey, Job Openings, Affirmative Action Planning Data, Annual Planning Information, Combined Annual Report of DET and JTPA, Directory of Labor Market Information Employment and Earnings, Labor Market Area Bulletins, Profile of Active Applicants, Vermont Labor Market, Employment and Wages Covered by Unemployment Insurance, Licensed Occupations in Vermont Mining and Quarrying, Construction, Unemployment Compensation Statistical Table, Vermont Economic and Demographic Profile Series, Vermont Industrial Projections to 2000, Vermont Occupational Projections to 2000*; Computer Readable Formats: Forthcoming; Custom Research: Upon request, limited time available.

Virginia

Virginia Employment Commission, Labor Market and Demographics Analysis Section, P.O. Box 1358, Richmond, VA 23211, 804-786-8222; Selected Publications: *Guide to Establishing a Business, LMI Directory, Business Registration Guide, Work Force 2000, Labor Force by Sex and Minority Status, Commuting Patterns, Data on Public Schools, Economic Assumptions for the U.S. and VA, Economically Disadvantaged Data, Employment and Training Indicators, Employment and Wages in Establishments, Employment and Wages in VA, Monthly Labor Market Review, Wage Survey Selected Manufacturers Occupation, Licensed Occupations in VA, List of Employers By Size, State and County Veteran Population, Trends in Employment-Hours and Earnings, Quarterly Virginia Economic Indicators, Virginia Business Resource Directory.* Computer Readable Formats: ALICE (Virginia based only); Custom Research: Limited for nominal fee.

Washington

Employment Security Group, Labor Market and Economic Analysis Branch, 605 Woodland Square Loop S.E., Lacey, WA 98503, mailing address P.O. Box 9046, Olympia, WA 98507-9046, 206-438-4804; Selected Publications: *Labor Area Summaries, Washington Labor Market, LMI Review, Affirmative Action Information, Annual Demographic Information, Area Wage Survey, Employment and Payrolls in Washington, Occupational Profiles and Projections, Labor Market Monthly*; Computer Readable Formats: Some; Custom Research: Large projects are charged on a contract basis.

West Virginia

Employment Security Department, Labor and Economic Research, 112 California Ave., Charleston, WV 25305, 304-558-2630; Selected Publications: *Affirmative Action, West Virginia Women in the Labor Force, Annual Planning Information, Metropolitan Statistical Areas Annual Planning Information, Job Training Partnership Act, West Virginia County Profiles, WV Economic Summary, Employment and Earnings Trends, Insured Workers Summary, Occupational Projections, Veterans Report, Wage Survey, Youth Report, Directory of Publications, Licensed Occupations in West Virginia*; Computer Readable Formats: Forthcoming; Custom Research: Limited amount available free.

Wisconsin

Department of Industry, Labor and Human Relations, Employment and Training Library, P.O. Box 7944, Madison, WI 53707, 608-267-9613; Selected Publications: *LMI: A Reference Guide of WI Publications, Labor Market Planning Information, Employment, Wages, Taxes Due Covered by Wisconsin U.C. Law, Wisconsin Projections 1988-2000, Affirmative Action Data, Career Connection, Monthly Wisconsin Economic Indicators, Civilian Labor Force Estimates, Consumer Price Index, Current Population Survey, Employment and Wages, Wage Survey, Covered Employment By Size of Industry and County, Wisconsin Employment Picture, Wisconsin Works, Inform Bi-Monthly*; Computer Readable Formats: Some; Custom Research: Charge for large projects.

Wyoming

Employment Security Commission, Research & Analysis, P.O. Box 2760, Casper, WY 82602, 307-235-3200; Selected Publications: *Occupational Employment Statistics: Manufacturing and Hospitals, Occupational Employment Statistics, Wyoming's Annual Planning Report, Wyoming's Covered Employment and Wage Data, Labor Force Trends, Applicants and Job Openings in Wyoming, Affirmative Action Package*; Computer Readable Format: No; Custom Research: Limited amount available.

State Statistical Abstracts

For years researchers have been aware of the importance of keeping around the latest edition of the *Statistical Abstract of the United States* (available for $25 from Superintendent of Documents, U.S. GPO, Washington, DC 20402, 202-783-3238). Now if you are interested in local or regional opportunities, trends or markets, almost every state government offers their own *State Statistical Abstract* or something comparable. Most of the states produce their abstract on an annual basis. There are only 11 states which do not publish abstracts: Alabama, Arkansas, Delaware, Kansas, Massachusetts, Michigan, New Hampshire, New Mexico, Texas, Virginia, and Wisconsin.

Tables and graphs are used to illustrate the performance of the economy. Where comparisons can be made, state, regional, and national data can be compared. Market analysts, businesses and researchers will find the following kinds of information in a statistical abstract:

- how many of Fortune magazine's top 500 companies have manufacturing plants in the state;
- the number of jobs directly or indirectly related to exports;
- largest sources of personal income;
- number of people employed in agricultural/non-agricultural jobs;
- how a state ranks in population and land size;
- number of acres of forest land;
- number of airports, number privately owned;
- number of registered aircraft;
- changes in population-age distribution;
- percentage of 17- and 18-year-olds graduating from high school;
- number of state universities, vocational schools;
- motor vehicle registrations;
- crime rates; and
- traffic fatalities.

Similar to the *Statistical Abstract of the U.S.* in providing important data in charts and tables, these state abstracts offer important leads to more detailed sources of information. Although the specific charts and tables may not offer the exact detail of data you require on a particular topic, they will identify the offices which generate this type of information. By contacting the specific office you are likely to get the precise data you require. They can't publish everything they have in a single statistical abstract, but they can dig it out of their files for you.

Statistical Abstract Offices

Alaska
Alaska Department of Labor, Research and Analysis, P.O. Box 25501, Juneau, AK 99802; 907-465-4500. Publication: *Employment and Earnings Report, Statistical Quarterly* (free).

Arizona
Arizona Department of Economic Security Research Administration, P.O. Box 6123, Phoenix, AZ 85005; 602-542-3871. Publication: *Labor Market Information-Annual Planning Information* (free).

California
Department of Finance, 915 L Street, 8th Floor, Sacramento, CA 95814; 916-322-2263. Publication: *California Statistical Abstract* (free).

Colorado
State Planning and Budget, Room 1111, State Capitol Building, Denver, CO 80203; 303-866-3386. Publication: *Economic Perspective* (free).

Connecticut
Office of Policy and Management, Budget and Financial Management Division, 80 Washington St., Hartford, CT 06106; 203-566-8342. Publication: *Economic Report of the Governor* (free).

District of Columbia
Office of Policy and Program Evaluation, Room 208, District Building, 1350 Pennsylvania Ave. NW, Washington, DC 20004; 202-727-6979. Publication: *Indices* ($21).

Florida
University Presses of Florida, 15 N.W. 15th St., Gainesville, FL 32603; 904-392-1351. Publication: *Florida Statistical Abstract* ($22.95).

Georgia
Georgia Office of Budget and Planning, 254 Washington St. SW, Suite 614, Atlanta, GA 30334-8500; 404-656-0911. Publications: *Georgia Descriptions and Data - A Statistical Abstract* ($10).

Hawaii
State of Hawaii, Business and Economic Development, P.O. Box 2359, Honolulu, HI 96804, Attention: Information Office; 808-586-2466. Publication: *State of Hawaii Statistical Abstract* ($8).

Idaho
Secretary of State, Room 203, State House, Boise, ID 83720; 208-334-2300. Publication: *Idaho Blue Book* ($5).

Illinois
University of Illinois, Bureau of Economic and Business Research, 1206 S. 6th St., 428 Commerce West, Champaign, IL 61820; 217-333-2330. Publication: *Illinois Statistical Abstract* ($40).

Indiana
Indiana Department of Commerce, Division of Economic Analysis, One North Capitol, Suite 200, Indianapolis, IN 46204; 317-264-3110. Publication: *Indiana: Its Economy, Its People* ($2).

Iowa
Iowa Development Commission, 200 East Grand Ave., Des Moines, IA 50309; 515-243-4871. Publication: *Statistical Profile of Iowa* (free).

Kentucky
Cabinet for Economic Development, 133 Holmes St., Frankfort, KY 40601; 502-564-4715. Publication: *Kentucky Economic Statistics* ($10).

Maine
Business Development Office, State House Station #59, Augusta, ME 04333; 207-289-3195. Publication: *Maine Statistical Summary* (free).

Maryland
Dept. of Economic & Employment Development, 217 East Redwood, 11th Floor, Baltimore, MD 21202, 410-333-6953. Publication: *Statistical Abstract* ($39).

Minnesota
Department of Trade and Economic Development, Business Development Analysis Division, 900 American Center Building, 150 East Kellogg, St. Paul, MN 55101; 612-297-2335 or 297-2872. Publication: *Compare Minnesota* (free). They do not have an abstract.

Market Studies, Demographics and Statistics

Mississippi

Mississippi State University, Division of Business Research, College of Business and Industry, Drawer 5288, Mississippi State, MS 39762; 601-325-3817. Publications: *Mississippi Statistical Abstract* ($35).

Missouri

University of Missouri, B & PA Research Center, 10 Professional Building, Columbia, MO 65211; 314-882-4805. Publications: *Statistical Abstract* ($25).

Montana

Department of Commerce, Census and Economic Information Center, 1424 9th Ave. Helena, MT 59620; 406-444-4393. Publication: *Montana Statistical Abstract* (from 1984, free). *State Summary Volume*, from the Montana County Profile Series.

Nebraska

Department of Economic Development, Research Division, P.O. Box 94666, Lincoln, NE 68509; 402-471-3111. Publication: *Nebraska Statistical Handbook* ($10).

Nevada

Vital Statistics, 505 East King Street, Room 102, Carson City, NV 89710; 702-687-4480. Publication: *Statistical Abstract* (free).

New Jersey

Office of Economic Policy, New Jersey Department of Commerce, 20 W. State St., Trenton, NJ; 609-292-3860.

New York

Rockefeller Institute of Government, 411 State St., Albany, NY 12203; 518-443-5522. Publication: *New York Statistical Yearbook* ($50 + $4 shipping and handling).

North Carolina

State Planning Office, Office of the State Budget, 116 W. Jones St., Raleigh, NC 27603; 919-733-4131. Publication: *North Carolina State Statistical Abstract* ($25 + tax).

North Dakota

The Bureau of Business and Economic Research, College of Business and Public Administration, Box 8255, University of North Dakota, Grand Forks, ND 58202; 701-777-3365. Publication: *North Dakota Statistical Abstract* ($20).

Ohio

Ohio Data Users, P.O. Box 1001, Columbus, OH 43266; 614-466-2115. Publication: *County Profiles* ($50).

Oklahoma

University of Oklahoma, CEMR (Center for Economic and Management Research), College of Business Administration, 307 W. Brooks St., Room 4, Norman, OK 73019; 405-325-2931. Publication: *Statistical Abstract* ($22).

Oregon

Economic Development Department, 775 Summer Street, Salem, OR 97310, Attn: Publications; 503-373-1290. Publication: *Oregon Economic Profile* ($3.50).

Pennsylvania

State Data Center, State University at Harrisburg, Capitol College, Middletown, PA 17057; 717-948-6336. Publication: *Statistical Abstract* ($35).

Rhode Island

Department of Economic Development, 7 Jackson Walkway, Providence, RI 02903; 401-277-2601. Publication: *Annual Economic Trend Series* (free).

South Carolina

Division of Research and Statistical Services, 1000 Assembly St., Rembert C. Dennis Building, Suite 425, Columbia, SC 29201; 803-734-3793. Publication: *South Carolina Statistical Abstract* ($20).

South Dakota

Businesses Research Bureau, School of Business, The University of South Dakota, 414 East Clark St., Vermillion, SD 57069-2390; 605-677-5287. Publication: *South Dakota Community Abstract* ($20).

Tennessee

University of Tennessee, Center for Business and Economic Research, S. 100 Glocker Hall, College of Business Administration, Knoxville, TN 37996; 615-974-5441. Publication: *Tennessee State Statistical Abstract* ($36 + $3 shipping and handling).

Texas

Department of Commerce, Research and Planning Division, State Data Center, P.O. Box 12728, Austin, TX 78711; 512-463-1166.

Utah

Office of Planning and Budget, Room 116, State Capitol Building, Salt Lake City, UT 84115; 801-538-1027. Publication: *Economic Report to the Governor* ($12).

Vermont

Agency of Development and Community Affairs, Montpelier, VT 05602; 802-828-3211. Publication: *Vermont Selected Statistics* (free).

Washington

Office of Forecast Council, Evergreen Plaza, Room 300, Mailstop FJ33, Olympia, WA 98504; 206-586-6785. Publication: *Economic and Revenue Forecast for Washington State* ($4.50 per issue in state, $9 per issue out of state; $18 per year in state subscription, $36 per year out of state subscription).

West Virginia

Chamber of Commerce, Research and Strategic Planning, P.O. Box 2789, Charleston, WV 25330; 304-342-1115.

Wyoming

Division of Economic Analysis, Room 327E, Emerson Building, Cheyenne, WY 82002-0060; 307-777-7504. Publication: *The Wyoming Data Handbook* (Free).

State Forecasting Agencies

State planning offices can provide vast quantities of local market information, demographic data, and company intelligence -- more than you would believe possible. Every state has a bureau equivalent to a planning office to assist the Governor in charting future economic change. Of course, the quantity of information varies from one state to the next as does the sophistication in methods of gathering and analyzing data. However, most information is generated to support decision making for policies and legislative initiatives which will affect the current and future status of the state economy. These blueprints for the future usually include plans for attracting new businesses and industries as well as improving the quality of housing, education and transportation.

It should be noted that there is a wide disparity in the research and strategic focus of these state planning offices. The position of this function within the state bureaucratic structure often provides clues about the scope of its mission. In most states this forecasting operation is housed in the Department of Economic Development or in a separate policy office under the Governor's office. However, in our survey of all fifty states, we discovered this crucial function in unexpected places. In South Carolina, for example, there is a special Commission on the Future within the Lieutenant Governor's office, and in Texas, a comparable office falls under the jurisdiction of the state comptroller.

The types of information available from these offices are outlined below.

Business Expansion and Economic Outlook

If you currently do business in a state or intend to establish a business there, it would be wise to learn about the Governor's long-term strategy. Keep in mind that no one is more concerned about the state's future than this elected official. If your company sells to farmers, inquire at the planning office about the Governor's agricultural policies. If your firm relies on high tech complementary businesses, see whether there is a plan to attract high tech companies. Or, if you are interested in consumer markets, be aware of demographic projections conducted by the planning agency for the state as well as for specific regions and counties. Many states appear to be charting future population patterns on a regular basis as is evident with the sampling of publications noted here.

Indiana: *Some Aspects of Demographic Change in Indiana from 1980 to 2000*
California: *California's Economic Future -- Building New Foundations for a Competitive Society*
Michigan: *Population Projections for Michigan to the Year 2010*
Utah: *Utah 2000*
Nebraska: *Nebraska Industry -- A Survey of Concerns, Needs and Future Plans*
New Jersey: *Annual Economic Forecast*

Demographics and Market Studies

Most of these offices are aware of the current demographic situation within their state. They also continually monitor the major industries in the state as well as emerging industries. Their data are usually derived from a combination of federal, state and locally generated information. Sometimes these offices are part of the state data center program run by the U.S. Bureau of the Census. Demographic studies as well as state statistical abstracts are readily available.

Arizona: *Community Profiles*
Montana: *County Profiles*
Washington DC: *Housing Monographs by Ward*
Nevada: *Community Profiles -- Demographic Facts*
New Hampshire: *Changes in Households and Households Size for Towns and Cities*
Iowa: *A Statistical Profile of Iowa*
Maryland: *State Statistical Abstract*

These state planning offices often produce in-depth market studies on diverse topics:

Arizona: *Aerospace in Arizona -- An Assessment of Market Opportunities*
Delaware: *Food Processors, Banking,* and *Automotive Just-In-Time Suppliers*
Maryland: *Impact of Professional Sports on the Maryland Economy*
Michigan: *Machine Tool Industry Update*
Missouri: *Home Health Care and the Homemaker*
Nebraska: *Profit Opportunities in Nebraska for Manufacturers of Pet Food*
New York: *Statistical Profile of the Printing and Publishing Industry*
Florida: *Monthly Tourist Surveys*
Virginia: *High Technology Communications in Virginia*

Company Information and Industry Directories

Many of these offices are responsible for maintaining information on the companies which are located within their state. It is not unusual for the state to collect the following data on every manufacturer and corporation:

- Name of company;
- Address and telephone number;
- Names of principal officers;
- Types of products or services produced;
- Number of employees; and
- Sales estimate.

You stand to learn more about a company, especially its financial picture, if the business in question received some type of economic assistance from the state. After all, once a company takes taxpayer money, the public has a right to know. There is a growing number of companies that fall into this category. Recently we received a list of over 100 firms which obtained financial assistance from Pennsylvania just during the past year.

Other handy resources available from many state planning offices are company directories. Many of them concentrate on one industry sector.

Kansas: *Directory of Kansas Warehouse and Distribution Centers*
Michigan: *Michigan Private 100*
Montana: *Consumer Products Buyer's Directory*
Oregon: *Directory of Oregon Electronic Products*

Databases and Special Services

Because these planning agencies share their forecasts and statistical data with other offices within the state government, often the data are readily available to the public, usually for free or on a cost recovery basis. Already many have established customized databases, some of which permit direct online access. Examples include:

- Idaho's database linking entrepreneurs with investors;
- Colorado's community profiles database covering 63 counties and 260 municipalities;
- Florida's nine public access databases; and
- Nevada's computerized databank on land availability, labor resources and economic statistics.

Difficulties Tracking Down Forecasting Data

Since numerous offices within a state are engaged in forecasting expect to run into some obstacles. Don't be discouraged if, when you contact one office for specific market data, you are told there is "no way" they would keep such information. The odds are that some other state bureaucrat has the information, so always patiently ask for other offices you could call. For example, practically every state publishes a directory of manufacturers, but it may not be produced by the planning office but by some other agency across town. This holds true when hunting for statistical information, market studies, and databases.

State Planning Offices

The address and telephone numbers are included for the primary planning offices in each state as well as the District of Columbia. The publications listed with the office do not represent the entire universe of hardcopy data available. These titles are included only when the office is capable of providing us with a current listing. There are states which have publications, but do not have any sort of catalog. For those states you must request data under specific topic headings.

Alabama

Alabama Department of Economic and Community Affairs, P.O. Box 25037, Montgomery, AL 36125-0347; 205-284-8910. Publications: *Annual Report*.

Alaska

State Planning Office, Division of Policy, Commerce & Economic Development, Office of Management and Budget, P.O. AM, Juneau, AK 99811; 907-465-3568.

Arizona

Arizona Department of Commerce, 3800 N. Central, Phoenix, AZ 85012; 602-280-1300. Publications: *Annual Report, Arizona Annual Economic Profile, Arizona Developments Quarterly Newsletter, Directory of High Technology Companies, Guide to Establishing a Business in Arizona, Arizona Agribusiness Profiles, Arizona Community Profiles* ($18), *Arizona Indian Profiles, Arizona Industrial Profiles* ($15), *Arizona Main Street Newsletter, Common Questions About Planning Newsletter, Planning and Zoning Handbook* ($20), *Rural Economic Development Resource Directory* ($5), *Financial Resources for Business Development, Request for Proposal Handbook, Bi-Weekly Report of Federal and State Proposals Under Review, Clearinghouse Manual, Federal Assistance Award Data System Report, Arizona Energy Data Report, Community Energy Profile Handbook, So-Easy Energy Saving Packet, Energy Checklist, Ease the Squeeze Driving Hints, Apartment Energy Conservation Guide, Home Energy Conservation Guide, Mobile Home Energy Conservation Guide, Energy Fact Sheets, Arizona Exporters Directory, Arizona World Trade Review Quarterly Newsletter, Directory of International Services, Twenty Questions about the Community Development Block Grants, Energy News, Local State Funding Report*.

Arkansas

Office of Industrial Development, State of Arkansas, #1 Capitol Mall, Little Rock, AR 72201; 501-682-1121. Publications: *Breaking Down Old Walls-Laying a New Foundation, Annual Report*.

California

Commission on Economic Development, State of California, State Capitol, Room 1028, Sacramento, CA 95814; 916-445-1025. Publications: *Annual Report* ($2.50), *Doing Business in California-A Guide for Establishing a Business* (old version $3, new version $1.67 postage), *An International Trade Policy for California* ($2, photocopy charged for postage), *Poisoning Prosperity-The Impact of Toxics in California's Economy* ($5, follow-up version $3), *Assessment of Reduced Revenue on California Local Law Enforcement* ($2, postage charged).

Colorado

State of Colorado, Division of Commerce and Development, Department of Local Affairs, 1313 Sherman St., Room 523, Denver, CO 80203; 303-866-2205. Publications: *Directory of Services* (free to state employees only), *Stateline* (state newsletter, only for state employees). Other Services: Community Profiles Database, covering 63 counties and 260 municipalities. More information on demographics can be obtained from State of Colorado, Division of Local Government, Department of Local Affairs, Room 521, Denver, CO 80203; 303-866-2156.

Connecticut

Connecticut Department of Economic Development, Marketing Department, 865 Brook Street, Rocky Hill, CT 06067; 203-258-4288. Publications: *Annual Report*.

Delaware

Delaware Development Office, State of Delaware, Executive Department, 99 Kings Highway, P.O. Box 1401, Dover, DE 19903, 302-739-4271. Publications: *Three-Year Capital Budget Plan, Delaware Data Book* ($25), *Comparison of Estimated State and Local Family Tax Burdens, Small Business Start-Up Guide*, and *Procurement Guide*. Other Services: Business Research Section maintains an extensive library of data resources and responds to requests for economic, demographic and travel information. Selective online access available to a computerized real estate file. A computerized hotel reservation system is also available.

District of Columbia

Office of Planning, Deputy Mayor for Economic Development, Government of the District of Columbia, Washington, DC 20004; 202-727-6492. Publications: *Census Tract Map* ($2), *Citizen's Guide to Zoning, Comprehensive Plan and Land Use Map, Development Process in the District of Columbia* ($50), *District of Columbia Zoning Map* ($3), *Market Assessment for Downtown Washington, Housing Monograph by Ward, Population Monograph by Ward, Land Use Monograph by Ward, 1982 Housing Unit Estimates Washington, DC, Planning for the Future/The Ward Planning Process, Proposal to Establish Development Zones East of the Anacostia River, Population Estimates Washington, DC, Connecticut Avenue Corridor Study, Anacostia Metro Station Action Plan, Benning Road Action Plan, Fort Totten Metro Station Action Plan, Fourteenth Street and Potomac Avenue Metro State Area Action Plan, Howard Gateway Action Plan, New York Avenue Industrial Corridor Action Plan, Rhode Island Avenue Metro Station Action Plan, Taylor and Upshur Street Action Plan, Street Address Directory* ($4), *The State of the Wards Report*.

Florida

Bureau of Economic Analysis, Florida Department of Commerce, Division of Economic Development, Tallahassee, FL 32301; 904-487-2971. Publications: *Monthly Tourist Surveys, County Comparisons, Florida and the Other Forty-Nine, Agency Functional Plan, A Guide to Florida Environmental Permitting.* Special Services: Five public access databases, and customized research requests; 909-488-4255.

Georgia

Office of Planning and Budget, 254 Washington Street, S.W., Atlanta, GA 30334-8500; 404-656-3820. Publications: *Governor's Policy Statement, Memos from Growth Issues Resources Council.*

Hawaii

Department of Business, Economic Development and Tourism, 11th floor, 220 S. King Street, Honolulu, HI 96813; 808-586-2406.

Idaho

Department of Commerce, Room 108, State Capitol, Boise, ID 83720; 208-334-3417. Publications: *Economic Development Agenda.*

Illinois

Illinois Department of Commerce and Community Affairs, 620 East Adams Street, Springfield, IL 62701; 217-782-3233. Publications: *Annual Report* (free).

Indiana

Indiana Economic Development Council, One North Capitol, Suite 425, Indianapolis, IN 46204; 317-631-0871. Publications: *The Futures of Indiana-Trends Affecting Economic Change 1986-2000, Indiana's Infrastructure Strategy-An Outline for Action, 1986 Indiana Economic Development Congress, Defining Vocational Education, Vocational Education: Who Are The Students, Vocational Education in Indiana, Vocational Education and Economic Development in Indiana, A Future of Learning and Work, The Investment Effects of Indiana's Preliminary Tax Abatement Programs, An Evaluation of Property Tax Abatement in Indiana, Looking Back-The Update of Indiana's Strategic Economic Development Plan.*

Iowa

Iowa Department of Economic Development, 200 East Grand Avenue. Des Moines, IA 50309; 515-281-3251. Publications: *Statistical Profile of Iowa, Economic Developments.*

Kansas

Department of Economic Development Research, 400 W 8th St. 5th Floor, Topeka, KS 66603; 913-296-3564. Department of Commerce; 913-296-3481. Publications: *Annual Report, Directory of Kansas Manufacturers and Products* ($10.53), *Directory of Kansas Warehouse and Distribution Centers, Directory of Kansas Job Shops, Fortune 500 Facilities in Kansas* (hasn't been revised since 1987), *Kansas Manufacturing Firms in Exports, Kansas Association Directory, Firms Headquartered In Kansas, Kansas New and Expanding Manufacturers, Kansas Economic Development Statutes* (being revised, may not be available to the public).

Kentucky

Center for Business & Economic Development, 302 Matthews Building, College of Business and Economics, University of Kentucky, Lexington, KY 40506; 606-257-7675. Publications: *Annual Economic Report.*

Louisiana

State Planning Office, Division of Administration, 1051 North Riverside Mall, Baton Rouge, LA 70804; 504-342-7410.

Maine

Economic and Community Development Office, State House Station 59, Augusta, ME 04333; 207-289-2656. Also, Data Census Manager, 20 Union Street, Augusta, ME 04330-6827; 207-289-2271.

Maryland

Division of Research, Department of Economic and Community Development, 45 Calvert St., Annapolis, MD 21401; 301-974-3629. Publications: *The Impact of Professional Sports on the Maryland Economy, An Econometric Analysis of Variations in Workers' Compensation Rates, The Fiscal Impact of Professional Sports, The Economic Impact of the Preakness on the Maryland Economy, Workers' Compensation Insurance, Competitive Rating in Workers' Compensation Insurance, The Economic Impact of the University of Maryland's Football Program, Report of the Special Advisory Committee on Professional Sports and the Economy, Maryland Statistical Abstract, Workers' Compensation in Maryland, Technical Notes on 27 Issues in Workers' Compensation, Workers' Compensation in Maryland, Workers' Compensation Summary of Major Studies, Prompt Payment of Temporary Total Disability Benefits, Maryland Workers' Compensation Claims Experience, Workers' Compensation Medical Claims and Benefits Written Opinions, A Comparative Analysis of Accident Patterns by Industry and by State, Report of the Governor's Commission to Study the Workers' Compensation System, Addendum to the Report of the Governor's Commission to Study the Workers' Compensation System, A Preliminary Feasibility Study of Ferry Service on the Chesapeake Bay, A Guide to the Calculation of Workers' Tax Payments, The Impact of the Commercial Fishing Industry on the Maryland Economy, Telecommunications Taxation, Selected Economic Indications-Monthly.*

Massachusetts

Executive Office of Economic Affairs, One Ashburton Place, Room 2101, Boston, MA 02108; 617-727-1130.

Michigan

Business Research Office, Department of Commerce, State of Michigan, P.O. Box 30225, Lansing, MI 48909; 517-373-7401. Publications: *Business Guide to Understanding Michigan Sales and Use Tax, Comparison with Illinois, Comparison with Indiana, Comparison with Kentucky, Comparison with Ohio, Comparison with Tennessee, Comparison with Wisconsin, County Business Climate Overview and Highlights for each of 83 Counties, Food Processing Overview, Michigan as a Place to do Business - A Review of Recent Studies, Michigan's Labor Force Characteristics, Michigan's Market Potential, Michigan Property Tax System - Overview of the, Ontario - Brief Look at Augusta, Ontario vs. Michigan - A Comparison, Review of Michigan Taxes, Crain's Detroit Business List of Top Privately Held Companies, Crain's Detroit Business List of Top Publicly Held Companies, Fortune 500 Companies Headquartered in Michigan, Michigan Private 100, The Michigan 100, Employment Size Study, Industrial Construction Trends by County, Industrial Real Estate Market Survey, Michigan Economic Update, Michigan Economy-Overview, New Business Incorporations, New Capital Expenditures in Michigan, Population Projections for Michigan to the Year 2010, Questions & Answers About Small Business, REMI Employment Multipliers, U.S. Dept. of Commerce, Bureau of Economic Analysis Projections, Metal Fabricating Industry Study, Michigan Chemical Industry-An Overview, Michigan Machine Tool Industry Update, Michigan Machinery Industry Overview, Michigan Service Industry Overview, Michigan-State of the Future, Plastics Industry, Basic Business Sources-SMU Business Library, Business Reference Sources-Library of Michigan, Business Taxes in Michigan, The Case for Michigan, Commercial Redevelopment Act, Community Growth Alliances, Export Assistance, Food Processing Opportunities in Michigan, Forest Products Opportunities in Michigan, Governor's Commission on Jobs and Economic Development Adopts Labor Training, Labor Training, Leader in Automated Systems Manufacturing, Michigan-The Leader in Metalworking, Michigan's Expanding Plastics Industry, Michigan's Improving Business Future, Michigan Main Street-Downtown Revitalization Assistance, Property Tax Incentives, Small Business Centers, State Financial Assistance.*

Minnesota

State Planning Agency, Administration, 300 Centennial Bldg., 658 Cedar St., St. Paul, MN 55155; 612-296-3985. Publications: *Minnesota State Hospital Facilities and Alternative Use, Minnesota State Hospital Use and Cost, A Profile of Minnesota State Hospital Employees, The Economic Impact of Minnesota State Hospitals, Public Opinions About State Hospitals, Residents/Patients in Minnesota State Hospitals, Opinions and Recommendations for the Minnesota State Hospital System, Minnesota State Hospitals-Executive Summary, Mental Health Commission Report, Studies of the Academies for the Deaf and the Blind, Disabilities and Technology, Real Homes Real Education Real Job: A New Way of Thinking.*

Department of Trade and Economic Development, 900 American Center Building, 150 East Kellogg, St. Paul, MN 55701; 612-296-8341. Publications: *Compare Minnesota* (free).

Mississippi

Mississippi Research and Development Center, 3825 Ridgewood Rd., Jackson, MS 39211; 601-325-3817. Publications: *Bibliography of Publications, Budget Facts: Facts on Financing Mississippi State Government, Catalog of Audiovisual Materials Available on Loan, Checklist for New Manufacturers in Mississippi, A Comparison of the 1980 Census Count in Mississippi with the Mississippi Research and Development Center's 1980 County Population Projections, Directory of Master Parent Companies of Mississippi Manufacturers, Electrical Peak Demand Control System, Factors Affecting the Location of Technology Intensive Industries, Facts and Figures, Handbook of Selected Data for Mississippi, Highlights of Mississippi's Changing Economy, How to Develop a Business Plan, Industrial Incentives, Major*

Market Studies, Demographics and Statistics

Government Regulations Affecting Small Retail Business in Mississippi, Mississippi County Data Bank, Mississippi Industrial Services Communicator, Mississippi Manufacturers Directory ($35), *Mississippi Manufacturing Atlas, Mississippi's Public Junior College Vocational-Technical Courses of Interest to Industry, R & D Economic Brief, R & D Annual Report, Services for Mississippi Businesses.*

Missouri

Missouri Office of Administration, Division of Budget and Planning, P.O. Box 809, Jefferson City, MO 65102; 314-751-2345. Publications: *Missouri Demographic and Economic Profile, An Analysis of the Missouri Agribusiness Sector, Missouri's Statewide Economic Development Planning Program, A Directory of Missouri Data Sources* ($23), *An Economic Analysis of Energy Supply and Demand in Missouri, Export Trade of the State of Missouri, Home Health Care and The Homemaker, Housing Program Utilization in Missouri, Missouri Housing Situation, Missouri Transportation System: Condition, Capacity and Impediments to Efficiency, Transportation Trends, Potential Industrial Opportunities for Missouri's Resource Base, A User's Guide to Missouri Maps.*

Montana

Business Assistance Division, Department of Commerce, State of Montana, 1424 9th Ave., Helena, MT 59620; 406-444-3923. Publications: *County Profiles, Montana Statistical Abstract, 1984, Montana Manufacturers and Products Directory, Business and Industrial Location Guide, Consumer Products Buyers' Directory.*

Nebraska

Nebraska Department of Economic Development, P.O. Box 94666-State Office Bldg., 301 Centennial Mall South, Lincoln, NE 98509; 402-471-3111, 1-800-426-6505. Publications: *The Ethanol Distilling Industry-An Industrial Opportunity in Nebraska, Pharmaceuticals and Related Industries: Opportunities in Nebraska, Threshold Estimates and Other Tools for Retail Analysis, Frozen Potato and Onion Processing Opportunities in Nebraska, Investment of Nebraska Public Pension Funds, Nebraska as a World Class Center for Communications Industry, Equity Capital for Nebraska Small Business, Nebraska Visitors Survey, Nebraska Industry: A Survey of Their Concerns, Needs & Future Plans, Characteristics of Nebraska Immigrants and Outmigrants, 1984 Nebraska Air Service Study, The Nebraska Economic Indicators Survey, Hazardous Waste in Nebraska, Profit Opportunities in Nebraska for Manufacturers of Pet Food, Opportunities for Nebraska Businesses in India, Nebraska Profit Opportunities for Manufacturers of Scientific, Measuring and Controlling Instruments, Vegetable Production, Processing and Marketing in Nebraska, Service as a Leading Sector in Economic Development, Nebraska's Economic Performance, Building Prosperity: Nebraska Economic Development Strategy, Nebraska Statistical Handbook* ($8), *Nebraska Facts and Figures, Nebraska Directory of Manufacturers and their Products* ($20), *Nebraska Community Profiles.*

Nevada

Commission on Economic Development, State of Nevada, Capitol Complex, Carson City, NV; 702-885-4325. Publications: *State Plan for Economic Diversification and Development, Nevada Industrial Directory, Community Profiles-Demographic Facts, Quarterly Newsletter, State Economic Development Brochure, The Nevada Development Handbook.* Other: Development of a statewide database to provide access to information about land availability, labor sources and economic statistics.

New Hampshire

Office of State Planning, State of New Hampshire, Executive Department, 2 1/2 Beacon St., Concord, NH 03301; 603-271-2155. Publications: *Current Year Population for New Hampshire Communities, Selected Economic Characteristics for New Hampshire Municipalities, Current Estimates and Trends in New Hampshire's Housing Supply Update-Annual, New Hampshire Population Projections for Counties and Municipalities, Current Estimates and Trends in New Hampshire's Housing Supply-1970-1981, New Hampshire Population Trends, Changes in Households and Household Size for Towns and Cities in New Hampshire, Taxable Valuation Per Person in New Hampshire Communities.*

New Jersey

Office of Economic Analysis, State of New Jersey, 1 West State St. Trenton, NJ 08625; 609-292-3860. Publications: *Economic Report of the Governor-Annual, Economic Forecast-Annual.*

New Mexico

Economic Development Department, 1100 St. Francis Drive, Santa Fe, NM 87503; 505-827-0302. Publications: *Annual Report, New Mexico USA (Economic Development), The New Mexico Rio Grande Research Corridor, New Mexico Magazine, The New Mexico Manufacturing Directory, The New Mexico Fact Book,* *Community Surveys, Brochure on International Trade, Brochure on Writing a Business Plan, Financial Resources in New Mexico.*

New York

Bureau of Business Research, NYS Department of Economic Development, Room 910, One Commerce Plaza, Albany, NY 12245; 518-443-5522. Publications: *The Alpine Ski Industry in New York State, The Apparel Industry in New York State-A Statistical Profile, Business Trends in New York State-Monthly, Economic Trends in Selected Metropolitan Areas of New York State, Financial Services Industries in New York State, Industrial Development Bond report, New York State Business Fact Book Supplement-Annual, New York State Tax Structure-State Taxes-Local Taxes outside NYC, Local Taxes New York City, Personal Income in Areas and Counties of New York State-Annual, Profile of People, Jobs and Housing for New York State-New York City-Each County, A Statistical Profile of the Printing and Publishing Industry in New York State, A Statistical Report on High Technology Industries in New York State, Summaries of Selected Business and Business Climate Surveys, Summary of Business Statistics-Quarterly and Annual, Tax Incentives and Financing for Industrial Location, Tax Incentives-New York State, Tax Incentives-New York City.*

North Carolina

Office of Policy and Planning, NC Department of Administration, 116 Jones St., Raleigh, NC 27603-8003; 919-733-4131.

North Dakota

North Dakota Scanning Network, State of North Dakota, Office of the Governor, Bismarck, ND 58505; 701-224-2810. Publications: *Prairie Scans,* a newsletter identifying important issues and problems the state may face in the future. North Dakota Economic Development Commission, Liberty Memorial Building, Bismarck, ND 58505, 701-224-2810---Publications: *Annual Planning Report, North Dakota Economic Indicators, New Wealth Creating in North Dakota, North Dakota Growth Indicators, North Dakota Taxes, Available Buildings in North Dakota, North Dakota Economic Development Commission Work Plan, Financial and North Dakota, Resources and North Dakota, Manufacturers and North Dakota, Network Newsletter.*

Ohio

State of Ohio, Department of Development, P.O. Box 1001, Columbus, OH 43216; 614-466-2609. Publications: *Annual Report.*

Oklahoma

Oklahoma Futures Commission, Department of Commerce, 6601 Broadway Extension, P.O. Box 26980, Oklahoma City, OK 73126-0980; 405-843-9770. Publications: *Five Year Plan.*

Oregon

Oregon Economic Development Department, 775 Summer Street NE, Salem, OR 97310; 503-373-1200. Publications: *Starting a Business in Oregon, A Summary of Oregon Taxes, Financial Incentives for Business Expansion:Building the Long-Term Financing Gap for Small Business, Directory of Manufacturing Plants, Oregon County Economic Indicators* ($3.50), *Oregon Economic Development Revenue Bonds, Directory of Oregon Manufacturers* ($60), *Oregon Industrial and Commercial Announced Investments, Oregon Economic Trends Project* ($50), *Oregon International Trade Directory* ($30), *Exporter's Handbook* ($25), *Helping Export Firms, Personalized Export Panel, Asia Representatives Office, Directory of Oregon Electronic Products, Directory of Oregon Industrial Equipment and Supplies, Directory of Forest Products Equipment and Services.*

Pennsylvania

Pennsylvania Department of Commerce, 446 Forum Bldg., Harrisburg, PA 17120; 717-783-1132. Publications: *Annual Report.*

Rhode Island

Rhode Island Statewide Planning Program, 265 Melrose St., Providence, RI 02907; 401-277-2601. Publications: *State Guide Plan and Strategic Plan, The Housing Report of the Governor's Human Services Advisory Council, Interim Ground Transportation Plan-Year 2010, Access Update-Telecommunications Device for the Deaf in State Government, Forensic Services Security Issues, Quonset State Airport Master Plan, Jerusalem Master Plan, Hazard Mitigation Plan, Ocean State Outdoors-Recreation and Conservation Strategies for Rhode Island, Highway Jurisdiction in Rhode Island, Methods for Calculating Vehicle Miles of Travel in Rhode Island, Transportation and Land Use, Rhode Island Coastal Resources Management Program, Water Resources Issues in Land Use Policy, Reevaluation of Statewide Travel Demand Model, Federally Assisted Rental Housing, Quonset State Airport Master Plan, Unified Work Program for Transportation Planning,*

Work Program 1987-1988, Policy Statement-Proposals for New or Restructured Public Transit Facilities or Service, Port of Galilee-A Case Study of Port Redevelopment, The Feasibility of Closing Ladd Center, Unified Work Program for Transportation Planning, Siting High-Level Nuclear Waste Repositories, Ocean State Outdoors-Recreation and Conservation Strategies for Rhode Island.

South Carolina
Commission on the Future of South Carolina, Office of Lieutenant Governor, Post Office Box 142, Columbia, SC 29202; 803-734-2080.

South Dakota
Governor's Office of Economic Development, Capitol Lake Plaza, 711 Wells Ave., Pierre, SD 57501-3369; 605-773-5032. Publications: *Economic Development Programs, Directory of Manufacturers and Processors* ($35).

Tennessee
Department of Economic and Community Development, 320 Sixth Ave., North, Nashville, TN 37219; 615-741-1888. Publications: *Economic Growth in Tennessee, Tennessee Economic Statistics, Tennessee Population.*

Texas
Comptroller of Public Accounts, LBJ State Office Building, Austin, TX 78774; 512-463-1778. Publications: *Annual Financial Report, 1988-1989 Biennial Revenue Estimate, Taxes and Texas: A National Survey on Alternatives and Comparisons, Texas Fees-Putting a Price on State Services, Quarterly Survey of Business Expectations in Texas, Sales and Franchise Tax Exemptions, Time of Change-Time of Choice, State Government's Use of Outside Services, Decontrolling Natural Gas-The Impact on Texas Prices and Tax Revenue, The High Finance of Higher Education, The Petroleum Industry and the Texas Sales Tax, The Geography of State Spending, Productivity Ideas and Cost Cutting Alternative to Control of State Budget Growth, Hazardous Waste in Texas, The Geography of Texas Taxes.*

Utah
State Data Center, Office of State Planning and Budget, State of Utah, 116 Capitol Bldg, Salt Lake City, UT 84114; 801-533-6082. Publications: *1987 Baseline Projections, Economic Report to the Governor, State of Utah Revenue Forecast* (quarterly), *Utah Data Guide* (quarterly), *Budget in Brief* (annual), *Capital Budget* (annual), *Historic and Projected Long Term Revenues and Expenditures, Historic Analysis of Preliminary Taxes, The Impact of the Gramm-Rudman-Hollings Deficit Reduction Act, The Import of the Tourism- Travel and Recreation Industry in Utah, The Importance of the Agricultural Industry in Utah, Retail Sales and Service Analysis, Flooding and Landslides in Utah-An Economic Impact Analysis, The Economic and Demographic Impacts of the Intermountain Power Project, Final Socio-economics Technical Report-Utah Basin Synfuels Development, Utah-2000, Energy-2000, Socioeconomic Impacts of the Boulder to Bullfrog Road Improvement, The Economic Issues Surrounding the Vitro Remedial Action Alternatives, Utah Facts, Utah Directory of Business and Industry, Utah Export Directory, Utah Economic Development Plan, Utah Economic and Business Review, Construction Report* (quarterly), *Statistical Abstract of Utah.*

Vermont
Office of Policy Research and Coordination, Pavillion Office Building, 109 State St., Montpelier, VT 05602; 802-828-3326. Services and Responsibilities: Monitor Trends and Anticipate the Impact of Evolving Technologies such as Telecommunications, Provide Staff for the Governor's Council of Economic Advisors, Data on Vermont's Economy.

Virginia
Governor's Office, Department of Economic Development, 1000 Washington Building, Richmond, VA 23219; 804-786-3791. Publications: *Virginia Facts and Figures 1987, Economic Developments-A Statistical Summary, Quarterly Economic Development Report, High Technology Communications in Virginia, Corporate Headquarters in Virginia, Metalworking Industries-Advantages of a Virginia Location, High Technology-Biomedical and Related Industries-Advantages of a Virginia Location, Printing Industry-Cost Savings in Virginia, Virginia Small Business Financing Authority, High Technology Applied Here, Virginia-Local Taxes on Manufacturers, Virginia-Export Management/Trading Companies, International Business Services Directory, Mountains of Hardwood-Virginia's Southern Mountain Region, Virginia-A Guide to Establishing a Business, Are You Ready? A Guide to Community Preparedness for Industrial Development in Virginia, Manufacturing in Virginia, Allegheny County-Clifton Forge-Covington-Virginia-A New Thrust for Industry, The Virginia Economy, Foreign Investment in Virginia.*

Washington
Washington State, Department of Trade and Economic Development, 101 General Administration Bldg., Olympia, WA 98504; 206-753-5630. Publications: *Foreign Exports and the Washington Economy, The Aquaculture Industry in Washington State-An Economic Overview, Washington State Department of Trade and Economic Development-The First Two Years.*

West Virginia
Research and Strategic Planning, Department of Industrial and Community Development, 1900 Washington St., East Bldg. 6, Room 504, Charleston, WV 25305; 304-348-3810.

Wisconsin
Bureau of Research, Department of Development, 123 West Washington Ave., P.O. Box 7970, Madison, WI 53707; 608-267-9214. Publications: *Profiles in Success-Wisconsin Business Developments, New Industries and Plant Expansions Reported in Wisconsin, Models of State Entrepreneurial Development Programs, Youth Unemployment in Wisconsin, Entrepreneurial Culture in Wisconsin, Out-of-State Certified Minority Businesses, Industrial Revenue Bond Financing in Wisconsin, Analysis of State Investment Board Investments to Enhance the Wisconsin Economy, Biennial Report on Tax Incremental Financing, Industrial Revenue Bond Financing, Economic Development Lending Activities of the Wisconsin Housing Development Authority, Wisconsin Long-range Economic Forecast 1985-1995, An Economic Analysis of Wisconsin Regions, Advertising Conversion Results 1983 and 1986, Ozone Air Quality Management and Economic Development in Southeastern Wisconsin, The Relationship of State and Local Government Spending and Taxing to Economic Performance-An Econometric Analysis of the States from 1972 to 1984, Labor Management Cooperation in Wisconsin, The Wisconsin Tourism Industry-Analysis of Market Share and Trends, The Economic Development Potential of the Service Sector Industries in Wisconsin, A Statistical Profile of Minority Population, Employment and Business Ownership in Wisconsin, Development Preparedness Task Force, Task Force Tourism Funding, The Flow of Federal Funds to Wisconsin, Exchange Rate and Interest Rates Effects on Wisconsin Employment, Management Assistance and Business Growth in Wisconsin, A Comparative Study of U.S. and Wisconsin Productivity-Analysis of Manufacturing Industries 1963-1982, Employment Potential of Wisconsin Industry Groups- An Analysis and Industry Classification, Local Economic Development in Wisconsin.*

Wyoming
Economic Development and Stabilization Board, Herschler Building, 2nd Floor West, Cheyenne, WY 82002; 307-777-7284. Publications: *Wyoming, Directory of Manufacturing and Mining, Business Development Kit, Mineral Yearbook.*

State Division of Motor Vehicles

Mailing lists galore and plentiful market research data derived from state motor vehicle departments offer the potential for increasing your bottom line. Did you ever want to know how many 40-year old males in Boston wear contact lenses, or perhaps obtain the names and addresses of all Arizonians who own Cadillacs? Well, it is within the realm of possibility.

Believe it or not, those long lines that drive us crazy when registering a car or renewing a driver's license have a bright side. Each person in line turns over to the state a wealth of information about him or herself. This data -- name, address, age, physical characteristics, and buying patterns -- are the stuff of which customer lists, market studies, and demographic analyses are made. While states charge you for this information, it will cost a fraction of what you would spend if you hired some sharp marketing consultant to unearth the data.

Take the example of my friend, Ron, a mechanic for expensive foreign cars in Wilmington, Delaware. One day Ron got tired of watching his boss laugh all the way to the bank and decided he wanted to open a shop of his own. Through the state he was able to obtain printouts of all owners of Audis, BMWs, and Mercedes in his area. Armed with this information, Ron ultimately was able to obtain a small business loan, open a shop, and now is making more than I'd care to admit.

Many states maintain files not only on autos, but also on boats and recreational vehicles. This data can be of further help in targeting potential customers. It doesn't take business brilliance to deduce that a person living in Palm Beach, who owns several high-ticket imported cars and has a 37-foot Hatteras yacht, is a potential customer for a home security company.

Many states will sort through their driver's license database by age and sex for an additional charge and provide a listing, for example, of all females between the ages of 18 and 45 years living in a particular district. If you are launching a magazine aimed at working women, this is priceless marketing intelligence. The same holds true for older persons who have special senior citizen identifiers and for young males who are eligible for the Selective Service.

This data is used in countless ways by researchers for compiling statistics on health issues, and of course, used by the government for manufacturer recalls or warranty programs, and emission studies. Insurance companies, financial institutions, and other businesses thrive on this cross-sectioning of the body public.

Information derived from a state's automobile owner registration master file is usually available in two formats -- magnetic tape or computer printouts. Most states prefer sending you a tape for larger files, while printouts are allowed for shorter sorts. In addition, some states offer mailing labels for an additional charge.

The most likely sorting options include: an entire state file; all

vehicles within a county; vehicle type (2-door, 4-door, 4-wheel drive) by state or county; and vehicle make or year by state or county.

Driver's license information can usually be extracted to provide: name and license number (only); name, license number, and address; and a variety of other factors regarding age or sex. All states charge for this information, usually per 1,000 entries plus a set-up fee, but the potential for increasing your profits by using this valuable data will far outweigh the costs.

There are a few states which do not allow access to this data. These are Connecticut, South Dakota, Rhode Island, New Jersey, Indiana, Hawaii, Georgia, and Arkansas. Utah, North Carolina, and Montana are the three states which will not divulge driver's license information but will turn over vehicle registration files. And three states, Pennsylvania, New Mexico and Kansas, will only give you the information under very specific circumstances. That leaves 38 states which are wide open.

Motor Vehicle Offices

Alabama
Drivers: Alabama Department of Public Safety, Drivers License Division, P.O. Box 1471, Montgomery, AL 36192; 205-242-4400. Services: Individual records can be retrieved for $5.75 per record.

Arizona
Drivers: Arizona Motor Vehicles Division, 1801 W. Jefferson St., Phoenix, AZ 85007; 602-255-7567. Request must be in writing with complete name, license number and date of birth. The cost is $3 for a 39 month check, $5 for a 5 year check.

Owners: Arizona Motor Vehicles Division, 1801 W. Jefferson St., Room 230M, Phoenix, AZ 85007; 602-255-7567. Database: Arizona Drivers - contains owner's name and address plus make, model, year, tag and license numbers for 1,655,833 cars and 875,000 other vehicles. Services: A mailing list is available for $3,300, or a computer tape can be purchased and data sorted by name and address. Tape cost is $30 per 1,000 names received.

Arkansas
Drivers: Arkansas Office of Motor Vehicle Registration, P.O. Box 1272, Little Rock, AR 72203; 501-682-7060. Services: license information is protected under the Privacy Act. A release must be signed by a driver before that data can be released.

Owners: Arkansas Office of Motor Vehicle Registration, P.O. Box 1272, Little Rock, AR 72203; 501-682-4603. Database: Arkansas Automobile Owners - contains owner's name and address plus make, model, year and license number for over 15 million automobiles and approximately 300,000 million other vehicles including motorcycles and boats. Services: No data tapes released. Records are open for public inspection at the office only.

California
Drivers: Department of Motor Vehicles, P.O. Box 944247, Sacramento, CA 94269; 916-657-6555. Services: Individual records can be requested; must identify the name, license number and date of birth of the driver.

Owners: Department of Motor Vehicles, P.O. Box 944247, MS-D-146, Sacramento, CA 94244-2470; 916-657-7669. Database: California Automobile

Owners - contains owner's name and address as well as make, model, year, tag and license numbers of 16.5 million automobiles and 631,000 motorcycles. Services: This file must be purchased in its entirety (i.e., information of all motorcycles and registration records for automobiles costs approximately $100 per 1,000 names).

Colorado

Drivers: Colorado Motor Vehicle Division, Traffic Records, 140 W. 6th Ave., #104, Denver, CO 80204; 303-572-5601. Database: Colorado Drivers - contains name, address, license number of 3,167,570 drivers. It is available in three files: minor, provisional and adult permits. Services: One time single run only of name, address and license number only. The cost of $25 per 1,000 names with a $1,000 minimum plus set-up fee.

Owners: Colorado Motor Vehicle Division, Traffic Records, 140 W. 6th Ave., #103, Denver, CO 80204; 303-623-9463. Database: Colorado Owners - contains name and address. Services: One time single run only of name, address and license number only. The cost of $25 per 1,000 names with a $1,000 minimum.

Connecticut

Drivers and Owners: Connecticut State Department of Motor Vehicles, 60 State Street, Wethersfield, CT 06109; 203-566-3830. Data is not released.

Delaware

Drivers: Delaware Motor Vehicles Division, P.O. Box 698, Dover, DE 19903; 302-739-4461. Database: Delaware Drivers - provides name, address, height, weight and other drivers license information except hair color of 494,035 drivers. Services: Some ready-made programs available. Any additional programming requires additional charges.

Owners: Delaware Motor Vehicle Division, P.O. Box 698, Dover DE 19903; 302-739-4421. Database: Delaware Drivers - provides owner's name and address along with make, model, year, title number, expiration date of 580,849 registration cars, motorcycles or trucks. Services: A data tape can be purchased with sorting of reportable variables for $375 plus $11 per 1,000 names.

District of Columbia

Drivers: District of Columbia, Department of Public Works Information Office, 301 C St., N.W., Room 1025, Washington, D.C. 20001; 202-727-6761. Database: District of Columbia Drivers - contains name, address, suspensions, sex, Social Security number, height, type of permit, license number, expiration dates, and restrictions of 800,000 drivers. Services: Computer tapes and printouts available. Data can be sorted by categories but not recommended. Cost is $1,700.

Owners: District of Columbia, Department of Public Works Information Office, 301 C St., NW, Room 1025, Washington, D.C. 20001; 202-727-1159. Database: District of Columbia Owners - contains owner's name, address, make, model, year, tag number, and registration number of 263,290 vehicles. Services: Computer tape available, data can be sorted by category. Cost is $900.

Florida

Drivers: Florida Highway Safety and Motor Vehicles Department, Neil Kirkman Building, Tallahassee, FL 32301; 904-488-6710. Database: Florida Drivers - contains name, address, and date of birth of over 12 million drivers. Services: No sorting is available. A computer tape or printout can be obtained for $.45 per second.

Owners: Florida Highway Safety and Motor Vehicles Department, Neil Kirkman Building, Tallahassee, FL 32301; 904-488-6710. Database: Florida Automobile Owners - provides owner's name and address plus make, model, year, tag number and class code for 7 million cars and 5 million other vehicles. Services: No sorting is available, data available on a computer tape or printout. Cost is $1.60 per second.

Georgia

Drivers: Motor Vehicle Records, 959 E. Confederate Ave., Atlanta, GA 30316; 404-624-7487. Data is not released.

Owners: Motor Vehicle Division, Trinity Washington Bldg., Atlanta, GA 30334; 404-656-4156. Data is not released.

Hawaii

Drivers and Owners: Division of Motor Vehicles and Licenses, 1455 S. Beretainia St., Honolulu, HI 96814; 808-973-2700. Data is not released.

Idaho

Drivers: Idaho Transportation Department, Economics & Research Section, P.O. Box 7129, Boise, ID 83707-1129; 208-334-8741. Database: Idaho Drivers - provides name, address, sex, date of birth, license type, expiration date, and county of residence of approximately 1,000,000 drivers. Services: Data may be selected by sex, age or range of ages, and county of residence. The cost is $75 plus computer charges (this varies depending on size of the file, sorts, etc.) and shipping charges.

Owners: Idaho Transportation Department, Economics & Research Section, P.O. Box 7129, Boise, ID 83707-1129; 208-334-8741. Database: Idaho Owners - provides registered owner, address, make, model, year, issue and expiration date. Approximately 1,300,000 records. Services: Data can be selected by registration type, and/or county of residence. The cost is $75 plus computer charges (this varies depending on the size of the file, sorts, etc.) and shipping charges. Computer tape or printouts are available.

Illinois

Drivers: Illinois Secretary of State, Drivers Services Division, 2701 S. Dirksen Parkway, Springfield, IL 62723; 217-782-1978. Database: Illinois Drivers - contains name, address, sex, date of birth, license issue and expiration date of 8 million drivers. Services: Data can be sorted by various categories and provided on a computer tape for $200 plus $20 per 1,000 names, or on a printout for $.50 per page (15,000 names or less).

Owners: Illinois Secretary of State, Centennial Building, Room 114, Springfield, IL 62756; 217-782-0029. Database: Illinois Automobile Owners - provides owner's name and address, make, model and year of over 6 million passenger cars and over 2 million other vehicles. Services: Complete records are available. Data can be sorted by various categories. Computer tapes available for $200 plus $20 per 1,000; computer printouts for $.50 per pate (15,000 names or less).

Indiana

Drivers and Owners: Indiana Bureau of Motor Vehicles, 100 N. Senate Ave., Indianapolis, IN 46204; 317-232-2798. Data is not released.

Iowa

Drivers: Iowa Department of Transportation, Drivers Services, Lucas State Office Building, Des Moines, IA 50319; 515-244-8725. Database: Iowa Drivers - provides name, address, date of birth, height, weight, restrictions, issue and expiration dates, license number, and restrictions of 2.5 million drivers. Services: Data is listed in order by license number. Data cannot be sorted. Computer tapes available, $370 (Tapes must be provided by requester).

Owners: Iowa Department of Transportation, Office of Vehicle Registration, P.O. Box 9204, Des Moines, IA 50306-9204; 515-237-3182. Database: Iowa Automobile Owners - provides complete description of vehicle for 4.2 million cars and other vehicles. Services: Data tapes available for $.39 per thousand names plus $14 for each tape, computer time charge for sorts and a $20 set up fee.

Kansas

Drivers: Topeka Drivers Licenses Bureau, 37th and Burlingame, Topeka, KS 66609; 913-266-7380. Data tapes not released for commercial purposes.

Owners: Kansas Titles and Registration Bureau, Room 123 S. Docking State Office Building, 915 Harrison, Topeka, KS 66626; 913-296-3621. Data tapes not released for commercial purposes.

Kentucky

Drivers: Kentucky Transportation Cabinet, Division of Driver Licensing, State Office Bldg., 501 High St., Frankfort, KY 40622; 502-564-4864. Database: Kentucky Drivers - provides name, address, and date of birth of over 2.4 million drivers. Services: Data can be sorted by various categories. Computer tapes or printouts are available for $.01 per name plus $510 for programming and computer costs. Mailing labels are available for $2.45 per 1,000 plus above charges.

Owners: Kentucky Transportation Cabinet, Division of Motor Vehicle Licensing, State Office Building, Room 205, Frankfort, KY 40622; 502-564-4864. Database: Kentucky Automobile Owners - provides owner's name and address along with make, model and year for over 2 million vehicles. Services: Data can be sorted by various categories. Computer tapes and printouts available for $.02 per name plus programming costs. Mailing labels can be purchased for $3.50 per 1,000 plus programming costs.

Louisiana

Drivers: Louisiana Department of Public Safety and Corrections, P.O. Box 66614, Baton Rouge, LA 70896; 504-925-6146. Database: Louisiana Drivers - provides name, address, height, weight, sex, date of birth of 2.7 million drivers. Services: Computer tape and printout available. Data can be sorted by variables. Cost is $.03 per name plus $500.

Owners: Louisiana Department of Public Safety and Corrections, P.O. Box 66614, Baton Rouge, LA 70896; 504-925-6146. Database: Louisiana Owners - provides owner's name, address, make, model and year, date of acquisition, color, new or used for 4.5 million vehicles. Services: Computer tape and printout available for $.03 per record and $500.

Maine

Drivers: Maine Motor Vehicle Division, 101 Hospital Street, Station 29, Augusta, ME 04333; 207-289-5553. Database: Maine Drivers - provides name, address, date of birth, and sex of 800,000 drivers. Services: Data available on computer tape, printout available for $.25 per name. Mailing labels are available for an extra charge.

Owners: Maine Motor Vehicles Division, 101 Hospital Street, Station 29, Augusta, ME 04333; 207-289-5553. Database: Maine Automobile Owners - contains owner's name and address, date of birth as well as make, model, year, identification number for 700,000 registered vehicles. Services: Data can be sorted by variables and can be purchased on computer tape, printout or mailing labels. Cost available on request.

Maryland

Drivers: Maryland Motor Vehicle Administration, 6601 Ritchie Highway, Room 200, Glen Burnie, MD 21062; 410-768-7665. Database: Maryland Drivers - contains name, address, date of birth, height, weight, and identification number of over 2 million drivers. Services: Data can be sorted by variables and available on computer tape for $500 (non-refundable) plus $.05 for each record.

Owners: Maryland Motor Vehicle Administration, 6601 Ritchie Highway, Room 200, Glen Burnie, MD 21062; 410-768-7665. Database: Maryland Automobile Owners - provides owner's name and address along with make, model and year for nearly 3,000,000 passenger cars and 3 million other vehicles. Some insurance information is included.

Massachusetts

Drivers: Massachusetts Registry of Motor Vehicles, 100 Nashua Street, Boston, MA 02114; 617-727-3716. Database: Massachusetts Automobile Drivers - provides name, address, and Social Security number of 4 million drivers. Services: Data can be sorted by all variables except sex. The cost is $1,000 for the first 1,000 names and $40 per 1,000 records thereafter. Data is available on computer tape or printout (for less than 30,000 names).

Owners: Massachusetts Registry of Motor Vehicles, 100 Nashua Street, Boston, MA 02114; 617-727-3716. Database: Massachusetts Automobile Owners - contains owner's name and address along with make, model and year of 5 million vehicles. Services: Sorting of data is available, for instance, by particular insurance company the owner carries. The cost is $1,000 for the first 1,000 names and $40 per 1,000 records thereafter. Data is available on computer tape or printout (for less than 30,000 names).

Michigan

Drivers: Michigan Systems Programming Division, 7064 Crowners Drive, Lansing, MI 48918; 517-322-1584. Database: Michigan Drivers - provides names, address, date of birth, and sex of 6,447,174 drivers. Services: Data may be selected by sex, date of birth, county, state, city, and zip code at a cost of $64 per 1,000 names versus $16 per 1,000 names unsorted. There is a $500 minimum charge. Data can be purchased on computer tape or printout. It is also available in limited amount on disc.

Owners: Michigan Department of State, Data Processing Division, 7064 Crowners Drive, Lansing, MI 48918; 517-322-1584. Database: Michigan Automobile Owners - provides owner's name and address with year, license number, make and model of 5,234,916 passenger cars and 2,261,688 other vehicles. Services: The cost for sorting is $64 per 1,000 names versus $16 per 1,000 unsorted names. There is a $500 minimum charge. Data can be purchased on computer tape or printout. It is also available in limited amount on disc.

Minnesota

Drivers: Minnesota Department of Public Safety, Driver/Vehicle Services Division, Transportation Building, 395 John Ireland Blvd., St. Paul, MN 55155; 612-297-2442. Database: Minnesota Drivers - provides name, address, and sex of 3.3 million drivers. Services: Data can be sorted; there is an extra fee if more information is required. Data is available on printout or computer tape or mailing labels for $8 to $10 per name with a $500 minimum. Custom programming cost varies depending on complexity of request.

Owners: Minnesota Department of Public Safety, Driver/Vehicle Services Division, Transportation Building, 395 John Ireland Blvd., St. Paul, MN 55155; 612-296-6911. Database: Minnesota Automobile Owners - contains owner's name and address along with make, model and year for 3.2 million cars and 1.2 million other vehicles. Services: Certain data can be sorted. Data is available on computer tape or printout. There is a $500 minimum plus $8 per 1,000 names.

Mississippi

Drivers: Mississippi Department of Public Safety/Data Processing, P.O. Box 958, Jackson, MS 39205; 601-987-1212. Database: Mississippi Drivers - contains name, address, date of birth, race and sex of over 1,924,696 drivers. Services: Data cannot be sorted. The entire file must be purchased for $250 plus $20 per reel.

Owners: Mississippi State Tax Commission Network, P.O. Box 960, Room 220, Jackson, MS 39205; 601-359-1117. Database: Mississippi Automobile Owners - provides a complete file, including owner's name and address, make, model, year of 1.6 million registered vehicles. Services: Data can be sorted and made available on computer tape or printout. Fees range from $1,000 - $2,000. Mailing labels available for an extra charge.

Missouri

Drivers: Missouri Department of Revenue, Information Services Bureau, P.O. Box 41, Jefferson City, MO 65105; 314-751-5486. Database: Missouri Drivers - contains name, address, sex, date of birth, height, weight, eye color, restrictions, license number, class, and county of 3.4 million drivers. Services: Data available on computer tape or printouts for $.018 per 50,000 records. Process fee is $85.26 and programming fee is $28.75 per hour. Mailing labels available for an extra charge $2 per 1,000.

Owners: Missouri Department of Revenue, Information Services Bureau, P.O. Box 41, Jefferson City, MO 65105; 314-751-5486. Database: Missouri Owners - provides name and address of registered owners plus make, model, year, number of cylinders, type of fuel, license ID number, license expiration date, and year for over 4.2 million cars and 3.4 million other vehicles. Services: Data available on computer tape or printout. Cost: $.018 per 50,000 records. Process fee is $85.26 and programming fee is $28.75 per hour. Mailing labels available for an extra fee of $2 per 1,000.

Montana

Drivers: Drivers Services, 303 North Roberts, Helena, MT 59620; 406-444-3275. Data is not released.

Owners: Montana Motor Vehicle Division, 925 Main St., Deer Lodge, MT 59722; 406-846-1423. Database: Montana Automobile Owners - provides owner's name and address along with year, make, model, body, color, serial number, second owner for over one million registered vehicles. Services: Data available on computer tape and printout. The cost is $300 for the first 10,000 names and $30 per 1,000 names thereafter on tape or disc. Cost for each additional 1,000 names on printout is $40.

Nebraska

Drivers: Nebraska Department of Motor Vehicles, P.O. Box 94789, Lincoln, NE 68509; 402-471-3909. To receive information you must provide the correct name, date of birth, or license number for each record requested. The cost is $1.75 per record.

Owners: Nebraska Department of Motor Vehicles, P.O. Box 94789, Lincoln, NE 68509; 402-471-3909. Database: Nebraska Automobile Owners - provides listing by make, model, and year which includes owner's name and address for 856,000 passenger cars and 650,000 other vehicle owners. Services: Data can be provided on computer tape and printout for $12 per 1,000 with a $300 minimum.

Nevada

Drivers: Nevada Department of Motor Vehicles, 555 Wright Way, Carson City, NV 89711; 702-687-5370. Database: Nevada Drivers - provides name, address, date of birth, height, weight, for more than one million drivers. Services: Data can be sorted by county, zip code, date of birth and make of car. Data available on computer tape or printout (up to 1,000,000 names). Mailing labels available for an extra fee. Cost is $2,500 for the entire file or $15 per 1,000 for a partial listing.

Owners: Nevada Department of Motor Vehicles, 555 Wright Way, Carson City, NV 89711; 702-687-5370. Database: Contains owner's name, address along with make, model and year for one million registered vehicles. Data may also be selected by county, zip code and make of car. Services: Computer tape is available for $2,500 or portions prorated $15 per thousand. A printout is available up to 1,000,000 records. Also available on mailing labels. (Prices are subject to change.)

New Hampshire

Drivers: New Hampshire Department of Safety, Data Processing, 10 Hazen Drive, Concord, NH 03305; 603-271-2314. Database: New Hampshire Drivers - consists of name, address, physical characteristics, Social Security number, class of license, issue and expiration date, and restriction of 843,000 drivers. Services: Data can be sorted by sex or age. Data provided on computer tape or printout. Prices vary, depending on data requested and size of the file.

Owners: New Hampshire Department of Safety, Data Processing, 10 Hazen Drive, Concord, NH 03305; 603-271-2314. Database: New Hampshire Owners - contains owner's name and address along with make, model and year for 815,628 passenger cars and 517,606 other vehicles. Services: Data can be sorted by zip code, model or make. Data available on computer tape or printout (extra charge). Fees vary depending on request. Entire file available on microfiche for $50.

New Jersey

Drivers and Owners: Data is not available for purchase. Must write in for individual records. New Jersey Division of Motor Vehicles, 25 S. Montgomery St., Trenton, NJ 08660; 609-588-2424.

New Mexico

Drivers and Owners: Data cannot be sold for commercial purposes. New Mexico Taxation and Revenue Department, Motor Vehicle Division, P.O. Box 1028, Santa Fe, NM 87504-1028; 505-827-2294.

New York

Drivers: NY State Department of Motor Vehicles, Data Preparation, Empire State Plaza, Albany, NY 12202. Printouts available by written request. Cost for individual record is $5 per search.

Owners: State Department of Motor Vehicles, Empire State Plaza, P.O. Box 2650, Room 433, Albany, NY 12202; 518-473-5595. Data tapes are not available for purchase. Must write in for individual records at $5 per record.

North Carolina

Drivers: No records released.

Owners: Transportation Data Service Center, Century Center, Bldg. B, 1020 Birchridge Rd., Raleigh, NC 27610; 919-250-4204. Database: North Carolina

Automobile Owners - provides owner's name and address, second owner's name, make, model, year, plate classification, license number and weight of vehicle for 5.5 million registered vehicles. Services: Data can be sorted by model, year, make, county, zip code and other variables. The cost is $250 for the first 12,500 records and $20 per 1,000 records thereafter.

North Dakota

Drivers: North Dakota Drivers License and Traffic Safety Division, 608 East Boulevard Avenue, Bismarck, ND 58505-0700; 701-224-2601. Database: North Dakota Drivers - provides name, address, date of birth, and license number of 450,000 drivers. Services: Special sort/extraction is available. The cost is $9 per 1,000 names with a $250 minimum. Mailing labels are also available for an extra fee.

Owners: North Dakota Department of Transportation, Motor Vehicle Service Division, 608 E. Boulevard, Bismarck, ND 58505; 701-224-2725. Database: North Dakota Automobile Owners - contains owner's name and address along with make, model and year of 369,010 passenger cars and 391,968 other vehicles. Services: Data can be sorted by variables and provided on computer printout tape for $50 plus $40 per 1,000 names. Mailing labels available for an extra fee.

Ohio

Drivers: Ohio Bureau of Motor Vehicles, Data Services, P.O. Box 16520, Columbus, OH 43266-0020; 614-752-7695. Database: Ohio Drivers - includes name, address, sex, date of birth, height, weight, hair color, eye color, zip code, and some restrictions for over 7.4 million registered drivers. Services: Data can be sorted by variables. Data is available on computer tape for $.075 per record. Mailing labels are $.08 each.

Owners: Ohio Bureau of Motor Vehicles, Data Services, P.O. Box 16520, Columbus, OH 43266-0020; 614-752-7695. Database: Ohio Automobile Owners - provides owner's name and address along with make, model, year, license number, and expiration date for over 9 million registered vehicles. Services: Data can be sorted by variables. Available on computer tape or printout at $.075 per record. Mailing labels provided for $.08 each.

Oklahoma

Drivers and Owners: Data tapes are not sold. Individual records available for $1 each. Oklahoma Tax Commission, Motor Vehicle Division, 2501 N. Lincoln Blvd., Oklahoma City, OK 73194; 405-521-3217.

Oregon

Drivers: Oregon Department of Transportation, Motor Vehicles Division, 1905 Lana Ave., NE, Salem, OR 97314; 503-378-6995. Database: Oregon Drivers - contains name, address, sex, age, and year of birth for over 2 million drivers. Services: Data can be sorted and provided on computer tape for $180 or printout for $180 for full file.

Owners: Oregon Department of Transportation, Motor Vehicles Division, 1905 Lana Ave., NE, Salem, OR 97314; 503-378-6995. Database: Oregon Automobile Owners - contains owner's name and address along with make, model and year for over two million registered vehicles. Services: Data can be selected by variables, data available on computer tape or printout for $180.

Pennsylvania

Drivers and Owners: Data only available with a special request. Not available for commercial purposes. Bureau of Drivers Licenses Information, Box 58691, Harrisburg, PA 17106; 717-787-2158.

Rhode Island

Drivers and Owners: Data not available to the public. Department of Motor Vehicles, State Office Building, Providence, RI 02903; 401-277-2970.

South Carolina

Drivers: South Carolina Highway Department, Public Transportation, P.O. Box 1498, Columbia, SC 29216-0028; 803-251-2940. Database: South Carolina Drivers - provides name, address, date of birth, license number, and restrictions for 1.8 million drivers. Services: Data may be sorted by last name, zip code, tag number as well as automobiles and/or motorcycles for 100,000 records. Computer tapes or printouts are available for $1,200.

Owners: South Carolina Highway Department, Public Transportation, P.O. Box 1498, Columbia, SC 29216-0019; 803-251-2960. Database: South Carolina Automobile Owners - contains name and address of 700,000 registered vehicle owners along with make, year and serial number. Services: Data may be sorted by last name, county, city, state, insurance information and tag number as well as automobile and/or motorcycles. Requests must be mailed in. Prices are available upon written request.

South Dakota

Drivers and Owners: Data is not released. Division of Motor Vehicles, 118 W. Capitol St., Pierre, SD 57501; 605-773-3545.

Tennessee

Drivers: Department of Safety Information System, 150 Foster Ave., Nashville, TN 37210; 615-251-5322. Database: Tennessee Drivers - contains name, address, date of birth, sex and physical characteristics of approximately 3.5 million drivers. Services: Data can be sorted by category. Computer tapes, printouts and mailing labels are available for a minimum $500 plus $.10 per record.

Owners: Department of Safety Information Systems, 1150 Foster Ave., Nashville, TN 37210; 615-251-5322. Database: Tennessee Automobile Owners - contains owner's name, address, model, make, year and tag number of approximately 4 million vehicles. Services: Computer tapes, printouts and mailing labels available for $300 minimum, plus $100 set up fee plus $20.05 per 1,000 names. (Prices subject to change.)

Texas

Drivers: Texas Department of Public Safety, Attn: L.I. and V.I., P.O. Box 4087, Austin, TX 78773; 512-465-2000. Database: Texas Drivers - provides name, address, date of birth, and license number for over 1.3 million drivers. Services: Data can be sorted by category. Data provided on computer tape for $30,000 for the entire file, or $2.25 per 1,000.

Owners: Texas Department of Transportation, Division of Motor Vehicles, 40th and Jackson, Austin, TX 78779-0001; 512-465-7531. Database: Texas Automobile Owners - contains owner's name and address along with make, model, year, previous owner, and lien holder for 14 million vehicles. Services: Sorting is not available. Data available on computer tape for $4,000 plus $.30 per 1,000 written records.

Utah

Drivers: Department of Public Safety, Drivers License Division, 4501 S. 2700 West, 3rd Floor, P.O. Box 30560, Salt Lake City, UT 84130-0560; 801-965-4437. Data is not released.

Owners: Utah State Tax Commission, Data Processing, 160 E. 300 South St., Salt Lake City, UT 84134; 801-530-4848. Database: Utah Automobile Owners - provides owner's name and address along with make, model and year for 1.9 million vehicles. Services: Data can be sorted and made available on computer tape for $300 to $400.

Vermont

Drivers: Vermont Department of Motor Vehicles, 120 State St., Montpelier, VT 05603; 802-828-2020. Database: Vermont Drivers - contains name, address, physical characteristics, license number and date of birth for 427,512 drivers. Services: Full identification must be provided in order to obtain information. Cost is $4 for each record up to 4 records.

Owners: Vermont Department of Motor Vehicles, 120 State Street, Montpelier, VT 05603; 802-828-2020. Database: Vermont Automobile Owners - provides owner's name and address along with make, model and year for 327,016 passenger cars and 207,684 other vehicles. Services: Must provide vehicle identification to obtain information. Cost is $4 for each record up to 4 records.

Virginia

Drivers: Data is not released.

Owners: Dealer & Information, P.O. Box 7412, Richmond, VA 23269,; 804-367-0455. If you provide the license number, they will provide the information. Initial fee of $3,000 plus $5 per record.

Washington

Drivers: Department of Licensing, Highways/Licensing Building, P.O. Box 3090, Olympia, WA 98507; 206-753-6961. Database: Washington Drivers - provides driver's name, date of birth and address of registered drivers. Services: Sorting is available. A written request is required and an agreement must be signed. Each program is custom made. The charge is $3,680 plus tax.

Owners: Department of Licensing, Highways/Licenses Building, Olympia, WA 98507; 206-753-6950. Database: Washington Automobile Owners - contains owner's name, address, make, model, year and class of vehicle. Services: Data can be sorted alphabetically by owner's name, address, make, model, year and class of vehicle. It can be sorted alphabetically by owner's name, state or county. A written request is required and an agreement must be signed. Each program is custom made. The charge is $3,680 plus tax.

West Virginia

Drivers: West Virginia Department of Motor Vehicles, Bldg. #3, Room 113, Charleston, WV 25317; 304-348-2723. Database: West Virginia Drivers - provides name, address, height, weight, race, sex, and date of birth for 1.4 million drivers. Services: Data can be sorted and provided on computer tape or printout. Cost is $5,040.

Owners: West Virginia Department of Motor Vehicles, Bldg. #3, Room 113, Charleston, WV 25317; 304-348-2723. Database: West Virginia Automobile Owners - contains owner's name and address along with make, model and year of 1.4 million passenger cars and 246,000 other vehicles. Services: Data can be sorted and provided on computer tape or printout for $5,040.

Wisconsin

Drivers: Wisconsin Department of Transportation, 4802 Sheybogan Ave., P.O. Box 7918, Madison, WI 53711; 608-266-2237. Database: Wisconsin Drivers - provides an alphabetical list of name, address, date of birth, sex and driver's record for 4.5 million drivers. Services: Data available on computer tape for $2,200.

Owners: Wisconsin Department of Transportation, 4802 Sheybogan Ave., P.O. Box 7911, Madison, WI 53707-7911; 608-266-1951. Database: Wisconsin Owners- provides owner's name and address plus make, model and year of 2.3 million passenger cars and 1.7 million other vehicles. Services: Data cannot be sorted. Entire file must be purchased on computer tape for $2,200.

Wyoming

Drivers: Wyoming Department of Transportation, Attn: Driver Control, P.O. Box 1708, Cheyenne, WY 82003; 307-777-5259. Database: Wyoming Driver - provides name, address, date of birth, Social Security number, status, expiration, and issuance date for 500,000 drivers. Services: Cost for magnetic tape: $1 per record with a $100 minimum. All requests must be approved by the Commission.

Owners: Wyoming Department of Transportation, Licensing Station, 5300 Bishop Blvd., Cheyenne, WY 82009; 307-777-6511. Individual record searches with a written request. Cost $5 per search.

Selling Overseas: Foreign Markets

There is probably more information in the United States about any country in the world than there is in the countries themselves. Expertise and assistance to exporters continue to increase at both the federal and state level.

Polypropylene In Countries That Don't Even Count People

A few years ago a Fortune 500 company asked us to identify the consumption of polypropylene resin for 15 lesser developed countries. It was a project they had been working on without success for close to a year. After telexing all over the world and contacting every domestic expert imaginable, we too came up empty-handed. The basic problem was that we were dealing with countries that did not even count people, let alone polypropylene resin.

Our savior was a woman at the U.S. Commerce Department named Maureen Ruffin, who was in charge of the World Trade Reference Room. Ms. Ruffin and her colleagues collect the official import/export statistical documents for every country in the world as soon as they are released by the originating countries. Although the data are much more current and more detailed than those published by such international organizations as the United Nations, the publications available at this federal reference room are printed in the language of origin. Because none of the 15 subject countries manufacture polypropylene resin, Ms. Ruffin showed us how to get the figures by identifying those countries which produce polypropylene and count up how much each of them exported to the countries in question. To help us even further, she also provided us with free in-house translators to help us work with the foreign documents.

Exporter's Hotline

The Trade Promotion Coordinating Committee has established this comprehensive "one-stop-shop" for information on U.S. Government programs and activities that support exporting efforts. This hotline is staffed by trade specialists who can provide information on seminars and conferences, overseas buyers and representatives, overseas events, export financing, technical assistance, and export counseling. They also have access to the National Trade Data Bank.

Trade Information Center
U.S. Department of Commerce
Washington, DC 20230
1-800-USA-TRADE
FAX: 202-377-4473
TDD: 1-800-833-8723

Country Experts

If you are looking for information on a market, company or most any other aspect of commercial life in a particular country, your best point of departure is to contact the appropriate country desk officer at the U.S. Department of Commerce. These experts often have the information you need right at their fingertips or they can refer you to other country specialists.

U.S. Foreign & Commercial Services (FCS)
Export Promotion Services
U.S. Department of Commerce
Room 2810
Washington, DC 20230   202-377-8220

All the Department of Commerce/US & FCS field offices around the country are listed later in this chapter. (You will also find a separate roster of international trade offices maintained by the states.)

A

Country	Expert	Phone	Room
ASEAN	George Paine	202-377-3875	2308
Afghanistan	Tim Gilman	202-377-2954	2029B
Albania	Lynn Fabrizio	202-377-2645	6043
Algeria	Jeffrey Johnson	202-377-4652	2039
Angola	Claude Clement	202-377-5148	3317
Anguilla	Michelle Brooks	202-377-2527	3021
Antigua /Barbuda	Michelle Brooks	202-377-2527	3021
Argentina	Randy Mye	202-377-1548	3021
Aruba	Michelle Brooks	202-377-2527	3020
Australia	Gary Bouck	202-377-3646	2308
Austria	Philip Combs	202-377-2920	3029

B

Country	Expert	Phone	Room
Bahamas	Rodrigo Soto	202-377-2527	3021
Bahrain	Claude Clement /Jeffrey Johnson	202-377-5545	2039
Baltic States	Pam Green	202-377-4915	3413
Bangladesh	Cheryl McQueen	202-377-2954	2029B
Barbados	Michelle Brooks	202-377-2527	3021
Belgium	Simon Bensimon	202-377-5041	3046
Belize	Michelle Brooks	202-377-2527	3021
Benin	Debra Henke	202-377-4228	3317
Bermuda	Michelle Brooks	202-377-2527	3021
Bhutan	Tim Gilman	202-377-2954	2029B
Bolivia	Laura Zeiger	202-377-2521	3029
Botswana	Vacant	202-377-5148	3317
Brazil	Larry Farris	202-377-3871	3017
Brunei	Raphael Cung	202-377-3875	2308
Bulgaria	Lynn Fabrizio	202-377-2645	6043
Burkina Faso	Philip Michelini	202-377-4388	3317
Burma	George Paine	202-377-3875	2308
Burundi	Debra Henke	202-377-4228	3317

C

Country	Expert	Phone	Room
Cambodia	Hong-Phong B. Pho	202-377-3875	2308
Cameroon	Debra Henke	202-377-4228	3317
Canada	Jonathan Don	202-377-3101	3033
Cape Verde	Philip Michelini	202-377-4388	3317

Country	Contact	Phone	Code
Caymans	Michelle Brooks	202-377-2527	3020
Central Africa Republic	Debra Henke	202-377-4228	3317
Chad	Debra Henke	202-377-4228	3317
Chile	Roger Turner	202-377-1495	3017
Columbia	Laurie MacNamara	202-377-1659	3025
Comoros	Chandra Watkins	202-377-4564	3317
Congo	Debra Henke	202-377-4228	3317
Costa Rica	Theodore Johnson	202-377-2527	3021
Cuba	Rodrigo Soto	202-377-2527	3021
Cyprus	Ann Corro	202-377-3945	3044
Czechoslovakia	Mark Mowrey	202-377-2645	6043

D

Country	Contact	Phone	Code
D'Jibouti	Chandra Watkins	202-377-4564	3317
Denmark	Maryanne Lyons	202-377-3254	3413
Dominica	Michelle Brooks	202-377-2527	3021
Dominican Republic	Rodrigo Soto	202-377-2527	3021

E

Country	Contact	Phone	Code
E. Caribbean	Michelle Brooks	202-377-2527	3021
Ecuador	Laurie McNamara	202-377-1659	3025
Egypt	Thomas Sams /Corey Wright	202-377-4441	2039
El Salvador	Theodore Johnson	202-377-2527	3020
Equatorial Guinea	Debra Henke	202-377-4228	3317
Ethiopia	Chandra Watkins	202-377-4564	3317
European Community	Charles Ludolph	202-377-5276	3036

F

Country	Contact	Phone	Code
Finland	Maryanne Lyons	202-377-3254	3413
France	Elena Mikalis	202-377-8008	3042

G

Country	Contact	Phone	Code
Gabon	Debra Henke	202-377-4228	3317
Gambia	Philip Michelin	202-377-4388	3317
Germany	Brenda Fisher	202-377-2434	3409
Germany	Joan Kloepfer	202-377-2841	3409
Ghana	Debra Henke	202-377-4228	3317
Greece	Ann Corro	202-377-3945	3044
Grenada	Michelle Brooks	202-377-2527	3021
Guadeloupe	Michelle Brooks	202-377-2527	3021
Guatemala	Ted Johnson	202-377-2527	3021
Guinea	Philip Michelini	202-377-4388	3317
Guinea-Bissau	Philip Michelini	202-377-4388	3317
Guyana	Michelle Brooks	202-377-2527	3021

H

Country	Contact	Phone	Code
Haiti	Rodrigo Soto	202-377-2527	3021
Honduras	Theodore Johnson	202-377-2527	3020
Hong Kong	JeNelle Matheson	202-377-3583	2317
Hungary	Brian Toohey	202-377-2645	6043

I

Country	Contact	Phone	Code
Iceland	Maryanne Lyons	202-377-3254	3037
India	John Simmons /John Crown /Tim Gilman	202-377-2954	2029B
Indonesia	Karen Goddin	202-377-3875	2308
Iran	Corey Wright	202-377-4652	2039

Country	Contact	Phone	Code
Iraq	Thomas Sams	202-377-4441	2039
Ireland	Boyce Fitzpatrick	202-377-2177	3039
Israel	Kate FitzGerald-Wilks /Doris Nelmes	202-377-4652	2039
Italy	Boyce Fitzpatrick	202-377-2177	3045
Ivory Coast	Philip Michelini	202-377-4388	3317

J

Country	Contact	Phone	Code
Jamaica	Rodrigo Soto	202-377-2527	3021
Japan	Ed Leslie /Cantwell Walsh /Eric Kennedy	202-377-2425	2324
Jordan	Claude Clement	202-377-2515	2039

K

Country	Contact	Phone	Code
Kenya	Chandra Watkins	202-377-4564	3317
Korea	Jeffrey Donius /Dan Duvall /Renato Amador	202-377-4957	2327
Kuwait	Corey Wright /Thomas Sams	202-377-2515	2039

L

Country	Contact	Phone	Code
Laos	Hong-Phong B. Pho	202-377-3875	2308
Lebanon	Corey Wright /Thomas Sams	202-377-2515	2039
Lesotho	Vacant	202-377-5148	3317
Liberia	Reginald Biddle	202-377-4388	3317
Libya	Claude Clement	202-377-5545	2039
Luxembourg	Simon Bensimon	202-377-5401	3046

M

Country	Contact	Phone	Code
Macao	JeNelle Matheson	202-377-2462	2323
Madagascar	Chandra Watkins	202-377-4564	3317
Malawi	Vacant	202-337-5148	3317
Malaysia	Raphael Cung	202-377-3875	2308
Maldives	John Simmons	202-377-2954	2029B
Mali	Philip Michelini	202-377-4388	3317
Malta	Robert McLaughlin	202-377-3748	3049
Mauritana	Philip Michelini	202-377-4564	3317
Mauritius	Chandra Watkins	202-377-4564	3317
Mexico	Andrew Lowry /Ingrid Mohn	202-377-4464	3028
Mongolia	JeNelle Matheson	202-377-2462	2323
Montserrat	Michelle Brooks	202-377-2527	3314
Morocco	Jeffrey Johnson	202-377-5545	2039
Mozambique	Vacant	202-377-5148	3317

N

Country	Contact	Phone	Code
Namibia	Emily Solomon	202-377-5148	3317
Nepal	Tim Gilman	202-377-2954	2029B
Netherlands	Simon Bensimon	202-377-5401	3039
Netherlands Antilles	Michelle Brooks	202-377-2527	3021
New Zealand	Gary Bouck	202-377-3647	2308
Nicaragua	Ted Johnson	202-377-2527	3021
Niger	Philip Michelini	202-377-4388	3317
Nigeria	Debra Henke	202-377-4228	3317
Norway	James Devlin	202-377-4414	3037

O

Country	Contact	Phone	Code
Oman	Kate		

	Fitzgerald-Wilks /Doris Nelmes	202-377-4652	2039
P			
Pacific Islands	Gary Bouck	202-377-3647	2308
Pakistan	Cheryl McQueen	202-377-2954	2029B
Panama	Theodore Johnson	202-377-2527	3020
Paraguay	Randy Mye	202-377-1548	3021
People/China	Robert Chu /Laura McCall	202-377-3583	2317
Peru	Laura Zeiger	202-377-2521	3029
Philippines	George Paine	202-377-3875	2308
Poland	Audrey A. Zuck	202-377-2645	6043
Portugal	Mary Beth Double	202-377-4508	3044
Puerto Rico	Rodrigo Soto	202-377-2527	3021
Q			
Qatar	Kate Fitzgerald-Wilks /Doris Nelmes	202-377-4652	2039
R			
Romania	Lynn Fabrizio	202-377-2645	6043
Russia CIS	Jack Brougher /Susan Lewens /Tim Smith	202-377-4655	3318
Rwanda	Debra Henke	202-377-4228	3317
S			
Sao Tome & Principe	Debra Henke	202-377-4228	3317
Saudi Arabia	Jeffrey Johnson /Claude Clement	202-377-4652	2039
Senegal	Philip Michelini	202-377-4388	3317
Seychelles	Chandra Watkins	202-377-4564	3317
Sierra Leone	Philip Michelini	202-377-4388	3317
Singapore	Raphael Cung	202-377-3875	2308
Somalia	Chandra Watkins	202-377-4564	3317
South Africa	Emily Solomon	202-377-5148	3317
Spain	Mary Beth Double	202-377-4508	3045
Sri Lanka	John Simmons	202-377-2954	2029B
St. Bartholomy	Michelle Brooks	202-377-2527	3021
St. Kitts-Nevis	Michelle Brooks	202-377-2527	3021
St. Lucia	Michelle Brooks	202-377-2527	3021
St. Martin	Michelle Brooks	202-377-2527	3021
St. Vincent Grenadines	Michelle Brooks	202-377-2527	3021
Sudan	Chandra Watkins	202-377-4564	3317
Suriname	Michelle Brooks	202-377-2527	3021
Swaziland	Vacant	202-377-5148	3317
Sweden	James Devlin	202-377-4414	3037
Switzerland	Philip Combs	202-377-2920	3039
Syria	Corey Wright /Thomas Sams	202-377-2515	2039
T			
Taiwan	Ian Davis /Dan Duvall /Paul Carroll	202-377-4957	2308
Tanzania	Vacant	202-377-5148	3317
Thailand	Jean Kelly	202-377-3875	2308
Togo	Debra Henke	202-377-4228	3021

Trinidad & Tobago	Michelle Brooks	202-377-2527	3021
Tunisia	Corey Wright /Thomas Sams	202-377-2515	2039
Turkey	Heidi Lamb	202-377-5373	3045
Turks & Caicos Islands	Rodrigo Soto	202-377-2527	3021
U			
Uganda	Chandra Watkins	202-377-4564	3317
United Arab Emirates	Claude Clement /Jeffrey Johnson	202-377-5545	2039
United Kingdom	Robert McLaughlin	202-377-3748	3045
Uruguay	Roger Turner	202-377-1495	3021
V			
Venezuela	Herbert Lindow	202-377-4303	3029
Vietnam	Hong-Phong B. Pho	202-377-3875	2308
Virgin Islands (UK)	Michelle Brooks	202-377-2527	3020
Virgin Islands (US)	Rodrigo Soto	202-377-2527	3021
Y			
Yemen, Rep of	Kate Fitzgerald-Wilks /Doris Nelmes	202-377-4652	2039
Yugoslavia	Jeremy Keller	202-377-2645	6043
Z			
Zaire	Debra Henke	202-377-4228	3317
Zambia	Vacant	202-377-5148	3317
Zimbabwe	Vacant	202-377-5147	3317

State Department Country Experts

If you need information that is primarily political, economic or cultural in nature, direct your questions first to the State Department Country Desk Officers.

U.S. Department of State
2201 C Street NW
Washington, DC 20520   202-647-6575

Foreign Specialists At Other Government Agencies

The following is a listing by subject area of other departments within the federal government which maintain country experts who are available to help the public:

1) **Mineral Resources:**
Bureau of Mines, U.S. Department of Interior, Division of International Minerals, 810 7th Street NW, Washington, DC 20241-0002, 202-501-9666

2) **Foreign Agriculture:**
Economic Research Service, Agriculture & Trade Analysis Division, U.S. Department of Agriculture, Room 732, 1301 New York Avenue, NW, Washington, DC 20005, 202-219-0700

Food Safety and Inspection Service, International Programs, U.S. Department of Agriculture, Room 341-E, 14th and Independence SW, Washington, DC 20250-3700, 202-720-3473

Animal and Plant Health Inspection Service, Import-Export, U.S. Department of Agriculture, 6505 Bellcrest Road, Hyattsville, MD 20782, 301-436-8590

Food Transportation, International Transportation Branch, U.S. Department of Agriculture, Room 1217 South Building, Washington, DC 20250, 202-690-1320

3) Energy Resources:
Office of Export Assistance, U.S. Department of Energy, 1000 Independence Avenue, SW, Washington, DC 20585, 202-586-0151

Office of Fossil Energy, U.S. Department of Energy, 1000 Independence Ave., SW, Washington, DC 20585, 202-586-7297

4) Economic Assistance to Foreign Countries:
Business Office, U.S. Agency for International Development, 320 21st Street NW, Washington, DC 20523, 703-875-1551

5) Information Programs and Cultural Exchange:
U.S. Information Agency, 301 4th Street SW, Washington, DC 20547, 202-619-4700

6) Seafood Certificates:
Inspection Certificates for Seafood Exports, National Oceanic and Atmospheric Administration, 1335 East-West Highway, Room 6120, Silver Spring, MD 20910, 301-443-8910

7) Metric:
Office of Metric Programs, National Institute of Standards and Technology, Gaithersburg, MD 20899, 202-377-0944

8) Telecommunications Information:
Bureau of International Communications and Information Policy, U.S. Dept of State, Washington, DC 20520, 202-647-5231

9) Fisheries:
Office of Trade and Industry Services, Fisheries Promotion and Trade Matters, National Marine Fisheries Service, 1335 East-West Highway, Silver Spring, MD 20910, 301-713-2351

Fax Directory
Of Overseas Commercial Counselors

You can FAX IT, if you are looking for a market study, a client or any other piece of information in a given country. Listed below are the fax numbers of the commercial officers who work at U.S. Embassies around the world. These officers are available to assist U.S. businesses succeed in selling their products overseas.

Algeria:
Algiers — 9-011-213-2-60-18-63
Argentina:
Buenos Aires — 9-011-54-1775-6040
Australia:
Sydney — 9-011-61-2-261-8148

Brisbane	9-011-61-7-832-6247
Melbourne	9-011-61-3-696-1820
Perth	9-011-61-9-325-3569
Austria:	
Vienna	9-011-43-222-341261
Barbados:	
Bridgetown	9-1-809-426-2275
Belgium:	
Brussels (Emb)	9-011-32-2-512-6653
Brussels (EC)	9-011-32-2-513-1228
Antwerp	9-011-32-3-234-3698
Brazil:	
Brasilia	9-011-55-61-225-3981
Belo Horizonte	9-011-55-31-224-6214
Rio de Janeiro	9-011-55-21-240-9738
Sao Paulo	9-011-55-11-853-2744
Cameroon:	
Douala	9-011-237-427-790
Yaounde	9-011-237-427-790
Canada:	
Ottawa	9-1-613-233-8511
Calgary	9-1-403-264-6630
Halifax	9-1-902-423-6861
Montreal	9-1-514-398-0711
Toronto	9-1-416-595-0051
Vancouver	9-1-604-685-5285
China:	
Beijing	9-011-86-1-532-3297
Guangzhou	9-011-86-20-666-409
Shanghai	9-011-86-21-433-1576
Shenyang	9-011-86-24-290-074
Columbia:	
Bogata	9-011-57-1-285-7945
Costa Rica:	
San Jose	9-011-506-31-47-83
Cote D'Ivoire:	
Abidjan	9-011-225-22-32-59
African Dev Bk	9-011-225-33-21-72
Czechoslovakia:	
Prague	9-011-42-2-532-457
Denmark:	
Copenhagen	9-011-45-31-42-01-75
Dominican Republic:	
Santa Domingo	9-1-809-688-4838
Ecuador:	
Quito	9-011-593-2-504-550
Guayaquil	9-011-593-4-324-558
Egypt:	
Cairo	9-011-20-2-355-8368
Alexandria	9-011-20-3-482-9199
Finland:	
Helsinki	9-011-358-0-635-332
France:	
Paris(EMB)	9-011-33-1-4266-4827
Paris (ORCD)	9-011-33-1-4524-7410
Bordeaux	9-011-33-56-51-60-42
Lyon	9-011-33-1-4266-4827
Marseille	9-011-33-1-4266-4827
Nice	9-011-33-1-4266-4827
Strasbourg	9-011-33-1-4266-4827
Germany:	
Bonn	9-011-49-228-334-649
Berlin	9-011-37-2-229-2167

Dusseldorf	9-011-49-211-594-897
Frankfurt	9-011-49-69-748-204
Hamburg	9-011-49-410-6598
Munich	9-011-49-89-285-261
Stuttgart	9-011-49-711-234-350

Greece:
Athens	9-011-30-1-723-9705

Guatemala:
Guatemala	9-011-502-2-317-373

Honduras:
Teguicigalpa	9-011-504-32-0027

Hong Kong:
Hong Kong	9-011-852-845-9800

Hungary:
Budapest	9-011-36-1-142-2529

India:
New Delhi	9-011-91-11-687-2391
Bombay	9-011-91-22-822-0350
Calcutta	9-011-91-33-283-823
Madras	9-011-91-44-825-0240

Indonesia:
Jakarta	9-011-62-21-360-644
Medan	9-011-62-21-360-644
Surabaya	9-011-62-21-360-644

Iraq:
Baghdad	9-011-964-1-718-9297

Ireland:
Dublin	9-011-353-1-608-469

Israel:
Tel Aviv	9-011-972-3-658-033

Italy:
Rome	9-011-39-6-4674-2113
Florence	9-011-39-55-283-780
Genoa	9-011-39-10-207-721
Milan	9-011-39-2-481-4161
Naples	9-011-39-81-761-1869

Jamaica:
Kingston	9-1-809-929-3637

Japan:
Tokyo	9-011-81-3-589-4235
Tokyo (TradeCtr)	9-011-81-3-987-2447
Fukuoka	9-011-81-9-271-3922
Osaka-Kobe	9-011-81-6-361-5978
Sapporo	9-011-81-11-641-0911

Kenya:
Nairobi	9-011-254-2-340-838

Korea:
Seoul	9-011-82-2-739-1628

Kuwait:
Kuwait	9-011-965-240-7368

Malaysia:
Kuala Lumpur	9-011-60-3-242-1866

Mexico:
Mexico City	9-011-52-5-207-8938
Mexico City (Trade Center)	9-011-52-5-566-1115
Guadalajara	9-011-52-36-26-6549
Monterrey	0-011-52-83-42-5172

Morocco:
Casablanca	9-011-212-22-02-59
Rabat	9-011-212-7-656-61

Netherlands:
The Hague	9-011-31-70-363-29-85

Amsterdam	9-011-64-4-781-701

Nigeria:
Lagos	9-011-234-1-619-856

Norway:
Oslo	9-011-47-2055-88-03

Pakistan:
Karachi	9-011-92-21-511-381

Panama:
Panama	9-011-507-27-1713

Peru:
Lima	9-011-51-14-33-4687

Philippines:
Manila	9-011-63-2-818-2684
Asian Dev Bank	9-011-63-2-834-4003

Poland:
Warsaw	9-011-48-22-21-63-27

Portugal:
Lisbon	9-011-351-1-726-8914
Oporto	9-011-351-2-600-2737

Romania:
Bucharest	9-011-40-0-110-474

Saudi Arabia:
Riyadh	9-011-966-1-488-3237
Dhahran	9-011-966-3-891-8332
Jeddah	9-011-966-2-665-8106

Singapore:
Singapore	9-011-65-338-5010

South Africa:
Johannesburg	9-011-27-11-331-6178
Cape Town	9-011-27-21-214-280

Spain:
Madrid	9-011-34-1-575-8655
Barcelona	9-011-34-3-319-5621

Sweden:
Stockholm	9-011-46-8-660-9181

Switzerland:
Bern	9-011-41-31-43-73-36
Geneva(GATT)	9-011-41-22-799-0885
Zurich	9-011-41-4-383-9814

Taiwan:
Taipei	9-011-886-2-757-7162
Kaohsiung	9-011-886-7-231-8237

Thailand:
Bangkok	9-011-66-2-255-2915

Trinidad & Tobago:
Port-of-Spain	9-1-809-622-9583

Turkey:
Ankara	9-011-90-4-167-1366
Istanbul	9-011-90-1-152-2417

United Arab Emirates:
Adu Dhabi	9-011-971-2-331-374
Dubai	9-011-971-4-375-121

United Kingdom:
London	9-011-44-71-491-4022

U.S.S.R.:
Moscow	9-011-7-095-230-2101

Venezuela:
Caracas	9-011-58-2-285-0336

Yugoslavia:
Belgrade	9-011-38-11-645-096
Zagreb	9-011-38-41-440-235

Selling Overseas: Foreign Markets

Money For Selling Overseas

1) State Government Money Programs:
Some state government economic development programs offer special assistance for those who need financial assistance in selling overseas. See the section presented later in this chapter entitled *State Government Assistance To Exporters*.

2) Export-Import Bank Financing:
The Export-Import Bank facilitates and aids in the financing of exports of U.S. goods and services. Its programs include short-term, medium-term, and long-term credits, small business support, financial guarantees and insurance. In addition, it sponsors conferences on small business exporting, maintains credit information on thousands of foreign firms, supports feasibility studies of overseas programs, and offers export and small business finance counseling. To receive *Marketing News* Fact Sheets, or the *Eximbank Export Credit Insurance* booklet, or the Eximbank's *Program Selection Guide,* contact: Export-Import Bank, 811 Vermont Ave. NW, Washington, DC 20571, 202-566-8860, 1-800-424-5201.

3) Small Business Administration (SBA) Export Loans:
This agency makes loans and loan guarantees to small business concerns as well as to small business investment companies, including those which sell overseas. It also offers technical assistance, counseling, training, management assistance, and information resources, including several excellent publications to small and minority businesses in export operations. Contact your local or regional SBA office listed in the blue pages of your telephone book under Small Business Administration, or Small Business Administration, 409 3rd St, SW, Washington, DC 20416, 202-205-6720.

4) Overseas Private Investment Corporation (OPIC):
This agency provides marketing, insurance, and financial assistance to American companies investing in 118 countries and 16 geographic regions. Its programs include direct loans, loan guarantees and political risk insurance. OPIC also sponsors seminars for investment executives as well as conducts investment missions to developing countries. The Investor Services Division offers a computer service to assist investors in identifying investment opportunities worldwide. A modest fee is charged for this service and it is also available through the LEXIS/NEXIS computer network. Specific Info-Kits are available identifying basic economic, business and political information for each of the countries covered. In addition, it operates:

> Program Information Hotline
> Overseas Private Investment Corporation
> 1100 New York Ave., NW
> Washington, DC 20527
> 1-800-424-OPIC (Hotline)
> 202-336-8400 (General Information)
> 202-457-7128 (Investor Services Division)
> 202-336-8636 (Public Affairs)
> 202-336-8680 (Press Information)

5) Agency For International Development (AID):
AID offers a variety of loan and financing guarantee programs for projects in developing countries that have a substantial developmental impact or for the exportation of manufactured goods to AID-assisted developing countries. Some investment opportunities are region specific, which include the Association of Southeast Asian National, the Philippines, and Africa. For more information contact the Office of Investment, Agency for International Development, 515 22nd Street NW, Room 301, Washington, DC 20523-0231, 202-663-2280.

Marketing Data, Custom Studies And Company Information

Further information on any of the following services and products can be obtained by contacting a U.S. Department of Commerce/US & FCS field office listed later in this chapter, or contact the US & FCS at: United States and Foreign Commercial Services, U.S. Department of Commerce, Room 3810, HCH Building, 14th & Constitution Ave., NW, Washington, DC 20230, 202-377-4767 or call 1-800-USA-TRADE.

1) International Industry Experts:
A separate Office of Trade Development at the Commerce Department handles special marketing and company problems for specific industries. Experts are available in the following international market sectors:

Aerospace:	202-377-2835
Automotive and Consumer Goods:	202-377-0823
Basic Industries:	202-377-0614
Capital Goods and International Construction:	202-377-5023
Science and Electronics and	
Telecommunications and Industries:	202-377-3548
Service:	202-377-5261
Textiles and Apparel:	202-377-3737

You can also talk to industry desk officers at the Department of Commerce. They can provide information on the competitive strengths of U.S. industries in foreign markets from abrasives to yogurt. They are listed in the "Experts" section at the end of this book and have "COMMERCE" after their name.

2) Trade Lists:
Directories of overseas customers for U.S. exports in selected industries and countries: They contain the names and product lines of foreign distributors, agents, manufacturers, wholesalers, retailers and other purchasers. They also provide the name and title of a key officials as well as telex and cable numbers, and company size data. Prices range up to $40 for a list of a category.

3) Country Trade Statistics:
Tables showing American exports of 100-150 industries to a selected country: Data are available for over 150 countries and include relative growth rates, percentage export shares and leading markets for specific U.S. products. Price is $25 per country.

4) Custom Statistical:
Export data for a particular country are presented according to customer's specifications. This service is broader in scope and more detailed in nature than the *Country Trade Statistics* service. Prices start at $50.

5) Customized Export Mailing Lists:
Selected lists of foreign companies in particular industries,

countries and types of business can be requested by a client. Gummed labels are also available. Prices start at $35.

6) World Traders Data Reports:
Background reports are available on individual firms containing information about each firm's business activities, its standing in the local business community, its credit-worthiness and overall reliability and suitability as a trade contact for exporters. The price is $75 per report.

7) Agent Distributor Service:
This is a customized search for interested and qualified foreign representatives on behalf of an American client. U.S. commercial officers overseas conduct the search and prepare a report identifying up to six foreign prospects which have personally examined the U.S. firm's product literature and have expressed interest in representing the firm. The price is $90 per market.

8) New Product Information Service:
This service is designed to help American companies publicize the availability of new U.S. products in foreign markets and simultaneously test market interest in these products. Product information which meets the criteria is distributed worldwide through Commercial News USA and Voice of America broadcasts. A fee is charged for participation.

9) Customized Market Studies:
At a cost of $500 per country per product, these studies are called "Comparison Shopping Service". They are conducted by the U.S. Embassy foreign commercial attaches and can target information on quite specific marketing questions.

- Does the product have sales potential in the country?
- Who is the supplier for a comparable product locally?
- What is the going price for a comparable product in this country?
- What is the usual sales channel for getting this type of product into the market?
- What are the competitive factors that most influence purchases of these products in the market (i.e., price, credit, quality, delivery, service, promotion, brand)?
- What is the best way to get sales exposure in the market for this type of product?
- Are there any significant impediments to selling this type of product?
- Who might be interested and qualified to represent or purchase this company's products?
- If a licensing or joint venture strategy seems desirable for this market, who might be an interested and qualified partner for the U.S. company?

10) Special Opportunities in the Caribbean Basin and Latin America:
Under the Caribbean Economic Recovery Act of 1983, the government has established special incentives for American firms wishing to do business with Latin American and Caribbean Basin companies. Seminars, workshops, business development missions, business counseling as well as marketing and competitive information are available.

Latin America/Caribbean Business Development Center
U.S. Department of Commerce   202-377-0841
Washington, DC 20230   FAX: 202-377-2218

11) New Markets In Eastern European Countries:
The Eastern Europe Business Information Center is stocked with a wide range of publications on doing business in Eastern Europe; these include lists of potential partners, investment regulations, priority industry sectors, and notices of upcoming seminars, conferences, and trade promotion events. It also serves as a referral point for programs of voluntary assistance to the region.

Eastern Europe Business Information Center
U.S. Department of Commerce   202-377-2645
Washington, DC 20230   FAX: 202-377-4473

12) Opportunities for Rebuilding The Gulf:
The Gulf Reconstruction Center coordinates the Department of Commerce's reconstruction activities and counsels the U.S. business community about rebuilding opportunities in Kuwait and the Gulf region. The center serves as an information clearinghouse for business investors. It also provides American firms with materials on doing business in Kuwait. The Center is compiling a database of companies interested in business opportunities in the region, which can also be used by the Kuwaiti Government and the U.S. Army Corps of Engineers to obtain information on companies interested in Kuwait's reconstruction effort.

Counseling and Referral Services
Gulf Reconstruction Center
U.S. Department of Commerce   202-377-5767
Washington, DC 20230   FAX: 202-377-0878

13) Exporting to Japan: Japan Export Information Center (JEIC)
JEIC provides business counseling services and accurate information on exporting to Japan. The JEIC is the point of contact for information on business in Japan, market entry alternatives, market information and research, product standards and testing, tariffs, and non-tariff barriers. The center maintains a commercial library and participates in seminars on various aspects of Japanese business. Contact: Japan Export Information Center, (202) 377-2425; FAX: (202) 377-0469.

Trade Fairs And Missions

Trade fairs, exhibitions, trade missions, overseas trade seminars and other promotional events and services are sponsored by the Export Promotion Services Group, US & FCS, U.S. Department of Commerce, 14th & E Streets, N.W., Room 2808, Washington, DC 20230, 202-377-8220. This office or one of its field offices which are listed later in this chapter can provide additional details on these activities.

1) Industry-Organized, Government-Approved Trade Missions:
Such missions are organized by trade associations, local Chambers of Commerce, state trade development agencies, and similar trade-oriented groups with U.S. Department of Commerce support.

2) Catalog Exhibitions:
Such exhibitions feature displays of U.S. product catalogs, sales brochures and other graphic sales materials at American

embassies and consulates or in conjunction with trade shows. A Commerce Department specialist assists in the exhibition. Call 202-377-3973; FAX: 202-377-0178.

3) Video Catalog:

This catalog is designed to showcase American products via video tape presentation. This permits actual product demonstrations giving the foreign buyer an opportunity to view applications of American products. Federal specialists participate in these sessions. Call 202-377-3973; FAX: 202-377-0178.

4) U.S. Specialized Trade Missions:

These missions are distinct from those mentioned above since the U.S. Department of Commerce plans the visits and accompanies the delegation. They are designed to sell American goods and services as well as establish agents or representation abroad. The Department of Commerce provides marketing information, advanced planning, publicity and trip organization. Call 1-800-USA-TRADE.

5) U.S. Seminar Missions:

The objective here is to promote exports and help foreign representation for American exporters. However, unlike trade missions, these are designed to facilitate the sales of state-of-the-art products and technology. This type of mission is a 1-2 day "seminar" during which team members discuss technology subjects followed by private, sales-oriented appointments. Call 1-800-USA-TRADE.

6) Matchmaker Trade Delegations:

These Commerce-recruited and planned missions are designed to introduce new-to-export or new-to-market businesses to prospective agents and distributors overseas. Trade Specialists from Commerce evaluate the potential firm's products, find and screen contacts and handle logistics. This is followed by an intensive trip filled with meetings and prospective clients and in-depth briefings on the economic and business climate of the countries visited. Call Office of Export Promotion Services, 202-377-3119; FAX: 202-377-0178.

7) Investment Missions:

These events are held in developing countries offering excellent investment opportunities for U.S. firms. Missions introduce U.S. business executives to key business leaders, potential joint venture partners and senior foreign government officials in the host country. Call Investment Missions, 202-457-7039; FAX: 202-223-3514.

8) Foreign Buyer Program:

This program supports major domestic trade shows featuring products and services of U.S. industries with high export potential. Government officials world-wide recruit qualified buyers to attend the shows. Call 202-377-8433; FAX: 202-377-0178.

9) Trade Fairs, Solo Exhibitions, and Trade Center Shows:

The Department of Commerce organizes a wide variety of special exhibitions. These events range from solo exhibitions representing U.S. firms exclusively at trade centers overseas to U.S. pavilions in the largest international exhibitions. Call 1-800-USA-TRADE.

10) Agent/Distributor Service (ADS):

Looking for overseas representatives to expand your business and boost your export sales? Commerce will locate, screen, and assess agents, distributors, representatives, and other foreign partners for your business. Call 1-800-USA-TRADE.

11) Trade Opportunities Program (TOP):

TOP provides companies with current sales leads from international firms seeking to buy or represent their products or services. TOP leads are printed daily in leading commercial newspapers and are also distributed electronically via the U.S. Department of Commerce Economic Bulletin Board. Call 202-377-1986; FAX: 202-377-2164.

12) Travel and Tourism:

The U.S. Travel and Tourism Administration promotes export earnings through trade in tourism. USTTA stimulates demand for travel to the U.S., encourages and facilitates promotion in international travel markets by U.S. travel industry concerns; works to increase the number of new-to-market travel businesses participating in the export market; forms cooperative marketing opportunities for private industry and regional state, and local government; provides timely data; and helps to remove government-imposed travel barriers. Call International Congress Programs, 202-377-4904.

13) Gold Key Service:

This customed tailored service is aimed at U.S. firms which are planning to visit a country. Offered by many overseas posts, it combines several services, such as market orientation briefings, market research, introductions to potential partners, and interpreters for meetings, assistance in developing a sound market strategy, and an effective follow-up plan. Call 1-800-USA-TRADE.

Special Programs For Agricultural Products

The following programs are specifically aimed at those who wish to sell agricultural products overseas. Agricultural exporters should also be sure not to limit themselves only to programs under this heading. Programs listed under other headings can also be used for agricultural products.

1) Office Space for Agricultural Exporters:

The Foreign Agriculture Service (FAS) maintains overseas agricultural trade offices to help exporters of U.S. farm and forest products in key overseas markets. The facilities vary depending on local conditions, but may include a trade library, conference rooms, office space, and kitchens for preparing product samples. Contact: Foreign Agriculture Service, U.S. Department of Agriculture, 12 Street and Jefferson Drive SW, Washington, DC 20250, 202-720-9509; FAX: 202-690-4374.

2) Research Services:

The Agricultural Research Service provides exporters with information, research and consultants on a wide array of topics including shipping, storage, insect control, pesticide residues, and market disorders. Contact: Agricultural Research Service, U.S. Department of Agriculture, 12th Street and Jefferson Drive SW, Washington, DC 20250, 202-504-5605; FAX: 301-504-5298.

3) Foreign Market Information:
A special office serves as a single contact point within the Foreign Agriculture Service for agricultural exporters seeking foreign market information. The office also counsels firms which believe they have been injured by unfair trade practices. Contact: Trade Assistance and Planning Office, U.S. Department of Agriculture, 12th Street and Jefferson Drive SW, Washington, DC 20250, 703-305-2771; FAX: 703-305-2788.

4) Export Connections:
The AgExport Action Kit provides information which can help put U.S. exporters in touch quickly and directly with foreign importers of food and agricultural products. The services include trade leads, a Buyer Alert newsletter, foreign buyer lists, and U.S. supplier lists. All services are free. Contact: AgExport Connections, U.S. Department of Agriculture, Washington, DC 20250, 202-720-7103; FAX: 202-690-4374.

5) Country Market Profiles:
Country-specific 2-4 page descriptions are available for 40 overseas markets for high value agricultural products. They provide market overview, market trends, and information on the U.S. market position, the competition, and general labeling and licensing requirements. Contact: Country Market Profiles, FAS Information Service, U.S. Department of Agriculture, Washington, DC 20250, 202-720-7937; FAX: 202-720-1727.

Export Regulations, Licensing, And Product Standards

Talk to ELVIS — Bureau of Export Administration (BXA)
BXA is responsible for controlling exports for reasons of national security, foreign policy, and short supply. Licenses on controlled exports are issued, and seminars on U.S. export regulations are held domestically and overseas.

Export license applications may be submitted and issued through computer via the Export License Application and Information Network (ELAIN). The System for Tracking Export License Application (STELA) provides instant status updates on license applications by the use of a touch-tone phone.

The Export Licensing Voice Information (ELVIS) is an automated attendant that offers a range of licensing information and emergency handling procedures. Callers may order forms and publications or subscribe to the *Office of Export Licensing (OEL) Insider Newsletter*, which provides regulatory updates. While using ELVIS, a caller has the option to speak to a consultant.

Office of Export Licensing	202-377-8536
	FAX: 202-377-3322
ELAIN	202-377-4811
STELA	202-377-2752
ELVIS	202-377-4811

The National Institute of Standards and Technology provides a free service which will identify standards for selling any product to any country in the world. This federal agency will tell you what the standard is for a given product or suggest where you can obtain an official copy of the standard.

National Center for Standards and Certification
National Institute of Standards and Technology
Building 411, Room A163
Gaithersburg, MD 20899   301-975-4040

Cheap Office And Conference Space Overseas

If you are travelling overseas on a business trip, you may want to look into renting office space and other services through the American Embassy. Depending on the country and the space available, the embassy can provide temporary office space for as low as $25 per day, along with translation services, printing and other services. Meeting rooms, seminar or convention space along with promotion services, mailings, freight handling, and even catering may be available in many countries. Contact the Department of Commerce/US & FCS field office which is listed later in this chapter or the appropriate country desk officer at the U.S. Department of Commerce in Washington, DC.

Other Services, Resources And Databases

The following is a description of some of the additional services and information sources that can be useful to anyone investigating overseas markets:

1) World Import/Export Statistics:
For the latest information on any product imported to or exported from any foreign country, contact: Foreign and U.S. Trade Reference Room, U.S. Dept. of Commerce, Room 2233, Washington, DC 20230, 202-377-4855.

2) Help In Selling To Developing Nations:
The U.S. Agency For International Development (AID) provides information to U.S. suppliers, particularly small, independent enterprises, regarding purchases to be financed with AID funds. U.S. small businesses can obtain special counseling and related services in order to furnish equipment, materials, and services to AID-financed projects. AID sponsors Development Technologies Exhibitions, where technical firms in the U.S. are matched up with those in lesser developed countries for the purpose of forming joint ventures or exploring licensing possibilities. AID provides loans and grants to finance consulting services that support project activities related to areas such as agriculture, rural development, health, and housing. Contact: Office of Business Relations, U.S. Agency for International Development, State Annex 14, Room 1400A, Washington, DC 20523, 703-875-1551.

3) Foreign Demographic Profiles:
The U.S. Bureau of the Census produces detailed statistical profiles of foreign trade and demographic topics, as well as import/export statistics, and can do marketing research consultation for American exporters. The cost of the latest edition, 1989, is $7.50 (GPO: 031-024-07074-0). Contact: Superintendent of Documents, U.S. Government Printing Office, Washington, D.C. 20402; 202-783-3238.

Also available from the Government Printing office is the CIA *World Factbook*. Produced annually by the CIA, this publication provides country-by-country data on demographics, economy, communications, and defense. The cost is $23 (GPO: 041-015-00169-8). Order from the above address by mail or by phone.

4) Help With Selling Commodities Abroad:

The Foreign Agricultural Service is charged with maintaining and expanding export sales of U.S. agricultural commodities and products. Staff can provide information on foreign agricultural production, trade and consumption, marketing research including areas of demand for specific commodities in foreign countries, and analyses of foreign competition in agricultural areas. Other services include financing opportunities, contributing to export promotion costs and testing market assistance. This office also handles U.S. representation to foreign governments and participates in formal trade negotiations. Contact: Foreign Agricultural Service, U.S. Department of Agriculture, 14th and Independence Avenue, S.W., Room 4647, South Bldg., Washington, DC 20250, 202-447-6343.

5) International Prices:

Export price indexes for both detailed and aggregate product groups on a quarterly basis, as well as price trends comparisons of U.S. exports with those of Japan and Germany, are available from:

International Prices Division, Bureau of Labor Statistics, U.S. Department of Labor, 2nd Massachusetts Ave., NE, Room 3955, Washington, DC 20212, 202-606-7100.

6) Identifying Overseas Opportunities:

The International Trade Administration (ITA) of the Commerce Department assists American exporters in locating and gaining access to foreign markets. It furnishes information on overseas markets available for U.S. products and services, requirements which must be fulfilled, economic conditions in foreign countries, foreign market and investment opportunities, etc. Operations are divided into four major areas:

- **International Economic Policy:** promotes U.S. exports geographically by helping American businesses market products in various locations abroad and by solving the trade and investment problems they encounter. This office is staffed by Country Desk Officers knowledgeable in marketing and business practices for almost every country in the world. (See details above). Contact: Office of International Economic Policy, ITA, U.S. Department of Commerce, Washington, DC 20230, 202-377-3022. See Appendix N for country marketing experts.

- **Export Administration:** supervises the enforcement provisions of the Export Administration Act, and administers the Foreign Trade Zone Program. Personnel in its export enforcement and its administration, policy and regulations offices can offer technical advice and legal interpretations of the various export legislation which affect American businesses. Assistance in complying with export controls can be obtained directly from the Exporter Counseling Division within the Bureau of Export Administration (BXA) Office of Export Licensing in Washington, DC, 202-377-4811.

BXA also has four field offices that specialize in counseling on export controls and regulations:
Western Regional Office   714-660-0144

Northern California Branch Office   408-748-7450
Portland Branch Office   503-326-5159
Eastern Regional Office   603-834-6300

- **Trade Development:** advises businesses on trade and investment issues, and promotes U.S. exports by industry or product classifications. Offices offer assistance and information on export counseling, statistics and trade data, licensing, trading companies, and other services. Contact: Office of Trade Development, ITA, U.S. Department of Commerce, Washington, DC 20230, 202-377-1461; FAX: 202-377-5697.

- **U.S. and Foreign Commercial Service:** provides information on government programs to American businesses, and uncovers trade opportunities for U.S. exporters. They also locate representatives and agents for American firms, assist U.S. executives in all phases of their exporting, and help enforce export controls and regulations. They operate through 47 district offices located in major U.S. cities and in 124 posts in 68 foreign countries. In addition, a valued asset of the US & FCS is a group of about 525 foreign nationals, usually natives of the foreign country, who are employed in the U.S. embassy or consulate and bring with them a wealth of personal understanding of local market conditions and business practices. U.S. exporters usually tap into these services by contacting the Department of Commerce/US & FCS field office in their state (listed later in this chapter), or Office of U.S. and Foreign Commercial Service, U.S. Department of Commerce, Washington, DC 20230; 202-377-4767.

Or contact regional directors at:
Africa, Near East and South Asia   202-377-4836
East Asia and Pacific   202-377-8422
Europe   202-377-1599
Western Hemisphere   202-377-2736

FAX (Europe and Western Hemisphere)   202-377-3159
FAX (All others)   202-377-5179

7) Latest News On Foreign Opportunities:

In addition to technical reports on foreign research and development, National Technical Information Service sells foreign market airgrams and foreign press and radio translations. A free video is available explaining NTIS services. Contact: National Technical Information Service, U.S. Department of Commerce, 5285 Port Royal Road, Springfield, VA 22161, 703-487-4650.

8) Planning Services for U.S. Exporters:

In its effort to promote economic development in Third World countries, the Trade and Development Program finances planning services for development projects leading to the export of U.S. goods and services. A free pamphlet is available that describes the planning services offered by the Trade and Development Program. To obtain a copy, contact: U.S. Trade and Development Program, Department of State, Room 309 SA-16, Washington, DC 20523-1602, 703-875-4357.

9) Terrorism Abroad:

Assistance is available to companies doing business abroad to assess the security conditions and risk in certain cities and countries which may pose a threat. Contact: Private Sector Liaison Staff, Bureau of Diplomatic Security, U.S. Dept. of State, 2216 Gallows Rd., Dunn Loring, VA 22027, 703-204-6210.

10) Trade Remedy Assistance Center:
The Center provides information on remedies available under the Trade Remedy Law. It also offers technical assistance to eligible small businesses to enable them to bring cases to the International Trade Commission. Contact: ITC Trade Remedy Assistance Center, U.S. International Trade Commission, 500 E Street SW, Washington, DC 20436, 202-205-2200.

11) International Expertise:
Staff in the following offices will prove helpful as information sources regarding the international scope of their respective subject areas:

Economics:
> International Economics, Bureau of Economic Analysis, U.S. Department of Commerce, 1401 K Street, N.W., Washington, DC 20230, 202-523-0695

Productivity and Technology Statistics:
> Bureau of Labor Statistics, U.S. Department of Labor, 2 Massachusetts Ave., NE, #2150, Washington, DC 20212, 202-606-5600.

Investments and Other Monetary Matters:
> Office of Assistant Secretary for International Affairs, U.S. Department of the Treasury, Room 3430, Washington, DC 20220, 202-622-0060.

European Lifestyles:
> European Community Information Service, 2100 M Street NW, Suite 707, Washington, DC 20037, 202-862-9500

Population:
> Barbara Boyle Torrey, Chief, Center for International Research, Bureau of Census, U.S. Department of Commerce, Room 709, Scuderi Building, Washington, DC 20233, 301-763-4811

> Population Reference Bureau, Inc., 1875 Connecticut Ave., NW, #520, Washington, DC 20009, 202-483-1100.

Country Development:
> Inter-American Development Bank, 1300 NY Ave., NW, Washington, DC 20577, 202-623-1000

> International Monetary Fund, 700 19th Street NW, Washington, DC 20431, 202-623-7000

> World Bank, 1818 H St NW, Washington, DC 20433, 202-477-1234

12) National Trade Data Bank:
This is a "one-stop" source for export promotion and international trade data collected by 15 U.S. government agencies. Updated each month and released on CD-ROM, the Data Bank enables a user with and IBM-compatible personal computer equipped with a CD-ROM reader to access over 100,00 trade documents. It contains the latest Census data on U.S. imports and exports by commodity and country; the complete CIA World Factbook; current market research reports compiled by the U.S. and Foreign and Commercial Service; the complete Foreign Traders Index which has over 45,000 names and addresses of individuals and firms abroad interested in importing U.S. products; and many other data services. It is available for free at over 700 Federal Dispository Libraries and can be purchased for $35 per disc or $360 for a 12-month subscription. Contact: Economics and Statistics Administration, U.S. Department of Commerce, Washington, DC 20230, 202-377-1986.

13) Global Demographics:
The Center for International Research at the Department of Commerce complies and maintains up-to-date global demographic and social information for all countries in its International Data Base, which is accessible to U.S. companies seeking to identify potential markets overseas. The database can be purchased for $175. Contact Systems Analysis and Programming Staff, 301-763-4811.

14) International Energy Data Base:
The Office of Fossil Energy forwards prospective energy-related leads to the Agency for International Development (AID) for inclusion in its growing trade opportunities data base in an effort to reach an extended audience seeking energy-related trade opportunities. For more information on the Fossil Energy-AID Data base contact: The Office of Fossil Energy, U.S. Department of Energy, 1000 Independence Ave SW, Washington, DC 20585, 202-586-9680.

15) Product Info On 25 World Markets:
The Small Business Administration has an Export Information System (XIS), which are data reports providing specific product or service information on the top 25 world markets and market growth trends for the past five years. Contact: Office of International Trade, Small Business Administration, 409 Third St. SW, Washington, DC 20416, 202-205-7264.

16) Monitoring Investments In Developing Countries:
The Agency for International Development maintains a Trade and Investment Monitoring System (TIMS) which is a user-friendly computer-based system, providing a broad array of trade and investment information to potential U.S. investors and exporters on 42 developing countries. Contact: International Business, Agency for International Development, Room 100 SA-2, Washington, DC 20253-0229, 202-663-2660.

17) On-Line Economic Bulletin Board (EBB):
This computer-based electronic bulletin board, is an on-line sources for trade leads as well as the latest statistical releases from the Bureau of Census, the Bureau of Economic Analysis, the Bureau of Labor Statistics, the Federal reserve Board, and other Federal Agencies. Subscribers pay an annual fee, plus cost per minute. Contact EBB, Office of Business Analysis, U.S. Department of Commerce, Washington, DC 20230, 202-377-1986.

Now use your FAX machine to get the latest economic, financial, and trade news available from the U.S. government. Just dial 1-900-786-2329 from your FAX machine's touch-tone telephone and follow the simple voice instructions. EBB/FAX™ stores the complete text of many government press releases and information files. The cost for this service is 65¢ per minute.

Charges will appear on your regular phone bill and there are no registration fees. The list of files is updated every business day and the service is available 24 hours per day, 7 days per week.

18) Free Legal Assistance:
The Export Legal Assistance Network (ELAN) is a nationwide group of attorneys with experience in international trade who provide free initial consultations to small businesses on export related matters. Contact: Export Legal Assistance Network, Small Business Administration, 409 Third St. SW, Washington, DC 20416, 202-778-3080.

19) Global Learning:
U.S. Department of Education, Business and International Education Programs. The business and international education program is designed to engage U.S. schools of business language and area programs, international study programs, public and private sector organizations, and U.S. businesses in a mutually productive relationship which will benefit the Nation's future economic interest. Approximately $2.3 million annually is available to assist U.S. institutions of higher education to promote the Nation's capacity for international understanding. Typical grantee activities include executive seminars, case studies and export skill workshops. For more information contact: Center for International Education, U.S. Department of Education, Room 3053, ROB-3, 7th and D Streets, SW, Washington, DC 20202; 202-708-8764.

20) Export Counseling — SCORE, ACE:
The Small Business Administration can provide export counseling to small business exporters by retired and active business executives. Members of the Service Corps of Retired Executives (SCORE) and the Active Corps of Executives (ACE), with years of practical experience in international trade, assist small firms in evaluating their export potential and developing and implementing basic export marketing plans. For more information, contact your local SBA office listed in the government pages of your telephone book, or National SCORE Office, 1825 Connecticut Ave., NW, Suite 503, Washington, DC 20009; 202-653-6279.

21) Department of Energy — Office of International Affairs and Energy Emergencies:
The Department of Energy (DOE) promotes U.S. exports of energy goods, services and technology primarily through participation in The Committee on Renewable Energy Commerce and Trade, and The Coal and Clean Technology Export Program. The following is a list of DOE's programs and the corresponding telephone numbers to call for more information.

Committee on Renewable Energy Commerce and Trade (CORECT): Through the concept of "one-stop shopping" potential exporters can receive comprehensive advice on potential markets, financing and information on export guidelines. Call 202-586-5517.

Coal and Technology Export Program (CTEP): CTEP serves as a reservoir for international information on U.S. coal and coal technologies, as DOE's intra-departmental coordinator, and as the USG inter-agency liaison for coal companies and technology firms. Call 202-586-7297.

Bureau of International Affairs and Energy Emergencies' Eastern European Development Program: Eastern Europe is now threatened with severe energy shortfalls due to circumstances such as the Persian Gulf situation, the concern over environmentally hazardous nuclear reactors, and the decrease in oil supplies from the former Soviet Union. Call 202-586-1189.

The Export Assistance Initiative: This entity in the Bureau of International Affairs has been designed to help identify overseas opportunities for U.S. companies, identify and attempt to alleviate discriminatory trade barriers, and identify possible financing alternatives for U.S. companies. Call 202-586-0153.

Read All About It:
Helpful Publications

Basic Guide to Exporting:
This publication outlines the sequence of steps necessary to determine whether to, and how to, use foreign markets as a source of profits. It describes the various problems which confront smaller firms engaged in, or seeking to enter, international trade as well as the types of assistance available. It also provides a guide to appraising the sales potential of foreign markets and to understanding the requirements of local business practices and procedures in overseas markets. The booklet is available for $8.50 from: Superintendent of Documents, U.S. Government Printing Office, Washington, DC 20402, 202-783-3238.

Exporter's Guide to Federal Resources for Small Business:
This free booklet describes the types of assistance available for small businesses interested in international trade opportunities. It is available from any of the Small Business Administration field offices or contact: Office of International Trade, U.S. Small Business Administration, 409 3rd St., SW, 6th Floor, Washington, DC 20416, 202-205-6720.

Markets Overseas with U.S. Government Help:
This booklet describes the various agencies of the federal government which offer programs to assist those businesses involved or contemplating international trade. It is available for 50 cents from the Small Business Administration, Box 30, Denver, CO 80201.

Commercial News USA:
This publication describes a free export promotion service that will publicize the availability of your new product to foreign markets, and test foreign market interest in your new product. There is a small fee. Contact: Marketing Programs Section, Room 2106, U.S. Department of Commerce, Washington, DC 20230, 202-377-4918.

Export Programs: A Business Directory of U.S. Government Resources:
This guide provides an overview of U.S. government export assistance programs and contact points for further information and expertise in utilizing these programs. Contact: Trade Information Center, U.S. Department of Commerce, Washington, DC 20230, 1-800-872-8723.

Business America:

The principal Commerce Department publication for presenting domestic and international business news. Each weekly issue includes a "how to" article for new exporters, discussion of U.S. trade policy, news of government actions that may affect trade, a calendar of upcoming trade show, exhibits, fairs and seminars. An annual subscription is $49. Contact: Superintendent of Documents, Government Printing Office, Washington, DC 20402, 202-783-3238.

Key Officers of Foreign Service Posts: A Guide for Business Representatives:

Lists the names of key State and Commerce officers at U.S. embassies and consulates. Cost is $5 per copy. Contact: Superintendent of Documents, Government Printing Office, Washington, DC 20402, 202-783-3238.

Export Trading Company (ETC) Guidebook:

This Guidebook is intended to assist those who are considering starting or expanding exporting through the various forms of an ETC. This Guidebook will also facilitate your review of the ETC Act and export trading options and serve as a planning tool for your business by showing you what it takes to export profitably and how to start doing it. Cost is $8. Contact: Superintendent of Documents, Government Printing Office, Washington, DC 20402, 202-783-3238.

Foreign Labor Trends:

Published by the Department of Labor, theses are a series of reports, issued annually, that describe and analyze labor trends in more than 70 countries. The reports, which are prepared by the American Embassy in each country, cover labor-management relations, trade unions, employment and unemployment, wages and working conditions, labor and government, international labor activities, and other significant developments. Contact: Office of Foreign Relations, Room S 5006, 200 Constitution Ave, NW, Washington, DC 20210, 202-523-6257.

ABC's of Exporting:

This is a special issue of Business America which goes step by step through the exporting process. It explains the federal agencies and how they can help as well as providing a directory of export sources. This publication is free and is available by contacting: Trade Information Center, U.S. Department of Commerce, Washington, DC 20230, 1-800-872-8723.

Ag Exporter:

Monthly magazine published by the U.S. Department of Agriculture's Foreign Agricultural Service (FAS). The annual subscription cost is $14. Contact: Trade Assistance and Planning Office, Foreign Agricultural Service, U.S. Department of Agriculture, Washington, DC 20250; 703-756-6001.

AID Procurement Information Bulletin:

This publication advertises notices of intended procurement of AID-financed commodities. The subscription cost is free. Contact: USAID's Office of Small and Disadvantaged Business Utilization/Minority Resource Center, Washington, DC 20523-1414; 703-875-1551.

The Government Printing Office (GPO) has many more titles to choose from. For a listing, contact the GPO (listed below) by mail, or phone and ask for the Foreign Trade and Tariff Subject Bibliography (SB-123).

Government Printing Office
Superintendent of Documents
Washington, DC 20402
202-783-3238

U.S. Department of Commerce/US & FCS Field Offices

Trade experts at these 64 offices advise companies on foreign markets.

Alabama
Birmingham: 2015 2nd Ave N., 35203, 205-731-1331

Alaska
Anchorage: 222 W. 7th Ave., P.O. Box 32, 99513, 907-271-5041

Arizona
Phoenix: 230 North 1st Avenue, Room 3412, 85025, 602-379-3285

Arkansas
Little Rock: 320 W. Capitol Avenue, Suite 811, 72201, 501-378-5794

California
Los Angeles: 11000 Wilshire Blvd., Room 9200, 90024, 213-209-7104
Santa Ana: 116-A W. 4th Street, Suite 1, 92701, 714-836-2461
San Diego: 6363 Greenwich Drive, 92122, 619-557-5395
San Francisco: 450 Golden Gate Ave, Box 36013, 94102, 415-556-5860

Colorado
Denver: 680 World Trade Center, 1625 Broadway, 80202, 303-844-3246

Connecticut
Hartford: 450 Main Street, Room 610-B, 06103, 203-240-3530

District of Columbia
Washington: 14th & Constitution Ave NW #1068 HCHB, 20230, 202-377-3181

Delaware
Served by Philadelphia, Pennsylvania

Florida
Miami: 51 S.W. First Avenue, Suite 224, 33130, 305-536-5267
Clearwater: 128 North Osceola Avenue, 34615, 813-461-0011
Jacksonville: 3100 University Blvd. South, Suite 200A, 32216, 904-791-2796
Orlando: U.S. Dept of Commerce, c/o College of Business Administration, CEBAII, Room 346, 32802, 407-648-1608
Tallahassee: 107 W. Gaines St., Collins Bldg., Room 401, 32304, 904-488-6469

Georgia
Atlanta: 4360 Chamber-Dunwoody Road, 30341, 404-452-9101
Savannah: 120 Barnard Street, A-107, 31401, 912-944-4204

Hawaii
Honolulu: 300 Ala Moana Blvd., Box 50026, 96850, 808-541-1782

Idaho
Boise: 700 W. State Street, Boise, 83720, 208-334-3857

Illinois
Chicago: 55 E Monroe, Room 1406, 60603, 312-353-4450
Rockford: 515 N Court Street, 61110-0247, 815-987-8123
Palatine: W.R. Harper College, Algonquin and Roselle Rd., 60067, 312-397-3000, ext. 2532.

Selling Overseas: Foreign Markets

Indiana
Indianapolis: One N. Capitol, Suite 520, 46204-2227, 317-226-6214.

Iowa
Des Moines: 210 Walnut Street, Room 817, 50309, 515-284-4222

Kansas
Wichita: 7591 River Park Pl., Suite 580, 727 N. Waco, 67203, 316-269-6160

Kentucky
Louisville: 601 West Broadway, Room 636B, 40202, 502-582-5066

Louisiana
New Orleans: 2 Canal Street, Room 432, 70130, 504-589-6546

Maine
Augusta: 77 Sewall Street, 04330, 207-622-8249

Maryland
Baltimore: U.S. Custom House, 40 South Bay, Room 413, 21202, 301-962-3560

Massachusetts
Boston: World Trade Center, Suite 307, 02210, 617-565-8563

Michigan
Detroit: 477 Michigan Avenue, Room 1140, 48226, 313-226-3650
Grand Rapids: 300 Monroe N.W., Room 409, 49503, 616-456-2411

Minnesota
Minneapolis: 110 S. 4th Street, Room 108, 55401, 612-348-1638

Mississippi
Jackson: 300 Woodrow Wilson Blvd., Room 328, Jackson Mall Office Center, 39213, 601-965-4388

Missouri
St. Louis: 7911 Forsyth Blvd., Suite 610, 63105, 314-425-3302
Kansas City: 601 East 12th Street, Room 635, 64106, 816-426-3141

Montana
Served by Boise, Idaho

Nebraska
Omaha: 11133 O Street, 68137, 402-221-3664

Nevada
Reno: 1755 E. Plumb Lane, #152, 89502, 702-785-5203

New Hampshire
Served by Boston, Massachusetts

New Jersey
Trenton: 3131 Princeton Pike Bldg. 6, Suite 100, 08648, 609-989-2100

New Mexico
Albuquerque: 625 Silver SW, 3rd Floor, 87102, 214-767-0542
Santa Fe: Economic Development and Tourism Department, 1100 St. Francis Dr., 87503, 505-827-0264

New York
Buffalo: 111 West Huron Street, Room 1312, Federal Building, 14202, 716-846-4191
Rochester: 111 East Avenue, 14604, 716-263-6480
New York: U.S. Dept. of Commerce, 26 Federal Plaza, Foley Square, 10278, 212-264-0634

North Carolina
Greensboro: 324 West Market Street, 27402, 919-333-5345

North Dakota
Served by Omaha, Nebraska

Ohio
Cincinnati: 550 Main Street, Room 9504, 45202, 513-684-2944
Cleveland: 668 Euclid Avenue, Suite 600, 44114, 216-522-4750

Oklahoma
Oklahoma City: 6601 Broadway Extension, 73116, 405-231-5302
Tulsa: 440 S. Houston Street, Room 505, 74127, 918-581-7650

Oregon
Portland: Suite 242, One World Trade Center, 121 SW Salmon Street, 97204, 503-326-3001

Pennsylvania
King of Prussia: 475 Allendale Road, 19406, 215-962-4980
Pittsburgh: 1000 Liberty Avenue, Room 2002, 15222, 412-644-2850

Puerto Rico
San Juan: Room 659 Federal Building, 00918, 809-766-5555

Rhode Island
Providence: 7 Jackson Walkway, 02903, 401-528-5104, ext. 22

South Carolina
Columbia: 1835 Assembly Street, Suite 172, 29201, 803-765-5345
Charleston: Room 128, JC Long Bldg, 9 Liberty Street, 29424, 803-724-4361

South Dakota
Served by Omaha, Nebraska

Tennessee
Nashville: 404 James Robertson Parkway, Suite 1114, 37219, 615-736-5161
Memphis: 22 North Front Street, Suite 200, 38103, 901-544-4137
Knoxville: 301 E. Church Ave., 37915, 615-549-9268

Texas
Dallas: 1100 Commerce Street, Room 7A5, 75242, 214-767-0542
Austin: 816 Congress, First City Center Bldg., Room 1200, 78701, 512-482-5939
Houston: 515 Rusk Street, Room 2625, 77002, 713-229-2578

Utah
Salt Lake City: Suite 105, 324 South State Street, 84111, 801-524-5116

Vermont
Served by Boston, Massachusetts

Virginia
Richmond: 400 North 8th Street, Room 8010, 23240, 804-771-2246

Washington
Seattle: 3131 Elliott Avenue, Suite 290, 98121, 206-442-5616
Spokane: West 808 Spokane Falls Blvd., Room 625, 99201, 509-353-2922

West Virginia
Charleston: 405 Capitol St., Suite 809, 25301, 304-347-5123

Wisconsin
Milwaukee: 517 E. Wisconsin Avenue, Room 606, 53202, 414-291-3473

Wyoming
Served by Denver, Colorado

State Government Assistance To Exporters

Last year state governments spent approximately $40,000,000 to help companies in their state sell goods and services overseas. This figure increased almost 50% over the previous two years. During the same period of time, federal monies devoted to maximizing companies' export capabilities remained virtually constant. This is another indicator of how the states are fertile sources of information and expertise for large and small businesses.

The underlying mission of these offices is to create jobs within their state. Usually their approach is to help companies develop overseas marketing strategies or to offer incentives to foreign companies to invest in their state. The major state trade development programs and services are outlined below.

1) Marketing Research and Company Intelligence:

All of the states can provide some degree of overseas marketing information. The level of detail will depend upon the resources of the state. Thirty-two states (except for Alabama, Arizona, California, Delaware, Hawaii, Idaho, Kansas, Maryland, Minnesota, Nebraska, Nevada, New Jersey, New York, South Dakota, Texas, Washington, West Virginia, and Wyoming) say they will do customized market studies for companies. Such studies are free or available for a small fee. For example, the Commonwealth of Virginia will do an in-depth market study for a company and charge $1,000. They estimate similar surveys done by the private sector cost up to $20,000. Virginia relies on MBA students and professors within the state university system who get credit for working on such projects.

Even if a state does not perform customized studies, the trade office within the department of economic development will prove to be an ideal starting place for marketing information. Some states which do not undertake comprehensive studies for prospective exporters will do a limited amount of research for free. These offices can also point to outside sources as well as the notable resources at the federal level which may be able to assist. And those states with offices overseas also can contact these foreign posts to identify sources in other countries. Moreover, many of the offices have people who travel abroad frequently for companies and also work with other exporters. Such bureaucrats can be invaluable for identifying the exact source for obtaining particular market or company intelligence.

2) Company and Industry Directories:

Many states publish directories which are helpful to both exporters and researchers. Some states publish export/import directories which show which companies in the state are exporters and what they sell as well as which are importers and what they buy. Because many of the trade offices are also interested in foreign investment within their state, many publish directories or other reference sources disclosing which companies in their state are foreign owned, and by whom. Other state publications may include export service directories which list organizations providing services to exporters such as banks, freight forwarders, translators, and world trade organizations. Some also publish agribusiness exporter directories which identify agricultural-related companies involved in exporting.

3) Free Newsletters:

All but 14 states (i.e., Alabama, Colorado, Delaware, Florida, Hawaii, Indiana, Louisiana, Minnesota, Mississippi, Michigan, Kentucky, Ohio, North Carolina, South Dakota, and Tennessee) generate international newsletters or publish a special section within a general newsletter on items of interest to those selling overseas. These newsletters are normally free and cover topics like new trade leads, new rules and regulations for exports, and details about upcoming overseas trade shows. Such newsletters can also be a source for mailing lists for those whose clients include exporters. We haven't specifically investigated the availability of such lists, but remember that all states have a law comparable to the federal Freedom of Information Act which allows public access to government data.

4) Overseas Contacts:

Finding a foreign buyer or an agent/distributor for a company is one of the primary functions of these state offices. How they do this varies from state to state. Many sponsor trade fairs and seminars overseas to attract potential buyers to products produced in their state. The more aggressive trade promotion offices may organize trade missions and escort a number of companies overseas and personally help them look for buyers or agents. Many will distribute a company's sales brochures and other literature to potential buyers around the world through their overseas offices. Some states work with the federal government and explore general trade leads and then try to match buyers with sellers. Others will cultivate potential clients in a given country and contact each directly.

5) Export Marketing Seminars:

Most all of the states conduct free or modestly priced seminars to introduce companies to selling overseas. Some of the courses are held in conjunction with the regional International Trade Administration office of the U.S. Commerce Department. The course may be general in nature, for example, *The Basics of Exporting*, or focused on specific topics such as *International Market Research Techniques, Letters of Credit, Export Financing*, or *How to do Business with Israel*.

6) State Grants & Loans for Exporters:

Many states offer financial assistance for those wishing to export. Some states even provide grants (money you do not have to pay back) to those firms which cannot afford to participate in a trade mission or trade fair. This means that they provide money to those companies which are just trying to develop a customer base overseas. More typically the state will help with financing of a sale through state-sponsored loans and loan guarantees, or assistance in identifying and applying for federal or commercial export financing.

7) Trade Leads Databases:

Because these offices provide mostly services, there are not many opportunities for them to develop databases. However, their trade leads program is one area where a number of offices have computerized. These databases consist of the names and addresses along with some background information on those overseas companies which are actively searching or might be interested in doing business with companies within the state. The number of leads in such a system could range from several hundred to five or ten thousand. None of these states seem to have made such information available on machine readable formats to those outside the office. But, in light of state Freedom of Information statutes, it may be worth making a formal inquiry if you have an interest. The states which have computerized their trade leads include: Alabama, California, Colorado, Connecticut, Florida, Georgia, Hawaii, Indiana, Iowa, Minnesota, Mississippi, Missouri, Nebraska, New Jersey, New York, North Carolina, North Dakota, Ohio, Pennsylvania, South Dakota, Tennessee, West Virginia, and Wisconsin.

State International Trade Offices

The foreign cities in parentheses after the telephone number are those locations where the state maintains a trade office.

Alabama
International Development and Trade Division, Alabama Development Office, State Capitol, Montgomery, AL 36130, 205-263-0048; FAX: 205-265-5078 (Hanover, **Germany**; Seoul, **Korea**; Tokyo, **Japan**;)

Alaska
International Trade Director, Office of International Trade, Department of Commerce and Economic Development, 3601 C Street, Suite 798, Anchorage, AK 99503, 907-561-5585; FAX: 907-561-4557 (Tokyo, **Japan**; Seoul, **Korea**)

Arizona
International Trade, Department of Commerce, 3800 N. Central, Phoenix, AZ 85012, 602-280-1371

Arkansas
International Marketing, Department of Economic Development, One State Capitol Mall, Little Rock, AR 72201, 501-682-7690 (Brussels, **Belgium**; Tokyo, **Japan**; Taipei, **Taiwan**)

California
California State World Trade Commission, 1121 L Street, Suite 310, Sacramento, CA 95814, 916-324-5511; FAX: 916-324-5791 (Tokyo, **Japan**; London, **England**; **Hong Kong**; Frankfort, **Germany**; Mexico City, **Mexico**)

Export Finance Office, 107 South Broadway, Room 8039, Los Angeles, CA 90012, 213-620-2433; FAX: 213-620-6102

Colorado
International Trade Office, Department of Commerce and Development, 1625 Broadway, Suite 680, Denver, CO 80202, 303-892-3850

Connecticut
International Division, Department of Economic Development, 865 Brook St., Hartford, CT 06067, 203-258-4256 (Frankfort, **Germany**; Tokyo, **Japan**)

Delaware
Delaware Development Office, Division of Economic Development, 99 Kings Highway, Box 1401, Dover, DE 19903, 302-736-4271; FAX: 302-736-5749

District of Columbia
D.C. Office of International Business, 1250 I St., Suite 1003, Washington, DC 20005, 202-757-1576

Florida
Florida Department of Commerce, 366 Collins Building, Tallahassee, FL 32399-2000, 904-488-6124; FAX: 904-487-1407 (Toronto, **Canada**; Brussels, **Belgium**; Seoul, **Korea**; Frankfort, **Germany**; Tokyo, **Japan**; London, **England**)

Georgia
Department of Industry, Trade and Tourism, Suite 1100, 285 Peachtree Center Ave., Atlanta, GA 30303, 404-656-3545; FAX: 404-656-3567 (Brussels, **Belgium**; Tokyo, **Japan**; Toronto, **Canada**; Seoul, **Korea**)

Hawaii
International Services Branch, Department of Planning and Economic Development, P.O. Box 2359, Honolulu, HI 96804, 808-548-7719

Idaho
Economic Development, Division of Economic and Community Affairs, 700 W. State Street, Boise, ID 83720, 208-334-2470; FAX: 208-334-2783

Illinois
International Business Division, Illinois Department of Commerce and Community Affairs, 100 W. Randolph Street, Suite 3-400, Chicago, IL 60601, 312-814-7166 (Brussels, **Belgium**; San Paulo, **Brazil**; Hong Kong; Osaka and Tokyo, **Japan**; Warsaw, **Poland**; Toronto, **Canada**; Shenyaang, **China**)

Illinois Export Council, 321 N. Clark St. #550, Chicago, IL 60610, 312-793-4995

Indiana
International Trade Division, Department of Commerce, One North Capitol, Suite 700, Indianapolis, IN 46204, 317-232-3527 (Brussels, **Belgium**; Tokyo, **Japan**; London, **England**; Toronto, **Canada**; Tiapie, **Taiwan**; Beijing, **China**; Seoul, **Korea**)

Iowa
International Trade, Iowa Department of Economic Development, 200 East Grand Avenue, Des Moines, IA 50309, 515-242-4743; FAX: 515-242-4749 (Frankfurt, **Germany**; Hong Kong; Tokyo, **Japan**)

Kansas
Kansas Department of Commerce, 400 W. 8th, Suite 500, Topeka, KS 66603, 913-296-4027 (Tokyo, **Japan**; Brussels, **Belgium**)

Kentucky
Office of International Marketing, Kentucky Commerce Cabinet, Capitol Plaza Tower, 24th Floor, Frankfort, KY 40601, 502-564-2170 (Tokyo, **Japan**; Brussels, **Belgium**)

Louisiana
Office of Commerce and Industry, P.O. Box 94185, Baton Rouge, LA 70804-9185, 504-342-9232; FAX: 504-342-5389 (Mexico City, **Mexico**; Tiapie, **Taiwan**; Seoul, **Korea**)

Maine
International Trade, Maine World Trade Commission, State House, Station 59, Augusta, ME 04333, 207-289-2656

Maryland
Maryland International Division, World Trade Center, 401 East Pratt Street, 7th Floor, Baltimore, MD 21202, 301-333-4295 (Brussels, **Belgium**; Tokyo, **Japan**; Hong Kong)

Massachusetts
Office of International Trade, 100 Cambridge Street, Room 902, Boston, MA 02202, 617-367-1830

Michigan
U.S./International Trade Division, Manufacturing Development Group, Michigan Department of Commerce, P.O. Box 30017, Lansing, MI 48909, 517-373-1054; FAX: 517-335-2521 (Toronto, **Canada**; Lago, **Nigeria**; Hong Kong; Brussels, **Belgium**; Tokyo, **Japan**)

Minnesota
Minnesota Trade Office, 1000 World Trade Center, 30 E. 7th Street, St. Paul, 55101, 612-297-4222; FAX: 612-296-3555 (Oslo, **Norway**; Stockholm, **Sweden**)

Mississippi
Department of Economic Development, P.O. Box 849, Jackson, MI 39205, 601-359-3552 (Seoul, **Korea**; Tokyo, **Japan**; Hong Kong; Frankfort, **Germany**; Tiapie, **Taiwan**)

Missouri
Export Development Office, Department of Commerce and Economic Development, P.O. Box 118, Jefferson City, MO 65102, 314-751-4855 (Tokyo, **Japan**; Dusseldorf, **Germany**; Seoul, **Korea**; Tiapie, **Taiwan**)

Montana
International Trade Office, Montana Department of Commerce, 1424 9th Avenue, Helena, MT 59620, 406-444-3923 (Tokyo, **Japan**; Calgary, **Canada**; Tiapie, **Taiwan**; Kumamoto, **Japan**)

Nebraska
Department of Economic Development, 301 Centennial Mall South, P.O. Box 94666, Lincoln, NE 68509, 402-471-3111

Nevada
Commission of Economic Development, Capital Complex, Carson, NV 89710, 702-687-4325

New Hampshire
Foreign Trade and Commercial Development, Department of Resources and

Economic Development, 172 Pembroke Street, P.O. Box 856, Concord, NH 03301, 603-271-2591

New Jersey
Division of International Trade, Department of Commerce and Economic Development, 153 Halsey Street, Newark, NJ 07102, 201-648-3518 (Tokyo, **Japan**)

New Mexico
Economic Development Division, Economic Development and Tourism Department, 1100 St. Francis Drive, Joseph Montoya Building, Santa Fe, NM 87503, 505-827-0307; FAX: 505-827-0263

New York
International Division, Department of Commerce, 1515 Broadway, 51st Floor, New York Department of Economic Development, New York, NY 10036, 212-827-6100 (Tokyo, **Japan**; Wiesbaden, **Germany**; London, **England**; Milan, **Italy**; Ontario and Montreal, **Canada**; **Hong Kong**)

North Carolina
International Division, Department of Commerce, 430 North Salisbury Street, Raleigh, NC 27611, 919-733-7193 (Dusseldorf, **Germany**; **Hong Kong**; Tokyo, **Japan**)

North Dakota
International Trade Consultant, Economic Development Commission, 1833 East Expressway, Bismarck, ND 58504, 701-224-2810

Ohio
International Trade Division, Department of Development, 77 S. High Street, P.O. Box 1001, Columbus, OH 43266, 614-466-5017 (Brussels, **Belgium**; Tokyo, **Japan Hong Kong**, Toronto, **Canada**)

Oklahoma
International Trade Division, Oklahoma Department of Commerce, 6601 Broadway Extension, Oklahoma City, OK 73116, 405-841-5220

Oregon
International Trade Division, Oregon Economic Development Department, #1 World Trade Center, Suite 300, 121 Salmon Street, Portland, OR 97204, 503-229-5625, or 1-800-452-7813 (Tokyo, **Japan**)

Pennsylvania
International Projects Manager, Bureau of International Commerce, 433 Forum Building, Harrisburg, PA 17120, 717-783-5107 (Frankfurt, **Germany**; Tokyo, **Japan**;)

Puerto Rico
P.R. Department of Commerce, P.O. Box 4275, San Juan, PR 00936, 809-721-3290

Rhode Island
Business and Industry Representative, Department of Economic Development, 7 Jackson Walkway, Providence, RI 02903, 401-277-2601 (**Hong Kong**)

South Carolina
International Business Development, South Carolina State Development Board, P.O. Box 927, Columbia, SC 29202, 803-737-0400; FAX: 803-737-0481 (Tokyo, **Japan**; Frankfort, **Germany**)

South Dakota
South Dakota International Trade Center, Capitol Lake Plaza, Pierre, SD 57501, 605-773-5032

Tennessee
Export Promotion Office, Department of Economic and Community Development, Rachel Jackson Building, 7th Floor, Nashville, TN 37219, 615-741-5870

Texas
International Business Development Department, Texas Department of Commerce, P.O. Box 12728, Austin, TX 78711, 512-472-5059 (Mexico City, **Mexico**)

Utah
Export Development Committee, Economic and Industrial Development Division, 324 S. State St., Salt Lake City, UT 84111, 801-538-3631 (Tokyo, **Japan**)

Vermont
International Business, Department of Economic Development, Pavilion Office Building, Montpelier, VT 05602, 802-828-3221

Virginia
Director of International Marketing, 2 James Center, P.O. Box 798, Richmond, VA 23206, 804-371-8100 (Tokyo, **Japan**; Brussels, **Belgium**)

Washington
Domestic and International Trade Division, Department of Trade and Economic Development, 2001 Sixth Ave, 26th Floor, Seattle, WA 98121, 206-464-7143; FAX: 206-464-7222 (Tokyo, **Japan**)

West Virginia
Governor's Office of Community and Industrial Development, State Capitol, Room 517, Charleston, WV 25305, 304-348-2243; FAX: 304-348-0449 (Tokyo, **Japan**)

Wisconsin
Bureau of International Business Development, Department of Development, 123 West Washington Avenue, Madison, WI 53702, 608-266-1767 (Frankfurt, **Germany**; **Hong Kong**)

Wyoming
International Trade Division, Department of Commerce, Herschler Building, Cheyenne, WY 82002, 307-777-6412; FAX: 307-777-5840

Overseas Travel: Business Or Pleasure

The following sources and services will be helpful to anyone who is on business or vacation in any foreign country.

1) **Arts America:**
The U.S. Information Agency assists qualified artists and performers in arranging private tours overseas. Its aim is to present a balanced portrayal of the American scene. Some of the past activities have included a major exhibition of American crafts shown in China, a modern dance company in the USSR, Spain, and Portugal, and a jazz ensemble in Nigeria, Senegal and Kenya. Contact: Program Manager, Office of the Associate Director for Programs, United States Information Agency, 301 4th Street SW, Room 567, Washington, DC 20547, 202-619-4779.

2) **Travel Overseas On Government Expense:**
The U.S. Speakers program will pay experts, who can contribute to foreign societies' understanding of the United States, to travel abroad and participate in seminars, colloquia or symposia. Subjects treated by the program include economics, international political relations, U.S. social and political processes, arts and humanities, and science and technology. To see if you qualify contact: U.S. Speakers, Office of Program Coordination and Development, U.S. Information Agency, 301 4th Street SW, Room 550, Washington, DC 20547, 202-619-4764.

3) **Citizens Arrested Overseas:**
The Arrest Unit at the State Department monitors arrests and trials to see that American citizens are not abused; acts as a liaison with family and friends in the United States; sends money or messages with written consent of arrestee; offers lists of lawyers; will forward money from the United States to

detainee; tries to assure that your rights under local laws are observed. The Emergency Medical and Dietary Assistance Program includes such services as providing vitamin supplements when necessary; granting emergency transfer for emergency medical care; and short-term feeding of two or three meals a day when arrestee is detained without funds to buy his or her own meals. Contact: Arrests Unit, Citizens Emergency Center, Overseas Citizens Service, Bureau of Consular Affairs, U.S. Department of State, 2201 C Street NW, Room 4811, Washington, DC 20520, 202-647-5225.

4) Citizens Emergency Center:
Emergency telephone assistance is available to United States citizens abroad under the following circumstances:

Arrests: 202-647-5225 (see details above)

Deaths: 202-647-5225; notification of interested parties in the United States of the death abroad of American citizens; assistance in the arrangements for disposition of remains.

Financial Assistance: 202-647-5225; repatriation of destitute nationals, coordination of medical evacuation of non-official nationals from abroad; transmission of private funds in emergencies to destitute United States nationals abroad when commercial banking facilities are unavailable (all costs must be reimbursed)

Shipping and Seamen: 202-647-5225; protection of American vessels and seamen

Welfare and Whereabouts: 202-647-5225; search for nonofficial United States nationals who have not been heard from for an undue length of time and/or about whom there is special concern; transmission of emergency messages to United States nationals abroad. For other help contact: Overseas Citizen Services, Bureau of Consular Affairs, U.S. Department of State, 2201 C Street NW, Washington, DC 20520, 202-647-5225

5) Country Information Studies:
For someone who wants more than what the typical travel books tell about a specific country, this series of books deals with more in depth knowledge of the country being visited. Each book describes the origins and traditions of the people and their social and national attitudes, as well as the economics, military, political and social systems. For a more complete listing of this series and price information, contact: Superintendent of Documents, U.S. Government Printing Office, Washington, DC 20402, 202-783-3238.

6) Foreign Country Background Notes:
Background Notes on the Countries of the World is a series of short, factual pamphlets with information on the country's land, people, history, government, political conditions, economy, foreign relations, and U.S. foreign policy. Each pamphlet also includes a factual profile, brief travel notes, a country map, and

a reading list. Contact: Public Affairs Bureau, U.S. Department of State, Room 4827A, 2201 C Street NW, Washington, DC 20520, 202-647-2518 for a free copy of *Background Notes* for the countries you plan to visit. This material is also available from the: Superintendent of Documents, U.S. Government Printing Office, Washington, DC 20402, 202-783-3238. Single copies cost in the range of $1.50 to $56 for a set.

7) Foreign Language Materials:
The Defense Language Institute Foreign Language Center (DLIFC) has an academic library with holdings of over 100,000 books and periodicals in 50 different foreign languages. These materials are available through the national interlibrary loan program which can be arranged through your local librarian.

8) Foreign Language Training:
The Foreign Service Institute is an in-house educational institution for foreign service officers, members of their families and employees of other government agencies. It provides special training in 50 foreign languages. Its instructional materials, including books and tapes, are designed to teach modern foreign languages. Instruction books must be purchased from Superintendent of Documents, U.S. Government Printing Office, Washington, DC 20402, 202-783-3238. Tapes must be purchased from the National Audiovisual Center, National Archive, Order Section/AV, 8700 Edgeworth Drive, Capitol Heights, MD 20743, 301-763-1891.

9) Free Booklets for Travelers:
The following booklets and guides are available free of charge:

Travel Information: Your Trip Abroad:
Contains basic information such as how to apply for a passport, customs tips, lodging information and how American consular officers can help you in an emergency. Publications Distribution, Bureau of Public Affairs, U.S. Department of State, 2201 C Street NW, Room 5815A, Washington, DC 20520, 202-647-9859.

Customs Information:
Provides information about custom regulations both when returning to the U.S. as well as what to expect when traveling to different parts of the world. Customs Office, P.O. Box 7118, Washington, DC 20044.

Visa Requirements of Foreign Governments:
Lists entry requirements of U.S. citizens traveling as tourists, where and how to apply for visas and tourist cards. Passport Services, Bureau of Consular Affairs, U.S. Department of State, 1425 K Street NW, Room G-62, Washington, DC 20524, 202-647-0518.

10) Passport Information:
A recorded telephone message provides general information on what is needed when applying for a U.S. passport. Call 202-647-0518. U.S. citizens and nationals can apply for passports at all passport agencies as well as those post offices and federal and state courts authorized to accept passport applications.

Legislation:
How To Monitor Federal Legislation

The U.S. Congress is accustomed to answering questions and sharing information with the public. Here is how you can quickly learn about any bill or resolution pending before the House of Representatives or Senate:

Free Legislation Database

This Bill Status Office can tell you within seconds the latest action on any federal legislation. Every bill and resolution for the current session as well as all House and Senate legislation dating back to 1975 are contained in LEGIS, a computerized database. When you call, it is best to give a key word or phrase (i.e., product liability, hazardous waste) which will help the congressional aides search LEGIS. This office can provide such detailed information as:

Have any bills been introduced covering a given topic?
Who is the sponsor of the bill?
How many cosponsors are there?
When was it introduced?
Which committees have the bills been referred to?
Have any hearings been held?
Has there been any floor action?
Has a similar bill been introduced in the other chamber?
Has there been any action on the other side of the Hill?
Have the House and Senate agreed to a compromise bill?
Has the bill been sent to the White House?
Has the President signed or vetoed the bill?
What is the PL (public law) number?

Telephone assistance is free, and printouts from LEGIS are available for $.20 per page but must be picked up at the Bill Status Office. However, by making arrangements with your Representative's or Senator's office, you can avoid this nominal charge and also have the printout mailed to your home or office. Contact: LEGIS, Office of Legislative Information, House Office Building Annex 2, 3rd & D Streets, SW, Room 696, Washington, DC 20515; 202-225-1772.

Bill Sponsor's Legislative Assistant

The aide to the Senator or Representative who is the sponsor of a particular bill is the best person to contact next. The Bill Status Office can tell you the sponsor, and the Capitol Hill Switchboard at 202-224-3121 can transfer you to the appropriate office; then ask to speak to the person in charge of the particular bill. Usually, this congressional aide will offer to send you a copy of the bill, a press announcement, and other background information. Don't loose this opportunity to get your first of many predictions about the likelihood of the bill becoming law.

Committee Staff

Committees and subcommittees are the real work centers of the Congress. After you touch base with the Bill Status Office (LEGIS), it is wise to double-check that information with the House or Senate committees which have jurisdiction over the legislation you are tracking. The Capitol Hill Switchboard at 202-224-3121 can connect you with any committee. Once you reach the committee staffer who handles the bill in question, you are now in a position of obtaining the following information:

Are hearings expected to be held?
Has the subcommittee or committee chair promised a vote on the measure?
What is the timetable for committee "markup" and consideration of amendments?
What is the Administration's position on the legislation?
Has the committee filed its report on the bill?
Is there any action on a similar proposal on the other side of the Hill?

You can get free copies of House bills, resolutions, and House committee reports by sending a self-addressed mailing label to the House Document Room, 2nd & D Sts., SW, Room B18, Washington, DC 20515; 202-225-3456. Similarly, you can direct your requests for Senate documents to the Senate Document Room, Senate Hart Bldg., Room B-04, Washington, DC 20510; 202-224-7860. Public laws, often called slip laws, can be obtained from either the House or Senate Document Rooms, but call the Bill Status Office to get the public law number. You can get printed copies of hearings by contacting the committee which conducted the inquiry, but expect several months lag time before it becomes available.

If the legislation you are concerned about is scheduled for action on the floor of the House or Senate, you can monitor its activity by the hour by listening to the following recorded messages:

House of Representatives Cloakroom
Democrat 202-225-7400
Republican 202-225-7430

Senate Cloakroom
Democrat 202-224-8541
Republican 202-224-8601

Play Constituent

Your Representative's or Senator's office also can help with your questions about specific bills, particularly when you have difficulty getting through to committee or subcommittee staffers. Remember that Members of Congress are eager to serve their constituents, especially for simple requests such as sending you copies of bills or new public laws. The Capitol Hill Switchboard Operator at 202-224-3121 can connect you with the Washington office of your Representative and Senators.

Additional Tools for Monitoring Federal Legislation

There are sophisticated variations of the free LEGIS database described above. One reason for the growth of commercial databases is that direct online access to LEGIS is limited to Members of Congress and their staff. The following databanks cover every bill or resolution pending before the current session:

* Electronic Legislative Search System

This online system tracks all current federal legislation (as well as all 50 states) and also provides introductory bill summaries and legislative histories. Contact: Commerce Clearinghouse, 4025 W. Peterson Avenue, Chicago, IL 60646, 312-583-8500.

* Legi-Slate

This computerized system provides information based primarily on the *Congressional Record*, the official edited transcript of the House and Senate floor proceedings. This database also contains committee schedules, all recorded votes and analyses voting patterns. Contact: Legi-Slate, 777 N.Capitol St.NE, Suite 900, Washington, DC 20002; 202-898-2300.

* Washington Alert Service

This database covers all bills introduced in the U.S. Congress and includes information on committee schedules, release of committee reports and other documents, all recorded votes as well as full text of the publication, *CQ Weekly Report*. Contact: Congressional Quarterly, 1414 22nd Street NW, Washington, DC 20037; 202-887-8500.

There are plenty of specialized trade publications designed to help lobbyists stay apprised of developments on the Hill. Online access is available to some of these newsletters, for instance, the Bureau of National Affairs' *Daily Tax Advance* and *Daily Congressional and Presidential Calendar* (BNA OnLine, 1227 25th St., NW, Room 3-268, Washington, DC 20037; 1-800-862-4636 or 202-452-4453). Another example is Budgetrack, a database produced by the editors of *Aviation Week and Space Technology*, which monitors the budget for the U.S. Defense Department and NASA from presidential submission to final congressional action (Budgetrack is available online from Data Resources, Inc., 1750 K St., NW, Washington DC 20006).

The American Enterprise Institute, the Brookings Institution, and other Washington-based think tanks generate position papers on specific legislative initiatives and often will share their information with the public. Other useful outside sources which can shed light on activities on the Hill are both small, specialized trade associations and large ones, for example, the National Paint and Coating Association and the U.S. Chamber of Commerce. How successful you are at getting these organizations to help you depends in large measure on how good you are on the telephone.

Congressional Experts

An estimated 4,000 legislative assistants and committee aides fall into the category of "professional staff." Because these congressional aides often draft bills and amendments and play a critical role in the negotiations with special interest groups, they are valuable sources of information, but some are much more open and candid than others. When dealing with these experts, remember they are at the beck and call of an elected official. It doesn't hurt to appeal to their egos and offer to call them when they aren't quite so busy.

Investigations and Special Reports

There are approximately 50 congressional committees and subcommittees which do not have legislative authority but serve as watchdogs with responsibility for reviewing existing laws. Some examples include the Senate Permanent Subcommittee on Investigations, House Select Committee on Aging, the Joint Economic Committee, and the House Science and Technology Subcommittee on Investigations and Oversight. These congressional panels conduct full-scale hearings on a wide range of subjects. A complete listing of these committees appears in the U.S. Congress Committees section. Some hearings conducted by the House Energy and Commerce Subcommittee on Oversight and Investigations during 100th Congress include the following examples:

"Biotechnology: Vaccine Development"
"EPA's Asbestos Regulations"
"Sulfites"
"Ground Water Monitoring"
"Unfair Foreign Trade Practices"
"SEC and Corporate Audits"
"SEC: Oversight of the Edgar System"

Several reports issued in 1985 by this House Subcommittee on Oversight and Investigations include:
The Computer Revolution and the US Labor Force
Drug Diversion: Prescription Drug Diversion and the American Consumer
Industrial Import Shock: Policy Challenges of the 80s

Many of these committees will put you on their mailing lists to receive notices of upcoming hearings as well as their *Committee Calendar*, which lists all of the hearings held during the previous year.

Congressional Caucuses

Approximately 100 non-legislative caucuses formed by Members of Congress serve as in-house think tanks. Some of these coalitions, such as the Congressional Clearinghouse on the Future provide information to the public. The House Steel Caucus, the Senate Coal Caucus, the Congressional Port Caucus, and others work to get their particular legislative initiatives through the Congress. The staff directors of these organizations can be good sources because these congressional aides have access to all government studies and also have close contact with industry and special interests that the caucus is going to bat for.

Many of these "informal groups" dissolve after work on its legislative priorities is completed, so you should expect that these organizations come and go. A list of these organizations appear next in U.S. Congress Committees section. Note that the Capitol Hill Switchboard at 202-224-3121 or your Member of Congress can help you find out if a particular special interest caucus exists. A list of the current caucuses appears in the U.S. Congress Committee section.

Federal Agencies Legislative Affairs Offices

Every federal department and agency has an office which makes the Administration's case for the President's proposed budget or legislation. These offices within the executive branch usually are termed the "Offices of Legislative Affairs," which concentrate on particular bills, in contrast to an agency's own Office of Congressional Relations, which tends to respond to requests made by lawmakers or their staff. The office of legislative affairs also makes available written testimony by agency officials who appeared as witnesses at congressional hearings.

Arms of Congress

In addition to the 47 House and Senate committees, the following four organizations produce volumes of information and reports to aid lawmakers. These studies and recommendations by these arms of Congress are available to the public.

* **Congressional Budget Office**
  House Office Building Annex 2
  2nd and D Streets, SW
  Washington, DC 20515   202-226-2800
Scorekeeping reports, special studies and other economic assessments are all available free to the public.

* **Congressional Research Service (CRS)**
  Library of Congress
See also the Current Events and Homework Chapter for a comprehensive listing of all CRS studies which cover practically every current event topic. You must arrange to get copies of any CRS publications through your Member of Congress.)

* **General Accounting Office**
  Office of Public Affairs Room 7049
  441 G Street NW
  Washington, DC 20548   202-275-2812
Reports and audit information about every government program.

* **Office of Technology Assessment**
  U.S. Congress
  Information Center
  Washington, DC 20510   202-228-6150
Studies and executive summaries are available on a whole range of subjects.

Tracking State Legislation

* See also Information Starting Places; State Information Starting Places Chapter
* See also Current Events and Homework Chapter

Bill Status Information

Most state legislatures maintain an office responsible for providing bill status information to the public. In Ohio, for example, a bank of telephone reference experts answer questions about current or past legislation on any given subject. The researchers rely on their own files and also have access to a computerized database updated by the Senate Clerk's office. Usually these offices can search their databases or indexes in several ways, by keyword or phrase, by specific subject, or by state senator or representative.

About half of the legislatures can send you this information in the form of a computer printout free of charge. In those states which do not operate a central bill status office, it is necessary to contact the Clerk of the House for information on bills pending before the House and similarly a call to the Secretary or Clerk of the Senate for updates on legislation pending before that body. Many legislatures have toll-free numbers which can be accessed only if you are calling from inside the state. Most of the State House hotlines operate just during the regular session of the legislature and, as you might expect, some of the "800" numbers change from one session to the next.

Your initial call to the bill status office will lead you to the appropriate committees, and if no action has been taken on a particular bill, this legislative information office can provide you with the sponsor of the legislation whom you can call directly for more details.

Copies of Bills and Other Legislative Documents

In most states, the legislative information office can send you copies of bills. Indiana is the only state that charges $.10 per page if the bill is more than 10 pages long. All states print the bills at the time of introduction. Over half reprint the amended legislation after committee action, and about two-thirds of all chambers print the legislation after the floor vote. Unlike the U.S. Congress, legislative documentation is skimpy when it comes to committee hearings as well as floor debate. Only about a third of all legislative bodies tape all committee sessions. You can make arrangements with the Clerk's office to listen to the tapes, and some states, like the Minnesota House, sell audio tapes of committee meetings and floor debates for $12.50 per copy.

Advanced Strategy for Monitoring One or All 50 State Legislatures

Coverage of a state legislature can be substantially enhanced in a number of ways; some are inexpensive; others can be costly:

* Clipping Service:
Newspapers, especially those published in the state capitol, can prove to be a cost effective way of staying informed provided the issues of concern with are controversial or of major significance to capture attention by the local media.

* Local Chamber of Commerce:
This organization may offer information about certain issues it is following on behalf of the business community.

* Stringers:
Often expensive, but there may be no substitute for hiring someone who is in frequent contact with legislators and is a familiar face in the document rooms and statehouse corridors.

* Governor's Legislative Liaison Office:
On major legislative initiatives and politically "hot" issues, try telephoning this office.

* National Conference of State Legislators (NCSL):
Although this organization serves legislators, the staff will respond to requests from the public. The Conference maintains a list of reports and studies by investigative committees in all 50 states. Access to its in-house database may be possible in the future. This national organization of state legislators and legislative staff whose aims are to improve the quality and effectiveness of state legislators, to ensure states a strong, cohesive voice in the federal decision-making process and to foster interstate communication and cooperation. Contact either of the two offices at 1560 Broadway, Suite 700, Denver, CO 80202; 303-830-2200; or 444 North Capitol St., NW, Suite 515, Washington, DC 20001; 202-624-5400.

* Council of State Governments/State Information Center:
This arm of the Council of State Governments publishes several useful directories, including *The Book of States, State Administration Officials Classified By Function*, and *State Legislative Leadership Committees and Staff*. Its database may soon be available to the public. Contact: State Information Center, Council of State Governments, P.O. Box 11910, Iron Works Pike, Lexington, KY 40578; 606-231-1830.

* Commerce Clearing House (CCH):
CCH offers the "State Legislative Reporting Service" as well as the Electronic Legislative Search System. The Reporting Service allows you to select only those legislatures you are interested in, whereas the online search system tracks all current legislation in all 50 states. Contact: CCH, 4025 West Peterson Avenue, Chicago, IL 60646; 312-583-8500.

* Information for Public Affairs:
This private firm offers online access to its database containing the status of legislation pending before the current session of

all 50 state legislatures. Contact: PAI, 1900 14th St., Sacramento, CA 95814; 916-444-0840.

* Other Private Legislative Reporting Services:
Legi-Tech Corporation and other firms specialize in tracking one or two statehouses. About half of the legislatures are covered by such information brokers.

Reports And Resources Available From State Legislatures

A trend among state legislatures is the creation of special investigative committees which have responsibility for oversight and often the power to subpoena. These watchdogs usually have permanent full-time staff and produce reports throughout the year. Frequent contact with these committees is necessary to stay informed about their activities.

Here is a sampling of reports issued by the Virginia Joint Legislative Audits and Review Committee:

Outpatient Care in Virginia
Medical Assistance Programs in Virginia: An Overview
Homes for Adults in Virginia
Social Services (including day care) in Virginia
Vehicle Cost Responsibility in Virginia
Highway Construction, Maintenance, and Transit Needs
The Occupational and Professional Regulatory System
Consolidation of Office Space in Northern Virginia
Special Report: Use of State-Owned Aircraft
Towns in Virginia
Virginia's Correctional System: Population Forecasting

Even those legislatures that compress their work into sixty or ninety day sessions are active year-round. Information about hearings, meetings, and reports produced throughout the Interim can be provided by each state house legislative information office.

State Legislatures: Bill Status Information Offices

You will find more than 50 information offices listed here because some state houses do not have one centralized legislature reference office.

Alabama

Senate Bill Status, 11 S.Union, Room 709, New State House, Montgomery, AL 36130; 205-242-7826. This office can respond to questions about all Senate bills and refer you to the appropriate committee, document room, etc.

House Bill Status, 11 S.Union, Room 512, New State House, Montgomery, AL 36130; 205-242-7630. This office can provide information on all bills pending before the House of Representatives and can refer you to the appropriate committees, document rooms, etc.

Alaska

Legislative Information, 130 Seward St., Suite 313, Juneau, AK 99801-2197; 907-465-4648. This office can provide information on the status of House and Senate bills. It can do subject searches by accessing a database but at this time Legislative Information cannot provide computer printouts. Copies of bills will be sent out by this office.

Arizona

Information Desk, House of Representatives, State House, 1700 West Washington Street, Phoenix, AZ 85007; 602-542-4221. This Information Desk is the best starting point to learn the status of all bills pending before the House of Representatives. This office will refer you to the appropriate committees, document room, etc.

Senate Information Desk, State House, 1700 West Washington Street, Phoenix, AZ 85007; 602-542-3559. This Information Desk maintains current information on all bills pending before the Arizona Senate. This office will refer you to the appropriate committees, document rooms, etc.

Arkansas

Office of Legislative Counsel, State Capitol Building, Room 315, Little Rock, AR 72201; 501-682-1937. This office can provide status information on all legislation pending before the House of Representatives and the Senate. It also has scheduling information and can you refer you to the appropriate committees, document rooms, etc.

California

Office of the Chief Clerk, State Assembly, State Capitol, Room 3196, Sacramento, CA 95814; 916-445-3614. This office can respond to questions regarding legislation pending before the State Assembly and Assembly committees. This office can refer you to the appropriate offices in the State Capitol, such as the document rooms.

Secretary of the Senate, State Capitol, Room 3044, Sacramento, CA 95814; 916-445-4251. This office can provide information about bills pending before the Senate and the Senate committees. The Secretary of the Senate also will refer you to appropriate offices in the State Capitol, such as where to obtain copies of Senate bills.

Colorado

Legislative Information Center, State Capitol Building, Room 0101, 200 E. Colfax Ave., Denver, CO 80203; 303-866-3055. This office can provide information on the status of both House and Senate bills. The Legislative Information Center also can send you copies of bills as well as mail out status sheets which target on bills pertaining to a specific subject.

Connecticut

Bill Information Room, Law & Legislative Reference Dept., State Library, 231 Capitol Avenue, Hartford, CT 06106; 203-566-5736. This office can provide information about both House and Senate bills and send you copies of bills. Besides doing a key word or subject search, this office can mail you a printout of all legislation pertaining to one topic.

Delaware

Division of Research, Legislative Counsel, Legislative Hall, Dover, DE 19901; 302-739-4114; 1-800-282-8545. This office can provide status information on both House and Senate bills and send you copies of bills. It can access a legislative computerized database and do searches for free. The toll-free number operates year-round.

Florida

Legislative Information Division, 11 W. Madison St., Room 704, Tallahassee, FL 32399-1400; 904-488-4371; 1-800-342-1827. This office can provide status information on all House and Senate bills. It can send you single copies of up to 10 bills and mail out printouts of all House and Senate bills pertaining to a specific subject.

Georgia

Clerk of the House, 309 State Capitol, Atlanta, GA 30334; 404-656-5015. This office can provide up-to-date information on all House bills and send you copies of House bills. The Clerk of the House also will search its database to tell you all legislation that has been introduced on a specific topic.

Secretary of the Senate, State Capitol, Room 353, Atlanta, GA 30334; 404-656-5040; 1-800-282-5803. This office can respond to questions about all bills

Legislation

pending before the Georgia Senate. The Secretary of the Senate can send you copies of Senate bills and search its database for legislation pertaining to a specific subject.

Hawaii

Clerk of the House, State Capitol of Hawaii, Honolulu, HI 96813; 808-586-6400. This office can respond to questions about bills pending before the House and refer you to appropriate offices in the State Capitol, such as the document room.

Clerk of the Senate, State Capitol of Hawaii, Honolulu, HI 96813; 808-586-6720. This office can provide status information on all legislation pending before the Hawaii Senate. It can refer you to the appropriate offices in the State Capitol, such as the document room.

Idaho

Legislative Information Center, State House Room 301, Boise, ID 83720; 208-334-2411. This office can give you information on the status of all House and Senate bills. It also can send you copies of bills as well as a printout of all legislation pertaining to a specific topic.

Illinois

Clerk of the House, State Capitol Building, Room 424, Springfield, IL 62706; 217-782-6010; 1-800-252-6300. This office can respond to questions about both House and Senate bills. It can provide you with copies of bills. The Clerk's office is able to send you printouts; for example, a list of all bills sponsored by one legislator.

Indiana

Legislative Information, Legislative Services Agency, 302 State House, Indianapolis, IN 46204; 317-232-9856. The agency can give you bill status information and do searches by key word, subject or legislator. Legislative Information can send you copies of bills, but charges $.15 per page.

Iowa

Legislative Public Information Office, State Capitol, Room 16, Des Moines, IA 50319; 515-281-5129. This office can provide information on all House and Senate bills and can send you copies of bills. It can access the computerized database and mail you a printout of all legislation pertaining to a specific subject.

Kansas

Legislative Reference, State Library, State Capitol Third Floor, Topeka, KS 66612; 913-296-2149; 1-800-432-3924. This office can tell you the status of all current House and Senate legislation as well as provide bill histories. Legislative Reference can send you copies of bills and voting records.

Kentucky

Bill Status, State Capitol, Room 80, Frankfort, KY 40601; 502-564-8100; 1-800-633-4171. This office can provide information on House and Senate bills pending before the legislature. It can also send you copies of bills.

Louisiana

Legislative Research Library, House of Representatives, P.O. Box 94012, Baton Rouge, LA 70804-9012; 504-342-2431; 1-800-272-8186. During the session call toll-free PULS Line (if out-of-state, 504-342-2425) for bill status information and send you copies of House and Senate bills. When the legislature is not in session contact the Legislative Research Library.

Maine

Legislative Information Office, State House, Room 314, Station 115, Augusta, ME 04333; 207-289-1692. This office can respond to questions about House and Senate bills and do key word or subject searches of its database.

Maryland

Legislative Information Desk, Dept. of Legislative Reference, 90 State Circle, Annapolis, MD 21401; 410-841-3886; 1-800-492-7122. This office can provide

status information on all House and Senate bills and send you copies of bills. It also can provide you with a printout of all bills which pertain to a specific subject area.

Massachusetts

Citizen Information Service, 1 Ashburton Place, 16th Floor, Boston, MA 02108; 617-727-7030. This office can provide bill status information and supply copies of bills but you must know the bill number. To obtain bill numbers and other information contact the Clerk of the House which is listed below.

Clerk of the House, House of Representatives, State House, Boston, MA 02133; 617-722-2356. This office can respond to questions about House and Senate bills and will refer you to the document room and other appropriate offices within the State House.

Michigan

Clerk of the House, State Capitol, Lansing, MI 48909; 517-373-0135. This office can provide information on the status of House bills and can do searches of its database to identify legislation which pertains to a specific subject. It will refer you to the House document room for copies of bills.

Secretary of the Senate, P.O. Box 30036, Lansing, MI 48933; 517-373-2400. This office can provide Senate bill status information and also can send you copies of bills.

Minnesota

House Index Office, State Capitol Building, Room 211, St Paul, MN 55155; 612-296-6646. This office can tell you the status of all House bills but will refer you to the Chief Clerk's office for copies of all House bills. It can search its database to identify all bills that pertain to a specific subject.

Senate Index Office, State Capitol Building, Room 231, St Paul, MN 55155, 612-296-2887-- This office can provide bill status information on all Senate legislation and will refer you to the Secretary of the Senate if you want to obtain copies of bills. It can search its database and identify all bills pertaining to a specific subject.

Mississippi

House Docket Room, PO Box 1018, New Capitol Room 305, Jackson, MS 39215; 601-359-3358. This office can tell you the status of all House bills and send you copies of proposed laws pending before the House.

Senate Docket Room, PO Box 1018, New Capitol Room 308, Jackson, MS 39215; 601-359-3229. This office can respond to questions about bills pending before the Mississippi Senate and send you copies of Senate bills.

Missouri

House Information Bill Status, State Capitol, Room 307B, Jefferson City, MO 65101; 314-751-3659. This office can provide information on bills pending before the House and will refer you to the appropriate offices within the State Capitol such as the document room.

Senate Research, State Capitol Room B-9, Jefferson City, MO 65101; 314-751-4666. This office can respond to questions about bills pending before the Senate and will refer you to the appropriate offices such as the document room.

Montana

Legislative Counsel, State Capitol, Room 138, Helena, MT 59620; 406-444-3064, 1-800-333-3408. The in-state toll-free number may change in subsequent sessions of the Montana legislature. The Legislative Counsel office can respond to inquiries year-round and send you copies of bills.

Nebraska

Hotline, Office of the Clerk, State Capitol, Room 2018, Lincoln, NE 68509; 402-471-2709; 1-800-742-7456. This office operates an in-state hotline during the session that can provide information on all bills pending before this unicameral legislature. The Clerk can respond to questions year-round.

Nevada

Chief Clerk of the Assembly, Legislative Building, Room 124, 401 S. Carson St., Carson City, NV 89710; 702-885-5739. This office can provide information about the status of bills pending before the Assembly. The Chief Clerk will refer you to the appropriate offices in the State Capitol such as the documents room or the Clerk of the Senate.

New Hampshire

State Library Government, Information Bureau, 20 Park Street, Concord, NH 03301; 603-271-2239. This office can respond to questions about House and Senate bills pending before the legislature. It can send you copies of bills and search its database for bills pertaining to specific subject areas.

New Jersey

Office of Legislative, Services - Bill Room, Executive Statehouse, Room #6, Statehouse CN068, Trenton, NJ 08625; 609-292-6395; 1-800-792-8630. This office can provide information about House and Senate legislation and can send you copies of bills. It will refer you to other offices within the State House if necessary.

New Mexico

Legislative Counsel, State Capitol, Room 334, Sante Fe, NM 87503; 505-986-4600. This office can provide bill status information on House and Senate legislation. It will refer you to the appropriate offices within the State Capitol such as the document room.

New York

Public Information Office, Room 202 LOB 2nd Floor Empire State Plaza, Albany, NY 12248; 518-455-4218; 1-800-342-9860. This office can provide information on the status of House and Senate bills and send you copies of bills. It may refer you to your local library if you want a search done to identify all bills which pertain to a specific subject.

North Carolina

Clerk of the House, State Legislative Building, Room 2320, Raleigh, NC 27601; 919-733-7760. This office can provide information about House and Senate bills and will refer you to the appropriate offices within the State Capitol such as where to obtain copies of bills.

North Dakota

Legislative Counsel Library, State Capitol, Bismarck, ND 58505; 701-224-2916. This office can provide information about House and Senate bills year-round and will refer you to appropriate offices in the State Capitol. The legislature maintains an in-state toll-free number during the biannual session.

Ohio

Legislative Information, State House, Columbus, OH 43266-0604; 614-466-8842; 1-800-282-0253. This office can provide information on the status of House and Senate legislation and do subject searches. This telephone bank of researchers will route your requests (i.e., copies of bills). In-state toll-free access is available throughout the year.

Oklahoma

Chief Clerk, House of Representatives, State Capitol Bldg., Oklahoma City, OK 73105; 405-521-2711, 1-800-522-8502. This office can respond to questions about bills pending before the House and Senate. It will refer you to the appropriate offices within the State Capitol.

Oregon

Legislative Library, State Capitol S-347, Salem, OR 97310; 503-378-8871, 1-800-332-2313. This office can provide information on House and Senate bills year-round. During the biannual session the legislature offers an in-state toll-free number for bill information.

Pennsylvania

Legislative Reference Bureau, History Room, Main Capitol Building, Room 648, Harrisburg, PA 17120-0033; 717-787-2342. This office can provide information on House and Senate bills be consulting its card index and computerized database. It will refer you to the appropriate offices, for example, where to obtain copies of bills.

Rhode Island

State Library, State House Room 208, Providence, RI 02903; 401-277-2473. This office can provide you with information on the status of House and Senate bills and send you copies of bills. It will refer you to the appropriate legislators or committees.

South Carolina

Legislative Information Systems, Room 112, Blatt Building, 1105 Pendleton St., Columbia, SC 29201; 803-734-2923, 1-800-922-1539. This office can respond to inquiries about House and Senate bills and will refer you to the appropriate offices such as where to obtain copies of bills. It can do subject searches but is unable to send out a printout.

South Dakota

Public Information Clerk, Legislative Research Counsel, State Capitol Building, 500 East Capitol, Pierre, SD 57501; 605-773-4498, 605-773-4296. Clare Cholik can provide information on the status of House and Senate bills. She can access a computerized database and do a search to identify legislation which pertains to a specific subject.

Tennessee

Office of Legislative Services, Room G-20, War Memorial Bldg, Nashville, TN 37243; 615-741-3511. This office can provide information on House and Senate bills and will send you copies of bills. It can identify all legislation pending on specific subjects.

Texas

Legislative Reference Library, PO Box 12488, Capitol Station, Austin, TX 78711; 512) 463-1252. This office can provide information on the status of all House and Senate bills. It can search its database to identify all legislation which pertains to a specific subject. It will refer you to the appropriate offices such as the document room.

Utah

Legislative Research and General Counsel, 436 State Capitol, Salt Lake City, UT 84114; 801-538-1032. This office can respond to questions about House and Senate bills. It will refer you to the appropriate offices within the State Capitol.

Vermont

Clerk of the House, Attn: Cathleen Cameron, State House, Montpelier, VT 05633-5501; 802-828-2247. Ms. Cameron can provide you with information on legislation pending before the House and do subject searches by accessing a computerized database. She will refer you to the appropriate offices in the State House.

Clerk of the Senate, State House, Montpelier, VT 05633-5501; 802-828-2241. This office can respond to questions about legislation pending before the Senate and will refer you to the appropriate legislators, committees, document rooms, etc.

Virginia

Legislative Information, House of Delegates, P.O. Box 406, Richmond, VA 23203; 804-786-6530. This office can provide information on House and Senate bills and can send you copies of bills. It can consult a printed index which is updated daily to identify bills which pertain to a specific subject.

Washington

House Workroom, Legislative Building, Third Floor Capitol Campus, Olympia, WA 98504; 206-786-7780; 1-800-562-6000. This office can provide information on the status of bills pending before the House. It can also provide copies of bills.

Legislation

The toll-free number (out of state should call 206-786-7763) is in operation only during the session.

Senate Workroom, Legislative Building AS32, Third Floor Capitol Campus, Olympia, WA 98504; 206-786-7592; 1-800-562-6000. This office can provide information on bills pending before the Senate and can supply you with copies of bills. An in-state toll-free number (out of state call 206-786-7763) provides both House and Senate bill information but only during the session.

West Virginia

Clerk of the House, House of Delegates, 1900 Kanawha Blvd. E, Bldg.1, Room M212, Charleston, WV 25305-0470; 304-340-3200. This office can respond to questions about legislation pending before the House of Delegates and House committees. It will refer you to the appropriate offices in the State Capitol such as where to obtain legislative documents.

Clerk of the Senate, 1900 Kanawha Blvd. E, Bldg., Room M-215, Charleston, WV 25305-0470; 304-357-7800. This office can provide information on the status of bills pending before the Senate. It will refer you to the appropriate offices in the State Capitol.

Wisconsin

Legislative Reference Bureau, 100 N. Hamilton St., POB 2037, Madison, WI 53701-2037; 608-266-0341; 1-800-362-9472. The legislature operates a Legislative Hotline during the session (if calling from inside Madison, dial 608-266-9960). The Legislative Reference Bureau can respond to questions year-round will refer you to the document room, etc.

Wyoming

Legislative Service Office, State Capitol Building, Room 213, Cheyenne, WY 82002; 307-777-7881, 1-800-342-9570 within Wyoming. When the Wyoming legislature is not in session it is necessary to contact this office. During the session, bill status questions are best directed to the two offices noted below.

Senate Information Clerk, State Capitol Building, Cheyenne, WY 82002; 307-777-6185; 307-777-7711. This office can respond to questions about the status of bill pendings before the Senate. It will refer you to the Bill Room to obtain copies of bills.

House Information Clerk, State Capitol Building, Cheyenne, WY 82002; 307-777-7765; 307-777-7852. This office can provide current information on legislation pending before the House. It will refer you to the proper offices in the State Capitol, for instance, the Bill Room.

Government Auctions and Surplus Property: Federal Auctions

Looking for a bargain? Year round, the federal government offers hundreds of millions of dollars worth of property and goods -- from animals to real estate -- at remarkable prices. The Customs Service sells seized property -- jewelry, camera, rugs -- anything brought in from another country. The IRS auctions off everything imaginable -- boats, cars, businesses. The U.S. Postal Service sells unclaimed merchandise, including lots of books.

There is one story to inspire: a New Yorker bought surplus parachutes from the Pentagon and became a supplier selling clothesline cord. If you are looking for a business, try the Small Business Administration, which sells equipment and businesses it has acquired through foreclosure. Want a good deal on a house? U.S. Department of Housing and Urban Development offers repossessed homes -- sometimes for practically nothing -- on government foreclosures.

Very few people know about these unique bargains because the federal government doesn't advertise them. Described below are 30 of Uncle Sam's Red Tag Specials. Contact the appropriate offices for more information. And remember, if you don't find what you want, stay at it. This is ongoing, and new merchandise and property are coming in all the time.

* Burros and Horses: Bureau of Land Management

Nevada State Office, Bureau of Land Management
U.S. Department of the Interior
850 Harvard Way   702-785-6400
Reno, NV 89520-0006   FAX: 702-673-6010

Or contact your local Bureau of Land Management office. The "Adopt-a-Horse" program is aimed at keeping wild herds at in the West at manageable levels, and allows individuals around the country to purchase a wild horse for $125 or a burro for $75. The animals usually have their shots. Aside from the purchase price you only need pay for shipping. If you live west of the Mississippi, call the Program Office above to find out which of the 12 adoption satellites are nearest you. If you live east of the Mississippi, call 703-461-1365 to arrange an adoption. Representatives of the BLM travel around the country, so you don't have to travel to Wyoming to participate. The only qualifications for adoption are that you have appropriate facilities to house the animal, that you are of legal age in your state, and that you have no record of offenses against animals. The horses and burros may not be used for any exploitative purposes such as rodeos or races, nor may they be re-sold. Upon adoption, you sign an agreement to that effect, and no title of ownership is given until one year after an adoption. Animals are usually from two to six years in age, and must be trained. The offices listed above have a brochure called *So You'd Like to Adopt a Wild Horse or Burro* on the "Adopt-a-Horse" program that gives more details.

* Christmas Trees, Seedling, Wooden Poles and Posts: Bureau of Land Management

U.S. Department of the Interior
Bureau of Land Management
Division of Forestry
1849 C Street, N.W.
Washington, DC 20240   202-653-8864
or   U.S. Forest Service   202-205-1389

Contact your local Bureau of Land Management (BLM), U.S. Department of Interior. In the 11 Western states, the Bureau of Land Management has a program for obtaining low-cost Christmas trees from Federal lands. By contacting your local BLM office, you may obtain a permit for a nominal fee (usually $10) to cut a tree for your own use. You will be given a map with directions as to which are permissible areas for tree-cutting. Non-profit organizations may also qualify. Non-profit may get free use permits and cut larger amounts. Trees must be for their own use and may not be resold at fundraisers.

In addition, under the Minor Forest Products program, you may collect or cut specified small trees for use as poles or posts; or, you may obtain cactus or plant seedlings from areas of natural growth where there are abundant supplies -- again at a very low cost. These items are free for non-profit organizations for their own use. Permits for commercial usage may also be available. Cost depends on market value. Below are the addresses and phone numbers of Regional Bureau of Land Management Offices.

Alaska
222 W. 7th Ave. #13, Anchorage, AK 99513-5076; 907-271-5555.

Arizona
3707 N. 7th Street, P.O. Box 16563, Phoenix, AZ 85011; 602-640-5504.

California
2800 Cottage Way, E-2841, Sacramento, CA 95825; 916-978-4746.

Colorado
2850 Youngfield St., Lakewood, CO 80215; 303-239-3670.

Eastern States
7450 Ballston Blvd., Springfield, VA 22153; 703-440-1700.

Idaho
3380 Americana Terrace, Boise, ID 83706; 208-384-3014.

Montana
Granite Tower, 222 N. 32nd St., P.O. Box 36800, Billings, MT 59107; 406-255-2913.

Nevada
850 Harvard Way, P.O. Box 12000, Reno, NV 89520-0006; 702-785-6586.

New Mexico
1474 Rodeo Road, P.O. Box 27115, Santa Fe, NM 87502-0115; 505-438-7508.

Oregon
1300 NE 44th Ave., P.O. Box 2965, Portland, OR 97208-2965; 503-280-7287.

Utah
324 South State Street, Suite 301, Salt Lake City, UT 84111-2303; 801-539-4019.

Wyoming
2515 Warren Ave., P.O. Box 1828, Cheyenne, WY 82003; 307-775-6011.

* Federal Depository Insurance Corporation (FDIC)

Federal Depository Insurance Corporation
550 17th St. NW
Washington, DC 20429   202-393-8400
or   Office of Liquidations
1776 F Street NW

Washington, DC 20429   202-898-7343

The FDIC sells at auctions the furnishings and equipment of failed commercial banks. Consult the blue pages in your phone directory for the regional FDIC office nearest you. Each regional office handles their own personal property disposal. Professional auctioneers are contracted to auction off the accumulation of desks, calculators, chairs, computers and other furnishings that banks normally have. These auctions will be advertised in the auction section or classifieds of local newspapers.

The FDIC also holds open for offers costly commercial property and real estate. For a full catalog of these listings across the country, which also includes homes over $250,000 call 1-800-678-3342 or 1-800-445-3683. They will send *The Liquidation Book* which is the marketing list that is most current. All the property the FDIC has to sell is in this book, but if you are interested in bidding on a house under $250,000, it is wise to ask them for the phone number of the FDIC sales office in your area that is in charge of selling them, and then contact them directly. About 97 percent of the listings in it are commercial offerings such as hotels, offices, and industries. Sales of commercial real estate are advertised nationally by the FDIC in such papers as *The Wall Street Journal*.

* FHA Money May Be Waiting For You

DHUD-Distributive Shares Division
451 7th Street, SW
Washington, DC 20410
HUD Locator   202-708-1422
DHUD-Insurance Operation Division   703-235-8117
                                                        1-800-697-6967

If you or someone in your family has successfully paid off a mortgage on a house, there may be money waiting for you at the Department of Housing and Urban Development. HUD oversees the Federal Housing Administration (FHA) which insures mortgages that your bank lends to house buyers. Each year FHA predicts how many people will default on their loans, and based on that prediction, they calibrate how much mortgage insurance home buyers will pay during that year. If it turns out that there are fewer loan defaults than FHA predicted, those borrowers that have continued to pay their mortgages have what are called "Mutual Mortgage Dividend" checks coming to them upon completion of the loan agreement. Call 703-235-8117 if you think you are due a one time mortgage insurance premium refund or a distributive share.

Another way you may qualify for an FHA insurance refund is to have taken out, say, a 30 year mortgage and paid the entire FHA insurance premium up front instead of in installments over the entire period of the loan. If you have completed the loan agreement in less than 30 years, you may have money coming back to you since you didn't use the insurance for the entire 30 years you've already paid for. In most cases, though, you have to carry a loan for at least 7 years to qualify for a dividend, and the longer you have a loan, the more likely it is that you will qualify for a dividend check.

In these cases where you prepay all of your mortgage insurance premium up front, your bank should let you know that you may eventually be eligible for a mutual mortgage refund upon fulfillment of the loan agreement. Also, after you have paid off your loan, your bank should notify HUD, who in turn should notify you if you have any refund coming, usually within six months. However, if HUD cannot locate you, they will add your name to a list of other individuals who cannot be located but have HUD money coming to them.

Through the Freedom of Information Act many individuals have gotten their hands on copies of this list from HUD and gone around the country tracking down the people and charging them fees to recover this HUD money. Depending on the size of the original loan, your dividend refund could be several thousand dollars, and since some of these "bounty hunters" may ask for up to 50% of the refund just for making a phone call that you could make yourself, you could be losing out on a substantial sum of money by letting them do it. In fact, all you have to do to get the same list the bounty hunters are using is to call 703-235-8117. DHUD staff will mail to you, free of charge, an "information package" which contains the names of all the mortgagors in the state in which you reside (or request the list for), forms and basic information you would need to apply for a refund.

If you feel you may have money coming to you, or if a member of your family who took out a mortgage is now deceased and you are an heir, try to locate the original loan contract number, and then make a few calls. To apply for a refund you will need the loan number and FHA case number, which you can find on the Recorded Deed of Purchase, kept at your local county courthouse.

* Firewood: U.S. Forest Service

U.S. Forest Service
Timber Management
Department of Agriculture
14th & Independence Ave. S.W.
Box 96090
Washington, DC 20090-6090
Operations and Technology Information   202-205-0855/0857

Contact your nearest National Forest Office (list below) to find out about the firewood program and to learn which national forest is near you. Also, ask these regional offices about firewood from state forestry organizations and private timber companies. Ask about availability of firewood before you make the trip. In any National Forest, you may pick up downed or dead wood for firewood for a nominal charge of $5 per cord, $10 minimum fee, after requesting a permit from the Forest of your choice. You may phone to request the permit, and must have it in your possession while collecting the wood. The Forest Service allows you to gather 2-10 cords worth of wood. Six cords are equal to 12 pick-up truck loads. Wood may not be collected for commercial purposes. All permits to cut wood are issued locally, so you must purchase permits directly from the district ranger. Regional offices do not sell permits.

Northern Region I
Federal Building, 200 East Broadway St., P.O. Box 7669, Missoula, MT 59807; 406-329-3316. Includes Northern Idaho and Montana.

Rocky Mountain Region II
11177 West Eighth Ave., P.O. Box 25127, Lakewood, CO 80225; 303-236-9427. Includes Colorado, Nebraska, South Dakota, Eastern Wyoming.

Southwestern Region III
Federal Building, 517 Gold Ave. S.W., Albuquerque, NM 87102; 505-842-3306. Includes New Mexico, Arizona.

Intermountain Region IV
Federal Building, 324 25th St., Ogden, UT 84401; 801-625-5605. Includes Southern Idaho, Nevada, Utah, and Western Wyoming.

Pacific Southwest Region V
630 Sansome St., San Francisco, CA 94111; 415-705-2870. Includes California, Hawaii, Guam, Trust Territories of the Pacific Islands.

Pacific Northwest Region VI
333 SW First Avenue, P.O. Box 3623, Portland, OR 97208; 503-326-3626. Includes Oregon and Washington. (Mt. Hood is the most popular national forest and may be sold out of permits. Call them in advance at 503-666-0700. Try also the state and private timber units at 503-326-2727 or the U.S. Forest Service at 503-326-2877 or 503-326-2957.)

Southern Region VIII
1720 Peachtree Rd. N.W., Atlanta, GA 30367; 404-347-4177. Includes Alabama, Arkansas, Florida, Georgia, Kentucky, Louisiana, Mississippi, North Carolina, Puerto Rico and the Virgin Islands, South Carolina, Tennessee, Texas, Virginia.

Eastern Region IX
310 West Wisconsin Ave., Room 500, Milwaukee, WI 53203; 414-297-3600. Includes Illinois, Indiana, Ohio, Michigan, Minnesota, Missouri, New Hampshire, Maine, Pennsylvania, Vermont, West Virginia, Wisconsin, and Fingerlakes section of New York.

Alaskan Region X
Federal Office Building, 709 West Ninth St., P.O. Box 21628, Juneau, AK 99802-1628; 907-586-7840. Abundance of wood results in extensive free-use permits.

* Homes: Department of Agriculture (USDA)

Farmers Home Administration (FmHA)
Single Family Housing Division
Loan Processing
14th & Independence Ave., S.W., Room 5334
Washington, DC 20250   202-720-1474

Contact your local Farmers Home Administration Office. There are 1900 around the country. The Farmers Home Administration, part of the Department of Agriculture, makes low-interest loans available to qualified applicants to purchase homes or farms in rural areas (among other things). Rural settings are small towns with a population under 10,000. Check to see if the locale you are interested in qualifies. Sometimes areas of up to 25,000 in population are approved. Farmers Home Administration is also charged with disposing of properties that are foreclosed. First, they make any necessary repairs to the properties, then offer them for sale to people who have the same qualifications as those applying for FmHA loans (based on income, credit worthiness and other criteria). Eligible applicants also qualify to purchase the properties at special low FmHA interest rates (as low as 1%). If no eligible applicants purchase a property, it is then put up for sale to the general public at competitive prices. If the property is not sold within 10 days, it may be reduced by 10%. Sales to the general public may be through FmHA offices or through private real estate brokers. FmHA "eligible applicants" must reside on the property purchased; but if no such eligible buyers are available, other buyers may use it for investment or rental purposes. A separate program applies for farms. This program is designed to serve people of modest income and good credit who don't have enough to make a down payment on a home. Credit evaluation is done on the most recent 12 months. Bankruptcy is not looked at after 36 months. The current loan budget is one-third of what is was in the 70's. This program is being changed to eventually act as insurers to guarantee loans from professional lenders. Applicants may work in a city if their home is rural.

* Homes: Department of Housing and Urban Development

U.S. Department of Housing and Urban Development (HUD)
451 7th St. S.W.
Washington, DC 20410-4000

HUD Locator	202-708-1422
Multi-Family Property Dispositions	202-708-1220
Single-Family Property Dispositions	202-708-1832

HUD homes are properties HUD owns as a result of paying the balance on foreclosed FHA insured home mortgages. Any qualified buyer can purchase a HUD home. Generally, your monthly mortgage payment should be no more than 29% of your monthly gross income. Many HUD homes require only a 3% down payment. You can move into some HUD homes with a $100 down payment. HUD will pay the real estate brokers commission up to the standard 6% of the sales price. HUD may also pay your closing costs. HUD homes are priced at fair market value. Consult your local newspapers for HUD listings; or, your regional HUD office, listed below; or, the real estate broker of your choice.

HUD's Property Disposition facilities are located within ten regional offices and various field offices around the country. Contact the nearest office for details (see listing below). Frequently, HUD will advertise upcoming auctions of foreclosed properties in a local newspaper. The properties may be apartments, condominiums, or various kinds of single-family homes. The condition of these properties varies widely, including some that are little more than shells; and that, of course, affects the price. Some may be located in less than desirable neighborhoods; but others may end up being bargains, either as investments or personal residences. Bids are placed through private real estate brokers, who then submit them to HUD. Some offers for HUD homes are made to the seller and there may be negotiations. Offers for other HUD homes are done by bids placed during an "Offer Period." If you bid the full asking price, it may be accepted immediately. Otherwise, all the bids are opened at the close of the "Offer Period." The highest bidder wins. Contact the participating broker of your choice to show you the property and submit your bid. HUD broker contracted services are free to prospective buyers. Earnest money is a flat scaled fee ranging from $500-$2000 and must accompany the bid. Bidders must furnish their own financing. HUD stresses that properties sell "as is," so HUD will not make any repairs. It is up to a potential buyer to determine the value and condition, although the listings will state major problems.

Newspaper ads list houses that will be available for the next ten days, as well as others that did not sell in previous auctions. Listings include addresses, number of bedrooms and bathrooms, and suggested prices. Remember that HUD contracts are binding and non-negotiable: once your bid has won, there's no turning back. For a step by step buying guide to purchasing HUD owned homes, call the HUD Homeline, 1-800-767-4483, and request the brochure, *A Home of Your Own.* To learn about other programs at HUD that may be useful to you, call 202-708-0685.

HUD Region I (Boston)
Thomas P. O'Neill Federal Building, 10 Causeway St., Room 375, Boston, MA 02222-1092; 617-565-5102. Field offices are located in: Bangor, ME; Burlington, VT; Hartford, CT; Manchester, NH; and Providence, RI. Ask for Property Distribution Division in these offices.

Region II (New York)
HUD New York Regional Office, 26 Federal Plaza, New York, NY 10278-0068; 212-264-4771. Field offices located in: Albany, NY; Buffalo, NY; Camden, NJ; Hato Rey, PR; and Newark, NJ.

Region III (Philadelphia)
HUD Philadelphia Regional Office, Liberty Square Building, 105 South Seventh St., Philadelphia, PA 19106-3392; 215-597-2645. Field offices located in: Baltimore, MD; Charleston, WV; Pittsburgh, PA; Richmond, VA; Washington, DC; and Wilmington, DE.

Region IV (Atlanta)
HUD Atlanta Regional Office, Richard B. Russell Building, 75 Spring St., S.W., Atlanta, GA 30303-3388; 404-331-4127. Field offices located in: Birmingham, AL; Columbia, SC; Coral Gables, FL; Greensboro, NC; Jackson, MS; Jacksonville, FL; Knoxville, TN; Louisville, KY; Memphis, TN; Nashville, TN; Orlando, FL; and Tampa, FL.

Region V (Chicago)
HUD Chicago Regional Office, 626 West Jackson Blvd., Chicago, IL 60606-5601; 312-353-6950. Field offices are located in: Cincinnati, OH; Cleveland, OH; Columbus, OH; Detroit, MI; Flint, MI; Grand Rapids, MI; Indianapolis, IN; Milwaukee, WI; Minneapolis/St. Paul, MN; and Springfield, IL.

Region VI (Fort Worth)
HUD Fort Worth Regional Office, 1600 Throckmorton, P.O. Box 2905, Fort Worth, TX 76113-2905; 817-885-5531. Field Offices are located in: Albuquerque, NM; Dallas, TX; Houston, TX; Little Rock, AR; Lubbock, TX; New Orleans, LA; Oklahoma City, OK; San Antonio, TX; Shreveport, LA; and Tulsa, OK.

Region VII (Kansas City)
HUD Kansas City Regional Office, Professional Building, 1103 Grand Ave., Kansas City, MO 64106-2496; 816-374-6438. Field offices are located in: Des Moines, IA; Omaha, NE; St. Louis, MO; Topeka, KS.

Region VIII (Denver)
HUD Denver Regional Office, Executive Tower Building, 1405 Curtis St., Denver, CO 80202-2349; 303-844-4959. Field offices are located in: Casper, WY; Fargo, ND; Helena, MT; Salt Lake City, UH; and Sioux Falls, SD.

Region IX (San Francisco)
HUD San Francisco Regional Office, Phillip Burton Federal Building and U.S. Courthouse, 450 Golden Gate Ave., P.O. Box 36003, San Francisco, CA 94102-3448; 415-556-0796. Field offices are located in: Fresno, CA; Honolulu, HI; Las Vegas, NV; Los Angeles, CA; Phoenix, AZ; Reno, NV; Sacramento, CA; San Diego, CA; Santa Ana, CA; and Tucson, AZ.

Indian Programs Office, One North First Street, 3rd Floor, P.O. Box 13468, Phoenix, AZ 85002-3468; 602-261-4434.

Region X (Seattle)
HUD Seattle Regional Office, Arcade Plaza Building, 1321 Second Ave., Seattle, WA 98101-2054; 206-442-4373. Field offices are located in: Anchorage, AK; Boise, ID; Portland, OR; and Spokane, WA.

Other HUD Programs
HUD offers over 100 housing programs. Some may be useful to you. To find out about all the programs offered, and what they do, call 202-708-1420 and request *Programs of HUD*. This 119 page booklet will be sent to you free of charge. HUD offers free counseling to HUD homebuyers, homeowners and tenants. Contact your nearest HUD field office to find an approved housing counseling agency.

* Homes: H.O.P.E. 3

U.S. Department of Housing and Urban Development
Office of Community Planning and Development
Office of Affordable Housing Programs
451 7th St., S.W
Washington, DC 20410-7000   202-708-0324

The HUD Urban Homesteading Program has been replaced by the HOPE 3 Program -- with a $95 million budget -- as of June 1991. It is designed to provide homeownership for low income families and individuals. The funds will be distributed to the 10 HUD regions and awarded to local governments and non-profit organizations on a competitive bidding basis. It will generally provide down payment assistance for groups to acquire or rehabilitate affordable low income housing. After June or July, 1992, call your regional HUD office to find out who has been awarded grants, and then contact them directly to see what is available.

Government Auctions and Surplus Property

You qualify for housing help through HOPE 3 under the Low Income Family Housing Act if you are a first time homebuyer and are below 80% of the median income in your area. You must also meet the affordability criteria -- which requires that the cost of principal interest, taxes and insurance for the home comes to no more than 30% of your income. Since the program is new, the quality of public dissemination of information about these programs remains to be seen. These programs are instituted to help you, so don't be afraid to be persistent in asking for information about what HOPE 3 programs are available in your area from the Community Planning and Development Office at the Field or Regional HUD office nearest you.

To find out what the programs will provide and how to apply for a grant, contact John Garrity, DHUD, Office of Urban Rehabilitation, Room 7158, 451 Seventh Street, SW, Washington, DC 20410-7000, 202-708-0324 or look up the Monday, February 4, 1991 issue of the *Federal Register*, Part X, DHUD, 24 CFR Subtitle A called *HOPE for Homeownership for Single Family Homes Program; Notice of Program Guidelines*.

* Homes: Veterans Administration

U.S. Veterans Administration (VA)
810 Vermont Ave., NW
Washington, DC 20420   202-233-4000

Contact the local Veterans Administration Office in your state, or a real estate broker. Watch newspaper ads in local papers for listings of foreclosed properties. The "For Sale" signs on VA foreclosed properties are distinctive. The National Veterans Administration office in Washington, DC is not directly involved in handling the sales; for any inquiries you will be referred to a real estate broker or local VA office.

The Veterans Administration sells foreclosed properties through private real estate brokers. Properties are frequently advertised in local newspapers, giving information such as address, number of bedrooms and bathrooms, particular defects in the property, and price. Almost any real estate agent can show you the property. No broker has an exclusive listing for any of these properties. Local VA offices are the best source of information on the procedures involved in purchasing these properties. Regional offices publish lists of foreclosed properties with descriptions in multiple listing code and phone numbers to call about the property. In some cases, they will also directly send you lists of properties currently available in your area. These offices will mail out a list each time you write in a request, but unless you are a broker, they will not send the list for foreclosures to you on a monthly basis. You can, however, have the agent of your choice put on the mailing list. Others will not mail lists to you, but allow you to pick up the list from their office and/or will refer you to a broker. In either case, you must go through an agent to purchase the house, since they have the keys to the premises, and the process is very much like a regular real estate transaction. The listing has the price on it the VA wants. It will also state if the VA is willing to entertain a lower price. Except, remember, once you have put a bid on a house and won, there is no negotiating or turning back. Houses come "as is" with no guarantees, so it is important to inspect them carefully. Some are located in less desirable neighborhoods, but there are bargains to be had as well. For the most part VA financed homes are mainstream suburban, not inner city. They are often found in neighborhoods located in economically hard hit areas -- such as the Southwest. Prices may drop on homes that are not sold in a certain period of time. VA financing is possible, but you get a 10% discount for paying cash. Also, if you plan on VA financing, in cases of a tie, the other bidder gets priority for cash offers (pre-approved financing through a commercial lender.) You must state at the time of the bid whether you intend to use VA financing or have found your own.

There are two basic avenues to arrange financing. You can be pre-qualified by lenders and then go shopping. More commonly, the real estate broker you are working with will tell you what is available in the mortgage market. The usual way it works is that you find a broker, find a house, bid on it, wind the bid and then the broker helps you to find financing.

If you should win a bid on a VA foreclosed home but be unable to procure financing, some regional offices will put the home up for bid again. Others hold backup offers and will contact the next highest bidder if the original successful bidder is unable to complete the purchase. Most listings offer to sell financing at the current rate of interest for GI loans, even if the buyer is not a GI. A purchaser who is a GI can get these rates without using his GI benefits. Call 202-233-6388, the Central Office, if you have questions. They will direct you to the appropriate department of your regional office. If you are a GI and wish to find out about a Certificate of Eligibility, whereby you can purchase a home worth up to $184,000 without a down payment, call 202-208-1325 or your regional office. To discuss VA loan qualifications generally, call 202-872-1151 or your

regional office.

Purchase is done through a sealed bidding process. Earnest money requirements are published in the listing, usually ranging from $500 to $1000 and are nonrefundable if the bid is accepted. This is a salvage program designed to recover what it can of the cost to the VA for purchasing the property, within a reasonable amount of time after foreclosure -- usually around 6 months.

* Miscellaneous Property: U.S. Customs Service

E.G.& G. Dynatrend
2300 Clarendon Blvd., Suite 705   703-351-7887
Arlington, VA 22201   703-351-7880

E.G.& G. Dynatrend, under contract with the U.S. Customs Service, auctions forfeited and confiscated general merchandise, including vehicles, on a nationwide basis. Items include everything from vessels--both pleasure and commercial--to aircraft, machinery, clothes (in both commercial and individual quantities), jewelry, household goods, precious stones, liquor, furniture, high technology equipment, and infrequently, real estate. Public auctions and sealed and open bid methods are all used. Items are sold only by lot and number of items in a lot vary from one to many. You must bid on the entire lot.

The U.S. Customs Public Auction Line is 703-351-7887. Call it to subscribe to the mailing list of locations and dates of sales, to obtain general information about the custom sales program, dates of sales in your region or information about real estate sales. For $50 dollars per year you can subscribe to a mailing list of items to be auctioned nationwide; or you may subscribe to a list limited to one region of the country for $25. You will then receive fliers with descriptions of items available in upcoming auctions. Regions are divided as follows: General, Northeast sales; Southeast Sales; Northwest sales; and Southwest sales. Send your name, address, telephone number, and a money order to the above address. Allow six to eight weeks for the first flier to arrive. The fliers will then arrive three weeks prior to the viewing period and will tell you when and where the items are available for inspection and details of auction procedures. Catalogs are also available a week before the sale with additional details. For sealed bids, a deposit in cashier's check for the total bid must be submitted along with the bid. Make the cashier's check payable to U.S. Customs Service/E.G.& G. Dynatrend, Agent. Indicate sale number on cashier's check and outside on the envelope.

U.S. Customs auctions are held every nine weeks in the following eight cities: Los Angeles, CA; Laredo, TX; Nogales, AZ; Miami, FL; Edinburg, TX; Houston, TX; Chula Vista, CA (San Diego, CA area); Jersey City, NJ; El Paso, TX. Other auctions are scheduled at different times at various other cities also.

* Miscellaneous Property: U.S. Department of Defense

The Defense Reutilization Marketing Service
P.O. Box 1370   616-961-7331
Battle Creek, MI 49016-1370   1-800-222-DRMS

Imagine what kinds of items are used, then discarded, by a government department as big as the Defense Department: literally everything from recyclable scrap materials and weapons accessories, to airplanes, ships, trains, and motor vehicles; to wood and metalworking machinery, agricultural equipment, construction equipment, communications equipment and medical, dental and veterinary supplies. Not to forget photographic equipment, chemical products, office machines, food preparation and serving equipment, musical instruments, textiles, furs, tents, flags, and sometimes live animals such as goats and horses. No activated items with military applications are included. Neither are real estate or confiscated items such as sports cars or luxury goods.

Goods sold are either surplus or not usable by other government agencies. First priority is given to designated groups which qualify for donations. The rest is then put up for public sale. By contacting the Defense Reutilization Marketing Service at the above address or telephone, you can receive a booklet called *How to Buy Surplus Personal Property* which explains what DOD has for sale and how to bid for it. The Defense Department also lists notices of Sealed Bid property sales in the Commerce Business Daily, available from the Superintendent of Documents, Government Printing Office, Washington, DC 20402-9325; 202-783-3238.

Sales are conducted by regional Defense Reutilization and Marketing Region (DRMR) sales offices which coordinate sales in their geographical area. Listed below are addresses and telephone numbers of the regional offices, which can direct you further as to exactly where items are physically sold. Local sales are by auction, spot bid, or on a retail basis. Auctions are held where there are relatively small quantities of a variety of items. Spot bids are made through forms submitted in the course of a sale--usually when the property is something with a high demand or interest. The retail sales offer small quantities at fixed, market-level prices. There are 214 retail sales offices, located on military bases.

Large quantities of goods are usually sold by sealed bid, which you submit by mail, along with a deposit, on a form you obtain in a catalog which describes the items. (You receive the catalogs once you are on the mailing list). Recyclable materials are sold through the Resource Recovery Recycling Program or through the Hazardous Property Program. Call the above listed number for further details. You can be put on a mailing list to receive advance notice of DOD sales in your region, but if you don't make any bids after two notifications it will probably be removed unless you make an additional request to remain on the list. You can also be placed on a National Bidders List for sales throughout the country. By contacting the DOD Bidders Control Office, P.O. Box 1370, Battle Creek, MI 49016-1370, 616-961-7331, 961-7332, or 1-800-222-DRMS. People under age 18 and members of the U.S. Armed Forces, including civilian employees, are not eligible to participate in these sales.

Following are the Defense Reutilization and Marketing sales offices:

DRMR: Columbus, P.O. Box 500, Blacklick, OH 43004-0500, 614-692-2114. This region includes: MN, WI, MI, IA, NE, KS, MO, IL, IN, OH, WV, VA, DE, NJ, PA, , MD, CT, NY, RI, MA, ME, VT, NH, and District of Columbia

DRMR: Memphis, 2163 Airways Blvd., Memphis, TN 38114-0716, 901-775-6417. This region includes: TX, OK, AR, LA, MS, AL, TN, KY, GA, FL, SC, NC.

DRMR: Ogden, P.O. Box 53, Defense Depot Ogden, Ogden, UT 84407-5001, 801-777-6557. This region includes: ND, SD, MT, WY, ID, UT, CO, AZ, NM, WA, OR, NV, CA.

You can also take advantage of DOD sales if you live outside the United States. The DOD booklet, *How to Buy Surplus Personal Property,* lists addresses for various regions in Europe and the Pacific.

* Miscellaneous Property: U.S. Postal Service

U.S. Postal Service
475 L'Enfant Plaza, S.W.
Washington, DC 20260-0001   202-268-2000
Vehicle Management Facility   202-268-2000

Contact the Dead Letter Branches listed below for undeliverable goods; or your local Postmaster for Vehicle Maintenance Facilities and surplus property auctions. To receive advance notice of the auctions you can write to a Dead Letter Branch and request that your name be put on the auction sales mailing list. To be on all of them, you must write to each one separately. Usually 10 days before the auction, you will be notified by postcard of the time, date and place. Viewing inspections are usually held 2 hours before the auction begins.

The Postal Service holds auctions of unclaimed merchandise which includes a wide range of property -- from electronic and household items -- to clothes, jewelry, linens, toys, all types of equipment, and lots of books. Sales are handled through five dead letter branches throughout the country listed below. However, any high value items such as art works, are sold at the New York auction. Contact your local Postmaster to ask about their auctions of surplus property and used vehicles. There are 225 post office vehicle maintenance facilities throughout the country. Their addresses and phone numbers are all listed at the back of the Zip Code Directory kept at post offices. The used vehicle sales can be good bargains, since the vehicles are somewhat fixed up, painted, and occasionally in good condition. Some jeeps, for instance, may sell for between $1200 and $1500. Recently a man bought 15 jeeps for $100 each at auction. Vehicles that do not sell off the storage lot are auctioned. Sometimes cars such as Pintos can be picked up for as little as $750. The sales conducted by the 225 Vehicle Maintenance Facilities around the country are usually fixed price sales, but 5 or 6 times per year auctions have been held at larger cities.

The dead letter items are usually sold in lots of similar goods, with the volume or quantity varying widely. Prices depend on what the goods are and the number of people bidding at a particular auction. There may be a minimum bid required, such as $20; and often cash is the only acceptable payment. Bidders are responsible for removing the items purchased.

A flier for a Postal Service auction of unclaimed and damaged merchandise in St. Paul, Minnesota advised that only those already on an established check register may pay by check; otherwise, cash is required. It also advised that potential bidders to bring their own containers -- boxes, crates, and bags -- for

packing. The Postal Service in San Francisco, California, announced that books, jewelry, sound recordings, speakers, and cabinets, as well as miscellaneous merchandise would be available.

Eastern Region
U.S. Postal Service Claims and Inquiry, Room 531 A, 2970 Market St., Philadelphia, PA 19104-9652; 215-895-8140 (auction information and number to call to be notified by postcard of next upcoming auction). Includes Pennsylvania, Southern New Jersey, Maryland, Delaware, Ohio, Kentucky, part of Indiana, Virginia, West Virginia, North Carolina, and South Carolina.

Central Region
U.S. Postal Service Dead Letter Office, 180 E. Kellogg St., Room 932, St. Paul, MN 55101-9511; 612-293-3083. Includes Minnesota, Michigan, Wisconsin, North Dakota, South Dakota, Wyoming, Colorado, Nebraska, Iowa, Indiana, and Illinois.

Northeast Region
U.S. Postal Service Dead Parcel Office, J.P. Farley Bldg., Room 209A, New York, NY 10099-9543; 212-330-3859. Includes New York, Massachusetts, Puerto Rico, Connecticut, New Hampshire, New Jersey, and Rhode Island.

Southern Region
U.S. Postal Service Undeliverable Mail Branch, 730 Great Southwest Parkway, Atlanta, GA 30304-9506; 404-344-1625. Includes Georgia, Florida, Louisiana, Tennessee, Arkansas, Mississippi, Oklahoma, Texas, and parts of South Carolina.

Western Region
U.S. Postal Service Claims and Inquiries, 1300 Evans Ave., Room 293, San Francisco, CA 94105-9501; 415-543-1826. Auctions are held at 228 Harrison St., San Francisco, CA. Includes: Alaska, Oregon, Idaho, California, Washington, Nevada, Utah, Arizona, New Mexico, part of Texas, and Hawaii.

* Miscellaneous Property: General Services Administration Property

William Tesh, Chief of Sales Branch
U.S. General Services Administration (GSA)
Property Management Division
Crystal Mall 4, Room 709
Washington, DC 20406   703-557-7785

Contact your local GSA office listed below. The GSA disposes of surplus property for most of the government agencies, and has items ranging from vehicles and scrap metals, to office furniture, office and industrial equipment, data processing equipment, boats, medical equipment, waste paper and computers; as well as aircraft, railroad equipment, agricultural equipment, textiles, food waste, photographic equipment, jewelry, watches, and clothing.

Some regional offices have no mailing list. Instead, there is a number they will give you to call that is a recorded message of all upcoming events. It will give the time, date, and location of the auction and type, such as warehouse, vehicles or office furniture. Other regions allow you to have your name placed on a mailing list to receive advance notices of auctions at no cost. Catalogs list the specific items and their condition. Sales are conducted as regular auctions, spot auctions (where bids are submitted on-the-spot in writing) and by sealed bid (written on a form and mailed in). For auctions and spot bids, you will have two days prior to the sale to view and inspect property, and one week prior for sealed bids. For sealed bid items you receive a catalog, once your are on the mailing list, describing the merchandise. If your region does not have a mailing list, you may pick up catalogs at the office or the sale. Announcements come out as property is accumulated, with March to October being the busiest period. The highest bidder wins in all cases.

Prices may range from way below wholesale for some items to close-to-market prices for others, especially automobiles and boats. Cars tend to be common American-made brands, such as Tempos, Citations, and Reliances. Prices for 4-6 year-old cars may range from around $1500 to $3000 depending on the condition. Seized cars may be newer and of a foreign make. A Mercedes-Benz was recently sold at a National Capitol Region auction. Payment may be by cash, cashier's checks, money orders, traveler's checks, government, or credit union checks; but any personal or business checks must be accompanied by an Informal Bank Letter guaranteeing payment. Full payment must be made by the following day, and bidders are responsible for removal of all property. To bid in GSA auctions, you must register at the site and obtain a bidder number. Once you are on the bidders mailing list, you must bid at least once while receiving five mailings or your name will be removed from the list. Then you must contact the appropriate office again to continue receiving mailings.

Some listings for a GSA sale in Bismarck, North Dakota included the following items: miscellaneous kitchen equipment, meat slicers, coffee makers, cameras, film, binoculars, screens, paper, postage meter, nuts and bolts, typewriters, lettering set, mailboxes, lamps, and a streetlight.

For information about GSA auctions in your area, contact one of the regional offices listed below:

National Capitol Region (Washington DC and vicinity)
6808 Loisdale Rd., Building A, Springfield, VA 22150; 703-557-7785, or 703-557-7796, for a recording.

Region I (Boston)
GSA, Surplus Sales Branch, 10 Causeway St., 9th Floor, Boston, MA, 02109; 617-565-7326, Auction Hotline.

Region II (New York)
GSA Surplus Sales Branch, 26 Federal Plaza, Room 20-112, New York, NY, 10278; 212-264-4824, or 212-264-4823, for a recording.

Region III (Philadelphia)
GSA Surplus Sales Branch, 841 Chestnut, Suite 540, Philadelphia, PA 19107; 215-597-5674 or 215-597-SALE for a recording. (This is NCR Headquarters).

Region IV (Atlanta)
GSA Surplus Sales Branch, Attn: 4FBPS, 401 West Peachtree St., Atlanta, GA 30354; 404-331-0972.

Region V (Chicago)
230 S. Dearborn St., Chicago, IL 60604; 312-353-6061, office or 312-353-0246, hotline for a recorded announcement.

Region VI (Kansas)
GSA Surplus Sales Branch, 4400 College Blvd., Suite 175, Overland Park, KS 66211; 913-236-2523.

Region VII (Ft. Worth)
GSA Surplus Sales Branch, 819 Taylor St., Ft. Worth, TX 76102-6105; 817-334-2352, office or 2351 for a recorded announcement.

Region VIII (Denver)
GSA Surplus Sales Branch, Denver Federal Center Building 41, Denver, CO 80225-0506; 303-236-7705 or 7698.

Region IX (San Francisco)
GSA Surplus Sales Section PMB 9FBP-S, 525 Market St., 33rd Floor, San Francisco, CA 94105; 415-744-5245 or 1-800-676-SALE for catalogs or mailing lists.

Region X (Washington)
GSA Surplus Sales Branch GSA Center, Auburn, WA 98001-6599; 206-931-7566, recording or 509-353-2544.

* Miscellaneous Property: Internal Revenue Service (IRS)

IRS National Information Hotline   1-800-829-1040
This office appears to be understaffed. Overloads are automatically put on busy. It is very difficult to get through. If you call before 3:30, Donica Davis may be able to help you.

The hotline can tell you which local office to call. It will tell you to consult your local newspaper, in classifieds, for a listing of IRS seized property to be sold. The listing will give phone number and details. The property sold by the IRS is seized from delinquent taxpayers rather than being used or surplus government property. Many kinds of merchandise are put up for auction, including real estate, vehicles, and office and industrial equipment. Sales are by both sealed bids and public auction. Regarding property sales, the IRS warns that land may still be redeemed by the original owner up to 180 days AFTER you, the bidder, purchase it at an auction; and therefore no deed is issued until this time period has elapsed. Buildings on land being sold by the IRS are NOT open for inspection by a potential buyer unless permission is granted by the taxpayer/owner.

Payment may be by cash, certified check, cashier's check, or money order. In some cases, full payment is required the day of the sale. Otherwise, a 20%

downpayment (or $200, whichever is greater) is needed to hold the property, with the balance due at a specified time from the date of the sale, not to exceed one month.

* Miscellaneous Property: U.S. Marshals Service

U.S. Marshals Service
Seized Assets Division
U.S. Department of Justice
600 Army-Navy Drive
Arlington, VA 22202   202-307-9237
Contact your local Sunday newspaper for auction notices in the legal section, or the nearest U.S. Marshals Office under U.S. Department of Justice. Usually the Marshals Office is located in the Federal Building of a city. The U.S. Marshals Service or a contracted commercial sales or auction service may handle disposal of the property. Sales are always listed every other Wednesday in *USA Today* newspaper.

In 1991, the Drug Enforcement Agency managed 1.4 billion dollars worth of property from convicted drug dealers. The U.S. Marshals Service, which holds crime-related property accumulated in Federal drug-related and other confiscations, auctions much of this off to the public through 94 offices around the country. Items sold include everything from entire working businesses, to cars, houses, copiers, jewelry, rare coin and stamp collections, apartment complexes, and restaurants. The government is not giving these properties away by any means, but bargains are possible as well as opportunities to purchase some exotic goodies. Confiscated viable businesses are managed by the Service until the time of the auction in order to keep up or increase the businesses' value.

Auctions are not scheduled regularly, but occur when items accumulate. Auctions may be conducted by private auctioneers or the Marshals Service itself. No mailing list is kept to notify you individually, and there is no national listing of items, since new properties are seized daily and adjudication of drug-related cases may take years. Payment at these auctions is by cash, certified check, or special arrangements when large amounts of money are involved. One note, the Marshals Service checks out people paying for large items with cash to make sure the government is not re-selling things to drug dealers. The Marshals Service also auctions off property seized by the Drug Enforcement Agency.

* Natural Resources Sales Assistance

Small Business Administration (SBA)
409 Third Street SW
8th Floor   1-800-827-5722
Washington, DC 20416   202-205-6600
The federal government sells surplus property and natural resources, such as timber. SBA works with government agencies which are selling the property and resources to assure that small businesses have an opportunity to buy a fair share of them. Occasionally natural resources that the federal government is releasing on the market are made available. Small fuel companies and producers may get the option to buy their fair share of federal government coal leases. The royalty oil program enables small and independent refineries to buy oil at valuations set by the federal government - which is in excess of spot market prices. Agricultural leases may be had for land on which to graze cattle or grow crops. This SBA program is designed to ensure that small businesses get their fair share of real and personal federal property put on the market. Don't expect bargains. Write for *The U.S. Government Purchasing and Sales Directory* at the above address. This book tells you how to sell to the U.S. government, how to be put on its bidder's list, and what agencies sell property. For more information, contact Bill Berry at 202-205-6470. To find out what SBA Natural Resources Sales Assistance programs are in your area, contact your nearest SBA office. For information on other SBA services, call 1-800-827-5722 (recorded listing from which you can order brochures.)

* Real Estate: General Services Administration
Property Sales

General Services Administration (GSA)
Office of Real Estate Sales   1-800-GSA-1313
Call this toll-free number for national listing of properties, and then contact local GSA office for the area you are interested in. You can also obtain the list by calling Asset Disposition, 202-501-0067. The phone number of the local GSA office to contact will be provided on the list that is mailed to you free of charge upon request.

* Real Estate: Small Business Administration (SBA)

U.S. Small Business Administration
Portfolio Management Division
409 Third Street, SW
Washington, DC 20416   202-205-6660
Recording from which to order brochures   1-800-827-5722

Contact your local SBA office located in 10 Regional Offices around the country, or any of the 68 District Offices. SBA does not maintain a mailing list. No district or regional SBA office is aware of what the other offices are offering. The SBA auctions off properties of people who have defaulted on home loan payments in SBA-sponsored programs. Listings of auctions are printed in local newspapers, usually in the Sunday edition in the classified section. Merchandise is identified as SBA property and sold by brokers, none of whom have the exclusive listing, or by private auctioneers. The auctioneers are chosen on a rotating basis. SBA attempts to sell to the highest bidder, but may reject a winning bid if too low. Sales are infrequent. Do not expect bargains. Items sold range from office furniture and equipment to buildings or entire bakeries, drycleaners, or other businesses. There may be parts or whole businesses available. The auctioneer may have an entire auction of SBA items, or a mixture of things from various sources. You may request to bid by sealed bid if you desire; and a deposit is required. Payment is by cash or certified check. If you are interested in certain categories of merchandise, you might want to be placed on the mailing list of one or more auctioneers who specialize in that particular type of item, such as farm equipment, for example. Since the SBA is often the guarantor of bank loans, SBA auctions are relatively infrequent and bargains are not easy to find. SBA Regional Offices follow:

Dallas: 8625 King George Dr., Dallas, TX 75235-3391; 214-767-7633

Kansas City: 911 Walnut St., 13th Floor, Kansas City, MO 64106; 816-426-3608

Denver: 999 18th St.,Suite 701, Denver, CO 80202; 303-294-7186

San Francisco: 71 Stevenson St., San Francisco, CA 94105-2939; 415-744-6402

Seattle: 2615 4th Ave.,Room 440, Seattle, WA 98121; 206-553-5676

Boston: 155 Federal Street, 9th Floor, Boston, MA 02110; 617-451-2023

New York: 26 Federal Plaza, Room 31-08, New York, NY 10278; 212-264-1450

King of Prussia: 475 Allendale Rd., Suite 201, King of Prussia, PA 19406; 215-962-3700

Atlanta: 1375 Peachtree St. N.E., 5th Floor, Atlanta, GA 30367-8102; 404-347-2797

Chicago: 300 South Riverside Plaza, Suite 1975 South, Chicago,IL 60606-6617; 312-353-5000

* Ships: Maritime Administration

U.S. Department of Transportation
Office of Ship Operations
Maritime Administration
400 7th St., S.W., Room 7324
Washington, DC 20590   202-366-5111

When the government decides that a merchant ship is no longer needed or useable, it may put that ship up for sale by auction, through a sealed bid procedure. A ten percent deposit is required. It is sold to the highest bidder usually for its scrap value. Contact the above address to be put on the auction mailing list.

* Timber Sales for Small Business

Small Business Administration (SBA)
409 3rd St., SW, #8800
Washington, DC 20416   202-205-6470

The U.S. Government regularly sells timber from the federal forests managed by the U.S. Forest Service, Department of Agriculture, and the Bureau of Land Management, Department of Interior. On occasion, timber also is sold from federally-owned forests which are under the supervision of the Department of Defense, the Department of Energy, and the Tennessee Valley Authority, and the Department of the Interior. The SBA and these agencies work together to ensure full opportunity for concerns to bid on federal timber sales. SBA and the sales agencies jointly set aside timber sales for bidding by small concerns when it appears that, under open sales, small business would not obtain a fair share at reasonable prices. Contact your local SBA office for further specific information. It is listed in the blue pages of the telephone directory. General information, if needed, is available from Bill Berry at 202-205-6470.

Donations To Non-Profit Organizations

* Art Exhibits

> Smithsonian Institution
> 1100 Jefferson Dr., SW
> Room 3146
> Washington, DC 20560   202-357-3168

The Smithsonian can bring art to you, whether you live in a major metropolitan area or a rural one. The Smithsonian Institute Traveling Exhibition Service (SITES) sponsors 80 to 100 different exhibits at any given time in museums and other locations around the country. The participation fee will range from $500 to $20,000. The exhibitions range from popular culture, to fine arts, photography, historical exhibits, or topics of interest to children. The collections are from other museums and institutions, sometimes including the Smithsonian, and are most frequently sent to other museums, libraries, historic homes, or even schools and community centers. More than half the locations are in rural settings. SITES estimates that more than 11 million people view the exhibits it circulates in this program. The bigger exhibits that require special security arrangements go only to museums equipped to handle them. If interested, call the above number for the SITES *Updates* catalog.

* Books

> Library of Congress
> Exchange and Gift Division
> 1st and C Street, SE
> Washington, DC 20540-4280   202-707-9511/9512

Government agencies, educational institutions, and other non-profit organizations may qualify to obtain free books from the U.S. Library of Congress. The books are largely technical and legal works, but from time to time contains entire collections from military installation lending libraries that have been closed. There is no way to tell what books will be available. Stock is constantly changing. Books are first offered on a competitive bidding basis. If they are not sold, they become available on a donation bidding basis. Commercial book dealers may compete in this bidding against non-profit organizations. The proceeds sustain the Book Preservation Program. Someone from the organization must choose which books are desired. He or she must have a letter from the organization or appropriate Congressional representative stating that the person it selected to choose the books acts for a non-profit organization. The Library will ship the books UPS at the organization's expense or the organization may supply the Library with pre-addressed franking labels. Congressional offices will help educational institutions such as universities and schools obtain these labels. Non-profit organizations may submit bids to purchase books. The Library will contact the organization if the bid is unacceptably low and give the bidder one chance to raise it. There is no limit on the number of books a group may order.

* Department of Housing and Urban Development (HUD)

> HUD Library and Information Service
> 451 7th Street SW
> Room 814
> Washington, DC 20743

To find out about the over 100 programs HUD offers to assist low and moderate income housing groups and individuals, obtain *Programs of HUD* by calling 202-708-1420.

* Food and Surplus Commodities

> USDA Food Distribution Programs
>   or Food Distribution Division
> Food and Nutrition Service
> 3101 Park Center Drive
> Room 503
> Alexandria, VA 22302   703-305-2680

Non-profit groups with tax-exempt status may apply for surplus commodities held by the Agriculture Department, such as grain (usually flour), oils, and sometimes milk and cheese. The large quantities of surplus cheese and milk that existed a couple of years ago are largely depleted. The items available depend somewhat on which foods are currently in surplus. Contact your state distribution agency, frequently the state Department of Agriculture, Department of Education, or Administrative Services, or the above address.

* Foreign Gifts

> General Services Administration
> Crystal Mall Building #4
> 1941 Jefferson Davis Highway
> Room 800
> Washington, DC 20406   703-308-0745

Non-Presidential gifts worth over $200 from foreign countries to U.S. government agencies or their representatives may be displayed by the recipient in his government office, then purchased by him at an officially assessed value. If the gift is not purchased, it may end up in a State Surplus Property office, where the general public can get a chance to buy it. Watches and jewelry are commonly available, along with books, sculptures, and various artifacts. But the souvenir from Anwar Sadat to Jimmy Carter during the Middle East peace talks goes to the U.S. Archives and possibly later to the Jimmy Carter Library.

When gifts are reported to the GSA, they first go through the federal screening cycle. Federal agencies have the first chance to purchase items at retail value price. If none exercise that option, then the recipient may purchase the item. If the item remains unsold, it enters the donation screening cycle. It may then be used for display purposes at state agencies such as libraries or museums. After that, it may be sold to the public at auction. At public auction, anyone can purchase the item. Non-profits have no special footing. Items are disposed of by GSA in basically the same way as other surplus and excess property.

Items desired by non-profit organizations should be requested through your local Surplus Property Office, which can then contact the GSA about a donation. You can find a list of foreign gifts given to government agencies published yearly in the *Federal Register*, State Department, Chief of Protocol, Washington, DC, 202-647-4169.

* Housing For The Homeless

> Judy Breitman
> Chief, Real Property Branch
> Division of Health Facilities Planning, ORM/OM
> Department of Health and Human Services
> Parklawn Building, Room 17A-10
> 5600 Fishers Lane   301-443-2265
> Rockville, MD 20857   FAX: 301-443-0084

The above will send you a helpful brochure entitled *Obtaining Federal Property for the Homeless: Questions and Answers About Federal Property Programs*. If you are part of a non-profit organization ministering to the homeless, the government is currently taking applications for eligible groups to receive excess or unused federal buildings or land for homeless people. The property is leased or deeded over. To find out what properties are available call the 24 hour hotline, 1-800-927-7588. Every Friday, *The Federal Register* (available from libraries or by subscription) will list which federal properties are available and where. You can also ask the National Coalition for the Homeless, 202-265-2371,to notify you when a property becomes available. The applying organization has 60 days after notice of property availability is published to submit a written expression of interest. It will then be sent an application packet and have 90 days after that to apply for the property. Criteria is outlined in *The Federal Register*. If you think your organization may qualify, call Public Health Service, 301-443-2265.

* Interagency Council on the Homeless

> 451 Seventh Street, SW
> Washington, DC 20410   202-708-1480

This is a coordinating counsel of 16 different Federal agencies, headed by the HUD Secretary. It works with State and local governments and private organizations on homeless-related efforts. Call it for information on homeless activities. For information on financing rehabilitation or support services, contact HUD's Office of Special Needs Assistance Program at 202-708-4300.

Title V of the McKinney Act is the "Federal Surplus Property Program." You can call 1-800-927-7588 to get answers about the Title V Program and properties 24 hours per day. Under this program, federally owned surplus or unused property may be deeded, leased or made available on an interim basis at no cost to homeless providers such as states, local governments and non-profit organizations. To find out about eligible properties, ask to be put on the mailing list that tells you of properties in your area as they are published by contacting your nearest field HUD office.

* Miscellaneous Property

Director, Property Management Division
Office of Transportation and Property Management
Federal Supply Service
Washington, DC 20406   703-308-0745

Or contact your local State Office of Surplus Property. The General Services Administration (GSA) will donate items it handles to qualifying non-profit organizations which request it. Items are "as is" and range from tools, office machines, supplies and furniture, clothes, hardware, medical supplies to cars, boats, and planes. Your State Agency for Surplus Property, also called Office of Purchasing, Property Control, or General Services, makes the determination whether your group qualifies, then contacts the GSA to obtain it. There may be a charge of 2% of the value and a fee for handling and service. Groups eligible can include public agencies, and non-profit educational, public health, elderly, or homeless organizations.

* Tools for Schools

Commander, Defense General Supply Center
Attn: DGSC-OMC
8000 Jefferson Davis Hwy.
Richmond, VA 23297-5501   804-279-3861

This program of the Defense Logistics Agency loans used industrial equipment no longer necessary to the military or military contractors to qualifying non-profit educational institutions. The equipment must be over $5000 in value and includes such things as saws, lathes, milling equipment, drilling equipment, and grinding equipment. Loans are for five year periods, but may be renewed indefinitely.

The receiving institution must pay for the cost of transportation, packaging and handling, plus any necessary repairs. Some equipment comes "as is" and may be inoperable; other items sometimes show up almost unused. The equipment generally dates from between 1950 to 1970, but in some cases it can be of superior quality than its modern equivalent. The Defense Industrial Plant Equipment Center advises looking first hand at equipment before ordering it. Contact the above for informational brochure and application.

* Travel Aboard An Icebreaker

Ice Operations Division
U.S. Coast Guard Headquarters
2100 2nd Street, SW
Washington, DC 20593   202-267-1450

The Coast Guard does not evaluates scientific projects to determine if they qualify. The group that qualifies as a primary user, because it is willing to pay for fuel and part of maintenance and helicopter costs on resupply trips, may send a scientist they select to ride along with one of the two Coast Guard Icebreakers that travel to the Arctic and Antarctica. At present, for the Antarctic trip, the National Science Foundation (1800 G St. N.W., Washington, DC 20550, 202-357-9859, Information Center or 202-357-7808, Polar Programs) is the primary user. For the Tooley, Greenland trip, the Military Sealift Command (202-433-6056 or 202-443-0083) is the primary user. Other interested parties who wish to send scientists or observers, such as scientific or environmental groups must obtain the consent of the primary user for that trip. Most travelers are sponsored by government or educational organizations, but the Coast Guard is interested in any appropriate, professional project and will consider other applications as well. They can also be flexible on their itinerary to accommodate projects. Sometimes scientists on short missions may travel at no cost. In addition, special expeditions are commissioned, such as the one in 1992 by the U.S. Geological Survey. If interested, contact the primary user.

Resolution Trust Corporation

As a result of the U.S. Savings and Loan failures, the U.S. Government has contracted the RTC to dispose of the thousands of real property and other assets it now possesses. Inventory constantly changes, but includes single family homes, as well as commercial properties, shopping centers, loans and undeveloped land.

* The Affordable Housing Disposition Program

Stephen Allen, Director
Barry Wides, Deputy Director
Resolution Trust Corporation (RTC)   202-416-7348
801 17th Street, NW   1-800-624-HOME
Washington, DC 20434   FAX: 202-416-2530

This program sells single and multi-family residences valued or sold at $67,500 or less. As of March 31, 1991, there were 18,816 RTC properties in the Affordable Housing Program with a total value of $1.6 billion. One to four family residences were 93% of that number and 84% of the single family properties were appraised at less than $50,000. Most of the properties are in the Southwest. More than half are in Texas. More properties in the east are becoming available. List prices are at fair market value but are negotiable. Offers are made to realtors for properties listed with clearinghouses. Such listing must be for 90 days during which only pre-qualified buyers can make offers. Generally to be eligible, your income must be less than $40,000 per year or no more than 115% of the area's median income. Contact the Housing Finance Agency in your State. You might also want to ask it about housing loans for low income persons.

The calendar gives the contact person who will show you the property and tell you the dates of the buyer's seminar you should attend to learn more about how to buy a home under the RTC Affordable Housing Program. RTC oversees the private sector auction companies who sell the homes. The auction company must set up a time for a "Buyer Awareness Seminar" to explain the process and the prerequisites of eligibility for the program and RTC financing. The auctions are usually open call; sometimes sealed bids are taken. One can bid up to the amount one has financing for. Earnest money is cash, usually $500 up front.

* Houses and Other Property From Failed Savings and Loan Companies

Resolution Trust Corporation (RTC)
801 17th Street, NW
Washington, DC 20434   202-416-7348

Call to have information on RTC programs mailed to you.
National Assets Specific Inquiry Program 1-800-431-0600
RTC National Sales Center 1-800-842-2970
Regional Assets Sales Hotline Numbers: 1-800-348-1484
    Property Listings 1-800-782-3006

* Housing for the Homeless

Resolution Trust Corporation (RTC)
801 17th Street, NW
Washington, DC 20434
Contact: Diane Case or Felisa Neuringer   202-416-7348

RTC offers real estate to public and non-profit organizations for public purposes such as day care, low and moderate income family housing and housing for the homeless. The property that is offered has been determined to not have a reasonable recovery value. When a property is deteriorated, of low value, holding costs are too high, or if there have been no offers made on it for a long time, RTC is authorized to transfer title to a designated public agency or non-profit organization which has its application for the property endorsed by a local governmental body.

RTC issues notices of properties available for public use that describes the condition, size and location of the property, gives a contact person, the public purpose for which it may be used, and date by which proposals to acquire the property must be received. The notices are sent to various agencies and to the RTC headquarters and regional offices. Upon acceptance of a proposal, the property is conveyed to the organization by quitclaim deed or deed without warranty.

* Real Estate and General Merchandise Anyone Can Buy

Call the Assets Sales Hotline number, 1-800-348-1484, to receive the calendar of events of all items such as fixtures, furniture and equipment, as well as property that is being auctioned around the country. The calendar is updated twice monthly and will be mailed to you free upon request. What type of auction it is, mixed where everyone can buy or "Affordable Housing Auctions" where only pre-qualified buyers can buy, will be stated in the calendar. It tells you what is being sold, where and who to contact. The auctioneer or contact person provides viewing locations of merchandise. Auctioneers may send you an inspection catalogue the week before the sale.

For real estate call 1-800-782-3006 to receive a list of all RTC properties around the country that are not being auctioned. Transactions are conducted like any regular real estate transaction where you make an offer.

* Tenant Programs

RTC often tries to arrange for the present occupiers of an RTC held property to buy the dwelling by arranging financing for two months rent equivalent in a down payment and mortgage payments like rent.

State Government Auctions

The following is a descriptive listing of state government offices which offer auctions or donations of surplus property.

Alabama

Alabama Surplus Property, P.O. Box 210487, Montgomery, AL 36121, 205-277-5866. Alabama auctions off a variety of items about three times per year, including office equipment, heavy machinery (such as milling machines and drill presses), and vehicles, including cars, trucks, boats, and tractors. Trailers, medical equipment, tires, dossiers, and lathes are also sold. The state advertises upcoming auctions in the classified section of local newspapers. Upon written request made to the above address, you can be put on a mailing list. You will then be notified 2 or 3 weeks in advance of each upcoming auction, but you won't receive a list of items. Lists of items can be picked up at the above office 2 days before the auction. Payment can be by cash, cashier's check, or personal check with a bank letter of credit. Items are available for viewing two days prior to the auction. No bids by mail.

Alaska

Surplus Property Management Office, 2400 Viking Dr., Anchorage, AK 99501, 907-279-0596. The Juno office is 907-465-2172. Call it for general information and mailing list information. Alaska's Division of General Services and Supply sells surplus office equipment, including furniture and typewriters, every Tuesday from 8:30 am to 12:00 pm, and from 1:00 pm to 4:00 pm in a garage sale fashion with prices marked for each item. For items costing over $100, cash or cashiers checks are required. Vehicles, at various locations throughout the state, are sold during sealed bid or outcry auctions twice a year, in the spring and fall. Payment is by cashiers check after you have been notified of your winning bid.

Arizona

Office of Surplus Property, 1537 W. Jackson St., Phoenix, AZ 85007, 602-542-5701. About four times per year, Arizona auctions off everything from vehicles to miscellaneous office equipment and computers. Items are sold by lots rather than individually; and prices, especially cars, can be below blue book price, depending upon opening bids. Vehicles range from empty frames to Jaguars. A mailing list is maintained. You can have it sent to you for no charge. Individual cities and county governments in Arizona also hold their own surplus auctions.

Arkansas

State Marketing and Redistribution Office, 6620 Young Rd., Little Rock, AR 72209, 501-565-8645. Arkansas conducts both sealed bid and retail, fixed price sales of surplus items. On Wednesdays, between 7:30 am and 3:00 pm, buyers may view and purchase items, which include office machines, tables, and tires, valued at under $500. Larger, more valuable items, including vehicles, medical equipment, mobile homes, and machine shop and automotive supplies, are sold by sealed bid. You can have your name placed on the mailing list for various categories such as computers, autos and miscellaneous equipment. You must bid three times to keep your name on the mailing list. The state also conducts sealed bids by mail. The bid fee is $1. No personal checks are accepted for sealed bids. All items are sold "as is," with no refunds or guarantees implied or stated.

California

State of California, Office of Fleet Administration, 1416 10th St., Sacramento, CA 95814, 916-657-2318. California sells surplus office equipment or other supplies only to schools and other non-profit or educational institutions. However, once a month on Saturdays, the General Services Department of the state holds open bid auctions at Sacramento or Los Angeles State Garages of surplus automobiles previously owned by state agencies. Vehicles can be viewed from 8:00 am to 10:00 am. The auction begins at 10:00 am. Vehicles may include sedans, cargo and passenger vans, pick-ups (mostly American-made). You can receive 2 weeks advance notice by getting on the mailing list. Auctions are occasionally advertised in the newspapers. Minimum bid prices are set for exceptionally nice cars. Only state agency vehicles are sold. Payment is by cash, cashiers check, or certified check. Personal checks are also accepted, but items may not be picked up until the check has cleared. Successful bidders have up to

one week to pay for and pick up the cars (the following Friday). Out-of-state checks are frowned upon. Prices vary greatly, and some vehicles have required minimum bids.

California Highway Patrol, Used Vehicle Sales Office, 2812 Meadowview Rd., Sacramento, CA 95832, 916-421-0285. Minimum bids are stated on a recorded telephone message. The auction is by sealed bids which are opened at 3:00 pm daily; winners may be present or notified by telephone. Payment is by cashiers check, certified check, or, money order only -- no personal checks or cash accepted. Bids may be submitted and inspection is available between 8:00 am and 3:00 pm.

Colorado

Department of Correctional Industries, State Surplus Agency, 4200 Garfield Street, Denver, CO 80216, 303-321-2200. Several times a year, Colorado auctions off its surplus property, except for motor vehicles, which are not sold to the public. Auctions are pre-announced in newspaper ads, and a mailing list is also maintained. To be put on the mailing list, call the above number. The auctions of state property are held the third Thursday of every month. If you are on the mailing list, you will receive a notice the weekend before the auction with a brief description of the items. Non-profit organizations have first choice of state surplus items, which can include typewriters, desks, computers, file cabinets, hospital beds, and much more. Payment may be made by cash, money order or personal checks with two IDs.

Connecticut

60 State St. Rear, Wethersfield, CT 06109, 203-566-7018, or 203-566-7190. Items vary from day to day. Vehicles are auctioned separately 8 or 9 times per year, with ads in the 4 largest newspapers and on 2 radio stations giving advance notice. There is no mailing list. These auctions are usually on the second Saturday of the month. Vehicles may be viewed one hour prior to the auction. Buyers may also purchase a brochure with vehicle descriptions when they pay the $3 registration fee. You may go Monday-Friday, noon to 3:45 to view and purchase smaller items in their warehouse.

Delaware

Division of Purchasing Surplus Property, P.O. Box 299, Delaware City, DE 19706, 302-834-4550. About two, sometimes three times each year, in May and in September, Delaware publicly auctions off vehicles, office furniture, and other surplus or used property. Vehicles include school buses, paddle boats, vans, pick-up trucks, heavy equipment, and sedans. Prices depend on the condition of the item and how many people are bidding for it. Vehicles may be inspected and started up prior to the auction, but may not be driven. You may get on a mailing list to be advised of upcoming auctions. A flyer with information and conditions of payment will be sent to you.

District of Columbia

District of Columbia Dept. of Public Works, 5001 Shepard Parkway, Washington, DC 20032, 202-404-1068. DC holds vehicle auctions every 1st and 3rd Tuesday of every month. Vehicles include cars, trucks, buses, ambulances, and boats. Inspection and viewing is available at 8:00 am, one hour prior to the 9:00 am open bid auction. Prices and conditions of vehicles vary greatly. No mailing list is kept. Auctions are posted 45 days in advance in the *Washington Times*. A $50 cash entry fee must be paid to attend an auction and is refunded if no car is purchased. Cars must be paid for in full at the auction by certified or cashier's check. Twice a year confiscated bikes and property found inside of cars go to auction.

District of Columbia Office of Property Control, 2250 Shannon Place SE, Washington, DC 20032, 202-767-7586. In the past, this office auctioned off items such as clothing, typewriters, cabinets, tools, refrigerators, and more at the DC Police Training Academy facility. Such auctions are becoming increasingly infrequent and may be discontinued altogether in the future. No mailing list is kept, but advance notices are placed in The Washington Post. Viewing of items is allowed the day of the sales. Cash only is accepted.

Florida

Department of Management Services, 813 A Lake Bradford Rd., Tallahassee, FL 32304, 904-488-5272. DGS holds no auctions. A retail store, located at the above address, is open from 12:30 pm to 4:30 pm on weekdays for public retail-type sales of various items, excluding vehicles. Items include office supplies, computers, medical equipment, mowers, calculators, typewriters, couches, desks, chairs, tables, air conditioners, black boards, and filing cabinets.

Department of Management Services, Division of Motor Pool Bureau of Motor Vehicles, 813 B Lake Bradford Rd., Tallahassee, FL 32304, 904-488-5178. Approximately once per month, somewhere in Florida, items are auctioned for the state by First Coast Auctions at 904-772-0110. Descriptive information and viewing schedules are published in newspapers. Surplus items, including motorcars, heavy equipment and boats are sold. Automobile auctions take place anywhere from 7 to 15 times per year, with dates set 4 to 6 weeks in advance at various auction locations throughout the state. The auctions are advertised. Some industrial equipment is also included, along with various kinds of used and confiscated vans, trucks, and cars. Pleasure and fishing boats are also auctioned. Items may be viewed prior to the auction. 1-800-766-9266 (in state).

Georgia

State of Georgia, Department of Administrative Services, Purchasing Division, Surplus Property Services, 1050 Murphy Avenue, SW, Atlanta, GA 30310, 404-756-4800. Georgia auctions vehicles, including sedans, wagons, trucks, vans, buses, and cement mixers. The state also auctions shop equipment, generators, typewriters, copiers, computers, tape recorders, and other office equipment, as well as audio-visual equipment, cameras, electronic equipment, and air conditioners. They keep a mailing list and also advertise the auctions in local newspapers. Merchandise may be inspected by pre-registered bidders two days before an auction. Auctions are held on the third Wednesday of a month -- but not necessarily every month. Auctions begin at 8:30 am if federal property is to be sold, otherwise they begin at 9-9:30 am. Vehicles may be started up, but not driven. Sealed bids are also used, and deposits are required with these. For auctions, items are payable with cash or check with sufficient I.D. if the amount is under $501.00. For personal or business checks in amounts over $501.00, property will be held until the check clears. Items must be paid for on the day of sale. A recent Georgia auction offered 40 sedans between 3 and 15 years old, 30 pick-up trucks from 5 to 22 years old, vans dating from 1965 to 1989, tires, tractors, farm equipment, shop equipment, office equipment, and 3 lots of televisions.

Hawaii

State Government Stock Control Department, 808-735-0348/0349. Hawaii does not conduct surplus sales at the state level. Federal public auctions are held by the Defense Reutilization Marketing Office, 808-476-6872.

Idaho

Division of Purchasing, 208-327-7465. In 1991 the Idaho state legislature dissolved centralized public auctions. Each state agency now holds its own auction or has a commercial auctioneer handle its surplus. If an agency decides to auction cars through sealed bids, it must advertise in 3 newspapers for 10 days. To find out if, when, and what an agency is disposing of through auction, contact that agency directly.

Illinois

Central Management Services, Division of Property Control, 3550 Great Northern Ave., Springfield, IL 62707, 217-793-1813. Two or three times per year this office auctions vehicles and property. Auctions are held at the Illinois state fairgrounds on Sangamon Avenue in Springfield. Auctions are always held on Saturdays. Property includes office equipment, desks, chairs, typewriters, restaurant equipment, calculators, cameras, refrigerators, and filing cabinets. Scrap metal and equipment not easily moved are sold by sealed bid. The office maintains a mailing list which costs $20/year to subscribe. Notices of auctions and bids are mailed out 3 weeks prior to the auction. The auctions are also advertised in advance in local newspapers. All the cars auctioned have a minimum mileage of 75,000 miles and were driven by state employees. Minimum bid begins at $300. Prices vary widely, but below-market prices are available.

Illinois auctions off vehicles by open bid auctions. (Confiscated cars are sold at federal auctions and may present greater possibility for a bargain.)

Indiana

State Surplus Property Section, 229 W. New York St., Indianapolis, IN 46202, 317-232-0134, warehouse; 317-232-1365, office. Indiana holds auctions as items accumulate through open cry auctions to the highest bidder. During the summer months, the state sells surplus from the Department of Transportation and the Department of Natural Resources. There is no mailing list. Auctions are advertised the first Thursday of every month in the Indianapolis Star. The auction date and selected auctioneer changes every year. The switch is made during July. Call the above office in May to obtain the new schedule. Sealed bids must contain 100% deposit. Payment is by cash, certified check, cashiers check, or money order. No personal checks or letters of credit are accepted. Items vary and are all state surplus.

Iowa

Department of Natural Resources, Wallace State Office Bldg., Des Moines, IA 50319, 515-281-5145. The Department of Natural Resources holds an auction when and if a sufficient number of items have accumulated, on the second Saturday of every May. Items disposed of include boats, fishing rods, tackle boxes, guns, and other fishing and hunting equipment, as well as office equipment. Payment is by cash or check with appropriate identification. There is no mailing list, but auctions are advertised in local newspapers.

Vehicle Dispatchers Garage, 301 E. 7th, Des Moines, IA 50319, 515-281-5121. The Department of Transportation holds auctions, if there is sufficient accumulation, three to four times per year at 9:00 am on Saturdays. The state disposes of approximately 500 vehicles yearly through these auctions. They mostly sell patrol cars, pickups and trucks. All have at least 81,000 miles of travel on them, and prices vary widely. A deposit of $200 is required on the day of the sale, with full payment due by the following Thursday. Payment may be made by cash or check with an accompanying letter of credit guaranteeing payment by the issuing institution. Viewing is possible Friday all day and Saturday morning prior to the sale. There is a mailing list. Auctions are advertised in the local papers.

Kansas

Kansas State Surplus Property, P.O. Box 19226, Topeka, KS 66619-0226, 913-296-2334, FAX: 913-296-7427. The State Surplus Property office sells sedans, snow plows, and everything they have, from staples to bulldozers. Property is first offered to other state agencies at set prices for 30 days. Whatever is left over is opened to public sale at the same prices. Prices tend to be competitive. Items not sold by auction are sold by sealed bids, with a catalog available containing descriptions of items and where they are located. Confiscated vehicles are not sold to the public. They are disposed of by county courthouses, usually to county agencies. To obtain copies of catalogs describing sealed bid items, write to the above address. It will be sent to you for 3 months, after which time your name will be purged unless you re-request it.

Kentucky

Kentucky Office of Surplus Property, 514 Barrett Ave., Frankfort, KY 40601, 502-564-4836. Kentucky holds public auctions on Saturdays every two or three months. Items may include vehicles, desks, chairs, calculators, typewriters, file cabinets, tape recorders, electronic equipment, couches, beds, and lawnmowers, to name a few. Merchandise may be viewed the day before an auction. The office maintains a mailing list and also advertises upcoming auctions in local newspapers. Some items are auctioned by sealed bids. Property is payable by cash, certified check, or money order.

Louisiana

Division of Administration, Louisiana Property Assistance Agency, P.O. Box 94095, 1059 Brickyard Lane, Baton Rouge, LA 70804-9095, 504-342-6849. Public auctions are held on the second Saturday of every month at 9:00 am at 1502 North 17th St. Items may be viewed at the warehouse from 8:00 am to 4:30 pm the week before. Property sold ranges from medical and office equipment, to boats, shop equipment, typewriters, file cabinets, pinball machines, bicycles, televisions, adding machines, and chairs, and vehicles. All items are sold "as is" and "where is." Payment is required in full the day of the auctions, but no personal or company checks are accepted. In addition, all merchandise must be removed within five days after the sale. Auctions are conducted by a different auctioneer each year, depending on who wins the bid for the annual contract.

Maine

Office of Surplus Property, Station 95, Augusta, ME 04333, 207-289-5750. Five or six times per year, Maine publicly auctions off vehicles on the grounds of the Augusta Mental Health Institute. You must register to be able to bid, and then you will automatically be notified of upcoming auctions. Vehicles may include police cruisers, pick-up trucks, snowmobiles, lawn mowers, and heavy equipment, such as large trucks, graders, and backhoes. Inspection is allowed between 1:00 pm and 3:00 pm on the Friday before, and 8:00 am and 10:00 am the day of the auctions, which are always held on Saturdays. The impound yard opens at 7:00 am. Vehicles may be started up but not driven. Personal checks, money orders, certified checks, and cash are all accepted. Office equipment and other non-vehicles items are sold by tag sale once per month, and prices are negotiable. Exact date, place, and time of auctions are announced in local newspapers, but there is no mailing list. Payment is due for both vehicles and other items the day of the auction or sale.

Maryland

Maryland State Department for Surplus Property, P.O. Box 122, 8037 Brock Bridge Rd., Jessup, MD 20794, 410-799-0440. Office furniture and the like are sold or donated to non-profit organizations or state agencies, and vehicles are sold to dealers only. The state maintains a retail store for surplus property at its warehouse at the above address. After a certain length of time, items that do not go to non-profits or state agencies become available to the public at set prices at its retail store.

Massachusetts

Massachusetts State Purchasing Agency, Department of Procurement and General Services, Surplus Property, One Ashburton Place, Boston, MA 02108, 617-727-7500. About six times per year, Massachusetts holds public auctions of surplus property. Bidders must register in the morning by filling out a card. The State Purchasing Agency places ads in The Boston Globe on the Sunday and Wednesday prior to each of the auctions, which are normally held on Saturdays. Vehicles are usually auctioned after about 60 or so accumulate. Vehicles sold include sedans, wagons, vans, and pick-ups with an average age of 7 years. The average car has over 100,000 miles. Conditions range from good to junk. Viewing is available the day before the auction from 9:00 am to 4:00 pm. Purchases are "as is". No start-ups allowed. The state does not auction other surplus property, in general, but occasionally special auctions are held for boats, parts from the Department of Public Works, and most recently, helicopters.

Michigan

State of Michigan, Department of Management and Budget, State Surplus Property, P.O. Box 30026, 3353 N. Logan, Lansing, MI 48913, 517-335-8444. The state auctions off all kinds of office furniture, household goods, machinery, livestock, and vehicles, such as sedans, buses, trucks, and boats. Auctions are held at different locations for different categories of property. The State Surplus Property Office sends out yearly calendars with auction dates and information. Contact them at the above address to have it sent to you. Double check dates because additions or changes may occur. Auctions are also published in the local newspapers. Payment may be made by cash or check and should include the 4% state sales tax. No refunds are made. Inspections of merchandise are available either the day before from 8:00 am to 3:00 pm or the morning of an auction from 8:00 am to 9:30 am. Auctions begin at 10:00 am. Items must be paid in full on the day of sale by cash or check. Buyer has 3 working days to remove the property.

Minnesota

Minnesota Surplus Operations Office, 5420 Highway 8, New Brighton, MN 55112, 612-639-4022; HOTLINE: 612-296-1056. Minnesota holds about 15 auctions per year at different locations around the state. They sell vehicles such as old patrol cars, passenger cars, trucks, vans, and trucks, as well as heavy machinery, boats, snowmobiles and outboard motors. The state also auctions off furniture, office equipment, kitchen equipment, tools, and confiscated items such as vehicles, computers, jewelry, car stereos and radios, and other personal effects. Many of these items are sold under market price. You may be put on a mailing list to receive a calendar for the schedule of upcoming auctions for the year. Auctions are advertised in the locale where they occur by radio, TV, and in Minneapolis and St. Paul newspapers. Inspection of property is held from 8:00 am to 9:30 am, an hour and a half before the auction begins; and payment is by personal check for in-state residents, cash, or money order.

Mississippi

Bureau of Surplus Property, P.O. Box 5778, Whitfield Rd., Jackson, MS 39288, 601-939-2050. Up to three times a year, Mississippi auctions such items as machinery, textiles, ammunition boxes, and unrepairable vehicles. Contact the above office to be put on the mailing list. Auctions are advertised in state newspapers. Inspections are allowed during the two days before the auction. Payment may be made by cash, bank draft, or check with bank letter of credit.

Department of Public Safety, Support Services, P.O. Box 958, Jackson, MS 39205, 601-987-1453. The state cars that are auctioned are mostly patrol cars, and only occasionally vans and other types of vehicles. State cars are usually wrecked or old. Most have at least 100,000 miles on them. Recent average prices have ranged from $1200 to $1500. The state is keeping cars longer, so less are being sold. These agency cars and others from the Department of Wildlife and Fisheries, military bases, Narcotics Division, and U.S. Marshal's Office -- which includes confiscated cars -- are auctioned the first Tuesday of every month by Mid South Auctions, 6655 N. State St., Jackson, MS 39213, 601-956-2700. Call to be put on the mailing list. Many car dealers as well as the public attend these auctions, so prices are competitive. Bargains are still possible. Payment must be in cash or cashiers check -- no personal checks. The balance is due the day of the auction.

Missouri

State Of Missouri, Surplus Property Office, Materials Management Section, P.O. Drawer 1310, 117 N. Riverside Dr., Jefferson City, MO 65102, 314-751-3415. At various times throughout the year, Missouri holds regular public auctions, as well as sealed bid auctions of merchandise located at various places in the state. The wide range of items include clothing, office equipment and vehicles. No confiscated or seized vehicles or other items are sold. You can be put on a mailing list to receive notices of upcoming auctions, plus they are advertised in local newspapers. For regular auctions, inspection is available the day before or on the day of the auction; and sealed bid items may be viewed two or three days before the deadline. Items may be sold by lot or individually. Payment may be made by cash or personal check.

Montana

Property and Supply Bureau, 930 Lyndale Ave., Helena, MT 59620-0137, 406-444-4514. Montana holds a vehicle auction once a year, of about 300 state vehicles. Contact the above to get on the mailing list. The auctions are by open cry and sealed bid. All items are from state surplus; nothing is seized or confiscated. These auctions are advertised in local newspapers prior to the auction. In addition, the state offers other property for sale each month on the second Friday of the month. The sales include items such as office supplies, computers, chairs, tables, and vehicles including trucks, vans, sedans, highway patrol cars, and more. Payment can be by cash up to $300. Higher amounts must be paid by certified or business check, or bank check.

Nebraska

Nebraska Office of Administrative Services, Material Division, Surplus Property, P.O. Box 94901, Lincoln, NE 68509, 402-479-4890. Three or four times a year, Nebraska auctions off office furniture, computers, couches, and more. Separate auctions are held for vehicles and heavy equipment -- also about three or four times per year. Auctions are advertised in newspapers and on radio, and a mailing list is also kept. Sealed bids for property such as scrap iron, wrecked vehicles, guard posts, and tires are taken. Items are available for viewing two days prior to the auctions, which are held on Saturdays at 5001 S. 14th St. All items are sold "as is". Payment, which can be made by cash or check, must be in full on the day of the auction.

Nevada

Nevada State Purchasing Division, Kinkead Bldg., Room 400 Capitol Complex, Carson City, NV 89710, 702-687-4070. The sales and auction are located at the warehouse at 2250 Barnett Way, Reno, NV 89512. About once a year, Nevada holds a sale on the second Saturday in August of such items as calculators, desks, cabinets, tables and chairs. Office equipment is released for sale to the public at a set price. The sale is held to clear the warehouse, and is on a first come, first serve basis, with minimum prices to cover service and handling marked on the property. Very few vehicles are confiscated. Most are surplus turned in by other state agencies for resale. Vehicles and motorcycles are auctioned. Public auctions are not served by mailing lists but are advertised in the newspapers. You can be put on a mailing list to receive notice of sealed bid sales of 19 categories of merchandise, including heavy equipment, boats, and planes. Once you have requested to place your name on the mailing list, if you do not subsequently bid on two consecutive occasions, it will be removed. Payment is by cash or local check with proper I.D. No out of state checks accepted. For vehicles, you can put down a 5% deposit with 5 days to complete payment. The county, city and University of Nevada also advertise and hold public auctions.

New Hampshire

Office of Surplus Property 78 Regional Dr., Building 3, Concord, NH 03301, 603-271-2126. New Hampshire holds two auctions per year of vehicles and other equipment, such as office furniture and machines, and refrigerators. Vehicles, which include cruisers, pickups, vans, and sometimes confiscated vehicles may be viewed the day before the auction, while other merchandise can be viewed on the same day just before the auction. A mailing list is maintained, and ads are also placed in local newspapers prior to the auctions. Acceptable payment includes cash and certified funds.

New Jersey

New Jersey Purchase and Property Distribution Center, CN-234, Trenton, NJ 08625-0234, 609-530-3300. New Jersey auctions used state vehicles such as vans, various types of compacts, and occasionally boats, buses and heavy equipment. Frequency of auctions depends on availability which currently averages once per month. Vehicles may be inspected and started up the day before the auction from 9:00 am to 3:00 pm. Payment is by cash, money order, or certified check. No personal checks. A 10% deposit is required to hold a vehicle, and then the successful bidder has 7 calendar days to complete payment and remove the vehicle by Friday. If an item is left after that, even if paid in full, a $20 per day storage fee is charged. To be advised of auctions, put your name on the mailing list by writing the address above. Phone calls to be put on the mailing list are not accepted. A recent vehicle auction in New Jersey offered a variety of Dodge and Chevy vehicles, ages ranging from three to thirteen years, with mileages from 50,000 to 130,000. Other surplus items are not put up for public auction; rather they are offered to other state agencies.

New Mexico

New Mexico Highway and Transportation Department, SB-2, 7315 Cerrillos Road, P.O. Box 1149, Santa Fe, NM 87504-1149, 505-827-5580. About once a year, on the last Saturday of September, New Mexico auctions off vehicles, including sedans, loaders, backhoes, snow removal equipment, pick-ups, vans, four-wheel drives, and tractors. They have some office equipment as well. The items come from state agencies. You may place your name on a mailing list to receive the exact date of the auction and descriptions of merchandise up for bidding. A public entity auction is held first. The published list of items to be publicly auctioned consists of what is left over. Everything is open auction; there are no sealed bids. Items may be inspected the day before the auction. Payment is by cash, checks with proper I.D., money orders, or cashier's checks. No credit cards.

Department of Public Safety, State Police Division, Attn: Major W.D. Morrow, P.O. Box 1628, Santa Fe, NM 87504. The above holds a public auction on the second Saturday in July at 4491 Cerrillos Road. Write the office above to be put on the mailing list. It is also advertised in local newspapers. Items sold include everything from calculators to cars. They come from seizures and surplus from other agencies. The vehicles may be viewed and started up the Friday before the auction. Payment may be by cash, money order, cashier's check or personal check with bank letter of guarantee.

New York

State of New York Office of General Service, Bureau of Surplus Property, Building #18, W.A. Harriman State Office Building Campus, Albany, NY 12226, 518-457-6335. The Office of General Services holds auctions continuously in locations around the state. The items are so numerous that the state finds it necessary to sell them by category. You can designate which categories you are interested in on the mailing list application. Items are sold as they become available. Sales are advertised one week in advance in local newspapers. These items include surplus and used office equipment, scrap material, agricultural items (even unborn cows). Most categories such as medical, photographic, institutional and maintenance equipment are sold through sealed bids, usually in lots of varying size. To participate in a sealed bid, you place your name on a mailing list for items in seven different categories, then make your bid by mail. The highest bidder wins and is notified by mail. Mailings give as much information as possible about the items being auctioned; but state officials stress that merchandise is sold "as is" and "where is". They advise viewing property in person before making a bid. A ten percent deposit is required with each sealed

bid. Vehicles are sold by public auction and may include cars, trucks, buses, tractors, bulldozers, mowers, compressors, plows, sanders, and other highway maintenance and construction equipment. Large items are sold individually, and smaller equipment, such as chain saws, is more likely to be sold in lots. These auctions take place about 55 times per year. It is always possible that enough surplus may not accumulate to warrant an auction. The state warns that just because an auction is scheduled is no guarantee that it will occur. Payment may be made by certified check or cash. A ten percent deposit will hold a vehicle until the end of the day.

North Carolina

State Surplus Property, P.O. Box 33900, Raleigh, NC 27636-3900, 919-733-3889. North Carolina sells through sealed bids surplus state merchandise including vehicles and office equipment. Office equipment includes furniture, typewriters, desks, and chairs. For a fee of $15 you can be placed on a mailing list to receive weekly advisories of what is for auction, with a description of the item and its condition. Otherwise, if you visit the warehouse in person, you can pick up free samples of bid listings and look at lists of prices that items sold for in previous auctions. The warehouse is located on Highway 54 - Old Chapel Hill Road. Payment is by money order or certified check, and you have 15 days to pay for your merchandise and 15 days to pick it up. Items may be inspected two weeks before an auction from Monday to Friday between 8:00 am and 5:00 pm. On Tuesdays, the warehouse is closed between 1:00 pm and 3:00 pm when the bids are opened and the public is then invited to attend. The state may reject bids that are too low. Vehicles vary greatly in type and condition.

North Dakota

Surplus Property Office, P.O. Box 7293, Bismarck, ND 58507, 701-224-2273. Once a year, usually in September, the Office of Surplus Property auctions through open bidding surplus office furniture and equipment, as well as vehicles and scrap materials. The auction is advertised the two days before and merchandise may be viewed the morning of the auction. The auction is held at Igo Industrial Park. Cash, cashiers checks, or money orders are acceptable forms of payment. Personal or business checks are accepted only with a bank letter of credit.

Ohio

Office of State and Federal Surplus Property, 4200 Surface Road, Columbus, OH 43228, 614-466-5052. Ohio holds public auctions and sealed bid sales on a wide range of office machines and equipment, furniture, and vehicles. The sealed bid sales are held at various locations around the state for inoperable vehicles. These may be inspected any time after you receive your bid invitation in the mail. No mailing list is maintained. Call or write for the information. When you attend an auction, you can fill out a label that will be used to notify you of the next auction. Other vehicle auctions are held three to four times a year, depending on the amount accumulated. Inspections are available the day before. Vehicles may include sedans, trucks, vans, 4x4s, boats, mowers, tractors, and chain saws. No seized or confiscated items are sold. At the time of the auction, a 25% downpayment is required, with the balance due by the following Monday (auctions are held on Saturdays). For the sealed bid auctions, payment must be by money order or certified check.

Oklahoma

Central Purchasing, Dept. Central Services, B-4, State Capitol, Oklahoma City, OK 73105, 405-521-3046; general information only for public auctions, 405-521-3835; for general information and information on sealed bids, 405-521-2110. The charge is $10 for which you will receive all the information and descriptions. Oklahoma auctions vehicles as they accumulate. The state advertises upcoming auctions in local newspapers. The state tells their condition. Vehicles often have from 80,000 to 120,000 miles on them and it is rare for a car to be rated as fair - - which means it is in running condition. They are usually bought by wholesalers. State agency cars are commonly sold, but occasionally seized or confiscated cars are sold. Agencies most likely to have auctions are: Department of Human Services (occasionally vehicles and other items, but they usually take their cars to public auctions); Wildlife Department (vehicles); Department of Public Safety (vehicles); and the Department of Transportation (vehicles). The Department of Transportation has four auctions per year. The cars and trucks can have 120,000 miles on them. They are usually not in good condition. The state advises that you contact each agency separately for details. Sealed bid auctions of all kinds of merchandise are also held. You may request your name to be placed on a mailing list, but if you do not bid three times, it will be removed. Otherwise, visit the office to view a catalog of listings.

Oregon

Department of General Services, Surplus Property, 1655 Salem Industrial Drive NE, Salem, OR 97310, 503-378-4714 (Salem area). Oregon auctions both vehicles and other equipment, such as office furniture. Merchandise may include snow plows, horse trailers, computer equipment, desks, chairs, tires or shop equipment. Some items are in excellent condition, and bargains may be found. Items come from state agency surplus and confiscations. On rare occasions exotic items such as a Porsche and hot tub have been sold. Public sales are held every Friday at set prices. Sealed bid sales are held separately. The frequency of auctions depends on the amount of items to be disposed. The numbers of vehicles for sale is increasing. Cars are also sold every week at set prices. For info call the 24 hour information line that is always kept current, 503-373-1392. Ads are also placed on radio and in local newspapers in the areas where the auction will be held, giving the date and location of the auction. The procedure is to register and obtain a bidder number, which you hold up when you are making a bid. The forms may be obtained at the auction site. At the same time as you register, you must show some form of identification. The conditions and terms of sale are always listed. At the public sales if you pay by Mastercard or Visa, title is immediately released. You can also pay 10% down at the auction site and pay the balance at the office with Mastercard or Visa in 3 days.

Pennsylvania

General Services Department, Bureau of Vehicle Management, 2221 Forster Street, Harrisburg, PA 17105, 717-783-3132. About 10 times per year, depending on the number of cars accumulated, the DGS auctions off all kinds of vehicles. Many have mileages under 100,000, and ages commonly range from 1979 to 1986. There are about 200 cars at each auction. They are mostly used state agency cars that have been replaced, but up to 3 seized cars are also sold each year. An inspection period begins two weeks before an auction on Monday through Friday from 9:00 am to 5:00 pm at the storage facility located at 22nd & Forster Sts. in Harrisburg. Inspection period ends 2 days before the auctions. Each car has a form detailing its condition. It will state if the car must be towed. All cars are sold "as is". Cars are started up the day of the auction, which is open cry. If you request an application, you may have your name put on a mailing list for advance advisories of auctions for a period of six months. A $100 deposit is required (cash only) if you win a bid, with full payment due within five working days by cashier's check, certified check, or postal money order. No personal or company checks accepted.

Bureau of Supplies and Surplus, Department of General Services, P.O. Box 1365, 2221 Forster Street, Harrisburg, PA 17105, 717-787-4083. The Bureau of Supplies and Surplus of the General Services Department sells such items as mainframe computers and off-loading equipment, office furniture and machines, including typewriters, desks, chairs, sectional furniture, filing cabinets, copy machines, dictaphones, and calculators. This merchandise is first offered to other state agencies, then municipalities, and is then put up for public sale after five days. There is no mailing list for notification of upcoming auctions, but ads are placed in the local newspapers in the area where an auction will be held and in the *Pennsylvania Bulletin*. You can be put on a mailing list for some specific items such as heavy equipment that is sold by sealed bid. State which categories of bidder's lists you are interested in. The notice you receive will give date, times and places to inspect and submit a bid. A $100 security deposit must accompany the bid. Property is sold at set prices. You may call to find out what items are currently for sale, or visit the warehouse which sells mostly office equipment such as computers, desks, chairs and file cabinets, between 10:00 am and 3:00 pm Monday through Friday.

Rhode Island

Department of Administration, Division of Purchase, 1 Capitol Hill, Providence, RI 02908, 401-277-2375. Rhode Island's Division of Purchase auctions off its surplus vehicles and office equipment, as well as other items, through sealed bid to a list of buyers who are usually in the business. Most of the cars sold have no plates and must be towed. They are sold primarily to wholesalers. Office equipment and supplies are primarily sold to suppliers. If the state ever does hold a public auction, it advertises two or three times in the local papers.

South Carolina

Surplus Property Office, Division of General Services, 1441 Boston Avenue, West Columbia, SC 29170, 803-822-5490. South Carolina sells items ranging from vehicles, to office and heavy equipment. Property is collected in monthly cycles and offered first to state agencies before being put up for sale to the public. No mailing list is kept for it, but you can visit the warehouse on 1441 Boston Avenue, in West Columbia, which is open between 8:00 am and 4:30 pm

Monday through Friday. Prices are tagged; there is no auction. Every 6 to 8 weeks, the General Services Division holds public auctions of items by lot for State, Federal, and Wildlife Department property. A mailing list is kept for advance advisories and property descriptions. There is a $15 fee, payable by check or money order, to receive the mailings annually. Items can be inspected two days prior to the sale. You are advised to make notes of the numbers of property you are interested in, then to check back to inquire if it is still available, since state agencies have first choice.

South Carolina Public Transportation Department, 1500 Shop Road, P.O. Box 191, Columbia SC 29202, 803-737-6635, for general information; 803-737-1488, for mailing list. About every five weeks, the South Carolina Department of Public Transportation holds auctions of its used and surplus vehicles, which include everything from patrol cars, trucks, and passenger cars, to highway equipment. To have your name put on a mailing list of upcoming auctions, call the number above. Payment is by cash, check or money order. Banking information will be requested for personal checks. Vehicles may be viewed from 9:00 am to 4:30 pm on the Monday and Tuesday before the auctions, which are always held on Wednesdays at 10 am. You may start up the cars. It is open bidding. Usually about 100 cars are sold at each auction.

South Dakota

Bureau of Administration, State Property Management, 701 East Sioux Ave., Pierre, SD 57501-3321, 605-773-4935. Twice a year, in the spring and fall, the Department of Transportation holds on its premises public auctions for office equipment and vehicles, including pick-ups. Most vehicles have over 85,000 miles on them and sell for well under market price. The cars usually sell for under $5000. Most are surplus or have been replaced at state agencies. A few are from seizures or confiscation. You may visually inspect the vehicles prior to the auction, but you may not enter them. However, during the auction, the vehicles are started and demonstrated. Auctions and special sales are located wherever the most property has accumulated in the state. Call or write the above office to have your name put on the mailing list. There is no charge. Terms are up to the auctioneer. Title is released only after checks clear, or immediately if accompanied by a bank letter.

Tennessee

Department of General Services Property Utilization, 6500 Centennial Boulevard, Nashville, TN 37243-0543, 615-741-1711. Tennessee auctions surplus vehicles, and machinery of various kinds -- milling machines, lathes, welders, and metal working equipment. The vehicles are of all types, including dump trucks, pick-ups, sedans, and station wagons. Auctions are held twelve times a year in Jackson, Dandridge, Nashville, and Chattanooga. A mailing list is kept, and auctions are advertised in local newspapers. Items are available for inspection the day before the auction. Keys are in the car, and start ups are allowed. Register at no charge the morning of the auction. Payment can be in cash, cashier's checks, or certified check. The state also conducts sealed bids usually 12 times a year and most commonly on office furniture.

Texas

Texas State Purchasing and General Services Commission, P.O. Box 13047, Capitol Station, Austin, TX 78711-3047, 512-463-3445. Every two months, Texas auctions off vehicles, office furniture and machines, and highway equipment. You must apply to be put on the mailing list, which will give you a brief description of items available at the next auction (call 512-463-3416). It will also tell you the location of the auction, which changes often. You may call the agency selling the property to arrange to inspect it; however, merchandise that is on site is available for inspection two hours before the auction. Items are mostly used state property, although some is confiscated as well. You must register to bid beforehand. Most registrations take place the day of the auction, beginning at 7:00 am. Payment on a winning bid is due at the end of the auction. Cash, cashiers check, certified check, money order, bank draft with Letter of Credit, or personal or company check with Letter of Credit are acceptable forms of payment. Items sold on site must be removed the day of the sale. For off-site items, 30 days are usually allowed for removal. Texas also holds sealed bid auctions, where you make a bid by mail. First, you indicate what category of property you are interested in, and they will send you bid forms and descriptions of items in that category. Sealed bid participants are notified by letter if winning bids and the exact amount due. Deposits for non-winners are returned. Also, each of the Texas state agencies hold local sales, for which each has its own mailing list and advertises in the local papers.

Government Auctions and Surplus Property

Utah

Utah State Surplus Office, 522 South 700 West, Salt Lake City, UT 84104, 801-533-5885. Four or five times a year, Utah auctions vehicles and office furniture, as well as heavy equipment, whenever property accumulates. Most items are sold by public auction, although sealed bid auctions are sometimes held as well. Mail-in bids are accepted if you can't attend in person. A 10% deposit is required. It is refunded unless you win the bid. Most of the public auctions are held in Salt Lake City at the address above, although some are occasionally held in other parts of the state. You may request your name be put on a mailing list to receive advance notice of auctions and a description of the items. Auctions are always held on Saturdays. Property may be viewed the Friday prior to an auction. Acceptable forms of payment are cash, cashier's check, and personal checks up to $100 with two forms of I.D. No business checks are accepted. Items must be removed and payments must be made in full on the day of the auction.

Vermont

Vermont Central Surplus Property Agency, RD #2, Box 520, Montpelier, VT 05602, 802-828-3394. Vermont sells low-priced surplus office furniture and machines on retail basis between 8:00 am and 4:00 pm daily at the Central Garage on Barre Montpelier Rd. Items include desks, chairs, file cabinets, and book shelves. Twice a year, vehicles, which may include police cruisers, dump trucks, and pick-ups, are sold by public auction, on a Saturday in late May and September. A mailing list is kept to advise you in advance of upcoming auctions. To have you name placed on it, contact the auctioneer. Local newspapers also advertise them. Vehicles may be inspected the Friday before an auction. The auctions are open bid, "as is", and "where is". There are no hold backs. The highest bid, even if it is far below market value, will take the item. A 25% deposit is due the day of the sale. The balance is due in 2 days, by the following Tuesday by 3:00 pm. Payment is up to the auctioneer, who is a private contractor. Usually, checks must be bank-certified, and a deposit is required to hold any vehicle not paid for in full the day of the auction.

Virginia

State Surplus Property, P.O. Box 1199, Richmond, VA 23231, 804-786-3876. Virginia auctions everything but land. It sells vehicles, office equipment and furniture, computers, tractors, bulldozers, dump trucks, pick-ups, and vans. Some of the cars are in good condition. Scrap metal, tires, and batteries are sold separately. Auctions may be held on any day of the week except Sunday. Sales are by both public auction and sealed bid. Agencies have the discretion to decide which way their surplus is sold. There are sealed bid offerings every week, and as many as two auctions per week. Twice a year there are auctions for cars only. The rest are mixed. Items are occasionally seized, such as jewelry. Auction sites are at various locations around the state. You may write to place your name on a mailing list for both public auctions and sealed bid auctions; phone call requests are not honored. For sealed bid, there are usually 100 to 200 items available. Inspections are encouraged. They are allowed the day before the auction and again for a couple of hours on the day of the auction. For sealed bid items, you may call for more details on the items offered for sale or to make an appointment to inspect the items.

Washington

Office of Commodity Redistribution, 2805 C St. S.W., Building 5, Door 49, Auburn, WA 98001-7401, 206-931-3931. Every Friday the public can visit the store at the central warehouse. It is open from 12:00 noon to 2:30 pm and purchases are for cash only. Washington holds auctions of used state vehicles, conducts "silent bids" (auctions where the bids are written rather than spoken), and also sells surplus materials by sealed bid (bids are placed through the mail) via catalogs. The vehicles are auctioned about every three months and include all kinds of used state conveyances, from patrol cars, to trucks and passenger cars, most having over 100,000 miles. There are few new luxury or confiscated type vehicles. The "silent bids" are held once a month, and include large quantities of office furniture sold by the pallet, with the exception of typewriters, which are sold individually. You may visit the warehouse to inspect the items beforehand. Payment may be made by cashiers check, money order, or cash, but no personal checks. For the sealed bids, you may request a catalog of merchandise, which includes everything from vehicles, to scrap material, office

equipment, computers, clothes, cleaning fluids, tools, and pumps. For any of these sales, you may request to be put on the mailing list at the address above.

West Virginia

West Virginia State Agency Surplus Property, 2700 Charles Ave., Dunbar, WV 25064, 304-766-2626. Contact the above to be put on the mailing list. Statewide sealed bids have a separate mailing list you must specifically request. For sealed bids, prospective buyers can inspect only by going to the site. Each month, West Virginia auctions such items as chairs, desks, telephones, computers, typewriters, office equipment and furniture, and other miscellaneous property, as well as vehicles. They are all auctioned at the same auction. The vehicles are in varying conditions. The auctions are always held on a Saturday. Inspection is available the week before the auction from 9:00 am to 6:00 pm. On auction day, the gate opens at 9:00 am. Miscellaneous property is sold until 12:00 noon. Then all the cars are sold. If time allows, any remaining miscellaneous property is auctioned. Payment may be by personal check, business check, or certified check, but no cash. Payment is due in full the same day. For sealed bids, payment is due within one week after a bid has won. Deposits, usually 20% of a bid, are returned to unsuccessful bidders, or in the case of winning bids, applied to the purchase price.

Wisconsin

Department of Transportation, P.O. Box 7396, Hill Farm Building, 4802 Sheboygan Ave., Madison, WI 53707-7396, 608-266-3965. Call 608-267-3620 to inquire whether a specific item is for sale. The Department of Transportation continuously sells a variety of merchandise from its warehouse in Madison. These items vary greatly from week to week, but may include work tables, desks, files, calculators and other office equipment and furniture, as well as vehicles. Call ahead before visiting the facility to view the property, which is sold at set prices. The few surplus items the state has are used up by other organizations or sold informally as parties express an interest. A small room stores all the items. Computers, however, and occasionally road finds accumulate. These are sold by sealed bid and you can call to get on the bid list.

Wisconsin Department of Administration, P.O. Box 7880, Madison, WI 53708, 608-266-8024. The Department of Administration holds vehicle auctions approximately every month -- usually with around 100 vehicles, including passenger vehicles, vans, trucks, and station wagons, all of different makes and models. Most are in running condition. Cars that need towing are rare and clearly designated. The vehicles are usually at least four years old, or have at least 70,000 miles on them. The auctions begin on Saturday at 10:00 am. Cars may be inspected the Friday before from 1:00 pm to 6:00 pm. The public may also inspect and start up the cars from 8:00 am to 10:00 am on the morning of the auction. You may have your name placed on a mailing list for advance notice of auctions; however, the auctions are also advertised in local newspapers. There are no sealed bids. Payment is by cash, personal check, cashiers check, or money order. No credit cards. The full amount is due the day of the auction. Occasionally, if the auctioneer is consulted at pre-registration, a small delay for bank loan arrangements are pre-approved so that the prospective buyer can bid.

Wyoming

State Motor Pool, 723 West 19th Street, Cheyenne, WY 82002, 307-777-7247. Although it first donates most of its surplus property to other state agencies, Wyoming does auction its remaining surplus vehicles, which may include pick-ups, vans, sedans, and jeeps, and also tires. Although most have high mileage -- from 80,000 to 100,000 miles, the majority are dependable vehicles. You can have your name placed on a mailing list to receive advance notices of auctions, which are held when items accumulate. On the average, one or two auctions are held each year. The state also advertises in local newspapers. Inspection of the vehicles is available between 3:00 pm and 6:00 pm the Friday before the auction, which is usually held on Saturdays and begins at 10:00 am. No start ups are allowed. Anything known to be wrong with the car will be on the list handed out at the auction, or sent if you are on the mailing list. Payment depends on the auctioneer who is a private contractor. Usually, cash or check with proper I.D. are acceptable. Some cars go for well below market value, but others may bid up in price, depending on the mood of the crowd.

Unclaimed Property: Does The Government Owe <u>You</u> Money?

In the United States today, experts believe that about $5 billion dollars in unclaimed money is collecting dust in state Abandoned Property offices. Some of the monetary items that end up in a state's possessions after being declared abandoned by the holding institution include:

- forgotten bank accounts
- uncashed stock dividends
- insurance payments
- safe deposit boxes
- utility deposits
- travelers checks
- money orders

People move away, lose track of investments, or die, and the accounts or funds, after a set amount of time -- frequently five years -- are reported to the state Treasurer's Escheats, Comptroller's, or Revenue office. The state then tries to track down the owners and return the money.

If you think financial property may be held by your state, the first step is to contact the appropriate office (a state-by-state listing follows) to find out whether your name is listed. Or, in the case of the estate of a deceased person, the listing would be under his/her name. You will then fill out a claim form which you must return together with the required identification or proof of ownership. Requirements for proving ownership may vary according to the amount of the claim and the complications involved, but frequently states will ask for such things as copies of driver's licenses, social security numbers, and bank account numbers and passbooks. Most require that the information be notarized. A few states have limitations on how long they keep abandoned property before turning it over to state coffers, but most keep it indefinitely. Some also pay interest on the money if the property was originally interest-bearing.

Honest Finders vs. Vultures

The states currently owe money from abandoned property to an estimated one in ten people in the country, according to attorney David Epstein. But many states do not have the resources to investigate every case, and do little more than advertise names of owners in local newspapers. The resulting gap is sometimes filled by professional "finders" or "heir searchers" who find the owners themselves and charge a fee or commission in exchange for returning it. They can obtain lists, legally in most cases but sometimes surreptitiously, of the names of the owners from the state offices, then conduct their own search. Some finders have charged commissions of 60% to 100%. The price of one finders fee in a past Colorado case was 30% of the dividends and all the shares of stock! Finders can, however, perform a valuable service by reuniting people with money that would have been lost to them forever. Because of cases where these finders have charged excessive fees to people for returning their own money, and because of the strain their

demands have put on some already over-burdened state offices, the finders have a shady reputation in some quarters. One state office, for example, refers to them as "bounty hunters," and another calls them "vultures." Many state offices feel that the finders infringe on the owner's right to have their money returned with no charge involved, which is the goal of the state.

The National Association of Abandoned Property Administrators says that since the states never find 100% of the owners, there is a place for honest finders. For example, if a state is unable to locate the owner of a sizable property that he didn't even know about, and a finder does the job, then a service has been performed. Many states, such as Texas, limit the amount of commission a finder may charge; and others have confidentiality laws that prevent them from aiding finders in any way.

One of the biggest obstacles states face is obtaining the cooperation of the banks, insurance companies, and other institutions in reporting properties to them. Despite laws that govern how a holding institution should deal with dormant accounts, they are often low priority items in a business. A state must sometimes work hard to convince them that the state is best qualified to return the money. Some states are passing laws that would penalize lax holding companies by charging them a fee.

With billions of dollars in property sitting around out there, clearly many people have an interest in what happens to it. Finders, keepers, states and businesses all have something at stake, and the losers will be those who fail to take advantage of the services that the states offer.

State Listing of Unclaimed Property Offices

Alabama
Department of Revenue and Unclaimed Property, 50 Ripley Street, Room 1116, Montgomery, AL 36104, or P.O. Box 327580, Montgomery, AL 36132-7580; 205-242-9614. Alabama sends notices to the last known addresses of people whose unclaimed property has reverted to the Department of Revenue. The state also advertises in local newspapers four times a year - in a total of 63 different publications. In Alabama only owners, heirs or those possessing power of attorney will receive the property once it has been rightfully claimed. It usually takes at least three weeks for the claimant to receive his money once the claim has been approved. The state has no statute of limitations on how long it can hold unclaimed property.

Alaska
Alaska Department of Revenue, Income and Excise Audit Division, Unclaimed Property Section, 1111 West 8th Street, Room 106, Juneau, AK 99801; 907-465-4653. Alaska publishes names of unclaimed property owners once a year in the three major newspapers, sends the information to state legislators, and contacts local news services in order to try to find the owners. They have a three person office, and the person in charge of refunds also makes efforts to investigate the whereabouts of owners. There is no full time locator. Alaska is currently holding an estimated 4.4 million dollars worth of unclaimed property.

Arizona
Arizona Department of Revenue, Unclaimed Property, 1600 West Monroe, Room 610, Phoenix, AZ 85007; 602-542-3908. Twice a year the state runs

Unclaimed Property: Does The Government Owe <u>You</u> Money?

advertisements in local newspapers with the names of people who have unclaimed property. Claimants need three pieces of I.D. to identify themselves as the rightful owners. In the case of an estate or property of a deceased person, a copy of the will and death certificate is also required. The cumulative number of people who once had, or still do have unclaimed property in Arizona is over 170,000.

Arkansas

Auditor of the State, Unclaimed Property Division, 230 State Capitol, Little Rock, AR 72201; 501-324-9670. Arkansas publishes the names of owners yearly in local newspapers once a week for two consecutive weeks. It also sends letters to the last known address of each person. Since 1988 the state has held "The Great Arkansas Treasure Hunt " which featured TV spots in an effort to locate owners. This year out of a total of $1,666,802 in unclaimed property, the state paid out $632,428. Arkansas is one of the few states where the unclaimed property reverts to a general fund after three years in the Unclaimed Property Office. This does not mean the money escheats to the state, but once the money goes into the fund, the owner must go to the State Claims Commissioner to claim it. The state will deal only with the actual owner of the property and not with other parties, including those endowed with power of attorney unless it is court ordered. Finders are restricted to a ten per-cent commission of the total retrieved. Refunds are usually sent out within about two weeks of approval.

California

Unclaimed Property Office, P.O. Box 942850, Sacramento, CA 94250-5873; 916-323-2827, toll free 1-800-992-4647 (CA only). In California the law requires the state to advertise unclaimed properties. However, according to Tom Holland, who heads the Unclaimed Property Office, they no longer have a special locator unit, due to budget cuts. The office uses radio and television advertisements, as well as newspaper advisories to locate owners every quarter. A person inquiring about abandoned property in California can get an instant answer by phone from the Office's computer. However, they still need to fill out a claim form and show proof of identity such as birth certificate and social security card once they have determined that the property they are looking for is in the hands of the state. There are hundreds of finders in California trying to get a piece of the considerable action in a state with over 1.6 million unclaimed properties worth seven hundred million dollars. They can come to the state's office or a public library and look up information on microfiche, but are limited to a ten per cent commission. In addition, the state will only make checks out amounting to 10 percent for a finder, while sending the remaining 90 percent directly to the owner.

Colorado

Colorado State Treasurer, Division of Unclaimed Property, 1560 Broadway, Suite 630, Denver, CO 80202; 303-894-2449. Colorado has no statute of limitations on unclaimed property. Once a year in March, the state places the names of owners whose accounts they received the previous year in local newspapers. Colorado will deal only with owners. Finders may obtain a list of property owners for $130, but no research is available to them. The list has 60,000 names on it. The Unclaimed Property Office will only send checks directly to owners. Returns usually go out within four to six weeks of approval. Colorado, like other states, also stipulates that no owner is obligated to pay a finder a commission until the funds have been held by the state for 24 months or longer. The state will not go through an intermediary. Claim forms are only sent to owners. The state currently holds 200,000 names on file of unclaimed property owners.

Connecticut

Treasury Department, 55 Elm St., Hartford, CT 06106; 203-566-5516. Accounts bearing interest are paid a 4 percent interest. Connecticut lists names of owners in local newspapers every quarter, rotating through two of the eight counties. The state has about 140 million dollars that is currently unclaimed - approximately 200,000 owners. This office is currently getting onto computer. Returns are made out to owners only. Finders are limited to a 50% commission, or 20% commission if the claim is under two years old.

Delaware

Delaware State Escheator, Abandoned Property Division, P.O. Box 8931, Wilmington, DE 19899; If you have a claim, write to Delaware State Escheator, P.O. Box 1039, Boston, MA 02103-1039; 302-577-3349. Delaware requires different kinds of proof of ownership, depending on the kind or amount of the claim. After approval, a return is usually mailed out in about six to eight weeks.

The state publishes names of owners in local newspapers and occasionally takes the lists to state fairs. On average, Delaware receives 20,000 items per year. Delaware will send returns in joint names of finder and owner.

District of Columbia

Department of Finance and Revenue, Unclaimed Property Division, 300 Indiana Ave. N.W., Room 5008, Washington, D.C. 20001; 202-727-0063. The District of Columbia requires the usual proof of ownership, plus social security numbers to identify owners. They get out the returns in about four to six weeks. D.C. places advertisements in newspapers in August and February, as well as sending out letters to owners. They do not have a locating unit. D.C. currently holds $11 million in unclaimed property. In 1991 two million dollars of unclaimed property has been returned. Finders are limited to 10% commission. Finders must wait until the District government has held an account for seven months before they can contract to recover it, and must have documentation and a contract that proves they have authority to act on behalf of the owner. The check is issued in the owner's name, but is sent to the address requested.

Florida

Office of Comptroller, Division of Finance, Abandoned Property Section, Tallahassee, FL 32399-0350; 904-487-0510. Florida deals with owners and other parties, but finders must be licensed private investigators. Claims are advertised in newspapers. Claims may be viewed on microfiche in the office. Lists of items are sold for $30. Returns are made out only to owners or investigators. They currently have about 141 million dollars worth of unclaimed property. There is no limit to the amount of commission finders may collect.

Georgia

Georgia Department of Revenue, Unclaimed Property Office, 270 Washington St. Room 405, Atlanta, GA 30334; 404-656-4244. Georgia is in the process of upgrading its office and soon hopes to speed up its return time on claims. Claimants may write, telephone, or come in and view lists on microfiche at the Georgia Department of Archives, 404-656-2393 in order to determine if they have property in the office. The next step is to fill out a claim form and return it with the necessary documentation and proof of identity. Checks are then sent out within a month. The office now has 4 employees. As part of its upgrading, the Georgia office also has more resources to locate owners, through records searches and outreach programs at state public events and placing lists in state Tax Commissioners' offices. They also place advertisements in 159 county newspapers and on television. Georgia holds property in perpetuity and does not pay interest. If you call to inquire about unclaimed property you may have coming to you, the office will check its records. However, nothing has been updated since 1987 on either microfiche or computer. If you think your claim originated after 1987, you must contact the holder directly to get the needed information. The office is currently holding about 65,000 names on file - a total of $45 million dating from 1973. However, they are also holding some safe deposit box items that date back to the 1800's. Finders are not dealt with. Checks are issued only to owners. Finders must wait for 24 months until they can contract to recover claims and they may charge no more than a 10 percent commission.

Hawaii

Director of Finance, State of Hawaii, Unclaimed Property Section, P.O. Box 150, Honolulu, HI 96810; 808-586-1590. Hawaii lists property owners names in local papers and attempts to locate people by phone. The state currently has about 200 thousand names of people who have not claimed their property. No interest is paid on accounts. The amounts range from a few cents to hundreds of thousands of dollars. Accumulation began in 1974. As of September 30, 1991, Hawaii is holding 21 million dollars of unclaimed property. Hawaii does deal with finders, in providing lists of owners names, etc, but the state will send out checks only to owners. People inquiring about unclaimed property may do so by phone, but a written request is required if there is more than one account. Records are kept on microfiche. Commission of finders is limited to 20 percent.

Idaho

Ms. Mary Weirick, State Tax Commission, Unclaimed Property Division, 700 West State St., P.O. Box 36, Boise, ID 83722-2240; 208-334-7623. Idaho publishes a list of names once a year in local newspapers, and puts circular inserts in all state and senior citizens papers. It advertises on 2 radio stations and 3 television stations. In addition, some local radio stations announce 25 names per day on weekdays. Also, they now have a full-time locator in the office to find potential owners. Idaho is currently holding approximately 11 million dollars in cash,

Unclaimed Property: Does The Government Owe <u>You</u> Money?

125,000 stock shares, 80,000 individual accounts, and thousands of safety deposit boxes. The state deals with finders and will sell them a list of properties worth $200 and above for $31.85. Property must be held for two years by the state before a commission may be charged. After that, checks may be mailed to finders, but they will be made out to the owner.

Illinois

Department of Financial Institutions, Unclaimed Property Division, 500 Iles Park Place, Suite 510, Springfield, IL 62718; 217-782-8463 or 217-782-6692. Illinois requests that inquiries to the office be in writing to facilitate their research. With sufficient detail, the search takes 3 to 4 weeks. Claim analysis takes 6 to 8 weeks. After approval, returns usually take about three months. The state advertises the names of owners twice a year in the newspapers of the county of each owner's last known address. Occasionally they advertise on radio and television. They currently have over two million names. Since 1971 over 270 million dollars have accumulated. Finders must be licensed detectives and are required to send the contract with the owners to the state office for approval. Items must be held by the state 2 years before finders make a contract on it. As of August 1990, finders are limited to a 10% commission. Checks are sent to owner and finder with power of attorney. Finders and holders are notified when claim is paid.

Indiana

Office of Attorney General Pearson, Unclaimed Property Division, 219 State House, Indianapolis, IN 46204-2794; 317-232-6348. Indiana has a statute of limitations of 25 years before unclaimed property reverts to the Common School Building Fund. After reversion, the property can no longer be claimed. The first time this will occur is in 1993. After approval, returns take about six to eight weeks. The whole claim process takes about 3 months. The state runs newspaper advertisements as well as television spots and a cable show called *Consumer Corner* in an effort to find owners. Finders must submit the contract with the owners for approval by the state, and checks are sent directly to the owners. Also, finders are limited to 10% commission and may collect nothing on items held for less than 24 months by the state.

Iowa

Great Iowa Treasure Hunt, Treasurer's Office, Hoover Building, State Capitol Complex, Des Moines, IA 50319; 515-281-5540/5366. You may write or call this office to see if you have unclaimed property. They will look it up on their computers. Iowa publishes owners' names in local newspapers twice a year, and has representatives at the State and County Fairs to disseminate information. Big books are brought and people can look through them. They use radio and TV advertisements for larger claims - $100 and over. Iowa currently has close to 74 thousand unclaimed properties. The office takes about two weeks to make the returns once the claim is approved. Finders must be private investigators. They may use the office's microfiche, but no lists are sold to them. Their commission is limited to 15 percent.

Kansas

State Treasurer's Office, Unclaimed Property Division, 900 Southwest Jackson, Suite 201, Topeka, KS 66612-1235; 913-296-3171, or toll free 1-800-432-0386 (KS only). Kansas will take phone or written inquiries about lost properties. They pay owners directly. Currently there are over 230,000 unclaimed properties in the state worth $22 million. The Treasurer's office makes attempts by mail and through public gatherings such as booths at state fairs to find owners. About 45 percent of properties are recovered. Finders commissions are limited to 15 percent and contracts for items held by the state for less than two years are not valid.

Kentucky

Abandoned Property Unit, Station 62, Frankfort, KY 40620; 502-564-6823. Kentucky successfully processes 250-300 claims per year. They place advertisements in local newspapers, produce press releases, and run radio, television announcements, and at state fairs in attempts to locate owners. In addition, they try to find people by mail. Kentucky requests all inquiries to be in writing. In the past, they have even discovered people attempting fraud by using fake letterhead. One man claimed to be Thomas Edison's heir and owed $25,000. Finders need a power of attorney or other legal document. Returns are issued to owners and sent to the address requested. The office says they hope to see new legislation soon to control finders' fees.

Louisiana

Louisiana Department of Revenue and Taxation, Unclaimed Property Section, P.O. Box 91010, Baton Rouge, LA 70821-9010; 504-925-7425. Louisiana holds unclaimed items into perpetuity. It holds about 42 million dollars worth of unclaimed items. About 1500-2000 items are successfully united with owners each year. To research records, call the office to make an appointment. You can take the whole day to view printouts. Printouts are not for sale. Claims are advertised in newspapers and letters are sent to last known address. Finders must wait two years before making contracts on items over $50. Finders commission is limited to 10 percent. The office has a locator program. Once a claim is approved, the check will be issued within 90 days.

Maine

Treasurer's Department, Abandoned Property Division, House Station 39, Augusta, ME 04333; 207-289-2771. Maine accepts either phone or written inquiries, and will have a return in about a month from approval, although stock returns take longer. There is about a two month backlog in running computer searches. Since 1979, there has been no statute of limitation on the length of time, and the office will hold funds in perpetuity. The state currently holds about 14 million dollars worth of unclaimed property from 7000 holders and 20,000 owners. Finders cannot collect commissions on properties held less than two years and after that they are limited to 15% for items over $50. Maine uses advertising, personal letters, and booths at fairs to try to locate owners. The office has had good results in locating people. Maine pays interest that item earned at the time it was turned over to the state for up to 10 years. The office has hired a national firm to locate property.

Maryland

Comptroller of the Treasury, Unclaimed Property Section, 301 West Preston St., Baltimore, MD 21201; 410-225-1700. Maryland has no statute of limitations governing the length of time property is held. Maryland advertises in the jurisdiction of the last known address twice a year and mails notices to the last known address. It also advertises on radio and television, and disseminates information at state fairs. The office has been in existence since 1966 and deals with both finders and owners. Claim forms must be signed by the owner if possible. Only owners may ask for claim forms. Finders cannot, even if they have a contract. Payment is made only to the claimant. As of July 1, 1991, finders need not be paid on items held by the state for less than 2 years. No limits are placed on the amount of commission finders may charge after the two years elapses.

Massachusetts

Commonwealth of Massachusetts, Treasury Department, Unclaimed Property Division, One Ashburton Place, Room 1207, Boston, MA 02108; 617-367-3900. Massachusetts, whose office has been in existence since 1955, pays interest to owners on interest-earning property. The state holds items belonging to more than 30,000 people. They publish names in local newspapers every year to try to locate owners. Safety deposit boxes held more than 7 years are sold at auction. Once ownership has been established, the office pays returns in about four to six weeks. The state does not give returns to finders, but sells microfiche to finders for $25. There is a 30 percent cap on finders fees.

Michigan

Michigan Department of the Treasury, Escheats Division, Lansing, MI 48922; 517-334-6550. Michigan has a statute of limitations of seven years after abandonment for amounts under $50. Michigan is a custodial state. Lists of items are advertised in each county after they go through probate. Since 1988 listings have been put on computer. Prior to 1988, unless you know the holder, it is difficult to trace a claim. Approximately 68 million dollars worth of property is being held. They get the returns out within several weeks. Finders must have a contract if they charge more than 5 percent commission. Finders need a private detective's license. The office makes out checks only to owners or heirs. Third parties are never issued checks even if they have power of attorney.

Minnesota

Minnesota Department of Commerce, Office of Unclaimed Property, 133 East 7th Street, St. Paul, MN 55101-2362; 612-296-2568, toll free 1-800-652-9747 within the state but outside Minneapolis/St.Paul area. Minnesota has about 150,000 properties currently unclaimed. Inquiries may be made by phone or in writing, and specific documentation will be required. Normally six weeks are needed to process returns. Lists are advertised in newspapers. Searchers can collect for

Unclaimed Property: Does The Government Owe <u>You</u> Money?

owners if proper documents are presented, but there is a 10% limit on commissions unless there is a prior agreement between the owner and the searcher. Finders may not enforce contracts for locating items that have been held by the state for less than one year.

Mississippi

Mississippi Treasurer's Office, Unclaimed Property Division, P.O. Box 138, Jackson, MS 39205; 601-359-3600. Mississippi pays interest on accounts - 5% on interest-bearing accounts and 1% on everything else. They currently hold $5.4 million in unclaimed funds. Holding period, called dormancy, is 5 years. After that time, the holding company must turn the property over to the state. The state sets a limit of 10% commission for finders, but expects new legislation to restrict that amount further. The state is required by law to publish the names of all owners every third year with items worth $100 or more. It usually takes 30 to 60 days for returns to be processed, if all the information has been properly supplied by the claimant.

Missouri

Department of Economic Development, Unclaimed Property, Box 1272, Jefferson City, MO 65102; 314-751-0840. Missouri pays interest on interest-bearing accounts; and finders can collect their percentages with no limitations. The office tries to locate owners through advertising twice per year in news publications, mailing postcards to last known addresses, and some searches, but they do not have investigative capability.

Montana

State Of Montana, Department of Revenue, Abandoned Property Section, Mitchell Bldg., Helena, MT 59620; 406-444-2425. Montana's two-person office cannot conduct extensive investigations to find property owners, but are exceptionally dedicated to finding owners and have an excellent return rate. They can access state's income tax records and drivers license records for addresses. They will soon be able to access the Federal Deed Check. This office has a refund rate of 33 percent. In 1990 it took in $1.5 million and refunded one-half million dollars. Items over $100 are advertised in the county of the person's last known address. There are currently between 70 and 100 thousand accounts unclaimed. Returns are made to finders with legal contracts or power of attorney. There are no limits on finders.

Nebraska

Nebraska State Treasurer's Office, Property Capitol Building, P.O. Box 94788, Lincoln, NE 68509; 402-471-2455. Nebraska publishes the names of property owners in local newspapers, sends out letters, and conducts research in an effort to locate the rightful owners. It does not pay interest on accounts. The office will deal with owners only and issues checks to them alone. For the first 90 days during which property is held by the state, finders may not charge more than 10 percent commission. After that there is no limit.

Nevada

State of Nevada, Unclaimed Property Division, State Mail Room, Las Vegas, NV 89158; 702-486-4140/3000, or toll free 1-800-521-0019 (NV only). Nevada currently has about 80 thousand unclaimed properties, the vast majority of which are under $500. The current unclaimed amount, which the state holds in perpetuity, is $29 million. This 9 person office is computer. They prefer inquiries to be made in writing and will make returns in about three weeks. No interest is paid on interest bearing accounts. The state allows finders to make claims after the state has tried for two years to locate the rightful owner. Computer printouts of lists can be viewed by researchers at the office, but they are not for sale. The finders are then limited to ten percent commission, and the checks are sent only to the owner. Nevada advertises in local papers and on television and radio as part of its efforts to locate the owners.

New Hampshire

New Hampshire State Treasurer's Office, Abandoned Property Division, 25 Capitol St., State House Annex Room 121, Concord, NH 03301; 603-271-2619. People can come to the office and look at the books. State expects to be entirely on microfiche or computer by 1993. After advertising an abandoned property for two years in a statewide newspaper and sending a letter to the last known address, New Hampshire can go to court and have the account escheated to the county involved, with 15% going to a general State Treasurer's fund. After the two year period, the owner needs a special bill in the state legislature to retrieve

his money. The State advertises once again in the newspaper prior to escheatment, and they research large accounts. New Hampshire does not recognize finders; any agreement between a finder and owner is unenforceable for 24 months after a property is turned over to the state, and then the escheatment process takes over.

New Jersey

Department of Treasurer, Unclaimed Property, CN-214, Trenton, NJ 08646; 609-292-9200. All requests must be in writing. No information on claims is given out by phone. New Jersey will not supply lists of owners' names to finders. They pay interest on interest bearing accounts as of April 14, 1989, and are a custodial state. Their efforts to find owners consist mostly of running newspaper advertisements. The state of New Jersey does not deal with finders.

New Mexico

New Mexico Taxation and Revenue Department, P.O. Box 25123, Santa Fe, NM 87504-5123; 505-827-0767. New Mexico puts funds from unclaimed property in a special account in the General Fund, but it is still accessible to owners who make a claim. Objects such as those found in safe deposit boxes can be auctioned when they are turned over to the state, after 25 years. So far that has never happened, but it may in the future. The state currently holds 200,000 names on cards, which date back to 1959, and 70,000 names on computer, which date from March 1989 when the office was automated. The properties held total about $8 million. The state advertises owners' names statewide and sends letters to the last known addresses. Finders are subject to a gross receipts tax, but there is no limit on the commission they may charge. As of November 1, 1991, no finders may contract on items held by the state for less than two years.

New York

Administrator, Office of Unclaimed Funds, Alfred E. Smith Bldg., 9th Floor, Albany, NY 12236; 518-474-4038, toll free 1-800-221-9311 (NY only). From New York's hotline or regular phone number, owners can find out immediately if their property has been turned over to the state and if anyone has ever successfully made a claim on it. Then they will need to fill out the appropriate forms with proof of identification, which will vary for different kinds of property. New York is not a forms state. No particular application is needed, just proof that the property belongs to the claimant. Interest is paid for the first five years at the U.S. Treasury rate. There are currently seven million names of unclaimed property owners in the state, with funds amounting to two billion dollars. New York is very active in its efforts to find owners. Besides sending out letters (about three thousand per week), they have a mobile outreach program, where office personnel travel to various locations with all the computerized information, and visit senior citizens centers, malls, fairs, etc. They say this has been very successful in locating owners, whereas pilot projects to try to match names with the Department of Motor Vehicles and the Taxation and Finance Department have been less successful. The state is "not thrilled" with finders and feels that owners should be able to reclaim their property free of charge. Finders fees are limited to 15% and the office encourages people to deal directly with them.

North Carolina

Administrator, Escheat and Abandoned Property Section, Department of State Treasurer, 325 N. Salisbury St., Raleigh, NC 27603-1388; 919-733-6876. In North Carolina, the Abandoned Property Section can return funds in less than two weeks in uncomplicated situations. By law, they must send lists of owners names to clerks of the State Supreme Court in each county and to local newspapers. They also use computer matches with the Department of Motor Vehicles and Department of Revenue, and they have a locator unit as well. Currently, North Carolina holds over 79 million dollars in abandoned monies. In 1990 they took in over ten million dollars worth. Finders must be licensed private investigators or detectives and licenses may not be transferred from state to state. Finders must state their fees in a contract with the owner. Commissions are limited to 25%.

North Dakota

North Dakota Unclaimed Property Division, 918 East Divide Ave., Suite 410, P.O. Box 5523, Bismarck, ND 58502; 701-224-2805. North Dakota publicizes abandoned properties in local newspapers, radio, television, through mailings to last known addresses, and booths at the State Fair. They accept inquiries by phone or mail, and then require claim forms to be filled out with appropriate documents attached. Once approved, returns usually take about two weeks. The state sends checks only to owners and has a two-year waiting period before finders can contract on a property. Finders' fees are limited to 25% of the total amount. Interest earned by abandoned properties goes to a common school fund.

Ohio

Chief, Division of Unclaimed Funds, Department of Commerce, 77 South High Street, 20th Floor, Columbus, OH 43266-0545; 614-466-4433. In Ohio, the published lists of owners' names includes a coupon in the larger newspapers that they can fill out to expedite their claim. Returns could take from eight weeks to three months, depending on the complications involved. Ohio also has an outreach program where the office sends representatives to state and county fairs, shopping malls and other public events. This includes visiting sites of the Governor's "Regional Cabinet Day" program where he picks a town to spend the day in to conduct business. The state currently has 2.8 million names on file, with funds amounting to 110 million dollars. It pays no interest on accounts and there is a 5 percent processing fee for payment of claims. Ohio is unusual in that the Unclaimed Funds Division operates on the money it is holding, at no cost to the government. The state's Department of Development also uses unclaimed funds to guarantee loans that stimulate economic development. In addition, the original holding institutions in Ohio are only required to turn 10% of the unclaimed funds over to the state, and they use the money to invest at market value. The holding company may retain the other 90 percent and invest it in secured stock in the name of the State of Ohio. The claimant still receives the full amount owed to him. The Ohio office must hold funds for two years before finders can make contracts on them, and their fees are restricted to 10%. Checks are paid to owners only unless another party has the power of attorney.

Oklahoma

Oklahoma Tax Commission, Unclaimed Property Section, 2501 Lincoln Blvd., Oklahoma City, OK 73194-0010; 405-521-4275. Oklahoma is a custodial state and keeps unclaimed properties in perpetuity. Requests about claims must be in writing. State does not pay interest on interest-bearing accounts. The state currently holds $60 million worth of these monies. Approximately $11 million has been returned to owners. They publicize names in local newspapers twice a year and intend to have a locator service in the near future. If a finder has a power of attorney, he can submit a claim and there is a 25 percent limit on the amount of commission he can charge.

Oregon

Oregon Division of State Lands, 775 Summer Street NE, Salem, OR 97310; 503-378-3805. Oregon will hold unclaimed property indefinitely while it is invested in the School District Fund. From the time property is reported by a holding company as unclaimed until the time it is advertised and remitted to the state, which is about 6 months duration, information about it is not public information. Inquiries during that time must be directed to the holding company. Interest earned also goes to the Fund. There is $29 million worth of unclaimed property belonging to 80,000 persons. No interest is paid on interest-bearing accounts. The state sends letters to the last known addresses of owners and advertises in local newspapers. They publish an information brochure for consumers explaining the procedures involved for claiming abandoned property. They also publish an information packet for researchers who want to find claims as a business. State emphasizes to owners that it will do the search for them. The state sends checks jointly to finders and owners and there are currently no restrictions on the amount of commission finders may charge.

Pennsylvania

Supervisor, Abandoned and Unclaimed Property Section, Pennsylvania Department of Revenue, 2850 Turnpike Industrial Park, Middletown, PA 17057; 717-986-4641, or toll free 1-800-222-2046 (PA only). Procedures and proof required to reclaim property depend on the type and size of the property, and whether the claimant is the owner, heir or estate. As of September 30, 1991, the state has collected $208 million from 500,000 accounts, of which $34 million, plus securities, has been returned. Pennsylvania checks its list of names against state tax records to help locate people and sends out notices for amounts over $100. The state also lists the names of owners in local newspapers, and passes lists on to General Assembly members. In addition, they have an outreach program that travels to public functions, such as the governor's "Capitol for the Day" program, around the state looking for owners, and they have found one in five people on their list in this manner. In Pennsylvania there are no restrictions on finders. However, before claim forms are sent to finders, they must have a notarized power of attorney.

Rhode Island

State Of Rhode Island, Unclaimed Property Division, 40 Fountain St., Providence, RI 02903; 401-277-6505. Rhode Island takes about three to four weeks to return lost funds once the claim is made. People with more recent claims may call the state office to find out immediately from the computerized listing if they actually have money there. Older claims take a day to research. No dollar amounts are given out. They must then follow up with the proper identification. The state pays simple interest - 5% on interest-bearing accounts. They send out letters to the last known addresses of owners, and place advertisements in all the state newspapers. They also have an outreach program, where representatives of the Unclaimed Property Office travel to public functions around the state to try to locate people. The state says this program has been very effective. In March of 1988 Rhode Island advertised six thousand names of property owners and was able to locate half of them. Finders are on their own here - they receive no help from the state, nor are there restrictions on the fees they may charge. Finders' contracts are null and void if item has been in state custody for under 24 months.

South Carolina

Abandoned Property Office, South Carolina Tax Commission, P.O. Box 125, Columbia, SC 29214; 803-737-4771. In South Carolina, a claimant looking for lost property can go to the holding institution - that is, the original business where the account or money was located - within the first sixty days after his funds have been declared abandoned. Then, he must look for them in the state office. Make an appointment. The hours are 9:00 am to 11:00 am and 2:30 pm to 4:30 pm weekdays. The information is kept on microfiche. Twice a year the office runs advertisements in county newspapers, with names of people known to have lived in each county. They also travel to the State Fair in October, as well as mail letters to the last known addresses. South Carolina currently holds $31 million in abandoned property, representing 403,000 accounts. In 1989, lists of owners' names were made available to the public for the first time, but the office will not duplicate or mail copies. Finders fees have also been limited to 15%, and the finder must be a licensed private investigator. The state now mandates it must hold a property for two years before a finder can contract to recover it.

South Dakota

Ms. Ruby Douglas, Abandoned Property, State Treasurer's Office, 500 East Capitol, Pierre, SD 57501; 605-773-3378. Inquiries may be by phone or in writing to the office, which can do an immediate computer search to determine if a claimant's property is being held there. South Dakota has, after returns taken out, 4 million dollars of unclaimed property that has accumulated since the inception of the program. The accounts belong to about 15,000 people. Then, the claimant must submit whatever proof is required and complete the necessary paperwork. South Dakota has a successful outreach program that travels to state and county fairs with a specially-made list of names that is posted so the public may easily read it. In the past two years, they have tripled their refunds as a result of the program. In addition, the office lists names in local newspapers. Finders are limited to 25% commission and the office pays returns directly to owners only. No lists of names are made available for heir-finding purposes, although anyone who wants to see the names may come to the office by appointment only.

Tennessee

State of Tennessee, Unclaimed Property Division, Andrew Jackson State Office Bldg., 11th Floor, Nashville, TN 37243-0242; 615-741-6499. In Tennessee the Unclaimed Property Division pays only to original owner or estates in the case of money belonging to a deceased person. In all cases, they require suitable proof identification such as proof of address, social security number, etc. Returns take approximately three weeks. Interest is paid only if the original holder paid it as well. Tennessee advertises names of owners in local newspapers, sends letters to last known addresses, matches its list with other state agencies, and searches current telephone directories in an effort to locate owners. Further efforts, such as consulting credit bureaus, may be made in cases of large accounts. Since 1979, $26 million worth of abandoned property has been reported to the state office, of which $13 million has been returned. The office currently holds $30 million worth of property. Finders must make appointments with the office to view lists of names, and they are frequently booked a week in advance. The records viewed at the office are on microfiche and can be purchased for $30. Any contract made between a finder and owner must be approved by the state; and contracts are only valid after the state has held the property for one year. Finders are restricted to 10% commission or $50, whichever is greater.

Unclaimed Property: Does The Government Owe <u>You</u> Money?

Texas

Unclaimed Money Fund, P.O. Box 12019, State Treasurer's Office, Austin, TX 78711; 512-444-7833, or toll free 1-800-321-CASH (TX only). This office has a full-time locator and aggressively pursues search for owners. Texas claimants follow procedures similar to those in most states - that is, filling out claim forms, providing notarized documentation of ownership, and submitting driver's license or social security numbers. Returns take about 90 days to process. The state advertises names in local newspapers, on radio and television, and sends notices to the last known address of the owner. The Treasurer's office has received two million accounts over the past 25 years, representing over $206 million. Of that, 25 percent has been returned to owners. Holding companies also return many items. No interest on interest-bearing accounts is paid. Finders are limited to 10% commission; and the Treasurer's office advises people who have been contacted by a finder to check with them first before paying someone a fee to return their money. Half of the money never claimed in Texas goes to a Foundation School Fund, and the other half goes to the State general revenue. However, the money is always available to the rightful owner and claimants can retrieve their funds at any time.

Utah

Utah Unclaimed Property Division, 341 South Main Street, 4th Floor, Salt Lake City, UT 84114; 801-533-4101. Utah pays interest on accounts that were interest-bearing when they came from the bank, such as certificates of deposit; but other items such as savings accounts are closed out by the bank. The state advertises one time in the paper names they received in the past six months and publicizes on radio and television. They also run a booth at the State Fair and maintain a locator in the office. The state has over 150,000 unclaimed properties worth over $20 million at the present time. Searchers or finders can apply with a valid power of attorney and checks are issued either to owners or those with power of attorney. No agreement between owners and fee-finders is enforceable until the state has held the property for two years.

Vermont

State Treasurer's Office, Unclaimed Property Division, 133 State St., Montpelier, VT 05633-6200; 802-533-4101. Vermont sends out letters to owners of property worth $25 or more. If the amount is over $50, the state runs advertisements in local newspapers for two consecutive weeks. They have no other investigative capability due to the very small size of the office. Books are open to the public view at the office. Vermont has collected about two million dollars worth of unclaimed property since 1965, and currently holds between 16 and 18 thousand properties. Finders can only contract with owners after the state has held a property for twelve months.

Virginia

Department of the Treasury, Division of Unclaimed Property, P.O. Box 2478, Richmond, VA 23207; 804-225-2393, or toll free 1-800-468-1088 (VA only). Virginia requires a claimant to submit proof of whatever information the state received from the holder. For example, someone claiming money in a savings account would have to produce a passbook or other proof of ownership of that account. In most cases, returns are made within two months. The state pays interest if the original holder was also paying it. There is a 5% limit. In Virginia, unclaimed property information is classified as confidential, so the state cannot release information to finders. The public is not invited to look at the office's records. Private agreements between finders and owners are limited to a 10% commission for the finder. In addition, the property must be held for 36 months before such a contract is recognized. Approximately 600 thousand names are currently on file with the abandoned property office, and the state is holding an accumulation of some $125 million.

Washington

State of Washington Department of Revenue, Unclaimed Property Division, P.O. Box 448, Olympia, WA 98507; 206-586-2736. Washington has an automated system enabling the office to respond immediately to inquiries about unclaimed property. Their list dates back to 1955. The office attends county and state fairs to locate owners, and will branch out soon to malls and other public locations as well. A full time locator will be added to the office who will do nothing but track down owners. A spokesperson for the office says it is anticipated this will double the amount of claims refunded. The staff searches telephone books. One found the owner of $149,000 by looking in the telephone directory. She had not even known the money was owed to her. They also place advertisements in local newspapers every six months and send out notices. Efforts to advertise through the broadcast media have been very successful. A recent television show brought 250 calls. Washington pays interest if an account was previously an interest-bearing bank and CD account, and continues to pay the same rate of interest for up to 10 years. The state currently holds about $100 million in unclaimed property, from about 600,000 owners. Last year, it paid out over five million dollars in returns, out of the fourteen million it received. Washington is one of the most restrictive states for finders, limiting them to 5% commission and subjecting them to the confidentiality law which limits what information the office can reveal about abandoned property owners. As a result, they say they have few problems with heir-finding.

West Virginia

Treasurer of the State, Unclaimed Property Division, Bldg. 1, Suite E145, State Capital, Charleston, WV 25305; 304-343-4000. West Virginia is currently holding 6 million dollars in unclaimed funds for some 70,000 accounts. No interest is paid on interest-bearing accounts. West Virginia has a five-person office for unclaimed property, so the efforts they can make to locate owners are minimal, and returns may take some time. By law, however, the state must advertise the names in local newspapers, and send notices to the last known address within 10 days. There are no regulations on finders, but the office does not supply lists of names. Finders can view the names by visiting the office, but no information except names and addresses is released unless an owner has authorized it.

Wisconsin

Office of the State Treasurer, Unclaimed Property Division, P.O. Box 2114, Madison, WI 53701-2114; 608-267-7977. The Wisconsin office prefers written inquiries about lost properties, including as accurate a description as possible. Once a claim is approved by the Unclaimed Property Division and the Attorney General's office, returns are made within six to eight weeks. The state pays interest if the account was interest-bearing in the first place. For properties over $50, Wisconsin runs newspaper advertisements listing the names of owners. The office is able to perform only limited research. They search current telephone directories, and try to check social security numbers with the Department of Revenue. The state holds $10 million of unclaimed property. Finders are limited to 20% commission as of May 1988. They may purchase a list of names and view the records in the office, but checks are made out only in the names of the owners.

Wyoming

Unclaimed Property Division, Wyoming State Treasury Office, State Capital, Cheyenne, WY 82002; 307-777-7408. Wyoming's Unclaimed Property Division currently deals mainly with lost insurance policies. At present, only insurance companies are required to file unclaimed property with the state. Other holders are not required to turn over or even tell the state about unclaimed property. However, new legislation is expected soon to bring the state in line with the uniform unclaimed property law. Wyoming holds about half a million dollars worth of unclaimed funds. The claim procedures for recovering the insurance money is similar to what other states require - that is, proof of policy number, address, etc. Returns are usually made in one week. Currently Wyoming holds 4000 names on its unclaimed list. They are all on a printout list that can be purchased for $60. Wyoming has a five year statute of limitations, after which funds that are still unclaimed revert to a Common School Fund and are no longer claimable. Finders can come into the office to view the list of names and there are no restrictions on the amount of commission they may charge. However, finders have no access to property until the account has been held by the state for two years. The state deals only with owners and will remit only to claimant.

Free Tax Help

Federal Tax Help

Why pay money to expensive tax preparers, tax accountants, and tax attorneys when you can get most of what they offer better and most likely free? Did you know the government has dozens of free tax help programs very few people know about? There is a special section at the end of this chapter for state tax assistance.

Interesting Facts

Gross internal revenue collections reached $1.01 trillion in 1989 (up 8.4%) and there were 199.6 million federal tax returns and supporting documents filed. IRS issued 82.6 million refunds totaling $93.6 billion, compared to $94.5 billion last year. Last year was the seventh year taxpayers were invited to make voluntary contributions to reduce the public debt. There were 529 contributions, totaling $204,000. For tax years beginning after 1990, unnecessary cosmetic surgery will not qualify as a deductible medical expense. Cosmetic surgery is any procedure that is directed at improving the patient's appearance and does not meaningfully promote the proper function of the body or prevent or treat illness or disease.

Taxpayers Affected by Operation Desert Shield

New Publication 945, Tax Information for Those Affected by Operation Desert Shield, contains answers to commonly asked questions that primarily apply to newly activated reservists, as well as all other active duty U.S. military personnel and their families, citizens who had been detained by Iraq, and citizens who had to leave the Middle East because of the adverse conditions. This publication covers many issues, such as available tax relief measures for suspending examinations or collection of back taxes, extending due dates for filing an income tax return, meeting the requirements for the foreign earned income exclusion, and seeking other tax assistance.

* Actuaries Enrollment Board
Joint Board for the Enrollment of Actuaries
Internal Revenue Service (IRS)
U.S. Department of the Treasury
1111 Constitution Ave., NW
Washington, DC 20220   202-523-8787

Individuals who wish to perform actuarial services must enroll with this Board within the IRS. The Board is also responsible for the supervision of actuaries and their enrollment revocation after fair hearings.

* Amending Your Tax Return
Service Center Directors
Deputy Commissioner, Operations
Internal Revenue Service
U.S. Department of the Treasury
1111 Constitution Ave, NW
Washington, DC 20224   202-622-4255

If you find that you did not report income on your tax form, did not claim deductions or credit you could have claimed, or you claimed deductions or credits that you should not have claimed, you can correct your return by filing a Form 1040X, Amended U.S. Individual Income Tax Return. Generally, this form must be filed within three years from the date of your original return or within two years from the date you paid your taxes, whichever is later. File Form 1040X with the IRS Service Center in your area, listed elsewhere in this book.

* Collection
Office of the Assistant Commissioner
Internal Revenue Service
1111 Constitution Ave., NW
Room 7238
Washington, DC 20224   202-622-5430

Collection is responsible for securing delinquent Federal tax returns and for collecting taxes where the amount owed is not in dispute, but remains unpaid. The Service Center Collection Branch (SCCB) is Collection's first point of contact with taxpayers who are delinquent in filing returns and paying taxes. They send notices to taxpayers and act on the replies to the notices. The SCCB also reviews selected Forms W-4, Employee's Withholding Allowance Certificate, to determine whether employees have the correct amount of tax withheld from their wages and directs employers to increase the amount withheld when appropriate.

* Corporation Tax Statistics
Statistics of Income Division
Internal Revenue Service (IRS)
P.O. Box 2608
Washington, DC 20013   202-874-0360

The following Statistics of Income reports and tapes can be purchased from the Statistics of Income Division. Prepayment is required, with checks made payable to the IRS Accounting section:

Corporation Source Book, 1987, Publication 1053, $175. This 480-page document presents detailed income statement, balance sheet, tax and investment credit items by major and minor industries and size of total assets. A magnetic tape containing the tabular statistics for 1986 can be purchased for $1,500.

Partnership Source Book, 1957-1983, Publication 1289, $30. This 291-page document shows key partnership data for 1957 through 1983, at the minor, major and division industry levels. It includes a historical definition of terms section and a summary of legislative changes affecting the comparability of partnership data during that period. A magnetic tape containing the tabular statistics for partnerships can be purchased for $300 from the National Technical Information Service, Springfield, VA 22161.

Sole Proprietorship Source Book, 1957-1984, Publication 1323, $95. This source book is a companion to that for partnerships, described above. It is a 244-page document showing key proprietorship data for 1957 through 1984. Each page contains statistics for a particular industry. A magnetic tape containing the tabular statistics can be purchased for $245.

Studies of International Income and Taxes, 1979-1983, Publication 1267, $45. This report presents information from 13 Statistics of Income studies in the international area.

Partnership Returns, 1978-1982, Publication 369, $22. This report presents previously unpublished Statistics of Income data for 1980, 1981, and 1982, as well as data previously issued in the SOI Bulletin and in other publications.

* Earned Income Credit
Taxpayer Service Division
Internal Revenue Service
1111 Constitution Ave., NW
Washington, DC 20224   202-874-1460

Low income taxpayers who keep a home for themselves and at least one child may claim the Earned Income Credit (EIC). Your earned income and adjusted gross income must each be less than $22,370. You may be entitled to a refundable credit of up to $2,211. Contact the toll-free hotline in your area for more information.

* Electronic Tax Filing

Electronic Filing Division
Internal Revenue Service
1111 Constitution Ave., NW
Washington, DC 20224   202-927-2400

Electronic returns take a much shorter time to process because there are fewer steps in electronic processing, and that saves time. Electronic returns have a much higher accuracy rate than paper returns. This is because electronic returns are verified by electronic filing software before they are accepted. Usually, only people who expect a refund can file electronically, but this year, the service will conduct a pilot test for accepting and processing Balance Due returns. The test is limited to taxpayers who reside in the states of Georgia, Iowa, Indiana, Kentucky, Michigan, Ohio, Utah, Washington, and West Virginia. You must file you taxes electronically through a qualified electronic filer. This office can provide you with information on how to become an electronic filer, including the procedures, tests, and applications necessary. The following publications set the procedures for the electronic filing of tax year 1990 individual income tax returns and Direct Deposit. They also provide procedures for balance due returns.

1345 - *Procedures for Electronic Filing of Individual Income Tax Returns (Tax Year 1990)*.

1346 - *Electronic Return File Specifications and Record Layouts for Individual Income Tax Returns*.

* Employee Plans and Exempt Organizations

Office of the Assistant Commissioner
Internal Revenue Service
1111 Constitution Ave., NW
Washington, DC 20224   202-622-6710

The Employee Plans function administers the tax laws governing pension plans by issuing letters determining whether a plan qualifies under the law, examining returns to ensure that plans are complying with the law, and publishing rulings to clarify the law. Speakers address various practitioner groups across the country to highlight new Employee Plans developments and receive insights first-hand from practitioners. This office also handles exempt organizations, and administers the tax laws governing these organizations and private foundations. The IRS monitors whether sponsors of charitable fundraising events are providing accurate information on the extent to which contributions are deductible. The IRS educates the soliciting organizations and conducts a special examination program to decrease the abusive and misleading fundraising practices of some charities. Publication 1391, *Deductibility of Payments made to Charities Conducting Fundraising Events*, is part of an on-going educational program that includes speeches, taxpayer assistance workshops, and revisions to forms and publications. IRS has established a telephone hotline to help charities make a determination of the value of premiums offered in fundraising activities and to help charities answer questions from donors on the deductibility of contributions made. Charitable organizations engaging in misleading or abusive practices are referred for examination.

* Estate and Gift Tax

Office of Passthroughs and Special Industries
Internal Revenue Service
1111 Constitution Ave., NW, Room 5427
Washington, DC 20224   202-622-3000

This office will help you on matters pertaining to the regulations of estate and gift tax. This office is most often used by lawyers who are helping people manage estates, but they will answer people's questions or direct them to appropriate sources for more information.

* Federal Tax Guide for Older Americans

Committee on Aging
U.S. House of Representatives
Washington, DC 20515   202-226-3375

The *Federal Income Tax Guide for Older Americans* is a free publication, which presents an introduction to the basic provisions of the Tax code benefiting older Americans. It is designed to address the needs of older Americans with moderate income. In addition to emphasizing issues directly affecting senior citizens, the Tax Guide also discusses this year's tax forms to better help taxpayers fully understand the entire process. It also identifies numerous Internal Revenue service publications and prerecorded telephone messages which give more detailed information on the subjects discussed.

* Foreign Language Assistance in Tax Preparation

Taxpayer Services, International
Internal Revenue Service
U.S. Department of the Treasury
950 L'Enfant Plaza
Washington, DC 20024   202-874-1470

Interpreters are available at the IRS in the major foreign languages to assist taxpayers who do not speak English. Written requests for help may be sent to the above office, and IRS interpreters will respond to the questions, but only in English. Sometimes the State Department assists in the interpretation of letters. Requests are received only for obtaining solutions to specific tax problems and not for the preparation of tax returns.

VITA centers in local area often have foreign interpreters if the population in that area warrants them. Contact your local IRS office in the white pages of your phone directory or your area's Taxpayer Education Coordinator, listed elsewhere in this book, for information.

Many of the IRS forms are also available in Spanish. They are:

1S *Derechos del contribuyente (Your Rights as a Taxpayer), 179 Circular PR, Guia Contributiva Federal Para Patronos Puertoriquenos (Federal Tax Guide for Employers in Puerto Rico)*

556S *Revision de las Declaraciones de Impuesto, Derecho de Apelacion y Reclamaciones de Reembolsos (Examination of Returns, Appeal Rights, and Claims for Refund)*

579S *Como Preparar la Declaracion de Impuesto Federal (How to Prepare the Federal Income Tax Return)*

596SP *Credito por Ingroso del Trabajo*

594S *Proceso de cobro (Deudas del impuesto por razon del empleo) (The Collection Process: Employment Tax Accounts)*

850 *English-Spanish Glossary of Words and Phrases Used in Publications Issued by the Internal Revenue Service.*

* Foreign Tax Credits

Assistant Commissioner (International)
Internal Revenue Service
U.S. Department of the Treasury
950 L'Enfant Plaza South, SW
Attn: IN:C:TPS
Washington, DC 20024   202-874-1470

If you need information or assistance in the guidelines for foreign tax credit allowed for income taxes paid to foreign governments, contact this office. Income in this situation is taxed by both the United States and the foreign country. Publication 514 from the IRS describes in detail the tax credit, who is eligible, and how to calculate the credit.

* Free Courses on How To Prepare Taxes

Volunteer and Education Branch
Taxpayer Service Division
Internal Revenue Service (IRS)
U.S. Department of the Treasury
1111 Constitution Ave., NW, Room 2706
Washington, DC 20224   202-622-7827

The Volunteer Income Tax Assistance (VITA) is a program within the IRS where training is provided to volunteers to help people prepare basic tax returns for older, handicapped and non-English speaking taxpayers. The volunteers serve in the community at neighborhood centers, libraries, churches and shopping malls. The IRS provides free instruction and materials and trains volunteers to prepare Forms 1040 EZ, 1040A, and the basic 1040. New volunteers generally receive four-to-five days instruction; experienced individuals, a one-to-two day refresher. There is also self-instruction. Training is usually available December through January at convenient locations. In exchange for the free training, VITA asks that you spend several hours a week on VITA from January 1 through April

15. To join VITA in your area, just call the Taxpayer Education Coordinator at the number listed below.

Taxpayer Education Coordinators

550 22d St., S, Stop 117, Birmingham, AL 35233; 205-731-0403
P.O. Box 101500, Anchorage, AK 99510; 907-261-4458
2120 N. Central Ave., Stop 6610-PX, Phoenix, AZ 85004; 602-261-3861
P.O. Box 3778, Stop 25, Little Rock, AR 72203; 501-378-5685
300 N. Los Angeles St., Room 5205, Los Angeles, CA 90012; 213-894-4574
1221 Broadway, 4th Fl. Oakland, CA 94612; 415-273-4233
Chet Holifield Federal Bldg., P.O. Box C-10, Laguna Niguel, CA 92677; 714-643-4060
P.O. Box 2900, Stop SA5650, Sacramento, CA 95812; 916-978-4083
55 S. Market St., Stop 77-01-6400, San Jose, CA 95113; 408-291-7114
600 17th St.,Stop 6610-DEN, Denver, CO 80202-2490; 303-844-3340
135 High St., Stop 115, Hartford, CT 06103; 203-240-4154
P.O. Box 28, Wilmington, DE 19899; 302-573-6270
(DC Office) P.O. Box 1076, Baltimore, MD 21203; 202-488-3100, ext. 2222
P.O. Box 292590, Stop 6030, Building B, Fort Lauderdale, FL 33329-2590; 305-424-2439
400 W. Bay St.,Stop 6250, Jacksonville, FL 32202 904-791-2514
P.O. Box 1037, Room 110, Federal Office Bldg., Atlanta, GA 30370; 404-331-3808
PJKK Federal Building, P.O. Box 50089, Honolulu, HI 96850; 808-541-3300
550 W. Fort St., Box 041, Boise, ID 83724; 208-554-9183
P.O. Box 1193, Stop 32-1, Chicago, IL 60690; 312-886-4609
P.O. Box 19201, Stop 8, Springfield, IL 62701; 217-492-4386
P.O. Box 44211, Stop 60, Indianapolis, IN 46244; 317-269-6216
P.O. Box 1337, Stop 30, Des Moines, IA 50305; 515-284-4870
412 S. Main, Stop 6610-WIC, Wichita, KS 67202; 316-291-6610
P.O. Box 1216, Stop 531, Louisville, KY 40201; 502-582-6259
501 Magazine St., Room 605, New Orleans, LA 70130; 504-589-2801
P.O. Box 1020, Augusta, ME 04330; 207-622-8328
31 Hopkins Plaza, Room 615A, Baltimore, MD 21201; 301-962-2222
JFK Federal Bldg., P.O. Box 9088, Boston, MA 02203; 617-565-1645
P.O. Box 330400, Room 2442, Detroit, MI 48232-6500; 313-226-3674
316 Robert St., Stop 26, St. Paul, MN 55101; 612-290-3320
100 W. Capitol St., Suite 504, Stop 30, Jackson, MS 39269; 601-965-4142
P.O. Box 1147, H.W. Wheeler Station, St. Louis, MO 63188; 314-539-5660
Federal Building, 301 S. Park Ave., Drawer 10016, Helena, MT 59626-0016; 406-449-5375
106 S. 15th St., Stop 27, Omaha, NE 68102; 402-221-3501
4750 Oakey Blvd., Las Vegas, NV 89102; 702-455-1029
80 Daniel St. Portsmouth, NH 03801; 603-436-7386
425 Raritan Center Pkwy., Edison, NJ 08818; 201-417-4071
517 Gold Ave, SW, Stop 6610-ALB, P.O. Box 1967, Albuquerque, NM 87103; 505-766-2537
Leo O'Brien Federal Bldg., Clinton Ave., and N. Pearl St., Room 614, Albany, NY 12207; 518-472-2886
P.O. Box 606, RM G-5D, Brooklyn, NY 11202; 718-780-6020
P.O. Box 1040, Niagara Sq. Station, Buffalo, NY 14201; 716-846-4007
P.O. Box 34036, Church St. Station, New York, NY 10008; 212-264-3310
320 Federal Pl., Room 128, Greensboro, NC 27401; 919-333-5620
P.O. Box 2461, Fargo, ND 58108; 701-239-5213
P.O. Box 3459, Cincinnati, OH 45201; 513-684-2828
P.O. Box 99184, Cleveland, OH 44199; 216-522-3414
200 Northwest 4th St., Stop 6610, Oklahoma City, OK 73102; 405-231-4989
P.O. Box 2709, Portland, OR 97208; 503-221-6565
600 Arch St., Room 6424, Philadelphia, PA 19106; 215-597-0512
P.O. Box 2488, Room 123, Pittsburgh, PA 15230; 412-644-6504
P.O. Box 6627, Providence, RI 02940; 401-528-4276
Strom Thurmond Federal Bldg., 1835 Assembly St., Room 408, Columbia, SC 29201; 803-253-3031
P.O. Box 370, Aberdeen, SD 57402-0370; 605-226-7230
P.O. Box 1107, MDP 46, Nashville, TN 37202; 615-251-2247
300 E. 8th St., Stop 6610-AUS, Austin, TX 78701; 512-499-5439
7839 Churchill Way, Stop 6610-DAL, Dallas, TX 75242; 214-767-1428
4100 Westheimer, Stop 6610H-SW, Suite 280, Houston, TX 77027; 713-541-7610
465 South 400 East, Stop 6610-SLC, Salt Lake City, UT 84111; 801-524-6095
Courthouse Plaza, 199 Main St., Burlington, VT 05401; 802-951-6473
P.O. Box 10049, Room 5223, Richmond, VA 23240; 804-771-2289
915 Second Ave., MS-425, Seattle, WA 98174; 206-443-4230
P.O. Box 1138, Stop 2108, Parkersburg, WV 26102; 304-420-6612
P.O. Box 493, Milwaukee, WI 53201; 414-291-3302
308 W. 21st St., Stop 6610-CHE, Cheyenne, WY 82001; 307-772-2325
Mercantile Plaza Bldg., 10th Fl., Ave. Ponce De Leon, Stop 271/2, Hato Rey, PR 00917; 809-498-5946

* Free Legal Help If You Get Audited

Volunteer and Education Branch
Taxpayer Service Division
Internal Revenue Service (IRS)
U.S. Department of the Treasury
1111 Constitution Ave., NW, Room 2706
Washington, DC 20224   202-622-7827

Under this program, law and graduate accounting school students are given special permission to practice before the IRS on behalf of taxpayers who cannot afford professional help. Volunteers are needed to help with the clinic operations or to serve as Student Tax Clinic Directors. Students work under the direction of their professors to handle legal and technical problems. Your local taxpayer education coordinator will inform you of tax clinics in your area.

* Free Tax Forms At Your Library

Volunteer and Education Branch
Taxpayer Service Division
Internal Revenue Service
1111 Constitution Ave., NW, Room 1315
Washington, DC 20224   202-622-7827

The IRS supplies over 30,000 libraries, technical schools, prisons, and other facilities with free tax forms, audiovisual aids, and reference materials. These facilities are in need of volunteers to assist in distribution and use of these aids. Contact your local library or center and volunteer to help.

* Future Tax Legislation

Director, Legislative Affairs
Internal Revenue Service
U.S. Department of the Treasury
1111 Constitution Ave., NW
Washington, DC 20224   202-622-3700

The Legislative Affairs Division is responsible for developing IRS legislative proposals, tracking pending legislation, analyzing and implementing new legislation, and preparing responses to General Accounting Office reports.

For further information regarding tax laws that have been introduced, or for an assessment of future laws, contact the following offices. Ask to speak with the person monitoring changes in the tax provision you are calling about.

U.S. Department of the Treasury, Legislative Affairs, 1500 Pennsylvania, Ave., Room 3134, Washington, DC 20224; 202-566-2037
Senate Committee on Finance, 205 Dirksen Senate Office Building, Washington, DC 20510; 202-224-4515
House Committee on Ways and Means, 1102 Longworth House Office Building, Washington, DC 20515; 202-225-3625
Joint Committee on Taxation, 1015 Longworth House Office Building, Washington, DC 20515; 202-225-3621

* Historian

Internal Revenue Service (IRS)
1111 Constitution Ave., NW
Washington, DC 20224   202-377-6456

The IRS decision to create this position follows a growing trend in both the government and corporate worlds to establish history offices, archives, and historic preservation efforts. This new function will help the IRS move into the future with an understanding and appreciation of its past. The historian will develop an archival collection of the most important historical documents created by the IRS, will research and write policy and management-related historical reports, prepare a full-length history of taxation in the U.S., establish a collection of oral history interviews, and assist IRS staff members in answering historical research questions.

* Hotline for Tax Aspects of Retirement Plans

Employee Plans Technical and Actuarial Division
Internal Revenue Service
U.S. Department of the Treasury
1111 Constitution Ave., NW
Washington, DC 20224   202-566-6783/6784

The above numbers are hotlines to attorneys within this division that are there to discuss tax questions relating to retirement and pension plans, such as 401(k) and 501(c3). The hours are 1:30 to 4:00 p.m., Monday through Thursday.

Free Tax Help

* How to Protect Older Americans From Overpayment

Special Committee on Aging
U.S. Senate
Washington, DC 20510   202-224-5364

This is a free information paper updated yearly, which is designed to assure that older Americans claim every legitimate income tax deduction, exemption, and tax credit. This publication is very easy to understand and provides many examples and checklists. Also included is a section of income tax items which will change in the following year.

* Individual Income Tax Statistics

Statistics of Income Division
Internal Revenue Service
P.O. Box 2608
Washington, DC 20013   202-874-0300

Statistics of Income - 1987, Individual Income Tax Returns, Publication 1304, is a report that presents information on sources of income, exemptions, itemized deductions, and tax computations, with the data presented by size of adjusted gross income and marital status. This publication is available from the Superintendent of Documents, Government Printing Office, Washington, D.C. 20402; 202-783-3238 (S/N 048-004-02296-6).

* Individual Tax Model

Statistics of Income Division
Internal Revenue Service
U.S. Department of the Treasury
1111 Constitution Ave., NW
Attn: R:S:P
Washington, DC 20224   202-874-0700

State tax officials determine rate structure and revenue yields through the use of *Individual Tax Model*. Public use tape files are available from the office above that include this tax model.

* Information for Tax Practitioners

Forms Distribution Centers
Internal Revenue Service (IRS)
U.S. Department of the Treasury
P.O. Box 85074, Richmond, VA 23261-5074
P.O. Box 8903, Bloomington, IN 61702
Rancho Cordova, CA 95743-0001   1-800-829-3676

Tax practitioners can benefit from the following information made available to them from the IRS. Publication 1045, *Information for Tax Practitioners*, contains orders blanks for ordering bulk supplies of federal income tax forms. Also within the publication is a form that allows one to be placed on a mailing list in his IRS district to receive a tax practitioner's newsletter. Package X is also available to practitioners with the most popular tax forms and instructions on how to prepare them.

* In-House IRS Audit Manuals

Freedom of Information Reading Room
Internal Revenue Service (IRS)
U.S. Department of the Treasury
1111 Constitution Ave., NW
Room 1569
Washington, DC 20224   202-622-5164

Tax audit manuals use by IRS staff and other in-house manuals are available to the public. Contact the office above for arrangements to use particular materials. For copies of manuals and written requests, write to: Internal Revenue Service, c/o Ben Franklin Station, P.O. Box 388, Washington, D.C. 20044, Attn: Freedom of Information Request.

Available IRS Technical Manuals:

Organization and Staffing (1100), $36.45
Policies of the Internal Revenue Service (1218), $14.55
Delegation Orders (1229), $17.10
Internal Management Document System (1230), $21.90
Disclosure of Official Information (1272), $63.15
Travel (1763), $29.85
General (4000), $20.10
Income Tax Examinations (4200), $74.85
Tax Audit Guidelines for Internal Revenue Examiners (4231), $27.20
Techniques Handbook for Specialized Industries (4232)

1. Insurance, $15.45
2. Auto Dealers, $2.55
3. Textiles, $4.80
4. Timber, $6.15
5. Brokerage Firms, $11.90
6. Railroads, $13.65
7. Construction, $4.65
8. Oil and Gas, $47.85
9. Financial Institution, $6.45
10. Public Utilities, $10.05
11. Barter Exchanges, -0-

Tax Audit Guidelines, Partnerships, Estates and Trusts, and Corporations (4233), $22.55
Techniques Handbook for In-Depth Examinations (4235), $25.65
Examination Tax Shelters (4236), $10.65
Report Writing Guide for Income Tax Examiners (4237), $21.30
Examination Techniques Handbook for Estate Tax Examiners (4350), $27.15
Handbook for Quality Review (4419), $11.40
Employment Tax Procedures (4600), $12.90
Excise Tax Procedure (4700), $17.55
Handbook for Examination Group Managers (4(10)20), $15.75
Classification (41(12)0), $8.10
General Procedural Guides (5100), $24.45
Collection Quality Review System (CQRS) (5190), $4.05
Delinquent Return Procedures (5200), $10.05
Balance Due Account Procedures (5300), $23.55
Service Center Collection Branch Procedures (5400), $93.90
Service Center Collection Branch Managers (5415), $9.90
Automated Collection Function Procedures (5500), $18.60
Automated Collection System Managers (5512), $21.30
Collection Field Function Techniques and Other Assignments (5600), $32.25
Employment Tax Examinations (5(10)00), $12.60
Collection Technical Review Handbook for Employment Tax Examination (5(10)20)), $2.25
Group Managers Handbook (5620)0), $8.40
Field Branch Chief's Handbook (5630)0), $3.75
Special Procedures (5700), $57
Special Procedures Function Managers (57(15)0), $3.90
Legal Reference Guide for Revenue Officers (57(16)0), $37.50
Records and Reports (5800), $9.60
Collection Reports for Field Managers (5890), $4.35
Collection Support Function (5900), $19.50
Taxpayer Service (6810), $51.45
Exempt Organizations (7751), $60.90
Private Foundations (7752), $40.05
Employee Plans Master File (7810), $10.50
Exempt Organizations Business Master File (7820), $26.70
Examination Procedures (7(10)00), $49.95
Employee Plans Examination Guidelines (7(10)54), $15
Exempt Organizations Exam. Guides Handbook (7(10)69)), $13.80
Actuarial Guidelines (7(10)5(10)), $5.70
Appeals (Part VIII), $51
Handbook for Special Agents (9781), $84.15
Criminal Investigation (Part IX) $67.50
Technical (Part XI), $49.35
Employee Plans Training Program Phase I, Revised 10/87 (4210-01), $60.45
Employee Plans EP/EO CPE Operational Topics for 1989, Revised 12/88 (4213-002), $12.15
Employee Plans EP/EO CPE Technical Topics for 1989, Revised 12/88 (4213-003), $18.75
Employee Plans EP/EO CPE Technical Topics for 1989, Revised 3/89 (4213-005), $4.05
Employee Plans Training Program Phase II, Revised 01/87 (4220-01), $51.60
Exempt Organizations Continuing Professional Education Technical Instruction Program for 1986, Revised 01/86 (4277-20), $43.80
Exempt Organizations Continuing Professional Education Technical Instruction Program for 1987, Revised 01/87 (4277-25), $44.70
Exempt Organizations Continuing Professional Education Technical Instruction Program for 1988, Revised 01/88 (4277-28), $37.65
Exempt Organizations EP/EO CPE Operational Topics for 1989, Revised 01/89 (4277-31), $10.05
Exempt Organizations Continuing Professional Education Technical Instruction Program for 1989, Revised 01/89 (4277-32), $43.35
Exempt Organization Continuing Professional Education Technical Instruction Program for 1989 Index, Revised 01/89 (4277-33), $9
Exempt Organization Continuing Professional Education Technical Instruction Program for 1990, Revised 1/90 (4277-039), $68.85

Exempt Organization Continuing Professional Education Technical Instruction Program for 1990 Index, Revised 1/90 (4277-040), $9.

* Internal Revenue Bulletin

Superintendent of Documents
Government Printing Office
Washington, DC 20402   202-783-3238

The *Internal Revenue Bulletin* announces official Internal Revenue Service rulings, Treasury decisions, Executive Orders, legislation, and court decisions pertaining to Internal Revenue matters. The price is $104 per year (S/N 748-004-00000-9). Twice yearly, the weekly issues of the *Internal Revenue Bulletin* are consolidated into the *Cumulative Bulletins* (Jan-June and July-Dec). These *Bulletins* are not included as part of this subscription, but are sold as separate subscriptions. The subject bibliography, *Internal Revenue Cumulative Bulletins*, lists the bulletins available, dating back to 1940. Prices range from $8 to $42, depending on the year.

* International Tax Assistance

Office of the Associate Chief Counsel, International
Internal Revenue Service (IRS)
950 L'Enfant Plaza, SW, IN:C:TPS
Washington, DC 20224   202-287-4311

The International Office plays the lead role in devising strategies to assure that worldwide revenues due the United States are assessed and collected. International maintains a high number of taxpayer service visits to U.S. embassies and consulates to help U.S. taxpayers living abroad and in U.S. territories and possessions. Year-round taxpayer assistance by IRS staff at 13 overseas posts is supplemented by these visits. International publicized worldwide undelivered refunds, attempting to reach 800 taxpayers owed over $1 million in refunds returned as undeliverable by the world's postal authorities. The specialists in this office will offer technical assistance concerning questions relating to foreign taxes and tax credits. Refer also to Publications 54, *Tax Guide for U.S. Citizens and Resident Aliens Abroad*, and 514, *Foreign Tax Credits for Individuals*. International's Office of International programs administers 35 income tax treaties, 16 estate tax treaties and 7 gift tax treaties worldwide. These treaties provide for relief from double taxation, exchanges of information, routine sharing of information, and simultaneous examinations. During the past year, this office successfully completed negotiations in 122 cases for U.S. taxpayers who requested relief from double taxation.

Overseas Posts:

Bonn, West Germany	339-2119
Caracas, Venezuela	285-4641
London, England	408-8076 or 408-8077
Mexico City, Mexico	211-0042, ext. 3559
Nassau, Bahamas	809-322-1181
Ottawa, Canada	613-238-5335
Paris, France	4296-1202, ext. 2214
Riyadh, Saudi Arabia	488-3800, ext. 210
Rome, Italy	4674-2560
Sao Paulo, Brazil	881-6511, ext. 287
Singapore	338-0251, ext. 247
Sydney, Australia	261-9275
Tokyo, Japan	3224-5466

* IRS Assistance Through the Media

Audio/Visual Branch
Public Affairs Division, Internal Revenue Service
U.S. Department of the Treasury
1111 Constitution Ave., NW
Washington, DC 20224   202-622-7541

To provide specialized tax information to targeted audiences, the IRS developed an alliance with various industry groups and Public Broadcasting Service stations to produce and market *Tax Tips on Tape*, a series of 27 videos. The programs were shown on 240 public broadcasting stations and coordinated with special Outreach Program events across the country. IRS also joined with Financial News Network to produce a weekly half-hour live show, *IRS Tax Beat*. Topics ranged from tax-exempt organizations to estate taxes and featured IRS executives and specialists answering call-in questions. As part of the continuing efforts to use the most efficient means to distribute information, the IRS began a weekly satellite transmission of tax programs, which were made available to cable outlets and television stations free of charge. Watch for these broadcasts in your local listings.

* IRS Collection of Delinquent Child Support Payments

Chief Operations Officer
Internal Revenue Service (IRS)
U.S. Department of the Treasury
1111 Constitution Ave, NW
Washington, DC 20224   202-622-6600

If a taxpayer fails to make support payments to a child or spouse who receives public assistance, Congress requires the IRS to withhold all or part of the taxpayer's income tax refund to cover the delinquent payments. Since 1986, the IRS has also been required to apply individual income tax refunds to child support payments for individuals who are not on welfare and to non-tax debts owed to some Federal agencies, such as student loans, military enlistment bonuses, and home mortgage loans, etc. Through an agreement with the Department of Health and Human Services, IRS acts as a collection agent for the state welfare agencies in all child or spousal support cases. The refund amounts are used to reimburse the agencies for the support they furnish through Aid to Families with Dependent Children, or are turned over to the parents having custody of the child or children in non-welfare cases. Other agreements with the Departments of Housing and Urban Development, Agriculture, Energy, Interior, Education, Defense, Treasury, Justice, Health and Human Services, and the Veterans Affairs, Railroad Retirement Board and Small Business Administration require the IRS to act as a collection agent for delinquent non-tax Federal debts.

* IRS Collections and Returns

Returns Processing and Accounting
Office of the Assistant Commissioner
Taxpayer Service and Returns Processing
Internal Revenue Service
U.S. Department of the Treasury
1111 Constitution Ave., NW
Washington, DC 20224   202-622-6860

This office is responsible for the processing of collection and returns within the IRS tax system. Statistics generated from this office are available in the *Commissioner's Annual Report*, available from the Government Printing Office, Washington, D.C. 20402, for $3.50 (S/N 048-004-02280-9).

* IRS Community Outreach Assistance

Volunteer and Education Branch
Taxpayer Service Division
Internal Revenue Service (IRS)
U.S. Department of the Treasury
1111 Constitution Ave., NW, Room 2706
Washington, DC 20224   202-622-7827

IRS employees and volunteers provide free tax help in coordination with local groups. The help is offered at places of business, community or neighborhood centers, libraries, colleges, and other popular locations. Within the Community Outreach program, line-by-line help with your income tax forms is provided. Tax information seminars are also held, including discussions, films or videotapes, and a question and answer period. The programs are aimed at particular interest groups, such as low-to-middle income people interested in preparing their own returns, or small business owners needing free tax assistance. Contact the taxpayer education coordinator in your area for additional information.

* IRS Criminal Investigation

Assistant Commissioner, Criminal Investigation
Internal Revenue Service (IRS)
U.S. Department of the Treasury
1111 Constitution Ave., NW
Washington, DC 20224   202-622-6190

The mission of criminal investigation within the IRS is to encourage and achieve the highest possible level of voluntary compliance with the law by conducting investigations and recommending criminal prosecutions when warranted. Special agents target their efforts in the areas such as organized crime, narcotics trafficking, money laundering, questionable refund schemes, and tax shelters, of both domestic and international scope.

* IRS Private Letter Rulings and Information Letters

Technical Branch, Communications
Internal Revenue Service
U.S. Department of the Treasury
1111 Constitution Ave., NW

Washington, DC 20224   202-622-7270

If your tax situation warrants special interpretation on a particular tax deduction you would like to take, you can ask the IRS for a private letter ruling. The tax laws are applied to your case which can make this procedure time-consuming. To apply for a private-letter ruling, pertinent information must be sent, including names, addresses, taxpayer identification numbers, your IRS district office, a statement on why you qualify for the deduction, and legal documents pertaining to the case. Contact the above office on the procedure to follow. Someone from the IRS will be assigned to your case, and a notification will be sent to you on how to check the status of your ruling. Publication 91-1 explains the private letter ruling process. There is now a user fee, usually $2500, for each ruling.

Determination letters are also issued by the IRS to businesses and organizations concerning questions related to employee pension plans and tax-exempt status. The procedure for submitting information for a determination letter is similar to filing for a private-letter ruling; however, both the IRS district offices and the national office receive these requests and make the determinations.

General information letters are frequently issued by the IRS, and the request for the information is not as formal as the above mentioned letters. Simply write a letter or postcard to either the IRS district office in your area or to the national office with your question or situation on which you would like advice.

If making an inquiry to the national office, all of the above letters should be addressed to: Internal Revenue Service (Attn: CC:CORP:T:U), P.O. Box 7604, Ben Franklin Station, Washington, DC 20224.

* IRS Research Efforts

Research Division
Assistant Commissioner, Planning, Finance, and Research
Internal Revenue Service (IRS)
U.S. Department of the Treasury
1111 Constitution Ave., NW
Washington, DC 20224   202-874-0100

IRS research efforts emphasize voluntary compliance, trend identification, and analysis. The IRS published estimates and projections of gross income owed but not voluntarily paid for individuals and corporations for selected years from 1973 through 1992. An analysis is also being completed on the net tax gap, the amount of income tax owed but not paid either voluntarily or involuntarily.

One of the primary objectives is to provide high quality service to taxpayers. IRS began conducting taxpayer opinion surveys in its functions that have direct contact with taxpayers to get initial or baseline measurements of taxpayer perceptions about the quality level of IRS service. A report has also been released on a new method for estimating taxpayer paperwork burden associated with preparation, recordkeeping, obtaining and learning materials, and filing forms associated with tax preparation.

IRS completed a second major study of the effects of refund offsets for non-tax debts on subsequent taxpayer behavior. IRS learned that taxpayers are more likely to file balance-due returns or not to file in the subsequent year.

* IRS Service Centers

Service Center Directors
Deputy Commissioner, Operations
Internal Revenue Service (IRS)
U.S. Department of the Treasury
1111 Constitution Ave, NW
Washington, DC 20224   202-622-4255

The following is a listing of the Internal Revenue Service Centers where taxpayers must mail their tax forms. If an addressed envelope comes with your return, the IRS asks that you use it. If you do not have one, or if you have moved during the year, mail your return to the Internal Revenue Service Center for the place where you live. No street address is needed.

Service Center Offices:

Andover, MA	617-474-5549
Atlanta, GA	404-455-2049
Austin, TX	512-462-7025
Austin Compliance Center	512-326-0816
Brookhaven (Holtsville), NY	516-654-6886
Cincinnati, OH	606-292-5316
Fresno, CA	209-488-6437
Kansas City, MO	816-926-6828

Memphis, TN	901-365-5419
Ogden, UT	801-625-6374
Philadelphia, PA	215-969-2499

Regional Offices:

North Atlantic	212-264-0839
Mid-Atlantic	215-597-3991
Southeast	404-331-4506
Central	513-684-2587
Midwest	312-886-4291
Southwest	214-767-5762
Western	415-556-3035

* IRS Speakers and Customized Seminars

District Offices
Internal Revenue Service (IRS)
U.S. Department of the Treasury
1111 Constitution Ave., NW
Washington, DC 20224   1-800-829-1040

The Internal Revenue Service provides trained speakers for area civic organizations and other interested groups. Tax clinics are often organized for special interest groups. The IRS has also sponsored call-in radio programs where you may inquire about specific tax information. Contact the district offices of the IRS listed in this publication and inquire through the Public Affairs Director if these programs are of interest to you.

* IRS Special Enrollment Agents

Office of the Director of Practice
Internal Revenue Service (IRS)
U.S. Department of the Treasury
1111 Constitution Ave, NW
Washington, DC 20224   202-376-1421

IRS has designed a special enrollment of persons, other than attorneys and certified public accountants, who wish to represent clients before the IRS. This includes all matters connected with presentations to the Service, relating to a client's rights, privileges, and liabilities under laws or regulations administered by the Service. Such presentations include the preparation and filing of documents, all communications with the Service, and the representation of a client at conferences, hearings, and meetings. Candidates should be able to answer income tax accounting questions on the intermediate college course level. The following IRS publications, listed elsewhere in this book, will assist you in preparing for the examination:

17	*Your Federal Income Tax*
216	*Conference and Practice Requirements*
334	*Tax Guide for Small Business*
541	*Tax Information on Partnerships*
542	*Tax Information on Corporations*
553	*Highlights of the 1989 Changes*
560	*Self-Employed Retirement Plans*
589	*Tax Information on S Corporations*
590	*Individual Retirement Arrangements (IRAs)*

Answers to the previous year's examination may be obtained from the above address to assist you in preparing for the exam. Publication 1470, available from this office, includes an application for the test, as well as a copy of last year's exam. The two-day exam is given once a year in the fall.

* IRS Tax Compliance Program

Assistant Commissioner, Collection
Internal Revenue Service (IRS)
U.S. Department of the Treasury
1111 Constitution Ave., NW
Washington, DC 20224   202-622-5100

The Information Returns Program (IRP) is a largely computerized compliance program used by the IRS to match third party information on items, such as wages, interest, dividends, and certain deductions, with the amounts reported by taxpayers on their income tax returns. The IRS also uses the information to identify people who are reported to have received income, but did not file returns. In 1988, the IRS sent out 3.8 million notices reflecting discrepancies, and 3 million notices were sent to taxpayers for failure to file a tax return based upon information returns filed.

* IRS Technical-Advice Memorandums

Technical Branch, Communications
Internal Revenue Service (IRS)
U.S. Department of the Treasury
1111 Constitution Ave., NW
Washington, DC 20224   202-622-7270

If you are audited by the IRS and are in disagreement with the IRS agent over interpretation of a tax law, you can ask the agent to request a technical-advice memorandum for you. These memorandums must be requested through the IRS district offices. The national office then makes the final determination. Dollar amounts cannot be disputed through these memorandums, only the interpretation of the tax laws and procedures.

* IRS Walk-In Service Centers

Taxpayer Services
Internal Revenue Service (IRS)
U.S. Department of the Treasury
1111 Constitution Ave., NW, Room 2422
Washington, DC 20224   202-566-6352

Assisters are available in most IRS offices throughout the country to help you prepare your own return. In this way you will be given the opportunity to learn how to research and prepare your own tax return. An assister will "walk through" a return with you and a number of other taxpayers in a group setting. If you want help with your tax return, you should bring in your tax package, forms W-2 and 1099, and any other information (such as a copy of last year's return) that will help the assister to help you. At most IRS offices you can also get tax forms, publications, and help with questions about IRS notices or bills.

* Learn What's New In Taxes

Volunteer and Education Branch
Taxpayer Service Division
Internal Revenue Service
U.S. Department of the Treasury
1111 Constitution Ave., NW, Room 2706
Washington, DC 20224   202-622-7827

Tax professionals can learn recent tax law changes at Practitioner Institutes, which will enhance the professional quality of the services they provide. These institutes are sponsored by qualified educational institutions, state and local governments, and professional and other non-profit organizations. Contact your local Taxpayer Education Coordinator regarding these institutes.

* Let the IRS Compute Your Taxes

District Offices
Internal Revenue Service (IRS)
U.S. Department of the Treasury
1111 Constitution Ave., NW
Washington, DC 20224   1-800-829-1040

If you use Form 1040A to compute your taxes, the IRS will complete the calculation for your taxes. You must complete the tax return through Line 20. All income must be from wages and interest. Other minor stipulations also apply. Contact the above number for specific details on completing your taxes in this way.

* Money Waiting for You: Unclaimed Refunds

Accounting Branch
Internal Revenue Service (IRS)
801 Pennsylvania Ave., NW
Washington, DC 20004   301-492-5400

This office processes returned refund checks. After an attempt has been made by the Post Office to track the taxpayer fails, the IRS computer checks names against W2 forms, employer records and Social Security records for a correct address. Regional Offices use the media to advertise names of taxpayers who are due refunds. If after three years the IRS has been unsuccessful in finding the taxpayer, the money is deposited into an unclaimed refund account where it remains until it is claimed. Should a taxpayer discover at any time that they did not receive their refund they should contact the Internal Revenue Service Center where they filed their claim, or the office listed above.

* Obtaining Prior Year Tax Returns

Service Center Directors
Chief Operations Officer
Internal Revenue Service

U.S. Department of the Treasury
1111 Constitution Ave., NW
Washington, DC 20224   202-622-4255

It is possible to obtain a copy of your prior year tax return by completing Form 4506, *Request for Copy of Tax Form*, and mailing it to the Service Center where you filed the return. The charge is $4.25 for each year's return and must accompany this request. If a taxpayer's authorized representative wishes to request a copy of a taxpayer's prior year return, he or she must attach a signed copy of Form 2848, *Power of Attorney and Declaration of Representative*, or other document authorizing him or her to act for the taxpayer. In lieu of Form 4506, you can send a written request to the Service Center including the following information: your name, your social security number, and if you filed a joint return, the name and social security number of your spouse, the form number, the tax period, and your current address. You must sign this request, and if a joint return was filed, only one signature is needed. Allow 45 days to process the request. However, you often only need certain information, such as the amount of your reported income, the number of your exemptions, and tax shown on the return. You can get this information free if you write or visit an IRS office or call the toll-free number for your area.

* Penalties and Interest

Taxpayer Services
Internal Revenue Service (IRS)
1111 Constitution Ave., NW
Washington, DC 20224   202-566-6352

The law requires that IRS charge penalties for failure to file returns, late payments, payments with bad checks, negligence, false withholding statements, fraud, and other violations. The Penalty and Interest Notice Explanation (PINEX) notices are available upon request. These information notices show exactly how assessed penalties and interest have been computed on specific taxpayer accounts. The explanatory PINEX notices can be quickly computer-generated in response to taxpayer inquiries received by district offices and service centers. Taxpayer Service representatives are trained to answer taxpayer questions about these notices.

* Practitioner Services

Volunteer and Education Branch
Taxpayer Service Division
Internal Revenue Service
1111 Constitution Ave., NW
Washington, DC 20224   202-622-7827

Each District Office puts out a newsletter (the frequency varies) designed for practitioners that provides information on a wide variety of tax topics. The district offices also have practitioner hotlines, which can answer questions regarding account questions their clients have.

* Small Business Tax Education Course

Volunteer and Education Branch
Taxpayer Service Division
Internal Revenue Service
U.S. Department of the Treasury
1111 Constitution Ave., NW, Room 2706
Washington, DC 20224   202-622-7827

Approximately 1,000 junior colleges and universities are now offering a new course designed by the IRS for tax education of those in small businesses. Course materials are designed by the IRS, and the college may present the material as either a credit or non-credit course. Nine areas are covered in the course, including business assets; use of the home for business; employment taxes; excise taxes; starting a business and recordkeeping; *Schedules C (Profit or Loss from a Business), SE (Social Security Self-Employment Tax)*, and *1040-ES (Estimated Tax for Individuals)*; self-employment retirement plans; partnerships; and tip reporting and allocation rules. Contact a taxpayer education coordinator in your area, listed in this publication, for information on courses in your area.

* Statistics of Income Bulletin

Statistics of Income Division
Internal Revenue Service
U.S. Department of the Treasury
P.O. Box 2608
Washington, DC 20013   202-874-0700

The *Statistics of Income Bulletin* provides the earliest published annual financial statistics from the various types of tax and information returns filed with the

Free Tax Help

Internal Revenue Service. The *Bulletin* also includes information from periodic or special analytical studies of particular interest to tax administrators. In addition, historical data is provided for selected types of taxpayers, as well as State data and gross internal revenue collections. The *SOI Bulletin* is published quarterly and is available from the Superintendent of Documents, Government Printing Office, Washington, D.C. 20402; 202-783-3238. The subscription service is $20 annually, $7.50 for single copies.

* Tax Analysis

    Office of Tax Analysis
    Office of the Assistant Secretary
       of the Treasury for Tax Policy
    U.S. Department of the Treasury
    1500 Pennsylvania Ave., NW
    Washington, DC 20220   202-622-0050

This departmental office within Treasury analyzes tax programs and legislation and looks for alternative programs depending on the current economic climate. Advisors are available in many areas, such as economic modeling, revenue estimating, international taxation, individual taxation, business taxation, and depreciation analysis.

* Tax Assistance for the Military

    Taxpayer Services, International
    Internal Revenue Service (IRS)
    U.S. Department of the Treasury
    950 L'Enfant Plaza
    Washington, DC 20024   202-287-4311

The IRS sends trained instructors to military bases here and overseas to train personnel on tax procedures. Through the VITA program, these military personnel then organize internal training sessions to assist others in the preparation of their tax returns. Those chosen to be instructors often have experience in taxation or accounting. If your tax situation is complex, the Legal Assistance offices at military bases can assist you. United States embassies and consulates are also accessible for those in need of their services.

The following international telephone numbers are the local numbers of the 14 U.S. Embassies and consulates with full-time permanent staff from the IRS. Please check with your telephone company for any country or city codes required if you are outside the local dialing area. The Nassau and Ottawa numbers include the United States area codes.

Bonn, West Germany	339-2119
Caracas, Venezuela	285-4641
London, England	408-8076 or 408-8077
Mexico City, Mexico	525-211-0042, ext. 3559
Nassau, Bahamas	809-322-1181
Ottawa, Canada	613-238-5335
Paris, France	4296-1202
Riyadh, Saudi Arabia	488-3800, ext. 210
Rome, Italy	4674-2560
Sao Paulo, Brazil	881-6511, ext. 287
Singapore	338-0251, ext. 245
Sydney, Australia	261-9275
Tokyo, Japan	3224-5466

Publication 3, *Tax Information for Military Personnel*, may also be useful to you. Write to your area's IRS forms and publications distribution center, listed elsewhere, for a copy or call 1-800-424-3676.

* Tax Audits

    Taxpayer Services
    Internal Revenue Service (IRS)
    U.S. Department of the Treasury
    1111 Constitution Ave., NW
    Washington, DC 20224   202-874-1460

If the IRS selects your return for examination, you may be asked to produce records such as canceled checks, receipts or other supporting documents to verify entries on your return. Not all examinations result in changes in tax liability. If the examination of your return shows that you overpaid your tax, you will receive a refund. If the examination of your return shows that you owe additional tax, payment is expected. If you don't agree with the Examiner's findings, you have the right to appeal them. During the examination process, you will be given information about your appeal rights. Publication 5, *Appeal Rights and*

Preparation of Protests for Unagreed Cases, explains your appeal rights in detail and tells you exactly what to do if you want to appeal. You can appeal the findings of an examination with the IRS through their Appeals Office. Most differences can be settled through this appeals system without expensive and time-consuming court trials. If the matter cannot be settled to your satisfaction in appeals, you can take your case to court. Depending on whether you first pay the disputed tax, you can take your case to the U.S. Tax Court, the U.S. Claims Court, or your U.S. District Court. These courts are entirely independent of the IRS. As always, you can represent yourself or have someone admitted to practice before the court represent you. If you disagree about whether you owe additional tax, you generally have the right to take your case to the U.S. Tax Court if you have not yet paid the tax. Ordinarily, you have 90 days from the time the IRS mails you a formal notice telling you that you owe additional tax, to file a petition with the U.S. Tax Court. You can request simplified small tax case procedures if your case is $10,000 or less for any period or year. A case settled under these procedures cannot be appealed. If you have already paid the disputed tax in full, you may file a claim for a refund. If the IRS disallows the claim or you do not take action within 6 months, then you may take your case to the U.S. Claims Court or your U.S. District Court. If the court agrees with you on most issues in your case, and finds that the IRS position was largely unjustified, you may be able to recover some of your administrative and litigation costs. To do this, you must have used all the administrative remedies available to you within the IRS. This includes going through the Appeals system and giving the IRS all the information necessary to resolve the case. Publication 556, *Examination of Returns, Appeal Rights, and Claims for Refund*, will help you more fully understand your appeal rights.

Internal Revenue Service Regional Offices
Central: 550 Main St., Cincinnati, OH 45202. Serving: IN, KY, MI, OH, WV

Mid-Atlantic: 841 Chestnut St., Philadelphia, PA 19107. Serving: DE, MD, NJ, PA, VA.

Midwest: One N. Wacker St., Chicago, IL 60606. Serving: IL, IA, MN, MO, MT, NE, ND, SD, WI.

North-Atlantic: 90 Church St., New York, NY 10007. Serving: CT, ME, MA, NH, NY, RI, VT.

Southeast: 275 Peachtree St., NE, Atlanta, GA 30043. Serving: AL, AR, GA, FL, LA, MS, NC, SC, TN.

Southwest: LB-70 Stop 1000 SWRO, 7839 Churchill Way, Dallas, TX 75251. Serving: AZ, CO, KS, NM, OK, TX, UT, WY.

Western: 1650 Mission St., 5th Fl., San Francisco, CA 94103. Serving: AK, CA, HI, ID, NV, OR, WA.

IRS Regional Directors of Appeals
Room 7514, 550 Main St., Cincinnati, OH 45202

841 Chestnut St., Philadelphia, PA 19107

230 N. Dearborn, 29th Fl., Room 2972, Chicago, IL 60604

90 Church St., New York, NY 10007

Room 625, 275 Peachtree St., NE, Atlanta, GA 30043

LB-70, Stop 8000 SWRO, 7839 Churchill Way, Dallas, TX 75251

1650 Mission St., 5th Fl., San Francisco, CA 94103

* Tax Counseling for the Elderly

    Volunteer and Education Branch
    Taxpayer Service Division
    Internal Revenue Service (IRS)
    U.S. Department of the Treasury
    1111 Constitution Ave., NW, Room 2706
    Washington, DC 20224   202-622-7827

Tax Counseling for the Elderly (TCE) provides free tax help to people aged 60 or older, especially those who are disabled or who have special needs. Volunteers who provide tax counseling are often retired individuals who are associated with non-profit organizations that receive grants from the IRS. The grants are used to help pay out-of-pocket expenses for the volunteers to travel wherever there are elderly who need help, whether they are homebound, in retirement homes, or at special TCE sites. Sites are located conveniently in neighborhood centers, libraries, churches and other places in the community. Contact your local taxpayer education coordinator for programs in your area.

The following IRS Publications, available free from the IRS (1-800-TAX-FORM), may be useful for the elderly.

Publication 524, *Credit for the Elderly or the Disabled*
Publication 554, *Tax Information for Older Americans*

* Tax Court

United States Tax Court
400 Second St., NW
Washington, DC 20217   202-376-2751

If your taxes are delinquent, the Internal Revenue Service will issue you a delinquency notice, whether you are a consumer or a corporation. If you wish to contest the delinquency, a petition for a hearing can be filed with the U.S. Tax Court. This court is an independent court and not part of the IRS. The court's decision is final and cannot be appealed.

* Tax Data

Statistics of Income Division
Internal Revenue Service
P.O. Box 2608
Washington, DC 20013   202-874-0700

The Statistics of Income Division has Public Use Magnetic Tape Microdata Files from which specific information requests can be filled on a cost reimbursable basis. These files include individual income tax returns for 1978-1986. (Individual income tax returns for 1966-1977 are available from the Center for Electronic Records of the National Archives and Records Administration, Washington, D.C., 20408.) Files containing more limited data for each State are also available for 1985. All of these files have been edited to protect the confidentiality of individual taxpayers. Private foundations for 1982, 1983 and 1985 and non-profit charitable organizations for 1983 and 1985 are also available. The individual private foundation and charitable organization files are the only microdata files that can be released to the public. This office also has Migration Data, with compilations showing migration patterns, from where to where, by State and county, based on year-to-year changes in the tax return address. Data are available for selected time periods (according to the years in which returns were filed) between 1978 and 1988 and include counts of the number of individual income tax returns and personal exemptions. In addition, county income totals are available for Income Years 1982 and 1984 through 1987.

* Tax Education for High School Students

Volunteer and Education Branch
Taxpayer Service Division
Internal Revenue Service (IRS)
U.S. Department of the Treasury
1111 Constitution Ave., NW, Room 2706
Washington, DC 20224   202-622-7827

The IRS sponsors an introductory tax education program, *Understanding Taxes*, for high school students. Since many of the students have part-time jobs, the material that is learned can be practiced immediately. Instructional materials include computer software and video programs. Volunteer instructors are those who enjoy teaching and helping others, and who are knowledgeable about taxation. Your local taxpayer education coordinator will assist you in organizing these courses.

* Tax Exempt Organizations

Exempt Organizations Technical Division
Internal Revenue Service (IRS)
U.S. Department of the Treasury
1111 Constitution Ave., NW, Room 6411
Washington, DC 20224   202-622-8100

This office within the IRS sets the qualifications of organizations seeking a tax exempt status. Compliance with the law is also monitored. For a listing of the names of exempt organizations through October 31, 1988, subscribe to *Cumulative List of Organizations*, as legislated through Section 170(c) of the Internal Revenue Code of 1954. The subscription is $41 annually and includes three cumulative quarterly supplements. Available from the Superintendent of Documents, Government Printing Office, Washington, DC 20402, 202-783-3238.

* Tax Help for the Hearing Impaired

Taxpayer Services Division
Internal Revenue Service (IRS)
U.S. Department of the Treasury
1111 Constitution Ave, NW
Washington, DC 20224
Teletypewriter Number   1-800-829-4059

Telephone tax service by way of a teletypewriter is available from the IRS to assist hearing impaired taxpayers. During the IRS filing season, the hours of operation are 8am to 6:45 pm EST. In the non-filing season, the hours are 8am to 4:30pm EST.

* Tax Help on Audio and Video Cassettes

Audio/Visual Branch
Public Affairs Division
Internal Revenue Service (IRS)
U.S. Department of the Treasury
1111 Constitution Ave., NW
Washington, DC 20224   202-622-7541

The IRS provides local libraries with audio cassettes and videocassettes, for loan to the public, on how to fill out Forms 1040EZ, 1040A, 1040, and Schedules A and B. These tax tapes contain simple, step-by-step instructions to the forms and tax tips. Contact this office or your local library for more information.

* Tax Information in Braille

National Library Service for the Blind
   and Physically Handicapped
1291 Taylor St.
Washington, DC 20542   202-707-5100

IRS materials are available in Braille. They include Publications 17, *Your Federal Income Tax*, and 334, *Tax Guide for Small Business*, and Forms 1040, 1040A, and 1040EZ and instructions. They may be obtained at Regional Libraries for the Blind and Physically Handicapped. For a regional library in your area, contact the National Library Service for a listing.

* Tax Matters Digest System

Superintendent of Documents
Government Printing Office
Washington, DC 20402   202-783-3238

The *Bulletin Index - Digest System* contains the *Finding List* and *Digests* of all permanent tax matters published in the Internal Revenue System. Each subscription service consists of a basic manual and cumulative supplements for an indefinite period.

Service No. 1 - Income Taxes, 1953-1987. ($42) (S/N 948-001-00000-4)
Service No. 2 - Estate and Gift Taxes, 1953-1986. ($17) (S/N 948-002-00000-1)
Service No. 3 - Employment Taxes, 1953-1986. ($17) (S/N 948-003-00000-7)
Service No. 4 - Excise Taxes, 1953-1986. ($17) (S/N 948-004-00000-3)

* Tax Returns Prepared Free for Low Income, Elderly and Handicapped

Volunteer and Education Branch
Taxpayer Service Division
Internal Revenue Service
U.S. Department of the Treasury
1111 Constitution Ave., NW, Room 2706
Washington, DC 20224   202-622-7827

The Volunteer Income Tax Assistance (VITA) Program offers free tax help to people who cannot afford professional assistance. Volunteers help prepare basic tax returns for older, handicapped, and non-English-speaking taxpayers. Assistance is provided in the community at libraries, schools, shopping malls, and at other convenient locations.

Volunteers may take part in various VITA program activities, such as directly preparing returns, teaching taxpayers to prepare their own returns, managing a VITA site, or arranging publicity. Volunteers generally include college students, law students, members of professional business and accounting organizations, and members of retirement, religious, military, and community groups. The IRS provides VITA training materials and instructors. Training is conducted at a time and location convenient to volunteers and instructors. Generally, these sessions are offered in December through January each year.

Free Tax Help

The emphasis in VITA is to teach taxpayers to complete their own tax returns. A volunteer's role becomes that of an instructor rather than a preparer. VITA volunteers will teach taxpayers to prepare their own Forms 1040EZ, 1040A, 1040, and W-4. Assistance with state and local returns can also be provided. If complicated questions or returns are introduced, professional assistance will be provided or the taxpayer will be referred to one of the IRS publications for guidance. Contact your local taxpayer education coordinator for additional information on programs in your district.

Contact your local library or IRS office for locations near you.

* Tax Workshops for Small Businesses

Volunteer and Education Branch
Taxpayer Service Division
Internal Revenue Service
U.S. Department of the Treasury
1111 Constitution Ave., NW, Room 2706
Washington, DC 20224   202-622-7827

Small businesses usually need help getting started and taxes are one important aspect of successful entrepreneurship. Small Business Tax Workshops help people understand their federal tax obligations. Free workshops explain withholding tax responsibilities and the completion of employment tax returns. Contact the Taxpayer Education Coordinator in your area for information regarding the meeting time and place. The following IRS publications are particularly useful to small business and are free by calling the IRS at 1-800-TAX-FORM:

Publication 334, *Tax Guide for Small Business*
Publication 583, *Taxpayers Starting a Business*

* Taxpayer Publications

Taxpayer Services
Internal Revenue Service (IRS)
1111 Constitution Ave., NW
Washington, DC 20224   1-800-829-3676

The IRS publishes over 100 free taxpayer information publications on various subjects. One of these, Publication 910, *Guide to Free Tax Services*, is a catalog of the free services and publications they offer.

* The Buck Stops Here

Problem Resolution Staff
Assistant to the Commissioner
Taxpayer Ombudsman
Internal Revenue Service (IRS)
U.S. Department of the Treasury
1111 Constitution Ave., NW
Washington, DC 20224   202-622-4300

A major goal of the Problem Resolution Program (PRP) is to solve tax problems that have not been resolved through normal procedures. PRP represents the interests and concerns of taxpayers within the IRS and seeks to prevent future problems by identifying the root causes of such problems. Each IRS district, service center and regional office has a Problem Resolution Officer (PRO). In resolving problems and protecting taxpayer rights, PROs have authority to intervene to assure IRS actions are correct and appropriate. Effective January 1, 1989, authority to issue Taxpayer Assistance Orders (TAOs) was granted to the Taxpayer Ombudsman. This authority was delegated to the Problem Resolution Officers, as field representatives of the Ombudsman. TAOs may be issued when, in the judgement of the Ombudsman or PRO, a taxpayer is suffering, or is about to suffer a significant hardship as a result of an IRS action or inaction. A TAO can order the function that is handling the taxpayer's case to take appropriate steps to relieve the hardship. The order can also suggest alternative actions to resolve the case. Requests for such relief may be made by taxpayers, their representatives, or by IRS employees on behalf of taxpayers. Contact the IRS toll-free information number regarding tax questions, and ask for Problem Resolution assistance.

* Videos and Films on IRS Topics

Audio/Visual Branch
Public Affairs Division
Internal Revenue Service (IRS)
U.S. Department of the Treasury
1111 Constitution Ave., NW

Washington, DC 20224   202-622-7541

The IRS provides audio cassettes and video cassettes for loan to the public on how to fill out Forms 1040EX, 1040A, 1040, and schedules A and B. These tax tapes contain simple step-by-step instructions to the forms and tax tips. Other titles include:

Hey, We're Being Audited! - light-hearted film of an average family after being called in for an IRS tax audit.

A Sensible Approach for the Future of Your Business? - explains what electronic filing is, how to register with the IRS to offer electronic filing, and how it will benefit business.

You've Got To Do This - explains how electronic filing works and how you may get quick refunds.

Form 8300: Why You Should File - informs businesses about their reporting requirements to the IRS for cast transactions over $10,000.

A Video Guide to Taxes-1992 - quick update of tax law changes and general tax information for individual tax returns.

Por Que Nosotros, Los Garcia? - Spanish language film explains taxpayers' examination and appeal rights.

Por Que Los Impuestos? - reporter uncovers the history of taxation, how taxes are used, the rights and responsibilities of taxpayers, and the different kinds of IRS assistance available.

The IRS has distributed these tapes to many local libraries, as well as IRS district offices. Contact an IRS office near you for more information regarding these videos.

* Voicing Opinions of IRS Tax Laws

Office of Chief Counsel, Corporate
Internal Revenue Service
U.S. Department of the Treasury
1111 Constitution Ave., NW
Attn: CC:CORP:T:R
Washington, DC 20224   202-622-7700

If you have a personal recommendation for changing a federal tax law, you may send written comments to the address above. The letter must include the section within the Internal Revenue Code in which the portion of the law appears. Please send an original and eight copies of the correspondence.

If you wish to comment on how to improve a tax form or instruction booklet, you may address correspondence to the Tax Forms Coordinating Committee, Internal Revenue Service, 1111 Constitution Avenue, NW, Washington, DC 20224.

Senators and members of the House of Representatives can also be contacted if you wish to voice your opinions of tax laws and procedures. Write to: The Honorable (the senator's name), U.S. Senate, Washington, DC 20510; or The Honorable (your representative's name), U.S. House of Representatives, Washington, DC 20515.

* Wage Reporting

Returns, Processing, and Accounting
Internal Revenue Service
U.S. Department of the Treasury
1111 Constitution Ave., NW, Room 7009
Washington, DC 20224   202-622-6860

The combined annual wage reporting system was designed to assist employers in the reporting of taxes. For more assistance in this area, contact your local field office listed in your phone directory or the office above.

* Where To File: Mailing Address

If an addressed envelope came with your return, please use it. If you do not have one, or if you moved during the year, mail your return to the Internal Revenue Service Center for the place where you live. No street address is needed.

Florida, Georgia, South Carolina
Use this address: Atlanta, GA 39901

New Jersey, New York (New York City and counties of Nassau, Rockland, Suffolk, and Westchester)
Use this address: Holtsville, NY 00501

New York (all other counties), Connecticut, Maine, Massachusetts, New Hampshire, Rhode Island, Vermont
Use this address: Andover, MA 05501

Illinois, Iowa, Minnesota, Missouri, Wisconsin
Use this address: Kansas City, MO 64999

Delaware, District of Columbia, Maryland, Pennsylvania, Virginia
Use this address: Philadelphia, PA 19255

Indiana, Kentucky, Michigan, Ohio, West Virginia
Use this address: Cincinnati, OH 45999

Kansas, New Mexico, Oklahoma, Texas
Use this address: Austin, TX 73301

Alaska, Arizona, California (counties of Alpine, Amador, Butte, Calaveras, Colusa, Contra Costa, Del Norte, El Dorado, Glenn, Humboldt, Lake, Lassen, Mendocino, Modoc, Napa, Nevada, Placer, Plumas, Sacramento, San Joaquin, Shasta, Sierra, Siskiyou, Solano, Sonoma, Sutter, Tehama, Trinity, Yolo, and Yuba), Colorado, Idaho, Montana, Nebraska, Nevada, North Dakota, Oregon, South Dakota, Utah, Washington, Wyoming
Use this address: Ogden, UT 84201

California (all other counties), Hawaii
Use this address: Fresno, CA 93888

Alabama, Arkansas, Louisiana, Mississippi, North Carolina, Tennessee
Use this address: Memphis, TN 37501

American Samoa
Use this address: Philadelphia, PA 19255

Guam
Use This address: Commissioner of Revenue and Taxation
                                855 West Marine Dr
                                Agana, GU 96910

Puerto Rico (or if excluding income under section 933), Virgin Islands (Nonpermanent residents)
Use this address: Philadelphia, PA 19255

Virgin Islands (Permanent residents)
Use this address: V.I. Bureau of Internal Revenue
                            Lockharts Garden No. 1A
                                Charlotte Amalie,
                            St. Thomas, VI 00802

Foreign country: U.S. citizens and those filing Form 2555 or Form 4563
Use this address: Philadelphia, PA 19255

All A.P.O. or F.P.O. addresses
Use this address: Philadelphia, PA 19255

Tax Hotlines

Toll-free telephone tax assistance is available in all 50 states, the District of Columbia, Puerto Rico, and the Virgin Islands. There is no long distance charge for your call. It is best to call early in the morning or later in the week for prompt service. The IRS offers these suggestions for using its services.

Call IRS With Your Tax Question:
If the instructions to the tax forms and our free tax publications have not answered your question, please call us Toll-Free. Toll-Free is a telephone call for which you pay only local charges.

Choosing the Right Number:
Use only the number listed below for your area. Use a local city number only if it is not a long distance call for you. Please do not dial 1-800 when using a local city number.

Before You Call:
Remember that good communication is a two-way process. IRS representatives care about the quality of the service we provide to you, our customer. You can help us provide accurate, complete answers to your tax questions by having the following information available.
1. The tax form, schedule, or notice to which your question relates.
2. The facts about your particular situation (the answer to the same question often varies from one taxpayer to another because of differences in their age, income, whether they can be claimed as a dependent, etc.).
3. The name of any IRS publication or other source of information that you used to look for the answer.

Before You Hang Up:
If you do not fully understand the answer you receive, or you feel our representative may not fully understand your question, our representative needs to know this. He or she will be happy to take the additional time required to be sure we have answered your question fully and in the manner which is most helpful to you.

By law, you are responsible for paying your fair share of Federal income tax. If the IRS should make an error in answering your question, you are still responsible for the payment of the correct tax. Should this occur, however, you will not be charged any penalty. To make sure that IRS representatives give accurate and courteous answers, a second IRS representative sometimes listens in on telephone calls. No record is kept of any taxpayer's identity.

Alabama
1-800-829-1040

Alaska
Anchorage, 561-7484
Elsewhere, 1-800-829-1040

Arizona
Phoenix, 640-3900
Elsewhere, 1-800-829-1040

Arkansas
1-800-829-1040

California
Oakland, 839-1040
Elsewhere, 1-800-829-1040

Colorado
Denver, 825-7041
Elsewhere, 1-800-829-1040

Connecticut
1-800-829-1040

Delaware
1-800-829-1040

District of Columbia
1-800-829-1040

Florida
Jacksonville, 354-1760
Elsewhere, 1-800-829-1040

Georgia
Atlanta, 522-0050
Elsewhere, 1-800-829-1040

Hawaii
Oahu, 541-1040
Elsewhere, 1-800-829-1040

Idaho
1-800-829-1040

Illinois
Chicago, 435-1040
In area code 708, 312-435-1040
Elsewhere, 1-800-829-1040

Indiana
Indianapolis, 226-5477
Elsewhere, 1-800-829-1040

Iowa
Des Moines, 283-0523
Elsewhere, 1-800-829-1040

Kansas
1-800-829-1040

Kentucky
1-800-829-1040

Louisiana
1-800-829-1040

Maine
1-800-829-1040

Maryland
Baltimore, 962-2590
Elsewhere, 1-800-829-1040

Massachusetts
Boston, 536-1040

Elsewhere, 1-800-829-1040

Michigan
Detroit, 237-0800
Elsewhere, 1-800-829-1040

Minnesota
Minneapolis, 644-7515
St. Paul, 644-7515
Elsewhere, 1-800-829-1040

Mississippi
1-800-829-1040

Missouri
St. Louis, 342-1040
Elsewhere, 1-800-829-1040

Montana
1-800-829-1040

Nebraska
Omaha, 422-1500
Elsewhere, 1-800-829-1040

Nevada
1-800-829-1040

New Hampshire
1-800-829-1040

New Jersey
1-800-829-1040

New Mexico
1-800-829-1040

New York
Bronx, 488-9150
Brooklyn, 488-9150
Buffalo, 685-5432
Manhattan, 732-0100
Nassau, 222-1131
Queens, 488-9150
Staten Island, 488-9150
Suffolk, 724-5000
Elsewhere, 1-800-829-1040

North Carolina
1-800-829-1040

North Dakota
1-800-829-1040

Ohio
Cincinnati, 621-6281
Cleveland, 522-3000
Elsewhere, 1-800-829-1040

Oklahoma
1-800-829-1040

Oregon
Portland, 221-3960
Elsewhere, 1-800-829-1040

Pennsylvania
Philadelphia, 574-9900
Pittsburgh, 281-0112
Elsewhere, 1-800-829-1040

Puerto Rico
San Juan Metro area, 766-5040
Isla, 766-5549

Rhode Island
1-800-829-1040

South Carolina
1-800-829-1040

South Dakota
1-800-829-1040

Tennessee
Nashville, 259-4601
Elsewhere, 1-800-829-1040

Texas
Dallas, 742-2440
Houston, 541-0440
Elsewhere. 1-800-829-1040

Utah
1-800-829-1040

Vermont
1-800-829-1040

Virginia
Richmond, 649-2361
Elsewhere, 1-800-829-1040

Washington
Seattle, 442-1040
Elsewhere, 1-800-829-1040

West Virginia
1-800-829-1040

Wisconsin
Milwaukee, 271-3780
Elsewhere, 1-800-829-1040

Wyoming
1-800-829-1040

Telephone Assistance Services for Hearing Impaired Taxpayers Who Have Access to TDD Equipment

Hours of Operation:

8:00 am to 6:30 pm EST (January 1 - April 4)	9:00 am to 7:30 pm EST (April 5 - April 15)
9:00 am to 5:30 pm EST (April 16 to October 31)	8:00 am to 4:30 pm EST (November 1 to December 31)

All locations in U.S., including Alaska, Hawaii, Virgin Islands, and Puerto Rico   1-800-829-4059

Recorded Messages

What is Tele-Tax?

Recorded Tax Information has about 140 topics of tax information that answer many Federal tax questions. You can hear up to three topics on each call you make.

Automated Refund Information is available so you can check the status of your refund.

To Call Tele-Tax Toll-Free, Use Only the Numbers Listed Below for Your Area

Long-distance charges apply if you call from outside the local dialing area of the numbers listed below. Do not dial "1-800" when using a local number. However, when dialing from an area that does not have a local number, be sure to dial "1-800" before calling the toll-free number. A complete list of these topics follows this section.

How Do I Use Tele-Tax?

Recorded Tax Information
Topic numbers are effective January 1, 1991. Push-button (tone signaling) service is available 24 hours a day, 7 days a week.
Rotary (dial)/Push-button (pulse dial) service is available Monday through Friday during regular office hours. (In Hawaii, from 6:30 am to 1:00 pm).
Select, by number, the topic you want to hear.
Have paper and pencil handy to take notes.
Call the appropriate phone number listed below. If you have a push-button (tone signaling) phone, immediately follow the recorded instructions or if you have a rotary (dial) or push-button (pulse dial) phone, wait for further recorded instructions.

Automated Refund Information
Be sure to have a copy of your tax return available since you will need to know the first social security number shown on your return, the filing status, and the exact amount of your refund.
Then, call the appropriate phone number listed below and follow the recorded instructions.
IRS updates refund information every 7 days. If you call to find out about the status of your refund and do not receive a refund mailing date, please wait 7 days before calling back.
Push-button (tone signaling) service is available Monday through Friday from 7:00 am to 11:30 pm. (Hours may vary in your area).
Rotary (dial)/push-button (pulse dial) service is available Monday through Friday during regular office hours. (In Hawaii, from 6:30 am to 1:00 pm.)

Alabama
1-800-829-4477

Alaska
1-800-829-4477

Arizona
Phoenix, 640-3933
Elsewhere, 1-800-829-4477

Arkansas
1-800-829-4477

California
Counties of Alpine, Amador, Butte, Calaveras, Colusa, Contra Costa, Del Norte, El Dorado, Glenn, Humboldt, Lake, Lassen, Marin, Mendocino, Modoc, Napa, Nevada, Placer, Plumas, Sacramento, San Joaquin, Shasta, Sierra, Siskiyou, Solano, Sonoma, Sutter, Tehama, Trinity, Yolo, Yuba, 1-800-829-4032
Oakland, 839-4245
Elsewhere, 1-800-829-4477

Colorado
Denver, 592-1118
Elsewhere, 1-800-829-4477

Connecticut
1-800-829-4477

Delaware
1-800-829-4477

District of Columbia
628-2929

Florida
1-800-829-4477

Georgia
Atlanta, 331-6572
Elsewhere, 1-800-829-4477

Hawaii
1-800-829-4477

Idaho
1-800-829-4477

Illinois
Chicago, 886-9614
In area code 708, 312-886-9614
Springfield, 789-0489
Elsewhere, 1-800-829-4477

Indiana
Indianapolis, 631-1010
Elsewhere, 1-800-829-4477

Iowa
Des Moines, 284-7454
Elsewhere, 1-800-829-4477

Kansas
1-800-829-4477

Kentucky
1-800-829-4477

Louisiana
1-800-829-4477

Maine
1-800-829-4477

Maryland
Baltimore, 244-7306
Elsewhere, 1-800-829-4477

Massachusetts
Boston, 536-0709
Elsewhere, 1-800-829-4477

Michigan
Detroit, 961-4282
Elsewhere, 1-800-829-4477

Minnesota
St. Paul, 644-7748
Elsewhere, 1-800-829-4477

Mississippi
1-800-829-4477

Missouri
St. Louis, 241-4700
Elsewhere, 1-800-829-4477

Montana
1-800-829-4477

Nebraska
Omaha, 221-3324
Elsewhere, 1-800-829-4477

Nevada
1-800-829-4477

New Hampshire
1-800-829-4477

New Jersey
1-800-829-4477

New Mexico
1-800-829-4477

New York
Bronx, 488-8432
Brooklyn, 488-8432
Buffalo, 685-5533
Manhattan, 406-4080
Queens, 488-8432
Staten Island, 488-8432
Elsewhere, 1-800-829-4477

North Carolina
1-800-829-4477

North Dakota
1-800-829-4477

Ohio
Cincinnati, 421-0329
Cleveland, 522-3037
Elsewhere, 1-800-829-4477

Oklahoma
1-800-829-4477

Oregon
Portland, 294-5363
Elsewhere, 1-800-829-4477

Pennsylvania
Philadelphia, 627-1040
Pittsburgh, 261-1040
Elsewhere, 1-800-829-4477

Puerto Rico
1-800-829-4477

Rhode Island
1-800-829-4477

South Carolina
1-800-829-4477

South Dakota
1-800-829-4477

Tennessee
1-800-829-4477

Texas
Dallas, 767-1792
Houston, 541-3400
Elsewhere, 1-800-829-4477

Utah
1-800-829-4477

Vermont
1-800-829-4477

Virginia
Richmond, 783-1569
Elsewhere, 1-800-829-4477

Washington
Seattle, 343-7221
Elsewhere, 1-800-829-4477

West Virginia
1-800-829-4477

Wisconsin
Milwaukee, 273-8100
Elsewhere, 1-800-829-4477

Wyoming
1-800-829-4477

Tele-Tax Topic Numbers and Subjects

IRS Procedures and Services
101   IRS help available: Volunteer tax assistance programs, toll-free telephone, walk-in assistance, and outreach program
102   Tax assistance for individuals with disabilities and the hearing impaired
103   Small business tax educations: Tax help for small businesses
104   Problem resolution program: Special help for problem situations
105   Public libraries: Tax information tapes and reproducible tax forms.
106   1040 PC tax return
107   The collection process
108   Tax fraud: How to report
109   Types of organizations that qualify for tax-exempt status
110   Organizations: How to apply for exempt status
111   Examination appeal rights
112   Electronic filing
113   Power of attorney information
114   Change of address: How to notify IRS
911   Hardship assistance applications
999   Local information

Filing Requirements, Filing Status, Exemptions
151   Who must file?
152   Which form: 1040, 1040A, or 1040EZ?
153   When, where, and how to file
154   What is your filing status?
155   Dependents
156   Estimated tax

IRS Tax Forms

All Federal Income Tax Forms are listed in numerical order after this state-by-state roster. To order any of the IRS forms, publications and instruction packets which are listed in the next section, call the toll-free IRS hotline at 1-800-424-3676. To send for forms through the mail, write to the appropriate state address below. Two copies of each form and one copy of each set of instructions will be sent.

Forms Distribution Centers

Alabama
P.O. Box 8903
Bloomington, IL 61703

Alaska
Rancho Cordova, CA 95743-0001

Arizona
Rancho Cordova, CA 95743-0001

Arkansas
P.O. Box 8903
Bloomington, IL 61703

California
Rancho Cordova, CA 95743-0001

Colorado
Rancho Cordova, CA 95743-0001

Connecticut
P.O. Box 85074
Richmond, VA 23261-5074

Delaware
P.O. Box 85074
Richmond, VA 23261-5074

District of Columbia
P.O. Box 85074
Richmond, VA 23261-5074

Florida
P.O. Box 85074
Richmond, VA 23261-5074

Georgia
P.O. Box 85074
Richmond, VA 23261-5074

Hawaii
Rancho Cordova, CA 95743-0001

Idaho
Rancho Cordova, CA 95743-0001

Illinois
P.O. Box 8903
Bloomington, IL 61703

Indiana
P.O. Box 8903
Bloomington, IL 61703

Iowa
P.O. Box 8903
Bloomington, IL 61703

Kansas
P.O. Box 8903
Bloomington, IL 61703

Kentucky
P.O. Box 8903
Bloomington, IL 61703

Louisiana
P.O. Box 8903
Bloomington, IL 61703

Maine
P.O. Box 85074
Richmond, VA 23261-5074

Maryland
P.O. Box 85074
Richmond, VA 23261-5074

Massachusetts
P.O. Box 85074
Richmond, VA 23261-5074

Michigan
P.O. Box 8903
Bloomington, IL 61703

Minnesota
P.O. Box 8903
Bloomington, IL 61703

Mississippi
P.O. Box 8903
Bloomington, IL 61703

Missouri
P.O. Box 8903
Bloomington, IL 61703

Montana
Rancho Cordova, CA 95743-0001

Nebraska
P.O. Box 8903
Bloomington, IL 61703

Nevada
Rancho Cordova, CA 95743-0001

New Hampshire
P.O. Box 85074
Richmond, VA 23261-5074

New Jersey
P.O. Box 85074
Richmond, VA 23261-5074

..

Free Tax Help

New Mexico
Rancho Cordova, CA 95743-0001

New York
P.O. Box 85074
Richmond, VA 23261-5074

North Carolina
P.O. Box 85074
Richmond, VA 23261-5074

North Dakota
P.O. Box 8903
Bloomington, IL 61703

Ohio
P.O. Box 8903
Bloomington, IL 61703

Oklahoma
P.O. Box 8903
Bloomington, IL 61703

Oregon
Rancho Cordova, CA 95743-0001

Pennsylvania
P.O. Box 85074
Richmond, VA 23261-5074

Puerto Rico
P.O. Box 85074
Richmond, VA 23261-5074

Rhode Island
P.O. Box 85074
Richmond, VA 23261-5074

South Carolina
P.O. Box 85074
Richmond, VA 23261-5074

South Dakota
P.O. Box 8903
Bloomington, IL 61703

Tennessee
P.O. Box 8903
Bloomington, IL 61703

Texas
P.O. Box 8903
Bloomington, IL 61703

Utah
Rancho Cordova, CA 95743-0001

Vermont
P.O. Box 85074
Richmond, VA 23261-5074

Virgin Islands
V.I. Bureau of Internal Revenue
Lockharts Garden No. 1A
Charlotte Amalie
St. Thomas, VI 00802

Virginia
P.O. Box 85074
Richmond, VA 23261-5074

Washington
Rancho Cordova, CA 95743-0001

West Virginia
P.O. Box 85074
Richmond, VA 23261-5074

Wisconsin
P.O. Box 8903
Bloomington, IL 61703

Wyoming
Rancho Cordova, CA 95743-0001

Foreign Addresses
Forms Distribution Center
P.O. Box 85074
Richmond, VA 23261-5074

Forms Distribution Center
Rancho Cordova, CA 95743-0001

Taxpayers with mailing addresses in foreign countries should send the order blank to either address. Send letter requests for other forms and publications to: Forms Distribution Center, P.O. Box 85074, Richmond, VA 23261-5074.

Numerical List of Federal Tax Return Forms and Related Forms

Timber/Forest Industries Schedules
Supplement to income tax return for taxpayers claiming a deduction for depletion of timber and for depreciation of plant and other timber improvements. IT-IRC sec. 631; Regs. sec. 1.611-3: IT-IRC sec. 6012; Pub. 17

Tax Forms Package 1
Federal Income Tax Forms
A package of income tax forms for nonbusiness and nonfarm taxpayers. Contains one copy of instructions for Form 1040 and two copies of the following: Form 1040, Schedule A, and Schedule B.
IT-IRC sec. 6012; Pub. 17

Tax Forms Package 1-X
Federal Income Tax Forms
A package of income tax forms for nonbusiness and nonfarm taxpayers. Contains one copy of instructions for Form 1040 and two copies of the following: Form 1040, Schedule A, Schedule B, Form 2106 and instructions, and Form 2441 and instructions.
IT-IRC sec. 6012; Pub. 17

Tax Forms Package 2
Federal Income Tax Forms
A package of income tax forms for nonbusiness and nonfarm taxpayers. Contains one copy of instructions for Form 1040 and two copies of the following: Form 1040, Schedule A, Schedule B, Schedule D, Schedule E, Form 2441 and instructions, and Form 4562 and instructions.
IT-IRC sec. 6012; Pub. 17

Tax Forms Package 2-R
Federal Income Tax Forms
A package of income tax forms for nonbusiness and nonfarm taxpayers. Contains one copy of instructions for Form 1040 and two copies of the following: Form 1040, Schedule A, Schedule B, Schedule D, Schedule E, Schedule R and instructions, and Form 4562 and instructions.
IT-IRC sec. 6012; Pub. 17

Tax Forms Package 3
Federal Income Tax Forms
A package of income tax forms for business taxpayers. Contains one copy of instructions for Form 1040 and two copies of the following: Form 1040, Schedule A, Schedule B, Schedule C, Schedule D, Schedule E, Schedule SE, Form 2441 and instructions, and Form 4562 and instructions.
IT-IRC sec. 6012; Pub. 17

Tax Forms Package 3-E
Federal Income Tax Forms
A package of income tax forms for business taxpayers. Contains one copy of instructions for Form 1040 and two copies of the following: Forms 1040, Schedule A, Schedule B, Schedule C, Schedule D, Schedule E, Schedule SE, and Form 4562 and instructions.
IT-IRC sec. 6012; Pub. 17

Tax Forms Package 4
Federal Income Tax Forms
A package of income tax forms for farm taxpayers. Contains one copy of instructions for Form 1040 and two copies of the following: Form 1040, Schedule A, Schedule B, Schedule C, Schedule D, Schedule E, Schedule F, Schedule SE, Form 2441 and instructions, Form 4136, and Form 4562 and instructions.
IT-IRC sec. 6012; Pub. 17

Tax Forms Package 5
Federal Income Tax Forms
A package of income tax forms for individual taxpayers. Contains one copy of instructions for Form 1040A and two copies each of Form 1040EZ, Form 1040A, and Schedule 1 (Form 1040A).

Package X
Informational Copies of Federal Tax Forms
A two-volume set of income tax and information return forms, substitute forms information, and other information needed by tax practitioners to service their clients.

CT-1
Employer's Annual Railroad Retirement and Unemployment Repayment Tax Return
Used to report employees' and employers' taxes under the RRTA and RURT. Emp-IRC secs. 3201, 3202, 3221, 3321, 3322, and 6011; Regs. secs. 31.6011(a)-2, 31.6011(a)-3AT, and 31.6302(c)-2; Separate instructions

CT-2
Employee Representative's Quarterly Railroad Tax Return
Used to report employee representative's tax under the RRTA and RURT.
Emp-IRC secs. 3211, 3321, and 6011; Regs. secs. 31.6011(a)-2 and 31.6011(a)-3AT

W-2
Wage and Tax Statement (For Use in Cities and States Authorizing Combined Form)
Used to report wages, tips and other compensation, allocated tips, employee social security tax, income tax, state or city income tax withheld; and to support credit shown on individual income tax return.
Emp-IRC sec 6051; Regs secs 1.6041-2 and 31.6051-1; Circular E; Separate instructions

W-2AS
American Samoa Wage and Tax Statement
Used to report wages, tips, and other compensation, employee social security tax, Samoan income tax withheld, and to support credit shown on American Samoa individual income tax return.
Emp-IRC sec. 6051; Regs. sec. 31.6051-1, Circular SS

W-2c
Statement of Corrected Income and Tax Amounts
Used to correct previously filed Forms W-2, W-2P, W-2AS, W-2CNMI, W-2GU, and W-2VI. Emp-IRC sec. 6051; Reg. sec. 1.6041-2 and 31.6051-1

499R-2/W-2PR
Puerto Rico Withholding Statement
Used to report social security wages, tips, and social security tax withheld for employees in Puerto Rico. Emp-IRC sec. 6051; Regs. sec. 31.6051-1; Circular PR

W-2G
Statement for Recipients of Certain Gambling Winnings
Used to report gambling winnings and any taxes withheld.
IT-IRC sec 3402(q) and 6041; Temp Regs sec 7.6041-1 and Regs sec 31.3402(q)-1(f); See separate Instructions for Forms 1099, 1098, 5498, 1096, and W-2G.

W-2GU
Guam Wage and Tax Statement
Used to report wages, tips and other compensation, employee social security tax, Guam income tax withheld, and to support credit shown on individual income tax return. Emp-IRC sec. 6051; Regs. sec. 31.6051-1; Circular SS

W-2CNMI
Commonwealth of Northern Mariana Islands Wage and Tax Statement
Used to report wages, tips and other compensation, employee social security tax, CNMI income tax withheld, and to support credit shown on individual income tax return. Emp-IRC sec. 6051; Regs. sec. 31.6050-1; Circular SS

W-2VI
U.S. Virgin Islands Wage and Tax Statement
Used to report wages, tips and other compensation, employee social security tax, VI income tax withheld, and to support credit shown on individual income tax return.
Emp-IRC sec. 6051; Regs. secs. 1.6041-2 and 31.6051-1; Circular SS

W-2P
Statement For Recipients of Annuities, Pensions, Retired Pay, or IRA Payments
Used to report periodic distributions from annuities, pensions, retirement pay, and payments from an IRA; Federal and state income tax withheld.
Emp-IRC sec. 3402(o); Regs. sec. 32.1-1; Circular E; Separate instructions

W-3
Transmittal of Income and Tax Statements
Used by employers and other payers to transmit Forms W-2 and W-2P to the Social Security Administration.
Emp-IRC sec. 6011; Reg. sec. 31.6051-2

W-3c
Transmittal of Corrected Income and Tax Statements
Used by employers and other payers to transmit corrected income and tax statements (Forms W-2c).
Emp-IRC sec. 6011; Reg. 31.6051-2

W-3PR
Transmittal of Withholding Statements
Used by employers to transmit Forms 499R-2/W-2PR.
Emp-IRC sec. 6011; Reg. sec. 31.6051-2; Circular PR

W-3SS
Transmittal of Wage and Tax Statements
Used by employers to transmit Forms W-2AS, W-2CNMI, W-2GU, and W-2VI.
Emp-IRC sec. 6011; Reg. sec. 31.6051-2; Circular SS

W-4
Employee's Withholding Allowance Certificate
Completed by employee and given to employer so that proper amount of income tax can be withheld from wages. Also used by employee to claim exemption from withholding by certifying that he or she had no liability for income tax for preceding tax year and anticipates that no liability will be incurred for current tax year. Emp-IRC secs. 3402(f), 3402(m) and 3402(n); Regs. secs. 31.3402(f)5-1 and 31.3402(n)-1; Circular E

W-4P
Withholding Certificate for Pension or Annuity Payments
Used to figure amount of Federal income tax to withhold from periodic pension or annuity payments or to claim additional withholding or exemption from withholding for periodic or nonperiodic payments. Emp-IRC sec. 3405

W-4S
Request for Federal Income Tax Withholding from Sick Pay
Filed with a third party payer of sick pay to request Federal income tax withholding.
Emp-IRC sec. 3402(o); Regs. sec. 31.3402(o)-3

W-5
Earned Income Credit Advance Payment Certificate
Used by employee to request employer to furnish advance payment of earned income credit with the employee's pay. IRC sec. 3507

W-8
Certificate of Foreign Status
Used by foreign persons to notify payers of interest, mortgage interest recipients, or middlemen, brokers, or barter exchanges not to withhold or report on payments of interest, or on broker transactions or barter exchanges.
IRC secs. 3406, 6042, 6044, 6045, and 6049

W-9
Request for Taxpayer Identification Number and Certification
Used by a person required to file certain information returns with IRS to obtain the correct taxpayer identification number (TIN) of the person for whom a return is filed. Also used to claim exemption from backup withholding and to certify that the person whose TIN is provided is not subject to backup withholding because of failure to report interest and dividends as income.

W-10
Dependent Care Provider's Identification and Certification
Used by taxpayers to certify that the name, address, and taxpayer identification number of their dependent care provider is correct.
IRS secs. 21, 129, 501(c)3)

SS-4
Application for Employer Identification Number
Used by employers and other entities to apply for an identification number.
Emp-IRC Regs. sec. 31.6011(b)-1; Circulars A and E

SS-4 PR
Solicitud de Numero de Identificacion Patronal
Used by employers and other entities in Puerto Rico to apply for an identification number. A variation of Form SS-4.
Emp-IR Regs. sec. 31.6011(b)-1; Circular PR

SS-5
Application for a Social Security Card
Used by an individual to obtain a social security number and card.
Emp-IR Regs. sec. 31.6011(b)-2; Circulars A and E

SS-8
Information for Use in Determining Whether a Worker Is an Employee for Federal Employment Taxes and Income Tax Withholding
Used to furnish information about services of an individual, generally selected as representative of a class of workers, to get written determination on status.
Emp-IRC sec. 3121; Regs. sec. 31.3121(d)-1

SS-16
Certificate of Election of Coverage Under the Federal Insurance Contributions Act
Used by religious orders, whose members are required to take a vow of poverty, to elect social security coverage.
Emp-IRC sec. 3121(r); Regs. sec. 31.3121(r)-1

11-C
Stamp Tax and Registration Return for Wagering
Used to report taxes due under IRC sections 4401 and 4411, and as an application for registry and wagering activity. Upon approval of the return, the Service will issue a Special Tax Stamp.
Ex-IRC secs. 4411 and 4412; Regs. secs. 44.4412 and 44.4901

56
Notice Concerning Fiduciary Relationship
Used by persons to notify IRS that they are acting in fiduciary capacity for other persons.
IT-IRC sec. 6903; Regs. sec. 301.6903-1

637
Registration for Tax-Free Transactions Under Chapters 31, 32, and 38 of the Internal Revenue Code
Used as an application and certificate; by manufacturers, refiners or importers who buy taxable articles tax-free for further manufacture of taxable articles, or for resale direct to a manufacturer for such purpose. The original of the application is validated and returned as the Certificate of Registry by the District Director. Ex-IRC secs. 4052, 4064(b)(1)(c), 4101, 4221, and 4661; Regs. secs. 48.4101-1, 48.4222(a)-1, and 48.4222(d)-1

637A
Registration for Tax-Free Sales and Purchases of Fuel Used in Aircraft
Used to register for tax-free sales under IRC section 4041(c). Filed by a seller who is a manufacturer, producer, importer, wholesaler, Jobber, or retailer; or by a seller that is a commercial airline, nonprofit educational organization, or other exempt user that wishes to sell or purchase tax-free fuel for use in aircraft. The original of the application is validated by the District Director and returned as the Certificate of Registry.
Ex-IRC sec. 4041(c); Regs. sec. 48.4041-11

706
United States Estate (and Generation-Skipping Transfer) Tax Return
Used for the estate of a deceased United States resident or citizen.
E&G-IRC sec. 6018; Regs. sec. 20.6018-1; Separate instructions

706-A
United States Additional Estate Tax Return
Used to report recapture tax under special use valuation.
E&G-IRC sec. 2032A; Separate instructions

706CE
Certificate of Payment of Foreign Death Tax
Used to report credit against United States estate tax for estate inheritance, legacy, or succession tax paid to a foreign government.
E&G-IRC sec. 2014; Regs. sec. 20.2014-5

706GS(D)
Generation-Skipping Transfer Tax Return for Distributions
Used by distributees to report generation-skipping transfer tax on taxable distributions from trusts subject to the tax.
E&G-IRC sec. 2601; Temp Regs. sec. 26.2662-1(b)(1); Separate instructions

706GS(D-1)
Notification of Distribution from a Generation-Skipping Trust
Used by trustees to report certain information to distributees regarding taxable distributions from a trust subject to the generation-skipping transfer tax.
E&G-IRC sec. 2601; Temp. Regs. sec. 26.2662-1(b)(1)

706GS(T)
Generation-Skipping Transfer Tax Return for Terminations
Used by trustees to report generation-skipping transfer tax on taxable terminations of trusts subject to the tax.
E&G-IRC sec. 2601; Temp. Regs. sec. 26.2662-1(b)2); Separate instructions

706NA
United States Estate (and Generation-Skipping Transfer) Tax Return, Estate of nonresident not a citizen of the United States
Used for United States nonresident alien decedent's estate to be filed within 9 months after date of death.
E&G-IRC sec. 6018; Regs. sec. 20.6018-1(b); Separate instructions

Schedule S (Form 706)
Increased Estate Tax on Excess Retirement Accumulations
Used to pay the section 4980A increased estate tax on excess retirement accumulations. E&G-IRC sec. 4980A(d)

709
United States Gift (and Generation-Skipping Transfer) Tax Return
Used to report gifts of more than $10,000 (or, regardless of value, gifts of a future interest in property).
E&G-IRC sec. 6019; Regs. sec. 25.6019-1; Separate instructions

709-A
United States Short Form Gift Tax Return
Used to report gifts of more than $10,000 but less than $20,000 if the gifts are nontaxable by reason of gift splitting.
E&G-IRC secs. 6019, 6075; Regs. sec. 25.6019-1

712
Life Insurance Statement
Used with Form 706 or Form 709.
E&G-IRC secs 6001 and 6018; Regs secs 20.6001-1, 20.6018-4(d), 25.6001-1(b)

720
Quarterly Federal Excise Tax Return
Used to report excise taxes due from retailers and manufacturers on sale or manufacture of various articles; taxes on facilities and services; taxes on certain products and commodities (gasoline, coal, etc); windfall profits and Inland waterways taxes. Ex-IRC sec. 6011; Separate instructions

730
Tax on Wagering
Used to report taxes due under IRC section 4401.
Ex-IRC sec. 4401; Regs. sec. 44.6011(a)-1

843
Claim
Used to claim refund of taxes (other than income taxes) which were illegally, erroneously or excessively collected; or to claim amount paid for stamps unused or used in error or excess; and for a refund or abatement of interest or penalties assessed.
Misc-IRC secs. 6402, 6404, 6511, 6404(e), and 6404(f); Regs. secs. 31.6413(c)-1, 301.6402-2, and 301.6404-1

851
Affiliations Schedule
Used with Form 1120 by parent corporation for affiliated corporations included in consolidated tax return. IT-IRC sec. 1502; Regs. sec. 1.1502-75(h)

872-C
Consent Fixing Period of Limitation Upon Assessment of Tax Under Section 4940 of the Internal Revenue Code
Used only with Form 1023, Application for Recognition of Exemption, by an organization described in Internal Revenue Code section 170(b)(1)(A)(vi) or section 509(a)2), to request the organization be treated as a publicly supported organization during an advance ruling period. IT-IRC sec. 6501(c)4)

926
Return by a Transferor of Property to a Foreign Corporation, Foreign Trust or Estate, or Foreign Partnership
Used to report transfers of property by a U.S. person to a foreign partnership, trust or estate, or corporation, and pay any excise tax due on the transfer.
IT-IRC sec. 1491; Regs. sec. 1.1491-2

928
Gasoline Bond
Used to post bond for excise tax on fuel.
Ex-IRC sec. 4101

940
Employer's Annual Federal Unemployment (FUTA) Tax Return
Used by employers to report Federal unemployment (FUTA) tax. Emp-IRC sec 6011; IRC Chapter 23; Regs sec 31.6011(a)-3; Circular E; Circular SS

940-EZ
Employer's Annual Federal Unemployment (FUTA) Tax Return
Used by employers to report Federal unemployment (FUTA) tax. This form is a simplified version of Form 940.
EMP-IRC sec. 6011; IRC Chapter 23; Regs. sec. 31.6011(a)-3; Circular E; Circular SS

940PR
Planilla Para La Declaracion Anual Del Patrono-La Contribucion Federal Para el Desempleo (FUTA)
Used by employers in Puerto Rico. A variation of Form 940.
Emp-IRC sec. 6011; IRC Chapter 23; Regs. sec. 31.6011(a)-3; Circular PR

941
Employer's Quarterly Federal Tax Return
Used by employer to report social security taxes and income taxes withheld, advance earned income credit (EIC), and back up withholding.
Emp-IRC secs. 3101, 3111, 3402, 3405 and 3406; Regs. secs. 31.6011(a)-1 and 31.6011(a)-4; Circular E

Sch. A (Form 941)
Record of Federal Backup Withholding Tax Liability
Used to report backup withholding liability when treated as a separate tax for depositing purposes.
Emp-IRC secs. 3406, 6302; Regs. secs. 31.6302 and 35a.9999-3

941c
Statement to Correct Information Previously Reported on the Employer's Federal Tax Return
Used by employers to correct wages, tips, and tax previously reported.
Emp-IRC secs. 6205 and 6402; Regs. secs. 31.6011(a)-1, 31.6205-1, and 31.6402(a)-2; Circulars A, E, and SS

941c PR
Planilla Para La Correccion De Informacion Facilitada Anteriormente En Complimiento Con La Ley Del Seguro Social
Used by employers in Puerto Rico. A variation of Form 941c.
Emp-IRC Chapter 21; Regs secs 31.6011(a)-1 and 31.6205-1, 31.6402(a)-2; Circular PR

941E
Quarterly Return of Withheld Federal Income Tax and Hospital Insurance (Medicare) Tax
Used by State and local government employers and by other organizations that are not liable for social security taxes. A variation of Form 941.
Emp-IRC secs. 3121(u) and 3402

941-M
Employer's Monthly Federal Tax Return
Used by employers to report withheld income tax and social security taxes (because they have not complied with the requirements for filing quarterly returns, or for paying or depositing taxes reported on quarterly returns).
Emp-IRC sec. 7512; Regs. sec. 31.6011(a)-5

941 PR
Planilla Para La Declaracion Trimestral Del Patrono-La Contribucion Federal al Seguro Social
Used by employers in Puerto Rico. A variation of Form 941.
Emp-IRC secs. 3101 and 3111; Regs. sec. 31.6011(a)-1; Circular PR

941SS
Employer's Quarterly Federal Tax Return
Used by employers in Virgin Islands, Guam, the Northern Mariana Islands, and American Samoa. A variation of Form 941.
Emp-IRC secs. 3101 and 3111; Regs. sec. 31.6011(a)-1; Circular SS

942
Employer's Quarterly Tax Return for Household Employees

Used by household employers quarterly to report social security and income taxes withheld from wages of household employees.
Emp-IRC secs. 3101 and 3111; Regs. sec. 31.6011(a)-1(a)(3)

942PR
Planilla Para La Declaracion Trimestral Del Patrono De Empleados Domesticos

Used by household employers in Puerto Rico to report social security taxes withheld from wages of household employees. A variation of Form 942.
Emp-IRC secs. 3101 and 3111; Regs. sec. 31.6011(a)-1(a)(3)

943
Employer's Annual Tax Return for Agricultural Employees

Used by Agricultural employers to report social security and income taxes withheld.
Emp-IRC secs. 3101, 3111 and 3402; Regs. sec. 31.6011(a)-1 and 31.6011(a)-4; Circular A

943A
Agricultural Employer's Record of Federal Tax Liability

Used by agricultural employers who have a tax liability of $3,000 or more during any month. Emp-IRC sec. 6302; Regs. sec. 6302(c)-1; Circular A

943 PR
Planilla Para La Declaracion Anual De La Contribucion Del Patrono De Empleados Agricolas

Used by agricultural employers in Puerto Rico. A variation of Form 943.
Emp-IRC secs 3101 and 3111; Regs sec 31.6011(a)-1, 31.6011(a)-4; Circular PR

943A-PR
Registro De La Obligacion Contributiva Del Patrono Agricola

Used by agricultural employers in Puerto Rico. A variation of Form 943A.
Emp-IRC sec. 6302; Regs. sec. 31.6302(c)-1; Circular PR

952
Consent to Fix Period of Limitation on Assessment of Income Taxes

Used when complete liquidation of a subsidiary is not accomplished within the tax year in which the first liquidating distribution is made. The receiving corporation is required to file this consent with its return for each tax year which falls wholly or partly within the period of liquidation.
IT-IRC sec. 332; Regs. sec. 1.332-4

966
Corporate Dissolution or Liquidation

Used (under IRC section 6043(a)) by corporations within 30 days after adoption of resolution or plan of dissolution, or complete or partial liquidation. (An information return.)
IT-IRC sec. 6043(a)

970
Application to Use LIFO Inventory Method

Used to change to the LIFO inventory method provided by section 472.
IT-IRC sec. 472; Regs. sec. 1.472-3

972
Consent of Shareholder to Include Specific Amount in Gross Income

Used by shareholders of a corporation who agree to include in their gross income for their taxable year a specific amount as a tax dividend.
IT-IRC sec. 565

973
Corporation Claim for Deduction for Consent Dividends

Used by corporations that claim a consent dividends deduction. Accompanied by filed consents of shareholders on Form 972. IT-IRC sec. 561

976
Claim for Deficiency Dividends Deduction by a Personal Holding Company, Regulated Investment Company, or Real Estate Investment Trust

Used by a personal holding company, regulated investment company, or real estate investment trust to claim a deficiency dividends deduction.
IT-IRC sec. 547 and 860; Regs. sec. 1.547-2(b)(2) and 1.860-2(b)(2)

982
Reduction of Tax Attributes Due to Discharge of Indebtedness

Used by a taxpayer who excludes from gross income under section 108 any amount of income attributable to discharge of indebtedness, in whole or in part, in the tax year, for which it is liable or subject. Also used as a consent of a corporation to adjustment of basis of its property under regulations prescribed under IRC section 1082(a)(2).
IT-IRC secs. 108, 1017, and 1082

990
Return of Organization Exempt From Income Tax (Except Private Foundation)

Used by organizations exempt under IRC section 501(a) and described in Code section 501(c), other than private foundations. (An information return.)
IT-IRC sec. 6033; Regs. sec. 1.6033-1(a)(2); Separate instructions

Package 990-1
Organizations Exempt from Income Tax under section 501(c) (other than sections 501(c)(3), (c)(4), (c)(6), and (c)(7), of the Internal Revenue Code)

A package of information forms for exempt organizations. Contains one copy each of Instructions for Forms 990, 990-EZ, and 990-T; two copies each of Forms 990, 990-EZ, and 990-T.
IT-IRC sec. 6033, one copy of Form 990-W, Form 1120-W, and instructions.

Package 990-2
Organizations Exempt from Income Tax under Section 501(c)(3) (other than Private Foundations as defined in Section 509(a), of the Internal Revenue Code)

A package of information forms for exempt organizations. Contains one copy each of Instructions for Forms 990, Schedule A (Form 990), 990-EZ, and 990-T; two copies each of Forms 990, Schedule A (Form 990), 990-EZ, and 990-T, one copy of Form 990-W, Form 1120-W, and instructions; one copy of Supplemental Instructions, and a sample filled-in Form 990 and Schedule A (Form 990).
IT-IRC sec. 6033

Package 990-3
Organizations Exempt from Income Tax under section 501(c)(4) of the Internal Revenue Code

A package of information forms for exempt organizations. Contains one copy each of Instructions for Forms 990, 990-EX, and 990-T; two copies each of Forms 990, 990-EX, and 990-T, one copy of Form 990-W, Form 1120-W, and instructions; one copy of Supplemental Instructions, and sample filled-in Forms 990-EZ and 990-T.
IT-IRC sec. 6033

Sch. A (Form 990)
Organization Exempt Under 501 (c)(3) (Supplementary Information)

Used by organizations described in IRC section 501(c)(3) (other than private foundations filing Form 990-PF).
IT-IRC sec. 6033; Separate instructions

990-BL
Information and Initial Excise Tax Return for Black Lung Benefit Trusts and Certain Related Persons

Used by Black Lung Benefit Trusts exempt under Section 501(c)(21) as an information return. Also used by these trusts and certain related persons for attaching Schedule A (Form 990-BL) when taxes under sections 4951 or 4952 are due.
IT/EX-IRC sec. 501 (c)(21); Chapter 42; Separate instructions

990-C
Farmers' Cooperative Association Income Tax Return
Used by Farmers' Cooperative Marketing and Purchasing Association.
IT-IRC secs. 521, 1381, 1382, 1383, 1385, 1388, and 6012; Regs. secs. 1.522-1, 1.1381-1, 2, 1.1382-1, 2, 3, 4, 5, 6, 7, 1.1383-1, 1.1385-1, 1.388-1, and 1.6012-2(f); Separate instructions

990-EZ
Short Form Return of Organization Exempt Form Income Tax
Used by organizations of gross receipts less than $100,000 and total assets of less than $250,000 at end of year.
IT-IRC sec. 6033; Regs. sec. 1.6033-1(a)(2); Separate instructions

990-PF
Return of Private Foundation or Section 4947(a)(1)Trust Treated as a Private Foundation
Used by private foundations and Section 4947(a)(1)trusts. (An information return.) IT/Ex-IRC sec. 6033; IRC Chapter 42; Separate instructions

Package 990-PF
Returns for Private Foundations or Section 4947(a)(1) Trusts Treated as Private Foundations
A package of information forms used by private foundations and Sections 4947(a)(1)trusts. In addition to Form 990-PF, this package includes Form 990-T and Form 4720, Form 990-W, Form 1120-W and instructions for each form, and filled-in samples of Form 990-PF. IT-IRC sec. 6033

990-T
Exempt Organization Business Income Tax Return
Used by exempt organization with unrelated business income (under IRC section 511). IT-IRC secs. 511 and 6012; Regs. secs. 1.6012-2(e) and 1.6012-3(a)(5); Separate instructions

990-W
Estimated Tax on Unrelated Business Taxable Income for Tax-Exempt Organization
Used as a worksheet by tax-exempt trusts and tax-exempt corporations to figure their estimated tax liability. Tax-exempt trusts and corporations should keep it for their records. IT-IRC sec. 6154

1000
Ownership Certificate
Used by a citizen, resident individual, fiduciary, partnership, or nonresident partnership all of whose members are citizens or residents who have interest in bonds of a domestic or resident corporation (containing a tax-free covenant and issued before January 1, 1934). IT-IRC sec. 1461; Regs. sec. 1.1461-1(h)

1001
Ownership, Exemption, or Reduced Rate Certificate
Used by a nonresident alien individual or fiduciary, foreign partnership, foreign corporation or other foreign entity, nonresident foreign partnership composed in whole or in part of nonresident aliens (applies to IRC section 1451 only), or nonresident foreign corporation (applies to Code section 1451 only), receiving income subject to withholding under Code section 1441, 1442, or 1451. IT-IRC sec. 1461; Regs. sec. 1.1461-1(i)

Package 1023
Application for Recognition of Exemption Under Section 501(c)3-of the Internal Revenue Code
Used to apply for exemption under section 501(a) IRC as organizations described in section 501(c)3-(also sections 501(e) and (f)). Includes 3 copies of Form 872-C. IT-IRC sec. 501; Regs. sec. 1.501(a)-1(a)3

Package 1024
Application for Recognition of Exemption Under Section 501(a) or Determination Under Section 120
Used by organizations to apply for exemption under IRC section 501(a) (as described in Code sections 501(c)2), 4), 5), 6), 7), 8), 9), (10), (12), (13), (15), (17), (19), 20) and 25). (Also used to apply for a determination as a qualified plan under section 120.) IT-IRC secs. 501, 120; Regs. sec. 1.501(a)-1(a)3

1028
Application for Recognition of Exemption Under Section 521 of the Internal Revenue Code
Used by farmers, fruit growers, or similar associations to claim exemption under IRC section 521. IT-IRC sec. 521; Regs. sec. 1.521-1, Separate instructions

1040
U.S. Individual Income Tax Return
Used by citizens or residents of the United States to report income tax. (Also see Form 1040A, and 1040EZ.) IT-IRC secs. 6012 and 6017; Regs. secs. 1.6012-1 and 1.6017-1; Pub. 17; Separate instructions

Sch. A (Form 1040)
Itemized Deductions
Used to report itemized deductions (medical and dental expense, taxes, contributions, interest, casualty and theft losses, moving expenses, miscellaneous deductions subject to the 2% AGI limit, and other miscellaneous deductions). IT-IRC secs. 67, 163, 164, 165, 166, 170, 211, 212, 213, and 217; Pub. 17; See the separate instructions for Form 1040.

Sch. B (Form 1040)
Interest and Dividend Income
Used to list gross dividends received (if more than $400) and interest income (if more than $400), and to ask questions about foreign accounts and foreign trusts. IT-IRC secs. 6012, 61, and 116; Pub. 17; See the separate Instructions for Form 1040.

Sch. C (Form 1040)
Profit or Loss From Business
Used to figure profit or (loss) from business or professions. IT-IRC sec. 6017; Regs. sec. 1.6017-1; Pubs. 17 and 334; See separate Instructions for Form 1040.

Sch. D (Form 1040)
Capital Gains and Losses
Used to report details of gain (or loss) from sales or exchanges of capital assets; to figure capital loss carry-overs from 1989 to 1990, and to reconcile Forms 1099-B with tax return. IT-IRC secs. 1202-1223, 6045; Pubs. 17 and 334; See the separate Instructions for Form 1040.

Sch. D-1 (Form 1040)
Continuation Sheet for Schedule D (Form 1040)
Used to attach to Schedule D (Form 1040) to list additional transactions in Parts 2a and 9a.

Sch. E (Form 1040)
Supplemental Income and Loss
Used to report income from rents, royalties, partnerships, S corporations, estates, trusts, REMICs, etc. IT-IRC secs. 6012 and 6017; Regs. secs. 1.6012-1 and 1.6017-1; Pub. 17; See the separate Instructions for Form 1040.

Sch. F (Form 1040)
Farm Income and Expenses
Used to figure profit or (loss) from farming. IT-IRC sec. 6012; Regs. sec. 1.61-4; Pub. 225; See the separate Instructions for Form 1040.

Sch. R (Form 1040)
Credit for the Elderly or the Disabled
Used to figure credit for the elderly and for persons under 65 who retired on permanent and total disability and received taxable disability benefits. IT-IRC sec. 22; Pub. 17 and 524; Separate instructions

Sch. SE (Form 1040)
Social Security Self-Employment Tax
Used to figure self-employment income and self-employment tax. IT-IRC secs. 1401 and 1402; See the separate Instructions for Form 1040.

1040A
U.S. Individual Income Tax Return
Used by citizens and residents of the United States to report income tax. (Also see Form 1040 and 1040EZ.) IT-IRC sec. 6012; Regs. sec. 1.6012-1; Pub. 17; Separate instructions

Free Tax Help

1040C
U.S. Departing Alien Income Tax Return
Used by aliens who intend to depart from the U.S., to report income received, or expected to be received for the entire taxable year, determined as nearly as possible by the date of intended departure. (Also see Form 2063.)
IT-IRC sec. 6851; Regs. sec. 1.6851-2; Pub. 519; Separate instructions

1040-ES
Estimated Tax for Individuals
Used to pay income tax (including self-employment tax and alternative minimum tax) due (the tax that is more than the tax withheld from wages, salaries, and other payments for personal services). It is not required unless the total tax is more than withholding (if any) by $500 or more. IT-IRC sec. 6654

1040-ES (Espanol)
Contribucion Federal Estimada Del Trabajo Por Cuenta Propia-Puerto Rico
Used in Puerto Rico. The payment vouchers are provided for payment of self-employment tax on a current basis.
IT-IRC sec. 6654

1040-ES (NR)
U.S. Estimated Tax for Nonresident Alien Individuals
Used by nonresident aliens to pay any income tax due in excess of the tax withheld. It is not required unless the total tax exceeds withholding (if any) by $500 or more.
IT-IRC sec. 6654

1040EZ
Income Tax Return for Single Filers With No Dependents
Used by citizens & residents of the United States to report income tax. (Also see Form 1040 and Form 1040A.)
IT-IRC sec. 6012; Reg. sec. 1.6012-1; Pub. 17; Separate instructions

1040NR
U.S. Nonresident Alien Income Tax Return
Used by all nonresident alien individuals, whether or not engaged in a trade or business within the United States, who file a U.S. tax return. Also used as required for filing nonresident alien fiduciary (estate and trusts) returns.
IT-IRC secs. 871 and 6012; Pub. 519; Separate instructions

1040 PR
Planilla Para La Declaracion De La Contribucion Federal Sobre El Trabajo Por Cuenta Propia-Puerto Rico
Used in Puerto Rico to compute self-employment tax in accordance with IRC Chapter 2 of Subtitle A, and to provide proper credit to taxpayer's social security account. IT-IRC secs. 6017 and 7651; Regs. sec. 1.6017-1; Circular PR

1040SS
U.S. Self-Employment Tax Return-Virgin Islands, Guam, and American Samoa
Used to compute self-employment tax in accordance with IRC Chapter 2 of Subtitle A, and to provide proper credit to taxpayer's social security account.
IT-IRC secs. 6017 and 7651; Regs. sec. 1.6017-1; Circular SS

1040X
Amended U.S. Individual Income Tax Return
Used to claim refund of income taxes, pay additional income taxes, or designate dollar(s) to a Presidential election campaign fund.
IT-IRC secs. 6402, 6404, 6511, and 6096; Separate instructions

1041
U.S. Fiduciary Income Tax Return
Used by a fiduciary of a domestic estate or domestic trust to report income tax.
IT-IRC sec. 6012; Regs. secs. 1.671-4, 1.6012-3(a), and 1.6041-1; Separate instructions

Sch. D (Form 1041)
Capital Gains and Losses
Used to report details of gain (or loss) from sales or exchanges of capital assets.
IT-IRC sec. 6012; Regs. sec. 1.6012-3(a); Separate instructions

Sch. J. (Form 1041)
Information Return Trust Allocation of an Accumulation Distribution (IRC section 665)
Used by domestic complex trusts to report accumulation distributions. IT-IRC secs. 665, 666, and 667

Sch. K-1 (Form 1041)
Beneficiary's Share of Income, Deductions, Credits, etc.
Used to report each beneficiary's share of the income, deductions, credits, and distributable net alternative minimum taxable income form the estate or trust.
IT-IRC sec. 6012; Regs. secs. 1.6012-3(a)

1041-A
U.S. Information Return-Trust Accumulation of Charitable Amounts
Used by a trust that claims a contribution deduction under IRC section 642(c), or by a trust described in Code section 4947(a)2). (An information return.)
IT-IRC secs. 6034 and 6104; Regs. sec. 1.6034-1

1041-ES
Estimated Income Tax for Fiduciaries
Used to figure and pay estimated tax for fiduciaries. IT-IRC sec. 6654

1041-T
Transmittal of Estimated Taxes Credited to Beneficiaries
Used by a trust to make an election under section 643(g) to credit an overpayment of estimated tax to beneficiaries. IT-IRC sec. 643(g)

1042
Annual Withholding Tax Return for U.S. Source Income of Foreign Persons
Used by withholding agents to report tax withheld at source on certain income paid to nonresident aliens, foreign partnerships, or foreign corporations not engaged in a trade or business in the U.S. IT-IRC secs. 1441, 1442, and 1461; Regs. secs. 1.1441-1 and 1.1461-2(b); Separate instructions

1042S
Foreign Person's U.S. Source Income Subject to Withholding
Used by a withholding agent to report certain income and tax withheld at source for foreign payees. (An information return.)
IT-IRC sec. 1461; Regs. sec. 1.1461-2(c); Separate instructions

1045
Application for Tentative Refund
Used by taxpayers (other than corporations) to apply for a tentative refund from the carryback of a net operating loss, unused general business credit, or overpayment of tax due to a claim of right adjustment under section 1341(b)(1).
T-IRC sec. 6411; Regs. sec. 1.6411-1

1065
U.S. Partnership Return of Income
Used by partnerships as an information return.
IT-IRC sec. 6031 and 6698; Regs. secs. 1.761-1(a), 1.6031-1, and 1.6033-1(a)5); Separate instructions

Package 1065
Federal Income Tax Forms
A package of income tax forms for partnerships. Contains one copy of instructions for Form 1065, two copies of Form 1065, six copies of Schedule K-1 (Form 1065) and two copies of instructions, two copies of Form 4562 and one copy of instructions. T-IRC sec. 6031

Sch. D (Form 1065)
Capital Gains and Losses
Used to show partnership's capital gains and losses. IT-IRC 6031

Sch. K-1 (Form 1065)
Partner's Share of Income, Credits, Deductions, Etc.
Used to show partner's share of income, credits, deductions, etc.
IT-IRC secs. 702 and 703; Separate instructions

1066
U.S. Real Estate Mortgage Investment Conduit Income Tax Return
Used to report income, deductions, gains and losses, and the tax on net income from prohibited transactions, of a real estate mortgage investment conduit. IT-IRC secs. 860D and 860F(e); Separate instructions

Sch. Q (Form 1066)
Quarterly Notice to Residual Interest Holder of REMIC Taxable Income or Net Loss Allocation
Used to show residual interest holder's share of taxable income (or net loss), excess inclusion, and section 212 expenses. IT-IRC sec. 860G(c)

1078
Certificate of Alien Claiming Residence in the United States
Used by an alien claiming residence in the U.S., for income tax purposes. Filed with the withholding agent.
IT-IRC secs. 871 and 1441; Regs. secs. 1.1441-5 and 1.871-3,4

1090
Statement of Income, and Profit and Loss Accounts
Used by a railroad company with Form 1120. IT-Instruction for Form 1120

1096
Annual Summary and Transmittal of U.S. Information Returns
Used to summarize and transmit Forms W-2G, 1098, 1099-A, 1099-B, 1099-DIV, 1099-G, 1099-INT, 1099-MISC, 1099-OID, 1099-PATR, 1099-R, 1099-S, and 5498. IT-IRC secs. 408(i), 6041, 6041A, 6042, 6043, 6044, 6045, 6047, 6049, 6050A, 6050B, 6050D, 6050E, 6050H, and 6050J

1098
Mortgage Interest Statement
Used to report $600 or more of mortgage interest from an individual in the course of a trade or business.
IT-IRC sec. 6050H; Regs. sec. 1.6050H-2; See the separate Instructions for Forms 1099, 1098, 5498, 1096, and W-2G

1099-A
Information Return for Acquisition or Abandonment of Secured Property
Used by lenders to report acquisitions by such lenders or abandonments of property that secures a loan.
IT-IRC sec. 6050J; Temp. Regs. sec. 1.6050J-1T; See the separate Instructions for Forms 1099, 1098, 5498, 1096, and W-2G

1099-B
Statement for Recipients of Proceeds From Broker and Barter Exchange Transactions
Used by a broker to report gross proceeds from the sale or redemption of securities, commodities or regulated futures contracts, or by a barter exchange to report the exchange of goods or services. IT-IRC sec. 6045; Regs. sec. 1.6045-1; See the separate instructions for Forms 1099, 1098, 5498, 1096, and W-2G

1099-DIV
Statement for Recipients of Dividends and Distributions
Used to report dividends and distributions. IT-IRC secs. 6042 and 6043; Regs. secs. 1.6042-2 and 1.6043-2; See the separate instructions for Forms 1099, 1098, 5498, 1096, and W-2G

1099-G
Statement for Recipients of Certain Government Payments
Used to report government payments such as unemployment compensation, state and local income tax refunds, credits, or offsets, discharges of indebtedness by the Federal Government, taxable grants, and subsidy payments form the Department of Agriculture.
IT-IRC secs. 6041, 6050B, 6050D, and 6050E; Regs. secs. 1.6041-1, 1.6050B-1, 1.6050D-1, and 1.6050E-1; See the separate Instructions for Forms 1099, 1098, 5498, 1096, and W-2G

1099-INT
Statement for Recipients of Interest Income
Used to report interest income. IT-IRC secs. 6041 and 6049; Regs. secs. 1.6041-1, 1.6049-4, and Temp. Regs. sec. 1.6049-7T; See the separate Instructions for Forms 1099, 1098, 5498, 1096, and W-2G

1099-MISC
Statement for Recipients of Miscellaneous Income
Used to report rents, royalties, prizes and awards, fishing boat proceeds, payments by health, accident and sickness insurers to physicians or other health service providers, fees, commissions or other compensation for services rendered in the course of the payer's business when the recipient is not treated as an employee, direct sales of $5,000 or more of consumer products for resale, substitute payments by brokers in lieu of dividends or tax-exempt interest, and crop insurance proceeds. IT-IRC secs. 6041, 6041A, 6045(d), and 6050A; Regs. secs. 1.6041-1, 1.6045-2, and 1.6050A-1; See the separate Instructions for Forms 1099, 1098, 5498, 1096, and W-2G

1099-OID
Statement for Recipients of Original Issue Discount
Used to report original issue discount. IT-IRC sec. 6049; Regs. sec. 1.6049-4; Temp. Regs. secs. 1.6049-4, 1.6049-5T, and 1.6049-7T; See the separate Instructions for Forms 1099, 1098, 5498, 1096, and W-2G

1099-PATR
Statement for Recipients (Patrons) of Taxable Distributions Received From Cooperatives
Used to report patronage dividends.
IT-IRC sec. 6044; Regs. sec. 1.6044-2; See the separate instructions for Forms 1099, 1098, 5498, 1096, and W-2G

1099-R
Statement for Recipients of Total Distributions From Profit-Sharing, Retirement Plans, Individual Retirement Arrangements, Insurance Contracts, Etc.
Used to report total distributions from profit-sharing, retirement plans and individual retirement arrangements, and certain surrenders of insurance contracts.
IT-IRC sec. 402, 408, and 6047; Temp Regs. sec. 35.3405-1; Regs. secs. 1.408-7 and 1.6047-1; See the separate Instructions for Forms 1099, 1098, 5498, 1096, and W-2G

1099-S
Statement for Recipients of Proceeds From Real Estate Transactions
Used by the person required to report gross proceeds from real estate transactions.
IT-IRC sec. 6045(e); Temp Regs. sec. 1.6045-3T; See the separate Instructions for Forms 1099, 1098, 5498, 1096, and W-2G

1116
Computation of Foreign Tax Credit (Individual, Fiduciary, or Nonresident Alien Individual)
Used to figure the foreign tax credit claimed for the amount of any income, war profits, and excess profits tax paid or accrued during the taxable year to any foreign country or U.S. possession. IT-IRC secs. 27, 901, and 904; Pub. 514; Separate instructions

1118
Computation of Foreign Tax Credit-Corporations
Used to support the amount of foreign tax credit claimed on corporation income tax returns.
IT-IRC secs. 901 through 906; Separate instructions

I (Form 1118)
Computation of Reduction of Oil and Gas Extraction Taxes
Used to compute the section 907(a) reduction for a corporation that is claiming a foreign tax credit with respect to any income taxes paid, accrued, or deemed to have been paid during the tax year with respect to foreign oil and gas extraction income.
IT-IRC sec. 907

Sch. J (Form 1118)
Separate Limitation Loss Allocations and Other Adjustments Necessary to Determine Numerators of Limitation Fractions, Year-End Recharacterization Balances and Overall Foreign Loss Account Balances

Used to show the adjustments to separate limitation income or losses in determining the numerators of the limitation fractions for each separate limitation; the year-end balances of separate limitation losses that were allocated among other separate limitations (in the current year or in prior years) that have yet to be recharacterized; and the balances in the overall foreign loss accounts at the beginning of the tax year, any adjustments to the account balances, and the balances, in the overall foreign loss accounts at the end of the tax year. IT-IRC sec. 904(f)

1120
U.S. Corporation Income Tax Return
Used by a corporation to report income tax. (Also see Form 1120-A.)
IT-IRC sec. 6012; Regs. secs. 1.1502-75(h), and 1.6012-2; Separate instructions

Package 1120
Federal Income Tax Forms
A package of income tax forms for corporations. Contains one copy of instructions for Forms 1120 and 1120-A, two copies of Form 1120, two copies of Form 1120-A, two copies of Schedule D, one copy of Form 1120-W, two copies of Form 3468, two copies of Form 7004, and two copies of Form 4562.
IT-IRC sec. 6012

Sch. D (Form 1120)
Capital Gains and Losses
Used with Forms 1120, 1120-A, 1120-DF, 1120-IC-DISC, 1120-F, 1120-FSC, 1120-H, 1120L, 1120-ND, 1120-PC, 1120-POL, 1120-REIT, 1120-RIC, 990-C and certain Forms 990-T to report details of gain (or loss) from sales or exchanges of capital assets, and to figure alternative tax. IT-IRC secs. 1201 and 1231

Sch. PH (Form 1120)
Computation of U.S. Personal Holding Company Tax
Used to figure personal holding company tax; filed with the income tax return of every personal holding company. IT-IRC secs. 541, 6012, and 6501(f); Separate instructions

1120-A
U.S. Corporation Short-Form Income Tax Return
Used by a corporation to report income tax.
IT-IRC sec. 6012; Regs. sec. 1.6012-2; Separate instructions

1120-DF
U.S. Income Tax Return for Designated Settlement Funds (Under Section 468B)
Used by designated settlement funds to report contributions received, income earned, the administration expenses of operating the fund, and the tax on its investment income. IT-IRC secs. 468B and 6012; Separate instructions

1120F
U.S. Income Tax Return of a Foreign Corporation
Used by foreign corporations to report income tax.
IT-IRC secs. 881, 882, 884, 887, and 6012; Separate instructions

1120-FSC
U.S. Income Tax Return of a Foreign Sales Corporation
Used by foreign sales corporations to report income tax.
IT-IRC secs. 922, 6011(c), and 6012; Separate instructions

Sch. P (Form 1120-FSC)
Computation of Transfer Price or Commission
Used to compute transfer price or commission under IRC sections 925(a)(1) and 2). IT-IRC sec. 6011(c)

1120-H
U.S. Income Tax Return for Homeowners Associations
Used by homeowner associations to report income tax. (An annual return.)
IT-IRC sec. 528 and Reg. sec. 1.528-8

1120-IC-DISC
Interest Charge Domestic International Sales Corporation Return
Used by domestic corporations that make the election under IRC section 992(b) to be a domestic international sales corporation.
IT-IRC secs. 6011(c) and 6072(b); Separate instructions

Sch. K (Form 1120-IC-DISC)
Shareholder's Statement of IC-DISC Distributions
Used to report deemed and actual distributions from an IC-DISC to shareholders and to report deferred DISC income and certain other information to shareholders.
IT-IRC secs. 6011(c)

Sch. P (Form 1120-IC-DISC)
Computation of Inter-company Transfer Price or Commission
Used to compute inter-company transfer prices or commissions under IRC sections 994(a)(1) and (2).
IT-IRC secs. 6011(c)

Sch. Q (Form 1120-IC-DISC)
Borrower's Certificate of Compliance with the Rules for Producer's Loans
Used by an IC-DISC to establish that the borrower is in compliance with the rules for producer's loans.
IT-Regs. sec. 1.993-4(d)

1120L
U.S. Life Insurance Company Income Tax Return
Used by life insurance companies to report income tax.
IT-IRC secs. 801 and 6012; Reg. sec. 1.6012-2; Separate instructions

1120-ND
Return for Nuclear Decommissioning Funds and Certain Related Persons
Used by nuclear decommissioning funds to report income, expenses, transfers of funds to the public utility that created it and to figure the taxes on income plus penalty taxes on trustees and certain disqualified persons. IT-IRC sec. 468A; Separate instructions

1120-PC
U.S. Property and Casualty Insurance Company Income Tax Return
Used by nonlife insurance companies to report income tax.
IT-IRC secs. 831 and 6012; Separate instructions

1120-POL
U.S. Income Tax Return for Certain Political Organizations
Used by certain political organizations to report income tax.
IT-IRC secs. 856 and 6012; Separate instructions

1120-REIT
U.S. Income Tax Return for Real Estate Investment Trusts
Used by real estate investment trusts to report income tax.
IT-IRC secs. 856 and 6012; Separate instructions

1120-RIC
U.S. Income Tax Return for Regulated Investment Companies
Used by regulated investment companies to report income tax.
IT-IRC secs. 851 and 6012; Separate instructions

1120S
U.S. Income Tax Return for an S Corporation
Used by S corporations that have made the election prescribed by IRC section 1362.
IT-IRC sec. 6037; IRC Subchapter S; Regs. sec. 1.6037-1; Separate instructions

Package 1120S
Federal Income Tax Forms

A package of income tax forms for S Corporations. Contains one copy of instructions for Form 1120S, two copies of Form 1120S, two copies of Schedule D (Form 1120S), two copies of Schedule K-1 (Form 1120S), two copies of shareholder's instructions for Schedule K-1 (Form 1120S), and two copies of Form 4562. IT-IRC sec. 6037

Sch. D (Form 1120S)
Capital Gains and Losses and Built-in Gains

Used by S corporations that have made the election prescribed by IRC section 1362. Sch. D is used to report details of gains (and losses) from sales, exchanges or distribution of capital assets and to figure the tax imposed on certain capital gains and certain built-in gains.
IT-IRC secs. 1201 and 1231; and IRC Subchapter S; Separate instructions

Sch. K-1 (Form 1120S)
Shareholder's Share of Income, Credits, Deductions, Etc.

Used to show shareholder's share of income, credits, deductions, etc. A four-part assembly: A copy is filed with Form 1120S, a copy is for S corporation records, and a copy is given to each shareholder along with the separate instructions. IT-IRC sec. 6037

1120-W
Corporation Estimated Tax

Used as a worksheet by corporations to figure estimated tax liability; not to be filed. Corporations should keep it for their records. IT-IRC sec. 6655

1120X
Amended U.S. Corporation Income Tax Return

Used by corporations to amend a previously filed Form 1120 or Form 1120-A. IT-Regs. sec. 301.6402-3

1122
Authorization and Consent of Subsidiary Corporation to be Included in a Consolidated Income Tax Return

Used as the authorization and consent of a subsidiary corporation to be included in a consolidated income tax return. IT-IRC sec. 1502; Regs. sec. 1.1502-75(h)

1128
Application for Change in Accounting Period

Used to obtain approval of a change, adoption or retention of an accounting period. IT-IRC sec. 442; Regs. secs. 1.442-1(b) and 1.1502-76; Separate instructions

1138
Extension of Time for Payment of Taxes by a Corporation Expecting a Net Operating Loss Carryback

Used by a corporation expecting a net operating loss carryback to request an extension of time for payment of taxes. IT-IRC sec. 6164

1139
Corporation Application for Tentative Refund

Used by corporations to apply for a tentative refund from the carryback of a net operating loss, net capital loss, unused general business credit, or overpayment of tax due to a claim or right adjustment under section 1341(b)(1).
IT-IRC sec. 6411

1310
Statement of Person Claiming Refund Due a Deceased Taxpayer

Used by claimant to secure payment of refund on behalf of a deceased taxpayer. IT-IRC sec. 6402; Regs. sec. 301.6402-2(e); Pubs. 17 and 559

1363
Export Exemption Certificate

Used by shipper or other person to suspend liability for the payment of the tax for a period of 6 months from the date of shipment from the point of origin. The original is filed with the carrier at time of payment of the transportation charges and the duplicate is retained with the shipping papers for a period of 3 years from the last day of the month during which the shipment was made from the point of origin. May also be used as a blanket exemption certificate, with approval of District Director. Ex-IRC secs. 4271 and 4272; Temp Regs. Part 154.2-1

2032
Contract Coverage Under Title II of the Social Security Act

Used to make an agreement pursuant to IRC section 3121(l).
Emp-IRC sec. 3121(l); Regs. sec. 36.3121(l)(1)-1

2063
U.S. Departing Alien Income Tax Statement

Used by a resident alien who has not received a termination assessment, or a nonresident alien who has no taxable income from United States sources. IT-IRC sec. 6851(d); Regs. sec. 1.6851-2; Rev. Rul. 55-468; C.B.1955-2, 501; Pub. 519

2106
Employee Business Expenses

Used by employees to support deductions for business expenses. IT-IRC secs. 62, 162, and 274; Instructions for Form 1040, Pub. 463; Separate instructions

2119
Sale of Your Home

Used by individuals who sold their principal residence whether or not they bought another one. Also used by individuals 55 or over who elect to exclude gain on the sale of their principal residence.
IT-IRC secs. 121 and 1034; Pub. 17; Separate instructions

2120
Multiple Support Declaration

Used as a statement disclaiming as an income tax exemption an individual to whose support the taxpayer and others have contributed.
IT-IRC sec. 152(c); Regs. sec. 1.152-3(c); Pub. 17

2210
Underpayment of Estimated Tax by Individuals and Fiduciaries

Used by individuals and fiduciaries to determine if they paid enough estimated tax. The form is also used to compute the penalty for underpayment of estimated tax.
IT-IRC sec. 6654; Regs. secs. 1.6654-1 and 1.6654-2; Separate instructions

2210F
Underpayment of Estimated Tax by Farmers and Fishermen

Used by qualified farmers and fishermen to determine if they paid enough estimated tax. Used only by individuals whose gross income from farming or fishing is at least two-thirds of their gross annual income. (All other individuals should use Form 2210.) The form is also used to compute the penalty for underpayment of estimated tax.
IT-IRC sec. 6654; Reg. secs. 1.6654-1 and 1.6654-2

2220
Underpayment of Estimated Tax by Corporations

Used by corporations to determine if they paid enough estimated tax. The form is also used to compute the penalty for underpayment of estimated tax.
IT-IRC sec. 6655; Separate instructions

2290
Heavy Vehicle Use Tax Return

Used to report tax due on use of any highway motor vehicle which falls within one of the categories shown in the tax computation schedule on the form or meets certain weight limitations. Ex-IRC sec. 4481; Regs. sec. 41.6011(a)-1(a)

2350
Application for Extension of Time to File U.S. Income Tax Return

Used by U.S. citizens and certain resident aliens abroad, who expect to qualify for special tax treatment to obtain an extension of time for filing an income tax return.
IT-IRC secs. 911 and 6081; Regs. sec. temporary 5b.911-6(b), 1.911-7(c), and 1.6081-2; Pub. 54

2438

Regulated Investment Company Undistributed Capital Gains Tax Return

Used to report tax payable on or before 30th day after close of company's taxable year. A copy is filed with Form 1120-RIC. (An annual return.)
IT-IRC sec. 852(b)3); Regs. sec. 1.852-9

2439

Notice to Shareholder of Undistributed Long-Term Capital Gains

Used as an annual statement to be distributed to shareholders of a regulated investment company. (Copy to be attached to Form 1120-RIC.)
IT-IRC sec. 852(b)(3)(D)(i); Regs. sec. 1.852-9

2441

Child and Dependent Care Expenses

Used to figure the credit for child and dependent care expenses and/or the exclusion of employer-provided dependent care benefits. (To be attached to Form 1040.) IT-IRC sec. 21 & 129; Regs. sec. 1.44A-1; Pubs. 17 and 503

2553

Election by A Small Business Corporation

Used by qualifying small business corporations to make the election prescribed by IRC section 1362. IT-IRC sec. 1362; Separate instructions

2555

Foreign Earned Income

Used by U.S. citizens and resident aliens who qualify for the foreign earned income exclusion and/or the housing exclusion or deduction. (To be filed with Form 1040.) IT-IRC secs. 911 and 6012(c); Regs. secs. 1.911-1 and 1.6012-1; Pub. 54; Separate instructions

2670

Credit or Refund-Exemption Certificate for Use by a Nonprofit Educational Organization

Used by certain nonprofit educational organizations to support a claim for credit or refund to the person who paid the manufacturers excise tax, or the exemption of these sales from the special fuels tax under IRC Chapter 31.
Ex-IRC secs. 4041, 4221, and 6416; Regs. sec. 48.4221-6

2688

Application for Additional Extension of Time To File U.S. Individual Income Tax Return

Used to apply for an extension of time to file Form 1040.
IT-IRC sec. 6081; Regs. sec. 1.6081-1(b)(5); T.D.6436

2758

Application for Extension of Time To File Certain Excise, Income, Information, and Other Returns

Used to apply for an extension of time to file Form 1041 and certain other returns. A separate Form 2758 must be filed for each return.
IT-IRC sec. 6081; Regs. sec. 1.6081-1(b)

2848

Power of Attorney and Declaration of Representative

Used as an authorization for one person to act for another in any tax matter (except alcohol & tobacco taxes and firearms activities).
IT-Title 26, CFR, Part 601; Separate instructions

2848-D

Tax Information Authorization and Declaration of Representative

Used by one person to authorize another to receive or inspect confidential tax information (except alcohol and tobacco taxes and firearms activities) when power of attorney is not filed.
IT-Title 26, CFR, Part 601; Separate instructions

3115

Application for Change in Accounting Method

Used to secure approval for change in accounting method.
IT-IRC sec. 446(e); Regs. sec. 1.446-1(e); Separate instructions

3206

Information Statement by United Kingdom Withholding Agents Paying Dividends From United States Corporations to Residents of the U.S. and Certain Treaty Countries

Used to report dividends paid by U.S. corporations to beneficial owners of dividends paid through United Kingdom Nominees. Used when the beneficial owners are residents of countries other than United Kingdom with which the U.S. has a tax treaty providing for reduced withholding rates on dividends.
IT secs. 7.507 and 7.508 of T.D. 5532

3468

Computation of Investment Credit

Used by individuals, estates, trusts, and corporations claiming an investment credit or business energy investment credit. Also see Form 3800.
IT-IRC secs. 38, 46, 47, 48, and 49; Separate instructions

3491

Consumer Cooperative Exemption Application

Used by certain consumer cooperatives that are primarily engaged in retail sales of goods or services generally for personal, living or family use to apply for exemption from filing Forms 1096 and 1099-PATR.
IT-IRC sec. 6044(c); Regs. sec. 1.6044-4

3520

U.S. Information Return-Creation of or Transfers to Certain Foreign Trusts

Used by a grantor in the case of an inter vivos trust, a fiduciary of an estate in the case of a testamentary trust, or a transferor to report the creation of any foreign trust by a U.S. person or the transfer of any money or property to a foreign trust by a U.S. person.
IT-IRC sec. 6048; Regs. secs. 16.3-1 and 301.6048-1

3520-A

Annual Return of Foreign Trust with U.S. Beneficiaries

Used to report the operation of foreign trust that has U.S. beneficiaries.
IT-IRC sec. 6048

3800

General Business Credit

Used to summarize investment credit (Form 3468), jobs credit (Form 5884), credit for alcohol used as fuel (Form 6478), credit for increasing research activities (Form 6765), and low-income housing credit (Form 8586).
IT-IRC secs. 38 and 39; Separate instructions

3903

Moving Expenses

Used to support itemized deductions for expenses of travel, transportation and certain expenses attributable to disposition of an old residence and acquisition of a new residence for employees and self-employed individuals moving to a new job location.
IT-IRC sec. 217; Regs. sec. 1.217; Pub. 521; Separate instructions

3903F

Foreign Moving Expenses

Used by U.S. citizens or resident aliens moving to a new principal workplace outside the United States or its possessions.
IT-IRC 217(h); Pub. 521; Separate instructions

4029

Application for Exemption from Social Security Taxes and Waiver of Benefits

Used by members of qualified religious groups to claim exemption from social security taxes.
IT-IRC sec. 1402(g)

4070

Employee's Report of Tips to Employer

Used by employees to report tips to employers.
Emp-IRC sec. 3102(c); Regs. sec. 31.6053-1(b)(2)

4070-A
Employee's Daily Record of Tips
Used by employees to keep a daily record of tips received.
Emp-IRC sec. 3102(c); Regs. sec. 31.6053-4

4070PR
Informe al Patrono de Propinas Recibidas por el Empleado
Used by employees in Puerto Rico. A variation of Form 4070.
Emp-IRC sec. 3102(c); Regs sec. 31.6053-1(b)(2)

4070A-PR
Registro Diario de Propinas Recibidas por el Empleado
Used by employees in Puerto Rico. A variation of Form 4070-A.
Emp-IRC sec. 3102(c); Regs. sec. 31.6053-4

4136
Computation of Credit for Federal Tax on Gasoline and Special Fuels
Used by individuals, estates, trusts, or corporations, including S corporations and domestic international sales corporations, to claim credit for Federal excise tax on the number of gallons of gasoline and special fuels used for business. Also used to claim the one-time credit allowed owners of qualified diesel-powered highway vehicles.
Ex-IRC secs. 34, 4041, 4081, 4091, 6420, 6421, and 6427

4137
Computation of Social Security Tax on Unreported Tip Income
Used by an employee who received tips subject to FICA tax but failed to report them to his or her employer.
IT/Emp-IRC sec. 3102; Regs. sec. 31.3102-3(d) and 31.6011(a)-1(d)

4224
Exemption From Withholding of Tax on Income Effectively Connected With the Conduct of a Trade or Business in the United States
Used to secure, at the time of payment, the benefit of exemption from withholding of the tax on certain income for nonresident alien individuals and fiduciaries, foreign partnerships, and foreign corporations.
IT-IRC secs. 1441 and 1442; Regs. sec. 1.1441-4

4255
Recapture of Investment Credit
Used by individuals, estates, trusts, or corporations to figure the increase in tax if regular or energy property was disposed of or ceased to qualify before the end of the property class life or life years used to figure the credit.
IT-IRC sec. 47

4361
Application for Exemption from Self-Employment Tax for Use by Ministers, Members of Religious Orders and Christian Science Practitioners
Used by members of qualified religious groups to claim exemption from tax on self-employment income.
IT-IRC sec. 1402(e)

4461
Application for Approval of Master or Prototype Defined Contribution Plan
Used by employers who want an opinion letter for approval of form of a master or prototype plan.
IT-IRC secs. 401(a), and 501(a)

4461-A
Application for Approval of Master or Prototype Defined Benefit Plan
Used by employers who want an opinion letter for approval of form of a master or prototype plan.
IT-IRC secs. 401(a) and 501(a)

4461-B
Application of Master or Prototype Plan, or Regional Prototype Plan Mass Submitter Adopting Sponsor
Used by mass submitters who want approval on a plan of adopting sponsoring organization or sponsor. IT-IRC secs. 401(a) and 501(a)

4466
Corporation Application for Quick Refund of Overpayment of Estimated Tax
Used to apply for a "quick" refund of overpaid estimated tax. (Must be filed before the regular tax return is filed.) IT-IRC sec. 6425; Regs. sec. 1.6425-1(b)

4469
Computation of Excess Medicare Tax Credit
Used by railroad employee representatives and medicare qualified Government employees to figure their credit of excess medicare (hospital insurance benefits) tax. IT-IRC sec. 6413(c)(3); P.L.80-248

4506
Request for Copy of Tax Form
Used by a taxpayer or authorized representative to request a copy of a tax return or Forms W-2 that were filed with the return. IT-Regs. sec. 601.702

4506-A
Request for Public-Inspection Copy of Exempt Organization Tax Form
Used by a third-party for a copy of an exempt organization tax form which may be inspected at an IRS office. IT-IRC sec. 6104(b)

4562
Depreciation and Amortization
Used by individuals, estates, trusts, partnerships, and corporations claiming depreciation and amortization. Also used to substantiate depreciation deductions for automobiles and other listed property.
IT-IRC secs. 167, 168, 179 and 280F; Separate instructions

4563
Exclusion of Income for Bona Fide Residents of American Samoa
Used by bona fide residents of American Samoa to exclude income from sources in American Samoa, Guam, and the Commonwealth of the Northern Mariana Islands, to the extent specified in IRC section 931.
IT-IRC sec. 931; Regs. sec. 1.931-1; Pub. 570

4626
Alternative Minimum Tax-Corporations
Used by corporations to figure their alternative minimum tax and their environmental tax.
IT-IRC secs. 55, 56, 57, 58, 59, and 291; Separate instructions

4684
Casualties and Thefts
Used by all taxpayers to figure gains (or losses) resulting from casualties and thefts. IT-IRC sec. 165; Separate instructions

4720
Return of Certain Excise Taxes on Charities and Other Persons Under Chapters 41 and 42 of the Internal Revenue Code
Used by charities and other persons to compute certain excise taxes which may be due under IRC Chapters 41 and 42.
Ex-IRC secs. 4911, 4912, 4941, 4942, 4943, 4944, 4945, and 4955; Separate instructions

4768
Application for Extension of Time To File U.S. Estate (and Generation-Skipping Transfer) Tax Return and/or Pay Estate (and Generation-Skipping Transfer) Tax(es)
Used to apply for estate tax extensions in certain cases.
E&G-IRC secs. 6081 and 6161; Regs. sec. 20.6081-1 and 20.6161-1

4782
Employee Moving Expense Information
Used by employers to show the amount of any reimbursement or payment made to an employee, a third party for the employee's benefit, or the value of services furnished in-kind, for moving expenses during the calendar year.
IT-IRC secs. 82 and 217; Regs. sec. 31.6051-1(e)

4789
Currency Transaction Report
Used by financial institutions to report deposit, withdrawal, exchange of currency, or other payment or transfer, by, through, or to such financial institution which involves currency transactions of more than $10,000.
P.L.92-508; Treasury Regs. 31CFR103

4797
Sales of Business Property
Used to report details of gain (or loss) from sales, exchanges, or involuntary conversions (from other than casualty and theft) of noncapital assets and involuntary conversions (other than casualty and theft) of capital assets, held in connection with a trade or business or a transaction entered into for profit. Also used to compute recapture amounts under sections 179 and 280F when the business use of section 179 or 280F property drops to 50% or less.
IT-IRC secs. 1231, 1245, 1250, 1252, 1254, and 1255; IT-IRC secs. 1202, 1211, and 1212; Separate instructions

4835
Farm Rental Income and Expenses
Used by landowner (or sublessor) to report farm rental income based on crops or livestock produced by the tenant where the landowner (or sublessor) does not materially participate in the operation or management of the farm. (Also see Schedule F (Form 1040).)
IT-IRC sec. 61

4868
Application for Automatic Extension of Time to File U.S. Individual Income Tax Return
Used to apply for an automatic 4-month extension of time to file Form 1040.
IT-IRC sec. 6081; Regs. sec. 1.6081-4; TD 7885

4876-A
Election To Be Treated as an Interest Charge DISC
Used by a qualifying corporation that wishes to be treated as an Interest Charge Domestic International Sales Corporation (Interest Charge DISC).
IT-Regs. sec. 1.921

4952
Investment Interest Expense Deduction
Used by an individual, estate, or trust to figure the deduction limitation for interest expense on funds borrowed that is allocable to property held for investment.
IT-IRC sec. 163(d)

4970
Tax on Accumulation Distribution of Trusts
Used by a beneficiary of a domestic or foreign trust to figure the tax attributable to an accumulation distribution.
IT-IRC sec. 667

4972
Tax on Lump-Sum Distributions
Used to determine the income tax on the income portion of lump-sum distributions.
IT-IRC sec. 402(e); Separate instructions

5074
Allocation of Individual Income Tax to Guam or the Commonwealth of the Northern Mariana Islands (CNMI)
Used as an attachment to Form 1040 filed by an individual who reports adjusted gross income of $50,000 or more, with gross income of $5,000 or more from Guam or CNMI sources.
IT-IRC sec. 935; Regs. sec. 301.7654-1(d)

5213
Election to Postpone Determination as to Whether the Presumption that an Activity is Engaged in for Profit Applies
Used by individuals, trusts, estates, and S corporations to postpone a determination as to whether an activity is engaged in for profit.
IT-IRC sec. 183(e)

5227
Split-Interest Trust Information Return
Used by section 4947(a)(2) trusts treated as private foundations.
Ex-IRC sec. 6011; Separate instructions

5300
Application for Determination for Defined Benefit Plan
Used to request a determination letter as to the qualification of a defined benefit plan (other than a collectively-bargained plan).
IT-IRC sec. 401(a); Separate instructions

Sch. T (Form 5300)
Supplemental Application for Approval of Employee Benefit Plans
Used as an attachment to Forms 5300, 5301, 5303, 5307, and 6406 to provide information on how the applicant meets the requirements of the Tax Equity and Fiscal Responsibility Act of 1982, the Tax Reform Act of 1984, and the Retirement Equity Act of 1984, and the Tax Reform Act of 1986.
IT-IRC 401(a); Separate instructions

5301
Application for Determination for Defined Contribution Plan
Used to request a determination letter as to the qualification of a defined contribution plan (other than a collectively-bargained plan).
IT-IRC sec. 401(a); Separate instructions

5302
Employee Census
Used as a schedule of the 25 highest paid participants of a deferred compensation plan, which is attached to Forms 5300, 5301, 5303, and 5307 (where applicable). IT-IRC sec. 401(a)

5303
Application for Determination for Collectively-Bargained Plan
Used to request a determination letter as to the qualification of a collectively-bargained plan. Also used by multi-employer plans covered by PBGC insurance to request a determination letter regarding termination.
IT-IRC sec. 401(a); Separate instructions

5305
Individual Retirement Trust Account
Used as an agreement between an individual and the individual's trustee for the establishment of an individual retirement account. IT-IRC sec. 408(a)

5305-A
Individual Retirement Custodial Account
Used as an agreement between an individual and the individual's custodian for the establishment of an individual retirement account. IT-IRC sec. 408(a)

5305-SEP
Simplified Employee Pension-Individual Retirement Accounts Contribution Agreement
Used as an agreement between an employer and his or her employees to establish a Simplified Employee Pension. IT-IRC 408(k)

5305-A-SEP
Salary Reduction and Other Elective Simplified Employee Pension - Individual Retirement Accounts Contribution Agreement
Used as an agreement between an employer and his or her employees to

establish a Simplified Employee Pension with an elective deferral. IT-IRC sec. 408(k)(6)

5306
Application for Approval of Prototype or Employer Sponsored Individual Retirement Account

Used by banks, savings and loan associations, federally insured credit unions, and such other persons approved by the Internal Revenue Service to act as trustee or custodian, insurance companies, regulated investment companies and trade or professional societies or associations, to get the approval as to form of a trust or annuity contract which is to be used for individual retirement accounts or annuities. Also to be used by employees, labor unions and other employee associations that want approval of a trust which is to be used for individual retirement accounts. IT-IRC sec. 408(a), (b), or (c)

5306-SEP
Application for Approval of Prototype Simplified Employee Pension-SEP

Used by program sponsors who want to get IRS approval of their prototype simplified employee pension (SEP) agreements. IT-IRC sec. 408

5307
Application for Determination for Adopters of Master or Prototype, Regional Prototype or Volume Submitter Plans

Used to request a determination letter as to the qualification of any defined benefit or defined contribution plan (the form of which has been previously approved) other than a collectively bargained plan. IT-IRC sec. 401(a); Separate instructions

5308
Request for Change in Plan/Trust Year

Used by employer or plan administrators to request approval of change in a plan year or a trust year. IT-IRC sec. 412(c)(5), sec. 442

5309
Application for Determination of Employee Stock Ownership Plan

Used by corporate employers who wish to get a determination letter regarding the qualification of an Employee Stock Ownership Plan under IRC 409 or 4975(e)(7). IT-IRC 409-4975(e)(7)

5310
Application for Determination Upon Termination; Notice of Merger, Consolidation or Transfer of Plan Assets or Liabilities; Notice of Intent to Terminate

Used by an employer who wishes a determination letter as to the effect of termination of a plan on its prior qualification under IRC section 401(a); by every employer or plan administrator (if designated) for any plan merger or consolidation; or to give notice to PBGC of intent, for any transfer of plan assets or liabilities to another plan to terminate a defined benefit pension plan. IT-IRC secs. 401(a), 6058(b), ERISA sec. 4041(a); Separate instructions

5329
Return for Additional Taxes Attributable to Qualified Retirement Plans (Including IRAs), Annuities, and Modified Endowment Contracts

Used to report excise taxes or additional income tax owed in connection with individual retirement arrangements, annuities, and qualified retirement plans. IT-IRC secs. 72, 4973, 4974, and 4980A; Separate instructions

5330
Return of Excise Taxes Related to Employee Benefits Plans

Used to report and pay the excise tax imposed by IRC section 4791 on a minimum funding deficiency, by Code section 4973(a)(2) on excess contributions to a section 403(b)(7)(A) custodial account, by section 4975 on prohibited transactions, by section 4976 on disqualified benefits from welfare plans, by section 4977 on certain fringe benefits, and by 4978 on certain ESOP transactions. Ex-IRC sec. 6011; Separate instructions

5452
Corporate Report of Nondividend Distributions

Used by corporations to report their nontaxable distributions. IT-CFR 1.301-1, 1.316-1, 1.333-1, and 1.6042-2

5471
Information Return With Respect to a Foreign Corporation

Used by U.S. persons to report their activities with related foreign corporations. IT-IRC secs. 951-972, 6035, 6038 and 6046; Separate instructions

Sch. M (Form 5471)
Foreign Corporation Controlled by a U.S. Person

Used by a U.S. person who controls a foreign corporation to report the activities between the U.S. person and the foreign corporation. IT-IRC sec. 6038

Sch. N (Form 5471)
Foreign Personal Holding Company

Used by officers, directors, and shareholders of foreign personal holding companies to report information concerning the foreign personal holding company. IT-IRC sec. 6035

Sch. O (Form 5471)
Organization or Reorganization of Foreign Corporation, and Acquisitions and Dispositions of its Stock

Used by U.S. persons to report acquisitions or dispositions of interests in foreign corporations. IT-IRC sec. 6046

5472
Information Return of a Foreign Owned Corporation

Used for reporting the activities between foreign owned corporations and persons related to transactions made by the corporations. IT-IRC sec. 6038A

5498
Individual Retirement Arrangement Information

Used to report contributions to individual retirement arrangements (IRAs) and the value of the account. IT-IRC sec. 408(i)(o); Prop. Regs. sec. 1.408-5; See the separate Instructions for Forms 1099, 1098, 5498, 1096, and W-2G

5500
Annual Return/Report of Employee Benefit Plan (with 100 or more participants)

Used to report on deferred compensation plans and welfare plans that have at least 100 participants. IT-IRC sec. 6058(a); ERISA section 103; Separate instructions

Sch. A (Form 5500)
Insurance Information

Used as an attachment to Forms 5500, 5500-C, or 5500-R to report information about insurance contracts that are part of a qualified deferred compensation plan. ERISA section 103(e)

Sch. B (Form 5500)
Actuarial Information

Used to report actuarial information for a defined benefit plan. (Attached to Forms 5500, 5500-C, or 5500-R.) IT-IRC sec. 6059; ERISA section 103(a); Separate instructions

Sch. C (Form 5500)
Service Provider Information

Used as an attachment to Form 5500 to report information about service providers and trustees of qualified deferred compensation plans. ERISA section 103.

Sch. P (Form 5500)
Annual Return of Fiduciary of Employee Benefit Trust

Used as an annual return for employee benefit trusts which qualify under section 401(a) and are exempt from tax under section 501(a). (Attach to Forms 5500, 5500-C or 5500-R.) IT-IRC secs. 6033(a) and 6501(a)

Sch. SSA (Form 5500)
Annual Registration Statement Identifying Separated Participants with Deferred Vested Benefits
Used to list employees who separated from employment and have a deferred vested benefit in the employer's plan of deferred compensation. (Attached to Forms 5500, 5500-C, or 5500-R.) IT-IRC sec. 6057

5500-C/R
Return/Report of Employee Benefit Plan (with fewer than 100 participants)
Used to report on deferred compensation plans and welfare plans that have fewer than 100 participants.
IT-IRC sec. 6058(a); ERISA section 103; Separate instructions

5500EZ
Annual Return of One-Participant Owners and Their Spouses Pension Benefit Plan
Used to report on pension profit-sharing, etc. plans that cover only an individual or an individual and the individual's spouse who wholly own a business.
IT-IRC sec. 6058(a); Separate instructions

5558
Application for Extension of Time to File Certain Employee Plan Returns
Used to provide a means by which a person may request an extension of time to file Forms 5500, 5500-C, 5500-R, or 5330.

5578
Annual Certification of Racial Nondiscrimination for a Private School Exempt from Federal Income Tax
Used by certain organizations exempt or claiming to be exempt under IRC section 501(c)(3) and operating, supervising, or controlling a private school (or schools) to certify to a policy of racial nondiscrimination.
IT-IRC sec. 6001; Rev. Proc. 75-50, 1975-2; C.B.587

5712
Election to be Treated as a Possessions Corporation Under Section 936
Used by a corporation to elect to be treated as a possessions corporation for the tax credit allowed under IRC section 936. IT-IRC sec. 936(e)

5712-A
Cost Sharing or Profit Split Method Under Section 936(h)(5): Election and Verification
Used by a domestic corporation if it elects to compute its taxable income under either the cost sharing method or the profit split method. IT-IRC sec. 936(h)(5)

5713
International Boycott Report
Used by persons with operations in or related to any country associated in carrying out an international boycott.
IT-IRC sec. 999; Separate instructions

Sch. A (Form 5713)
Computation of the International Boycott Factor
Used by taxpayers in computing the loss of tax benefits under the international boycott factor method.
IT-IRC sec. 999

Sch. B (Form 5713)
Specifically Attributable Taxes and Income
Used by taxpayers in computing the loss of tax benefits under the specifically attributable taxes and income method.
IT-IRC sec. 999

Sch. C (Form 5713)
Tax Effect of the International Boycott Provisions
Used to summarize the loss of tax benefits resulting from the application of the international boycott provisions.
IT-IRC sec. 999

5735
Computation of Possessions Corporation Tax Credit Under Section 936
Used by qualified possessions corporations to compute credit allowed by IRC section 936.
IT-IRC sec. 936

Sch. P (Form 5735)
Allocation of Income and Expenses Under Section 936(h)(5)
Used by corporations that have elected the cost sharing or profit split method of computing taxable income. The form is attached to Form 5735.
IT-IRC sec. 935(h)(5)

5754
Statement By Person(s) Receiving Gambling Winnings
Used to list multiple winners of certain gambling proceeds.
IT-IRC sec. 3402(q); Regs. secs. 31.3402(q)-1(e) and 1.6011-3; See the separate Instructions for Forms 1099, 1098, 5498, 1096, and W-2G

5768
Election/Revocation of Election by an Eligible Section 501(c)3-Organization to Make Expenditures to Influence Legislation
Used by certain eligible IRC section 501(c)3-organizations to elect or revoke election to apply the lobbying expenditures provisions of code section 501(h).
IT-IRC secs. 501 and 4911

5884
Jobs Credit
Used by individuals, estates, trusts, and corporations claiming a jobs credit and any S corporation, partnership, estate or trust which apportion the jobs credit among their shareholders, partners, or beneficiaries. See also Form 3800.
IT-IRC secs. 38, 51, 52, and 53

6008
Fee Deposit for Outer Continental Shelf Oil
Used to deposit fees on oil that is produced on the Outer Continental Shelf.
IRC sec. 7805, sec. 302(d) of P.L.95-372

6009
Quarterly Report of Fees Due on Oil Production
Used to compute fees due on oil that is produced on the Outer Continental Shelf. IRC sec. 7805, sec. 302(d) of P.L.95-372

6069
Return of Excise Tax on Excess Contributions to Black Lung Benefit Trust Under Section 4953 and Computation of Section 192 Deduction
Used by exempt Black Lung Benefit Trusts as a worksheet to determine deduction under section 192 and to report tax under section 4953.
IT/Ex-IRC secs. 192 and 4953

6088
Distributable Benefits from Employee Pension Benefit Plans
Used to report the 25 highest paid participants of a deferred compensation plan, which is attached to Form 5310.
IT-IRC sec. 401(a)

6118
Credit for Income Tax Return Preparers
Used by income tax return preparers to file for refund of penalties paid.
IT-IRC sec. 6696

6177
General Assistance Program Determination
Used by a General Assistance Program of a state or political subdivision of a state in order to be designated as a Qualified General Assistance Program for purposes of certifying individual recipients of the program for the jobs credit.
IT-IRC sec. 51(d)(6)(B)

6197
Gas Guzzler Tax
Used by automobile manufacturers and importers to report the tax on "gas guzzler" types of automobiles. The form is filed as an attachment to Form 720. Ex-IRC sec. 4064

6198
At-Risk Limitations
Used by individuals, partners, S corporation shareholders, and certain closely-held corporations to figure the overall profit (loss) from an at-risk activity for the tax year, the amount at-risk, and the deductible loss for the tax year. IT-IRC sec. 465; Separate instructions

6199
Certification of Youth Participating in a Qualified Cooperative Education Program
Used by a qualified school to certify that a student meets the requirements of Sec. 51(d)8-as a member of a targeted group eligible for the jobs credit. IT-IRC sec. 51

6251
Alternative Minimum Tax-Individuals
Used by individuals to figure their alternative minimum tax. IT-IRC secs. 55, 56, 57, 58, and 59; Separate instructions

6252
Installment Sale Income
Used by taxpayers other than dealers, who sell real or personal property, and receive a payment in a tax year after the year of sale. IT-IRC sec. 453; Pub. 537; Separate instructions

6406
Short Form Application for Determination for Amendment of Employee Benefit Plan
Used for amending a plan on which a favorable determination letter has been issued under ERISA. IRC secs. 401(a) and 501(a); Separate instructions

6478
Credit for Alcohol Used as Fuel
Used by taxpayers to figure their credit for alcohol used as fuel. The credit is allowed for alcohol mixed with other fuels and for straight alcohol fuel. See also Form 3800. IT-IRC sec. 38 and 40

6497
Information Return of Nontaxable Energy Grants or Subsidized Energy Financing
Used by every person who administers a government program for a Federal, state, or local governmental entity or agent thereof, that provides grants or subsidized financing under programs a principal purpose of which is energy production or conservation if the grant or financing is not taxable to the recipient. IT-IRC sec. 6050D; Regs. sec. 1.6050D-1

6627
Environmental Taxes
Used to report environmental taxes on petroleum and certain chemicals. Ex-IRC secs. 4611, 4661, and 4671

6765
Credit for Increasing Research Activities (or for claiming the orphan drug credit)
Used by individuals, estates, trusts, and corporations claiming a research credit for increasing the research activities of a trade or business. Also used to claim the orphan drug credit. See also Form 3800. IT-IRC secs. 28 and 41; Separate instructions

6781
Gains and Losses From Section 1256 Contracts and Straddles
Used by all taxpayers that held section 1256 contracts or straddles during the tax year. IT-IRC secs. 1092 and 1256

7004
Application for Automatic Extension of Time to File Corporation Income Tax Return
Used by corporations and certain exempt organizations to request an automatic extension of 6 months to file corporate income tax return. IT-IRC sec. 6081(b); Regs. sec. 1.6081-3

8023
Corporate Qualified Stock Purchase Election
Used by a purchasing corporation to elect section 338 treatment for the purchase of another corporation. IT-IRC sec. 338(g); Temp. Regs. sec. sf 338-1

8027
Employer's Annual Information Return of Tip Income and Allocated Tips
Used by large food or beverage employers to report each establishment's gross receipts, charge receipts and charge tips, and allocated tips of employees. IT-IRC sec. 6053(c); Regs. sec. 31.6053-3; Separate instructions

8027-T
Transmittal of Employer's Annual Information Return of Tip Income and Allocated Tips
Used by large food or beverage employers with more than one establishment to transmit Forms 8027. IT-IRC sec. 6053(c); Regs. sec. 31.6053-3

8038
Information Return for Tax-Exempt Private Activity Bond Issues
Used by issuers of tax-exempt private activity bonds to provide IRS with information required by section 149(e). IT-IRC sec. 149(e); Temp. Regs. sec. 1.149(e)-1T; Separate instructions

8038-G
Information Return for Tax-Exempt Governmental Bond Issues
Used by the issuers of tax-exempt governmental bonds (with issue prices of $100,000 or more) to provide IRS with information required by section 149(e). IT-IRC sec. 149(e); Temp. Regs. sec. 1.149(e)-1T; Separate instructions

8038-GC
Consolidated Information Return for Small Tax-Exempt Governmental Bond Issues, Leases and Installment Sales
Used by the issuers of tax-exempt governmental bonds (with issue prices of less than $100,000) to provide IRS with information required by section 149(e). IT-IRC sec. 149(e); Temp. Regs. sec. 1.149(e)-1T

8082
Notice of Inconsistent Treatment or Amended Return
Used by partners, S corporation shareholders and residual holders of an interest in a REMIC to report inconsistent treatment of partnership, S corporation or REMIC items or to report amendment of partnership, S corporation or REMIC items. Form 8082 is also used by the TMP (tax matters partner or tax matters person) to make an administrative adjustment request (AAR) on behalf of the partnership, S corporation, or REMIC. IT-IRC sec. 6222 and 6227(c); Separate instructions

8109
Federal Tax Deposit Coupon
Twenty-three preprinted deposit coupons for making deposits of Federal taxes (such as social security, Federal unemployment, and excise taxes) are contained in a coupon book. Instructions are in the coupon book, along with a reorder form (Form 8109A, FTD Reorder Form). IT/Emp/Ex-IRC sec. 6302; Regs. secs. 1.6302-1, 1.6302-2, 31.6302(c)-1, 31.6302(c)-2, 31.6302(c)-3, 46.6302(c)-1, 48.6302(c)-1, 49.6302(c)-1, 51.4995-3, and 52.6302-1

8109-B
Federal Tax Deposit Coupon
An over-the-counter Federal tax deposit coupon for making Federal tax deposits when Form 8109 deposit coupons have been reordered but not yet received or

when a new entity has received its employer identification number but has not yet received its initial order of Forms 8109.
IT/Emp/Ex-IRC sec. 6302; Regs. secs. 1.6302-1, 1.6302-2, 31.6302(c)-1, 31.6302(c)-2, 31.6302(c)-3, 46.6302(c)-1, 48.6302(c)-1, 49.6302(c)-1, 51.4995-3 and 52.6302-1

8210

Self-Assessed Penalties Return

Used by payers of certain interest and dividends to figure and pay penalties imposed with regard to the filing of certain information returns and the furnishing of certain payee statements.
PA-IRC secs. 6676(b), 6721, 6722, 6723, and 6724; Temp. Regs. sec. 301.6723-1T

8233

Exemption From Withholding on Compensation for Independent Personal Services of a Nonresident Alien Individual

Used by nonresident alien individuals to claim exemption from withholding on compensation for independent personal services because of an income tax treaty or the personal exemption amount. Also used by nonresident alien students, teachers, and researchers to claim exemption from withholding under a U.S. tax treaty on compensation for services.
IT-IRC sec. 1441; Reg. sec. 1.1441-4

8264

Application for Registration of a Tax Shelter

Used by tax shelter organizers to register certain tax shelters with the IRS, for purposes of receiving a tax shelter registration number.
IT-IRC sec. 6111; Regs. secs. 301.6111-1T; Separate instructions

8271

Investor Reporting of Tax Shelter Registration Number

Used by persons who have purchased or otherwise acquired an interest in a tax shelter required to be registered to report the tax shelter registration number. Form is attached to any tax return on which a deduction, credit, loss, or other tax benefit is claimed, or any income reported, from a tax shelter required to be registered. IT-IRC sec. 6111; Regs. secs. 301.6111-1T

8274

Certification by Churches and Qualified Church-Controlled Organizations Electing Exemption from Employer Social Security Taxes

Used by churches and certain church-controlled organizations to elect exemption from social security taxes by certifying the organization is opposed to these taxes for religious purposes.
Emp-IRC sec. 3121(w)

8275

Disclosure Statement Under Section 6661

Used to disclose items which could cause a substantial understatement of income and is filed to avoid the penalty imposed by section 6661; Separate instructions
PA-IRC sec. 6661; Regs. sec. 1.6661; Separate instructions

8279

Election To Be Treated as a FSC or as a Small FSC

Used by qualifying corporations that wish to be treated as a Foreign Sales Corporation (FSC) or Small Foreign Sales Corporation (Small FSC).
IT-IRC sec. 927

8281

Information Return for Publicly Offered Original Issue Discount Instruments

Used by issuers of publicly offered debt instruments having OID to provide the information required by section 1275(c).
IT-IRC sec. 1275(c); Temp. Regs. sec. 1.1275-3T

8282

Donee Information Return

Used by exempt organizations who sells, exchanges, transfers, or otherwise disposes of the charitable property within 2 years after the date of the receipt of the contribution. The return is filed with the IRS and a copy is given to the donor. IT-IRC sec. 6050L

8283

Noncash Charitable Contributions

Used by individuals, closely held corporations, personal service corporations, partnerships, and S corporations to report contributions of property other than cash in which the total claimed value of all property exceeds $500.
IT-IRC secs. 170; 1.170A-13 and 1.170A-13T; Separate instructions

8288

U.S. Withholding Tax Return for Dispositions by Foreign Persons of U.S. Real Property Interests

Used to transmit the withholding on the sale of U.S. real property by foreign persons. IT-IRC sec. 1445; Regs. secs. 1.1445-1 through 1.1445-7; Temp. Regs. secs. 1.1445-9T through 1.1445-11T

8288-A

Statement of Withholding on Dispositions by Foreign Persons of U.S. Real Property Interests

Anyone filing Form 8288 must attach copies A and B of Form 8288-A for each person subject to withholding. IT-IRC sec. 1445; Regs. secs. 1.1445-1 through 1.1445-7, Temp. Regs. secs. 1.1445-9T through 1.1445-11T

8288-B

Application for Withholding Certificate for Dispositions by Foreign Persons of U.S. Real Property Interests

Used to apply for a withholding certificate based upon certain criteria to reduce or eliminate withholding under section 1445.
IT-IRC sec. 1445; Regs. secs. 1.1445-3 and 1.1445-6 and Rev. Proc. 88-23

8300

Report of Cash Payments Over $10,000 Received in a Trade or Business

Used by a trade or business to report receipt of more than $10,000 cash in a transaction in the course of such trade or business.
IT-IRC sec. 6050I; Regs. sec. 1.6050I-1

8308

Report of a Sale or Exchange of Certain Partnership Interests

Used by partnerships to report the sale or exchange of a partnership interest where a portion of any money or other property given in exchange for the interest is attributable to unrealized receivables or substantially appreciated inventory items (section 751(a) exchange). IT-IRC sec. 6050K

8328

Carryforward Election of Unused Private Activity Bond Volume Cap

Used by the issuing authority of tax-exempt private activity bonds to elect under section 146(f) to carryforward the unused volume cap for specific projects.
IT-IRC sec. 146(f)

8329

Lender's Information Return for Mortgage Credit Certificates

Used by lenders of certified indebtedness amounts to report information regarding the issuance of mortgage credit certificates under section 25.
IT-IRC sec. 25; Regs. sec. 1.25-8T

8330

Issuer's Quarterly Information Return for Mortgage Credit Certificates

Used by issuers of mortgage credit certificates to report information required under section 25. IT-IRC sec. 25; Regs. secs. 1.25-8T

8332

Release of Claim to Exemption for Child of Divorced or Separated Parents

Used to release claim to a child's exemption by a parent who has custody of his or her child and is given to the parent who will claim the exemption. The parent who claims the child's exemption attaches this form to his or her tax return.
IT-IRC sec. 152(e)(2); Temp. Regs. sec. 1.152-4T; Pub. 504

8362
Currency Transaction Reported by Casinos
Used by casinos licensed by a state or local government having annual gaming revenues in excess of $1 million to report each deposit, withdrawal, exchange of currency or gambling tokens or chips or other payment or transfer, by, through, or to such casino, involving currency of more than $10,000.
P.L.91-508; Treasury Regs. secs. 31 CFR 103.22; 31 CFR 103.26; and 31 CFR 103.36

8390
Information Return for Determination of Life Insurance Company Earnings Rate Under Section 809
Used by certain life insurance companies to gather information to compute various earnings rates required by section 809.
IT-IRC sec. 809; Separate instructions

8396
Mortgage Interest Credit
Used by qualified mortgage credit certificate holders to figure their mortgage interest credit and any carryover to a subsequent year.
IT-IRC sec. 25

8404
Computation of Interest Charge on DISC-Related Deferred Tax Liability
Used by shareholders of Interest Charge Domestic International Sales Corporations (IC-DISCs) to figure and report their interest on DISC-related deferred tax liability. ITC 995(f); Treasury Regs. 1.995(f)

8453
U.S. Individual Income Tax Declaration for Electronic Filing
Used by qualified filers who file Forms 1040 and certain related schedules, 1040A and 1040EZ via electronic transmission on magnetic media. These filers must file Form 8453 to transmit the individual taxpayer's and return preparer's signature(s) for the return.
IT-IRC secs. 6012 and 6017

8453-E
Annual Return/Report of Employee Benefit Plan Magnetic Media/Electronic Filing
Used by qualified filers who file Forms 5500, 5500-C or 5500-R via electronic transmission.
IT-IRC sec. 6058

8453-F
U.S. Fiduciary Income Tax Declaration for Magnetic Tape/Electronic Filing
Used by qualified filers who file Form 1041 and related schedules via electronic transmission.
IT-IRC sec. 6012

8453-P
U.S. Partnership Declaration for Magnetic Tape/Electronic Filing
Used by qualified filers who file Form 1065 and related schedules via electronic transmission.
IT-IRC sec. 6031

8582
Passive Activity Loss Limitations
Used by individuals, estates, and trusts to figure the amount of any passive activity loss for the current tax year for all activities and the amount of the passive activity loss allowed on their tax returns.
IT-IRC sec. 469; Separate instructions

8582-CR
Passive Activity Credit Limitations
Used by individuals, estates, and trusts to figure the amount of any passive activity credit for the current year and the amount allowed on their tax returns.
IT-IRC sec. 469; Separate instructions

8586
Low-Income Housing Credit
Used by owners of residential rental projects providing low-income housing to claim the low-income housing credit. IT-IRC sec. 42

8594
Asset Acquisition Statement
Used by the buyer and seller of assets used in a trade or business involving goodwill or a going concern value.
IT-IRC 1060, Temp. Regs. sec. 1.1060-1T

8606
Nondeductible IRA Contributions, IRA Basis, and Nontaxable IRA Distributions
Used by individuals to report the amount of IRA contributions they choose to be nondeductible and to figure their basis in their IRA(s) at the end of the calendar year and the nontaxable part of any distributions they received.
IT-IRC sec. 408(o)

8609
Low-Income Housing Credit Allocation Certification
Used by housing credit agencies to allocate a low-income housing credit dollar amount. Also, used by low-income housing building owners to make elections and certify certain necessary information.
IT-IRC sec. 42

8610
Annual Low-Income Housing Credit Agencies Report
Used by housing credit agencies to transmit Forms 8609 and to report the dollar amount of housing credit allocations issued during the calendar year.
IT-IRC sec. 42

8611
Recapture of Low-Income Housing Credit
Used by taxpayers to recapture low-income housing credit taken in a prior year because there is a decrease in the qualified basis of a residential low-income housing building from one year to the next.
IT-IRC sec. 42(j)

8612
Return of Excise Tax on Undistributed Income of Real Estate Investment Trusts
Used by real estate investment trusts to report the excise tax on undistributed income. EX-IRC sec. 4981

8613
Return of Excise Tax on Undistributed Income of Regulated Investment Companies
Used by regulated investment companies to report the excise tax on undistributed income.
EX-IRC sec. 4982

8615
Computation of Tax for Children Under Age 14 Who Have Investment Income of More Than $1,000
Used to see if any of a child's investment income in excess of $1,000 is taxed at his or her parent's rate and, if so, to figure the child's tax.

8621
Return by a Shareholder of a Passive Foreign Investment Company or Qualified Electing Fund
Used by U.S. persons who own an interest in a foreign investment company to report elections, terminations of elections, and amounts to be included in gross income.
IT-IRC secs. 1291, 1293, and 1294

8645
Soil and Water Conservation Plan Certification
Used by taxpayers to certify that the plan under which they are claiming conservation expenses is an approved plan.
IT-IRC sec. 175(c)(3)

8656

Alternative Minimum Tax-Fiduciaries

Used by a fiduciary of an estate or trust to compute the alternative minimum taxable income, distributable net alternative minimum taxable income, and to report any alternative minimum tax due.
IT-IRC secs. 55 - 59; Separate instructions

8689

Allocation of Individual Income Tax to the Virgin Islands

Used as an attachment to Form 1040 filed by an individual who reports adjusted gross income from Virgin Islands sources.
IT-IRC sec. 932

8693

Low-Income Housing Credit Disposition Bond

Used to post a bond to avoid recapture of the low-income housing credit under section 42(j)(6). IT-IRC secs. 42 and 42(j)(6)

8697

Interest Computation Under the Look-Back Method for Completed Long-Term Contracts

Used by taxpayers to figure the interest due or to be refunded under the look-back method of section 460(b)3-on certain long-term contracts entered into after February 28, 1986, that are accounted for under either the percentage of completion-capitalized cost method or the percentage of completion method.
IT-IRC secs. 460(a) and 460(b)(2)(B); Separate instructions

8703

Annual Certification by Operator of a Residential Rental Project

Used by operators of residential rental projects to provide annual information the IRS will use to determine whether the projects continue to meet the requirements of section 142(d). Operators indicate on the form the specific test the bond issuer elected for the project period and also indicate the percentage of low-income units in the residential rental project.
IT-IRC secs. 142

8709

Exemption From Withholding on Investment Income of Foreign Governments

Used by foreign governments or international organizations to claim exemption from withholding under sections 1441 and 1442 on items of income qualifying for tax exemption under section 892.
IT-IRC secs. 892

8716

Election To Have a Tax Year Other Than a Required Tax Year

Used by partnerships, S corporations, and personal service corporations to elect to have a tax year other than a required tax year.
IT-IRC sec. 444

Sch. H (Form 8716)

Section 280H Limitations for a Personal Service Corporation (PSC)

Used by personal service corporations to determine their compliance with the distribution requirements of Section 280H.
IRC secs. 280H and 444

8717

User Fee for Employee Plan Determination Letter Request

Used by applicants for Employee Plan determination letters to transmit the appropriate user fee. Rev. Proc. 89-4, 1983-3 I.R.B. 18

8718

User Fee for Exempt Organization Determination Letter Request

Used by applicants for Exempt Organization determination letters to transmit the appropriate user fee.
Rev. Proc. 89-4. 1989-3 I.R.B. 18

8736

Application for Automatic Extension of Time to File Returns for a Partnership, a REMIC, or for Certain Trusts

Used to apply for an automatic three-month extension of time to file Form 1041 (trust), Form 1041S, or Form 1065.
IT-IRC sec. 6081; Regs. secs. 1.6081-2T and 1.6081-3T

8743

Information on Fuel Inventories and Sales

Used by refiners and importers to report information on fuel inventories and sales. The form is filed as an attachment to Form 720.
EX-IRC secs. 4041, 4081, and 4091

8800

Application for Additional Extension of Time to File Return for a U.S. Partnership, REMIC, or for Certain Trusts

Used to apply for an additional extension of up to three months of time to file Form 1041 (trust), Forms 1041S, or Form 1065. A separate Form 8800 must be filed for each return.
IT-IRC sec. 6081; Regs. secs. 1.6081-2T and 1.6081-3T

8801

Credit for Prior Year Minimum Tax

Used by taxpayers to figure the minimum tax credit allowed for tax year.
IT-IRC sec. 53; Separate instructions

8802

Annual Summary of Capital Construction Fund Activity

Used by taxpayers who maintain a capital construction fund under section 607 of the Merchant Marine Act of 1936, to report deposits to and withdrawals from the fund and to report the balances of the memorandum accounts required by Internal Revenue Code section 7518(d).
IT-IRC sec. 7518; Separate instructions

8803

Limit on Alternative Minimum Tax For Children Under Age 14

Used by children under age 14 to see if the alternative minimum tax figured on Form 6251 can be reduced.
IT-IRC sec. 59(j)

8804

Annual Return for Partnership Withholding Tax (Section 1446)

Used to report the total liability under section 1446 for the partnership's tax year. Form 8804 is also a transmittal form for Form 8805.
IT-IRC sec. 1446; Rev. Proc. 89-31; Separate instructions

8805

Foreign Partner's Information Statement of Section 1446 Withholding Tax

Used to show the amount of effectively connected taxable income and the tax payments allocable to the foreign partner for the partnership's tax year.
IT-IRC sec. 1446; Rev. Proc. 89-31; Separate instructions

8807

Computation of Certain Manufacturers and Retailers Excise Taxes

Used by manufacturers, producers, and importers to figure the tax on the sale of fishing equipment, bows and arrows, pistols and revolvers, firearms, and shells and cartridges. And, used by retailers to figure the excise tax on the sale of truck, trailer, and semitrailer chassis and bodies, and tractors.
EX-IRC secs. 4161, 4181, and 4051

8809

Request for Extension of Time To File Information Returns

Used to request an extension of time to file Forms W-2, W-2G, W-2P, 1098, 1099, or 5498.
PA-IRC sec. 6081; Regs. sec. 1.6081-1

8810

Corporate Passive Activity Loss and Credit Limitations

Used by closely held C corporations and personal service corporations that have passive activity losses and/or credits. IT-IRC sec. 469; Separate instructions

8811

Information Return for Real Estate Mortgage Investment Conduits (REMICs) and Issuers of Collateralized Debt Obligations

Used by REMICs and issuers of Collateralized Debt Obligations to report entity information needed to compile Publication 938, *Real Estate Mortgage Investment Conduit (REMIC) Reporting Information.*
IT-IRC secs. 860A-G and 1272(a)(6)(C)(ii)

8813

Partnership Withholding Tax Payment (Section 1446)

Used to make payment to the Internal Revenue Service of withholding tax under section 1446. Each payment of section 1446 taxes made during the partnership's tax year must be accompanied by Form 8813.
IT-IRC sec. 1446; Rev. Proc. 89-31; Separate instructions

8814

Parent's Election to Report Child's Interest and Dividends

Used by parents who elect to report the interest and dividends of their child under age 14 on their own tax return. The form is used to figure the amount of the child's income to report on the parent's return and the amount of additional tax that must be added to the parent's tax.
IT-IRC 1(i)(7)

8816

Special Loss Discount Account and Special Estimated Tax Payments for Insurance Companies

Used by insurance companies that elect to take an additional deduction under section 847.
IT-IRC sec. 847

8817

Allocation of Patronage and Nonpatronage Income and Dividends

Used by taxable farmers cooperatives to show income and deductions by patronage and nonpatronage sources.

TD F 90-22.1

Report of Foreign Bank and Financial Accounts

Used by individuals, trusts, partnerships or corporations having a financial interest in, or signature authority or other authority over, bank, securities, or other financial accounts in a foreign country, when the accounts were more than $10,000 in aggregate value at any time during the calendar year.
P.L.91-508; Treasury Regs. 31CFR103

Free Tax Publications

The Internal Revenue Service publishes many free publications to help you "make your taxes less taxing." The publications listed in this section give general information about taxes for individuals, small businesses, farming, fishing, and recent tax law changes. (Forms and schedules related to the subject matter of each publication are indicated after each listing.) You may want to order one of these publications, and then, if you need more detailed information on any subject, order the specific publication about it.

IRS Forms and Publications Distribution

Taxpayer Services
Internal Revenue Service (IRS)
U.S. Department of the Treasury
1111 Constitution Ave., NW, Room 2422
Washington, DC 20224   1-800-829-3676

Tax forms and publications can be obtained by calling the toll-free number. To send for forms through the mail, write to the state IRS address listed below. Two copies of each form and one copy of each set of instructions will be sent.

Alabama
P.O. Box 8903
Bloomington, IL 61703

Alaska
Rancho Cordova, CA 95743-0001

Arizona
Rancho Cordova, CA 95743-0001

Arkansas
P.O. Box 8903
Bloomington, IL 61703

California
Rancho Cordova, CA 95743-0001

Colorado
Rancho Cordova, CA 95743-0001

Connecticut
P.O. Box 85074
Richmond, VA 23261-5074

Delaware
P.O. Box 85074
Richmond, VA 23261-5074

District of Columbia
P.O. Box 85074
Richmond, VA 23261-5074

Florida
P.O. Box 85074
Richmond, VA 23261-5074

Georgia
P.O. Box 85074
Richmond, VA 23261-5074

Hawaii
Rancho Cordova, CA 95743-0001

Idaho
Rancho Cordova, CA 95743-0001

Illinois
P.O. Box 8903
Bloomington, IL 61703

Indiana
P.O. Box 8903
Bloomington, IL 61703

Iowa
P.O. Box 8903
Bloomington, IL 61703

Kansas
P.O. Box 8903
Bloomington, IL 61703

Kentucky
P.O. Box 8903
Bloomington, IL 61703

Louisiana
P.O. Box 8903
Bloomington, IL 61703

Maine
P.O. Box 85074
Richmond, VA 23261-5074

Maryland
P.O. Box 85074
Richmond, VA 23261-5074

Massachusetts
P.O. Box 85074
Richmond, VA 23261-5074

Michigan
P.O. Box 8903
Bloomington, IL 61703

Minnesota
P.O. Box 8903
Bloomington, IL 61703

Mississippi
P.O. Box 8903
Bloomington, IL 61703

Missouri
P.O. Box 8903
Bloomington, IL 61703

Montana
Rancho Cordova, CA 95743-0001

Nebraska
P.O. Box 8903
Bloomington, IL 61703

Nevada
Rancho Cordova, CA 95743-0001

New Hampshire
P.O. Box 85074
Richmond, VA 23261-5074

New Jersey
P.O. Box 85074
Richmond, VA 23261-5074

New Mexico
Rancho Cordova, CA 95743-0001

New York
P.O. Box 85074
Richmond, VA 23261-5074

North Carolina
P.O. Box 85074
Richmond, VA 23261-5074

North Dakota
P.O. Box 8903
Bloomington, IL 61703

Ohio
P.O. Box 8903
Bloomington, IL 61703

Oklahoma
P.O. Box 8903
Bloomington, IL 61703

Oregon
Rancho Cordova, CA 95743-0001

Pennsylvania
P.O. Box 85074
Richmond, VA 23261-5074

Puerto Rico
P.O. Box 85074
Richmond, VA 23261-5074

Rhode Island
P.O. Box 85074
Richmond, VA 23261-5074

South Carolina
P.O. Box 85074
Richmond, VA 23261-5074

South Dakota
P.O. Box 8903
Bloomington, IL 61703

Tennessee
P.O. Box 8903
Bloomington, IL 61703

Texas
P.O. Box 8903
Bloomington, IL 61703

Utah
Rancho Cordova, CA 95743-0001

Vermont
P.O. Box 85074
Richmond, VA 23261-5074

Virgin Islands
V.I. Bureau of Internal Revenue
Lockharts Garden No. 1A
Charlotte Amalie
St. Thomas, VI 00802

Virginia
P.O. Box 85074
Richmond, VA 23261-5074

Washington
Rancho Cordova, CA 95743-0001

West Virginia
P.O. Box 85074
Richmond, VA 23261-5074

Wisconsin
P.O. Box 8903
Bloomington, IL 61703

Wyoming
Rancho Cordova, CA 95743-0001

Foreign Addresses

Forms Distribution Center
P.O. Box 85074
Richmond, VA 23261

Forms Distribution Center
Rancho Cordova, CA 95743-0001

Taxpayers with mailing addresses in foreign countries should send requests or the order blank to whichever address is closer. Send letter requests for other forms and publications to: Forms Distribution Center, P.O. Box 85074, Richmond, VA 23261.

Free IRS Publications and Forms

The forms and schedules related to the subject matter of each publication are indicated after each listing.

1   Your Rights as a Taxpayer

To ensure that you always receive fair treatment in tax matters, you should know what your rights are. This publication clarifies your rights at each step in the tax process.

1S   Derechos del Contribuyente (Your Rights as a Taxpayer)

Spanish version of Publication 1.

2   The ABC's of Income Tax

This publication gives the basic tax rules that can help you prepare your individual tax return. It explains who must file a return, which tax form to use, when the return is due, and other general information. It will help you decide which filing status you qualify for, whether you can claim any dependents, and whether the income you are receiving is taxable. The publication goes on to explain the kinds of expenses you may be able to deduct and the various kinds of credits you may be able to take to reduce your tax.
Forms 1040, 1040A, 1040EZ, Schedules A, B, D, E, R, SE, Forms W-2. 2106. 2119, 2441, and 3903.

3   Tax Information for Military Personnel

This publication gives information about the special tax situations of active members of the Armed Forces. It includes information on items that are includible in and excludable from gross income, alien status, dependency exemptions, sale of residence, itemized deductions, tax liability, and filing returns.
Forms 1040, 1040A, 1040EZ, 1040NR, 1040X, 1310, 2106, 2688, 2848, 3903, 3903F, 4868 and W-2.

4   Student's Guide to Federal Income Tax

This publication explains the federal tax laws that apply to high school and college students. It describes the student's responsibilities to file and pay taxes, how to file, and how to get help.
Forms 1040EZ, W-2 and W-4.

17   Your Federal Income Tax

This publication can help you prepare your individual tax return. It takes you through the individual tax return and explains the tax laws that cover salaries and wages, interest and dividends, rental income, gains and losses, adjustments to income (such as alimony, and IRA contributions), and itemized deductions. Forms 1040, 1040A, 1040EZ, Schedules A, B, D, E, R, SE, Forms W-2, 2106, 2119, 2441, 3903.

225 Farmer's Tax Guide
This publication explains the federal tax laws that apply to farming. It gives examples of typical farming situations and discusses the kinds of farm income you must report and the different deductions you can take. Schedules A, D, F, SE (Form 1040), and Forms 1040, 4136, 4255, 4562, 4684, 4797, 6251.

334 Tax Guide for Small Business
This book explains some federal tax laws that apply to businesses. It describes the four major forms of business organizations: sole proprietorship, partnership, corporation, and S corporation: and explains the tax responsibilities of each. Schedule C (Form 1040), Schedule K-1 (Form 1065 and 1120S), Forms 1065, 1120, 1120-A, 1120S, 4562.

595 Tax Guide for Commercial Fishermen
This publication will familiarize you with the federal tax laws as they apply to the fishing industry. It is intended for sole proprietors who use Schedule C (Form 1040) to report profit or loss from fishing. This guide does not cover corporations or partnerships. Schedule C (Form 1040), Forms 1099-MISC, 4562, 4797.

15 Circular E, Employer's Tax Guide
Every employer automatically receives this publication on its revision and every person who applies for an employer identification number receives a copy. Forms 940, 941, and 941E.

51 Circular A, Agricultural Employer's Tax Guide
Form 943.

54 Tax Guide for U.S. Citizens and Resident Aliens Abroad
This publication discusses the tax situations of U.S. citizens and resident aliens who live and work abroad. In particular, it explains the rules for excluding income and excluding or deducting certain housing costs. Answers are provided to questions that taxpayers abroad most often ask. Forms 2555, 1116, and 1040, Schedule SE (Form 1040).

80 Circular SS, Federal Tax Guide for Employers in the Virgin Islands, Guam, American Samoa, and the Commonwealth of the Northern Mariana Islands
Forms 940, 941SS, and 943.

179 Circular PR, Guia Contributiva Federal Para Patronos Puertorriquenos (Federal Tax Guide for Employers in Puerto Rico)
Forms W-3PR, 940PR, 941PR, 942PR, and 943PR.

349 Federal Highway Use Tax on Heavy Vehicles
This publication explains which trucks, truck-tractors, and buses are subject to the federal use tax on heavy highway motor vehicles, which is one source of funds for the national highway construction program. The tax is due from the person in whose name the vehicle is either registered or required to be registered. The publication tells how to figure and pay the tax due. Form 2290.

378 Fuel Tax Credits and Refunds
This publication explains the credit or refund allowed for the federal excise taxes paid on certain fuels, and the income tax credit available when alcohol is used as a fuel. Forms 843, 4136 and 6478.

448 Federal Estate and Gift Taxes
This publication explains federal estate and gift taxes. Forms 706 and 709.

463 Travel, Entertainment, and Gift Expenses
This publication explains what expenses you may deduct for business-related travel, meals, entertainment, and gifts and it discusses the reporting and recordkeeping requirements for these expenses. The publication also summarizes the deduction and substantiation rules for employees, self-employed persons (including independent contractors), and employers (including corporations and partnerships). Form 2106.

501 Exemptions, Standard Deduction, and Filing Information
This publication provides answers to some basic tax questions: who must file; what filing status to choose; how many exemptions to claim; and how to figure the amount of the standard deduction. It also covers rules for foster care providers. Form 2120 and 8332.

502 Medical and Dental Expenses
This publication tells you how to figure your deduction for medical and dental expenses. You may take this deduction only if you itemize your deductions on Schedule A (Form 1040).
Schedule A (Form 1040).

503 Child and Dependent Care Expenses
This publication explains the credit you may be able to take if you pay someone to care for your dependent who is under 13, your disabled dependent, or your disabled spouse. For purposes of the credit, "disabled" refers to a person physically or mentally unable to care for himself or herself. Schedule 1 (Form 1040A), and Form 2441.

504 Tax Information for Divorced or Separated Individuals
This publication explains tax rules of interest to divorced or separated individuals. It covers filing status, dependency exemptions, and the treatment of alimony and property settlements.

505 Tax Withholding and Estimated Tax
This publication explains the two methods of paying tax under our pay-as-you-go system. They are (1) Withholding. Your employer will withhold income tax from your pay. Tax is also withheld from certain other types of income. You can have more or less withheld, depending on your circumstances. (2) Estimated tax. If you do not pay your tax through withholding, or do not pay enough tax that way, you might have to pay estimated tax. Forms W-4, W-4P, W-4S, 1040-ES, 2210, and 2210F.

508 Educational Expenses
This publication explains what work-related educational expenses qualify for deduction, how to report your expenses and any reimbursement you receive, and which forms and schedules to use. Form 2106 and Schedule A (Form 1040).

509 Tax Calendars for 1993

510 Excise Taxes for 1993
This publication covers in detail the various federal excise taxes reported on Form 720. These include the following groupings: environmental taxes; facilities and service taxes on communication and air transportation; fuel taxes; manufacturers taxes; vaccines; and heavy trucks, trailers and tractors. In addition, it briefly describes other excise taxes and tells which forms to use in reporting and paying the taxes. Forms 720, 8743, and 8807.

513 Tax Information for Visitors to the United States
This publication briefly reviews the general requirements of U.S. income tax laws for foreign visitors. You may have to file a U.S. income tax return during your visit. Most visitors who come to the United States are not allowed to work in this country. Please check with the Immigration and Naturalization Service before you take a job. Forms 1040C, 1040NR, 2063, and 1040-ES (NR).

514 Foreign Tax Credit for Individuals
This publication may help you if you paid foreign income tax. You may be able to take a foreign tax credit or deduction to avoid the burden of double taxation. The publication explains which foreign taxes qualify and how to figure your credit or deduction. Form 1116.

515 Withholding of Tax on Nonresident Aliens and Foreign Corporations
This publication provides information for withholding agents who are required to withhold and report tax on payments to nonresident aliens and foreign corporations. Included are three tables listing U.S. tax treaties and some of the treaty provisions that provide for reduction of or exemption from withholding for certain types of income. Forms 1042 and 1042S, 1001, 4224, 8233, 1078, 8288, 8288-B, 8804, 8805, 8288-A and W-8, 8813, and 8709.

516 Tax Information for U.S. Government Civilian Employees Stationed Abroad

This publication covers the tax treatment of allowances, reimbursements, and business expenses that U.S. government employees, including foreign service employees, are likely to receive or incur.

517 Social Security for Members of the Clergy and Religious Workers

This publication discusses social security coverage and the self-employment tax for the clergy. It also tells you how, as a member of the clergy (minister, member of a religious order, or Christian Science practitioner), you may apply for an exemption from the self-employment tax that would otherwise be due for the services you perform in the exercise of your ministry. Net earnings from self-employment are explained and sample forms are shown.
Form 2106, Form 1040, Schedule SE (Form 1040), and Schedule C (Form 1040).

519 U.S. Tax Guide for Aliens

This comprehensive publication gives guidelines on how to determine your U.S. tax status and figure your U.S. tax.
Forms 1040, 1040C, 1040NR, 2063, and Schedule A (Form 1040).

520 Scholarships and Fellowships

This publication explains the tax laws that apply to U.S. citizens and resident aliens who study, teach or conduct research in the United States or abroad under scholarships and fellowship grants.

521 Moving Expenses

This publication explains how, if you changed job locations last year or started a new job, you may be able to deduct your moving expenses. You may qualify for a deduction whether you are self-employed or an employee. The expenses must be connected with starting work at your new job location. You must meet a distance test and a time test. You also may be able to deduct expenses of moving to the United States if you retire while living and working overseas or if you are a survivor or dependent of a person who died while living and working overseas. Forms 3903, 3903F, 4782.

523 Tax Information on Selling Your Home

This publication explains how you report gain from selling your home, how you may postpone the tax on part or all of the gain, and how you may exclude part or all of the gain from your gross income if you are 55 or older. Form 2119.

524 Credit for the Elderly or the Disabled

This publication explains how to figure the credit for the elderly or the disabled. You may be able to claim this credit if you are 65 or older, or if you are retired on disability and were permanently and totally disabled when you retired. Figure the credit on Schedule R (Form 1040), Credit for the Elderly or the Disabled. To take the credit you must file a Form 1040.
Schedule R (Form 1040).

525 Taxable and Nontaxable Income

This publication discusses wages, salaries, fringe benefits, and other compensation received for services as an employee. In addition, it discusses items of miscellaneous taxable income as well as items that are exempt from tax.

526 Charitable Contributions

If you make a charitable contribution or gift to, or for the use of, a qualified organization, you may be able to claim a deduction on your tax return. This publication explains how the deduction is claimed, and the limits that apply.
Schedule A (Form 1040), Form 2106.

527 Residential Rental Property

This publication defines rental income, discusses rental expenses, and explains how to report them on your return. It also discusses casualty losses on rental property, passive activity limits, at-risk rules pertaining to rental property, and the sale of rental property.
Schedule E (Form 1040), and Forms 4562 and 4797.

529 Miscellaneous Deductions

This publication discusses expenses you generally may take as miscellaneous deductions on Schedule A (Form 1040), such as unreimbursed employee expenses and expenses of producing income. It does not discuss other itemized deductions, such as the ones for charitable contributions, moving expenses, interest, taxes, or medical and dental expenses.
Schedule A (Form 1040), Form 2106.

530 Tax Information for Homeowners (Including Owners of Condominiums and Cooperative Apartments)

This publication gives information about home ownership and federal taxes. It explains how to determine basis, how to treat settlement and closing costs, and how to treat repairs and improvements you make. The publication discusses itemized deductions for mortgage interest, real estate taxes, and casualty and theft losses. It also explains the mortgage interest credit.

531 Reporting Income From Tips

This publication gives advice about keeping track of cash and charge tips and explains that all tips received are subject to federal income tax. The publication also explains the rules about the information that employers must report to the Internal Revenue Service about their employees' tip income.
Forms 4070 and 4070A.

533 Self-Employment Tax

This publication explains the self-employment tax, which is a social security tax for people who work for themselves. It is similar to the social security tax withheld from the pay of wage earners. Schedule SE (Form 1040).

534 Depreciation

This publication discusses the various methods of depreciation, including the modified accelerated cost recovery system (MACRS). Form 4562.

535 Business Expenses

This publication discusses business expenses such as: fringe benefits; rent; interest; taxes; insurance; and employee benefit plans. It also outlines the choice to capitalize certain business expenses; discusses amortization and depletion; covers some business expenses that may be deductible in some circumstances and not deductible in others; and points out some expenses that are not deductible.

536 Net Operating Losses

537 Installment Sales

This publication discusses sales arrangements that provide for part or all of the selling price to be paid in a later year. These arrangements are "installment sales." If you finance the buyer's purchase of your property, instead of having the buyer get a loan or mortgage from a bank, you probably have an installment sale. Form 6252.

538 Accounting Periods and Methods

This publication explains which accounting periods and methods can be used for figuring federal taxes, and how to apply for approval to change from one period or method to another. Most individual taxpayers use the calendar year for their accounting period and the cash method of accounting. Forms 1128 and 3115.

541 Tax Information on Partnerships

Forms 1065 and Schedules D, K, and K-1 (Form 1065).

542 Tax Information on Corporations

Forms 1120 and 1120-A

544 Sales and Other Dispositions of Assets

This publication explains how to figure gain and loss on various transactions, such as trading or selling an asset used in a trade or business, and it explains the tax results of different types of gains and losses. Not all transactions result in taxable gains or deductible losses, and not all gains are taxed the same way.
Schedule D (Form 1040) and Form 4797.

545 Interest Expense

This publication explains what items may and may not be deducted as interest. (Interest is an amount paid for the use of borrowed money.) This publication also explains how much interest you may deduct and how to figure this amount. Where you deduct interest expense depends on why you borrowed the money. Schedule A (Form 1040).

547 Nonbusiness Disasters, Casualties, and Thefts

This publication explains when you can deduct a disaster, casualty, or theft loss. Casualties are events such as hurricanes, earthquakes, tornadoes, fire, floods, vandalism, loss of deposits in a bankrupt or insolvent financial institution, and car accidents. The publication also explains how to treat the reimbursement you receive from insurance or other sources. Form 4684.

Free Tax Help

550 Investment Income and Expenses
This publication explains which types of investment income are and are not taxable, when the income is taxed, and how to report it on your tax return. The publication discusses the treatment of tax shelters and investment-related expenses. The publication also explains how to figure your gain and loss when you sell or trade your investment property.
Forms 1099-INT and 1099-DIV, Schedules B and D (Form 1040).

551 Basis of Assets
This publication explains how to determine the basis of property. The basis of property you buy is usually its cost. If you received property in some other way, such as by gift or inheritance, you normally must use a basis other than cost.

552 Recordkeeping for Individuals
This publication can help you decide what records to keep and how long to keep them for tax purposes. These records will help you prepare your income tax returns so that you will pay only your correct tax. If you keep a record of your expenses during the year, you may find that you can reduce your taxes by itemizing your deductions. Deductible expenses include medical and dental bills, interest, contributions, and taxes.

553 Highlights of 1992 Tax Changes
This publication discusses the more important changes in the tax rules brought about by recent legislation, rulings, and administrative decisions. It does not discuss all new tax rules or detail all changes. It highlights the important recent changes that taxpayers should know about when filing their 1989 tax forms and when planning for 1990.

554 Tax Information for Older Americans
This publication gives tax information of special interest to older Americans. An example takes you through completing a tax return and explains such items as the sale of a home, the credit for the elderly or the disabled, the supplemental Medicare premium, and pension and annuity income. The publication includes filled-in forms and schedules that show how these and other items are reported. Schedules B, D, and R (Form 1040), and Forms 1040 and 2119.

555 Community Property and the Federal Income Tax
This publication may help married taxpayers who are domiciled in one of the following community property states: Arizona, California, Idaho, Louisiana, Nevada, New Mexico, Texas, Washington or Wisconsin. If you wish to file a separate tax return, you should understand how community property laws affect the way you figure your tax before completing your federal income tax return.

556 Examination of Returns, Appeal Rights, and Claims for Refund
This publication may be helpful if your return is examined by the Internal Revenue Service. It explains that returns are normally examined to verify the correctness of reported income, exemptions, or deductions, and it describes what appeal rights you have if you disagree with the results of the examination.
This publication also explains the procedures for the examination of items of partnership income, deduction, gain, loss, and credit. Information is given on how to file a claim for refund, the time for filing a claim for refund, and any limit on the amount of refund. Forms 1040X and 1120X

556S Revision de las Declaraciones de Impuesto, Derecho de Apelacion y Reclamaciones de Reembolsos (Examination of Returns, Appeal Rights, and Claims for Refund)
(Spanish version of Publication 556) Forms 1040X and 1120X

557 Tax-Exempt Status for Your Organization
This publication discusses how organizations become recognized as exempt from federal income tax under section 501(a) of the Internal Revenue Code. (These include organizations described in Code section 501(c).) The publication explains how to get a ruling or determination letter recognizing the exemption, and it gives other information that applies generally to all exempt organizations. Forms 990, 990PF, 1023, and 1024.

559 Tax Information for Survivors, Executors, and Administrators
This publication can help you report and pay the proper federal income and estate taxes if you are responsible for settling a decedent's estate. The publication also answers many questions that a spouse or other survivor faces when a person dies. Form 1040, Form 1041, Form 706, and Form 4810.

560 Self-Employed Retirement Plans
This publication discusses retirement plans for self-employed persons and certain partners in partnerships. These retirement plans are sometimes called Keogh plans or HR-10 plans.

561 Determining the Value of Donated Property
This publication can help donors and appraisers determine the value of property (other than cash) that is given to qualified organizations. It explains what kind of information you need to support a charitable deduction you claim on your return. Form 8283.

564 Mutual Fund Distributions
This publication discusses the federal income tax treatment of distributions paid or allocated to you as an individual shareholder of a mutual fund. A comprehensive example shows distributions made by a mutual fund and an illustration of Form 1040.
Forms 1040, Schedule B (Form 1040), and Form 1099-DIV.

570 Tax Guide for Individuals in U.S. Possessions
This publication is for individuals with income from American Samoa, Guam, the Commonwealth of the Northern Mariana Islands, Puerto Rico, and the U.S. Virgin Islands. Forms 4563, 5074, and 8689.

571 Tax-Sheltered Annuity Programs for Employees of Public Schools and Certain Tax-Exempt Organizations
This publication explains the rules concerning employers qualified to buy tax-sheltered annuities, eligible employees who may participate in the program, and the amounts that may be excluded from income. Form 5330.

575 Pension and Annuity Income (Including Simplified General Rule)
This publication explains how to report pension and annuity income on your federal income tax return. It also explains the special tax treatment for lump-sum distributions from pension, stock bonus, or profit-sharing plans.
Forms 1040, 1099-R and 4972.

578 Tax Information for Private Foundations and Foundation Managers
This publication covers tax matters of interest to private foundations and their managers, including the tax classification of the foundations, filing requirements, the tax on net investment income, and various excise taxes on transactions that violate the foundation rules. Form 990-F

579S Como Preparar la Declaracion de Impuesto Federal (How to Prepare the Federal Income Tax Return)
Forms 1040, 1040A, 1040EZ.

583 Taxpayers Starting a Business
This publication shows sample records that a small business can use if it operates as a sole proprietorship. Records like these will help you prepare complete and accurate tax returns and make sure you pay only the tax you owe. This publication also discusses the taxpayer identification number businesses must use, information returns businesses may have to file, and the kinds of business taxes businesses may have to pay.
Schedule C (Form 1040), and Form 4562.

584 Nonbusiness Disaster, Casualty, and Theft Loss Workbook
This workbook can help you to figure your loss from a disaster, casualty or theft. It will help you most if you list your possessions before any losses occur. The workbook has schedules to help you figure the loss on your home and its contents. There is also a schedule to help you figure the loss on your car, truck, or motorcycle.

586A The Collection Process (Income Tax Accounts)
This publication explains your rights and duties as a taxpayer who owes tax. It also explains the legal obligation of the Internal Revenue Service to collect overdue taxes, and the way we fulfill this obligation. It is not intended to be a precise and technical analysis of the law in this area.

586S Proceso de cobro (Deudas del impuesto sobre ingreso)
(Spanish version of Publication 586A)

587 Business Use of Your Home

This publication can help you decide if you qualify to deduct certain expenses for using part of your home in your business. You must meet specific tests and your deduction is limited. Deductions for the business use of a home computer are also discussed. Schedule C (Form 1040), and Form 4562.

589 Tax Information on S Corporations

This publication discusses the way corporations are taxed under subchapter S of the Internal Revenue Code. In general, an "S" corporation does not pay tax on its income. Instead, it passes through its income and expenses to its shareholders, who then report them on their own tax returns. Forms 1120S and Schedule K-1 (Form 1120S)

590 Individual Retirement Arrangements (IRAs)

This publication explains the rules for and the tax benefits of having an individual retirement arrangement (IRA). An IRA is a savings plan that lets you set aside money for your retirement. Generally, your contributions to an IRA are tax deductible in part or in full and the earnings in your IRA are not taxed until they are distributed to you. Forms 1040, 5329 and 8606.

593 Tax Highlights for U.S. Citizens and Residents Going Abroad

This publication briefly reviews various U.S. tax provisions that apply to U.S. citizens or resident aliens who live or work abroad and expect to receive income from foreign sources.

594 The Collection Process (Employment Tax Accounts)

This booklet explains your rights and duties as a taxpayer who owes employer's quarterly federal taxes. It also explains how we fulfill the legal obligation of the Internal Revenue Service to collect these taxes. It is not intended as a precise and technical analysis of the law.

594S Proceso de cobro (Deudas del impuesto por razon del empleo) (Spanish version of Publication 594.)

596 Earned Income Credit

This publication discusses who may receive the earned income credit, and how to figure and claim the credit. It also discusses how to receive advance payments of the earned income credit. Forms W-5, 1040, and 1040A.

597 Information on the United States-Canada Income Tax Treaty

This publication reproduces the entire text of the U.S.-Canada income tax treaty, and also gives an explanation of provisions that often apply to U.S. citizens or residents who have Canadian source income. There is also a discussion that deals with certain tax problems that may be encountered by Canadian residents who temporarily work in the United States.

598 Tax on Unrelated Business Income of Exempt Organizations

This publication explains the unrelated business income tax provisions that apply to most tax-exempt organizations. An organization that regularly operates a trade or business that is not substantially related to its exempt purpose may be taxed on the income from this business. Generally, a tax-exempt organization with gross income of $1,000 or more from an unrelated trade or business must file a return. Form 990-T.

686 Certification for Reduced Tax Rates in Tax Treaty Countries

This publication explains how U.S. citizens, residents, and domestic corporations may certify to a foreign treaty country that they are entitled to treaty benefits.

721 Tax Guide to U.S. Civil Service Retirement Benefits

This publication explains how the federal income tax rules apply to the benefits that retired federal employees or their survivors receive under the U.S. Civil Service Retirement System or Federal Employees Retirement System. There is also information on estate taxes. Form 1040.

850 English-Spanish Glossary of Words and Phrases Used in Publications Issued by the Internal Revenue Service

901 U.S. Tax Treaties

This publication includes information about the reduced tax rates and exemptions from U.S. taxes provided under U.S. tax treaties with other countries. This publication is intended for residents of those countries who receive income from U.S. sources. Information for foreign workers and students is emphasized. Form 1040NR

904 Interrelated Computations for Estate and Gift Taxes

Forms 706 and 709.

907 Tax Information for Handicapped and Disabled Individuals

This publication explains tax rules of interest to handicapped and disabled people and to taxpayers with disabled dependents. For example, you may be able to take a tax credit for certain disability payments, you may be able to deduct medical expenses, and you may be able to take a credit for expenses of care for disabled dependents. Schedule A (Form 1040), Schedule R (1040), and Form 2441.

908 Bankruptcy and Other Debt Cancellation

This publication explains the income tax aspects of bankruptcy and discharge of debt for individuals and small businesses. Forms 982, 1040, 1041, 1120.

909 Alternative Minimum Tax for Individuals

This publication discusses the alternative minimum tax, which applies to individuals. Forms 6251, 8801, and 8803.

911 Tax Information for Direct Sellers

This publication may help you if you are a "direct seller," a person who sells consumer products to others on a person-to-person basis. Many direct sellers sell door-to-door, at sales parties, or by appointment in someone's home. Information on figuring your income from direct sales as well as the kinds of expenses you may be entitled to deduct is also provided. Schedules C and SE (Form 1040).

915 Social Security Benefits and Equivalent Railroad Retirement Benefits

This publication explains when you have to include part of your social security or equivalent railroad retirement benefits in income on Form 1040. It also explains how to figure the amount to include. Forms SSA-1099 and RRB-1099, Social Security Benefits Worksheet, Notice 703, Forms SSA-1042S and RRB-1042S.

917 Business Use of a Car

This publication explains the expenses that you may deduct for the business use of your car. Car expenses that are deductible do not include the cost of commuting expenses (driving from your home to your workplace). The publication also discusses the taxability of the use of a car provided by an employer and rules on leasing a car for business. Form 2106

919 Is My Withholding Correct for 1991?

To help employees check their withholding, this publication has worksheets that will help them estimate both their 1990 tax and their total 1990 withholding. The employees can then compare the two amounts. The publication tells employees what to do if too much or too little tax is being withheld. Form W-4.

924 Reporting of Real Estate Transactions to IRS

This publication informs sellers of certain real estate about the information they must provide to the real estate reporting person in order that the reporting person can complete the Form 1099-S that must be filed with the IRS.

925 Passive Activity and At-Risk Rules

This publication covers the rules that limit passive activity losses and credits and the at-risk limits. Form 8582.

926 Employment Taxes for Household Employers

This publication shows how a household employer reports federal income tax withholding, social security (FICA), and unemployment taxes (FUTA). You may be a household employer if you have a babysitter, maid, or other employee who works in your house. The publication also shows what records you must keep. Forms W-2, W-3, 940, 940EZ, and 942.

929 Tax Rules for Children and Dependents

This publication describes the tax law affecting certain children and dependents. No personal exemption is allowed to a taxpayer who can be claimed as a dependent by another taxpayer. The standard deduction for dependents may be limited. Minor children may have to pay tax at their parent's tax rate.
Form 8615, Form 8814, and Form 8803.

936 Limits on Home Mortgage Interest Deduction

This publication covers the rules governing the deduction of home mortgage interest if your acquisition cost exceeds $1 million ($500,000 if you are married filing separately) or your home equity debt exceeds $100,000 ($50,000 if you are married filing separately). Worksheets are provided to determine what interest expenses qualify as home mortgage interest.

937 Business Reporting

The first part of this publication explains your responsibilities, if you have employees, to withhold federal income taxes and social security taxes (FICA) from their wages, and to pay social security taxes and federal unemployment taxes (FUTA). It also discusses the rules for advance payment of the earned income credit, and for reporting and allocating tips.

The second part provides general information about the rules for reporting payments to nonemployees and transactions with other persons. It also provides information on taxpayer identification numbers, backup withholding, and penalties relating to information returns.
Forms W-2, W-2G, W-4, 940, 941, 1098, 1099 series, 4789, 5498, 8300, and 8308.

938 Real Estate Mortgage Investment Conduits (REMICS) Reporting Information (And Other Collateralized Debt Obligations (CDOs))

This publication discusses reporting requirements for issuers of real estate mortgage investment conduits (REMICS) and collateralized debt obligations (CDOs). This publication also contains a directory of REMICS and CDOs to assist brokers and middlemen in fulfilling reporting requirements.

939 Pension General Rule (Nonsimplified Method)

This publication covers the nonsimplified General Rule for the taxation of pensions or annuities, which must be used if the Simplified General Rule is not applicable or is not chosen. For example, the nonsimplified method must be used for payments under commercial annuities. The publication also contains the necessary actuarial tables for this method.

945 Tax Information for Those Affected by Operation Desert Shield

This publication covers many issues, such as available tax relief measures for suspending examinations or collection of back taxes, extending due dates for filing an income tax return, meeting the requirements for the foreign earned income exclusion, and seeking other tax assistance. This publication applies to newly activated reservists, as well as all other active duty U.S. military personnel and their families, citizens who had been detained by Iraq, and citizens who had to leave the Middle East because of the adverse conditions.

946 How to Begin Depreciating your Property

Publication for people who are depreciating property for the first time.

953 International Tax information for Businesses

Covers topics of interest to U.S. citizens and resident aliens with foreign investments and nonresident aliens who want to invest in U.S. businesses.

1004 Identification Numbers Under ERISA

1045 Information for Tax Practitioners

1212 List of Original Discount Instruments

This publication explains the tax treatment of original issue discount (OID). It describes how (1) Brokers and other middlemen, who may hold the debt instruments as nominees for the owners, should report OID to IRS and to the owners on Forms 1099-OID or 1099-INT, and (2) Owners of OID debt instruments should report OID on their income tax returns. The publication gives rules for figuring the discount amount to report each year, if required. It also gives tables showing OID amounts for certain publicly-traded OID debt instruments, including short-term U.S. Government securities.
Schedule B (Form 1040) and Forms 1099-OID and 1099-INT.

1244 Employee's Daily Record of Tips (Form 4070-A) and Employee's Report of Tips to Employer (Form 4070)

This publication explains how you must report tips if you are an employee who receives tips. Copies of the monthly tip report you must give your employer are included, as well as a daily list you can use for your own records.
Forms 4070 and 4070-A.

1544 Reporting Cash Payments of Over $10,000 (Received in a Trade or Business)

This new publication was developed to assist the government in the war against drugs. It contains information for filing Form 8300 and includes an example with a filled-in Form 8300.

State Tax Assistance

These state taxpayer service departments are the basic starting place for free assistance and guidance pertaining to your state taxes.

Alabama

Taxpayer Assistance
Alabama Income Tax Division
P.O. Box 327465
Montgomery, AL 36132-7465 — 205-242-1000

Alaska

(No individual income tax; corporation tax only)
Alaska Department of Revenue
Income and Excise Audit Division
Attn: Corporations Unit
P.O. Box SA
Juneau, AK 99801 — 907-465-2370

Arizona

Personal Income Tax
Arizona Department of Revenue
P.O. Box 29002
Phoenix, AZ 85038

Corporation Tax
Arizona Department of Revenue
P.O. Box 29079
Phoenix, AZ 85038

Information and fewer than 6 forms	602-255-3381
6 or more forms	602-542-4260

Arkansas

Arkansas Department of Finance Administration
Attn: Income Tax
P.O. Box 3628
Little Rock, AR 72203

General Information	501-682-7250
Refund Information	501-682-7280
Forms	501-682-7255

California

Personal
Franchise Tax Board
P.O. Box 942840
Sacramento, CA 942857-0000 — 800-852-5711

Corporate
Franchise Tax Board
P.O. Box 942857
Sacramento, CA 94257-0500 — 916-369-0500

Colorado

Taxpayer Services
Department of Revenue
1375 Sherman Street
Denver, CO 80261

Personal	303-534-1209
Corporate	303-534-1209

Connecticut

Department of Revenue Services
92 Farmington Avenue
Hartford, CT 06105

Information and Forms	1-800-321-7829
Information	203-566-8520
Forms	203-297-5773

Delaware

Delaware Division of Revenue
820 North French Street — 1-800-292-7826
Wilmington, DE 19899 — 302-577-3300

Florida

Florida Taxpayer Assistance — 1-800-872-9909
P.O. Box 5139 — 904-488-6800
Tallahassee, FL 32314-5139

Bulk form orders — 904-488-8422

Georgia

Income Tax Division
P.O. Box 38007
Atlanta, GA 30334

Personal	404-656-4293
Corporate	404-656-4165

Hawaii

Taxpayer Services Branch
Hawaii State Tax Collector
P.O. Box 259
Honolulu, HI 96809-02559 — 808-548-4242

Information	1-800-222-3229
Forms	1-800-222-7572

Idaho

Idaho Department of Revenue and Taxation
P.O. Box 36
Boise, ID 83722 — 208-334-7787

Illinois

Illinois Department of Revenue
P.O. Box 19015
Springfield, IL 62794-9015 — 217-785-6760

Information all year, Forms July - December	1-800-732-8866
Forms January - June	1-800-624-2459

Indiana

Indiana Department of Revenue
Taxpayer Services Division
Room 104-B, 100 North Senate Street
Indianapolis, IN 46204 — 317-232-2240

Iowa

Iowa Department of Revenue and Finance
Hoover State Office Building
Des Moines, IA 50319

Information and forms	515-218-3114
Bulk form orders	515-281-5370

Free Tax Help

Kansas

Kansas Department of Revenue
Box 12001
Topeka, KS 66612-2001

Personal	913-296-0222
Business	913-296-1711

Kentucky

Kentucky Revenue Cabinet
Frankfort, KY 40618

Information	502-564-4580
Forms	502-564-3658

Louisiana

Louisiana Department of Revenue and Taxation
P.O. Box 201
Baton Rouge, LA 70821

Information	504-925-4611
Forms	504-925-7532
Refund information	504-925-4611

Maine

State of Maine
Department of Taxation
Station 24
Augusta, ME 04333

	207-626-8475
Information	1-800-452-1983
Forms	1-800-338-5811

Maryland

Comptroller of the Treasury
Income Tax Information
301 W. Preston St.
Baltimore, MD 21201

	410-974-3951

Massachusetts

Massachusetts Department of Revenue
100 Cambridge Street
Boston, MA 02204
Attention: Correspondence Unit

	617-727-4392

Michigan

Department of Treasury
430 West Allegan Street
Lansing, MI 48922

Information	1-800-877-MICH
Information	517-373-2910
Information	517-373-3386
Forms	1-800-FORM-2-ME
Forms	517-373-6598
Forms	517-335-1144

Minnesota

Minnesota Taxpayer Assistance
10 River Park Plaza
St. Paul, MN 55146

Personal	1-800-652-9094
Personal	612-296-3781
Corporate	1-800-657-3777
Corporate	612-296-6181

Mississippi

Mississippi State Tax Commission
P.O. Box 1033
Jackson, MS 39215

	601-359-1141

Missouri

Taxpayer Assistance
Missouri Department of Revenue
P.O. Box 2200
Jefferson City, MO 65105-2200

Information	314-751-3503
Forms	314-751-4695

Montana

Montana Department of Revenue
Income Tax Division
P.O. Box 5803
Helena, MT 59604

Personal	406-444-2837
Corporate	406-444-3388

Nebraska

Nebraska Department of Revenue
Taxpayer Assistance
P.O. Box 94818
Lincoln, NE 68509

Personal Income Tax information, in season	1-800-422-4618
Personal Information, all year	402-471-5729
Corporate Information, all year	1-800-742-7474

Nevada

No Income Tax

	702-687-4820

New Hampshire

No Income Tax

	603-271-2191

New Jersey

New Jersey Division of Taxation
50 Barrack Street
CN 269
Trenton, NJ 08646

	1-800-323-4400
	609-292-6400

New Mexico

New Mexico Taxation and Revenue
P.O. Box 630
Santa Fe, NM 87509-0630

	505-827-0909

New York

New York State Department of Taxation and Finance
Taxpayer Assistance Bureau
W. A. Harriman Campus
Albany, NY 12227

General Information	1-800-225-5829
Refund Information	1-800-443-3200
Forms	1-800-462-8100
All	518-438-6777

North Carolina

Information:
North Carolina Department of Revenue
P.O. Box 25000
Raleigh, NC 27640

Refund Information:
North Carolina Department of Revenue
P.O. Box R
Raleigh, NC 27634

Information	1-800-222-9965
Forms	1-800-451-1404
All	919-733-3450

North Dakota

Office of State Tax Commissioner
600 East Boulevard Avenue
Bismarck, ND 58505-0599   701-224-3017

Ohio

Taxpayer Services
Ohio Department of Taxation
P.O. Box 2476   1-800-282-1782
Columbus, Ohio 43266-0076   614-846-6712

Oklahoma

Oklahoma Tax Commission
2501 Lincoln Boulevard   1-800-522-8165
Oklahoma City, OK 73194   405-521-4321

Oregon

Oregon Department of Revenue
Tax Help Section
955 Center Street, NE
Salem, OR 97310   503-378-4988

Pennsylvania

Personal:
Pennsylvania Department of Revenue
Taxpayer Services
Department 280101
Harrisburg, PA 17128-0101   717-986-4621

Corporate:
Pennsylvania Department of Revenue
Business Trust Fund Taxes
Department 280904
Harrisburg, PA 17128-0904   717-787-2416

Rhode Island

Rhode Island Division of Taxation
1 Capitol Hill
Providence, RI 02908
Information   401-277-2905
Forms   401-277-3934

South Carolina

South Carolina Department of Revenue
P.O. Box 125
Columbia, SC 29214
Information   803-737-4709
Forms   803-737-5084

South Dakota

No Income Tax   605-773-3311

Tennessee

Tennessee Taxpayer Services
504 Andrew Jackson Building
Nashville, TN 37242
Information   615-741-3581
Forms   615-741-2481

Texas

No Income Tax   512-463-4600

Utah

Utah State Tax Commission
160 East 3rd South
Salt Lake City, UT 84134   801-530-4848

Vermont

Personal:
Vermont Department of Taxes
Pavillion Office Building
Montpelier, VT 05602   802-828-2515

Corporate:
Vermont Department of Taxes
P.O. Box 547
Montpelier, VT 05602   802-828-2865

Virginia

Virginia Department of Taxation
P.O. Box 6L
Richmond, VA 23282
* Place attention notation to what it concerns
Personal   804-367-8031
Corporate   804-367-8038
Forms   804-367-8055

Washington

No Income Tax   800-233-6349

West Virginia

West Virginia Department of Revenue
P.O. Box 3784   1-800-642-9016
Charleston, WV 25337-3784   304-344-2068

Wisconsin

Taxpayer Services
Wisconsin Department of Revenue
P.O. Box 8906
Madison, WI 53708
Personal, information and forms   608-266-2486
Corporate, information and forms   608-266-2772
Bulk form orders   608-267-2025

Wyoming

No Income Tax   307-777-7961

Free Experts:
Free Help in Finding A Free Expert

* See also Experts Chapter

Not only is the world full of experts who are willing to help resolve your information problems for free, there are organizations whose mission it is to put you in touch with these experts. Here is a list of some of these clearinghouses arranged by subject area. Don't forget to use the Experts Chapter which includes the name and phone number of experts by keyword from aquaculture to zinc. Remember that these experts spend their lives studying specific areas and are waiting to help you for free as long as you treat them right.

* Agriculture and Commodities

Office of Public Affairs
U.S. Department of Agriculture
Room 413A
Washington, DC 20250   202-720-4623

A staff of research specialists are available to provide specific answers or direct you to an expert in any agricultural-related topic.

National Agricultural Library
10301 Baltimore Boulevard
Beltsville, MD 20705-2351   301-504-5755

This library serves as an information clearinghouse.

National Agricultural Statistics Service (ASS)
U.S. Department of Agriculture, NAS
14th & Independence Avenue SW
Room 4117 S. Bldg.
Washington, DC 20250   202-720-3896

ASS provides contacts for agricultural production, stocks, prices and other data.

* Arts and Entertainment

Performing Arts Library
John F. Kennedy Center
Washington, DC 20566   202-707-6245

This center which works jointly with the Library of Congress offers reference services on any aspect of the performing arts.

* Best and Worst Industries and Companies

U.S. Department of Commerce
Washington, DC 20230   202-482-2000

Over 100 analysts monitor all the major industries in the U.S. and the companies within these industries ranging from athletic products to truck trailers.

Office of Industries
U.S. International Trade Commission
500 E Street SW, Room 504
Washington, DC 20436   202-205-3296

Experts analyze impact of world trade on U.S. industries ranging from audio components to x-ray apparatus.

* Business Advice

Roadmap Program
U.S. Department of Commerce
14th & Constitution Avenue NW
Washington, DC 20230   202-482-3176

Roadmap Program provides reference services on all aspects of commerce and business.

Library
U.S. Department of Commerce
14th & Constitution Avenue NW
Washington, DC 20230   202-482-5511

This library also provides reference services on all aspects of business.

* Country Experts

Country Officers
U.S. Department of State
2201 C Street NW
Washington, DC 20520   202-647-4000

Hundreds of experts are available to provide current political, economic, and other background information on the country they study. Call to ask for number of specific country officer.

U.S. Department of Commerce
International Trade Administration
Washington, D.C. 20230   202-482-2000

Teams of experts from these regions can provide information on marketing and business practices for every country in the world.

Agricultural and Trade Analysis Division
Economics Research Service
U.S. Department of Agriculture
14th and Independence Ave.
Washington, DC 20005-4788   202-720-8732

This office provides information on agricultural-related aspects of foreign countries.

Foreign Agricultural Services
Information Division
U.S. Department of Agriculture
14th and Independence Avenue, SW
Washington, DC 20250   202-720-9461

FAS provides data on world crops, agricultural policies, and markets.

Division of International Minerals
Bureau of Mines
U.S. Department of Interior
810 7th Street, NW, MS 5205
Washington, DC 20241   202-501-9666

Foreign country experts monitor all aspects of foreign mineral industries.

* Crime

National Criminal Justice Reference Service
National Institute of Justice
Box 6000
Rockville, MD 20850   301-251-5500

Database and reference service provide bibliographies and expertise free or sometimes for a nominal fee.

Uniform Crime Reporting Section
FBI
U.S. Department of Justice
409 7th St., NW
Washington, DC 20535   202-324-3000

Statistics are available on eight major crimes against person and property.

* Demographics, Economic and Industry Statistics

Data Users Service Division
Bureau of the Census
Customer Service
Washington, DC 20233   301-763-4100

Staff will guide you to the billions of dollars worth of taxpayer supported data.

* Economics: National, Regional and International

Bureau of Economic Analysis
U.S. Department of Commerce
Washington, DC 20230   202-523-0777

This is the first place to call for economic data.

* Education

Office of Educational Research and Improvement
U.S. Department of Education
555 New Jersey Ave., NW
Washington, DC 20208-1235   202-708-5366

A network of 16 information clearinghouses that identify literature, experts, audiovisuals, funding, etc.

Educational Information Branch
Department of Education/OERI
555 New Jersey Avenue, NW
Washington, DC 20208   1-800-424-1616

Hotline provides referrals to other information sources on any aspect of education.

* Energy

National Energy Information Center
U.S. Department of Energy
1F048 Forrestal Building
1000 Independence Ave., SW
Washington, DC 20585   202-586-8800

This office provides general reference services on Department of Energy data.

Conservation and Renewable Energy Inquiry and Referral Service
PO Box 8900
Silver Spring, MD 20907   1-800-523-2929

Free help on how to save energy as well as information on solar, wind, or any other aspect of renewable energy.

U.S. Department of Energy
Office of Scientific and Technical Information
PO Box 62
Oak Ridge, TN 37831   615-576-1301

This office provides research and other information services on all energy related topics.

* Health

ONHIC
National Health Information Center
PO Box 1133   1-800-336-4797
Washington, DC 20013-1133   301-565-4167 in MD

For leads to both public and private sector health organizations, research centers and universities.

National Center for Health Statistics
U.S. Department of Health and Human Services
6525 Belcrest Rd., Room 1064
Presidential Building
Hyattsville, MD 20782   301-436-8500

This clearinghouse can provide data on any aspect of health.

* Housing

Library and Information Services Center
U.S. Department of Housing and Urban Development
451 7th Street SW
Washington, DC 20410   202-708-2370

This library provides information on all aspects of housing and staff will direct you to a program which meets your needs.

* Import and Export Statistics

Foreign Trade Reference Room
U.S. Department of Commerce
14th and Constitution Ave., NW

Washington, DC 20230   202-482-2185

This library can provide data on many aspects of U.S. trade.

* Metals and Minerals

Division of Mineral Commodities (Domestic)
Bureau of Mines
U.S. Department of the Interior
810 7th Street, NW
Washington, DC 20241   202-501-9450

Dozens of commodity specialists collect, analyze, and disseminate information on the adequacy and availability of the mineral base for the national economy.

* Prices, Employment, Productivity And Living Conditions Statistics

U.S. Department of Labor
Bureau of Labor Statistics
Washington, DC 20212   202-606-7828

There are subject specialists in such areas as plant closings, labor force projections, producer price indexes, work stoppages.

* World Import and Export Statistics

World Trade Statistics
U.S. Department of Commerce
Room 2233, Herbert Hoover Building
14th and Constitution Ave.
Washington, DC 20230   202-482-5242

This is place for numbers concerning most country's trade.

General Sources

These three offices are the places to get help in locating experts in government as well as the private sector and trade associations.

* Associations

Information Central
American Society of Association Executives
1575 Eye Street NW
Washington, DC 20005   202-626-2723

If you cannot find a relevant association after referring to *Gale's Encyclopedia of Associations* (which is available in most libraries) this organization will help find the right one.

* Government Experts

Federal Information Center
P.O. Box 600
Cumberland, MD 21501-0600   301-722-9000

Centers are located throughout the country and the staff will find you an expert in the government on most any topic.

* Technical Research

Science and Technology Division
Reference Section, Library of Congress
1st and Independence, SE
Washington, DC 20540   202-707-5639

This reference section offers both free and fee-based reference and bibliographic services.

State Starting Places For Finding Experts

If you have trouble locating the exact office you need from the listings elsewhere in the book, this is the section for you. The first place you should start is with State Information Offices listed below. The operators at these offices are normally trained to handle information requests from people who don't know where to go within the state bureaucracy. If you are not successful, try either or both of the other offices listed.

Governor's Office

Because the responsibilities of various state offices often overlap, it may be helpful to begin your data search by contacting the state governor's office. While every state has a central switchboard to field inquiries regarding state business, the number is usually helpful only if you already know which agency is responsible for gathering and interpreting the information you are after. If you are hazy in this regard, the state governor's office will certainly know the appropriate agency department and, if you are lucky, even the name of the special contact person to call.

State Library

A vast amount of research information is available from the state library. After all, it is the official repository of state agency documents and the first place to start if you want to do all of the footwork yourself. In addition, most state libraries also shelve copies of federal government documents and publications.

State libraries are paid for with tax dollars and are open to the public. Collections usually include state legal codes, state historical documents, archival records, genealogy type information, business and economic records, statistical abstracts and annual reports.

In each library these is generally a government information person who can provide telephone and personal assistance to researchers. In addition, there is often a staff specialist to help with statistical questions.

The following is a list of state operators, librarians, and governor's offices.

State Information and Governor's Offices

Alabama
State Information: 205-242-8000

Governor's Office: Office of the Governor, Statehouse, 11 South Union St., Montgomery, AL 36130; 205-242-7100.

State Library: Alabama Public Library Service, 6030 Monticello Drive, Montgomery, AL 36130; 205-277-7330.

Alaska
State Information: 907-465-2111

Governor's Office: Office of the Governor, P.O. Box 110001, Juneau, AK 99811; 907-465-3500.

State Library: Libraries and Museums, P.O. Box 110571, Juneau, AK 99811-0571; 907-465-2920.

Arizona
State Information: 602-542-4900

Governor's Office: Office of Office of the Governor, 1700 West Washington St., Phoenix, AZ 85007; 602-542-4331.

State Library: Department of Library Archives and Public Records, State Capitol, Room 442, 1700 W. Washington, St., Phoenix, AZ 85007; 602-542-4159.

Arkansas
State Information: 501-682-3000

Governor's Office: Office of the Governor, State Capitol Building, Room 250, Little Rock, AR 72201; 501-682-2345.

State Library: Arkansas State Library, 1 Capitol Mall, Little Rock, AR 72201; 501-682-1527.

California
State Information: 916-322-9900

Governor's Office: Office of the Governor, State Capitol, Sacramento, CA 95814; 916-445-2841.

State Library: California State Library, Library and Courts Building, Sacramento, CA 95814; 916-654-0261.

Colorado
State Information: 303-866-5000

Governor's Office: Office of the Governor, 136 State Capitol Building, Denver, CO 80203-1792; 303-866-2471.

State Library: Colorado State Library, 201 East Colfax Ave., Denver, CO 80203; 303-866-4799.

Connecticut
State Information: 203-240-0222

Governor's Office: Office of the Governor, Executive Chambers, Room 202, Hartford, CT 06106; 203-566-4840.

State Library: Connecticut State Library, 231 Capitol Ave., Hartford, CT 06115; 203-566-3056.

Delaware
State Information: 302-739-4000

Governor's Office: Office of the Governor, Tatnall Bldg., William Penn Street, Dover, DE 19901; 302-739-4101.

State Library: Delaware State Library, 43 South DuPont Highway, Dover, DE 19901; 302-739-4748.

District of Columbia
Information: 202-727-1000

Mayor's Office: Executive Office of the Mayor, 441 4th NW, Room 1100, 1 Judiciary Square, Washington, DC 20001; 202-727-2980.

Central Library: Martin Luther King, Jr. Memorial Library, 901 G St. NW, Washington, DC 20001; 202-727-1101.

Florida
State Information: 904-488-1234

Governor's Office: Office of the Governor, The Capitol, Tallahassee, FL 32399-0001; 904-488-4441.

State Library: Florida State Library, R.A. Gray Building, 500 Bruno St., Tallahassee, FL 32399; 904-487-2651.

Georgia
State Information: 404-656-2000

Governor's Office: Office of the Governor, 203 State Capitol, Atlanta, GA 30334; 404-656-1776.

State Library: Georgia State Library, 156 Trinity Ave, Atlanta, GA 30303; 404-656-2462.

Hawaii
State Information: 808-548-6222

Governor's Office: Office of the Governor, State Capitol, Honolulu, HI 96813; 808-548-5420.

State Library: Hawaii State Library, 478 South King St., Honolulu, HI 96813; 808-548-4775.

Idaho
State Information: 208-334-2411

Governor's Office: Office of the Governor, State House, Boise, ID 83720; 208-334-2100.

State Library: Idaho State Library, 325 West State St., Boise, ID 83720; 208-334-5124.

Illinois
State Information: 217-782-2000

Governor's Office: Office of the Governor, State Capitol, Springfield, IL 62706; 217-782-6830.

State Library: Illinois State Library, 300 S. 2nd Street, Springfield, IL 62701; 217-782-7848.

Indiana
State Information: 317-232-1000

Governor's Office: Office of the Governor, State House, 100 N. Capitol Ave. Indianapolis, IN 46204; 317-232-4567.

State Library: Indiana State Library, 140 North Senate, Indianapolis, IN 46204; 317-232-3675.

Iowa
State Information: 515-281-5011

Governor's Office: Office of the Governor, State Capitol, Des Moines, IA 50319; 515-281-5211.

State Library: Iowa State Library, East 12th and Grand Streets, Des Moines, IA 50319; 515-281-4118.

Kansas
State Information: 913-296-0111

Governor's Office: Office of the Governor, State House, Topeka, KS 66612; 913-296-3232.

State Library: Kansas State Library, State House, Topeka, KS 66612; 913-296-3296.

Kentucky
State Information: 502-564-3130

Governor's Office: Office of the Governor, State Capitol Building, Frankfort, KY 40601; 502-564-2611.

State Library: Kentucky State Library, 700 Capitol Ave., #200, Frankfort, KY 40601-3489; 502-564-4848.

Louisiana
State Information: 504-342-6600
Governor's Office: Office of the Governor, P.O. Box 94004, Baton Rouge, LA 70804; 504-342-7015.

State Library: Louisiana State Library, P.O. Box 131, Baton Rouge, LA 70821; 504-342-4923.

Maine
State Information: 207-582-9500

Governor's Office: Office of the Governor, State House Station 1, Augusta, ME 04333; 207-287-3531.

State Library: Maine State Library, State House, Station 83, Augusta, ME 04333; 207-287-5600.

Maryland
State Information: 410-974-2000

Governor's Office: Office of the Governor, State House, Annapolis, MD 21404; 410-974-3901.

State Library: Maryland State Archives, Hall of Records, 350 Rowe Boulevard, Annapolis, MD 21404; 410-974-3914.

Massachusetts
State Information: 617-722-2000

Governor's Office: Office of the Governor, State House, Boston, MA 02133; 617-727-3600.

State Library: 341 State Street, Boston, MA 02133; 617-727-2590.

Michigan
State Information: 517-373-1837

Governor's Office: Office of the Governor, State Capitol Building, Lansing, MI 48913; 517-373-3400.

State Library: Michigan State Library, 717 W. Allegan, Lansing, MI 48909; 517-373-5400.

Minnesota
State Information: 612-296-6013

Governor's Office: Office of the Governor, 130 State Capitol, St. Paul, MN 55155; 612-296-3391.

State Library: Legislative Reference Library, State Office Building, St. Paul, MN 55155; 612-296-3398.

Mississippi
State Information: 601-359-1000

Governor's Office: Office of the Governor, P.O. Box 139, Jackson, MS 39205; 601-359-3150.

State Library: Department of Archives and History Library, P.O. Box 571, Jackson, MS 39205; 601-359-6850.

Missouri
State Information: 314-751-2000

Governor's Office: Office of the Governor, State Capitol, P.O. Box 720, Jefferson City, MO 65102-0720; 314-751-3222.

State Library: Missouri State Library, P.O. Box 387, Jefferson City, MO 65102-0387; 314-751-3615.

Montana
State Information: 406-444-2511

Governor's Office: Office of the Governor, State Capitol, Helena, MT 59620; 406-444-3111.

State Library: Montana State Library, 1515 East 6th Ave., Helena, MT 59620; 406-444-3115.

Nebraska
State Information: 402-471-2311

Governor's Office: Office of the Governor, State Capitol, P.O. Box 94848, Lincoln, NE 68509-4848; 402-471-2244.

State Library: Nebraska State Library, P.O. Box 98910, Lincoln, NE 68509-8910; 402-471-3189.

Nevada
State Information: 702-687-5000

Governor's Office: Office of the Governor, State Capitol Bldg., Carson City, NV 89710; 702-687-5670.

State Library: Nevada State Library, 100 Sewart St., Carson City, NV 89710; 702-687-5160.

New Hampshire
State Information: 603-271-1110

Governor's Office: Office of the Governor, State House, Concord, NH 03301; 603-271-2121.

State Library: New Hampshire State Library, 20 Park St., Concord, NH 03301; 603-271-2394.

New Jersey
State Information: 609-292-2121

Governor's Office: Office of the Governor, 125 West State St., State House, Trenton, NJ 08625; 609-292-6000.

State Library: New Jersey State Library, State House Annex, CN 520, Trenton, NJ; 609-292-6220.

New Mexico
State Information: 505-827-4011

Governor's Office: Office of the Governor, State Capitol Building, Santa Fe, NM 87503; 505-827-3000.

Governor's Office: State Library: New Mexico State Library, 325 Don Gaspar, Santa Fe, NM 87503; 505-827-3800.

New York
State Information: 518-474-2121

Governor's Office: Office of the Governor, State Capitol, Albany, NY 12224; 518-474-5355.

State Library: New York State Library, Empire State Plaza, Madison Avenue, Albany, NY 12230; 518-474-5355.

North Carolina
State Information: 919-733-1110

Governor's Office: Office of the Governor, State Capitol, Raleigh, NC 27603; 919-733-5811.

State Library: North Carolina State Library, 109 East Jones St., Raleigh, NC 27611; 919-733-2570.

North Dakota
State Information: 701-224-2000

Governor's Office: Office of the Governor, State Capitol, Bismarck, ND 58505; 701-224-2200.

State Library: North Dakota State Library, State Capitol, Bismarck, ND 58505; 701-224-2490.

Ohio
State Information: 614-466-2000

Governor's Office: Office of the Governor, State House, Columbus, OH 43215; 614-466-3555.

State Library: Ohio State Library, 65 South Front St., Columbus, OH 43266; 614-644-7061.

Oklahoma
State Information: 405-521-1601

Governor's Office: Office of the Governor, 212 State Capitol, Oklahoma City, OK 73105; 405-521-2342.

State Library: Oklahoma State Library, 200 N.E. 18th St., Oklahoma City, OK 73105; 405-521-2502.

Oregon
State Information: 503-378-3131

Governor's Office: Office of the Governor, 254 State Capitol, Salem, OR 97310; 503-378-3100.

State Library: Oregon State Library, State Library Building, Salem, OR 97310; 503-378-4274.

Pennsylvania
State Information: 717-787-2121

Governor's Office: Office of the Governor, 225 Main Capitol Bldg., Harrisburg, PA 17120; 717-787-5962.

State Library: Pennsylvania State Library, P.O. Box 1601, Harrisburg, PA 17105; 717-787-5718.

Rhode Island
State Information: 401-277-2000

Governor's Office: Office of the Governor, 222 State House, Providence, RI 02903; 401-277-2080.

State Library: Rhode Island State Library, Room 208, State House, Providence, RI 02903; 401-277-2473.

South Carolina
State Information: 803-734-1000

Governor's Office: Office of the Governor, P.O. Box 11369, Columbia, SC 29211; 803-734-9818.

State Library: South Carolina State Library, P.O. Box 11469, Columbia, SC 29225; 803-734-8666.

South Dakota
State Information: 605-773-3011

Governor's Office: Office of the Governor, State Capitol, Pierre, SD 57501; 605-773-3212.

State Library: South Dakota State Library, 500 E. Capitol, Pierre, SD 57501; 605-773-3131.

Tennessee
State Information: 615-741-3011

Governor's Office: Office of the Governor, State Capitol, Nashville, TN 37219; 615-741-2001.

State Library: Tennessee State Library, 403 7th Ave. North, Nashville, TN 37243; 615-741-2764.

Texas
State Information: 512-463-4630

Governor's Office: Office of the Governor, P.O. Box 12428, Austin, TX 78711; 512-463-2000.

State Library: Texas State Library, P.O. Box 12927, Austin, TX 78711; 512-463-5455.

Utah
State Information: 801-538-3000

Governor's Office: Office of the Governor, Room 210, State Capitol, Salt Lake City, UT 84114; 801-538-1000.

State Library: Utah State Library, 2150 South 300 West, Suite 16, Salt Lake City, UT 84115; 801-466-5888.

Vermont
State Information: 802-828-1110

Governor's Office: Office of the Governor, 109 State Street, Montpelier, VT 05609-0101; 802-828-3333.

State Library: Vermont State Library, 109 State Street, Montpelier, VT 05609-0601; 802-828-3261.

Virginia
State Information: 804-786-0000

Governor's Office: Office of the Governor, P.O. Box 1475, Richmond, VA 23212; 804-786-2211.

State Library: Virginia State Library, 11th St and Capitol Square, Richmond, VA 23219; 804-786-8929.

Washington
State Information: 206-753-5000

Governor's Office: Office of the Governor, Legislative Building, Olympia, WA 98504; 206-753-6780.

State Library: Washington State Library, Capitol Campus, Mail Stop AJ-11, Olympia, WA 98504; 206-753-5590.

West Virginia
State Information: 304-558-3456

Governor's Office: Office of the Governor, Main Capitol Complex, Charleston, WV 25305; 304-558-2000.

State Library: West Virginia State Library, Cultural Center, Charleston, WV 25305; 304-558-2041.

Wisconsin
State Information: 608-266-2211

Governor's Office: Office of the Governor, 115 E. Capitol, Madison, WI 53702; 608-266-1212.

State Library: State Historical Society, 816 State St., Madison, WI 53706; 608-264-6534.

Wyoming
State Information: 307-777-7011

Governor's Office: Office of the Governor, State Capitol, Cheyenne, WY 82002; 307-777-7434.

State Library: Wyoming State Library, Supreme Court Building, 23rd and Capitol, Cheyenne, WY 82002; 307-777-7283.

8,000 Free Experts

You may have heard of the "seven-phone call rule" for tracking down an expert who will help you for free. Well, now you can throw that phrase out the window. With this handy list of 8,000 government experts you are likely to find the right subject specialist in only ONE phone call.

Do you have a new idea to revolutionize the crayon market? Shetty Sundar at the U.S. International Trade Commission has spent her career analyzing this market. Want to know how many women-owned businesses there are in the United States? Contact Leonel Miranda at the Bureau of Census and she will give you the official data. You'll find 60 bureaucrats listed in this chapter who are experts in computers and the computer industry. You will also find experts on sewing machines, eggs, fish nets, and robots. Remember each of these professionals has devoted his or her life work to studying a specific area and will share their knowledge without charging a penny **just as long as you treat them right.** (Refer to the *Tips on Finding Information* chapter, specifically "The Art of Getting a Bureaucrat to Talk" and "Case Study: Jelly Beans", for guidance on how to deal with bureaucrats.)

The abbreviations for the federal agency which precede an expert's telephone number are spelled out below. If you have trouble with a telephone number, after all, numbers change all the time, simply contact the agency directly.

ACYF =	Administration for Children and Youth and Families, HHS, 901 D St., SW, Washington, DC 20447
ADAMHA =	Alcohol, Drug Abuse, and Mental Health Administration, HHS, 5600 Fishers Lane, Room 13C05, Rockville, MD 20857
AGRI =	National Agriculture Statistics Service, U.S. Department of Agriculture, 14th and Independence Avenue, SW, Washington, DC 20250
AHCPR =	Agency for Health Care Policy and Research, HHS, 2101 East Jefferson St., Ste. 501, Rockville, MD 20852
AOA =	Administration on Aging, HHS, 330 Independence Avenue, Washington, DC 20201
ASH =	Assistant Secretary for Health, HHS, 200 Independence Avenue, SW, Room 719-H, Hubert Humphrey Bldg., Washington, DC 20201
ATSDR =	Agency for Toxic Substances and Disease Registry, HHS, 1600 Clifton Rd., NE, Mail Stop 828, Atlanta, GA 30333
BEIB =	Biomedical Engineering and Instrumentation Branch, NIH, 9000 Rockville Pike, Bldg. 13, Bethesda, MD 20892
BHCDA =	Bureau of Health Care Delivery and Assistance, HHS, 5600 Fishers Lane, Room 7-05, Rockville, MD 20857
BJSCONTA =	U.S. Department of Justice, 10th and Constitution Avenue, NW, Washington, DC 20530
CC =	Clinical Center, NIH, 9000 Rockville Pike, Bldg. 10, Bethesda, MD 20892
CDC =	Centers for Disease Control, HHS, Room 2067, Bldg. 1, Atlanta, GA 30333
CENSUS =	Data Users Service Division, Customer Service, Bureau of Census, U.S. Department of Commerce, Washington, DC 20233
CNTYCOM =	Country Desk Officers, International Trade Administration, U.S. Department of Commerce, Washington, DC 20230
CNTYMINE =	Bureau of Mines, U.S. Department of Interior, 810 7th St., NW, Washington, DC 20241
CNTY STATE =	United States Department of State, 2201 C St., NW, Washington, DC 20520
COMMERCE =	Industry Experts, Public Affairs, International Trade Administration, U.S. Department of Commerce, Washington, DC 20230
CPSC =	Consumer Product Safety Commission, 5401 Westbard Avenue, N.W., Washington, DC 20816
CUSTOMS =	U.S Customs Service, Department of the Treasury, Customs Information Exchange, U.S. Customhouse, Code 20437, 6 World Trade Center, New York, NY 10048
DAS =	Division of Administrative Services, NIH, Building 1, 9000 Rockville Pike, Bethesda, MD 20892
DC =	District of Columbia
DCRT =	Division of Computer Research and Technology, NIH, 9000 Rockville Pike, Bethesda, MD 20892
DEO =	Division of Equal Opportunity, NIH, 9000 Rockville Pike, Bldg. 31, Bethesda, MD 20892
DMCH =	Division of Maternal and Child Health, HHS, 5600 Fishers Lane, Rockville, MD 20857
DN =	Division of Nursing, HHS, 5600 Fishers Lane, Rockville, MD 20857
DPCS =	Division of Primary Care Services, HHS, 5600 Fishers Lane, Rockville, MD 20857
DPM =	Division of Personnel Management, NIH, 9000 Rockville Pike, Bldg. 1, Bethesda, MD 20892
DRG =	Division of Research Resources, NIH, 9000 Rockville Pike, Bldg. 31, Bethesda, MD 20892
DRR =	Division of Research Resources, NIH, 9000 Rockville Pike, Bldg. 31, Bethesda, MD 20892
DRS =	Division of Research Services, NIH, 9000 Rockville Pike, Bldg. 12, Room 4007, Bethesda, MD 20892
ECONOMICS =	Bureau of Economic Analysis, U.S. Department of Commerce, Washington, DC 20230
EPA =	Environmental Protection Agency, 401 M St., Washington, DC 20460
FAES =	Foundation for Advanced Education in the Sciences, Inc., NIH, One Cloister Court, Building 60, Suite 230, Bethesda, MD 20814-1460
FCC =	Federal Communications Commission, 1919 M St., NW, Room 734, Washington, DC 20554-0001
FDA =	Food and Drug Administration, HHS, 5600 Fishers Lane, Room 1505 Parklawn Bldg., Rockville, MD 20857
FIC =	Fogarty International Center, NIH, 9000 Rockville Pike, Bldg. 38, Bethesda, MD 20892

FS =	Forest Service, U.S. Department of Agriculture, Auditors Building, 201 14th Street, S.W., Washington, DC 20250
FWS =	Fish and Wildlife Service, Department of the Interior, 1849 C Street, N.W., Washington, DC 20240
FTC =	Federal Trade Commission, 6th St. and Pennsylvania Avenue, NW, Washington, DC 20580
HCFA =	Health Care Financing Administration, HHS, 200 Independence Avenue, SW, Room 435-H, Hubert Humphrey Bldg., Washington, DC 20201
HHS =	Regional Directors, Health and Human Services, Room 638-E, Hubert Humphrey Bldg., 200 Independence Avenue, SW, Washington, DC 20201
HHSREG =	Regional Directors, Health and Human Services, Room 638-E, Hubert Humphrey Bldg., 200 Independence Avenue, SW, Washington, DC 20201
HRSA =	Health Resources and Services Administration, HHS, 5600 Fisher Lane, Room 1443, Parklawn Bldg., Rockville, MD 20857
IHS =	Indian Health Service, HHS, Room 6-35, Parklawn Bldg., Rockville, MD 20857
IG =	Inspector General, Office of, HHS, 330 Independence Avenue, SW, Room 5259, HHS Cohen Bldg., Washington, DC 20201
LABOR =	Bureau of Labor Statistics, U.S. Department of Labor, 2 Massachusetts Avenue, NE, Washington, DC 20212
MAPB =	Medical Arts and Photography Branch, 9000 Rockville Pike, Bldg. 10, Bethesda, MD 20892
MD =	Maryland
MINES =	Division of Mineral Commodities, U.S. Department of Interior, 810 7th St., NW, Washington, DC 20241
NASA =	National Aeronautics and Space Administration, Washington, DC 20546
NCDB =	National Center for Drugs and Biolgics, NIH, 9000 Rockville Pike, Bldg. 29, Bethesda, MD 20892
NCHS =	National Center for Health Statistics, HHS, 6525 Bellcrest Rd., Hyattsville, MD 20782
NCI =	National Cancer Institute, NIH, 9000 Rockville Pike, Bldg. 31, Bethesda, MD 20892
NCNR =	National Center for Nursing Research, NIH, 9000 Rockville Pike, Bldg. 31, Bethesda, MD 20892
NEA =	National Endowment for the Arts, 1100 Pennsylvania Avenue, N.W., Washington DC 20506
NEH =	National Endowment for the Humanities, 1100 Pennsylvania Avenue, N.W., Washington, DC 20506
NEI =	National Eye Institute, NIH, 9000 Rockville Pike, Bldg. 31, Bethesda, MD 20892
NEIC =	National Energy Information Center, Energy Information Administration, U.S. Department of Energy, E1-231, Forrestal Building, Washington, DC 20585
NHLBI =	National Heart, Lung, and Blood Institute, NIH, 9000 Rockville Pike, Bldg. 31, Bethesda, MD 20892
NIA =	National Institute on Aging, NIH, 9000 Rockville Pike, Bldg. 31, Bethesda, MD 20892
NIAID =	National Institute of Allergy and Infectious Diseases, NIH, 9000 Rockville Pike, Bldg. 31, Bethesda, MD 20892
NIAMS =	National Institute of Arthritis and Musculoskeletal and Skin Diseases, 9000 Rockville Pike, Bldg. 31, Bethesda, MD 20892
NICHD =	National Institute of Child Health and Human Development, NIH, 9000 Rockville Pike, Bldg. 31, Bethesda, MD 20892
NIDA =	National Institute on Drug Abuse, HHS, 5600 Fishers Lane, Rockville, MD 20857
NIDDK =	National Institute of Diabetes and Digestive and Kidney Diseases, NIH, 9000 Rockville Pike, Bldg. 31, Bethesda, MD 20892
NIDR =	National Institute of Dental Research, NIH, 9000 Rockville Pike, Bldg. 31, Bethesda, MD 20892
NIEHS =	National Institute of Environmental Health Sciences, NIH, Research Triangle Park, NC 27709
NIGMS =	National Institute of General Medical Sciences, NIH, 5333 Westbard Avenue, Room 926, Bethesda, MD 20892
NIH =	National Institutes for Health, 9000 Rockville Pike, Bldg 1, Room 126, Bethesda, MD 20892
NIMH =	National Institute of Mental Health, NIH, 5600 Fishers Lane, Rockville, MD 20857
NINDS =	National Institute of Neurological Disorders and Stroke, 9000 Rockville Pike, Bldg. 31, Bethesda, MD 20892
NLM =	National Library of Medicine, 8600 Rockville Pike, Bethesda, MD 20894
OB =	Office of Biologics, NIH, 9000 Rockville Pike, Bldg. 29, Bethesda, MD 20892
OCA =	Office of Consumer Affairs, HHS, 1620 L St., NW, Ste. 700, Washington, DC 20036
OC =	Office of Communications, NIH, 9000 Rockville Pike, Bldg. 1, Bethesda, MD 20892
OCR =	Office for Civil Rights, HHS, 300 Independence Avenue, SW, Room 5044, HHS Cohen Bldg., Washington, DC 20201
OD =	Office of the Director, NIH, 9000 Rockville Pike, Bldg. 1, Bethesda, MD 20892
OERT =	Office of Extramural Research and Training, NIH, P.O. Box 12233, Research Triangle Park, NC 27709
OHDS =	Office of Human Development Services, HHS, 200 Independence Avenue, SW, Washington DC 20201
OPRR =	Office for Protection from Research Risks, NIH, 9000 Rockville Pike, Bldg. 31, Bethesda, MD 20892
ORS =	Office of Research Services, NIH, 9000 Rockville Pike, Bldg. 1, Bethesda, MD 20892
PEC =	Peace Corps, 1990 K St., NW, Washington, DC 20526
PHS =	Public Health Service, HHS, Office of Communication, 200 Independence Avenue, SW, Washington, DC 20201
SSA =	Social Security Administration, HHS, 6401 Security Blvd., Room 932, Altmeyer Bldg., Baltimore, MD 21235
SSAREG =	Public Information Contacts, Social Security Administration, HHS, 6401 Security Blvd., Room 932, Altmeyer Bldg., Baltimore, MD 21235
TRADREP =	Office of the U.S. Trade Representative, 600 17th St., NW, Washington, DC 20506
USITC =	Office of Industries, U.S. International Trade Commission, 500 E. St., SW, Washington, DC 20436
UMD =	University of Maryland, University of Maryland-College Park, College Park, MD 20742
UVA =	University of Virginia, Office of Television News, Booker House, PO Box 9018, Charlottesville, VA 22906-9018
VA =	Virginia
VIC =	Visitor Information Center, NIH, 9000 Rockville Pike, Bldg.10, Bethesda, MD 20892
VRP =	Veterinary Resources Program, NIH, 9000 Rockville Pike, Bldg. 14, Bethesda, MD 20892

Experts

A

ABS resins....Misurelli, Denby USITC 202-205-3362
ABS resins....Taylor, Ed USITC 202-205-3362
ACTH, Excessive Secretion....Staff NHLBI 301-496-4236
AG Indexes with options....Fichert, David CFT 312-353-3181
AIDS....Staff PHS Hotline 800-342-2437
AIDS....Staff NIAID 301-496-5717
AIDS....Staff NCI 301-496-5583
AIDS (Acquired Immune Deficiency Syndrome)....Kytle, Rayford PHS 202-690-6867
AIDS - PHS....Staff PHS 800-843-9388
AIDS Dementia....Staff NINDS 301-496-5751
AIDS, Neurological Symptoms or Effects of....Staff NINDS 301-496-5751
AIDS, Neurological Symptoms or Effects of....Staff NIDCD 301-496-7243
AIDS, Pediatric....Staff NICHD 301-496-5133
AIDS, Research Facilities....Staff NCRR 301-496-5545
AIDS/HIV....Jaffe, Harold W. CDC 404-639-2000
AM Intercity Relays--FCC....Staff FCC 202-634-6307
AM Radio Advertising....Staff FCC 202-632-7551
AM Radio Assignment & Transfer Applications....Staff FCC 202-254-9470
AM Radio Construction Permit Applications....Staff FCC 202-254-9570
AM Radio--Radio Programming....Staff FCC 202-632-7048
AM Radio Station--New....Staff FCC 202-254-9570
AM Radio Stations....Staff FCC 202-632-7010
AM Remote Pickups....Staff FCC 202-634-6307
ARC (AIDS-Related Complex)....Staff NIAID 301-496-5717
ASEAN....Paine, George Cnty Commerce 202-482-3875
Abaca....Cook, Lee USITC 202-205-3471
Abetalipoproteinemia....Staff NHLBI 301-496-4236
Abortion (Research Relating to)....Staff NCHS 301-436-8500
Abortion (Research Relating to)....Staff CDC 404-639-3286
Abortion (Research Relating to)....Staff NICHD 301-496-5133
Abortion/Surveillance Data....Berreth, Don CDC 404-639-3286
Above Ground Storage Tanks....Staff EPA 202-260-1130
Abrasion (Corneal)....Staff NEI 301-496-5248
Abrasive....White, Linda USITC 202-205-3427
Abrasive Products....Presbury, Graylin COMMERCE 202-482-5158
Abrasives, Manmade....Austin, Gordon MINES 202-501-9388
Abrasives, Natural....Austin, Gordon MINES 202-501-9388
Absences from Work, Empl/Unempl Statistics....Staff LABOR 202-606-6378
Access Charge Rules and Policies....Staff FCC 202-632-9342
Access Charge Tariff....Staff FCC 202-632-6387
Accessories....Schiazzano, Patricia CUSTOMS 212-466-5881
Accident Prevention and the Elderly....Staff NIA 301-496-1752
Accident Statistics....Staff NCHS 301-496-8500
Accident Statistics....Staff CDC 404-329-3286
Accounting....Chittum, J. Marc COMMERCE 202-482-0345
Accounting and Related Issues....Lee, Ronald CENSUS 301-763-4270
Accreditation (Health Professions)....Staff HRSA/BHPr 301-443-3376
Accreditation (Nurse Training)....Staff HRSA/BHPr 301-443-5786
Acetal resins....Misurelli, Denby USITC 202-205-3362
Acetates....Michels, David USITC 202-205-3352
Acetic acid....Michels, David USITC 202-205-3352
Acetone....Michels, David USITC 202-205-3352
Acetoricinoleic acid ester....Johnson, Larry USITC 202-205-3351
Achondroplasia....Staff NICHD 301-496-5133
Achondroplasia....Staff NIAMS 301-496-8188
Acid Rain....Staff EPA 202-233-9150
Acid Rain....Swink, Denise NEIC 202-586-9680
Acid, oleic....Randall, Rob USITC 202-205-3366
Acid, stearic....Randall, Rob USITC 202-205-3366
Acidosis....Staff NICHD 301-496-5133
Acids, inorganic....Trainor, Cynthia USITC 202-205-3354
Acne....Staff NIAMS 301-496-8188
Acne (Cystic)....Staff NIAMS 301-496-8188
Acoustic Neuroma....Staff NINDS 301-496-5751
Acoustic Neuroma....Staff NIDCD 301-296-7243
Acquired Immune Deficiency Syndrome (AIDS)....Staff NIAID 301-496-5717
Acquired Immune Deficiency Syndrome (AIDS)....Staff NCI 301-496-5583

Acquired Immune Deficiency Syndrome (AIDS)....Staff PHS 800-342-2437
Acquisitions, Land....Staff FWS 202-358-2200
Acromegaly....Staff NIDDK 301-496-3583
Acrylates....Michels, David USITC 202-205-3352
Acrylic resins....Misurelli, Denby USITC 202-205-3362
Acrylonitrile....Michels, David USITC 202-205-3352
Actinide Chemistry....Marianelli, Robert NEIC 301-903-5804
Activated carbon....Randall, Bob USITC 202-205-3366
Acupuncture....Staff NINDS 301-496-5751
Acute Hemorrhagic Conjunctivitis....Staff NEI 301-496-5248
Acute Leukemia....Staff NCI 301-496-5583
Acyclic plasticizers....Johnson, Larry USITC 202-205-3351
Adding Machines....Baker, Scott USITC 202-205-3386
Addison's Disease....Staff NIDDK 301-496-3583
Addressing Machines....Taylor, Kayla USITC 202-205-3390
Addressing machines....Baker, Scott USITC 202-205-3386
Adenoma of the Thyroid....Staff NIDDK 301-496-3583
Adherence to Therapeutic Regimens....Staff NCNR 301-496-0526
Adhesives....Jonnard, Aimison USITC 202-205-3350
Adhesives/Sealants....Prat, Raimundo COMMERCE 202-482-0128
Adipic acid esters....Johnson, Larry USITC 202-205-3351
Adjudication....Langan, Patrick Justice Stat 202-616-3490
Adjudication....Gaskins, Carla Justice Stat 202-508-8850
Administration, Director, Office of....Carney, Kenneth G. NLM 301-496-6491
Administrative Law Judges....Cabell, Henry B. FTC 202-326-3642
Administrative Law Judges....Harriger, Patricia A. FTC 202-326-3626
Administrative Law Judges....Jones, Shirley J. FTC 202-326-3634
Administrative Law Judges....Parker, Lewis, F. FTC 202-326-3632
Administrative Law Judges....Timony, James P. FTC 202-326-3635
Admission (Health Professions Schools)....Staff BHPr 301-443-3376
Admission Procedures (Patient)....Staff CC 301-496-4891
Admissions (Patient)....Staff CC 301-496-3315
Adolescence....Staff NIMH 301-443-4515
Adolescence....Staff NICHD 301-496-5133
Adolescent Drug Use....Brown, Mona ADAMHA 301-443-6245
Adolescent Pregnancy....Staff NICHD 301-496-5133
Adoption....Long, Susan ACF 202-401-9215
Adrenal Gland....Staff NIDDK 301-496-3583
Adrenal Insufficiency....Staff NICHD 301-496-5133
Adrenoleukodystrophy....Staff NINDS 301-496-5751
Adult Education....Staff FAES 301-496-7976
Advanced Industrial Concepts....Gunn, Marvin NEIC 202-586-5377
Advanced Solid Rocket Motor....Staff NASA 205-544-7061
Advanced Space Transportation Systems....Staff NASA 814-864-6170
Advanced Studies....Staff FIC 301-496-2516
Advanced Training (Registered Nurse)....Staff BHPr 301-443-5786
Advertising....Chittum, J. Marc COMMERCE 202-482-0345
Advertising....Zanot, Eric J. UMD 301-405-2429
Advertising services....Sweet, Mary Elizabeth USITC 202-205-3455
Adynamia....Staff NINDS 301-496-5751
Aerial Cable....Staff FCC 202-634-1800
Aerodynamic Research....Staff NASA 804-864-3305
Aeroelasticity Research....Staff NASA 804-864-6120
Aeronautics....Andersen, Drucella NASA 202-453-8613
Aeronautics....Ellis, Linda NASA 216-433-2900
Aeronautics....Koehler, Keith NASA 804-824-1579
Aeronautics Research....Schauer, Catherine NASA 804-864-3314
Aerospace - Space Marketing Support....Vacant COMMERCE 202-482-1228
Aerospace - Space Programs....Pajor, Peter LABOR 202-482-2122
Aerospace Financing Issues....Bender, Juliet COMMERCE 202-482-4222
Aerospace Industry Analysis....Walsh, Hugh COMMERCE 202-482-4222
Aerospace Industry Data....Walsh, Hugh COMMERCE 202-482-4222
Aerospace Information and Analysis....Walsh, Hugh COMMERCE 202-482-4222
Aerospace Market Development....Vacant COMMERCE 202-482-1228
Aerospace Market Promo.....Vacant COMMERCE 202-482-1228
Aerospace Policy and Analysis....Bath, Sally H. COMMERCE 202-482-4222
Aerospace Technology....Ellis, Linda NASA 216-433-2900
Aerospace Trade Policy Issues....Bath, Sally COMMERCE 202-482-2124
Aerospace Trade Promo.....Vacant COMMERCE 202-482-1228

Aerospace- Marketing Support....Driscoll, George COMMERCE 202-482-1228
Afghanistan....Gilman, Timothy Cnty Commerce 202-482-2954
Afghanistan (Kabul)....Staff Cnty State 202-647-9552
Afghanistan/Minerals....Kuo, Chin Cnty Mines 202-501-9693
Africa/trade matters....Frechette, Myles US Trade Rep 202-395-6135
Agamaglobulinemia....Staff NIAID 301-496-5717
Agar agar....Jonnard, Aimison USITC 202-205-3350
Age Search (Access to Personal Census Records)....Staff CENSUS 301-763-7936
Age and Sex (U.S.)....Staff CENSUS 301-763-7950
Ageism....Staff NIA 301-496-1752
Agent Orange....Berreth, Don CDC 404-639-3286
Agglomerating machinery....Greene, William USITC 202-205-3405
Aging....Staff NIA 301-496-1752
Aging....Sprott, Richard L. FAES 301-496-4996
Aging (Mental Health)....Staff NIMH 301-443-4515
Aging, Administration on....McCarthy, Jack AOA 202-619-0556
Aging, National Institute on....Shure, Jane AOA 301-496-1752
Aging-Related Maculopathy....Staff NEI 301-496-5248
Agreements--Collective Bargaining/Public File....Cimini, Michael LABOR 202-606-6275
Agribusiness, Major Proj.....Bell, Richard COMMERCE 202-482-2460
Agricultural Affairs/trade matters....Early, Suzanne US Trade Rep 202-395-6127
Agricultural Chemicals....Maxey, Francis P. COMMERCE 202-482-0128
Agricultural Finances....Morehart, Mitch Agri 202-219-0801
Agricultural Finances....Hacklander, Duane Agri 202-219-0798
Agricultural Finances - Cash Receipts....Williams, Roberts Agri 202-219-0804
Agricultural Finances - Cash Receipts....Dixon, Connie Agri 202-219-0804
Agricultural Finances - Costs & Returns....Morehart, Mitch Agri 202-219-0801
Agricultural Finances - Costs & Returns....Dismukes, Robert Agri 202-219-0801
Agricultural Finances - Credit & Fin. Mrkts- World....Baxter, Tim Agri 202-219-0706
Agricultural Finances - Credit & Financial Markets....Stam, Jerry Agri 202-219-0892
Agricultural Finances - Credit & Financial Markets....Ryan, Jim Agri 202-219-0798
Agricultural Finances - Credit & Financial Markets....Sullivan, Pat Agri 202-219-0719
Agricultural Finances - Farm Household....Ahearn, Mary Agri 202-219-0807
Agricultural Finances - Farm Real Estate Taxes....DeBraal, Peter Agri 202-219-0425
Agricultural Finances - Farm, Annual....Strickland, Roger Agri 202-219-0804
Agricultural Finances - Future Markets....Heifner, Richard Agri 202-219-0868
Agricultural Finances - Futures Markets - Crops....Evans, Sam Agri 202-219-0841
Agricultural Finances - Futures Markets-Livestock....Jessee, W.B. Agri 202-219-0767
Agricultural Finances - Income - Farm Forecast....McElroy, Bob Agri 202-219-0800
Agricultural Finances - Prices, Parity & Indexes....Milton, Bob Agri 202-720-3570
Agricultural Finances - Prices, Parity & Indexes-Recev'd....Vanderberry, Herb Agri 202-720-5446
Agricultural Finances - Prices, Parity & Indexes - Paid....Kleweno, Doug Agri 202-720-4214
Agricultural Finances - Production Costs- Tob/Sweeteners....Clauson, Annette Agri 202-219-0890
Agricultural Finances - Production Costs....Kleweno, Doug Agri 202-720-4214
Agricultural Finances - Production Costs - Crops....Dismukes, Robert Agri 202-219-0801
Agricultural Finances - Production Costs - Dairy....Matthews, Ken Agri 202-219-0770
Agricultural Finances - Subsidies....Mabbs-Zeno, Carl Agri 202-219-0631
Agricultural Finances - Subsidies....Nelson, Fred Agri 202-219-0896
Agricultural Finances - Taxes....Durst, Ron Agri 202-219-0896
Agricultural Finances - Wages & Labor....Kurtz, Tom Agri 202-690-3228
Agricultural Finances - Wages & Labor....Duffield, James Agri 202-219-0033
Agricultural Finances - Wages & Labor....Oliveira, Victor Agri 202-219-0033
Agricultural Finances - Production Costs - Livestock....Shapouri, H. Agri 202-219-0770
Agricultural Finances - Production Costs - Sweeteners....Lord, Ronald Agri 202-219-0888
Agricultural Lands....Staff FWS 703-358-1713
Agricultural Machinery....Weining, Mary COMMERCE 202-482-4708
Agricultural machinery....Vacant USITC 202-205-3380
Agriculture - State - Delaware, Dover....Feurer, T.W. Agri 302-736-4811
Agriculture, Crop Statistics....Jahnke, Donald CENSUS 301-763-8567

Agriculture, Data Requirements and Outreach....Miller, Donald CENSUS 301-763-8561
Agriculture, Farm Economics....Liefer, James A. CENSUS 301-763-8566
Agriculture, General Information....Manning, Tom CENSUS 301-763-1113
Agriculture, Guam....Hoover, Kent CENSUS 301-763-8564
Agriculture, Livestock Statistics....Hutton, Linda CENSUS 301-763-8569
Agriculture, No. Marianas....Hoover, Kent CENSUS 301-763-8564
Agriculture, Puerto Rico....Hoover, Kent CENSUS 301-763-8564
Agriculture, State - Alabama, Montgomery....Kleweno, Dave Agri 205-223-7263
Agriculture, State - Alaska, Palmer....Brown, D.A. Agri 907-745-4272
Agriculture, State - Arizona, Phoenix....Bloyd, B. L. Agri 602-640-2573
Agriculture, State - Arkansas, Little Rock....Klugh, B.F. Agri 501-324-5145
Agriculture, State - California, Sacramento....Tippett, H.J. Agri 916-551-1533
Agriculture, State - Colorado, Lakewood....Hudson, C.A. Agri 303-236-2300
Agriculture, State - Florida, Orlando....Freie, R.L. Agri 407-648-6013
Agriculture, State - Georgia, Athens....Snipes, L.E. Agri 404-546-2236
Agriculture, State - Hawaii, Honolulu....Rowley, H.K. Agri 808-973-9588
Agriculture, State - Idaho, Boise....Gerhardt, D.G. Agri 208-334-1507
Agriculture, State - Illinois, Springfield....Clampet, J.L. Agri 217-492-4295
Agriculture, State - Indiana, West Lafayette....Gann, R.W. Agri 317-494-8371
Agriculture, State - Iowa, Des Moines....Skow, D.M. Agri 515-284-4340
Agriculture, State - Kansas, Topeka....Bryam, T.J. Agri 913-233-2230
Agriculture, State - Kentucky, Louisville....Williamson, D. D. Agri 502-582-5293
Agriculture, State - Louisiana, Baton Rouge....Frank, A.D. Agri 504-922-1362
Agriculture, State - Maryland, Annapolis....West, M.B. Agri 301-841-5740
Agriculture, State - Michigan, Lansing....Fedewa, D.J. Agri 517-377-1831
Agriculture, State - Minnesota, St. Paul....Rock, C.C. Agri 612-296-2230
Agriculture, State - Mississippi, Jackson....Knight, G.R. Agri 601-965-4575
Agriculture, State - Missouri, Columbia....Walsh, P.A. Agri 314-876-0950
Agriculture, State - Montana, Helena....Sands, J. Agri 406-449-5303
Agriculture, State - Nebraska, Lincoln....Aschwege, J.L. Agri 402-437-5541
Agriculture, State - Nevada, Reno....Lies, C. R. Agri 702-784-5584
Agriculture, State - New England - Concord, NH....Davis, A.R. Agri 603-224-9639
Agriculture, State - New Jersey, Trenton....Battaglia, R.J. Agri 609-292-6385
Agriculture, State - New Mexico, Las Cruces....Gore, C.E. Agri 505-522-6023
Agriculture, State - New York, Albany....Schooley, R.E. Agri 518-457-5570
Agriculture, State - North Carolina, Raleigh....Murphy, R.M. Agri 919-856-4394
Agriculture, State - North Dakota, Fargo....Wiyatt, S.D. Agri 701-239-5306
Agriculture, State - Ohio, Columbus....Ramey, J.E. Agri 614-469-5590
Agriculture, State - Oklahoma, Oklahoma City....Bellinghausen, R. P. Agri 405-525-9226
Agriculture, State - Oregon, Portland....Williamson, P. M. Agri 503-326-2131
Agriculture, State - Pennsylvania, Harrisburg....Evans, W.C. Agri 717-787-3904
Agriculture, State - South Carolina, Columbia....Power, H.J. Agri 803-765-5333
Agriculture, State - South Dakota, Sioux Falls....Ranek, J.C. Agri 605-330-4235
Agriculture, State - Tennessee, Nashville....Brantner, K. Agri 615-781-5300
Agriculture, State - Texas, Austin....Findlay, D. S. Agri 512-482-5581
Agriculture, State - Utah, Salt Lake City....Gneiting, D.J. Agri 801-524-5003
Agriculture, State - Virginia, Richmond....Bass, R. Agri 804-786-3500
Agriculture, State - Washington, Tumwater....Hasslen, D.A. Agri 206-586-8919
Agriculture, State - West Virginia, Charleston....Loos, Dave Agri 304-558-2217
Agriculture, State - Wisconsin, Madison....Pratt, L.H. Agri 608-264-5317
Agriculture, State - Wyoming, Cheyenne....Coulter, R.W. Agri 307-772-2181
Agriculture, Virgin Islands....Hoover, Kent CENSUS 301-763-8564
Agroforestry....Huke, Susan FS 202-205-1589
Aid to Families with Dependent Children (AFDC)....Long, Susan ACF 202-401-9215
Aids and IV drug abuse....Brown, Mona ADAMHA 301-443-6245
Air Compressors, Gas....McDonald, Edward COMMERCE 202-482-2107
Air Conditioners....Rocks, Michael CUSTOMS 212-466-5669
Air Conditioning Equipment....Vacant COMMERCE 202-482-3509
Air Enforcement Division....Staff EPA 202-26-=2820
Air Environmental Laws....Wallo, Andrew NEIC 202-586-4996
Air Gas Compressors, Trade Promo.....Heimowitz, Leonard COMMERCE 202-482-0558
Air Pollution....Staff EPA 301-382-7645
Air Pollution....Staff EPA 301-382-5575
Air Pollution Control Equipment....Jonkers, Loretta COMMERCE 202-482-0564
Air Pollution and Respiratory Health....Etzel, Ruth CDC 404-488-7320
Air Quality (Outdoor Cities)....Staff EPA 202-26-=5575
Air Quality Management Division....Staff EPA 202-541-5621
Air Quality Planning and Standards....Staff EPA 202-541-5616
Air Risc Hotline....Staff EPA 919-541-0888
Air Traffic Control Equipment (Market Support)....Driscoll, George COMMERCE 202-482-1228

Air Transportation Services....Lahey, Kathleen USITC 202-205-3409

Air and Energy Policy Division....Staff EPA 202-260-5490

Air and Radiation....Staff EPA 202-260-7400

Air conditioners....Mata, Ruben USITC 202-205-3403

Air transportation services....Lahey, Kathleen USITC 202-205-3409

Airborne Science and Applications....Staff NASA 415-604-3934

Aircraft....Dicerbo, Mario CUSTOMS 212-466-5672

Aircraft....Andersen, Peder USITC 202-205-3409

Aircraft & Aircraft Engines, Market Support....Driscoll, George COMMERCE 202-482-1228

Aircraft Auxiliary Equipment, Market Support....Driscoll, George COMMERCE 202-482-1228

Aircraft Engines, Trade Promo.....Vacant COMMERCE 202-482-1228

Aircraft Fuel Economy Research....Ellis, Linda NASA 216-433-2900

Aircraft Noise Abatement Research....Ellis, Linda NASA 216-433-2900

Aircraft Operating Problems Research....Koehler, Keith NASA 804-824-1579

Aircraft Parts, Market Support....Driscoll, George COMMERCE 202-482-1228

Aircraft Parts, Trade Promo/Aux Equipment....Vacant COMMERCE 202-482-1228

Aircraft Propulsion....Ellis, Linda NASA 216-433-2900

Aircraft Reliability Research....Peto, Mary Ann NASA 216-433-2902

Aircraft Testing....Staff NASA 804-864-3314

Aircraft and Aircraft Engines, Trade Promo.....Vacant COMMERCE 202-482-1228

Airlines....Johnson, C William COMMERCE 202-482-5012

Airport Equipment, Market Support....Driscoll, George COMMERCE 202-482-1228

Airport Equipment, Trade Promo.....Vacant COMMERCE 202-482-1228

Airports, Ports, Harbors, Major Projects....Piggot, Deborne COMMERCE 202-482-3352

Alarms, burglar and fire....Scott, Baker USITC 202-205-3386

Alaska Natural Gas Transportation System (ANGTS)....Bayer, Michael NEIC 202-586-4669

Albania....Fabrizo, Lynn Cnty Commerce 202-482-4915

Albania....Becker, Margaret Peace Corps 202-606-3547

Albania....Sowry, Jenny Peace Corps 202-606-3547

Albania....Staff Cnty State 202-647-3187

Albania\Minerals....Plachy, Josef Cnty Mines 202-501-9673

Albinism (Eyes)....Staff NEI 301-496-5248

Albright's Syndrome....Staff NIAMS 301-496-8188

Albright's Syndrome....Staff NICHD 301-496-5133

Albums (autograph, photograph)....Stahmer, Carsten USITC 202-205-3321

Alcohol....Staff ADAMHA 301-443-4883

Alcohol....Staff NCALI 301-468-2600

Alcohol (and Cancer)....Staff NCI 301-496-5583

Alcohol Abuse and Alcoholism, National Institute on....Miller, Diane ADAMHA 301-443-3860

Alcohol Fuels....Staff NEIC 202-586-9920

Alcohol Fuels....Russell, John NEIC 202-536-8053

Alcohol Fuels....Detchon, Reid NEIC 202-586-4220

Alcohol and Aging....Staff NIA 301-496-1752

Alcohol and Aging....Staff NCALI 301-468-2600

Alcohol and Aging....Staff ADAMHA 301-443-4883

Alcohol, Drug Abuse, & Mental Health Block Grants....Hurley, Joan ADAMHA 301-443-6549

Alcohol, oleyl....Randall, Rob USITC 202-205-3366

Alcoholic Beverages....Kenney, Cornelius COMMERCE 202-482-2428

Alcoholism....Staff ADAMHA 301-443-4883

Alcoholism....Staff NCALI 301-468-2600

Alcohols....Michels, David USITC 202-205-3352

Alcohols, polyhydric, fatty acids....Land, Eric USITC 202-205-3349

Aldehydes....DiMaria, Joseph CUSTOMS 212-466-4769

Aldehydes....Michels, David USITC 202-205-3352

Aldosteronism....Staff NHLBI 301-496-4236

Alexander's Syndrome....Staff NINDS 301-496-5751

Algeria....Johnson, Jeffrey/Clement, Claude/Cerone, Chris Cnty Commerce 202-482-1870

Algeria (Algiers)....Staff Cnty State 202-647-4680

Algeria/Minerals....Michalski, Bernadette Cnty Mines 202-501-9699

Alien Restricted Permits....Staff FCC 202-632-7240

Alkali metals....Connant, Kenneth USITC 202-205-3346

Alkaloids....Nesbitt, Elizabeth USITC 202-205-3355

Alkaptonuria....Staff NHLBI 301-496-4236

Alkylating Agents....Staff NCI 301-496-5583

Allergic Diseases....Kaliner, Michael A. FAES 301-496-9314

Allergies....Staff NIAID 301-496-5717

Allergies (Eyes)....Staff NEI 301-496-5248

Allergy & Infectious Diseases, National Inst. of....Randall, Patricia NIH 301-496-5717

Allied Health Professions....Staff HRSA/BHPr 301-443-3376

Almonds....Burket, Stephen USITC 202-205-3318

Alopecia....Staff NIAMS 301-496-8188

Alpaca....Shelton, Linda USITC 202-205-3457

Alpers Syndrome....Staff NINDS 301-496-5751

Alpha-1-antitrypsin Deficiency (liver)....Staff NIDDK 301-496-3583

Alpha-1-antitrypsin Deficiency (lung)....Staff NHLBI 301-496-4236

Alternate Fuels Statistics....Geidl, John NEIC 202-254-5570

Alternate energy....Foreso, Cynthia USITC 202-205-3348

Alternative Fuels....Allsup, Jerry NEIC 202-586-9118

Alternative Fuels Data Center....Eberhardt, James NEIC 202-586-9837

Alternative Motor Fuels....Bower, Marc NEIC 202-586-3891

Alum. Forgings, Electro....Cammarota, David COMMERCE 202-482-0575

Alum. Sheet, Plate/Foil....Cammarota, David COMMERCE 202-482-0575

Alumina....Conant, Kenneth USITC 202-205-3346

Aluminum....Plunkert, Patricia MINES 202-501-9419

Aluminum....McNay, Deborah USITC 202-205-3425

Aluminum Extrud. Alum Rolling....Cammarota, David COMMERCE 202-482-0575

Aluminum compounds....Greenblatt, Jack USITC 202-205-3353

Alveolar Bone (Regeneration/Resorption)....Staff NIDR 301-496-4261

Alveolar Microlithiasis....Staff NHLBI 301-496-4236

Alveolar Proteinosis....Staff NHLBI 301-496-4236

Alzheimer's Disease....Staff NIA 301-496-1752

Alzheimer's Disease....Staff NINDS 301-496-5751

Alzheimer's Disease....Staff NIMH 301-443-4515

Alzheimer's Disease....Staff NIDCD 301-496-7243

Alzheimer's Disease....Baldwin, Elaine ADAMHA 301-443-4536

Amateur Licenses....Staff FCC 717-337-1212

Amaurotic Idiocy....Staff NINDS 301-496-5751

Ambergris....Land, Eric USITC 202-205-3349

Ambiguous Genitalia....Staff NICHD 301-496-5133

Amblyopia....Staff NEI 301-496-5248

Ambulance & Rescue Squads....Staff FCC 717-337-1212

Ambulatory Patient Centers....Staff CC 301-496-3141

Amebiasis....Staff NIAID 301-496-5717

American Nurses' Association....Staff NIH 816-474-5720

American fisheries products....Corey, Roger USITC 202-205-3327

Amides....Michels, David USITC 202-205-3352

Amides, fatty acids of (surface-active agents)....Land, Eric USITC 202-205-3349

Amines....Michels, David USITC 202-205-3352

Amines, fatty acids of (surface-active agents)....Land, Eric USITC 202-205-3349

Amino Acid Disorders....Staff NICHD 301-496-5133

Amino acids....Michels, David USITC 202-205-3352

Ammonia....Trainor, Cynthia USITC 202-205-3354

Ammonium nitrate, fuel-sensitized....Johnson, Larry USITC 202-205-3351

Ammonium nitrate, non-explosive or non-fertilizer....Greenblatt, Jack USITC 202-205-3353

Ammonium phosphate....Greenblatt, Jack USITC 202-205-3353

Ammonium sulfate....Greenblatt, Jack USITC 202-205-3353

Ammunition....Robinson, Hazel USITC 202-205-3496

Ammonium nitrate, fertilizer....Trainor, Cynthia USITC 202-205-3354

Amplifiers....Sherman, Thomas USITC 202-205-3389

Amplifiers....Taylor, Kayla USITC 202-205-3390

Amyloid Polyneuropathy....Staff NINDS 301-496-5751

Amyloidosis....Staff NIDDK 301-496-3583

Amyloidosis....Staff NIAMS 301-496-8188

Amyloidosis....Staff NEI 301-496-5248

Amyotonia Congenita....Staff NINDS 301-496-5751

Amyotrophic Lateral Sclerosis....Staff NIDCD 301-496-7243

Amyotrophic Lateral Sclerosis....Staff NINDS 301-496-5751

Analgesic-Associated Nephropathy....Staff NIDDK 301-496-3583

Analgesics....Nesbitt, Elizabeth USITC 202-205-3355

Analysis and Data, Producer Price Indexes....Howell, Craig LABOR 202-606-7705

Analytical Chemistry....Staff NIGMS 301-496-7301

Analytical Instrument (Trade Promo)....Manzolino, Frank COMMERCE 202-482-2991

Analytical Instruments....Nealon, Marquarite COMMERCE 202-482-2991

Anaplasia....Staff NCI 301-496-5583

Andalusite....DeSapio, Vincent USITC 202-205-3435

Andorra....Staff Cnty State 202-647-1412

Anemia....Staff NIDDK 301-496-3583

Anemia (Hemolytic and Aplastic)....Staff NCI 301-496-5583

Anemia (Hemolytic and Aplastic)....Staff NHLBI 301-496-4236
Anencephaly....Staff NINDS 301-496-5751
Anesthesiology....Staff NIGMS 301-496-7301
Anesthesiology (Dental)....Staff NIDR 301-496-4261
Aneurysm....Staff NHLBI 301-496-4236
Aneurysm (Brain or Spinal)....Staff NINDS 301-496-5751
Angelman's Disease....Staff NINDS 301-496-5751
Angina Pectoris....Staff NHLBI 301-496-4236
Angioedema....Staff NIAID 301-496-5717
Angiography....Staff NHLBI 301-496-4236
Angioplasty....Staff NHLBI 301-496-4236
Angles, shapes, and sections (steel)....Vacant USITC 202-205-3419
Angola....Holm-Olsen, Finn Cnty Commerce 202-482-4228
Angola (Luanda)....Staff Cnty State 202-647-8252
Angola/Minerals....King, Audie L. Cnty Mines 202-501-9674
Angora....Shelton, Linda USITC 202-205-3467
Anguilla....Brooks, Michelle Cnty Commerce 202-482-2527
Aniline Dyes (and Cancer)....Staff NCI 301-496-5583
Animal (Caging, Housing, Watering)....Staff NCRR 301-496-5175
Animal Bedding....Staff OD/DL 301-496-1160
Animal Colonies and Models (Special)....Staff DRR 301-496-5175
Animal Feeds...Janis, William V. COMMERCE 202-482-2250
Animal Feeds....Conte, Ralph CUSTOMS 212-466-5759
Animal Food....Staff OD/DL 301-496-1160
Animal Genetics....Staff NCRR/VRP 301-496-5255
Animal Health....Staff NCRR/VRP 301-496-4463
Animal Husbandry....Staff NCRR/VRP 301-496-2527
Animal Models for Aging Research....Staff NIA 301-496-1752
Animal Nutrition....Staff NCRR/VRP 301-496-4481
Animal Research....Staff NCRR 301-496-5545
Animal Research....Staff OD/DC 301-496-8740
Animal Research (Intramural)....Staff NCRR 301-496-5795
Animal Research (Intramural)....Staff OD/DC 301-496-8740
Animal Resources Program....Staff NCRR 301-496-5175
Animal Sanitation....Staff OD/ORS 301-496-2960
Animal Welfare....Staff NCRR 301-496-5545
Animal Welfare....Staff OD/DC 301-496-8740
Animal Welfare Policy....Staff OPRR 301-496-7163
Animal feeds....Pierre-Benoist, John USITC 202-205-3320
Animal oil, fats, greases....Reeder, John USITC 202-205-3319
Animals: Guide for the Care and Use of Lab Animals....Staff NCRR 301-496-5545
Aniridia....Staff NEI 301-496-5248
Ankylosing Spondylitis....Staff NIAMS 301-496-8188
Anorexia Nervosa....Staff NICHD 301-496-5133
Anorexia Nervosa....Staff NIMH 301-496-4515
Anosmia....Staff NINDS 301-496-5751
Anosmia....Staff NIDCD 301-496-7243
Anoxia....Staff NHLBI 301-496-4236
Antarctica/Minerals....Doan, David Cnty Mines 202-501-9678
Antenatal Diagnosis....Staff NICHD 301-496-5133
Antenna....Kitzmiller, John USITC 202-205-3387
Antenna Structures & Towers....Staff FCC 202-634-7521
Anthracite....Foreso, Cynthia USITC 202-205-3348
Anthrax....Staff NIAID 301-496-5717
Anti-infective agents....Nesbitt, Elizabeth USITC 202-205-3355
Anti-inflammatory agents....Nesbitt, Elizabeth USITC 202-205-3355
Antialphatrypsin....Staff NIDDK 301-496-3583
Antibiotics....Staff NIAID 301-496-5717
Anticoagulant Drugs....Staff NHLBI 301-496-4236
Anticonvulsants....Nesbitt, Elizabeth USITC 202-205-3355
Antidiuretic Hormone....Staff NIDDK 301-496-3583
Antidiuretic Hormone....Staff NHLBI 301-496-4236
Antigua and Barbuda (St. John's)....Staff Cnty State 202-647-2621
Antigua/Barbuda....Brooks, Michelle Cnty Commerce 202-482-2527
Antigua/Minerals....Torres, Ivette Cnty Mines 202-501-9680
Antihistamines....Nesbitt, Elizabeth USITC 202-205-3355
Antimetabolites....Staff NCI 301-496-5583
Antimony....Llewellyn, Thomas MINES 202-501-9395
Antimony....Lundy, David USITC 202-205-3439
Antimony compounds....Greenblatt, Jack USITC 202-205-3353
Antipyretics....Nesbitt, Elizabeth USITC 202-205-3355
Antiques....Mushinske, Larry CUSTOMS 212-466-5739
Antiques....Spalding, Josephine USITC 202-205-3498
Antisocial Behavior....Staff NIMH 301-496-4515
Antiviral Substances....Staff NIAID 301-496-5717
Aorta....Staff NHLBI 301-496-4236

Aortic Insufficiency/Stenosis....Staff NHLBI 301-496-4236
Aortic Valve....Staff NHLBI 301-496-4236
Aortitis....Staff NHLBI 301-496-4236
Apes and Monkeys (Medical Research)....Staff NCRR 301-496-5545
Aphakia....Staff NEI 301-496-5248
Aphasia....Staff NINDS 301-496-5751
Aphasia (due to Stroke)....Staff NINDS 301-496-5751
Aphthous Stomatitis-Recurrent....Staff NIDR 301-496-4261
Aplastic Anemia....Staff NHLBI 301-496-4236
Apparatus, Filtering/Purifying....Rocks, Michael CUSTOMS 212-466-5669
Apparel....Dulka, William COMMERCE 202-482-4058
Apparel, Body Supporting....Burtnik, Brian CUSTOMS 212-466-5880
Apparel, Food and Raw Materials, Intl. Price Ind....Frumkin, Rob LABOR 202-606-7106
Apparel, Knit Wearing: Boys'....Ryan, Mary CUSTOMS 212-466-5877
Apparel, Knit Wearing: Men's....Ryan, Mary CUSTOMS 212-466-5877
Apparel, Leather....Schiazzano, Patricia CUSTOMS 212-466-5881
Apparel, Miscellaneous....DeGaetano, Angela CUSTOMS 212-466-5540
Apparel, Plastic Wearing....Schiazzano, Patricia CUSTOMS 212-466-5881
Apparel, Women's Woven Wearing....Crowley, Eileen CUSTOMS 212-466-5866
Apparel, Woven Wearing: Boys'....Shea, Gerard CUSTOMS 212-466-5878
Apparel, Woven Wearing: Men's....Shea, Gerard CUSTOMS 212-466-5878
Appliances, Small....Smyth, James CUSTOMS 212-466-2084
Appraisals, Land....Staff FWS 703-358-1713
Apraxia....Staff NINDS 301-496-5751
Aquaculture....Little, Robert Agri 202-720-6147
Aquaculture....Moore, Joel Agri 202-720-3244
Aquaculture....Harvey, Dave Agri 202-219-0890
Aquaculture....Staff FWS 703-358-1715
Aquatic Resource Education....Staff FWS 703-358-2156
Aquatic Species Management....Staff FWS 703-358-1710
Arachnoiditis....Staff NINDS 301-496-5751
Aran Duchenne Spinal Muscular Dystrophy....Staff NINDS 301-496-5751
Arch Glazing Petition....Giles, Ken CPSC 301-504-0580
Archaeology Research....Staff NEH 202-606-8210
Archeology....Staff FWS 703-358-2043
Architecture....Harris, William M. UVA 701-924-6450
Architecture Services....Stonitsch, Laura USITC 202-205-3408
Architecture, Urban Planning....Beatley, Timothy UVA 701-924-6459
Area Measurement....Hirschfeld, Don CENSUS 301-763-3827
Argentina....Mye, Randolph Cnty Commerce 202-482-1548
Argentina....Eschelman, Michael Peace Corps 202-606-3376
Argentina....Lustumbo, Julie Peace Corps 202-606-3575
Argentina (Buenos Aires)....Staff Cnty State 202-647-2401
Argentina/Minerals....Velasco, Pablo Cnty Mines 202-501-9677
Argon....Conant, Kenneth USITC 202-205-3346
Armenia....Staff Cnty State 202-647-8671
Arms....Robinson, Hazel USITC 202-205-3496
Arnold-Chiari Malformations....Staff NINDS 301-496-5751
Arrhythmias....Staff NHLBI 301-496-4236
Arsenic....Loebenstein, Roger MINES 202-501-9416
Arsenic....Conant, Kenneth USITC 202-205-3346
Arsenic compounds....Greenblatt, Jack USITC 202-205-3353
Art, works of....Spalding, Josephine USITC 202-205-3498
Arteriosclerosis....Staff NHLBI 301-496-4236
Arteriosclerosis (Cerebral)....Staff NINDS 301-496-5751
Arteriovenous Malformations (Cerebral & Spinal)....Staff NINDS 301-496-5751
Arteritis (eyes)....Staff NEI 301-496-5248
Arthritis....Staff NIAMS 301-496-8188
Arthritis....Staff NIA 301-496-1752
Arthritis & Musculoskeletal & Skin Dis., Nat'l Ins....Raab, Connie NIH 301-496-8118
Arthritis Information Clearinghouse....Staff NIAMS 301-495-4484
Arthrogryposis Multiplex Congenita....Staff NIAMS 301-496-8188
Arthrogryposis Multiplex Congenita....Staff NICHD 301-496-5133
Artificial Blood Vessels....Staff NHLBI 301-496-4236
Artificial Heart....Staff NHLBI 301-496-4236
Artificial Heart Valves....Staff NHLBI 301-496-4236
Artificial Insemination....Staff NICHD 301-496-5133
Artificial Intelligence....Staff NLM 301-496-9300
Artificial Intelligence....Kader, Victoria COMMERCE 202-482-0571
Artificial Intelligence Research....Staff NASA 713-483-5111
Artificial Joints....Staff NIAMS 301-496-8188
Artificial Lung....Staff NHLBI 301-496-4236
Artificial Skin....Staff NIGMS 301-496-7301
Artificial flowers....Spalding, Josephine USITC 202-205-3498
Artificial flowers of man-made fibers....Cook, Lee USITC 202-205-3471

Artificial mixtures of fatty substances....Randall, Rob USITC 202-205-3366

Aruba....Brooks, Michelle Cnty Commerce 202-482-2527

Aruba/Minerals....Torres, Ivette Cnty Mines 202-501-9680

Asbestos....Virta, Robert MINES 202-501-9384

Asbestos....White, Linda USITC 202-205-3427

Asbestos & the Workplace....Berreth, Don CDC 404-639-3286

Asbestos (and Cancer)....Staff NCI 301-496-5583

Asbestos Action Program (Technical Questions)....Staff EPA 202-260-3949

Asbestos Clearinghouse....Staff EPA 800-368-5838

Asbestos Ombudsman & Small Business Clearinghouse....Staff EPA 202-305-5938

Asbestos Ombudsman Clearinghouse/Hotline....Staff EPA 800-368-5888

Asbestos Publications....Staff EPA 202-554-1404

Asbestos/Cement Products....Pitcher, Charles COMMERCE 202-482-0132

Asbestosis....Staff NHLBI 301-496-4236

Asbestosis....Staff CDC/NIOSH 404-639-3286

Asia/trade matters....Lake, Charles US Trade Rep 202-395-3900

Asparagus....Nunis, Kelly USITC 202-205-3324

Aspartame, Neurological Effects of....Staff NINDS 301-496-5751

Asperger's Syndrome....Staff NINDS 301-496-5751

Aspergillosis....Staff NIAID 301-496-5717

Asphalt....White, Linda USITC 202-205-3427

Asphalt, Natural....Solomon, Cheryl C. MINES 202-501-9393

Asphyxia....Staff NINDS 301-496-5751

Aspirin Allergy....Staff NIAID 301-496-5717

Aspirin-Myocardial Infarction Study (AMIS)....Staff NHLBI 301-496-4236

Assembly Equipment....Abrahams, Edward COMMERCE 202-482-0312

Assist. Commissioner, Consumer Prices & Price Index....Armknecht, Paul LABOR 202-606-6952

Assistant Commis., Empl/Unempl. Stats, Curr. Empl. An....Bregger, John E. LABOR 202-606-6388

Assistant Commiss., Empl/Unempl. Stats, Fed/State....Ziegler, Martin LABOR 202-606-6500

Assistant Commissioner, Compensation Levels & Trnd....MacDonald, Kathleen M. LABOR 202-606-6302

Assistant Commissioner, Industry Prices & Pr. Index....Tibbetts, Thomas LABOR 202-606-7700

Assistant Commissioner, Intl. Price Indexes....Reut, Katrina LABOR 202-606-7100

Assistant Commissioner, Safety, Health & Work. Cond....Eisenberg, William M. LABOR 202-606-6304

Associate Commissioner, Compensation & Work. Cond.....Stelluto, George LABOR 202-606-6300

Associate Commissioner, Empl/Unempl Stats....Plewes, Thomas J. LABOR 202-606-6400

Associate Commissioner, Employment Projections....Kutscher, Ronald LABOR 202-606-5700

Associate Commissioner, Prices & Living Cond.....Dalton, Kenneth LABOR 202-606-6960

Associate Commissioner, Productivity & Technology.....Dean, Edwin R. LABOR 202-606-5600

Asthma....Staff NIAID 301-496-5717

Asthma....Staff NHLBI 301-496-4236

Astigmatism....Staff NEI 301-496-5248

Astronaut Training....Staff NASA 713-483-5111

Astronomy....Chevalier, Roger A. UVA 701-924-7494

Astronomy Research....Gundy, Cheryl NASA 301-338-4707

Astrophysical Research....Katz, Jessie NASA 301-286-5566

Asymmetric Septal Hypertrophy (ASH)....Staff NHLBI 301-496-4236

Ataxia....Staff NINDS 301-496-5751

Ataxia Telangiectasia....Staff NCI 301-496-5583

Ataxia Telangiectasia....Staff NINDS 301-496-5751

Atelectasis....Staff NHLBI 301-496-4236

Atherosclerosis....Staff NHLBI 301-496-4236

Atherosclerosis (Cerebral)....Staff NINDS 301-496-5751

Atherosclerosis (Effect on Vision)....Staff NEI 301-496-5248

Athetosis....Staff NINDS 301-496-5751

Athletic equipment....Robinson, Hazel USITC 202-205-3496

Atmospheric Science Research....Staff NASA 804-864-6122

Atmospheric and Indoor Air Programs....Staff EPA 202-233-9140

Atomic Vapor Laser Isotope Separation Plant....Forsythe, Larry NEIC 301-903-4610

Atopic Dermatitis....Staff NIAMS 301-496-8188

Atrial Fibrillation....Staff NHLBI 301-496-4236

Atrophy....Staff NINDS 301-496-5751

Attention Deficit Disorder....Staff NINDS 301-496-5751

Attention Deficit Disorder....Staff NICHD 301-496-5133

Attention Deficit Disorder....Staff NIMH 301-443-4515

Auctions....Staff FCC 202-633-5940

Audio Visual Services....Siegmund, John COMMERCE 202-482-4781

Audio components....Taylor, Kayla USITC 202-205-3390

Audiology (Clinical Center patients)....Staff CC 301-496-5368

Audiovisual Material (For Health Prof. Education)....Staff NLM 301-496-6095

Audiovisual Materials (Nursing)....Staff HRSA/BHPr 301-443-5786

Australia....Bouck, Gary (Bus.)/Golike, William (Policy) Cnty Commerce 202-482-3646

Australia....Lyday, Travis Cnty Mines 202-501-9695

Australia (Canberra)....Staff Cnty State 202-647-9691

Austria....Combs, Philip Cnty Commerce 202-482-2920

Austria (Vienna)....Staff Cnty State 202-647-1484

Austria/Minerals....Buck, Donald E. Cnty Mines 202-501-9670

Autism....Staff NINDS 301-496-5751

Autism....Staff NICHD 301-443-5133

Autism....Staff NIMH 301-443-4515

Auto Ind. Affairs Parts/Suppliers....Reck, Robert O. COMMERCE 202-482-1419

Auto Industry Affairs....Keitz, Stuart COMMERCE 202-482-0554

Auto Parts/Suppliers (Trade Promotions)....White, John C. COMMERCE 202-482-0671

Autoimmune Disease....Staff NIAID 301-496-5717

Autoimmune Disease....Staff NIAMS 301-496-8188

Automatic Teller Machine Theft....Kaplan, Carol Justice Stat 202-307-0759

Automation (Laboratory Apparatus and Processes)....Staff NCRR/BEIB 301-496-4426

Automobile - Catalytic Converters....Staff EPA 202-233-9090

Automobile - Imports....Staff EPA 202-233-9660

Automobile Emissions....Staff EPA 202-260-7647

Automobile Emissions- Recalls....Staff EPA 202-233-9260

Automobile Parts....Topolansky, Adam USITC 202-205-3394

Automobile Warranty Information....Staff EPA 202-233-9100

Automobiles....Desoucey, Robert CUSTOMS 212-466-5667

Automobiles....Hagey, Manuel USITC 202-205-3392

Autonomic drugs....Nesbitt, Elizabeth USITC 202-205-3355

Average Retail Food Prices--Monthly, CPI....Cook, William LABOR 202-606-6988

Average Retail Prices & Indexes of Fuels & Utls.....Adkins, Robert LABOR 202-606-6985

Average Retail Prices & Indexes, Motor Fuels Only....Chelena, Joseph LABOR 202-606-6982

Aversives....Giles, Ken CPSC 301-504-0580

Aviation Licenses....Staff FCC 717-337-1212

Aviation Rules & Hearings....Staff FCC 202-632-7175

Aviation Services (Rules)....Staff FCC 202-632-7175

Aviation and Helicopter Services....Johnson, William C. COMMERCE 202-482-5012

Avionics Marketing....Driscoll, George COMMERCE 202-482-1228

Avionics Testing....Deason, Billie A. NASA 713-483-5111

Azides....Johnson, Larry USITC 202-205-3351

B

B-19 Infection (Human Parvovirus)....Staff NICHD 301-496-5133

BCG (Bacillus Calmette-Guerin)....Staff NCI 301-496-5583

Baby Bottle Tooth Decay....Staff NIDR 301-496-4261

Baby Walkers....Tyrrell, Elaine CPSC 301-504-0580

Baby carriages, strollers, and parts....Seastrum, Carl USITC 202-205-3493

Baccalaureate Nursing Schools....Staff HRSA/BHPr 301-443-2134

Back Problems....Staff NINDS 301-496-5751

Back Problems....Staff NIAMS 301-496-8188

Bacterial Meningitis....Staff NIAID 301-496-5717

Bacterial Meningitis....Staff NIDCD 301-496-7243

Bacteriologic Media....Staff OD/ORS 301-496-6017

Bacteriology....Staff NIAID 301-496-5717

Bags....Gorman, Kevin CUSTOMS 212-466-5893

Bags or sacks....Cook, Lee USITC 202-205-3471

Bahamas....Soto, Rodrigo Cnty Commerce 202-482-2527

Bahamas (Nassau)....Staff Cnty State 202-647-2621

Bahamas/Minerals....Torres, Ivette Cnty Mines 202-501-9680

Bahrain....Clement, Claude Cnty Commerce 202-482-5545

Bahrain (Manama)....Staff Cnty State 202-647-6572

Bahrain/Minerals....Michalski, Bernadette Cnty Mines 202-501-9699

Bail (Federal)....Kaplan, Carol Justice Stat 202-307-0759

Bakery Products....Janis, William V. COMMERCE 202-482-2250

Balance of Payments, Chief....Bach, Christopher L., ECONOMIC 202-523-0620
Ball Bearings....Reise, Richard COMMERCE 202-482-3489
Balls, sports and play....Robinson, Hazel USITC 202-205-3496
Baltic States....Staff Cnty State 202-647-3187
Baltics....Taylor, Jeff Peace Corps 202-606-5519
Baltics Republic Desk....Green, Pam/Lewens, Susan Cnty Commerce 202-482-3952
Baltimore Longitudinal Study of Aging....Staff NIA 301-496-1752
Baltimore Longitudinal Study of Aging....Staff NIA 301-550-1766
Bamboo....Vacant USITC 202-205-3306
Bandages, impregnated w/ medicinals....Randall, Rob USITC 202-205-3366
Banding, Bird....Staff FWS 703-358-1714
Bangladesh....McQueen, Cheryl Cnty Commerce 202-482-2954
Bangladesh (Dhaka)....Staff Cnty State 202-647-9552
Bangladesh/Minerals....Vacant Cnty Mines 202-501-9694
Banking....Candilis, Wray O. COMMERCE 202-482-0339
Banking services....Brown, Richard USITC 202-205-3438
Banking services....Holoyda, Olha USITC 202-205-3436
Barbados....Brooks, Michelle Cnty Commerce 202-482-2527
Barbados....Staff Cnty State 202-647-2621
Barbados/Minerals....Torres, Ivette Cnty Mines 202-501-9680
Barbasco....Wanser, Stephen USITC 202-205-3363
Barbiturates....Nesbitt, Elizabeth USITC 202-205-3355
Barbuda/Minerals....Torres, Ivette Cnty Mines 202-501-9680
Barge Freight Index....Sepsey, Judy CFT 312-353-9025
Barite....Searls, James, P. MINES 202-501-9407
Barite....Johnson, Larry USITC 202-205-3351
Barium....Lundy, David USITC 202-205-3439
Barium carbonate....Johnson, Larry USITC 202-205-3351
Barium compounds....Greenblatt, Jack USITC 202-205-3353
Barium pigments....Johnson, Larry USITC 202-205-3351
Barium sulfate....Johnson, Larry USITC 202-205-3351
Barlow's Syndrome (Mitral Valve Prolapse)....Staff NHLBI 301-496-4236
Barrettes....Burns, Gail USITC 202-205-3501
Bars (steel)....Vacant USITC 202-205-3419
Bartter's Syndrome....Staff NHLBI 301-496-4236
Basal Cell....Staff NCI 301-496-5583
Basic Energy Sciences....Stull, Diane NEIC 301-903-5565
Basic Paper & Board Mfg....Smith, Len COMMERCE 202-482-0375
Basic Research....Staff NIGMS 301-496-7301
Basketwork, wickerwork, related products....Ruggles, Fred USITC 202-205-3325
Bathing caps....Jones, Jackie USITC 202-205-3466
Bathing caps....Hamey, Amy USITC 202-205-3465
Batten's Disease....Staff NINDS 301-496-5751
Battered Spouses....Staff NIMH 301-443-4515
Battered Spouses....Staff Hot-Line 301-654-1881
Batteries....Miller, Julius CUSTOMS 212-466-4680
Batteries....Eaton, Russell NEIC 202-586-0205
Batteries....Kolberg, Mary USITC 202-205-3401
Batteries, Storage....Larrabee, David COMMERCE 202-377-0575
Battery-Driven Vehicles....Alpaugh, Richard NEIC 202-586-1477
Bauxite....Sehnke, Errol D. MINES 202-501-9421
Bauxite (for metal)....McNay, Deborah USITC 202-205-3425
Bauxite calcined....White, Linda USITC 202-205-3427
Bauxite, Alumina, Prim Alum....Cammarota, David COMMERCE 202-482-0575
Bay rum or bay water....Land, Eric USITC 202-205-3349
Beads....Witherspoon, Ricardo USITC 202-205-3489
Beads, articles of....Witherspoon, Ricardo USITC 202-205-3489
Beans, ex oilseed....McCarty, Timothy USITC 202-205-3324
Bearings....Riedl, Karl CUSTOMS 212-466-5493
Bearings, ball and roller....Stonitsch, Laura USITC 202-205-3408
Bed Wetting....Staff NICHD 301-443-5133
Bedding....Hansen, John CUSTOMS 212-466-5854
Bedspreads....Sweet, Mary Elizabeth USITC 202-205-3455
Beef....Ludwick, David USITC 202-205-3329
Beer....Salin, Victoria USITC 202-205-3331
Behavioral and Social Sciences....Staff NICHD 301-496-6832
Behcet's Disease (Neurological Effects of)....Staff NINDS 301-496-5751
Behcet's Disease (Systemic)....Staff NIDR 301-496-4261
Behcet's Disease (Systemic)....Staff NIAMS 301-496-8188
Belarus....Staff Cnty State 202-647-6764
Belgium....Bensimon, Simon Cnty Commerce 202-482-5041
Belgium (Brussels)....Staff Cnty State 202-647-6071
Belgium/Minerals....Newman, Harold R. Cnty Mines 202-501-9669
Belize....Brooks, Michelle Cnty Commerce 202-482-2527
Belize....Brown, Brenda L. Peace Corps 202-606-3624
Belize (Belize City)....Staff Cnty State 202-647-4980

Belize/Minerals....Mobbs, Philip Cnty Mines 202-501-9679
Bell's Palsy....Staff NINDS 301-496-5751
Belting and Hose....Prat, Raimundo COMMERCE 202-482-0128
Belting of rubber or plastics (for machinery)....Johnson, Larry USITC 202-205-3351
Belting, industrial....Cook, Lee USITC 202-205-3471
Belts, apparel: Leather....Jones, Jackie USITC 202-205-3466
Belts, apparel: Other mens and boys....Linkins, Linda USITC 202-205-3469
Belts, apparel: Other womens and girls....Linkins, Linda USITC 202-205-3467
Bemiconductor Prod. Equipment & Materials....Finn, Erin COMMERCE 202-482-2795
Benign Congenital Hypotonia....Staff NINDS 301-496-5751
Benign Mucosal Pemphigoid....Staff NIAMS 301-496-8188
Benign Prostatic Hyperplasia....Staff NIDDK 301-496-3583
Benin....Henke, Debra Cnty Commerce 202-482-4228
Benin....Olson, Susan Peace Corps 202-606-3136
Benin....Sanchez, Patricia Peace Corps 202-606-3237
Benin (Cotonou)....Staff Cnty State 202-647-2865
Benin/Minerals....van Oss, Hendrik Cnty Mines 202-501-9687
Bensenoid intermediates, miscellaneous....Matusik, Ed USITC 202-205-3356
Bentonite....Lukes, James USITC 202-205-3426
Benzene....Raftery, Jim USITC 202-205-3365
Benzenoid paints....Johnson, Larry USITC 202-205-3351
Benzenoid plasticizers....Johnson, Larry USITC 202-205-3351
Benzenoid plastics....Misurelli, Denby USITC 202-205-3362
Benzenoid varnishes....Johnson, Larry USITC 202-205-3351
Benzo(a)pyrene....Staff NCI 301-496-5583
Benzoic acid....Matusik, Ed USITC 202-205-3356
Berger's Disease....Staff NIDDK 301-496-3583
Beriberi (Neurological)....Staff NINDS 301-496-5751
Beriberi (Nutritional)....Staff NIDDK 301-496-3583
Bermuda....Brooks, Michelle Cnty Commerce 202-482-2527
Bermuda (Hamilton)....Staff Cnty State 202-647-8027
Bermuda/Minerals....Torres, Ivette Cnty Mines 202-501-9680
Bernard-Soulier Syndrome....Staff NIDDK 301-496-3583
Beryllium....Duggan Brian COMMERCE 202-482-0575
Beryllium....Kramer, Deborah A. MINES 202-501-9394
Beryllium....Lundy, David USITC 202-205-3439
Beryllium compounds....Greenblatt, Jack USITC 202-205-3353
Beta-thalassemia (Cooley's Anemia)....Staff NHLBI 301-496-4236
Betatron....Staff NCI 301-496-5583
Beverages....Kenney, Cornelius COMMERCE 202-482-2428
Beverages, Alcoholic....Maria, John CUSTOMS 212-466-5730
Beverages, Alcoholic....Salin, Victoria USITC 202-205-3331
Beverages, Non-alcoholic....Dennis, Alfred USITC 202-205-3316
Bhutan....Gilman, Timothy Cnty Commerce 202-482-2954
Bhutan....Staff Cnty State 202-647-2141
Bhutan/Minerals....Vacant Cnty Mines 202-501-9694
Bicycles....Vanderwolf, John COMMERCE 202-482-0348
Bicycles....Tyrrell, Elaine CPSC 301-504-0580
Bicycles....Desoucey, Robert CUSTOMS 212-466-5667
Bicycles and parts....Seastrum, Carl USITC 202-205-3493
Bilateral Agreements....Staff FIC 301-496-5903
Biliary Cirrhosis....Staff NIDDK 301-496-3583
Bilirubinemia....Staff NICHD 301-496-5133
Billfolds....Seastrum, Carl USITC 202-205-3493
Billiard cloth....Cook, Lee USITC 202-205-3471
Binocular Vision....Staff NEI 301-496-5248
Binswanger's Disease....Staff NINDS 301-496-5751
Bio-related Chemistry....Staff NIGMS 301-496-7301
Biochemistry Instrumentation....Staff DRR 301-496-5545
Biodegradable Plastics....Staff EPA 202-260-5649
Bioethics....Bonkovsky, Frederick O. FAES 301-496-2429
Biofeedback....Staff NIMH 301-443-4515
Biofeedback....Staff NHLBI 301-496-4236
Biofuels....Morrer, Richard NEIC 202-586-8072
Biogasoline....Moorer, Richard NEIC 202-586-8072
Biohazard Control....Staff OD/ORS 301-496-2960
Biohazard Identification....Staff OD/ORS 301-496-2960
Biohazards (Cancer Research)....Staff NCI 301-496-5583
Biological Community Profiles....Staff FWS 703-358-1710
Biological Information Services....Goshorn, Jeanne C. NLM 301-496-1131
Biological Models & Materials Resources Program....Staff NCRR 301-402-0630
Biology....Block, Gene D. UVA 701-982-5255
Biomedical Communications....Staff NLM 301-496-6308
Biomedical Computer Centers....Staff NCRR 301-496-5411
Biomedical Engineering....Staff NIGMS 301-496-7301

Biomedical Engineering....Staff NCRR/BEIB 301-496-4741
Biomedical Information Services....Spann, Melvin L. NLM 301-496-1131
Biomedical Research Development Grant Programs....Staff NCRR 301-496-6743
Biomedical Research Support Program....Staff NCRR 301-496-5411
Biomedical Research Support Program....Staff DRR 301-496-6743
Biomedical Research Training and Fellowships....Staff NIGMS 301-496-7301
Biomedical Research Training and Fellowships....Staff DRG 301-496-7441
Bioorganic Chemistry....Kirk, Kenneth L. FAES 301-496-2619
Biophysics....Staff NIGMS 301-496-7301
Biopsy....Staff NCI 301-496-5583
Biotechnology....Arakaki, Emily COMMERCE 202-482-3888
Biotechnology Information....Staff NLM 301-496-4441
Biotechnology, Trade Promo.....Gwaltney, G. P. COMMERCE 202-482-3090
Bird meat....Newman, Douglas USITC 202-205-3328
Birth....Staff NICHD 301-496-5133
Birth Defects (Developmental)....Staff NICHD 301-496-5133
Birth Defects (Neurological)....Staff NINDS 301-496-5751
Birth Defects and Developmental Disabilities....Oakley, Godfrey P. CDC 404-488-7150
Birth Defects and Genetic Diseases....Erickson, David J. CDC 404-488-7160
Birth Place....Hansen, Kristin CENSUS 301-763-3850
Birth Weight....Staff NICHD 301-496-5133
Bismuth....Jasinski, Stephen MINES 202-501-9418
Bismuth....Lundy, David USITC 202-205-3439
Bismuth compounds....Greenblatt, Jack USITC 202-205-3353
Bituminous coal....Foreso, Cynthia USITC 202-205-3348
Black Holes....Staff NASA 205-544-0034
Black Lung Disease....Berreth, Don CDC 404-639-3286
Black Lung Disease....Gambino, Phil SSA 410-965-8904
Black powder....Johnson, Larry USITC 202-205-3351
Blankets....Sweet, Mary Elizabeth USITC 202-205-3455
Blasting caps....Johnson, Larry USITC 202-205-3351
Blastomycosis....Staff NIAID 301-496-5717
Bleaching machines....Greene, William USITC 202-205-3405
Blepharitis....Staff NEI 301-496-5248
Blepharospasm....Staff NINDS 301-496-5751
Blepharospasm....Staff NEI 301-496-5248
Blind (Rehabilitation and Research)....Staff NEI 301-496-5248
Bloch-Sulzberger Syndrome (Neurological Effects)....Staff NINDS 301-496-5751
Blood Brain Barrier....Staff NINDS 301-496-5751
Blood Cells....Staff NHLBI 301-496-4236
Blood Coagulation....Staff NHLBI 301-496-4236
Blood Diseases....Staff NHLBI 301-496-4236
Blood Donations....Staff CC 301-496-1048
Blood Fractions....Staff NHLBI 301-496-4236
Blood Groups....Staff NHLBI 301-496-4236
Blood Plasma....Staff FDA/NCDB/OB 301-496-4396
Blood Plasma....Staff NHLBI 301-496-4236
Blood Pressure....Staff NHLBI 301-496-4236
Blood Resources (National)....Staff NHLBI 301-496-4236
Blood Substitutes....Staff NHLBI 301-496-4236
Blood Vessels....Staff NHLBI 301-496-4236
Blouses....Holoyda, Olha USITC 202-205-3467
Blowers....Riedl, Karl CUSTOMS 212-466-5493
Blowers and Fans....Jonkers, Loretta COMMERCE 202-482-0564
Boat Building, Major Proj.....Piggot, Deborne COMMERCE 202-482-3352
Boats....Wholey, Patrick CUSTOMS 212-466-5668
Boats, Craft....Vanderwolf, John COMMERCE 202-482-0348
Boats, Pleasure....Vanderwolf, John COMMERCE 202-482-0348
Boats, Pleasure....Lahey, Kathleen USITC 202-205-3409
Body Weight....Staff NIDDK 301-496-3583
Body-supporting garments, includes corset/brassieres....Linkins, Linda USITC 202-205-3469
Boilers....Rocks, Michael CUSTOMS 212-466-5669
Boilers....Vacant USITC 202-205-3380
Bolivia....Lindow, Herbert Cnty Commerce 202-482-2521
Bolivia....Godbey, Maria Elena Peace Corps 202-606-3198
Bolivia....Erlandson, Barbara Peace Corps 202-606-3499
Bolivia (La Paz)....Staff Cnty State 202-647-3076
Bolivia/Minerals....Velasco, Pablo Cnty Mines 202-501-9677
Bolivian Hemorrhagic Fever....Staff NIAID 301-496-5717
Bolting cloth....Cook, Lee USITC 202-205-3471
Bolts....Brandon, James USITC 202-205-3433
Bone Disorders....Staff NIAMS 301-496-8188
Bone Marrow Failure....Staff NHLBI 301-496-4236
Bone Marrow Transplantation....Staff NCI 301-496-5583
Bone Marrow Transplantation....Staff NIAID 301-496-5717

Bone Marrow Transplantation....Staff NHLBI 301-496-4236
Bone black...Johnson, Larry USITC 202-205-3351
Bone char....Randall, Rob USITC 202-205-3366
Bone, articles of....Spalding, Josephine USITC 202-205-3498
Book Store (Clinical Center)....Staff FAES 301-496-5274
Bookbinding machinery....Slingerland, David USITC 202-205-3400
Books....Lofquist, William S. COMMERCE 202-482-0379
Books....Abramowitz, Carl CUSTOMS 212-466-5733
Books....Stahmer, Carsten USITC 202-205-3321
Books (Export Promo)....Kimmel, Edward COMMERCE 202-482-3640
Books-Information-NIH Library....Staff NCRR 301-496-2184
Books-Information-NIH Library....Staff NLM 301-496-6095
Borax....Greenblatt, Jack USITC 202-205-3353
Boric acid....Trainor, Cynthia USITC 202-205-3354
Boron....Lyday, Phyllis A. MINES 202-501-9405
Boron....Lundy, David USITC 202-205-3439
Boron compounds....Greenblatt, Jack USITC 202-205-3353
Botswana....Holm-Olsen, Finn Cnty Commerce 202-482-4228
Botswana....Grimmett, Michael Peace Corps 202-606-3246
Botswana....Woodfork, Jacqueline Peace Corps 202-606-3247
Botswana (Gaborone)....Staff Cnty State 202-647-8252
Botswana/Minerals....Antonides, Lloyd Cnty Mines 202-501-9686
Bottles, pails and dishes, of rubber of plastics....Raftery, Jim USITC 202-205-3365
Botulism....Staff NIAID 301-496-5717
Boundaries of Legal Areas, Boundary Changes....Goodman, Nancy CENSUS 301-763-3827
Boundaries of Legal Areas, State Boundary Certifica....Stewart, Louise CENSUS 301-763-3827
Bowel Diseases, Inflammatory....Staff NIDDK 301-496-3583
Bowen's Disease....Staff NCI 301-496-5583
Brachial Plexus Injuries....Staff NINDS 301-496-5751
Bradycardia....Staff NHLBI 301-496-4236
Braids, other....Shelton, Linda USITC 202-205-3457
Brain....Staff NINDS 301-496-5751
Brain Banks....Staff NINDS 301-496-5751
Brain Injury....Staff NINDS 301-496-5751
Brain Tumor....Staff NCI 301-496-5583
Brain Tumor....Staff NINDS 301-496-5751
Brain Tumor....Staff NIDCD 301-496-7243
Brass....Lundy, David USITC 202-205-3439
Brazil....Farris, Larry Cnty Commerce 202-482-3871
Brazil (Brasilia)....Staff Cnty State 202-647-8252
Brazil/Minerals....Gurmendi, Alfredo Cnty Mines 202-501-9681
Bread and other baked goods....Schneider, Greg USITC 202-205-3326
Breast Cancer....Staff NCI 301-496-5583
Breast Milk....Staff NICHD 301-496-5133
Breeder reactor....Greenblatt, Jack USITC 202-205-3353
Brick, ceramic....White, Linda USITC 202-205-3427
British Indian Ocean Territories (BIOT)....Staff Cnty State 202-647-8913
British Pound with options....Lang, Dawn M. CFT 312-35-39018
Broadcast Allocation....Staff FCC 202-634-6530
Broadcast Call Letters....Staff FCC 202-634-1923
Broadcast News....Barkin, Steve UMD 301-405-2412
Broadcast Station Inspections....Staff FCC 202-632-7014
Broadcasting services....R-Archila, Laura USITC 202-205-3411
Broiler with options....Fichert, David CFT 312-353-3181
Bromine....Lyday, Phyllis A. MINES 202-501-9405
Bromine....Conant, Kenneth USITC 202-205-3346
Bronchiectasis....Staff NHLBI 301-496-4236
Bronchitis (Chronic)....Staff NHLBI 301-496-4236
Brooms....Burns, Gail USITC 202-205-3501
Brucellosis....Staff NIAID 301-496-5717
Brunei....Cung, Raphael Cnty Commerce 202-482-3875
Brunei (Bandar Seri Begawan)....Staff Cnty State 202-647-3276
Brunei/Minerals....Vacant Cnty Mines 202-501-9694
Brushes....Brownchweig, Gilbert CUSTOMS 212-466-5744
Brushes....Burns, Gail USITC 202-205-3501
Bruxism....Staff NIDR 301-496-4261
Bubonic Plague....Staff NIAID 301-496-5717
Buckets....Kaplan, Kathy CPSC 301-504-0580
Buckles....Shildneck, Ann USITC 202-205-3499
Buerger's Disease (Thromboangiitis Obliterans)....Staff NHLBI 301-496-4236
Builders Hardware....Williams, Franklin COMMERCE 202-482-0132
Builders' Wares....Mazzola, Joan CUSTOMS 212-466-5880
Building Materials and Construction....Pitcher, Charles B. COMMERCE 202-482-0132

Building Materials, Trade Policy....Smith, Mary Ann COMMERCE 202-482-0132

Building boards....Ruggles, Fred USITC 202-205-3325

Building components (wood)....Ruggles, Fred USITC 202-205-3325

Buildings, Energy Efficient....Kapus, Theodore NEIC 202-586-9123

Bulbar Palsy....Staff NINDS 301-496-5751

Bulgaria....Sowry, Jenny Peace Corps 202-606-3547

Bulbs (lamps)....Cutchin, John USITC 202-205-3396

Bulgaria....Fabrizio, Lynn Cnty Commerce 202-482-4915

Bulgaria....Becker, Margaret Peace Corps 202-606-3547

Bulgaria (Sofia)....Staff Cnty State 202-647-3188

Bulgaria/Minerals....Plachy, Joseph Cnty Mines 202-501-9673

Bulimia....Staff NIMH 301-443-4513

Bulimia....Staff NICHD 301-496-5133

Bulletin Board....Staff CENSUS 301-763-1580

Bullous Pemphigoid....Staff NIAMS 301-496-8188

Bunker "C" fuel oil....Foreso, Cynthia USITC 202-205-3348

Bureau of Competition - Accounting....Broberg, Evelyn S. FTC 202-326-2569

Bureau of Competition - Accounting....Painter, David T. FTC 202-326-2574

Bureau of Competition - Accounting....Rowe, Ronald Baylor FTC 202-326-2610

Bureau of Competition - Accounting....Steffen, Boris J. FTC 202-326-2573

Bureau of Competition - Administration....Baumgartner, Phillip A. FTC 202-326-2546

Bureau of Competition - Administration....Foster, Patricia A. FTC 202-326-2852

Bureau of Competition - Administration....Kennedy, Chandra FTC 202-326-2547

Bureau of Competition - Administration....Kereszturi, Joyce A. FTC 202-326-2541

Bureau of Competition - Administration....McGraw, Jeanne M. FTC 202-326-2565

Bureau of Competition - Administration....Onley, Essie FTC 202-326-2544

Bureau of Competition - Administration....Salters, Willie FTC 202-326-2561

Bureau of Competition - Administration....Saltzman, Harold E. FTC 202-326-3459

Bureau of Competition - Administration....Shelton, Joyce A. FTC 202-326-2856

Bureau of Competition - Compliance....Baruch, Roberta S. FTC 202-326-2861

Bureau of Competition - Compliance....Brown, Renee FTC 202-326-2687

Bureau of Competition - Compliance....Chosid, Robin S. FTC 202-326-2031

Bureau of Competition - Compliance....Davidson, Kenneth FTC 202-326-2863

Bureau of Competition - Compliance....Dietrich, Diana L. FTC 202-326-3512

Bureau of Competition - Compliance....Ducore, Daniel P. FTC 202-326-2526

Bureau of Competition - Compliance....Eckhaus, Joseph FTC 202-326-2687

Bureau of Competition - Compliance....Gill, Pamela A. FTC 202-326-2765

Bureau of Competition - Compliance....Lawler, Stewart FTC 202-326-3181

Bureau of Competition - Compliance....Libby, Kenneth A. FTC 202-326-2694

Bureau of Competition - Compliance....Lippincott, Holly FTC 202-326-3237

Bureau of Competition - Compliance....Miller, Joseph FTC 202-326-3361

Bureau of Competition - Compliance....Ortiz, Rafael A. FTC 202-326-2687

Bureau of Competition - Compliance....Piotrowski, Elizabeth A. FTC 202-326-2623

Bureau of Competition - Compliance....Pozen, Sharis Arnold FTC 202-326-2937

Bureau of Competition - Compliance....Randall, Raymond L. FTC 202-326-2768

Bureau of Competition - Compliance....Rohlck, Eric C. FTC 202-326-2681

Bureau of Competition - Compliance....Scott, Pauline FTC 202-326-2670

Bureau of Competition - Compliance....Seymour, Jane R. FTC 202-326-2687

Bureau of Competition - Compliance....Von Nirschel, David FTC 202-326-3213

Bureau of Competition - Compliance....Youngwood, Gordon FTC 202-326-2682

Bureau of Competition - Gen. Lit. (Assoc & Business)....Banks, Jonathan FTC 202-326-2773

Bureau of Competition - Gen. Lit. (Assoc & Business)....Boynton, Evelyn B. FTC 202-326-2737

Bureau of Competition - Gen. Lit. (Assoc & Business)....Brandon, Jeff FTC 202-326-2929

Bureau of Competition - Gen. Lit. (Assoc & Business)....Catt, Malcolm L. FTC 202-326-2911

Bureau of Competition - Gen. Lit. (Assoc & Business)....Cox, Kent FTC 202-326-2058

Bureau of Competition - Gen. Lit. (Assoc & Business)....Draluck, Jonathan FTC 202-326-2564

Bureau of Competition - Gen. Lit. (Assoc.& Business)....Harcketts, J. Dennis FTC 202-326-2783

Bureau of Competition - Gen. Lit. (Assoc & Business)....Hoagland, John R. FTC 202-326-2893

Bureau of Competition - Gen. Lit. (Assoc & Business)....Leviton, Lenore FTC 202-326-2779

Bureau of Competition - Gen. Lit. (Assoc & Business)....Lomax, Joan C. FTC 202-326-2901

Bureau of Competition - Gen. Lit. (Assoc & Business)....Marks, Randall FTC 202-326-2571

Bureau of Competition - Gen. Lit. (Assoc & Business)....McCartney, P. Abbott FTC 202-326-2695

Bureau of Competition - Gen. Lit. (Assoc & Business)....McNeely, Michael FTC 202-326-2904

Bureau of Competition - Gen. Lit. (Assoc & Business)....Middleton, Judith A. FTC 202-326-2915

Bureau of Competition - Gen. Lit. (Assoc & Business)....Oppenheim, Martha H. FTC 202-326-2941

Bureau of Competition - Gen. Lit. (Assoc & Business)....Sesnowitz, Douglas K. FTC 202-326-2901

Bureau of Competition - Gen. Lit. (Assoc & Business)....Veney, Wanda M. FTC 202-326-2895

Bureau of Competition - Gen. Lit. (Assoc & Business)....Zimmerman, Seth B. FTC 202-326-2800

Bureau of Competition - Gen. Lit. (Energy & Food)....Carrington, Daveene FTC 202-326-2619

Bureau of Competition - Gen. Lit. (Energy & Food)....Casey, Christopher FTC 202-326-2652

Bureau of Competition - Gen. Lit. (Energy & Food)....Chung, Cecil FTC 202-326-3204

Bureau of Competition - Gen. Lit. (Energy & Food)....Dodson, Beverly A. FTC 202-326-2939

Bureau of Competition - Gen. Lit. (Energy & Food)....Fishkin, James FTC 202-326-2663

Bureau of Competition - Gen. Lit. (Energy & Food)....Frumin, Jill M. FTC 202-326-2758

Bureau of Competition - Gen. Lit. (Energy & Food)....Henning, Renee S. FTC 202-326-2621

Bureau of Competition - Gen. Lit. (Energy & Food)....Hershey, Micheline FTC 202-326-2191

Bureau of Competition - Gen. Lit. (Energy & Food)....Hevener, Carl D. FTC 202-326-2843

Bureau of Competition - Gen. Lit. (Energy & Food)....Johnson, Dennis F. FTC 202-326-2712

Bureau of Competition - Gen. Lit. (Energy & Food)....Jones, Robert FTC 202-326-2740

Bureau of Competition - Gen. Lit. (Energy & Food)....Joseph, Anthony Low FTC 202-326-2910

Bureau of Competition - Gen. Lit. (Energy & Food)....Krulla, Rhett R. FTC 202-326-2608

Bureau of Competition - Gen. Lit. (Energy & Food)....Lawrence, Jo Ann FTC 202-326-2642

Bureau of Competition - Gen. Lit. (Energy & Food)....Licker, Naomi FTC 202-326-2851

Bureau of Competition - Gen. Lit. (Energy & Food)....Liedquist-Scott, Philo FTC 202-326-2631

Bureau of Competition - Gen. Lit. (Energy & Food)....Lipson, Frank FTC 202-326-2617

Bureau of Competition - Gen. Lit. (Energy & Food)....McDonald, Carol E. FTC 202-326-2616

Bureau of Competition - Gen. Lit. (Energy & Food)....Nolan, Arthur J. FTC 202-326-2770

Bureau of Competition - Gen. Lit. (Energy & Food)....Petrizzi, Maribeth FTC 202-326-2646

Bureau of Competition - Gen. Lit. (Energy & Food)....Proctor, Barbara FTC 202-326-2630

Bureau of Competition - Gen. Lit. (Energy & Food)....Richman, Peter FTC 202-326-2563

Bureau of Competition - Gen. Lit. (Energy & Food)....Robinson, Emily K. FTC 202-326-2640

Bureau of Competition - Gen. Lit. (Energy & Food)....Salemi, Constance M. FTC 202-326-2643

Bureau of Competition - Gen. Lit. (Energy & Food)....Schildkraut, Marc G. FTC 202-326-2622

Bureau of Competition - Gen. Lit. (Energy & Food)....Schneider, Marc FTC 202-326-2062

Bureau of Competition - Gen. Lit. (Energy & Food)....Shapiro, Barbara K. FTC 202-326-2633

Bureau of Competition - Gen. Lit. (Energy & Food)....Silver, Daniel FTC 202-326-3102

Bureau of Competition - Gen. Lit. (Energy & Food)....Skubel, Marmichael O. FTC 202-326-2611

Bureau of Competition - Gen. Lit. (Energy & Food)....Tovsky, Robert S. FTC 202-326-2634

Bureau of Competition - Gen. Lit. (Energy & Food)....Villavicencio, Alice M.

FTC 202-326-3155

Bureau of Competition - Gen. Lit. (Energy & Food)....Washington, Norris FTC 202-326-2606

Bureau of Competition - Gen. Lit. (Energy & Food)....Wilensky, Steven FTC 202-326-2650

Bureau of Competition - Gen. Lit. (Health Care)....Bellack, George R. FTC 202-326-2763

Bureau of Competition - Gen. Lit. (Health Care)....Blumenreich, Linda FTC 202-326-2751

Bureau of Competition - Gen. Lit. (Health Care)....Brownman, Joseph S. FTC 202-326-2605

Bureau of Competition - Gen. Lit. (Health Care)....Bruno, Marian FTC 202-326-2846

Bureau of Competition - Gen. Lit. (Health Care)....Clark-Coleman, Sheila FTC 202-326-2759

Bureau of Competition - Gen. Lit. (Health Care)....Connelly-Draper, Molly FTC 202-326-2760

Bureau of Competition - Gen. Lit. (Health Care)....Davis, Rendell A., Jr. FTC 202-326-2894

Bureau of Competition - Gen. Lit. (Health Care)....Day, Robert FTC 202-326-2772

Bureau of Competition - Gen. Lit. (Health Care)....Friedman, Alan J. FTC 202-326-2742

Bureau of Competition - Gen. Lit. (Health Care)....Gibbs, Garry FTC 202-326-2767

Bureau of Competition - Gen. Lit. (Health Care)....Greene, Stephanie FTC 203-326-2925

Bureau of Competition - Gen. Lit. (Health Care)....Hilder, Elizabeth FTC 202-326-2545

Bureau of Competition - Gen. Lit. (Health Care)....Holmes, Deborah A. FTC 202-326-2752

Bureau of Competition - Gen. Lit. (Health Care)....Horoschak, Mark J. FTC 202-326-2756

Bureau of Competition - Gen. Lit. (Health Care)....Jones, Patricia Y. FTC 202-326-2942

Bureau of Competition - Gen. Lit. (Health Care)....Kenyon, Kathleen FTC 202-326-2429

Bureau of Competition - Gen. Lit. (Health Care)....Maxwell, Sally L. FTC 202-326-2674

Bureau of Competition - Gen. Lit. (Health Care)....McDuffie, Lourine FTC 202-326-2735

Bureau of Competition - Gen. Lit. (Health Care)....Meier, Markus FTC 202-326-2781

Bureau of Competition - Gen. Lit. (Health Care)....Moreland, Judith A. FTC 202-326-2776

Bureau of Competition - Gen. Lit. (Health Care)....Narrow, David M. FTC 202-326-2744

Bureau of Competition - Gen. Lit. (Health Care)....Osnowitz, Steve FTC 202-326-2746

Bureau of Competition - Gen. Lit. (Health Care)....Ostheimer, Michael FTC 202-326-2699

Bureau of Competition - Gen. Lit. (Health Care)....Pender, David FTC 202-326-2549

Bureau of Competition - Gen. Lit. (Health Care)....Porter, Dora L. FTC 202-326-2752

Bureau of Competition - Gen. Lit. (Health Care)....Schorr, Gary FTC 202-326-3063

Bureau of Competition - Gen. Lit. (Health Care)....Soudakoff, Alan FTC 202-326-2747

Bureau of Competition - Gen. Lit. (Health Care)....Tucker, Deborah FTC 202-326-2766

Bureau of Competition - Gen. Lit. (Health Care)....Voss, Oscar M. FTC 202-326-2750

Bureau of Competition - Gen. Lit. (Non-Mergers)....Antalics, Michael FTC 202-326-4821

Bureau of Competition - Gen. Lit. (Non-Mergers)....Arthridge, Thomas FTC 202-326-4824

Bureau of Competition - Gen. Lit. (Non-Mergers)....Barnes, Rosenna FTC 202-326-2796

Bureau of Competition - Gen. Lit. (Non-Mergers)....Bauer, Mark, D. FTC 202-326-2723

Bureau of Competition - Gen. Lit. (Non-Mergers)....Bloom, Morris A. FTC 202-326-2707

Bureau of Competition - Gen. Lit. (Non-Mergers)....Cole, Judith A. FTC 202-326-2693

Bureau of Competition - Gen. Lit. (Non-Mergers)....Cook, Robert FTC 202-326-2771

Bureau of Competition - Gen. Lit. (Non-Mergers)....Constantini, Amie M. FTC 202-326-3186

Bureau of Competition - Gen. Lit. (Non-Mergers)....Costilo, L. Barry FTC 202-326-2748

Bureau of Competition - Gen. Lit. (Non-Mergers)....Cunningham, Linda FTC 202-326-2638

Bureau of Competition - Gen. Lit. (Non-Mergers)....Dagen, Richard FTC 202-326-2628

Bureau of Competition - Gen. Lit. (Non-Mergers)....Doyle, Robert W., Jr. FTC 202-326-2819

Bureau of Competition - Gen. Lit. (Non-Mergers)....Dugan, John, F. FTC 202-326-2715

Bureau of Competition - Gen. Lit. (Non-Mergers)....Easterling, Wallace W. FTC 202-326-2936

Bureau of Competition - Gen. Lit. (Non-Mergers)....Gray, Jessica FTC 202-326-3342

Bureau of Competition - Gen. Lit. (Non-Mergers)....Hackley, Jacqueline FTC 202-326-2729

Bureau of Competition - Gen. Lit. (Non-Mergers)....Horwitz, Reid B. FTC 202-326-2053

Bureau of Competition - Gen. Lit. (Non-Mergers)....Inglefield, David L. FTC 202-326-2637

Bureau of Competition - Gen. Lit. (Non-Mergers)....Johnson, Joyce FTC 202-326-2576

Bureau of Competition - Gen. Lit. (Non-Mergers)....Klein, Deborah E. FTC 202-326-2813

Bureau of Competition - Gen. Lit. (Non-Mergers)....Menna, Mark FTC 202-326-2722

Bureau of Competition - Gen. Lit. (Non-Mergers)....Mills, Karen FTC 202-326-2052

Bureau of Competition - Gen. Lit. (Non-Mergers)....Moscatelli, Catharine FTC 202-326-2749

Bureau of Competition - Gen. Lit. (Non-Mergers)....Nagata, Ernest A. FTC 202-326-2714

Bureau of Competition - Gen. Lit. (Non-Mergers)....Nolan, Paul FTC 202-326-2770

Bureau of Competition - Gen. Lit. (Non-Mergers)....Oxenham, Sarah FTC 202-326-2226

Bureau of Competition - Gen. Lit. (Non-Mergers)....Parker, Patrice FTC 202-326-2837

Bureau of Competition - Gen. Lit. (Non-Mergers)....Potts, Agnes FTC 202-326-3186

Bureau of Competition - Gen. Lit. (Non-Mergers)....Ragano, James M. FTC 202-326-3186

Bureau of Competition - Gen. Lit. (Non-Mergers)....Ramadhan, Allee A. FTC 202-326-2716

Bureau of Competition - Gen. Lit. (Non-Mergers)....Riddell, Stephen FTC 202-326-2721

Bureau of Competition - Gen. Lit. (Non-Mergers)....Schultheiss, Patricia FTC 202-326-2877

Bureau of Competition - Gen. Lit. (Non-Mergers)....Seesel, John H. FTC 202-326-2702

Bureau of Competition - Gen. Lit. (Non-Mergers)....Stone, David J. FTC 202-326-3186

Bureau of Competition - Gen. Lit. (Non-Mergers)....Sockwell, Stephen W., Jr. FTC 202-326-2950

Bureau of Competition - Gen. Lit. (Non-Mergers)....Spriggs, Valicia A. FTC 202-326-2839

Bureau of Competition - Gen. Lit. (Non-Mergers)....Stevens, Peer L. FTC 202-326-3154

Bureau of Competition - Gen. Lit. (Non-Mergers)....Waldeck, Cecelia FTC 202-326-3669

Bureau of Competition - Gen. Lit. (Non-Mergers)....Weber, John C. FTC 202-326-2682

Bureau of Competition - Gen. Lit. (Non-Mergers)....Williams, Tonya FTC 202-326-2752

Bureau of Competition - Gen. Lit. (Non-Mergers)....Woodard, Carolyn FTC 202-326-2706

Bureau of Competition - General Litigation....Berg, Karen E. FTC 202-326-2960

Bureau of Competition - General Litigation....Bernstein, Steven K. FTC 202-326-2423

Bureau of Competition - General Litigation....Brooks, Sylvia M. FTC 202-326-5916

Bureau of Competition - General Litigation....Dadoun, David FTC 202-326-3103

Bureau of Competition - General Litigation....Elmore, Ernest FTC 202-326-3109

Bureau of Competition - General Litigation....Heydenreich, Melissa FTC

202-326-2543

Bureau of Competition - General Litigation....Higgins, Claudia R. FTC 202-326-2682

Bureau of Competition - General Litigation....Holden, James FTC 202-326-2963

Bureau of Competition - General Litigation....Jex, Elizabeth FTC 202-326-3273

Bureau of Competition - General Litigation....Levy, Richard A. FTC 202-326-2682

Bureau of Competition - General Litigation....Lingos, Annthalia FTC 202-326-2682

Bureau of Competition - General Litigation....Malester, Ann B. FTC 202-326-2682

Bureau of Competition - General Litigation....Mendel, Jacqueline FTC 202-326-2603

Bureau of Competition - General Litigation....Moiseyev, Michael FTC 202-326-3106

Bureau of Competition - General Litigation....Paige, Margaret C. FTC 202-326-2682

Bureau of Competition - General Litigation....Person, Brenda W. FTC 202-326-2682

Bureau of Competition - General Litigation....Pettee, Susan P. FTC 202-326-2682

Bureau of Competition - General Litigation....Pickett, Robert FTC 202-326-2682

Bureau of Competition - General Litigation....Piercy, Carey FTC 202-326-2962

Bureau of Competition - General Litigation....Tahyar, Benjamin FTC 202-326-2889

Bureau of Competition - General Litigation....Triggs, Casey FTC 202-326-2804

Bureau of Competition - General Litigation....Yahia, Terri FTC 202-326-2602

Bureau of Competition - General Litigation....Wilkinson, Laura FTC 202-326-2830

Bureau of Competition - General Litigation....Wilmer, Bobbie J. FTC 202-326-2836

Bureau of Competition - International Antitrust....Briseno, Liliana O. FTC 202-326-2731

Bureau of Competition - International Antitrust....Crise, Cameron J. FTC 202-326-2731

Bureau of Competition - International Antitrust....Feuillan, Jacques C. FTC 202-326-2379

Bureau of Competition - International Antitrust....Karlsson, Paul FTC 202-326-2566

Bureau of Competition - International Antitrust....Lindstrom, Talbot S. FTC 202-326-2717

Bureau of Competition - International Antitrust....Parisi, John J. FTC 202-326-2133

Bureau of Competition - International Antitrust....Schimpff, Kirsten M. FTC 202-326-2731

Bureau of Competition - International Antitrust....Shanahan, Deirdre E. FTC 202-326-2951

Bureau of Competition - International Antitrust....White, Roxanne FTC 202-326-2954

Bureau of Competition - Office of the Director....Arquit, Kevin J. FTC 202-326-2556

Bureau of Competition - Office of the Director....Clark, Barbara A. FTC 202-326-2562

Bureau of Competition - Office of the Director....Egan, James C., Jr. FTC 202-326-2886

Bureau of Competition - Office of the Director....Forster, Mary C. FTC 202-326-2551

Bureau of Competition - Office of the Director....Green, Geoffrey FTC 202-326-2641

Bureau of Competition - Office of the Director....Greenbaum, Joan S. FTC 202-326-2629

Bureau of Competition - Office of the Director....Rowe, Ronald A. FTC 202-326-2575

Bureau of Competition - Office of the Director....Snider, Virginia L. FTC 202-326-2682

Bureau of Competition - Office of the Director....Steptoe, Mary Lou FTC 202-326-2584

Bureau of Competition - Office of the Director....Taylor, Mildred E. FTC 202-326-2553

Bureau of Competition - Office of the Director....Whitener, Mark D. FTC 202-326-2845

Bureau of Competition - Office of the Director....Winslow, Walter T., Jr. FTC 202-326-2560

Bureau of Competition - Policy & Evaluation....Averitt, Neil W. FTC 202-326-2885

Bureau of Competition - Policy & Evaluation....Cariaga, Frances P. FTC 202-326-2882

Bureau of Competition - Policy and Evaluation....Kattan, Joseph FTC 202-326-2884

Bureau of Competition - Policy & Evaluation....Mongoven, James F. FTC 202-326-2879

Bureau of Competition - Policy & Evaluation....Morse, Howard FTC 202-326-2949

Bureau of Competition - Policy and Evaluation....Doying, William A.E. FTC 202-326-2582

Bureau of Competition - Premerger Notification....Bellamy, Lottie FTC 202-326-3100

Bureau of Competition - Premerger Notification....Cohen, Victor FTC 202-326-2849

Bureau of Competition - Premerger Notification....Colding, Dollie FTC 202-326-2866

Bureau of Competition - Premerger Notification....Crouse, Lynda M. FTC 202-326-2880

Bureau of Competition - Premerger Notification....Epps, Melea R.C. FTC 202-326-2705

Bureau of Competition - Premerger Notification....Hancock, Thomas F. FTC 202-326-2946

Bureau of Competition - Premerger Notification....Horton, Renee A. FTC 202-326-2842

Bureau of Competition - Premerger Notification....Kaplan, Jeffrey FTC 202-326-2943

Bureau of Competition - Premerger Notification....Owen, Deborah K. FTC 202-326-2151

Bureau of Competition - Premerger Notification....Rubenstein, Hy David FTC 202-326-2887

Bureau of Competition - Premerger Notification....Schechter, William I. FTC 202-326-3119

Bureau of Competition - Premerger Notification....Sharpe, Patrick FTC 202-326-2848

Bureau of Competition - Premerger Notification....Sipple, John M., Jr. FTC 202-326-2862

Bureau of Competition - Premerger Notification....Smith, Richard B. FTC 202-326-2850

Bureau of Competition - Premerger Notification....Speed, Bernice L. FTC 202-326-2280

Bureau of Competition - Premerger Notification....Wolfe, Mary E. FTC 202-326-2880

Bureau of Competition - Premerger Notification....Peay, Sandra M. FTC 202-326-2844

Bureau of Consumer Affairs - Advertising Practices....Bloom, Jeffrey I. FTC 202-326-3327

Bureau of Economics - Antitrust....Ferguson, James M. FTC 202-326-3386

Bureau of Economics - Office of the Director....Painter, Susan FTC 202-326-3370

Burkina Faso....Michelini, Philip Cnty Commerce 202-482-4388

Burkina Faso (Ouagadougou)....Staff Cnty State 202-647-3066

Burkina Faso/Minerals....Van Oss, Hendrik Cnty Mines 202-501-9687

Burkitt's Lymphoma....Staff NCI 301-496-5583

Burma (Myanmar)....Paine, George Cnty Commerce 202-482-3875

Burma (Rangoon)....Staff Cnty State 202-647-7108

Burma/Minerals....Vacant Cnty Mines 202-501-9694

Burn Research....Staff NIGMS 301-496-7301

Burning Mouth Syndrome....Staff 301-496-4261

Bursitis....Staff NIAMS 301-496-8188

Burundi....Michelini, Philip Cnty Commerce 202-482-4388

Burundi (Bujumbura)....Staff Cnty State 202-647-3139

Burundi/Minerals....Antonides, Lloyd Cnty Mines 202-501-9686

Buses....Hagey, Michael USITC 202-205-3392

Business Administration....Allen, Brandt R. UVA 701-924-4842

Business Cycle Indicators....Statistical Indicators Staff ECONOMIC 202-523-0500

Business Data Centers....Rowe, John CENSUS 301-763-1580

Business Establishment List, Empl/Unempl. Stats....Searson, Michael LABOR 202-606-6469

Business Forms....Bratland, Rose Marie COMMERCE 202-492-0380

Business Licenses....Staff 717-337-1212

Business Opportunities, Small and Woman-Owned....Staff HUD 202-708-1428

Business Outlook, Chief....Green, George R. ECONOMIC 202-523-0701

Business Radio....Staff FCC 717-337-1212

Business Statistics, Business Owners' Characterist....McCutcheon, Donna CENSUS 301-763-5517

Business Statistics, Minority Businesses....McCutcheon, Donna CENSUS 301-763-5517

Business, Statistics, County Business Patterns....Decker, Zigmund CENSUS

301-763-5430
Business/Industry Data Centers....Rowe, John CENSUS 301-763-1580
Businesses, Disadvantaged....Miranda, Leonel NEIC 202-254-5583
Businesses, Minority-Owned....Miranda, Leonel NEIC 202-254-5583
Businesses, Women-Owned....Miranda, Leonel NEIC 202-254-5583
Butadiene....Raftery, Jim USITC 202-205-3365
Butane....Land, Eric USITC 202-205-3349
Butter....Warren, J Fred USITC 202-205-3311
Buttons....Shildneck, Ann USITC 202-205-3499
Butyl alcohol....Michels, David USITC 202-205-3352
Butyl benzyl phthalate....Johnson, Larry USITC 202-205-3351
Butyl oleate....Johnson, Larry USITC 202-205-3351
Butyl rubber....Misurelli, Denby USITC 202-205-3362
Butyl stearate....Johnson, Larry USITC 202-205-3351
Butylene....Raftery, Jim USITC 202-205-3365
Byssinosis (Brown Lung Disease)....Staff NHLBI 301-496-4236

C

CAD/CAM/CAE Software....Swann, Vera A. COMMERCE 202-482-0396
CD Players....Dicerbo, Mario CUSTOMS 212-466-5672
CD-ROM....Staff CENSUS 301-763-4673
CDC Information Center....Kennedy, Joan U. CDC 404-639-1601
CDC Information Center (Library).... CDC 404-639-3396
CEA (Carcinoembryonic Antigen)....Staff NCI 301-496-5583
CENDATA....Staff CENSUS 301-763-2074
CO/Fuel Gas Detectors....Mesa, Stacey Reuben CPSC 301-504-0580
Cable Access Policy....Staff FCC 202-632-7480
Cable Broadcasting....Siegmund, John COMMERCE 202-482-4781
Cable Pole Attachments....Staff FCC 202-632-1861
Cable Telephone....Staff FCC 202-634-1830
Cable Television Complaints....Staff FCC 202-632-7048
Cable Television Cross Ownership....Staff FCC 202-634-1830
Cable Television Franchising....Staff FCC 202-632-7076
Cablegrams....Staff FCC 202-632-7265
Cadastral Surveys....Staff FWS 703-358-1713
Cadmium....Llewellyn, Thomas MINES 202-501-9395
Cadmium....Lundy, David USITC 202-205-3439
Caffeine and its compounds....Nesbitt, Elizabeth USITC 202-205-3355
Calcium....Miller, Michael MINES 202-501-9409
Calcium....Lundy, David USITC 202-205-3439
Calcium carbonate....Tepordei, Valentin V. MINES 202-501-9392
Calcium carbonate....Johnson, Larry USITC 202-205-3351
Calcium compounds....Greenblatt, Jack USITC 202-205-3353
Calcium pigments....Johnson, Larry USITC 202-205-3351
Calcium sulfate....Johnson, Larry USITC 202-205-3351
Calculators....Baker, Scott USITC 202-205-3386
Calculus....Staff NIDR 301-496-4261
Calendaring machines....Slingerland, David USITC 202-205-3400
Call Sign Block Allocation....Staff FCC 202-653-8126
Call Signs Allocation....Staff FCC 202-634-1923
Calligraphy....Staff FWS 202-208-4111
Cambodia....Pho, Hong-Phong B. Cnty Commerce 202-482-3875
Cambodia (Phom Penh)....Staff Cnty State 202-647-3133
Cambodia/Minerals....Vacant Cnty Mines 202-501-9694
Cameos....Witherspoon, Ricardo USITC 202-205-3489
Cameras....Kiefer, Barbara CUSTOMS 212-466-5685
Cameroon....Henke, Debra Cnty Commerce 204-482-5149
Cameroon....Blackwell, Gloria Peace Corps 202-606-3998
Cameroon....Swezy, Virginia Peace Corps 202-606-3998
Cameroon (Yaounde)....Staff Cnty State 202-647-1707
Cameroon/Minerals....Dolley, Thomas Cnty Mines 202-501-9690
Camphor....Randall, Rob USITC 202-205-3366
Campus Radio Stations....Staff FCC 202-653-6288
Canada....Don, Jonathan Cnty Commerce 202-482-3101
Canada (Ottawa)....Staff Cnty State 202-647-2170
Canada/Minerals....Doan, David Cnty Mines 202-501-9678
Canada/trade matters....Weiss, David US Trade Rep 202-395-5663
Canadian Dollar with options....Bice, David CFT 312-353-7880
Canavan's Disease....Staff NINDS 301-496-5751
Cancer (Reproductive Tract)....Staff NCI 301-496-5583
Cancer (Reproductive Tract)....Staff NICHD 301-496-5133
Cancer Control Program....Staff NCI 301-496-5583
Cancer Institute, National....Nealon, Eleanor NIH 301-496-6631
Cancer Institute, National....Newman, Patricia NIH 301-496-6641
Cancer Prevention....Wyatt, Stephen W. CDC 404-488-5496

Cancer Research....Staff NCI 301-496-5583
Cancer and Aging....Staff NIA 301-496-1752
Candida....Staff NIAID 301-496-5717
Candida....Staff NIDR 301-496-4261
Candidiasis....Staff NIAID 301-496-5717
Candidiasis....Staff NIDR 301-496-4261
Candles....Brownchweig, Gilbert CUSTOMS 212-466-5744
Candles....Randall, Rob USITC 202-205-3366
Candy....Maria, John CUSTOMS 212-466-5730
Canes....Burns, Gail USITC 202-205-3501
Canker Sores....Staff NIDR 301-496-4261
Canned Goods....Hodgen, Donald A. COMMERCE 202-482-3346
Canoes....Lahey, Kathleen USITC 202-205-3409
Capacitors....Josephs, Irwin CUSTOMS 212-466-5673
Capacitors....Malison, Andrew USITC 202-205-3391
Cape Verde....Michelini, Philip Cnty Commerce 202-482-4388
Cape Verde....Fossum, Linnea Peace Corps 202-606-3708
Cape Verde (Praia)....Staff Cnty State 202-647-3391
Cape Verde Islands/Minerals....King, Audie L. Cnty Mines 202-501-9674
Capital Goods (Trade Prom)....Brandis, Jay COMMERCE 202-482-0560
Capital Measurement, Productivity Research....Harper, Michael LABOR 202-606-5603
Capital Punishment....Greenfeld, Lawrence Justice Stat 202-616-3281
Capitation Grants for Health Professions Schools....Staff HRSA/BHPr 301-443-5794
Capitation Grants for Nurse Training....Staff HRSA/BHPr 301-443-5786
Caprolactam monomer....Matusik, Ed USITC 202-205-3356
Caps....Jones, Jackie USITC 202-205-3466
Caps....Hamey, Amy USITC 202-205-3465
Carbon....Johnson, Larry USITC 202-205-3351
Carbon Black....Prat, Raimundo COMMERCE 202-482-0128
Carbon Products....Brownchweig, Gilbert CUSTOMS 212-466-5744
Carbon activated....Randall, Bob USITC 202-205-3366
Carbon and graphite electrodes....Cutchin, John USITC 202-205-3396
Carbon black....Johnson, Larry USITC 202-205-3351
Carbon dioxide....Conant, Kenneth USITC 202-205-3346
Carbon disulfide....Conant, Kenneth USITC 202-205-3346
Carbon tetrachloride....Michels, David USITC 202-205-3352
Carboxylic acids....Michels, David USITC 202-205-3352
Carboxymethyl cellulose salts (surface active)....Land, Eric USITC 202-205-3349
Carcalon (Krebiozen)....Staff NCI 301-496-5583
Carcinogen....Staff NCI 301-496-5583
Carcinogen Assessment....Staff EPA 202-260-5898
Carcinoma....Staff NCI 301-496-5583
Card cases....Seastrum, Carl USITC 202-205-3493
Cardiac Disease....Staff NHLBI 301-496-4236
Cardiac Pacemakers....Staff NHLBI 301-496-4236
Cardiomegaly....Staff NHLBI 301-496-4236
Cardiomyopathy (Hypertrophic, Dilated)....Staff NHLBI 301-496-4236
Cardiopulmonary Resuscitation (CPR)....Staff NHLBI 301-496-4236
Cardiovascular Disease....Staff NHLBI 301-496-4236
Cardiovascular drugs....Nesbitt, Elizabeth USITC 202-205-3355
Carditis....Staff NHLBI 301-496-4236
Career Criminals....Langan, Patrick Justice Stat 202-616-3490
Career Criminals....Greenfeld, Lawrence Justice Stat 202-616-3281
Careers in Nursing....Staff DRR 301-443-5786
Caribbean....Frechette, Myles US Trade Rep 202-395-6135
Caribbean Basin....Dowling, Jay Cnty Commerce 202-482-1648
Caribbean Primate Research Center....Staff NCRR 301-496-5411
Caries....Staff NIDR 301-496-4261
Carpal Tunnel Syndrome....Staff NINDS 301-496-5751
Carpal Tunnel Syndrome....Staff NIAMS 301-496-8188
Carpets....Sweet, Mary Elizabeth USITC 202-205-3455
Carrier Equipment....Staff FCC 202-634-1800
Carrots....McCarty, Timothy USITC 202-205-3324
Carrying Cases....Gorman, Kevin CUSTOMS 212-466-5893
Cartography....Staff FWS 703-358-1713
Case....Swann, Vera COMMERCE 202-482-4936
Casein....Randall, Rob USITC 202-205-3366
Cash registers....Baker, Scott USITC 202-205-3386
Castile soap....Land, Eric USITC 202-205-3349
Casting machines....Greene, William USITC 202-205-3405
Cat Cry Syndrome (Cri Du Chat)....Staff NICHD 301-496-5133
Cat Scratch Fever....Staff NIAID 301-496-5717
Catalytic Converters....Staff EPA 202-233-9090
Cataplexy....Staff NINDS 301-496-5751
Cataract....Staff NEI 301-496-5248

Catheterization (Cardiac or Heart)....Staff NHLBI 301-496-4236

Cathode-Ray tubes....Kitzmiller, John USITC 202-205-3351

Cattle (Feeder) with options....Fichert, David CFT 312-353-3181

Cattle with options....Fichert, David CFT 312-353-3181

Caulking compounds....Johnson, Larry USITC 202-205-3351

Caulks....Johnson, Larry USITC 202-205-3351

Caustic potash....Conant, Kenneth USITC 202-205-3346

Caustic soda....Conant, Kenneth USITC 202-205-3346

Caymans....Brooks, Michelle Cnty Commerce 202-482-2527

Cedar leaf....Land, Eric USITC 202-205-3349

Celiac Disease....Staff NIDDK 301-496-3583

Celiac Disease....Staff NIAID 301-496-5717

Cell Aging....Staff NIA 301-496-1752

Cell Bank....Staff NIGMS 301-496-7301

Cell Biology....Staff NIGMS 301-496-7301

Cellular Function....Staff NIGMS 301-496-7301

Cellular Immunology....Finerty, John FAES 301-496-7815

Cellular Mobile Radio....Staff FCC 202-653-6400

Cellular Structure....Staff NIGMS 301-496-7301

Cement....Pitcher, Charles COMMERCE 202-482-0132

Cement....Solomon, Cheryl C. MINES 202-501-9393

Cement Plants, Major Proj.....White, Barbara COMMERCE 202-482-4160

Cement, hydraulic....White, Linda USITC 202-205-3427

Cements of rubber, vinyl, etc.....Jonnard, Aimison USITC 202-205-3350

Cements, dental....Randall, Rob USITC 202-205-3366

Census Awareness (Regional Offices)....Staff CENSUS 301-763-4683

Census Catalog....McCall, John CENSUS 301-763-1584

Census Customer Service Fax Number....Staff CENSUS 301-763-4794

Census Geographic Concepts....Staff CENSUS 301-763-5720

Census History....Bohme, Frederick CENSUS 301-763-7936

Census Personnel Locator....Staff CENSUS 301-763-7662

Census and You (Monthly Newsletter)....Morton, Jackson CENSUS 301-763-1584

Census and You (Monthly Newsletter)....Tillman, Neil CENSUS 301-763-1584

Census of Retail Trade, Guam....Larson, Odell CENSUS 301-763-8226

Census of Retail Trade, Guam....Hoover, Kent CENSUS 301-763-8564

Census of Retail Trade, Puerto Rico....Larson, Odell CENSUS 301-763-8226

Census of Retail Trade, Puerto Rico....Hoover, Kent CENSUS 301-763-8564

Census of Retail Trade, Virgin Islands....Larson, Odell CENSUS 301-763-8226

Census of Retail Trade, Virgin Islands....Hoover, Kent CENSUS 301-763-8564

Census of Selected Service Industries, Guam....Larson, Odell CENSUS 301-763-8226

Census of Selected Service Industries, Guam....Hoover, Kent CENSUS 301-763-8564

Census of Selected Service Industries, Puerto Rico....Larson, Odell CENSUS 301-763-8226

Census of Selected Service Industries, Puerto Rico....Hoover, Kent CENSUS 301-763-8564

Census of Selected Service Industries, Virgin Isl....Larson, Odell CENSUS 301-763-8226

Census of Selected Service Industries, Virgin Isl....Hoover, Kent CENSUS 301-763-8564

Census of Wholesale Trade, Guam....Larson, Odell CENSUS 301-763-8226

Census of Wholesale Trade, Guam....Hoover, Kent CENSUS 301-763-8564

Census of Wholesale Trade, Puerto Rico....Larson, Odell CENSUS 301-763-8226

Census of Wholesale Trade, Puerto Rico....Hoover, Kent CENSUS 301-763-8564

Census of Wholesale Trade, Virgin Islands....Larson, Odell CENSUS 301-763-8226

Census of Wholesale Trade, Virgin Islands....Hoover, Kent CENSUS 301-763-8564

Centenarians....Staff NIA 301-496-1752

Center for Hazardous Materials Hotline....Staff EPA 800-334-2467

Centers for Disease Control....Staff CDC 404-329-3291

Centers of Population....Hirschfeld, Don CENSUS 301-763-3827

Central Africa Republic....Michelini, Philip Cnty Commerce 202-482-4388

Central African Republic (Bangui)....Staff Cnty State 202-647-3139

Central African Republic/Minerals....Dolley, Thomas Cnty Mines 202-501-9690

Central Core Disease....Staff NINDS 301-496-5751

Central Storeroom....Staff OD/DL 301-496-9156

Centrifuges....Slingerland, David USITC 202-205-3400

Ceramic Gas Turbines....Alpaugh, Richard NEIC 202-586-8012

Ceramic construction articles....White, Linda USITC 202-205-3427

Ceramic sanitary fixtures....Fulcher, Nancy USITC 202-205-3434

Ceramic table, kitchen articles....McNay, Deborah USITC 202-205-3425

Ceramics....Kalkines, George CUSTOMS 212-466-5794

Ceramics (Advanced)....Shea, Moira COMMERCE 202-482-0128

Ceramics Machinery....Shaw, Eugene COMMERCE 202-482-3494

Cereal breakfast foods....Schneider, Greg USITC 202-205-3326

Cereal grains....Pierre-Benoist, John USITC 202-205-3320

Cereals....Janis, William V. COMMERCE 202-482-2250

Cerebellar Arteriosclerosis....Staff NINDS 301-496-5751

Cerebellar Arteriovenous Malformations....Staff NINDS 301-496-5751

Cerebellar Ataxia....Staff NINDS 301-496-5751

Cerebellar Lesions....Staff NINDS 301-496-5751

Cerebral Death....Staff NINDS 301-496-5751

Cerebral Degeneration....Staff NINDS 301-496-5751

Cerebral Palsy....Staff NINDS 301-496-5751

Cerebral Palsy....Staff NIDCD 301-496-7243

Cerebrotendious Xanthomatosis....Staff NINDS 301-496-5751

Cerebrovascular Disease....Staff NINDS 301-496-5751

Cerium....DeSapio, Vincent USITC 202-205-3435

Cerium compounds....Greenblatt, Jack USITC 202-205-3353

Ceroid Lipofuscinosis....Staff NINDS 301-496-5751

Cesium....Reese, Robert G., Jr. MINES 202-501-9413

Cesium compounds....Greenblatt, Jack USITC 202-205-3353

Chad....Michelini, Philip Cnty Commerce 202-482-4388

Chad....Hanson, Julie Peace Corps 202-606-3004

Chad (N'Djamena)....Staff Cnty State 202-647-1707

Chad/Minerals....Dolley, Thomas Cnty Mines 202-501-9690

Chagas' Disease....Staff NIAID 301-496-5717

Chain, of base metal....Vacant USITC 202-205-3419

Chairs....Spalding, Josephine USITC 202-205-3498

Chalazion....Staff NEI 301-496-5248

Chalk (pigment grade)....Johnson, Larry USITC 202-205-3351

Chalks....Shetty, Sundar USITC 202-205-3486

Channel black....Johnson, Larry USITC 202-205-3351

Chaparral Tea....Staff NCI 301-496-5583

Characteristics of Injuries and Illnesses, Comp. Wk....Biddle, Elyce LABOR 202-606-6170

Charcoal Broiling of Meat....Staff NCI 301-496-5583

Charcot-Marie-Tooth Disease....Staff NINDS 301-496-5751

Charge Syndrome....Staff NICHD 301-496-5133

Check-writing machines....Scott, Baker USITC 202-205-3386

Chediak-Higashi Syndrome....Staff NIAID 301-496-5717

Cheese....Warren, J Fred USITC 202-205-3311

Chelation Therapy (For Arterios., Hemosiderosis)....Staff NHLBI 301-496-4236

Chemical Elements....DiMaria, Joseph CUSTOMS 212-466-4769

Chemical Emergency Preparedness and Prevention....Staff EPA 202-260-8600

Chemical Hazards....Staff OD/ORS 301-496-2960

Chemical Information Services....Hazard, George F. NLM 301-496-1131

Chemical Measurement Techniques....Patrinus, Aristides NEIC 301-903-5348

Chemical Plants, Major Proj.....Haraguchi, Wally COMMERCE 202-482-4877

Chemical Sciences....Marianelli, Robert NEIC 301-903-5804

Chemical Spills....Staff FWS 703-358-1713

Chemical Spills National Response Center....Staff EPA 202-426-2675

Chemical and Petroleum Branch....Staff EPA 919-541-5874

Chemical and Physical Hazards....Kapolka, Robert J. CDC 404-639-3147

Chemical elements....Conant, Kenneth USITC 202-205-3346

Chemicals....Kelly, William J. COMMERCE 202-482-0128

Chemicals (Technical and Non-Technical Questions)....Staff EPA 202-554-1404

Chemicals and Allied Products....Siesseger, Frederic COMMERCE 202-482-0128

Chemotherapy (Cancer)....Staff NCI 301-496-5583

Chemotherapy (Effect on Teeth)....Staff NIDR 301-496-4261

Chesapeake Bay Program....Staff EPA 301-267-0061

Chicken pox....Staff NIAID 301-496-5717

Chief Economist, BEA....Triplett, Jack E. ECONOMIC 202-523-0759

Child Abuse....Staff OHDS/ACYF 301-245-2859

Child Abuse & Neglect....Long, Susan ACF 202-401-9215

Child Care, Population....O'Connell, Martin CENSUS 301-763-5303

Child Care, Population....Bachu, Amara CENSUS 301-763-5303

Child Development....Staff OHDS/ACYF 301-775-7782

Child Rearing....Staff NIMH 301-443-4515

Child Welfare....Staff OHDS/ACYF 301-775-8888

Childbirth....Staff NICHD 301-496-5133

Childbirth....Staff HRSA/BHCDA/DMCH 301-443-2170

Childhood Malignancies....Staff NCI 301-496-5583

Childhood Mental Illness....Staff NIMH 301-443-4515

Childhood Progressive Dementia....Staff NINDS 301-496-5751

Children (Gifted)....Staff NIMH 301-443-4515

Children's Attitudes Towards Aging....Staff NIA 301-496-1752

Chile....Turner, Randy Cnty Commerce 202-482-1495

Chile....Eschelman, Michael Peace Corps 202-606-3376
Chile....Lustumbo, Julie Peace Corps 202-606-3575
Chile....Staff Cnty State 202-647-2407
Chile/Minerals....Velasco, Pablo Cnty Mines 202-501-9677
China, People's Republic of (Beijing)....Staff Cnty State 202-647-6300
China/Minerals....Tse, Pui-Kwan Cnty Mines 202-501-9696
China/trade matters....Lake, Charles US Trade Rep 202-395-3900
Chinaware....Harris, John COMMERCE 202-482-1178
Chinaware....Kalkines, George CUSTOMS 212-466-5794
Chinaware articles....McNay, Deborah USITC 202-205-3425
Chlamydial Infections....Staff NIAID 301-496-5717
Chlorides, nonmetallic....Conant, Kenneth USITC 202-205-3346
Chlorine....Conant, Kenneth USITC 202-205-3346
Chlorofluorocarbons....Michels, David USITC 202-205-3352
Chlorofluorocarbons (CFC)....Staff EPA 202-233-9190
Chloroform....Michels, David USITC 202-205-3352
Chocolate....Maria, John CUSTOMS 212-466-5730
Chocolate....Gallagher, Joan USITC 202-205-3317
Cholera....Staff NIAID 301-496-5717
Cholesterol....Staff NHLBI/IC 301-951-3260
Chondrocalcinosis....Staff NIAMS 301-496-8188
Chondrosarcoma....Staff NCI 301-496-5583
Chordoma....Staff NCI 301-496-5583
Choriocarcinoma....Staff NCI 301-496-5583
Chorionic Villus Sampling (CVS)....Staff 301-496-5133
Choroiditis....Staff NEI 301-496-5248
Christmas Decorations....Rauch, Theodore CUSTOMS 212-466-5892
Christmas Island/Minerals....Lyday, Travis Cnty Mines 202-501-9695
Chrome pigments....Johnson, Larry USITC 202-205-3351
Chromium....Presbury, Graylin COMMERCE 202-482-5158
Chromium....Papp, John F. MINES 202-501-9438
Chromium....Vacant USITC 202-205-3419
Chromium compounds....Greenblatt, Jack USITC 202-205-3353
Chronic Bronchitis....Staff NHLBI 301-496-4236
Chronic Disease Nutrition....Byers, Tim E. CDC 404-488-5121
Chronic Disease Prevention....Koplan, Jeffrey P. CDC 404-488-5401
Chronic EBV....Staff NIAID 301-496-5717
Chronic Fatigue Syndrome....Staff NIAID 301-496-5717
Chronic Granulomatous Disease....Staff NIAID 301-496-5717
Chronic Hepatitis with Rheumatic Disease....Staff NIAMS 301-496-8188
Chronic Infections....Staff NIAID 301-496-5717
Chronic Myelogenous Leukemia....Staff NCI 301-496-5583
Chronic Obstructive Lung Disease (COPD)....Staff NCNR 301-496-0526
Chronic Obstructive Lung Disease (COPD)....Staff NHLBI 301-496-4236
Cicatricial Pemphigoid....Staff NEI 301-496-5248
Cigarette Lighters....Maruggi, Al CPSC 301-504-0580
Cigarette Safety....Kaplan, Kathy CPSC 301-504-0580
Cigarettes (Research)....Staff NCI 301-496-5583
Cigars and cigarettes....Salin, Victoria USITC 202-205-3331
Cigars and cigarettes holders....Burns, Gail USITC 202-205-3501
Cigars and cigarettes lighters....Burns, Gail USITC 202-205-3501
Cinchona bark alkaloids and their salts....Nesbitt, Elizabeth USITC 202-205-3355
Cinnamon oil (essential oil)....Land, Eric USITC 202-205-3349
Circulation/Circulatory System....Staff NHLBI 301-496-4236
Circumcision....Staff NICHD 301-496-5133
Cirrhosis....Staff NIDDK 301-496-3583
Citizenship....Staff CENSUS 301-763-7955
Citral....Land, Eric USITC 202-205-3349
Citrates....Michels, David USITC 202-205-3352
Citric acid....Michels, David USITC 202-205-3352
Citrus fruits....Dennis, Alfred USITC 202-205-3316
Civet....Land, Eric USITC 202-205-3349
Civil Air Patrol (Rules)....Staff FCC 202-632-7175
Civil Aircraft Agreement....Bender, Juliet COMMERCE 202-482-1228
Civil Aviation....Johnson, C William COMMERCE 202-482-5012
Civil Cases (Federal)....Kaplan, Carol Justice Stat 202-307-0759
Civil Engineering....Demetsky, Michael J. UVA 701-924-6362
Civil Money Penalties....Holtz, Judy IG 202-619-1142
Clackerballs....Tyrell, Elaine CPSC 301-504-0850
Classification....Hartman, Frank CENSUS 301-763-2474
Classification System, Standard Industrial, Em/Un....Bennott, William LABOR 202-606-6464
Claudication....Staff NHLBI 301-496-4236
Clays....Virta, Robert MINES 202-501-9384
Clays....DeSapio, Vincent USITC 202-205-3435
Clean LAN/Waste Lan Hotline....Staff EPA 202-260-0056

Clean Lakes Program....Staff EPA 202-260-7840
Cleaners, under 10 lbs each....Randall, Rob USITC 202-205-3366
Cleaning....Bedore, James USITC 202-205-3424
Cleaning machinery....Slingerland, David USITC 202-205-3400
Cleaning machines (textile)....Greene, William USITC 202-205-3405
Cleanwater Act....Staff EPA 202-260-5882
Clearances (News Releases)....Staff OD/OC 301-496-2535
Clearinghouse for Census Data Services....Staff CENSUS 301-763-1580
Cleft Lip....Staff NIDR 301-496-4261
Cleft Palate....Staff NIDR 301-496-4261
Climate Change Division....Staff EPA 202-260-8825
Clocks....Piropato, Louis CUSTOMS 212-466-5895
Clocks....Luther, Dennis USITC 202-205-3497
Closures, stoppers, seals, lids, caps, rubber or plastic....Trainor, Cynthia USITC 202-205-3354
Clotting Disorders....Staff NHLBI 301-496-4236
Clove oil (essential oil)....Land, Eric USITC 202-205-3349
Coal....Biggerstaff, Margie NEIC 202-586-3867
Coal....Karsteter, Dorothy NEI~C 202-586-8800
Coal....Foreso, Cynthia USITC 202-205-3348
Coal Exports....Oddenino, Charles COMMERCE 202-482-1466
Coal Exports....Yancik, Joseph J. COMMERCE 202-482-1466
Coal Statistics....Geidl, John NEIC 202-254-5570
Coal Technology Export Program....Swink, Denise NEIC 202-586-9680
Coal Workers' Pneumoconiosis (Black Lung Disease)....Staff NHLBI 301-496-4236
Coal and Electricity....Como, Anthony NEIC 202-586-5935
Coal and Minerals....Staff FWS 703-358-2183
Coal tar, crude....Foreso, Cynthia USITC 202-205-3348
Coal, Technology....Siegel, Jack NEIC 202-586-1650
Coal-tar pitch....Foreso, Cynthia USITC 202-205-3348
Coarctation of the Aorta....Staff NHLBI 301-496-4236
Coast Station Licenses....Staff FCC 717-337-1212
Coast Station Rules & Hearings....Staff FCC 202-632-7175
Coastal Anadromous Fish....Staff FWS 703-358-1718
Coastal Barrier Coordination....Staff FWS 703-358-2183
Coastal Barrier Research....Staff FWS 703-358-1710
Coated Garments: Boys'....Raftery, William CUSTOMS 212-466-5851
Coated Garments: Men's....Raftery, William CUSTOMS 212-466-5851
Coated Garments: Women's....Raftery, William CUSTOMS 212-466-5851
Coated fabric apparel....Jones, Jackie USITC 202-205-3466
Coating machines....Greene, William USITC 202-205-3405
Coats' Disease....Staff NEI 301-496-5248
Coats, Women's Knit....Crowley, Michael CUSTOMS 212-466-5852
Coaxial/Underground Cable....Staff FCC 202-634-1800
Cobalt....Staff NCI 301-496-5583
Cobalt....Cammmarota, David COMMERCE 202-482-0575
Cobalt....Shedd, Kim B. MINES 202-501-9420
Cobalt....Lundy, David USITC 202-205-3439
Cobalt compounds....Greenblatt, Jack USITC 202-205-3353
Cockayne's Syndrome....Staff NIA 301-496-1752
Cocks and valves....Mata, Ruben USITC 202-205-3403
Cocoa....Gallagher, Joan USITC 202-205-3317
Coffee....Maria, John CUSTOMS 212-466-5730
Coffee....Schneider, Greg USITC 202-205-3326
Coffee & Tea....Gray, Fred Agri 202-219-0888
Cogan's Syndrome....Staff NEI 301-496-5248
Cogeneration Energy Systems....Eustis, John NEIC 202-586-2098
Cognition....Staff NIMH 301-496-5133
Cognition....Staff NIMH 301-443-4515
Coin purses....Seastrum, Carl USITC 202-205-3493
Coke for fuel....Foreso, Cynthia USITC 202-205-3348
Coke, calcined (non-fuel)....White, Linda USITC 202-205-3427
Cold Storage....Lange, John Agri 202-720-0585
Coley's Mixed Toxins....Staff NCI 301-496-5583
Colitis....Staff NIDDK 301-496-3583
Collagen Disease....Staff NIAMS 301-496-8188
Collagen/Collagenase....Staff NIDR 301-496-4261
Collapsed Lung....Staff NHLBI 301-496-4236
Collective Bargaining Agreements Analysis....Cimini, Michael LABOR 202-606-6275
Collective Bargaining Settlements, Major, Comp/Wk....Devine, Janice M. LABOR 202-606-6276
Collective Bargaining--Public File, Agreements....Cimini, Michael LABOR 202-606-6275
Colombia (Bogota)....Staff Cnty State 202-647-3023
Colombia/Minerals....Mobbs, Philip Cnty Mines 202-501-9679

Color Blindness (Deficiency)....Staff NEI 301-496-5248

Colorectal Neoplasms....Staff NCI 301-496-5583

Coloring Matter....Joseph, Stephanie CUSTOMS 212-466-5768

Colostomy....Staff NIDDK 301-496-3583

Columbia....MacNamara, Laura Cnty Commerce 202-482-1659

Columbium....Presbury, Graylinn, C. COMMERCE 202-482-5158

Columbium....Cunningham, Larry D. MINES 202-501-9443

Columbium....Lundy, David USITC 202-205-3439

Coma....Staff NINDS 301-496-5751

Combs....Brownchweig, Gilbert CUSTOMS 212-466-5744

Combs....Burns, Gail USITC 202-205-3501

Commerce....DeMong, Richard F. UVA 701-924-3227

Commercial Development of Space....Selby, Barbara NASA 703-557-5609

Commercial Lighting Fixtures....Whitley, Richard A. COMMERCIAL 202-482-0682

Commercial Operator Licenses....Staff FCC 202-632-7240

Commercial Operators....Staff FCC 202-632-7240

Commercial Printing....Lofquist, William COMMERCE 202-482-0379

Commercial Space Ventures....Selby, Barbara NASA 703-556-5609

Commercial/Indus Refrig....Bodson, John COMMERCIAL 202-482-3509

Commercial Aircraft (Trade Policy)....Bath, Sally COMMERCE 202-482-4222

Commissioner's Office....Starek, Roscoe B., III FTC 202-326-2150

Commissioner's Office....Steiger, Janet D. FTC 202-326-2100

Commissioner's Office....Yao, Dennis A. FTC 202-326-2171

Commissioner's Office - Azcuenaga, Mary L.....Blumenthal, Don M. FTC 202-326-3797

Commissioner's Office - Azcuenaga, Mary L.....Blunt, Deborah M. FTC 202-326-2145

Commissioner's Office - Azcuenaga, Mary L.....Bokat, Karen G. FTC 202-326-2912

Commissioner's Office - Azcuenaga, Mary L.....Buek, Alexandra P. FTC 202-326-2145

Commissioner's Office - Azcuenaga, Mary L.....Heim, Joan L. FTC 202-326-2145

Commissioner's Office - Azcuenaga, Mary L.....Jeter, LaJuan J. FTC 202-326-2145

Commissioner's Office - Azcuenaga, Mary L.....Parrish, Pearl D. FTC 202-326-2145

Commissioner's Office - Azcuenaga, Mary L.....Warden, John B. FTC 202-326-2145

Commissioner's Office - Owen, Deborah K.....Clayborne, Delores M. FTC 202-326-2152

Commissioner's Office - Owen, Deborah K.....Eisenstat, Philip FTC 202-326-2157

Commissioner's Office - Owen, Deborah K.....Felder, Clayrine K. FTC 202-326-2153

Commissioner's Office - Owen, Deborah K.....Hogue, Cynthia A. FTC 202-326-2158

Commissioner's Office - Owen, Deborah K.....Plyler, Joyce FTC 202-326-2155

Commissioner's Office - Starek, Roscoe B., III....Cook, Barbara A. FTC 202-326-2150

Commissioner's Office - Starek, Roscoe B., III....Evans, Janet M. FTC 202-326-2125

Commissioner's Office - Starek, Roscoe B., III....Hobson, Paula Ann FTC 202-326-2124

Commissioner's Office - Starek, Roscoe B., III....Krauss, Joseph FTC 202-326-2713

Commissioner's Office - Starek, Roscoe B., III....Norris, Catherine FTC 202-326-2123

Commissioner's Office - Starek, Roscoe B., III....Samter, Nadine S. FTC 202-326-2129

Commissioner's Office - Starek, Roscoe B., III....Stockum, Steve FTC 202-326-3376

Commissioner's Office - Steiger, Janet D.....Anderson, Emily FTC 202-326-2109

Commissioner's Office - Steiger, Janet D.....Armstrong, Katherine FTC 202-326-3250

Commissioner's Office - Steiger, Janet D.....Cohen, William E. FTC 202-326-2110

Commissioner's Office - Steiger, Janet D.....Cohn, Susan FTC 202-326-3053

Commissioner's Office - Steiger, Janet D.....Conn, David FTC 202-326-2114

Commissioner's Office - Steiger, Janet D.....Crist, Sandy FTC 202-326-2105

Commissioner's Office - Steiger, Janet D.....Ewing, Faye FTC 202-326-2111

Commissioner's Office - Steiger, Janet D.....Hamill, James C., Jr. FTC 202-326-2107

Commissioner's Office - Steiger, Janet D.....Miles, Elizabeth D. FTC 202-326-2108

Commissioner's Office - Steiger, Janet D.....Oas, Julia FTC 202-326-2483

Commissioner's Office - Steiger, Janet D.....Washington, Monica FTC 202-326-2111

Commissioner's Office - Steiger, Janet D.....White, Robert S. FTC 202-326-2102

Commissioner's Office - Yao, Dennis A.....Corley, Derry L. FTC 202-326-2168

Commissioner's Office - Yao, Dennis A.....Dahdouh, Thomas FTC 202-326-2263

Commissioner's Office - Yao, Dennis A.....DeSanti, Susan S. FTC 202-326-2167

Commissioner's Office - Yao, Dennis A.....Harris, LaVerne H. FTC 202-326-2170

Commissioner's Office - Yao, Dennis A.....Murphy, R. Dennis FTC 202-326-3524

Commissioner's Office - Yao, Dennis A.....Thompson, Patricia V. FTC 202-326-2169

Commissioner's Office - Yao, Dennis A.....Vecchi, Christa Van Anh FTC 202-326-3166

Commissioner, Special Assistant to Office of....Barkume, Anthony J. LABOR 202-606-7808

Commissioner, Special Assistant to Office of....Parks, William LABOR 202-606-7807

Commodity and Programs & Policies - Crops....Evans, Sam Agri 202-219-0840

Common Carrier Development Stations....Staff FCC 202-634-1706

Common Carrier Radio Microwave Services....Staff FCC 202-634-1706

Common Carrier Radio Mobile Services....Staff FCC 202-632-6400

Common Carrier Statistics....Staff FCC 202-632-0745

Common Cold....Staff NIAID 301-496-5717

Commonwealth of Independent States....Levine, Richard Cnty Mines 202-501-9685

Commonwealth of Independent States....Lester, Toby Peace Corps 202-606-3973

Commonwealth of Independent States....Hirsch, Roderick Peace Corps 202-606-3973

Commonwealth of Independent States....Staff Cnty State 202-647-9559

Communicable and Infectious Diseases....Staff CDC 404-639-3286

Communicable and Infectious Diseases....Staff NIAID 401-496-5717

Communication Human (Disorders)....Staff NINDS 401-496-5751

Communication Human (Disorders)....Staff NIMH 401-443-4515

Communication Human (Disorders)....Staff NIDCD 401-496-7243

Communication Human (Normal)....Staff NICHD 301-496-5133

Community Corrections and Detention....Clark, John R. Justice Stat 202-514-8585

Community Energy Systems....Klunder, Kurt NEIC 202-586-2826

Community Health Centers....Mehuron, Charlotte HRSA 301-443-3376

Community Planning and Development....Staff HUD 202-708-0270

Community Services Program....Long, Susan ACF 202-401-9215

Commuting, Population....Boertein, Celia CENSUS 301-763-3850

Commuting....Salopek, Phil CENSUS 301-763-3850

Comoros....Walkins, Chandra Cnty Commerce 202-482-3317

Comoros....Schmitz, Virginia Peace Corps 202-606-3334

Comoros (Moroni)....Staff Cnty State 202-647-5684

Comoros/Minerals....King, Audie L. Cnty Mines 202-501-9674

Compensation and Working Conditions, Asst. Commis.....Stelluto, George LABOR 202-606-6300

Compensation and Working Conditions, Employee Ben.....Staff LABOR 202-606-6222

Compensation and Working Conditions, Employer Costs....Rogers, Brenda LABOR 202-606-6199

Compensation and Working Conditions, Industry injuries & illness....Staff LABOR 202-606-6180

Compensation and Working Conditions, Recorded Message....24-hour hotline LABOR 202-606-7828

Compensation and Working Conditions, Supp. Data....Biddle, Elyce LABOR 202-606-6275

Compensation and Working Conditions, Supp. Data....Biddle, Elyce LABOR 202-606-6170

Compensation and Working Conditions, Work Injury Report Surveys....Jackson, Ethel LABOR 202-606-6180

Compensation Levels & Trends, Asst. Commis.....MacDonald, Kathleen M. LABOR 202-606-6302

Composites, Advanced....Manion, James COMMERCE 202-482-5157

Composting (Yardwaste and Municipal Solid Waste)....Staff EPA 202-262-4745

Computational Aerodynamics....Farrar, Diane NASA 415-604-3934

Computational Molecular Biology....Staff DRCT 301-496-1141

Computer Consulting....Adkins, Robert COMMERCE 202-482-4781

Computer Crime....Kaplan, Carol Justice Stat 202-307-0759

Computer Networks....Spathopoulos, Vivian COMMERCE 202-482-0572

Computer Professional Services....Atkins, Robert COMMERCE 202-482-4781

Computer Systems and Services, Chief....Doyle, James P. ECONOMIC 202-523-0978

Computer and Communication Systems, Director of....Bennett, Harry D. NLM

301-496-1351
Computer and DP Services....Inoussa, Mary COMMERCE 202-482-5820
Computer and DP Services....Atkins, Robert G. COMMERCE 202-482-4781
Computer, Midrange....Hoffman, Heidi M. COMMERCE 202-482-2053
Computer, Personal....Woods, R. Clay COMMERCE 202-482-3013
Computer, Personal....Miles, Timothy O. COMMERCIAL 202-482-2990
Computer, Portable....Hoffman, Heidi M. COMMERCE 202-482-2053
Computer, Super....Streete, Jonathan P. COMMERCE 202-482-0572
Computer/data processing services....Xavier, Neil USITC 202-205-3450
Computers & Business Equipment, Office of....McPhee, John E. COMMERCE 202-482-0572
Computers in Medical Research....Staff DCRT 301-496-6203
Computers in Medical Research....Staff NCRR 301-496-5411
Computers, Midrange....Hoffman, Heidi M. COMMERCE 202-482-2053
Computers, Trade Promo.....Fogg, Judy A. COMMERCE 202-482-4936
Computing Device Emission Standards....Staff FCC 202-653-6288
Consumer Protection Bureau - Enforcement....Ecklund, Stephen C. FTC 202-326-3034
Concrete and products....White, Linda USITC 202-205-3427
Condensate, lease....Foreso, Cynthia USITC 202-205-3348
Conductors....Cutchin, John USITC 202-205-3396
Conduit....Cutchin, John USITC 202-205-3396
Conduits....Miller, Julius CUSTOMS 212-466-4680
Confectionery....Gallagher, Joan USITC 202-205-3317
Confectionery Products....Kenney, Cornelius COMMERCE 202-482-2428
Confidentiality of Data....Kaplan, Carol Justice Stat 202-307-0759
Confidentiality and Privacy Issues....Gates, Jerry CENSUS 301-763-5062
Congenital Abnormalities....Staff NICHD 301-496-5133
Congenital Abnormalities....Staff NINDS 301-496-5751
Congenital Abnormalities....Staff NEI 301-496-5248
Congenital Adrenal Hyperplasia....Staff NIDDK 301-496-3583
Congenital Adrenal Hyperplasia....Staff NICHD 301-496-5133
Congenital Heart Disease....Staff NHLBI 301-496-4236
Congenital Infections....Staff NIAID 301-496-5717
Congestive Heart Failure....Staff NHLBI 301-496-4236
Congo....Henke, Debra Cnty Commerce 202-482-5149
Congo (Brazzaville)....Staff Cnty State 202-647-3139
Congo/Minerals....Dolley, Thomas Cnty Mines 202-501-9690
Congressional Affairs....Staff CENSUS 301-763-2446
Congressional Districts, Address Locations....Swapshur, Ernie CENSUS 301-763-5692
Congressional Districts, Boundaries....Hammill, Robert CENSUS 301-763-5720
Congressional Districts, Component Areas....Hamill, Robert CENSUS 301-763-5720
Congressional Relations Office....Drummy, Maureen FTC 202-326-2149
Conjunctivitis....Staff NEI 301-496-5248
Connective Tissue Diseases....Staff NIAMS 301-496-8188
Conservation....King, Marion NEIC 202-586-8800
Constipation....Staff NIDDK 301-496-3583
Constipation and Aging....Staff NIA 301-496-1752
Construction Machinery....Heimowitz, L. COMMERCE 202-482-0558
Construction Statistics, Census/Industry Surveys....Visnansky, Bill CENSUS 301-763-7546
Construction Statistics, Constr Authorzd by Bldg Permit....Hoyle, Linda CENSUS 301-763-7244
Construction Statistics, New Residential, Charact....Berman, Steve CENSUS 301-763-7842
Construction Statistics, New Residential, House Complet....Fondelier, David CENSUS 301-763-5731
Construction Statistics, New Residential, Housing Start....Fondelier, David CENSUS 301-763-5731
Construction Statistics, New Residential, In Select MSA....Jacobson, Dale CENSUS 301-763-7842
Construction Statistics, New Residential, Sales....Berman, Steve CENSUS 301-763-7842
Construction Statistics, Residential Alterations....Roff, George CENSUS 301-763-5705
Construction Statistics, Residential Repairs....Roff, George CENSUS 301-763-5705
Construction Statistics, Value New Constr Put in Place....Meyer, Allan CENSUS 301-763-5717
Construction and Forestry, PPI, Prices/Lv. Cond....Davies, Wanda LABOR 202-606-7713
Construction paper....Rhodes, Richard USITC 202-205-3322
Construction services....Stonitsch, Laura USITC 202-205-3408
Construction, Domestic....MacAuley, Patrick COMMERCE 202-482-0132
Construction, Machinery....Heimowitz, L. COMMERCE 202-482-0558

Consulting services....SeSapio, Vincent USITC 202-205-3435
Consumer Affairs (all press inquiries)....Shaw Crouse, Janice OCA 202-634-4310
Consumer Affairs, Energy Affairs....Buchan, Douglas NEIC 202-586-5373
Consumer Expenditure Survey....Hoff, Gail CENSUS 301-763-2063
Consumer Expenditure Survey, Prices, Data Tapes....Passero, William LABOR 202-606-6900
Consumer Expenditure Survey, Prices & Liv. Cond....Jacobs, Eva LABOR 202-606-6900
Consumer Expenditure Survey, Surv. Data & Tapes....Passero, William LABOR 202-606-6900
Consumer Expenditure Survey, Surv. Oper., Pr/Lv.....Dietz, Richard LABOR 202-606-6872
Consumer Goods....Bodansky, Harry COMMERCE 202-482-4783
Consumer Price Index, Prices & Liv. Cond.....Jackman, Patrick LABOR 202-606-6952
Consumer Price Indexes, Avg. Retail Food Pr--Mo.....Cook, William LABOR 202-606-6988
Consumer Price Indexes, Pr/Lv. Con, Data Diskettes....Gibson, Sharon LABOR 202-606-6968
Consumer Price Indexes, Prices & Living Cond.....Jackman, Patrick LABOR 202-606-6952
Consumer Price Indexes, Prices & Living Conditions....Staff LABOR 202-606-7000
Consumer Price Indexes, Recorded CPI Detail....24-Hour Hotline LABOR 202-606-7828
Consumer Price Indexes, Avg. Ret. Pr., Fuels & Util.....Adkins, Robert LABOR 202-606-6985
Consumer Prices and Price Indexes, Asst. Comm....Armknecht, Paul LABOR 202-606-6952
Consumer Protection Bureau - Service Industry....Jones-Thompson, Gwendolyn L. FTC 202-326-3305
Consumer Protection Bureau - Service Industry Practices....Bash, Eric FTC 202-326-2892
Consumer Protection Bureau - Service Industry Practices.....Daynard, Matthew FTC 202-326-3291
Consumer Protection Bureau....Blickman, Neil J. FTC 202-326-3038
Consumer Protection Bureau....George, Jeanne FTC 202-326-3226
Consumer Protection Bureau....Hanson, Jean R. FTC 202-326-3236
Consumer Protection Bureau....Jackson, Howard R. FTC 202-326-3170
Consumer Protection Bureau....Lefevre, John F. FTC 202-326-3209
Consumer Protection Bureau....Vickers, Kate FTC 202-326-3670
Consumer Protection Bureau - Advertising....Amundsen, Jeri FTC 202-326-3180
Consumer Protection Bureau - Advertising Practices....Andrews, John C. FTC 202-326-2613
Consumer Protection Bureau - Advertising Practices....Bank, Kevin M. FTC 202-326-2675
Consumer Protection Bureau - Advertising Practices....Cheek, Robert C. FTC 202-326-3045
Consumer Protection Bureau - Advertising Practices....Cleland, Richard FTC 202-326-3088
Consumer Protection Bureau - Advertising Practices....Colbert, Lynne J. FTC 202-326-3571
Consumer Protection Bureau - Advertising Practices....Dahl, Brian A. FTC 202-326-3182
Consumer Protection Bureau - Advertising Practices....Del Borello, Michael FTC 202-326-3051
Consumer Protection Bureau - Advertising Practices....Dershowitz, Michael FTC 202-326-3158
Consumer Protection Bureau - Advertising Practices....Downs, Linda S. FTC 202-326-3147
Consumer Protection Bureau - Advertising Practices....Embrack, Kenneth A. FTC 202-326-3247
Consumer Protection Bureau - Advertising Practices....Engle, Mary Koelbel FTC 202-326-3161
Consumer Protection Bureau - Advertising Practices....Fair, Lesley A. FTC 202-326-3081
Consumer Protection Bureau - Advertising Practices....Fink, Duane E. FTC 202-326-3145
Consumer Protection Bureau - Advertising Practices....Forbes, Dean C. FTC 202-326-2831
Consumer Protection Bureau - Advertising Practices....Forbes, Georgianna A. FTC 202-326-3183
Consumer Protection Bureau - Advertising Practices....Fremont, Laura FTC 202-326-2649
Consumer Protection Bureau - Advertising Practices....Greisman, Lois C. FTC 202-326-3404
Consumer Protection Bureau - Advertising Practices....Guelzow, Lynn F. FTC

202-326-2386

Consumer Protection Bureau - Advertising Practices....Hoppock, Theodore H. FTC 202-326-3087

Consumer Protection Bureau - Advertising Practices....Johnson, Barbara J. FTC 202-326-3149

Consumer Protection Bureau - Advertising Practices....Kando, Carol A. FTC 202-326-3152

Consumer Protection Bureau - Advertising Practices....Kastriner, Marianne FTC 202-326-3165

Consumer Protection Bureau - Advertising Practices....Knight, Sydney FTC 202-326-2162

Consumer Protection Bureau - Advertising Practices....Koff, Karen J. FTC 202-326-2687

Consumer Protection Bureau - Advertising Practices....Kolish, Elaine D. FTC 202-326-3042

Consumer Protection Bureau - Advertising Practices....Kopchik, Lisa B. FTC 202-326-3139

Consumer Protection Bureau - Advertising Practices....Kull, Michael D. FTC 202-326-3467

Consumer Protection Bureau - Advertising Practices....Levin, Toby M. FTC 202-326-3156

Consumer Protection Bureau - Advertising Practices....Maher, Anne FTC 202-326-2987

Consumer Protection Bureau - Advertising Practices....Matthews, Cynthia I. FTC 202-326-3151

Consumer Protection Bureau - Advertising Practices....Murray, Joanna C. FTC 202-326-3256

Consumer Protection Bureau - Advertising Practices....Peeler, C. Lee FTC 202-326-3090

Consumer Protection Bureau - Advertising Practices....Pillsbury, Harold C. FTC 202-326-3194

Consumer Protection Bureau - Advertising Practices....Priesman, Phillip FTC 202-326-2484

Consumer Protection Bureau - Advertising Practices....Robinson, Henrietta FTC 202-326-3043

Consumer Protection Bureau - Advertising Practices....Rosso, Rosemary FTC 202-326-2174

Consumer Protection Bureau - Advertising Practices....Rusk, Michelle K. FTC 202-326-3148

Consumer Protection Bureau - Advertising Practices....Skidmore, Patricia A. FTC 202-326-3050

Consumer Protection Bureau - Advertising Practices....Sneed, Devenette FTC 202-326-3360

Consumer Protection Bureau - Advertising Practices....Thomas, Sheri FTC 202-326-3398

Consumer Protection Bureau - Advertising Practices....Warder, Nancy S. FTC 202-326-3048

Consumer Protection Bureau - Advertising Practices....Washington, Janice C. FTC 202-326-3332

Consumer Protection Bureau - Advertising Practices....Watts, Marianne R. FTC 202-326-3074

Consumer Protection Bureau - Advertising Practices....Weinstein, Loren FTC 202-326-2687

Consumer Protection Bureau - Advertising Practices....Wilkenfeld, Judith D. FTC 202-326-3150

Consumer Protection Bureau - Advertising Practices....Winston, Joel FTC 202-326-3153

Consumer Protection Bureau - Consumer & Bus. Educ....Andrean, Michael D. FTC 202-326-3650

Consumer Protection Bureau - Consumer & Bus. Educ.....Carter, Joanne B. FTC 202-326-2446

Consumer Protection Bureau - Consumer & Bus. Educ.....Moss, Betty W. FTC 202-326-3650

Consumer Protection Bureau - Consumer & Bus. Educ.....Sachs, Nancy L. FTC 202-326-3270

Consumer Protection Bureau - Consumer & Bus. Educ.....Tressler, Colleen P. FTC 202-326-2368

Consumer Protection Bureau - Consumer & Bus. Educ.....Vawter, Irene FTC 202-326-3268

Consumer Protection Bureau - Credit Practices....Baheri, Leila M. FTC 202-326-5610

Consumer Protection Bureau - Credit Practices....Berrelez, Rolando FTC 202-326-3211

Consumer Protection Bureau - Credit Practices....Brinckerhoff, Clarke FTC 202-326-3208

Consumer Protection Bureau - Credit Practices....Brown, Connie FTC 202-326-3212

Consumer Protection Bureau - Credit Practices....Carroll, Millicent FTC 202-326-2696

Consumer Protection Bureau - Credit Practices....Childs, Beverly R. FTC 202-326-3174

Consumer Protection Bureau - Credit Practices....Cohen, Stephen FTC 202-326-3222

Consumer Protection Bureau - Credit Practices....Credle, Lillie R. FTC 202-326-2975

Consumer Protection Bureau - Credit Practices....D'Entremont, Donald FTC 202-326-2736

Consumer Protection Bureau - Credit Practices....Fitzpatrick, Roger J. FTC 202-326-3172

Consumer Protection Bureau - Credit Practices....Flanigan, Stephanie P. FTC 202-326-2382

Consumer Protection Bureau - Credit Practices....Grimes, David G. FTC 202-326-3171

Consumer Protection Bureau - Credit Practices....Grissett, Heide FTC 202-326-3008

Consumer Protection Bureau - Credit Practices....Isaac, Ronald G. FTC 202-326-3231

Consumer Protection Bureau - Credit Practices....Kane, Thomas E. FTC 202-326-2304

Consumer Protection Bureau - Credit Practices....Keller, Christopher W. FTC 202-326-3159

Consumer Protection Bureau - Credit Practices....Lamb, Cynthia S. FTC 202-326-3001

Consumer Protection Bureau - Credit Practices....Levin, Arthur, B. FTC 202-326-3040

Consumer Protection Bureau - Credit Practices....Medine, David FTC 202-326-3224

Consumer Protection Bureau - Credit Practices....Morris, Lucy Eggersten FTC 202-326-3295

Consumer Protection Bureau - Credit Practices....Nixon, Judith M. FTC 202-326-3173

Consumer Protection Bureau - Credit Practices....Reynolds, Carole L. FTC 202-326-3230

Consumer Protection Bureau - Credit Practices....Sheelor, Margaret A. FTC 202-326-3007

Consumer Protection Bureau - Credit Practices....Szurgot, Charles F. FTC 202-326-3229

Consumer Protection Bureau - Credit Practices....Taylor, Brenda A. FTC 202-326-3125

Consumer Protection Bureau - Credit Practices....Twohig, Peggy FTC 202-326-3210

Consumer Protection Bureau - Credit Practices....Wahl, Hughes E. FTC 202-326-2999

Consumer Protection Bureau - Credit Practices....Wilmore, Sandra FTC 202-326-3169

Consumer Protection Bureau - Credit Practices....Wilson, Laura FTC 202-326-3236

Consumer Protection Bureau - Enforcement....Boyle, Terrence J. FTC 202-326-3016

Consumer Protection Bureau - Enforcement....Brewer, Joel N. FTC 202-326-2967

Consumer Protection Bureau - Enforcement....Dingfelder, Justin FTC 202-326-3017

Consumer Protection Bureau - Enforcement....Dublin, Brenda J. FTC 202-326-2976

Consumer Protection Bureau - Enforcement....Easton, Robert E. FTC 202-326-3029

Consumer Protection Bureau - Enforcement....Feinstein, Jeffrey E. FTC 202-326-2372

Consumer Protection Bureau - Enforcement....Frankle, Janice Podoll FTC 202-326-3022

Consumer Protection Bureau - Enforcement....Frisby, Robert FTC 202-326-2098

Consumer Protection Bureau - Enforcement....Graybill, Dean C. FTC 202-326-3284

Consumer Protection Bureau - Enforcement....Koman, Joseph J., Jr. FTC 202-326-3014

Consumer Protection Bureau - Enforcement....Lewis, Ronald D. FTC 202-326-2985

Consumer Protection Bureau - Enforcement....Martin, Vada L. FTC 202-326-3002

Consumer Protection Bureau - Enforcement....Massie, Thomas D. FTC 202-326-2982

Consumer Protection Bureau - Enforcement....McDonald, Jerry R. FTC 202-326-2971

Consumer Protection Bureau - Enforcement....Metrinko, Peter FTC 202-326-2104

Consumer Protection Bureau - Enforcement....Mickum, George B. FTC 202-326-3132

Consumer Protection Bureau - Enforcement....Mills, James G. FTC 202-326-3035

Consumer Protection Bureau - Enforcement....O'Brien, George T. FTC 202-326-2972

Consumer Protection Bureau - Enforcement....Patch, Susanne S. FTC 202-326-2981

Consumer Protection Bureau - Enforcement....Phillips, Joyce D. FTC 202-326-3041

Consumer Protection Bureau - Enforcement....Proctor, Deloris FTC 202-326-2349

Consumer Protection Bureau - Enforcement....Sacks, Ruth S. FTC 202-326-3033

Consumer Protection Bureau - Enforcement....Simpson, Robert M. FTC 202-326-2974

Consumer Protection Bureau - Enforcement....Sizemore, Diana H. FTC 202-326-3027

Consumer Protection Bureau - Enforcement....Tatum, Barbara FTC 202-326-2978

Consumer Protection Bureau - Enforcement....Thomas, Beverly J. FTC 202-326-2938

Consumer Protection Bureau - Enforcement....Toufexis, Rose FTC 202-326-3011

Consumer Protection Bureau - Enforcement....Vecellio, Constance M. FTC 202-326-2966

Consumer Protection Bureau - Enforcement....Witkowski, Wallace A. FTC 202-326-3015

Consumer Protection Bureau - Enforcement....Wright, Janet FTC 202-326-2980

Consumer Protection Bureau - Enforcement....Wilenzick, Marc B. FTC 202-326-2442

Consumer Protection Bureau - Marketing Practices....Bresnahan, Linda Jean FTC 202-326-3129

Consumer Protection Bureau - Marketing Practices....Cohn, Thomas A. FTC 202-326-3352

Consumer Protection Bureau - Marketing Practices....Cook, John M. FTC 202-326-2056

Consumer Protection Bureau - Marketing Practices....Danielson, Carole I. FTC 202-326-3115

Consumer Protection Bureau - Marketing Practices....Donohue, Richard C. FTC 202-326-3112

Consumer Protection Bureau - Marketing Practices....Feinstein, Mary S. FTC 202-326-3064

Consumer Protection Bureau - Marketing Practices....Grant, Elizabeth FTC 202-326-3299

Consumer Protection Bureau - Marketing Practices....Guerard, Collot FTC 202-326-3338

Consumer Protection Bureau - Marketing Practices....Harrington, Eileen FTC 202-326-3127

Consumer Protection Bureau - Marketing Practices....Haynes, William L. FTC 202-326-3107

Consumer Protection Bureau - Marketing Practices....Hile, Allen FTC 202-326-3122

Consumer Protection Bureau - Marketing Practices....Hodapp, Lawrence FTC 202-326-3105

Consumer Protection Bureau - Marketing Practices....Howard, Patricia S. FTC 202-326-2321

Consumer Protection Bureau - Marketing Practices....Howerton, Kent C. FTC 202-326-3013

Consumer Protection Bureau - Marketing Practices....Ireland, Robert S. FTC 202-326-3114

Consumer Protection Bureau - Marketing Practices....Jennings, Carol FTC 202-326-3010

Consumer Protection Bureau - Marketing Practices....Johnson, Delores M. FTC 220-326-3124

Consumer Protection Bureau - Marketing Practices....Jones, Cotie W. FTC 202-326-2047

Consumer Protection Bureau - Marketing Practices....Kresses, Mamie FTC 202-326-2070

Consumer Protection Bureau - Marketing Practices....Laden, Gary M. FTC 202-326-3118

Consumer Protection Bureau - Marketing Practices....Modell, Shira D. FTC 202-326-3116

Consumer Protection Bureau - Marketing Practices....Pitofsky, Sally Forman FTC 202-326-3318

Consumer Protection Bureau - Marketing Practices....Quaresima, Richard A.

FTC 202-326-3130

Consumer Protection Bureau - Marketing Practices....Reznek, Sarah FTC 202-326-2213

Consumer Protection Bureau - Marketing Practices....Salsburg, Daniel FTC 202-326-3032

Consumer Protection Bureau - Marketing Practices....Samley, Deborah FTC 202-326-2709

Consumer Protection Bureau - Marketing Practices....Shikiar, Robert FTC 202-326-3009

Consumer Protection Bureau - Marketing Practices....Smith, Arlene FTC 202-326-2390

Consumer Protection Bureau - Marketing Practices....Stamps, Shirley L. FTC 202-326-3099

Consumer Protection Bureau - Marketing Practices....Stone, Christopher FTC 202-326-3138

Consumer Protection Bureau - Marketing Practices....Toporoff, Steven FTC 202-326-3135

Consumer Protection Bureau - Marketing Practices....Torok, David FTC 202-326-3075

Consumer Protection Bureau - Marketing Practices....Tregillus, Craig FTC 202-326-2970

Consumer Protection Bureau - Marketing Practices....Vera, Martha W. FTC 202-326-3096

Consumer Protection Bureau - Office of Director....Betts, Raymond L. FTC 202-326-3163

Consumer Protection Bureau - Office of Director....Broder, Betsy FTC 202-326-3968

Consumer Protection Bureau - Office of Director....Brown, Gloria FTC 202-326-3047

Consumer Protection Bureau - Office of Director....Chung, Jock K. FTC 202-326-2984

Consumer Protection Bureau - Office of Director....Cutler, Barry J. FTC 202-326-3238

Consumer Protection Bureau - Office of Director....Damtoft, Russel W. FTC 202-326-3312

Consumer Protection Bureau - Office of Director....Enright, Maureen FTC 202-326-3160

Consumer Protection Bureau - Office of Director....Gorss, Janel A. FTC 202-326-3246

Consumer Protection Bureau - Office of Director....Hutchins, Clovia FTC 202-326-3215

Consumer Protection Bureau - Office of Director....Jung, Louise R. FTC 202-326-2989

Consumer Protection Bureau - Office of Director....Legal, Sharon V. FTC 202-326-3240

Consumer Protection Bureau - Office of Director....Maronick, Thomas J. FTC 202-326-2291

Consumer Protection Bureau - Office of Director....McDowell, Heather FTC 202-326-3356

Consumer Protection Bureau - Office of Director....Parnes, Lydia B. FTC 202-326-2676

Consumer Protection Bureau - Operations....Allen, Theodoshia FTC 202-326-3251

Consumer Protection Bureau - Operations....Burruss, James S., Jr. FTC 202-326-3261

Consumer Protection Bureau - Operations....Clayborne, Leroy, Jr. FTC 202-326-3252

Consumer Protection Bureau - Operations....Comtois, Joseph D. FTC 202-326-3255

Consumer Protection Bureau - Operations....Cossette, Darlene M. FTC 202-326-3255

Consumer Protection Bureau - Operations....Miller, Sylvia FTC 202-326-3258

Consumer Protection Bureau - Operations....Milton, Kathleen FTC 202-326-3253

Consumer Protection Bureau - Operations....Peterson, Mark D. FTC 202-326-3731

Consumer Protection Bureau - Operations....Ross, Michelle FTC 202-326-3260

Consumer Protection Bureau - Operations....Shapr, Kanili FTC 202-326-6196

Consumer Protection Bureau - Operations....Soranno, Donatos S. FTC 202-326-3255

Consumer Protection Bureau - Service Industry Pract....Crowley, John A. FTC 202-326-3280

Consumer Protection Bureau - Service Industry....Chambers, Sylvia J. FTC 202-326-3286

Consumer Protection Bureau - Service Industry....Dolan, James Reilly FTC 202-326-3292

Consumer Protection Bureau - Service Industry....Feinberg, Melissa FTC

202-326-3315

Consumer Protection Bureau - Service Industry....Fields, Mary C. FTC 202-326-3098

Consumer Protection Bureau - Service Industry....Fix, David FTC 202-326-3298

Consumer Protection Bureau - Service Industry....Frankel, David P. FTC 202-326-2166

Consumer Protection Bureau - Service Industry....Friedman, Robert D. FTC 202-326-3297

Consumer Protection Bureau - Service Industry....Gordimer, Douglas FTC 202-326-3003

Consumer Protection Bureau - Service Industry....Gross, Walter, III FTC 202-326-3319

Consumer Protection Bureau - Service Industry....Gurwitz, Stephen FTC 202-326-3272

Consumer Protection Bureau - Service Industry....Hippsley, Heather FTC 202-326-3285

Consumer Protection Bureau - Service Industry....Jones, Elaine FTC 202-326-3622

Consumer Protection Bureau - Service Industry....Katz, Michael A. FTC 202-326-3123

Consumer Protection Bureau - Service Industry....Kelly, Deborah H. FTC 202-326-3004

Consumer Protection Bureau - Service Industry....Kelly, Richard F. FTC 202-326-3304

Consumer Protection Bureau - Service Industry....Kinscheck, Renate FTC 202-326-3283

Consumer Protection Bureau - Service Industry....Lamberton, Peter W. FTC 202-326-3274

Consumer Protection Bureau - Service Industry....McCarey, Michael C. FTC 202-326-3303

Consumer Protection Bureau - Service Industry....Mereu, Richard FTC 202-326-3245

Consumer Protection Bureau - Service Industry....Osinbajo, Deborah A. FTC 202-326-3316

Consumer Protection Bureau - Service Industry....Owens, Denise FTC 202-326-3277

Consumer Protection Bureau - Service Industry....Rich, Jessica FTC 202-326-2148

Consumer Protection Bureau - Service Industry....Rosenfeld, Dana FTC 202-326-2113

Consumer Protection Bureau - Service Industry....Rothchild, John FTC 202-326-3307

Consumer Protection Bureau - Service Industry....Rushkoff, Bennett FTC 202-326-3439

Consumer Protection Bureau - Service Industry....Sheer, Alain FTC 202-326-3321

Consumer Protection Bureau - Service Industry....Spiegel, David R. FTC 202-326-3281

Consumer Protection Bureau - Service Industry....Spiro, Daniel A. FTC 202-326-3288

Consumer Protection Bureau - Service Industry....Stevenson, Hugh FTC 202-326-3511

Consumer Protection Bureau - Service Industry....Tait, Monica FTC 202-326-3505

Consumer Protection Bureau - Service Industry....Toone, Cassandra L. FTC 202-326-3276

Consumer Protection Bureau - Service Industry....Vidas, Sandra M. FTC 202-326-2456

Consumer Protection Bureau - Service Industry....Wagner, Connie FTC 202-326-3309

Consumer Protection Bureau - Service Industry....Williams, Gwendolyn C. FTC 202-326-3311

Consumer Protection Bureau - Service Industry Prac....Buckley, John D. FTC 202-326-3317

Consumer Protection Bureau - Service Industry Prac....Curtin, Theodore C. FTC 202-326-2311

Contact Lenses....Staff NEI 301-496-5248

Containers (of wood)....Ruggles, Fred USITC 202-205-3325

Containers, of base metal....Fulcher, Nancy USITC 202-205-3434

Contaminants, Environmental....Staff FWS 703-358-2148

Continental Shelf, Outer....Staff FWS 202-358-2183

Continuous Ambulatory Peritoneal Dialysis (CAPD)....Staff NIDDK 301-496-3583

Contraception....Staff NICHD 301-496-5133

Contraceptives....Staff NICHD 301-496-5133

Contraceptives....Cruzan, Susan FDA 301-443-3285

Control Devices (non-licenses)....Staff FCC 202-653-6288

Conventional Fossil Fuel Power (Major Projects)....Dollison, Robert COMMERCE 202-482-2733

Conventions, Exhibits....Dickinson, Joanne CENSUS 301-763-2370

Converted Paper Prod....Stanley, Gary COMMERCE 202-482-0375

Converters....Greene, William USITC 202-205-3405

Cook Islands....Lagoy, Michele Peace Corps 202-606-3227

Cook Islands....Staff Cnty State 202-647-3546

Cooley's Anemia....Staff NHLBI 301-496-4236

Cooperative Forestry....Liu, Karen FS 202-205-1378

Copper....Jolly, Janice L. MINES 202-501-9414

Copper....Edelstein, Daniel MINES 202-501-9415

Copper....Lundy, David USITC 202-205-3439

Copper Wire Mills....Duggan, Brain COMMERCE 202-482-0575

Copper compounds....Greenblatt, Jack USITC 202-205-3353

Copper/Brass Mills....Duggan, Brian COMMERCE 202-482-0575

Copra and coconut oil....Reeder, John USITC 202-205-3319

Cor Pulmonale....Staff NHLBI 301-496-4236

Cordage....Konzet, Jeffrey CUSTOMS 212-466-5885

Cordage machines....Greene, William USITC 202-205-3405

Cordless Telephone....Staff FCC 202-653-6288

Cork and cork products....Ruggles, Fred USITC 202-205-3325

Corn Products....Janis, William V. COMMERCE 202-482-2250

Corn with options....Gore, Philip CFT 312-886-3044

Corn, field....Pierre-Benoist, John USITC 202-205-3320

Corneal Disorders....Staff NEI 301-496-5248

Corneal Transplantation....Staff NEI 301-496-5248

Cornelia deLange Syndrome....Staff NICHD 301-496-5133

Coronary Angioplasty....Staff NHLBI 301-496-4236

Coronary Artery Surgery Study (CASS)....Staff NHLBI 301-496-4236

Coronary Bypass....Staff NHLBI 301-496-4236

Coronary Disease....Staff NHLBI 301-496-4236

Corrections....Innes, Christopher Justice Stat 202-724-3121

Corrections....Beck, Allen Justice Stat 202-616-3277

Corrections....Greenfeld, Lawrence Justice Stat 202-616-3281

Corrections....Huggins, Wayne M. Justice Stat 202-307-3106

Corrections....Baunach, Phyllis Jo Justice Stat 202-307-0361

Corrections - Community....Baunach, Phyllis Jo Justice Stat 202-307-0361

Corrections - General....Greenfeld, Lawrence Justice Stat 202-616-3281

Corrections - General....Baunach, Phyllis Jo Justice Stat 202-307-0361

Corrections - General....Beck, Allen Justice Stat 202-616-3277

Corrections - General....Stephan, James Justice Stat 202-616-7273

Corrections - General....Innes, Christopher Justice Stat 202-724-3121

Corrections - General....Kline, Susan Justice Stat 202-724-3118

Corrections - General....Kane, Patrick R. Justice Stat 202-307-3226

Corrections - State....Shipley, Bernard Justice Stat 202-307-7703

Corundum-Emery....Austin, Gordon MINES 202-501-9388

Cosmetic Allergy....Staff FDA 301-245-1061

Cosmetic and Toiletry Preparations....Joseph, Stephanie CUSTOMS 212-466-5768

Cosmetic creams....Land, Eric USITC 202-205-3349

Cosmetics....Hurt, William COMMERCE 202-482-0128

Cosmetics....Lecos, Chris FDA 202-205-4144

Cosmetics (Export Promo)....Kimmel, Ed COMMERCE 202-482-3460

Cosmetics, perfumery, toilet preparations....Land, Eric USITC 202-205-3349

Cost Rica....Stanton, Dan Peace Corps 202-606-3620

Cost of Crime - General....Lindgren, Sue Justice Stat 202-307-0760

Cost of Crime - General....Rand, Michael Justice Stat 202-616-3494

Cost of Crime - To Government....Lindgren, Sue Justice Stat 202-307-0760

Cost of Crime - To Victims....Klaus, Patsy Justice Stat 202-307-0776

Cost-of-Living Abroad, Productivity & Technology....Capdevielle, Patricia LABOR 202-606-5654

Costa Rica....Subrin, Laura Cnty Commerce 202-482-2527

Costa Rica....Tumaylle, Carol Peace Corps 202-606-3321

Costa Rica (San Jose)....Staff Cnty State 202-647-3381

Costa Rica/Minerals....Mobbs, Richard Cnty Mines 202-501-9679

Costochondritis....Staff NIAMS 301-496-8188

Costume Jewelry, Trade Promo....Beckham, R. COMMERCE 202-482-5478

Cote d'Ivoire....Strozier, Maisha Peace Corps 202-606-3185

Cote d'Ivoire (Abidjan)....Staff Cnty State 202-647-2865

Cote d'Ivoire (Ivory Coast)....van Oss, Hendrik Cnty Mines 202-501-9687

Cotton....Latham, Roger Agri 202-720-5944

Cotton....Skinner, Robert Agri 202-219-0841

Cotton....Meyer, Leslie Agri 202-219-0840

Cotton....Sweet, Mary Elizabeth USITC 202-205-3455

Cotton - World....Whitton, Carolyn Agri 202-219-0826

Cotton Seed Oil....Janis, William V. COMMERCE 202-482-2250

Cottonseed and cottonseed oil....Reeder, John USITC 202-205-3319

Council of Europe....Staff Cnty State 202-647-1708

County Business Patterns....Decker, Zigmund CENSUS 301-763-5430

County and City Data Books....Cevis, Wanda CENSUS 301-763-1034

Courier Services....Elliot, Fred COMMERCE 202-482-1134

Court Appeals....Gaskins, Carla Justice Stat 202-508-8550

Court Appeals....Langan, Patrick Justice Stat 202-616-3490

Court Appeals....Lindgren, Sue Justice Stat 202-307-0760

Court Case Processing Time....Gaskins, Carla Justice Stat 202-508-8550

Court Case Processing Time - Federal....Kaplan, Carol Justice Stat 202-307-0759

Court Caseload....Gaskins, Carla Justice Stat 202-508-8550

Court Caseload....Langan, Patrick Justice Stat 202-616-3490

Court Organization....Gaskins, Carla Justice Stat 202-508-8550

Court Organization....Langan, Patrick Justice Stat 202-616-3490

Courts....Langan, Patrick Justice Stat 202-616-3490

Courts....Gaskins, Carla Justice Stat 202-508-8550

Coxsackie Virus (Hand-Food & Mouth Disease)....Staff NIAID 301-496-5717

Coxsackie Virus (Hand-Foot & Mouth Disease)....Staff NICHD 301-496-5133

Cranes....Greene, William USITC 202-205-3405

Craniofacial Malformations....Staff NIDR 301-496-4261

Crayons....Sundar, Shetty USITC 202-205-3486

Creams, cosmetic....Land, Eric USITC 202-205-3349

Cretinism....Staff NIDDK 301-496-3583

Creutzfeldt-Jakob Disease....Staff NINDS 301-496-5751

Cri Du Chat (Cat Cry Syndrome)....Staff NICHD 301-496-5133

Crib Death (SIDS)....Staff NICHD 301-496-5133

Crib Toys....Tyrrell, Elaine CPSC 301-504-0580

Crigler-Najar Syndrome....Staff NIDDK 301-496-3583

Crime Incidence, Rates, and Trends....Dillingham, Steven Justice Stat 202-307-0765

Crime Incidence, Rates, and Trends....Klaus, Patsy Justice Stat 202-307-0776

Crime Incidence, Rates, and Trends....Taylor, Bruce Justice Stat 202-616-3498

Crime Measurement Methods....Dodge, Richard Justice Stat 202-616-3485

Crime Measurement Methods....Taylor, Bruce Justice Stat 202-616-3498

Crime Measurement Methods....Rand, Michael Justice Stat 202-616-3494

Crime Prevention Measures....Shields, Stephanie Justice Stat 202-466-6272

Crime Seasonality....Dodge, Richard Justice Stat 202-616-3485

Crime Severity....Klaus, Patsy Justice Stat 202-307-0776

Crime Types: Homicide....Zawitz, Marianne Justice Stat 202-616-3499

Crime Types: Homicide....White, Paul Justice Stat 202-307-0771

Crime Types: Federal, Bank Robbery, Computer....Kaplan, Carol Justice Stat 202-307-0759

Crime Types: Rape, Robbery, Assault, Theft....Klaus, Patsy Justice Stat 202-307-0776

Crime Types: Rape, Robbery, Assault, Theft....Rand, Michael Justice Stat 202-616-3494

Crime Types: Rape, Robbery, Assault, Theft....Harlow, Catherine Justice Stat 202-307-0757

Crime and the Elderly....Staff NIA 301-496-1752

Crime, Incidence, Rates, and Trends....Rand, Michael Justice Stat 202-616-3494

Crime, Location of....Dodge, Richard Justice Stat 202-616-3485

Crime, Population....McGinn, Larry CENSUS 301-763-1735

Criminal Defendants....Gaskins, Carla Justice Stat 202-508-8550

Criminal Defendants....Langan, Patrick Justice Stat 202-616-3490

Criminal Defendants - Federal....Kaplan, Carol Justice Stat 202-307-0759

Criminal History Data Quality....Kaplan, Carol Justice Stat 202-307-0759

Criminal Justice Agencies....Lindgren, Sue Justice Stat 202-307-0760

Criminal Justice Expenditure and Employment....Lindgren, Sue Justice Stat 202-307-0760

Critical Care Medicine Department....Staff CC 301-496-9565

Crohn's Disease....Staff NIDDK 301-496-3583

Crohn's Disease....Staff NIAID 301-496-5717

Crop Protection....Staff FWS 703-358-2043

Cross-Eye....Staff NEI 301-496-5248

Crude Oil....Heath, Charles NEIC 202-586-6860

Crude Oil Markets....Cook, John NEIC 202-586-5214

Crude cresylic acid....Foreso, Cynthia USITC 202-205-3348

Crude petroleum....Foreso, Cynthia USITC 202-205-3348

Crushing machines....Greene, William USITC 202-205-3405

Cryolite....White, Linda USITC 202-205-3427

Cryosurgery (Eyes)....Staff NEI 301-496-5248

Cryptococcosis....Staff NIAID 301-496-5717

Cryptosporidiosis....Staff NIAID 301-496-5717

Cuba....Soto, Rodrigo Cnty Commerce 202-482-2527

Cuba (Havana)....Staff Cnty State 202-647-9272

Cuba/Minerals....Gurmendi, Alfredo Cnty Mines 202-501-9681

Cucumbers....McCarty, Timothy USITC 202-205-3324

Culm....Foreso, Cynthia USITC 202-205-3348

Cupric oxide....Conant, Kenneth USITC 202-205-3346

Cuprous oxide....Conant, Kenneth USITC 202-205-3346

Current Analysis of U.S. Export & Import Price Ind....Vachris, Michelle LABOR 202-606-7155

Current Business Analysis, (Acting Chief)....Fox, Douglas R. ECONOMIC 202-523-0697

Current Business Statistics....Statistical Series Staff ECONOMIC 202-523-6336

Current Employment Analysis, Assist. Comm. Empl/Unempl....Bregger, John E. LABOR 202-606-6378

Current Wage Developments, Comp. & Working Cond....Cimini, Michael LABOR 202-606-6275

Current-Carrying Wiring Devices....Whitley, Richard A. COMMERCE 202-482-0682

Curtains....Sweet, Mary Elizabeth USITC 202-205-3455

Cushing's Syndrome....Staff NIDDK 301-496-3583

Cushing's Syndrome....Staff NINDS 301-496-5751

Cushing's Syndrome....Staff NICHD 301-496-5133

Cushions....Spalding, Josephine USITC 202-205-3498

Customer Service....Staff CENSUS 301-763-4100

Cut Flowers....Conte, Ralph CUSTOMS 212-466-5759

Cut flowers....Burket, Stephen USITC 202-205-3318

Cutis Laxa....Staff NHLBI 301-496-4236

Cutlery....Harris, John COMMERCE 202-482-1178

Cutlery....Preston, Jacques CUSTOMS 212-466-5488

Cutlery....MacKnight, Peggy USITC 202-205-3431

Cutting machines textile....Greene, William USITC 202-205-3405

Cyclic Idiopathic Edema....Staff NHLBI 301-496-4236

Cyclitis....Staff NEI 301-496-5248

Cyprus....Corro, Ann Cnty Commerce 202-482-3945

Cyprus (Nicosia)....Staff Cnty State 202-647-6113

Cyprus/Minerals....King, Audie L. Cnty Mines 202-501-9674

Cystic Acne....Staff NIAMS 301-496-8188

Cystic Fibrosis (Pancreas)....Staff NIDDK 301-496-3583

Cystinosis....Staff NICHD 301-496-5133

Cystinuria....Staff NIDDK 301-496-3583

Cystitis....Staff NIDDK 301-496-3583

Cytology....Staff NCI 301-496-5583

Cytomegalic Inclusion Disease....Staff NINDS 301-496-5751

Cytomegalic Inclusion Disease....Staff NIDCD 301-496-7243

Cytomegalovirus (Congenital)....Staff NHLBI 301-496-4236

Cytomegalovirus (Congenital)....Staff NICHD 301-496-5133

Cytomegalovirus (Congenital)....Staff NIAID 301-496-5717

Czechoslovakia....Mowrey, Mark Cnty Commerce 202-482-2645

Czechoslovakia (Prague)....Staff Cnty State 202-647-3298

Czechoslovakia/Minerals....Plachy, Josef Cnty Mines 202-501-9673

D

D'Jibouti....Watkins, Chandra Cnty Commerce 202-482-4564

D-Mark with options....Bice, David CFT 312-35-37880

DES (Diethylstilbestrol)....Staff NCI 301-496-5583

DES (Diethylstilbestrol)....Staff NICHD 301-496-5133

DES (Diethylstilbestrol)....Staff FDA 301-443-3170

DMSO (Dimethylsulfoxide)....Staff NCI 301-496-5583

DMSO (Dimethylsulfoxide)....Staff FDA/NCDB 301-443-1016

DNA....Staff NCI 301-496-5583

DNA....Staff NIGMS 301-496-7301

Dairy Products....Janis, William V. COMMERCE 202-482-2250

Dairy Products - Milk, Ice Cream, etc.....Buckner, Dan Agri 202-720-4448

Dairy Products - Milk, Ice Cream, etc.....Miller, Jim Agri 202-219-0770

Dairy Products - Milk, Ice Cream, etc.....Short, Sara Agri 202-219-0769

Dairy products....Warren, J Fred USITC 202-205-3311

Dam Safety....Staff FWS 703-35801719

Dance....Butler, Jeanne NEA 202-682-5435

Dandy-Walker Syndrome....Staff NINDS 301-496-5751

Darier's Disease....Staff NIAMS 301-496-8188

Data Acquisition Systems....Brown, Dwayne NASA 202-543-8956

Data Base Services....Inoussa, Mary COMMERCE 202-482-5820

Data Diskettes & Tapes, State & Area Labor Force....Marcus, Jessie LABOR 202-606-6392

Data Diskettes and Tapes, Empl. & Wages, Empl/Unempl....Buso, Michael LABOR 202-606-6378

Data Diskettes, Consumer Price Indexes, Pr/Lv. Con....Gibson, Sharon LABOR 202-606-6968

Data Diskettes, Employment Projections....Bowman, Charles LABOR 202-606-5702

Data Diskettes, Prices and Living Conditions....Rosenberg, Elliott LABOR 202-606-7728

Data Processing Services....Atkins, Robert G. COMMERCE 202-482-4781

Data Tapes, Industry-Occup. Matrix, Empl. Proj.....Turner, Delores LABOR 202-606-5730

Data Tapes, Productivity & Technology....Kriebel, Bertram LABOR 202-606-5606

Data and Tapes, Consumer Expend. Survey, Prices....Passero, William LABOR 202-606-6900

Data processing machines....Bringe, Julie USITC 202-205-3390

Data processing services....Xavier, Neil USITC 202-205-3450

Day Care....Long, Susan ACF 202-401-9215

Deafness....Staff NIDCD 301-496-7243

Deafness, National Institute of....Allen, Marin NIH 301-496-7243

Death and Dying....Staff NIMH 301-443-4515

Death and Dying....Staff NIA 301-443-1752

Decalcomanias (decals)....Stahmer, Carsten USITC 202-205-3321

Decennial Census, 1990 Counts f/Current Boundaries....Miller, Joel CENSUS 301-763-5720

Decennial Census, Content & Tabula, Program Design....Berman, Patricia CENSUS 301-763-7094

Decennial Census, Content, General....Paez, Al CENSUS 301-763-4251

Decennial Census, Content, General....Lichtman-Panzer, Paulette CENSUS 301-763-5270

Decennial Census, Count Information....Staff CENSUS 301-763-5002

Decennial Census, Count Information....Staff CENSUS 301-763-5020

Decennial Census, Count Questions, 1990 Census....Kobilarcik, Ed CENSUS 301-763-4894

Decennial Census, Demographic Analysis....Robinson, Gregg CENSUS 301-763-5590

Decennial Census, Housing Data, Special Tabuls. of....Downs, Bill CENSUS 301-763-8553

Decennial Census, Litigation....Gregg, Valerie CENSUS 301-763-7787

Decennial Census, Population Data, Special Tab. of....Cowan, Rosemarie CENSUS 301-763-7947

Decennial Census, Post-Enumeration Surveys....Hogan, Howard CENSUS 301-763-1794

Decennial Census, Publications, General....Landman, Cheryl CENSUS 301-763-3938

Decennial Census, Publications, General....Porter, Gloria CENSUS 301-763-4908

Decennial Census, Reapportionment....Turner, Marshall CENSUS 301-763-5820

Decennial Census, Redistricting....Talbert, Cathy CENSUS 301-763-4070

Decennial Census, Sampling Methods....Woltman, Henry CENSUS 301-763-5987

Decennial Census, Tabulations, General....Landman, Cheryl CENSUS 301-763-3938

Decennial Census, Tabulations, General....Porter, Gloria CENSUS 301-763-4908

Decennial Census, User-Defined Area Program....Quasney, Adrienne CENSUS 301-763-4282

Decennial Management....Walsh, Thomas CENSUS 301-763-2682

Decennial Planning Division....Vacant CENSUS 301-763-7670

Decontamination....Staff OD/ORS 301-496-2960

Decontamination (Radioactive Spills)....Staff OD/ORS 301-496-2254

Decubitus Ulcers....Staff NIA 301-496-1752

Deep Space Communications Complex....Wood, Alan S. NASA 818-354-5011

Defense Energy Projects....Carroll, Wade NEIC 301-903-3321

Degenerative Basal Ganglia Disease....Staff NINDS 301-496-5751

Degenerative Joint Disease....Staff NIAMS 301-496-8188

Deglutition....Staff NIDR 301-496-4261

Dejerine-Sottas Disease....Staff NINDS 301-496-5751

Delivery of Nursing Care....Staff NCNR 301-496-0526

Dementia....Staff NINDS 301-496-5751

Dementia....Staff NIA 301-496-1752

Demographic Programs, Statistical Research....Ernst, Lawrence CENSUS 301-763-7880

Demographic Studies, Center for....Wetzel, James R. CENSUS 301-763-7720

Demography....Staff NICHD 301-496-5133

Demography of Aging....Staff NIA 301-496-1752

Demyelinating Diseases....Staff NINDS 301-496-5751

Dengue....Staff NIAID 301-496-5717

Denmark....Lyons, Maryanne Cnty Commerce 202-482-3254

Denmark (Copenhagen)....Staff Cnty State 202-647-5669

Denmark/Minerals....Rabchevsky, George Cnty Mines 202-501-9672

Dental Assistants (Education)....Staff HRSA/BHPr 301-443-6837

Dental Care Programs (Aged, Handicapped, Prepaid)....Staff HRSA 301-443-6853

Dental Diseases/Disorders....Staff NIDR 301-496-4261

Dental Research, National Institute of....Jacquet, Brent NIH 301-496-4261

Dental Restorative Materials....Staff NIDR 301-496-4261

Dental cements....Randall, Rob USITC 202-205-3366

Dentobacterial Plaque Infection....Staff NIDR 301-496-4261

Dentures....Staff NIDR 301-496-4261

Depreciation Rules....Staff FCC 202-632-7500

Depression....Staff NIMH 301-443-4515

Depression and Aging....Staff NIMH 301-443-1185

Depression and Aging....Staff NIA 301-496-1752

Depth Perception....Staff NEI 301-496-5248

Deputy Commissioner, Office of....Barron, William G. LABOR 202-606-7802

Deputy Director (Acting), BEA....Young, Allan H. ECONOMIC 202 523-0693

Dermatitis Herpetiformis....Staff NIAMS 301-496-8188

Dermatological agents....Nesbitt, Elizabeth USITC 202-205-3355

Dermatology....Staff NIAMS 301-496-8188

Dermatology....Staff NCI 301-496-5583

Dermatomyositis....Staff NIAMS 301-496-8188

Dermatomyositis....Staff NINDS 301-496-5751

Dermographism....Staff NIAID 301-496-5717

Desalination/Water Reuse....Wheeler, Frederica COMMERCE 202-482-3502

Design Arts....Kriegsman, Sali Ann NEA 202-682-5435

Detergents....Joseph, Stephanie CUSTOMS 212-466-5768

Detergents....Land, Eric USITC 202-205-3349

Developmental Disabilities....Long, Susan ACF 202-401-9215

Developmental Disabilities and Birth Defects....Oakley, Godfrey P. CDC 404-488-7150

Developmental Disorders....Staff NINDS 301-496-5751

Developmental Disorders....Staff NIDCD 301-496-7243

Developmental Disorders....Staff NICHD 301-496-5133

Developmental Endocrinology....Chrousos, George P. FAES 301-496-5800

Developmental Endocrinology....Vamvakopoulos, Nicholas FAES 301-496-6994

Devic's Syndrome....Staff NINDS 301-496-5751

Dextrine....Randall, Rob USITC 202-205-3366

Di(2-ethylhexyl) adipate....Johnson, Larry USITC 202-205-3351

Di(2-ethylhexyl) phthalate....Johnson, Larry USITC 202-205-3351

Diabetes....Taylor, Simeon FAES 301-496-2596

Diabetes (And Arteriosclerosis)....Staff NHLBI 301-496-4236

Diabetes (Juvenile)....Staff NIDDK 301-496-3583

Diabetes Clearinghouse....Staff NIDDK 301-468-2162

Diabetes Insipidus....Staff NIDDK 301-496-3583

Diabetes Mellitus....Staff NIDDK 301-496-3583

Diabetes and Aging (Type 1 and Type 2)....Staff NIDDK 301-496-3583

Diabetes and Aging (Type 1 and Type 2)....Staff NIA 301-496-1752

Diabetes and Pregnancy....Staff NICHD 301-496-5133

Diabetes with Insulin Allergy or Resistance....Staff NIAID 301-496-5717

Diabetes with Insulin Allergy or Resistance....Staff NIDDK 301-496-3583

Diabetes, Digestive & Kidney Disorders, Nat'l Inst....Singer, Betsy NIH 301-496-3583

Diabetic Neuropathy....Staff NINDS 301-496-5751

Diabetic Retinopathy....Staff NEI 301-496-5248

Diagnostic Laboratories for Animal Disease....Staff NCRR 301-496-5175

Diagnostic Radiology....Staff CC 301-496-7700

Dial-a-Porn Complaints....Staff FCC 202-632-7553

Dialysis, Kidney....Staff NIDDK 301-496-3583

Diamond....Austin, Gordon MINES 202-501-9388

Diamond, Industrial....Prebury, Graylin COMMERCE 202-482-5158

Diamonds....DeSapio, Vincent USITC 202-205-3435

Diarrheal Illnesses....Staff NIDDK 301-496-3583

Diarrheal Illnesses....Staff NIAID 301-496-5717

Diathermy Approval....Staff FCC 301-725-1585

Diatomite....Davis, Lawrence L. MINES 202-501-9386

Diatomite....White, Linda USITC 202-205-3427

Dictation machines....Sherman, Thomas USITC 202-205-3389

Diego Garcia....Staff Cnty State 202-647-8913

Diethylstilbestrol (DES)....Staff NCI 301-496-5583

Diethylstilbestrol (DES)....Staff FDA 301-443-3170

Diethylstilbestrol (DES)....Staff NICHD 301-496-5133

Diffuse Sclerosis....Staff NINDS 301-496-5751

Digestive Diseases....Staff NIDDK 301-496-3583

Digestive Diseases Clearinghouse....Staff NIDDK 301-468-6344

Digital Electronic Message Service....Staff FCC 202-634-1706

Digital Terminations Systems....Staff FCC 202-634-1706

Dilsobutylene....Raftery, Jim USITC 202-205-3365

Dilsodecyl phthalate....Johnson, Larry USITC 202-205-3351

Dinnerware of ceramic....McNay, Deborah USITC 202-205-3425

Dioctyl phthalates....Johnson, Larry USITC 202-205-3351

Diphtheria....Staff NIAID 301-496-5717

Diploma Schools of Nursing....Staff HRSA/BHPr 301-443-2134

Direct Broadcasting Satellites....Staff FCC 202-632-9356

Direct Distance Dialing....Staff FCC 202-632-5550

Direct Mail....Elliot, Fred COMMERCE 202-482-3574

Director, BEA....Carson, Carol S. ECONOMIC 202-523-0707

Director, Office of the....Lindberg, Donald A. NLM 301-496-6221

Disability Benefits, Social Security....Gambino, Phil SSA 410-965-8904

Disc Drives, Diskettes....Kader, Victoria COMMERCE 202-482-0571

Discoid Lupus Erythematosus....Staff NIAMS 301-496-8188

Discouraged Workers, Empl./Unempl. Stats....Hamel, Harvey LABOR 202-606-6378

Discouraged Workers, Employment Statistics....Hamel, Harvey LABOR 202-606-6378

Disease Information Hotline.... CDC 404-322-4555

Disease Prevention....Staff NCNR 301-496-0526

Disinfection....Staff OD/ORS 301-496-2960

Displaced Workers, Empl/Unempl Statistics....Gardner, Jennifer LABOR 202-606-6378

Disposal (Animal Waste, Dead Animal, Infect. Materials)....Staff OD/ORS 301-496-2960

Distillate fuel oil....Foreso, Cynthia USITC 202-205-3348

Distilled Water....Staff OD/ORS 301-496-2960

Distribution services....Xavier, Neil USITC 202-205-3450

Diuretics....Staff NHLBI 301-496-4236

Diurnaldystonia....Staff NINDS 301-496-5751

Diverticulitis....Staff NIDDK 301-496-3583

Divorce Statistics....Heuser, Robert CDC 301-436-8954

Dizziness....Staff NINDS 301-496-5751

Dizziness....Staff NIDCD 301-496-7243

Djibouti, Republic of (Djibouti)....Staff Cnty State 202-647-8852

Djibouti/Minerals....Antonides, Lloyd Cnty Mines 202-501-9686

Doll carriages, stroller, and parts....Seastrum, Carl USITC 202-205-3493

Dolls....Vacant COMMERCE 202-482-0338

Dolls....Wong, Alice CUSTOMS 212-466-5538

Dolls....Luther, Dennis USITC 202-205-3497

Dolomite, dead burned....DeSapio, Vincent USITC 202-205-3435

Domestic Oil Reserves Statistics....Lique, Diane Q. NEIC 202-586-6090

Domestic Satellite Licenses....Staff FCC 301-634-1624

Domestic Violence....Klaus, Patsy Justice Stat 202-307-0776

Domestic Violence....Rand, Michael Justice Stat 202-616-3494

Domestic Violence....Langan, Patrick Justice Stat 202-616-3490

Dominica....Brooks, Michelle Cnty Commerce 202-482-2527

Dominica (Roseau)....Staff Cnty State 202-647-2621

Dominica/Minerals....Torres, Ivette Cnty Mines 202-501-9680

Dominican Republic....Soto, Rodrigo Cnty Commerce 202-482-2527

Dominican Republic....Pauk, Jennifer L. Peace Corps 202-606-3323

Dominican Republic (Santo Domingo)....Staff Cnty State 202-647-2620

Dominican Republic/Minerals....Doan, David Cnty Mines 202-501-9678

Down Syndrome....Staff NICHD 301-496-5133

Down apparel....Jones, Jackie USITC 202-205-3466

Draperies....Sweet, Mary Elizabeth USITC 202-205-3455

Drawing instruments....Shetty, Sundar USITC 202-205-3486

Dresses....Crowley, Michael CUSTOMS 212-466-5852

Dresses....Holoyda, Olha USITC 202-205-3467

Dressing machines (textile)....Greene, William USITC 202-205-3405

Drilling Mus/Soft Compounds....Vacant COMMERCE 202-482-0564

Drink-preparing machines....Jackson, Georgia USITC 202-205-3399

Drinking Water Branch....Staff EPA 202-260-5526

Drinking Water Standards....Staff EPA 202-260-7575

Drinking and Cancer....Staff NCI 301-496-5583

Drug Abuse Treatment....Hurley, Joan ADAMHA 301-443-6549

Drug Abuse, National Institute on....Brown, Mona ADAMHA 301-443-6245

Drug Abuse, Prenatal....Brown, Mona ADAMHA 301-443-6549

Drug Abuse, Treatment....Hurley, Joan ADAMHA 301-443-6549

Drug Abuse, in Workplace....Brown, Mona ADAMHA 301-443-6245

Drug Allergy....Staff NIAID 301-496-5717

Drug Enforcement Administration....Staff EPA 202-307-1000

Drug Hemolytic Anemia....Staff NIDDK 301-496-3583

Drug Purpura....Staff NIDDK 301-496-3583

Drug Resistance....Staff NIAID 301-496-5717

Drug Test Guidelines....Brown, Mona ADAMHA 301-443-6245

Drugs....Hurt, William COMMERCE 202-482-0128

Drugs & Drug Labeling....Lecos, Chris FDA 202-205-4144

Drugs & Drug Labeling: AIDS Drugs....Peterson, Faye FDA 301-443-3285

Drugs & Drug Labeling: Generic....Shaffer, Michael FDA 301-443-3285

Drugs & Drug Labeling: Orphan Drugs....Cruzan, Susan FDA 301-443-3285

Drugs & Drug Labeling: Over-the Counter....Snider, Sharon FDA 301-443-3285

Drugs & Drug Labeling: Women's Issues (Drugs)....Cruzan, Susan FDA 301-443-3285

Drugs & Drug Labeling:Prescription Drugs, Biologic....Peterson, Faye FDA 301-443-3285

Drugs (Cancer)....Staff NCI 301-496-5583

Drugs (Cardiac)....Staff NHLBI 301-496-4236

Drugs (Eyes)....Staff NEI 301-496-5248

Drugs (Use and Abuse)....Staff NIDA 301-443-6500

Drugs - General....Lindgren, Sue Justice Stat 202-307-0760

Drugs and Aging....Staff NIA 301-496-1752

Drugs and Prisoners....Baunach, Phyllis Jo Justice Stat 202-307-0361

Drugs and Prisoners....Stephan, James Justice Stat 202-616-7273

Drugs, natural....Nesbitt, Elizabeth USITC 202-205-3355

Drugs, synthetic....Nesbitt, Elizabeth USITC 202-205-3355

Drunk Driving....Zawitz, Marianne Justice Stat 202-616-3499

Dry Edible Beans....Budge, Arvin Agri 202-720-4285

Dry Edible Beans....Lucier, Gary Agri 202-219-0884

Dry Edible Beans....Greene, Catherine Agri 202-219-0886

Dry Eyes....Staff NEI 301-496-5248

Dry-cleaning machines....Jackson, Georgia USITC 202-205-3399

Drying machines....Jackson, Georgia USITC 202-205-3399

Duchenne Muscular Dystrophy....Staff NINDS 301-496-5751

Duchenne Muscular Dystrophy....Staff NIAMS 301-496-8188

Duck Stamps....Staff FWS 202-208-4354

Dumping Toxic Waste....Staff EPA 202-260-4627

Dupuytren's Contracture....Staff NIAMS 301-496-8188

Dupuytren's Contracture....Staff NINDS 301-496-5751

Durable Consumer Goods....Ellis, Kevin M. COMMERCE 202-482-1176

Dust Inhalation Diseases (Pneumoconioses)....Staff NHLBI 301-496-4236

Dust Inhalation Diseases (Pneumoconioses)....Staff FDA 301-443-3170

Dust Inhalation Diseases (Pneumoconioses)....Staff CDCW/NIOSH 404-639-3286

Dwarfism....Staff NICHD 301-496-5133

Dyeing machines....Greene, William USITC 202-205-3405

Dyes....Wanser, Stephen USITC 202-205-3363

Dynamite....Johnson, Larry USITC 202-205-3351

Dysautonomia....Staff NINDS 301-496-5751

Dysentery....Staff NIAID 301-496-5717

Dyskinesia....Staff NINDS 301-496-5751

Dyslexia....Staff NICHD 301-496-5133

Dyslexia....Staff NINDS 301-496-5751

Dyslexia....Staff NIMH 301-443-4513

Dyslexia....Staff NIDCD 301-496-7243

Dysmenorrhea....Staff NICHD 301-496-5133

Dystonia....Staff NINDS 301-496-5751

Dystonia Musculorum Deformans (Torsion Dystonia)....Staff NINDS 301-496-5751

E

E. Caribbean....Brooks, Michelle Cnty Commerce 202-482-2527

ECG....Staff NHLBI 301-496-4236

EKG....Staff NHLBI 301-496-4236

EPA Action Line....Staff EPA 800-223-0425

EPA Journal....Staff EPA 202-260-4359

EPA Recycling Program....Staff EPA 202-260-6980

ERIP (Energy-Related Inventions Program)....Staff NEIC 202-586-1479

Ear Infection....Staff NDCD NINDS 301-496-7243

Earnings Publication....Green, Gloria LABOR 202-606-6373

Earnings, Employment and Earnings Publication....Green, Gloria LABOR 202-606-6373

Earnings, Foreign Countries, Productivity & Tech.....Capdevielle, Patricia LABOR 202-606-5654

Earnings, Population Survey....Mellor, Earl LABOR 202-606-6378

Earnings, Real--News Release, Empl/Unempl. Stats....Hiles, David LABOR 202-606-6547

Earth Observing System (EOS)....Staff NASA 301-286-5566

Earth-moving machines....Stonitsch, Laura USITC 202-205-3408

Earthenware....Harris, John COMMERCE 202-482-1178

Earthenware....Kalkines, George CUSTOMS 212-466-5794

Earthenware, articles of....McNay, Deborah USITC 202-205-3425

East Caribbean....Almaguer, Antoinette Peace Corps 202-606-3322

Eastern European Health Scientist Exchange Program....Staff FIC 301-496-4784

Eaton-Lambert Myasthenic Syndrome....Staff NINDS 301-496-5751

Echocardiography....Staff NHLBI 301-496-4236

Eclampsia/Preeclampsia....Staff NICHD 301-496-5133

Ecological Effects Branch....Staff EPA 202-305-7347

Econometrics, Assistant to Director....Hirsch, Albert A. ECONOMIC 202-523-0729

Economic Accounts, Associate Director for National....Parker, Robert P. ECONOMIC 202-523-0517

Economic Bureau - Antitrust....Boner, Roger FTC 202-326-3455

Economic Bureau - Antitrust....Creswell, Jay S., Jr. FTC 202-326-3519

Economic Bureau - Consumer Protection....Cox, Carolyn FTC 202-326-3434

Economic Bureau - Office of the Director....Brown,Mary FTC 202-326-3429

Economic Bureau - Office of the Director....Deyak, Timothy FTC 202-326-3379

Economic Census Products....Zeisset, Paul CENSUS 301-763-1792

Economic Growth/Empl Proj, Occupational Outlook Quarterly....Fountain, Melvin LABOR 202-606-5707

Economic Growth/Empl Proj, Associate Commissioner....Kutscher, Ronald LABOR 202-606-5700

Economic Growth/Empl Proj, Data Diskettes....Bowman, Charles LABOR 202-606-5702

Economic Growth/Empl Proj, Economic Growth Proj....Saunders, Norman LABOR 202-606-5723

Economic Growth/Empl Proj, Ind-Occpl Empl Matrix....Turner, Delores LABOR 202-606-5730

Economic Growth/Empl Proj, Labor Force Projection....Fullerton, Howard LABOR 202-606-5711

Economic Growth/Empl Proj, Occupational Outlook Hand....Pilot, Michael LABOR 202-606-5703

Economic Growth/Empl Proj, Occupational Projections....Rosenthal, Neal LABOR 202-606-5701

Economic Programs, Statistical Research....Monsour, Nash J. CENSUS 301-763-5702

Economic Projections, Employment Projections....Saunders, Norman LABOR 202-606-5723

Economics....Elzinga, Kenneth G. UVA 701-924-6752

Economics Bureau....Cahill, Patricia FTC 202-326-3346

Economics Bureau....Duke, Richard M. FTC 202-326-3453

Economics Bureau....Schumann, Lawrence FTC 202-326-3359

Economics Bureau....Ward, Michael R. FTC 202-326-2096

Economics Bureau - Antitrust....Brashears, Nicole K. FTC 202-326-2455

Economics Bureau - Antitrust....Breen, Denis A. FTC 202-326-3447

Economics Bureau - Antitrust....Brogan, Robert D. FTC 202-326-3508

Economics Bureau - Antitrust....Bustamante, Rene FTC 202-326-3396

Economics Bureau - Antitrust....Callison, Elizabeth FTC 202-326-3521

Economics Bureau - Antitrust....Coate, Malcolm FTC 202-326-3351

Economics Bureau - Antitrust....Coleman, Mary FTC 202-326-3617

Economics Bureau - Antitrust....Cucinelli, Ieva P. FTC 202-326-3450

Economics Bureau - Antitrust....Dobson, Douglas C. FTC 202-326-3465

Economics Bureau - Antitrust....Fisher, Alan A. FTC 202-326-3516

Economics Bureau - Antitrust....Freeman, Barry FTC 202-326-3372

Economics Bureau - Antitrust....Gessler, Geary A. FTC 202-326-3463

Economics Bureau - Antitrust....Gessler, Kevin O. FTC 202-326-2306

Economics Bureau - Antitrust....Glasner, David FTC 202-326-3345

Economics Bureau - Antitrust....Grinshteyn, Ilona FTC 202-326-3355

Economics Bureau - Antitrust....Gulyn, Peter FTC 202-326-2194

Economics Bureau - Antitrust....Harmon, Bernadette D. FTC 202-326-3449

Economics Bureau - Antitrust....Howell, John M. FTC 202-326-3456

Economics Bureau - Antitrust....Iosso, Thomas FTC 202-326-2720

Economics Bureau - Antitrust....Jaynes, Philip W. FTC 202-326-3507

Economics Bureau - Antitrust....John, Tammy FTC 202-326-3462

Economics Bureau - Antitrust....Kneuper, Robert FTC 202-326-3469

Economics Bureau - Antitrust....Layher, William N. FTC 202-326-3515

Economics Bureau - Antitrust....Levinson, Robert FTC 202-326-3517

Economics Bureau - Antitrust....Levy, Roy FTC 202-326-3353

Economics Bureau - Antitrust....Martin, Fred FTC 202-326-3514

Economics Bureau - Antitrust....Megna, Pamela FTC 202-326-3491

Economics Bureau - Antitrust....Nelson, Steven R. FTC 202-326-3523

Economics Bureau - Antitrust....Patterson, Margaret A. FTC 202-326-3472

Economics Bureau - Antitrust....Pegram, William M. FTC 202-326-3336

Economics Bureau - Antitrust....Pidano, Charles FTC 202-326-3454

Economics Bureau - Antitrust....Rodriguez, Armando FTC 202-326-3616

Economics Bureau - Antitrust....Sacher, Seth B. FTC 202-326-3612

Economics Bureau - Antitrust....Silvia, Louis FTC 202-326-3471

Economics Bureau - Antitrust....Simpson, John D. FTC 202-326-3451

Economics Bureau - Antitrust....Tatem, Lewis FTC 202-326-3373

Economics Bureau - Antitrust....Wadbrook, Clare FTC 202-326-3420

Economics Bureau - Antitrust....Wagner, Curtis FTC 202-326-3348

Economics Bureau - Antitrust....Zichterman, Elizabeth C. FTC 202-326-3410

Economics Bureau - Antitrust....Williams, Mark FTC 202-326-3374

Economics Bureau - Consumer Protection....Butters, Gerald R. FTC 220-326-3393

Economics Bureau - Consumer Protection....Daniel, Lisa M. FTC 202-326-3394

Economics Bureau - Consumer Protection....Dulisse, Brian FTC 202-326-3614

Economics Bureau - Consumer Protection....Fahnline, Kathryn FTC 202-326-3611

Economics Bureau - Consumer Protection....Foster, Susan W. FTC 202-326-3482

Economics Bureau - Consumer Protection....Lacko, James FTC 202-326-3387

Economics Bureau - Consumer Protection....Lean, David F. FTC 202-326-3480

Economics Bureau - Consumer Protection....Mulholland, Joseph FTC 202-326-3378

Economics Bureau - Consumer Protection....Pappalardo, Janis K. FTC 202-326-3380

Economics Bureau - Consumer Protection....Porter, Russell FTC 202-326-3460

Economics Bureau - Consumer Protection....Sciolli, Stefano FTC 202-326-3388

Economics Bureau - Consumer Protection....Silversin, Louis FTC 202-326-3385

Economics Bureau - Consumer Protection....Small, Helen W. FTC 202-326-3375

Economics Bureau - Consumer Protection....VanderNat, Peter FTC 202-326-3518

Economics Bureau - Consumer Protection....Wells, Pamela L. FTC 202-326-3371

Economics Bureau - Economic Policy Analysis....Chase, Vera FTC 202-326-3354

Economics Bureau - Economic Policy Analysis....Daniel, Tim FTC 202-326-3520

Economics Bureau - Economic Policy Analysis....Fitzpatrick, M.E. (Keety) FTC 202-326-3427

Economics Bureau - Economic Policy Analysis....Grawe, Oliver FTC 202-326-3445

Economics Bureau - Economic Policy Analysis....Hilke, John C. FTC 202-326-3483

Economics Bureau - Economic Policy Analysis....Howarth, Dolly A. FTC 202-326-3382

Economics Bureau - Economic Policy Analysis....Ippolito, Pauline M. FTC 202-326-3477

Economics Bureau - Economic Policy Analysis....Kelly, Kenneth H. FTC 202-326-3358

Economics Bureau - Economic Policy Analysis....Kleit, Andrew FTC 202-326-3481

Economics Bureau - Economic Policy Analysis....Kobayashi, Bruce FTC 202-326-3363

Economics Bureau - Economic Policy Analysis....Metzger, Michael FTC 202-326-3367

Economics Bureau - Economic Policy Analysis....Morkre, Morris E. FTC 202-326-3365

Economics Bureau - Economic Policy Analysis....Reiffen, David FTC 202-326-2027

Economics Bureau - Economic Policy Analysis....Reitzes, James FTC 202-326-3349

Economics Bureau - Economic Policy Analysis....Vita, Mike FTC 202-326-3493

Economics Bureau - Economic Policy Analysis....Wellford, Charissa FTC 202-326-3020

Economics Bureau - Economics Policy Analysis....Rogers, Robert FTC 202-326-3368

Economics Bureau - Office of the Director....Altrogge, Phyllis D. FTC 202-326-3464

Economics Bureau - Office of the Director....Anderson, Keith B. FTC 202-326-3428

Economics Bureau - Office of the Director....Bond, Ronald S. FTC 202-326-3424

Economics Bureau - Office of the Director....Carpenter, Lynn J. FTC 202-326-3390

Economics Bureau - Office of the Director....Langenfeld, James FTC 202-326-3423

Economics Bureau - Office of the Director....Meadows, Chrystal E. FTC 202-326-3489

Economics Bureau - Office of the Director....Munson, Delores A. FTC 202-326-3613

Economics Bureau - Office of the Director....Pautler, Paul A. FTC 202-326-3357

Economics Bureau - Office of the Director....Peterman, John L. FTC 202-326-3431

Economics Bureau - Office of the Director....Richards, Karin F. FTC 202-326-2601

Economics Bureau - Office of the Director....Rosano, William V. FTC 202-326-3422

Economics Bureau - Office of the Director....Samuels, Carolyn FTC

202-326-3412

Economics Bureau - Office of the Director....Simmons, Gwendolynn FTC 202-326-3395

Economics Bureau - Office of the Director....Williams, Cheryl G. FTC 202-326-3418

Economics Bureau- Office of the Director....Farber, Leslie FTC 202-326-3510

Economizers.... USITC 202-205-3380

Ectodermal Dysplasias....Staff NIAMS 301-496-8188

Ectodermal Dysplasias....Staff NIDR 301-496-4261

Ectopic Hormones....Staff NIDDK 301-496-3583

Ecuador....MacNamara, Laura Cnty Commerce 202-482-1659

Ecuador....Godbey, Maria Elena Peace Corps 202-606-3198

Ecuador....Erlandson, Barbara Peace Corps 202-606-3499

Ecuador (Quito)....Staff Cnty State 202-647-3338

Ecuador/Minerals....Velasco, Pablo Cnty Mines 202-501-9677

Eczema....Staff NIAID 301-496-5717

Eczema....Staff NIAMS 301-496-8188

Edema....Staff NHLBI 301-496-4236

Edible gelatin....Jonnard, Aimison USITC 202-205-3350

Edible preparations....Schneider, Greg USITC 202-205-3326

Education....Bunker, Linda K. UVA 701-924-0740

Education....Gibbs, Anette UVA 701-924-3880

Education (Nursing)....Staff HRSA/BHPr/DN 301-443-5786

Education Facilities, Major Proj.....White, Barbara COMMERCE 202-482-4160

Education Services....Reeder, John USITC 202-205-3319

Education and Curriculum Support Projects....Staff CENSUS 301-763-1510

Education, Energy Management....Duane, Jerry NEIC 202-586-2366

Education, Environmental....Staff FWS 703-358-2029

Educational Attainment, Empl/Unempl. Stats....Staff LABOR 202-606-6378

Educational Attainment, Employment Statistics....Staff LABOR 202-606-6378

Educational Programs....Sindelar, Terri NASA 202-453-8400

Educational Television....Staff FCC 202-632-6908

Educational Television....Staff FCC 202-632-6357

Educational/Training....Francis, Simon COMMERCE 202-482-0345

Eggs....Newman, Douglas USITC 202-205-3328

Egypt....Sams, Thomas/Wright, Corey Cnty Commerce 202-482-4441

Egypt, Arab Republic of (Cairo)....Staff Cnty State 202-647-1228

Egypt/Minerals....Dolley, Thomas Cnty Mines 202-501-9690

Ehlers-Danlos Syndrome....Staff NIAMS 301-496-8188

Eisenmenger's Syndrome....Staff NHLBI 301-496-4236

El Salvador....Lee, Helen Cnty Commerce 202-482-2527

El Salvador (San Salvador)....Staff Cnty State 202-647-4961

El Salvador/Minerals....Mobbs, Philip Cnty Mines 202-501-9679

Elastic fabrics....Shelton, Linda USITC 202-205-3457

Elastomers....Misurelli, Denby USITC 202-205-3362

Elderly Victims....Klaus, Patsy Justice Stat 202-307-0776

Elec/Power Gen/Transmission & Dist Eqt (Trade Pro)....Brandes, Jay COMMERCE 202-482-0560

Electric Energy Statistics....Geidl, John NEIC 202-254-5570

Electric Industrial Apparatus Nec....Whitley, Richard A. COMMERCE 202-482-0682

Electric Machinery & Trans., Producer Price Index....Yatsko, Ralph LABOR 202-606-7745

Electric Networks....Brewer, Robert H. NEIC 202-586-2828

Electric Vehicles....Barber, Kenneth NEIC 202-586-2198

Electric Vehicles....Alpaugh, Richard NEIC 202-586-8012

Electric and Hybrid Propulsion Systems....Barber, Kenneth NEIC 202-586-2198

Electric and Nuclear Power....Welch, Thomas NEIC 202-586-8800

Electric and Nuclear Power....Jeffers, William NEIC 202-586-8800

Electric sound and visual signalling apparatus....Baker, Scott USITC 202-205-3386

Electric-Magnetic Field Technical Questions....Staff EPA 301-260-9640

Electrical Articles....Miller, Julius CUSTOMS 212-466-4680

Electrical Engineering....Papantoni-Kazakos, Panayota UVA 701-924-6102

Electrical Power Plants, Major Proj.....Dollison, Robert COMMERCE 202-482-2733

Electrical Structures....Miller, Julius CUSTOMS 212-466-4680

Electrical Vol Standards....Mesa, Stacey Reuben CPSC 301-504-0580

Electricity....Sugg, William COMMERCE 202-482-1466

Electricity Transmission....Brewer, Robert NEIC 202-586-2828

Electricity Transmission, Health Effects of....Brewer, Robert NEIC 202-586-2828

ElectroOptical Instruments, Trade Promo.....Gwaltney, G. P. COMMERCE 202-482-2991

Electrocardiogram....Staff NHLBI 301-496-4236

Electromechanical appliances....Jackson, Georgia USITC 202-205-3399

Electron Microscopy....Staff NCRR 301-496-5545

Electron Microscopy....Staff NIDR 301-496-4261

Electron Microscopy....Staff DRS/BEIB 301-496-2599

Electronic Components/Prod & Test Eqt, Trade Promo....Burke, Joseph J. COMMERCE 202-482-5014

Electronic Database Services....Inoussa, Mary COMMERCE 202-482-5820

Electronic Eavesdropping....Staff FCC 202-632-7260

Electronic Fund Transfer Crime....Kaplan, Carol Justice Stat 202-307-0759

Electronic Prod. and Test.....Finn, Erin COMMERCE 202-482-3360

Electronic Prod. and Test (Export Promo)....Ruffin, Marlene COMMERCE 202-482-0570

Electronic Telephone Switching....Staff FCC 202-634-1800

Electronic technology....Puffert, Douglas USITC 202-205-3402

Electronic tubes....Malison, Andrew USITC 202-205-3391

Electronic, (Legislation)....Donnelly, Margaret COMMERCE 202-482-5466

Electrothermic appliances....Jackson, Georgia USITC 202-205-3399

Elementary and Secondary Education Programs....Staff NEH 202-606-8377

Elements, chemical....Conant, Kenneth USITC 202-205-3346

Elephantiasis....Staff NIAID 301-496-5717

Elevators....Greene, William USITC 202-205-3405

Elevators, Moving Stairways....Weining, Mary COMMERCE 202-482-4708

Eligibility Criteria (Grants)....Staff DRG 301-496-7441

Embolism....Staff NHLBI 301-496-4236

Embroidery machines....Greene, William USITC 202-205-3405

Emergency Broadcasting System....Staff FCC 202-632-3906

Emergency Medical Services....Staff FCC 717-337-1212

Emergency Plan. & Community Right-to-Know Hotline....Staff EPA 800-535-0202

Emigration....Woodrow, Karen CENSUS 301-763-5990

Emission Standards....Staff EPA 202-541-5571

Emissions Standards Division....Staff EPA 919-541-5544

Emphysema....Staff NHLBI 301-496-4236

Empl.& Wages, Empl/Unempl, Data Diskettes and Tapes....Buso, Michael LABOR 202-606-6567

Empl/Unempl Stats, (ES202), Empl/Wgs Ind....Bush, Joseph LABOR 202-606-6373

Empl/Unempl Stats, Assistant Commis.....Plewes, Thomas J. LABOR 202-606-6400

Empl/Unempl Stats, Occl Empl/Unempl, Occpl Empl Sv....Johnson, Lawrence LABOR 202-606-6569

Empl/Unempl Stats, State Data, Demographic Charact....Biederman, Edna LABOR 202-606-6392

Empl/Unempl Stats, Std Industrial Classification....Bennott, William LABOR 202-606-6474

Empl/Unempl Stats, Std Occupational Classification....McElroy, Michael LABOR 202-606-6516

Empl/Unempl Stats, Unempl Ins Stats, Claimant Data....Terwilliger, Yvonne LABOR 202-606-6392

Empl/Unempl Stats, Unempl Ins Stats, Establ Record....Cimini, Michael LABOR 202-606-6275

Empl/Unempl Stats., Benchmarks....Getz, Patricia LABOR 202-606-6521

Empl/Unempl, National Data, Data Diskettes....Singleton, Christopher LABOR 202-606-6551

Empl/Unempl. Stats, Business Establishment List....Searson, Michael LABOR 202-606-6479

Empl/Unempl.Stats, Curr. Empl. An, Assistant Commis.....Bregger, John E. LABOR 202-606-6388

Employee Benefit Survey, General Info., Comp./Wk. Con....Staff LABOR 202-606-6222

Employee Benefit Survey, Health & Life Insur.....Blostin, Allan LABOR 202-606-6240

Employee Benefit Survey, Retirement & Capital Acc....Houff, James LABOR 202-606-6238

Employee Benefits,Compensation & Working Condition....Staff LABOR 202-606-6199

Employer Costs for Employe Comp, Comp & Working....Rogers, Brenda LABOR 202-606-6199

Employment....Palumbo, Thomas CENSUS 301-763-8574

Employment & Unempl. Statistics, Flexitime & Shift....Mellor, Earl LABOR 202-606-6378

Employment & Unempl. Statistics, Older Workers....Rones, Philip LABOR 202-606-6378

Employment & Unempl. Statistics, Part-time Workers....Nardone, Thomas LABOR 202-606-6378

Employment & Unempl. Statistics, Working Poor....Herz, Diane LABOR 202-606-6378

Employment & Unempl. Stats, Labor Force Data Disk....Marcus, Jessie LABOR 202-606-6392

Employment & Unempl. Stats, Longitud. Data/Gr.Flow....Horvath, Francis

LABOR 202-606-6345

Employment & Unempl. Stats, States Est. Surv. Data....Podgornik, Guy LABOR 202-606-6559

Employment & Unempl. Stats. Earnings, Pop. Survey....Mellor, Earl LABOR 202-606-6378

Employment & Unempl. Stats., Mass Layoff Stats.....Siegel, Lewis LABOR 202-606-6404

Employment & Unempl. Stats., Minimum Wage Data....Haugen, Steve LABOR 202-606-6378

Employment & Unempl. Stats., Multiple Jobholders....Stinson, John LABOR 202-606-6373

Employment & Unempl. Stats., States Est. Surv.....Shipp, Kenneth LABOR 202-606-6559

Employment Analysis, Current, Assist. Comm. Empl/Unempl....Bregger, John E. LABOR 202-606-6388

Employment Cost Index, Comp. & Working Cond.....Shelly, Wayne LABOR 202-606-6199

Employment Projections, Assistant Commis.....Kutscher, Ronald LABOR 202-606-5700

Employment Projections, Data Diskettes....Bowman, Charles LABOR 202-606-5702

Employment Projections, Economic Growth....Saunders, Norman LABOR 202-606-5723

Employment Projections, Productivity & Technology....Fullerton, Howard LABOR 202-606-5711

Employment Projections, Productivity & Technology....Franklin, James LABOR 202-606-5709

Employment Requirements Tables, Productivity & Tech....Franklin, James LABOR 202-606-5709

Employment Statistics....Palumbo, Thomas CENSUS 301-763-8574

Employment Stats, Area Data, Demog Charact....Biederman, Edna LABOR 202-606-6392

Employment Stats, Area Data, Employment....Shipp, Kenneth LABOR 202-606-6559

Employment Stats, Curr Empl Anal., Assist. Commis.....Bregger, John E. LABOR 202-606-6388

Employment Stats, Discouraged Workers....Hamel, Harvey LABOR 202-606-6378

Employment Stats, Displaced Workers....Horvath, Francis LABOR 202-606-6345

Employment Stats, Dropouts....Cohany, Sharon LABOR 202-606-6378

Employment Stats, Earn Stats, Qrtly Empl and Wage....Bush, Joseph LABOR 202-606-6567

Employment Stats, Earnings Publication....Green, Gloria LABOR 202-606-6373

Employment Stats, Educational Attainment....Staff LABOR 202-606-6378

Employment Stats, Employment Publication....Green, Gloria LABOR 202-606-6373

Employment Stats, Family Charactr of Labor Force....Hayghe, Howard LABOR 202-606-6378

Employment Stats, Ind Earn Stats, Mthly Payr Surv....Seifert, Mary Lee LABOR 202-606-6552

Employment Stats, Ind Empl Stats, Mthly Payr Surv....Seifert, Mary Lee LABOR 202-606-6552

Employment and Earnings Period. Empl/Unempl. Stats....Green, Gloria LABOR 202-606-6373

Employment and Unemployment Statistics, Est. Surv.....Seifert, Mary Lee LABOR 202-606-6552

Employment, Area Data....Shipp, Kenneth LABOR 202-606-6559

Employment/Unempl Stats, Minorities....Cattan, Peter LABOR 202-606-6378

Employment/Unempl Stats, Permanent Plant Closings....Siegel, Lewis LABOR 202-606-6404

Employment/Unempl Stats, State Data, Employment....Shipp, Kenneth LABOR 202-606-6559

Employment/Unempl Stats, Students....Cohany, Sharon LABOR 202-606-6378

Employment/Unempl Stats, Veterans....Cohany, Sharon LABOR 202-606-6378

Employment/Unempl Stats, Women....Hayghe, Howard LABOR 202-606-6378

Employment/Unempl Stats, Work-life Estimates....Horvath, Francis LABOR 202-606-6345

Employment/Unempl Stats, Permanent Mass Layoffs....Siegel, Lewis LABOR 202-606-6404

Employment/Unemployment Stats, Older Workers....Rones, Philip LABOR 202-606-6378

Employment/Unempl Stats, Machine Readable Data....Green, Gloria LABOR 202-606-6373

Employment/Unempl Stats, Associate Commissioner....Plewes, Thomas J. LABOR 202-606-6400

Employment/Unempl Stats, Real Earnings, News Release....Hiles, David

LABOR 202-606-6547

Employment/Unempl Statistics, Trends....Staff LABOR 202-606-6378

Enamel....Staff NIDR 301-496-4261

Enamels....Johnson, Larry USITC 202-205-3351

Encephalitides....Staff NINDS 301-496-5751

Encephalitis....Staff NIAID 301-496-5717

Encephalitis....Staff NINDS 301-496-5751

Encephalitis Lethargica....Staff NINDS 301-496-5751

Encephalomyelitis....Staff NINDS 301-496-5751

Encopresis....Staff NICHD 301-496-5133

Endangered Species Bulletins, Tech.....Staff FWS 703-358-2166

Endangered Species Permits....Staff FWS 703-358-2104

Endangered Species Recovery Plans....Staff FWS 703-358-2171

Endangered Species Research....Staff FWS 703-358-1710

Endangered Species Listing....Staff FWS 703-358-2171

Endocarditis....Staff NHLBI 301-496-4236

Endocardium....Staff NHLBI 301-496-4236

Endocrine Gland....Staff NICHD 301-496-5133

Endocrinologic Muscle Disease....Staff NINDS 301-496-5751

Endocrinology....Staff NIDDK 301-496-3583

Endocrinology (Sexual Development)....Staff NICHD 301-496-5133

Endocrinology of Aging....Staff NIA 301-496-1752

Endodontics....Staff NIDR 301-496-4261

Endometriosis....Staff NICHD 301-496-5133

Energy & Environ. Sys.....Greer, Damon COMMERCE 202-482-5456

Energy Assist. Block Grant/For Low Income Families....Long, Susan ACF 202-401-9215

Energy Assist. Block Grant/For Low Income Families....Long, Susan ACF 202-401-9215

Energy Biosciences Research....Rabson, Robert NEIC 301-903-2873

Energy Conservation....Davis, Michael J. NEIC 202-586-9220

Energy Conservation....Freedman, Karen NEIC 202-586-8800

Energy Conservation Programs....Staff FWS 703-358-1719

Energy Consumption Surveys....Carlson, Lynda NEIC 202-586-1112

Energy Demand Forecasts....Rodekohr, Mark NEIC 202-586-1130

Energy Efficient Buildings....Oliver, Robert NEIC 202-586-9190

Energy Efficient Buildings....Kapus, Theodore NEIC 202-586-9123

Energy Information Statistical Standards....Bishop, Yvonne NEIC 202-254-5419

Energy Information Statistics....Bishop, Yvonne NEIC 202-254-5419

Energy Inventions....Staff NEIC 202-586-1479

Energy Management Education....Duane, Jerry NEIC 202-586-2366

Energy Markets Short-Term Forecasting....Staff NEIC 202-586-1441

Energy Pollutant Research....Smith, David NEIC 301-903-5468

Energy Supply and Conversion Forecasts....Hutzler, Mary J. NEIC 202-586-2222

Energy Technical Assistance....Bowes, Ronald NEIC 202-586-5517

Energy, Commodities....Yancik, Joseph J. COMMERCE 202-482-1466

Energy, Commodities....Oddenino, Charles L. COMMERCE 202-482-1466

Energy, Producer Price Index....Caswell, Maria LABOR 202-606-7722

Energy, Renewable....Rasmussen, John COMMERCE 202-482-1466

Energy, Renewable....Davis, Michael J. NEIC 202-586-9220

Energy, Solar....San Martin, Robert NEIC 202-586-9275

Energy-Related Business Assistance....Lane, Harry NEIC 202-586-9104

Energy-Related Inventions Program (ERIP)....Staff NEIC 202-586-1479

Energy-Related Inventions and Innovations....Staff NEIC 202-586-1479

Engine Design....Eberhardt, James NEIC 202-586-9387

Engineering (Biomedical)....Staff NCRR/BEIP 301-496-4426

Engineering (Biomedical)....Staff DCRT 301-496-1111

Engineering (Biomedical)....Staff NIGMS 301-496-7301

Engineering Surveys--Field Strength....Staff FCC 202-632-7040

Engineering resins....Misurelli, Denby USITC 202-205-3362

Engineering services....Stonitsch, Laura USITC 202-205-3408

Engineering/Construction Services, Trade Promo.....Ruan, Robert COMMERCE 202-482-0359

Engines....Josephs, Irwin CUSTOMS 212-466-5673

Engines....Anderson, Peder USITC 202-205-3388

Enterprise Statistics....Monaco, Johnny CENSUS 301-763-1758

Enterprise Statistics....Staff CENSUS 301-763-1758

Entertainment Industries....Siegmund, John COMMERCE 202-482-4781

Entertainment services....R-Archila, Laura USITC 202-205-3488

Environment services....DeSapio, Vincent USITC 202-205-3435

Environment, Safety and Health Concerns....Ziemer, Paul NEIC 202-586-6151

Environmental Carcinogens....Staff NCI 301-496-5583

Environmental Contaminants....Staff FWS 703-358-2148

Environmental Control....Staff OD/ORS 301-496-3537

Environmental Economics, Chief....Rutledge, Gary L. ECONOMIC 202-523-0687

Environmental Education....Staff EPA 202-260-4958
Environmental Education....Staff FWS 703-358-2029
Environmental Hazards and Health Effects....Falk, Henry CDC 404-488-7300
Environmental Health....Staff NIEHS 919-541-3345
Environmental Health Sciences, Nat'l Institute of....Lee, Hugh NIH 919-541-3345
Environmental Health, National Center for....Houk, Vernon N. CDC 404-488-7000
Environmental Issues - General Information Hotline....Staff EPA 800-759-4372
Environmental Law....Staff FCC 202-632-6990
Environmental Mutagenesis....Staff NIEHS 919-541-3345
Environmental Requirements for Laboratory Animals....Staff OD 301-496-1357
Environmental Safety....Staff OD/ORS 301-496-3537
Environmental Sciences....Allen, Ralph O. UVA 701-982-4922
Environmental Statistics and Information....Staff EPA 202-260-2680
Environmental Teratology....Staff NIEHS 919-541-3345
Environmental Toxicology....Zeeman, Maurice G. FAES 202-260-1237
Environmental Toxicology....Staff FWS 703-358-1710
Enzymes....Nesbitt, Elizabeth USITC 202-205-3355
Eosinophilic Granuloma of the Lung....Staff NHLBI 301-496-4236
Eosinophilic Syndrome....Staff NIAID 301-496-5717
Epidemic Aid/Disease Outbreaks....Berreth, Don CDC 404-639-3286
Epidemiology....Friedman, Lawrence M. FAES 301-496-2533
Epidemiology/Biostatistics....Hirsch, Robert FAES 202-994-7778
Epidemiology....Thacker, Stephen B. CDC 404-639-3661
Epidemiology of Aging....Staff NIA 301-496-1752
Epidermodysplasia Verruciformis....Staff NIAMS 301-496-8188
Epidermolysis Bullosa....Staff NIAMS 301-496-8188
Epikeratophakia....Staff NEI 301-496-5248
Epilepsy....Staff NINDS 301-496-5751
Epilepsy....Chandler, Jerry L. FAES 301-496-1846
Epistaxis (Nosebleed)....Staff NHLBI 301-496-4236
Epoxides....Michels, David USITC 202-205-3352
Epoxidized ester....Johnson, Larry USITC 202-205-3351
Epoxidized linseed oils....Johnson, Larry USITC 202-205-3351
Epoxidized soya oils....Johnson, Larry USITC 202-205-3351
Epoxy resins....Misurelli, Denby USITC 202-205-3362
Epstein-Barr Syndrome....Staff NIAID 301-496-5717
Epstein-Barr Virus....Staff NIAID 301-496-5717
Equal Employment Opportunity....Staff OD/DEO 301-496-6301
Equatorial Guinea....Henke, Debra Cnty Commerce 202-482-4228
Equatorial Guinea (Malabo)....Staff Cnty State 202-647-3139
Equatorial Guinea/Minerals....Dolley, Thomas Cnty Mines 202-501-9690
Equipment Measurement Authorization....Staff FCC 301-725-1585
Equipment leasing....Bedore, James USITC 202-205-3424
Equatorial Guinea....Blackwell, Gloria Peace Corps 202-606-3998
Equatorial Guinea....Swezey, Virginia Peace Corps 202-606-3998
Erythema Elevatum Diutinum....Staff NIAMS 301-496-8188
Erythema Nodosum....Staff NIAID 301-496-5717
Erythroblastosis Fetalis....Staff NICHD 301-496-5133
Erythrocytes (Red Blood Cells)....Staff NHLBI 301-496-4236
Erythrocytes (Red Blood Cells)....Staff FDA/NCDB 301-496-3556
Esophagus, Carcinoma....Staff NCI 301-496-5583
Esotropia....Staff NEI 301-496-5248
Essential Hypertension....Staff NHLBI 301-496-4236
Essential oils....Land, Eric USITC 202-205-3349
Establishment Survey, Data Disk....Podgornik, Guy LABOR 202-606-6559
Establishment Survey, Emp/Unemp....Shipp, Kenneth LABOR 202-606-6559
Establishment Survey, National, Empl/Unempl.....Seifert, Mary Lee LABOR 202-606-6552
Establishment Survey, Natl., Indus. Classif. Empl/Unempl.....Getz, Patricia LABOR 202-606-6521
Establishment Survey, States & Areas, Data Diskette....Podgornik, Guy LABOR 202-606-6559
Establishment Survey, States & Areas, Empl/Unemp....Shipp, Kenneth LABOR 202-606-6559
Esters, fatty-acid, of polyhydric alcohols....Land, Eric USITC 202-205-3349
Estimates & Incidence/Industry Injuries & Illness....Staff LABOR 202-606-6180
Estonia....Staff Cnty State 202-647-3187
Estrogen Replacement Therapy....Staff NICHD 301-496-5133
Estrogen Replacement Therapy....Staff NCI 301-496-5583
Estrogen Replacement Therapy....Staff FDA 301-443-3170
Estrogen Replacement Therapy....Staff NIAMS 301-496-8188
Estrogen Replacement Therapy....Staff NIA 301-496-1752
Estrogen Therapy....Staff NIA 301-496-1752
Ethane....Land, Eric USITC 202-205-3349
Ethanol....DiMaria, Joseph CUSTOMS 212-466-4769

Ethanolamines....Michels, David USITC 202-205-3352
Ethers....DiMaria, Joseph CUSTOMS 212-466-4769
Ethers....Michels, David USITC 202-205-3352
Ethers, fatty-acid, of polyhydric alcohols....Land, Eric USITC 202-205-3349
Ethiopia....Watkins, Chandra Cnty Commerce 202-482-4564
Ethiopia (Addis Ababa)....Staff Cnty State 202-647-8852
Ethiopia/Minerals....Antonides, Lloyd Cnty Mines 202-501-9686
Ethyl alcohol (ethanol) for nonbeverage use....Michels, David USITC 202-205-3352
Ethylene....Raftery, Jim USITC 202-205-3365
Ethylene dibromide....Michels, David USITC 202-205-3352
Ethylene glycol....Michels, David USITC 202-205-3352
Ethylene oxide....Michels, David USITC 202-205-3352
Ethylene-propylene rubber....Misurelli, Denby USITC 202-205-3362
Eurodollars with options....SIA Manasses CFT 312-353-9027
Europe/trade matters....Marcich, Christopher US Trade Rep 202-395-4620
European Assistance....Balfour, Michele FTC 202-326-2371
European Community....Ludolph, Charles Cnty Commerce 202-482-5276
European Economic Community (EEC)....Staff Cnty State 202-647-1708
Ewing's Sarcoma....Staff NCI 301-496-5583
Ex Parte Rules....Staff FCC 202-632-6990
Exec. Director's Office - Procurement & Gen. Services....Bussard, Clyde FTC 202-326-2266
Exec. Director's Bureau - Procurement & Gen. Services....Rice, Melvin L. FTC 202-326-2297
Exec. Director's Office - Procurement & Gen. Services.....Stokes, Akyva L. FTC 202-326-2278
Exec. Director's Office - Procurement & Gen. Services.....Wells, Ernest L. FTC 202-326-2248
Exec. Director's Office - Procurement & Gen. Services....Duncan, Mary A. FTC 202-326-2248
Exec. Director's Office - Procurement & Gen. Services....Fuehrerh, Carl E., Jr. FTC 202-326-2270
Exec. Director's Office - Procurement & Gen. Services....Wilson, Ricardo M. FTC 202-326-2261
Exec. Director's Office - Procurement & Gen. Services....Meritt, Claude O., Jr. FTC 202-326-2286
Exec. Director's Office - Procurement & Gen. Services.....Simpson, Flossie I. FTC 202-326-2297
Exec. Director's Office - Procurement & Gen Services....Royster, Lawrence D., Sr. FTC 202-326-2251
Exec. Director's Office - Procurement & Gen. Services.....Sefchick, Jean FTC 202-326-2258
Exec. Director's Office - Procurement & Gen. Services....Felder, J. Allen FTC 202-326-2269
Exec. Director's Office - Procurement & Gen. Services....Short, Francis G. FTC 202-326-2251
Exec. Director's Office - Procurement & Gen. Services.....Goines, Russell E. FTC 202-326-2267
Exec. Director's Office - Procurement & Gen. Services....Cox, Donald W. FTC 202-326-2274
Exec. Director's Office - Procurement & Gen. Services....Dickerson, William F. FTC 202-326-3735
Exec. Director's Office - Procurement & Gen. Services....Hayes, Ronald FTC 202-326-3734
Exec. Director's Office - Procurement & Gen. Services....Thorton, Kristy FTC 202-326-2533
Exec. Director's Office - Procurement & Gen. Services....Vasser, Robert M. FTC 202-326-2245
Exec. Director's Office - Procurement & Gen. Services.....Scott, John T. FTC 202-326-2297
Exec. Director's Office - Procurement & Gen. Services....Armstead, Gloria FTC 202-326-2262
Executive Director's Office....Baugh, Elaine H. FTC 202-326-2196
Executive Director's Office....Giffin, James M. FTC 202-326-2209
Executive Director's Office....Holland, Peggy FTC 202-326-3426
Executive Director's Office....Hunter, Nancy L. FTC 202-326-2202
Executive Director's Office....Kelsey, Teresa J. FTC 202-326-2196
Executive Director's Office....Letalik, Kitsie E. FTC 202-326-2259
Executive Director's Office....Lewis, Andrea FTC 202-326-2647
Executive Director's Office....Manley, Bernita L. FTC 202-326-3533
Executive Director's Office....Proctor, Alan FTC 202-326-2204
Executive Director's Office....Straight, Rosemarie FTC 202-326-2207
Executive Director's Office....Stultz, Rachel FTC 202-326-2199
Executive Director's Office....Walton, Robert, III FTC 202-326-2205
Executive Director's Office....Zytnick, Joseph FTC 202-326-2224
Executive Director's Office....Wiggs, Barbara B. FTC 202-326-2196

Executive Director's Office - Automated Systems....Chambers, Michael D. FTC 202-326-2379

Executive Director's Office - Automated Systems....Chmielewski, Richard FTC 202-326-2402

Executive Director's Office - Automated Systems....Clark, Randal S. FTC 202-326-3500

Executive Director's Office - Automated Systems....Condor, Karen FTC 202-326-3402

Executive Director's Office - Automated Systems....DeVaughn, Willetta FTC 202-326-2233

Executive Director's Office - Automated Systems....Donovan, Tammy M. FTC 202-326-2588

Executive Director's Office - Automated Systems....Edwards, Kathleen N. FTC 202-326-2240

Executive Director's Office - Automated Systems....Feldmann, Lester A. FTC 202-326-2216

Executive Director's Office - Automated Systems....Frank, F. Michael FTC 202-326-2217

Executive Director's Office - Automated Systems....Gabriel, Jack FTC 202-326-2250

Executive Director's Office - Automated Systems....Hales, Gregory E. FTC 202-326-2795

Executive Director's Office - Automated Systems....Haley, Brian FTC 202-326-2226

Executive Director's Office - Automated Systems....Hines, David C. FTC 202-326-3527

Executive Director's Office - Automated Systems....Horne, Dawn R. FTC 202-326-2281

Executive Director's Office - Automated Systems....Jaye, Jeffrey A. FTC 202-326-3136

Executive Director's Office - Automated Systems....Johnson, Gracie E. FTC 202-326-2211

Executive Director's Office - Automated Systems....Johnson, Loretta FTC 202-326-3624

Executive Director's Office - Automated Systems....Krim, Mead Ann FTC 202-326-3407

Executive Director's Office - Automated Systems....Krupinski, Robert FTC 202-326-2231

Executive Director's Office - Automated Systems....Lewis, Matthew FTC 202-326-2791

Executive Director's Office - Automated Systems....Lynch, Dennis FTC 202-326-2840

Executive Director's Office - Automated Systems....Mills, Mark C. FTC 202-326-3214

Executive Director's Office - Automated Systems....Momeni, Ali FTC 202-326-2232

Executive Director's Office - Automated Systems....Morris, Derrick FTC 202-326-2235

Executive Director's Office - Automated Systems....Moser, William E. FTC 202-326-2227

Executive Director's Office - Automated Systems....Nguyen, Kim FTC 202-326-2283

Executive Director's Office - Automated Systems....Overholt, Roberta FTC 202-326-2228

Executive Director's Office - Automated Systems....Pascoe, George FTC 202-326-3405

Executive Director's Office - Automated Systems....Passarelli, Joseph FTC 202-326-2394

Executive Director's Office - Automated Systems....Pinegar, Timothy S. FTC 202-326-2570

Executive Director's Office - Automated Systems....Pitt, Julia K. FTC 202-326-2369

Executive Director's Office - Automated Systems....Robertson, Diana FTC 202-326-2230

Executive Director's Office - Automated Systems....Russo, Jim FTC 202-326-2218

Executive Director's Office - Automated Systems....Seelinger, Douglas A. FTC 202-326-2237

Executive Director's Office - Automated Systems....Smith, Susan D. FTC 202-326-2220

Executive Director's Office - Automated Systems....Snyder, I. Michael FTC 202-326-2298

Executive Director's Office - Automated Systems....Travis, Robin FTC 202-326-3539

Executive Director's Office - Automated Systems....Vaughn, Brooks FTC 202-326-2215

Executive Director's Office - Automated Systems....Veneroso, Carmela FTC 202-326-2254

Executive Director's Office - Automated Systems....Wu, John FTC 202-326-2238

Executive Director's Office - Automated Systems....West, Harold D. FTC 202-326-2011

Executive Director's Office - Automated Systems....Williams, Ken FTC 202-326-2082

Executive Director's Office - Budget & Finance....Arnold, Richard D., II FTC 202-326-2314

Executive Director's Office - Budget & Finance....Farmer, Melissa S. FTC 202-326-2244

Executive Director's Office - Budget & Finance....Fielding, Parcellena FTC 202-326-2312

Executive Director's Office - Budget & Finance....Gates, Dawn M. FTC 202-326-2314

Executive Director's Office - Budget & Finance....Gee, Jennifer C. FTC 202-326-2433

Executive Director's Office - Budget & Finance....Graham, Otto C. FTC 202-326-2315

Executive Director's Office - Budget & Finance....Hailes, Gail E. FTC 202-326-2318

Executive Director's Office - Budget & Finance....Hendershot, Alec R. FTC 202-326-3334

Executive Director's Office - Budget & Finance....Hodge, Denise D. FTC 202-326-2324

Executive Director's Office - Budget & Finance....Jefferson, Betty A. FTC 202-326-2327

Executive Director's Office - Budget & Finance....King, Linda G. FTC 202-326-2323

Executive Director's Office - Budget & Finance....Lancaster, Dorothy M. FTC 202-326-2488

Executive Director's Office - Budget & Finance....Mason, Dorothy T. FTC 202-326-2329

Executive Director's Office - Budget & Finance....Simms, Anthony FTC 202-326-2325

Executive Director's Office - Budget & Finance....Smith, Deona J. FTC 202-326-2330

Executive Director's Office - Budget & Finance....Smith, Virginia FTC 202-326-2339

Executive Director's Office - Budget & Finance....Spyres, Julie K. FTC 202-326-3301

Executive Director's Office - Budget & Finance....Squalls, Cora L. FTC 202-326-2322

Executive Director's Office - Budget & Finance....Savell, Toby Sunshine FTC 202-326-2422

Executive Director's Office - Budget & Finance....Thompson, Carl M. FTC 202-326-2337

Executive Director's Office - Budget & Finance....Thorpe, Wilhelmina FTC 202-326-2219

Executive Director's Office - Information Services....Bolden, Sandra B. FTC 202-326-2406

Executive Director's Office - Information Services....Booker, Lance FTC 202-326-2523

Executive Director's Office - Information Services....Bush, Edgar A. FTC 202-326-2421

Executive Director's Office - Information Services....Carter-Johnson, Jean FTC 202-326-2405

Executive Director's Office - Information Services....Chambers, Dewayne W. FTC 202-326-2222

Executive Director's Office - Information Services....Coleman, Kwame S. FTC 202-326-2528

Executive Director's Office - Information Services....Eperson, Patricia C. FTC 202-326-2420

Executive Director's Office - Information Services....Golden, Keith G. FTC 202-326-2410

Executive Director's Office - Information Services....Harewood, Stanley M. FTC 202-326-2222

Executive Director's Office - Information Services....Harris, Diane FTC 202-326-2528

Executive Director's Office - Information Services....Johnson, Dana FTC 202-326-2431

Executive Director's Office - Information Services....Johnson, Phyllis A. FTC 202-326-2507

Executive Director's Office - Information Services....Jones, Deborah A. FTC 202-326-2222

Executive Director's Office - Information Services....Jones, Michael J. FTC 202-326-2660

Executive Director's Office - Information Services....Kelly, Eldora FTC

202-326-2404
Executive Director's Office - Information Services....Long, Marcus D. FTC 202-326-2660
Executive Director's Office - Information Services....Maisel, Theodore A. FTC 202-326-2415
Executive Director's Office - Information Services....Moore, Joyce M. FTC 202-326-2872
Executive Director's Office - Information Services....Musser, Franklin L. FTC 202-326-2411
Executive Director's Office - Information Services....Pearson, Drake A. FTC 202-326-2412
Executive Director's Office - Information Services....Pierce, Marilyn S. FTC 202-326-2659
Executive Director's Office - Information Services....Proctor, Jerusha E. FTC 202-326-2408
Executive Director's Office - Information Services....Reese, Genevieve E. FTC 202-326-2409
Executive Director's Office - Information Services....Titzer, Kristine L. FTC 202-326-2407
Executive Director's Office - Information Services....Tucker, Francenia FTC 202-326-2430
Executive Director's Office - Information Services....Verter, DeShonda L. FTC 202-326-2013
Executive Director's Office - Information Services....Wise, Taleiha FTC 202-326-2508
Executive Director's Office - Information Services....Woodson, Margaret B. FTC 202-326-2417
Executive Director's Office - Information Services....Wiley, Bessie M. FTC 202-326-2416
Executive Director's Office - Library....Anderson, Rita D. FTC 202-326-2834
Executive Director's Office - Library....Bacon, Geraldine G. FTC 202-326-2380
Executive Director's Office - Library....Blades, Donna L. FTC 202-326-3005
Executive Director's Office - Library....Conrad, Jean FTC 202-326-2378
Executive Director's Office - Library....Cunningham, Jack FTC 202-326-2387
Executive Director's Office - Library....Curtin, Frank FTC 202-326-2280
Executive Director's Office - Library....Douglass, Franklin S. FTC 202-326-2376
Executive Director's Office - Library....Dowdle, Walter D. FTC 202-326-2505
Executive Director's Office - Library....Hammonds, Estelle FTC 202-326-2388
Executive Director's Office - Library....Hynes, Barbara A. FTC 202-326-2389
Executive Director's Office - Library....Jennings, Bruce FTC 202-326-2383
Executive Director's Office - Library....Knott, Margie FTC 202-326-2395
Executive Director's Office - Library....Ottie, Denise B. FTC 202-326-2381
Executive Director's Office - Library....Sims, Shirlene FTC 202-326-2395
Executive Director's Office - Library....Smith, Ayanna FTC 202-326-2390
Executive Director's Office - Library....Sullivan, R. Elaine FTC 202-326-2385
Executive Director's Office - Library....Watts, David V. FTC 202-326-2241
Executive Director's Office - Personnel....Allen, Gelinda A. FTC 202-326-2658
Executive Director's Office - Personnel....Axelrod, Harold FTC 202-326-2790
Executive Director's Office - Personnel....Berry, Chrishania R. FTC 202-326-2363
Executive Director's Office - Personnel....Brooks, Judy FTC 202-326-2347
Executive Director's Office - Personnel....Carter, Carole A. FTC 202-326-2550
Executive Director's Office - Personnel....Caton, Kathleen FTC 202-326-2342
Executive Director's Office - Personnel....Clark, Vivian Renee FTC 202-326-2365
Executive Director's Office - Personnel....Cooper, Erica FTC 202-326-2021
Executive Director's Office - Personnel....Coote, Sharon FTC 202-326-2348
Executive Director's Office - Personnel....Crayton, Erika L. FTC 202-326-2022
Executive Director's Office - Personnel....Davis, Elliot FTC 202-326-2022
Executive Director's Office - Personnel....Harris, Barbara A. FTC 202-326-2428
Executive Director's Office - Personnel....Holmes, Ann FTC 202-326-2345
Executive Director's Office - Personnel....La Veille, Monica FTC 202-326-2361
Executive Director's Office - Personnel....McCoy, Catherine M. FTC 202-326-2358
Executive Director's Office - Personnel....Schwarz, Mae FTC 202-326-2341
Executive Director's Office - Personnel....Smith, Del FTC 202-326-2357
Executive Director's Office - Personnel....Steinberg, Sharon FTC 202-326-2364
Executive Director's Office - Personnel....Hines, Calvin FTC 202-326-2273
Executive Director's Office - Proc. & Gen. Services....Clayborne, Charles FTC 202-326-2272
Executive Director's Office - Proc. & Gen. Services....Lorette, Barbara D. FTC 202-326-2260
Executive Director's Office - Proc. & Gen. Services.....Haines, John, P. FTC 202-326-2252
Executive Director's Office - Proc. & Gen. Services.....Hymon, James F. FTC 202-326-3736
Executive Director's Office - Proc. & Gen. Services.....Justice, Julius FTC

202-326-2275
Executive Director's Office - Proc. & Gen. Services.....Moore, David L. FTC 202-326-2277
Executive Director's Office - Proc. & Gen. Services.....Moore, Francenia K. FTC 202-326-2872
Executive Director's Office - Proc. & Gen. Services.....Hutcherson, Willie S. FTC 202-326-2297
Executive Director's Office - Proc. & Gen. Services.....Greulich, Sherron FTC 202-326-2271
Executive Director's Office - Starek, Roscoe B. III....Riley, Katherine E. FTC 202-326-2127
Exercise and Aging....Staff NIA 301-496-1752
Exercise and the Heart....Staff NHLBI 301-496-4236
Exhibits and Publications (Printing)....Charuhas, Joseph NLM 301-496-6308
Exhibits, Conventions....Dickinson, Joanne CENSUS 301-763-2370
Exotic Fish....Staff FWS 703-358-1718
Exotic Species....Staff FWS 703-358-1718
Exotropia....Staff NEI 301-496-5248
Experimental Aerodynamics....Mewhinney, Michael NASA 415-604-3937
Experimental Aerodynamics....Hutchison, Jane NASA 415-604-4698
Experimental Allergic Encephalomyelitis (EAE)....Staff NINDS 301-496-5751
Experimental Development Stations....Staff FCC 202-653-8141
Experimental Immunology....O'Shea, John FAES 301-846-1330
Explosives....Maxey, Francis P. COMMERCE 202-482-0128
Explosives....Preston, Jacques CUSTOMS 212-466-5488
Explosives....Cantrell, Raymond L. MINES 202-501-9581
Explosives....Johnson, Larry USITC 202-205-3351
Export & Import Price Indexes, Curr. Anal.....Vachris, Michelle LABOR 202-606-7155
Export Trading Company Affairs....Muller, George COMMERCE 202-482-5131
Exposure Evaluation Division....Staff EPA 202-260-1866
Express Delivery Service....Elliott, Fred COMMERCE 202-482-1134
Extramural Associates Program....Staff OD/OERT 301-496-9728
Extrapyramidal Disorders....Staff NINDS 301-496-5751
Eye (Radiation and Ultra Violet Effect)....Staff FDA/NCDRH 301-443-4690
Eye (Statistics)....Staff NCHS 301-436-8500
Eye Banks....Staff NEI 301-496-5248
Eye Care....Staff NEI 301-496-5248
Eye Diseases....Staff NEI 301-496-5248
Eye Exercises....Staff NEI 301-496-5248
Eye Institute, National....Stein, Judith NIH 301-496-5248
Eye Strain....Staff NEI 301-496-5248
Eye glasses....Johnson, Christopher USITC 202-205-3488
Eyeglasses....Staff NEI 301-496-5248

F

FAES (Foundation for Adv. Educa. in the Sciences)....Staff FAES 301-496-7976
FM Radio Advertising....Staff FCC 202-632-7551
FM Radio Intercity Relays....Staff FCC 202-634-6307
FM Radio Remote Pickup....Staff FCC 202-634-6307
FM Radio Stations....Staff FCC 202-632-6908
FM Radio Stations--New....Staff FCC 202-632-6908
FM Translators/Boosters....Staff FCC 202-634-6307
Fabric folding machines....Greene, William USITC 202-205-3405
Fabricated Metal Construction Materials....Williams, Franklin COMMERCE 202-482-0132
Fabrics, Coated or Laminated....Barth, George CUSTOMS 212-466-5884
Fabrics, Embroidered....Konzet, Jeffrey CUSTOMS 212-466-5885
Fabrics, Knit....Konzet, Jeffrey CUSTOMS 212-466-5885
Fabrics, Non-Woven....Barth, George CUSTOMS 212-466-5884
Fabrics, Technical....Barth, George CUSTOMS 212-466-5884
Fabrics, Woven....Tytelman, Alan CUSTOMS 212-466-5896
Fabrics, woven: cotton....Freund, Kimberlie USITC 202-205-3456
Fabrics, woven: glass....McNay, Deborah USITC 202-205-3425
Fabrics, woven: jute....Cook, Lee USITC 202-205-3471
Fabrics, woven: manmade fibers....Freund, Kimberlie USITC 202-205-3456
Fabrics, woven: pile....Freund, Kimberlie USITC 202-205-3456
Fabrics, woven: silk....Freund, Kimberlie USITC 202-205-3456
Fabrics: Tufted....Freund, Kimberlie USITC 202-205-3456
Fabrics: billiard cloth....Cook, Lee USITC 202-205-3471
Fabrics: bolting cloth....Cook, Lee USITC 202-205-3471
Fabrics: coated....Cook, Lee USITC 202-205-3471
Fabrics: elastic....Freund, Kimberlie USITC 202-205-3456
Fabrics: impression....Freund, Kimberlie USITC 202-205-3456
Fabrics: knit....Freund, Kimberlie USITC 202-205-3456

Fabrics: narrow....Freund, Kimberlie USITC 202-205-3456

Fabrics: nonwoven....Sussman, Donald USITC 202-205-3470

Fabrics: oil cloths....Cook, Lee USITC 202-205-3471

Fabrics: tapestry, woven....Freund, Kimberlie USITC 202-205-3456

Fabrics: tire....Cook, Lee USITC 202-205-3471

Fabrics: tracing cloth....Cook, Lee USITC 202-205-3471

Fabrics: embroidered....Freund, Kimberlie USITC 202-205-3456

Fabrics: woven, wool....Fruend, Kimberlie USITC 202-205-3456

Fabry's Disease....Staff NINDS 301-496-5751

Fabry's Disease....Staff NICHD 301-496-5133

Facial Neuralgia (Tic Douloureux)....Staff NINDS 301-496-5751

Facilities Management....Bass, Robert C. FTC 202-326-2265

Facilities Management....Glisson, Thomas A. FTC 202-326-2308

Facilities Management....Lampkins, Gladys M. FTC 202-326-2307

Facilities Management....Morris, J. Wayne FTC 202-326-2310

Facilities Management....Morris, Patrick A. FTC 202-326-2309

Facilities Management....Singleton, Frieda FTC 202-326-2580

Facsimile (FAX)--Wire....Staff FCC 202-634-1800

Fainting (Syncope)....Staff NHLBI 301-496-4236

Fair Housing and Equal Opportunity....Staff HUD 202-708-3735

Falconry....Staff FWS 703-358-1821

Falls and Frailty....Staff NIA 301-496-1752

Familial Ataxia Telangiectasia....Staff NCI 301-496-5583

Familial Ataxia Telangiectasia....Staff NINDS 301-496-5751

Familial Dysautonomia (Riley-Day Syndrome)....Staff NINDS 301-496-5751

Familial Hypertension....Staff NHLBI 301-496-4236

Familial Periodic Paralysis....Staff NINDS 301-496-5751

Familial Spastic Paraparesis....Staff NINDS 301-496-5751

Families....Staff CENSUS 301-763-7987

Family Characteristics of Labor Force....Hayghe, Howard LABOR 202-606-6378

Family Issues....Long, Susan ACF 202-401-9215

Family Medicine Training....Staff HRSA/BHPr 301-443-6837

Family Nursing Practitioner....Staff HRSA/BHPr 301-443-6333

Family Planning....Staff NCNR 301-496-0526

Family Planning....Eddinger, Lucy ASH 202-690-8335

Family Planning (Research)....Staff NICHD 301-496-5133

Family Size....Staff NICHD 301-496-5133

Family and Aging....Staff NIA 301-496-1752

Fanconi's Anemia....Staff NHLBI 301-496-4236

Fans....Mata, Ruben USITC 202-205-3403

Farm Bill....Staff FWS 703-358-2043

Farm Machinery....Weining, Mary COMMERCE 202-482-4708

Farm Population....Dahmann, Don CENSUS 301-763-5158

Farmlands....Staff FWS 703-358-2043

Farms & Land - Corporate & Family Farms....Reimund, Donn Agri 202-219-0522

Farms & Land - Farm Numbers....Ledbury, Dan Agri 202-720-1790

Farms & Land - Farm Output & Productivity....Douvelis, George Agri 202-219-0432

Farms & Land - Farm Real Estate....Hexem, Roger Agri 202-219-0419

Farms & Land - Foreign Land Ownership....DeBraal, Peter Agri 202-219-0425

Farms & Land - Land Ownership & Tenure....Wunderlich, Gene Agri 202-219-0425

Farms & Land - Land Use....Daugherty, Arthur Agri 202-219-0424

Farms & Land - World....Urban, Francis Agri 202-219-0717

Farsightedness....Staff NEI 301-496-5248

Fasteners (Industrial)....Reise, Richard COMMERCE 202-482-3489

Fasteners (Nails, Screws, Etc.)....Fitzgerald, John CUSTOMS 212-466-5492

Fats and Oils....Janis, William V. COMMERCE 202-482-2250

Fats and vegetable oils and their products....Reeder, John USITC 202-205-3319

Fatty acids....Randall, Rob USITC 202-205-3366

Fatty alcohols of animal or vegetable origin....Randall, Rob USITC 202-205-3366

Fatty and Aromatic Substances....Joseph, Stephanie CUSTOMS 212-466-5768

Fatty ethers of animal or vegetable origin....Randall, Rob USITC 202-205-3366

Fatty substances derived from animal, marine, veg....Randall, Rob USITC 202-205-3366

Fatty-acid amides....Land, Eric USITC 202-205-3349

Fatty-acid esters of polyhydric alcohols....Land, Eric USITC 202-205-3349

Fatty-acid quaternary ammonium salts (surface act)....Land, Eric USITC 202-205-3349

Fear of Crime....Lindgren, Sue Justice Stat 202-307-0760

Fear of Crime....Klaus, Patsy Justice Stat 202-307-0776

Fear of Crime....Rand, Michael Justice Stat 202-616-3494

Feather products....Spalding, Josephine USITC 202-205-3498

Feathers....Steller, Rose USITC 202-205-3323

Febrile Convulsions....Staff NINDS 301-496-5751

Febrile Seizures....Staff NICHD 301-496-5133

Federal Justice....Kaplan, Carol Justice Stat 202-307-0759

Feed Grains - Corn, Sorghum, Barley, Oats....Van Lahr, Charles Agri 202-720-7369

Feed Grains - Corn, Sorghum, Barley, Oats....Tice, Thomas Agri 202-219-0840

Feed Grains - Corn, Sorghum, Barley, Oats....Cole, James Agri 202-219-0840

Feed Grains - Corn, Sorghum, Barley, Oats - World....Riley, Peter Agri 202-219-0824

Feeds, animal....Pierre-Benoist, John USITC 202-205-3320

Feldspar....Potter, Michael J. MINES 202-501-9387

Feldspar....White, Linda USITC 202-205-3427

Female Offenders....Conley, Joyce Justice Stat 202-633-2214

Female Offenders - Federal....Kaplan, Carol Justice Stat 202-307-0759

Female Victims....Klaus, Patsy Justice Stat 202-307-0776

Fencing, Metal....Shaw, Robert COMMERCE 202-482-0132

Ferments....Nesbitt, Elizabeth USITC 202-205-3355

Ferricyanide blue....Johnson, Larry USITC 202-205-3351

Ferrites....Cutchin, John USITC 202-205-3396

Ferroalloys....Staff USITC 202-205-3419

Ferroalloys Products....Presbury Greylin COMMERCE 202-482-0609

Ferrocerium....Johnson, Larry USITC 202-205-3351

Ferrocyanide blue....Johnson, Larry USITC 202-205-3351

Ferrous Scrap....Sharkey, Robert COMMERCE 202-482-0606

Fertility....Staff NICHD 301-496-5133

Fertility Drugs....Staff NICHD 301-496-5133

Fertility/Births....Bachu, Amara CENSUS 301-763-5303

Fertility/Births....O'Connell, Martin CENSUS 301-763-5303

Fertilizers....Maxey, Francis P. COMMERCE 202-482-0128

Fertilizers....Brownchweig, Gilbert CUSTOMS 212-466-5744

Fertilizers....Trainor, Cynthia USITC 202-205-3354

Fetal Alcohol Syndrome....Staff NICHD 301-496-5133

Fetal Alcohol Syndrome Prevention....Floyd, Louise CDC 404-488-7370

Fetal Monitoring....Staff NICHD 301-496-5133

Fetus....Staff NICHD 301-496-5133

Fever....Staff NIAID 301-496-5717

Fever Blisters....Staff NIDR 301-496-4261

Fibers....Konzet, Jeffrey CUSTOMS 212-466-5885

Fibers: abaca....Cook, Lee USITC 202-205-3471

Fibers: alpaca....Warlick, William USITC 202-205-3459

Fibers: camel hair....Warlick, William USITC 202-205-3459

Fibers: cashmere....Warlick, William USITC 202-205-3459

Fibers: cotton....Sweet, Mary Elizabeth USITC 202-205-3455

Fibers: flax....Cook, Lee USITC 202-205-3471

Fibers: jute....Cook, Lee USITC 202-205-3471

Fibers: wool....Warlick, William USITC 202-205-3459

Fibers: angora....Warlick, William USITC 202-205-3459

Fibers: manmade....Warlick, William USITC 202-205-3459

Fibers: silk....Warlick, William USITC 202-205-3459

Fibers: sisal and henequen....Cook, Lee USITC 202-205-3471

Fibrillation....Staff NHLBI 301-496-4236

Fibrin....Randall, Rob USITC 202-205-3366

Fibrinolysis....Staff NHLBI 301-496-4236

Fibroid Tumors....Staff NICHD 301-496-5133

Fibromuscular Hyperplasia....Staff NHLBI 301-496-4236

Fibromuscular Hyperplasia....Staff NIAMS 301-496-8188

Fibromyalgia....Staff NIAMS 301-496-8188

Fibrositis....Staff NIAMS 301-496-8188

Fibrotic Lung Diseases....Staff NHLBI 301-496-4236

Field Disturbance....Staff FCC 202-653-7313

Fifth Disease....Staff NIAID 301-496-5717

Fiji....Lagoy, Michele Peace Corps 202-606-3227

Fiji (Suva)....Staff Cnty State 202-647-3546

Fiji/Minerals....Lyday, Travis Cnty Mines 202-501-9695

Filariasis....Staff NIAID 301-496-5717

Filberts....Burket, Stephen USITC 202-205-3318

Film....Brownchweig, Gilbert CUSTOMS 212-466-5744

Film (photographic)....Bishop, Kate USITC 202-205-3494

Film, plastics....Misurelli, Denby USITC 202-205-3362

Films, Wildlife Video....Staff FWS 202-205-5611

Filters/Purifying Equipment....Jonkers, Loretta COMMERCE 202-482-0564

Finance and Management Ind.....Candilis, Wray O. COMMERCE 202-482-0339

Financial services....Brown, Richard USITC 202-205-3438

Finland....Lyons, Maryanne Cnty Commerce 202-482-3254

Finland (Helsinki)....Staff Cnty State 202-647-6071

Finland/Minerals....Buck, Donald E. Cnty Mines 202-501-9670

Fire....Staff FCC 717-337-1212

Fire Management....Staff FWS 703-358-2043

Fire Safety....Cowart, Everett CDC 404-639-3148

Firearms....Preston, Jacques CUSTOMS 212-466-5488

Firearms....Robinson, Hazel USITC 202-205-3496

Firewood....Ruggles, Fred USITC 202-205-3325

Fireworks....Glover, Stephanie CPSC 301-504-0580

Fireworks....Johnson, Larry USITC 202-205-3351

First aid kits....Randall, Rob USITC 202-205-3366

Fish....Brady, Thomas CUSTOMS 212-466-5790

Fish....Corey, Roger USITC 202-205-3327

Fish & Wildlife Law Enforcement....Staff FWS 703-358-1949

Fish Broodstock Program....Staff FWS 703-358-1715

Fish Conservation and Management Act....Staff 703-358-1715

Fish Control Chemicals....Staff FWS 703-358-1715

Fish Culture Information....Staff FWS 703-358-1715

Fish Disease Diagnosis/Control....Staff FWS 703-358-1715

Fish Diseases/Research....Staff FWS 703-358-1715

Fish Ecology....Staff FWS 703-358-1710

Fish Habitat Research....Lennartz, Michael R. FS 202-205-1524

Fish Hatcheries....Staff FWS 703-358-1715

Fish Health Inspections....Staff FWS 703-358-1715

Fish Husbandry....Staff FWS 703-358-1718

Fish Law Enforcement....Staff FWS 703-358-1949

Fish Nets and Nettings....Barth, George CUSTOMS 212-466-5884

Fish Propagation....Staff FWS 703-358-1715

Fish and Wildlife News....Staff FWS 202-208-5634

Fish and Wildlife Reference Service....Staff FWS 703-358-2156

Fish and Wildlife Service....Staff EPA 703-208-4111

Fish nets and netting....Cook, Lee USITC 202-205-3471

Fish oils....Reeder, John USITC 202-205-3319

Fish, Exotic....Staff FWS 703-358-1718

Fisheries, Major Proj.....Bell, Richard COMMERCE 202-482-2460

Fishery Information Systems....Staff FWS 703-558-1861

Fishing on Refuges....Staff FWS 703-358-1718

Fishing tackle....Robinson, Hazel USITC 202-205-3496

Flags....Cook, Lee USITC 202-205-3471

Flares....Johnson, Larry USITC 202-205-3351

Flashlights....Cutchin, John USITC 202-205-3396

Flat glass and products....Lukes, James USITC 202-205-3426

Flat goods....Seastrum, Carl USITC 202-205-3493

Flat panel displays....Malison, Andrew USITC 202-205-3391

Flatgoods....Gorman, Kevin CUSTOMS 212-466-5893

Flaxseed and linseed oil....Reeder, John USITC 202-205-3319

Flight Control Research....Witherspoon, John NASA 804-864-6170

Flight Research Programs....Lovato, Nancy NASA 805-258-3448

Flight Simulation Research....Hutchison, Jane NASA 415-604-4968

Flight simulating machines....Andersen, Peder USITC 202-205-3388

Floaters....Staff NEI 301-496-5248

Floating structures....Lahey, Kathleen USITC 202-205-3409

Floor Coverings....Hansen, John CUSTOMS 212-466-5854

Floor coverings, textile....Sweet, Mary Elizabeth USITC 202-205-3465

Flooring (wood)....Ruggles, Fred USITC 202-205-3325

Floppy Baby (Nemaline Myopathy)....Staff NINDS 301-496-5751

Floral waters....Land, Eric USITC 202-205-3349

Floriculture....Brewster, Jim Agri 202-720-7688

Floriculture....Johnson, Doyle Agri 202-219-0884

Flour....Janis, William V. COMMERCE 202-482-2250

Flour (grain)....Pierre-Benoist, John USITC 202-205-3320

Flowers....Janis, William V. COMMERCE 202-482-2250

Flowers, Artificial....Rauch, Theodore CUSTOMS 212-466-5892

Fluid Power....McDonald, Edward COMMERCE 202-482-0680

Fluorescein Angiography....Staff NEI 301-496-5248

Fluoridation....Staff CDC 404-639-3286

Fluoridation....Staff NIDR 301-496-4261

Fluoridation....Berreth, Don CDC 404-639-3286

Fluoride Research....Staff NIDR 301-496-4261

Fluorine....Conant, Kenneth USITC 202-205-3346

Fluorocarbons....Michels, David USITC 202-205-3352

Fluorosis....Staff NIDR 301-496-4261

Fluorspar....Miller, Michael MINES 202-501-9409

Fluorspar....DeSapio, Vincent USITC 202-205-3435

Fluxes....White, Linda USITC 202-205-3427

Fogarty Publications....Staff FIC 301-496-2075

Fogarty Scholars....Staff FIC 301-496-4161

Foil, metal: aluminum....Yost, Charles USITC 202-205-3432

Foil, metal: other....Lundy, David USITC 202-205-3439

Folk Arts....Sheehy, Daniel NEA 202-682-5449

Food - Food Assistance and Nutrition....Smallwood, Dave Agri 202-219-0864

Food - Food Assistance and Nutrition....Smallwood, Dave Agri 202-219-0867

Food - Food Away From Home....Price, Charlene Agri 202-219-0866

Food - Food Consumption....Putnam, Judy Agri 202-219-0870

Food - Food Demand & Expenditures....Blaylock, James Agri 202-219-0862

Food - Food Demand & Expenditures....Haidacher, Richard Agri 202-219-0870

Food - Food Demand & Expenditures (World)....Stallings, Dave Agri 202-219-0708

Food - Food Manufacturing....Gallo, Tony Agri 202-219-0866

Food - Food Manufacturing & Retailing....Handy, Charles Agri 202-219-0866

Food - Food Policy....Myers, Les Agri 202-219-0860

Food - Food Policy....Smallwood, Dave Agri 202-219-0864

Food - Food Policy (World)....Westcott, Paul Agri 202-219-0840

Food - Food Policy - World....Lynch, Loretta Agri 202-219-0689

Food - Food Safety & Quality....Roberts, Tanya Agri 202-219-0864

Food - Food Safety & Quality....Lin, Bina-Hwah Agri 202-219-0459

Food - Food Wholesaling....Epps, Walter Agri 202-219-0866

Food - Marketing Margins & Statistics....Haidacher, Richard Agri 202-219-0870

Food - Marketing Margins & Statistics....Dunham, Denis Agri 202-219-0870

Food - Marketing Margins & Statistics....Elitzak, Howard Agri 202-219-0870

Food - Marketing Margins & Statistics....Handy, Charles Agri 202-219-0866

Food - Price Spreads (Meat)....Duewer, Larry Agri 202-219-0712

Food - Retailing....Kaufman, Phil Agri 202-219-0866

Food Additives....Staff FDA 301-472-4750

Food Additives/Dyes....Corwin, Emil FDA 202-205-4144

Food Grains - Rice....Owens, Marty Agri 202-720-2157

Food Grains - Wheat....Siegenthaler, Vaughn Agri 202-720-8068

Food Grains - Wheat....Allen, Ed Agri 202-219-0841

Food Labeling....Staff FDA 301-472-4750

Food Labeling....Lecos, Chris FDA 202-205-4144

Food Prices & Consumer Index....Parlett, Ralph Agri 202-219-0870

Food Prices & Consumer Price Index....Dunham, Denis Agri 202-219-0870

Food Prices Retail, Consumer Expenditure Survey....Cook, William LABOR 202-606-6988

Food Products Machinery....Shaw, Gene COMMERCE 202-482-3494

Food Retailing....Kenney, Cornelius COMMERCE 202-482-2428

Food and Chemicals, Prices/Lv. Cond....Hippen, Roger LABOR 202-606-7723

Food, Apparel, & Raw Materials, Intl. Price Ind.....Frumkin, Rob LABOR 202-606-7106

Food, Raw Materials, and Apparel, Intl. Price Ind....Frumkin, Rob LABOR 202-606-7106

Food-preparing machines....Jackson, Georgia USITC 202-205-3399

Footwear with Uppers of Rubber, Plastic or Leather....Francke, Eric CUSTOMS 212-466-5890

Footwear....Byron, James E. COMMERCE 202-482-4034

Footwear....Shildneck, Ann USITC 202-205-3499

Forecasting Prison Populations....Shipley, Bernard Justice Stat 202-307-7703

Foreign Born Population....Staff CENSUS 301-763-7955

Foreign Countries, Labor Force & Unemployment....Sorrentino, Constance LABOR 202-606-5654

Foreign Countries--Hourly Compensation Costs....Capdevielle, Patricia LABOR 202-606-5654

Foreign Countries--Prices, Prod. & Tech.....Godbout, Todd LABOR 202-606-5654

Foreign Countries--Productivity, Unit Labor Costs....Neef, Arthur LABOR 202-606-5654

Foreign Language Education....Staff NEH 202-606-8373

Foreign Medical Students....Mehuron, Charlotte HRSA 301-443-3376

Foreign Scientists Assistance....Staff FIC 301-472-6166

Foreign Trade Data Services....Mearkle, Hayden CENSUS 301-763-7754

Foreign Trade Data Services....Staff CENSUS 301-763-5140

Foreign Trade, Shippers Export Declaration....Blyweiss, Hal CENSUS 301-763-5310

Foreign trade zones....Burns, Gail USITC 202-205-2501

Forest Diseases....Smith Richard S. FS 202-205-1532

Forest Fire Sciences....Donoghue, Linda R. FS 202-205-1561

Forest Insects....Lyon, Robert L. FS 202-205-1532

Forest Products....Smith, Len COMMERCE 202-482-0375

Forest Products....Fitzgerald, Richard O. FS 202-205-1753

Forest Products, Domestic Construction....Kristensen, Chris COMMERCE 202-482-0384

Forest Products, Trade Policy....Hicks, Michael COMMERCE 202-482-0375

Forest Protection....Staff FWS 703-358-2043

Forest Radio Service....Staff FCC 717-337-1212

Forest Recreation and Urban Forestry....Ewert, Alan FS 202-205-1092

Forestry & Construction, Prices and Living Cond.....Davies, Wanda LABOR

202-606-7713
Forestry Atmospheric Deposition Research....Dunn, Paul H. FS 202-205-1524
Forestry Ecosystem Research....Szaro, Robert FS 202-205-1524
Forestry Wetlands Research....Bartuska, Ann M. FS 202-205-1524
Forestry and Construction, Prices/Lv. Cond....Davies, Wanda LABOR 202-606-7713
Forestry, Global Change Research....Niebla, Elvia E. FS 202-205-1561
Forestry, Land Reclamation....Duscher, Karl FS 202-205-1224
Forestry, Lands and Resource Information....Holmes, Chris FS 202-205-1006
Forestry, Mineral Materials....Marshall, Steve FS 202-205-1242
Forestry, Oil and Gas Analysis....Holm, Melody FS 303-236-9376
Forestry, Pesticide Use....Staff FS 202-205-1600
Forestry, Soils Program....Avers, Peter FS 202-205-1473
Forestry, Solid Leasable Minerals....Kurcaba FS 202-205-1243
Forestry, Water Rights....Glasser, Steve FS 202-205-1473
Forestry, Water Rights Program....Glasser, Steve FS 202-205-1473
Forfeiture....Zawitz, Marianne Justice Stat 202-616-3499
Forged-steel grinding balls....Stonitsch, Laura USITC 202-205-3408
Forgings Semifinished Steel....Bell, Charles COMMERCE 202-482-0609
Fork-lift trucks....Murphy, Mary USITC 202-205-3401
Formaldehyde....Michels, David USITC 202-205-3352
Fossil Energy....Stuntz, Linda NEIC 202-586-6660
Fossil Fuel Power Generation, Major Proj.....Dollison, Robert COMMERCE 202-482-2733
Foster Care....Long, Susan ACF 202-401-9215
Foundry Equipment....Kemper, Alexis COMMERCE 202-482-5956
Foundry Industry....Bell, Charles COMMERCE 202-482-0609
Foundry products....Vacant USITC 202-205-3419
Fracture Healing....Staff NIAMS 301-496-8188
Fragile X Syndrome....Staff NICHD 301-496-5133
France....Mikalis, Elana Cnty Commerce 202-482-6008
France (Paris)....Staff Cnty State 202-647-2633
France/Minerals....Newman, Harold R. Cnty Mines 202-501-9669
Franchising....Staff FCC 202-254-3407
Franchising services....Bedore, James USITC 202-205-3424
Fraud (Scientific)....Staff OD/OSI 301-496-2624
Fraud Hotline, HUD....Staff HUD 800-347-3735
Fraud, Waste & Abuse-Investigations, Audits....Holtz, Judy IG 202-619-1149
Freedom of Information....Staff OD/DC 301-496-5633
Freedom of Information Office....Coleman, Gary PHS 202-690-7453
Freedom of Information, Office of....Leathers, Laura CDC 404-639-2388
French Antilles....Staff Cnty State 202-647-2620
French Guinea/Minerals....Mobbs, Philip Cnty Mines 202-501-9679
French Polynesia....Staff Cnty State 202-647-3546
Freon (chlorofluorocarbons)....Michels, David USITC 202-205-3352
Frequencies Allocations, Government....Staff FCC 202-653-8141
Frequencies Allocations, International....Staff FCC 202-653-8126
Frequencies Allocations, Non-Government....Staff FCC 202-653-8108
Friedreich's Ataxia....Staff NINDS 301-496-5751
Frohlich's Syndrome (Adiposogenital Dystrophy)....Staff NINDS 301-496-5751
Frohlich's Syndrome (Adiposogenital Dystrophy)....Staff NIDDK 301-496-3583
Frohlich's Syndrome (Adiposogenital Dystrophy)....Staff NICHD 301-496-5133
Frozen Fruits, Vegetables & Specialties....Hodgen, Donald A. COMMERCE 202-482-3346
Fructose....Randall, Rob USITC 202-205-3366
Fruit, edible, ex citrus....Vacant USITC 202-205-3306
Fruits and Tree Nuts....Hintzman, Kevin Agri 202-720-5412
Fruits and Tree Nuts - Tree Nuts....Johnson, Doyle Agri 202-219-0884
Fruits and Tree Nuts....Shields, Dennis Agri 202-219-0884
Fruits and Tree Nuts....Bertelsen, Diane Agri 202-219-0884
Fruits and Vegetables....Hopartd, Stanley CUSTOMS 212-466-5760
Fuchs' Dystrophy....Staff NEI 301-496-5248
Fuel oil (nos. 1, 2, 3, 4, 5, 6)....Foreso, Cynthia USITC 202-205-3348
Fuel oil, bunker "C"....Foreso, Cynthia USITC 202-205-3348
Fuel oil, navy special....Foreso, Cynthia USITC 202-205-3348
Fuel, jet....Foreso, Cynthia USITC 202-205-3348
Fuels and Utls. Retail Prices, Consumer Price Index...Adkins, Robert LABOR 202-606-6985
Fuels and Chemical Analysis....Staff EPA 313-668-4245
Fuels and Utilities Index, Monthly....Adkins, Robert LABOR 202-606-6985
Fulminates....Johnson, Larry USITC 202-205-3351
Fumes (Hazardous)....Staff OD/ORS 301-496-2960
Fungal Diseases (Eyes)....Staff NEI 301-496-5248
Fungal Infections....Staff NIAID 301-496-5717
Funnel Chest (Pectus Excavatum)....Staff NHLBI 301-496-4236
Fur Goods....Byron, James E. COMMERCE 202-482-4034
Fur and furlike apparel....Jones, Jackie USITC 202-205-3466

Fur and furlike apparel....Hamey, Amy USITC 202-205-3465
Furfural....Michels, David USITC 202-205-3352
Furnace black...Johnson, Larry USITC 202-205-3351
Furnaces....Mesa, Stacey Reuben CPSC 301-504-0580
Furnaces....Rocks, Michael CUSTOMS 212-466-5669
Furnaces....Mata, Ruben USITC 202-205-3403
Furnishings....Hansen, John CUSTOMS 212-466-5854
Furniture....Vacant COMMERCE 202-482-0338
Furniture....Mushinske, Larry CUSTOMS 212-466-5739
Furniture....Spalding, Josephine USITC 202-205-3498
Furskins....Steller, Rose USITC 202-205-3323
Fuse/Burn....Glover, Stephanie CPSC 301-504-0580
Fused Alumina, (Abrasive)....Austin, Gordon MINES 202-501-9388
Fuses: Blasting....Vacant USITC 202-205-3343
Fuses: electrical....Malison, Andrew USITC 202-205-3391
Fusion Energy....Davies, Anne NEIC 301-903-4941
Fusion Energy....Greenblatt, Jack USITC 202-205-3353
Fusion Plasma....Crandall, David NEIC 301-903-4596
Fuzzy Logic....Kader, Victoria COMMERCE 202-482-0571

G

G. Bissaue....Fossum, Linnea Peace Corps 202-606-3708
G6PD Deficiency....Staff NHLBI 301-496-4236
GBF/DIME System....Staff CENSUS 301-763-1580
Gabon....Henke, Debra Cnty Commerce 202-482-5149
Gabon....Blackwell, Gloria Peace Corps 202-606-3998
Gabon....Swezey, Virginia Peace Corps 202-606-3998
Gabon (Libreville)....Staff Cnty State 202-647-1707
Gabon/Minerals....King, Audie L. Cnty Mines 202-501-9674
Galactorrhea....Staff NIDDK 301-496-3583
Galactosemia....Staff NIDDK 301-496-3583
Galactosemia....Staff NICHD 301-496-5133
Galactosemia....Staff NINDS 301-496-5751
Galileo Flight Project....Wilson, James NASA 818-354-5011
Gallbladder....Staff NIDDK 301-496-3583
Gallium....Kramer, Deborah A. MINES 202-501-9394
Gallium....Lundy, David USITC 202-205-3439
Gallstones....Staff NIDDK 301-496-3583
Gambia....Michelin, Philip Cnty Commerce 202-482-4388
Gambia....McCormick, Michael L. Peace Corps 202-606-3644
Gambia....Herring, Debra Peace Corps 202-606-3644
Gambia, The (Banjul)....Staff Cnty State 202-647-3395
Gambia/Minerals....van Oss, Hendrick Cnty Mines 202-501-9687
Game animals....Steller, Rose USITC 202-205-3323
Games....McKenna, Thomas CUSTOMS 212-466-5475
Games....Robinson, Hazel USITC 202-205-3496
Games and Childrens' Vehicles....Vanderwolf, John COMMERCE 202-482-0348
Gamma Ray Observatory....Beasley, Dolores NASA 301-286-2806
Gamma Ray Observatory....Staff NASA 301-286-5565
Garage Door Openers--Licenses....Staff FCC 717-337-1212
Garage Door Openers--Not Licensed....Staff FCC 202-653-6288
Garage Door Operators....Mesa, Stacey Reuben CPSC 301-504-0580
Garnet....Austin, Gordon MINES 202-501-9388
Garters and suspenders....Linkins, Linda USITC 202-205-3469
Gas Reserves Statistics....Lique, Diane NEIC 202-586-6090
Gas Vol Standards....Mesa, Stacey Reuben CPSC 301-504-0580
Gas generators....Vacant USITC 202-205-3380
Gas oil....Foreso, Cynthia USITC 202-205-3348
Gas-operated metalworking appliances....Vacant USITC 202-205-3380
Gaseous Diffusion Plants (GDP)....Bennett, John NEIC 301-903-5832
Gases, Greenhouse....Patrinus, Aristides NEIC 301-903-5348
Gaskets/Gasketing Materials....Reiss, Richard COMMERCE 202-482-3489
Gasoline....Foreso, Cynthia USITC 202-205-3348
Gasoline, Retail Prices....Chelena, Joseph LABOR 202-606-6982
Gastric Hypersecretion....Staff NIDDK 301-496-3583
Gastrinoma....Staff NIDDK 301-496-3583
Gastrointestinal Disorders....Staff NIDDK 301-496-3583
Gastrointestinal Tract Diseases....Staff NIDDK 301-496-3583
Gaucher's Disease....Staff NINDS 301-496-5751
Gauze, impregnated with medicinals....Randall, Rob USITC 202-205-3366
Gears....Riedl, Karl CUSTOMS 212-466-5493
Gelatin....Brownchweig, Gilbert CUSTOMS 212-466-5744
Gelatin, articles of....Spalding, Josephine USITC 202-205-3498
Gelatin, edible....Jonnard, Aimison USITC 202-205-3350
Gelatin, inedible....Jonnard, Aimison USITC 202-205-3350

Gelatin, photographic....Jonnard, Aimison USITC 202-205-3350

Gem Stones....Austin, Gordon MINES 202-501-9388

Gems....DeSapio, Vincent USITC 202-205-3435

Gemstones, imitation....Witherspoon, Ricardo USITC 202-205-3489

Gen. Indus. Mach. Nec, Exc 35691....Shaw, Eugene COMMERCE 202-482-2204

GenBank (Genetic Sequence Data Bank)....Staff NIGMS 301-496-7301

General Agreement on Trade and Tariffs (GATT)....Klein, Cecelia US Trade Rep 202-395-3063

General Aviation Aircraft (Market Support)....Driscoll, George COMMERCE 202-482-1228

General Clinical Research Centers Program....Staff DRR 301-496-6595

General Counsel's Office....Ballard, Sonia D. FTC 202-326-2669

General Information....Staff CENSUS 301-763-4100

General Information - Environmental Issues Hotline....Staff EPA 800-759-4372

General Litigation (Assoc. & Business Practices)....Abrahamsen, Dana FTC 202-326-2906

General Litigation (Assoc. and Business Practices)....Alexander, Janice FTC 202-326-2891

General Litigation (Health Care)....Allen, Patricia A. FTC 202-326-3176

General Mobile Licenses....Staff FCC 717-337-1212

General Mobile Radio Service....Staff FCC 717-337-1212

General, Medical Sciences, National Institute of....Dieffenbach, Ann NIH 301-496-7301

Generator Sets/Turbines (Major Proj)....Dollison, Robert C0MMERCE 202-482-2733

Generators....Cutchin, John USITC 202-205-3396

Genetic Pancrea. Involv. not due to Cystic Fibrosis....Staff NIDDK 301-496-3583

Genetics....Staff NINDS 301-496-5751

Genetics....Staff NIGMS 301-496-7301

Genetics....Staff NIDR 301-496-4261

Genetics....Staff NICHD 301-496-5133

Genetics....Parry, Dilys M. FAES 301-496-4947

Genetics (Animal Monitoring)....Staff NCRR/VRP 301-496-9188

Genetics of Aging....Staff NIA 301-496-1752

Genetics, Developmental....Adhya, Sankar L. FAES 301-496-2495

Genital Herpes....Staff NIAID 301-496-5717

Genital Warts....Staff NIAID 301-496-5717

Geothermal Energy....Mock, John E. NEIC 202-586-5340

Geology....Goodell, Grant UVA 701-924-0559

Geophysical Phenomena Research....Staff NASA 415-604-3937

Geophysical Research....Beasley, Dolores NASA 301-286-2806

Georgia....Staff 202-647-8671

Geoscience Research....Coleman, James NEIC 301-903-5822

Geothermal Loan Guarantee Program....Staff NEIC 202-586-1539

Geriatric Medicine....Staff NIA 301-496-1752

Geriatric Medicine....Roth, Jesse FAES 301-558-8198

Geriatric Psychiatry....Staff NIMH 301-443-4515

Geriatric Psychiatry....Staff NIA 301-496-1752

Geriatrics....Staff NIA 301-496-1752

German Measles (Rubella)....Staff NIAID 301-496-5717

Germanium....Llewellyn, Thomas O. MINES 202-501-9395

Germanium....Lundy, David USITC 202-205-3439

Germanium oxides....Conant, Kenneth USITC 202-205-3346

Germany....Fisher, Brenda Cnty Commerce 202-482-2434

Germany....Kloepfer, Joan Cnty Commerce 202-482-2841

Germany....Staff Cnty State 202-647-2005

Germany, East/Minerals....Rabchevsky, George Cnty Mines 202-501-9672

Germfree Rodents....Staff NCRR/VRP 301-496-5255

Gerontology....Staff NIA 301-496-1752

Gerson Method....Staff NCI 301-496-5583

Gerstmann's Syndrome....Staff NICHD 301-496-5133

Gestation....Staff NICHD 301-496-5133

Ghana....Henke, Debra Cnty Commerce 202-482-5149

Ghana....McCormick, Michael L. Peace Corps 202-606-3644

Ghana....Herring, Debra Peace Corps 202-606-3644

Ghana (Accra)....Staff Cnty State 202-647-4567

Ghana/Minerals....van Oss, Hendrik Cnty Mines 202-501-9687

Giardiasis....Staff NIAID 301-496-5717

Gibraltar....Staff Cnty State 202-647-8027

Giftware (Export Promo)....Beckham, Reginald COMMERCE 202-482-5478

Gigantism....Staff NIDDK 301-496-3583

Gilbert's Syndrome....Staff NIDDK 301-496-3583

Gilles de la Tourette's Disease....Staff NINDS 301-496-5751

Gingivitis....Staff NIDR 301-496-4261

Glace fruit and vegetable substances....Frankel, Lee USITC 202-205-3315

Glands....Staff NIDDK 301-496-3583

Glass....Bunin, Jacob CUSTOMS 212-566-5796

Glass (flat)....Lukes, James USITC 202-205-3426

Glass articles, nspf....Lukes, James USITC 202-205-3426

Glass containers....Lukes, James USITC 202-205-3426

Glass fiber....Lukes, James USITC 202-205-3426

Glass yarn....Lukes, James USITC 202-205-3426

Glass, Flat....Williams, Franklin COMMERCE 202-482-0132

Glassblowing....Staff NCRR/BEIP 301-496-5195

Glassware....Harris, John COMMERCE 202-482-0348

Glassware....McNay, Deborah USITC 202-205-3425

Glassware (Issue and Washing)....Staff OD/ORS 301-496-4595

Glassworking machines....Vacant USITC 202-205-3380

Glaucoma....Staff NEI 301-496-5248

Glazing compounds....Johnson, Larry USITC 202-205-3351

Gliomas....Staff NINDS 301-496-5751

Global Change Division....Staff EPA 202-233-9190

Global Climate Change....Galas, David J. NEIC 301-903-3251

Globoid Cell Leukodystrophy....Staff NINDS 301-496-5751

Glomerulonephritis....Staff NIDDK 301-496-3583

Gloves....Burtnik, Brian CUSTOMS 212-466-5880

Gloves....Jones, Jackie USITC 202-205-3466

Gloves (Work)....Byron, James E. COMMERCE 202-482-3459

Glucose Intolerance....Staff NIDDK 301-496-3583

Glue....Brownchweig, Gilbert CUSTOMS 212-466-5744

Glue size....Jonnard, Aimison USITC 202-205-3350

Glue, articles of....Spalding, Josephine USITC 202-205-3498

Glue, of animal or vegetable origin....Jonnard, Aimison USITC 202-205-3350

Gluten Intolerance....Staff NIDDK 301-496-3583

Glycerine....Michels, David USITC 202-205-3352

Glycogen Storage Disease....Staff NIDDK 301-496-3583

Glycogen Storage Disease....Staff NICHD 301-496-5133

Glycols....Michels, David USITC 202-205-3352

Goats....Steller, Rose USITC 202-205-3323

Goiter....Staff NIDDK 301-496-3583

Gold....Lucus, John M. MINES 202-501-9417

Gold....McNay, Deborah USITC 202-205-3425

Gold compounds....Greenblatt, Jack USITC 202-205-3353

Gold with options....Rosenfeld, David CFT 312-353-9026

Golf equipment....Robinson, Hazel USITC 202-205-3496

Gonads....Staff NICHD 301-496-5133

Gonorrhea....Staff NIAID 301-496-5717

Goodpasture's Syndrome....Staff NHLBI 301-496-4236

Goodpasture's Syndrome....Staff NIDDK 301-496-3583

Gout....Staff NIAMS 301-496-8188

Government and Foreign Affairs....Abraham, Henry J. UVA 701-924-3958

Government and Foreign Affairs....Cooper, Alice H. UVA 701-924-4660

Government and Foreign Affairs....Jordan, David C. UVA 701-924-3298

Government, (Acting Chief)....Ziemer, Richard C. ECONOMIC 202-523-0715

Government, Productivity in, Prod. & Tech.....Forte, Darlene J. LABOR 202-606-5621

Government-Press Relations, Broadcast Journalism....Holman, Ben UMD 301-405-2420

Government-Press relations....Hiebert, Ray E. UMD 301-405-2419

Governments, Criminal Justice Statistics....Cull, Diana CENSUS 301-763-7789

Governments, Employment....Stevens, Alan CENSUS 301-763-5086

Governments, Federal Expenditure Data....Kellerman, David CENSUS 301-763-5276

Governments, Finance....Wulf, Henry CENSUS 301-763-7664

Governments, Governmental Organization....Cull, Diana CENSUS 301-763-7789

Governments, Operations Support and Analysis....Fanning, William CENSUS 301-763-4403

Governments, Survey Operations....Speight, Genevieve CENSUS 301-763-7783

Governments, Taxation....Keffer, Gerard CENSUS 301-763-5356

Graduate Courses....Staff FAES 301-496-7976

Grain....Conte, Ralph CUSTOMS 212-466-5759

Grain Mill Products....Janis, William V. COMMERCE 202-482-2250

Grain products, milled....Pierre-Benoist, John USITC 202-205-3320

Grains....Pierre-Benoist, John USITC 202-205-3320

Granite....White, Linda USITC 202-205-3427

Granulocytopenia....Staff NIDDK 301-496-3583

Granulomatous Diseases....Staff NIAID 301-496-5717

Grape Cure....Staff NCI 301-496-5583

Grapefruit oil (essential oil)....Land, Eric USITC 202-205-3349

Graphite....Taylor, Harold A. MINES 202-501-9754

Graphite....White, Linda USITC 202-205-3427

Grasslands....Staff FWS 703-358-2043

Grateful Med (Software for Information Retrieval)....Staff NLM 301-496-3583

Grave's Disease (Eye Complications)....Staff NEI 301-496-5248

Grave's Disease (General Information)....Staff NIDDK 301-496-3583
Grease, lubricating....Foreso, Cynthia USITC 202-205-3348
Great Lakes Fisheries....Staff FWS 703-358-1718
Greece....Corro, Ann Cnty Commerce 202-482-3945
Greece (Athens)....Staff Cnty State 202-647-6113
Greece/Minerals....Rabchevsky, George Cnty Mines 202-501-9672
Greenhouse Gases....Patrinus, Aristides NEIC 301-903-5348
Greenland....Staff Cnty State 202-647-5669
Greenland/Minerals....Rabchevsky, George Cnty Mines 202-501-9672
Greensand....Searls, James P. MINES 202-501-9407
Greeting Cards....Bratland, Rose Marie COMMERCE 202-482-0380
Grenada....Brooks, Michelle Cnty Commerce 202-482-2527
Grenada (St. George's)....Staff Cnty State 202-647-2621
Grinding machines....Greene, William USITC 202-205-3405
Ground Water Exploration and Development....Wheeler, Frederica
    COMMERCE 202-482-3509
Ground Water Protection....Staff EPA 202-260-7077
Ground Water and Drinking Water....Staff EPA 202-250-5543
Ground fish....Corey, Roger USITC 202-205-3327
Group Quarters, Population....Smith, Denise CENSUS 301-763-7883
Growth Hormone Deficiency....Staff NIDDK 301-496-3583
Growth and Development....Staff NICHD 301-496-5133
Guadeloupe/Minerals....Torres, Ivette Cnty Mines 202-501-9680
Guadeloupe....Brooks, Michelle Cnty Commerce 202-482-2527
Guadeloupe (Basse-Terre)....Staff Cnty State 202-647-2620
Guatemala....Lee, Helen Cnty Commerce 202-482-2527
Guatemala....Brown, Brenda L. Peace Corps 202-606-3624
Guatemala (Guatemala City)....Staff Cnty State 202-647-4980
Guatemala/Minerals....Mobbs, Philip Cnty Mines 202-501-9679
Guatemalan Rain Forest....Bauer, Gerald FS 703-235-1676
Guide for the Care and Use of Laboratory Animals....Staff NCI 301-496-5545
Guides....Young, Gary CENSUS 301-763-1584
Guillain-Barre Syndrome (Polyneuritis)....Staff NINDS 301-496-5751
Guinea....Michelin, Philip Cnty Commerce 202-482-4388
Guinea....Strozier, Maisha Peace Corps 202-606-3185
Guinea (Conakry)....Staff Cnty State 202-647-2865
Guinea-Bissau....Michelin, Philip Cnty Commerce 202-482-4388
Guinea-Bissau (Bissau)....Staff Cnty State 202-647-4567
Guinea-Bissau/Minerals....Izon, David Cnty Mines 202-501-9692
Guinea/Minerals....Izon, David Cnty Mines 202-501-9692
Gum Disease....Staff NIDR 301-496-4261
Gums and resins....Reeder, John USITC 202-205-3319
Gun cotton....Johnson, Larry USITC 202-205-3351
Gunpowder....Johnson, Larry USITC 202-205-3351
Guns and Ammunition....Vanderwolf, John COMMERCE 202-482-0348
Gut, articles of....Spalding, Josephine USITC 202-205-3498
Gut; catgut, whip gut, oriental gut, and wormgut....Ludwick, David USITC
    202-205-3329
Guyana....Brooks, Michelle Cnty Commerce 202-482-2527
Guyana (Georgetown)....Staff Cnty State 202-647-4195
Guyana/Minerals....Mobbs, Philip Cnty Mines 202-501-9679
Gynecological Research....Nelson, Lawrence FAES 301-496-4686
Gynecology....Staff NICHD 301-496-5133
Gynecomastia....Staff NICHD 301-496-5133
Gynecomastia....Staff NIDDK 301-496-3583
Gypsum....Davis, Lawrence L. MINES 202-501-9386
Gypsum....White, Linda USITC 202-205-3427
Gypsum board....Ruggles, Fred USITC 202-205-3325
Gyrate Atrophy....Staff NEI 301-496-5248

H

HIV Infection....Staff NIAID 301-496-5717
HIV Infection....Staff NCI 301-496-5583
HIV/AIDS....Jaffe, Harold W. CDC 404-639-2000
HIV: Oral Complications....Staff NIDR 301-496-4261
HUD Fraud Hotline....Staff HUD 800-347-3735
Habeas Corpus....Kaplan, Carol Justice Stat 202-307-0759
Habitat Management....Staff FWS 703-358-1718
Habitat Models....Staff FWS 703-358-1710
Habitat Resources Research....Staff FWS 703-358-1710
Hafnium....Templeton, David A. MINES 202-501-9391
Hafnium....Lundy, David USITC 202-205-3439
Hailey's Disease....Staff NIDDK 301-496-3583
Hair....Steller, Rose USITC 202-205-3323
Hair Loss....Staff NIAMS 301-496-8188

Hair Ornaments....Brownchweig, Gilbert CUSTOMS 212-466-5744
Hair Spray....Staff FDA 301-245-1061
Hair curlers, nonelectric....Burns, Gail USITC 202-205-3501
Hair ornaments....Burns, Gail USITC 202-205-3501
Hair, articles of....Burns, Gail USITC 202-205-3501
Haiti....Soto, Rodrigo Cnty Commerce 204-482-2527
Haiti....Almaguer, Antoinette Peace Corps 202-606-3322
Haiti (Port-au-Prince)....Staff Cnty State 202-647-4195
Haiti/Minerals....Torres, Ivette Cnty Mines 202-501-9680
Halides, nonmetallic....Conant, Kenneth USITC 202-205-3346
Hallervorden-Spatz Disease....Staff NINDS 301-496-5751
Halogenated hydrocarbons....Michels, David USITC 202-205-3352
Halogens....Conant, Kenneth USITC 202-205-3346
Hand Saws, Saw Blades....Shaw, Eugene COMMERCE 202-482-3494
Hand Tools....Schulberg, Martin CUSTOMS 212-466-5487
Hand tools with self-contained motor....Cutchin, John USITC 202-205-3396
Hand tools: household....Brandon, James USITC 202-205-3433
Hand tools: other....Brandon, James USITC 202-205-3433
Hand, Foot, and Mouth Disease....Staff NIAID 301-496-5717
Hand/Edge Tools Ex Mach TI/Saws....Shaw, Eugene COMMERCE
    202-482-3494
Handbags....Byron, James E. COMMERCE 202-482-4034
Handbags....Gorman, Kevin CUSTOMS 212-466-5893
Handbags....Seastrum, Carl USITC 202-205-3493
Handbook, Occupational Outlook, Empl. Projections....Pilot, Michael LABOR
    202-606-5703
Handicapped Discrimination....Haynes, Marcella OCR 202-619-0671
Handkerchiefs....Jones, Jackie USITC 202-205-3466
Handkerchiefs....Hamey, Amy USITC 202-205-3465
Handwork yarns: cotton....Warlick, William USITC 202-205-3459
Handwork yarns: manmade fibers....Warlick, William USITC 202-205-3459
Handwork yarns: wool....Shelton, Linda USITC 202-205-3457
Hansen's Disease....Staff NIAID 301-496-5717
Happy Puppet Syndrome....Staff NINDS 301-496-5751
Harada's Disease....Staff NEI 301-496-5248
Hard Surfaced Floor Coverings....Shaw, Robert COMMERCE 202-482-0132
Hardboard....Ruggles, Fred USITC 202-205-3325
Hardening of the Arteries....Staff NHLBI 301-496-4236
Harassing Telephone Calls....Staff FCC 202-632-7553
Hashimoto's Disease....Staff NIDDK 301-496-3583
Hats....Jones, Jackie USITC 202-205-3466
Hats....Hamey, Amy USITC 202-205-3465
Hay....Eldridge, Herb Agri 202-720-7621
Hay....Tice, Thomas Agri 202-219-0840
Hay Fever....Staff NIAID 301-496-5717
Hazard Screening....Giles, Ken CPSC 301-504-0580
Hazard Waste Publications....Staff EPA 202-260-8864
Hazardous Chemical Spills....Staff FWS 703-358-2148
Hazardous Site Evaluation Division....Staff EPA 202-603-8800
Hazardous Substances Information....Staff NLM 301-496-1131
Hazardous Substances Information Office....Siegel, Sidney NLM 301-496-5022
Hazardous Waste - Superfund....Staff EPA 202-920-9810
Hazardous Waste Cleanups....Staff EPA 202-260-8864
Hazardous Waste Disposal....Lytle, Jill NEIC 202-586-0370
Hazardous Waste Disposal Unit....Staff EPA 202-307-8833
Hazardous Waste Enforcement - General....Staff EPA 202-260-9810
Hazardous Waste Ombudsman Hotline....Staff EPA 800-262-7937
Hazardous Waste Spills - Emergency Response....Staff EPA 202-260-8720
Hazardous Waste Transporting Generating or Permits....Staff EPA 202-260-4627
Hazardous Wastes....Berreth, Don CDC 404-639-3286
Head Injury....Staff NINDS 301-496-5751
Head Injury....Staff NIDCD 301-496-7243
Head Lice (Pediculosis)....Staff NIAID 301-496-5717
Head Start....Long, Susan ACF 202-401-9215
Headache....Staff NINDS 301-496-5751
Headwear....Schiazzano, Patricia CUSTOMS 212-466-5881
Headwear....Hamey, Amy USITC 202-205-3465
Headwear....Jones, Jackie USITC 202-205-3466
Health....Francis, Simon COMMERCE 202-482-2697
Health & Life Insurance, Comp. & Working Condition....Blostin, Allan LABOR
    202-606-6240
Health Care - Nurse....Brooke, Joan FTC 202-326-2120
Health Care Policy & Research, Agency for....Isquith, Bob AHCPR
    301-227-8364
Health Care Policy & Research, Agency for....Isquith, Bob AHCPR
    301-227-8364
Health Care Resources....Mehuron, Charlotte HRSA 301-443-3376

Health Care Technology....Isquith, Bob AHCPR 301-227-8674

Health Effects Division....Staff EPA 202-305-7351

Health Effects of Electricity Transmission....Brewer, Robert NEIC 202-586-2828

Health Expenditures (U.S. Totals)....Hardy, Robert HCFA 202-690-6145

Health Information Programs Development, Dir. of....Siegel, Elliot R. NLM 301-496-8834

Health Maintenance Organizations (HMOs)....Hardy, Robert HCFA 202-690-6145

Health Manpower Education....Staff HRSA/BHPr 301-443-2060

Health Professionals....Staff HRSA/BHPr 301-443-2060

Health Professions and Health Profession Loans....Mehuron, Charlotte HRSA 301-443-3376

Health Promotion and Disease Prevention....Harris, Linda ASH 202-205-9370

Health Promotion and Disease Prevention....Berreth, Don CDC 404-639-3286

Health Research, Office of....Staff EPA 202-260-5900

Health Services Research Information....Cahn, Marjorie NLM 301-496-0176

Health Start....Mehuron, Charlotte HRSA 301-443-3376

Health Statistics, National Center for....Sandra, Smith NCHS/CDC 301-436-7551

Health Surveys....Mangold, Robert CENSUS 301-763-5508

Health and Environmental Research....Galas, David J. NEIC 301-903-3251

Health and medical services....R-Archila, Laura USITC 202-205-3411

Hearing Disorders....Staff NINDS 301-496-5751

Hearing Disorders....Staff NIDCD 301-496-7243

Hearing Loss and Aging....Staff NINDS 301-496-5751

Hearing Loss and Aging....Staff NIA 301-496-1752

Hearing Loss and Aging....Staff CC 301-496-5368

Heart Attacks....Staff NHLBI 301-496-4236

Heart Block....Staff NHLBI 301-496-4236

Heart Disease....Staff NHLBI 301-496-4236

Heart Pacemaker....Staff NHLBI 301-496-4236

Heart Transplantation....Staff NHLBI 301-496-4236

Heart Valves....Staff NHLBI 301-496-4236

Heart, Lung and Blood Inst.....Bellicha, Terry NIH 301-496-4236

Heart-Lung Machines....Staff NHLBI 301-496-4236

Heat Stroke and Aging....Staff NIA 301-496-1752

Heat Tapes....Mesa, Stacey Reuben CPSC 301-504-0580

Heat Treating Equipment....Kemper, Alexis COMMERCE 202-482-5956

Heat process equipment....Slingerland, David USITC 202-205-3400

Heat-Resistant Materials....Staff NASA 804-864-6120

Heat-insulating articles....DeSapio, Vincent USITC 202-205-3435

Heating Equipment Ex. Furnaces....Bodson, John COMMERCE 202-482-3509

Heavy Metals (Cadmium, Zinc, Mercury)....Staff NIEHS 919-541-3345

Helicopter Services....Johnson, C. William COMMERCE 202-482-5012

Helicopters....Walsh, Hugh COMMERCE 202-482-4222

Helicopters (Trade Promo)....Vacant COMMERCE 202-482-1228

Helicopters, Market Support....Driscoll, George COMMERCE 202-482-1228

Heliotropin....Land, Eric USITC 202-205-3349

Helium....Conant, Kenneth USITC 202-205-3346

Helium, Division of Helium Field Operations....Leachman, William D. MINES 806-376-2604

Hematology....Finlayson, John FAES 301-496-5544

Hemiplegia....Staff NINDS 301-496-5751

Hemodialysis....Staff NIDDK 301-496-3583

Hemoglobin Genetics....Staff NIDDK 301-496-3583

Hemoglobinopathies....Staff NIDDK 301-496-3583

Hemolytic Anemia....Staff NIDDK 301-496-3583

Hemolytic Disease (Newborn)....Staff NICHD 301-496-5133

Hemolytic Disease (Newborn)....Staff NHLBI 301-496-4236

Hemophilia....Staff NHLBI 301-496-4236

Hemophilus Influenzae....Staff NIAID 301-496-5717

Hemorrhagic Diseases....Staff NIDDK 301-496-3583

Hemorrhagic Diseases....Staff NHLBI 301-496-4236

Hemorrhoids....Staff NHLBI 301-496-4236

Hemorrhoids....Staff NIDDK 301-496-3583

Hemosiderosis....Staff NHLBI 301-496-4236

Henoch-Schonlein Purpura....Staff NIAID 301-496-5717

Henoch-Schonlein Purpura....Staff NICHD 301-496-5133

Hepatitis....Staff NIAID 301-496-5717

Hepatitis....Staff NIDDK 301-496-3583

Hepatitis....Herrmann, Kenneth L. CDC 404-639-2339

Hepatitis (Treatment of Acute or Chronic)....Staff NIDDK 301-496-3583

Hepatitis (Treatment of Acute or Chronic)....Staff NIAID 301-496-5717

Herbicide-Fungicides....Staff EPA 202-305-6250

Hereditary Angioedema....Staff NIAID 301-496-5717

Hereditary Cerebellar Ataxia....Staff NINDS 301-496-5751

Hereditary Emphysema....Staff NHLBI 301-496-4236

Hereditary Movement Disorders....Staff NINDS 301-496-5751

Hereditary Nervous System Tumors....Staff NINDS 301-496-5751

Heredity and Cancer....Staff NCI 301-496-5583

Heritable Disorders of Connective Tissue....Staff NHLBI 301-496-4236

Heritable Disorders of Connective Tissue....Staff NIAMS 301-496-8188

Hernias (Abdominal, Bladder)....Staff NIDDK 301-496-3583

Herniated Disc....Staff NIAMS 301-496-8188

Herpes (Nervous System Involvement)....Staff NINDS 301-496-5751

Herpes Simplex (Eye Effects)....Staff NEI 301-496-5248

Herpes Simplex Virus (Oral Lesions)....Staff NIDR 301-496-4261

Herpes Simplex Virus (Type II)....Staff NIAID 301-496-5717

Herpes Zoster (Shingles)....Staff NINDS 301-496-5751

Herpes Zoster-Varicella Infections....Staff NIAID 301-496-5717

Heterocyclic Compounds....Winters, William CUSTOMS 212-466-5747

Hiatal Hernia....Staff NIDDK 301-496-3583

Hiccups....Staff NHLBI 301-496-4236

Hide cuttings....Trainor, Cynthia USITC 202-205-3354

Hides....Steller, Rose USITC 202-205-3323

High Alpha Technology....Nolan, Donald NASA 805-258-3447

High Blood Pressure....Staff NHLBI 301-496-4236

High Blood Pressure....Staff NIA 301-496-1752

High Blood Pressure....Staff NHLBI/IC 301-951-3260

High Energy Fuel Research....Ellis, Linda NASA 216-443-2900

High Tech Trade, U.S. Competitiveness....Hatter, Victoria L. COMMERCE 202-482-3913

High Voltage Electron Microscopy....Staff NCRR 301-496-5411

High Voltage Transmission Lines....Klunder, Kurt NEIC 202-586-2826

High-Density Lipoproteins (HDL)....Staff NHLBI 301-496-4236

Hill-Burton Health Facilities....Mehuron, Charlotte HRSA 301-443-3376

Hirsutism....Staff NIAMS 301-496-8188

Hispanic and Other Ethnic Population Statistics....Staff CENSUS 301-763-7955

Histiocytosis....Staff NCI 301-496-5583

Histiocytosis....Staff NHLBI 301-496-4236

Histoplasmosis....Staff NIAID 301-496-5717

Histoplasmosis (Eye)....Staff NEI 301-496-5248

Historical Medical Prints and Photographs....Staff NLM 301-496-5961

Historical Prints and Photographs....Keister, Lucinda NLM 301-496-5961

Historical Statistics....Staff CENSUS 301-763-7936

History....Braun, Herbert UVA 701-924-6397

History of Medicine....Staff NLM 301-496-5405

History of Medicine....Teigen, Philip NLM 301-496-5405

Hives....Staff NIAID 301-496-5717

Hodgkin's Disease....Staff NCI 301-496-5583

Hogs....Ludwick, David USITC 202-205-3329

Hogs (live) with options....Prentice, Jon CFT 312-353-8647

Hoists/Overhead Cranes....Wiening, Mary COMMERCE 202-482-4708

Home & Community Based Care (Medicaid)....Hardy, Robert HCFA 202-690-6145

Home Care, Nursing Home Care, Hospital Care....Staff NCNR 301-496-0526

Home Health Care....Hardy, Robert HCFA 202-690-6145

Home furnishings....Sweet, Mary Elizabeth USITC 202-205-3455

Homeless....Long, Susan ACF 202-401-9215

Homeless....Staff HUD 202-708-1480

Homeless Population....Taeuber, Cynthia CENSUS 301-763-7883

Homocystinuria....Staff NICHD 301-496-5133

Homocystinuria....Staff NHLBI 301-496-4236

Honduras....Lee, Helen Cnty Commerce 202-482-2527

Honduras....Stanton, Dan Peace Corps 202-606-3620

Honduras....Tumaylle, Carol Peace Corps 202-606-3321

Honduras (Tegucigalpa)....Staff Cnty State 202-647-3381

Honduras/Minerals....Mobbs, Philip Cnty Mines 202-501-9679

Honey....Hoff, Fred Agri 202-219-0883

Honey - Prices....Schuchardt, Rick Agri 220-690-3236

Honey - Prod.....Kruchten, Tom Agri 202-690-4870

Hong Kong....Bakar, Sheila Cnty Commerce 202-482-3932

Hong Kong....Staff Cnty State 202-647-6300

Hong Kong/Minerals....Tse, Pui-Kwan Cnty Mines 202-501-9696

Hoof, articles of....Spalding, Josephine USITC 202-205-3498

Hoofs, crude....Ludwick, David USITC 202-205-3329

Hooks and eyes....Shildneck, Ann USITC 202-205-3499

Hormone Distribution....Staff NIDDK 301-496-3583

Hormones....Staff NIDDK 301-496-3583

Hormones....Nesbitt, Elizabeth USITC 202-205-3355

Hormones (Sex)....Staff NICHD 301-496-5133

Hormones and Cancer....Staff NCI 301-496-5583

Horn, articles of....Spalding, Josephine USITC 202-205-3498

Horn, crude....Ludwick, David USITC 202-205-3329

Horse Racing Programming and Advertising....Staff FCC 202-632-7048

Horses....Steller, Rose USITC 202-205-3323

Horticultural machinery....Vacant USITC 202-205-3380

Hose and Belting....Prat, Raimundo COMMERCE 202-482-0128

Hose, industrial....Cook, Lee USITC 202-205-3471

Hose, of rubber or plastics....Johnson, Larry USITC 202-205-3351

Hoses....Mazzola, Joan CUSTOMS 212-466-5880

Hosiery....Linkins, Linda USITC 202-205-3469

Hospice....Hardy, Robert HCFA 202-690-6145

Hospice Care....Staff NIA 301-496-1752

Hospital Administrators....Staff HRSA/BHPr 301-443-2134

Hospital Care Statistics....Pokras, Robert CDC 301-436-7125

Hospital Infections....Staff NIAID 301-496-5717

Hospital-Based Schools of Nursing....Staff HRSA/BHPr 301-443-2134

Hotel & Restaurant Eq., Export Promo.....Kimmel, Edward K. COMMERCE 202-482-3640

Hotels and Motels....Sousane, J. Richard COMMERCE 202-482-4582

Hotline (Fraud & Abuse)....Holtz, Judy IG 202-619-1142

Hourly Compensation Costs, Foreign Countries....Capdevielle, Patricia LABOR 202-606-5654

Household Appliances....Harris, John M. COMMERCE 202-482-0348

Household Articles Plastic....Rauch, Theodore CUSTOMS 212-466-5892

Household Articles, Metal....Smyth, James CUSTOMS 212-466-2084

Household Estimates for States and Counties....Staff CENSUS 301-763-5221

Household Furniture....Vacant COMMERCE 202-482-0338

Household Hazardous Waste....Staff EPA 202-260-5649

Household Wealth....Lamas, Enrique CENSUS 301-763-8578

Households Touched by Crime....Rand, Michael Justice Stat 202-616-3494

Housewares....Harris, John COMMERCE 202-482-1178

Housing Construction....Cosslett, Patrick COMMERCE 202-482-0132

Housing and Urban Development. Major Proj.....White, Barbara COMMERCE 202-482-4160

Housing, American Housing Survey....Montfort, Edward CENSUS 301-763-8551

Housing, Components of Inventory Change Survey....Maynard, Jane CENSUS 301-763-8551

Housing, Decennial Census....Downs, Bill CENSUS 301-763-8553

Housing, Income Statistics....Staff CENSUS 301-763-8576

Housing, Indian....Staff HUD 202-708-0950

Housing, Information....Downs, Bill CENSUS 301-763-8553

Housing, Market Absorption....Smoler, Anne CENSUS 301-763-8552

Housing, Multifamily....Staff HUD 202-708-2495

Housing, New York City Housing & Vacancy Survey....Harper, Margaret CENSUS 301-763-8552

Housing, Public....Staff HUD 202-708-0950

Housing, Single Family....Staff HUD 202-708-3175

Housing, Vacancy Data....Fraser, Wallace CENSUS 301-763-8165

Hubble Space Telescope....Villard, Ray NASA 301-338-4514

Hubble Space Telescope (HST)....Katz, Jesse NASA 301-286-5566

Human Development....Staff NICHD 301-443-5133

Human Genetic Mutant Cell Repository....Staff NIGMS 301-496-7301

Human Papilloma Virus (HPV)....Staff NCI 301-496-5583

Human Papilloma Virus (HPV)....Staff NIAID 301-496-5717

Humane Transport of Fish and Wildlife....Staff FWS 703-358-2095

Hungary....Touhey, Brian Cnty Commerce 202-482-2645

Hungary....Becker, Margaret Peace Corps 202-606-3547

Hungary....Sowry, Jenny Peace Corps 202-606-3547

Hungary (Budapest)....Staff Cnty State 202-647-3298

Hungary/Minerals....Steblez, Walter Cnty Mines 202-501-9671

Hunt's Disease....Staff NINDS 301-496-5751

Hunter Education Programs....Staff FWS 703-358-2156

Hunter's Syndrome....Staff NIDDK 301-496-3583

Hunting and Fishing Survey, National....Staff FWS 703-358-2156

Hunting, Refuges....Staff FWS 703-358-2043

Huntington's Disease....Staff NINDS 301-496-5751

Hurler's Syndrome....Staff NICHD 301-496-5133

Hurler's Syndrome....Staff NIDDK 301-496-3583

Hyaline Membrane Disease....Staff NICHD 301-496-5133

Hyaline Membrane Disease....Staff NHLBI 301-496-4236

Hydraulics....Riedl, Karl CUSTOMS 212-466-5493

Hydrazine....Conant, Kenneth USITC 202-205-3346

Hydro Power Plants, Major Proj.....Healey, Mary Alice COMMERCE 202-482-4333

Hydrocarbon Geoscience Research....Juckett, Donald NEIC 202-586-5600

Hydrocarbons....Winters, William CUSTOMS 212-466-5747

Hydrocarbons....Raftery, Jim USITC 202-205-3365

Hydrocephalus....Staff NINDS 301-496-5751

Hydrocephalus....Staff NICHD 301-496-5133

Hydrochloric acid....Trainor, Cynthia USITC 202-205-3354

Hydroelectric Energy....Loose, Ronald NEIC 202-586-8086

Hydroelectric Power....Loose, Ronald NEIC 202-586-8066

Hydroelectric Power Projects....Staff FWS 703-358-2183

Hydrofluoric acid....Trainor, Cynthia USITC 202-205-3354

Hydrogen....Conant, Kenneth USITC 202-205-3346

Hydroxides, inorganic....Conant, Kenneth USITC 202-205-3346

Hygienists (Education)....Staff HRSA/BHPr 301-443-6837

Hyperactivity....Staff NIMH 301-443-4515

Hyperactivity....Staff NICHD 301-496-5133

Hyperactivity....Staff NINDS 301-496-5751

Hyperbaric Chamber - UMD Shock Trauma Center....Staff 301-528-6294

Hyperbaric Oxygenation....Staff NHLBI 301-496-4236

Hyperbilirubinemia....Staff NICHD 301-496-5133

Hyperbilirubinemia....Staff NIDDK 301-496-3583

Hypercalcemia....Staff NIDDK 301-496-3583

Hypercalciuria....Staff NIDDK 301-496-3583

Hypercholesterolemia....Staff NHLBI 301-496-4236

Hyperglycemia....Staff NIDDK 301-496-3583

Hyperkinesis....Staff NIMH 301-443-4515

Hyperlipidemia....Staff NHLBI 301-496-4236

Hyperlipoproteinemia....Staff NHLBI 301-496-4236

Hyperparathyroidism....Staff NIDDK 301-496-3583

Hyperpyrexia (heat stroke/heat exhaustion)....Staff NIA 301-496-1752

Hypersensitivity Pneumonitis....Staff NIAID 301-496-5717

Hypersonic Aircraft....James, Donald G. NASA 415-604-3935

Hypersonic Engines....Staff NASA 804-864-3305

Hypertension....Staff NHLBI/IC 301-951-3260

Hypertension....Staff NCNR 301-496-0526

Hyperthermia....Staff NCI 301-496-5583

Hyperthermia (heat stroke/heat exhaustion)....Staff NIA 301-496-1752

Hyperthyroidism....Staff NIDDK 301-496-3583

Hypertriglyceridemia....Staff NHLBI 301-496-4236

Hyperuricemia....Staff NIDDK 301-496-3583

Hyperventilation....Staff NHLBI 301-496-4236

Hypnotics....Nesbitt, Elizabeth USITC 202-205-3355

Hypobetalipoproteinemia....Staff NHLBI 301-496-4236

Hypocomplementemic Glomerulonephritis....Staff NIAID 301-496-5717

Hypoglycemia....Staff NHLBI 301-496-4236

Hypoglycemia....Staff NIDDK 301-496-3583

Hypogonadism....Staff NIDDK 301-496-3583

Hypogonadism....Staff NICHD 301-496-5133

Hypokalemia....Staff NHLBI 301-496-4236

Hypokalemic Periodic Paralysis....Staff NINDS 301-496-5751

Hypolipoproteinemia....Staff NIDDK 301-496-3583

Hypoparathyroidism....Staff NIDDK 301-496-3583

Hypopituitarism....Staff NIDDK 301-496-3583

Hypospadias....Staff NICHD 301-496-5133

Hypotension....Staff NHLBI 301-496-4236

Hypothalamus....Staff NIDDK 301-496-3583

Hypothalamus....Staff NICHD 301-496-5133

Hypothermia (Accidental)....Staff NIA 301-496-1752

Hypothyroidism, Goitrous....Staff NIA 301-496-3583

Hypotonia....Staff NINDS 301-496-5751

Hypoventilation....Staff NHLBI 301-496-4236

Hypoxia....Staff NHLBI 301-496-4236

Hypsarrhythmia....Staff NINDS 301-496-5751

I

IGE....Staff NIAID 301-496-5717

Iceland....Lyons, Maryanne Cnty Commerce 202-482-3254

Iceland (Reykjavik)....Staff Cnty State 202-647-5669

Iceland Disease....Staff NINDS 301-496-5751

Iceland/Minerals....Buck, Donald E. Cnty Mines 202-501-9670

Ichthyosis....Staff NIAMS 301-496-8188

Idiopathic Hypertrophic Subaortic Stenosis (IHSS)....Staff NHLBI 301-496-4236

Idiopathic Inflammatory Myopathy....Staff NINDS 301-496-5751

Idiopathic Osteoporosis....Staff NIAMS 301-496-8188

Idiopathic Thrombocytopenic Purpura (ITP)....Staff NHLBI 301-496-4236

Idiopathic Thrombocytopenic Purpura (ITP)....Staff NIDDK 301-496-3583

IgE....Staff 301-496-5717

Ignition equipment....Kolberg, Mary USITC 202-205-3401

Ileitis....Staff NIDDK 301-496-3583

Image Processing....Staff DCRT 301-496-2250

Image Processing....Staff DCRT 301-496-7963

Immigration....Dye, Larry ACF 202-401-9215

Immigration (Legal/Undocumented)....Woodrow, Karen CENSUS 301-763-5590

Immune Deficiency Diseases....Staff NIAID 301-496-5717

Immunization....Berreth, Don CDC 404-639-3286

Immunization, Disease....Orenstein, Walter A. CDC 404-639-180

Immunizations (Foreign Travel)....Staff CDC 404-639-3286

Immunology....Staff NIAID 301-496-5717

Immunology (Cancer)....Staff NCI 301-496-5583

Immunotherapy (Cancer)....Staff NCI 301-496-5583

Implantable Defibrillator....Staff NHLBI 301-496-4236

Implants, Lens....Staff NEI 301-496-5248

Impotence....Staff NIMH 301-443-4515

Impotence....Staff NIDDK 301-496-3583

In Vitro Fertilization....Staff NICHD 301-496-5133

Inactive Waste Site Management....Duffy, Leo P. NEIC 202-586-7710

Inactive Waste Site Cleanup....Duffy, Leo P. NEIC 202-586-7710

Inappropriate Antidiuretic Hormone Syndrome....Staff NHLBI 301-496-4236

Inborn Errors of Metabolism....Staff NICHD 301-496-5133

Inborn Errors of Metabolism....Staff NINDS 301-496-5751

Inborn Errors of Metabolism....Staff NHLBI 301-496-4236

Inborn Errors of Metabolism....Staff NICHD 301-496-5133

Inborn Heart Defects....Staff NHLBI 301-496-4236

Incapacitation....Langan, Patrick Justice Stat 202-616-3490

Incapacitation....Greenfeld, Lawrence Justice Stat 202-616-3281

Incidental Radiation Devices....Staff FCC 202-653-6288

Incinerators....Staff EPA 202-308-8461

Incontinence....Staff NIA 301-496-1752

Indexes of Fuels and Utilities, Monthly....Adkins, Robert LABOR 202-606-6985

India....Simmons, John/Crown, John/Gilman, Tim Cnty Commerce 202-482-2954

India (New Delhi)....Staff Cnty State 202-647-2351

India/Minerals....Vacant Cnty Mines 202-501-9694

Indian Fisheries Resources/Treaties....Staff FWS 703-358-1718

Indian Health....DeAsis, Patricia IHS 301-44-3593

Indian Health....Stone, Hardy IHS 301-443-3593

Indian Housing....Staff HUD 202-708-0950

Indian Hunting, Migratory Birds....Staff FWS 703-358-1773

Indian Wildlife Assistance....Staff FWS 703-358-1718

Indians - Administration for Native Americans....Long, Susan ACF 202-401-9215

Indigent Defense....Gaskins, Carla Justice Stat 202-508-8550

Indium....Jasinski, Stephen M. MINES 202-501-9418

Indium....Lundy, David USITC 202-205-3439

Indonesia....Goddin, Karen Cnty Commerce 202-482-3875

Indonesia (Jakarata)....Staff Cnty State 202-647-3276

Indonesia/Minerals....Kuo, Chin Cnty Mines 202-501-9693

Indoor Air Division....Staff EPA 202-233-9030

Indoor Air Division, National Program....Staff EPA 202-233-9030

Induced Movement Disorders....Staff NINDS 301-496-5751

Industrial Chemicals....Whitley, Richard A. COMMERCE 202-482-0682

Industrial Chemicals (Effects on Human Health)....Staff NIEHS 919-541-3345

Industrial Chemicals and Cancer....Staff NCI 301-496-5583

Industrial Classification, Est. Surv, Natl. Emp/Unemp....Getz, Patricia LABOR 202-606-6521

Industrial Drives/Gears....Reiss, Richard COMMERCE 202-482-3489

Industrial Gases....Kostalas, Antonios COMMERCE 202-482-0128

Industrial Heating Equipment....Staff FCC 202-653-6288

Industrial Hygiene....Staff OD/ORS 301-496-2960

Industrial Hygiene....Gaunce, Jean A. CDC 404-639-3415

Industrial Minerals, Assistant Branch Chief....Morse, D. MINES 202-501-9402

Industrial Minerals, Assistant Branch Chief....Mozian, Z. MINES 202-501-9396

Industrial Minerals, Chief, Branch of....Barsotti, Aldo F. MINES 202-501-9399

Industrial Organic Chemicals....Hurt, William COMMERCE 202-482-4333

Industrial Prices & Price Indexes, Asst. Commis.....Tibbetts, Thomas LABOR 202-606-7700

Industrial Process Controls....Nealon, Marguerite COMMERCE 202-482-0411

Industrial Process Controls (Export Promo)....Manzolilo, Frank COMMERCE 202-482-2991

Industrial Productivity....Streb, Alan NEIC 202-586-9232

Industrial Solid (Non Hazardous) Waste....Staff EPA 202-260-4807

Industrial Structure....Davis, Lester A. COMMERCE 202-482-4924

Industrial Technology Transfer....Duane, Jerry NEIC 202-586-2366

Industrial Trucks....Wiening, Mary COMMERCE 202-482-4608

Industrial ceramics....DeSapio, Vincent USITC 202-205-3435

Industrial diamonds....DeSapio, Vincent USITC 202-205-3435

Industrial gases....Conant, Kenneth USITC 202-205-3346

Industrial licenses....Staff FCC 717-337-1212

Industrial, Scientific, & Medical Equipment....Staff FCC 202-653-6288

Industry Data Centers....Rowe, John CENSUS 301-763-1580

Industry Projections and Economic Growth, Empl. Pro....Bowman, Charles LABOR 202-606-5702

Industry Wage Surveys, Comp. & Work. Conditions....Kellinson, Jonathan LABOR 202-606-6245

Industry and Commodity Classification....Venning, Alvin CENSUS 301-763-1935

Industry-Occupational Employment Matrix....Turner, Delores LABOR 202-606-5730

Industry/trade matters....Phillips, Don 202-385-5656

Inedible gelatin....Jonnard, Aimison USITC 202-205-3350

Inertial Confinement Fusion....Kahalas, Sheldon NEIC 301-903-5491

Infant Formula....Corwin, Emil FDA 202-205-4144

Infant Mortality....Staff NICHD 301-496-5133

Infant Mortality....Staff NCHS 301-436-8500

Infant Mortality....Staff CDC 404-639-3286

Infant Mortality/"Health Start"....Smith, Sandra CDC 301-436-7135

Infant Mortality/"Healthy Start"....Mehuron, Charlotte HRSA 301-443-3376

Infant Nutrition....Staff NICHD 301-496-5133

Infant Suffocation....Tyrrell, Elaine CPSC 301-504-0580

Infantile Muscular Atrophy....Staff NINDS 301-496-5751

Infantile Muscular Atrophy....Staff NIAMS 301-496-8188

Infantile Spinal Muscular Atrophy....Staff NINDS 301-496-5751

Infants (Care)....Staff HRSA 301-443-2086

Infants' accessories or apparel....Holoyda, Olha USITC 202-205-3469

Infections....Staff NIAID 301-496-5717

Infectious Arthritis....Staff NIAMS 301-496-8188

Infectious Eye Disease....Staff NEI 301-496-5248

Infectious Materials (Disposal)....Staff OD/ORS 301-496-2960

Infectious Mononucleosis....Staff NIAID 301-496-5717

Infectious Wastes....Staff EPA 202-260-8551

Infertility....Staff NICHD 301-496-5133

Inflammatory Bowel Disease....Staff NIDDK 301-496-3583

Inflammatory Bowel Disease....Staff NIAID 301-496-5717

Inflatable Articles....McKenna, Thomas CUSTOMS 212-466-5475

Influenza....Staff NIAID 301-496-5717

Influenza....Berreth, Don CDC 404-639-3286

Information Industries....Inoussa, Mary C. COMMERCE 202-482-5820

Information Services, Chief,....DiCesare, Constance LABOR 202-606-5886

Information Specialists, Publ. & Special Studies....Staff LABOR 202-606-7828

Information services....Xavier, Neil USITC 202-205-3450

Infraction Reports--International....Staff FCC 202-653-8138

Infrared Astronomy....Hutchison, Jane NASA 415-604-4968

Ingot molds....Greene, William USITC 202-205-3405

Inherited Blood Abnormalities....Staff NHLBI 301-496-4236

Inherited Blood Abnormalities....Staff NIDDK 301-496-3583

Inherited Metabolic Disorders....Staff NIDDK 301-496-3583

Inherited Neurologic Abnormalities....Staff NINDS 301-496-5751

Injunctions....Staff FCC 202-632-7112

Injuries (Eye)....Staff NEI 301-496-5248

Injury Prevention and Control....Broome, Claire V. CDC 404-488-4690

Ink....Brownchweig, Gilbert CUSTOMS 212-466-5744

Ink powders....Johnson, Larry USITC 202-205-3351

Inks....Johnson, Larry USITC 202-205-3351

Inland Fish and Reservoirs....Staff FWS 703-358-1710

Innovative Energy Research....Polansky, Walter NEIC 301-903-5995

Inorganic Chemicals....Kostallas, Anthony COMMERCE 202-482-0128

Inorganic Compounds & Mixtures....DiMaria, Joseph CUSTOMS 212-466-4769

Inorganic Pigments....Kostallas, Anthony COMMERCE 202-482-0128

Inorganic acids....Trainor, Cynthia USITC 202-205-3354

Inorganic compounds and mixtures....Greenblatt, Jack USITC 202-205-3353

Inorganic hydroxides....Conant, Kenneth USITC 202-205-3346

Inorganic oxides....Conant, Kenneth USITC 202-205-3346

Insanity Defense....Baunach, Phyllis Jo Justice Stat 202-307-0361

Insect Stings Allergy....Staff NIAID 301-496-5717

Insecticide-Rodenticides....Staff EPA 202-305-5200

Insects, Forest....Lyon, Robert FS 202-205-1532

Insomnia....Staff NIMH 301-443-4515

Inspector General Whistle Blower Hotline....Staff EPA 800-424-4000

Institutional Conservation Methods....Volk, Robert NEIC 202-586-8034

Instrument Development....Staff DRS/BEIB 301-496-4741

Instrument Development....Staff NCRR/BEIP 301-496-4741

Instruments, Drafting....Losche, Robert CUSTOMS 212-466-5670

Instruments, Measuring and Controlling....Riedl, Karl CUSTOMS 212-466-5493

Instruments, Navigational....Losche, Robert CUSTOMS 212-466-5670

Instruments: controlling....Moller, Ruben USITC 202-205-3495

Instruments: dental....Johnson, Christopher USITC 202-205-3488

Ischemic Heart Disease....Staff NHLBI 301-496-4236
Isinglass....Jonnard, Aimison USITC 202-205-3350
Islet Cell Hyperplasia....Staff NIDDK 301-496-3583
Islet Cell Transplants....Staff NIDDK 301-496-3583
Isobutane....Raftery, Jim USITC 202-205-3365
Isobutylene....Raftery, Jim USITC 202-205-3365
Isoprene....Raftery, Jim USITC 202-205-3365
Isopropyl myristate....Johnson, Larry USITC 202-205-3351
Isotope Production....Erb, Donald NEIC 301-903-2593
Isotopes....Staff NCI 301-496-5583
Israel....Fitzgerald-Wilkes, Kate/Thanos, Paul Cnty Commerce 202-482-1870
Israel (Tel Aviv)....Staff Cnty State 202-647-3672
Israel/Minerals....King, Audie L. Cnty Mines 202-501-9674
Italy....Fitzpatrick, Boyce Cnty Commerce 202-482-2177
Italy (Rome)....Staff Cnty State 202-647-2453
Italy/Minerals....Rabchevsky, George Cnty Mines 202-501-9672
Ivory Coast....Michelini, Paul Cnty Commerce 202-482-4388
Ivory Coast/Minerals....van Oss, Hendrik Cnty Mines 202-501-9687
Ivory, articles of....Spalding, Josephine USITC 202-205-3498
Ivory, tusks....Ludwick, David USITC 202-205-3329

J

Jackets: mens and boys....Linkins, Linda USITC 202-205-3469
Jackets: womens and girls....Holoyda, Olha USITC 202-205-3467
Jails, Inmates, and Crowding....Baunach, Phyllis Jo Justice Stat 202-307-0361
Jails, Inmates, and Crowding....Stephan, James Justice Stat 202-616-7273
Jails, Inmates, and Crowding....Greenfeld, Lawrence Justice Stat 202-616-3281
Jails, Inmates, and Crowding....DeWitt, Charles Justice Stat 202-307-2942
Jakob-Creutzfeldt Disease....Staff NINDS 301-496-5751
Jamaica....Soto, Rodrigo Cnty Commerce 202-482-2527
Jamaica....Almaguer, Antoinette Peace Corps 202-606-3322
Jamaica (Kingston)....Staff Cnty State 202-647-2620
Jamaica/Minerals....Torres, Ivette Cnty Mines 202-501-9680
Jams and Jellies....Hodgen, Donald A. COMMERCE 202-482-3346
Jams, jellies, and marmalades....Vacant USITC 202-205-3306
Japan....Cantall, W./Leslie, E./Kennedy, E./Christian, A. Cnty Commerce 202-482-2425
Japan (Tokyo)....Staff Cnty State 202-647-3152
Japan/Minerals....Wu, John Cnty Mines 202-501-9697
Japan/trade matters....Lake, Charles US Trade Rep 202-395-3900
Japanese Yen with options....Bice, David CFT 312-353-7880
Jet fuel....Foreso, Cynthia USITC 202-205-3348
Jewelry, Export Promo.....Beckham, Reginald COMMERCE 202-482-5478
Jewelry....Harris, John M. COMMERCE 202-482-1178
Jewelry....Piropato, Louis CUSTOMS 212-466-5895
Jewelry....Witherspoon, Ricardo USITC 202-205-3489
Job Vacancy Stats, Employment Statistics....Devens, Richard LABOR 202-606-6402
Jordan....Fitzgerald-Wilkes, Kate/Thanos, Paul Cnty Commerce 202-482-1857
Jordan (Amman)....Staff Cnty State 202-647-1022
Jordan/Minerals....Dolley, Thomas Cnty Mines 202-501-9690
Joseph's Disease....Staff NINDS 301-496-5751
Journal, EPA....Staff EPA 202-260-4659
Journalism research methods....Newhagan, John D. UMD 301-405-2417
Judges....Gaskins, Carla Justice Stat 202-508-8550
Judges....Langan, Patrick Justice Stat 202-616-3490
Judiciary....Gaskins, Carla Justice Stat 202-508-8550
Judiciary....Langan, Patrick Justice Stat 202-616-3490
Juices....Maria, John CUSTOMS 212-466-5730
Juices, fruit....Dennis, Alfred USITC 202-205-3316
Juices, vegetable....Dennis, Alfred USITC 202-205-3316
Juvenile Corrections....Baunach, Phyllis Jo Justice Stat 202-307-0361
Juvenile Corrections....Kline, Susan Justice Stat 202-724-3118
Juvenile Delinquency....Staff NIMH 301-443-4515
Juvenile Diabetes....Staff NIDDK 301-443-3583
Juvenile Rheumatoid Arthritis....Staff NIAMS 301-496-8188
Juvenile Spin. Musc. Atrophy (Kug.-Wel. Disease)....Staff NINDS 301-496-5751
Juveniles - General....Lindgren, Sue Justice Stat 202-307-0760
Juxtaglomerular Hyperplasia (Bartter's Syndrome)....Staff NHLBI 301-496-4236

K

Kanner's Syndrome....Staff NINDS 301-496-5751
Kaolin....Lukes, James USITC 202-205-3426

Kaposi's Sarcoma....Staff NCI 301-496-5583
Kawasaki Disease....Staff NIAID 301-496-5717
Kawasaki Disease....Staff CDC 401-639-3286
Kearns-Sayre Syndrome....Staff NINDS 301-496-5751
Kenya....Watkins, Chandra Cnty Commerce 202-482-4564
Kenya....Schmitz, Virginia Peace Corps 202-606-3334
Kenya (Nairobi)....Staff Cnty State 202-647-5684
Kenya/Minerals....Izon, David Cnty Mines 202-501-9692
Keratitis....Staff NEI 301-496-5248
Keratoconus....Staff NEI 301-496-5248
Keratomileusis....Staff NEI 301-496-5248
Keratoplasty....Staff NEI 301-496-5248
Kerosene....Foreso, Cynthia USITC 202-205-3348
Ketones....Michels, David USITC 202-205-3352
Key cases....Seastrum, Carl USITC 202-205-3493
Kidney....Staff NIDDK 301-496-3583
Kidney Dialysis....Hardy, Robert HCFA 220-690-6145
Kidney Stones....Staff NIDDK 301-496-3583
Kidney, Urology Clearinghouse....Staff NIDDK 301-468-6345
Kiribati (Tarawa)....Staff Cnty State 202-647-3546
Kiribati (Gilbert Islands)/Minerals....Lyday, Travis Cnty Mines 202-501-9695
Kitchen Cabinets....Auerbach, Mitchel COMMERCE 202-482-0375
Kleine-Levin Syndrome....Staff NINDS 301-496-5751
Klinefelter's Syndrome....Staff NICHD 301-496-5133
Knitting machines....Greene, William USITC 202-205-3405
Knotted Netting....Konzet, Jeffrey CUSTOMS 212-466-5885
Koch Antitoxins....Staff NCI 301-496-5583
Korea....Donius, Jeffrey/ Amador, Ranato/ Duvall, Dan Cnty Commerce 202-482-4957
Korea, North and South....Staff Cnty State 202-647-7717
Korea, North/Minerals....Kuo, Chin Cnty Mines 202-501-9693
Korea, South/Minerals....Kuo, Chin Cnty Mines 202-501-9693
Krabbe's Disease....Staff NINDS 301-496-5751
Krebiezen (Carcalon)....Staff NCI 301-496-5583
Kugelberg-Welander Disease (Juv. Spi. Mus. Atoph.)....Staff NINDS 301-496-5751
Kuru....Staff NINDS 301-496-5751
Kuwait....Wright, Corey/Sams, Thomas Cnty Commerce 202-482-1680
Kuwait (Kuwait)....Staff Cnty State 202-647-6562
Kuwait/Minerals....Michalski, Bernadette Cnty Mines 202-501-9699
Kyanite....DeSapio, Vincent USITC 202-205-3435
Kyanite-Mullite....Potter, Michael J. MINES 202-501-9387
Kyrgyzstan....Staff Cnty State 202-647-6859

L

LNG Plants (Major Proj)....Thomas, Janet COMMERCE 202-482-4146
Labels....Cook, Lee USITC 202-205-3471
Labor Composition, Multifactor Productivity, Hrs.....Rosenblum, Larry LABOR 202-606-5606
Labor Force Data, Data Disk & Tapes....Marcus, Jessie LABOR 202-606-6392
Labor Force Data, Machine-readable data, Empl/Un....Green, Gloria LABOR 202-606-6373
Labor Force Projections....Fullerton, Howard LABOR 202-606-5711
Labor Force and Unemployment, Foreign Countries....Sorrentino, Constance LABOR 202-606-5654
Labor Force, State and Area Tapes and Diskettes....Marcus, Jessie LABOR 202-606-6392
Laboratory Animals....Staff NCRR 301-496-5545
Laboratory Animals....Staff NCRR 301-496-2527
Laboratory Glassware....Staff OD/ORS 301-496-4595
Laboratory Instruments....Nealon, Marguerite COMMERCE 202-482-3411
Laboratory Instruments, Trade Promo.....Gwaltney, G.P. COMMERCE 202-482-3090
Labyrinthitis....Staff NINDS 301-496-5751
Labyrinthitis....Staff NIDCD 301-496-7243
Lace....Konzet, Jeffrey CUSTOMS 212-466-5885
Lace....Sweet, Mary Elizabeth USITC 202-205-3455
Lacemaking machines....Greene, William USITC 202-205-3405
Lacings....Cook, Lee USITC 202-205-3471
Lacquers....Johnson, Larry USITC 202-205-3351
Lacrimal Glands....Staff NEI 301-496-5248
Lactation....Staff NIDDK 301-496-3583
Lactose....Randall, Rob USITC 202-205-3366
Lactose Intolerance....Staff NIDDK 301-496-3583
Laetrile....Staff NCI 301-496-5583

Lakes....Wanser, Stephen USITC 202-205-3363

Lamb....Steller, Rose USITC 202-205-3323

Laminar Flow Rooms....Staff OD/ORS 301-496-2960

Lamp black....Johnson, Larry USITC 202-205-3351

Lamps....Kalkines, George CUSTOMS 212-466-5794

Lamps (bulbs)....Cutchin, John USITC 202-205-3396

Land Disposal....Staff EPA 202-260-4687

Land Disposition, Fish and Wildlife....Staff FWS 703-358-1713

Land Fields....Staff EPA 202-260-4687

Land Mobile Common Carrier....Staff FCC 202-653-0914

Land Mobile Frequent Assignment Techniques....Staff FCC 717-337-1411

Land Mobile Operational Review of Radio....Staff FCC 202-632-6497

Land Resource Usage and Analysis....Staff FWS 703-358-1706

Land Transportation....Staff FCC 717-337-1212

Land and Space Based Remote Sensing Instruments....Staff NASA 804-864-6170

Land and Water Conservation Fund....Staff FWS 703-358-1713

Language....Staff NINDS 301-496-5751

Language....Staff NIDCD 301-496-7243

Language....Staff CENSUS 301-763-1154

Language Development....Staff NICHD 301-496-5133

Language and journalism....McAdams, Katherine C. UMD 301-405-2423

Laos....Pho, Hong-Phong B. Cnty Commerce 202-482-3875

Laos (Vientiane)....Staff Cnty State 202-647-3133

Laos/Minerals....Vacant Cnty Mines 202-501-9694

Laser (Cancer Surgery)....Staff NCI 301-496-5583

Laser (Tatoo Removal/Dermatology)....Staff 301-496-8188

Laser Angioplasty....Staff NHLBI 301-496-4236

Laser Energy Conversion Techniques....Staff NASA 804-864-6122

Laser Treatment (Eyes)....Staff NEI 301-496-5248

Lasers, Trade Promo.....Manzolilo, Frank COMMERCE 202-482-2991

Lassa Fever....Staff NIAID 301-496-5717

Latin America/trade matters....Frechette, Myles US Trade Rep 202-395-6135

Latvia....Staff Cnty State 202-647-3187

Launch Vehicles....Brown, Dwayne C. NASA 202-453-8956

Laundry machines....Jackson, Georgia USITC 202-205-3399

Laurence-Moon-Bardet-Biedl Syndrome....Staff NINDS 301-496-5751

Law Enforcement, Prosecution & Courts - State....Manson, Donald Justice Stat 202-616-3491

Law Suits Litigation....Staff FCC 202-632-7112

Lawn & Garden Equipment....Vanderwof, John COMMERCE 202-482-0348

Layoff Statistics, Empl/ Unempl. Stats.....Siegel, Lewis LABOR 202-606-6404

Lead....Woodbury, William D. MINES 202-501-9444

Lead....White, Linda USITC 202-205-3427

Lead Based Paints....Staff CDC 404-639-3286

Lead Encephalopathy....Staff NINDS 301-496-5751

Lead Poisoning....Staff CDC 404-639-3286

Lead Poisoning....Staff NIEHS 919-541-3345

Lead Poisoning....Grigg, Bill PHS 202-690-6867

Lead Poisoning Prevention....Binder, Suzanne CDC 404-488-7330

Lead Poisoning Prevention....Giles, Ken CPSC 301-504-0580

Lead Products....Larrabee, David COMMERCE 202-482-0575

Lead compounds....Greenblatt, Jack USITC 202-205-3353

Lead for pencils....Shetty, Sundar USITC 202-205-3486

Lead pigments....Johnson, Larry USITC 202-205-3351

Lead-Poisoning Anemia....Staff NHLBI 301-496-4236

Learning Center for Interactive Technology....Staff NLM 301-496-6280

Learning Disabilities....Staff NINDS 301-496-5751

Learning Disabilities....Staff NICHD 301-496-5133

Learning Disabilities....Staff NIMH 301-443-4515

Learning Disabilities....Staff NIDCD 301-496-7243

Lease condensate....Foreso, Cynthia USITC 202-205-3348

Leasing Equipment and Vehicles....Shuman, John COMMERCE 202-482-3050

Leather....Steller, Rose USITC 202-205-3323

Leather Products....Byron, James E. COMMERCE 202-482-4034

Leather Tanning....Byron, James E. COMMERCE 202-482-4034

Leather apparel....Jones, Jackie USITC 202-205-3466

Leather apparel....Hamey, Amy USITC 202-205-3465

Leather footwear parts....Shildneck, Ann USITC 202-205-3499

Leather, Producer Price Index....Paik, Soon LABOR 202-606-7714

Lebanon....Wright, Corey/Sams, Thomas Cnty Commerce 202-482-4441

Lebanon (Beirut)....Staff Cnty State 202-647-1030

Lebanon/Minerals....Michalski, Bernadette Cnty Mines 202-501-9699

Leber's Disease....Staff NEI 301-496-5248

Left Ventricular Assist Device (LVAD)....Staff NHLBI 301-496-4236

Legal Services....Chittum, J. Marc. COMMERCE 202-482-0345

Legal Services....Posey, Melanie USITC 202-205-3303

Legg-Perthes Disease....Staff NIAMS 301-496-8188

Legionella Pneumophila....Staff NIAID 301-496-5717

Legionella Pneumophila....Staff CDC 404-639-3286

Legionnaire's Disease....Staff NIAID 301-496-5717

Legionnaire's Disease....Staff CDC 404-639-3286

Legislation....Gregg, Valerie CENSUS 301-763-7787

Legislation....Lacy, Velma CENSUS 301-763-4001

Legislative Information....Staff OD/DLA 301-496-3471

Leigh's Disease (Subacute Necrotizing Encephal.)....Staff NINDS 301-496-5751

Leishmaniasis....Staff NIAID 301-496-5717

Lemon oil (essential oil)....Land, Eric USITC 202-205-3349

Lennox-Gastaut Syndrome....Staff NINDS 301-496-5751

Lens....Staff NEI 301-496-5248

Lens Implants....Staff NEI 301-496-5248

Lenses....Johnson, Christopher USITC 202-205-3488

Leprosy....Staff NIAID 301-496-5717

Lesch-Nyhan Disease....Staff NIDDK 301-496-3583

Lesch-Nyhan Disease....Staff NINDS 301-496-5751

Lesch-Nyhan Disease....Staff NIMH 301-443-4515

Lesotho....Holm-Olsen, Finn Cnty Commerce 202-482-4228

Lesotho....Grimmett, Michael Peace Corps 202-606-3246

Lesotho....Woodfork, Jacqueline Peace Corps 202-606-3247

Lesotho (Maseru)....Staff Cnty State 202-647-8252

Lesotho/Minerals....King, Audie L. Cnty Mines 202-501-9674

Leukemia....Staff NCI 301-496-5583

Leukoaraiosis....Staff NINDS 301-496-5751

Leukodystrophy....Staff NINDS 301-496-5751

Leukoencephalopathy....Staff NINDS 301-496-5751

Leukoplakia....Staff NIDR 301-496-4261

Levulose....Randall, Rob USITC 202-205-3366

Liberia....Michelini, Philip/Cerone, Chris Cnty Commerce 202-482-4388

Liberia (Monrovia)....Staff Cnty State 202-647-3391

Liberia/Minerals....van Oss, Hendrik Cnty Mines 202-501-9687

Librarians Office....Staff DRS 301-496-2447

Library....Staff CENSUS 301-763-5042

Library (National Library of Medicine)....Staff NLM 301-496-6095

Library - Toxic Substances....Staff EPA 202-260-3944

Libya....Clement, Claude Cnty Commerce 202-482-5545

Libya (Tripoli)....Staff Cnty State 202-647-4674

Libya/Minerals....Dolley, Thomas Cnty Mines 202-501-9690

Lice....Staff NIAID 301-496-5717

Licenses, Federal Permits....Staff FWS 703-358-2183

Lichen Planus....Staff NIDR 301-496-4261

Lichen Planus....Staff NIAMS 301-496-8188

Liechtenstein....Staff Cnty State 202-647-1484

Life Cycle....Staff NIA 301-496-1752

Life Expectancy....Staff NIA 301-496-1752

Life Extension....Staff NIA 301-496-1752

Life Insurance and Health, Comp. & Working Cond.....Blostin, Allan LABOR 202-606-6240

Life Review....Staff NIA 301-496-1752

Life Sciences Research....Staff NASA 713-438-5111

Life on Other Planets....Staff NASA 415-604-3934

Light Water Reactor Safety....Giessing, Daniel NEIC 301-903-3456

Light oil....Foreso, Cynthia USITC 202-205-3348

Lighting Devices....Staff FCC 202-653-6288

Lighting Fixtures....Kalkines, George CUSTOMS 212-466-5794

Lighting equipment....Kolberg, Mary USITC 202-205-3401

Ligninsulfonic acid and its salts....Land, Eric USITC 202-205-3349

Lignite....Foreso, Cynthia USITC 202-205-3348

Lime....Miller, Michael MINES 202-501-9409

Lime....White, Linda USITC 202-205-3427

Limestone....White, Linda USITC 202-205-3427

Linear Accelerator....Staff NCI 301-496-5583

Lipid Research Clinics....Staff NHLBI 301-496-4236

Lipid Storage Diseases....Staff NINDS 301-496-5751

Lipid Transport Disorders....Staff NHLBI 301-496-4236

Lipidemia....Staff NHLBI 301-496-4236

Lipidosis....Staff NINDS 301-496-5751

Lipoproteins....Staff NHLBI 301-496-4236

Liquefied natural gas (LNG)....Land, Eric USITC 202-205-3349

Liquefied petroleum gas (LPG)....Land, Eric USITC 202-205-3349

Liquefied refinery gas (LRG)....Land, Eric USITC 202-205-3349

Liquid Metal Reactors (LMR)....Rosen, Sol NEIC 301-903-3218

Liquid Waste....Staff OD/ORS 301-496-2960

Liquid Waste (Radioactive)....Staff OD/ORS 301-496-2254

Listeriosis....Staff NIAID 301-496-5717

Literature....Bradford, Gigi NEA 202-682-5451

Experts

Literature of journalism....Paterson, Judith UMD 301-405-2425
Lithium....Ober, Joyce A. MINES 202-501-9406
Lithium....Conant, Kenneth USITC 202-205-3346
Lithium compounds....Greenblatt, Jack USITC 202-205-3353
Lithium stearate....Randall, Rob USITC 202-205-3366
Lithuania....Staff Cnty State 202-647-3187
Liver....Staff NIDDK 301-496-3583
Livestock - Cattle....Shepler, Glenda Agri 202-720-3040
Livestock - Cattle & Sheep....Gustafson, Ron Agri 202-219-1286
Livestock - Hogs....Hamer, Hubert Agri 202-720-3106
Livestock - Hogs....Southard, Leland Agri 202-219-0767
Livestock - Sheep....Simpson, Linda Agri 202-720-3578
Livestock - World....Bailey, Linda Agri 202-219-1286
Livestock - World....Shagam, Shayle Agri 202-219-0767
Livestock Damage Control....Staff FWS 703-358-1718
Living Arrangements, Population....Saluter, Arlene CENSUS 301-763-7987
Local Government Radio....Staff FCC 717-337-1212
Local Television Transmission....Staff FCC 202-634-1706
Locked-In Syndrome....Staff NINDS 301-496-5751
Locks....Smyth, James CUSTOMS 212-466-2084
Locks and Keys....Staff OD/ORS/Locksmith 301-496-3507
Loeffler's Syndrome....Staff NIAID 301-496-5717
Logs, Wood....Hicks, Michael COMMERCE 202-482-0375
Logs, rough....Ruggles, Fred USITC 202-205-3325
Long-Term Care & Alternatives....Hardy, Robert HCFA 202-690-6145
Longevity (Statistics)....Staff NCHS 301-436-8500
Longevity (Statistics)....Staff NIA 301-496-1752
Longitudinal Data/Gross Flows, Empl/Unempl. Stats.....Horvath, Francis LABOR 202-606-6345
Lotteries....Staff FCC 202-632-6990
Lou Gehrig's Disease....Staff NINDS 301-496-5751
Loudspeakers....Sherman, Thomas USITC 202-205-3389
Low Back Pain....Staff NIAMS 301-496-8188
Low Back Pain (Sciatica)....Staff NINDS 301-496-5751
Low Birth Weight....Staff NICHD 301-496-5133
Low Blood Pressure....Staff NHLBI 301-496-4236
Low Energy Nuclear Research....Hendrie, David NEIC 301-902-3610
Low Power Television Stations....Staff FCC 202-632-7426
Low Power Transmitters....Staff FCC 202-653-6288
Low Vision Aids....Staff NEI 301-496-5248
Low fuming brazing rods....Lundy, David USITC 202-205-3439
Low-Density Lipoproteins (LDL)....Staff NHLBI 301-496-4236
Low-Income Weatherization Assistance....Staff NEIC 202-586-2204
Lowe Syndrome (Oculocerebrorenal)....Staff NICHD 301-496-5133
Lowe's Syndrome....Staff NEI 301-496-5248
Lube fittings....Fravel, Dennis USITC 202-205-3404
Lubricating grease....Foreso, Cynthia USITC 202-205-3348
Lubricating oil....Foreso, Cynthia USITC 202-205-3348
Luggage....Byron, James E. COMMERCE 202-482-3034
Luggage....Gorman, Kevin CUSTOMS 212-466-5893
Luggage....Seastrum, Carl USITC 202-205-3493
Lumber....Wise, Barbara COMMERCE 202-482-0375
Lumber....Ruggles, Fred USITC 202-205-3325
Lumber with options....Rosenfeld, Donald CFT 312-353-9026
Lunar Landing Research Vehicle....Haley, Donald E. NASA 805-258-3456
Lunar Landing Research Vehicle....Nolan, Donald A. NASA 805-358-3447
Lunar Samples Research....Staff NASA 713-483-5111
Lung Cancer....Staff NCI 301-496-5583
Lung Disease (Asbestosis)....Staff NIEHS 919-541-3345
Lung Disease (Infectious/Allergenic)....Staff NIAID 301-496-5717
Lung Disease (Non-infec., Non-aller., Non-tumor.)....Staff NHLBI 301-496-4236
Lung Disease (Tumorous/Cancerous)....Staff NCI 301-496-5583
Lupus Erythematosus....Staff NIAMS 301-496-8188
Lupus Erythematosus....Staff NINDS 301-496-5751
Lupus Erythematosus....Staff NIAID 301-496-5717
Luxembourg....Bensimon, Simon Cnty Commerce 202-482-5401
Luxembourg (Luxembourg)....Staff Cnty State 202-647-6664
Luxembourg/Minerals....Newman, Harold R. Cnty Mines 202-501-9699
Lyme Arthritis/Lyme Disease....Staff NIAID 301-496-5717
Lyme Arthritis/Lyme Disease....Staff NIAMS 301-496-8188
Lymphadenopathy Syndrome (LAD)....Staff NIAID 301-496-5717
Lymphedema....Staff NCI 301-496-5583
Lymphoblastic Lymphosarcoma....Staff NCI 301-496-5583
Lymphoma....Staff NCI 301-496-5583
Lymphosarcoma....Staff NCI 301-496-5583

M

MARC (Minority Access to Research Careers)....Staff NIGMS 301-496-7301
MBS resins....Misurelli, Denby USITC 202-205-3362
Macao....Matheson, JeNelle Cnty Commerce 202-482-2462
Macaroni and other alimentary pastes....Schneider, Greg USITC 202-205-3326
Macau....Staff Cnty State 202-647-6300
Machine Belts and Clothing....Barth, George CUSTOMS 212-466-5884
Machine Tool Accessories....McGibbon, Patrick COMMERCE 202-482-0314
Machine-readable Data, Labor Force Data, Empl/Unempl....Green, Gloria LABOR 202-606-6373
Machinery, Agricultural....Wholey, Patrick CUSTOMS 212-466-5668
Machinery, Excavating....Wholey, Patrick CUSTOMS 212-466-5668
Machinery, Heavy Industrial....Horowitz, Alan CUSTOMS 212-466-5494
Machinery, International Price Indexes....Costello, Brian LABOR 202-606-7107
Machinery, Intl. Price Ind., Prices & Liv. Cond....Costello, Brian LABOR 202-606-7107
Machinery, Office and Textile....Brodbeck, Arthur CUSTOMS 212-466-5490
Machinery, Prices and Living Conditions....Alterman, William LABOR 202-606-7108
Machinery, Printing....Rocks, Michael CUSTOMS 212-466-5669
Machines & machinery: agricultural or horticultural....Vacant USITC 202-205-3380
Machines and machinery: adding....Baker, Scott USITC 202-205-3386
Machines and machinery: addressing....Baker, Scott USITC 202-205-3386
Machines and machinery: agglomerating....Greene, William USITC 202-205-3405
Machines rolling (textile)....Greene, William USITC 202-205-3405
Machines, spraying: agricultural/horticultural....Vacant USITC 202-205-3380
Machines, spraying: other....Slingerland, David USITC 202-205-3400
Machines, textile: bleaching....Greene, William USITC 202-205-3405
Machines, textile: calendaring and rolling....Greene, William USITC 202-205-3405
Machines, textile: cleaning....Greene, William USITC 202-205-3405
Machines, textile: coating....Greene, William USITC 202-205-3405
Machines, textile: drying....Greene, William USITC 202-205-3405
Machines, textile: dyeing....Greene, William USITC 202-205-3405
Machines, textile: embroidery....Greene, William USITC 202-205-3405
Machines, textile: knitting....Greene, William USITC 202-205-3405
Machines, textile: lacemaking....Greene, William USITC 202-205-3405
Machines, textile: printing....Greene, William USITC 202-205-3405
Machines, textile: spinning....Greene, William USITC 202-205-3405
Machines, textile: tobacco....Jackson, Georgia USITC 202-205-3399
Machines, textile: tools, machine....Fravel, Dennis USITC 202-205-3404
Machines, textile: vending....Jackson, Georgia USITC 202-205-3399
Machines, textile: washing....Greene, William USITC 202-205-3405
Machines, textile: weaving....Greene, William USITC 202-205-3405
Machines, textile: weighing....Slingerland, David USITC 202-205-3400
Machines: agricultural or horticultural....McCarty, Timothy USITC 202-205-3398
Machines: bookbinding....Slingerland, David USITC 202-205-3400
Machines: calculators....Baker, Scott USITC 202-205-3386
Machines: cash registers....Baker, Scott USITC 202-205-3386
Machines: casting machines....Greene, William USITC 202-205-3405
Machines: checkwriting....Baker, Scott USITC 202-205-3386
Machines: cleaning (heat process equipment)....Slingerland, David USITC 202-205-3400
Machines: cleaning (textiles)....Greene, William USITC 202-205-3405
Machines: coating....Greene, William USITC 202-205-3405
Machines: converters....Greene, William USITC 202-205-3405
Machines: cordage....Greene, William USITC 202-205-3405
Machines: crushing....Greene, William USITC 202-205-3405
Machines: cutting....Greene, William USITC 202-205-3405
Machines: data processing....Bringe, Julie USITC 202-205-3390
Machines: dressing....Greene, William USITC 202-205-3405
Machines: drink preparing....Jackson, Georgia USITC 202-205-3399
Machines: dry cleaning....Jackson, Georgia USITC 202-205-3399
Machines: drying....Jackson, Georgia USITC 202-205-3399
Machines: dyeing....Greene, William USITC 202-205-3405
Machines: earth moving....Stonitsch, Laura USITC 202-205-3408
Machines: embroidery....Greene, William USITC 202-205-3405
Machines: fabric folding....Greene, William USITC 202-205-3405
Machines: farm....Vacant USITC 202-205-3380
Machines: flight simulators....Anderson, Peder USITC 202-205-3388
Machines: food preparing....Jackson, Georgia USITC 202-205-3399
Machines: horticultural....Vacant USITC 202-205-3380
Machines: mining....Stonitsch, Laura USITC 202-205-3408
Machines: office copying....Baker, Scott USITC 202-205-3386

Machines: packaging....Slingerland, David USITC 202-205-3400

Machines: paper....Slingerland, David USITC 202-205-3400

Machines: paperboard....Slingerland, David USITC 202-205-3400

Machines: postage franking....Baker, Scott USITC 202-205-3386

Machines: printing....Slingerland, David USITC 202-205-3400

Machines: pulp....Slingerland, David USITC 202-205-3400

Machines: reeling....Greene, William USITC 202-205-3405

Machines: rolling (metal)....Fravel, Dennis USITC 202-205-3404

Machines: rolling nes....Slingerland, David USITC 202-205-3400

Machines: screening....Greene, William USITC 202-205-3405

Machines: sealing....Slingerland, David USITC 202-205-3400

Machines: sewing....Greene, William USITC 202-205-3405

Machines: shoe....Vacant USITC 202-205-3380

Machines: sorting....Greene, William USITC 202-205-3405

Machines: stone processing....Greene, William USITC 202-205-3405

Machines: stoneworking....Vacant USITC 202-205-3380

Machines: Rolling (textile)....Greene, William USITC 202-205-3405

Macroglobulinemia and Myeloma....Staff NCI 301-496-5583

Macular Degeneration....Staff NEI 301-496-5248

Madagascar....Watkins, Chandra Cnty Commerce 202-482-4564

Madagascar, Republic of (Antananarivo)....Staff Cnty State 202-647-5684

Madagascar/Minerals....Dolley, Thomas Cnty Mines 202-501-9690

Magazines....Bratland, Rose Marie COMMERCE 202-482-0380

Magnesite: crude....White, Linda USITC 202-205-3427

Magnesite: dead burned....DeSapio, Vincent USITC 202-205-3435

Magnesium....Cammarota, David COMMERCE 202-482-0575

Magnesium....DeSapio, Vincent USITC 202-205-3435

Magnesium & Mg Comps....Kramer, Deborah A. MINES 202-501-9394

Magnesium compounds....Greenblatt, Jack USITC 202-205-3353

Magnetic Confinement....Willis, John NEIC 301-903-4095

Magnetic Fusion....Finn, Thomas G. NEIC 202-586-5444

Magnetic Resonance Imaging....Staff NINDS 301-496-5751

Magnetic devices....Cutchin, John USITC 202-205-3396

Mailing services....Xavier, Neil USITC 202-205-3450

Mainframes....Miles, Tim COMMERCE 202-482-2990

Maintenance services....Bedore, James USITC 202-205-3424

Major Industries, Technological Trends in....Riche, Richard LABOR 202-606-5626

Major Market Index with options....Fedinets, Robert P. CFT 312-353-9016

Major Projects....Thiebeault, Robert COMMERCE 202-482-5225

Malabsorptive Diseases....Staff NIDDK 301-496-3583

Malaria....Staff NIAID 301-496-5717

Malaria....Campbell, Carlos C. CDC 404-488-4046

Malawi....Holm-Olsen, Finn Cnty Commerce 202-482-4228

Malawi....Brill, Terry Peace Corps 202-606-3535

Malawi (Lilongwe)....Staff Cnty State 202-647-8433

Malawi/Minerals....King, Audie L. Cnty Mines 202-501-9690

Malaysia....Cung, Raphael Cnty Commerce 202-482-3875

Malaysia (Kuala Lumpur)....Staff Cnty State 202-647-3276

Malaysia/Minerals....Wu, John Cnty Mines 202-501-9697

Maldives....Simmons, John Cnty Commerce 202-482-2954

Maldives....Staff Cnty State 202-647-2351

Mali....Michelini, Philip Cnty Commerce 202-482-4388

Mali....Hanson, Julie Peace Corps 202-606-3004

Mali Republic (Bamako)....Staff Cnty State 202-647-3066

Mali/Minerals....van Oss, Hendrik Cnty Mines 202-501-9687

Malignancy....Staff NCI 301-496-5583

Malnutrition....Staff NIDDK 301-496-3583

Malnutrition....Staff NICHD 301-496-5133

Malocclusion....Staff NIDR 301-496-4261

Malpractice (Medical)....Mehuron, Charlotte HRSA 301-443-3376

Malta....McLaughlin, Robert Cnty Commerce 202-482-3748

Malta....DiMeo, Pam Peace Corps 202-606-3196

Malta....Schildwachter, Christy Peace Corps 202-606-3196

Malta (Valletta)....Staff Cnty State 202-647-2453

Malta/Minerals....Plachy, Josef Cnty Mines 202-501-9673

Malts....Pierre-Benoist, John USITC 202-205-3320

Mammals, Marine....Staff FWS 703-358-1718

Mammography....Staff NCI 301-496-5583

Management Consulting....Chittum, J. Marc COMMERCE 202-482-0345

Management consulting services....DeSapio, Vincent USITC 202-205-3435

Manganese....Presbury, Graylin COMMERCE 202-482-5158

Manganese....Jones, Thomas S. MINES 202-501-9428

Manganese....Vacant USITC 202-205-3419

Manganese compounds....Greenblatt, Jack USITC 202-205-3353

Mania....Staff NIMH 301-443-4515

Manifold Business Forms....Bratland, Rose Marie COMMERCE 202-482-0380

Manmade Fiber....Dulka, William COMMERCE 202-482-4058

Manmade fibers....Freund, Kimberlie USITC 202-205-3456

Manmade fibers....Shelton, Linda USITC 202-205-3457

Manmade fibers....Warlick, William USITC 202-205-3459

Manned Flight....Phelps, Patti NASA 407-867-4444

Mantles....Vacant USITC 202-205-3343

Manufacturers Operations Division....Staff EPA 202-233-9240

Manufacturers, Prod Data, Durables, Census/Annl Svy....Hansen, Kenneth CENSUS 301-763-7304

Manufacturers, Prod Data, Nondurables, Cur Indrl Rp....Flood, Thomas CENSUS 301-763-5911

Manufacturers, Special Topics, Concentration....Goldhirsch, Bruce CENSUS 301-763-1503

Manufacturers, Special Topics, Inventories....Runyan, Ruth CENSUS 301-763-2502

Manufacturers, Special Topics, Pollution Abatement....Champion, Elinor CENSUS 301-763-5616

Manufactures, Nondurables....Zampogna, Michael CENSUS 301-763-2510

Manufactures, Special Topics, Monthly Shipments....Runyan, Ruth CENSUS 301-763-2502

Manufactures, Special Topics, Orders....Runyan, Ruth CENSUS 301-763-2502

Manufactures, Special Topics, Research/Develop Capa....Champion, Elinor CENSUS 301-763-5616

Manufactures, Prod Data, Nondurables, Census/Annual Svy....Zampogna, Michael CENSUS 301-763-2510

Manufacturing, Durables (Census/Annual Survey)....Hansen, Kenneth CENSUS 301-763-7304

Maple Syrup Urine Disease....Staff NIDDK 301-496-3583

Maps, 1980 Census Map Orders....Baxter, Leila CENSUS 812-288-3192

Maps, 1990 Census....Staff CENSUS 301-763-4100

Maps, Cartographic Operations....Staff CENSUS 301-763-3973

Maps, Computer Mapping....Broome, Fred CENSUS 301-763-3973

Marble, breccia, and onyx....White, Linda USITC 202-205-3427

Marfan's Syndrome....Staff NIAMS 301-496-8188

Marfan's Syndrome....Staff NHLBI 301-496-4236

Margarine....Janis, William V. COMMERCE 202-482-2250

Marijuana (Effect on Glaucoma)....Staff NEI 301-496-5248

Marijuana (In Urine)....Staff NIDA 301-443-6245

Marine Insurance....Johnson, C. William COMMERCE 202-482-5012

Marine Mammal Research....Staff FWS 703-358-1710

Marine Mammals....Staff FWS 703-358-1718

Marine Recreational Equipment, Export Promo.....Beckham, Reginald COMMERCE 202-482-5478

Marine Services....Staff FCC 717-337-1212

Marine and Estuarine Protection....Staff EPA 202-260-7166

Marital Characteristics of Labor Force....Hayghe, Howard LABOR 202-606-6378

Marital Status....Saluter, Arlene CENSUS 301-763-7987

Maritime Services....Lahey, Kathleen USITC 202-205-3409

Maritime Shipping....Johnson, C. William COMMERCE 202-482-5012

Marker (Cancer)....Staff NCI 301-496-5583

Marketing....Morin, Bernard A. UVA 701-924-3477

Marketing Promo., Basic Ind.....Trafton, Donald R. COMMERCE 202-482-2493

Marriage Statistics....Heuser, Robert CDC 301-436-8954

Mars Exploration....Keegan, Sarah NASA 703-271-5591

Marsh Land....Staff FWS 703-358-2043

Marshall Islands (Majuro)....Staff Cnty State 202-647-0108

Martinique....Brooks, Michelle Cnty Commerce 202-482-2527

Martinique (Fort-de-France)....Staff Cnty State 202-647-2620

Martinique/Minerals....Torres, Ivette Cnty Mines 202-501-9680

Mass Layoff Statistics, Empl/Unempl. Stats.....Siegel, Lewis LABOR 202-606-6404

Mass Layoff Statistics, Employment/Unemployment....Siegel, Lewis LABOR 202-606-6404

Mass Layoffs, Employment Statistics....Siegel, Lewis LABOR 202-606-6404

Mass Spectrometers....Staff NCRR 301-496-5411

Mass media and society....Stepp, Jr., Carl UMD 301-405-2428

Mastectomy....Staff NCI 301-496-5583

Mastication....Staff NIDR 301-496-4261

Matches....Johnson, Larry USITC 202-205-3351

Materials, Advanced....Cammarota, David COMMERCE 202-482-0575

Maternal & Child Health....Mehuron, Charlotte HRSA 301-443-3376

Maternal and Child Nutrition....Wong, Faye L. CDC 404-488-5099

Mattresses....Spalding, Josephine USITC 202-205-3498

Mauritania....Michelini, Philip Cnty Commerce 202-482-4388

Mauritania....Hanson, Julie Peace Corps 202-606-3004

Mauritania (Nouakchott)....Staff Cnty State 202-647-2865

Mauritania/Minerals....Michalski, Bernadette Cnty Mines 202-501-9699

Mauritius....Watkins, Chandra Cnty Commerce 202-482-4564

Mauritius (Port Louis)....Staff Cnty State 202-647-5684

Mauritius/Minerals....Antonides, Lloyd Cnty Mines 202-501-9686

McArdle's Disease....Staff NINDS 301-496-5751

Measles....Staff NIAID 301-496-5717

Measles Encephalitis....Staff NINDS 301-496-5751

Measles Immunization....Staff CDC 404-329-3534

Meat Products....Hodgen, Donald A. COMMERCE 202-482-3346

Meat and Dairy Products....Brady, Thomas CUSTOMS 212-466-5790

Meat, inedible....Ludwick, David USITC 202-205-3329

Mech. Power Transmission Eqmt. Nec.....Reise, Richard COMMERCE 202-482-3489

Mechanical and Aerospace Engineering...Jacobson, Ira D. UVA 701-924-6217

Meconium Aspiration Syndrome....Staff NICHD 301-496-5133

Media (Bacteriologic)....Staff OD/ORS 301-496-6017

Media Arts....O'Doherty, Brian NEA 202-682-5452

Medicaid....Hardy, Robert HCFA 202-690-6145

Medical Care for Aged....Staff NIA 301-496-1752

Medical Devices....Cruzan, Susan FDA 301-443-3285

Medical Equipment....Staff FCC 202-653-6288

Medical Facilities, Major Proj....White, Barbara COMMERCE 202-482-4160

Medical Fraud/Quackery....Adams, Betsy FDA 301-443-4177

Medical Information System (MIS)....Staff CC 301-496-7946

Medical Instruments....Fuchs, Michael COMMERCE 202-482-0550

Medical Instruments....Preston, Jacques CUSTOMS 212-466-5488

Medical Instruments, Trade Promo.....Keen, George B. COMMERCE 202-482-2010

Medical Monitoring Program....Staff EPA 202-260-1640

Medical Photography....Staff NCRR/MAPB 301-496-5995

Medical School Grants....Mehuron, Charlotte HRSA 301-443-3376

Medical Scientist Training Program....Staff NIGMS 301-496-7301

Medical Staff Fellowship Training Program....Staff CC 301-496-2427

Medical Statistics....Flegal, Katherine CDC 301-436-7075

Medical Subject Headings....Schuyler, Peri L. NLM 301-496-1495

Medical Waste....Staff EPA 202-260-8551

Medical apparatus....Johnson, Christopher USITC 202-205-3488

Medically Underserved Areas....Mehuron, Charlotte HRSA 301-443-3376

Medicare....Hardy, Robert HCFA 202-690-6145

Medicine for the Public (Lect., Videos, Booklets)....Staff CC 301-496-2563

Medicine, National Library of....Baldwin, Elaine ADAMHA 301-443-4536

Mediterranean Fever....Staff NIAID 301-496-5717

Mediterranean Fever....Staff NIAMS 301-496-8188

Mediterranean/trade matters....Marcich, Christopher US Trade Rep 202-395-4620

Medlars/Medline....Staff NLM 301-496-6193

Meige's Syndrome (Facial Dystonia)....Staff NINDS 301-496-5751

Meige's Syndrome (Facial Dystonia)....Staff NIDCD 301-496-7243

Melamine....Michels, David USITC 202-205-3352

Melamine resins....Misurelli, Denby USITC 202-205-3362

Melanoma....Staff NCI 301-496-5583

Melanoma....Staff NEI 301-496-5248

Melkerson's Syndrome....Staff NINDS 301-496-5751

Memory....Staff NINDS 301-496-5751

Memory....Staff NIMH 301-443-4515

Memory Loss....Staff NIA 301-496-1752

Meniere's Disease....Staff NINDS 301-496-5751

Meniere's Disease....Staff NIDCD 301-496-7243

Meningitis....Staff NIAID 301-496-5717

Meningitis....Staff NINDS 301-496-5751

Meningitis....Wenger, Jay d. CDC 404-639-2215

Meningocele....Staff NINDS 301-496-5751

Meningocele....Staff NICHD 301-496-5133

Meningococcal Meningitis....Staff NIAID 301-496-5717

Menkes' Disease....Staff NINDS 301-496-5751

Menopause....Staff NIA 301-496-1752

Menstruation....Staff NICHD 301-496-5133

Mental Health and Aging....Staff NIMH 301-443-4515

Mental Health and Aging....Staff NIA 301-496-1752

Mental Retardation....Staff NICHD 301-496-5133

Mental Retardation (PCMR)....Long, Susan ACF 202-401-9215

Menthol....Land, Eric USITC 202-205-3349

Mercury....Reese, Jr., Robert MINES 202-501-9413

Mercury....Conant, Kenneth USITC 202-205-3346

Mercury Poisoning....Staff NINDS 301-496-5751

Mercury compounds....Greenblatt, Jack USITC 202-205-3353

Mercury in Fish....Staff EPA 301-755-0100

Mercury, Fluorspar....Manion, James J. COMMERCE 202-482-5157

Mergers and Acquisitions....Staff FCC 202-632-4887

Metabolic (Nervous System)....Staff NINDS 301-496-5751

Metabolic Disorders....Staff NIDDK 301-496-3583

Metabolism (Inborn Errors)....Staff NICHD 301-496-5133

Metabolism (Inborn Errors)....Staff NINDS 301-496-5751

Metachromatic Leukodystrophy....Staff NINDS 301-496-5751

Metal Articles....Schulberg, Martin CUSTOMS 212-466-5487

Metal Building Products....Williams, Franklin COMMERCE 202-482-0132

Metal Cookware....Harris, John COMMERCE 202-482-0348

Metal Cutting Machine Tools....Vacant COMMERCE

Metal Cutting Tools Fr Mach Tools....Vacant COMMERCE

Metal Foils....Fitzgerald, John CUSTOMS 212-466-5492

Metal Forming Machine Tools....Vacant COMMERCE

Metal Metabolism....Staff NIDDK 301-496-3583

Metal Powders....Duggan, Brian COMMERCE 202-482-0575

Metal rolling mills....Fravel, Dennis USITC 202-205-3404

Metal working machines....Fravel, Dennis USITC 202-205-3404

Metallurgy Research....Thomas, Iran NEIC 301-903-3426

Metals....Fitzgerald, John CUSTOMS 212-466-5492

Metals, Assistant Branch Chief....Butterman, W. MINES 202-501-9425

Metals, Assistant Branch Chief....Sibley, S.F. MINES 202-501-9344

Metals, Chief, Branch of....Makar, Harry MINES 202-501-9432

Metals, Prices & Living Conditions....Kazanowski, Edward LABOR 202-606-7735

Metals, Secondary....Manion, James J. COMMERCE 202-482-5157

Metalworking....Mearman, John COMMERCE 202-482-0315

Metalworking Equipment Nec.....McGibbon, Patrick COMMERCE 202-482-0314

Metastases....Staff NCI 301-496-3583

Metastic Tumors (Central Nervous System)....Staff NINDS 301-496-5751

Meteorological Research....Loughlin, John NASA 301-286-5565

Meteorological instruments....Shetty, Sundar USITC 202-205-3486

Metered Service--Message Units....Staff FCC 202-632-7553

Methacrylates....Michels, David USITC 202-205-3352

Methane....Moorer, Richard NEIC 202-586-8072

Methane....Land, Eric USITC 202-205-3349

Methanol....DiMaria, Joseph CUSTOMS 212-466-4769

Methodology, Prices and Living Conditions....Rosenberg, Elliott LABOR 202-606-7728

Methyl alcohol (methanol)....Michels, David USITC 202-205-3352

Methyl ethyl ketone....Michels, David USITC 202-205-3352

Methyl oleate...Johnson, Larry USITC 202-205-3351

Methylene Chloride....Giles, Ken CPSC 301-504-0580

Metropolitan Areas....Forstall, Richard/Fitzsimmons, James CENSUS 301-763-5158

Metropolitan Areas (MSA's), Population....Forstall, Richard CENSUS 301-763-5158

Mexico....Bannister, Rebeccaw Lowry/Ingrid Mohn Cnty Commerce 202-482-0300

Mexico (Mexico, D.F.)....Staff Cnty State 202-647-9894

Mexico/Minerals....Torres, Ivette Cnty Mines 202-501-9680

Mexico/trade matters....Roh, Charles US Trade Rep 202-395-5663

Mica....Presbury, Graylin COMMERCE 202-482-5158

Mica....Davis, Lawrence L. MINES 202-501-9386

Mica....White, Linda USITC 202-205-3427

Miscellaneous Reimbursable....Godoy, Francisco FTC 202-326-3757

Microbiological Monitoring....Staff OD/ORS 301-496-2960

Microbiology....Garges, Susan FAES 301-496-2095

Microcephaly....Staff NINDS 301-496-5751

Microcephaly....Staff NICHD 301-496-5133

Microorganisms Control....Staff OD/ORS 301-496-2960

Microphones....Sherman, Thomas USITC 202-205-3389

Microscopes...Johnson, Christopher USITC 202-205-3488

Microtropia....Staff NEI 301-496-5248

Microvascular Surgery....Staff NINDS 301-496-5751

Microwave Auxiliary--Common Carrier....Staff FCC 202-634-1706

Microwave Auxiliary--Mass Media....Staff FCC 202-634-6307

Microwave Cable Television Relay Service....Staff FCC 202-254-3420

Microwave Closed Loop....Staff FCC 202-634-1706

Microwave Common Carrier Licenses....Staff FCC 202-634-1706

Microwave Licenses....Staff FCC 202-634-1706

Microwave Monitoring Stations....Staff FCC 202-632-7593

Microwave Multipoint Distribution....Staff FCC 202-634-1706

Microwave Ovens....Staff FCC 202-653-6288

Microwave Radio Relay....Staff FCC 202-634-1706

Microwave Television--Pickup....Staff FCC 202-634-1706

Microwave, Protection from Interference....Staff FCC 202-632-7593
Middle Ear Infections....Staff NINDS 301-496-5751
Middle Ear Infections....Staff NIDCD 301-496-7243
Migraine (Headache)....Staff NINDS 301-496-5751
Migrant Health....Mehuron, Charlotte HRSA 301-44303376
Migration, Current Statistics....DeAre, Diana CENSUS 301-763-3850
Migratory Bird Research....Staff FWS 703-358-1710
Mild Retardation Prevention.... CDC 404-488-7370
Military Lands, Wildlife....Staff FWS 703-358-1718
Military Stations....Staff FCC 202-653-8141
Milk....Warren, J Fred USITC 202-205-3311
Milk Intolerance....Staff NIDDK 301-496-3583
Millinery ornaments....Spalding, Josephine USITC 202-205-3498
Millwork....Wise, Barbara COMMERCE 202-482-0375
Minamata Disease (Mercury Poisoning)....Staff NINDS 301-496-5751
Mineral Based Cons. Materials, Asphalt....Pitcher, Charles B. COMMERCE 202-482-0132
Mineral Based Cons. Mats., Gypsum....Pitcher, Charles B. COMMERCE 202-482-0132
Mineral Based Cons. Mats., Stone....Pitcher, Charles B. COMMERCE 202-482-0132
Mineral Based Const. Mats., Clay....Pitcher, Charles B. COMMERCE 202-482-0132
Mineral Based Const. Mats., Concrete....Pitcher, Charles B. COMMERCE 202-482-0132
Mineral Industries....McNamee, John CENSUS 301-763-5938
Mineral Metabolism....Staff NIDDK 301-496-3583
Mineral oil....Foreso, Cynthia USITC 202-205-3348
Mineral salts....Randall, Rob USITC 202-205-3366
Mineral substances, miscellaneous....Lundy, David USITC 202-205-3439
Mineral wool....White, Linda USITC 202-205-3427
Minerals in the World Economy/Minerals....Kimbell, Charles Cnty Mines 202-501-9659
Minerals, Non-Metallic....Bunin, Jacob CUSTOMS 212-566-5796
Minimal Brain Dysfunction....Staff NINDS 301-496-5751
Minimal Brain Dysfunction....Staff NIMH 301-443-4515
Minimum Wage Data, Empl/Unempl. Stats.....Haugen, Steve LABOR 202-606-6378
Minimum Wage Data, Employment/Unemployment....Haugen, Steve LABOR 202-606-6378
Mining....Staff FCC 717-337-1212
Mining....Stonitsch, Laura USITC 202-205-3408
Mining Machinery....McDonald, Edward COMMERCE 202-482-0680
Mining Machinery, Trade Promo....Zanetakos, George COMMERCE 202-482-0552
Mining machines....Stonitsch, Laura USITC 202-205-3408
Mink....Kruchten, Tom Agri 202-690-4870
Minorities, Empl./ Unempl. Stats.....Cattan, Peter LABOR 202-606-6378
Minority Access to Research Careers (MARC)....Staff NIGMS 301-496-7301
Minority Aging....Staff NIA 301-496-1752
Minority Biomedical Research Support (MBRS)....Staff NIGMS 301-496-7301
Minority Health....Crawford, Blake ASH 301-443-5224
Minority High School Student Research Apprentices....Staff NCRR 301-496-6743
Mirror Fusion Systems....Brewer, Robert NEIC 202-586-2828
Misc. Textile and Related Articles....Falcone, Anthony CUSTOMS 212-466-5886
Miscellaneous animal products....Ludwick, David USITC 202-205-3329
Miscellaneous articles of pulp and paper....Rhodes, Richard USITC 202-205-3322
Miscellaneous benzenoid intermediates....Matusik, Ed USITC 202-205-3356
Miscellaneous fish products....Corey, Roger USITC 202-205-3327
Miscellaneous products....Spalding, Josephine USITC 202-205-3498
Miscellaneous vegetable products....Pierre-Benoist, John USITC 202-205-3320
Miscellaneous wood products....Ruggles, Fred USITC 202-205-3325
Mitochondrial Myopathies....Staff NINDS 301-496-5751
Mitral Valve....Staff NHLBI 301-496-4236
Mixed Connective Tissue Disease....Staff NIAMS 301-496-8188
Mixtures (artificial) of fatty substances....Randall, Rob USITC 202-205-3366
Mixtures of inorganic compounds....Greenblatt, Jack USITC 202-205-3353
Mixtures of organic compounds....Michels, David USITC 202-205-3352
Mobile Homes....Cosslett, Patrick COMMERCE 202-482-0132
Mobile Services Licenses....Staff FCC 202-632-6400
Mobile Telephone Services....Staff FCC 202-653-5560
Mobilization Planning....Staff FCC 202-632-7025
Moccasins....Shildneck, Ann USITC 202-205-3499
Model Airplanes....Staff FCC 717-337-1212
Model Rocket Motors....Tyrrell, Elaine CPSC 301-504-0580

Models....Luther, Dennis USITC 202-205-3497
Models (Mathematical)....Staff NCRS/BEIB 301-496-5771
Modular High Temperature Reactors....Rosen, Sol NEIC 301-903-3218
Molasses....Williams, Joan USITC 202-205-3313
Molders' boxes, forms, and patterns....Greene, William USITC 202-205-3405
Molding....Rocks, Michael CUSTOMS 212-466-5669
Moldings, wooden....Ruggles, Fred USITC 202-205-3325
Molecular Biology....Staff NIGMS 301-496-7301
Molecular Biology....Davies, David R. FAES 301-496-4295
Molecular Genetics....Staff NIGMS 301-496-7301
Molecular Hematology....Anderson, W. French FAES 301-496-5844
Molecular Immunogenetics and Vaccine Research....Berzofsky, Jay A. FAES 301-496-6874
Molecular Pharmacology....Kohn, Kurt W. FAES 301-496-1924
Molybdenum....Cammarota, David COMMERCE 202-482-0575
Molybdenum....Blossom, John MINES 202-501-9435
Molybdenum....DeSapio, Vincent USITC 202-205-3435
Molybdenum compounds....Greenblatt, Jack USITC 202-205-3353
Monaco....Staff Cnty State 202-647-2633
Mongolia....Matheson, Jenell Cnty Commerce 202-482-2462
Mongolia....Swanson, Alan Peace Corps 202-606-3040
Mongolia....Huston, Christine Peace Corps 202-606-3040
Mongolia....Staff Cnty State 202-647-6300
Mongolia/Minerals....Wu, John Cnty Mines 202-501-9697
Mongolism (Down Syndrome)....Staff NICHD 301-496-5133
Monitoring Stations, Protection from Interference....Staff FCC 202-632-7593
Monitoring Telephone Service....Staff FCC 202-632-5550
Monofilaments, manmade....Sweet, Mary Elizabeth USITC 202-205-3455
Mononucleosis....Staff NIAID 301-496-5717
Monorails....Wiening, Mary COMMERCE 202-482-4708
Monserrat/Minerals....Torres, Ivette Cnty Mines 202-501-9680
Monosodium glutamate....Land, Eric USITC 202-205-3349
Monthly Labor Review,Exec. Ed., Public & Spec Stud....Fisher, Robert W. LABOR 202-606-5903
Monthly Product Announcement....Baker, Bernice L. CENSUS 301-763-1584
Montserrat....Brooks, Michelle Cnty Commerce 202-482-2527
Moon Exploration....Keegan, Sarah NASA 703-271-5591
Morocco....Clement, Claude/Cerone, Chris Cnty Commerce 202-482-2527
Morocco....DiMeo, Pam Peace Corps 202-606-3196
Morocco....Schildwachter, Christy Peace Corps 202-606-3196
Morocco (Rabat)....Staff Cnty State 202-647-4675
Morocco/Minerals....Dolley, Thomas Cnty Mines 202-501-9690
Mortality Rates (Cancer)....Staff NCI 301-496-5583
Mortality Statistics....Rosenbery, Harry CDC 301-436-8884
Mortgage Backed Securities....Lang, Dawn M. CFT 312-353-9018
Motion Pictures....Seigmund, John COMMERCE 202-482-4781
Motion pictures....R-Archila, Laura USITC 202-205-3411
Motor Carrier....Staff FCC 717-337-1212
Motor Fuels, Only, Avg. Ret. Prices and Indexes....Chelena, Joseph LABOR 202-606-6982
Motor Neuron Disease....Staff NINDS 301-496-5751
Motor Vehicles....Warner, Albert T. COMMERCE 202-482-0669
Motor Vehicles Auto Ind. Affairs....Gaines, Robin COMMERCE 202-482-0669
Motor oil....Foreso, Cynthia USITC 202-205-3348
Motor transportation services....Lahey, Kathleen USITC 202-205-3409
Motor vehicles: armored vehicles....Kolberg, Mary USITC 202-205-3401
Motor vehicles: buses....Hagey, Michael USITC 202-205-3392
Motor vehicles: fork-lift/self-propelled trucks....Hagey, Michael USITC 202-205-3392
Motor vehicles: passenger autos....Hagey, Michael USITC 202-205-3392
Motor vehicles: snowmobiles....Kolberg, Mary USITC 202-205-3401
Motor vehicles: tractors, extruck tractors....Vacant USITC 202-205-3380
Motor vehicles: trucks (includes truck tractors)....Hagey, Michael USITC 202-205-3392
Motorcycles....Vanderwolf, John COMMERCE 202-482-0348
Motorcycles....Desoucey, Robert CUSTOMS 212-466-5667
Motorcycles....Murphy, Mary USITC 202-205-3401
Motors....Smyth, James CUSTOMS 212-466-2084
Motors, Elect....Whitley, Richard A. COMMERCE 202-482-0682
Motors: electric....Cutchin, John USITC 202-205-3396
Motors: non-electric....Andersen, Peder USITC 202-205-3388
Moya-Moya Disease....Staff NINDS 301-496-5751
Mozambique....Holm-Olsen, Finn Cnty Commerce 202-482-5148
Mozambique (Maputo)....Staff Cnty State 202-647-8252
Mozambique/Minerals....van Oss, Hendrik Cnty Mines 202-501-9687
Mucopolysaccharidosis....Staff NIAMS 301-496-8188
Mufflers (apparel)....Jones, Jackie USITC 202-205-3466

Mufflers (apparel)....Hamey, Amy USITC 202-205-3465
Multi-Infarct Dementia....Staff NIA 301-496-1752
Multi-Infarct Dementia....Staff NINDS 301-496-5751
Multifactor Productivity, Labor Composition, Hrs.....Rosenblum, Larry LABOR 202-606-5606
Multifamily Housing....Staff HUD 202-708-2495
Multilateral trade negotiations....Lavoral, Warren US Trade Rep 202-395-3324
Multiple Basal Cell Carcinoma....Staff NCI 301-496-5583
Multiple Myeloma....Staff NCI 301-496-5583
Multiple Risk Factor Intervention Trial....Staff NHLBI 301-496-4236
Multiple Sclerosis....Staff NINDS 301-496-5751
Multiple Sclerosis....Staff NIDCD 301-496-7243
Multiple Warts....Staff NCI 301-496-5583
Multipoint Distribution Service....Staff FCC 202-634-1706
Mumps....Staff NIAID 301-496-5717
Muni Bonds with options....SIA Manasses CFT 312-35-39027
Municipal Solid Waste Management....Staff EPA 202-260-9872
Municipal Solid Waste Management - Combustion....Staff EPA 202-260-4745
Municipal Waste....Gross, Thomas J. NEIC 202-586-9497
Murmurs (Heart)....Staff NHLBI 301-496-4236
Muscle Disease....Staff NINDS 301-496-5751
Muscle Disease....Staff NIAMS 301-496-8188
Muscle Wasting....Staff NINDS 301-496-5751
Muscle Wasting....Staff NIAMS 301-496-8188
Muscular Dystrophy....Staff NINDS 301-496-5751
Muscular Fatigue....Staff NINDS 301-496-5751
Musculoskeletal Fitness....Staff NIAMS 301-496-8188
Museums and Historic Orgns. Projects....Staff NEH 202-606-8284
Mushrooms....McCarty, Timothy USITC 202-205-3324
Music....Siegmund, John COMMERCE 202-482-4781
Music....Handy, D. Antoinette NEA 202-682-5445
Musical Instruments....Harris, John COMMERCE 202-482-0348
Musical Instruments....Kalkines, George CUSTOMS 212-466-5794
Musical instruments, accessories....Witherspoon, Ricardo USITC 202-205-3489
Musical instruments, parts....Witherspoon, Ricardo USITC 202-205-3489
Musk, grained or in pods....Land, Eric USITC 202-205-3349
Mutual Funds....Muir, S. Cassin COMMERCE 202-482-0343
Myasthenia Gravis....Staff NINDS 301-496-5751
Mycoplasma....Staff NIAID 301-496-5717
Mycosis Fungoides....Staff NCI 301-496-5583
Mycotoxins....Staff NIEHS 919-541-3345
Myelodysplastic Syndromes....Staff NHLBI 301-496-4236
Myelofibrosis....Staff NHLBI 301-496-4236
Myelofibrosis....Staff NCI 301-496-5583
Myeloma....Staff NCI 301-496-5583
Myocardial Infarction....Staff NHLBI 301-496-4236
Myocardium....Staff NHLBI 301-496-4236
Myoclonus....Staff NINDS 301-496-5751
Myofascial Pain Syndrome....Staff NIAMS 301-496-8188
Myopia....Staff NEI 301-496-5248
Myositis....Staff NIAMS 301-496-8188
Myositis....Staff NINDS 301-496-5751
Myositis Ossificans....Staff NIAMS 301-496-8188
Myotonia Atrophica....Staff NINDS 301-496-5751
Myotonia Atrophica....Staff NIAMS 301-496-8188
Myotonia Congenita....Staff NINDS 301-496-5751
Myotonia Congenita....Staff NIAMS 301-496-8188
Myotonia Congenita....Staff NICHD 301-496-5133
Myotonia Dystrophica....Staff NINDS 301-496-5751
Myths on Aging....Staff NIA 301-496-1752

N

NASA Engineering....Peto, Mary Ann NASA 216-433-2902
NASA Industrial Applications Centers....Selby, Barbar NASA 703-557-5609
NASA Mission Safety....Brown, Dwayne C. NASA 202-453-8956
NASA Science and Engineering Labs....Sahli, Jim NASA 205-544-6528
NASA Scientific Balloon Program....Koehler, Keith NASA 804-824-1579
NASA Sounding Rocket Program....Koehler, Keigh NASA 804-824-1579
NASA Tethered Satellite....Berg, Jerry NASA 205-544-6540
NATO (North Atlantic Treaty Organization)....Staff Cnty State 202-647-1622
Nails....Yost, Charles USITC 202-205-3442
Namibia....Holm-Olsen, Finn Cnty Commerce 202-482-4228
Namibia....Grimmett, Michael Peace Corps 202-606-3246
Namibia....Woodfork, Jacqueline Peace Corps 202-606-3247
Namibia....Staff Cnty State 202-647-8252

Namibia/Minerals....Heydari, Michael Cnty Mines 202-501-9688
Naphtha....Foreso, Cynthia USITC 202-205-3348
Naphthalene (refined)....Matusik, Ed USITC 202-205-3356
Napkins, cloth....Sweet, Mary Elizabeth USITC 202-205-3455
Narcolepsy....Staff NINDS 301-496-5751
Narrow fabrics....Shelton, Linda USITC 202-205-3457
Nat'l, Input-Output Tables, Computer Tapes, Disks & Print....Carter, Esther M. ECONOMIC 202-523-0792
Nat'l, Fed. Govt Defense Purchases of Goods & Services....Galbraith, Karl D. ECONOMIC 202-523-3472
Nat'l, State & Local Govt, Purchases of Goods & Services.....Peters, Donald L. ECONOMIC 202-523-0726
Nat'l, Fed. Govt Nondefense Purchases-Goods & Services....Mangan, Robert ECONOMIC 202-523-5017
Nat'l, Input-Output Tables, Goods-Producing Industry....Bonds, Belinda ECONOMIC 202-523-0843
Nat'l, Input-Output Tables, Services Producing Industry....Horowitz, Karen ECONOMIC 202-523-3505
Natality Statistics....Heuser, Robert CDC 301-436-8954
Natality, Marriage and Divorce Statistics....Heuser, Robert CDC 301-436-8954
National Air Data Branch....Staff EPA 919-541-5583
National Air Toxic Information Clearinghouse....Staff EPA 919-541-0850
National Cancer Program....Staff NCI 301-496-5583
National Cholesterol Education Program....Staff NHLBI 301-496-0554
National Crime Survey....DeBarry, Marshall Justice Stat 202-307-0775
National Crime Survey....Rand, Michael Justice Stat 202-616-3494
National Crime Survey....Taylor, Bruce Justice Stat 202-616-3498
National Crime Survey - Data Tapes....DeBerry, Marshall Justice Stat 202-307-0775
National Crime Survey - Data Tapes....Rand, Michael Justice Stat 202-616-3494
National Crime Survey - Data Tapes....Taylor, Bruce Justice Stat 202-616-3498
National Crime Survey - General....Klaus, Patsy Justice Stat 202-307-0776
National Crime Survey - General....Rand, Michael Justice Stat 202-616-3494
National Crime Survey - General....Taylor, Bruce Justice Stat 202-616-3498
National Crime Survey - General....DeBerry, Marshall Justice Stat 202-307-0775
National Crime Survey - General....Dodge, Richard Justice Stat 202-616-3485
National Crime Survey - General....Harlow, Caroline Justice Stat 202-307-0757
National Crime Survey - Redesign....Taylor, Bruce Justice Stat 202-616-3498
National Crime Survey - Redesign....Dodge, Richard Justice Stat 202-616-3485
National Crime Survey - Supplements....Kindermann, Charles Justice Stat 202-616-3489
National Environmental Policy Act....Staff FCC 202-632-6990
National Environmental Policy Act (NEPA)....Borgstrom, Carol NEIC 202-586-4600
National Establishment Survey, Empl/Unempl....Seifert, Mary Lee LABOR 202-606-6552
National Establishment Survey, Indust. Classif. E/Un....Getz, Patricia LABOR 202-606-6521
National Fish Hatchery System....Staff FWS 703-358-1715
National Health Service Corps....Mehuron, Charlotte HRSA 201-443-3376
National High Blood Pressure Education Program....Staff NHLBI 301-496-0554
National Hunting and Fishing Survey....Staff FWS 703-358-2156
National Income and Wealth, Auto Output....McCully, Clint ECONOMIC 202-523-0819
National Income and Wealth, Chief....Donahoe, Gerald F. ECONOMIC 202-523-0669
National Pesticides Survey....Staff EPA 202-260-7176
National Pesticides Telecommunications Network....Staff EPA 800-858-7378
National Pollutant Discharge Elimination System....Staff EPA 703-821-4660
National Projections, States & Metro. Areas....Johnson, Kenneth P. ECONOMIC 202-523-0971
National Radon Hotline....Staff EPA 800-767-7236
National Services Information Centers....Johnson, Sam CENSUS 301-763-1384
National, Business Cycle Indicators....Green, George R. ECONOMIC 202-523-0800
National, Capital Consumption....John C. Musgrave ECONOMIC 202-523-0837
National, Capital Expenditures....Cartwright, David W. ECONOMIC 202-523-0791
National, Capital Stock....Musgrave, John C. NATIONAL 101-523-0837
National, Composite Indexes....Robinson, Charles S. ECONOMIC 202-523-0800
National, Computer Price Index....Won, Gregory U. ECONOMIC 202-523-5421
National, Construction....Robinson, Brooks B. ECONOMIC 202-523-0592
National, Corporate Profits and Taxes....Petrick, Kenneth A. ECONOMIC 202-523-0888
National, Cyclically-Adjusted Budget....Michael Well ECONOMIC 202-523-3470
National, Depreciation....Musgrave, John W. ECONOMIC 202-523-0837
National, Disposable Personal Income....Cybert, Pauline M. ECONOMIC

202-523-0832

National, Dividends....Petrick, Kenneth A. ECONOMIC 202-523-0888

National, Employee Benefit Plans....Sensenig, Arthur L. ECONOMIC
202-523-0809

National, Employee Compensation....Sensenig, Arthur L. ECONOMIC
202-523-0809

National, Environmental Studies....Rugledge, Gary L. ECONOMIC
202-523-0687

National, Farm Output, Product, and Income....Smith, George ECONOMIC
202-523-0821

National, Federal Govt., Contributions & Transfers....Tsehaye, Benyam
ECONOMIC 202-523-0885

National, Federal Govt., Receipts and Expenditures....Dobbs, David T.
ECONOMIC 202-523-0744

National, GNP by Industry....Mohr, Michael W. ECONOMIC 202-523-0795

National, GNP, Computer Tapes, Disks and Printouts....Blue, Eunice V.
ECONOMIC 202-523-0804

National, GNP, Current Estimates....Mannering, Virginia H. ECONOMIC
202-523-0824

National, Gross Private Domestic Investment....Cartwright, David W.
ECONOMIC 202-523-0791

National, Input-Output Annual Tables....Planting, Mark A. ECONOMIC
202-523-0867

National, Input-Output, Benchmark Tables....Maley, Leo C. ECONOMIC
202-523-0683

National, Interest Income and Payments....Weadock, Teresa L. ECONOMIC
202-523-0833

National, Inventories....Baldwin, Steven ECONOMIC 202-523-0784

National, Inventory/Sales Ratios....Stiller, Jean M. ECONOMIC 202-523-6585

National, Methodology....Beckman, Barry A. ECONOMIC 202-523-0800

National, National Income....Seskin, Eugene P. ECONOMIC 202-523-0848

National, Net Exports....Ehemann, Christian ECONOMIC 202-523-0699

National, Output Measures....Ehemann, Christian ECONOMIC 202-523-0669

National, Personal Consumpt. Expenditures, Prices....McCully, Clint
ECONOMIC 202-523-0819

National, Personal Consumption Expend, Other Goods....Key, Greg
ECONOMIC 202-523-0778

National, Personal Consumption Expend., Services....McCully, Clint
ECONOMIC 202-523-0819

National, Personal Consumption Expenditures....McCully, Cling ECONOMIC
202-523-0819

National, Personal Consumption Expenditures, Autos....Johnson, Everette P.
ECONOMIC 202-523-0807

National, Personal Income....Cypert, Pauline M. ECONOMIC 202-523-0832

National, Plant and Equipment Expenditures....Crawford, Jeffrey W.
ECONOMIC 202-523-0782

National, Pollution Abatement & Control Spending....Rutledge, Gary L.
ECONOMIC 202-523-0687

National, Price Measures (Fixed-Weighted)....Herman, Shelby A. ECONOMIC
202-523-0828

National, Producers' Durable Equipment....Crawford, Jeffrey W. ECONOMIC
202-523-0782

National, Proprietors' Income, Nonfarm....Abney, Willie J. ECONOMIC
202-523-0811

National, Rental Income....Smith, George ECONOMIC 202-523-0821

National, Residential Construction....Robinson, Brooks, B. ECONOMIC
202-523-0592

National, Savings....Donahoe, Gerald F. ECONOMIC 202-523-0669

National, State & Local Govt., Receipts & Expend.....Sullivan, David F.
ECONOMIC 202-523-0725

National, Statistical Series....Young, Mary D. ECONOMIC 202-523-0500

National, Structures....Robinson, Brooks B. ECONOMIC 202-523-0592

National, UN and OCED System of National Accounts....Honsa, Jeanette M.
ECONOMIC 202-523-0839

National, Wages and Salaries....Sensenig, Arthur L. ECONOMIC 202-523-0809

National, Wealth Estimates....Musgrave, John C. ECONOMIC 202-523-0837

Natural Gas....Gillett, Tom COMMERCE 202-482-1466

Natural Gas....Tomaszewski, Clifford NEIC 202-586-9482

Natural Gas....Altman, Paula NEIC 202-586-8800

Natural Gas....Cogan, Jonathan NEIC 202-586-8800

Natural gas....Land, Eric USITC 202-205-3349

Natural gas liquids (NGL)....Land, Eric USITC 202-205-3349

Natural pearls....Witherspoon, Ricardo USITC 202-205-3489

Natural rubber....Misurelli, Denby USITC 202-205-3362

Natural, Synthetic Rubber....Hurt, William COMMERCE 202-482-0128

Nauru....Staff Cnty State 202-647-3546

Nauru/Minerals....Lyday, Travis Cnty Mines 202-501-9695

Naval Reactor Propulsion....Staff NEIC 301-903-3465

Navigation, Air or Water....Staff FCC 202-632-7175

Navigational instruments....Shetty, Sundar USITC 202-205-3486

Navy special fuel oil....Foreso, Cynthia USITC 202-205-3348

Nearsightedness....Staff NEI 301-496-5248

Neckties....Linkins, Linda USITC 202-205-3469

Nemaline Myopathy (Floppy Baby)....Staff NINDS 301-496-5751

Neonatal Adaptation....Staff NICHD 301-496-5133

Neonatal Asphyxia....Staff NINDS 301-496-5751

Neoplasms (Trophoblastic)....Staff NCI 301-496-5583

Nepal....Gilman, Timothy Cnty Commerce 202-482-2954

Nepal....Ordonez, Miguel Peace Corps 202-606-3118

Nepal (Kathmandu)....Staff Cnty State 202-647-1450

Nepal/Minerals....Vacant Cnty Mines 202-501-9694

Nepheline Syenite....Potter, Michael J. MINES 202-501-9387

Nephritis....Staff NIDDK 301-496-3583

Nephrocalcinosis....Staff NIDDK 301-496-3583

Nephrolithiasis....Staff NIDDK 301-496-3583

Nephrotic Syndrome....Staff NIDDK 301-496-3583

Nerve Damage....Staff NINDS 301-496-5751

Netherlands....Bensimon, Simon Cnty Commerce 202-482-5401

Netherlands (The Hague)....Staff Cnty State 202-647-6664

Netherlands Antilles....Brooks, Michelle Cnty Commerce 202-482-2527

Netherlands Antilles (Curacao)....Staff Cnty State 202-647-2620

Netherlands Antilles/Minerals....Torres, Ivette Cnty Mines 202-501-9680

Netherlands/Minerals....Rabchevsky, George Cnty Mines 202-501-9672

Nettings: fish....Cook, Lee USITC 202-205-3471

Nettings: other....Sweet, Mary Elizabeth USITC 202-205-3455

Neural Stimulation....Staff NINDS 301-496-5751

Neural Stimulation....Staff NIDCD 301-496-7243

Neural Tube Defects....Staff NINDS 301-496-5751

Neural Tube Defects....Staff NICHD 301-496-5133

Neuralgia....Staff NINDS 301-496-5751

Neuritis (Peripheral Neuropathy)....Staff NINDS 301-496-5751

Neuro-Ophthalmology....Staff NEI 301-496-5248

Neuroaxonal Dystrophy....Staff NINDS 301-496-5751

Neuroblastoma....Staff NEI 301-496-5248

Neuroendocrinology....Bondy, Caroline FAES 301-496-6664

Neurofibromatosis (von Recklinghausen's)....Staff NINDS 301-496-5751

Neurofibromatosis (von Recklinghausen's)....Staff NIDCD 301-496-7243

Neurogenic Arthropathy....Staff NINDS 301-496-5751

Neurogenic Disability (Mouth and Pharynx)....Staff NIDR 301-496-4261

Neuroimaging....Alger, Jeffry R. FAES 301-496-6801

Neurologic Disease....Staff NINDS 301-496-5751

Neurological Disorders & Stroke, Nat'l Inst. of....Emr, Marian NIH
301-496-5924

Neurology....Grafman, Jordan FAES 301-496-0220

Neuromuscular Disease....Staff NINDS 301-496-5751

Neuromyopathies....Staff NINDS 301-496-5751

Neuromyositis....Staff NINDS 301-496-5751

Neuronal Ceroid Lupofuscinoses....Staff NINDS 301-496-5751

Neuropathies....Staff NINDS 301-496-5751

Neuropharmacology....Staff NINDS 301-496-5751

Neurosclerosis....Staff NINDS 301-496-5751

Neurosyphilis....Staff NINDS 301-496-5751

New Caledonia....Staff Cnty State 202-647-3546

New Caledonia/Minerals....Lyday, Travis Cnty Mines 202-501-9695

New Zealand....Bouck, Gary (Bus.)/Golike, William (Policy) Cnty Commerce
202-482-3647

New Zealand (Wellington)....Staff Cnty State 202-647-9691

New Zealand/Minerals....Lyday, Travis Cnty Mines 202-501-9695

Newborn....Staff NICHD 301-496-5133

News Gathering and Publishing....Staff FCC 717-337-1212

Newspaper management....Smith, Michael V. UMD 301-405-2427

Newspapers....Bratland, Rose Marie COMMERCE 202-482-0380

Newsprint....Stahmer, Carsten USITC 202-205-3321

Nicaragua....Subrin, Laura Cnty Commerce 202-482-2527

Nicaragua....Brown, Brenda L. Peace Corps 202-606-3624

Nicaragua (Managua)....Staff Cnty State 202-647-4975

Nicaragua/Minerals....Mobbs, Philip Cnty Mines 202-501-9679

Nickel....Kuck, Peter H. MINES 202-501-9436

Nickel....Lundy, David USITC 202-205-3439

Nickel Products....Presbury, Graylin COMMERCE 202-482-0575

Nickel compounds....Greenblatt, Jack USITC 202-205-3353

Niemann-Pick Disease....Staff NINDS 301-496-5751

Niemann-Pick Disease....Staff NEI 301-496-5248

Niger....Michelini, Philip Cnty Commerce 202-482-4388

Niger....Hanson, Julie Peace Corps 202-606-3004
Niger (Niamey)....Staff Cnty State 202-647-3066
Niger/Minerals....Izon, David Cnty Mines 202-501-9692
Nigeria....Henke, Degra Cnty Commerce 202-482-4228
Nigeria....McCormick, Michael L. Peace Corps 202-606-3644
Nigeria....Herring, Debra Peace Corps 202-606-3644
Nigeria (Abuja)....Staff Cnty State 202-647-3395
Nigeria/Minerals....Izon, David Cnty Mines 202-501-9692
Night Blindness....Staff NEI 301-496-5248
Nightwear....DeGaetano, Angela CUSTOMS 212-466-5540
Nitric acid....Trainor, Cynthia USITC 202-205-3354
Nitrites....Michels, David USITC 202-205-3352
Nitrogen....Cantrell, Raymond MINES 202-501-9581
Nitrogen....Conant, Kenneth USITC 202-205-3346
Nitrogen Compounds...Joseph, Stephanie CUSTOMS 212-466-5768
Nitrogenous fertilizers....Trainor, Cynthia USITC 202-205-3354
Nitrosamines....Staff NCI 301-496-5583
Nobel Prize....Staff NIGMS 301-496-7301
Noise....Staff NIDCD 301-496-7243
Noise....Staff NINDS 301-496-5751
Noise Information....Staff EPA 202-260-1089
Non-Game Wildlife....Staff FWS 703-358-1718
Non-Hodgkins Malignant Lymphoma....Staff NCI 301-496-5583
Non-Toxic Shot....Staff FWS 703-358-1773
Non-alcoholic Beverages....Kenney, Cornelius COMMERCE 202-482-2428
Non-benzenoid resins....Misurelli, Denby USITC 202-205-3362
Non-electric Machinery, Prices and Living Cond.....Dickerson, Bryant LABOR 202-606-7734
Non-electric motors and engines....Andersen, Peder USITC 202-205-3388
NonFarm Proprietors' Income & Employment....Levine, Bruce ECONOMIC 202-254-6634
Noncurrent Carrying Wiring Devices....Whitley, Richard A. COMMERCE 202-482-0682
Nondurable Goods....Simon, Leslie B. COMMERCE 202-482-0341
Nonenumerated products....Spalding, Josephine USITC 202-205-3498
Nonferrous Foundries....Duggan, Brian COMMERCE 202-482-0610
Nonferrous Metals....Marion, James J. COMMERCE 202-482-0575
Noninfectious Chemical Agents (Eff. on Human Hea.)....Staff NIEHS 919-541-3345
Nonmetallic Minerals Nec....Manion, James J. COMMERCE 202-482-0575
Nonresidential Constr (Domestic)....MacAuley, Patrick COMMERCE 202-482-0132
Norwalk Agent....Staff NIAID 301-496-5717
Norway....Devlin, James Cnty Commerce 202-482-4414
Norway (Oslo)....Staff Cnty State 202-647-5669
Norway/Minerals....Buck, Donald E. Cnty Mines 202-501-9670
Nosebleed (Epistaxis)....Staff NHLBI 301-496-4236
Nuclear (Heart Pacemaker)....Staff NHLBI 301-496-4236
Nuclear Energy....Greenblatt, Jack USITC 202-205-3353
Nuclear Energy....Staff NEIC 301-903-5447
Nuclear Energy Statistics....Geidl, John NEIC 202-254-5570
Nuclear Facility Safety....Kornack, Wallace NEIC 202-586-4400
Nuclear Fusion....Davies, Anne NEIC 301-903-4941
Nuclear Magnetic Resonance....Becker, Edwin D. FAES 301-496-1024
Nuclear Magnetic Resonance Spectrometers....Staff NCRR 301-496-5411
Nuclear Medicine Department....Staff CC 301-496-6455
Nuclear Physics....Hess, Wilmot NEIC 301-903-3713
Nuclear Power Plants....Werner, Thomas NEIC 301-903-3773
Nuclear Power Plants, Major Proj.....Dollison, Robert COMMERCE 202-482-2733
Nuclear Power Projects....Staff FWS 703-358-2183
Nuclear Safety Issues....Staff NEIC 301-903-3465
Nuclear Safety Regulations....Blush, Steven NEIC 202-586-2407
Nuclear Weapons Stockpiles....Mistretta, Michael J. NEIC 301-903-6699
Number Research, Price and Index, Pr/Lv. Cond....Zieschang, Kimberly LABOR 202-606-6573
Numerical Contrls. Fr. Mach. Tools....McGibbon, Patrick COMMERCE 202-482-0314
Numerical controls....Malison, Andrew USITC 202-205-3391
Nursing Homes....Staff NIA 301-496-1752
Nursing Homes....Hardy, Robert HCFA 202-690-6145
Nursing Homes and Care....Staff HRSA/DPCS 301-443-2270
Nursing Interventions....Staff NCNR 301-496-0526
Nursing Research, National Center for....Pollin, Geraldine NIH 301-496-0207
Nursing Research, National Center for....McBride, Esther NIH 301-496-0207
Nursing Systems....Staff NCNR 301-496-0526

Nutrition....Staff NICHD 301-496-5133
Nutrition....Staff HRSA/DMCH 301-443-4026
Nutrition....Staff NIDDK 301-496-3583
Nutrition....Meyers, Linda ASH 202-205-9007
Nutrition....Trowbridge, Frederick L. CDC 404-488-5090
Nutrition....Hubbard, Van S. FAES 301-496-7823
Nutrition....Meyers, Linda ASH 202-205-9007
Nutrition Research Coordination....Staff OD 301-496-9281
Nutrition and Aging....Staff NIA 301-496-1752
Nutrition, Maternal and Child....Wong, Faye L. CDC 404-488-5099
Nutritional Statistics....Looker, Ann CDC 301-436-7072
Nuts....Conte, Ralph CUSTOMS 212-466-5759
Nuts, Bolts, Washers....Reise, Richard COMMERCE 202-482-3489
Nuts, Edible...Janis, William V. COMMERCE 202-482-2250
Nuts, Edible....Burket, Stephen USITC 202-205-3318
Nystagmus....Staff NEI 301-496-5248

O

Oakum....Cook, Lee USITC 202-205-3471
Oats with options....Gore, Philip CFT 312-886-3044
Obesity....Staff NIDDK 301-496-3583
Obesity....Staff NIMH 301-496-4515
Obesity in Children....Staff NICHD 301-496-5133
Obstruction Markings--Antenna....Staff FCC 202-632-7521
Occupation Statistics....Priebe, John/Masumura, Wilfred CENSUS 301-763-8574
Occupational Data/Current Survey, Empl/Unempl.St.....Staff LABOR 202-606-6378
Occupational Diseases....Staff CDC/NIOSH 404-639-3286
Occupational Lung Disease....Staff NHLBI 301-496-4236
Occupational Medicine....Pettengill, Harry NEIC 301-903-7030
Occupational Mobility, Occup. Data, Empl/Unempl. Data....Rones, Philip LABOR 202-606-6378
Occupational Outlook Handbook, Employment Proj.....Pilot, Michael LABOR 202-606-5703
Occupational Outlook Quarterly, Empl. Proj.....Fountain, Melvin LABOR 202-606-5707
Occupational Projections....Rosenthal, Neal LABOR 202-606-5701
Occupational Safety....Gibbs, Roy NEIC 301-903-4343
Occupational Safety & Health, National Institute for....Berreth, Don CDC 404-639-3286
Occupational Safety and Health....Millar, J. Donald CDC 404-639-3771
Ocean Biological Experiments....Koehler, Keith NASA 802-824-1579
Ocean Energy....Loose, Ronald NEIC 202-586-8086
Ocean Physics Research....Koehler, Keith NASA 804-824-1579
Ocean Shipping....Johnson, William C. COMMERCE 202-482-5012
Ocean Thermal Energy....Loose, Ronald NEIC 202-586-8086
Oceans and Coastal Protection Division....Staff EPA 202-260-1952
Oceans and Watersheds....Staff EPA 202-260-7166
Ocular Hypertension....Staff NEI 301-496-5248
Oculocraniosomatic Neuromuscular Disease....Staff NINDS 301-496-5751
Odor....Staff NINDS 301-496-5751
Odor....Staff NIDCD 301-496-7243
Odoriferous Compounds....Joseph, Stephanie CUSTOMS 212-466-5768
Odoriferous or aromatic substances....Land, Eric USITC 202-205-3349
Off-Track Betting....Staff FCC 202-632-7048
Off-the-Air Pickup....Staff FCC 202-634-1706
Offal....Ludwick, David USITC 202-205-3329
Offender-based Transaction Statistics....Manson, Donald Justice Stat 202-616-3491
Offender-based Transaction Statistics....Langan, Patrick Justice Stat 202-616-3490
Offenders....Baunach, Phyllis Jo Justice Stat 202-307-0361
Offenders....Greenfeld, Lawrence Justice Stat 202-616-3281
Offenders....Stephan, James Justice Stat 202-616-7273
Offenders....Beck, Allen Justice Stat 202-616-3277
Offenders - Federal....Kaplan, Carol Justice Stat 202-307-0759
Offenders, Female....Baunach, Phyllis Jo Justice Stat 202-307-0361
Offenders, Female - Federal....Kaplan, Carol Justice Stat 202-307-0759
Office copying machines....Baker, Scott USITC 202-205-3386
Office machines....Baker, Scott USITC 202-205-3386
Office of Congressional Relations....Hall, Dorian J. FTC 202-326-2186
Office of Congressional Relations....Leslie, Louise M. FTC 202-326-2195
Office of Congressional Relations....Prendergast, William B. FTC 202-326-2195
Office of Consumer and Competition Advocacy....Laney, Veronica FTC 202-326-2249

Office of Consumer and Competition Advocacy....Wise, Michael O. FTC 202-326-3444

Office of Inspector General....Treitsch, Dennis R. FTC 202-326-2581

Office of Inspector General....Trzeciak, Adam R. FTC 202-326-2435

Office of Inspector General....Zirkel, Frederick J. FTC 202-326-2800

Office of Inspector General....Williams, Joyce E. FTC 202-326-2313

Office of Public Affairs....Elder, Donald FTC 202-326-2181

Office of Public Affairs....Jansen, Bonnie FTC 202-326-2161

Office of Public Affairs....Leslie, John T. FTC 202-326-2178

Office of Public Affairs....Mack, Brenda A. FTC 202-326-2182

Office of Public Affairs....Shaipro, Howard FTC 202-326-2176

Office of the Commissioner....Azcuenaga, Mary L. FTC 202-326-2145

Office of the General Counsel....Coleman, Jill E. FTC 202-326-2414

Office of the General Counsel....Cox, John H. FTC 202-326-2568

Office of the General Counsel....Crockett, Elaine FTC 202-326-2453

Office of the General Counsel....Cummins, Jerold D. FTC 202-326-2471

Office of the General Counsel....Dawson, Rachel Miller FTC 202-326-2463

Office of the General Counsel....DeLuca, Nancy F. FCC 202-326-2440

Office of the General Counsel....DeMille-Wagman, Lawrence FTC 202-326-2448

Office of the General Counsel....Dooley, Frederick E. FTC 202-326-2443

Office of the General Counsel....DuPree, Scott E. FTC 202-326-2479

Office of the General Counsel....Etheridge, Monica M. FTC 202-326-2666

Office of the General Counsel....Fields, Kwasi A. FTC 202-326-2452

Office of the General Counsel....Freedman, Bruce G. FTC 202-326-2464

Office of the General Counsel....Golden, William P. FTC 202-326-2494

Office of the General Counsel....Goosby, Consuella M. FTC 202-326-2486

Office of the General Counsel....Greenfield, Gary M. FTC 202-326-2753

Office of the General Counsel....Hurwitz, James D. FTC 202-326-2847

Office of the General Counsel....Isenstadt, Ernest J. FTC 202-326-2473

Office of the General Counsel....Kane, Maryanne S. FTC 202-326-2450

Office of the General Counsel....Kaye, Ira S. FTC 202-326-2426

Office of the General Counsel....Levine, Joanne L. FTC 202-326-2474

Office of the General Counsel....Lewis, Tina M. FTC 202-326-2465

Office of the General Counsel....Melman, Leslie R. FTC 202-326-2478

Office of the General Counsel....Miller, Rachel Dawson FTC 202-326-2463

Office of the General Counsel....Murphy, John T. FTC 202-326-2457

Office of the General Counsel....Neal, Valary FTC 202-326-2066

Office of the General Counsel....Orlans, Melvin H. FTC 202-326-2475

Office of the General Counsel....Pahl, Thomas B. FTC 202-326-2115

Office of the General Counsel....Polydor, Cheryl L. FTC 202-326-2279

Office of the General Counsel....Pressley, Doris P. FTC 202-326-2916

Office of the General Counsel....Rittner, Kathleen FTC 202-326-2498

Office of the General Counsel....Shaffer, Jay C. FTC 202-326-2557

Office of the General Counsel....Shonka, David C. FTC 202-326-2436

Office of the General Counsel....Spears, James M. FTC 202-326-2480

Office of the General Counsel....Tang, Alexander FTC 202-326-2447

Office of the General Counsel....Wagman, Lawrence FTC 202-326-2448

Office of the General Counsel....Worthy, Betty J. FTC 202-326-2459

Office of the General Counsel....White, Christian S. FTC 202-326-2476

Office of the General Counsel....Winerman, Marc L. FTC 202-326-2451

Office of the Secretary....Ashe, Maurice FTC 202-326-2516

Office of the Secretary....Berman, Benjamin I. FTC 202-326-2960

Office of the Secretary....Carson, Diane B. FTC 202-326-2501

Office of the Secretary....Clark, Donald S. FTC 202-326-2514

Office of the Secretary....Dickerson, Eunice L. FTC 202-326-3347

Office of the Secretary....Foster, Elizabeth M. FTC 202-326-2187

Office of the Secretary....Liebman, Marvin FTC 202-326-2069

Office of the Secretary....Lofty, Bernita V. FTC 202-326-3117

Office of the Secretary....Parker, Shalena FTC 202-326-2512

Office of the Secretary....Pierce, Diane E. FTC 202-326-2519

Office of the Secretary....Plummer, C. Landis FTC 202-326-2520

Office of the Secretary....Reynolds, Ronald H. FTC 202-326-2521

Office of the Secretary....Tanner, Trina A. FTC 202-326-2517

Office of the Secretary....Thielen, John J. FTC 202-326-2506

Office of the Secretary....Tinker, Wallace FTC 202-326-2192

Office of the Secretary....Wood, Dolores A. FTC 202-326-2518

Office of the Secretary....Williams, Linda A. FTC 202-326-2515

Offshore Radio Telecommunications Service....Staff FCC 202-653-5560

Oil & Gas (Fuels Only)....Gillett, Tom COMMERCE 202-482-1466

Oil & Gas Development & Refining, Maj. Proj.....Bell, Richard COMMERCE 202-482-2460

Oil Field Machinery....McDonald, Edward COMMERCE 202-482-0680

Oil Field Machinery, Trade Promo.....Zanetakos, George COMMERCE 202-482-0552

Oil Pollution....Staff EPA 202-260-6862

Oil Shale Reserves Management....Furiga, Richard NEIC 202-586-4410

Oil Shale, Major Proj.....Bell, Richard COMMERCE 202-482-2460

Oil Spills....Staff FWS 703-358-2148

Oil Spills - Emergency Response Division....Staff EPA 202-260-6862

Oil and Gas Leasing on Fish and Wildlife Refuges....Staff FWS 703-358-2043

Oil and Gas Statistics....Peterson, Jimmie NEIC 202-586-6401

Oil and Hazardous Material Spills....Staff EPA 202-267-2675

Oil and Hazardous Material Spills Response Hotline....Staff EPA 800-424-8802

Oil, Used....Staff EPA 202-260-6261

Oil, lubricating....Foreso, Cynthia USITC 202-205-3348

Oilcloth....Cook, Lee USITC 202-205-3471

Oils, Animal and Vegetable....Maria, John CUSTOMS 212-466-5730

Oils, essential....Land, Eric USITC 202-205-3349

Oilseeds....Reeder, John USITC 202-205-3319

Oilseeds - Soybeans, Sunflowers....Kerestes, Dan Agri 202-270-9526

Oilseeds - Soybeans, Sunflowers....Hoskin, Roger Agri 202-219-0840

Oilseeds - Soybeans, Sunflowers....McCormick, Ian Agri 202-219-0840

Oilseeds - Soybeans, Sunflowers - World....Morgan, Nancy Agri 202-219-0826

Older Women....Staff NIA 301-496-1752

Older Workers, Empl/Unempl. Stats.....Rones, Philip LABOR 202-606-6378

Oleic acid....Randall, Rob USITC 202-205-3366

Oleic acid ester....Johnson, Larry USITC 202-205-3351

Oleyl alcohols....Randall, Rob USITC 202-205-3366

Olivopontocerebellar Atrophy....Staff NINDS 301-496-5751

Oman....Fitzgerald-Wilks, Kate/Thanos, Paul Cnty Commerce 202-482-2039

Oman (Muscat)....Staff Cnty State 202-647-6558

Oman/Minerals....Michalski, Bernadette Cnty Mines 202-501-9699

On Site Contractor Employees....Baxter, Robert L., II FTC 202-326-2243

On Site Contractor Employees....Cassagnol, Pascale FTC 202-326-2088

On Site Contractor Employees....Gardner, Kevin P. FTC 202-326-2243

On Site Contractor Employees....Hallman, Kevin J. FTC 202-326-2243

On Site Contractor Employees....Lathern, Ronald C. FTC 202-326-2290

On Site Contractor Employees....Saunders, Paristina FTC 202-326-2243

Onchocerciasis....Staff NEI 301-496-5248

Oncology....Staff NCI 301-496-5583

One-Way Paging and Signaling....Staff FCC 202-653-5560

Ophthalmia Neonatorum....Staff NEI 301-496-5248

Ophthalmic....Johnson, Christopher USITC 202-205-3488

Ophthalmic Congenital and Genetic Disease....Staff NEI 301-496-5248

Ophthalmology Research....Staff NEI 301-496-5248

Oppenheim's Disease (Amyotonia Congenita)....Staff NINDS 301-496-5751

Optic Atrophy....Staff NEI 301-496-5248

Optic Neuritis....Staff NEI 301-496-5248

Optical Equipment....Kiefer, Barbara CUSTOMS 212-466-5685

Optical elements....Johnson, Christopher USITC 202-205-3488

Optical goods....Johnson, Christopher USITC 202-205-3488

Optometry Research....Staff NEI 301-496-5248

Oral Cancer....Staff NIDR 301-496-4261

Oral Contraceptives....Staff NICHD 301-496-5133

Oral Health....Marianos, Donald W. CDC 404-488-4452

Oral Surgery-Intravenous Sedation....Staff NIDR 301-496-4261

Orange oil (essential oil)....Land, Eric USITC 202-205-3349

Ordering Info (Computer Software, Publications)....Customer Services Staff CENSUS 301-763-4100

Ores....Fitzgerald, John CUSTOMS 212-466-5492

Organ Donations (Eyes)....Staff NEI 301-496-5248

Organ Transplants....Mehuron, Charlotte HRSA 301-443-3376

Organ Transplants/Medicare, Medicaid Funding....Hardy, Robert HCFA 202-690-6145

Organic Chemicals....Hurt, William COMMERCE 202-482-0128

Organic acids....Michels, David USITC 202-205-3352

Organization for Economic Cooperation & Develop.....Staff Cnty State 202-647-2469

Organo-Sulfur Compounds....Winters, William CUSTOMS 212-466-5747

Organo-metallic compounds....Michels, David USITC 202-205-3352

Original Telephone & Telephone Plant Cost....Staff FCC 202-632-3772

Orotic Aciduria....Staff NIDDK 301-496-3583

Orphan Drugs....Staff NINDS 301-496-5751

Orphan Drugs....Staff OD 301-496-1454

Orphan Drugs....Staff FDA 301-443-4903

Orphan Drugs....Cruzan, Susan FDA 301-443-3285

Orthodontics....Staff NIDR 301-496-4261

Orthognathic Surgery....Staff NIDR 301-496-4261

Orthokeratology....Staff NEI 301-496-5248

Orthopedic Implants....Staff NIAMS 301-496-8188

Orthostatic Hypotension....Staff NHLBI 301-496-4236

Orthostatic Hypotension....Staff NINDS 301-496-5751

Orthotics....Staff NIAMS 301-496-8188

Ossein....Jonnard, Aimison USITC 202-205-3350

Osteitis Deformans....Staff NIAMS 301-496-8188
Osteoarthritis....Staff NIAMS 301-496-8188
Osteoarthritis....Staff NIA 301-496-1752
Osteoarthritis with Age....Staff NIA 301-496-1752
Osteogenesis....Staff NIAMS 301-496-8188
Osteogenesis Imperfecta....Staff NIAMS 301-496-8188
Osteogenesis Imperfecta....Staff NICHD 301-496-5133
Osteogenic Sarcoma....Staff NCI 301-496-5583
Osteomalacia....Staff NIAMS 301-496-8188
Osteomyelitis....Staff NIAMS 301-496-8188
Osteoporosis....Staff NIAMS 301-496-8188
Osteoporosis....Staff NICHD 301-496-5133
Osteoporosis with Age....Staff NIAMS 301-496-8188
Osteosclerosis (Osteopetrosis)....Staff NIAMS 301-496-8188
Osteosclerosis (Osteopetrosis)....Staff NICHD 301-496-5133
Ostomy....Staff NIDDK 301-496-3583
Otitis Media....Staff NINDS 301-496-5751
Otitis Media....Staff NIAID 301-496-5717
Otitis Media....Staff NIDCD 301-496-7243
Otosclerosis....Staff NINDS 301-496-5751
Otosclerosis....Staff NIDCD 301-496-7243
Outdoor Air - Cities....Staff EPA 202-260-5575
Outdoor Lightning Fixtures....Whitley, Richard A. COMMERCE 202-482-0682
Outdoor Power (Export Promo)....Beckham, Reginald COMMERCE 202-482-5478
Outer Continental Shelf....Staff FWS 703-358-2183
Ovarian Cancer....Staff NCI 301-496-5583
Ovens....Mata, Ruben USITC 202-205-3403
Oviduct....Staff NICHD 301-496-5133
Ovulation....Staff NICHD 301-496-5133
Ovum....Staff NICHD 301-496-5133
Oxalosis & Hyperoxaluria....Staff NIDDK 301-496-3583
Oxides, inorganic....Conant, Kenneth USITC 202-205-3346
Oxygen....Conant, Kenneth USITC 202-205-3346
Oxygenators (Artificial Lungs)....Staff NHLBI 301-496-4236
Ozone - Stratospheric....Staff EPA 292-233-9190

P

PCB's (Polychlorinated Biphenyl) Chem. Regulations....Staff EPA 202-260-3933
PHS Commissioned Corps....Simmons, Paul B. ASH 202-690-6867
PKU (Phenylketonuria)....Staff NICHD 301-496-5133
PMS (Premenstrual Syndrome)....Staff NICHD 301-496-5133
PMS (Premenstrual Syndrome)....Staff NIMH 301-443-4515
Pacemaker (Cardiac/Heart)....Staff NHLBI 301-496-4236
Pacemakers....Cruzan, Susan FDA 301-443-3285
Pacific Islands....Bouck, Gary (Bus.)/Golike, William (Policy) Cnty Commerce 202-482-3647
Pacific Islands (General)....Staff Cnty State 202-647-3546
Pacific/trade matters....Lake, Charles US Trade Rep 202-395-3900
Packaging machinery....Shaw, Gene COMMERCE 202-482-3494
Packaging machines....Slingerland, David USITC 202-205-3400
Paget's Disease of Bone (Osteitis Deformans)....Staff NIAMS 301-496-8188
Paging--Common Carrier....Staff FCC 202-652-0914
Paging--One Way....Staff FCC 717-337-1212
Pain....Staff NIDR 301-496-1752
Pain....Staff NINDS 301-496-5751
Pain (Cancer Related)....Staff NCI 301-496-5583
Pain (Oral-Facial)....Staff NIDR 301-496-4261
Pain and the Elderly....Staff NIA 301-496-1752
Paint....Brownchweig, Gilbert CUSTOMS 212-466-5744
Paint rollers....Burns, Gail USITC 202-205-3501
Paint sets, artist's....Johnson, Larry USITC 202-205-3351
Paintings....Mushinske, Larry CUSTOMS 212-466-5739
Paints....Johnson, Larry USITC 202-205-3351
Paints/Coatings....Prat, Raimundo COMMERCE 202-482-0128
Pajamas....Linkins, Linda USITC 202-205-3469
Pakistan....McQueen, Cheryl Cnty Commerce 202-482-2954
Pakistan....Ordonez, Miguel Peace Corps 202-606-3118
Pakistan (Islamabad)....Staff Cnty State 202-647-9823
Pakistan/Minerals....Kuo, Chin Cnty Mines 202-501-9693
Palau (Koror)....Staff Cnty State 202-647-0108
Palm oil....Reeder, John USITC 202-205-3319
Palmitic acid esters....Johnson, Larry USITC 202-205-3351
Palpitation....Staff NHLBI 301-496-4236
Palsy, Cerebral....Staff NINDS 301-496-5751

Panama....Subrin, Laura Cnty Commerce 202-482-2527
Panama....Stanton, Dan Peace Corps 202-606-3620
Panama....Tumaylle, Carol Peace Corps 202-606-3321
Panama (Panama City)....Staff Cnty State 202-647-4986
Panama/Minerals....Mobbs, Philip Cnty Mines 202-501-9679
Pancreatic Diseases....Staff NIDDK 301-496-3583
Panencephalitis....Staff NINDS 301-496-5751
Panty hose....Linkins, Linda USITC 202-205-3469
Pantyhose....DeGaetano, Angela CUSTOMS 212-466-5540
Pap Smear....Staff NCI 301-496-5583
Paper....Stanley, Gary COMMERCE 202-482-0375
Paper....Rhodes, Richard USITC 202-205-3322
Paper & Board Packaging....Smith, Leonard S. COMMERCE 202-482-0375
Paper Industries Machinery....Abrahams, Edward COMMERCE 202-482-0312
Paper and Paper Products....Abromowitz, Carl CUSTOMS 212-466-5733
Paper machines....Slingerland, David USITC 202-205-3400
Paper, products of....Stahmer, Carsten USITC 202-205-3321
Paperboard....Rhodes, Richard USITC 202-205-3322
Paperboard machines....Slingerland, David USITC 202-205-3400
Paperboard, products of....Stahmer, Carsten USITC 202-205-3321
Papermakers' felts....Cook, Lee USITC 202-205-3471
Papermaking materials....Rhodes, Richard USITC 202-205-3322
Papilloma Virus and Cancer....Staff NCI 301-496-5583
Papua New Guinea....Nagle, Douglas Peace Corps 202-606-3290
Papua New Guinea....Jefferson, Mary Peace Corps 202-606-3231
Papua New Guinea....Schell, Russell Peace Corps 202-606-3231
Papua New Guinea (Port Moresby)....Staff Cnty State 202-647-3546
Papua New Guinea/Minerals....Lyday, Travis Cnty Mines 202-501-9695
Paraguay....Mye, Randolph Cnty Commerce 202-482-1548
Paraguay....Godbey, Maria Elena Peace Corps 202-606-3198
Paraguay....Erlandson, Barbara Peace Corps 202-606-3499
Paraguay (Asuncion)....Staff Cnty State 202-647-2296
Paraguay/Minerals....Gurmendi, Alfredo Cnty Mines 202-501-9681
Paralysis Agitans....Staff NINDS 301-496-5751
Paralysis, Periodic....Staff NINDS 301-496-5751
Paramedical Training....Staff HRSA/BHPr 301-443-5794
Paramyotonia Congenita....Staff NINDS 301-496-5751
Paraplegia....Staff NINDS 301-496-5751
Parasitic Disease....Staff NIAID 301-496-5717
Parasitic Diseases....Collery, Daniel G. CDC 404-488-4050
Parasitology....Staff NIAID 301-496-5717
Parathyroid Disorders....Staff NIDDK 301-496-3583
Parachutes....Andersen, Peder USITC 202-205-3388
Parkinson's Disease....Staff NINDS 301-496-5751
Parkinson's Disease....Staff NIDCD 301-496-7243
Parkinsonism-Dementia....Staff NINDS 301-496-5751
Parole and Parolees....Huggins, M. Wayne Justice Stat 202-307-3106
Parole and Parolees....Greenfeld, Lawrence Justice Stat 202-616-3281
Paroxysmal Atrial Tachycardia (PAT)....Staff NHLBI 301-496-4236
Paroxysmal Nocturnal Hemoglobinuria....Staff NHLBI 301-496-4236
Paroxysmal Nocturnal Hemoglobinuria....Staff NIAID 301-496-5717
Pars Planitis....Staff NEI 301-496-5248
Part-time Workers, Employment/Employment....Nardone, Thomas LABOR 202-606-6378
Particle Beams....Wood, Robert NEIC 301-903-5535
Particle board....Ruggles, Fred USITC 202-205-3325
Party favors....Luther, Dennis USITC 202-205-3497
Parvovirus Infections....Staff NIAID 301-496-5717
Passenger autos, trucks, and buses....Hagey, Michael USITC 202-205-3392
Pasta...Janis, William V. COMMERCE 202-482-2250
Patents, Fish and Wildlife....Staff FWS 703-358-1730
Pathogen-Free Mice and Rats....Staff DRS/VRB 301-496-5255
Patient Dumping....Holtz, Judy IG 202-619-1142
Paving Materials, Asphalt....Pitcher, Charles COMMERCE 202-482-0132
Paving Materials, Concrete....Pitcher, Charles COMMERCE 202-482-0132
Pay Cable Television....Staff FCC 202-632-7480
Peanuts....Latham, Roger Agri 202-720-5944
Peanuts....Sanford, Scott Agri 202-219-0840
Peanuts....Burket, Stephen USITC 202-205-3318
Peanuts - World....McCormick, Ian Agri 202-219-0840
Pearl essence....Johnson, Larry USITC 202-205-3351
Pearls....Witherspoon, Ricardo USITC 202-205-3489
Peat....Cantrell, Raymond MINES 202-501-9581
Peat moss....Trainor, Cynthia USITC 202-205-3354
Pectin....Janis, William V. COMMERCE 202-482-2250
Pectin....Jonnard, Aimison USITC 202-205-3350
Pectus Excavatum (Funnel Chest)....Staff NHLBI 301-496-4236

Pedodontics....Staff NIDR 301-496-4261

Peer Review Organizations (PROs)....Hardy, Robert HCFA 202-690-6145

Peer Review Orgs./Sanctions....Holtz, Judy IG 202-619-1142

Pelizaeous-Merzbacher Disease....Staff NINDS 301-496-5751

Pelvic Inflammatory Disease....Staff NIAID 301-496-5717

Pemphigus Vulgaris....Staff NIAMS 301-496-8188

Pemphigoid....Staff NIAMS 301-496-8188

Pencils....Smyth, James CUSTOMS 212-466-2084

Pencils....Shetty, Sundar USITC 202-205-3486

Pencils/Pens, etc.....Vacant COMMERCE 202-482-0338

Penicillin....Nesbitt, Elizabeth USITC 202-205-3355

Pens....Smyth, James CUSTOMS 212-466-2084

People/China....Chu, Robert Cnty Commerce 202-482-2462

People/China....McCall, Laura Cnty Commerce 202-482-3583

Peptic Ulcers....Staff NIDDK 301-496-3583

Perchloroethylene....Michels, David USITC 202-205-3352

Perfumery, cosmetics, and toilet preps....Land, Eric USITC 202-205-3349

Periarteritis Nodosa....Staff NHLBI 301-496-4236

Periarteritis Nodosa....Staff NIAID 301-496-5717

Pericardial Tamponade....Staff NHLBI 301-496-4236

Pericarditis....Staff NHLBI 301-496-4236

Pericardium....Staff NHLBI 301-496-4236

Perinatal Biology....Staff NICHD 301-496-5133

Periodic Paralysis....Staff NINDS 301-496-5751

Periodicals....Bratland, Rose Marie COMMERCE 202-482-0380

Periodontal Diseases....Staff NIDR 301-496-4261

Peripheral Nerve Tumor....Staff NINDS 301-496-5751

Peripheral Neuropathy (Neuritis)....Staff NINDS 301-496-5751

Peripheral Vascular Disease....Staff NHLBI 301-496-4236

Perlite....Bolen, Wallace P. MINES 202-501-9389

Permit Information, Fish and Wildlife....Staff FWS 703-358-2104

Pernicious Anemia....Staff NIDDK 301-496-3583

Peroneal Muscular Atrophy....Staff NINDS 301-496-5751

Peroxides and Acetals....DiMaria, Joseph CUSTOMS 212-466-4769

Peroxides, inorganic....Conant, Kenneth USITC 202-205-3346

Personal leather goods....Seastrum, Carl USITC 202-205-3493

Personality....Staff NIMH 301-443-4515

Pertussis....Staff NIAID 301-496-5717

Peru....Lindow, Herbert Cnty Commerce 202-482-2521

Peru (Lima)....Staff Cnty State 202-647-3360

Peru/Minerals....Mobbs, Philip Cnty Mines 202-501-9679

Pesticide Hotline....Staff EPA 806-743-3095

Pesticide Information....Staff EPA 202-305-5919

Pesticide Monitoring....Staff FWS 703-358-2148

Pesticide Monitoring Programs, National....Staff FWS 703-358-2148

Pesticides....Staff NIEHS 919-541-3345

Pesticides....Wanser, Stephen USITC 202-205-3363

Pesticides Information Center....Staff EPA 202-305-5805

Pesticides and Toxic Enforcement....Staff EPA 202-260-8690

Pesticides and Toxic Substances....Staff EPA 202-235-5300

Pesticides....Reilly, Cornelius CUSTOMS 212-466-5770

Pet Food....Janis, William V. COMMERCE 202-482-2250

Pet Products (Export Promo)....Kimmel, Edward K. COMMERCE 202-482-3640

Pet animals (live)....Steller, Rose USITC 202-205-3323

Petrochemicals....Hurt, William COMMERCE 202-482-0128

Petrochemicals Plants, Major Proj.....Haraguchi, Wally COMMERCE 202-482-4877

Petrochemicals, Cyclic Crudes....Hurt, William COMMERCE 202-482-0128

Petroleum....Winters, William CUSTOMS 212-466-5747

Petroleum....Withrow, Leola NEIC 202-586-8800

Petroleum....Christian, Trisha NEIC 202-586-8800

Petroleum....Foreso, Cynthia USITC 202-205-3348

Petroleum (Ground Level)....Staff EPA 919-541-5526

Petroleum Offshore Drilling....Staff FCC 717-337-1212

Petroleum Products Markets....Cook, John NEIC 202-586-5214

Petroleum Statistics....Heath, Charles NEIC 202-586-6860

Petroleum, Crude and Refined Products....Gillett, Tom COMMERCE 202-482-1466

Peyronie's Disease....Staff NIDDK 301-496-3583

Phacoemulsification....Staff NEI 301-496-5248

Pharmaceuticals....Hurt, William COMMERCE 202-482-0128

Pharmaceuticals....Reilly, Cornelius CUSTOMS 212-466-5770

Pharmacology Information System (PROPHET)....Staff DRR 301-496-5411

Pharmacology Research Associate Training Program....Staff NIGMS 301-496-7301

Pharmacology/Toxicology....Staff NIGMS 301-496-7301

Pharmacology/Toxicology....Staff NIEHS 919-541-3345

Pharynx....Staff NIDR 301-496-4261

Phenol....Matusik, Ed USITC 202-205-3356

Phenolic resins....Misurelli, Denby USITC 202-205-3362

Phenylketonuria (PKU)....Staff NICHD 301-496-5133

Pheochromocytema....Staff NHLBI 301-496-4236

Philippines....Paine, George Cnty Commerce 202-482-3875

Philippines (Manila)....Staff Cnty State 202-647-1221

Philippines/Minerals....Lyday, Travis Cnty Mines 202-501-9695

Phlebitis....Staff NHLBI 301-496-4236

Phlebothrombosis....Staff NHLBI 301-496-4236

Phobias....Staff NIMH 301-496-4513

Phonograph and parts....Sherman, Thomas USITC 202-205-3389

Phonograph records....Sherman, Thomas USITC 202-205-3389

Phonographic equipment....Sherman, Thomas USITC 202-205-3389

Phonographs....Sherman, Thomas USITC 202-205-3389

Phosphate Rock....Stowasser, William F. MINES 202-501-9408

Phosphatic fertilizers....Trainor, Cynthia USITC 202-205-3354

Phosphoric acid....Trainor, Cynthia USITC 202-205-3354

Phosphoric acid esters....Johnson, Larry USITC 202-205-3351

Phosphorus....Trainor, Cynthia USITC 202-205-3354

Phosphorus compounds....Conant, Kenneth USITC 202-205-3346

Photocells....Malison, Andrew USITC 202-205-3391

Photocoagulation....Staff NEI 301-496-5248

Photocopy Services....Staff NIH Library/DRS 301-496-2983

Photocopying apparatus....Baker, Scott USITC 202-205-3386

Photographic Equipment & Supplies....Watson, Joyce COMMERCE 202-482-0574

Photographic chemicals....Wanser, Stephen USITC 202-205-3363

Photographic film: scrap....Bishop, Kathryn USITC 202-205-3494

Photographic film: waste....Bishop, Kathryn USITC 202-205-3494

Photographic gelatin....Jonnard, Aimison USITC 202-205-3350

Photographic supplies....Bishop, Kathryn USITC 202-205-3494

Photographs....Stahmer, Carsten USITC 202-205-3321

Photographs (Historical)....Staff NLM 301-496-5961

Photography....Staff NCRRR/MAPB 301-496-5995

Photovoltaics....Rannels, James E. NEIC 202-586-1720

Phthalic acid esters....Johnson, Larry USITC 202-205-3351

Phthalic anhydride....Matusik, Ed USITC 202-205-3356

Physical Environment. Agents (Effect on Hum. Hea.)....Staff NIEHS 919-541-3345

Physical Fitness & Sports, President's Council on....Guback, Steve ASH 202-272-3430

Physician's Assistant....Staff HRSA/BHPr 301-443-5794

Physicians Radio--Private....Staff FCC 202-632-1212

Physics....McCarthy, James UVA 701-924-6783

Physiology....Staff NIGMS 301-496-7301

Pi-Mesons (Cancer Treatment)....Staff NCI 301-496-5583

Pick's Disease....Staff NINDS 301-496-5751

Pick's Disease....Staff NIA 301-496-1752

Pig iron....Vacant USITC 202-205-3419

Pigments....Brownchweig, Gilbert CUSTOMS 212-466-5744

Pigments, inorganic....Johnson, Larry USITC 202-205-3351

Pigments, organic....Wanser, Stephen USITC 202-205-3363

Pillow blocks....Fravel, Dennis USITC 202-205-3404

Pillowcases....Sweet, Mary Elizabeth USITC 202-205-3455

Pillows....Spalding, Josephine USITC 202-205-3498

PinWorms....Staff NIAID 301-496-5717

Pinball machines....Robinson, Hazel USITC 202-205-3496

Pinene....Michels, David USITC 202-205-3352

Pink Eye....Staff NEI 301-496-5248

Pipe, of rubber or plastics....Johnson, Larry USITC 202-205-3351

Pipelines (Major Promo)....Bell, Richard COMMERCE 202-482-2460

Pipes, tobacco....Johnson, Christopher USITC 202-205-3488

Pitch from wood....Randall, Rob USITC 202-205-3366

Pituitary Tumors....Staff NINDS 301-496-5751

Pituitary Tumors....Staff NIDDK 301-496-3583

Pituitary Tumors....Staff NICHD 301-496-5133

Pityriasis Rosea....Staff NIAMS 301-496-8188

Pityriasis Rubra Pilaris....Staff NIAMS 301-496-8188

Placenta....Staff NICHD 301-496-5133

Plant Closings Statistics....Siegel, Lewis LABOR 202-606-6404

Plants....Conte, Ralph CUSTOMS 212-466-5759

Plants, live....Burket, Stephen USITC 202-205-3318

Plaque (Dental)....Staff NIDR 301-496-4261

Plasma Cell Cancer....Staff NCI 301-496-5583

Plaster products....White, Linda USITC 202-205-3427

Poultry - Broilers, Turkeys and Eggs....Little, Robert Agri 202-720-6147
Poultry - Broilers, Turkeys, Eggs....Krutchen, Tom Agri 202-690-4870
Poultry - Broilers, Turkeys, Eggs....Christensen, Lee Agri 202-219-0714
Poultry - Broilers, Turkeys, Eggs....Perez, Agnes Agri 202-219-0714
Poultry - Broilers, Turkeys, Eggs - World....Witucki, Larry Agri 202-219-0766
Poultry Products....Hodgen, Donald A. COMMERCE 202-482-3346
Poverty Statistics, Current Surveys....Staff CENSUS 301-763-8578
Powder, smokeless....Johnson, Larry USITC 202-205-3351
Powered-Lift Technology....Waller, Peter NASA 415-604-3938
Prader-Willi Syndrome....Staff NICHD 301-496-5133
Precious Metal Jewelry....Harris, John M. COMMERCE 202-482-1178
Precious stones....White, Linda USITC 202-205-3427
Precocious Puberty....Staff NICHD 301-496-5133
Predator Control, Fish and Wildlife....Staff FWS 703-358-1718
Prefabricated Buildings, Metal....Williams, Franklin COMMERCE 202-482-0132
Prefabricated Buildings, Wood....Cosslett, Patrick COMMERCE 202-482-0132
Pregnancy....Staff NICHD 301-496-5133
Pregnancy....Staff NCNR 301-496-0526
Pregnancy and Infant Health....Atrash, Hani K. CDC 404-488-5147
Prematurity....Staff NICHD 301-496-5133
Prenatal Care....Staff NICHD 301-496-5133
Prenatal Nutrition....Staff NICHD 301-496-5133
Prepared Meats....Hodgen, Donald A. COMMERCE 202-482-3346
Presbycusis....Staff NINDS 301-496-5751
Presbycusis....Staff NIDCD 301-496-7243
Presbycusis/Hearing and Aging....Staff NINDS 301-496-5751
Presbycusis/Hearing and Aging....Staff NIA 301-496-1752
Presbycusis/Hearing and Aging....Staff NIDCD 301-496-7243
Presbyopia....Staff NEI 301-496-5248
Presenile Dementia....Staff NIA 301-496-1752
Presenile Dementia....Staff NINDS 301-496-5751
Presenile Dementia....Staff NIMH 301-443-4515
Press Information....Staff CENSUS 301-763-4040
Pretrial Release and Crime - Federal....Kaplan, Carol Justice Stat 202-307-0759
Preventive Health Block Grant....Berreth, Don CDC 404-639-3286
Price Indexes (Consumer) Prices & Liv. Cond.....Jackman, Patrick LABOR 202-606-6952
Price Indexes, International, Assist. Commiss.....Reut, Katrina LABOR 202-606-7100
Price and Index Number Research, Prices/Lv. Cond....Zieschang, Kimberly LABOR 202-606-6573
Prices & Liv. Cond, Consumer Expenditure Survey....Jacobs, Eva LABOR 202-606-6900
Prices & Living Conditions, Assist. Commis.....Dalton, Kenneth LABOR 202-606-6960
Prices & Living Conditions, Consumer Price Indexes....Staff LABOR 202-606-7000
Prices & Living Conditions, Food, Raw Matls, Apprl....Frumkin, Rob LABOR 202-606-7106
Prices & Living Conditions, Intl. Prices, Revision....Reut, Katrina LABOR 202-606-7100
Prices & Living Conditions, Intl. Pr., Machinery....Costello, Brian LABOR 202-606-7107
Prices and Living Conditions, Data Diskettes....Rosenberg, Elliott LABOR 202-606-7728
Prices and Living Conditions, Non-electric mach.....Dickerson, Bryandt LABOR 202-606-7734
Prices and Living Conditions, Services....Gerduk, Irwin LABOR 202-606-7748
Prices and Living Conditions, Statistical Methods....Hedges, Brian LABOR 202-606-6897
Prices, Foreign Countries, Prod. & Technol.....Godbout, Todd LABOR 202-606-5654
Prices/Living Cond, Asst Commr, Consumer Price Index...Armknecht, Paul LABOR 202-606-6952
Prices/Living Cond., Recorded PPI Detail....24-hour hotline LABOR 202-606-7828
Prices/Living Conditions, Dept. Store Inventory....Gibson, Sharon LABOR 202-606-6968
Prices/Living Conds, Associate Commissioner....Dalton, Kenneth LABOR 202-606-6960
Prices/Living Conds, Asst Commr, Consumer Prices....Armknecht, Paul LABOR 202-606-6952
Prices/Living Conds, CPI Recorded Detail....24-Hour Hotline LABOR 202-606-7828
Prices/Living Conds, CPI, Data Diskettes....Gibson, Sharon LABOR 202-606-6968
Prices/Living Conds, Consumer Expend Survey....Jacobs, Eva LABOR

202-606-6900
Prices/Living Conds, Consumer Expend Survey Data....Passero, William LABOR 202-606-6900
Prices/Living Conds, Consumer Expend Survey Operations....Dietz, Richard LABOR 202-606-6872
Prices/Living Conds, Consumer Expend Survey Tapes....Passero, William LABOR 202-606-6900
Prices/Living Conds, Consumer Price Indexes....Jackman, Patrick LABOR 202-606-6952
Prices/Living Conds, Data Diskettes....Rosenberg, Elliott LABOR 202-606-7728
Prices/Living Conds, Electric machinery & Transpor....Yatsko, Ralph LABOR 202-606-7745
Prices/Living Conds, Estd Retail Food Price, Mthly....Cook, William LABOR 202-606-6988
Prices/Living Conds, Forestry and Construction....Davies, Wanda LABOR 202-606-7713
Prices/Living Conds, Index Number Research Studies....Zieschang, Kimberly LABOR 202-606-6573
Prices/Living Conds, Indexes, Fuels, Mthly....Adkins, Robert LABOR 202-606-6985
Prices/Living Conds, Indexes, Utils, Mthly....Adkins, Robert LABOR 202-606-6985
Prices/Living Conds, Intl Price Indexes....Reut, Katrina LABOR 202-606-7100
Prices/Living Conds, Leather....Paik, Soon LABOR 202-606-7714
Prices/Living Conds, Machinery....Alterman, William LABOR 202-606-7108
Prices/Living Conds, Metals....Kazanowski, Edward LABOR 202-606-7735
Prices/Living Conds, Non-electric Machinery....Dickerson, Bryandt LABOR 202-606-7734
Prices/Living Conds, PPI, Current Analysis....Howell, Craig LABOR 202-606-7705
Prices/Living Conds, PPI, Forestry....Davies, Wanda LABOR 202-606-7713
Prices/Living Conds, Price Research Studies....Zieschang, Kimberly LABOR 202-606-6753
Prices/Living Conds, Producer Price Indexes....Tibbetts, Thomas LABOR 202-606-7700
Prices/Living Conds, Recorded CPI Summary....24-Hour quickline LABOR 202-606-6994
Prices/Living Conds, Retail Prices, Fuels, Mthly....Adkins, Robert LABOR 202-606-6985
Prices/Living Conds, Retail Prices, Gasoline....Chelena, Joseph LABOR 202-606-6982
Prices/Living Conds, Retail Prices, Utils, Mthly....Adkins, Robert LABOR 202-606-6985
Prices/Living Conds, Textiles....Paik, Soon LABOR 202-606-7714
Prices/Living Conds, Transportation Equipment....Yatsko, Ralph LABOR 202-606-7745
Primary Lateral Sclerosis....Staff NINDS 301-496-5751
Primary Plastics....Reilly, Cornelius CUSTOMS 212-466-5770
Primate Research....Staff NCRR 301-496-5545
Primate Research Centers Program....Staff NCRR 301-496-5175
Principe....Blackwell, Gloria Peace Corps 202-606-3998
Principe....Swezey, Virginia Peace Corps 202-606-3998
Printed Matter....Abramowitz, Carl CUSTOMS 212-466-5733
Printed circuit boards....Malison, Andrew USITC 202-205-3391
Printed matter....Stahmer, Carsten USITC 202-205-3321
Printing & Publishing....Lofquist, William COMMERCE 202-482-0379
Printing Trade Services....Bratland, Rose Marie COMMERCE 202-482-0380
Printing Trades Machines/Equipment....Kemper, Alexis COMMERCE 202-482-5956
Printing ink....Johnson, Larry USITC 202-205-3351
Printing machines....Slingerland, David USITC 202-205-3400
Printing machines (textiles)....Greene, William USITC 202-205-3405
Prisoner Surveys, National Prisoner Statistics....McGinn, Larry CENSUS 301-763-1735
Prisons, Prisoners, and Crowding....Beck, Allen Justice Stat 202-616-3277
Prisons, Prisoners, and Crowding....Innes, Christopher Justice Stat 202-724-3121
Prisons, Prisoners, and Crowding....Baunach, Phyllis Jo Justice Stat 202-307-0361
Prisons, Prisoners, and Crowding....Greenfeld, Lawrence Justice Stat 202-616-3281
Prisons, Prisoners, and Crowding....Huggins, Wayne M. Justice Stat 202-307-3106
Prisons, Prisoners, and Crowding....Stephan, James Justice Stat 202-616-7273
Privacy and Security of Data....Kaplan, Carol Justice Stat 202-307-0759
Private Carriers Communications....Staff FCC 717-337-1212
Private Operational Fixed Services....Staff FCC 717-337-1212
Private Security....Zawitz, Marianne Justice Stat 202-616-3499

Private Wire Systems--Telephone & Telegraph....Staff FCC 202-634-1800

Privatization of Corrections....Lindgren, Sue Justice Stat 202-307-0760

Probation and Probationers....Greenfeld, Lawrence Justice Stat 202-616-3281

Procaine....Staff NIA 301-496-1752

Process Control Instruments....Nealon, Margaret COMMERCE 202-482-3411

Process Control Instruments, Trade Promo.....Manzolilo, Frank COMMERCE 202-482-2991

Producer Price Indexes Prices/Living Cond.....Tibbetts, Thomas LABOR 202-606-7700

Producer Price Indexes, Analysis and Data....Howell, Craig LABOR 202-606-7705

Producer Price Indexes, Analysis and Data....Howell, Craig LABOR 202-606-7705

Producer Price Indexes, Electric Machinery & Trans....Yatsko, Ralph LABOR 202-606-7745

Producer Price Indexes, Forestry & Construction....Davies, Wanda LABOR 202-606-7713

Producer Price Indexes, Metals....Kazanowski, Edward LABOR 202-606-7735

Producer Price Indexes, Textiles & Leather....Paik, Soon LABOR 202-606-7714

Productivity & Technology, Assist. Commis.....Dean, Edwin R. LABOR 202-606-5600

Productivity & Technology, Data Diskettes....Fulco, Lawrence J. LABOR 202-606-5604

Productivity & Technology, Data Tapes....Kriebel, Bertram LABOR 202-606-5606

Productivity & Technology, Employment Projections....Franklin, James LABOR 202-606-5709

Productivity & Technology, Employment Requirement Tbls....Franklin, James LABOR 202-606-5709

Productivity/Techlgy, Compensation, For. Countries....Capdevielle, Patricia LABOR 202-606-5654

Productivity/Techlgy, Data Tapes....Kriebel, Bertram LABOR 202-606-5606

Productivity/Techlgy, Earnings, Foreign Countries....Capdevielle, Patricia LABOR 202-606-5654

Productivity/Techlgy, For Countries, Other Econ In....Neef, Arthur LABOR 202-606-5654

Productivity/Techlgy, Foreign Countries, Labor For....Sorrentino, Constance LABOR 202-606-5654

Productivity/Techlgy, Foreign Countries, Productivity....Neef, Arthur LABOR 202-606-5654

Productivity/Techlgy,ForeignCountries,Unemployment....Sorrentino,Constance LABOR 202-606-5654

Productivity/Techlgy, Productivity Research....Harper, Michael LABOR 202-606-5603

Productivity/Techlgy, Productivity in Government....Forte, Darlene J. LABOR 202-606-5621

Productivity/Techlgy, Productivity & Costs-News Release....Fulco, Lawrence J. LABOR 202-606-5604

Productivity/Techlgy, Productivity Trends Federal Govt....Ardolini, Charles W. LABOR 202-606-5618

Productivity/Technlgy, Associate Commissioner....Dean, Edwin R. LABOR 202-606-5600

Productivity/Technlgy, Cost-of-Living Abroad....Capdevielle, Patricia LABOR 202-606-5654

Productivity/Technlgy, Tech Trends, Major Ind....Riche, Richard LABOR 202-606-5626

Productivity Research, Capital Measurement, Pr/Tch....Harper, Michael LABOR 202-606-5603

Productivity Trends Selected Industries....Ardolini, Charles W. LABOR 202-606-5618

Productivity Trends in Selected Ind. & Fed. Gov't....Ardolini, Charles W. LABOR 202-606-5618

Productivity in Government, Productivity & Tech.....Forte, Darlene J. LABOR 202-606-5621

Productivity, Multifactor, Labor Composition, Hrs.....Rosenblum, Larry LABOR 202-606-5606

Productivity, Unit Labor Costs, Foreign Countries....Neef, Arthur LABOR 202-606-5654

Professional services....Xavier, Neil USITC 202-205-3450

Progeria....Staff NIA 301-496-1752

Progestins and Progesterone....Staff NICHD 301-496-5133

Progestins and Progesterone....Staff HRSA/DMCH 301-443-4026

Progressive Cerebral Degeneration....Staff NINDS 301-496-5751

Progressive Dementia in Children....Staff NINDS 301-496-5751

Progressive Infantile Spinal Muscular Atrophy....Staff NINDS 301-496-5751

Progressive Leukodystrophy....Staff NINDS 301-496-5751

Progressive Multifocal Leukoencephalopathy....Staff NINDS 301-496-5751

Progressive Muscular Atrophy....Staff NINDS 301-496-5751

Progressive Supranuclear Palsy....Staff NINDS 301-496-5751

Progressive Systemic Sclerosis....Staff NINDS 301-496-5751

Progressive Systemic Sclerosis....Staff NIAMS 301-496-8188

Project LASER Discovery Lab....Armstrong, Pat NASA 205-544-1798

Project LASER Volunteer Programs....Widenhofer, Karen NASA 205-544-3234

Projections, Labor Force, Employment Projections....Fullerton, Howard LABOR 202-606-5711

Projections, Occupational, Empl. Proj.....Rosenthal, Neal LABOR 202-606-5701

Projectors (photographic)....Bishop, Kathryn USITC 202-205-3494

Propagation Research, Fish and Wildlife....Staff FWS 703-358-1710

Propagation--Radio Waves....Staff FCC 202-632-7025

Propane....Land, Eric USITC 202-205-3349

Property Records--Common Carrier....Staff FCC 202-634-1861

Propulsion Systems....Brogan, John NEIC 202-586-1477

Propylene....Raftery, Jim USITC 202-205-3365

Propylene glycol....Michels, David USITC 202-205-3352

Propylene oxide....Michels, David USITC 202-205-3352

Prosecution....Gaskins, Carla Justice Stat 202-508-8550

Prosecution....Langan, Patrick Justice Stat 202-616-3490

Prostaglandins....Staff NICHD 301-496-5133

Prostaglandins....Staff NHLBI 301-496-4236

Prostate Enlargement....Staff NIDDK 301-496-3583

Prostate/Hyperplasia of the Prostate....Staff NIA 301-496-1752

Prostate/Hyperplasia of the Prostate....Staff NIDDK 301-496-3583

Prostatitis....Staff NIDDK 301-496-3583

Prostheses (Heart and Blood Vessel)....Staff NHLBI 301-496-4236

Prostheses (Orthotics)....Staff NIAMS 301-496-8188

Prosthodontics....Staff NIDR 301-496-4261

Protein Abnormalities with Neurologic Disease....Staff NINDS 301-496-5751

Protein Engineering....Staff DCRT 301-496-1100

Prurigo Nodularis....Staff NIAMS 301-496-8188

Pseudogout....Staff NIAMS 301-496-8188

Pseudohypoparathyroidism....Staff NIDDK 301-496-3583

Pseudosenility....Staff NIA 301-496-1752

Pseudotumor Cerebri....Staff NEI 301-496-5248

Pseudotumor Cerebri....Staff NINDS 301-496-5751

Pseudoxanthoma Elasticum....Staff NHLBI 301-496-4236

Psittacosis....Staff NIAID 301-496-5717

Psoriasis....Staff NIAMS 301-496-8188

Psoriatic Arthritis....Staff NIAMS 301-496-8188

Psychology....Allen, Joseph P. UVA 701-982-4727

Psychology....McCarty, Richard UVA 701-924-4730

Psychoneuroimmunomodulation....Staff NINDS 301-496-5751

Psychopharmacology....Staff NIMH 301-443-4515

Psychotherapeutic agents....Nesbitt, Elizabeth USITC 202-205-3355

Psychotic Episodes....Staff NIMH 301-443-4515

Pterygium....Staff NEI 301-496-5248

Ptosis....Staff NEI 301-496-5248

Public Affairs Office....Banks, Valarie FTC 202-326-2177

Public Affairs, Office of....Berreth, Donald CDC 404-639-3286

Public Cellular Radio....Staff FCC 202-632-6400

Public Defense....Gaskins, Carla Justice Stat 202-508-8550

Public Health Practice Program....Baker, Edward L. CDC 404-639-1900

Public Health and Safety....Ziemer, Paul NEIC 202-586-6151

Public Housing....Staff HUD 202-708-0950

Public Information Center....Staff EPA 202-260-7751

Public Information Office....Dye, Larry ACF 202-401-9215

Public Information Office....Miller, James ADAMHA 301-443-8956

Public Information Office....Isquith, Bob AHCPR 301-227-8364

Public Information Office....Grigg, Bill ASH 202-690-6867

Public Information Office....Fendler, Gary FDA 301-443-1130

Public Information Office....Erbe, Kevin L. HCFA 202-690-8390

Public Information Office....Mehuron, Charlotte HRSA 301-443-3376

Public Information Office....Holtz, Judy IG 202-619-1142

Public Information Office....DeAsis, Patricia IHS 301-443-3593

Public Information Office....Velez, Larry OCR 202-619-1587

Public Information Office....Gambino, Phil SSA 410-965-8904

Public Information Office - Atlanta....Mull, Daryl SSAREG 404-331-0612

Public Information Office - Boston....Czarnowski, Kurt SSAREG 617-565-2881

Public Information Office - Chicago....Mahler, Mary SSAREG 312-353-7092

Public Information Office - Dallas....O'Neil, Dee SSAREG 214-767-4191

Public Information Office - Denver....Shellhamer, Janice SSAREG 303-844-4441

Public Information Office - Kansas City....Bischof, Ken SSAREG 816-426-6191

Public Information Office - New York....Clark, John SSAREG 212-264-2500

Public Information Office - Philadelphia....Edward, Dana SSAREG 215-596-6981

Public Information Office - San Francisco....Walker, Leslie SSAREG 415-744-4664

Public Information Office - Seattle....Farrell, Dan SSAREG 206-399-4256

Public Information Office, Chief....Howenstine, Barbara W. ECONOMIC 202-523-0777

Public Information, Director, Office of....Mehnert, Robert NLM 301-496-6308

Public Information, Fish and Wildlife Service....Staff FWS 202-208-5634

Public Land Mobile Radio Service....Staff FCC 202-653-5560

Public Microwave....Staff FCC 202-634-1706

Public Opinion About Crime....Lindgren, Sue Justice Stat 202-307-0760

Public Opinion About Crime....Zawitz, Marianne Justice Stat 202-616-3499

Public Relations....Grunig, James E. UMD 301-405-2416

Public Rural Radio....Staff FCC 202-653-5560

Public Services Division....Lacroix, Eve-Marie NLM 301-496-5501

Public Surveys, Fish and Wildlife Service....Staff FWS 703-358-1730

Public Use, Fish and Wildlife Hatcheries....Staff FWS 703-358-1715

Public Use, Fish and Wildlife Refuges....Staff FWS 703-358-2029

Public relations....R-Archila, Laura USITC 202-205-3411

Public relations theory and techniques....Zerbinos, Eugenia UMD 301-405-2430

Public relations, magazine journalism....Grunig, Larissa A. UMD 301-405-2431

Public-Use Microdata Samples....Campbell, Carmen CENSUS 301-763-2005

Publications (Inquiries) and NLM Photos/Slides....Beckwith, Frances NLM 301-496-6308

Publications Information, Public. & Spec. Studies....Staff LABOR 202-606-7828

Publications Office, Press Officer....Hoyle, Kathryn LABOR 202-606-5902

Publications Office, Recorded Current....24-Hour Hotline LABOR 202-606-7828

Publications Office, TDD (Telecom. Device for Deaf)....TDD LABOR 202-606-5897

Publications and Special Studies, Assoc. Com....Klein, Deborah P. LABOR 202-606-5900

Publishing....Lofquist, William COMMERCE 202-482-0379

Puerto Rico....Soto, Rodrigo Cnty Commerce 202-482-2527

Pulleys....Vacant USITC 202-205-3380

Pulmonary Alveolar Proteinosis....Staff NHLBI 301-496-4236

Pulmonary Angiomyomatosis....Staff NHLBI 301-496-4236

Pulmonary Diseases (Infectious/Allergenic)....Staff NIAID 301-496-5717

Pulmonary Diseases (Non-Inf., Non-All., Non-Tum.)....Staff NHLBI 301-496-4236

Pulmonary Diseases (Tumorous/Cancerous)....Staff NCI 301-496-5583

Pulmonary Edema....Staff NHLBI 301-496-4236

Pulmonary Embolism....Staff NHLBI 301-496-4236

Pulmonary Emphysema....Staff NHLBI 301-496-4236

Pulmonary Fibrosis....Staff NHLBI 301-496-4236

Pulp Mills, Major Proj.....White, Barbara COMMERCE 202-482-4160

Pulp machines....Slingerland, David USITC 202-205-3400

Pulp, articles of....Rhodes, Richard USITC 202-205-3322

Pulpmills....Stanley, Gary COMMERCE 202-482-0375

Pulpwood....Ruggles, Fred USITC 202-205-3325

Pumice....Bolen, Wallace P. MINES 202-501-9389

Pumice....White, Linda USITC 202-205-3427

Pumps....Riedl, Karl CUSTOMS 212-466-5493

Pumps, Pumping Eqmt....McDonald, Edward COMMERCE 202-482-0680

Pumps, Valves, Comp (Trade Promo.)....Heimowitz, Leonard COMMERCE 202-482-0558

Pumps, air and vacuum....Mata, Ruben USITC 202-205-3403

Pumps, liquid....Mata, Ruben USITC 202-205-3403

Pure Red Cell Aplasia....Staff NHLBI 301-496-4236

Purpura....Staff NIAMS 301-496-8188

Purpura....Staff NIDDK 301-496-3583

Putty....Johnson, Larry USITC 202-205-3351

Puzzles....Luther, Dennis USITC 202-205-3497

Pyelonephritis....Staff NIDDK 301-496-3583

Pyorrhea....Staff NIDR 301-496-4261

Pyrethrum....Wanser, Stephen USITC 202-205-3363

Pyridine....Foreso, Cynthia USITC 202-205-3348

Q

Qatar....Fitzgerald-Wilks, Kate/Thanos, Paul Cnty Commerce 202-482-1870

Qatar (Doha)....Staff Cnty State 202-647-6572

Qatar/Minerals....Izon, David Cnty Mines 202-501-9692

Quadriplegia....Staff NINDS 301-496-5751

Quality Control--Common Carrier....Staff FCC 202-634-1800

Quarantine, Disease....McCance, Charles R. CDC 404-639-1455

Quarterly Financial Report....Zarrett, Paul CENSUS 301-763-2718

Quarterly, Occupational Outlook, Empl. Proj.....Fountain, Melvin LABOR

202-606-5707

Quartz Crystal....Ober, Joyce A. MINES 202-501-9406

Quartzite....White, Linda USITC 202-205-3427

Quasars....Staff NASA 205-544-0034

Quaternary ammonium salts, fatty acids....Land, Eric USITC 202-205-3349

Quebracho....Wanser, Stephen USITC 202-205-3363

Quill, articles of....Spalding, Josephine USITC 202-205-3498

Quilts....Sweet, Mary Elizabeth USITC 202-205-3455

R

RCRA Information Hotline....Staff EPA 415-744-2074

RCRA/Superfund (OUST Hotline)....Staff EPA 800-424-9346

Rabies....Staff NIAID 301-496-5717

Race Statistics....Staff CENSUS 301-763-2607

Racing shells....Hagey, Michael USITC 202-205-3392

Radar Intrusion Alarms (unlicensed)....Staff 202-653-6288

Radar apparatus....Kitzmiller, John USITC 202-205-3387

Radial Keratotomy....Staff NEI 301-496-5248

Radiation....Staff NCI 301-496-5583

Radiation (Effect on Eyes)....Staff NEI 301-496-5248

Radiation (Effect on Teeth)....Staff NIDR 301-496-4261

Radiation (Nervous System)....Staff NINDS 301-496-5751

Radiation (Nonionizing)....Staff OD/ORS 301-496-2960

Radiation (Nonionizing)....Staff NIEHS 919-541-3345

Radiation (X-ray) Effects on Fetus....Staff FDA 301-443-2356

Radiation Environmental Laws....Wallo, Andrew NEIC 202-586-4996

Radiation Hazards....Staff FCC 202-653-8169

Radiation Programs, Office of....Staff EPA 202-233-9320

Radiation Protection....Simpson, Paul D. CDC 404-639-3145

Radiation Questions....Staff EPA 202-233-9280

Radiation Safety....Cruzan, Susan FDA 301-443-3285

Radiation Safety (Radio. Spills, Lab. Surveys)....Staff OD/ORS 301-496-5774

Radiation Safety Badges....Staff OD/ORS 301-496-2254

Radiation Safety Officer....Staff NIH 301-496-2254

Radiation Studies....Smith, James M. CDC 404-488-7040

Radiation Studies Division....Staff EPA 202-233-9340

Radio & TV Broadcast Eqpmt....Rettig, Theresa COMMERCE 202-482-4466

Radio Broadcasting Advisory Committee....Staff FCC 202-632-6485

Radio Control Devices (licensed)....Staff FCC 202-632-4964

Radio Control Devices (non-licensed)....Staff FCC 202-653-6288

Radio Frequency Devices....Staff FCC 202-653-6288

Radio Noise....Staff FCC 301-725-1585

Radio Propagation....Staff FCC 202-632-7025

Radio apparatus and parts....Kitzmiller, John USITC 202-205-3387

Radio navigational apparatus....Kitzmiller, John USITC 202-205-3387

Radio receivers....Kitzmiller, John USITC 202-205-3387

Radioactive Materials (Shipping & Receiving)....Staff OD/ORS 301-496-2254

Radioactive Waste Disposal....Lytle, Jill NEIC 202-586-0370

Radioactive Waste Disposal at NIH (Solid & Liquid)....Staff OD/ORS 301-496-2254

Radiograms....Staff FCC 202-632-7265

Radiolocation--Industrial....Staff FCC 717-337-1212

Radionuclide Techniques in CV Diagnosis....Staff NHLBI 301-496-4236

Radios....Dicerbo, Mario CUSTOMS 212-466-5672

Radioscope Power Systems....Lane, Robert NEIC 301-903-4362

Radiotelegraph Common Carrier....Staff FCC 202-632-7265

Radiotelegraph Operator License....Staff FCC 202-632-7240

Radiotelephone Common Carrier Services....Staff FCC 202-652-6400

Radiotelephone Equipment....Staff FCC 301-725-1585

Radiotherapy (Cancer)....Staff NCI 301-496-5583

Radium....Staff NCI 301-496-5583

Radon Division....Staff EPA 202-233-9370

Radon Information....Staff EPA 202-233-9370

Radon Publications....Staff EPA 202-260-8366

Rags....Cook, Lee USITC 202-205-3471

Rail, locomotives....Lahey, Kathleen USITC 202-205-3409

Railroad Equipment....Wholey, Patrick CUSTOMS 212-466-5668

Railroad Services....Sousane, J. Richard COMMERCE 202-482-4582

Railroads....Staff FCC 717-337-1212

Railroads (Major Proj)....Smith, Jay L COMMERCE 202-482-4642

Railway rolling stock....Lahey, Kathleen USITC 202-205-3409

Rain Forests....Martin, R. Michael FS 703-235-1676

Rainwear....Shetty, Sundar USITC 202-205-3457

Ramsey Hunt Syndrome....Staff NINDS 301-496-5751

Ramsey Hunt Syndrome....Staff NIDCD 301-496-7243

Range Research....Lennartz, Michael R. FS 202-205-1524
Rape....Baldwin, Elaine ADAMHA 301-443-4536
Rare Disorders (Neurological)....Staff NINDS 301-496-5751
Rare Earths....Hedrick, James B. MINES 202-501-9412
Rare saccharides....Randall, Rob USITC 202-205-3366
Rare-earth compounds....Greenblatt, Jack USITC 202-205-3353
Rare-earth metals....Conant, Kenneth USITC 202-205-3346
Rate Base (International, Telegraph & Telephone)....Staff FCC 202-632-3772
Rate Level (International, Telegraph & Telephone)....Staff FCC 202-632-5550
Rate Structure (International, Telegraph & Telephone....Staff FCC 202-632-5550
Rate of Return (International, Telegraph & Telephone)....Staff FCC 202-632-3772
Rattan....Ruggles, Fred USITC 202-205-3325
Raw Materials, Food, & Apparel, Intl. Price Ind.....Frumkin, Rob LABOR 202-606-7106
Raynaud's Disease....Staff NHLBI 301-496-4236
Raynaud's Disease....Staff NIAMS 301-496-8188
Reading Development....Staff NINDS 301-496-5751
Reading Development....Staff NICHD 301-496-5133
Reading Disorders....Staff NICHD 301-496-5133
Reading Disorders....Staff NINDS 301-496-5751
Reading Disorders....Staff Dept. of Education 202-245-8707
Reading Disorders....Staff NIDCD 301-496-7243
Real Earnings--News Release, Empl/Unempl. Stats....Hiles, David LABOR 202-606-6547
Recalls (Automobile Emissions)....Staff EPA 202-233-9260
Recalls (drugs)....Adams, Betsy FDA 301-443-3285
Recalls (food)....Corwin, Emil FDA 202-205-4144
Recidivism....Beck, Allen Justice Stat 202-616-3277
Recidivism....Greenfeld, Lawrence Justice Stat 202-616-3281
Recidivism....Shipley, Bernard Justice Stat 202-307-7703
Recombinant DNA....Staff NIAID 301-496-5717
Recombinant DNA....Staff NIGMS 301-496-7301
Recombinant DNA Activity....Staff OD 301-770-0131
Reconstituted crude petroleum....Foreso, Cynthia USITC 202-205-3348
Recorded CPI Detail, Prices & Living Cond.....24-Hour Hotline LABOR 202-606-7828
Recorded Messages, Compensation & Working Condition....24-hour hotline LABOR 202-606-7828
Records, tapes and recording media....Sherman, Thomas USITC 202-205-3389
Recovery Plans, Endangered Species....Staff FWS 703-358-2183
Recreation, Fish and Wildlife Recreation....Staff FWS 703-358-1715
Recreation, Refuges....Staff FWS 703-358-2029
Recreational Equipment, Export Promo.....Beckham, Reginald COMMERCE 202-482-5478
Rectifiers....Josephs, Irwin CUSTOMS 212-466-5673
Recurrent Fever....Staff NIAID 301-496-5717
Recurrent Pyogenic Infections....Staff NIAID 301-496-5717
Recycling (General Issues)....Staff EPA 202-260-6261
Recycling Program (EPA)....Staff EPA 202-260-6980
Red Blood Cells (Erythrocytes)....Staff FDA/NCDB 301-496-3556
Red Blood Cells (Erythrocytes)....Staff NHLBI 301-496-4236
Reduction of Carrier Service....Staff FCC 202-632-7553
Reeling machines....Greene, William USITC 202-205-3405
Reflex Sympathetic Dystrophy Syndrome....Staff NIAMS 301-496-8188
Reflux Nephropathy....Staff NIDDK 301-496-3583
Refractive Errors....Staff NEI 301-496-5248
Refractories....DeSapio, Vincent USITC 202-205-3435
Refractory Anemia....Staff NHLBI 301-496-4236
Refractory Products....Duggan, Brian COMMERCE 202-482-0610
Refrigeration....Rocks, Michael CUSTOMS 212-466-5669
Refrigeration equipment....Mata, Ruben USITC 202-205-3403
Refsum's Disease....Staff NINDS 301-496-5751
Refugee Resettlement....Long, Susan ACF 202-401-9215
Regional Director - Atlanta....Williams, Thomas T. HHSREG 404-331-2442
Regional Director - Boston....Davenport, Sue Winthrop HHSREG 617-565-1500
Regional Director - Chicago....Brummet-Flaum, Delilah HHSREG 312-353-5160
Regional Director - Dallas....Standefer, Paulette HHSREG 214-767-3301
Regional Director - Denver....Artist, Jane HHSREG 303-844-4545
Regional Director - Kansas City....Petrowsky, Dana HHSREG 816-426-2821
Regional Director - New York...Johnson, Jr., Cleveland HHSREG 212-264-4600
Regional Director - Philadelphia...Jacobs, Alma HHSREG 215-596-6492
Regional Director - San Francisco....Phelon, Ronald W. FTC 415-744-7920
Regional Director - San Francisco....Dana, III, Deane HHSREG 415-556-6746

Regional Director - Seattle....Kelly, Bernard E. HHSREG 206-553-0420
Regional Economic Analysis, Chief....Kort, John R. ECONOMIC 202-523-0946
Regional Economic Measurement, Chief....Hazen, Linnea ECONOMIC 202-254-6642
Regional Economics, Associate Director....Knox, Hugh W. ECONOMIC 202-523-0751
Regional Economics, Associate Director....Knox, Hugh W. ECONOMIC 202-523-0751
Regional Enteritis....Staff NIDDK 301-496-3583
Regional Medical Libraries....Staff NLM 301-496-4777
Regional Office - Atlanta....Staff CENSUS 404-347-2274
Regional Office - Atlanta....Alphin, Katherine B. FTC 404-347-7520
Regional Office - Atlanta....Bolen, Ida FTC 404-347-7046
Regional Office - Atlanta....Brennan, Virginia FTC 404-347-7540
Regional Office - Atlanta....Couillou, Chris M. FTC 404-347-7517
Regional Office - Atlanta....Davis, Paul K. FTC 404-347-4836
Regional Office - Atlanta....Dowdy, Lemuel W. FTC 404-347-7538
Regional Office - Atlanta....Foster, Andrea FTC 404-347-7516
Regional Office - Atlanta....House, Nicole L. FTC 404-347-7541
Regional Office - Atlanta....Kirtz, Harold E. FTC 404-347-7522
Regional Office - Atlanta....Laitsch, Ronald E. FTC 404-347-7535
Regional Office - Atlanta....Liebes, Cinday A. FTC 404-347-7514
Regional Office - Atlanta....Ozburn, Chris Edmonds FTC 404-347-7515
Regional Office - Atlanta....Powell, Saundra FTC 404-347-4836
Regional Office - Atlanta....Rohrer, James T. FTC 404-347-7534
Regional Office - Atlanta....Schanker, Barbara S. FTC 404-347-7518
Regional Office - Atlanta....Taylor, Mark FTC 404-347-7512
Regional Office - Atlanta....Wallace, Cheryl J. FTC 404-347-7521
Regional Office - Atlanta....Walton, Doris P. FTC 404-347-7532
Regional Office - Atlanta....Whittaker, Ingrid FTC 404-347-7536
Regional Office - Atlanta....Williams, Addie L. FTC 404-347-7510
Regional Office - Boston....Staff CENSUS 617-565-7078
Regional Office - Boston....Block, Paul G. FTC 617-565-7240
Regional Office - Boston....Bolton, Barbara E. FTC 617-565-7240
Regional Office - Boston....Caverly, Andrew FTC 617-565-7240
Regional Office - Boston....Cooper, Joanne FTC 617-565-7240
Regional Office - Boston....Cooper, Gary S. FTC 617-565-7240
Regional Office - Boston....Greenberg, Sara FTC 617-565-7240
Regional Office - Boston....Haley, Mary G. FTC 617-565-7240
Regional Office - Boston....Harrington, Diane J. FTC 617-565-7240
Regional Office - Boston....Keniry, David I., Jr. FTC 617-565-7240
Regional Office - Boston....La Due, Charles M. FTC 617-565-7240
Regional Office - Boston....McDonough, William P. FTC 617-565-7240
Regional Office - Boston....Morse, Phoebe D. FTC 617-565-7240
Regional Office - Boston....Robertson, Terry L. FTC 617-565-7240
Regional Office - Boston....Schultz, Cornelia FTC 617-565-7240
Regional Office - Boston....Sexton, Colleen FTC 617-565-7240
Regional Office - Boston....Sica, Joseph P. FTC 617-565-7240
Regional Office - Boston....Wood, Kristie FTC 617-565-7240
Regional Office - Boston....Wood, Pamela J. FTC 617-565-7240
Regional Office - Chicago....Staff CENSUS 312-353-0980
Regional Office - Chicago....Baker, Steven C. FTC 312-353-8156
Regional Office - Chicago....Daniels, Janice A. FTC 312-353-1156
Regional Office - Chicago....DiGiulio, Barbara A. FTC 312-353-4445
Regional Office - Chicago....Dodge, Karen D. FTC 312-353-4448
Regional Office - Chicago....Franczyk, Nicholas J. FTC 312-353-7957
Regional Office - Chicago....Fuller, Catherine R. FTC 312-353-5576
Regional Office - Chicago....Genda, Christine M. FTC 312-353-5261
Regional Office - Chicago....Hallerud, John C. FTC 312-353-5575
Regional Office - Chicago....Hughes, Timothy T. FTC 312-353-4431
Regional Office - Chicago....Krause, Alan E. FTC 312-353-4441
Regional Office - Chicago....McGrew, Theresa M. FTC 312-353-5532
Regional Office - Chicago....Miller, Michael T. FTC 312-353-5260
Regional Office - Chicago....Olson, Mary E. FTC 312-353-4427
Regional Office - Chicago....Owen, Nathan P. FTC 312-353-4435
Regional Office - Chicago....Russell, Thomas J. FTC 312-353-4523
Regional Office - Chicago....Smith, Michele FTC 312-353-5045
Regional Office - Chicago....Wronka, Kathleen F. FTC 312-353-4442
Regional Office - Chicago....Williams, Vassoria L. FTC 312-353-4426
Regional Office - Cleveland....Amdur, Ilene FTC 216-522-4210
Regional Office - Cleveland....Balster, Steven W. FTC 216-522-4210
Regional Office - Cleveland....Broyles, Phillip FTC 216-522-4210
Regional Office - Cleveland....Doubrava, Brenda W. FTC 216-522-4210
Regional Office - Cleveland....Greene, Willie L. FTC 216-522-4210
Regional Office - Cleveland....Griffiths, Stephanie M. FTC 216-522-4210
Regional Office - Cleveland....Hessoun, Bonnie T. FTC 216-522-4210
Regional Office - Cleveland....King, Michael L. FTC 216-522-4210

Regional Office - Cleveland....Lerner, Louis L. FTC 312-353-5528
Regional Office - Cleveland....Mendenhall, John M. FTC 216-522-4210
Regional Office - Cleveland....Milgrom, Michael FTC 216-522-4210
Regional Office - Cleveland....Pirrone, Jaclyn S. FTC 216-522-4210
Regional Office - Cleveland....Plottner, David V. FTC 216-522-4210
Regional Office - Cleveland....Powell, Catherine F. FTC 216-522-4210
Regional Office - Cleveland....Rose, Michael B. FTC 216-522-4210
Regional Office - Cleveland....Sternlicht, Melissa FTC 216-522-4210
Regional Office - Cleveland....Vantusko, Mary Jo. FTC 216-522-4210
Regional Office - Cleveland....Zeman, Gerald C. FTC 216-522-4210
Regional Office - Cleveland....Williams, Brinley H. FTC 216-522-4210
Regional Office - Dallas....Staff CENSUS 214-767-7105
Regional Office - Dallas....Arthur, Susan E. FTC 214-767-5503
Regional Office - Dallas....Black, Michael R. FTC 202-326-3457
Regional Office - Dallas....Blackman, Claire R. FTC 214-767-5503
Regional Office - Dallas....Donsky, Robin L. FTC 214-767-5503
Regional Office - Dallas....Elliott, James E. FTC 214-767-5503
Regional Office - Dallas....Garcia, Ernestina FTC 214-767-5503
Regional Office - Dallas....Golder, James R. FTC 214-767-5503
Regional Office - Dallas....Gosha-Nelson, Jannette FTC 214-767-5503
Regional Office - Dallas....Griggs, W. David FTC 214-767-5503
Regional Office - Dallas....Kennedy, Gary D. FTC 214-767-5503
Regional Office - Dallas....Lenamond, Leslee A. FTC 214-767-5503
Regional Office - Dallas....Malmberg, Kristin L. FTC 214-767-5503
Regional Office - Dallas....McCowan, Curtistene S. FTC 214-767-5503
Regional Office - Dallas....Morgan, Maridel S. FTC 214-767-5503
Regional Office - Dallas....Shepherd, Judith A. FTC 214-767-5503
Regional Office - Dallas....Spears, Debby H. FTC 214-767-5503
Regional Office - Dallas....Weart, Steven E. FTC 214-767-5503
Regional Office - Denver....Staff CENSUS 303-969-7750
Regional Office - Denver....Burns, Michael D. FTC 303-844-3565
Regional Office - Denver....Carter, Thomas B. FTC 214-767-5503
Regional Office - Denver....Charter, Janice FTC 303-844-2868
Regional Office - Denver....Cole, Pamela M. FTC 303-844-2255
Regional Office - Denver....Cramer, Norman FTC 303-844-2275
Regional Office - Denver....Dahnke, Jeffrey FTC 303-844-2254
Regional Office - Denver....Farrand, Kelli A. FTC 303-844-2253
Regional Office - Denver....Gomez, Cynthia FTC 303-844-3082
Regional Office - Denver....Keese, Deborah C. FTC 303-844-2271
Regional Office - Denver....Kessler, Jonathan FTC 303-844-2276
Regional Office - Denver....Kraus, Loretta FTC 303-844-2273
Regional Office - Denver....Mooers, Elizabeth FTC 303-844-2274
Regional Office - Denver....Naylor, Sharon L. FTC 303-844-3576
Regional Office - Denver....Redd, Patricia R. FTC 303-844-3590
Regional Office - Denver....Wild, Claude C., III FTC 303-844-3571
Regional Office - Detroit....Staff CENSUS 313-354-4654
Regional Office - Kansas City....Staff CENSUS 816-891-7562
Regional Office - Los Angeles....Dawson, Darlene FTC 310-575-7974
Regional Office - Los Angeles....Deitch, Russell S. FTC 310-575-7965
Regional Office - Los Angeles....Donaldson, Nancy D. FTC 310-575-7890
Regional Office - Los Angeles....Frauens, Sue L. FTC 310-575-7890
Regional Office - Los Angeles....French, Kathy S. FTC 310-575-6138
Regional Office - Los Angeles....Guler, Ann M. FTC 310-575-7966
Regional Office - Los Angeles....Jacobs, John D. FTC 310-575-6602
Regional Office - Los Angeles....McKown, Raymond E. FTC 310-575-7962
Regional Office - Los Angeles....Roark, Paul R. FTC 310-575-7870
Regional Office - Los Angeles....Sekovich, Dale S. FTC 310-575-7572
Regional Office - Los Angeles....Smart, Bret S. FTC 310-575-7975
Regional Office - Los Angeles....Staples, Greg FTC 310-575-7990
Regional Office - Los Angeles....Stock, Linda M. FTC 310-575-7896
Regional Office - Los Angeles....Syta, Thomas J. FTC 310-575-7879
Regional Office - Los Angeles....Updegrove, Paul M. FTC 310-575-2420
Regional Office - Los Angeles....Watenmaker Dorothy N. FTC 310-575-7890
Regional Office - Los Angeles....Williams, Daylan M. FTC 310-575-7890
Regional Office - Los Angeles....Willis, Elizabeth M. FTC 310-575-7971
Regional Office - Los Angles....Staff CENSUS 818-904-6339
Regional Office - New York....Staff CENSUS 212-264-4730
Regional Office - New York....Au, Alice FTC 212-264-1210
Regional Office - New York....Bloom, Michael J. FTC 212-264-1201
Regional Office - New York....D'Amato, Donald G. FTC 212-264-1223
Regional Office - New York....Eichen, Robin E. FTC 212-264-1250
Regional Office - New York....Fischman, Ethel B. FTC 212-264-4688
Regional Office - New York....Freeman, Debra A. FTC 212-264-1229
Regional Office - New York....Goldsmith, Harriet S. FTC 212-264-1208
Regional Office - New York....Lipkowitz, Eugene FTC 212-264-1230
Regional Office - New York....Loughnan, Alan FTC 212-264-1232
Regional Office - New York....McLean, Rhonda J. FTC 212-264-1211

Regional Office - New York....Oteri, Patricia FTC 212-264-9804
Regional Office - New York....Presti, Angelo M. FTC 212-264-1220
Regional Office - New York....Roth, Marc S. FTC 212-264-8855
Regional Office - New York....Thompson, Luvennia H. FTC 212-264-0287
Regional Office - New York....Waldman, Ronald FTC 212-264-1242
Regional Office - San Francisco....Badger, Linda K. FTC 415-744-7920
Regional Office - San Francisco....Davis, Venita L. FTC 415-744-7920
Regional Office - San Francisco....Dominguez-Aldama, Rosa FTC 415-744-7920
Regional Office - San Francisco....Ehrenreich, Eric FTC 415-744-7920
Regional Office - San Francisco....Gold, Matthew FTC 415-744-7920
Regional Office - San Francisco....Kauffman, Craig D. FTC 415-744-7920
Regional Office - San Francisco....Klurfeld, Jeffrey A. FTC 415-744-7920
Regional Office - San Francisco....Kundig, Sylvia J. FTC 415-744-7920
Regional Office - San Francisco....Newmann, David M. FTC 415-744-7920
Regional Office - San Francisco....O'Brien, Kerry FTC 415-744-7920
Regional Office - San Francisco....Sodergren, Harold G. FTC 415-744-7920
Regional Office - San Francisco....Steiner, Jerome M., Jr. FTC 415-744-7920
Regional Office - San Francisco....Steinitz, Sidney FTC 202-326-3282
Regional Office - San Francisco....Stone, Ralph E. FTC 415-744-7920
Regional Office - San Francisco....Wodinsky, Erika R. FTC 415-744-7920
Regional Office - San Francisco....Wright, Gerald E. FTC 415-744-7920
Regional Office - San Francisco....Weigand, John FTC 415-744-7920
Regional Office - Seattle....Staff CENSUS 206-728-5314
Regional Office - Seattle....Benfield, Mary T. FTC 206-553-4656
Regional Office - Seattle....Brook, Randall H. FTC 206-553-4656
Regional Office - Seattle....Durham, Eleanor FTC 206-553-4656
Regional Office - Seattle....Fournier, Dean A. FTC 206-553-4656
Regional Office - Seattle....France, Laureen FTC 206-553-4656
Regional Office - Seattle....Harwood, Charles A. FTC 206-553-4656
Regional Office - Seattle....Hensley, Patricia A. FTC 202-553-4656
Regional Office - Seattle....Kirkwood, John B. FTC 206-553-4646
Regional Office - Seattle....Koester, Brian J. FTC 206-553-4656
Regional Office - Seattle....Leigh, Patricia FTC 206-553-4656
Regional Office - Seattle....McPeek, Zhenin FTC 206-553-4656
Regional Office - Seattle....Nielsen, Kathryn C. FTC 206-553-5656
Regional Office - Seattle....Schroeder, Robert J. FTC 206-553-4656
Regional Office - Seattle....Schuller, Stella A. FTC 206-553-4656
Regional Office - Seattle....Stansell, Maxine FTC 206-553-4656
Regional Office - Seattle....Thorleifson, Tracy S. FTC 206-553-4656
Regional Office - Seattle....Woods, K. Shane FTC 206-553-4656
Regional Office - Seattle....Zerbe, Richard O. FTC 206-553-4656
Regional Office - Seattle....Zweibel, George J. FTC 206-553-4656
Regional Office -Charlotte....Staff CENSUS 704-371-6142
Regional Office- Dallas....Hickman, Joseph L. FTC 214-767-5503
Regional, BEA Economic Areas....Trott, Jr., Edward A. ECONOMIC 202-523-0973
Regional, Disposable Personal Income....Brown, Robert ECONOMIC 202-254-6632
Regional, Dividends, Interest & Rental Income....Jolley, Charles A. ECONOMIC 202-254-6637
Regional, Economic Situation, Current....Friedenberg, Howard L. ECONOMIC 202-523-0979
Regional, Farm Proprietors' Income & Employment....Zavrel, James M. ECONOMIC 202-254-6638
Regional, Gross State Product Estimates....Dunbar Ann E. ECONOMIC 202-523-9180
Regional, Methodology....Bailey, Wallace K. ECONOMIC 202-254-6635
Regional, Personal Income & Employment, Metro Area....Hazan, Linnea ECONOMIC 202-254-6642
Regional, Personal Income and Employment, States....Hazan, Linnea ECONOMIC 202-254-6642
Regional, Personal Income and Employment, Counties....Hazan, Linnea ECONOMIC 202-254-6642
Regional, Projections-States & Metropolitan Areas....Pigler, Carmen C. ECONOMIC 202-523-0586
Regional, Shift-Share Analysis....Kort, John R. ECONOMIC 202-523-0946
Regional, State Ecometric Modeling....Lienesch, C. Thomas ECONOMIC 202-523-0943
Regional, State Quarterly Personal Income....Whiston, Isabelle B. ECONOMIC 202-254-6672
Regional, Transfer Payments....Levine, Bruce ECONOMIC 202-254-6634
Regional, Wage & Salary Income & Employment....Carnevale, Sharon ECONOMIC 202-254-7703
Regional, Requests for Pers. Income & Employment Data....Information System Staff ECONOMIC 202-254-6630
Regulators....Vacant USITC 202-205-3380
Rehabilitation....Staff NIA 301-496-1752

Experts

Reiter's Syndrome....Staff NIAMS 301-496-8188
Relays....Miller, Julius CUSTOMS 212-466-4680
Religious Studies....Childress, James F. UVA 701-924-3741
Remission....Staff NCI 301-496-5583
Remote Sensing Techniques....Sullivan, Nancy NASA 601-688-3341
Remote Sensor Systems....Koehler, Keith NASA 804-824-1579
Renal Disorders in Children....Staff NIDDK 301-496-3583
Renal Glycosuria....Staff NIDDK 301-496-3583
Renal Hypertension....Staff NHLBI 301-496-4236
Renal Tubular Acidosis....Staff NHLBI 301-496-4236
Renal Vascular Disease....Staff NHLBI 301-496-4236
Renewable Energy....Davis, Michael J. NEIC 202-586-9220
Renewable Energy Conversion....Kessler, Roland NEIC 202-586-8089
Renewable Energy Eqpmt....Garden, Les COMMERCE 202-482-0556
Renewable Energy Resources....King, Marion NEIC 202-586-8800
Renewable Energy Resources....Freedman, Karen NEIC 202-586-8800
Renovascular Hypertension....Staff NHLBI 301-496-4236
Rental (Scientific)....Staff DRS 301-496-4131
Reporting Crime to Police....Harlow, Caroline Justice Stat 202-307-0757
Reproductive Disorders....Staff NICHD 301-496-5133
Rescue Squads....Staff FCC 717-337-1212
Research & Development....Price, James B. COMMERCE 202-482-4781
Research (ethical issues)....Staff OD/OERT 301-496-7005
Research Aircraft....Brown, Dwayne C. NASA 202-453-8956
Research Career Development....Staff DRG 301-496-7441
Research Grants....Staff DRG 301-496-7441
Research Training....Staff DRG 301-496-7441
Research Training....Staff NIGMS 301-496-7301
Residence Adjustment....Zabronsky, Daniel ECONOMIC 202-254-6639
Residential Lighting Fixtures....Whitley, Richard A. COMMERCE 202-482-0682
Residual fuel oil....Foreso, Cynthia USITC 202-205-3348
Resistors....Josephs, Irwin CUSTOMS 212-466-5673
Resistors....Malison, Andrew USITC 202-205-3391
Resource Conservation and Reclamation Act (RCRA)....Traceski, Thomas NEIC 202-586-2481
Respiratory Diseases....Good, Robert C. CDC 404-639-3052
Respiratory Diseases (Infectious/Allergenic)....Staff NIAID 301-496-5717
Respiratory Diseases (Non-In., Non-All., Non-Tum.)....Staff NHLBI 301-496-4236
Respiratory Diseases (Tumorous/Cancerous)....Staff NCI 301-496-5583
Respiratory Syncytial Virus....Staff NIAID 301-496-5717
Restless Leg Syndrome....Staff NINDS 301-496-5751
Restricted Radiation Devices....Staff FCC 202-653-6288
Retail Trade....Margulies, Marvin J. COMMERCE 202-482-5086
Retail Trade, Advance Monthly Sales....Piencykoski, Ronald CENSUS 301-763-5294
Retail Trade, Annual Sales....Piencykoski, Ronald CENSUS 301-763-5294
Retail Trade, Census....Russell, Anne CENSUS 301-763-7038
Retail Trade, Monthly Inventories....Piencykoski, Ronald CENSUS 301-763-5294
Retail Trade, Monthly Trade Report....True, Irving CENSUS 301-763-7128
Retinal Degeneration....Staff NEI 301-496-5248
Retinal Detachment....Staff NEI 301-496-5248
Retinal Diseases....Staff NEI 301-496-5248
Retinal Diseases....Dudley, Peter A. FAES 301-496-5884
Retinal Vascular Disease....Staff NEI 301-496-5248
Retinitis Pigmentosa....Staff NEI 301-496-5248
Retinoblastoma....Staff NEI 301-496-5248
Retinopathies....Staff NEI 301-496-5248
Retirement....Staff NIA 301-496-1752
Retirement & Capital Acc, Employee Benefit Survey....Houff, James LABOR 202-606-6238
Retirement of Telephone Plants....Staff FCC 202-634-1861
Rett's Syndrome....Staff NINDS 301-496-5751
Reunion....Staff Cnty State 202-647-2453
Reunion/Minerals....Antonides, Lloyd Cnty Mines 202-501-9686
Reye's Syndrome....Staff NINDS 301-496-5751
Rh Factor....Staff NHLBI 301-496-4236
Rhabdomyosarcoma and Undifferentiated Sarcomas....Staff NCI 301-496-5583
Rhenium....Blossom, John W. MINES 202-501-9435
Rhenium....Lundy, David USITC 202-205-3439
Rheumatic Fever....Staff NIAID 301-496-5717
Rheumatic Heart....Staff NHLBI 301-496-4236
Rheumatoid Arthritis....Staff NIAMS 301-496-8188
Rhinitis....Staff NIAID 301-496-5717

Rhodium compounds....Greenblatt, Jack USITC 202-205-3353
Ribbons: inked....Cook, Lee USITC 202-205-3471
Ribbons: other....Shelton, Linda USITC 202-205-3457
Ribbons: typewriter....Shelton, Linda USITC 202-205-3457
Rice....Pierre-Benoist, John USITC 202-205-3320
Rice Milling....Janis, William V. COMMERCE 202-482-2250
Rice with options....Sepsey, Judy CFT 312-353-9025
Ricinoleic acid esters....Johnson, Larry USITC 202-205-3351
Rickets, Vitamin-D Resistant....Staff NIDDK 301-496-3583
Rickettsial Diseases....Staff NIAID 301-496-5717
Riding Mowers....Mesa, Stacey Reuben CPSC 301-504-0580
Riding crops....Burns, Gail USITC 202-205-3501
Rifles....Robinson, Hazel USITC 202-205-3496
Riley-Day Syndrome....Staff NINDS 301-496-5751
Ringworm....Staff NIAID 301-496-5717
River Blindness....Staff NEI 301-496-5248
River Blindness....Staff NIAID 301-496-5717
Roads, Railroads, Mass Trans (Major Proj)....Smith, Jay L. COMMERCE 202-482-4642
Robotics Research....Staff NASA 713-483-5111
Robots....Vacant COMMERCE 202-482-0314
Rocky Mountain Spotted Fever....Staff NIAID 301-496-5717
Rods, plastics....Misurelli, Denby USITC 202-205-3362
Roller Bearings....Reise, Richard COMMERCE 202-482-3489
Rolling Mill Machinery....Abrahams, Edward COMMERCE 202-482-0312
Rolling machines, except metal....Slingerland, David USITC 202-205-3400
Rollings mills, metal....Fravel, Dennis USITC 202-205-3401
Romania....Fabrizio, Lynn Cnty Commerce 202-482-2645
Romania....Becker, Margaret Peace Corps 202-606-3547
Romania....Sowry, Jenny Peace Corps 202-606-3547
Romania (Bucharest)....Staff Cnty State 202-647-3187
Romania/Minerals....Steblez, Walter Cnty Mines 202-501-9671
Roofing, Asphalt....Pitcher, Charles COMMERCE 202-482-0132
Root Caries....Staff NIDR 301-496-4261
Rope....Cook, Lee USITC 202-205-3471
Rosemary oil (essential oil)....Land, Eric USITC 202-205-3349
Rotavirus....Staff NIAID 301-496-5717
Rouges....Land, Eric USITC 202-205-3349
Rubber....Prat, Raimundo COMMERCE 202-482-0128
Rubber Products....Prat, Raimundo COMMERCE 202-482-0128
Rubber Sheet....Mazzola, Joan CUSTOMS 212-466-5880
Rubber and Plastic Articles....Mazzola, Joan CUSTOMS 212-466-5880
Rubber, Synthetic and Natural....Joseph, Stephanie CUSTOMS 212-466-5768
Rubber, natural....Misurelli, Denby USITC 202-205-3362
Rubber, synthetic....Misurelli, Denby USITC 202-205-3362
Rubella....Staff NIAID 301-496-5717
Rubeola....Staff NIAID 301-496-5717
Rubidium....Reese, Jr., Robert MINES 202-501-9413
Rugs....Hansen, John CUSTOMS 212-466-5854
Rugs....Sweet, Mary Elizabeth USITC 202-205-3455
Runaway Youth/Homeless....Long, Susan ACF 202-401-9215
Rural Aged....Staff NIA 301-496-1752
Rural Development....Mazie, Sara Agri 202-219-0530
Rural Development....McGranahan, David Agri 202-219-0532
Rural Development - Agric. & Community Linkages....Hines, Fred Agri 202-219-0525
Rural Development - Business & Industry....Bernat, Andrew Agri 202-219-0540
Rural Development - Community Development....Sears, David Agri 202-219-0544
Rural Development - Credit & Financial Markets....Sullivan, Pat Agri 202-219-0719
Rural Development - Employment....Swaim, Paul Agri 202-219-0552
Rural Development - Employment....Parker, Tim Agri 202-219-0541
Rural Development - Local Government Finance....Reeder, Richard Agri 202-219-0542
Rural Development - Local Government Finance...Jansen, Anicca Agri 202-219-0542
Rural Health....Mehuron, Charlotte HRSA 301-443-3376
Rural Residence....Staff CENSUS 301-763-7962
Russia....Brougher, J./Lewens, S./Smith, T./Johnson, P. Cnty Commerce 202-482-0354
Russia....Staff Cnty State 202-647-9806
Rwanda....Michelini, Philip Cnty Commerce 202-482-4388
Rwanda (Kigali)....Staff Cnty State 202-647-3139
Rwanda/Minerals....Antonides, Lloyd Cnty Mines 202-501-9686

S

Sewing thread: wool....Shelton, Linda USITC 202-205-3457

Sex Change....Staff NICHD 301-496-5133

Sex Determination....Staff NICHD 301-496-5133

Sex Hormones....Staff NICHD 301-496-5133

Sex and Aging....Staff NIA 301-496-1752

Sexual Development....Staff NICHD 301-496-5133

Sexually Transmitted Diseases....Staff NIAID 301-496-5717

Sexually Transmitted Diseases and HIV Prevention....Wasserheit, Judith N. CDC 404-639-2552

Seychelles....Watkins, Chandra Cnty Commerce 202-482-4564

Seychelles....Schmitz, Virginia Peace Corps 202-606-3334

Seychelles (Victoria)....Staff Cnty State 202-647-5684

Seychelles/Minerals....Antonides, Lloyd Cnty Mines 202-501-9686

Sezary Syndrome....Staff NIAMS 301-496-8188

Shale oil....Foreso, Cynthia USITC 202-205-3348

Shared Energy Cooperatives....Klunder, Kurt NEIC 202-586-2826

Shared Instrumentation Grant....Staff NCRR 301-496-6743

Shawls....Jones, Jackie USITC 202-205-3466

Sheep....Steller, Rose USITC 202-205-3323

Sheet, plastics....Misurelli, Denby USITC 202-205-3362

Sheets, bed....Sweet, Mary Elizabeth USITC 202-205-3455

Shell, articles of....Spalding, Josphine USITC 202-205-3498

Shellac and other lacs....Reeder, John USITC 202-205-3319

Shellac, varnish....Johnson, Larry USITC 201-205-3351

Shellfish....Brady, Thomas CUSTOMS 212-466-5790

Shellfish....Newman, Douglas USITC 202-205-3328

Shells, crude....Steller, Rose USITC 202-205-3323

Shingles (Herpes Zoster)....Staff NINDS 301-496-5751

Shingles (Herpes Zoster)....Staff NIAID 301-496-5717

Shingles and shakes (wood)....Ruggles, Fred USITC 202-205-3325

Shingles, Wood....Wise, Barbara COMMERCE 202-482-0375

Shingles, asphalt....Rhodes, Richard USITC 202-205-3322

Ship Earth Stations....Staff FCC 202-632-7175

Ship Inspections....Staff FCC 202-632-7014

Ship Licensing....Staff FCC 717-337-1212

Ship Rules/Exemptions....Staff FCC 202-632-7175

Shirts....Holoyda, Olha USITC 202-205-3467

Shock (Cardiogenic)....Staff NHLBI 301-496-4236

Shock (Hemorrhagic)....Staff NHLBI 301-496-4236

Shock Trauma Center....Staff UMD 301-528-6294

Shoe machinery....Vacant USITC 202-205-3380

Shoe parts....Shildneck, Ann USITC 202-205-3499

Shoes....Shildneck, Ann USITC 202-205-3499

Short-Term Forecasts of Energy Markets....Kilgore, Calvin NEIC 202-586-1617

Shorts....DeGaetano, Angela CUSTOMS 212-466-5540

Shorts: mens and boys....Linkins, Linda USITC 202-205-3469

Shorts: womens and girls....Holoyda, Olha USITC 202-205-3467

Shotguns....Robinson, Hazel USITC 202-205-3496

Shrimp....Newman, Douglas USITC 202-205-3328

Shy-Drager Syndrome....Staff NINDS 301-496-5751

Shy-Drager Syndrome....Staff NIMH 301-443-4515

Sickle Cell Anemia....Staff NHLBI 301-496-4236

Sideroblastic Anemia....Staff NHLBI 301-496-4236

Siding (wood)....Ruggles, Fred USITC 202-205-3325

Sierra Leone....Michelini, Philip Cnty Commerce 202-482-4388

Sierra Leone....McCormick, Michael L. Peace Corps 202-606-3644

Sierra Leone....Herring, Debra Peace Corps 202-606-3644

Sierra Leone (Freetown)....Staff Cnty State 202-647-3395

Sierra Leone/Minerals....Michalski, Bernadette Cnty Mines 202-501-9699

Sight Substitution Systems....Staff NEI 301-496-5248

Silica....White, Linda USITC 202-205-3427

Silicon....Cunningham, Larry D. MINES 202-501-9443

Silicon....Conant, Kenneth USITC 202-205-3346

Silicon Carbide Abrasive....Austin, Gordon MINES 202-501-9388

Silicone resins....Misurelli, Denby USITC 202-205-3362

Silicones....Michels, David USITC 202-205-3352

Silk....Freund, Kimberlie USITC 202-205-3456

Silk....Shelton, Linda USITC 202-205-3457

Silk....Warlick, William USITC 202-205-3459

Sillimanite....DeSapio, Vincent USITC 202-205-3435

Silver....Reese, Jr., Robert G. MINES 202-501-9413

Silver....McNay, Deborah USITC 202-205-3425

Silver compounds....Greenblatt, Jack USITC 202-205-3353

Silver with options....Rosenfeld, David CFT 312-353-9026

Silverware....Harris, John COMMERCE 202-482-1178

Singapore....Cung, Raphael Cnty Commerce 202-482-3875

Singapore (Singapore)....Staff Cnty State 202-647-3278

Singapore/Minerals....Tse, Pui-Kwan Cnty Mines 202-501-9696

Single Family Housing....Staff HUD 202-708-3175

Single Side Band--Standards....Staff FCC 202-653-6288

Sinusitis....Staff NIAID 301-496-5717

Sirups....Williams, Joan USITC 202-205-3313

Sjogren's Syndrome....Staff NIAMS 301-496-8188

Sjogren's Syndrome....Staff NIAID 301-496-5717

Sjogren's Syndrome....Staff NINDS 301-496-5751

Sjogren's Syndrome....Staff NEI 301-496-5248

Sjogren's Syndrome....Staff NIDR 301-496-4261

Ski equipment....Robinson, Hazel USITC 202-205-3496

Skin Cancer....Staff NCI 301-496-5583

Skin Diseases....Staff NIAMS 301-496-8188

Skin and Aging....Staff NIA 301-496-1752

Skin and Aging....Staff NIAMS 301-496-8188

Skin and Sunlight....Staff NIAMS 301-496-8188

Skin and Sunlight....Staff NCI 301-496-5583

Skins (animal)....Steller, Rose USITC 202-205-3323

Skirts....Holoyda, Olha USITC 202-205-3467

Skirts, Knit and Woven....DeGaetano, Angela CUSTOMS 212-466-5540

Slack....Foreso, Cynthia USITC 202-205-3348

Slacks, mens and boys....Linkins, Linda USITC 202-205-3467

Slacks, womens and girls....Holoyda, Olha USITC 202-205-3467

Slate....White, Linda USITC 202-205-3427

Sleep Disorders....Staff NINDS 301-496-5751

Sleep Disorders....Staff NIMH 301-443-4515

Sleep Disturbances....Staff NIMH 301-443-4515

Sleep and Aging....Staff NIA 301-496-1752

Sleep and Aging....Staff NIMH 301-443-1185

Sleepwear....Kaplan, Kathy CPSC 301-504-0580

Slide fasteners....Shildneck, Ann USITC 202-205-3499

Slippers....Shildneck, Ann USITC 202-205-3499

Slow Viruses....Staff NINDS 301-496-5751

Small Business Innovation Research Program....Selby, Barbara NASA 703-557-5609

Small Business Trade Policy....Burroughs, Helen COMMERCE 202-482-4806

Small Cell Carcinoma....Staff NCI 301-496-5583

Small and Woman-Owned Business Opportunities....Staff HUD 202-708-1428

Smallpox....Staff NIAID 301-496-5717

Smell (Disorders)....Staff NINDS 301-496-5751

Smell (Disorders)....Staff NIDCD 301-496-7243

Smoke Detectors....Glover, Stephanie CPSC 301-504-0580

Smokeless Tobacco (Oral Complications)....Staff NIDR 301-496-4251

Smokeless powder....Johnson, Larry USITC 202-205-3351

Smokers' Articles....Conte, Ralph CUSTOMS 212-466-5759

Smokers' articles....Burns, Gail USITC 202-205-3501

Smoking & Health....Hensley, Timothy CDC 404-488-5705

Smoking (Cancer related)....Staff NCI 301-496-5583

Smoking and Health....Staff Off. on Smok. and Health 301-443-1575

Smoking and Health....Eriksen, Michael P. CDC 404-488-5701

Smoking and Health, Public Information....McKenna, Jeffrey P. CDC 404-488-5705

Smoking and Heart Disease....Staff NHLBI 301-496-4236

Snackfood....Janis, William V. COMMERCE 202-482-2250

Snap fasteners....Shildneck, Anna USITC 202-205-3499

Soap, castile....Land, Eric USITC 202-205-3349

Soap, surface-active agents, synthetic detergent....Land, Eric USITC 202-205-3349

Soap, toilet....Land, Eric USITC 202-205-3349

Soaps....Joseph, Stephanie CUSTOMS 212-466-5768

Soaps, Detergents, Cleansers....Hurt, William COMMERCE 202-482-0128

Soapstone....White, Linda USITC 202-205-3427

Social Services Block Grant....Long, Susan ACF 202-401-9215

Social Work Department....Staff CC 301-496-2381

Social and Behavioral Research on Aging....Staff NIA 301-496-1752

Social and Behavioral Sciences....Staff NICHD 301-496-6832

Sociology....Caplow, Theodore UVA 703-924-6397

Sociology of Journalism....Levy, Mark R. UMD 301-405-2389

Soda ash....Conant, Kenneth USITC 202-205-3346

Sodium....Lecos, Chris FDA 202-205-4144

Sodium....Conant, Kenneth USITC 202-205-3346

Sodium Compounds....Kostick, Dennis S. MINES 202-501-9410

Sodium and potassium salts of oils, greases, fat....Land, Eric USITC 202-205-3349

Sodium benzoate....Matusik, Ed USITC 202-205-3356

Sodium bicarbonate....Conant, Kenneth USITC 202-205-3346

Sodium carbonate....Conant, Kenneth USITC 202-205-3346

Sodium compounds....Greenblatt, Jack USITC 202-205-3353

Sodium hydroxide....Conant, Kenneth USITC 202-205-3346

Soft Drink....Kenney, Cornelius COMMERCE 202-482-2428

Software....Smolenskni, Mary COMMERCE 202-482-2053

Software....Hijikata, Heidi C. COMMERCE 202-482-0571

Software services....Xavier, Neil USITC 202-205-3450

Software, Export Promo.....Fogg, Judy COMMERCE 202-482-4936

Solar Burns (Eye Effects)....Staff NEI 301-496-5248

Solar Cells/Photovoltaic Devices/Small Hydro....Garden, Les COMMERCE 202-482-0556

Solar Energy Conversion....San Martin, Robert NEIS 202-586-9275

Solar Energy Conversion....Annan, Robert H. NEIC 202-586-1720

Solar Eqmt. Ocean/Biomass....Garden, Les COMMERCE 202-482-0556

Solar Equipment, Geoth....Garden, Les COMMERCE 202-482-0556

Solar Phenomena Research....Staff NASA 415-604-3937

Solar System Exploration....Farrar, Diane NASA 415-604-3934

Solar Thermal and Biomass Power....Burch, Gary NEIC 202-586-8121

Solar energy....Foreso, Cynthia USITC 202-205-3348

Solid Waste Disposal....Staff OD/ORS 301-496-3537

Solid Waste Disposal (Radioactive)....Staff OD/ORS 301-496-2254

Solid Waste Information Clearinghouse Hotline....Staff EPA 800-677-9424

Solid Waste Management (Municipal)....Staff EPA 202-260-9872

Solid Waste Office of....Staff EPA 202-260-4627

Solomon Islands....Nagle, Douglas Peace Corps 202-606-3290

Solomon Islands....Jefferson, Mary Peace Corps 202-606-3231

Solomon Islands....Schell, Russell Peace Corps 202-606-3231

Solomon Islands (Honiara)....Staff Cnty State 202-647-3546

Solomon Islands/Minerals....Lyday, Travis Cnty Mines 202-501-9695

Somalia....Watkins, Chandra Cnty Commerce 202-482-4564

Somalia (Mogadishu)....Staff Cnty State 202-647-8852

Somalia/Minerals....Antonides, Lloyd Cnty Mines 202-501-9686

Sorbitol....Randall, Rob USITC 202-205-3366

Sorting machines....Greene, William USITC 202-205-3405

Sound signaling apparatus....Baker, Scott USITC 202-205-3386

Sounding Rocket Program....Koehler, Keith NASA 804-824-1579

Sounding Rockets....Brown, Dwayne C. NASA 202-453-8956

South Africa....Solomon, Emily Cnty Commerce 202-482-5148

South Africa, Republic of (Pretoria)....Staff Cnty State 202-647-8432

South Africa/Minerals....Heydari, Michael Cnty Mines 202-501-9688

South Pacific Commission....Staff Cnty State 202-647-3546

Soy Products....Janis, William V. COMMERCE 202-482-2250

Soybean Meal with options....Sweet, Margie CFT 312-353-3288

Soybean oil with options....Sweet, Margie CFT 312-353-3288

Soybeans and soybean oil....Reeder, John USITC 202-205-3319

Soybeans with options....Sweet, Margie CFT 312-353-3288

Space Communications....Brown, Dwayne C. NASA 202-453-8956

Space Derived Technology....Dunbar, Brian NASA 202-453-1547

Space Exploration....Keegan, Sarah NASA 703-271-5591

Space Flight....Cast, Jim NASA 202-453-1142

Space Flight....Campion, Edward S. NASA 202-453-1134

Space Flight Systems....Peto, Mary Ann NASA 216-433-2902

Space Industry Machinery, Nec....Shaw, Eugene COMMERCE 202-482-3494

Space Policy Development....Pajor, Pete COMMERCE 202-482-4222

Space Propulsion....Ellis, Linda NASA 216-433-2900

Space Remote Sensing Commercialization....Sullivan, Nancy NASA 601-688-3341

Space Science and Applications....Cleggett-Haleim, Paula NASA 202-453-1547

Space Science and Applications....Braukus, Michael NASA 202-453-1549

Space Shuttle....James, Donald G. NASA 415-604-3935

Space Shuttle....Malone, June NASA 205-544-7061

Space Shuttle Engine Testing....Sullivan, Nancy NASA 601-688-3341

Space Shuttle Program....Staff NASA 713-483-5111

Space Shuttle Propulsion Testing....Sullivan, Nancy NASA 601-688-3341

Space Shuttle Research....Staff NASA 804-864-6122

Space Station Freedom....Peto, Mary Ann NASA 216-433-2902

Space Station Freedom....Simmons, Mike NASA 205-544-6537

Space Technology....Staff NASA 205-544-6538

Space Vehicle Testing....Buckingham, Bruce NASA 407-867-2468

Space technology....Anderen, Drucella NASA 202-453-8613

Spacecraft....Anderson, Peder USITC 202-205-3388

Spacelab....Hess, Mark NASA 202-453-4164

Spacelab Missions Operations....Drachlis, David NASA 205-544-6538

Spain....Double, Mary Beth Cnty Commerce 202-482-4508

Spain (Madrid)....Staff Cnty State 202-647-1412

Spain/Minerals....Newman, Harold R. Cnty Mines 202-501-9669

Spanish, Italian and Portuguese languages....Opere, Fernando UVA 701-924-7159

Spasmodic Dysphonia....Staff NINDS 301-496-5751

Spasmodic Torticollis....Staff NINDS 301-496-5751

Spastic Hemiplegia....Staff NINDS 301-496-5751

Spastic Paraplegia....Staff NINDS 301-496-5751

Spastic Quadriplegia....Staff NINDS 301-496-5751

Spasticity....Staff NINDS 301-496-5751

Special Industry Machinery, Nec....Shaw, Eugene COMMERCE 202-482-3494

Special Population Censuses....Dopkowski, Ronald CENSUS 301-763-2767

Special Topics - Agricultural History....Bowers, Douglas Agri 202-219-0787

Special Topics - Alternative Crops....Glaser, Lewrene Agri 202-219-0888

Special Topics - Biotechnology....Reilly, John Agri 202-219-0450

Special Topics - Biotechnology (Dairy)....Fallert, Richard Agri 202-219-0712

Special Topics - Commodity Programs & Policies....Harwood, Joy Agri 202-219-0840

Special Topics - Commodity Programs & Policies-Honey....Hoff, Fred Agri 202-219-0883

Special Topics - Commodity Programs & Policies-Tobacco....Grise, Verner Agri 202-219-0890

Special Topics - Commodity Programs & Policies-Crops....Westcott, Paul Agri 202-219-0840

Special Topics - Commodity Programs & Policies-Dairy....Fallert, Richard Agri 202-219-0712

Special Topics - Commodity Programs & Policies-Sugar....Lord, Ron Agri 202-219-0888

Special Topics - Commodity Programs & Policies-World....Dixit, Praveen Agri 202-219-0632

Special Topics - Economic Linkages to Agriculture....Edmondson, William Agri 202-219-0785

Special Topics - Energy....Gill, Mohinder Agri 202-219-0464

Special Topics - Farm Labor Laws....Runyan, Jack Agri 202-219-0932

Special Topics - Farm Labor Market....Whitener, Leslie Agri 202-219-0932

Special Topics - Farm Machinery....Vesterby, Marlow Agri 202-219-0422

Special Topics - Farm Structure....Reimund, Donn Agri 202-219-0522

Special Topics - Fertilizer....Taylor, Harold Agri 202-219-0464

Special Topics - Fertilizer....Rives, Sam Agri 202-720-2324

Special Topics - Macroeconomic Conditions....Monaco, Ralph Agri 202-219-0872

Special Topics - Macroeconomic Conditions (World)....Baxter, Tim Agri 202-219-0706

Special Topics - Natural Resource Policy....Osborn, Tim Agri 202-219-0401

Special Topics - Natural Resource Policy....Ribaudo, Marc Agri 202-219-0444

Special Topics - Natural Resource Policy (World)....Urban, Francis Agri 202-219-0717

Special Topics - Pesticides....Padgitt, Merritt Agri 202-219-0433

Special Topics - Pesticides....Vandeman, Ann Agri 202-219-0433

Special Topics - Pesticides....Delvo, Herman Agri 202-219-0456

Special Topics - Pesticides....Love, John Agri 202-219-0886

Special Topics - Pesticides....Rives, Sam Agri 202-720-2324

Special Topics - Population....Beale, Calvin Agri 202-219-0535

Special Topics - Population....Swanson, Linda Agri 202-219-0535

Special Topics - Population - World....Urban, Francis Agri 202-219-0705

Special Topics - Seeds....Gill, Mohinder Agri 202-219-0464

Special Topics - Soil Conservation....Osborn, Tim Agri 202-219-0405

Special Topics - Soil Conservation....Magleby, Richard Agri 202-219-0435

Special Topics - Sustainable Agriculture....Gajewski, Greg Agri 202-219-0883

Special Topics - Sustainable Agriculture....Vandeman, Ann Agri 202-219-0433

Special Topics - Transportation....Hutchinson, T.Q. Agri 202-219-0840

Special Topics - Water & Irrigation....Gollehon, Noel Agri 202-219-0410

Special Topics - Water & Irrigation....Hostetler, John Agri 202-219-0410

Special Topics - Water Quality....Ribaudo, Marc Agri 202-219-0444

Special Topics - Water Quality....Crutchfield, Steve Agri 202-219-0444

Special Topics - Water Quality....Rives, Sam Agri 202-720-2324

Special Topics - Weather....Owens, Marty Agri 202-720-2157

Special Topics - Weather....Teigan, Lloyd Agri 202-219-0705

Special classification provisions....Shetty, Sundar USITC 202-205-3486

Species Profiles, Fish and Wildlife....Staff FWS 703-358-1710

Spectacles....Johnson, Christopher USITC 202-205-3488

Speech....Staff NIDR 301-496-4261

Speech and Language Disorders....Staff NINDS 301-496-5751

Speech and Language Disorders....Staff NICHD 301-496-5133

Speech and Language Disorders....Staff NIDCD 301-496-7243

Speed Changers....Reise, Richard COMMERCE 202-482-3489

Speed changers....Fravel, Dennis USITC 202-205-3404

Sphingolipidoses....Staff NINDS 301-496-5751

Sphingolipidoses Mucopolysaccaridoses & Stor. Dis......Staff NINDS 301-496-5751

Spices....Conte, Ralph CUSTOMS 212-466-5759

Spices....Schneider, Greg USITC 202-205-3326
Spielmeyer-Sjogren's Disease....Staff NINDS 301-496-5751
Spina Bifida....Staff NINDS 301-496-5751
Spina Bifida....Staff NICHD 301-496-5133
Spina Bifida....Staff NIDCD 301-496-7243
Spinal Arachnoiditis....Staff NINDS 301-496-5751
Spinal Cord Injury....Staff NINDS 301-496-5751
Spinal Cord Lesions....Staff NINDS 301-496-5751
Spinal Cord Tumors....Staff NINDS 301-496-5751
Spinal Muscular Atrophy....Staff NINDS 301-496-5751
Spinning machines....Greene, William USITC 202-205-3405
Spinocerebellar Degeneration....Staff NINDS 301-496-5751
Split Channel Operations....Staff FCC 202-653-5560
Sponge, articles of....Spalding, Josephine USITC 202-205-3498
Sponges, marine....Ludwick, David USITC 202-205-3329
Sporting Goods....McKenna, Thomas CUSTOMS 212-466-5475
Sporting Goods and Athletic....Vanderwolf, John COMMERCE 202-482-0348
Sporting Goods, Export Promo.....Beckham, Reginald COMMERCE 202-482-5478
Sporting goods....Robinson, Hazel USITC 202-205-3496
Sports Blackouts....Staff FCC 202-632-7048
Sports Medicine....Staff NIAMS 301-496-8188
Spraying machinery: agricultural/horticultural....Vacant USITC 202-205-3380
Spraying machinery: other....Slingerland, David USITC 202-205-3400
Squamous Cell....Staff NCI 301-496-5583
Sri Lanka....Simmons, John Cnty Commerce 202-482-2954
Sri Lanka....Ordonez, Miguel Peace Corps 202-606-3118
Sri Lanka (Colombo)....Staff Cnty State 202-647-2351
Sri Lanka/Minerals....Vacant Cnty Mines 202-501-9694
St. Bartholomey....Brooks, Michelle Cnty Commerce 202-482-2527
St. Kitts-Nevis....Brooks, Michelle Cnty Commerce 202-482-2527
St. Lucia....Brooks, Michelle Cnty Commerce 202-482-2527
St. Martin....Brooks, Michelle Cnty Commerce 202-482-2527
St. Vincent Grenadines....Brooks, Michelle Cnty Commerce 202-482-2527
Stained Teeth (Tetracycline)....Staff NIDR 301-496-4261
Stains....Johnson, Larry USITC 202-205-3351
Standard Industrial Classification, Empl/Unempl....Bennott, William LABOR 202-606-6474
Standard Occupational Classification, Empl/Unempl....McElroy, Michael LABOR 202-606-6516
Staphylococcal Infections....Staff NIAID 301-496-5717
Staple fibers, manmade....Sweet, Mary Elizabeth USITC 202-205-3455
Starches....Pierre-Benoist, John USITC 202-205-3320
Starches, chemically treated....Randall, Rob USITC 202-205-3366
State Data Center Program....Carbaugh, Larry CENSUS 301-763-1580
State Energy Programs....Demetrops, James NEIC 202-586-9187
State Projections....Staff CENSUS 301-763-1902
State and Area Labor Force Data, Data Disk & Tapes....Marcus, Jessie LABOR 202-606-6392
State and Area Labor Force Data, Demog. Char. E/Un....Biederman, Edna LABOR 202-606-6392
State and Metropolitan Area Data Books....Cevis, Wanda CENSUS 301-763-1034
State and Outlying Area Estimates....Staff CENSUS 301-763-5072
States & Areas Establishment Survey, Data Disk.....Podgornik, Guy LABOR 202-606-6559
States & Areas Establishment Survey, Empl/Unempl....Shipp, Kenneth LABOR 202-606-6559
Statistical Abstract....King, Glenn CENSUS 301-763-5299
Statistical Areas....Staff CENSUS 301-763-3827
Statistical Briefs....Bernstein, Robert CENSUS 301-763-1584
Statistical Methods, Prices & Living Cond.....Hedges, Brian LABOR 202-606-6897
Statistical Research for Demographic Programs....Ernst, Lawrence CENSUS 301-763-7880
Statistical Research for Economic Programs....Monsour, Nash J. CENSUS 301-763-5702
Statistical Surveys, National Fish and Wildlife....Staff FWS 703-358-1730
Statistician, Chief....Young, Allan H. ECONOMIC 202-523-0693
Statistics....Dillingham, Steven Justice Stat 202-307-0765
Statistics (Blindness and Visual Disorders)....Staff NEI 301-496-5248
Statistics (Health)....Staff NCHS 301-496-8500
Statistics (Health)....Staff CDC 404-639-3286
Staurolite....Austin, Gordon MINES 202-501-9388
Stearic acid....Randall, Rob USITC 202-205-3366
Stearic acid esters....Randall, Rob USITC 202-205-3366
Steatite....White, Linda USITC 202-205-3427

Steel Industry Products....Bell, Charles COMMERCE 202-482-0608
Steel, Basic Shapes and Forms....Ilardi, Paula CUSTOMS 212-466-5476
Steel: Ingots, blooms, and billets....Mascola, Robert USITC 202-205-3428
Steel: angles, shapes, and sections....Vacant USITC 202-205-3419
Steel: bars....Vacant USITC 202-205-3419
Steel: pipe and tube and fittings....MacKnight, Peggy USITC 202-205-3431
Steel: plate....Mascola, Robert USITC 202-205-3428
Steel: rails....Yost, Charles USITC 202-205-3432
Steel: sheet....Mascola, Robert USITC 202-205-3428
Steel: strip....Mascola, Robert USITC 202-205-3428
Steel: tubes....Laney-Cummings, Karen USITC 202-205-3431
Steel: waste and scrap....Vacant USITC 202-205-3419
Steel: wire....Yost, Charles USITC 202-205-3442
Steel: wire rods....Yost, Charles USITC 202-205-3442
Steel: Pipes....MacKnight, Peggy USITC 202-205-3431
Steele-Richardson Disease....Staff NINDS 301-496-5751
Stereo apparatus....Sherman, Thomas USITC 202-205-3389
Sterilization....Staff NICHD 301-496-5133
Steroid Contraceptives....Staff NICHD 301-496-5133
Steroid Hormones....Stoney, Simons S. FAES 301-496-6797
Steroid Hypertension....Staff NHLBI 301-496-4236
Stevens-Johnson Syndrome....Staff NIAID 301-496-5717
Stiff Man Syndrome....Staff NINDS 301-496-5751
Still's Disease....Staff NIAMS 301-496-8188
Stomach Cancer....Staff NCI 301-496-5583
Stone....Bunin, Jacob CUSTOMS 212-566-5796
Stone and products....White, Linda USITC 202-205-3427
Stone, Crushed....Tepordei, Valentin V. MINES 202-501-9392
Stone, Dimension....Taylor, Harold A. MINES 202-501-9754
Stone-processing machines....Greene, William USITC 202-205-3405
Stoneware articles....McNay, Deborah USITC 202-205-3425
Stoneworking machines....Vacant USITC 202-205-3380
Storage Batteries....Larrabee, David COMMERCE 202-482-0575
Storm Water....Staff EPA 703-821-4823
Storm Water Hotline....Staff EPA 703-821-4823
Stoves/Woodburning....Staff EPA 919-541-2821
Strabismus....Staff NEI 301-496-5248
Stranger-to-Stranger Crime....Rand, Michael Justice Stat 202-616-3494
Streptococcal Infections....Staff NIAID 301-496-5717
Streptokinase....Staff NHLBI 301-496-4236
Stress....Staff NIMH 301-496-4513
Stress (EKG)....Staff NHLBI 301-496-4236
Stress and Aging....Staff NIA 301-496-1752
Striatonigral Degeneration....Staff NINDS 301-496-5751
Stroke....Staff NINDS 301-496-5751
Stroke (Hypertension)....Staff NHLBI 301-496-4236
Strontium....Ober, Joyce A. MINES 202-501-9406
Strontium....Lundy, David USITC 202-205-3439
Strontium compounds....Greenblatt, Jack USITC 202-205-3353
Strontium pigments....Johnson, Larry USITC 202-205-3351
Structures of base metals....Yost, Charles USITC 202-205-3442
Student Conservation Programs, Fish and Wildlife....Staff FWS 703-358-2029
Students, Youth, and Dropouts, Empl/Unempl. Stats.....Cohany, Sharon LABOR 202-606-6378
Studio Transmitter Links, Common Carrier....Staff FCC 202-634-1706
Studio Transmitter Links, Mass Media....Staff FCC 202-634-6307
Sturge-Weber Syndrome....Staff NINDS 301-496-5751
Stuttering....Staff NINDS 301-496-5751
Stuttering....Staff NIDCD 301-496-7243
Sty....Staff NEI 301-496-5248
Styrene (monomer)....Matusik, Ed USITC 202-205-3356
Styrene resins....Misurelli, Denby USITC 202-205-3362
Subacute Necrotizing Encephalomyelopathy (Leighs')....Staff NINDS 301-496-5751
Subacute Sclerosing Panencephalitis....Staff NINDS 301-496-5751
Subarachnoid Hemorrhage....Staff NINDS 301-496-5751
Submarine Cable....Staff FCC 202-632-7265
Subscription Television....Staff FCC 202-632-6357
Subseabed Disposal Research....Warnick, Walter NEIC 301-903-3122
Substance Abuse Prevention, Office of....Setal, Mel ADAMHA 301-443-9936
Sudan....Watkins, Chandra Cnty Commerce 202-482-4564
Sudan (Khartoum)....Staff Cnty State 202-647-9742
Sudan/Minerals....Antonides, Lloyd Cnty Mines 202-501-9686
Sudanophilic Leukodystrophy....Staff NINDS 301-496-5751
Sudden Cardiac Death....Staff NHLBI 301-496-4236
Sudden Infant Death Syndrome....Staff NICHD 301-496-5133
Sugar....Maria, John CUSTOMS 212-466-5730

Sugar....Williams, Joan USITC 202-205-3313

Sugar and Sweeteners....Eldridge, Herb Agri 202-720-7621

Sugar and Sweeteners....Lord, Ronald Agri 202-219-0888

Sugar and Sweeteners....Buzzanell, Peter Agri 202-219-0888

Suicide....Staff NIMH 301-443-4513

Suicide....Baldwin, Elaine ADAMHA 301-443-4536

Suit-Jackets....Crowley, Michael CUSTOMS 212-466-5852

Suits....Crowley, Michael CUSTOMS 212-466-5852

Suits: men's and boys'....Linkins, Linda USITC 202-205-3469

Suits: women's and girls'....Holoyda, Olha USITC 202-205-3467

Sulfides, nonmetallic....Conant, Kenneth USITC 202-205-3346

Sulfiting Agents....Lecos, Chris FDA 202-205-1144

Sulfur....Ober, Joyce MINES 202-501-9406

Sulfur....Trainor, Cynthia USITC 202-205-3354

Sulfur dioxide....Conant, Kenneth USITC 202-205-3346

Sulfuric acid....Trainor, Cynthia USITC 202-205-3354

Sulfuryl chloride....Conant, Kenneth USITC 202-205-3346

Summer Research Fellowship Program....Staff CC 301-496-2427

Sunlight and Skin Cancer....Staff NCI 301-496-5583

Sunspot Cycle....Staff FCC 202-653-8166

Supercomputers....Streeter, Jonathan COMMERCE 202-482-0572

Superconducting Super Collider Project....Cipriano, Joseph NEIC 214-708-2521

Superconductivity....Eaton, Russell NEIC 202-586-0205

Superconductors....Chiarado, Roger COMMERCE 202-482-0402

Superfund....Staff EPA 202-260-2180

Superfund....Berreth, Don CDC 404-639-3286

Superfund Hazardous Waste....Staff EPA 800-346-5009

Superphosphates....Trainor, Cynthia USITC 202-205-3354

Supersonic (Mach 1-5) Engine Testing....Staff NASA 804-864-6125

Supplemental Security Income (SSI)....Gambino, Phil SSA 410-965-8904

Supplies (Central Storeroom)....Staff OD/DAS 301-496-9156

Surface Active Agents....Joseph, Stephanie CUSTOMS 212-466-5768

Surface-active agents....Land, Eric USITC 202-205-3349

Surgeon General....Fingland, Mary Jane PHS 202-690-7163

Surgery (Cancer)....Staff NCI 301-496-5583

Surgery (Oral)....Staff NIDR 301-496-4261

Surgical Treatment of Heart Disease....Staff NHLBI 301-496-4236

Surgical apparatus....Johnson, Christopher USITC 202-205-3488

Suriname....Brooks, Michelle Cnty Commerce 202-482-2527

Suriname (Paramaribo)....Staff Cnty State 202-647-4195

Suriname/Minerals....Mobbs, Philip Cnty Mines 202-501-9679

Survey Data and Tapes, Consumer Expend. Surv.....Passero, William LABOR 202-606-6900

Survey Operations, Consumer Expend. Survey. Pr/Lv....Dietz, Richard LABOR 202-606-6872

Survey of Income and Program Participation (SIPP)....Staff CENSUS 301-763-2764

Surveys, Migratory Birds....Staff FWS 703-358-1714

Surveys, National Fish and Wildlife....Staff FWS 703-358-1730

Surveys, Waterfowl Harvest....Staff FWS 703-358-1714

Surveys, Waterfowls Population....Staff FWS 703-358-1714

Sutures, surgical....Randall, Rob USITC 202-205-3366

Swaziland....Holm-Olsen, Finn Cnty Commerce 202-482-5148

Swaziland....Brill, Terry Peace Corps 202-606-3535

Swaziland (Mbabane)....Staff Cnty State 202-647-8252

Swaziland/Minerals....van Oss, Hendrik Cnty Mines 202-501-9687

Sweat Gland Disorders....Staff NIAMS 301-496-8188

Sweaters....Crowley, Michael CUSTOMS 212-466-5852

Sweaters....Holoyda, Olha USITC 202-205-3467

Sweatshirts....Crowley, Michael CUSTOMS 212-466-5852

Sweatshirts....Holoyda, Olha USITC 202-205-3467

Sweden....Devlin, James Cnty Commerce 202-482-4414

Sweden (Stockholm)....Staff Cnty State 202-647-6071

Sweden/Minerals....Buck, Donald E. Cnty Mines 202-501-9670

Swimwear....Jones, Jackie USITC 202-205-3466

Swimwear....Hamey, Amy USITC 202-205-3465

Swimwear, Adult....Shea, Gerard CUSTOMS 212-466-5878

Swimwear, Childrens'....Kirschner, Bruce CUSTOMS 212-566-5865

Swimwear: womens and girls....Linkins, Linda USITC 202-205-3469

Swine Flu....Staff NIAID 301-496-5717

Switches, Electric....Malison, Andrew USITC 202-205-3391

Switches, telephone....Bien, William USITC 202-205-3398

Switchgear & Switchboard Apparatus....Whitley, Richard A. COMMERCE 202-482-0682

Switzerland....Combs, Philip/Wright, Corey Cnty Commerce 202-482-2920

Switzerland (Bern)....Staff Cnty State 202-647-1484

Switzerland/Minerals....Buck, Donald E. Cnty Mines 202-501-9670

Sydenham's Chorea....Staff NINDS 301-496-5751

Syncope (Fainting)....Staff NHLBI 301-496-4236

Synfuel Plants....Frye, Keith NEIC 301-903-2098

Synovitis....Staff NIAMS 301-496-8188

Synthesis Gas....Der, Victor NEIC 301-903-2877

Synthetic detergents....Land, Eric USITC 202-205-3349

Synthetic iron oxides and hydroxides....Johnson, Larry USITC 202-205-3351

Synthetic natural gas (SNG)....Land, Eric USITC 202-205-3349

Synthetic rubber....Misurelli, Denby USITC 202-205-3362

Syphilis....Staff NIAID 301-496-5717

Syria....Wright, Corey/Sams, Thomas Cnty Commerce 202-482-4441

Syria/Minerals....Michalski, Bernadette Cnty Mines 202-501-9699

Syrian Arab Republic (Damascus)....Staff Cnty State 202-647-1131

Syringomyelia....Staff NINDS 301-496-5751

System Integration....Atkins, Robert COMMERCE 202-482-4781

Systemic Lupus Erythematosus....Staff NIAMS 301-496-8188

Systolic Hypertension in the Elderly (SHEP)....Staff NHLBI 301-496-4236

Systolic Hypertension in the Elderly (SHEP)....Staff NIA 301-496-1752

T

T-Bills with options....SIA Manasses CFT 312-353-9027

T-Bonds with options....Redheffer, Nancy L. CFT 312-353-9015

T-Cell Deficiency....Staff NIAID 301-496-5717

T-Notes (2,5, 6-10) with options....Redheffer, Nancy L. CFT 312-353-9015

T-Notes/Bonds (Zeros) with options....Redheffer, Nancy L. CFT 312-353-9015

T-Shirts....Holoyda, Olha USITC 202-205-3467

T-Shirts, Knit....DeGaetano, Angela CUSTOMS 212-466-5540

TELEX, International & Domestic....Staff FCC 202-632-7265

TIGER System Products....Staff CENSUS 301-763-4100

TIGER, Applications....Carbaugh, Larry CENSUS 301-763-1580

TIGER, Future Plans....Staff CENSUS 301-763-4664

TSH, Excessive Secretion....Staff NIDDK 301-496-3583

TTY - Population Information....Staff CENSUS 301-763-5020

TV Broadcasting....Siegmund, John COMMERCE 202-482-4781

TV Communications Eqmt....Gossack, Linda COMMERCE 202-482-4466

TV Violence....Baldwin, Elaine ADAMHA 301-443-4536

Tablecloths....Sweet, Mary Elizabeth USITC 202-205-3455

Tachycardia....Staff NHLBI 301-496-4236

Taiwan....Davis, Ian/Carroll, Paul/Duvall, Dan Cnty Commerce 202-482-4957

Taiwan Coordination....Staff Cnty State 202-647-7711

Taiwan/Minerals....Tse, Pui-Kwan Cnty Mines 202-501-9696

Tajikistan....Staff Cnty State 202-647-8671

Takayasu's Arteritis....Staff NIAID 301-496-5717

Take Pride in America Program, Fish and Wildlife....Staff FWS 703-358-2156

Talc....Virta, Robert MINES 202-501-9384

Talc....White, Linda USITC 202-205-3427

Tall oil....Randall, Rob USITC 202-205-3366

Tangier Disease....Staff NHLBI 301-496-4236

Tangier Disease....Staff NINDS 301-496-5751

Tanning products and agents....Wanser, Stephen USITC 202-205-3363

Tantalum....Presbury, Graylin COMMERCe 202-482-5158

Tantalum....Cunningham, Larry D. MINES 202-501-9443

Tantalum....Lundy, David USITC 202-205-3439

Tanzania....Holm-Olsen, Finn Cnty Commerce 202-482-4228

Tanzania....Hohman, Eric Peace Corps 202-606-3709

Tanzania (Dar es Salaam)....Staff Cnty State 202-647-5684

Tanzania/Minerals....Izon, David Cnty Mines 202-501-9692

Tape Players....Dicerbo, Mario CUSTOMS 212-466-5672

Tape players....Sherman, Thomas USITC 202-205-3389

Tape recorders and players, audio....Sherman, Thomas USITC 202-205-3389

Tape recordings....Sherman, Thomas USITC 202-205-3389

Tapestries....Hansen, John CUSTOMS 212-466-5854

Tapestries....Sweet, Mary Elizabeth USITC 202-205-3455

Taping of Telephone Calls....Staff FCC 202-632-7260

Taps....Mata, Ruben USITC 202-205-3403

Tar Sands....Der, Victor NEIC 301-903-2877

Tar sands oil....Foreso, Cynthia USITC 202-205-3348

Tardive Dyskinesia....Staff NIMH 301-443-4515

Tardive Dyskinesia....Staff NINDS 301-496-5751

Tarsal Tunnel Syndrome....Staff NINDS 301-496-5751

Taste....Staff NIDR 301-496-4261

Taste and Smell Dysfunction....Staff NINDS 301-496-5751

Taste and Smell Dysfunction....Staff NIDCD 301-496-7243

Tay-Sach's Disease....Staff NINDS 301-496-5751

Tea....Janis, William V. COMMERCE 202-482-2250

Tea....Maria, John CUSTOMS 212-466-5730

Tea....Schneider, Greg USITC 202-205-3326

Technological Developments and Nursing Care....Staff NCNR 301-496-0526

Technology Centers, Fish....Staff FWS 703-358-1714

Technology Transfer, Office of....Adler, Reid FAES 301-496-0750

Technology Trends In Major Industries....Riche, Richard LABOR 202-606-5626

Teenage Pregnancy....Eddinger, Lucy ASH 202-690-8335

Teenage Pregnancy....Staff NICHD 301-496-5133

Teeth....Staff NIDR 301-496-4261

Telangiectasis (Rendu-Osler-Weber Dis., Syndrome)....Staff NHLBI 301-496-4236

Telecommunications for Deaf, Public & Spec. Studies....TDD LABOR 202-606-5897

Telecommunication Devices for the Deaf....Staff FCC 202-632-6999

Telecommunications....Stechschulte, Roger COMMERCE 202-482-4466

Telecommunications (Network Eqpt)....Henry, John COMMERCE 202-482-4466

Telecommunications (TV Broadcast Equip.)....Rettig, Thersa E. COMMERCE 202-482-4466

Telecommunications Services....Shefrin, Ivan COMMERCE 202-48244661

Telecommunications, CPE....Edwards, Dan COMMERCE 202-482-4466

Telecommunications, Cellular....Gossack, Linda COMMERCE 202-482-4466

Telecommunications, Fiber Optics...Judge, Paulames COMMERCE 202-482-4466

Telecommunications, Major Projects....Paddock, Rick COMMERCE 202-482-4466

Telecommunications, Network Equipment....Henry, John COMMERCE 202-482-4466

Telecommunications, Radio....Gossack, Linda COMMERCE 202-482-4466

Telecommunications, Satellites....Cooper, Patricia COMMERCE 202-482-4466

Telecommunications, Services....Shefrin, Ivan COMMERCE 202-482-4466

Telecommunications, Trade Promo.....Rettig, Theresa E. COMMERCE 202-482-4466

Telegraph Service....Staff FCC 202-632-7876

Telegraph and Telephone Rates....Staff FCC 202-632-5550

Telegraph and telephone apparatus....Bien, William USITC 202-205-3398

Telephone Equipment Interconnection....Staff FCC 202-634-1800

Telephone Lines....Staff FCC 202-632-1800

Telephone Telegraph Rates....Staff FCC 202-632-5550

Telephone services....Posey, Melanie USITC 202-205-3303

Telephones....Josephs, Irwin CUSTOMS 212-466-5673

Telephones, Wireless....Dicerbo, Mario CUSTOMS 212-466-5672

Teleprinter (Telephone, Telegraph)....Staff FCC 202-634-1800

Telescopes....Johnson, Christopher USITC 202-205-3488

Teletext Services....Inoussa, Mary COMMERCE 202-482-5820

Television Advertising....Staff FCC 202-632-7551

Television Advertising Intercity Relays....Staff FCC 202-634-6307

Television Political Broadcasting Fairness....Staff FCC 202-632-7586

Television Programming....Staff FCC 202-632-7048

Television Religious Petition....Staff FCC 202-632-7000

Television Remote Pickups....Staff FCC 202-634-6307

Television Stations--New....Staff FCC 202-632-6495

Television Translators....Staff FCC 202-632-7698

Television equipment....Kitzmiller, John USITC 202-205-3387

Television programming....Staff FCC 202-632-7551

Televisions....Dicerbo, Mario CUSTOMS 212-466-5672

Tellurium....Edelstein, Daniel MINES 202-501-9415

Tellurium compounds....Greenblatt, Jack USITC 202-205-3353

Temporal Arteritis (Eyes)....Staff NEI 301-496-5248

Temporal Arteritis (Neurological Aspects of)....Staff NINDS #01-496-5751

Temporomandibular Joint Disorders....Staff NIDR 301-496-4261

Tendonitis....Staff NIAMS 301-496-8188

Tennis equipment....Robinson, Hazel USITC 202-205-3496

Tents and tarpaulins....Freund, Kimberlie USITC 202-205-3456

Test Tube Babies....Staff NICHD 301-496-5133

Testicular Cancer....Staff NCI 301-496-5583

Tetanus....Staff NIAID 301-496-5717

Tetraethyl lead....Michels, David USITC 202-205-3352

Tetralogy of Fallot....Staff NHLBI 301-496-4236

Tetramer of proplyene....Raftery, Jim USITC 202-205-3365

Tetramethyl lead....Michels, David USITC 202-205-3352

Tetrapropylene....Raftery, Jim USITC 202-205-3365

Textile Machinery....Vacant COMMERCE 202-482-0679

Textile calendaring and rolling machines....Greene, William USITC 202-205-3405

Textile finishing agents....Land, Eric USITC 202-205-3349

Textile machines....Greene, William USITC 202-205-3405

Textile washing, bleaching, dyeing, machines....Greene, William USITC 202-205-3405

Textiles....Dulka, William A. COMMERCE 202-482-4058

Textiles and Leather, Prices and Living Conditions....Paik, Soon LABOR 202-606-7714

Textiles, Trade Promo....Molnar, Ferenc COMMERCE 202-482-2043

Thailand....Kelly, Jean Cnty Commerce 202-482-3875

Thailand....Swanson, Alan Peace Corps 202-606-3040

Thailand....Huston, Christine Peace Corps 202-606-3040

Thailand....Hower, Mark Peace Corps 202-606-5517

Thailand (Bangkok)....Staff Cnty State 202-647-7108

Thailand/Minerals....Vacant Cnty Mines 202-501-9694

Thalassemia....Staff NHLBI 301-496-4236

Thalassemia....Staff NIDDK 301-496-3583

Thallium....Llewellyn, Thomas MINES 202-501-9395

Thallium compounds....Greenblatt, Jack USITC 202-205-3353

Theater....McCord, Karyl NEA 202-682-5425

Theories of Aging....Staff NIA 301-496-1752

Thoracic-Outlet Syndrome....Staff NINDS 301-496-5751

Thorium....Hedrick, James B. MINES 202-501-9412

Thorium....DeSapio, Vincent USITC 202-205-3435

Thorium compounds....Greenblatt, Jack USITC 202-205-3353

Thread: cotton....Warlick, William USITC 202-205-3459

Thread: manmade fibers....Warlick, William USITC 202-205-3459

Thread: silk....Shelton, Linda USITC 202-205-3467

Threatened Species Permits, Fish and Wildlife....Staff FWS 703-358-2104

Thrombasthenia....Staff NIDDK 301-496-3583

Thrombocytopenia....Staff NIDDK 301-496-3583

Thromboembolism....Staff NHLBI 301-496-4236

Thrombolysis....Staff NHLBI 301-496-4236

Thrombophlebitis....Staff NHLBI 301-496-4236

Thrombosis....Staff NHLBI 301-496-4236

Thyroid (Adenoma of)....Staff NIDDK 301-496-3583

Thyroiditis....Staff NIDDK 301-496-3583

Thyroma....Staff NCI 301-496-5583

Thyroxine-iodine....Staff NIDDK 301-496-3583

Tic Douloureux (Trigeminal Neuralgia)....Staff NINDS 301-496-5751

Ticks....Staff NIAID 301-496-5717

Tie-line--Telegraph Telephone....Staff FCC 202-632-5550

Tiger, Products....Staff CENSUS 301-763-4100

Tights....DeGaetano, Angela CUSTOMS 212-466-5540

Tiles, ceramic....McNay, Deborah USITC 202-205-3425

Timber Management....Staff FS 303-498-1803

Timber Management, Fish and Wildlife....Staff FWS 703-358-2043

Time Served in Prison....Beck, Allen Justice Stat 202-616-3277

Time Served in Prison....Innes, Christopher Justice Stat 202-724-3121

Time Served in Prison....Greenfeld, Lawrence Justice Stat 202-616-3281

Time Served in Prison - Federal....Kaplan, Carol Justice Stat 202-307-0759

Time switches....Luther, Dennis USITC 202-205-3497

Timing apparatus....Luther, Dennis USITC 202-205-3497

Tin....Carlin, Jr., James F. MINES 202-501-9411

Tin....DeSapio, Vincent USITC 202-205-3435

Tin Products....Presbury, Graylin COMMERCE 202-482-5158

Tin compounds....Greenblatt, Jack USITC 202-205-3353

Tinnitus....Staff NINDS 301-496-5751

Tinnitus....Staff NIDCD 301-496-7243

Tires....Prat, Raimundo COMMERCE 202-482-0128

Tires....Rauch, Theodore CUSTOMS 212-466-5892

Tires and tubes, of rubber of plastics....Raftery, Jim USITC 202-205-3365

Tissue Culture Cells (Freezing and Storage)....Staff OD/ORS 301-496-2960

Tissue Culture Media....Staff OD/ORS 301-496-6017

Tissue Plasminogen Activator (TPA)....Staff NHLBI 301-496-4236

Tissue Typing....Staff NIAID 301-496-5717

Titanium....Gambogi, Joseph MINES 202-501-9390

Titanium....DeSapio, Vincent USITC 202-205-3435

Titanium compounds....Greenblatt, Jack USITC 202-205-3353

Titanium dioxide....Johnson, Larry USITC 202-205-3351

Titanium pigments....Johnson, Larry USITC 202-205-3351

Tobacco....Eldridge, Herb Agri 202-720-7621

Tobacco....Grise, Verner Agri 202-219-0890

Tobacco....Capehart, Tom Agri 202-219-0890

Tobacco....Conte, Ralph CUSTOMS 212-466-5759

Tobacco Products....Kenney, Cornelius COMMERCE 202-482-2428

Tobacco and tobacco products....Salin, Victoria USITC 202-205-3351

Tobacco machines....Jackson, Georgia USITC 202-205-3399

Tobacco pipes....Burns, Gail USITC 202-205-3501

Togo....Henke, Debra Cnty Commerce 202-482-5149

Turntables....Sherman, Thomas USITC 202-205-3389

Turpentine....Reeder, John USITC 202-205-3319

Turtles (Salmonellosis)....Staff CDC 404-639-3286

Tuvalu....Lagoy, Michele Peace Corps 202-606-3227

Tuvalu (Funafuti)....Staff Cnty State 202-647-3546

Twine....Cook, Lee USITC 202-205-3471

Typewriters....Baker, Scott USITC 202-205-3386

Typhoid Fever....Staff NIAID 301-496-5717

U

US Trade & Foreign Agriculture....Baxter, Tim Agri 202-219-0706

US Trade & Foreign Agriculture....Stallings, David Agri 202-219-0688

US Trade & Foreign Agriculture - Africa & Mideast....Kurtzig, Mike Agri 202-219-0680

US Trade & Foreign Agriculture - Asia - East....Coyle, William Agri 202-219-0610

US Trade & Foreign Agriculture - Asia - South....Landes, Rip Agri 202-219-0664

US Trade & Foreign Agriculture - Canada....Simone, Mark Agric 202-219-0610

US Trade & Foreign Agriculture - China....Tuan, Francis Agri 202-219-0626

US Trade & Foreign Agriculture - Developing Economies....Mathia, Gene Agri 202-219-0680

US Trade & Foreign Agriculture - Eastern Europe....Koopman, Robert Agri 202-219-0621

US Trade & Foreign Agriculture - Eastern Europe....Cochrane, Nancy Agri 202-219-0621

US Trade & Foreign Agriculture - Exports....MacDonald, Steve Agri 202-219-0822

US Trade & Foreign Agriculture - Exports & Imports....Warden, Thomas Agri 202-219-0822

US Trade & Foreign Agriculture - Food Aid....Kurtzig, Mike Agri 202-219-0680

US Trade & Foreign Agriculture - Food Aid Programs....Suarez, Nydia Agri 202-219-0821

US Trade & Foreign Agriculture - Latin America....Link, John Agri 202-219-0660

US Trade & Foreign Agriculture - Pacific Rim....Coyle, William Agri 202-219-0610

US Trade & Foreign Agriculture - Programs....Ackerman, Karen Agri 202-219-0821

US Trade & Foreign Agriculture - Trade & Finance....Magiera, Steve Agri 202-219-0633

US Trade & Foreign Agriculture - Trade & Finance....Roningen, Vern Agri 202-219-0631

US Trade & Foreign Agriculture - USSR....Zeimetz, Kathryn Agri 202-219-0624

US Trade & Foreign Agriculture - Western Europe....Coyle, William Agri 202-219-0610

USSR (Moscow)....Staff Cnty State 202-647-8671

Uganda....Watkins, Chandra Cnty Commerce 202-482-4564

Uganda....Fossum, Linnea Peace Corps 202-606-3708

Uganda (Kampala)....Staff Cnty State 202-647-5684

Uganda/Minerals....Izon, David Cnty Mines 202-501-9692

Ukraine....Hower, Mark Peace Corps 202-606-5517

Ukraine....Taylor, Jeff Peace Corps 202-606-5519

Ulcerative Colitis....Staff NIDDK 301-496-3583

Ulcerative Lesions (Oral)....Staff NIDR 301-496-4261

Ulcers....Staff NIDDK 301-496-3583

Ultrasonics Equipment....Staff FCC 202-653-8247

Umbrellas....Burns, Gail USITC 202-205-3501

Underground Nuclear Testing....Williams, Irvin NEIC 301-903-5341

Underwear....Burtnik, Brian CUSTOMS 212-466-5880

Underwear....Linkins, Linda USITC 202-205-3469

Unemployment Statistics....Palumbo, Thomas CENSUS 301-763-8574

Unemployment and Labor Force, Foreign Countries....Sorrentino, Constance LABOR 202-606-5654

Unfinished oils....Foreso, Cynthia USITC 202-205-3348

Uniform Crime Reports - Redesign Implementation....White, Paul Justice Stat 202-307-0771

Uniform Crime Reports - Redesign Implementation....Manson, Donald Justice Stat 202-616-3491

Unions, Employee Associations, Membership, Comp/Wk....Cimini, Michael LABOR 202-606-6275

Unit Labor Costs, Productivity....Neef, Arthur LABOR 202-606-5654

United Arab Emirates....Clement, Claude Cnty Commerce 202-482-5545

United Arab Emirates (Abu Dhabi)....Staff Cnty State 202-647-6558

United Arab Emirates/Minerals....King, Audie L. Cnty Mines 202-501-9674

United Kingdom....McLaughlin, Robert Cnty Commerce 202-482-3748

United Kingdom (London)....Staff Cnty State 202-482-8027

United Kingdom/Minerals....Newman, Harold R. Cnty Mines 202-501-9669

Universal joints....Topolansky, Adam USITC 202-205-3394

Unresectable Chrondosarcoma or Osteogenic Sarcoma....Staff NCI 301-496-5583

Upholstery fabrics....Freund, Kimberlie USITC 202-205-3456

Upper Atmosphere Research Satellite....Loughlin, John NASA 301-286-5565

Upper Atmosphere Research Satellite....Staff NASA 301-286-2806

Uranium....Sugg, William COMMERCE 202-482-1466

Uranium....DeSapio, Vincent USITC 202-205-3435

Uranium Enrichment....Swell, Philip NEIC 301-903-4321

Uranium compounds....Greenblatt, Jack USITC 202-205-3353

Uranium oxide....Greenblatt, Jack USITC 202-205-3353

Urban Residence....Staff CENSUS 301-763-7962

Urban and Community Forestry Programs....Conrad Robert FS 202-205-0823

Urban/Rural Residence....Staff CENSUS 301-763-7962

Urea....Trainor, Cynthia USITC 202-205-3354

Urea resins....Misurelli, Denby USITC 202-205-3362

Uremia....Staff NIDDK 301-496-3583

Uric Acid Kidney Stones....Staff NIDDK 301-496-3583

Urinary Incontinence....Staff NIA 301-496-1752

Urinary Tract Diseases....Staff NIDDK 301-496-3583

Urinary Tract Infections....Staff NIDDK 301-496-3583

Urinary Tract Tumors....Staff NIDDK 301-496-3583

Urine Volume....Staff NIDDK 301-496-3583

Urokinase....Staff NHLBI 301-496-4236

Urolithiasis....Staff NIDDK 301-496-3583

Urticaria....Staff NIAID 301-496-5717

Uruguay....Turner, Roger Cnty Commerce 202-482-1495

Uruguay....Eschelman, Michael Peace Corps 202-606-3376

Uruguay....Lustumbo, Julie Peace Corps 202-606-3575

Uruguay (Montevideo)....Staff Cnty State 202-647-2296

Uruguay/Minerals....Gurmendi, Alfredo Cnty Mines 202-501-9681

Uterus....Staff NICHD 301-496-5133

Utility, Retail Prices....Adkins, Robert LABOR 202-606-6985

Uveitis....Staff NEI 301-496-5248

Uzbekistan....Staff Cnty State 202-647-6731

V

VCR's....Dicerbo, Mario CUSTOMS 212-466-5672

VD....Staff NIAID 301-496-5717

VD (Control and Treatment)....Staff CDC 404-639-3286

Vacancies, NIH Recording....Staff NIH 301-496-1209

Vaccine Licensing....Peterson, Faye FDA 301-443-3285

Vaccines....Staff FDA/NCDB/OB 301-496-3556

Vaccines....Staff NIAID 301-496-5717

Vaccines....Nesbitt, Elizabeth USITC 202-205-3355

Vacuum cleaners....Jackson, Georgia USITC 202-205-3399

Vaginitis....Staff NIAID 301-496-5717

Valves....Riedl, Karl CUSTOMS 212-466-5493

Valves (Heart)....Staff NHLBI 301-496-4236

Valves and cocks....Mata, Ruben USITC 202-205-3403

Valves, Pipefittings Ex Brass....Reise, Richard COMMERCE 202-482-3489

Valvular Heart Disease....Staff NHLBI 301-496-4236

Vanadium....Hilliard, Henry E. MINES 202-501-9429

Vanadium....Lundy, David USITC 202-205-3439

Vanadium compounds....Greenblatt, Jack USITC 202-205-3353

Vanatu (Port Vila)....Staff Cnty State 202-647-3546

Vanillin....Land, Eric USITC 202-205-3349

Vanuatu....Nagle, Douglas Peace Corps 202-606-3290

Vanuatu....Jefferson, Mary Peace Corps 202-606-3231

Vanuatu....Schell, Russell Peace Corps 202-606-3231

Vanuatu/Minerals....Lyday, Travis Cnty Mines 202-501-9695

Varicella, Congenital....Staff NINDS 301-496-5751

Varicose Veins....Staff NHLBI 301-496-4236

Varnish....Brownchweig, Gilbert CUSTOMS 212-466-5744

Varnishes....Johnson, Larry USITC 202-205-3351

Vascular Collapse....Staff NHLBI 301-496-4236

Vasculitis....Staff NHLBI 301-496-4236

Vasculitis....Staff NIAID 301-496-5717

Vasculitis....Staff NHLBI 301-496-4236

Vasectomy....Staff NICHD 301-496-5133

Vatican....Staff Cnty State 202-647-2453

Vector-Borne Infectious Diseases....Gubler, Duane J. CDC 303-221-6428

Vegetable fibers (except cotton)....Cook, Lee USITC 202-205-3471

Vegetable glue....Jonnard, Aimison USITC 202-205-3350

Vegetables....Hintzman, Kevin Agri 202-720-5412

Vegetables....Lucier, Gary Agri 202-219-0884

Vegetables....Greene, Catherine Agri 202-219-0886

Vegetables....Hamm, Shannon Agri 202-219-0886

Vegetables....Hodgen, Donald A. COMMERCE 202-482-3346

Vegetables....Nunis, Kelly USITC 202-205-3324

Vegetables - Fresh....Brewster, Jim Agri 202-720-7688

Vegetables - Proc.....Budge, Arvin Agri 202-720-4285

Vehicle Propulsion Systems....Allsup, Jerry NEIC 202-586-9118

Vehicles, Special Purpose....Desoucey, Robert CUSTOMS 212-466-5667

Veiling....Sweet, Mary Elizabeth USITC 202-205-3455

Vending machines....Jackson, Georgia USITC 202-205-3399

Venereal Disease....Staff NIAID 301-496-5717

Venereal Disease (Control and Treatment)....Staff CDC 404-639-3286

Venezuela....Lindow, Herbert Cnty Commerce 202-482-4303

Venezuela (Caracas)....Staff Cnty State 202-647-3338

Venezuela/Minerals....Torres, Ivette Cnty Mines 202-501-9680

Ventilation....Staff OD/ORS 301-496-2960

Vermiculite....Potter, Michael J. MINES 202-501-9387

Vertigo....Staff NINDS 301-496-5751

Vertigo....Staff NIDCD 301-496-7243

Vests, mens'....Jones, Jackie USITC 202-205-3466

Veterans Status....Palumbo, Thomas CENSUS 301-763-8574

Veterans Status....Jones, Selwyn CENSUS 301-763-8574

Veterans, Employment Statistics....Cohany, Sharon LABOR 202-606-6378

Veterinary Medicine....Snider, Sharon FDA 301-443-3285

Veterinary instruments...Johnson, Christopher USITC 202-205-3488

Victim and Witness Assistance Programs....Kaplan, Carol Justice Stat 202-307-0759

Victim and Witness Assistance Programs....Zawitz, Marianne Justice Stat 202-616-3499

Victims of Crime....Meister, Brenda G. Justice Stat 202-307-5983

Victims of Crime....Rand, Michael Justice Stat 202-616-3494

Victims of Crime....Klaus, Patsy Justice Stat 202-307-0776

Victims of Crime....Taylor, Bruce Justice Stat 202-616-3498

Video Services....Plock, Ernest COMMERCE 202-482-4781

Video Transmission--Common Carrier....Staff FCC 202-634-1706

Video games....Robinson, Hazel USITC 202-205-3496

Videotex Services....Inoussa, Mary C. COMMERCE 202-482-5820

Vietnam....Pho, Hong-Phong B. Cnty Commerce 202-482-3875

Vietnam....Staff Cnty State 202-647-3132

Vietnam/Minerals....Vacant Cnty Mines 202-501-9694

Vincent's Infection....Staff NIDR 301-496-4261

Vinyl chloride monomer....Michels, David USITC 202-205-3352

Vinyl resins or plastics....Taylor, Ed USITC 202-205-3362

Violations, Fish and Wildlife Laws....Staff FWS 703-358-1949

Virgin Islands (UK)....Brooks, Michelle Cnty Commerce 202-482-2527

Virgin Islands (US)....Soto, Rodrigo Cnty Commerce 202-482-2527

Virology....Staff NIAID 301-496-5717

Virus (Cancer Related)....Staff NCI 301-496-5583

Virus Tumor Biology....Brady, John FAES 301-496-0988

Vision Care (Statistics)....Staff NCHS 301-436-8500

Vision and Aging....Staff NEI 301-496-5248

Vision and Aging....Staff NIA 301-496-1752

Visitor Centers, Hatcheries....Staff FWS 703-358-1715

Visual Arts....Staff NEA 202-682-5448

Visual communications....Roche, James M. UMD 301-405-2408

Visual signaling apparatus....Baker, Scott USITC 202-205-3386

Vital Statistics, Division of....Patterson, John E. CDC 301-436-8951

Vital Statistics, Family Growth Survey.... CDC 301-436-8731

Vitamin E (and Cardiovascular Disease)....Staff NHLBI 301-496-4236

Vitamin Supplements and Aging....Staff NIA 301-496-1752

Vitamins....Nesbitt, Elizabeth USITC 202-205-3355

Vitamins C,D,E, (and CVD)....Staff NHLBI 301-496-4236

Vitamins/Minerals....Corwin, Emil FDA 202-205-4144

Vitiligo....Staff NIAMS 301-496-8188

Vitrectomy....Staff NEI 301-496-5248

Vocal Cord Paralysis....Staff NINDS 301-496-5751

Vocal Cord Paralysis....Staff NIDCD 301-496-7243

Vogt-Koyanagi Disease....Staff NEI 301-496-5248

Volunteerism....Long, Susan ACF 202-401-9215

Von Recklinghausen's Disease....Staff NINDS 301-496-5751

Von Willebrand's Disease....Staff NHLBI 301-496-4236

Voting Districts....McCully, Cathy CENSUS 301-763-3827

Voting and Registration....Jennings, Jerry CENSUS 301-763-4547

Voyager Flight Project....Doyle, Jim NASA 818-354-5011

W

WARC Frequency Allocations....Staff FCC 202-632-7025

WARC Frequency Coordination....Staff FCC 202-653-8126

WARC Frequency lists, Notification & Registration....Staff FCC 202-653-8126

WARC Interference....Staff FCC 202-653-8126

Wage Developments, Current, Comp. & Working Cond....Cimini, Michael LABOR 202-606-6275

Wages/Indl Rels, Collect Barg Agreements Analysis....Cimini, Michael LABOR 202-606-6275

Wages/Indl Rels, Collect Barg Settlements, Major....Devine, Janice M. LABOR 202-606-6276

Wages/Indl Rels, Empl Benefit Surv, Other Benefits....Houff, James LABOR 202-606-6238

Wages/Indl Rels, Empl Benefit Surv, Pension Plans....Houff, James LABOR 202-606-6238

Wages/Indl Rels, Employment Cost Index....Shelly, Wayne LABOR 202-606-6199

Wages/Indl Rels, Health Studies....Webber, William LABOR 202-606-6161

Wages/Industrial Relations, Current Wage Developments....Cimini, Michael LABOR 202-606-6275

Wages/Industrial Relations, Special Projects....Webber, William LABOR 202-606-6162

Wages/Industrial Relations, Unions, Membership....Cimini, Michael LABOR 202-606-6275

Wages/Industrial Relations, Work Stoppages....Cimini, Michael LABOR 202-606-6275

Waldenstroms Macroglobulinemia....Staff NCI 301-496-5583

Walkie-Talkies (unlicensed)....Staff FCC 202-653-6288

Walking sticks....Burns, Gail USITC 202-205-3501

Wall coverings, of rubber or plastics....Raftery, Jim USITC 202-205-3365

Wallets....Seastrum, Carl USITC 202-205-3493

Wallets, Billfolds, Flatgoods....Byron, James E. COMMERCE 202-482-4034

Walleye....Staff NEI 301-496-5248

Wallpaper....Stahmer, Carsten USITC 202-205-3321

Warm Air Heating Eqmt....Vacant COMMERCE 202-482-3509

Warts....Staff NIAID 301-496-5717

Washington issues....Callahan, Christopher UMD 301-405-2432

Waste Detoxification....Gross, Thomas J. NEIC 202-586-9497

Waste Heat Recovery....Gross, Thomas J. NEIC 202-586-9497

Waste Material Management....Walter, Donald K. NEIC 202-586-6750

Waste Products Utilization....Gross, Thomas J. NEIC 202-586-9497

Waste Reduction Technologies....Gross, Thomas J. NEIC 202-586-9497

Waste Treatment and Disposal....Staff EPA 301-382-4627

Waste and Chemical Policy Division....Staff EPA 202-26--2747

Waste and scrap (metals)....Lundy, David USITC 202-205-3439

Waste or scrap....Spalding, Josephine USITC 202-205-3498

Waste, textile: cotton....Sweet, Mary Elizabeth USITC 202-205-3455

Waste, textile: manmade fiber....Sweet, Mary Elizabeth USITC 202-205-3455

Waste, textile: silk....Shelton, Linda USITC 202-205-3457

Waste, textile: wool....Shelton, Linda USITC 202-205-3457

Wastepaper....Stanley, Gary COMMERCE 202-482-0375

Watches....Harris, John COMMERCE 202-482-1178

Watches....Piropato, Louis CUSTOMS 212-466-5895

Watches....Luther, Dennis USITC 202-205-3497

Water Division....Staff EPA 202-260-7700

Water Enforcement Division....Staff EPA 202-260-8180

Water Environmental Laws....Staff NEIC 202-586-4996

Water Hardness (and CVD)....Staff NHLBI 301-496-4236

Water Pollution....Staff EPA 301-382-5508

Water Projects, Federal....Staff FWS 703-358-1719

Water Resource Equipment....Vacant COMMERCE 202-482-3509

Water Resource Usage and Analysis....Staff FWS 703-358-1710

Water Rights Agreements, Fish and Wildlife....Staff FWS 703-358-1719

Water Supply....Staff OD/ORS 301-496-3537

Water and Sewage Treatment Plants....Vacant COMMERCE 202-482-4643

Wave Energy....Loose, Ronald NEIC 202-586-8086

Wax, articles of....Spalding, Josephine USITC 202-205-3498

Waxes....Brownchweig, Gilbert CUSTOMS 212-466-5744

Waxes....Randall, Rob USITC 202-205-3366

Weapons Testing....Staff NEIC 301-903-3441

Weapons and Crime....Rand, Michael Justice Stat 202-616-3494

Weapons and Crime....Taylor, Bruce Justice Stat 202-616-3498

Wearing Apparel: Boys (sizes 2-7 only)....Kirschner, Bruce CUSTOMS

212-466-5865

Wearing Apparel: Girls (sizes 2-7 only)....Kirschner, Bruce CUSTOMS 212-466-5865

Wearing Apparel: Infants....Kirschner, Bruce CUSTOMS 212-466-5865

Weatherization Assistance....Staff NEIC 202-586-2204

Weatherization Assistance - Elderly....Staff NEIC 202-586-2204

Weatherization Assistance - Handicapped....Staff NEIC 202-586-2204

Weatherization Assistance - Low Income Individuals....Staff NEIC 202-586-2204

Weaving machines....Greene, William USITC 202-205-3405

Weber-Christian Disease....Staff NIAMS 301-496-8188

Weber-Christian Disease....Staff NIAID 301-496-5717

Weekly and Annual Earnings--Current Pop. Survey....Mellor, Earl LABOR 202-606-6378

Wegener's Granulomatosis....Staff NIAMS 301-496-8188

Wegener's Granulomatosis....Staff NIAID 301-496-5717

Wegener's Granulomatosis....Staff NIAMS 301-496-8188

Weighing machinery....Slingerland, David USITC 202-205-3400

Welding apparatus....Mata, Ruben USITC 202-205-3403

Welding/Cutting Apparatus....Kemper, Alexis COMMERCE 202-482-5956

Welfare and AFDC JOBS Programs....Long, Susan ACF 202-401-9215

Werdnig-Hoffmann Disease....Staff NINDS 301-496-5751

Werner's Syndrome....Staff NIDDK 301-496-3583

Wernicke's Disease....Staff NINDS 301-496-5751

Western European Union (WEU)....Staff Cnty State 202-647-8050

Western Hemisphere Programs, Fish and Wildlife....Staff FWS 703-358-1767

Western Sahara....Dolley, Thomas Cnty Mines 202-501-9690

Western Samoa....Lagoy, Michele Peace Corps 202-606-3227

Western Samoa (Apia)....Staff Cnty State 202-647-3546

Wetlands Division....Staff EPA 202-260-9916

Wetlands Inventory, National....Staff FWS 703-358-1744

Wetlands Protection Hotline....Staff EPA 800-832-7828

Whalebone, articles of....Spalding, Josephine USITC 202-205-3498

Wheat....Pierre-Benoist, John USITC 202-205-3320

Wheat with options....Sepsey, Judy CFT 312-353-9025

Wheel goods: motorized....Hagey, Michael USITC 202-205-3392

Wheel goods: non-motorized....Seastrum, Carl USITC 202-205-3493

Whiplash....Staff NINDS 301-496-5751

Whips....Burns, Gail USITC 202-205-3501

Whiskey....Salin, Victoria USITC 202-205-3331

Whistleblower Hotline....Staff EPA 800-424-4000

White Collar Crime....Kaplan, Carol Justice Stat 202-307-0759

Wholesale Trade....Margulies, Marvin COMMERCE 202-482-5086

Wholesale Trade, Census....Trimble, John CENSUS 301-763-5281

Wholesale Trade, Current Sales and Inventories....Gordon, Dale CENSUS 301-763-3916

Wholesale services....Bedore, James USITC 202-205-3424

Whooping Cough....Staff NIAID 301-496-5717

Wilderness Planning....Twiss, John FS 202-205-1404

Wilderness Planning, Fish and Wildlife....Staff FWS 703-358-2043

Wildlife Assistance....Staff FWS 703-358-1713

Wildlife Ecology....Staff FWS 703-358-1710

Wildlife Health Research....Staff FWS 703-358-1710

Wildlife Management, Refuges....Staff FWS 703-358-2043

Wildlife Permits....Staff FWS 703-358-1744

Wildlife Research....Lennartz, Michael R. FS 202-205-1524

Wildlife, Exotic....Staff FWS 703-358-1718

Wildlife, Injurious....Staff FWS 703-358-1718

Wildlife, Law Enforcement....Staff FWS 703-358-1949

Wildlife, Non-Game....Staff FWS 703-358-1718

Wildlife, Range and Fish Habitat Research....Lennartz, Michael R. FS 202-205-1424

Wilms' Tumor....Staff NCI 301-496-5583

Wilson Disease....Staff NIDDK 301-496-3583

Wilson Disease....Staff NINDS 301-496-5751

Wind Energy....Loose, Ronald NEIC 202-586-8086

Windmill Components....Garden, Les COMMERCE 202-482-0556

Wines....Salin, Victoria USITC 202-205-3331

Wire....Fitzgerald, John CUSTOMS 212-466-5492

Wire....Yost, Charles USITC 202-205-3442

Wire Cloth....Williams, Franklin COMMERCE 202-482-0132

Wire Cloth, Industrial....Reise, Richard COMMERCE 202-482-3489

Wire Facilities....Staff FCC 202-634-1800

Wire Rods....Fitzgerald, John CUSTOMS 212-466-5492

Wire and Wire Products....Vacant COMMERCE 202-482-0606

Wire or Cable Licenses....Staff FCC 202-634-1800

Wire rods....Yost, Charles USITC 202-205-3442

Wireless Microphones (licensed)....Staff FCC 717-337-1212

Wireless Microphones (non-licensed)....Staff FCC 202-653-6288

Wiretapping....Staff FCC 202-632-7260

Wiring sets....Cutchin, John USITC 202-205-3396

Wiskott-Aldrich Syndrome....Staff NCI 301-496-5583

Wolff-Parkinson-White Syndrome (WPW)....Staff NHLBI 301-496-4236

Wollastonite....Potter, Michael J. MINES 202-501-9387

Women in journalism....Beasley, Maurine UMD 301-405-2413

Women's Health Issues....Staff OD 301-496-5787

Women's Health and Fertility....Peterson, Herbert B. CDC 404-488-5250

Women, Employment/Unemployment Statistics....Hayghe, Howard LABOR 202-606-6378

Women, Population....Smith, Denise CENSUS 301-763-7883

Wood (densified)....Ruggles, Fred USITC 202-205-3325

Wood Containers....Hicks, Michael COMMERCE 202-482-0375

Wood Preserving....Hicks, Michael COMMERCE 202-482-0375

Wood Products....Stanley, Gary COMMERCE 202-482-0375

Wood Products....Garretto, Paul CUSTOMS 212-466-5779

Wood Products, Misc....Stanley, Gary COMMERCE 202-482-0375

Wood Technology....Staff FS 202-205-1565

Wood Working Machinery....McDonald, Edward COMMERCE 202-482-0680

Wood products, rough primary....Ruggles, Fred USITC 202-205-3325

Wood pulp....Rhodes, Richard USITC 202-205-3322

Wood veneers....Ruggles, Fred USITC 202-205-3325

Wool....Freund, Kimberlie USITC 202-205-3456

Wool....Shelton, Linda USITC 202-205-3457

Wool....Warlick, William USITC 202-205-3459

Wool and Mohair....Lawler, John Agri 202-219-0840

Wool and Mohair....Skinner, Robert Agri 202-219-0841

Wool and Mohair....Simpson, Linda Agri 202-720-3578

Wool grease, sulfonated or sulfated....Land, Eric USITC 202-205-3349

Word processors....Baker, Scott USITC 202-205-3386

Work Experience, Employment/Unemployment Stats....Mellor, Earl LABOR 202-606-6378

Work Injuries, Reports & Surveys of, Comp. & Work....Jackson, Ethel LABOR 202-606-6180

Work Injury, Report Surveys, Comp & Working Cond.....Jackson, Ethel LABOR 202-606-6180

Work Stoppages, Compensation & Working Conditions....Cimini, Michael LABOR 202-606-6275

Work-life Estimates, Employment Statistics....Horvath, Francis LABOR 202-606-6345

Workers, Older, Empl/Unempl. Stats.....Rones, Philip LABOR 202-606-6378

Working Conditions....Cimini, Michael LABOR 202-606-6275

Working Conditions, Employment Cost Data....Shelly, Wayne LABOR 202-606-6199

Working Conditions, Safety & Health, Asst.Comm.....Eisenberg, William M. LABOR 202-606-6304

Working Poor, Employment/Unemployment Statistics....Herz, Diane LABOR 202-606-6378

Works of Art....Mushinske, Larry CUSTOMS 212-466-5739

Wound Healing (LDBA)....Staff NIDR 301-496-4261

Woven Outerwear: Boys'....Raftery, William CUSTOMS 212-466-5851

Woven Outerwear: Men's....Raftery, William CUSTOMS 212-466-5851

Woven Outerwear: Women's....Raftery, William CUSTOMS 212-466-5851

Wryneck (Torticollis)....Staff NINDS 301-496-5751

X

X-ray (Radiation Effects on Fetus)....Staff FDA 301-443-2356

X-ray Technician....Staff HRSA/BHPr 301-443-5794

X-ray apparatus....Johnson, Christopher USITC 202-205-3488

Xanthinuria....Staff NIDDK 301-496-3583

Xanthomatosis....Staff NHLBI 301-496-4236

Xeroderma Pigmentosum....Staff NCI 301-496-5583

Xerophthalmia....Staff NEI 301-496-5248

Xeroradiography....Staff NCI 301-496-5583

Xerostomia (Dry Mouth)....Staff NIDR 301-496-4261

Xylene....Raftery, Jim USITC 202-205-3365

Xylenol....Matusik, Ed USITC 202-205-3356

Y

YAG Laser....Staff NEI 301-496-5248

Yarns....Konzet, Jeffrey CUSTOMS 212-466-5885

Yarns....Shelton, Linda USITC 202-205-3457

Year 2000 Research and Development....Staff CENSUS 301-763-8601

Yeast....Janis, William V. COMMERCE 202-482-2250

Yeast Infections....Staff NIAID 301-496-5717

Yellow Fever....Staff NIAID 301-496-5717

Yellow Page Advertising....Staff FCC 202-632-7553

Yellowcake....Greenblatt, Jack USITC 202-205-3353

Yemen....DiMeo, Pam Peace Corps 202-606-3196

Yemen....Schildwachter, Christy Peace Corps 202-606-3196

Yemen (Aden)/Minerals....Michalski, Bernadette Cnty Mines 202-501-9699

Yemen (Sana)/Minerals....Michalski, Bernadette Cnty Mines 202-501-9699

Yemen Arab Republic (Sanaa)....Staff Cnty State 202-647-6571

Yemen, Republic of....Fitzgerald-Wilkes, Kate/Thanos, Paul Cnty Commerce 202-482-1870

Youth Conservation Corps, Fish and Wildlife....Staff FWS 703-358-2029

Youth, Employment Statistics....Cohany, Sharon LABOR 202-606-6378

Youth, Students, and Dropouts, Empl./Unempl. Stats....Cohany, Sharon LABOR 202-606-6378

Yttrium....Hedrick, James B. MINES 202-501-9412

Yugoslavia....Keller, Jeremy Cnty Commerce 202-482-2645

Yugoslavia (Belgrade)....Staff Cnty State 202-647-4138

Yugoslavia/Minerals....Steblez, Walter Cnty Mines 202-501-9671

Z

Zaire....Henke, Debra Cnty Commerce 202-482-5149

Zaire, Republic of (Kinshasa)....Staff Cnty State 202-647-2080

Zaire/Minerals....Heydari, Michael Cnty Mines 202-501-9688

Zambia....Holm-Olsen, Finn Cnty Commerce 202-482-4228

Zambia (Lusaka)....Staff Cnty State 202-647-8433

Zambia/Minerals....Antonides, Lloyd Cnty Mines 202-501-9686

Zeolites....Virta, Robert MINES 202-501-9384

Zimbabwe....Holm-Olsen, Finn Cnty Commerce 202-482-4228

Zimbabwe....Brill, Terry Peace Corps 202-606-3535

Zimbabwe (Harare)....Staff Cnty State 202-647-9429

Zimbabwe/Minerals....Izon, David Cnty Mines 202-501-9692

Zinc....Jolly, James H. MINES 202-501-9422

Zinc....White, Linda USITC 202-205-3427

Zinc compounds....Greenblatt, Jack USITC 202-205-3353

Zip Codes, Demographic Data....Staff CENSUS 301-763-4100

Zip Codes, Economic Data....Russell, Anne CENSUS 301-763-7038

Zip Codes, Geographic Relationships....Quarato, Rose CENSUS 301-763-4667

Zippers....Shildneck, Ann USITC 202-205-3499

Zirconium....Templeton, David A. MINES 202-501-9391

Zirconium....DeSapio, Vincent USITC 202-205-3435

Zirconium compounds....Greenblatt, Jack USITC 202-205-3353

Zollinger-Ellison Syndrome....Staff NIDDK 301-496-3583

Zoonoses....Staff NIAID 301-496-5717

Zoris....Shildneck, Ann USITC 202-205-3499

The 8,000 Listings in the EXPERTS CHAPTER are <u>not</u> included in this Index.

Index

G
_____

H_____

M_____

Q

W